The United States and Sub-Saharan Africa
Guide to U.S. Official Documents and Government-Sponsored Publications, 1976–1980

Compiled by
Julian W. Witherell
African and Middle Eastern Division
Research Services

Library of Congress
Washington 1984

Library of Congress Cataloging in Publication Data

Witherell, Julian W.
  The United States and sub-Saharan Africa.

  Supt. of Doc. no.: LC 41.12: Un3
  1. Africa, Sub-Saharan—Bibliography—Union lists.
2. United States—Government publications—Bibliography—
Union lists. 3. Catalogs, Union—United States.
I. Title.
Z3501.W58 1984 [DT3] 016.967 84-600009
ISBN 0-8444-0448-9

For sale by the Superintendent of Documents, U.S. Government
Printing Office, Washington, D.C. 20402

Contents

CONTENTS

CONTENTS

CONTENTS ——————————————————————————

Preface

This guide focuses on publications relating to sub-Saharan Africa issued by or for United States government agencies in the period 1976–80. It updates that part of the Library of Congress's 1978 study, *The United States and Africa: Guide to U.S. Official Documents and Government-Sponsored Publications on Africa, 1785–1975* (entry 27 of the present guide) concerning nations south of the Sahara and cites a number of titles issued in 1973–75 that were not recorded in the earlier compilation. Also included is a selection of documents with 1981 or 1982 imprints that cover events, programs, or developments of the 1976–80 period. The guide is based on holdings of the Library of Congress, other collections in the Washington, D.C. area, and selected titles in other American libraries. Material in the Library of Congress is indicated by call numbers for cataloged works in the general collections, by the symbol DLC for uncataloged items, or by symbols showing locations in special collections (see Key to Symbols). *National Union Catalog* symbols are used to indicate the location of many titles not in the Library of Congress but held by other libraries.

As access to a number of collections cited in this guide is restricted, the user should consult the holding library concerning the availability of the material for reference, photocopying, or interlibrary loan. Information on the accessibility of collections in the Washington area is given in the tenth edition of *Library and Reference Facilities in the Area of the District of Columbia*[1] and in two studies of the Woodrow Wilson International Center for Scholars, *Scholars' Guide to Washington, D. C., for African Studies* (entry 29) and *Scholars' Guide to Washington, D.C., for Middle Eastern Studies* (entry 29, note). Additional data on titles not identified as held by libraries in and around the nation's capital has been gathered from published guides such as the *Monthly Catalog of United States Government Publications* and *A Survey of the United States Government's Investment in Africa* (see Key to Sources), or from information supplied by forty-nine American libraries and documentation centers.

Entries are grouped by region, as in *The United States and Africa*, with further division by country and subject.[2] As in the earlier guide, the term *government-sponsored publications* has been interpreted broadly to include a wide range of studies issued under official contract by universities and other research centers, prepared with financial support from one or more government agencies, or reproduced or translated by the government. Many contract studies indicate that authors are given wide latitude in expressing their own views, interpretations, and conclusions. As an example, the preface of *The Uprooted of the Western Sahel* (entry 3440), financed by the United States Agency for International Development (AID), notes that the authors had a "liberal mandate to treat the subject with intellectual independence. Neither the data nor the views expressed in the study represent the official views of the Agency for International Development or the U.S. Government."

The guide is limited to unclassified documents. Titles marked *restricted, confidential*, or *official use only*, with no indication that they were subsequently declassified, are not included. Also omitted are congressional bills and resolutions, reports prepared for Congress by the Congressional Research Service, Library of Congress,[3] most preliminary or progress reports on government contracts, and material on the United States issued by American cultural centers in Africa. For background information on various government agencies cited in this bibliography and on their publications, useful guides are *CIS Annual*; *Checklist of Congressional Hearings & Committee Prints*; *Government Reference Books*; *Guide to U.S. Government Publications*; *Index to U.S. Government Periodicals*; *U.S. Federal Official Publications: the International Dimension*; and *United States Government Manual* (for full citations, see Key to Sources).

Documents recorded here reflect both the wide range and the depth of official American interest in nations south of the Sahara and in broad issues having an impact on Africa, such as drought relief, human rights, refugees, and the role of women in national development. Congressional concern is indicated by frequent references to African economic, political, and social problems in the *Congressional Record*, identified through its sessional indexes.[4] Reports on hearings and congressional study missions further express American policy and provide background material on major issues, among them the civil war in Angola, South African apartheid, conditions in Uganda, the evolution of Zimbabwe, and the Sahelian drought.

American economic, military, social, and technical assistance programs south of the Sahara are documented in printed and mimeographed studies issued by or for AID and other federal departments and agencies. Most documents prepared by AID's bureaus and offices or produced under their auspices by other agencies or nongovernment contractors have been identified from catalogs held by AID's Development Information Center and the Documentation Center of its Sahel Development Program. Additional citations have been supplied by libraries of various contractors, primarily universities and other research centers.

A major bibliographic development of the late 1970s and early 1980s has been the marked increase in the number of these contract studies available to researchers in microform. Many have been identified through *A.I.D. Research & Development Abstracts* (see Key to Sources), an annotated list indicating how copies can be obtained in paper form or microfiche, or through *Sahel, a Guide to the Microfiche Collection of Documents and Dissertations* (see Key to Sources), a guide primarily to material in the Sahel Documentation Center, Michigan State University, reproduced by University Microfilms International. Major sources of microforms of documents prepared by or for other government agencies were *Resources in Education*, issued by the Educational Resources Information Center (ERIC), *American Statistics Index*, by the Congressional Information Service, and *Government Reports Announcements & Index*, by the National Technical Information Service (NTIS) (see Key to Sources).[5] Citations to material prepared under military auspices have been taken in part from *Africa; Selected References. Supplement* (see Key to Sources), issued by the Air University Library.

Government-sponsored translations into English of periodical and newspaper articles constitute a major component of citations on certain regions and countries. Material translated or reproduced by the Joint Publications Research Service (JPRS) provides information on a wide range of economic, military, and political topics. As most of the articles come from Arabic, French, and Portuguese-language serials, a high proportion of the translations concern Sudan, French-speaking, or Portuguese-speaking states. As an aid to researchers in locating titles from which the translations were taken, a list of the major periodicals covered by JPRS is noted in JPRS Newspapers and Periodicals (p. xxi).[6]

Given the volume of documentation on sub-Saharan Africa issued by or for government agencies in recent years, there is little doubt that some important publications were inadvertently omitted from this compilation. As supplements are under consideration to bring it up to date, additions, corrections, or suggestions would be welcome.

During the course of this study, the compiler was aided by Library of Congress staff and by librarians and area specialists in other research centers. The Library's Science and Technology Division, Serial and Government Publications Division, Near Eastern and African Law Division, Microform Reading Room, and Congressional Research Service were especially supportive. Special thanks also go to the staffs of the following libraries and documentation centers in the Washington, D.C., area who facilitated the compiler's bibliographic research in their collections: African Bibliographic Center; Bureau of the Census Library; Center for International Research, Bureau of the Census; Development Information Center, AID; Division of Research Grants, and Library, National Endowment for the Humanities; Documentation Center, Sahel Development Program, AID; Export-Import Bank of the United States; Foreign Service Institute; General Accounting Office; Geological Survey; National Agricultural Library; National Library of Medicine; National Museum of African Art; Office of Women in Development, AID; Overseas Private Investment Corporation; Smithsonian Institution; United States Information Agency; and libraries of the departments of Commerce, Energy, Health and Human Services, Housing and Urban Development, Labor, State, and Transportation.

The compiler expresses his deep appreciation to the following universities and other research centers that contributed citations or other information to this study: Auburn University; California Institute of Technology; California State Library; California State Personnel Board; Center for Research on Economic Development, University of Michigan; Center for Technology, Environment, and Development, Clark University; Cornell University; Department of Anthropology, University of New Mexico; Food and Feed Grain Institute, Kansas State University; Georgia Institute of Technology; Hoover Institution on War, Revolution, and Peace; Indiana University; Institute for Communication Research, Stanford University; Institute for Development Anthropology; Institute for Health Policy Studies, University of California, San Francisco; International Center for Marine Resource Development, University of Rhode Island; International Fertilizer Development Center;

International Plant Protection Center, Oregon State University; Johns Hopkins University; Lesotho Agricultural Sector Analysis Project, Colorado State University; Lincoln Laboratory, Massachusetts Institute of Technology (MIT); Meharry Medical College; Michigan State University; Mississippi State University; Ohio State University; Purdue University; Rand Corporation; Research Triangle Institute; Rice University; School of Architecture and Planning, MIT; South Dakota State University; Texas A&M University; Tufts University; Tuskegee Institute; University of Arizona; University of California, Berkeley; University of California, Los Angeles; University of Illinois, Urbana-Champaign; University of Iowa; University of Massachusetts, Amherst; University of Michigan; University of Missouri, Columbia; University of New Hampshire; University of North Carolina, Chapel Hill; University of Wisconsin, Madison; Utah State University; Vanderbilt University; West Virginia University; and Yale University.

Julian W. Witherell
July 1983

Notes

1.

U.S. *Library of Congress. Loan Division.* Library and reference facilities in the area of the District of Columbia. [1st]+ ed.; 1943+ [Washington]
Z732.D62U63
Tenth ed., edited by Margaret S. Jennings and published for the American Society for Information Science in cooperation with Joint Venture by Knowledge Industry Publications, White Plains, N.Y. (1979. 258 p.)

2.

The arrangement of the guide follows the same basic geographic pattern as in *The United States and Africa* except that Chad is entered in the West Africa section because of that country's close involvement with programs relating to Sahelian drought relief and economic development. Western Sahara, usually identified with North Africa, is covered here because of its relationship to Mauritania.

3.

Studies of the Library's Congressional Research Service (CRS) are prepared exclusively for members and committees of Congress. Many are subsequently issued as committee prints, entered into published hearings of congressional committees, inserted into the *Congressional Record*, or on occasion published by private institutions. CRS documents made available in the public domain are cited in its *CRS Studies in the Public Domain*, which is available for sale from the Superintendent of Documents, U.S. Government Printing Office, Washington, D.C. 20402.

4.

U.S. *Congress.* Congressional record; proceedings and debates of the Congress. 43d+ Mar. 4/26, 1873+ Washington, U.S. Govt. Print. Off.
J11.R5
Permanent ed. Issued for each session; the text is revised and rearranged from the daily ed.
An index is issued for each session which includes History of Bills and Resolutions.
At the time this guide was compiled, the index to the permanent edition was available through the 95th Congress, 2d session (1978). For subsequent sessions through the 96th Congress, 2d session (1980), the biweekly index to the daily edition (J11.R7) was used.
Citations in this guide taken from the *Congressional Record* (both permanent and daily editions) are limited to statements and extensions of remarks two pages or more in length.

5.

With the growing availability of contract studies and other government reports through the microform distribution services of such organizations as AID, Educational Resources Information Center (ERIC), National Technical Information Service (NTIS), Congressional Information Service, and University Microfilms International, researchers may find that microfiche or microfilm copies of some documents cited in this guide are held by libraries in their areas, both in the United States and abroad. Researchers in Great Britain, for example, will find an excellent collection of U.S. government and government-sponsored publications at the Library, Institute of Development Studies, University of Sussex.

6.

With some exceptions, only JPRS titles four or more pages in length are cited in this guide. Among the sources that index JPRS material, the most useful in this compilation were the *Monthly Catalog of United States Government Publications* (see Key to Sources) and the *Bell & Howell Transdex Index*, issued monthly with annual cumulations in microfiche (cumulations for 1974+ held by the Library of Congress). JPRS reports are held by the Library as follows: 1958–75 (no. 1– 65,120) in bound form in the general collections (AS36.U57);

1975+ (no. 65,120+) on microfiche in the Microform Reading Room; 1977+ (no. 68,872+) on microfiche in the Newspaper and Current Periodical Reading Room. Very recent issues (approximately the last two to three months) are held on paper, until replaced by microfiche, in the Newspaper and Current Periodical Reading Room.

Key to Symbols

AMAU	Air University, Maxwell Air Force Base, Ala. 36112
AMuI	International Fertilizer Development Center, Muscle Shoals, Ala. 35660
ATT	Tuskegee Institute, Tuskegee, Ala. 36088
AzU	University of Arizona, Tucson, Ariz. 85721
C	California State Library, Sacramento, Calif. 95814
CLU	University of California, Los Angeles, Main Library, Los Angeles, Calif. 90024
CPT	California Institute of Technology, Pasadena, Calif. 91109
CoDBW	United States Bureau of Sport Fisheries and Wildlife, Wildlife Research Center, Denver, Colo. 80203
CoFS	Colorado State University, Fort Collins, Colo. 80521
CtY	Yale University, New Haven, Conn. 06520
DBC	United States Bureau of the Census, Suitland, Md. 20233
DEI	Export-Import Bank of the United States, Washington, D.C. 20571
DI	United States Department of the Interior, Washington, D.C. 20240
DI-GS	United States Geological Survey, Reston, Va. 22092
DL	United States Department of Labor, Washington, D. C. 20210
DLC	Library of Congress, Washington, D.C. 20540
DLC-G&M	Library of Congress, Geography and Map Division, Washington, D.C. 20540
DLC-LL	Library of Congress, Law Library, Washington, D.C. 20540
DLC-Micro	Library of Congress, Microform Reading Room, Washington, D.C. 20540
DLC-Sci RR	Library of Congress, Science Reading Room, Washington, D.C. 20540
DNAL	National Agricultural Library, Beltsville, Md. 20250
DNAS-NAE	National Academy of Sciences, National Academy of Engineering Library, Washington, D.C. 20418
DPC	Peace Corps Information Services, Washington, D.C. 20525
DS	United States Department of State Library (Division of Library and Reference Services), Washington, D.C. 20520
DSI	Smithsonian Institution, Washington, D.C. 20560
GAT	Georgia Institute of Technology, Atlanta, Ga. 30332
IEN	Northwestern University, Evanston, Ill. 60201
IU	University of Illinois, Urbana, Ill. 61803
IaU	University of Iowa, Iowa City, Iowa 52240
InLP	Purdue University, Lafayette, Ind. 47907
InU	Indiana University, Bloomington, Ind. 47401
MMeT-F	Tufts University, Fletcher School of Law and Diplomacy, Medford, Mass. 02155
MWC	Clark University, Worcester, Mass., 01610
MiEM	Michigan State University, East Lansing, Mich. 48823
MiU	University of Michigan, Ann Arbor, Mich. 48104
MiU-RE	Center for Research on Economic Development, University of Michigan, Ann Arbor, Mich. 48109
MoU	University of Missouri, Columbia, Mo. 65201
MsSM	Mississippi State University, Mississippi State University, Miss. 39762
NIC	Cornell University, Ithaca, N.Y. 14850
OU	Ohio State University, Columbus, Ohio 43210

OrCS	Oregon State University, Corvallis, Or. 97331
TxHR	Rice University, Houston, Tex. 77001
ULA	Utah State University, Logan, Utah 84321
WU	University of Wisconsin, Madison, Wis. 53706
WvU	West Virginia University, Morgantown, W.Va. 26505

Key to Sources

Duffy. Survey

    Duffy, David L. A survey of the United States Government's investment in Africa. [Waltham, Mass.], Crossroads Press, [c1978]   DLC

Month. Cat.

    U.S. *Superintendent of Documents.* Monthly catalog of United States Government publications. no. [1]+ Jan. 1895+ Washington, U.S. Govt. Print. Off.   Z1223.A18

In addition, the following guides and lists have been of value in the preparation of this study:

U.S. *Agency for International Development. Sahel Development Program. Documentation Center.* Accessions list. [Washington] monthly (irregular)   DLC
    See full citation in entry 3285.

U.S. *Library of Congress. Library of Congress Office, Nairobi.* Accessions list, Eastern Africa. v. 1+ Jan. 1958+ Nairobi.   Z3516.U52
    See full citation in entry 19.   Z663. 28.A5

U.S. *President.* Public papers of the Presidents of the United States. Washington, [published by the Office of the Federal Register, National Archives and Records Service, General Services Administration; for sale by the Supt. of Docs.], U.S. Govt. Print. Off.   J80.A283
    A companion publication, *Weekly Compilation of Presidential Documents*, was also of value.

U.S. *Treaties, etc.* United States treaties and other international agreements. [Washington, Dept. of State; for sale by the Supt. of Docs., U.S. Govt. Print. Off.]   JA231.A34
    Vols. 26–31 (1975/76–1979) were used in this study.

A.I.D. research & development abstracts. 1973+ [Washington], U.S. Agency for International Development. quarterly.   DLC

Africa: selected references. Supplement. no. 1+ 1961+ Maxwell Air Force Base, Ala., Air University Library. annual. (Air University. Library. Special bibliography, no. 159)   DLC
    See full citation in entry 21.

Africa: special studies, 1962–1980; edited by Paul Keraris. Frederick, Md., University Publications of America, 1981. 21 p.   DLC
    An annotated list of studies, including U.S. Government documents, issued on microfilm by the publisher.

American statistics index; a comprehensive guide and index to the statistical publications of the U.S. Government. 1974+ Washington, Congressional Information Service.   Z7554. U5A46
    Monthly lists with annual cumulations; each issue appears in two sections—Abstracts and Index.

Checklist of congressional hearings & committee prints. Lanham, Md., Bernan Associates. semiannual
KF49.C70

Congressional Information Service. CIS annual. Washington.　　　　　　　　　KF49.C62
　　　Each issue appears in two sections—Abstracts of congressional publications and legislative history citations; Index to congressional publications and public laws.

Congressional quarterly almanac. Washington, Congressional Quarterly, inc. annual　　　JK1.C66
　　　Vols. 31–36 (1975–80) were used in this study to trace the course of legislation relating to African issues.

Downey, James A. U.S. federal official publications: the international dimension; prepared by James A. Downey, with a foreword by Leroy C. Schwarzkopf. Oxford, New York, Pergamon Press, 1978. 352 p. (Guides to official publications, v. 2)　　　　　　　　　　　Z1223.Z7D68　1978

Government reference books. 1st + ed.; 1968/69 + Littleton, Colo., Libraries Unlimited. biennial.
Z1223.Z7G68

　　　The 7th ed. (1980/81), compiled by Walter L. Newsome, was used in this compilation.

Government reports announcements & index. [Springfield, Va.], U.S. Dept. of Commerce, National Technical Information Service. biweekly.　　　　　　　　　　　　　Z7916.G78

Guide to U.S. Government publications; edited by John L. Andriot [et al.] McLean, Va., Documents Index, [1982] 2 v.　　　　　　　　　　　　　　　　Z1223.Z7A574

Index to U.S. Government periodicals. [Chicago], Infordata International inc.　　　Z1223.Z915
　　　Quarterly, with annual cumulations.
　　　Among the titles with coverage of sub-Saharan Africa regularly indexed are *Agenda*, Background Notes (series), *Department of State Bulletin*, *Development Digest*, *Foreign Agriculture*, and *World Agricultural Situation*.

Resources in education. [Washington], Educational Resources Information Center; [for sale by the Supt. of Docs., U.S. Govt. Print. Off.] monthly.　　　　　　　　　　Z5813.R4
　　　Semiannual indexes are also available.

Sahel, a guide to the microfiche collection of documents and dissertations. Ann Arbor, Mich., University Microfilms International, 1981. 324 p. (in various pagings) illus.　　　Z7165.S23S2　1981
　　　"The Sahel collection produced by University Microfilms International (UMI) consists of over 900 documents from the Sahel Documentation Center ... 100 American doctoral dissertations drawn from UMI files, and documents from numerous other public, quasi-public, and private organizations...."
　　　English or French.
　　　A preliminary title list, *Sahel Documents and Dissertations* (Ann Arbor, 1980? [79] p.) was also of value.

Sahel bibliographic bulletin. Sahel bulletin bibliographique. v. 1 + 1977 + East Lansing, Sahel Documentation Center, Michigan State University Libraries. quarterly.　　　Z7165.S23S23
　　　See full citation in entry 3287.

United States Government manual. Washington, Office of the Federal Register, National Archives and Records Service; for sale by the Supt. of Docs., U.S. Govt. Print. Off. annual.　　　JK421.A3

Abbreviations

As a reference aid, a selection of abbreviations used in the text and index of this guide is listed below:

ADB	African Development Bank
AFR	Bureau for Africa, United States Agency for International Development
AFR/CWR	Office of Central/West Africa Regional Affairs, United States Agency for International Development
AID	United States Agency for International Development
ANC	African National Congress of South Africa
ANRD	Alianza Nacional de Restoración Democrática
CILSS	Comité permanent inter-états de lutte contre la sécheresse dans le Sahel
CODESRIA	Council for the Development of Economic and Social Research in Africa
DEIDS	Development and Evaluation of Integrated Delivery Systems
DIAMANG	Companhia de Diamentes de Angola
EARTHSAT	Earth Satellite Corporation
ECOWAS	Economic Community of West African States
ELF	Eritrean Liberation Front
ELF-PLF	Eritrean Liberation Front-People's Liberation Forces
EPLF	Eritrean People's Liberation Front
ERTS	Earth Resources Technology Satellite
FAN	Forces armées du nord (Chad)
FAPLA	Forcas Armadas Populares de Libertação de Angola
FLEC	Frente de Libertação do Enclave de Cabinda
FNLA	Frente Nacional de Libertação de Angola
FPLM	Forcas Populares de Libertação de Moçambique
FRELIMO	Frente de Libertação de Moçambique
FROLINAT	Front de liberation national du Tchad
GUNT	Gouvernement d'union nationale de transition (Chad)
ILCA	International Livestock Centre for Africa
LASA	Lesotho Agricultural Sector Analysis Project
LDC	"Less Developed Countries"
MMM	Mouvement militant mauricien
MOJA	Movement for Justice in Africa (Liberia)
MPLA	Movimento Popular de Libertação de Angola—Partido de Trabalho
OECD	Organization for Economic Cooperation and Development
OMVS	Organisation pour la mise en valeur du fleuve sénégal
ORD	Organisme régional de développement (Upper Volta)
PAC	Pan Africanist Congress of Azania
PAI	Parti africain de l'indépendence (Senegal)
PAL	Progressive Alliance of Liberia
PDG	Parti démocratique gabonais
PDS	Parti démocratique sénégalais
PETROANGOL	Companhia de Petróleos de Angola
PFP	Progressive Federal Party (South Africa)

PMSD	Parti mauricien social démocrate
PRC	People's Republic of China
PS	Parti socialiste sénégalais
Polisario	Frente Popular para la Liberación de Saguia el Hamra y Rio de Oro
R&R	Relief & Recovery, *or* Recovery & Rehabilitation
REDSO/EA	Regional Economic Development Services Office, East Africa, United States Agency for International Development (Nairobi, Kenya)
REDSO/WA	Regional Economic Development Services Office, West Africa, United States Agency for International Development (Abidjan, Ivory Coast)
RPP	Rassemblement populaire pour le progrès (Djibouti)
SADAP	Southern Africa Development Analysis Project
SADEX	Southern Africa Development Information/Documentation Exchange
SADR	Saharan Arab Democratic Republic
SAFGRAD	Semi-Arid Food Grain Research and Development Program
SASOL	South African Coal, Oil, and Gas Corporation
SCAUL	Standing Conference of African University Libraries
SDAR	*See* SADR
SFWA	Office of Sahel & Francophone West Africa Affairs, Bureau for Africa, United States Agency for International Development
SNIM	Société nationale industrielle et minière (Mauritania)
SWAPO	South-West Africa People's Organization
TAICH	Technical Assistance Information Clearing House
TAMS	Tippetts-Abbett-McCarthy-Stratton
TANU	Tanganyika African National Union
TEFL	Teaching English as a Foreign Language
UDI	Unilateral Declaration of Independence (Rhodesia)
UDV-RDA	Union démocratique voltaïque-Rassemblement démocratique africaine
UNDP	United Nations Development Program
UNESCO (or Unesco)	United Nations Educational, Scientific and Cultural Organization
UNLF	Ugandan National Liberation Front
UNITA	União Nacional para a Independência Total de Angola
UPV	Union progressiste voltaïque
USAID	United States Agency for International Development
VOA	Voice of America
VOA-CAAP	Voice of America–Continuing Audience Analysis Program
WARDA	West Africa Rice Development Association
WSLF	Western Somali Liberation Front
ZANU	Zimbabwe African National Union
ZAPU	Zimbabwe African People's Union

JPRS Newspapers and Periodicals

As a reference aid in locating periodicals from which Joint Publications Research Service (JPRS) articles have been taken, a selection of those titles held by the Library of Congress is noted below. For information on the Library's holdings of newspapers translated by JPRS, the user should consult *African Newspapers in the Library of Congress* ([Washington], Newspaper Section, Serial Division, Library of Congress, 1977. 97 p.; a revised edition is in preparation); *Arab-World Newspapers in the Library of Congress* (entry 25); and the eighth edition (1982) of *Newspapers Received Currently in the Library of Congress* ([Washington], Serial and Government Publications Division, Library of Congress, 1982, 46 p. Z6945.U5N42). Information on holdings of major African studies centers, including the Library of Congress, can be gathered from *Africana Newspapers Currently Received by American Libraries*, compiled by Maidel K. Cason (Evanston, Ill., Melville J. Herskovits Library of African Studies, Northwestern University Library, 1983. 18 p.).

Periodicals translated or reproduced by JPRS and held by the Library of Congress are:

Actuel développement. Paris. bimonthly.	HC59.7.A28
L.C. has 1974+	
Africa. Dakar. monthly.	DT1.A13
L.C. has 1961+	
Afrique défense. Paris. monthly.	UA855.A37
L.C. has 1978+	
L'Afrique et l'Asie modernes. Paris. quarterly.	DT1.A85
L.C. has 1974+	
Afrique industrie infrastructures. Paris. semimonthly.	HC541.A54
L.C. has 1972+	
Afrique nouvelle. Dakar. weekly	AP27.A58
L.C. has 1947–77 on microfilm (DLC-Micro Microfilm 01864 AP); 1978+ in paper copy.	
Aviation Magazine International. Paris. biweekly.	TL502.A854
L.C. has 1951+	
Bohemia. La Habana. weekly.	AP63.B7
L.C. has 1944+	
Bulletin de l'Afrique noire. Paris. weekly.	DT348.B84
L.C. has 1967+	
Courrier diplomatique de l'Océan indien. Antananarivo. quarterly.	DT468.C68
L.C. has 1975/76+	
Croissance des jeunes nations. Paris. monthly.	HC59.7.C73
L.C. has 1962+	
Cuadernos del Tercer Mundo. México. monthly.	HC59.7.C77
L.C. has 1977+	
Défense nationale. Paris. monthly.	D410.R45
L.C. has 1972+	
Est & ouest. Paris. monthly.	D839.A822
L.C. has 1949+	

Eurafrica; tribune du tiers-monde. Bruxelles. monthly.   DT1.E84
    L.C. has 1957–76
Europe outremer. Paris. monthly.   JV1801.E65
    L.C. has 1973+
L'Express. Paris. weekly.   AP20.E926
    L.C. has 1953+
France-Eurafrique. Paris. monthly.   JV1801.U53
    L.C. has 1949–80
al-Ḥawādith. Beirut. weekly.   AP95.A6H29
    L.C. has 1962+ (June–Sept. 1976 lacking)
Le Monde diplomatique. Paris. monthly.   JX3.M65
    L.C. has 1964+
Le Moniteur africain. Dakar. weekly.   HF46.M6
    L.C. has 1974–78 (scattered issues lacking)
Mundo Obrero. Madrid. weekly.   HD8581.M66
    L.C. has 1977+ (scattered issues lacking)
Le Politicien. Dakar. monthly.   DLC
    L.C. has 1977+ (scattered issues lacking)
Politique hebdo. Paris.   D839.P64
    L.C. has 1970+
Remarques africaines. Bruxelles.   DT1.R34
    Frequency varies.
    Continued by *Remarques arabo-africaines.*
    L.C. has 1962–78
Remarques arabo-africaines. Bruxelles. monthly (irregular)   DT1.R34
    Continues *Remarques africaines.*
    L.C. has 1978+ (scattered issues lacking)
Révolution africaine. Alger. weekly.   AP27.R38
    L.C. has 1963+ ; issues for 1963–78 on microfilm (DLC-Micro
    PR no. 03013 AP)
Revue africaine de strategie. Paris. quarterly.   UA855.R48
    L.C. has 1979+
Revue française d'études politiques africaines. Paris.
    monthly.   DT1.R4
    L.C. has 1966–81
Semanário. Luanda.   DLC
    L.C. has issues of Apr.–Aug. 1978.
South African digest. Pretoria. weekly.   DT751.S599
    L.C. has 1954+
Spécial. Bruxelles. weekly.   AP22.S66
    L.C. has 1970–79
Spiegel. Hamburg. weekly.   AP30.S66
    L.C. has 1947+
Sudanow. Khartoum. monthly.   DT154.1.S92
    L.C. has 1976+
Tempo. Maputo. weekly.   AP68.T45
    L.C. has 1974+
Tricontinental. Havana. monthly.   D843.T7
    L.C. has 1966+
Verde Olivo. La Habana. weekly.   AP63.V435
    L.C. has 1959+
Weekly review. Nairobi.   HF1410.W4
    L.C. has 1975+
West Africa. London. weekly.   DT491.W4
    L.C. has 1917+

Zaire. Journal officiel de la République du Zaire.   DLC-LL
  Kinshasa. semimonthly.
    L.C. has 1971 + ; vols. for 1971–77 held also on microfilm
    (Microfilm LL-02103 Law)
Zaire. Kinshasa. weekly.   AP27.Z35
    L.C. has 1969 +

Sub-Saharan Africa

General

1

U.S. *Central Intelligence Agency*. National basic intelligence factbook. 1975?–80. [Washington] maps.   G122.U56a
   Semiannual, 1975?–79; annual, 1980.
   Continues: *National Basic Intelligence Factbook*, issued by the U.S. Office of Geographic and Cartographic Research.
   Superseded by *The World Factbook* (entry 15).
   For each African country, basic data is given on population, political organization, economic conditions, communications, and military forces, plus information on the influence of Communist and "other political or pressure groups" and a list of those international organizations with which the country is affiliated.
   L.C. has 1975–80.

2

U.S. *Foreign Broadcast Information Service*. Daily report: Middle East & Africa. Apr. 1, 1980+ [Washington?]   DLC-Micro
   Supersedes its *Daily Report: Middle East & North Africa* and *Daily Report: Sub-Saharan Africa*, both issued in the period Apr. 1, 1974–Mar. 31, 1980.

3

AF press clips. v. 1+ May 20, 1966+ Washington, Bureau of African Affairs, U.S. Dept. of State. weekly.   DLC
   Each issue reproduces press clippings on Africa "for reference use by the Bureau of African Affairs."
   L.C. has 1974+; held by the African Section.

4

Adelman, Kenneth L. U.S. security interests and options in Central Africa; final report. [Arlington, Va.] SRI International, Strategic Studies Center, 1977. 42 p. (SRI International. Strategic Studies Center. Technical note, SSC-TN-6576-1)

"SRI project 6576."
   Prepared for the Office, Assistant Secretary of Defense, International Security Affairs.
   "This study analyzes the impact of recent political, economic, and military developments in Central Africa—Zaire, Angola, and Zambia— and relates them to U.S. security interests in the region, on the continent, and worldwide."—p. ii.
   Abstract in *Government Reports Announcements & Index*, Jan. 5, 1979, p. 24.
   Microfiche. [s.l., Defense Documentation Center, 1978] 1 sheet.   DLC-Sci RR AD-A059280

5

Bailey, Norman A. Some reflections on Portuguese Africa in the year of decision 1974. [s.l.] 1974. 8 leaves. (FAR 20600-N)
   Prepared for the Colloquium on Portuguese Africa, sponsored by the U.S. Dept. of State, Oct. 1974.
   Examined in the former Foreign Affairs Research Documentation Center, U.S. Dept. of State.

6

Basic data on sub-Saharan Africa. Washington, Bureau of Public Affairs, U.S. Dept. of State, 1979. 13 p.   DLC
   "Special report, no. 61."
   Data is provided for 47 "political entities" south of the Sahara on population, ethnic groups, religions, languages, education, labor force, economic conditions, commerce, and United States economic assistance.
   Abstract in *American Statistics Index*, 1979, Abstracts, p. 655.
   Issued also in microfiche. [Washington, Congressional Information Service, 1979?] 1 sheet.
                 DLC-Micro ASI-79 7008-17

7

Clark, G. Edward. Sub-Saharan Africa and the United States: discussion paper. Washington, Office of Public Communication, U.S. Dept. of

7 (cont.)

State; for sale by the Supt. of Docs., U.S. Govt Print. Off., 1980. 46 p., 1 leaf of plates. illus., maps. (United States Department of State publication, 9112)   DT353.5.U6C55   1980

A general introduction to the history, ethnology, languages, political development, and economic conditions of sub-Saharan Africa, with an outline of United States relations with nations of this region.

Table (p. 18), arranged by country, provides information on U.S. official development assistance under Agency for International Development, Public Law 480, Peace Corps, and Export-Import Bank programs for the period 1974–78, plus figures for the same period on assistance from other western nations (e.g., France, Great Britain, Federal Republic of Germany, Canada), oil-producing (OPEC) nations, and Communist states (Soviet Union, China, Eastern European countries).

Other tables give figures on Communist military personnel and economic technicians in certain sub-Saharan nations as of 1978 (p. 31) and on U.S. economic assistance to Africa in the 1979–81 period in terms of bilateral aid and the American share of multilateral aid programs (p. 33).

The Appendix (p. 35–45) includes tables, by country, on population growth rates, population density, life expectancy, major ethnic and religious groups, literacy levels, labor force, gross domestic product, and trade.

Note: The text of this *Discussion Paper*, with an added introduction but without the appendix, appears also in *The Department of State Bulletin*, v. 80, no. 2036, Mar. 1980, p. 1–28, and v. 80, no. 2037, Apr. 1980, p. 1–30 (JX232.A33, v. 80).

8

Country fact sheets. 1975+ [Washington], Foreign Affairs Document and Reference Center, [U.S. Dept. of State] [5] v. (loose-leaf)   DS
    Partial contents: v. 5. Africa.
    For each country covered in vol. 5, basic data is given on the government, legal system, population, economy, military expenditures, balance of payments, commerce, United States assistance programs, U.S. Agency for International Development projects, educational and cultural exchange programs with the United States, and the "foreign investment climate."

9

Eyadema analyzes conditions in Africa, African personality. *In U.S. Joint Publications Research Service.* JPRS 75091. [Springfield, Va., National Technical Information Service, 1980] (Sub-Saharan Africa report, no. 2211) p. 1–4.

Translation of interview with President Gnassingbé Eyadéma of Togo in *Africa*, Dakar, Dec. 1979, p. 50, 51.
    Microfiche. [s.l., 1980]
                          DLC-Micro JPRS 75091

10

Hounsell, John W. A plan for a system to provide developmental information in Africa. Springfield, Va., National Technical Information Service, 1980. 41 p.

Prepared for the U.S. Agency for International Development.

"Outlines the functions and components of an African Information Network that would provide scientific, technical, economic, social, and other information for development to planners, administrators, extension workers, businesses, and individuals."—Abstract.

Abstract in *Government Reports Announcements & Index*, Sept. 12, 1980, p. 3897.

Microfiche. [Springfield, Va., National Technical Information Service, 1980] 1 sheet.
                          DLC-Sci RR PB 80 189806

11

Lilley, Robert J. Africa and change. Carlisle Barracks, Pa., Strategic Studies Institute, U.S. Army War College, 1981. 23 p. (Strategic issues research memorandum)

"The author analyzes present trends and projects these trends through the decade of the 1980's which will be a time of increasing economic woes and political instability throughout the African continent. The author sees three issues which will impact on US interests in the coming decade: the expansion of East-West competition in Africa, racial confrontation in South Africa, and access to resources."—Foreword.

Microfiche. [s.l., Defense Technical Information Center, 1981] 1 sheet. DLC-Sci RR AD-A098679

12

McGee, Gale W. Congress for Peace through Law. Congressional record, 94th Congress, 2d session, v. 122, July 1, 1976: 22114-22117.   J11.R5 v. 122
    Remarks in the U.S. Senate.
    Includes text of statement before the Congress by Paul Bomani, Tanzanian Ambassador to the United States, on African economic and political problems.

13

Reference aid: abbreviations in the African press. [Springfield, Va., National Technical Information Service], 1975. 162 p. (U.S. Joint Publications Research Service. JPRS 64918)
                          AS36.U57 JPRS 64918

14

Socio-economic indicators of basic needs, progress and commitment for 92 developing countries. [Washington?], Bureau for the Near East, [U.S. Agency for International Development], 1978. 60 p.

Covers 33 sub-Saharan African nations.

Includes tables on distribution of wealth, economic growth, utilization and productivity of labor, agricultural productivity, health and nutrition conditions, population and fertility, and basic education.

Abstract in *American Statistics Index*, 1979, Abstracts, p. 663–664.

Microfiche. [Washington, Congressional Information Service, 1979?]

DLC-Micro ASI:79 7208-16

15

The World factbook. 1981+ Washington, Directorate of Intelligence, Central Intelligence Agency. maps. annual. DLC

Supersedes the Agency's *National Basic Intelligence Factbook* (entry 1); includes the same basic data.

L.C. has 1981+

Bibliographies

16

U.S. *Dept. of State. Office of External Research.* Foreign affairs research special papers available: Africa, sub-Sahara. [Washington?], 1976. 128 p. (U.S. Dept. of State. Department of State publication, no. 8879) DLC

"This publication is a cumulative listing of papers on Sub-Saharan Africa collected by the Foreign Affairs Research Documentation Center between June 1971 and August 1976. These studies represent research done by individual scholars, universities, and research centers either independently or with Government funds. Subjects covered deal primarily with social sciences and humanities as they relate to foreign affairs and include such topics as education, leadership, and colonialism."

The former Documentation Center's cumulative lists complemented its monthly publication, *Foreign Affairs Research Papers Available.*

Many citations in the Sub-Saharan Africa list are to papers delivered at academic conferences.

17

U.S. *Dept. of State. Office of Long-Range Assessments and Research.* Government-sponsored research on foreign affairs. 1976/77+ Washington.

JX1293.U6U47a

Annual, 1976/77; quarterly, July/Sept. 1977–

Continues: *Government-Supported Research on Foreign Affairs; Inventory of Research Projects Completed and in Progress.*

Vols. for 1976/77–Mar. 1980 issued by the Office of External Research, U.S. Dept. of State.

"Describes the external research projects reported by sponsoring Agencies of the Federal Government. Projects included are those supported by research contracts and grants that deal with some aspect of a foreign society or of international relations."—Dec. 1981 issue, p. iii.

L.C. has 1976/77+

Note: A number of American research studies on various topics concerning sub-Saharan Africa are recorded in the following U.S. Government periodicals: *A.I.D. Research & Development Abstracts* (DLC-Sci RR), issued quarterly since July 1973 by the Agency for International Development; *Government Reports Announcements & Index* (Z7916.G58), a biweekly publication of the National Technical Information Service, and *Resources in Education* (Z5813.R4), issued monthly by the Educational Resources Information Center. Another source, *Foreign Affairs Research Papers Available* (Z7163.F73a), a monthly list of the former Foreign Affairs Research Documentation Center, Department of State, ceased publication in Feb. 1979; (an "informal" supplementary list appeared in Apr. 1979).

18

U.S. *Dept. of the Army.* Africa, problems and prospects: a bibliographic survey. Washington, for sale by the Supt. of Docs., U.S. Govt. Print. Off., 1977. xv, 577 p. maps (3 fold. in pocket)

Z3501.U47 1977

"DA pam 550-17-1."

Annotated guide to books, documents, and periodical literature, updating the agency's 1973 guide, *Africa: A Bibliographic Survey of Literature.*

Appendixes (p. 117–577) include "Military Power in Africa: Regional and Country-by-Country Surveys," reprinted from *Almanac of World Military Power*, "Mineral Industries of Africa," excerpted from *Mineral Industries of Africa*, and reprints of the Background Notes series issued by the Department of State covering each country.

Abstract in *Government Reports Announcements & Index*, Sept. 28, 1979, p. 27.

Issued also in microfiche. [s.l., Defense Documentation Center, 1979] 6 sheets.

DLC-Sci RR AD-A068837

19

U.S. *Library of Congress. Library of Congress Office, Nairobi.* Accessions list, Eastern Africa. v. 1+ Jan. 1968+ Nairobi. Z3516.U52
Z663.28.A5

Quarterly, 1968–71; bimonthly, 1972+

19 (cont.)

Includes Annual Serial Supplement and Annual Publishers Directory.

A record of publications acquired by the Office from Burundi, Comoros, Djibouti, Ethiopia, Kenya, Madagascar, Malawi, Mauritius, Réunion, Rwanda, Seychelles, Somalia, Sudan, Tanzania, Uganda, and Zambia, with occasional acquisitions from adjacent African countries.

Inclusion of a publication in the *Accessions List* does not assure permanent retention by the Library of Congress.

L.C. has 1968+

20

Africa. Washington, Supt. of Docs., U.S. Govt. Print. Off., 1981. 13 p.　　　　　DLC

"Subject bibliography. SB-284."

A list of publications about Africa available from the Superintendent of Documents, U.S. Government Printing Office, Washington, D.C. It includes citations to the "Country Studies" prepared under Government auspices by Foreign Area Studies, American University, the "Background Notes" and "Post Report" series of the Department of State, together with a listing of monographs issued by the Department of Commerce, Library of Congress, and other Government agencies.

L.C. has also lists issued in 1977, 1978, and 1980.

21

Africa: selected references. Supplement. no. 1+ 1961+ Maxwell Air Force Base, Ala., Air University, Library. annual. (U.S. Air University. Library. Special bibliography, no. 159)　　DLC

A list of monographs, periodical articles, and U.S. Government documents arranged by subject, region, and/or country. Includes citations to studies issued by United States armed forces training schools and to material prepared by the Joint Publications Research Service (JPRS).

L.C. has 1961+; held by the African & Middle Eastern Division.

22

African newspapers in the Library of Congress. [Washington], Newspaper Section, Serial Division, [Library of Congress], 1977. 97 p.　　DLC

Compiled by Frank J. Carroll and John Pluge.

Includes citations to 609 newspapers, indicating holdings.

23

Duisin, Xenia W. Sources of African government documents: a working list. *In* Regan, Muriel.

Information sources on international and foreign national documents. [s.l., 1977] p. 15–18.

Paper prepared for the Social Science and Education Divisions, Special Libraries Association, 1977.

Abstracts in *Resources in Education*, Oct. 1979, p. 124–125, and *Government Reports Announcements & Index*, June 6, 1980, p. 1959.

Microfiche. [Arlington, Va., ERIC Document Reproduction Service; prepared for Educational Resources Information Center, National Institute of Education, 1979] 1 sheet.

DLC-Micro ED171287

24

Mullan, Anthony P. Africana serials in microform in the Library of Congress. [Washington], Microform Section, Library of Congress, 1978. 36 leaves.

DLC

167 entries.

25

Selim, George D. Arab-world newspapers in the Library of Congress. Washington, Near East Section, Library of Congress; [for sale by the Supt. of Docs., U.S. Govt. Print. Off.], 1980. 85 p. (Near East series)　　　　　DLC

Includes holdings statements for Arabic, English, French, and/or Italian newspapers from Djibouti, Ethiopia, Mauritania, Somalia, and Sudan.

26

South, Aloha. Guide to Federal archives relating to Africa, researched and compiled by Aloha South. [Honolulu], Crossroads Press, [c1977] xx, 556 p. (The Archives and bibliographic series)

Z3509.S67

A part of the series of "Guides to the Sources of African History" sponsored by the International Council of Archives.

Compiled by the U.S. National Archives and Records Service under the auspices of the African Studies Association, the guide is "designed to make available the vast quantity of Africa-related material housed in the National Archives."— p. xiii.

27

Witherell, Julian W. The United States and Africa: guide to U.S. official documents and Government-sponsored publications on Africa, 1785–1975. [Washington], African Section, Library of Congress; [for sale by the Supt. of Docs., U.S. Govt. Print. Off.], 1978. xix, 949 p.　　Z3501.W57

8,827 entries.

Directories

28

African Bibliographic Center. AF-LOG: African interests of American organizations. Washington, 1975. 886 p. (Current reading list series, v. 11, no. 2)   DT2.A28 1975

Preparation of the directory supported by a contract between the U.S. Dept. of State and Development Alternatives, inc.

"Describes the current programs of more than 1,600 American non-governmental organizations and institutions interested in Africa."

Note: Updated and supplemented by *AF-LOG II: African Affairs in Washington, D.C., 1980–81* (DT2.5.A33), issued by the African Bibliographic Center as vol. 12, no. 2 in its Current Reading List Series.

29

Bhatt, Purnima M. Scholars' guide to Washington, D.C. for African studies; consultants, Daniel G. Matthews, Michael R. Winston, Julian W. Witherell. Washington, Smithsonian Institution Press, 1980. 347 p. (Scholars' guide to Washington, D.C., no. 4)   Z3501.B48

Developed under a grant from the U.S. Office of Education.

At head of title: Woodrow Wilson International Center for Scholars.

Note: Additional information on Washington-area collections, especially for northeastern Africa, can be found in *Scholars' Guide to Washington, D.C. for Middle Eastern Studies* (Z3013.6.D67), by Steven R. Dorr (Washington, Smithsonian Institution Press, 1981).

30

Duffy, David, *and* Barbara Jacobs. Directory of Third World studies in the United States. Waltham, Mass., Crossroads Press, c1981. 463 p.
                    HC59.7.D78

"Preparation of this work was made possible through a grant from the Program of Research Tools and Reference Works of the National Endowment for the Humanities."

"Third World" is defined as including Africa and the Middle East, Asia (excluding the Soviet Union), and Latin America.

Agriculture

31

U.S. *Dept. of Agriculture. Economic Research Service.* Africa and West Asia agricultural situation: review and outlook. 1976/77. [Washington] map. annual. (Foreign agricultural economic report)
                    HD1411.F59

Vol. for 1976/77 issued as Foreign Agricultural Economic Report, no. 138.

Continues: *Africa and West Asia Agricultural Situation: Review and Outlook* (entry 33).

Issued as a supplement to *World Agricultural Situation* (entry 58).

Superseded by *Africa & West Asia Agricultural Situation: Review and Outlook* (entry 32), issued by the Economics, Statistics, and Cooperatives Service, U.S. Dept. of Agriculture.

L.C. has 1976/77.

Note: Individual issues of this and other U.S. Government periodicals concerned with African agriculture can be identified through *American Statistics Index: A Comprehensive Guide and Index to the Statistical Publications of the U.S. Government* (Washington, Congressional Information Service; Z7554.U5A46).

32

———— Agricultural situation: Africa and the Middle East; review and outlook. 1977/78+ [Washington] map. annual.   HD1411.U624a

Continues: *Africa and West Asia Agricultural Situation: Review and Outlook* (entry 31).

Title varies: 1977/78–1978/79, *Africa and West Asia Agricultural Situation: Review and Outlook.*

Vols. for 1977/78–1978/79 issued by the Economics, Statistics, and Cooperatives Service, U.S. Dept. of Agriculture.

Issued as a supplement to *World Agricultural Situation* (entry 58).

L.C. has 1977/78+

33

———— The agricultural situation in Africa and West Asia. 1963?–1975/76. [Washington] annual. (Foreign agricultural economic report)
                    HD2117.U5

Title varies: 1963?–67, *The Africa and West Asia Agricultural Situation.*

Issued as a supplement to *World Agricultural Situation* (entry 58).

Superseded by the agency's *Africa and West Asia Agricultural Situation: Review and Outlook* (entry 31).

L.C. has 1963–1975/76.

34

U.S. *Dept. of Agriculture. Economics, Statistics, and Cooperatives Service.* Alternative futures for world food in 1985 [by Anthony Rojko, and others] Washington, 1978– (Foreign agricultural economic report, no. 146, 149,   )
                    HD1411.F59 no. 146, etc.

Bibliography: v. 1, p. 113–137.

Some statistical tables include data on African regions.

34 (cont.)

Contents: v. 1. World GOL [Grain, Oilseeds, Livestock] model analytical report.—v. 2. World GOL model supply-distribution and related tables.

35

U.S. *Presidential Commission on World Hunger.* Overcoming world hunger: the challenge ahead: report. Washington, The Commission; for sale by the Supt. of Docs., U.S. Govt. Print. Off., 1980. 251 p.   HD9000.5.U55   1980a

Sol M. Linowitz, chairman.

Occasional brief references to African conditions.

36

Addis Ababa Conference on Soybean Production, Protection, and Utilization, 1974. Soybean production, protection, and utilization: proceedings of a conference for scientists of Africa, the Middle East, and South Asia, October 14–17, 1974, Addis Ababa, Ethiopia; edited by D. K. Whigham; sponsored by the Ethiopian Institute of Agricultural Research and the International Soybean Program. Urbana, College of Agriculture, University of Illinois at Urbana-Champaign, 1975. 266 p. illus. (International agricultural publications)
SB205.S7A32   1974

INTSOY series, no. 6.

Supported by the U.S. Agency for International Development.

Includes country reports for Ethiopia, Ghana, Ivory Coast, Mauritius, Nigeria, Rhodesia, Rwanda, Sierra Leone, and Tanzania.

Issued also in microfiche. [Washington, U.S. Agency for International Development, 1975?] 3 sheets.   DLC-Sci RR PN-AAB-269

37

Agricultural development in Africa: issues of public policy; edited by Robert H. Bates [and] Michael F. Lofchie. [New York], Praeger, 1980. 451 p. map.
HD2117.A35

"The editors wish to acknowledge the support of the African Studies Center, University of California, Los Angeles; the Division of Social Sciences, California Institute of Technology; and the National Science Foundation."

Based on a colloquium sponsored by the African Studies Center at the University of California, Los Angeles, in 1978.

Bibliography: p. 425–440.

Note: Selected chapters of the publication are cited separately in this guide; they can be identified through the index under *Agricultural Development in Africa.*

38

Berry, Leonard, Richard Ford, *and* Richard

Hosier. The impact of irrigation on development: issues for a comprehensive evaluation study. [Washington?] Studies Division, Bureau for Program and Policy Coordination, U.S. Agency for International Development, 1980. 70 p. (A.I.D. program evaluation discussion paper, no. 9)

Bibliography: p. 52–60.

Includes tables on irrigation in Africa.

Examined in the Documentation Center, Sahel Development Program, AID, Washington, D.C.

39

Cohen, John M. Land tenure and rural development in Africa. *In* Agricultural development in Africa: issues of public policy; edited by Robert H. Bates [and] Michael F. Lofchie [New York], Praeger, 1980. p. 349–400.   HD2117.A35

Publication supported in part by the National Science Foundation.

40

Development Alternatives, inc. Strategies for small farmer development: an empirical study of rural development projects in The Gambia, Ghana, Kenya, Lesotho, Nigeria, Bolivia, Colombia, Mexico, Paraguay and Peru: a study, prepared under contract to Office of Development Administration, Technical Assistance Bureau, Agency for International Development, U.S. Department of State, Washington, D.C.; Elliott R. Morss [and others] Boulder, Colo., Westview Press, 1976– [2] v. maps.   HD1417.D48   1976

Includes bibliographical references.

Vol. 2 includes case studies on The Gambia, Ghana, Kenya, Lesotho, and Nigeria.

An "executive summary" ([56] p. FAR 26683-N) examined in the former Foreign Affairs Research Documentation Center, Department of State.

41

Farming Systems Research Unit—SAFGRAD; report of progress, December 8, 1978 – December 7, 1979 and plan of work for 1980. West Lafayette, Ind., Division of International Programs in Agriculture, Purdue University, 1980. 1 v. (loose-leaf)

Prepared for the U.S. Agency for International Development under contract AID/afr-C-1492.

SAFGRAD: Semi-Arid Food Grain Research and Development Program.

Examined in the Development Information Center, AID, Washington, D.C.

42

Food for development in sub-Saharan Africa, [by] Paul Russell [et al.] [Washington], Office of Development Resources, [U.S. Agency for International Development], 1980. [216] p.

42 (cont.)

Includes chapters on food availability, the role of the Public Law 480 program in Africa, assessment of food assistance programs in sub-Saharan Africa in the 1970s, and the outlook for food assistance in the 1980s. This is followed by statistical tables for individual countries indicating gross national product, inflation rate, external debt, trade balance, and food supply and production.

Examined in the Documentation Center, Sahel Development Program, AID, Washington, D.C.

43

Guide for field crops in the tropics and the subtropics, edited by Samuel C. Litzenberger. Washington, Office of Agriculture, Technical Assistance Bureau, Agency for International Development, 1974. 321 p. maps.   SB111.G84

Bibliography: p. 313–315.

Includes occasional references to crops in sub-Saharan Africa.

44

Interafrican Committee for Hydraulic Studies. Savanna regional water resources and land use: Ouagadougou, Upper Volta. New York, TAMSADG, 1978–79. 7 v. maps.

GB812.I57   1978

Includes bibliographies.

Prepared under a grant from the U.S. Agency for International Development; vol. 6 prepared under subcontract by the Earth Satellite Corporation.

Issued also in a French and/or English edition.

TAMSADG: Tippetts-Abbett-McCarthy-Stratton Agricultural Development Group.

Contents: v. 1. Report.—v. 2. Mapfolio.—v. 3. Appendices.—v. 4. Study proposals.—v. 5. Existing and planned water use.—v. 6. Existing land use.—v. 7. Water requirements.

L.C. has v. 1, 4–6; has also v. 4 and 7 in the French and/or English edition (TC519.S18I57 1975). All seven volumes have been examined on microfiche in the Development Information Center, Agency for International Development, Washington, D.C.; the identification number for each volume is as follows: v. 1 (PN-AAG-643); v. 2 (PN-AAG-645); v. 3 (PN-AAG-646); v. 4 (PN-AAG-647); v. 5 (PN-AAG-649); v. 6 (PN-AAG-879); v. 7 (PN-AAG-881).

45

Johnston, Bruce F. Agricultural production potentials and small farmer strategies in sub-Saharan Africa. *In* Agricultural development in Africa: issues of public policy; edited by Robert H. Bates [and] Michael F. Lofchie. [New York], Praeger, 1980. p. 67–97.   HD2117.A35

Publication supported in part by the National Science Foundation.

46

Lateef, Noel V. The in-between technology; animal power may be 'appropriate' for much of the African greenhouse. War on hunger, Nov. 1977: [11–13] illus.   HD9000.1.W37 v. 11

"Sub-Saharan Africa has the largest area of arable land with year-round growing potential of any continent: 724 million hectares, of which over 90% lies in the tropical belt.... The key to economic development for countries in sub-Saharan Africa lies in raising the productivity of the small farmer, who constitutes 70–80% of the population."—p. [11]

47

Lele, Uma J. Designing rural development programmes: lessons from past experience in Africa. Nairobi, Institute for Development Studies, University of Nairobi, 1974. 29 p. (Nairobi. University. Institute of Development Studies. Discussion paper, no. 213)   HD2118 1974.L44

Abstract in *A.I.D. Research and Development Abstracts*, Jan. 1977, p. 38.

Issued also by the Rural Development Committee, Center for International Studies, Cornell University, as its Rural Development Occasional Paper no. 5 (Ithaca, N.Y., 1975. 54 p.); in microfiche ([Washington, U.S. Agency for International Development, 1975?] 1 sheet)

DLC-Sci RR PN-AAC-186

Note: The author's research paper of the same title, prepared for the Second International Seminar on Change in Agriculture, Reading, Eng., 1974, abstracted in *Government Reports Announcements & Index*, Oct. 12, 1979, p. 29, is also available in microfiche ([Springfield, Va., National Technical Information Service, 1979] 1 sheet).   DLC-Sci RR PB-297664

48

National Research Council. *Committee on African Agricultural Research Capabilities*. African agricultural research capabilities [by the] Committee on African Agricultural Research Capabilities, Board on Agriculture and Renewable Resources of the Commission on Natural Resources and the Board on Science and Technology for International Development of the Commission on International Relations, National Research Council. Washington, National Academy of Sciences, 1974, xv, 221 p. illus., map (fold. in pocket)   S535.A2N37

Bibliography: p. 203–205.

Supported by the U.S. Agency for International Development under contract no. AID/csd-2584.

Emphasis is on sub-Saharan Africa.

48 (cont.)

Abstract in *Appropriate Technology Information for Developing Countries*, 2d ed., 1979, p. 109.

Issued also in microfiche. [Washington, U.S Agency for International Development, 1974?] 3 sheets.   DLC-Sci RR PN-AAB-051

49

Pelletier, Renée. Irrigation projects reported. *In* U.S. *Joint Publications Research Service*. JPRS 74585. [Springfield, Va., National Technical Information Service, 1979] (Sub-Saharan Africa report, no. 2178) p. 2–7.

Translation of article in *Africa*, Dakar, Oct. 1979, p. 61–63.

Microfiche. [s.l., 1979]
DLC-Micro JPRS 74585

50

Percy, Charles H. Shortage of food reserves and production in developing countries. Congressional record, 94th Congress, 2d session, v. 122, May 6, 1976: 12809-12813.   J11.R5 v. 122

Remarks in the U.S. Senate.

Senator Percy notes drought and famine conditions in Ethiopia and West Africa; includes articles describing this situation from the *Chicago Tribune*.

51

Reidinger, Richard B. World fertilizer review and prospects to 1980/81. Washington, Economic Research Service, U.S. Dept. of Agriculture, 1976. 34 p. (Foreign agricultural economic report, no. 115)   HD1411.F59 no. 115

Includes bibliographical references.

The situation in sub-Saharan Africa is covered in brief reports and in statistical tables.

52

Savanna regional water resources and land use project; semi-annual report. July/Dec. 1973?–Jan./Mar. 1979? [New York], TAMS Agricultural Development Group.

Prepared for the Comité interafricain d'études hydrauliques, Ouagadougou, under contract AID/afr-C-1041 with the U.S. Agency for International Development.

Frequency varies: no. 12 covers period Jan./Mar. 1979.

No more published?

Vols. for Jan./June 1974, July/Dec. 1976, July/Dec. 1977, July/Dec. 1978, and Jan./Mar. 1979 examined in the Development Information Center, AID, Washington, D.C.

The following reports, issued also in microfiche, are held by DLC-Sci RR:

July/Dec. 1977. 1 sheet. PN-AAG-182.
July/Dec. 1978. 1 sheet. PN-AAG-343.

53

Seminar in Food Storage and Handling Practices, *Dakar, Senegal*, Nov. 4–8, 1974. [Report] [Washington, Agency for International Development, 1974] 81 p. illus.

Microfiche. [Washington, U.S. Agency for International Development, 1974?] 1 sheet (DLC-Sci RR PN-AAB-369); and [Sahel Documents and Dissertations. Ann Arbor, Mich., University Microfilms International, 1980] 2 sheets (DLC-Micro 5357 AS302).

54

Swanson, Richard A. Beekeeping and development programs; apiculture in tropical climates conference report. Ouagadougou, Upper Volta, U.S. Agency for International Development, 1976. 79 p. illus.

Bibliography: p. 78–79.

Microfiche. [Sahel Documents and Dissertations. Ann Arbor, Mich., University Microfilms International, 1980] 1 sheet.
DLC-Micro Microfiche 5357 AS 026

55

University of Michigan. *Center for Research on Economic Development*. Francophone Africa program; annual report. 1969/70?–1980/81. Ann Arbor.   MiU-RE

Program sponsored by the U.S. Agency for International Development under contract AID/csd-2547.

Primarily concerned with agricultural development in Central and West Africa.

MiU-RE has 1977/78+; reports for 1975/76–1976/77 examined in the Documentation Center, Sahel Development Program, AID, Washington, D.C.

56

Weather-crop yield relationships in drought-prone countries of sub-Saharan Africa: final report to U.S. Department of State, Agency for International Development, Office of Foreign Disaster Assistance. [s.l.], 1979. 2 v. (177, 235 p.)

At head of title: U.S. National Oceanic and Atmospheric Administration, Center for Environmental Assessment Services, Climatic Impact Assessment Division, Models Branch.

Prepared in cooperation with the University of Missouri-Columbia.

Covers Benin, Central African Republic, Chad,

56 (cont.)

The Gambia, Mali, Mauritania, Niger, Nigeria, Senegal, Sudan, and Upper Volta.

Microfiche. [Sahel Documents and Dissertations. Ann Arbor, Mich., University Microfilms International, 1980] 6 sheets (DLC-Micro Microfiche 5357 AS358); vol. 2 (appendix) issued in microfiche by the Defense Technical Information Agency (1980. 3 sheets. DLC-Sci RR AD-A085248).

57

Whigham, D. K. International soybean variety experiment; first report of results. Urbana, College of Agriculture, University of Illinois at Urbana-Champaign, 1975. 161 p. map. (International Soybean Program. INTSOY series, no. 8)
SB205.S7W47

"Support for the research reported and the preparation of this publication was provided by the United States Agency for International Development under Contract No. AID/cm/ta-c-73-19 and the College of Agriculture, University of Illinois at Urbana-Champaign."

Agronomic data on Africa is given on p. 26–41.

58

World agricultural situation. [Washington], Economics, Statistics, and Cooperatives Service, U.S. Dept. of Agriculture.   HD1401.W63

Issued three times a year—June, September, and December.

Includes brief reports and statistical tables on the African agricultural situation.

59

World food aid needs and availabilities, 1981. [Washington], Economic Research Service, U.S. Dept. of Agriculture, [1981] 114 p. illus. (Foreign agricultural economic report, no. 168)
HD1411.F59 no. 168

Africa and the Middle East are covered specifically on p. 26–41, 73–96.

Bibliographies

60

Baron, Donald. Land reform in sub-Saharan Africa: an annotated bibliography; a report prepared for the Office of Rural Development, Agency for International Development, under RSSA USDA 4.77. [Washington, Dept. of Agriculture], 1978. 46 p.   DNAL

Issued also in microfiche. [Washington, U.S. Agency for International Development, 1978?] 1 sheet (DLC-Sci RR PN-AAG-726).

Note: Citations to U.S. Government-sponsored studies in this field are also found in *Land Tenure and Agrarian Reform in Africa and the Near East: an Annotated Bibliography, Compiled by the Staff of the Land Tenure Center Library under the Direction of Teresa J. Anderson, Librarian* (Boston, G. K. Hall, 1976. xxiv, 423p. Z7164.L3W56 1976).

61

Catalogue of research literature for development, produced under programs of the Bureau for Technical Assistance, U.S. Agency for International Development (A.I.D.), Washington, U.S. Agency for International Development, 1976–1977. 2 v.
Z7164.U5C38

Contents: v. 1. Food production and nutrition. —v. 2. Food production and nutrition, development and economics, education and human resources, health, selected development areas.

62

Dejene, Tekola, *and* Scott E. Smith. Experience in rural development: a selected, annotated bibliography of planning, implementing, and evaluating rural development in Africa. [Washington, Overseas Liaison Committee, American Council on Education], 1973. 48 p. (American Council on Education. Overseas Liaison Committee. OLC paper, no. 1)   Z5075.A4D44

At head of title: Development from below.

Activities of the Overseas Liaison Committee are supported in part through a contract with the U.S. Agency for International Development.

63

Landberg, Leif C. W. A bibliography for the anthropological study of fishing industries and marine communities. Kingston, University of Rhode Island, 1973. 572 p.   Z5118.M3L35

Supported by a research grant from the International Center for Marine Resources Development, which was established with a grant from the U.S. Agency for International Development.

Africa is specifically covered on p. 363-408.

64

——— ——— Supplement, 1973–1977. Kingston, International Center for Marine Resource Development, University of Rhode Island, 1979.

Held by the Library, International Center for Marine Resource Development, University of Rhode Island.

65

Lawani, S. M., *and* M. O. Odubanjo. A bibliography of yams and the genus *Dioscorea* Ibadan, Nigeria, International Institute of Tropical Agriculture, 1976. 192 p.

1,562 entries.

65 (cont.)

Abstract in *A.I.D. Research and Development Abstracts*, Jan. 1978, p. 38.

Microfiche. [Washington, U.S. Agency for International Development, 1976?] 3 sheets.

DLC-Sci RR PN-AAC-745

66

Morris, Robert F. Postharvest food losses in developing countries: a bibliography. Washington, National Academy of Sciences, 1978. 356 p.

Prepared for the Steering Committee on Postharvest Food Losses in Developing Countries, Board on Science and Technology for International Development, Commission on International Relations, National Research Council, for the Office of Agriculture, Bureau for Development Support, U.S. Agency for International Development.

Published to accompany *Postharvest Food Losses in Developing Countries* (HD9000.4.N37 1978), issued by the Board on Science and Technology for International Development of the National Research Council.

Includes numerous citations to monographs and periodical articles on conditions in sub-Saharan Africa.

Abstract in *A.I.D. Research and Development Abstracts*, v. 7, no. 2, 1979, p. 2.

Microfiche. [Washington, U.S. Agency for International Development, 1978?] 4 sheets.

DLC-Sci RR PN-AAG-345

67

Newman, Mark D. Changing patterns of food consumption in tropical Africa; a working bibliography. East Lansing, Dept. of Agricultural Economics, Michigan State University, 1978. 12 p. (African Rural Economy Program. Working paper, no. 23) MiEM

Prepared for the U.S. Agency for International Development.

Abstract in *A.I.D. Research and Development Abstracts*, July 1978, p. 40–41.

Issued also in microfiche. [Washington, U.S. Agency for International Development, 1978?] 1 sheet. DLC-Sci RR PN-AAF-043

The following items (entries 68–72) include citations to studies on agricultural credit in various sub-Saharan countries:

68

Ohio. State University, *Columbus. Dept. of Agricultural Economics and Rural Sociology*. Agricultural credit and rural savings II, prepared in cooperation with the A.I.D. Reference Center. Washington, Agency for International Development, Dept. of

State, 1976. 70 p. (U.S. Agency for International Development. A.I.D. bibliography series: Agriculture, no. 8) Z5074.C7034 1976

First ed., 1972, by Ohio State University Capital Formation and Technological Change Project.

69

———— Agricultural credit and rural savings III. Washington, Agency for International Development, 1977. 56 p. (U.S. Agency for International Development. A.I.D. bibliography series: Agriculture, no. 9) OU

70

———— Annotated bibliography on agricultural credit and rural savings IV. [Columbus?], 1980. 160 p. DLC

Prepared by the Department's Agricultural Finance Program.

Abstract in *A.I.D. Research & Development Abstracts*, v. 9, no. 3, 1981, p. 33–34.

Issued also in microfiche. [Washington, U.S. Agency for International Development, 1980?] 2 sheets. DLC-Sci RR PN-AAJ-340

71

———— Annotated bibliography on agricultural credit and rural savings V. [Columbus?], 1980. 60 p. OU

Prepared by the Department's Agricultural Finance Program.

Issued also in microfiche. [Washington, U.S. Agency for International Development, 1980?] 1 sheet (PN-AAJ-031); examined in the Development Information Center, Agency for International Development, Washington, D.C.

72

———— Annotated bibliography on agricultural credit and rural savings VI. [Columbus?] 1980. 65 p. DLC

Prepared by the Department's Agricultural Finance Program.

Abstract in *A.I.D. Research & Development Abstracts*, v. 9, no. 4, p. 35.

Issued also in microfiche. [Washington, U.S. Agency for International Development, 1980?] 1 sheet. DLC-Sci RR PN-AAJ-341

73

Orvedal, Arnold C. Bibliography of soils of the tropics. Vol. 1. Tropics in general and tropical Africa. [Washington], U.S. Agency for International Development, Technical Assistance Bureau, Office of Agriculture, [1975] 225 p. (Agriculture technology for developing countries. Technical series bulletin, no. 17) Z5074.S7078

73 (cont.)

"The Agronomy Department of Cornell University arranged for, and monitored, the preparation of this bibliography."

Abstract in *A.I.D. Research and Development Abstracts*, July 1976, p. 14.

Issued also in microfiche. [Washington, U.S. Agency for International Development, 1975?] 3 sheets. DLC-Sci RR PN-AAB-703

74

Riley, Peter, *and* Michael T. Weber. Food and agricultural marketing in developing countries, an annotated bibliography of doctoral research in the social sciences, 1969–1979. East Lansing, Dept. of Agricultural Economics, Michigan State University, 1979. 49 p. (MSU rural development series. Working paper, no. 5) MiEM

Funded by the U.S. Agency for International Development under contract AID/ta-CA-3.

Cited in the *Sahel Bibliographic Bulletin*, no. 3, 1980, p. 171, as including abstracts to 189 American dissertations.

75

Schatzberg, Michael G. Bibliography of small urban centers in rural development in Africa; cover photo, by Jean Tabachnick; edited by Aidan Southall. Madison, African Studies Program, University of Wisconsin-Madison, 1979. 246 p. Z7164.U7S25

Supported in part by a grant from the Office of Urban Development, U.S. Agency for International Development.

76

Utah. State University of Agriculture and Applied Science, *Logan*. Bibliography of water management, compiled by Diane Polchow, Mary Jo Lindberg, [and] Lynne C. Gabrish. Logan, Dept. of Agricultural and Irrigation Engineering, Utah State University, [1974] 352 p. Z5074.W3U83 1974

"Contract AID/csd-2459."

Includes occasional citations to sub-Saharan Africa.

77

VanDyk, David. Audio-visual techniques for rural development: a working bibliography. East Lansing, Dept. of Agricultural Economics, Michigan State University, 1980. 17 p. (African rural economy program. Working paper: special number)

Prepared for the U.S. Agency for International Development under grant agreement AID/afr-G-1261.

Examined in the Documentation Center, Sahel Development Program, AID, Washington, D.C.

Agricultural Education and Extension

78

Association for the Advancement of Agricultural Sciences in Africa. Proceedings of the Second General Conference, Dakar, Senegal, 24–28 March 1975: theme, Making agricultural research more meaningful to farmers. Rapport de la deuxième conférence générale: thème, Comment rendre la recherche agricole plus profitable aux paysans. [Addis Ababa, 1975] 884 p. (in 2 v.) S542.A4A87 1975

Supported in part by the U.S. Agency for International Development.

79

Barwell, Cyril. Farmer training in East-Central and Southern Africa. Rome, Food and Agriculture Organization of the United Nations, 1975. 123 p.

Project sponsored by the Danish International Development Agency.

Bibliography: p. 117–123.

Covers Ethiopia, Kenya, Tanzania, Uganda, Malawi, Zambia, Botswana, Lesotho, and Swaziland.

Abstract in *Resources in Education*, June 1976, p. 45.

Microfiche. [Arlington, Va., ERIC Document Reproduction Service; prepared for Educational Resources Information Center, National Institute of Education, 1976] 2 sheets.
DLC-Sci RR ED117547

80

Hanson, John W. Is the school the enemy of the farm? The African experience. East Lansing, African Rural Economy Program, Dept. of Agricultural Economics, Michigan State University, [1980] 97 p. (African rural economy paper, no. 22) DLC

Bibliography: p. 89–97.

"This paper has been published under the Sahel Secretariat and Documentation Center grant (AID/afr-G-1261) from the U.S. Agency for International Development."

Concerns the role played by primary education in rural development.

Abstract in *A.I.D. Research & Development Abstracts*, v. 9, no. 3, 1981, p. 39–40.

Issued also in microfiche. [Arlington, Va., ERIC Document Resources Information Center, National Institute of Education, 1980] 2 sheets (DLC-Micro ED197928); and [Washington, U.S.

80 (cont.)

Agency for International Development, 1980?] 2 sheets (DLC-Sci RR PN-AAJ-275).

Note: The African Rural Economy Program was established in 1976, succeeding the African Rural Employment Research Network which had functioned in the period 1971–76. In the introduction to *Is the School the Enemy of the Farm?*, the primary mission of the Program is described as furthering "comparative analysis of the development process in Africa with emphasis on both micro and macro level research on the rural economy."

81

Road to the village. Case studies in African community development, [by] James R. Sheffield [et al.] New York, African-American Institute, 1974. 146 p.

Case studies include Partnership for Productivity, a Kenyan pilot project; Tutume Community College, Botswana; Brigades in Botswana, an attempt to provide skills training to primary school leavers; development orientation in rural Ethiopia; and educational opportunities for rural and urban communities in Kenya.

Microfiche. [Arlington, Va., ERIC Document Reproduction Service; prepared for Educational Resources Information Center, National Institute of Education, 1975] 2 sheets.

DLC-Micro ED104753

82

Thimm, H. U. Postgraduate training in agricultural economics at African universities. Bonn, Division of Education, Science and Documentation, German Foundation for International Development, 1976. 153 p.

Cover title.

Based on a seminar held in Nairobi, Kenya, July 22–Aug. 4, 1976.

Includes statements on training programs at individual universities.

Microfiche. [Arlington, Va., ERIC Document Reproduction Service; prepared for Educational Resources Information Center, National Institute of Education, 1977] 2 sheets.

DLC-Micro ED134123

Bird and Insect Control

83

Barr, Barbara A., Carlton S. Koehler, *and* Ray F. Smith. Crop losses, rice: field losses to insects, diseases, weeds, and other pests. Berkeley, UC/AID Pest Management and Related Environmental Protection Project, 1975. 64 p.

SB608.R5B37

"This report was prepared for the United States Agency for International Development by the UC/AID Pest Management and Related Environmental Protection Project at the University of California, Berkeley, under Contract No. AID/csd 3296."

Bibliography: p. 54–64.

Emphasis is on Eastern and Southern Asia with occasional references to Sub-Saharan Africa.

84

DeGrazio, John W., *and* Jerome F. Besser. Bird damage to crops in Africa and Latin America. Denver, Denver Wildlife Research Center, 1974. 8 p.

Abstract in *A.I.D. Research and Development Abstracts*, Sept. 1975, p. 6.

Microfiche. [Washington, U.S. Agency for International Development, 1975?] 1 sheet.

DLC-Sci RR PN-AAB-095

85

Denver Wildlife Research Center. Annual progress report. 1968?+ Denver. illus.   SB993.D44

Cover title: 1970?– Annual report.

Work conducted with funds provided to the U.S. Fish and Wildlife Service by the U.S. Agency for International Development.

Includes occasional reports on research in several African countries, particularly Sudan.

Abstract of 1976 report in *A.I.D. Research and Development Abstracts*, v. 5, no. 4, Apr. 1978, p. 15.

L.C. has 1970+; vols. for 1976–77 held by DLC-Sci RR in microfiche ([Washington, Agency for International Development]) under the following identification numbers: 1976: PN-RAB-687; 1977: PN-AAG-017.

86

Quelea: control of damage to small grains; annual report. 1974?–75? [Denver], Denver Wildlife Research Center. illus.   CoDBW

Issued in cooperation with the U.S. Agency for International Development and the Tropical Pesticides Research Institute, Arusha, Tanzania.

No more published?

CoDBW has 1974–75; these issues also examined in the Development Information Center, U.S. Agency for International Development, Washington, D.C.

87

Vertebrate damage control research: Quelea bird problems in African agriculture; annual report. 1971?–74? [Denver?], Denver Wildlife Research Center.   CoDBW

87 (cont.)

No more published?

Title varies slightly.

Report for 1973 issued in cooperation with the Government of Ethiopia, the Government of Kenya, and the United Nations Development Program in Chad.

Report for 1974 issued in cooperation with the U.S. Agency for International Development and the United Nations Development Program.

Abstract for 1974 report in *A.I.D. Research and Development Abstracts*, v. 3, no. 4, Apr. 1976, p. 6.

CoDBW has 1973–74.

Report for 1974 issued in microfiche. [Washington, U.S. Agency for International Development, 1975?] 1 sheet.　　　DLC-Sci RR PN-RAB-172

Economic Aspects

88

U.S. *Dept. of Agriculture. Economic Research Service.* Indices of agricultural production in Africa and the Near East, 1956 [sic]–75. Washington, 1976. 101 p. (U.S. Dept. of Agriculture. Statistical bulletin, no. 556)　　　HD1751.A5 no. 556

Prepared by the Service's Foreign Demand and Competition Division.

Summary statistical tables on population, total and per capita agricultural output, and total and per capita food production are followed by tables on each African country indicating the output and value of various agricultural commodities, with an average total for period 1961–65 and annual figures for 1966–75.

89

———— Indices of agricultural production in Africa and the Near East, 1967–1976. [Washington, 1977] 52 p. (U.S. Dept. of Agriculture. Economic Research Service. Statistical bulletin, no. 572)

HD1751.A5 no. 572

Tables for each country indicate annual production of various commodities.

90

U.S. *Dept. of Agriculture. Economics, Statistics, and Cooperatives Service.* Indices of agricultural production in Africa and the Near East, 1968–77. [Washington, 1978] 52 p. (U.S. Dept. of Agriculture. Statistical bulletin, no. 610)

HD1751.A5 no. 610

Country tables include statistics on production by commodity, value, and indices of total agricultural and food production, with an average for the period 1961–65 and annual figures for 1968–77.

91

———— Indices of agricultural production in Africa and the Near East, 1969–78. [Washington, 1979] 52 p. map. (U.S. Dept. of Agriculture. Statistical bulletin, no. 623)　　　HD1751.A5 no. 623

Includes, by country, statistics on agricultural output for the base period 1961–65 and annual figures for 1969–78.

Abstract in *Government Reports Announcements & Index*, Oct. 12, 1979, p. 8.

Issued also in microfiche. [Springfield, Va., National Technical Information Service, 1979] 1 sheet.　　　DLC-Sci RR PB–297312

92

———— Indices of agricultural production in Africa and the Near East, 1970–79. [Washington, 1980] 54 p. (U.S. Dept. of Agriculture. Statistical bulletin, no. 637)　　　HD1751.A5 no. 637

Includes, by country, statistics on agricultural output for the base period 1961–65 and annual figures for 1970–79.

Abstract in *Government Reports Announcements & Index*, Oct. 10, 1980, p. 4392.

Issued also in microfiche. [Springfield, Va., National Technical Information Service, 1980] 1 sheet.　　　DLC-Sci RR PB80-198419

93

U.S. *Dept. of Agriculture. Economics, Statistics, and Cooperatives Service.* Global food assessment, 1980. Washington, 1980. 119 p. (Foreign agricultural economic report, no. 159)

HD1411.F59 no. 159

Sub-Saharan Africa is covered on p. 27–60; for each country, there are brief reports on agricultural production, consumption, and trade, and on general economic conditions, together with statistics on U.S. food assistance programs.

Issued also for the Subcommittee on Foreign Agricultural Policy, Committee on Agriculture, Nutrition, and Forestry, U.S. Senate (96th Congress, 2d session. Committee print).

94

U.S. *General Accounting Office.* Coffee, production and marketing systems: report to the Congress by the Comptroller General of the United States. [Washington] 1977. 91 p.

HD9199.A2U564　1977

"B-175530."

Includes occasional references to Africa.

95

African Rural Employment Research Network. African rural employment study: progress report and plan of work, 1972–76. East Lansing, Dept.

95 (cont.)

of Agricultural Economics, Michigan State University, 1974. 110 p. (African Rural Employment Research Network. Working paper, no. 1)

HD1536.A2A34   1974

Bibliography: p. 91–94.

"AID research contract AID/csd 3625."

"African Rural Employment Library, acquisition list no. 22": p. 102–110.

"The Working Paper describes comparative micro-level research being undertaken on the demand for and supply of labor in agricultural production, employment in the rural nonfarm sector and rural-urban migration in Sierra Leone, Nigeria, Ethiopia, as well as detailed plans for a comprehensive analysis of the employment problem based on integrated micro-level research in one country—Sierra Leone."—Preface.

Issued also in microfiche. [Washington, U.S. Agency for International Development, 1974?] 2 sheets.   DLC-Sci RR PN-RAA-520

95a

Bates, Robert H. The commercialization of agriculture and the rise of rural political protest in Black Africa. *In* Food, politics and agricultural development: case studies in the public policy of rural modernization, edited by Raymond F. Hopkins, Donald J. Puchala, and Ross B. Talbot. Boulder, Colo., Westview Press, c1979. p. 227–260.

HD1415.F64

Cited by the Millikan Library, California Institute of Technology, as a study supported by the U.S. Government.

96

―――― Markets and states in tropical Africa: the political basis of agricultural policies. Berkeley, University of California Press, c1981. 178 p.

HD2118   1981.B37

Research supported by a grant from the National Science Foundation.

Bibliography: p. 147–166.

97

―――― Pressure groups, public policy, and agricultural development: a study of divergent outcomes. *In* Agricultural development in Africa: issues of public policy; edited by Robert H. Bates [and] Michael F. Lofchie. [New York], Prager, 1980. p. 170–217.   HD2117.A35

Publication supported in part by the National Science Foundation.

98

Byerlee, Derek. Human resources in rural development: some theoretical issues. [East Lansing, Dept.

of Agricultural Economics, Michigan State University, 1973] [11] p.

Concerns the African Rural Employment Project at Michigan State University.

Microfiche. [Washington, U.S. Agency for International Development, 1973?] 1 sheet.

DLC-Sci RR PN-AAA-987

99

―――― Rural-urban migration in Africa: theory, policy and research implications. [East Lansing, Dept. of Agricultural Economics, Michigan State University, 1973] 44 p.

"Research for this paper was financed by the U.S. Agency for International Development under a contract with Michigan State University to study rural employment in Africa."—p. 1.

Abstract in *A.I.D. Research and Development Abstracts*, July 1975, p. 16–17.

Microfiche. [Washington, U.S. Agency for International Development, 1973?] 1 sheet.

DLC-Sci RR PN-AAA-995

100

Coffee supply and distribution in producing countries, 1960/61–1979/80. Washington, Foreign Agricultural Service, U.S. Dept. of Agriculture, 1979. 60 p. (Foreign agriculture circular. Coffee. FCOF 4–79)   S21.F615

Includes statistics on a number of African countries.

101

Collins, Keith J., Robert B. Evans, *and* Robert D. Barry. World cotton production and use: projections for 1985 and 1990. [Washington] Economics, Statistics, and Cooperatives Service and Foreign Agricultural Service, U.S. Dept. of Agriculture, [1979] 100 p. (Foreign agricultural economic report, no. 154)   HD1411.F59 no. 154

Africa is covered on p. 49–55.

102

DeWilde, John C. Case studies: Kenya, Tanzania, and Ghana. *In* Agricultural development in Africa: issues of public policy; edited by Robert H. Bates [and] Michael F. Lofchie. [New York], Praeger, 1980. p. 113–169.   HD2117.A35

Publication supported in part by the National Science Foundation.

Emphasizes "actual evidence concerning the influence of prices on the production of agricultural commodities in Africa."—p. 113.

103

―――― Price incentives and African agricultural development. *In* Agricultural development in Africa:

103 (cont.)

issues of public policy: edited by Robert H. Bates [and] Michael F. Lofchie. [New York], Praeger, 1980. p. 46–66.   HD2117.A35

Publication supported in part by the National Science Foundation.

104

Due, Jean M. The allocation of credit to small farmers in Tanzania and Zambia. [Urbana, Dept. of Agricultural Economics, University of Illinois at Urbana-Champaign] 1978. 28 p. (Illinois agricultural economics staff paper, 78 E-55)

FAR 29356-N.

Research supported in part by the U.S. AID Mission to Tanzania.

Examined in the former Foreign Affairs Research Documentation Center, U.S. Dept. of State.

105

Eicher, Carl K., *and* Merritt Sargent. The evolution of the African Rural Employment Research Network. East Lansing, African Rural Employment Research Network, Dept. of Agricultural Economics, Michigan State University [1974] 31 p.

On cover: "Paper prepared for 'Workshop on Information Networking,' Office of Research and Institutional Grants, Agency for International Development, Washington, D.C., October 24–25, 1974."

"African Rural Employment Library, acquisition list no. 22: p. 22–30."

Microfiche. [Washington, U.S. Agency for International Development, 1974?] 1 sheet.

DLC-Sci RR PN-RAA-513

106

Food problems and prospects in sub-Saharan Africa: the decade of the 1980's [by] Cheryl Christensen [et al.] [Washington, Africa and Middle East Branch, Economic Research Service, U.S. Dept. of Agriculture, 1981] 293 p. (Foreign agricultural economic report, no. 166)   HD1411.F59 no. 166

"This study examines the long-term trends in food production, consumption, and trade in sub-Saharan Africa, the structure of both demand and production, and policies designed to improve productivity in this region."—Abstract.

Reviewed in *Sahel Bibliographic Bulletin*, Jan. – Mar. 1982, p. 3–4.

107

———— [Washington], African and Middle East Branch, Economics, Statistics, and Cooperatives Service, U.S. Dept. of Agriculture, [1980] 414 p. maps.

Prepared for the U.S. Agency for International Development.

Abstract in *A.I.D. Research & Development Abstracts*, v. 9, no. 3, 1981, p. 4.

Microfiche. [Washington, U.S. Agency for International Development, 1981] 5 sheets.

DLC-Sci RR PN-AAJ-159

108

Gemmill, Gordon, *and* Carl K. Eicher. A framework for research on the economics of farm mechanization in developing countries. East Lansing, Dept. of Agricultural Economics, Michigan State University, 1973. 67 p. illus. (African rural employment paper, no. 6)   HD1417.G44

"This paper has been developed as part of a three year study of rural employment problems in Africa which is being financed under an AID/Washington Contract (AID/csd 3625) with the Department of Agricultural Economics at Michigan State University."

Emphasis is on Sierra Leone, Nigeria, Ethiopia, and Ghana.

Issued also in microfiche. [Washington, U.S. Agency for International Development, 1973?] 1 sheet.   DLC-Sci RR PN-AAA-361

109

Jacqz, Jane W. The absolute poor. Report of a donor agencies meeting on rural development in Africa. [New York], African-American Institute, 1974. 50 p.

"The need for rural change in Africa and strategies for achieving change were the principal topics discussed at a meeting convened on April 3, 1974 by the African-American Institute."

Microfiche. [Arlington, Va., ERIC Document Reproduction Service; prepared for Educational Resources Information Center, National Institute of Education, 1975] 1 sheet.

DLC-Micro ED103338

110

Jessee, David L., *and* Russell H. Brannon. Unemployment and underemployment in rural sectors of the less developed countries: a bibliography. [Lexington?] University of Kentucky, 1977. 148 p. (U.S. Agency for International Development. Economics and Sector Planning Division. Occasional paper, no. 6)

Prepared under contract for the U.S. Agency for International Development.

Each section of the guide, e.g. "Agrarian Sector Policy to Increase Employment and Income," includes citations to monographs and periodical articles on Africa.

110 (cont.)

Abstract in *A.I.D. Research and Development Abstracts*, v. 7, no. 4, 1980, p. 4.

Microfiche. [Washington, U.S. Agency for International Development, 1977?] 2 sheets.

DLC-Sci RR PN-AAD-793

111

Jones, William O. Agricultural trade within tropical Africa: achievements and difficulties. *In* Agricultural development in Africa: issues of public policy; edited by Robert H. Bates [and] Michael F. Lofchie. [New York], Praeger, 1980. p. 311–348.

HD2117.A35

Publication supported in part by the National Science Foundation.

112

—— Agricultural trade within tropical Africa: historical background. *In* Agricultural development in Africa: issues of public policy; edited by Robert H. Bates [and] Michael F. Lofchie. [New York], Praeger, 1980. p. 10–45. HD2117.A35

Publication supported in part by the National Science Foundation.

113

King, David J. Land reform and participation of the rural poor in the development process of African countries. Madison, Land Tenure Center, University of Wisconsin, 1974. 66 p. (Wisconsin. University-Madison. Land Tenure Center. LTC, no. 101) HD966.K55

Prepared for the U.S. Agency for International Development under contract no. AID/csd-2263.

Abstract in *A.I.D. Research and Development Abstracts*, Jan. 1975, p. 32.

114

Liedholm, Carl, *and* Enyinna Chuta. Report on the rural non-farm component of the African Rural Employment Research Project, Njala University College. [East Lansing, Mich.?], 1974. [23] p. (in various pagings)

"This paper has been developed as part of a three year study of rural employment problems in Africa which is being financed under an AID/Washington contract (Aid/csd 3625) with the Department of Agricultural Economics at Michigan State University."

Microfiche. [Washington, U.S. Agency for International Development, 1974?] 1 sheet.

DLC-Sci RR PN-RAA-519

115

Mottin, Marie-France. Mechanization of agriculture results in increased dependency. *In* U.S.

Joint Publications Research Service. JPRS 75314. [Springfield, Va., National Technical Information Service, 1980] (Sub-Saharan Africa report, no. 2223) p. 17–24.

Translation of interview with René Dumont, a French agronomist, in *Demain l'Afrique*, Paris, Jan. 28, 1980, p. 31–35.

Microfiche. [s.l., 1980]

DLC-Micro JPRS 75314

116

1979/80 world sugar crop prospects down. Washington, Foreign Agricultural Service, U.S. Dept. of Agriculture, 1980. 20 p. (Foreign agriculture circular. Sugar. FS 2-80) S21.F615

Includes reports and statistics on a number of African nations.

Note: Reports and statistics on worldwide sugar production, including Africa, are issued periodically in the Foreign Agricultural Service's Sugar series, appearing in its Foreign Agriculture Circular.

117

OAU's food plan examined. *In* U.S. *Joint Publications Research Service*. JPRS 75957. [Springfield, Va., National Technical Information Service, 1980] (Sub-Saharan Africa report, no. 2260) p. 19–24.

Article on a recommendation of the Organization of African Unity's special summit, Lagos, Nigeria, Apr. 1980, calling for "a drive towards self-sufficiency in food production," in *West Africa*, London, May 26, 1980, p. 915–918.

Microfiche. [s.l., 1980]

DLC-Micro JPRS 75957

118

Ogunfowora, O. Income and employment potential of credit and technology in peasant farming. [East Lansing, Dept. of Agricultural Economics, Michigan State University, 1973] 18 p.

Paper presented at the Second Annual Conference of African Rural Employment Research Network, Njala University, Sierra Leone, Nov. 28–Dec. 2, 1973.

Microfiche. [Washington, U.S. Agency for International Development, 1973?] 1 sheet.

DLC-Sci RR PN-AAA-879

119

Record world tea crop harvested in 1978. Washington, Foreign Agricultural Service, U.S. Dept. of Agriculture, 1979. 9 p. (Foreign agriculture circular. Tea and spices. FTEA 4–79)

S21.F615

Includes statistics on African production.

120

Rourk, J. Phillip. Coffee production in Africa. [Washington] Foreign Agricultural Service, U.S. Dept. of Agriculture, 1975. 24 p. (U.S. Foreign Agricultural Service. FAS-M, 266)

S21.Z2383 no. 266

Emphasis is on production, marketing, government policy, and research in the major producing countries: Ethiopia, Ivory Coast, Angola, Uganda, Zaire, Cameroon, Madagascar, Kenya, Tanzania, Burundi, and Rwanda.

Issued also in microfiche. [Washington, Congressional Information Service, 1975?] 1 sheet.

DLC-Micro ASI:75 1926-1.65

121

—— Uptrend in coffee output unlikely in six countries in Asia and Africa. Foreign agriculture, Nov. 1, 1976: 2–4. illus. HD1401.F65 1976

Issued by the U.S. Foreign Agricultural Service.

Includes brief summaries on Kenya, Zaire, Cameroon, and Ivory Coast.

122

Rural employment in tropical Africa: a network approach. Annual report. [1972/73?–1975/76?] [East Lansing, Dept. of Agricultural Economics, Michigan State University] DLC

Report for 1974/75, issued as African Rural Employment Research Network Working Paper no. 8, includes notation that it was "developed as part of a three-year study of rural employment problems in Africa which is being financed under an AID/Washington Contract (AID/csd 3625) with the Department of Agricultural Economics at Michigan State University."

Focus of the 1974/75 report is on Sierra Leone, Ethiopia, and Nigeria.

L.C. has 1974/75.

Vol. for 1974/75 is abstracted in *A.I.D. Research and Development Abstracts*, July 1976, p. 19.

Vol. for 1974/75 issued also in microfiche. [Washington, U.S. Agency for International Development, 1975?] 1 sheet.

DLC-Sci RR PN-AAB-714

123

Small farmer credit in Africa. Washington, Agency for International Development, 1973. 225 leaves. illus., maps. DLC

Issued as vol. 6, Feb. 1973, of *A.I.D. Spring Review of Small Farmer Credit*.

Text of all chapters in English.

Partial contents: Banque nationale pour le développement agricole, *Abidjan*. Banque nationale pour le développement agricole: prêts de soudure (leaves 1–17).—Nnebe, Samuel. Centre national de promotion des entreprises cooperatives (CENAPEC) [Ivory Coast] (leaves 18–36).—Ijose, A. Institutional credit for small-holder farmers: a case study of the Western Nigeria Agricultural Credit Corporation (WNACC) (leaves 37–58).—Ugoh, Sylvester. Small holder agricultural credit in Eastern Nigeria: an analysis of the Fund for Agricultural and Industrial Development (leaves 59–71).—Osuntogun, Adeniyi. Agricultural credit strategies for Nigerian farmers (leaves 72–83).—Goodwin, Joseph B. A review of small farmer credit in Ghana: the rice and maize scheme of the Agricultural Development Bank (leaves 84–130).—Goodman, Daniel. Organizational structure and administrative procedures appropriate for supervised agricultural credit institutions in developing countries (leaves 131–158).

124

Southall, Aidan. Small urban centers in rural development in Africa. Madison, African Studies Program, University of Wisconsin-Madison, 1979. 409 p. maps.

A grant from the Office of Urban Development, U.S. Agency for International Development, assisted in the preparation for publication of the papers collected in this study.

Papers contributed to the study are cited separately in this guide under the names of their individual authors; these contributions can be identified by consulting the index under the title, *Small Urban Centers in Rural Development in Africa.*

Microfiche. [Washington, U.S. Agency for International Development, 1980?] 5 sheets (PN-AAJ-064); examined in the Development Information Center, Agency for International Development, Washington, D.C.

125

Timms, Daniel E. World demand prospects for coffee in 1980, with emphasis on trade by less developed countries. Washington, U.S. Dept. of Agriculture, Economic Research Service; for sale by the Supt. of Docs., U.S. Govt. Print. Off., 1973. 111 p. (Foreign agricultural economic report, no. 86)

HD1411.F59 no. 86

Includes statistics and projections on African coffee production, trade, and value.

126

Todaro, Michael P. Policies affecting rural-urban migration in Africa. Development digest, Apr. 1975: 8–23. HC10.D44 1975

Prepared by the National Planning Association for the U.S. Agency for International Development.

127

World cocoa bean production to be above record 1979/80 harvest. Washington, U.S. Dept. of Agriculture, Foreign Agricultural Service, 1980. 17 p. (Foreign agriculture circular. Cocoa. FCB 3–80) S21.F615

Tables indicate cocoa production in specified African countries in the 1975/76–1979/80 period, with forecast for 1980/81.

Note: Additional reports and statistics on cocoa production in Africa are given in other numbers in the Cocoa subseries of the Foreign Agriculture Circular.

128

World coffee crop for 1980/81 up marginally from initial estimate. Washington, U.S. Dept. of Agriculture, Foreign Agricultural Service, 1980. 17 p. (Foreign agriculture circular. Coffee. FCOF 5–80) S21.F615

Includes data on African production.

Note: Addition reports and statistics on coffee production and trade in Africa are given in other numbers in the Coffee subseries of the Foreign Agriculture Circular.

129

World cotton situation. Washington, U.S. Dept. of Agriculture, Foreign Agricultural Service. monthly. (Foreign agriculture circular. Cotton) S21.F615

Includes tables on cotton production in Africa.

130

World oilseeds situation and outlook. Washington, Foreign Agricultural Service, U.S. Dept. of Agriculture, 1980. [12] p. (Foreign agriculture circular. Oilseeds and products. FOP 5–80) S21.F615

Prepared by the Service's Oilseeds and Products Division.

Includes statistics on peanut production in Senegal, South Africa, and Sudan.

Note: Reports and statistics on worldwide oilseed production, including peanut output in Africa, are issued regularly in the Foreign Agricultural Service's Oilseeds and Products series, appearing in its Foreign Agriculture Circular.

131

World sisal and abaca production up slightly in 1980. Washington, Foreign Agricultural Service, U.S. Dept. of Agriculture, 1980. 18 p. (Foreign agriculture circular. Vegetable fibers. FVF 2–80) S21.F615

Includes reports and statistics on sisal production and trade in Kenya, Tanzania, Angola, Mozambique, and Madagascar.

Note: Reports and statistics on worldwide vegetable fiber production, including Africa, are issued regularly in the Foreign Agricultural Service's Vegetable Fibers series, appearing in its Foreign Agriculture Circular.

132

World sugar supply and distribution, 1955/56–1979/80. Washington, U.S. Department of Agriculture, Foreign Agricultural Service, 1980. 50 p. (Foreign agriculture circular. Sugar. FS 3–80) S21.F615

Africa is covered on p. 32–40 with specific reference to the following sub-Saharan producers: Angola, Ethiopia, Kenya, Madagascar, Mauritius, Mozambique, Réunion, Zimbabwe, South Africa, Swaziland, Tanzania, Uganda, and Zaire.

133

World tobacco production up 2.6 percent; stock increase expected in 1978. Washington, Foreign Agricultural Service, U.S. Dept. of Agriculture, 1979. 19 p. (Foreign agriculture circular. Tobacco. FT 2–79) S21.F615

Includes statistics on production of major tobacco-growing countries in Africa for the period 1972–1978.

Note: Reports and statistics on worldwide tobacco production, including Africa, are issued periodically in the Foreign Agricultural Service's Tobacco series, appearing in its Foreign Agriculture Circular.

134

Young, M. Crawford. The state and the small urban center in Africa. *In* Southall, Aidan. Small urban centers in rural development in Africa. Madison, African Studies Program, University of Wisconsin-Madison, 1979. p. 313–333.

Bibliography: p. 330–333.

A grant from the Office of Urban Development, U.S. Agency for International Development, assisted in the preparation for publication of the papers collected in the study.

Includes examples from Ghana, Uganda, and Zaire.

Microfiche. [Washington, U.S. Agency for International Development, 1980?] (PN-AAJ-064); examined in the Development Information Center, AID, Washington, D.C.

Fisheries

135

Craib, Kenneth E., *and* Warren R. Ketler. Fisheries and aquaculture collaborative research in the developing countries; a priority planning approach. Los Altos, Calif., Research Development Associates, 1978. [288] p.

Prepared for the U.S. Agency for International Development.

Bibliography on Africa: p. 235–241.

Includes occasional references to sub-Saharan Africa.

135 (cont.)

Abstract in *A.I.D. Research and Development Abstracts*, v. 8, no. 2, 1980, p. 3.

Microfiche. [Washington, U.S. Agency for International Development, 1978?] 4 sheets.

DLC-Sci RR PN-AAH-011

136

Grover, John H., Donald R. Street, *and* Paul D. Starr. Review of aquaculture development activities in Central and West Africa. Auburn University, Ala., International Center for Aquaculture, Agricultural Experiment Station, Auburn University, 1980. 31 p. illus. DLC

"Research and development series, no. 28."

Prepared for the U.S. Agency for International Development.

Emphasis is on Cameroon, Liberia, Nigeria, and Zaire.

Earlier version, lacking illustrations, issued in microfiche. [Washington, U.S. Agency for International Development, 1980?] 2 sheets.

DLC-Sci RR PN-AAH-936

137

Klimaj, Andrzej. Fishery atlas of the southwest African shelf; bottom and pelagic catches. (Atlas rybacki szelfu Afryki południowo-zachodniej Połowy denne i pelagiczne) Warsaw, Poland, Published for the National Marine Fisheries Service, U.S. Dept. of Commerce, and the National Science Foundation, Washington, D.C., by the Foreign Scientific Publications Dept. of the National Center for Scientific, Technical and Economic Information; [available from the National Technical Information Service, U.S. Dept. of Commerce, Springfield, Va.], 1978. 173 p. illus., maps. SH312.W47K5813 v. 3

Translation of vol. 3 of *Atlas Rybacki Szelfu Afryki Południowo-Zachodniej.*

Covers the coast from Gabon to Port Elizabeth, South Africa.

Forests and Forestry

138

U.S. *Congress. House. Committee on Foreign Affairs. Subcommittee on International Organizations.* Tropical deforestation: hearings, Ninety-sixth Congress, second session: an overview, the role of international organizations, the role of the multinational corporations, May 7, June 19, and September 18, 1980. Washington, U.S. Govt. Print. Off., 1981. 446 p. illus., maps.

KF27.F648 1980d
J74.A23, 96th
Cong., House
Comm. For. Aff.
no. 124

Don Bonker, chairman.

Includes occasional references to sub-Saharan Africa.

139

Forestry activities and deforestation problems in developing countries [by] John I. Zerbe [et al.] [s.l.] Forest Products Laboratory, U.S. Dept. of Agriculture, 1980. 196 p.

Prepared for the Office of Science and Technology, U.S. Agency for International Development.

Includes statistical data on assistance programs in forestry development in sub-Saharan Africa (p. 17–21).

Abstract in *A.I.D. Research & Development Abstracts*, July 1981, p. 42.

Microfiche. [Washington, U.S. Agency for International Development, 1980?] 3 sheets.

DLC-Sci RR PN-AAH-919

140

Pelletier, Renée. Timber crisis in Black Africa reported. *In* U.S. *Joint Publications Research Service*. JPRS 73450. [Springfield, Va., National Technical Information Service, 1979] (Translations on Sub-Saharan Africa, no. 2104) p. 4–10.

Translation of article in *Africa*, Dakar, Mar. 1979, p. 51–54.

Microfiche. [Washington, Supt. of Docs., U.S. Govt. Print. Off., 1979] DLC-Micro JPRS 73450

141

Weber, Fred R. Economic & ecologic criteria: proposed Club des Amis du Sahel agro-forestry/anti-desertification program. [s.l.], 1977. 1 v. (various foliations of leaves)

Paper prepared for the Office of Sahel and Francophone West Africa Affairs, U.S. Agency for International Development.

Examined in the Development Information Center, Agency for International Development, Washington, D.C.

142

The World's tropical forests: a policy, strategy, and program for the United States. Report to the President by a U.S. Interagency Task Force on Tropical Forests. [Washington, for sale by the Supt. of Docs., U.S. Govt. Print. Off., 1980] 52 p. illus., maps. (U.S. Dept. of State. International organization and conference series, 145) DLC

142 (cont.)
United States Department of State publication, 9117.

Grain and Grain Storage

143
U.S. *Dept. of Agriculture. Economic Research Service. Foreign Demand and Competition Division.* 26 years of world cereal statistics; area, yield, production, 1950–75 by country and region. [Washington?], 1976. 261 p.
Includes tables for most sub-Saharan African countries.
Examined in the Documentation Center, Sahel Development Program, Agency for International Development, Washington, D.C.

144
U.S. *General Accounting Office.* Hungry nations need to reduce food losses caused by storage, spillage, and spoilage; Department of State and other agencies: report to the Congress by the Comptroller General of the United States. Washington, 1976. 29 p.   HD9000.6.U65   1976a
"B-159652."
Publication data stamped on cover.
Bibliography: p. 28.
Includes frequent brief references to Africa.

145
Dalrymple, Dana G. Development and spread of high-yielding varieties of wheat and rice in the less developed nations. 6th ed. Washington, U.S. Dept. of Agriculture, Office of International Cooperation and Development, 1978. 134 p. (Foreign agricultural economic report, no. 95)
                    HD1411.F59 no. 95, 1978
Issued in cooperation with the U.S. Agency for International Development.
First published in 1969 under title: *Imports and Plantings of High-Yielding Varieties of Wheat and Rice in the Less Developed Nations.*
Includes bibliographical references.
Brief summaries on wheat cultivation in Ethiopia, Kenya, Nigeria, Rhodesia, Sudan, and Tanzania (p. 57–61), and on rice cultivation in Benin, Cameroon, The Gambia, Ghana, Ivory Coast, Liberia, Mali, Mauritania, Niger, Nigeria, Senegal, Sierra Leone, Togo, Upper Volta, and Zaire (p. 97–102).
L.C. has also editions of 1971 (HD1407.F68 no. 8), 1972 (HD1407.F68 no. 14), 1974 (HD1411.F59 no. 95), and 1976 (HD1411.F59 no. 95, 1976).

146
Frederiksen, R. A., S. B. King, *and* N. V. Sundaram.

A comparison of sorghum diseases in temperate and tropical environments. [Washington, Agriculture Research Service, U.S. Dept. of Agriculture], 1974. 20 p.
Discusses sorghum diseases in Africa, India, and North America.
Abstract in *A.I.D. Research and Development Abstracts*, July 1978, p. 19.
Microfiche. [Washington, U.S. Agency for International Development, 1974?] 1 sheet.
                    DLC-Sci RR PN-AAD-890

147
Kugler, Harold L. Report of AID activities related to grain storage and marketing problems in Africa. [Washington] Bureau for Africa, Agency for International Development, 1975. 20 p.
Prepared for the Group for Assistance on Storage of Grains in Africa (GASGA).
Examined in the Development Information Center, Agency for International Development, Washington, D.C.

148
McSwain, Arlan B. Semi-Arid Food Grain Research and Development Program (SAFGRAD) in Africa. End of contract report. [s.l.], 1977. 9 p.
Prepared for the U.S. Agency for International Development under contract AID/afr-C-1326.
Examined in the Development Information Center, Agency for International Development, Washington, D.C.

149
Rachie, Kenneth O., *and* LeRoy V. Peters. The Eleusines: a review of world literature. Hyderabad, India, International Crops Research Institute for the Semi-Arid Tropics, foreword 1977. 179 p.
                    SB191.R3R3
Bibliography: p. 156–179.
A review of information on finger millet which "plays an important part in the nutrition of millions of people in the semi-arid tropics, particularly in India and East Africa."—foreword.
Abstract in *A.I.D. Research & Development Abstracts*, July 1981, p. 1.
Issued also in microfiche. [Washington, U.S. Agency for International Development, 1977] 2 sheets.   DLC-Sci RR PN-AAH-492

150
Sears, Horace E. World grain trade statistics, 1950–51/1972–73. [Washington] Foreign Agricultural Service, U.S. Dept. of Agriculture, 1974. 92 p. (U.S. Foreign Agricultural Service. FAS-M; 258)
                    S21.Z2383 no. 258
Includes statistics for African countries.

151

Seed production and industry development; annual report. [State College, Seed Technology Laboratory, Mississippi State University]   MsSM

Prepared for the U.S. Agency for International Development.

Among the countries covered in the 1976/77 issue are Central African Republic, Chad, Niger, and Rwanda.

Abstract of the 1976/77 report in *A.I.D. Research and Development Abstracts*, Oct. 1978, p. 12.

MsSM has 1976/77; this report issued also in microfiche ([Washington, U.S. Agency for International Development, 1977?] PN-AAF-588).

152

Status of grain storage in developing countries. Manhattan, Food & Feed Grain Institute, Kansas State University, rev. 1975. 246 p. maps. (Kansas. State University of Agriculture and Applied Science, Manhattan. Food & Feed Grain Institute. Special report, no. 3)   DLC

Prepared for the U.S. Agency for International Development under contract AID/otr-C-1331.

Sub-Saharan Africa is specifically covered on p. 25–93.

153

Vaughan, Charles E., *and* James M. Beck. Report to AID/W and USAID/Cameroun on the First International Seed Technology Training Course for Central and West Africa, Maroua, Cameroun, Sept. 19–Oct. 5, 1977. [State College?], Seed Technology Laboratory, Mississippi State University, 1977. 29 p.   MsSM

Prepared for the U.S. Agency for International Development under contract AID/ta-C-1219.

Livestock and Range Management

154

U.S. *AID Mission to Chad*. Central African livestock production and marketing project: Assale (Chad)/Serbewel (Cameroon): evaluation report. N'Djamena, 1975. [35] p.   MiEM

155

Abercrombie, Frank D. Range development and management in Africa. [Washington], Agency for International Development, 1974 [i.e. 1975] 59 p. illus., maps.   SF85.4.A4A23

"The purpose of the paper is to provide guidelines on basic data gathering necessary for the design and implementation of range/livestock pro-

jects applicable to social and environmental conditions encountered in the beef producing areas of Africa."—Foreword.

Abstract in *A.I.D. Research and Development Abstracts*, Jan. 1976, p. 16–17.

Issued also in microfiche. [Washington, U.S. Agency for International Development, 1975?] 1 sheet.   DLC-Sci RR PN-AAB-229

156

Hoben, Allan. Lessons from a critical examination of livestock projects in Africa. [Washington], Studies Division, Bureau for Program and Policy Coordination, U.S. Agency for International Development, 1979. 30 leaves.

Examined in the Documentation Center, Sahel Development Program, AID, Washington, D.C.

157

Horowitz, Michael M. The sociology of pastoralism and African livestock projects. [Washington?], Office of Evaluation, Bureau for Program and Policy Coordination, Agency for International Development, 1979. 102 p. map. (A.I.D. program evaluation discussion paper, no. 6)

Abstract in *A.I.D. Research & Development Abstracts*, July 1981, p. 9.

Microfiche. [Washington, U.S. Agency for International Development, 1979?] 2 sheets.
          DLC-Sci RR PN-AAG-922

158

International Rangeland Congress, *1st, Denver, Colo.*, Aug. 14–18, 1978. Proceedings; edited by Donald N. Hyder. Denver, Society for Range Management, [1978] 742 p. illus., maps.

The U.S. Agency for International Development, U.S. Dept. of Agriculture, and the National Science Foundation are cited as "contributors."

Includes numerous contributions on conditions in sub-Saharan Africa.

Abstract in *A.I.D. Research and Development Abstracts*, v. 7, no. 1, 1979, p. 8.

Microfiche. [Washington, U.S. Agency for International Development, 1978?] 8 sheets.
          DLC-Sci RR PN-AAG-426

Note: The abstracts of the papers are issued also in microfiche ([Washington, U.S. Agency for International Development, 1978?] 1 sheet. DLC-Sci RR PN-AAG-427).

159

Livestock production and marketing; Chad basin. [s.l., U.S. Agency for International Development, 197–?] [49] p. map.

Microfiche. [Sahel Documents and Disserta-

159 (cont.)

tions. Ann Arbor, Mich., University Microfilms International, 1980] 1 sheet.

DLC-Micro Microfiche 5357 CD 031

160

McLeroy, George B. An overview of trypano-tolerant cattle development potentialities within the main tse-tse fly belt. [Washington], Agency for International Development, 1974. 5 p.

"AID/AFR/CWR technical staff paper."

Examined in the Development Information Center, AID, Washington, D.C.

161

Project review paper: Lake Chad livestock and mixed agriculture. N'Djamena, Chad, [U.S. Agency for International Development], 1975. [40] leaves.

Examined in the Documentation Center, Sahel Development Program, AID, Washington, D.C.

162

Reyna, Stephen P. The Assale-Serbewel social economic study. [s.l.], 1974. 113 p. maps.

"This report has been written as a contribution to the program constituting the preliminary phase of the project Animal Production Development in the Assale (Chad) and Serbewel (Cameroun) Districts (USAID 625/11/130-803) for the Lake Chad Basin Commission."

Microfiche. [Washington, U.S. Agency for International Development, 1974?] 2 sheets.

DLC-Sci RR PN-RAB-607

163

Trypanotolerant livestock in West and Central Africa. Addis Ababa, International Livestock Centre for Africa, 1979. 2 v. illus., maps. (ILCA monograph, 2)

Includes bibliographies.

The Centre's programs are funded in part by the U.S. Government.

Contents: v. 1. General study.—v. 2. Country studies.

In vol. 2, the livestock programs in the following countries are briefly described: Senegal, The Gambia, Guinea-Bissau, Guinea, Sierra Leone, Liberia, Mali, Upper Volta, Ivory Coast, Ghana, Togo, Benin, Nigeria, Cameroon, Central African Republic, Gabon, Congo, and Zaire.

Microfiche. [Washington, U.S. Agency for International Development, 1979?] 6 sheets (PN-AAJ-222–PN-AAJ-223); examined in the Development Information Center, Agency for International Development, Washington, D.C.

164

Workshop on Pastoralism and African Livestock Development, *Harpers Ferry, W. Va.*, Sept. 23–26, 1979. Report. Binghamton, N.Y., Institute for Development Anthropology, 1980. [81] p. (in various pagings) (A.I.D. program evaluation report, no. 4)

Supported by the U.S. Agency for International Development.

Abstract in *A.I.D. Research and Development Abstracts*, Feb. 1981, p. 19.

Microfiche. [Washington, U.S. Agency for International Development, 1980?] 1 sheet.

DLC-Sci RR PN-AAH-238

Arts

165

U.S. *Congress. House. Committee on House Administration.* Authorizing the Smithsonian Institution to acquire the Museum of African Art and for other purposes, August 2, 1978: report (to accompany H. R. 10792) [Washington, U.S. Govt. Print. Off., 1978] 7 p. DLC-LL

At head of title: 95th Congress, 2d session. House of Representatives. Report no. 95-1233.

Report submitted by Representative Lucien N. Nedzi.

166

U.S. *Congress. Senate. Committee on Rules and Administration.* Acquisition of the Museum of African Art by the Smithsonian Institution: hearing, Ninety-fifth Congress, second session, on S. 2507 ... April 25, 1978. Washington, U.S. Govt. Print. Off., 1978. 41 p.　　　KF26.R8　1978a
J74.A23 95th
Cong., Sen. Comm.
Rules, v. 2

Claiborne Pell, chairman.

List of publications and exhibitions of the Museum, 1964–1978: p. 37–41.

167

——— Authorizing the Smithsonian Institution to acquire the Museum of African Art: report (to accompany S. 2507) [Washington, 1978] 14 p.

DLC-LL

Report submitted by Senator Claiborne Pell.

At head of title: 95th Congress, 2d session. Senate. Report no. 95–793.

168

Acquisition of the Museum of African Art by the Smithsonian Institution. Statement on signing S. 2507 into law. Oct. 5, 1978. *In U.S. President.*

168 (cont.)

Public papers of the Presidents of the United States. Jimmy Carter. 1978. Washington, U.S. Govt. Print. Off., 1979. p. 1712–1713.

J80.A283 1978

169

Davies, Mary K. African influence in modern art: a select, annotated bibliography. Washington, Smithsonian Institution Libraries, Museum of African Art Library, 1980. 2 leaves. DLC

Held by the African Section.

170

——— Twin images in Africa: an introductionary bibliography. Washington, Smithsonian Institution Libraries, Museum of African Art Branch Library, 1981. 7 leaves. map. DLC

A listing of "a few selected sources which deal with twin-related practices in Africa, particularly that of producing carved wooden images."

Held by the African Section.

171

Life ... afterlife: African funerary sculpture. [Washington], National Museum of African Art, Smithsonian Institution, 1981. 15 p. illus. DLC

172

Mazonowicz, Douglas. On the rocks: the story of prehistoric art. Washington, published by the Smithsonian Institution Press for the Smithsonian Institution Traveling Exhibition Service, 1980. 32 p. illus.

"The silkscreens and line drawings illustrated in this book were made by the author from prehistoric images."

Accompanies an exhibition on the ice age and its art, circulated by the Smithsonian Traveling Exhibition Service. Describes prehistoric pictures from different parts of the world and examines what those pictures reveal about the way in which ancient people lived.

Citation received from the Museum of African Art, Smithsonian Institution, Washington, D.C.

173

Smithsonian Institution. *Museum of African Art Branch Library*. Library acquisitions list. Apr. 1980+ Washington. monthly. DLC

Held by the African Section.

L.C. has Apr. 1980+ (scattered issues wanting).

174

Smithsonian Institution. *Traveling Exhibition Service*. The image of the Black in Western art. [Washington?, c1980] [10] p. illus. DLC

Assistance Programs

175

U.S. *Congress. House. Committee on Foreign Affairs. Subcommittee on Africa*. U.S. interests in Africa: hearings, Ninety-sixth Congress, first session. Washington, U.S. Govt. Print. Off., 1980. 540 p.

KF27.F625 1979i
J74.A23 House
Comm. For. Aff.
v. 61

Stephen J. Solarz, chairman.

Hearings held Oct. 16 – Nov. 14, 1979.

A study of America's economic, strategic, and military interests.

Includes tables indicating assistance to sub-Saharan Africa in dollars by international donors, the United States, Communist countries, and other nations (p. 90–95), and a *Public Opinion Poll of American Attitudes Toward South Africa* prepared by the Carnegie Endowment for International Peace (p. 401–442).

Among the appendixes are the following:

2. Tables submitted by the Bureau of Mines showing dependency on African minerals by the United States, Europe, and Japan. p. 478–535.

4. Letter and tables submitted by the Department of the Treasury, listing U.S. aid to Africa, World Bank and IDA lending by region, and World Bank, IDA and African Development Bank lending to African countries. p. 537–540.

IDA: International Development Association.

Abstract in *American Statistics Index*, 1980, Abstracts, p. 965.

Issued also in microfiche. [Washington, Congressional Information Service, 1980?] 6 sheets.

DLC-Micro ASI:80 21388-30

176

U.S. *Congress. Senate. Committee on the Judiciary. Subcommittee to Investigate Problems Connected with Refugees and Escapees*. World hunger, health, and refugee problems: hearings, Ninety-third Congress, first session-Ninety-fourth Congress, second session. Washington, U.S. Govt. Print. Off., 1973–76. 7 v. maps.

KF26.J869 1973a
J74.A23 93d
Cong., Sen. Jud.
Comm. Ref., v. 1
(pt. 1–5); 94th
Cong., Sen. Jud.
Comm. Ref., v. 2
(pt. 6–7)

Parts 2–7 are hearings before the Subcommittee to Investigate Problems Connected with Refugees and Escapees of the Committee on the Judiciary

176 (cont.)

and the Subcommittee on Health of the Committee on Labor and Public Welfare.

Edward M. Kennedy, chairman of both subcommittees.

Partial contents: Pt. 1. Crisis in West Africa.—Pt. 2. Food scarcity, nutrition, and health.—Pt. 3. Development and food needs.—Pt. 4. Famine in Africa.—Pt. 5. Human disasters in Cyprus, Bangladesh, Africa.—Pt. 6. Special study mission to Africa, Asia & Middle East.

Among the appendixes to the various parts are the following:

Pt. 1:

Appendix 3. Text of a Food and Agriculture Organization (FAO) report on Sahelian problems, April 1973. p. 67–75.

Appendix 4. Catholic Relief Services field reports on Sahelian drought. p. 77–99.

Pt. 3:

Appendix 2. A listing of U.S. nonprofit organizations in medical and public health assistance abroad. p. 35–67.

Pt. 4:

Appendix 3. A review of implications of the drought in the striken areas of Tigre and Wollo provinces in Ethiopia. p. 101–110.

Appendix 4. Center for Disease Control. Nutritional surveillance in West Africa. p. 111–115.

Appendix 5. League of Red Cross Societies report on the drought in Africa, Geneva, January 17, 1974. p. 117–127.

Pt. 5:

Appendix 1. U.S. *Agency for International Development*. Background information on relief and rehabilitation programs in the African Sahel. p. 59–69.

Appendix 2. U.S. *Agency for International Development*. Report to the Congress on the famine in sub-Saharan Africa. p. 71–120.

Pt. 6:

Appendix 1. U.S. *Agency for International Development*. Special report to the Congress on the drought situation in sub-Sahara [*sic*] Africa, 1975. p. 125–149.

Appendix 2. Cahill, Kevin M. Report on Somalia. p. 151–166.

177

The Development impact of private voluntary organizations: Kenya and Niger; final report [by] A. H. Barclay [et. al.] [s.l.], Development Alternatives, inc., 1979. 98 p.

Prepared for the U.S. Agency for International Development under contract AID/otr-C-1383.

Microfiche. [Washington, U.S. Agency for International Development, 1979] 2 sheets (PN-AAG-894); held by the Development Information Center, AID, Washington, D.C.

178

Development of Lake Chad basin area: briefing paper. [s.l.], Ad Hoc Committee, UNDP/USAID, 1977. 112 leaves, 47 p. maps.

Microfiche. [Sahel Documents and Dissertations. Ann Arbor, Mich., University Microfilms International, 1980] 3 sheets.

DLC-Micro 5357 CD 005

179

Directory of development resources: on-call technical support services, information clearinghouses, field research facilities, newsletters, data banks, training. [Washington], Office of Development Information and Utilization, Resource Utilization Division, Agency for International Development, 1979. [343] p. (in various pagings) maps. HD82.D5165

Includes profiles of four centers in Africa: International Livestock Center for Africa (p. IO-1–IO-3); Technology Consultancy Center, University of Science and Technology, Kumasi, Ghana (p. IO-4–IO-6); West Africa Rice Development Association (p. IO-7–IO-9); and International Institute of Tropical Agriculture (p. IO-10–IO-12).

180

Reyna, Stephen P. Social soundness of four projects proposed by the United Nations Development Program/Lake Chad Basin Commission multidonor, multi-disciplinary mission. Durham, Dept. of Sociology and Anthropology, University of New Hampshire, [1978?] 105 leaves.

Study supported in part by the U.S. Agency for International Development.

Bibliography: leaves 103–105.

The four projects under consideration:

Kousseri (Cameroon) Integrated Rural Development Project.

Malo (Chad) Integrated Rural Development Project.

Diffa (Niger) Integrated Rural Development Project.

Development of the Chari Delta Project (Cameroon/Chad).

Microfiche. [Sahel Documents and Dissertations. Ann Arbor, Mich., University Microfilms International, 1980] 2 sheets.

DLC-Micro 5357 AS 197

181

Sperling, Philip. Evaluation of the Yaounde Seminar II. Washington, Office of International Training, Bureau for Program and Management Services,

181 (cont.)

Agency for International Development, 1974. [44] leaves.   T56.8.S64

In English or French.

"The Seminar on Project Management held in Yaounde, Cameroon from January 31, 1974 through March 6, 1974 was the first of the introductory seminars to be held under the auspices of the Pan-African Institute for Development."— p. [1]

Development Banks and Funds

182

U.S. *Congress. House. Committee on Banking, Currency and Housing. Subcommittee on International Development Institutions and Finance.* Development institution lending for palm oil production: hearing. Ninety-fourth Congress, second session on House Resolutions 1399, 1419, and 1445 ... September 15, 1976. Washington, U.S. Govt. Print. Off., 1976. 364 p. illus.   KF27.B3974   1976a

Henry B. Gonzalez, chairman.

Includes occasional references to Africa.

183

———— The African Development Fund: hearing, Ninety-fourth Congress, first session ... July 15, 1975. Washington, U.S. Govt. Print. Off., 1975. 259 p.   KF27.B3974   1975a
                                     J74.A23 94th
                                     Cong., House Comm.
                                     Bank., v. 22

Henry B. Gonzalez, chairman.

Among the "additional material submitted for the record" are the following items:

Report by the Board of Directors of the African Development Fund covering the period from 1st January to 31st December 1974. p. 127–163.

Agreement establishing the African Development Bank. p. 176–214.

184

U.S. *Congress. House. Committee on Banking, Finance, and Urban Affairs.* International Development Association and the African Development Bank: report, together with dissenting views (to accompany H. R. 6811) [Washington, U.S. Govt. Print. Off., 1980] 20 p.   DLC-LL

Report submitted by Representative Henry S. Reuss.

At head of title: 96th Congress, 2d session. House of Representatives. Report no. 96-1015.

The bill would authorize the United States "to take up membership in the African Development Bank."

185

U.S. *Congress. House. Committee on Banking, Finance and Urban Affairs. Subcommittee on International Development Institutions and Finance.* International Development Association sixth replenishment and African Development Bank membership: hearing, Ninety-sixth Congress, second session, on H. R. 6811 ... March 26, 27, and April 16, 1980. Washington, U.S. Govt. Print. Off., 1980. 325 p. illus.
                          KF27.B573   1980
                          J73.A24 96th
                          Cong., House Comm.
                          Bank., v. 54

Henry B. Gonzalez, chairman.

"Serial no. 96-54."

186

———— To provide for increased participation by the United States in the Inter-American Development Bank, the Asian Development Fund, and the African Development Fund: hearing, Ninety-sixth Congress, first session, March 21, and April 24, 1979. Washington, U.S. Govt. Print. Off., 1979. 596 p. illus.   KF27.B547   1979
                          J74.A23 96th
                          Cong., House Comm.
                          Bank., v. 13

Henry B. Gonzalez, chairman.

187

———— U.S. participation in multilateral development institutions: hearings, Ninety-fifth Congress, second session. Washington, U.S. Govt. Print. Off., 1978. 647 p. illus.   KF27.B547   1978
                          J74.A23 95th
                          Cong., House Comm.
                          Bank., v. 62

Henry B. Gonzalez, chairman.

Among the appendixes is the following:

Appendix 1. African Development Fund: annual report, 1976. p. 479–518.

188

U.S. *Congress. House. Committee on International Relations.* Rethinking United States foreign policy toward the developing world: hearing before the Committee on International Relations and its Subcommittee on International Development, House of Representatives, Ninety-fifth Congress, first session ... August 4, October 12, and November 1, 1977. Washington, U.S. Govt. Print. Off., 1977. 214 p.   KF27.I549   1977c
                          J74.A23 95th
                          Cong., House Comm.
                          Inter. Rel., v. 30

Clement J. Zablocki, chairman.

188 (cont.)

Michael Harrington, chairman, Subcommittee on International Development.

Witnesses are from the U.S. Agency for International Development.

Among the appendixes is the following:

Appendix C. Fordwor, Kwame D. Remarks [by President, African Development Bank] on "An assessment of development assistance strategies." p. 148–154.

189

U.S. *Congress. House. Committee on International Relations. Subcommittee on Africa.* To establish an African Development Foundation: hearings, Ninety-fifth Congress, first session, on H. R. 8130, October 13 and 26, 1977. Washington, U.S. Govt. Print. Off., 1978. 96 p.   KF27.I54914   1977b

Charles C. Diggs, Jr., chairman.

An examination of the operations of the Inter-American Foundation as a possible model for a similar organization for Africa.

Summary of H. R. 8130, a bill to establish an African Development Foundation: p. 2–4.

190

U.S. *Congress. Senate. Committee on Foreign Relations.* Multilateral development banks: hearing, Ninety-sixth Congress, first session, on S. 662 ... March 12, 1979. Washington, U.S. Govt. Print. Off., 1979. 220 p.   KF26.F6   1979c
J74.A23 96th
Cong., Sen. Comm.
For. Rel., v. 6

Frank Church, chairman.

Special report to the President and to Congress on the proposed second general replenishment of the resources of the African Development Bank, by the National Advisory Council on International Monetary and Financial Policies, March 1979: p. 189–220.

191

—— Providing for increased participation by the United States in the Inter-American Development Bank, the Asian Development Bank, and the African Development Fund: report (to accompany S. 662). [Washington, 1979] 32 p.   DLC-LL

Report submitted by Senator Frank Church.

At head of title: 96th Congress, 1st session. Senate. Report no. 96-135.

192

U.S. *Congress. Senate. Committee on Foreign Relations. Subcommittee on African Affairs.* African Development Fund: hearing before the Subcommittee on African Affairs and the Subcommittee on Foreign Assistance of the Committee on Foreign Relations, United States Senate, Ninety-fifth Congress, first session on H. R. 5262 ... April 18, 1977. Washington, U.S. Govt. Print. Off., 1977. 46 p.   KF26.F625   1977a
J74.A23 95th Cong.
Sen. Comm. For. Rel.,
v. 16

Dick Clark, chairman, Subcommittee on African Affairs.

Hubert H. Humphrey, chairman, Subcommittee on Foreign Assistance.

193

U.S. *Congress. Senate. Committee on Foreign Relations. Subcommittee on Foreign Assistance.* IDB and AFDF authorization: hearing, Ninety-fourth Congress, first session, on H. R. 9721 ... January 28, 1976. Washington, U.S. Govt. Print. Off., 1976. 86 p.   KF26.F6357   1976
J74.A23 94th
Cong., Sen. Comm.
For. Rel., v. 24

Hubert H. Humphrey, chairman.

IDB: Inter-American Development Bank.

AFDF: African Development Fund.

Principal witness on the African Development Fund is Edward W. Mulcahy, Deputy Assistant Secretary of State for African Affairs.

194

U.S. [*Treaties, etc. 1976 Nov. 18*] Agreement establishing the African Development Fund. Accord portant création du Fonds africain de développement. *In* U.S. *Treaties, etc.* United States treaties and other international agreements, v. 28, 1976–77. [Washington, Dept. of State; for sale by the Supt. of Docs., U.S. Govt. Print. Off., 1978] p. 4547–4606. ([Treaties and other international acts series, 8605])   JX231.A34 v. 28

Agreement done at Abidjan Nov. 29, 1972; signed on behalf of the United States Nov. 18, 1976.

195

Administration supports increased U.S. contributions to the African Development Fund. *In* U.S. *Dept. of State.* The Department of State bulletin, v. 76, no. 1976, May 9, 1977: 471–474.   JX232.A33 v. 76

Statements by Andrew Young, U.S. Ambassador to the United Nations, and David B. Bolen, Deputy Assistant Secretary of State for African Affairs, before the Subcommittee on African Affairs, Committee on Foreign Relations, Senate, Apr. 18, 1977.

196

African Development Bank. [*Treaties, etc. United States, 1976 June 30*] Grant agreement between the United States of America and the African Development Bank (regional onchocerciasis area land satellite (Landsat) related study in Benin, Ghana, and Upper Volta). *In U.S. Treaties, etc.* United States treaties and other international agreements, v. 28, 1976–77. [Washington, Dept. of State; for sale by the Supt. of Docs., U.S. Govt. Print. Off., 1978] p. 6963–6970. ([Treaties and other international acts series, 8698]) JX231.A34 v. 28
    Signed at Abidjan June 30, 1976.

197

Bushnell, John A. Statement on proposed replenishment and expansion of membership of the Inter-American Development Bank and U.S. membership in the African Development Fund. [Washington], Dept. of the Treasury, 1976. [38] p.
    Abstract in *American Statistics Index*, 1976, Abstracts, p. 705–706.
    Microfiche. [Washington, Congressional Information Service, 1976?] 1 sheet.
                    DLC-Micro ASI:76 8008-26

198

Collins, Cardiss. African Development Foundation. Congressional record [daily ed.], 96th Congress, 2d session, v. 126, July 31, 1980: E3743–E3744.
                    J11.R7 v. 126
    Extension of remarks in the U.S. House of Representatives.
    Includes text of statement by President Carter on Mar. 27, 1980, "The new situation in Zimbabwe."

199

Davis, Nathaniel. Department urges U.S. participation in African Development Fund. *In U.S. Dept. of State.* The Department of State bulletin, v. 73, no. 1885, Aug. 11, 1975: 213–215.
                    JX232.A33 v. 73
    Statement by the Assistant Secretary of State for African Affairs before the Subcommittee on International Development Institutions and Finance, Committee on Banking, Currency, and Housing, House of Representatives, July 15, 1975.

200

Foreign Assistance Appropriations, 1980. Congressional record [daily ed.], 96th Congress, 1st session, v. 125, July 19, 1979: H6266–H6277.
                    J11.R7 v. 125
    Debate in the U.S. House of Representatives includes frequent references to Africa.

A list of contributors to the African Development Fund is given on p. H6268.

201

Gray, William H. The African Development Foundation Act of 1979. Congressional record [daily ed.], 96th Congress, 1st session, v. 125, Oct. 9, 1979: E4913–E4915. J11.R7 v. 125
    Extension of remarks in the U.S. House of Representatives.
    Includes text of a bill to create the Foundation.

202

International financial institutions. Congressional record, 95th Congress, 1st session, v. 123, Apr. 6, 1977: 10759–10794. J11.R5 v. 123
    Remarks in the U.S. House of Representatives.
    Includes debate on increased United States participation in the African Development Fund.

203

Kriesberg, Martin. International organizations and agricultural development. [Washington], Economic Research Service, U.S. Dept. of Agriculture, [1977] 135 p. (Foreign agricultural economic report, no. 131) HD1411.F59 no. 131
    "An update of the earlier publication, Multilateral assistance for agriculture development, ERS-521."
    Bibliography: p. 132–135.
    The role of the African Development Bank is presented in Chapter 10 (p. 103–106).

204

Landfield, Sherwin. The African Development Bank and its AID grants: evaluation report. [Abidjan?], Regional Economic Development Services Office/West Africa, U.S. Agency for International Development, 1977. 48 p.
    Bibliography: p. 47–48.
    Examined in the Development Information Center, AID, Washington, D.C.

205

Ngwube, Douglas. ADB's new president profiled. *In U.S. Joint Publications Research Service.* JPRS 76124. [Springfield, Va., National Technical Information Service, 1980] (Sub-Saharan Africa report, no. 2272) p. 8–12.
    Article on Willa D. Mung'omba, President of the African Development Bank, in *West Africa*, London, July 7, 1980, p. 1225–1231.
    Microfiche. [s.l., 1980]
                    DLC-Micro JPRS 76124

206

———— African Development Bank looks outward. *In U.S. Joint Publications Research Service.* JPRS

206 (cont.)

73660. [Springfield, Va., National Technical Information Service, 1979] (Translations on Sub-Saharan Africa, no. 2118) p. 1–4.

From article in *West Africa*, London, May 21, 1979, p. 883–884.

Microfiche. [s.l., 1979]

DLC-Micro JPRS 73660

207

Omnibus Multilateral Development Institutions Act of 1977. Congressional record, 95th Congress, 1st session, v. 123, June 14, 1977: 18924–19008.

J11.R5 v. 123

Includes debate in the U.S. Senate on increased American participation in the African Development Fund.

208

Report on activities of Arab Bank for Economic Development in Africa. *In* U.S. *Joint Publications Research Service.* JPRS 67070. [Springfield, Va., National Technical Information Service, 1976] (Translations on Sub-Saharan Africa, no. 1642) p. 1–5.

Translation of article in *Europe Outremer*, Paris, Nov. 1975, p. 35, 36, 47.

Microfiche. [s.l., 1976]

DLC-Micro JPRS 67070

209

Roundtable discussion on African development. *In* U.S. *Joint Publications Research Service.* JPRS 76952. [Springfield, Va., National Technical Information Service, 1980] (Sub-Saharan Africa report, no. 2329) p. 2–7.

Translation of article in *Le Point*, Paris, Oct. 20, 1980, p. 95–98.

Among the participants were Chedly Ayari, President of the Arab Bank for Economic Development in Africa, and Edem Kodjo, Secretary-General of the Organization of African Unity.

Microfiche. [s.l., 1980]

DLC-Micro JPRS 76952

210

U.S. participation in the International Development Association and the African Development Bank. Congressional record [daily ed.], 96th Congress, 2d session, v. 126, June 16, 1980: S7073–S7078.

J11.R7 v. 126

Remarks in the U.S. Senate, primarily by Senators Frank Church and Samuel I. Hayakawa.

211

United Nations. Economic Commission for Africa. [*Treaties, etc. United States, 1976 June 17*] Basic agreement governing grants by the United States of America to the United Nations (United Nations Trust Fund for Africa). *In* U.S. *Treaties, etc.* United States treaties and other international agreements, v. 28, 1976–77. [Washington, Dept. of State; for sale by the Supt. of Docs., U.S. Govt. Print. Off., 1978] p. 6886–6897. ([Treaties and other international acts series, 8694])   JX231.A34 v. 28

Agreement of June 17, 1978 between the U.S. Agency for International Development and the United Nations Economic Commission for Africa.

212

Wider role for expanded ADB envisioned. *In* U.S. *Joint Publications Research Service.* JPRS 73820. [Springfield, Va., National Technical Information Service, 1979] (Sub-Saharan Africa report, 2129) p. 9–12.

Article from *West Africa*, London, June 11, 1979, p. 1012, 1018, 1019.

ADB: African Development Bank.

Microfiche. [Washington, Supt. of Docs., U.S. Govt. Print. Off., 1979]   DLC-Micro JPRS 73820

United States Programs

213

U.S. *Agency for International Development.* Accelerated impact program (AIP), [by] Irving H. Licht [et. al.] [Washington?], 1976.

An evaluation report of Agency for International Development assistance programs.

Examined in the Development Information Center, AID, Washington, D.C.

214

———— Accelerated impact program; Phase II [by] Herbert N. Miller, Yvonne John and Robert Elliott. [Washington?], 1977. 49 p.

Examined in the Development Information Center, AID, Washington, D.C.

215

———— Annual budget submission, AFR/CWR regional programs and summary. [Washington?]

AFR/CWR: Office of Central/West Africa Regional Affairs, U.S. Agency for International Development.

Vol. for 1977 examined in the Documentation Center, Sahel Development Program, AID, Washington, D.C.

216

———— Annual budget submission, Africa regional. Washington.

216 (cont.)

Vols. for 1972+ examined in the Development Information Center, AID, Washington, D.C.

217

———— Annual budget submission, Portuguese speaking Africa. [Washington?]

Title varies: 1977/78, *Annual Budget Submission: Angola, Cape Verde, Guinea-Bissau, Mozambique, and Sao Tome/Principe.*

In the 1979 report, it is noted that emphasis is on Cape Verde and Guinea-Bissau "where A.I.D. efforts are concentrated."—p. 1.

Vols. for 1977/78–1979 examined in the Development Information Center, Agency for International Development, Washington, D.C.

218

———— Briefing on African drought and related programs for senatorial delegation. Rabat, 1975. [100] p.   MiEM

219

———— Congressional presentation. Annex 1; Africa. [Washington] map. annual.   DLC

Supplements information on Africa contained in AID's annual *Congressional Presentation. Main Volume.* In recent years, each country section in *Annex 1; Africa* has included statistics on "economic and social data" plus a brief statement outlining current demographic, economic, agricultural, and employment trends, together with an overview of AID's programs.

Abstract of 1981 volume in *Government Reports Announcements & Index*, June 6, 1980, p. 1954.

Vols. for 1980, 1982+ held by the Library's African Section; vol. for 1981 issued in microfiche ([Springfield, Va., National Technical Information Service, 1980] 7 sheets. DLC-Sci RR PB80-150014).

220

———— Development assistance program, 1976–1980. Central-West African region. Washington, 1975. 2 v. maps.

Contents: v. 1. Overview and conclusions.— v. 2. [Country annexes].

Vol. 2 includes information on Cameroon, Central African Republic, Chad, Dahomey, Gabon, The Gambia, Guinea, Mali, Mauritania, Niger, Senegal, Togo, and Upper Volta.

Examined in the Development Information Center, AID, Washington, D.C.

221

———— Proposal for a program in appropriate technology: transmitted by the Agency for International Development, pursuant to Section 107 of the Foreign Assistance Act. Rev. ed. Washington, U.S. Govt. Print. Off., 1977. 382 p.

HC60.U6I48   1977

At head of title: Committee print. 95th Congress 1st session.

"Printed for the use of the Committee on International Relations.

Includes bibliographies.

A study of what could usefully be done to implement section 107 of the Foreign Assistance Act of 1961 which authorized the Agency for International Development "to support an expanded and coordinated private effort to promote the development and dissemination of technologies appropriate for developing countries."—p. iii. Some African examples are used to support the document's recommendations.

222

U.S. *Agency for International Development. Bureau for Africa.* Agricultural development strategy statement, with policy guidelines. [Washington], 1977. 51 p.

Microfiche. [Washington, U.S. Agency for International Development, 1977?] 1 sheet (PN-AAG-463); examined in the Development Information Center, AID, Washington, D.C.

223

———— Manpower and cost estimates for conducting environmental assessments of proposed FY 76 program. [Washington?], 1975. 1 v. (various pagings)

Examined in the Development Information Center, AID, Washington, D.C.

224

———— Report on AFR Mission Directors/Program Officers Conference, Senegal, Oct. 20–24, 1975. [Washington] 1975. 46 p.

Examined in the Development Information Center, AID, Washington, D.C.

225

U.S. *Agency for International Development. Bureau for Program and Policy Coordination. Office of Planning and Budgeting.* U.S. overseas loans and grants and assistance from international organizations. 1945/59+ [Washington] annual.

HC60.U48425

Title varies: 1945/59, *U.S. External Assistance: Obligations and Other Commitments;* 1945/60–1945/62, *U.S. Foreign Assistance and Assistance from International Organizations: Obligations and Loan Authorizations* (varies slightly).

Other slight variations in title.

Vols. for 1945/59–1945/60 issued by the Office of Statistics and Reports of the International Co-

225 (cont.)

operation Administration; 1945/61–1945/76 by the Statistics and Reports Division of the Agency for International Development.

For each country, dollar amounts are given for U.S. Government loans and grants under AID, Food for Peace, and other economic assistance programs, military assistance programs, Export-Import Bank loans, and other loan agreements.

L.C. has 1945/59+

226

U.S. *Agency for International Development. Office of Contract Management. Support Division.* Current technical service contracts and grants. 1975?+ Washington. annual.   HC60.U48427

Continues its *Current Technical Service Contracts.*

Includes information on AID contracts concerning Africa with universities, associations, and other research centers.

L.C. has 1975+

227

U.S. *Congress. House.* International Development and Food Assistance Act of 1978. Conference report (to accompany H. R. 12222). [Washington?] 1978. 47 p.   DLC-LL

At head of title: 95th Congress, 2d session. House of Representatives. Report no. 95-1545.

Submitted by Representative Clement J. Zablocki.

Includes brief references to Africa, such as the United Nations Trust Fund for Africa and the United Nations Institute for Namibia.

The following items (entries 228–268) are listed in chronological order by fiscal year

1976

228

U.S. *Congress. House. Committee on Appropriations. Subcommittee on Departments of State, Justice, Commerce, the Judiciary, and Related Agencies.* Departments of State, Justice, and Commerce, the judiciary, and related agencies appropriations for 1976: hearings before a subcommittee of the Committee on Appropriations, House of Representatives, Ninety-fourth Congress, first session. Washington, U.S. Govt. Print. Off., 1975. 9 v.

KF27.A664 1975
J74.A23 94th
Cong., House Comm.
Approp., v. 22

John M. Slack, chairman.

Testimony by Nathaniel Davis, Assistant Secretary of State for African Affairs, p. 232–268.

229

U.S. *Congress. House. Committee on Appropriations. Subcommittee on Foreign Operations and Related Agencies.* Foreign assistance and related agencies appropriations for 1976: hearings before a subcommittee of the Committee on Appropriations, House of Representatives, Ninety-fourth Congress, first session. Washington, U.S. Govt. Print. Off., 1975–1976. 4 v. illus.   KF27A646 1975a
J74.A23 94th
Cong., House Comm.
Approp., v. 15

Otto E. Passman, chairman.

Pt. 1 includes scattered references to Peace Corps programs in Africa; in Pt. 2, African programs of the U.S. Agency for International Development are discussed (p. 700–984); Pt. 4 includes references to U.S. economic and military assistance to African nations.

230

U.S. *Congress. House. Committee on International Relations.* Peace Corps authorization for fiscal year 1976 and transition quarter: hearings, Ninety-fourth Congress, first session, on H. R. 6334 ... May 13 and 15, 1975. Washington, U.S. Govt. Print. Off., 1975. 87 p.   KF27.I549 1975
J74.A23 94th
Cong., House Comm.
Inter. Rel., v. 15

Thomas E. Morgan, chairman.

Includes occasional references to Africa.

231

U.S. *Congress. Senate. Committee on Appropriations.* Foreign assistance and related programs appropriations for fiscal year 1976: hearings before a subcommittee of the Committee on Appropriations, United States Senate, Ninety-fourth Congress, first session. Washington, U.S. Govt. Print. Off., 1975. 1518, xxi p.   KF26.A6 1975o
J74.A23 94th
Cong., Sen. Comm.
Approp., v. 13

Daniel K. Inouye, chairman of subcommittee.

Includes frequent references to Africa, especially in sections relating to programs of the Peace Corps and Agency for International Development; tables indicating expenditures on United States military, economic and other assistance to African countries for fiscal years 1975 and 1976 are given on p. 1450–1469.

1977

232

U.S. *Congress. House. Committee on Appropriations.* Foreign assistance and related programs appropriation bill, 1977; report together with additional and supplemental views (to accompany H. R. 14260) [Washington, 1976] 76 p.

J66 serial 13134-8

Report submitted by Representative Otto E. Passman.

At head of title: 94th Congress, 2d session. House of Representatives. Report no. 94-1228.

Frequent references to Africa; most sub-Saharan nations are cited in a table, "Total Net Foreign Assistance to 137 Nations and 9 Territories of the World, Fiscal Year 1946 through Fiscal Year 1976, Estimated" (p. 8–9).

233

U.S. *Congress. House. Committee on Appropriations. Subcommittee on Departments of State, Justice, Commerce, the Judiciary, and Related Agencies.* Departments of State, Justice, and Commerce, the judiciary, and related agencies appropriations for 1977: hearings before a subcommittee of the Committee on Appropriations, House of Representatives, Ninety-fourth Congress, second session. Washington, U.S. Govt. Print. Off., 1976. 9 v.

KF27.A664 1976
J74.A23 94th
Cong., House Comm.
Approp., v. 38

John M. Slack, chairman.

Pt. 5, on the Dept. of State, includes occasional references to Africa.

234

U.S. *Congress. House. Committee on Appropriations. Subcommittee on Foreign Operations and Related Agencies.* Foreign assistance and related agencies appropriations for 1977: hearings before a subcommittee of the Committee on Appropriations, House of Representatives, Ninety-fourth Congress, second session. Washington, U.S. Govt. Print. Off., 1876. 2 v.

KF27.A646 1976
J74.A23 94th
Cong., House Comm.
Approp., v. 30

Otto E. Passman, chairman.

Pt. 1 includes brief references to the African Development Fund, family planning projects in various African nations are noted in Pt. 2.

235

U.S. *Congress. Senate. Committee on Appropriations.* Departments of State, Justice, and Commerce, the judiciary, and related agencies appropriations for fiscal year 1977: hearings before a subcommittee of the Committee on Appropriations, United States Senate, Ninety-fourth Congress, second session. Washington, U.S. Govt. Print. Off., 1976. 4 v. illus.

KF26.A6 1976
J74.A23 94th
Cong., Sen. Comm.
Approp., v. 46

John O. Pastore, chairman of subcommittee.

Vol. 1 includes tables indicating the staffing situation of American diplomatic posts in Africa.

236

U.S. *Congress. Senate. Committee on Appropriations. Subcommittee on Foreign Operations.* Foreign assistance and related programs appropriations for fiscal year 1977: hearings before a subcommittee of the Committee on Appropriations, United States Senate, Ninety-fourth Congress, second session, on H. R. 14260. Washington, U.S. Govt. Print. Off., 1876. 1194, xxi p. illus. KF26.A647 1976

J74.A23 94th
Cong., Sen. Comm.
Approp., v. 39

Daniel K. Inouye, chairman.

Includes occasional references to Africa, especially in sections relating to programs of the Agency for International Development (p. 883–896) and of the Peace Corps; tables indicating expenditures on United States military, economic, and other assistance to African countries for fiscal years 1975–1977 are given on p. 1119–1140.

237

U.S. *Congress. Senate. Committee on Foreign Relations.* International Development Assistance Act of 1977: report to accompany S. 1520. [Washington, U.S. Govt. Print. Off., 1977] 73 p. DLC-LL

Report submitted by Senator John Sparkman.

At head of title: 95th Congress, 1st session. Senate. Report no. 95–161.

"Calendar no. 135."

Table of U.S. economic assistance to Africa, by country, proposed for fiscal year 1978, including dollar amounts for the Agency for International Development, Public Law 480, and the Peace Corps. p. 4.

1978

238

U.S. *Congress.* [Hearings] Foreign assistance and related programs appropriations for fiscal year 1978: hearings before a subcommittee of the Committee on Appropriations, United States Senate, Ninety-fifth Congress, first session on H. R. 7797.

238 (cont.)

Washington, U.S. Govt. Print. Off., 1977. 1386, xvii p.   J74.A23, 95th Cong., Sen. Comm. Approp., v. 10

Daniel K. Inouye, chairman.

Among the occasional references to Africa is a statement by W. Haven North, Acting Assistant Administrator, Bureau for Africa, Agency for International Development, on the Sahel Development Program (p. 733–745).

239

U.S. *Congress. House. Committee on Appropriations. Subcommittee on Departments of State, Justice, Commerce, the Judiciary, and Related Agencies.* Departments of State, Justice, and Commerce, the judiciary, and related agencies appropriations for 1978: hearings before a subcommittee of the Committee on Appropriations, House of Representatives, Ninety-fifth Congress, first session. Washington, U.S. Govt. Print. Off., 1977. 7 v.   KF27.A664 1977 J74.A23 95th Cong., House Comm. Approp., v. 18

John M. Slack, chairman.

In Pt. 2, on the Dept. of State, there is a section on the activities of the Bureau of African Affairs (p. 286–289); Pt. 6 covers the African programs of the U.S. Information Agency (p. 732–743).

240

U.S. *Congress. House. Committee on Appropriations. Subcommittee on Foreign Operations and Related Agencies.* Foreign assistance and related agencies appropriations for 1978: hearings before a subcommittee of the Committee on Appropriations, House of Representatives, Ninety-fifth Congress, first session. Washington, U.S. Govt. Print. Off., 1977. 4 v.   KF27.A646 1977 J74.A23 95th Cong., House Comm. Approp., v. 11

Clarence D. Long, chairman.

Includes frequent references to Africa, particularly in Pt. 2, which includes discussions on Agency for International Development programs in education, health, and nutrition, plus comments on the Sahel Development Program and the Zimbabwe Development Fund (p. 22–55).

241

U.S. *Congress. House. Committee on International Relation.* Foreign assistance legislation for fiscal year 1978: hearings, Ninety-fifth Congress, first

session.... Washington, U.S. Govt. Print. Off., 1977. 9 v.   KF27.I549 1977 J74. A23 95th Cong. House. Comm. Inter. Rel., v. 91

Clement J. Zablocki, chairman.

Partial contents: Pt. 3. Economic and military assistance programs in Africa. 286 p.

Hearing held Mar. 17 – Apr. 28, 1977 before the Subcommittee on Africa; Charles C. Diggs, Jr., chairman. The subcommittee's report and recommendations are given in Pt. 9 (p. 229–231).

242

U.S. *Congress. House. Committee on International Relations. Subcommittee on International Development.* Peace Corps authorization for fiscal year 1978: hearing, Ninety-fifth Congress, first session, March 17, 1977. Washington, U.S Govt. Print. Off., 1977. 30 p.   KF27.I54923 1977 J74.A23 95th Cong., House Comm. Inter. Rel., v. 5

Michael Harrington, chairman.

Includes frequent references to Africa.

243

U.S. *Congress. House. Committee on International Relations. Subcommittee on International Operations.* Foreign relations authorization for fiscal year 1978: hearings, Ninety-fifth Congress, first session. Washington, U.S. Govt. Print Off., 1977. [456] p. maps.   KF27.I5493 1977 J74.A23 95th Cong. House Comm. Inter. Rel., v. 4

Dante B. Fascell, chairman.

Hearings held Mar. 22 – Apr. 21, 1977.

Frequent brief references to Africa.

244

U.S. *Congress. Senate. Committee on Foreign Relations.* The International Development Assistance Act of 1978: report, together with additional views on S. 3074. Washington, U.S. Govt. Print. Off., 1978. 122 p.   DLC-LL

John Sparkman, chairman.

At head of title: 95th Congress, 2d session. Senate. Report no. 95-840.

Table on proposed U.S. economic assistance programs to African nations in fiscal year 1979: p. 3.

245

——— The International Security Assistance Act of 1978: report (to accompany S. 3075) [Washington, U.S. Govt. Print. Off., 1978] 67 p.   DLC-LL

245 (cont.)

Report submitted by Senator John Sparkman.

At head of title: 95th Congress, 2d session. Senate. Report no. 95-841.

"Calendar no. 772."

Tables indicate U.S. military assistance programs in various African countries, with actual and proposed expenditures, for the period 1977–79.

1979

246

U.S. *Congress. House. Committee on Appropriations. Subcommittee on Departments of State, Justice, Commerce, the Judiciary, and Related Agencies.* Departments of State, Justice, and Commerce, the judiciary, and related agencies appropriations for 1978 [i.e., 1979]: hearings before a subcommittee of the Committee on Appropriations, House of Representatives, Ninety-fifth Congress, second session. Washington, U.S. Govt. Print. Off., 1978. 8 v.   KF27.A664 1978a
J74.A23 95th
Cong., House Comm.
Approp., v. 31

John M. Slack, chairman.

Title corrected in manuscript on t.p. of v. 1; printed correctly in subsequent volumes.

Pt. 2, on the Dept. of State, includes scattered references to Africa, while Pt. 7 covers African programs of the International Communication Agency (p. 635–646).

247

U.S. *Congress. House. Committee on Appropriations. Subcommittee on Foreign Operations and Related Agencies.* Foreign assistance and related agencies appropriations for 1979: hearings before a subcommittee of the Committee on Appropriations, House of Representatives, Ninety-fifth Congress, second session. Washington, U.S. Govt. Print. Off., 1978. 8 v.   KF27.A646 1978
J74.A23 95th
Cong., House Comm.
Approp., v. 24

Clarence D. Long, chairman.

Pt. 1 includes references to the African Development Fund (p. 581–618), while the refugee situation in Botswana, Zambia, and Mozambique is covered in Pt. 2 (p. 1–36).

248

U.S. *Congress. House. Committee on International Relations.* Foreign assistance legislation for fiscal year 1979: hearings, Ninety-fifth Congress, second

session. Washington, U.S. Govt. Print. Off., 1978. 9 v.   KF27.I549 1978
J74.A23 95th
Cong., House. Comm.
Inter. Rel., v. 92

Clement J. Zablocki, chairman.

Partial contents: Pt. 3. Economic and military assistance programs in Africa. 227 p.

Hearings held Feb. 7 – Mar. 2, 1978 before the Subcommittee on Africa; Charles C. Diggs, Jr., chairman. The subcommittee's report is given in Pt. 9 (p. 91–118).

249

U.S. *Congress. House. Committee on International Relations. Subcommittee on International Operations.* Foreign relations authorization for fiscal year 1979: hearings, Ninety-fifth Congress, second session. Washington, U.S. Govt. Print. Off., 1978. 671 p.   KF27.I5493 1978b
J74.A23 95th Cong.,
House Comm. Inter.
Rel., v. 67

Dante B. Fascell, chairman.

Hearings held Jan. 31 – Apr. 5, 1978.

Includes occasional references to Africa.

250

U.S. *Congress. Senate. Committee on Appropriations. Subcommittee on Foreign Operations.* Foreign assistance and related programs appropriations for fiscal year 1979: hearings before a subcommittee of the Committee on Appropriations, United States Senate, Ninety-fifth Congress, second session, on H. R. 12931. Washington, for sale by the Supt. of Docs., U.S. Govt. Print. Off., 1978. 1596 p.
KF26.A647 1978
J74.A23 95th Cong.
Sen. Comm. Approp.,
v. 23

Daniel K. Inouye, chairman.

Includes occasional references to Africa in discussions on Agency for International Development programs.

251

U.S. *Congress. Senate. Committee on Foreign Relations.* International Development Assistance Act of 1979: hearings, Ninety-sixth Congress, first session on S. 588 . . . and S. Res 92. Washington, U.S. Govt. Print. Off., 1979. 501 p.
KF26.F6 1979g
J74.A23 96th
Cong., Sen. Comm.
For. Rel., v. 5

Frank Church, chairman.

251 (cont.)

Hearings held Mar. 14–23, 1979.

Includes occasional references to Africa.

252

———— The International Development Assistance Act of 1979: report (to accompany S. 588) [Washington, 1979] 66 p.   DLC-LL

Report submitted by Senator Frank Church.

At head of title: 96th Congress, 1st session. Senate. Report no. 96-137.

"Calendar no. 145."

Table on proposed U.S. economic assistance programs to African countries in fiscal year 1980: p. 5.

253

———— The International Security Assistance Act of 1979: report (to accompany S. 584) [Washington, 1979] 44 p.   DLC-LL

Report submitted by Senator Frank Church.

At head of title: 96th Congress, 1st session. Senate. Report no. 96-136.

"Calendar no. 144."

Tables indicate U.S. military assistance programs in various African countries proposed for fiscal 1980.

The Committee's views on security assistance to Zaire are presented on p. 11.

1980

254

U.S. *Congress. House. Committee on Appropriations.* Foreign assistance and related programs appropriations bill, 1980; report, together with additional and Minority views (to accompany H. R. 4473) [Washington?], 1979. 100 p.   DLC-LL

Report submitted by Clarence D. Long, chairman of the committee's Subcommittee on Foreign Operations and Related Programs.

At head of title: 96th Congress, 1st session. House report no. 96-273.

Includes frequent references to Africa.

255

U.S. *Congress. House. Committee on Appropriations. Subcommittee on Departments of State, Justice, Commerce, the Judiciary, and Related Agencies.* Departments of State, Justice and Commerce, the judiciary, and related agencies appropriations for 1980: hearings before a subcommittee of the Committee on Appropriations, House of Representatives, Ninety-sixth Congress, first session. Washington, U.S. Govt. Print. Off., 1979. 9 v.

KF27.A664   1979
J74.A23 96th
Cong., House Comm.
Approp., v. 15

John M. Slack, chairman.

The Africa program of the International Communication Agency is discussed in Pt. 7, p. 216–226.

The programs of the Bureau of African Affairs, U.S. Dept. of State, are discussed in Pt. 8, p. 399–408, with testimony by Richard M. Moose, Assistant Secretary of State for African Affairs.

256

U.S. *Congress. House. Committee on Appropriations. Subcommittee on Foreign Operations and Related Programs.* Foreign assistance and related programs appropriations for 1980: hearings, Ninety-sixth Congress, first session. Washington, U.S. Govt. Print. Off., 1979. 6 v.   KF27.A6463   1979
J74.A23 96th Cong.,
House Comm. Approp.,
v. 9

Clarence D. Long, chairman.

African programs of various agencies are discussed in the following volumes:

Pt. 1. Refugee programs (p. 323–409), with testimony by Dick Clark, U.S. Coordinator for Refugee Affairs, and Peace Corps activities (p. 410–594).

Pt. 2. Includes brief statement on African Development Fund (p. 121–123).

Pt. 4. Economic assistance to Africa is covered specifically on p. 183–337.

Pt. 6 Covers the African Development Fund (p. 184–211) and the African Development Bank (p. 212–217).

257

U.S. *Congress. Senate. Committee on Foreign Relations.* Fiscal year 1980 international security assistance authorization: hearings, Ninety-sixth Congress, first session on S. 584, to amend the Foreign Assistance Act of 1961 and the Arms Export Control Act, and for other purposes. Washington, U.S. Govt. Print. Off., 1979. 523 p.   KF26.F6 1979i
J74.A23 96th
Cong., Sen.
Comm. For. Rel.,
v. 4

Frank Church, chairman.

Hearings held Feb. 28–Apr. 30, 1979.

Africa is covered specifically on p. 171–191; principal witness is Goler T. Butcher, Assistant Administrator, Bureau for Africa, Agency for International Development.

258

Moose, Richard M. Africa: FY 1980 assistance proposals.. *In* U.S. *Dept. of State.* The Department of State bulletin, v. 79, no. 2025, Apr. 1979: 9–11.

JX232.A33 v. 79

Statement by the Assistant Secretary of State for African Affairs before the Subcommittee on Africa, Committee on Foreign Affairs, House of Representatives, Feb. 14, 1979.

1980–1981

259

U.S. *Congress. House. Committee on Foreign Affairs.* Foreign assistance legislation for fiscal years 1980–81: hearings, Ninety-sixth Congress, first session. Washington, U.S. Govt. Print. Off., 1979. 7 v.

KF27.F6 1979e

Clement J. Zablocki, chairman.

Partial contents: Pt. 6. Economic and military assistance programs in Africa. 612 p.

Hearings held Feb. 13–Mar. 12, 1979 before the Subcommittee on Africa; Stephen J. Solarz, chairman.

Among the appendixes to Pt. 6 are the following:

Appendix 1. Additional questions submitted to AID by Representative Solarz and response thereto. p. 545–549.

Appendix 2. Section 102(d) of Public Law 480—progress and commitment data—Kenya. p. 550–568.

In Pt. 7, there are references to southern Africa in hearings before the Subcommittee on International Organizations; Don Bonker, chairman.

260

U.S. *Congress. Senate. Committee on Foreign Relations.* Foreign relations authorization act, fiscal years 1980 and 1981: hearings, Ninety-sixth Congress, first session, on S. 586 ... March 28 and 29, 1979. Washington, U.S. Govt. Print. Off., 1979. 282 p.

KF26.F6 1979e
J74.A23 96th
Cong., Sen. Comm.
For. Rel., v. 8

Frank Church, chairman.

Includes frequent references to Africa.

1981

261

U.S. *Congress.* [Hearings] Foreign assistance and related programs appropriations for fiscal year 1981: hearings before a subcommittee of the Committee on Appropriations, United States Senate, Ninety-sixth Congress, second session. Washing-

ton, for sale by the Supt. of Docs., U.S. Govt. Print. Off., 1980. 2 v.

J74.A23 96th
Cong., Sen.
Comm. Approp.,
v. 26

Daniel K. Inouye, chairman, Subcommittee on Foreign Operations.

The Sahel Development Program, Agency for International Development, is reviewed in part 1, p. 562–578; principal witness is Goler T. Butcher, the Agency's Assistant Administrator for Africa. In part 2, there are statistical tables indicating AID programs in various African countries for fiscal years 1979–1981 (p. 327–340).

262

U.S. *Congress. House. Committee on Appropriations.* Foreign assistance and related programs appropriations bill, 1981. Report, together with minority views (to accompany H. R. 7854). [Washington?] 1980. 103 p.

DLC

Report submitted by Clarence D. Long, chairman of the committee's Subcommittee on Foreign Operations and Related Agencies.

At head of title: 96th Congress, 2d session. House of Representatives. Report no. 96-1207.

Includes occasional references to Africa.

263

U.S. *Congress. House. Committee on Appropriations. Subcommittee on Departments of State, Justice, and Commerce, the Judiciary, and Related Agencies.* Departments of State, Justice, and Commerce, the judiciary, and related agencies appropriations for fiscal year 1981: hearings before a subcommittee of the Committee on Appropriations, House of Representatives, Ninety-sixth Congress, second session. Washington, U.S. Govt. Print. Off., 1980. 8 v.

KF27.A664 1980

John M. Slack, chairman; Neal Smith, acting chairman.

In Pt. 2, the budget of the Bureau of African Affairs, Dept. of State, is reviewed on p. 514–521.

In Pt. 8, the African program of the International Communication Agency is reviewed on p. 374–386.

264

U.S. *Congress. House. Committee on Appropriations. Subcommittee on Foreign Operations and Related Agencies.* Foreign assistance and related programs appropriations for 1981: hearings before a subcommittee of the Committee on Appropriations, House of Representatives, Ninety-sixth Congress, second session. Washington, U.S. Govt. Print. Off., 1980. 6 v.

KF27.A463 1980

Clarence D. Long, chairman.

In Pt. 6, there is a statement by Richard M.

264 (cont.)

Moose, Assistant Secretary of State for African Affairs, on U.S.-Liberian relations, Aug. 19, 1980, plus a discussion on Liberia: p. 118–143. Also included is testimony and discussion on Somalia, Sept. 16, 1980: p. 146–211.

265

U.S. *Congress. House. Committee on Foreign Affairs.* Foreign assistance legislation for fiscal year 1981: hearings, Ninety-sixth Congress, second session ... Washington, U.S. Govt. Print. Off., 1980. 9 v.

KF27.F6   1980

Clement J. Zablocki, chairman.

Partial contents: Pt. 7. Economic and security assistance programs in Africa. 705 p.

Hearings held Feb. 7–Mar. 6, 1980 before the Subcommittee on Africa; Stephen J. Solarz, chairman.

Among the appendixes to Pt 7 are the following:

Appendix 1. Summary of *U.S. Foreign Assistance to Africa: A New Institutional Approach*, by the Development Group for Alternative Policies. p. 665–669.

Appendix 6. Loy, Frank. U.S. refugee assistance in Africa. p. 675–681.

Pt. 8. U.S. voluntary contributions to international organizations. 310 p.

Hearing held Feb. 19–26, 1980 before the Subcommittee on International Organizations; Don Bonker, chairman.

Includes remarks on southern Africa.

Among the appendixes to Pt. 8 is the following:

Appendix 11. Easum, Donald B. Statement by the President, the African-American Institute, on behalf of UNETPSA, the U.N. Institute for Namibia, and the U.N. Trust Fund for South Africa. p. 291–297.

UNETPSA: United Nations Educational Training Program for Southern Africa.

266

U.S. *Congress. House. Committee on Foreign Affairs. Subcommittee on International Operations.* Authorizing appropriations for fiscal year 1980–81 for the Department of State, the International Communication Agency, and the Board for International Broadcasting: hearings, Ninety-sixth Congress, first session. Washington, U.S. Govt. Print. Off., 1979. 315 p.   KF27.F647   1979

Dante B. Fascell, chairman.

Hearings held Feb. 7–22, 1979.

In Appendix 1, the Dept. of State provides tables on official employment profiles of U.S. diplomatic missions, including Dept. of State, Agency for International Development, and Peace Corps personnel, as of Dec. 31, 1978 (p. 218–229), plus statistics by country of U.S. nationals arrested during 1978 (p. 253–254).

267

U.S. *Congress. Senate. Committee on Foreign Relations.* FY 1981 foreign assistance legislation: hearing, Ninety-sixth Congress, second session, on S. 2423 ... S. 2422 ... S. 2588. Pt. 1. Washington, U.S. Govt. Print. Off., 1980. 470 p.

KF26.F6   1980b

Frank Church, chairman.

Hearings held Mar. 12–Apr. 16, 1980.

Africa is covered specifically on p. 451–470.

268

U.S. *Congress. House. Committee on International Relations. Subcommittee on Africa.* Toward a more responsive aid policy for Africa: hearing, Ninety-fifth Congress, first session, October 5, 1977. Washington, U.S. Govt. Print. Off., 1978. 24 p.

KF27.I54914   1977f
J74.A23 95th Cong.,
House Comm. Inter.
Rel., v. 65

Charles C. Diggs, Jr., chairman.

In his opening remarks, Chairman Diggs noted that the purpose of the hearing was to obtain a preview of the kind of creative response that the Carter administration and the Agency for International Development under new leadership will bring to bear on African economic problems.—p. 1.

Witnesses are Goler T. Butcher, Assistant Administrator, and W. Haven North, Deputy Assistant Administrator, Bureau for Africa, Agency for International Development.

269

U.S. *Congress. House. Committee on International Relations. Subcommittee on International Resources, Food, and Energy.* Food problems of developing countries: implications for U.S. policy; hearings, Ninety-fourth Congress, first session, May 21, June 3 and 5, 1975. Washington, U.S. Govt. Print. Off., 1975. 355 p.   KF27.I54947   1975a
J74.A23 94th
Cong., House Comm.
Inter. Rel., v. 18

Charles C. Diggs, Jr., chairman.

Tables indicating Public Law 480 assistance to African nations: p. 138–141.

Abstract in *American Statistics Index*, 1975, Abstracts, p. 907.

Issued also in microfiche. [Washington, Congressional Information Service, 1975?] 4 sheets.

DLC-Micro ASI:75 21388-24

270

U.S. *Congress. Senate. Committee on Agriculture, Nutrition, and Forestry. Subcommittee on Foreign Agricultural Policy.* Public law 480 aid for refugees: hearing, Ninety-sixth Congress, second session, March 4, 1980. Washington, U.S. Govt. Print. Off., 1980. 29 p.   KF26.A3549 1980

Richard B. Stone, chairman.

In an appended statement, Vincent H. Palmieri, U.S. Coordinator for Refugee Affairs, U.S. Dept. of State, describes the needs of refugees in Somalia, Sudan, and Zimbabwe (p. 21–27).

271

U.S. *Congress. Senate. Committee on Foreign Relations.* Peace Corps act amendments of 1979: hearing, Ninety-sixth Congress, first session on S. 802 ... March 21, 1979. Washington, U.S. Govt. Print. Off., 1979. 108 p. map. KF26.F6 1979k
J74.A23 96th
Cong., Sen. Comm.
For Rel., v. 7

Frank Church, chairman; Richard B. Stone, presiding officer.

Includes occasional references to the Peace Corp's Africa programs.

272

U.S. *Congress. Senate. Committee on Foreign Relations. Subcommittee on Foreign Assistance.* Foreign assistance authorization, examination of U.S. foreign aid programs and policies: hearings, Ninety-fourth Congress, first session, on S. 1816 ... and H. R. 9005. Washington, U.S. Govt. Print. Off., 1975. 778 p. illus.   KF26.F6357 1975b
J74.A23 94th
Cong., Sen. Comm.
For. Rel., v. 9

Hubert H. Humphrey, chairman.

Includes occasional references to Africa.

273

—— International development assistance authorization and S. Res. 118: hearings, Ninety-fifth Congress, second session, on S. 2646 ... S. 2420 ... and S. Res. 118 ... March 2, 3, and April 28, 1978. Washington, U.S. Govt. Print. Off., 1978. 1179 p. illus.   KF26.F6359 1978b
J74.A23 95th
Cong., Sen. Comm.
For. Rel., v. 42

John Sparkman, chairman.

Summaries of Agency for International Development projects in Botswana, The Gambia, Lesotho, Mali, Mauritania, and Zaire, p. 1076–1083.

274

—— International security assistance programs: hearings, Ninety-fifth Congress, second session on S. 2846. Washington, U.S. Govt. Print. Off., 1978. 385 p.   KF26.F6357 1978
J74.A23 95th
Cong., Sen. Comm.
For. Rel., v. 43

John Sparkman, chairman.

Testimony and prepared statement of Richard M. Moose, Assistant Secretary of State for African Affairs: p. 9–13.

275

U.S. *Congressional Budget Office.* Assisting the developing countries: foreign aid and trade policies of the United States. Washington, for sale by the Supt. of Docs., U.S. Govt. Print. Off., [1980] xviii, 126 p. (*Its* Background paper)

HC60.U6C66 1980

"September 1980."

Includes bibliographical references.

Prepared for the U.S. Senate.

Includes occasional brief references to Africa.

276

U.S. *Dept. of Agriculture.* Programs in Africa. [Washington?] 1977. 1 v. (unpaged)

Cited as an "unpublished document" in Duffy. *Survey.*

277

U.S. *Joint Chiefs of Staff.* United States military posture for FY 1979. Statement by General George S. Brown to the Congress. Washington, 1978. 124 p.
AMAU

Theatre appraisals: Africa, p. 53–55.

278

U.S. *Office of Education. Institute of International Studies. International Services and Research Staff.* A survey of A.I.D. educational cooperation with developing countries [prepared for the Office of Education and Human Resources, Bureau for Technical Assistance, Agency for International Development by the International Services and Research Staff, Institute of International Studies, U.S. Office of Education, Department of Health, Education, and Welfare] [Washington], Agency for International Development, Dept. of State, [1973] 115 p.   LC2605.U56 1973

Includes regional reports on Africa and on the following sub-Saharan countries: Ethiopia, Liberia, Nigeria, Tanzania, and Uganda.

Issued also in microfiche. [Washington, U.S. Agency for International Development, 1973?] 2 sheets.   DLC-Sci RR PN-AAD-467

279

U.S. *Peace Corps*. Africa region country briefing papers, 1980–1981. [Washington?, 1981?] 75 p. maps. DLC

Brief programs overviews are given for the following countries: Benin, Botswana, Cameroon, Central African Republic, Gabon, The Gambia, Ghana, Ivory Coast, Kenya, Lesotho, Liberia, Malawi, Mali, Mauritania, Niger, Rwanda, Senegal, Seychelles, Sierra Leone, Swaziland, Tanzania, Togo, Upper Volta, and Zaire.

280

U.S. *Treasury Dept*. Report on developing countries external debt and debt relief provided by the United States. Washington, U.S. Govt. Print. Off., 1976. 91 p. HG4517.U58a 1973

At head of title: 94th Congress, 2d session. Committee print.

"Printed for the use of the Committee on International Relations."

Includes tables listing the debts of African nations.

281

U.S. [*Treaties, etc. 1975 Apr. 17*] Agreement for Phase I of the project for strengthening of public health delivery systems in Central and West Africa among the United States of America and the World Health Organization and governments of Central and West Africa. *In* U.S. *Treaties, etc.* United States treaties and other international agreements, v. 28, 1976–77. [Washington, Dept. of State; for sale by the Supt. of Docs., U.S. Govt. Print. Off., 1978] p. 3743–3785. ([Treaties and other international acts series, 8597]) JX231.A34 v. 28

Entered into force Apr. 17, 1975.

In English and French.

282

AID-financed university contracts and grants active during the period October 1, 1977 through September 30, 1978. Washington, [1978?] 29 p. DLC

Includes a section on contracts relating to Africa (general) and to specific sub-Saharan countries.

283

Action. Annual report. 1972+ [Washington] illus. HC60.A395a

Includes an overview of Peace Corps programs in Africa plus descriptions of its activities in sub-Saharan countries; for example, the 1980 report highlights programs in Upper Volta and Sierra Leone.

L.C. has 1972–75, 1978+

284

Action Programs International. Results of the CWR/Niamey Operations Planning Workship, Dec. 9–13, 1974. [Abidjan?, AID/REDSO/WA, 1974] 77 p.

CWR: Central West Region.

Microfiche. [Washington, U.S. Agency for International Development, 1974?] 1 sheet (PN-AAG-518); examined in the Development Information Center, AID, Washington, D.C.

285

Belcher, Marjorie S. Guidelines for AID's regional activities in Africa. [s.l.], 1980. [69] p. (in various pagings)

Includes bibliography.

Prepared for the U.S. Agency for International Development under contract AID/afr-C-1554.

Abstract in *A.I.D. Research and Development Abstracts*, Feb. 1981, p. 29.

Microfiche. [Washington, U.S. Agency for International Development, 1980?] 1 sheet.

DLC-Sci RR PN-AAH-502

286

Bennet, Douglas J. The U.S. and Africa: a growing partnership. Agenda, Mar. 1980: 15–19. HC59.7.A742 1980

Issued by the U.S. Agency for International Development.

A look at possible American responses to the economic and social problems facing African nations in the 1980s and 1990s.

287

Berg, Elliot. African external debt and AID policy: a diagnosis and proposal. [s.l.] 1973. 6 p. (FAR 17122-G)

Prepared for the Conference on African Trends Through the 70's, sponsored by the U.S. Dept. of State.

Examined in the former Foreign Affairs Research Documentation Center, Dept. of State.

288

Butcher, Goler T. Africa: far behind, pushing forward; U.S. assistance must serve as a catalyst in troubled years ahead. Agenda, Apr. 1980: 5–11. illus. HC59.7.A742 1980

Issued by the U.S. Agency for International Development.

Adapted from testimony by the Assistant Administrator, Bureau for Africa, Agency for International Development, before the Committee on Foreign Affairs, U.S. House of Representatives, Feb. 7, 1980.

289

———— Africa: new successes and new challenges. Agenda, Apr. 1979: 20–24. illus.

HC59.7.A742 1979

Issued by the U.S. Agency for International Development.

Condensed from a statement before the Subcommittee on Africa, Committee on Foreign Affairs, U.S. House of Representatives, Feb. 13, 1979.

290

Chernush, Kay. Corralling the tsetse fly; Leroy Williamson is "making things happen" in Africa's battle with the tsetse fly. Agenda, July/Aug. 1978: 5–10. illus.   HC59.7.A742 1978

Issued by the U.S. Agency for International Development.

Describes the work of Dr. Williamson and others concerned with the Agency's tsetse research project.

291

Compendium of energy-technology-related assistance programs for less-developed countries; final report. Columbia, Md., Hittman Associates, inc., 1976. 50 leaves.   DLC

Prepared for the Bureau of Oceans and International Environmental and Scientific Affairs, U.S. Dept. of State.

Sub-Saharan African countries included are Cameroon, Ethiopia, Ghana, Lesotho, Liberia, Mauritius, Nigeria, Sudan, Tanzania, and Upper Volta.

292

Cornman, Ron. The prospects for Peace Corps in urban Africa: an analysis and recommendations. [Washington?, Peace Corps, 1980] 101 p.   DLC

On cover: "Submitted to: Director, Africa Region, Peace Corps."

293

Councils for development: an international directory of councils and associations of voluntary agencies and other non-profit organizations in development assistance. New York, Technical Assistance Information Clearing House. American Council of Voluntary Agencies for Foreign Service, inc., 1981. 66 p.   DLC

Since 1955, the Clearing House "has been operated by the American Council of Voluntary Agencies for Foreign Service, inc. (ACVAFS) with support from the U.S. Government, currently a grant from the Agency for International Development."

Issued in cooperation with the International Agricultural Development Service.

Includes profiles of the following sub-Saharan organizations:

Christian Relief and Development Association, Ethiopia (p. 16–17).

Zambia Council for Social Development (p. 55–57).

294

Dalsimer, Isabel P., Ralph H. Faulkingham, *and* William H. Rusch. Evaluation of AID development program and support grants to Africare. McLean, Va., General Research Corporation, 1978. 79 leaves.

Submitted to the U.S. Agency for International Development under contract AID/afr-C-1142.

Examined in the Development Information Center, A.I.D. Washington, D.C.

295

Development issues: U.S. actions affecting the development of developing countries. 1975+ [Washington, International Development Cooperation Agency] annual.

A report to the U.S. Congress by the Development Coordination Committee.

Vols. for 1975+ examined in the Development Information Center, Agency for International Development, Washington, D.C.

296

Evaluation of ASPAU, AFGRAD, and INTERAF: impact of regional scholarship programs on manpower needs in Africa, [by] M. Hageboeck [et al.] Washington, Practical Concepts Incorporated, 1973. 1 v. (various pagings)   DLC

Prepared for the U.S. Agency for International Development under contract AID/csd-3375.

An evaluation of the effectiveness and impact of the African Scholarship Program of American Universities (ASPAU), African Graduate Scholarship Program (AFGRAD), and the Inter-African University, Scholarship Program (INTERAF).

297

Food and agriculture: a listing of U.S. non-profit organizations in food production and agricultural assistance abroad. New York, American Council of Voluntary Agencies for Foreign Service, Technical Assistance Information Clearing House, 1981. 165 p.   HD1431.F66

The Clearing House is operated by the Center under a grant from the U.S. Agency for International Development.

For each organization—primarily religious

297 (cont.)

groups—the "countries of assistance" are indicated.

298

Food for Peace; annual report on activities carried out under Public Law 480, 83d Congress, as amended. 1956+ [Washington], U.S. Dept. of Agriculture.   DNAL

Semiannual, 1956–72?

Title varies.

Report examined (1977/78) includes statistical tables on programs in Africa.

299

Gilligan, John J., *and* Talcott W. Seelye. U.S. economic and military assistance to Africa. Washington, Office of Media Services, Bureau of Public Affairs, U.S. Dept. of State, 1977. 5 p.   DLC

Statement by Mr. Gilligan, Administrator of the U.S. Agency for International Development, and Mr. Seelye, Deputy Assistant Secretary of State for African Affairs, U.S. Dept. of State, before the Subcommittee on Africa, Committee on International Relations, U.S. House of Representatives.

A report on the Carter Administration's proposals for economic assistance to Sahelian nations, for military aid to various African countries, and for development programs in southern Africa, including a Zimbabwe Development Fund.

300

An Integrated management information system for the Africa Bureau. Washington, Practical Concepts, inc., 1975. 2 v.   DLC

"Submitted to the Bureau for Africa, Agency for International Development."

L.C. has v. 1; both vols. examined in the Development Information Center, AID, Washington, D.C.

301

Irvine, Martha, *and* Judith Gilmore. Report on the trip to Ethiopia, Kenya, Ghana, and Senegal, July 2–August 3, 1974. [Washington, Agency for International Development, 1974] 25 p.

Report on the Agency's evolving relationships with voluntary agencies.

Examined in the Development Information Center, AID Washington, D.C.

302

Montgomery, John D., Paul A. Schwarz, *and* Charles A. Murray. Project management needs and project management training: a review of the AID exper-

ience in Africa. Washington, American Institutes for Research, 1974. 54 p.

Prepared for the U.S. Agency for International Development under contract AID/CM/otr-C-73-201.

Abstract in *A.I.D. Research and Development Abstracts*, Jan. 1976, p. 30.

Microfiche. [Washington, U.S. Agency for International Development, 1974?] 1 sheet.

DLC-Sci RR PN-AAB-234

303

Moose, Richard M. Africa: security assistance to the sub-Sahara. *In* U.S. *Dept. of State*. The Department of State bulletin, v. 78, no. 2013: 30–31.

JX232.A33, v. 78

Statement by the Assistant Secretary of State for African Affairs before the Subcommittee on Africa, Committee on International Relations, House of Representatives, Feb. 28, 1978.

304

Peace Corps staff list for Africa; 1977. [Washington? 1977?]

Source: Duffy. *Survey*.

305

Personnel requirements for project development in East and Southern Africa, [by] Donald R. Mickelwait [et al.] [Washington?], Development Alternatives, inc., 1977. 1 v. (various pagings)

Prepared for the Regional Economic Development Services Office/East Africa, U.S. Agency for International Development.

Examined in the Development Information Center, AID, Washington, D.C.

306

Pinder, Frank E. ECA/USAID/Ethiopia—final report. [s.l., 1976?] 55 leaves.

Report on a three-year period of service as advisor to the Executive Secretary of the United Nations Economic Commission for Africa under a U.S. Agency for International Development grant.

Examined in the Development Information Center, Agency for International Development, Washington, D.C.

307

The President's news conference of May 25, 1978 held in Chicago, Illinois. *In* U.S. *President*. Public papers of the Presidents of the United States. Jimmy Carter. 1978. Washington, U.S. Govt. Print. Off., 1979. p. 972–979.   J80.A283   1978

Includes frequent references to U.S. assistance programs in Africa.

308

Problems and potentials of minorities and women as AID/AFR contractors and grantees. [Washington, MATCH Institution], 1977. 3 v.

Prepared for the Bureau for Africa, U.S. Agency for International Development, under contract AID/afr-C-1290.

Contents: v. 1. Report findings, analysis and recommendations.—v. 2. Technical appendices. —v. 3. Evaluation and summary of seminar proceedings.

Examined in the Development Information Center, AID, Washington, D.C.

309

The Regional Economic Development Services Offices in Africa. [Washington], Office of the Auditor General, U.S. Agency for International Development, 1 v. (various pagings)

Examined in the Development Information Center, AID, Washington, D.C.

310

Regional rural development training (PAID) [Washington?, Agency for International Development, 1976?] [144] leaves (in various foliations)

Concerns AID-support for the work of the Pan-African Institute for Development.

Examined in the Documentation Center, Sahel Development Program, AID, Washington, D.C.

311

Report on examination of AID grants to the Association for the Advancement of Agricultural Sciences in Africa. [Washington], Office of the Auditor General, U.S. Agency for International Development, 1976. 13 p.

Examined in the Development Information Center, AID, Washington, D.C.

312

Sobhan, Iqbal. The planning and implementation of rural development projects: an empirical analysis. [Washington?], 1976. 100 p.

Bibliography: p. 97–100.

Prepared for the U.S. Agency for International Development under contract AID/CM/ta-147-533.

Covers 22 projects in Africa and 14 in Latin America.

Abstract in *A.I.D. Research and Development Abstracts*, July 1978, p. 6.

Microfiche. [Washington, U.S. Agency for International Development, 1976?] 2 sheets.

DLC-Sci RR PN-AAD-639

313

Stacy, Roy A. Africa: world's poorest struggle for survival. Agenda, May 1981: 12–15. illus.

HD59.7.A742   1981

Issued by the U.S. Agency for International Development.

Statement by the Acting Assistant Administrator, Bureau for Africa, Agency for International Development.

314

A Survey of institutional development activities and needs in sub-Saharan Africa: country reports. [New York?], Population Council, 1975. 283 p.

Covers health and population policies and programs, training facilities, and foreign assistance projects in Cameroon, Ethiopia, Ghana, Ivory Coast, Kenya, Liberia, Nigeria, Senegal, Sierra Leone, Tanzania, Zaire, and Zambia.

Microfiche. [Washington, U.S. Agency for International Development, 1975?] 3 sheets.

DLC-Sci RR PN-AAG-915

315

Technical Assistance Information Clearing House. U.S. non-profit organizations in development assistance abroad; Wynta Boynes, editor. New York, 1979. xvi, 525 p.   HC60.T4432   1979

The Clearing House is operated by the American Council of Voluntary Agencies for Foreign Service with funding by the U.S. Agency for International Development.

"TAICH directory 1978."

"This directory is an updated edition of part I (organization profile information) of the 1971 TAICH directory—U.S. non-profit organizations in development assistance abroad. Part II of the 1971 directory has been expanded and updated through a series of periodically revised country reports."

Errata sheets inserted.

Includes index.

A "country index" lists those organizations active in sub-Saharan Africa.

316

———— U.S. non-profit organizations in development assistance abroad. TAICH directory, supplement I, August 1980. New York, American Council of Voluntary Agencies for Foreign Service, [1980?] 54 p.   DLC

Note: A second supplement was issued in Jan. 1982.

317

Towers, Wayne M. U.S. Government programs for training African broadcasters, 1961–1971. [s.l.] 1976. [23] p.

317 (cont.)

Paper presented at a meeting of the International Communication Division, International Communication Association, 1976.

Microfiche. [Arlington, Va., ERIC Document Reproduction Service; prepared for Educational Resources Information Center, National Institute of Education 1976] 1 sheet.

DLC-Sci RR ED122339

318

U.S. economic assistance to Zaire, Kenya, and Zimbabwe. Foreign assistance programs in the South Pacific: the U.S. role. Reports of staff study missions to the Committee on Foreign Affairs, U.S. House of Representatives. Washington, U.S. Govt. Print. Off., 1982. 83 p. maps. DLC

At head of title: 96th Congress, 2d session. Committee print.

The report on assistance to the three African nations (p. 3–58) was prepared by Lewis Gulick, Gerald E. Pitchford, and Stephen D. Nelson, members of a staff mission which visited Africa in October 1980.

319

Wagner, Thomas W., *and* Donald S. Lowe. AID's Remote Sensing Grant Program: final report. Ann Arbor, Environmental Research Institute of Michigan, 1978. 118 p. illus., maps.

Prepared for the Office of Science and Technology, U.S. Agency for International Development under contract AID/ta-c-1148.

"This report summarizes a three-year program sponsored by the U.S. Agency for International Development (AID) to assist developing countries in testing and evaluating remote sensing techniques for varied natural resource assessment and planning activities."

Includes reports on Lesotho and Zaïre.

Microfiche. [Washington, U.S. Agency for International Development, 1978?] 2 sheets.

DLC-Sci RR PN-AAG-089

320

Zedalis, John P. Country roads ... AID builds them in Africa. War on hunger, Dec. 1976: 6–7, 11–13. illus.

HD9000.1.W37 1976

Issued by the U.S. Agency for International Development.

Programs of Communist Nations

321

U.S. *Central Intelligence Agency*. Communist aid to less developed countries of the free world, 1975.

[Washington], 1976. 33 p. illus. HC60.U6C45

"ER 76–10372U."

The term "Communist countries" refers to the Soviet Union, China, Bulgaria, Czechoslovakia, German Democratic Republic, Hungary, Poland, and Romania. Included in the term "less developed" countries of the free world are all African nations except South Africa.

322

—— Communist aid to the less developed countries of the free world, 1976. [Washington], 1977. 33 p. HC60.U6C45 1977

"ER 77-10296."

323

U.S. *Central Intelligence Agency. National Foreign Assessment Center*. Communist aid to less developed countries of the free world, 1977. [Washington] 1978. 38 p. (*Its* Research paper)

"ER 78-10478U." HC60.U6C45 1978a

324

—— Communist aid activities in non-Communist less developed countries in 1978; a research paper. Washington, 1979. 40 p. DLC

"ER 79-10412U."

325

—— Communist aid activities in non-Communist less developed countries, 1979 and 1954–79; a research paper. [Washington], 1980. 45 p. illus. col. maps. DLC

"ER 80-10318U."

Includes reports and statistical tables on both economic and military assistance programs; tables indicate the number of students from various non-Communist regions studying in the Soviet Union, other Eastern European nations, and China.

326

Butcher, Bradley A. PRC aid to Black Africa: an assessment; a research report submitted to the faculty. Maxwell Air Force Base, Ala., Air War College, Air University, 1976. 91 leaves.

AMAU

"Professional study no. 5865."

PRC: People's Republic of China.

327

Newsom, David D. Communism in Africa. *In* U.S. *Dept. of State*. The Department of State bulletin, v. 79, no. 2033, Dec. 1979: 29–32.

JX232.A33, v. 79

Statement by the Under Secretary of State for Political Affairs before the Subcommittee on

327 (cont.)

Africa, Committee on Foreign Affairs, House of Representatives, Oct. 18, 1979.

Includes statistical data on military personnel and economic technicians from the Soviet Union and East Europe, China, and Cuba in sub-Saharan nations as of 1978.

Other Programs

328

Charreau, C. An outline of French research and development organizations for technical assistance in tropical countries. Ithaca, N.Y. Dept. of Agriculture, Cornell University, 1974. 19 p. (Agronomy mimeo 74–15)　　　　　　　　　　MiEM

Prepared for the U.S. Agency for International Development under contract AID/csd-2834.

329

Forrester, Veronica. Extent of EEC aid to Africa noted. *In* U.S. *Joint Publications Research Service.* JPRS 76791. [Springfield, Va., National Technical Information Service, 1980] (Sub-Saharan Africa report, no. 2317) p. 1–5.

Article in *West Africa*, London, Oct. 20, 1980, p. 2060–2061, 2063.

EEC: European Economic Community.

Microfiche. [s.l., 1980]

DLC-Micro JPRS 76791

330

Madeley, John. UN strategy for African development examined. *In* U.S. *Joint Publications Research Service.* JPRS 74200. [Springfield, Va., National Technical Information Service, 1979] (Sub-Saharan Africa report, no. 2154) p. 1–4.

From article in *West Africa*, London, Aug. 13, 1979.

Microfiche. [Washington, Supt. of Docs., U.S. Govt. Print. Off., 1979]

DLC-Micro JPRS 74200

331

Takieddine, Randa. OPEC Special Fund director general discusses aid to Africa. *In* U.S. *Joint Publications Research Service.* JPRS 73357. [Springfield, Va., National Technical Information Service, 1979] (Translations on Sub-Saharan Africa, no. 2098) p. 2–5.

Interview with Ibrahim Shihata, Director General of the Organization of Petroleum Exporting Countries' Special Fund, in *An-Nahar Arab Report & Memo*, Mar. 12, 1979, p. 12–15.

Microfiche. [Washington, Supt. of Docs., U.S. Govt. Print. Off., 1979]

DLC-Micro JPRS 73357

332

Text of OAU economic action plan published. *In* U.S. *Joint Publications Research Service.* JPRS 75862. [Springfield, Va., National Technical Information Service, 1980] (Sub-Saharan Africa report, no. 2256) p. 1–4.

Article on the Organization of African Unity's special economic summit, Lagos, Nigeria, Apr. 1980, in *West Africa*, London, May 19, 1980, p. 869, 871–872.

Microfiche. [s.l., 1980]

DLC-Micro JPRS 75862

Commerce

Note: Basic statistics on United States trade with sub-Saharan Africa, together with data on grants and credits, are given in the *Statistical Abstract of the United States* (HA202), issued annually by the U.S. Bureau of the Census. Other periodicals of this agency provide more detailed coverage of trading patterns, such as *Highlights of U.S. Export and Import Trade* (HF105.C1332), *U.S. Exports: Schedule E Commodity by Country* (HF3031.U53a), and *U.S. General Imports: Schedule A, Commodity by Country* (HF105.C13733). *Survey of Current Business* (HC101.A13), issued monthly by the Bureau of Economic Analysis, U.S. Dept. of Commerce, includes tables on American trade with Africa plus data on United States assets there. These publications are available for sale from the Superintendent of Documents, U.S Government Printing Office, Washington, D.C. Related titles can be identified through the *Serials Supplement* to the *Monthly Catalog of United States Government Publications* (Z1223.A18). Agricultural trade between the United States and Africa is covered specifically in publications of the Economics and Statistics Service of the U.S. Dept. of Agriculture: *FATUS: Foreign Agricultural Trade of the United States* (monthly; HD9004.U553a) and its annual supplement, *Foreign Agricultural Trade Statistics Report*. Many issues of official statistical publications relating to commerce between the United States and Africa can be identified through the *American Statistics Index: A Comprehensive Guide and Index to the Statistical Publications of the U.S. Government (Washington, Congressional Information Service. Z7554.U5A46).*

333

U.S. *Central Intelligence Agency.* Non-OPEC LDCs: terms of trade since 1970. [Washington], 1976. 28 p. (*Its* Research aid)　　HF1413,U54　1976
"ER 76-10383."

OPEC: Organization of Petroleum Exporting Countries.

LDCs: "less developed countries."

Covers the following sub-Saharan African countries: Benin, Cameroon, Central African Republic, Chad, Congo, Ethiopia, Gambia, Ghana, Ivory Coast, Kenya, Liberia, Malagasy Republic, Malawi, Mali, Mauritania, Mauritius, Mozambique,

333 (cont.)

Niger, Réunion, Rwanda, Senegal, Sierra Leone, Somalia, Sudan, Tanzania, Togo, Uganda, Upper Volta, Zaïre, and Zambia.

334

U.S. *Central Intelligence Agency. National Foreign Assessment Center.* Non-OPEC LDC terms of trade, 1970–77. [Washington], 1979. 24 p. (*Its* Research paper)   HF1413.U54 1979

Covers the same African countries cited in entry 333, plus Angola.

335

U.S. *Congress. House. Committee on Agriculture. Subcommittee on Oilseeds and Rice.* Palm oil import review: hearings before the Subcommittee on Oilseeds and Rice, and Subcommittee on Cotton of the Committee on Agriculture, House of Representatives, Ninety-fourth Congress, second session, March 18, 1976, Washington, D. C. and May 15, 1976, Memphis, Tenn. Washington, U.S. Govt. Print. Off., 1976. 177 p.   KF27.A367 1976

Dawson Mathis, chairman, Subcommittee on Oilseeds and Rice.

David R. Bowen, chairman, Subcommittee on Cotton.

Includes occasional references to Africa.

336

African need for more internal trade reported. *In* U.S. *Joint Publications Research Service.* JPRS 76075. [Springfield, Va., National Technical Information Service, 1980] (Sub-Saharan Africa report, no. 2270) p. 8–11.

Extract from a "plan of action" adopted by a special summit of the Organization of African Unity, Lagos, Nigeria, Apr. 1980, in *West Africa*, London, June 23, 1980, p. 1111–1114.

Microfiche. [s.l., 1980]

      DLC-Micro JPRS 76075

337

Bolen, David B. Trade and investment: another dimension in U.S.-Africa relations. *In* U.S. *Dept. of State.* The Department of State bulletin, v. 75, no. 1951, Nov. 15, 1976: 616–622.

      JX232.A33 v. 75

Address by the Deputy Assistant Secretary of State for African Affairs before the Conference on American Public Policy and Private Enterprise in Africa, University of Houston, Texas, Oct. 14, 1976.

338

Chittum, J. Marc. Trade regulations for Burundi, Central African Empire, Chad, Gambia, Malawi,

Mali, Rwanda, Seychelles and Somalia. [Washington], U.S. Dept. of Commerce, Domestic and International Business Administration; [for sale by the Supt. of Docs., U.S. Govt. Print. Off.], 1977. 30 p. (Overseas business reports. OBR 77-59)

      HF91.U482 1977, no. 59

International marketing information series.

Issued also in microfiche. [Washington, Congressional Information Service, 1977?] 1 sheet.

      DLC-Micro ASI: 77 2026-5.64

339

——— Trade regulations of Benin, Guinea, Malagasy Republic, Mauritania, Mauritius, Mozambique, Niger, Togo, Uganda, and Upper Volta. [Washington], U.S. Dept. of Commerce, Domestic and International Business Administration; [for sale by the Supt. of Docs., U.S. Govt. Print. Off.] 1977. 34 p. (Overseas business reports. OBR 77-28)

      HF91.U482 1977, no. 28

International marketing information series.

Abstract in *American Statistics Index*, 1977, Abstracts, p. 158.

Issued also in microfiche. [Washington, Congressional Information Service, 1977?] 1 sheet.

      DLC-Micro ASI:77 2026-5.43

340

Howland, Kenneth E., *and* Daniel J. Stevens. A summary of tariff and nontariff barriers on tobacco in free world markets, 1973. Washington, Foreign Agricultural Service, U.S. Dept. of Agriculture, 1974. 49 p. (U.S. Foreign Agricultural Service. FAS-M, 257)   S21.Z2383 no. 257

Includes data on import duties and nontariff barriers to tobacco and tobacco products imposed by African nations.

341

International Coffee Council. [*Treaties, etc. 1975 Dec. 3*] International coffee agreement, 1976. *In* U.S. *Treaties, etc.* United States treaties and other international agreements, v. 28, 1976–77. [Washington, Dept. of State; for sale by the Supt. of Docs., U.S. Govt. Print. Off., 1978] p. 6401–6707. ([Treaties and other international acts series, 8683])   JX231.A34 v. 28

Approved by the International Coffee Council at London, Dec. 3, 1975; ratified by the United States Sept. 21, 1976.

In English, French, Portuguese, and Spanish.

African members of the Council: Burundi, Cameroon, Central African Republic, Congo, Dahomey, Ethiopia, Gabon, Ghana, Ivory Coast, Kenya, Liberia, Madagascar, Nigeria, Rwanda, Sierra Leone, Tanzania, Togo, Uganda, and Zaire.

342

Magyar, Karl P. United States trade with Africa: a critical perspective. [s.l., 1980?] 16 leaves.

DLC

On cover: "This paper was prepared for the Department of State as part of its external research program."

343

Market profiles for Africa. Washington, Office of International Marketing, Bureau of International Commerce; [for sale by the Supt. of Docs., U.S. Govt. Print. Off.], 1976. 41 p. (Overseas business reports. OBR 76-05)   HF91.U482 1976, no. 5

One-page reports on 40 African nations include information on foreign trade and investment, finance, economic conditions, natural resources, and population.

344

Market profiles for Africa. [Washington], U.S. Dept. of Commerce, Domestic and International Business Administration; [for sale by the Supt. of Docs., U.S. Govt. Print. Off.], 1976. 47 p. map. (Overseas business reports. OBR 76-51)

HF91.U482 1976, no. 51

International marketing information series.

Superseded by a publication with the same title (Overseas business reports. OBR 78-20; entry 345).

One-page reports on 44 sub-Saharan states include information on foreign trade and investment, finance, economic conditions, natural resources, and population.

345

Market profiles for Africa. [Washington], U.S. Dept. of Commerce, Industry and Trade Administration; [for sale by the Supt. of Docs., U.S. Govt. Print. Off.], 1978. 46 p. (Overseas business reports. OBR 78–20)   HF91.U482 1978, no. 20

International marketing information series.

Supersedes a publication with the same title (Overseas business reports. OBR 76-51; entry 344).

Superseded by a publication with the same title (Overseas business reports. 80-04; entry 346).

For a description of the contents of this publication, see entry 346.

346

Market profiles for Africa. [Washington], U.S. Dept. of Commerce, International Trade Administration; [for sale by the Supt. of Docs., U.S. Govt. Print. Off.], 1980. 47 p. (Overseas business reports. OBR 80-04)   HF91.U482 1980, no. 4

International marketing information series.

Supersedes a publication with the same title (OBR 78-20; entry 345).

Superseded by a publication with the same title (OBR 81-14; entry 347).

One-page reports on 45 sub-Saharan states include information on foreign trade and investment, finance, economic conditions, natural resources, and population.

347

Market profiles for Africa. Washington, U.S. Dept. of Commerce, International Trade Administration; [for sale by the Supt. of Docs., U.S. Govt. Print. Off.], 1981. 45 p. (Overseas business reports. OBR 81-14)   HF91.U482 1981, no. 14

International marketing information series.

Supersedes a publication with the same title (OBR 80-04; entry 346).

One-page reports on 45 sub-Saharan states include information on foreign trade and investment, finance, economic conditions, natural resources, and population.

348

Marx, Robert E. U.S. farm exports to Africa at record level in 1975. Foreign agriculture, June 7, 1976: 9, 12.   HD1401.F65 1976

Issued by the U.S. Foreign Agricultural Service.

349

Moore and Young lead "most successful" U.S. trade mission. Eximbank record, v. 4, no. 1, Oct. 1979: 1, 3. illus.   DEI

Report on a trade mission to Africa in September 1979 led by John L. Moore, Jr., chairman, Export-Import Bank of the United States, and Andrew Young, U.S. Ambassador to the United Nations.

Note: Export-Import Bank credit authorizations to sub-Saharan African countries are recorded in its *Annual Report* (HG3754.U5E95a). The 1979 report, for example, includes information on authorizations for Cameroon, Ethiopia, Ivory Coast, Nigeria, Togo, Zaire, and Zambia.

350

Morris, David. African exports to Japan increase. *In* U.S. *Joint Publications Research Service.* JPRS 76806. [Springfield, Va., National Technical Information Service, 1980] (Sub-Saharan Africa report, no. 2319) p. 6–9.

Article in *West Africa*, London, Oct. 27, 1980, p. 2122–2123.

Microfiche. [s.l., 1980]

DLC-Micro JPRS 76806

351

Pearson, Scott R. Notes on the contributions of exports to African development. [s.l., 1973] [4] leaves. (FAR 17123-N)

351 (cont.)

"These notes have been prepared as background material for use in a conference sponsored by the Department of State on African Trends Through the 70's, Washington, .D.C, April 1973."

Examined in the former Foreign Affairs Research Documentation Center, U.S. Dept. of State.

352

President of Club de Dakar interviewed. *In* U.S. *Joint Publications Research Service.* JPRS 73416. [Springfield, Va., National Technical Information Service, 1979] (Translations on Sub-Saharan Africa, no. 2101) p. 10–19.

Translation of interview with Mohamed T. Diawara in *Le Libre Belgique*, Feb. 27, 1979, p. 14, concerning the Club's focus on international trade and African economic development.

Microfiche. [Washington, Supt. of Docs., U.S. Govt. Print. Off., 1979]

DLC-Micro JPRS 73416

353

Riley, Harold M., *and* Michael T. Weber. Marketing in developing countries. East Lansing, Dept. of Agricultural Economics, Michigan State University, 1979. 29 p. (MSU rural development series. Working paper, no. 6)   MiEM

Prepared for the U.S. Agency for International Development under contract AID/ta-CA-3.

Cited in *Sahel Bibliographic Bulletin*, v. 4, no. 3, 1980, p. 171.

354

Sabatini, Omero. The EC and its special third-country partnerships. Foreign agriculture, Feb. 21, 1977: 2–5, 11–12. illus.   HD1401.F65 1977

At head of title: "Part 1—the Lomé Convention."

Issued by the U.S. Foreign Agricultural Service. EC: European Community.

355

Schaufele, William E. The climate for doing business in Africa: statement before the International Business Forum, April 15, 1977, Philadelphia, Pa. Washington, Office of Media Services, Bureau of Public Affairs, Dept. of State, 1977. 5 p.

Source: *Month. Cat.*, 1977, 77-16534.

356

———— United States economic relations with Africa. *In* U.S. *Dept. of State.* The Department of State bulletin, v. 74, no. 1915, Mar. 8, 1976: 295–299.

JX232.A33 v. 74

Address of the Assistant Secretary of State for African Affairs before the African-American Chamber of Commerce, New York, Feb. 18, 1976.

357

Thomason, James S. Seaport dependence and interstate cooperation: the case of sub-Saharan Africa. Alexandria, Va., Center for Naval Analyses, Institute of Naval Studies, 1980. 139 p. (Center for Naval Analyses. Professional paper, 268)

Bibliography: p. 128–129.

A study of cooperation among 18 sub-Saharan nations in the period 1962–68.

Microfiche. [s.l., Defense Documentation Center, 1980] 2 sheets.   DLC-Sci RR AD-A081193

358

United States foreign trade annual, 1973–1979. [Washington], U.S. Dept. of Commerce, International Trade Administration; [for sale by the Supt. of Docs., U.S. Govt. Print. Off.], 1980. 34 p. (Overseas business reports. OBR 80-23)

HF91.U482 1980, no. 23

International marketing information series.

Includes statistics on U.S. trade with individual African nations and on the U.S. share of manufactured products supplied to these states.

359

United States trade with major world areas, 1969–1975. [Washington], U.S. Dept. of Commerce, Bureau of International Economic Policy and Research; [for sale by the Supt. of Docs., U.S. Govt. Print. Off.], 1976. 85 p. (Overseas business reports. OBR 76-42)

HF91.U482 1976, no. 42

International marketing information series.

Tables indicate U.S. trade in dollars with African nations (excluding South Africa), divided by exports and imports of major commodities; trade figures for South Africa are combined with those for Australia and New Zealand.

360

United States trade with major world areas, 1971–1977. [Washington], U.S. Dept. of Commerce, Industry and Trade Administration; [for sale by the Supt. of Docs., U.S. Govt. Print. Off.], 1978. [90] p. (Overseas business reports. OBR 78-45)

HF91.U482 1978, no. 45

International marketing information series.

For a description of the contents of this publication, see entry 359.

361

World trade outlook for Africa. Washington, U.S. Dept. of Commerce, Domestic and International Business Administration; [for sale by the Supt. of

361 (cont.)

Docs., U.S. Govt. Print. Off.], 1976. 6 p. (Overseas business reports. OBR 76-10)

              HF91.U482   1976, no. 10

Brief reports on sub-Saharan Africa (general), South Africa, Nigeria, Ivory Coast, Kenya, Sudan, Zaire, and Zambia, all reprinted from *Commerce America*, Feb. 2, 1976.

362

World trade outlook for Africa. [Washington], U.S. Dept. of Commerce, Bureau of International Commerce; [for sale by the Supt. of Docs., U.S. Govt. Print. Off.] 1976. [8] p. (Overseas business reports, OBR 76-36)

              HF91.U482   1976, no. 36

International marketing information series.

Brief reports on sub-Saharan Africa (general), South Africa, Nigeria, Gabon, Ivory Coast, Kenya, Sudan, and Zaire, all reprinted from *Commerce America*, Aug. 2, 1976.

363

World trade outlook for Africa. [Washington], U.S. Dept. of Commerce, Bureau of International Commerce; [for sale by the Supt. of Docs., U.S. Govt. Print. Off.] 1977. 8 p. (Overseas business reports. OBR 77-12)

              HF91.U482   1977, no. 12

International marketing information series.

Supersedes a publication with the same title (Overseas business reports. OBR 76-32; entry 362).

Brief reports on sub-Saharan Africa (general), South Africa, Nigeria, Gabon, Ivory Coast, Kenya, Sudan, and Zaire, all reprinted from *Commerce America*, Jan. 31, 1977.

364

World trade outlook for Africa. [Washington], U.S. Dept. of Commerce, Bureau of International Commerce; [for sale by the Supt. of Docs., U.S. Govt. Print. Off.], 1977. 8 p. (Overseas business reports. OBR 77-44)

              HF91.U482   1977, no. 44

International marketing information series.

Brief reports on sub-Saharan Africa (general), South Africa, Nigeria, Cameroon, Ivory Coast, Kenya, Sudan, and Zaire, all reprinted from *Commerce America*. Aug. 1, 1977.

365

World trade outlook for Africa. [Washington], U.S. Dept. of Commerce, Industry and Trade Administration; [for sale by the Supt. of Docs., U.S. Govt. Print. Off.], 1978. 7 p. (Overseas business reports. OBR 78-11)   HF91.U482   1978, no. 11

International marketing information series.

Supersedes a publication with the same title (Overseas business reports. OBR 77-44; entry 364).

Superseded by a publication with the same title (Overseas business reports. OBR 78-35; entry 366).

Brief reports on sub-Saharan Africa (general), Nigeria, Gabon, Ivory Coast, Kenya, Liberia, Sudan, and Zambia, all reprinted from *Commerce America*, Jan. 30, 1978.

366

World trade outlook for Africa. [Washington], U.S. Dept. of Commerce, Industry and Trade Administration; [for sale by the Supt. of Docs., U.S. Govt. Print. Off.], 1978. 8 p. (Overseas business reports. OBR 78-35)   HF91.U482   1978, no. 35

International marketing information series.

Supersedes a publication with the same title (Overseas business reports. OBR 78-11; entry 365).

Superseded by a publication with the same title (Overseas business reports. OBR 79-06; entry 367).

Brief reports on Cameroon, Gabon, Ivory Coast, Liberia, Nigeria, Sudan, and South Africa, all reprinted from *Commerce America*, July 31, 1978.

367

World trade outlook for Africa. [Washington], U.S. Dept. of Commerce, Industry and Trade Administration; [for sale by the Supt. of Docs., U.S. Govt. Print. Off.], 1979. 7 p. (Overseas business reports. OBR 79-06)   HF91.U482   1979, no. 6

International marketing information series.

Supersedes a publication with the same title (Overseas business reports. OBR 78-35; entry 366).

Superseded by a publication with the same title (Overseas business reports. OBR 79-25; entry 368).

Brief reports on sub-Saharan Africa (general), Nigeria, Cameroon, Gabon, Ivory Coast, Kenya, and South Africa, all reprinted from *Business America*, Jan. 29, 1979.

368

World trade outlook for Africa. [Washington], U.S. Dept. of Commerce, Industry and Trade Administration; [for sale by the Supt. of Docs., U.S. Govt. Print Off.], 1979. 8 p. (Overseas business reports. OBR 79-25)   HF91.U482   1979, no. 25

International marketing information series.

Supersedes a publication with the same title (Overseas business reports. OBR 79-06; entry 367).

Superseded by a publication with the same title (Overseas business reports. OBR 80-12; entry 369).

Brief reports on sub-Saharan Africa (general), Nigeria, Cameroon, Gabon, Ivory Coast, Kenya, Liberia, Sudan, and South Africa, all reprinted from *Business America*, July 30, 1979.

369

World trade outlook for Africa. [Washington], U.S. Dept. of Commerce, International Trade Administration; [for sale by the Supt. of Docs., U.S. Govt. Print. Off.], 1980. 8 p. (Overseas business reports. OBR 80-12)   HF91.U482   1980, no. 12

International marketing information series.

Supersedes a publication with the same title (Overseas business reports. OBR 79-25; entry 368).

Brief reports on sub-Saharan Africa (general), Nigeria, Gabon, Cameroon, Ivory Coast, Kenya, Liberia, Sudan, and South Africa, all reprinted from *Business America*, Feb. 11, 1980.

Communications and Transportation

370

[*U.S. Central Intelligence Agency*] The Tan-Zam Railroad. 10–75. [Washington, 1975] col. map.
          G8442.T3   1975.U5

Scale 1 : 10,230,000.

Shows mineral resources and agricultural areas found along the railway between Dar es Salaam, Tanzania, and Kitwe, Zambia.

"502797."

371

Badibanga, André. African press adulation of national leaders analyzed. *In* U.S. *Joint Publications Research Service.* JPRS 73489. [Springfield, Va., National Technical Information Service, 1979] (Translations on Sub-Saharan Africa, no. 2107) p. 1–14.

Translation of article in *Revue française d'études politiques africaines*, Paris, Mar. 1979, p. 40–57, based on an analysis of *Elima* (Kinshasa), *Togo-Presse* (Lomé), *Fraternité-Matin* (Abidjan), and *Sahel* (Niamey).

Microfiche. [Washington, Supt. of Docs., U.S. Govt. Print. Off., 1979]
          DLC-Micro JPRS 73489

372

Carter, Anne F. Ship and port developments, 1967 through 1972. China Lake, Calif., Naval Weapons Center, 1973. [254] p. illus., maps.

"NWC TP 5590."

Africa is covered on p. 82–97.

Microfiche. [s.l. 1974] 3 sheets.
          DLC-Sci RR AD-918654

373

Decupper, Joel. Air Afrique problems discussed. *In* U.S. *Joint Publications Research Service.* JPRS

75418. [Springfield, Va., National Technical Information Service, 1980] (Sub-Saharan Africa report, no. 2228) p. 58–63.

Translation of article in *Africa*, Dakar, Feb. 1980, p. 48–49.

Microfiche. [s.l., 1980]
          DLC-Micro JPRS 75418

374

Dodson, Don, *and* William A. Hachten. Communication and development: African and Afro-American parallels. [Minneapolis?], 1973. 37 p. (Journalism monographs, no. 28)

Issued by the Association for Education in Journalism.

Abstract in *Resources in Education*, Feb. 1975, p. 45.

Microfiche. [Arlington, Va., ERIC Document Reproduction Service; prepared for Educational Resources Information Center, National Institute of Education, 1975] 1 sheet.
          DLC-Micro ED096680

375

Gaudio, Attilio. Freedom of expression in Africa examined. *In* U.S. *Joint Publications Research Service.* JPRS 73044. [Springfield, Va., National Technical Information Service, 1979] (Translations on Sub-Saharan Africa, no. 2078) p. 10–19.

Translation of article on press freedom with particular reference to Cameroon, Ivory Coast, and Senegal, in *Africa*, Dakar, Feb. 1979, p. 47–50, 90.

Microfiche. [Washington, Supt. of Docs., U.S. Govt. Print. Off., 1979]
          DLC-Micro JPRS 73044

376

Harbridge House, inc. African shipping patterns: final report, prepared for the Supply and Transportation Division of the Department of State. Boston, 1975. 114 p. (in various pagings) illus.
          HE901.H37   1975

377

Harrow, Kenneth. Sembene Ousmane's Xala: an analysis of the use of film and novel in the communication of ideology. East Lansing, Michigan State University, [1977?] [18] p.

Abstract in *Resources in Education*, Mar. 1978, p. 108.

Microfiche. [Arlington, Va., ERIC Document Reproduction Service; prepared for Educational Resources Information Center, National Institute of Education, 1978] 1 sheet.
          DLC-Micro ED145819

378

Kurtz, Camille, *and* Daniel G. Matthews. "Africa speaks, America responds": a report on the African Council on Communication Education Dialogue, "Communication Education/Training Needs in Africa," April 11–13, 1979, Washington, D.C. Washington, African Bibliographic Center, 1979. [122] p. illus.

Cosponsored by the African Bibliographic Center, the African Council on Communication Education, and the Overseas Liaison Committee, American Council on Education.

In English and French.

Abstract in *Resources in Education*, 1980 annual cumulation, p. 620.

Microfiche. [Arlington, Va., ERIC Document Reproduction Service; prepared for Educational Resources Information Center, National Institute of Education, 1980] 2 sheets.

DLC-Micro ED178978

379

Lake Chad Basin Commission. [*Treaties, etc. United States, 1976 June 25*] Grant agreement between the Agency for International Development and the Lake Chad Basin Commission (final engineering design of two road links). *In* U.S. *Treaties, etc.* United States treaties and other international agreements, v. 28, 1976–77. [Washington, Dept. of State; for sale by the Supt. of Docs., U.S. Govt. Print. Off., 1978] p. 6098–6118. ([Treaties and other international acts series, 8671])

JX231.A34 v. 28

Signed at N'Djamena, Chad June 25, 1976.

In English and French.

Concerns funding for the construction of road links between Kousseri and Fotokol, Cameroon, and between Magada, Cameroon, and Bongor, Chad.

380

Mamoudou, Mahammadou. Air Afrique president notes company's progress. *In* U.S. *Joint Publications Research Service*. JPRS 74448. [Springfield, Va., National Technical Information Service, 1979] (Sub-Saharan Africa report, no. 2169) p. 1–7.

Translation of interview with Aoussou Koffi, director of Air Afrique, in *Sahel Hebdo*, Niamey, Sept. 3, 1979, p. 11–14.

Microfiche. [Washington, Supt. of Docs., U.S. Govt. Print. Off., 1979] DLC-Micro JPRS 74448

381

Nettleton, John G. The Tanzam Railroad: the PRC in Africa versus United States interests; a research study submitted to the faculty. Maxwell Air Force Base, Ala., Air Command and Staff College, Air University, 1974. 109 leaves. maps. AMAU

Bibliography: leaves 104-108.

PRC: People's Republic of China.

Abstract in *Air University Abstracts of Research Papers*, 1974, no. 668.

Issued also in mcirofiche. [s.l., 1974] 2 sheets (AD-920593L).

382

Nwankwo, Robert I. Political culture or professional underdevelopment? Indentity and leadership among Afro-American and African press. [s.l., 1978] [30] p.

Speech prepared for presentation at the annual meeting of the Association for Education in Journalism, 1978.

Abstract in *Resources in Education*, July 1979, p. 60.

Microfiche. [Arlington, Va., ERIC Document Reproduction Service; prepared for Educational Resources Information Center, National Institute of Education, 1979] 1 sheet.

DLC-Micro ED166711

383

Review of civil aviation projects. *In* U.S. *Joint Publications Research Service*. JPRS 71295. [Springfield, Va., National Technical Information Service, 1978] (Translations on Sub-Saharan Africa, no. 1947) p. 5–12.

Translation of article on the Agence pour la sécurité de la navigation aérienne en Afrique et à Madagascar (ASECNA), in *Africa*, Dakar, Apr. 1978, p. 57, 59, 61, 90.

Microfiche. [Washington, Supt. of Docs., U.S. Govt. Print. Off., 1978] DLC-Micro JPRS 71295

Drought Conditions— Desertification

384

U.S. *Agency for International Development*. Drought damage and famine in Sub-Sahara Africa. [Washington], Bureau of Public Affairs, Dept. of State, Office of Media Services, 1974. 54 p. maps. (U.S. Dept. of State. African series, 58)

HC591.S253F39

U.S. Dept. of State. Office of Media Services. Special report, no. 10.

United States Departments of State publication, 8792.

Contains the text of AID's *Report to the Congress on Famine in Sub-Sahara [sic] Africa* (1974).

384 (cont.)

The focus is on Mali, Chad, Mauritania, Senegal, Upper Volta, The Gambia, Niger, and Ethiopia, with additional assessments on the situation in Nigeria, Sudan, Ghana, Central African Republic, Cameroon, Tanzania, and Kenya.

385

U.S. *Agency for International Development. Bureau for Africa.* Special report to the Congress on the drought situation in Sub-Saharan Africa. [Washington], 1975. [48] p. illus., map.

Abstract in *American Statistics Index*, 1975, Abstracts, p. 595.

Microfiche. [Washington, U.S. Agency for International Development, 1975?] 1 sheet (DLC-Sci RR PN-AAG-148); and [Washington, Congressional Information Service, 1975?] 1 sheet (DLC-Micro ASI: 75 7208-3).

Issued also as Appendix 1, Pt. 6 of *World Hunger, Health, and Refugee Problems* (entry 176).

386

Berry, Leonard, *and* Richard B. Ford. Recommendations for a system to monitor critical indicators in areas prone to desertification. Worcester, Mass., Program for International Development, Clark University, 1977. [187] leaves (in various foliations) DLC

A report submitted to the United States Agency for International Development and the Department of State under Contract Number AID/ta-C-1407 on behalf of the United States Task Force on Desertification."

Includes the Sahel and Eastern Africa.

387

Desertification project; final report. Washington, American Association for the Advancement of Science, [1978] 20 p.

In the "acknowledgement to donors," the Association expresses its gratitude to the U.S. Agency for International Development's Sahel Development Program which provided funds for planning the project in grant AID/afr-G-1322.

Examined in the Documentation Center, Sahel Development Program. AID, Washington, D.C.

388

Eckholm, Erik, *and* Lester R. Brown. The spreading desert. War on Hunger, Aug. 1977: 1–11. illus., map. HD9000.1.W37 1977

Issued by the U.S. Agency for International Development.

Emphasis is on desertification in Africa.

389

——— The spreading desert: part II. War on hunger, Sept. – Oct. 1977: 1–8. illus.

HD9000.1.W37 1977

Issued by the U.S. Agency for International Development.

Includes descriptions on conditions in West Africa, Sudan, Ethiopia, and Somalia.

390

MacLeod, N. H., J. S. Schubert, *and* P. Anaejionu. Report on the Skylab 4 African drought and arid lands experiment. *In* Skylab explores the Earth; prepared by NASA Lyndon B. Johnson Space Center. Washington, Scientific and Technical Information Office, National Aeronautics and Space Administration, 1977. (U.S. National Aeronautics and Space Administration. NASA SP, 380) p. 263–286. illus., maps. QC808.5.S48

391

Paylore, Patricia. Desertification: a world bibliography, compiled and edited by Patricia Paylore for 23d International Geographical Congress, Moscow, 1976, pre-conference meeting of the IGU Working Group on Desertification, Desert Research Institute, Ashkhabad, Turkmen SSR, July 20–26, 1976. Tucson, University of Arizona, Office of Arid Lands Studies, c1976. 644 p.

Z6004.D4P35

Africa is covered specifically on p. 45–272.

Issued also in microfiche. [Washington, U.S. Agency for International Development, 1976?] 3 sheets. DLC-Sci RR PN-AAC-381

392

Reining, Priscilla. Desertification papers prepared before and as a sequel to the Science Associations' Nairobi Seminar on Desertification. Washington, American Association for the Advancement of Science, [1978] 141 p. illus., maps.

In *Desertification Project; Final Report* (entry 387), the Association expresses its gratitude to the U.S. Agency for International Development's Sahel Development Program which provided funds for planning the project through grant AID/afr-G-1322.

Examined in the Documentation Center, Sahel Development Program, AID, Washington, D.C.

393

——— Handbook on desertification indicators based on the Science Associations' Nairobi Seminar on Desertification. Washington, American Association for the Advancement of Science, [1978] 141 p.

Examined in the Documentation Center, Sahel Development Program, AID, Washington D.C.

Ecology

394

U.S. *Congress. Joint Economic Committee. Subcommittee on International Economics.* The global 2000 report: hearing, Ninety-sixth Congress, second session, September 4, 1980. Washington, for sale by the Supt. of Docs., U.S. Govt. Print. Off., 1980. 57 p.   KF25.E253 1980
                    J74.A23 96th
                    Cong., Joint Econ.
                    Comm., v. 45

Henry S. Reuss, chairman.

Includes a summary of the *Report* (entry 400).

395

U.S. *Environmental Protection Agency.* Africa, international environmental bibliographies; environmental legislation. [Washington?, 1975?] 31 p.

"Draft."

Source: *Month. Cat.*, 1975, no. 15427.

396

——— Environmental reports summaries. Vol. 1. Africa, Asia, Australia, September [sic] through June 1976. [Washington?, 1976?] 185 p.

Covers the period 1970–76.

For each country, there are summaries of laws and regulations and information on activities of national environmental control organizations; Africa is covered on p. 1–38.

Abstract in *Government Reports Announcements & Index*, May 13, 1977, p. 180.

Microfiche. [Springfield, Va., National Technical Information Service, 1977] 3 sheets.

                    DLC-Sci RR PB-259891

Note: Summaries of environmental reports from Africa are also given in the Agency's monthly publication, *Summaries of Foreign Government Environment Reports* (TD172.S77).

397

African overview, [by] Leonard Berry [et al.] [Worcester, Mass.?], Clark University, 1978. 28 leaves. map. (Workshops in Environmental Investigation. Techniques and procedures for project development. Overview, no. 1)   DLC

"Training course for preparing initial environmental examinations conducted on behalf of AID Training Contract RFP/50106 and prepared for workshops in February and May, 1978."

Includes "National environmental profiles" for Kenya, Tanzania, Zambia, Botswana, Ethiopia, and Malawi.

398

Berry, Leonard, *and* Richard B. Ford. The environmental context of development; [final report. Worcester. Mass., Clark University, 1977] [136] leaves (in various foliations) col. map.   DLC

"A project to analyze environmental issues and trends in Eastern and Southern Africa; project document 1223.4. A report on activities from May, 1976 through April, 1977. Submitted to US-AID by the Program for International Development, Clark University, in conjunction with Contract no. AID/afr-C-1223."

Focus is on Kenya, Tanzania, Botswana, Zambia, Ethiopia, Malawi, and Sudan.

399

Environmental and natural resource management in developing countries: a report to Congress. Washington, U.S. Agency for International Development, Dept. of State, 1979. 2 v.   HC59.7.E6475

"This report is the final product of a project organized, in close collaboration with the Agency for International Development (A.I.D.), by the Science and Technology Division of the Library of Congress."

Includes bibliographies.

Contents: v. 1. Report.—v. 2. Appendix.

In vol. 1, Africa is covered on p. 30–65; vol. 2 consists of environmental reports on Sri Lanka and Mauritania (see entry 4125).

400

Global 2000 Study (U.S.) The global 2000 report to the President—entering the twenty-first century: a report, prepared by the Council on Environmental Quality and the Department of State; Gerald O. Barney, study director. [Washington, for sale by the Supt. of Docs., U.S. Govt. Print. Off., 1980] 3 v.   HC79.E5G59 1980b

Includes bibliographies.

Contains frequent references to projections concerning environmental conditions and the use of resources in Africa.

Issued also by Pergamon Press, New York (HC79.E5G59 1980).

Note: A summary of the report is included in a hearing on it held on Sept. 4, 1980 by the Joint Economic Committee, U.S. Congress (see entry 394). Subsequently, in Jan. 1981, the Council issued *Global Future: Time to Act; Report to the President on Global Resources, Environment and Population* (HC79.E5C68 1981), an assessment of existing government programs and recommendations for improvements.

401

Leary, John C. Protection of the human environment—the African perspective; case study. [Washington, U.S. Foreign Service Institute], 1973. 14 p.

"Senior Seminar in Foreign Policy, 1972/73."

Examined in the Foreign Service Institute Library, Rosslyn, Va.

402

McKee, Edwin D., Carol S. Breed, *and* Steven G. Fryberger. Desert sand seas. *In* Skylab explores the Earth; prepared by NASA Lyndon B. Johnson Space Center. Washington, Scientific and Technical Information Office, National Aeronautics and Space Administration, 1977. (U.S. National Aeronautics and Space Administration. NASA SP, 380) p. 5–47. illus. maps.   QC808.5.S48

Includes descriptions of sand deposits in the Sahelian zone and in southwestern Africa.

403

Network for environment & development. v. 1+ Feb. 1979+ [Worcester, Mass., International Development Program, Center for Technology, Environment, and Development, Clark University] irregular.   DLC

Issues for Feb. 1979–Mar. 1980 indicate that the publication was prepared under a U.S. Agency for International Development contract.

Each issue includes at least one article on sub-Saharan Africa; the March 1982 issue focuses on East Africa.

L.C. has Feb. 1979+

404

Regional meeting of experts on environmental education in Africa, Brazzaville, People's Republic of the Congo, 11–16 September 1976. Final report. [Paris, United Nations Educational, Scientific, and Cultural Organization, 1977] 56 p.

"ED-76/COF.665/COL.2."

Abstract in *Resources in Education*, Apr. 1978, p. 114.

Microfiche. [Arlington, Va., ERIC Document Reproduction Service; prepared for Educational Resources Information Center, National Institute of Education, 1978] 1 sheet.

   DLC-MICRO ED147112

405

A Study of global sand seas; Edwin D. McKee, editor: prepared in cooperation with the National Aeronautics and Space Administration. Washington, U.S. Govt. Print. Off., 1979. 429 p. illus. maps. (U.S. Geological Survey. Professional paper, 1052)

   QE71.2.S88

Frequent references to deserts and sand-dunes in Africa, particularly the Sahara and the Namib.

Economic Conditions

406

U.S. *Agency for International Development. Office of Science and Technology*. Small and medium in-

dustry development, prepared in cooperation with A.I.D. Reference Center. Washington, Agency for International Development, Dept. of State, 1974. 131 p. (A.I.D. bibliography series: Science and technology, no. 1)   Z7164.U5U54 1974

Annotated bibliography, including citations to publications on Africa.

407

U.S. *Agency for International Development. Statistics and Reports Division*. Africa economic growth trends. [Washington] annual.   HA1955.U54a

Primarily statistical tables with an emphasis on production of selected commodities, electric power output, total foreign trade, and United States trade.

L.C. has 1969, 1972, 1974, and 1976; more complete holdings in the Development Information Center, AID, Washington, D.C.

Note: Individual issues of many U.S. Government periodicals concerned with economic conditions in Africa or in specific African countries can be identified through the *American Statistics Index: A Comprehensive Guide and Index to the Statistical Publications of the U.S. Government* (Washington, Congressional Information Service. Z7554. U5A46).

408

——— Selected economic data for the less developed countries. Washington. annual.   HC59.7.U516a

Statistical tables for African nations (including South Africa) indicate leading exports, literacy, student enrollment by age group, infant mortality, life expectancy, and number of persons per physician.

Cataloged in L.C. under U.S. Agency for International Development. Office of Statistics and Reports.

L.C. has 1970–73, 1976; more complete holdings examined in the Development Information Center, AID, Washington, D.C.

409

U.S. *Central Intelligence Agency. National Foreign Assessment Center*. Handbook of economic statistics, 1980; a research aid. Washington, for sale by the Supt. of Docs., U.S. Govt, Print. Off., 1980. 237 p. col. maps.   DLC

"ER 80-10452."

Selected African nations are listed in several statistical tables indicating production and economic development by years over the period 1960–79. For example, the tables on crude oil reserves and production include data for Gabon, Nigeria, and South Africa (p. 123–124), while those on mineral production cite figures for Gabon, Ghana, Guinea, Rhodesia, Rwanda, South Africa, Zaire, and Zambia (p. 138–154).

409 (cont.)

Note: Supplementary statistics on crude oil production in Angola, Gabon, and Nigeria are regularly cited in *International Energy Statistical Review* (HD9560.4.U485a), issued approximately monthly by the National Foreign Assessment Center.

410

—— Least developed countries: economic characteristics and stakes in north-south issues. [Washington], 1978. 48 p. illus. (*Its* Research paper)   HC59.7.U52 1978
"ER 78-10253."

African countries included in the report: Benin, Botswana, Burundi, Cape Verde, Central African Empire, Chad, Comoros, Ethiopia. The Gambia, Guinea, Lesotho, Malawi, Niger, Rwanda, Somalia, Sudan, Tanzania, Uganda, and Upper Volta.

411

U.S. *Congress. House. Committee on Foreign Affairs. Subcommittee on International Economic Policy and Trade.* Review of activities of the Overseas Private Investment Corporation: hearings, Ninety-sixth Congress, July 17, 1979, and February 7, 1980. Washington, U.S. Govt. Print. Off., 1980. 111p.   KF27.F6465 1979d
J74.A23 96th
Cong., House Comm.
For. Aff., v. 70

Jonathan B. Bingham, chairman.

Includes occasional references to OPIC's involvement in American investment in Africa.

412

U.S. *Congress. House. Committee on International Relations. Subcommittee on Africa.* Underdevelopment in Africa: hearings, Ninety-fifth Congress, first session. Washington, U.S. Govt. Print. Off., 1978. 279 p.   KF27.I54914 1977j
J74.A23 95th
Cong., House Comm.
Inter. Rel., v. 39

Charles C. Diggs, Jr., chairman.

Hearing held Sept. 7–20, 1977.

In his opening remarks, Chairman Diggs noted that "Despite the vast mineral wealth and great agricultural and energy resources potential, the African continent remains one of the least developed regions of the world. Therefore, this series of hearings will concentrate on economic growth and development in Africa."—p. 1. Sessions were held on health and development, population, agriculture and industry, and urbanization.

413

U.S. *Congress. House. Committee on International Relations. Subcommittee on International Economic*

Policy. To require certain actions by the Overseas Private Investment Corporation: hearings, Ninety-fourth Congress, second session. Washington, U.S. Govt. Print. Off., 1976. 2 v.
KF27.I54924 1976a
J74.A23 94th Cong.,
House Comm. Inter.
Rel., v. 74

Robert N. C. Nix, chairman.

Hearings held May 25–Aug. 9, 1976.

Part 2 has subtitle: Hearings and markup sessions of the Committee on International Relations, House of Representatives, Ninety-fourth Congress, second session, on H. R. 14681.

Includes bibliographical references.

Concerns allegations that TAW International Leasing Corporation, a company leasing equipment and facilities in ten African countries, was directed by OPIC to transfer local currencies in nine African countries in a manner which violated local foreign exchange regulations.

414

U.S. *Congress. House. Committee on International Relations. Subcommittee on International Economic Policy and Trade.* Extension and revision of Overseas Private Investment Corporation programs: hearings and markup, Ninety-fifth Congress, first session. Washington, U.S. Govt. Print. Off., 1977. 443 p. illus.   KF27.I54924 1977
J74.A23 95th
Cong., House Comm.
Inter. Rel., v. 24

Jonathan B. Bingham, chairman.

Hearings held June 21–Sept. 16, 1977.

Includes tables indicating the risk insurance and financial assistance provided by OPIC to American investors in various African countries.

415

U.S. *Congress. Senate. Committee on Finance. Subcommittee on Taxation and Debt Management Generally.* Foreign indebtedness to the United States: hearing, Ninety-sixth Congress, first session, February 5, 1979. Washington, U.S. Govt. Print. Off., 1979. 45 p.   KF26.F5695 1979a
J74.A23 96th
Cong., Sen. Comm.
Fin., v. 2

Harry F. Byrd, Jr., chairman.

Includes occasional references to Africa.

416

The African graduate fellowship program (AFGRAD) operation search, 1975. New York, African-American Institute, 1976. [196] leaves.

416 (cont.)

Study funded by the U.S. Agency for International Development.

An evaluation of "the manner and extent to which former AFGRAD participants are contributing to African economic development."

Examined in the Development Information Center, AID, Washington, D.C.

417

Baaklini, A. I. Afro-Arab economic relations. [s.l.] 1980. 30 leaves. DLC

On cover: "Presented at a conference on 'African-Arab Relations,' May 2–3, 1980, United States State Department, Washington, D.C."

Abstract in *Government Reports Announcements & Index*, Jan. 2, 1981, p. 26.

Issued also in microfiche. [s.l., Defense Technical Information Center, 1980] 1 sheet.

DLC-Sci RR AD-A089013

418

Cronje, Suzanne. Lonrho empire in Africa considered. *In* U.S. *Joint Publications Research Service.* JPRS 72555. [Springfield, Va., National Technical Information Service, 1979] (Translations on Sub-Saharan Africa, no. 2046) p. 6–11.

Translation of article in *Demain l'Afrique*, Paris, Nov. 1978, p. 94–95.

Microfiche. [Washington, Supt. of Docs., U.S. Govt. Print. Off., 1979]

DLC-Micro JPRS 72555

419

Diggs, Charles C. The plea of the poor: an address by President Julius Nyerere of Tanzania. Congressional record, 95th Congress, 1st session, v. 123, Oct. 5, 1977, p. 32532–32535. J11.R5 v.123

Remarks in the U.S. House of Representatives.

Includes text of address by President Nyerere delivered at Howard University.

420

Due, Jean M. Africa—twenty years after independence—what happened? [Urbana, Dept. of Agricultural Economics, University of Illinois at Urbana-Champaign, 1981] 8 p. (Illinois agricultural economics staff paper, 81 E-175) IU

Supported in part by U.S. Agency for International Development Title XII funds.

Discusses problems involved in economic development.

421

Economic and social development in West Africa. Abidjan, Ivory Coast, Regional Economic Development Support Office-West Africa, Agency for International Development, 1979. [70] p. (in various pagings)

Region of coverage is from Cape Verde to Zaire.

Abstract in *A.I.D. Research & Development Abstracts*, v. 9, no. 4, 1981, p. 23.

Microfiche. [Washington, U.S. Agency for International Development, 1979?] 1 sheet.

DLC-Sci RR PN-AAJ-924

422

Economic development and social change: four case studies from Africa. New York, School Services Division, African-American Institute, 1975. 20 p. map.

Examples are from Tanzania, Egypt, Nigeria, and South Africa.

Abstract in *Resources in Education*, Apr. 1977, p. 129.

Microfiche. [Arlington, Va., ERIC Document Reproduction Service; prepared for Educational Resources Information Center, National Institute of Education, 1977] 1 sheet.

DLC-Micro ED132085

423

Economic development versus military expenditures in countries receiving U.S. aid: priorities and the competition for resources: report, submitted to the Committee on Foreign Affairs, U.S. House of Representatives and Committee on Foreign Relations, U.S. Senate, by the Agency for International Development in accordance with section 620(s) of the Foreign Assistance Act of 1961, as amended. Washington, U.S. Govt. Print. Off., 1980 i.e. 1981. 93 p. HC60.E25

At head of title: 96th Congress, 2d session. Joint committee print.

Chiefly tables.

"December 1980."

"Basic economic data" tables for African countries include statistics on gross national product, current government expenditures, military expenditures, total imports, and international reserves (p. 11–21). These are followed by tables indicating defense costs and military imports by country as percentages of total expenditures and total imports (p. 22–32).

424

Edwards, Ralph S. Digest of eastern and southern Africa development plans. Washington, U.S. Dept. of Commerce, Domestic and International Business Administration, 1976. 14 p. (Overseas business reports. OBR 76-16)

HF91.U482 1976, no. 16

Supersedes in part *Digest of African Countries'*

424 (cont.)

Economic Development Plans (Overseas business reports. OBR 73-21).

Covers Kenya, Madagascar, Mauritius, Somalia, South Africa, Sudan, Tanzania, and Zambia.

425

———— Digest of Western Africa development plans. Washington, U.S. Dept. of Commerce, Domestic and International Business Administration; for sale by the Supt. of Docs., U.S. Govt. Print. Off., 1975. 17 p. (Overseas business reports. OBR 75-50)
HF91.U482   1975, no. 50

Supersedes in part *Digest of African Countries Economic Development Plans* (Overseas business reports. OBR 73-21).

Covers Cameroon, Gabon, Ivory Coast, Mali, Nigeria, Senegal, Sierra Leone, and Togo.

Abstract in *American Statistics Index*, 1975, Abstracts, p. 147.

Issued also in microfiche. [Washington, Congressional Information Service, 1975?] 1 sheet.
DLC-Micro ASI:75 2026-4:50

426

Fields, Nate. U.S. economic role in Africa. *In* The U.S. role in changing world political economy: major issues for the 96th Congress: a compendium of papers submitted to the Joint Economic Committee, Congress of the United States. Washington, U.S. Govt. Print. Off., 1979. p. 553–564.   HF1455.U54

427

Gruhn, Isebill V. Regional integration in Africa: lessons of history. [s.l.], 1980. 11 leaves.   DLC

Paper prepared for a conference on the Economic Community of West African States, U.S. Dept. of State, June 9, 1980.

At head of title: "This paper was prepared for the Department of State as part of its external research program."

428

Jacka, Thomas R. Development projects in eight African countries. [Washington], U.S. Dept. of Commerce, Domestic and International Business Administration, 1977. 12 p. (Overseas business reports. OBR 77-03)
HF91.U482   1977, no. 3

International marketing information series.

"This report contains brief descriptions of development projects presently in their initial stages of implementation or proposed for undertaking between 1978 and 1982. It attempts to identify specific projects and development within the framework of development plans as outlined in OBR

75-50, 'Digest of Western Africa Development Plans, [entry 425] issued in November 1975 and OBR 76-16, 'Digest of Eastern and Southern Africa Development Plans [entry 424] issued in March 1976."

Covers Botswana, Cameroon, Gabon, Ivory Coast, Kenya, Liberia, Senegal, and Sudan.

429

Ladd, William C., *and* James F. McClelland. Francophone Africa. [Washington], Overseas Private Investment Corp., 1975. 6 v.   HF3921.L33

A survey of nine French-speaking states in early 1974 with the cost shared by the Overseas Private Investment Corp. and "five American companies who have an interest in increasing their own and other American trade and investment in the area."

Contents: [1] A report on business opportunities in Cameroon (83 p.).—[2] A report on business opportunies in Mali, Niger, Upper Volta (8 p.).—[3] A report on business opportunities in Senegal (81 p.).—[4] A report on business opportunities in Togo (50 p.).—[5] A report on business opportunities in Ivory Coast (74 p.).—[6] A report on business opportunities in Gabon (64 p.).

L.C. has reports on Cameroon, Senegal, Togo, and the combined study on Mali, Niger, and Upper Volta. Reports on Ivory Coast (FAR 23262-N) and Gabon (FAR 23409-N) were examined in the former Foreign Affairs Research Documentation Center, U.S. Dept. of State, Washington, D.C. An additional report was prepared on Dahomey "prior to recent nationalization by the present Government and is being withheld from publication until the foreign investment climate can be gauged."

430

Lavroff, Dmitri-Georges. Foreign economic, strategic interests in Africa examined. *In* U.S. *Joint Publications Research Service*. JPRS 72570. [Springfield, Va., National Technical Information Service, 1979] (Translations on Sub-Saharan Africa, no. 2048) p. 1–10.

Translation of article in *Demain l'Afrique*, Paris, Dec. 1978, p. 5–18.

Microfiche. [Washington, Supt. of Docs., U.S. Govt. Print. Off., 1979]
DLC-Micro JPRS 72570

431

Messe, Xavier. Secretary General discusses OCAM operations. *In* U.S. *Joint Publications Research Service*. JPRS 73939. [Springfield, Va., National Technical Information Service, 1979] (Sub-Saharan Africa report, no. 2138) p. 10–14.

Translation of interview with Sydney Moutia,

431 (cont.)

Secretary-General of the Organisation commune africaine et mauricienne, in *Demain l'Afrique*, Paris, June 18, 1979, p. 71–72.

Microfiche. [Washington, Supt. of Docs., U.S. Govt. Print. Off., 1979]

DLC-Micro JPRS 73939

432

Phillips, Adedotun O. Review of income distribution data: Ghana, Kenya, Tanzania and Nigeria. Princeton, N.J., Research Program in Economic Development, Woodrow Wilson School, Princeton University, 1975. 43 leaves. (Princeton University. Woodrow Wilson School of Public and International Affairs. Research Program in Economic Development. Discussion paper, no. 58)

DLC

"This research was supported by the U.S. Agency for International Development under the joint Princeton/Brookings Income Distribution Project."

Abstract in *A.I.D. Research and Development Abstracts*, Sept. 1975, p. 14.

Issued also in microfiche. [Washington, U.S. Agency for International Development, 1975?] 1 sheet. DLC-Sci RR PN-AAB-132

433

Quick, Elsie M. Africa's resources: patterns of production and trade. [Washington?], 1975. [36] leaves. (FAR 22490-S)

"A contract study prepared for the Department of State under its External Research Program."

Examined in the former Foreign Affairs Research Documentation Center, U.S. Dept. of State.

434

Regional organizations development: Africa Co-operative Savings and Credit Association/Directed Agricultural Production Credit (ACOSCA/DAPC); evaluation, [by] Russell W. Bierman [et al.] [s.l.] 1977. 85 p.

Prepared for the U.S. Agency for International Development.

Examined in the Development Information Center, AID, Washington, D.C.

435

Report on Arab banking activities in sub-Saharan Africa. *In* U.S. *Joint Publications Research Service*. JPRS 66792. [Springfield, Va., National Technical Information Service, 1976] (Translations on Sub-Saharan Africa, no. 1638) p. 1–8.

Translation of article in *Afrique industrie infra-structures*, Jan. 1, 1976, p. 62–65.

Microfiche. [s.l., 1976]

DLC-Micro JPRS 66792

436

Resource transfer in a world market economy: Sub-Saharan Africa. [Carlisle Barracks, Pa., Strategic Studies Institute, U.S. Army War College, 1977?]

Cited in *African Development: International and Regional Paradigms; Special Report.*

437

Salacuse, Jeswald W. Arab investment in Africa and the trilateral venture. [s.l., 1980?] 13 leaves.

DLC

On cover: "This paper was prepared for the Department of State as part of its external research program."

Issued also in microfiche. [s.l., Defense Technical Information Center, 1981] 1 sheet.

DLC-Sci RR AD-A093685

438

Schatz, Sayre P. U.S. investment in Black Africa. [s.l.], 1980. 3 leaves. DLC

On cover: "Paper for the Colloquium on U.S. Trade and Investment Activities in Black Africa, U.S. State Department, January 23, 1980."

439

Sherwin, Walter J. Decentralization for development; the concept and its application in Ghana and Tanzania. [Washington, Agency for International Development] 1977. 31 p. (U.S. Agency for International Development. Development Studies Program. Occasional paper, no. 2)

Abstract in *A.I.D. Research and Development Abstracts*, Apr. 1978, p. 23–24.

Microfiche. [Washington, U.S. Agency for International Development, 1977?] 1 sheet.

DLC-Sci RR PN-AAE-543

440

Von der Mehden, Fred R. Communalism, wealth, and income in Afro-Asia. [Houston, Tex., Program of Development Studies, William Marsh Rice University], 1977. 259 p.

"This paper reports research conducted under AID contract AID/otr-C-1394 on 'Distribution of Gains, Wealth and Income from Development'."

Appendixes include statistical data on communal factors in Ghana, Uganda, and Kenya.

Abstract in *A.I.D. Research and Development Abstracts*, Apr. 1978, p. 24.

Microfiche. [Washington, U.S. Agency for International Development, 1977?] 3 sheets.

DLC-Sci RR PN-AAE-459

Education

441

U.S. *Office of Education. Division of International Education.* Programs concerning Africa. [Washington?, 1977?]

Source: Duffy. *Survey.*

442

The Admission and academic placement of students from selected sub-Saharan African countries; a workshop report, July–August 1973. [Washington], National Association for Foreign Student Affairs [and] American Association of Collegiate Registrars and Admissions Officers, [1973] 258 p. map.

Sponsored in part by the U.S. Agency for International Development.

Report on sessions of a workshop held in Ghana, Togo, and Nigeria to review educational structures in African nations; includes reports on 19 countries: Botswana, Ethiopia, The Gambia, Ghana, Ivory Coast, Kenya, Lesotho, Liberia, Malawi, Mali, Nigeria, Senegal, Sierra Leone, Swaziland, Tanzania, Togo, Uganda, Zaire, and Zambia.

Abstract in *Resources in Education*, Feb. 1975, p. 81.

Microfiche. [Arlington, Va., ERIC Document Reproduction Service; prepared for Educational Resources Information Center, National Institute of Education, 1975] 3 sheets.

DLC-Micro ED096936

443

Ampene, E. Kwasi. Persistent issues in African education. Vancouver, Centre for Continuing Education, University of British Columbia, 1978. 23 p. (British Columbia. University. Centre for Continuing Education. Occasional papers in continuing education, no. 16)

Abstract in *Resources in Education*, Apr. 1979, p. 23.

Microfiche. [Arlington, Va., ERIC Document Reproduction Service; prepared for Educational Resources Information Center, National Institute of Education, 1979] 1 sheet.

DLC-Micro ED162172

444

Association of African Universities. Directory of African universities. Répertoire des universités africaines. Accra, 1974. 512 p.

In English and /or French.

Abstract in *Resources in Education*, Feb. 1976, p. 123.

Microfiche. [Arlington, Va., ERIC Document Reproduction Service; prepared for Educational Resources Information Center, National Institute of Education, 1976] 6 sheets.

DLC-Micro ED112778

Note: L.C. has also a 2d ed., issued in 1976 (LA1503.A85 1976).

445

Basic training course in systematic curriculum development. Course Seven: Education and Development Unit 2. Nairobi, African Curriculum Organization, 1979. 64 p.

On cover: "Organized and run on behalf of ACO by Kenya Institute of Education (KIE), the University of Nairobi, and the German Agency for Technical Co-operation (GTZ)."

"The linkage between formal education and the development efforts of third world nations is examined."—Abstract.

Abstract in *Resources in Education*, Apr. 1981, p. 126.

Microfiche. [Arlington, Va., ERIC Document Reproduction Service; prepared for Educational Resources Information Center, National Institute of Education, 1981] 1 sheet.

DLC-Micro ED195496

446

Basic training course in systematic curriculum development; information brochure. [Nairobi?], African Curriculum Organization, [1979] 22 p.

"This manual provides background information, program organization descriptions, and guidelines for preparing and reporting projects undertaken by students enrolled for the postgraduate diploma in curriculum development at the University of Nairobi, under the direction of the African Curriculum Organization (ACO)."—Abstract.

On cover: "Organized and run on behalf of ACO by Kenya Institute of Education (KIE), the University of Nairobi, and the German Agency for Technical Cooperation (GTZ)."

Abstract in *Resources in Education*, May 1981, p. 182.

Microfiche. [Arlington, Va., ERIC Document Reproduction Service; prepared for Educational Resources Information Center, National Institute of Education, 1981] 1 sheet.

DLC-Micro ED196815

447

Benjamin, Theodore D., and John J. Koran. End of project review: SEPA/EDC/APSP (Science Education Programme for Africa/Education Development Center/African Primary Science Pro-

447 (cont.)
gram) [s.l.], Overseas Liaison Committee, American Council on Education, 1975. 45 p.

Prepared for the Bureau for Africa, U.S. Agency for International Development.

Examined in the Development Information Center, AID, Washington, D.C.

448
Bigelow, Ross E., *and* Eliza T. Dresang. African education research. Madison, Wisc., 1974. 3 v. map.

Abstract in *Research in Education*, Nov. 1974, p. 170.

Contents: pt. 1. Issues and patterns.—pt. 2. Project classification.—pt. 3. Continuing research resources.

Microfiche. [Arlington, Va., ERIC Document Reproduction Service; prepared for Educational Resources Information Center, National Institute of Education, 1974] 3 sheets.

DLC-Micro ED093849-ED093851

449
Chaytor, D. E. B. Source book for science teachers. Accra, Science Education Programme for Africa, 1976. 139 p. illus.

"This *Sourcebook* has been produced with funds provided by the United States Agency for International Development through Education Development Center, Newton, Massachusetts, U.S.A."

Microfiche. [Washington, U.S. Agency for International Development, 1976?] 2 sheets.

DLC-Sci RR PN-AAG-060

450
Conference of Ministers of Education of African Member States, *4th, Lagos, Nigeria, 1976*. Final report, Conference of Ministers of Education of African Member States, organized by Unesco with the co-operation of OAU and ECA, Lagos (Nigeria), 27 January–4 February 1976. Paris, Unesco, 1976. 98 p. (United Nations Educational, Scientific, and Cultural Organization. Document, ED/MD/41) AS4.U8A15 ED/MD/41

Abstract in *Resources in Education*, Nov. 1977, p. 89.

Issued also in microfiche. [Arlington, Va., ERIC Document Reproduction Service; prepared for Educational Resources Information Center, National Institute of Education, 1977] 1 sheet.

DLC-Micro ED140493

451
Duckworth, Eleanor R. The African primary science program; an evaluation and extended thoughts, [by] Eleanor Duckworth, North Dakota Study Group on Evaluation. Grand Forks, University of North Dakota, 1978. 135 p. illus.

LB1585.5.A25D8

Abstract in *Resources in Education*, Oct. 1979, p. 191.

Issued also in microfiche. [Arlington, Va., ERIC Document Reproduction Service; prepared for Educational Resources Information Center, National Institute of Education, 1979] 2 sheets.

DLC-Micro ED171741

452
Dyasi, Hubert M. The teaching-learning strategy of the primary science project of the Science Education Programme for Africa. Paris, International Institute for Educational Planning, c1977. 21 p. (International Institute for Educational Planning. IIEP seminar paper, no. 30)

On cover: "A contribution to the IIEP Seminar on 'Teaching-Learning Strategies and Educational Planning,' 8–12 March 1976."

Abstract in *Resources in Education*, June 1979, p. 192.

Microfiche. [Arlington, Va., ERIC Document Reproduction Service; prepared for Educational Resources Information Center, National Institute of Education, 1979] 1 sheet.

DLC-Micro ED165996

453
Education Development Center, *Newton, Mass*. Final report to USAID on African mathematics program, contract no. USAID afr-711, June 26, 1970 to May 31, 1975. Newton, Mass., 1975. 87 leaves.

DLC

454
Environmental science education for pre-service primary teacher education. Report of a workshop on environmental science education, July 1974, Nairobi, Kenya. [s.l., 1974] 66 p.

Sponsored in part by the United Nations Educational, Scientific, and Cultural Organization, and the Science Education Programme for Africa.

Abstract in *Resources in Education*, Oct. 1977, p. 135.

Microfiche. [Arlington, Va., ERIC Document Reproduction Service; prepared for Education Resources Information Center, National Institute of Education, 1977] 1 sheet.

DLC-Micro ED139652

455
Feasibility study for an international evaluation of the effectiveness of bilingual approaches in educating rural poor linguistic minorities; final report to Agency for International Development. Arling-

455 (cont.)

ton, Va., Center for Applied Linguistics, 1978. 256 p.

Prepared for the Agency under grant AID/ta-G-1396.

"This report summarizes a study on the feasibility of conducting a coordinated international evaluation of models of vernacular educations for rural poor, linguistic minority populations in LDCs.... In all the countries surveyed, the expansion of educational opportunity implies the need for strategies to cope with children who do not speak the official or national language."—Abstract.

Covers seven countries, including Ghana, Nigeria, and Sudan.

Abstract in *A.I.D. Research and Development Abstracts*, Oct. 1978, p. 29.

Microfiche. [Washington, U.S. Agency for International Development, 1978?] 3 sheets.

DLC-Sci RR PN-AAF-527

456

Hanson, John W. Report on the supply of secondary level teachers in Africa: shifting the locus and focus to Africa: summary, [by] John W. Hanson and D. J. S. Crozier, with the cooperation on tabular data and appendices of Richard Hovey [and others]; cooperating organizations, Midwest Universities Consortium for International Activities [and others] East Lansing, Institute for International Studies in Education, Michigan State University, c1974. 379 p. illus. (Report on the supply of secondary level teachers in English-speaking Africa, [16]) LB2833.4.S87H35

Summarizes the reports on a project of the Overseas Liaison Committee of the American Council on Education.

Bibliography: p. 315–378.

Emphasis is on 15 nations or regions in which English is used extensively in secondary education —Botswana, Ethiopia, The Gambia, Ghana, Kenya, Lesotho, Liberia, Malawi, Nigeria, Sierra Leone, Swaziland, Tanzania, Uganda, West Cameroon, and Zambia.

Issued also in microfiche. [Washington, U.S. Agency for International Development, 1974?] 5 sheets. DLC-Sci RR PN-AAD-587

457

Leavitt, Howard B., *and* Robert F. Schenkkan. Asian, Middle Eastern and African reactions to the feasibility of international educational technology networks. [Washington?], Academy for Educational Development, 1975. [24] p.

On cover: Asia, Middle East and Africa trip report. Report no. 2.

Prepared for the U.S. Agency for International Development under contract AID/ta-BOA-1060.

Microfiche. [Washington, U.S. Agency for International Development, 1975?] 1 sheet.

DLC-Sci RR PN-AAD-542

458

McSwain, Martha I. B. Opportunities to use family resource for reading in the developing countries of Africa. [s.l.], 1978. [21] p.

Paper presented at the annual meeting of the International Reading Association World Congress on Reading, 1978.

"As the strongest, most cohesive, and most viable societal unit, the African family, has a great impact on literacy and reading."—Abstract.

Abstract in *Resources in Education*, May 1979, p. 41.

Microfiche. [Arlington, Va., ERIC Document Reproduction Service; prepared for Educational Resources Information Center, National Institute of Education, 1979] 1 sheet.

DLC-Micro ED163416

459

Matiru, Barbara, *and* Peter Sachsenmeier. Basic training course in systematic curriculum development; course one: background to curriculum development in Africa. [Nairobi?], African Curriculum Organization, 1979. 27 p.

On cover: "Organized and run on behalf of ACO by Kenya Institute of Education (KIE), the University of Nairobi, and the German Agency for Technical Co-operation (GTZ)."

Abstract in *Resources in Education*, Apr. 1981, p. 182.

Microfiche. [Arlington, Va., ERIC Document Reproduction Service; prepared for Educational Resources Information Center, National Institute of Education, 1981] 1 sheet.

DLC-Micro ED196816

460

———— Basic training course in systematic curriculum development; course two: introduction to methods and processes of curriculum development. Unit 3: translating national goals into educational programmes. Nairobi, African Curriculum Organization, 1979. 38 p.

On cover: "Organized and run on behalf of ACO by Kenya Institute of Education (KIE), the University of Nairobi, and the German Agency for Technical Co-operation (GTZ)."

Abstract in *Resources in Education*, May 1981, p. 182.

Microfiche. [Arlington, Va., ERIC Document Reproduction Service; prepared for Educational

460 (cont.)
Resources Information Center, National Institute of Education, 1981] 1 sheet.

DLC-Micro ED196817

461
——— Basic training course in systematic curriculum development. Study guide. [s.l.], 1979. 13 p.

On cover: "Organized and run on behalf of ACO [African Curriculum Organization] by Kenya Institute of Education (KIE), the University of Nairobi, and the German Agency for Technical Co-operation (GTZ)."

"This booklet consists of introductory statements to prospectives students in the University of Nairobi's Postgraduate Diploma in Curriculum Development Program."—Abstract.

Abstract in *Resources in Education*, May 1981, p. 183.

Microfiche. [Arlington, Va., ERIC Document Reproduction Service; prepared for Educational Resources Information Center, National Institute of Education, 1981] 1 sheet.

DLC-Micro ED196814

462
Obanya, Pai, Vinesh Y. Hookoomsing, *and* Lucia Omondi. Basic training course in systematic curriculum development; course six: curriculum development in subject areas: languages. Nairobi, African Curriculum Organization, 1979. 163 p.

Bibliography: p. 157–163.

On cover: "Organized and run on behalf of ACO by Kenya Institute of Education (KIE), the University of Nairobi, and the German Agency for Technical Cooperation (GTZ)."

Microfiche. [Arlington, Va., ERIC Document Reproduction Service; prepared for Educational Resources Information Center, National Institute of Education, 1981] 2 sheets.

DLC-Micro Ed197585

463
Panyako, David E. M. African education: new strategies in curriculum development. Storrs, World Education Project, University of Connecticut, 1979. 22 p. (Connecticut. University. World Education Project. World education monograph series, 1979, no. 1)

Abstract in *Resources in Education*, Oct. 1979, p. 64.

Microfiche. [Arlington, Va., ERIC Document Reproduction Service; prepared for Educational Resources Information Center, National Institute of Education, 1979] 1 sheet.

DLC-Micro ED170880

464
Science Education Programme for Africa. Handbook for teachers. Accra, 1974. 341 p. illus.

Produced by the Education Development Center, Newton, Mass., with funding by the U.S. Agency for International Development.

Abstract in *Resources in Education*, Nov. 1977, p. 169.

Microfiche. [Arlington, Va., ERIC Document Reproduction Service; prepared for the Educational Resources Information Center, National Institute of Education, 1977] 5 sheets.

DLC-Micro ED141074

465
Sine, Babacar. Education and mass media in Black Africa. The development of educational methods and techniques suited to the specific conditions of the developing countries. Problems presented by the adaptation of educational technologies. Paris, Division of Methods, Materials, and Techniques, United Nations Educational, Scientific, and Cultural Organization, 1975. [41] p. illus.

Abstract in *Resources in Education*, Sept. 1976, p. 114.

Microfiche. [Arlington, Va., ERIC Document Reproduction Service; prepared for Educational Resources Information Center, National Institute of Education, 1976] 1 sheet.

DLC-Micro ED122729

466
Taska, Betty K. Teacher training for the non-native speaker in francophone Africa. [s.l.], 1974. 10 p.

Concerns teaching English as a second language.

Abstract in *Resources in Education*, Feb. 1975, p. 64–65.

Microfiche. [Arlington, Va., ERIC Document Reproduction Service; prepared for Educational Resources Information Center, National Institute of Education, 1975] 1 sheet.

DLC-Micro ED096812

467
Thompson, Kenneth W., *and* Barbara R. Fogel. Higher education and social change: promising experiments in developing countries. New York, Praeger, 1976–77. 2 v. (Praeger special studies in international economics and development)

LC2605.T45

Vol. 2 edited by K. W. Thompson, B. R. Fogel, and H. E. Danner.

Includes bibliographic references and indexes.

"Published in cooperation with the International Council for Educational Development."

Contents: v. 1. Reports.—v. 2, Case studies.

In vol. 1, Africa is covered specifically on p. 87–

467 (cont.)

107 and 139–165; in vol. 2, African case studies are presented on p. 3–214.

Abstract in *A.I.D. Research and Development Abstracts*, Jan. 1978, p. 21–22.

Issued also in microfiche. [Washington, U.S. Agency for International Development, 1977?] 9 sheets.

DLC-Micro PN-AAD-619-PN-AAD-620

Academic Exchange Programs

468

American Council on Education. *Overseas Liaison Committee.* A review of the Fulbright-Hays Senior Academic Exchange Program in Africa: policies and procedures. Washington, 1975. 114 p. (FAR 22886-S)

"This report has been prepared under grant no. 1069-487100 from the United States Department of State, Bureau of Cultural Affairs, Office of Policy and Plans."

Examined in the former Foreign Affairs Research Documentation Center, U.S. Dept. of State.

469

Brady, Mary W., *and* Georgette J. Garner. An African view of an American experience. [Luxembourg?, Miami University, European Center, 1975?] [50] p. (FAR 25742-N)

Based on interviews with Africans who had completed exchange programs in the United States; survey conducted under the auspices of the Office of African Programs, Bureau of Educational and Cultural Affairs, U.S. Dept. of State.

Examined in the former Foreign Affairs Research Documentation Center, U.S. Dept. of State.

Adult Education

470

U.S. *Agency for International Development. Office of Education and Human Resources.* Non-formal education, prepared by Office of Education and Human Resources, Bureau for Technical Assistance, in cooperation with A.I.D. Reference Center. Washington, Agency for International Development, Dept. of State, 1975. 70 p. (U.S. Agency for International Development. A.I.D. bibliography series. Education and human resources, no. 2)

LB1026.U54 1975

195 annotated citations, including 28 on Africa.

471

African Adult Education Association. Seminar on

"Structures of Adult Education in Developing Countries, with Special Reference to Africa;" report. [Nairobi?], 1975. 37 p.

Issued in cooperation with the United Nations Educational, Scientific, and Cultural Organization.

Seminar supported by the Danish International Development Agency.

Abstract in *Resources in Education*, Mar. 1976, p. 9.

Microfiche. [Arlington, Va., ERIC Document Reproduction Service; prepared for Educational Resources Information Center, National Institute of Education, 1976] 1 sheet.

DLC-Micro ED113460

472

Bown, Lalage. "A rusty person is worse than rusty iron"—adult education and the development of Africa. [Syracuse, N.Y.?], Syracuse University, 1975. 29 p.

Bibliography: p. 25–29.

"Address delivered by Lalage Bown, Professor of Adult Education, Ahmadu Bello University, Zaria, Nigeria, upon being awarded the William Pearson Tolley Medal for Distinguished Leadership in Adult Education."—p. 4.

Abstract in *Resources in Education*, June 1976, p. 30.

Microfiche. [Arlington, Va., ERIC Document Reproduction Service; prepared for Educational Resources Information Center, National Institute of Education, 1976] 1 sheet.

DLC-Micro ED117450

473

Directory of adult education centers in Africa. Répertoire des centres de l'éducation des adultes en Afrique. Dakar, [United Nations Educational, Scientific, and Cultural Organization] Regional Office for Education in Africa, Documentation and Information Section, 1974. 82 p.

At head of title: "Draft copy."

Text in English or French.

Abstract in *Resources in Education*, Aug. 1975, p. 28.

Microfiche. [Arlington, Va., ERIC Document Reproduction Service; prepared for Educational Resources Information Center, National Institute of Education, 1975] 1 sheet.

DLC-Micro ED103719

474

Ewert, D. Merrill. Formal vs. nonformal education: the African experience. [s.l.], 1980. 24 p.

Bibliography: p. 21–24.

Paper presented at the International Adult

474 (cont.)

Education Section, National Adult Education Conference, 1980.

Microfiche. [Arlington, Va., ERIC Document Reproduction Service; prepared for Educational Resources Information Center, National Institute of Education, 1981] 1 sheet.

DLC-Sci RR ED197065

475

Lenglet, Frans, *and* Emile G. McAnany. Rural adult education and the role of mass media: a comparative analysis of four projects. Washington, Academy for Educational Development, inc., 1977. 62 p.

Prepared for the U.S. Agency for International Development under contract AID/afr-C-1158.

Bibliography: p. 60–62.

Issued in cooperation with the Institute for Communication Research, Stanford University.

A description and comparison of rural education projects using television in Tanzania, Ivory Coast, Dominican Republic, and Guatemala.

Abstracts in *Resources in Education*, Nov. 1979, p. 131, and A.I.D. Research and Development Abstracts, Feb. 1981, p. 42.

Microfiche. [Arlington, Va., ERIC Document Reproduction Service; prepared for the Educational Resources Information Center, National Institute of Education, 1979] 1 sheet (DLC-Micro ED172754); and [Washington, U.S. Agency for International Development, 1977?] 1 sheet (DLC-Micro PN-AAG-834).

African Studies in the United States

476

African Curriculum Workshop for Public School Teachers; final report, July 1, 1976 through June 30, 1980, [by] Victor C. Uchendu [et al.] Urbana, African Studies Program, University of Illinois at Urbana-Champaign, 1980. 420 p.

Sponsored by the National Endowment for the Humanities.

"This report describes a major project in African curriculum development for public school teachers in the three state area of Illinois, Missouri, and Arkansas."—Abstract.

Abstract in *Resources in Education*, Mar. 1981, p. 155–156.

Microfiche. [Arlington, Va., ERIC Document Reproduction Service; prepared for Educational Resources Information Center, National Institute of Education, 1981] 5 sheets.

DLC-Micro ED194423

477

African Curriculum Workshop for Public School Teachers; Sec. Ed. 459A, Summer 1977. Urbana, African Studies Program, University of Illinois at Urbana-Champaign, 1977. 8 pieces, map.

"This workshop is made possible by a grant from the National Endowment for the Humanities."

Under constant revision.

Contents: Handout A. Children's books about Africa (listed topically).—B. Annotated summaries of children's books about Africa.—Reading list for teachers' background.—D. Books on reserve.—E. Articles on reserve (Education and Social Science Library): an annotated list.—F. Periodicals.—G. Bibliography on African literature (not on reserve).—H. A guide to audiovisual resources for use in schools.

Held by the Office of the Africana Bibliographer, Library, University of Illinois at Urbana-Champaign, Urbana, Ill.

478

African heritage curriculum materials; teacher's manual. Washington, Museum of African Art, 1975. 112 p.

Produced with the support of a grant from the U.S. Office of Education, Ethnic Heritage Studies Program.

A guide for secondary school teachers.

Abstract in *Resources in Education*, June 1976, p. 171.

Microfiche. [Arlington, Va., ERIC Document Reproduction Service; prepared for Educational Resources Information Center, National Institute of Education, 1976] 2 sheets.

DLC-Micro ED118479

479

African music in an American context. New York, School Services Division, African-American Institute, [1975] 7 p.

Abstract in *Resources in Education*, Apr. 1977, p. 130.

Microfiche. [Arlington, Va., ERIC Document Reproduction Service; prepared for Educational Resources Information Center, National Institute of Education, 1977] 1 sheet.

DLC-Micro ED132093

The following items (entries 480–483) are reports developed as part of an interdisciplinary workshop project in African curriculum development at the University of Illinois, Urbana-Champaign, funded by the National Endowment for the Humanities.

480

Anderson, A. John. "The African family;" an instruc-

480 (cont.)

tional unit for tenth grade world history. Urbana, African Studies Program, University of Illinois, [1977] 28 p.

Microfiche. [Arlington, Va., ERIC Document Reproduction Service; prepared for Educational Resources Information Center, National Institute of Education, 1980] 1 sheet.

DLC-Micro ED188989

481

Britton, Enid. "African art and culture for high school students of art;" an instructional unit for tenth through twelfth grade art. Urbana, African Studies Program, University of Illinois, [1979] 48 p. illus.

Abstract in *Resources in Education*, 1980 annual cumulation, p. 2125.

Microfiche. [Arlington, Va., ERIC Document Reproduction Service; prepared for Educational Resources Information Center, National Institute of Education, 1980] 1 sheet.

DLC-Micro ED189008

482

Campbell, Margaret H. "Africa, roots and pride for Afro-Americans;" an instructional unit for high school anthropology. Urbana, African Studies Program, University of Illinois, [1977] 32 p.

Abstract in *Resources in Education*, 1980 annual cumulation, p. 2125.

Microfiche. [Arlington, Va., ERIC Document Reproduction Service; prepared for Educational Resources Information Center, National Institute of Education, 1980] 1 sheet.

DLC-Micro ED189007

483

Dobbs, Sherry. "The African folktale;" an instructional unit for seventh grade English. Urbana, African Studies Program, University of Illinois, [1977] 56 p.

Bibliography: p. 48–52.

Abstract in *Resources in Education*, 1980 annual cumulation, p. 2123.

Microfiche. [Arlington, Va., ERIC Document Reproduction Service; prepared for Educational Resources Information Center, National Institute of Education, 1980] 1 sheet.

DLC-Micro ED188998

484

Foreign language and international studies specialists: the marketplace and national policy, prepared for the National Endowment for the Humanities [by] Sue E. Berryman [et al.]; with the assistance of Ellen H. Gelbard and Priscilla M. Schlegel. Santa Monica, Calif., Rand, 1979. xxxii, 223 p. (Rand Corporation. Rand report; R-2501-NEH)

AS36.R3 R-2501

Bibliography: p. 217–223.

Includes the following tables relating to the study of sub-Saharan Africa:

Table 2.1. Percent of center budgets furnished through NDEA [National Defense Education Act] support, by world area. p. 45.

Table 3.1. Foreign languages used by the United States Government [arranged by language and by agency]. p. 101–110.

485

Hall, Susan J. Africa in U.S. educational materials: thirty problems and responses. [New York], School Services Division, African-American Institute, [c1976] 62 p.

Bibliography: p. 55–62.

Abstract in *Resources in Education*, Dec. 1977, p. 139–140.

Microfiche. [Arlington, Va., ERIC Document Reproduction Service; prepared for Educational Resources Information Center, National Institute of Education, 1977] 1 sheet.

DLC-Micro ED142449

486

——— Africa in U.S. schools, K–12: a survey. New York, African-American Institute, 1978. 30 p.

Abstract in *Resources in Education*, June 1979, p. 201.

Microfiche. [Arlington, Va., ERIC Document Reproduction Service; prepared for Educational Resources Information Center, National Institute of Education, 1979] 1 sheet.

DLC-Micro ED166070

487

Hawkins, John N., *and* Jon Maksik. Teacher's resource handbook for African studies: an annotated bibliography of curriculum materials, preschool through grade twelve. Los Angeles, African Studies Center, University of California, [c1976] 68 p. (California. University. University at Los Angeles. African Studies Center. Reference series, v. 16)

DT19.95.C3A34 no. 16

662 entries.

List of publishers and distributors: p. 62–65.

Abstract in *Resources in Education*, Aug. 1977, p. 185.

Issued also in microfiche. [Arlington, Va., ERIC Document Reproduction Service; prepared for Educational Resources Information Center, National Institute of Education, 1977] 1 sheet.

DLC-Micro ED137213

488

Hayward, Fred M., *and* Paul A. Beckett. The cost of teaching African languages: major problems and their national implications. [s.l.], 1978. 9 p.

Paper on teaching African languages in the United States presented at a Conference on African Languages, East Lansing, Mich., 1979.

Abstract in *Resources in Education*, 1980 annual cumulation, p. 638.

Microfiche. [Arlington, Va., ERIC Document Reproduction Service; prepared for Educational Resources Information Center, National Institute of Education, 1980] 1 sheet.

DLC-Micro ED179102

489

Herborn, Peter M. "African studies curriculum project;" an instructional unit for seventh grade world cultures. Urbana, African Studies Program, University of Illinois, [1977] 27 p.

Bibliography: p. 26–27.

Report developed as part of an interdisciplinary workshop project in African curriculum development funded by the National Endowment for the Humanities.

Abstract in *Resources in Education*, 1980 annual cumulation, p. 2123.

Microfiche. [Arlington, Va., ERIC Document Reproduction Service; prepared for Educational Resources Information Center, National Institute of Education, 1980] 1 sheet.

DLC-Micro ED188997

490

Kenski, Henry C., *and* Margaret C. Kenski. Teaching African politics at American colleges and universities: a survey. [s.l.], 1975. 20 p.

Paper prepared for a meeting of the Western Social Science Association, 1975.

Abstract in *Resources in Education*, Mar. 1977, p. 140–141.

Microfiche. [Arlington, Va., ERIC Document Reproduction Service; prepared for Educational Resources Information Center, National Institute of Education, 1977] 1 sheet.

DLC-Micro ED130960

491

Key competencies: African and African and Afro-American studies, elementary schools. [Philadelphia], Division of African and Afro-American Studies, School District of Philadelphia, 1980. 17 p.

Abstract in *Resources in Education*, Feb. 1981, p. 168–169.

Microfiche. [Arlington, Va., ERIC Document Reproduction Service; prepared for Educational Resources Information Center, National Institute of Education, 1981] 1 sheet.

DLC-Micro ED193111

492

Key competencies: African and Afro-American studies (Junior High) (J-AAS) and African and Afro-American studies (Senior High) (S-AAS) [Philadelphia], Division of African and Afro-American Studies, School District of Philadelphia, 1980. 21 p.

Abstract in *Resources in Education*, Feb. 1981, p. 169.

Microfiche. [Arlington, Va., ERIC Document Reproduction Service; prepared for Educational Resources Information Center, National Institute of Education, 1981] 1 sheet.

DLC-Micro ED193112

The following items (entries 493–495) are reports developed as part of an interdisciplinary workshop project in African curriculum development at the University of Illinois, Urbana-Champaign, funded by the National Endowment for the Humanities.

493

Lewis, Elaine. "African unit;" an instructional unit for sixth grade. Urbana, African Studies Center, University of Illinois, [1977] 36 p. maps.

Abstract in *Resources in Education*, 1980 annual cumulation, p. 2122–2123.

Microfiche. [Arlington, Va., ERIC Document Reproduction Service; prepared for Educational Resources Information Center, National Institute of Education, 1980] 1 sheet.

DLC-Micro ED188994

494

McKenzie, Karen S. "Introducing Africa in the classroom;" an instructional unit for seventh grade social studies. Part 1. Urbana, African Studies Program, University of Illinois, [1979] 80 p. map.

Abstract in *Resources in Education*, 1980 annual cumulation, p. 2123.

Microfiche. [Arlington, Va., ERIC Document Reproduction Service; prepared for Educational Resources Information Center, National Institute of Education, 1980] 1 sheet.

DLC-Micro ED188996

495

Miller, Shirley A. "Kusema;" an instructional unit for language arts, K-7. Urbana, African Studies Program, University of Illinois, [1977] 44 p.

Abstract in *Resources in Education*, 1980 annual cumulation, p. 2123.

Microfiche. [Arlington, Va., ERIC Document

495 (cont.)

Reproduction Service; prepared for Educational Resources Information Center, National Institute of Education, 1980] 1 sheet.

DLC-Sci RR ED188995

496

The New American mathematics and the old African mathematics: an adventure in comparative mathematics. New York, School Services Division, African-American Institute, [1976] 6 p.

Abstract in *Resources in Education*, Apr. 1977, p. 130.

Microfiche. [Arlington, Va., ERIC Document Reproduction Service; prepared for Educational Resources Information Center, National Institute of Education, 1977] 1 sheet.

DLC-Micro ED132090

497

Patterson, Ruth P. "African studies curriculum unit;" the cycle of life in the African family; an instructional unit for senior high school home economics. Urbana, African Studies Program, University of Illinois, [1978] 18 p.

Report developed as part of an interdisciplinary workshop project in African curriculum development funded by the National Endowment for the Humanities.

Abstract in *Resources in Education*, 1980 annual cumulation, p. 2124–2125.

Microfiche. [Arlington, Va., ERIC Document Reproduction Service; prepared for Educational Resources Information Center, National Institute of Education, 1980] 1 sheet.

DLC-Micro ED189006

498

Priebe, Richard. African literature and the American university. [s.l., 1973] 14 p.

Paper presented at annual meeting of the American Sociological Association, 1973.

Abstract in *Resources in Education*, Apr. 1975, p. 90.

Microfiche. [Arlington, Va., ERIC Document Reproduction Service; prepared for Educational Resources Information Center, National Institute of Education, 1975] 1 sheet.

DLC-Micro ED098908

499

Schmidt, Nancy J. African outreach workshop, 1974. Urbana, African Studies Program, University of Illinois, 1975. 68 p.

Funded by the U.S. Office of Education under grant OEG-074-0354.

The primary objective of the workshop "was to assist teachers in developing curriculum units on Africa using materials available in their local community."—Preface.

Abstract in *Resources in Education*, Oct. 1975, p. 177–178.

Microfiche. [Arlington, Va., ERIC Document Reproduction Service; prepared for Educational Resources Information Center, National Institute of Education, 1975] 1 sheet.

DLC-Micro ED107644

500

——— Evaluating materials about Africa for children. [s.l.], 1975. 24 p.

Paper presented at a meeting of the Illinois Association of School Librarians, 1975.

Abstract in *Resources in Education*, Oct. 1975, p. 120.

Microfiche. [Arlington, Va., ERIC Document Reproduction Service; prepared for Educational Resources Information Center, National Institute of Education, 1975] 1 sheet.

DLC-Micro ED107262

501

——— Selected bibliographies for teaching children about Subsaharan Africa. Urbana, Publications Office, College of Education, University of Illinois, 1975. 50 p.

Prepared under a contract with the National Institute of Education, U.S. Dept. of Health, Education and Welfare.

Abstract in *Resources in Education*, Apr. 1976, p. 132.

Microfiche. [Arlington, Va., ERIC Document Reproduction Service; prepared for Educational Resources Information Center, National Institute of Education, 1976] 1 sheet.

DLC-Micro ED115369

502

Smith Allie E. "Instructional materials on Africa for primary grades;" an instructional unit for grade one. Urbana, African Studies Program, University of Illinois, [1978] 38 p.

Report developed as part of an interdisciplinary workshop project in African curriculum development funded by the National Endowment for the Humanities.

Abstract in *Resources in Education*, 1980 annual cumulation, p. 2122.

Microfiche. [Arlington, Va., ERIC Document Reproduction Service; prepared for Educational Resources Information Center, National Institute of Education, 1980] 1 sheet.

DLC-Micro ED188989

503

Spanjer, Allan, *and* Eugene Bales. Africa and Iberia to the Americas (Brazil): a curriculum development and teacher training project. [Atlanta, Georgia State University, 1978] 74 p.

"This report provides a description of a Fulbright-Hays Group Projects Abroad study trip to Brazil. The central purpose of the trip was to establish a basis for further development of curricula which promotes intercultural understanding through study of cultural influences of minority groups. The focus was on African and Iberian carryover into the Americas with special emphasis on Brazil."–Abstract.

Abstract in *Resources in Education*, Feb. 1981, p. 162.

Microfiche. [Arlington, Va., ERIC Document Reproduction Service; prepared for Educational Resources Information Center, National Institute of Education, 1981] 1 sheet.

DLC-Micro ED194459

504

Stumpff, Marcelle. "An African curriculum unit;" an instructional unit for tenth through twelfth grades world civilization. Urbana, African Studies Program, University of Illinois, [1979] 21 p.

Report developed as part of an interdisciplinary workshop project in African curriculum development funded by the National Endowment for the Humanities.

Abstract in *Resources in Education*, 1980 annual cumulation, p. 2124.

Microfiche. [Arlington, Va., ERIC Document Reproduction Service; prepared for Educational Resources Information Center, National Institute of Education, 1980] 1 sheet.

DLC-Micro ED189005

505

Teaching African geography from a global perspective. New York, School Services Division, African-American Institute, [1975] 10 p. map.

Abstract in *Resources in Education*, Apr. 1977, p. 131.

Microfiche. [Arlington, Va., ERIC Document Reproduction Service; prepared for Educational Resources Information Center, National Institute of Education, 1977] 1 sheet.

DLC-Sci RR ED132095

The following items (entries 506–507) are reports developed as part of an interdisciplinary workshop in African curriculum development at the University of Illinois, Urbana-Champaign, funded by the National Endowment for the Humanities.

506

Volkmann, Roberta. "Africa: a unit for an arts in general education curriculum;" an instructional unit for sixth grade. Urbana, African Studies Program, University of Illinois, [1979] 75 p. illus., map.

Abstract in *Resources in Education*, 1980 annual cumulation, p. 2122.

Microfiche. [Arlington, Va., ERIC Document Reproduction Service; prepared for Educational Resources Information Center, National Institute of Education, 1980] 1 sheet.

DLC-Micro ED188993

507

Wilcox, Elizabeth A. "A curriculum unit on Africa for the seventh grade;" an instructional unit for seventh grade language arts and eighth grade remedial English. Urbana, African Studies Program, University of Illinois, [1979] 26 p.

Abstract in *Resources in Education*, 1980 annual cumulation, p. 2123.

Microfiche. [Arlington, Va., ERIC Document Reproduction Service; prepared for Educational Resources Information Center, National Institute of Education, 1980] 1 sheet.

DLC-Micro ED188999

508

Wiley, David, and David Dwyer. African language instruction in the United States: directions and priorities for the 1980s. East Lansing, African Studies Center, Michigan State University, 1980. 33 p.

Abstract in *Resources in Education*, May 1981, p. 98.

Microfiche. [Arlington, Va., ERIC Document Reproduction Service; prepared for Educational Resources Information Center, National Institute of Education, 1981] 1 sheet.

DLC-Micro ED196272

509

Williams, John A., *and* Brenda Coven. A brief guide to preparing an undergraduate research paper in African history. [Stony Brook, State University of New York, 1975] 19 p.

Prepared for the American Historical Association.

Abstract in *Resources in Education*, Jan. 1976, p. 167.

Microfiche. [Arlington, Va., ERIC Document Reproduction Service; prepared for Educational Resources Information Center, National Institute of Education, 1975] 1 sheet.

DLC-Micro ED111747

510

Wisconsin. University-Madison. *African Studies Program.* Films on Africa: an educator's guide to 16 mm films available in the Midwest. Madison, 1974. 68 p.   DT19.8Z9W57 1964

"Funding for the preparation and production of this material was provided through grants from the U.S. Office of Education."—p. i.

Abstract in *Resources in Education*, Dec. 1976, p. 146.

Issued also in microfiche. [Arlington, Va., ERIC Document Reproduction Service; prepared for Educational Resources Information Center, National Institute of Education, 1976] 1 sheet.
     DLC-Micro ED127246

511

Zekiros, Astair, *and* Marylee Wiley. Africa in social studies textbooks. Madison, Wisc., Dept. of Public Instruction, 1978. 30 p.

Sponsored by the U.S. Office of Education.

Abstract in *Resources in Education*, Nov. 1979, p. 208.

Microfiche. [Arlington, Va., ERIC Document Reproduction Service; prepared for Educational Resources Information Center, National Institute of Education, 1979] 1 sheet.
     DLC-Micro ED173260

Energy Resources— Production & Consumption

512

U.S. *Central Intelligence Agency.* Free world oil refineries. [Washington, available from the Library of Congress], 1975. 59 p. (*Its* Research aid)
     TP690.3.U52 1975

"A (ER) 75-67."

Chiefly tables.

Crude oil refineries and ownership in Africa: p. 11–14.

Note: Statistical information on oil production, costs, prices, exports, and probable reserves is recorded in the Agency's periodical, *International Energy Statistical Review* (title varies slightly) (HD9560.4.U485a), a continuation of its *International Oil Developments: Statistical Survey.*

Individual issues of various U.S. Government periodicals concerned with foreign petroleum production and trade can be identified in *American Statistics Index: A Comprehensive Guide and Index to the Statistical Publications of the U.S. Government* (Washington, Congressional Information Service; Z7554.U5A46).

513

────── Major oil and gas fields of the free world. [McLean, Va.], 1976. 30 p. maps. (*Its* Research aid)   TN870.U45 1976

"ER 76-10001."

Major oil and gas fields of sub-Saharan Africa; p. 12–15.

514

────── Major oil and gas fields of the free world. [McLean, Va.], CIA; [Washington] available from the Library of Congress, 1977. 30 p. col. maps (1 fold.)   TN870.U45 1977

"ER 77-10313."

Major oil and gas fields of sub-Saharan Africa: p. 20–23.

515

────── OPEC countries: current account trends, 1975–76. [Langley, Va.], 1976. 21 p. (*Its* Research aid)   HD9560.1.066U55 1976

Cover title.

"ER 76-10370."

Includes statistics on the petroleum exports and total trade of Gabon and Nigeria.

516

────── West-Central Africa, oil and gas prospects. [Washington, 1977] col. map.
     G8631.H8 1977.U5

Scale ca. 1:12,500,000.

Shows oil fields in coastal areas of Nigeria, Cameroon, Gabon, Congo, Zaire, and Angola.

517

────── World oil refineries. [Washington], 1974. 46 p. (*Its* Reference aid) HD9560.4.U485 1974

"A (ER 74-61."

Includes data on the capacity and ownership of African refineries.

518

U.S. *Congress. House. Committee on International Relations. Subcommittee on International Security and Scientific Affairs.* United States energy policy toward developing countries: hearing before the Subcommittees on International Security and Scientific Affairs and on International Economic Policy and Trade of the Committee on International Relations, House of Representatives, Ninety-fifth Congress, first session, October 28, 1977. Washington, U.S. Govt. Print. Off., 1978. 47 p.   KF27.I5495 1977b
     J74.A23 95th Cong.,
     Comm. Inter. Rel.,
     v. 55

Clement J. Zablocki, chairman, Subcommitee on International Security and Scientific Affairs.

Jonathan B. Bingham, chairman, Subcommittee on International Economic Policy and Trade.

Includes occasional references to Africa.

519

U.S. *Congress. House. Committee on Science and Technology.* Oversight of energy development in Africa and the Middle East: report, Ninety-sixth Congress, second session. Washington, for sale by the Supt. of Docs., U.S. Govt. Print. off., 1980. 132 p.   DLC

At head of title: Committee print.

"Serial QQ."

Don Fuqua, chairman.

A staff analysis based on discussions in South Africa, Saudi Arabia, Ivory Coast, and Nigeria.

520

U.S. *Dept. of Energy. Office of International Affairs.* The role of foreign governments in the energy industries. Washington; for sale by the Supt. of Docs., U.S. Govt. Print. Off., 1977. 409 p.

HD9502.A2U56 1977

Government regulation of the petroleum industry is surveyed in the following African countries (p. 251–309): Algeria, Angola, Egypt, Gabon, Libya, Nigeria, and South Africa.

521

Africa energy survey methodology. Washington, Donovan, Hamester, and Rattien, [1979] 2 v. illus.

Submitted to the Office of Development Resources, Bureau of Africa, U.S. Agency for International Development.

"The purpose of the Africa Energy Survey Methodology is to assist planners to assess energy resources, uses and suitable conversion technologies."—p. 1.

Abstracts in *A.I.D. Research & Development Abstracts*, v. 9, no. 4, 1981, p. 62–63.

Microfiche. [Washington, U.S. Agency for International Development, 1979?] 4 sheets.

DLC-Sci RR PN-AAJ-209-PN-AAJ-210

522

African Solar Energy Workshop, *Atlanta*, May 21–26, 1979. Summary report. [Nairobi], United Nations Development Programme, 1980. 43 p. (United Nations Development Programme. Energy report series, ERS-5-80)   DLC

Sponsored in part by the U.S. Agency for International Development and the U.S. Dept. of Energy.

Organized by the Georgia Institute of Technology.

523

Ashworth, John H. Renewable energy sources for the world's poor: a review of current international development assistance programs. Golden, Colo.,

Solar Energy Research Institute, 1979. [69] p. (in various pagings)   DLC

Prepared for the U.S. Dept. of Energy under contract no. EG-77-C-01-4042.

Includes brief references to various energy sources (e.g., charcoal, firewood, solar power) in sub-Saharan Africa.

524

Bever, James A., *and* Barbara M. Bever. Energy and related development assistance activities in EA and BLS areas (East and Southern Africa); recommendations to U.S. Agency for International Development (with special attention to renewable & improved traditional energy to meet rural needs) [s.l.], 1979. 100 p. illus.

Prepared under contract AID/afr-C-1543 for the Agency's Special Development Problems Division, Bureau for Africa, and its Regional Economic Development Services Office for East & Southern Africa.

EA: East Africa.

BLS: Botswana, Lesotho, and Swaziland.

Abstract in *A.I.D. Research and Development Abstracts*, v. 8, no. 2, 1980, p. 24.

Microfiche. [Washington, U.S. Agency for International Development, 1979?] 2 sheets.

DLC-Sci RR PN-AAH-007

525

A Brief description of the Developing Country Energy Project. Upton, N.Y., Policy Analysis Division, National Center for Analysis of Energy Systems, Brookhaven National Laboratory, 1976. 5 p.

Prepared under contract to the U.S. Energy Research and Development Administration.

Among the countries considered are Ghana and Kenya.

Microfiche. [Washington?, Technical Information Center, U.S. Energy Research & Development Administration, 1977] 1 fiche.

DLC-Sci RR BNL21874

526

Cherif, Messaoud. Impact of Iranian oil crisis on Africa studied. *In* U.S. *Joint Publications Research Service.* JPRS 73268. [Springfield, Va., National Technical Service, 1979] (Translations on sub-Saharan Africa, no. 2092) p. 1–4.

Translation of article in *Demain l'Afrique*, Paris, Mar. 26, 1979, p. 40–42.

Microfiche. [Washington, Supt. of Docs., U.S. Govt. Print. Off., 1979]

DLC-Micro JPRS 73268

527

Firewood crops: shrub and tree species for energy production: report of an ad hoc panel of the Advisory Committee on Technology Innovation, Board on Science and Technology for International Development, Commission on International Relations. Washington, National Academy of Sciences, 1980. 237 p. illus.   SD536.5.F57

Bibliography: p. 191–202.

Includes information on African flora.

528

French, David. Firewood in Africa: discussion paper for the Africa Bureau Firewood Workshop, June 12–14, 1978. Washington, 1978. 53 p.

Prepared for the Bureau for Africa, U.S. Agency for International Development.

Includes also the "Summary of Proceedings" of the workshop, p. 6–15.

Abstract in *Government Reports Announcements & Index*, Oct. 12, 1979, p. 10.

Microfiche. [Springfield, Va., National Technical Information Service, 1979] 1 sheet.
                DLC-Sci RR PB-297178

529

———— The economics of renewable energy systems for developing countries. Washington, 1979. 68 p.

Research supported in part by the U.S. Agency for International Development.

Includes analyses of a solar thermal irrigation pump near Bakel, Senegal, and a solar cell irrigation pump on Lake Chad.

Microfiche. [Washington, U.S. Agency for International Development, 1979?] 1 sheet.
                DLC-Sci RR PN-AAG-864

530

French, David, *and* Patricia Larson. Energy for Africa: selected readings. Washington, Special Development Problems Division, Bureau for Africa, Agency for International Development, 1980. 199 p.

"During 1979 and 1980, the Africa Bureau of the U.S. Agency for International Development worked to establish guidelines for its energy program. As part of this process, papers were commissioned on the following issues: the relationship of energy to African development, energy surveys, the economics of energy systems, technology transfer, community involvement in fuelwood activities, and the monitoring of energy projects."—p. [1].

Abstract in *A.I.D. Research & Development Abstracts*, v. 9, no. 3, 1981, p. 63.

Microfiche. [Washington, U.S. Agency for International Development, 1980?] 3 sheets.
                DLC-Sci RR PN-AAJ-432

531

Hoskins, Marilyn W. Community participation in African fuelwood production, transformation, and utilization. [s.l., 1979] [67] p.

Bibliography p. [63–67].

On cover: Overseas Development Council; Agency for International Development.

Prepared for the Workshop on Fuelwood and Other Renewable Fuels in Africa, Paris, 1979.

Abstract in *A.I.D. Research & Development Abstracts*, July 1981, p. 41.

Microfiche. [Washington, U.S. Agency for International Development, 1979?] 1 sheet.
                DLC-Sci RR PN-AAH-466

532

Howe, James W. Energy for the villages of Africa: recommendations for African governments and outside donors. [s.l.], Overseas Development Council, 1977. 136 p. maps.

Prepared for the U.S. Agency for International Development.

Bibliography: p. 128–136.

Abstracts in *Government Reports Announcement & Index*, June 22, 1979, p. 133, and *A.I.D. Research and Development Abstracts*, v. 8, no. 2, 1980, p.

Among the appendixes are the following:

1. Tarrant, James J. Energy needs and tasks in Debarek, Ethiopia. p. 54–73.

2. Holtzman, John S. Energy needs and tasks in a Sahelian village. p. 74–90.

3. The Gelebs of Ethiopia: Omo River project. p. 91–93.

Describes the introduction of windmills for agricultural irrigation.

4. Africa's conventional energy resources. p. 94–100.

Microfiche. [Springfield, Va., National Technical Information Service, 1979] 2 sheets (DLC-Sci RR PB292790), and [Washington, U.S. Agency for International Development, 1979?] 2 sheets (DLC-Sci RR PN-AAG-968).

533

Larson, Patricia S. Energy activities supported by the Africa Bureau. [Washington?], 1981. 62 p.

Submitted to the Selected Development Problems Division, Office of Development Resources, Bureau for Africa, U.S. Agency for International Development.

Examined in the Development Information Center, AID, Washington, D.C.

534

Maachou, Abdelkader. Oil's impact on developing countries discussed. *In* U.S. *Joint Publications Research Service*. JPRS 76637. [Springfield, Va.,

534 (cont.)

National Technical Information Service, 1980] (Sub-Saharan Africa report, no. 2307) p. 1–7.

Translation of article in *Revue africaine de stratégie*, Paris, July–Sept. 1980, p. 15–18.

Microfiche. [s.l., 1980]

DLC-Micro JPRS 76637

535

OAU's energy plan examined. *In* U.S. *Joint Publications Research Service.* JPRS 75957. [Springfield, Va., National Technical Information Service, 1980] (Sub-Saharan Africa, report, no. 2260) p. 11–18.

Article on the energy plan discussed at the Organization of African Unity's special summit, Lagos, Nigeria, Apr. 1980, in *West Africa*, London, June 2, 1980, p. 960–963.

Microfiche. [s.l., 1980]

DLC-Micro JPRS 75957

536

An Overview of alternative energy sources for LDCs: report to U.S. Agency for International Development, Technical Assistance Bureau, Office of Science and Technology. [s.l.], Arthur D. Little, inc., 1974. 372 p.

LDCs: Lesser-developed countries.

Country profiles, indicated economic conditions and energy resources, are presented, including Ivory Coast and Kenya.

Microfiche. [Springfield, Va., National Technical Information Service, 1975] 4 sheets.

DLC-Sci RR PB-239465

537

PRC Energy Analysis Company. Solar energy commercialization for African countries, prepared by PRC Energy Analysis Company for U.S. Department of Energy, Assistant Secretary for Conservation and Solar Applications, Office of Solar Applications and Commercialization. Washington, The Office; [Springfield, Va., available from National Technical Information Service, U.S. Dept. of Commerce], 1978. 103 p. maps.

TJ810.P27 1978

Prepared under contract no. EG-77-C-01-2522. "HCP/CS-2522."

Based on a survey of Kenya, Cameroon, Nigeria, Niger, Ivory Coast, and Senegal.

Issued also in microfiche. [s.l., Technical Information Center, Dept. of Energy, 1979] 2 sheets.

DLC-Sci RR HCP/CS-2522

538

Pelletier, Renée. Increased price of oil hits Africa. *In* U.S. *Joint Publications Research Service.* JPRS

72986. [Springfield, Va., National Technical Information Service, 1979] (Translations on Sub-Saharan Africa, no. 2074) p. 10–19.

Translation of article in *Africa*, Dakar, Jan. 1979, p. 35–38.

Microfiche. [Washington, Supt. of Docs., U.S. Govt. Print. Off., 1979]

DLC-Micro JPRS 72986

539

Posmowski, Pierrette. Current use of solar energy in Africa discussed. *In* U.S. *Joint Publications Research Service.* JPRS 65372. [Springfield, Va., National Technical Information Service, 1975] (Translations on Africa, no. 1606) p. 35–39.

Translation of interview with Abdou Moumouni, director of solar energy for Niger, in *Afrique nouvelle*, Dakar, June 11–12, 1975, p. 16, 17, 23.

Microfiche. [s.l., 1975]

DLC-Micro JPRS 65372

540

Ratajczak, A. F., *and* W. J. Bifano. Description of photovoltaic village power systems in the United States and Africa. Cleveland, Lewis Research Center, National Aeronautics and Space Administration, [1979?] [10] p. illus.   DLC
"NASA TM-79149."

541

Sigisbert, Geneviève. Oil problems in African nations analyzed. *In* U.S. *Joint Publications Research Service.* JPRS 74171. [Springfield, Va., National Technical Information Service, 1979] (Sub-Saharan Africa report, no. 2151) p. 7–21.

Translation of article in *Europe Outremer*, Paris, Apr. 1979.

Microfiche. [Washington, Supt. of Docs., U.S. Govt. Print. Off., 1979]

DLC-Micro JPRS 74171

542

The Socio-economic context of the fuelwood use in small rural communities, [by] Dennis H. Wood [et al.] [s.l.], 1980. xxv, 293 p. (A.I.D. evaluation special study, no. 1)

Prepared for the Bureau for Program and Policy Coordination, U.S. Agency for International Development.

Includes frequent references to Africa.

Abstract in *A.I.D. Research & Development Abstracts*, July 1981, p. 27.

Microfiche. [Washington, U.S. Agency for International Development, 1980?] 4 sheets.

DLC-Sci RR PN-AAH-747

543

UPDEA Abidjan seminar on electric-power interconnection reported. *In* U.S. *Joint Publications Research Service.* JPRS 75862. [Springfield, Va., National Technical Information Service, 1980] (Sub-Saharan Africa report, no. 2256) p. 29–38.

Translation of article on a meeting of the Union of Producers and Distributors of Electric Power in Africa, a group of 18 electric power companies from 17 French-speaking nations of Central and West Africa, in *Fraternité-Matin*, Abidjan, May 5–9, 1980.

Microfiche. [s.l., 1980]

DLC-Micro JPRS 75862

544

Ulinski, Carol A. Fuelwood and other renewable energies in Africa: a brief summary of U.S.—supported programs. [s.l.], 1979. 48 p.

Bibliography: p. 43–48.

Prepared under a U.S. Agency for International Development contract for the Workshop on Fuelwood and Other Renewable Fuels in Africa, Paris, 1979.

Abstract in *A.I.D. Research & Development Abstracts*, July 1981, p. 39–40.

Microfiche. [Washington, U.S. Agency for International Development, 1979?] 1 sheet.

DLC-Sci RR PN-AAH-450

Fauna and Flora

545

U.S. *Congress. House. Committee on Merchant Marine and Fisheries.* Elephants: hearings, Ninety-sixth Congress, first session, on H.R. 4685 ... July 25, 26, 1979. Washington, U.S. Govt. Print. Off., 1979. 253 p. illus.   KF27.M4 1978a
J74.A23 96th
Cong., House
Comm. Merchant
Marine, v. 13

John M. Murphy, chairman.

Hearings were on "a bill to provide for the control of the importing into, and the exporting from, the United States of elephants and elephant products."

Emphasis is on the survival of the African elephant.

Abstract in *American Statistics Index*, 1980, Abstracts, p. 975.

Issued also in microfiche. [Washington, Congressional Information Service, 1980?] 3 sheets.

DLC-Micro ASI:80 21568-19

546

U.S. *Congress. Senate. Committee on Environment and Public Works. Subcommittee on Resource Protection.* Elephant Protection Act of 1979 and the International Wildlife Resources Conservation Act of 1980: hearing, Ninety-sixth Congress, second session, on H.R. 4685 ... June 30, 1980. Washington, U.S. Govt. Print. Off., 1980. 220 p.
KF26.E675   1980a
J74.A23 96th
Cong., Sen. Comm.
Envir., v. 53

John C. Culver, chairman; John H. Chafee, presiding officer.

Hearing were called "to discuss ways in which our country can assist other nations in overall wildlife and habitat conservation as well as efforts to halt the decline of a particular species; namely, the elephant."—p. 1.

Foreign Relations

547

U.S. *Congress. House. Committee on Foreign Affairs. Subcommittee on Africa.* Briefing on OAU summit at Monrovia: hearing, Ninety-sixth Congress, first session. July 27, 1979. Washington, U.S. Govt. Print. Off., 1979. 16 p.   KF27.F625 1979h
J74.A23 96th Cong.,
House Comm. For, Aff.,
v. 46

Stephen J. Solarz, chairman.

OAU: Organization of African Unity.

Witness is William C. Harrop, Deputy Assistant Secretary of State.

548

Bozhilov, Lyubomir. Western manipulations in Africa analyzed. *In* U.S. *Joint Publications Research Service.* JPRS 74413. [Springfield, Va., National Technical Information Service, 1979] (Sub-Saharan Africa report, no. 2167) p. 1–17.

Translation of article in *Novo Vreme*, Sofia, Aug. 1979, p. 110–123.

Microfiche. [Washington, Supt. of Docs., U.S. Govt. Print. Off., 1979]

DLC-Micro JPRS 74413

549

Dekersat, Jean. Senghor discusses foreign intervention in Africa. *In* U.S. *Joint Publication Research Service.* JPRS 75862. [Springfield, Va., National Technical Information Service, 1980] (Sub-Saharan Africa report, no. 2256) p. 129–135.

Translation of interview with President Léopold

549 (cont.)

S. Senghor of Senegal, in *Le Figaro Magazine*, Paris, May 10, 1980, p. 88–93.

Microfiche. [s.l., 1980]

DLC-Micro JPRS 75862

550

Morris, David R. The Organization of African Unity; a report submitted to the faculty. Maxwell Air Force Base, Ala., Air War College, Air University, 1974. 35 leaves. (FAR 19932-N)

"Preofessional study no. 5357."

Examined in the former Foreign Affairs Research Documentation Center, U.S. Dept. of State.

Issued also in microfiche. [s.l., 1974] 1 sheet (AD-919227L).

551

Mozambique, Zaire, issue joint communique on cooperation. *In* U.S. *Joint Publications Research Service.* JPRS 75990. [Springfield, Va., National Technical Information Service, 1980] (Sub-Saharan Africa report, no. 2263) p. 3–6.

Translation of article in *Notícias*, Maputo, June 10, 1980, p. 3.

Microfiche. [s.l., 1980]

DLC-Micro JPRS 75990

552

The Organization of African Unity and peacekeeping; a group research project, [by] Mack L. Gibson [et al.] Carlisle Barracks, Pa., U.S. Army War College, 1974. 299 p.

At head of title: USAWC military research program paper.

"This research paper was designed to evaluate the capabilities of the Organization of African Unity (OAU) to function as a regional peacekeeping force and to determine whether such a force is considered to be in the best interests of the United States."—p. iii.

Microfiche. [Springfield, Va., National Technical Information Service, 1975] 4 sheets (DLC-Sci RR A003178); issued in microfilm by University Publications of America (cited in its *Africa: Special Studies, 1962–1980*, p. 4).

553

Pelcovits, Nathan A. The OAU in comparative perspective. [Washington?] 1978. 17 leaves. (FAR 28919-S)

Prepared for the Conference on the OAU and Conflict Management, sponsored by the U.S. Dept. of State, May 1978.

Examined in the former Foreign Affairs Re-search Documentation Center, U.S. Dept. of State.

554

President discusses relations with Soviets, Chinese, west. *In* U.S. *Joint Publications Research Service.* JPRS 69395. [Springfield, Va., National Technical Information Service, 1977] (Translations on Sub-Saharan Africa, no. 1768) p. 8–13.

In an interview, President Félix Houphouët-Boigny of Ivory Coast discusses Africa's political and economic relations with world powers; in *Fraternité-Matin*, Abidjan, May 13, 1977, p. 20–21.

Microfiche. [s.l., 1977]

DLC-Micro JPRS 69359

555

Rigobert, Kongo S. Outlook for pan-Africanism tied to OAU. *In* U.S. *Joint Publications Research Service.* JPRS 72565. [Springfield, Va., National Technical Information Service, 1979] (Translations on Sub-Saharan Africa, no. 2047) p. 1–7.

Translation of article in *L'Observateur*, Ouagadougou, Nov. 23, 1978, p. 1, 6–7, 9.

Microfiche. [Washington, Supt. of Docs., U.S. Govt. Print. Off., 1979]

DLC-Micro JPRS 72565

United States Policy

556

[U.S. *Central Intelligence Agency*] U.S. foreign service posts, Bureau of African Affairs (AF). 1–75. [Washington, 1975] col. map.

G8201.F55 1975.U5

Scale not given.

Shows locations of U.S. embassies, consulates general and consulates in Africa.

"564061."

"Source: Office of the Geographer, April 1975."

557

U.S. *Congress.* [Hearings] Nomination of Hon. Andrew Young as U.S. representative to U.N.: hearing before the Committee on Foreign Relations, United States Senate, Ninety-fifth Congress, first session on the nomination of Congressman Andrew Young to be the United States representative to the United Nations, with the rank of ambassador, and representative in the Security Council of the United Nations, January 25, 1977. Washington, U.S. Govt. Print. Off., 1977. 58 p.

J74.A23, 95th
Cong., Sen. Comm.
For. Rel., v. 64

Includes frequent references to South Africa.

558

U.S. *Congress. House.* Foreign relations authorization act, fiscal year 1979; conference report (to accompany H.R. 12598) [Washington], 1978. 66 p.
DLC-LL
Report submitted by Representative Dante B. Fascell.

At head of title: 95th Congress, 2d session. House of Representatives. Report no. 95-1535.

Includes frequent references to Africa.

559

U.S. *Congress. House. Committee on Foreign Affairs.* Congress and foreign policy. 1978+ Washington, for sale by the Supt. of Docs., U.S. Govt. Print. Off. annual. KF4651.A6133
Includes bibliographies.

At head of title, 1978– : Committee print.

Vols. for 1978– prepared by the Foreign Affairs and National Defense Division in cooperation with other divisions of the Congressional Research Service, Library of Congress.

Continues *Congress and Foreign Policy* issued by the Committee on International Relations, House of Representatives, U.S. Congress (KF4651. A6133; L.C. has 1974–77).

L.C. has 1978+

Note: Since 1974, each annual volume issued by the Committee on International Relations and its successor, the Committee on Foreign Affairs, has included a chapter analyzing the role of Congress in the formulation of United States foreign policy toward Africa; these appear as follows:
1974. Mowle, Susan M. Africa. p. 57–59.
1975. Mowle, Susan M. Congress and Africa. p. 174–181.
1976. Mowle, Susan M. Africa. p. 179–190.
1978. Copson, Raymond W. Congress and Africa policy. p. 171–180.
1979. Copson, Raymond W. Congress and Africa policy, 1979: focus on Rhodesia. p. 85–99.
Includes also brief sections on Zaire, Sudan, Uganda, Nigeria, Angola, and Mozambique.
At the end of each chapter is a list of recent Congressional hearings and other documents on Africa plus citations to pertinent Issue Briefs of the Congressional Research Service.
Note: Other publications of the Committee on Foreign Affairs also provide an overview of legislative activity on Africa; among them are the following: *Chronologies of Major Developments in Selected Areas of Foreign Affairs*, issued quarterly with annual cumulations (DLC; L.C. retains current issues only) *Survey of Activities*, issued annually (JK 1430.F575; L.C. has 1949+); and *Legislation on Foreign Relations through [year]*, issued jointly with the Senate Committee on Foreign Relations (KF 4650.A29F67; L.C. has 1957+).

560

U.S. *Congress. House. Committee on International Relations.* Report of Secretary of State Kissinger on his visits to Latin America, Western Europe, and Africa hearing, Ninety-fourth Congress, second session, June 17, 1976. Washington, U.S. Govt. Print. Off., 1976. 31 p.

KF27.I549 1976g
J74.A23 94th
Cong., House Comm.
Inter. Rel., v. 78
Thomas E. Morgan, chairman.

561

U.S. *Congress. Senate. Committee on Appropriations. Subcommittee on Departments of State, Justice, and Commerce, the Judiciary, and Related Agencies.* Departments of State, Justice, and Commerce, the judiciary, and related agencies appropriations for fiscal year 1978: hearings before a subcommittee of the Committee on Appropriations, United States Senate Ninety-fifth Congress, first session. Washington, U.S. Govt. Print. Off., 1977. 6 v.

KF26.A659 1977
J74.A23 95th
Cong., Sen. Comm.
Approp., v. 17
Ernest F. Hollings, chairman.

Part 1 includes budget estimates of the Bureau of African Affairs, Dept. of State, and of American diplomatic posts in Africa, plus tables indicating the staffing situation of these posts.

562

—— Departments of State, Justice, and Commerce, the judiciary and related agencies appropriations for fiscal year 1980: hearings before a subcommittee of the Committee on Appropriations, United States Senate, Ninety-sixth Congress, first session, on H. R. 4473. Washington, for sale by the Supt. of Docs., U.S. Govt. Print. Off., 1979. 2 v. KF26.A659 1979
J74.A23 96th
Cong., Sen. Comm.
Approp., v. 17
Ernest F. Hollings, chairman.

Pt. 1 includes budget estimates of the Bureau of African Affairs, Dept. of State, and of American diplomatic posts in Africa, plus tables indicating the staffing situation of these posts.

563

U.S. *Congress. Senate. Committee on Foreign Relations.* Nomination of Nathaniel Davis to be Assistant Secretary of State for African Affairs: hearing, Ninety-fourth Congress, first session ... February 19, 1975. 86 p. KF26.F6 1975a
J74.A23 94th
Cong., Sen. Comm.
For. Rel., v. 36
John Sparkman, chairman.

564

—— U.S. policy toward Africa: report (to accom-

564 (cont.)
pany S. Res. 436) [Washington, 1976] 13 p.
J66 serial 13130-4
Report submitted by Senator John Sparkman.
At head of title: 94th Congress, 2d session. Senate. Report no. 94-780.
"The purposes of S. Res. 436, as amended, is to express the support of the Senate to the basic principles of the new American policy toward Africa as outlined by Secretary of State Kissinger in his address at Lusaka, Zambia, on April 27, 1976."
The text of Secretary Kissinger's address is given on p. 5–13.

565
——— Vance nomination: hearing, Ninety-fifth Congress, first session ... January 11, 1977. Washington, U.S. Govt. Print. Off., 1977. 126 p.
KF27.F6 1977
J74.A23 95th
Cong., Sen. Comm.
For. Rel., v. 65
John Sparkman, chairman.
Comments by Cyrus R. Vance, Secretary of State-designate, on U.S. policy toward Africa are given on p. 27–29.

566
U.S. *Congress. Senate. Committee on Foreign Relations. Subcommittee on African Affairs.* Ambassador Young's African trip: hearing, Ninety-fifth Congress, first session ... June 6, 1977. Washington, U.S. Govt. Print. Off., 1977. 29 p.
KF26.F625 1977b
J74.A23 95th
Cong., Sen. Comm.
For Rel., v. 21
Dick Clark, chairman.
A report on Ambassador Andrew J. Young's 18-day trip to Ivory Coast, Ghana, Liberia, Gabon, Mozambique, South Africa, Zambia, and Sudan.

567
——— U.S. policy toward Africa: hearing, Ninety-fifth Congress, second session ... May 12, 1978. Washington, U.S. Govt. Print. Off., 1978. 35 p.
KF26.F625 1978a
J74.A23 95th
Cong., Sen. Comm.
For. Rel., v. 50
Dick Clark, chairman.
Includes statements by Cyrus R. Vance, Secretary of State, Andrew J. Young, U.S. Representative to the United Nations, and Richard M. Moose, Assistant Secretary of State for African Affairs.
"The hearing was held the day before the Katangan attack on Shaba province in Zaire. Although certain classified information has been deleted for publication, nothing was removed from the testimony that relates to that issue. The committee feels that publication of the hearings [sic] will contribute to a better understanding of the evolution of U.S. policy toward Africa, particularly in light of subsequent controversies which arose over the Katangan attack, the role of Cuba in Africa and alleged shifts in the direction of American policy goals."—p. iii.

568
Africa: general policies of the United States toward Africa. *In* U.S. *Dept. of State.* Foreign relations of the United States. 1951, v. 5. Washington, U.S. Govt. Print Off., 1982. p. 1199–1236. (U.S. Dept. of State. Department of State publication 9114)
JX233.A3 1951, v. 5
Paper prepared in the Bureau of Near Eastern, South Asian, and African Affairs, U.S. Dept. of State, Dec. 29, 1950.

569
Correspondent reports on shaping of U.S. African policy. *In* U.S. *Joint Publications Research Service.* JPRS 72791. [Springfield, Va., National Technical Information Service, 1979] (Translations on Sub-Saharan Africa, no. 2062) p. 4–7.
Article in *West Africa*, London, Jan. 22, 1979, p. 116–117.
Microfiche. [Washington, Supt. of Docs., U.S. Govt. Print. Off., 1979]
DLC-Micro JPRS 72791

570
Diggs, Charles C. Kissinger in Africa. Congressional record, 94th Congress, 2d session, v. 122, Apr. 27, 1976: 11419–11421. J11.R5 v. 122
Remarks in the U.S. House of Representatives.
Includes text of address by Secretary of State Kissinger at a luncheon in Lusaka hosted by Zambian President Kenneth D. Kaunda.

Note: The Kissinger speech is also included as part of remarks in the U.S. Senate, Apr. 27, 1976, by Senator Gale W. McGee (*Congressional Record*, v. 122, Apr. 27, 1976: 11323–11326. J11.R5 v. 122).

571
Dole, Robert. Carter in Africa: a sorry safari. Congressional record, 95th Congress, 2d session, v. 124, Apr. 5, 1978: 8717–8718. J11.R5 v. 124
Remarks in the U.S. Senate.
Includes article from the *Washington Post*.

572
Drinan, Robert F. Representative Solarz outlines challenge of new administration in Africa. Con-

572 (cont.)

gressional record [daily ed.], 96th Congress, 2d session, v. 126, Dec. 5, 1980: E5279–E5280.

J11.R7 v. 126

Extension of remarks in the U.S. House of Representatives.

Includes article, "Reagan and Africa," by Representative Stephen J. Solarz, in the *New York Times*.

572a

Foltz, William J. U.S. national interests in Africa. *In* The National interests of the United States in foreign policy: seven discussions at the Wilson Center, December 1980, February 1981; edited by Prosser Gifford. Washington, Woodrow Wilson International Center for Scholars, University Press of America, c1981. p. 93–103.   E876.N37

573

Habib, Philip C. U.S. interests in Africa. [Washington], Office of Public Communications, Bureau of Public Affairs, Dept. of State, 1978. 4 p. (U.S. Dept. of State. Current policy, no. 48)   DLC

Speech by the Diplomat-in-Residence, Stanford University, before the World Affairs Council of Northern California, San Francisco, Oct. 31, 1978.

574

Interview with the President. *In* U.S. *President.* Public papers of the Presidents of the United States. Jimmy Carter. 1977. Washington, U.S. Govt. Print. Off., 1977. p. 643–651.   J80.A283 1977

During a question-and-answer session with a group of publishers, editors, and broadcasters on Apr. 15, 1977, President Carter outlined his administration's policy toward Africa and its views on Cuban intervention there.

574a

Jonah, James O. C. The relationship between U.S. national interests and various countries and/or areas in Africa. *In* The National interests of the United States in foreign policy: seven discussions at the Wilson Center, December 1980, February 1981; edited by Prosser Gifford. Washington, Woodrow Wilson International Center for Scholars, University Press of America, c1981. p. 104–111.   E876.N37

575

Key officers of foreign service posts; guide for business representatives. 1964?+ [Washington, Publishing Services Division, Dept. of State; for sale by the Supt. of Docs., U.S. Govt. Print. Off.] three times a year.   JX1705.A255

Title varies slightly.

A list of the principal officers of U.S. diplomatic posts, including those in Africa.

L.C. has 1965+

Note: For information on African diplomats assigned to the United States, see *Diplomatic List* (JX1705.A22), issued quarterly by the Dept. of State. Supplementary information is provided in the department's *Employees of Diplomatic Missions* (quarterly; JX1705.A235) and in its *Foreign Consular Offices in the United States* (annual; JX1705.A28).

576

Kissinger, Henry A. America and Africa. *In* U.S. *Dept. of State.* The Department of State bulletin, v. 74, no. 1927, May 31, 1976: 679–684.

JX232.A33 v. 74

Address made at a dinner hosted by President William R. Tolbert of Liberia, Monrovia, Apr. 30, 1976.

577

—— Secretary Kissinger reports to Congress on his visits to Latin America, Western Europe, and Africa. *In* U.S. *Dept. of State.* The Department of State bulletin, v. 75, no. 1933, July 12, 1976: 41–48.

JX232.A33 v. 75

Report to the Committee on International Relations, House of Representatives, June 17, 1976.

Africa is covered on p. 46–48.

578

—— Strengthening the relationship between the United States and Africa. *In* U.S. *Dept. of State.* The Department of State bulletin, v. 75, no. 1949, Nov. 1, 1976: 559–562.   JX232.A33 v. 75

Toast given at a luncheon in honor of African foreign ministers and permanent representatives to the United Nations, New York, Oct. 8, 1976.

579

—— The relationship between America and Africa. *In* U.S. *Dept. of State.* Newsletter, no. 180, June 1976: 10–14.   JX1.U542 1976

Testimony by the Secretary of State before the Committee on Foreign Relations, U.S. Senate, May 13, 1976.

580

—— The United States and Africa. *In* U.S. *Dept. of State.* The Department of State bulletin, v. 74, no. 1928, June 7, 1976: 713–719.

JX232.A33 v. 74

Statement by the Secretary of State before the Committee on Foreign Relations, Senate, May 13, 1976.

581

—— The United States and Africa: strengthening the relationship. *In* U.S. *Dept. of State.* The Department of State bulletin, v. 73, no. 1894, Oct. 13, 1975: 571–575.　　　　JX232.A33 v. 73

Toast by the Secretary of State at the U.S. Mission to the United Nations in honor of foreign ministers and permanent representatives of the United Nations of member nations of the Organization of African Unity.

582

—— The United States and Africa: strengthened ties for an era of challenge. *In* U.S. *Dept. of State.* The Department of State bulletin, v. 75, no. 1939, Aug. 23, 1976: 257–265.　　　JX232.A33 v. 75

Address by the Secretary of State before the annual conference of the National Urban League, Boston, Aug. 2, 1976.

583

Lake, Anthony. Africa in a global perspective. *In* U.S. *Dept. of State.* The Department of State bulletin, v. 77, no. 2007, Dec. 12, 1977: 842–848.

JX232.A33 v. 77

Address by the Director of Policy Planning Staff, Dept. of State, for the Christian A. Herter Lecture at Johns Hopkins University School of Advanced International Studies, Washington, Oct. 27, 1977.

Focus is on U.S.-African relations.

584

Macebuh, Stanley. U.S., Nigerian policies on Zimbabwe, Namibia discussed. *In* U.S. *Joint Publications Research Service.* JPRS 72503. [Springfield, Va., National Technical Information Service, 1978] (Translations on Sub-Saharan Africa, no. 2043) p. 55–58.

Article in *Daily Times*, Lagos, Nov. 30, 1978, p. 3.

Microfiche. [Washington, Supt. of Docs., U.S. Govt. Print. Off., 1979?]

DLC-Micro JPRS 72503

585

McGee, Gale W. Secretary Kissinger's trip to Africa. Congressional record, 94th Congress, 2d session, v. 122, May 13, 1976: 13916–13925.

J11.R5 v. 122

Remarks in the U.S. Senate.

Includes texts of the Secretary of State's speeches in Monrovia, Apr. 30, Dakar, May 1, and Nairobi, May 6, 1976.

586

McGovern, George S. Senator Kennedy on Africa policy. Congressional record, [daily ed.], 96th

Congress, 2d session, v. 126, May 30, 1980: S6013–S6015.　　　　　　　　　　J11.R7 v. 126

Remarks in the U.S. Senate.

Includes text of Senator Edward M. Kennedy's interview with *Africa Report*.

587

Mondale, Walter F. Africa and the U.S.: shared values. Washington, Bureau of Public Affairs, U.S. Dept. of State, 1980. 3 p. (U.S. Dept. of State. Current policy, no. 203)　　　　　　　DLC

Address by the Vice President in Lagos, Nigeria, July 22, 1980.

588

Muskie, Edmund S. Africa and U.S. policy. *In* U.S. *Dept. of State.* The Department of State bulletin, v. 81, no. 2046, Jan. 1981: 1–3.

JX232.A33 v. 81

Address by the Secretary of State before the African-American Historical and Cultural Society and the World Affairs Council of Northern California, San Francisco, Dec. 4, 1980.

Issued also as no. 250 in the Dept. of State's Current Policy series.

589

Newsom, David D. Africa: U.S. policy and Africa. *In* U.S. *Dept. of State.* The Department of State bulletin, v. 79, no. 2027, June 1979: 20–21.

JX232.A33 v. 79

Address by the Under Secretary of State for Political Affairs at the George Washington University Institute for Sino-Soviet Studies, Washington, Mar. 14, 1979.

590

Percy, Charles H. African-American Conference. Congressional record, 96th Congress, 1st session, v. 125, Mar. 7, 1979: 4076–4079.

J11.R5 v. 125

Remarks in the U.S. Senate on the conference's session in Khartoum, Sudan, Nov. 27–Dec. 1, 1978.

Includes the Senator's statement during the conference.

591

—— Senate Resolution 436—submission of a resolution supporting the new U.S. policy toward Africa. Congressional record, 94th Congress, 2d session, v. 122, Apr. 29, 1976: 11827–11830.

J11.R5 v. 122

Remarks in the U.S. Senate.

On behalf of a number of Senators, Senator Percy introduces a resolution of support for the

591 (cont.)

policy expounded by Secretary of State Kissinger in Lusaka on Apr. 26.

592

The Presidential campaign, 1976; compiled under the direction of the Committee on House Administration, U.S. House of Representatives. Washington, U.S. Govt. Print. Off., 1978–1979. 3 v. in 5, ports.

E868.P73

Contents: v. 1. Jimmy Carter. 2 v.—v. 2. President Gerald R. Ford. 2 v.—v. 3. The debates.

Frequent references by both candidates to conditions in Africa and to American policy concerning African nations can be identified in the indexes to each volume; an example of the contents is the following:

Carter, Jimmy. Policy on Africa. v. 1, p. 684–688. A position paper on African policy.

593

The President's trip to Africa. Remarks during a briefing for reporters on board Air Force One en route to Monrovia, Liberia; April 3, 1978. *In* U.S. *President.* Public papers of the Presidents of the United States. Jimmy Carter. 1978. Washington, U.S. Govt. Print. Off., 1979. p. 667–671.

J80.A283 1978

Briefing by President Carter and Secretary of State Vance.

594

Secretary Kissinger visits six African nations. *In* U.S. *Dept. of State.* The Department of State bulletin, v. 74, no. 1927, May 31, 1976: 688–710.

JX232.A33 v. 74

Reports on the Secretary's statements and news conferences during his trip to the United Kingdom, Kenya, Tanzania, Zambia, Zaire, Liberia, Senegal, and France, Apr. 23–May 7, 1976.

595

Spencer, John M. A situational analysis of United States' foreign policy toward Africa; a research study submitted to the faculty. Maxwell Air Force Base, Ala., Air Command and Staff College, Air University, 1975. 54 leaves. (U.S. Air University. Air Command and Staff College. Research study).

AMAU

"FAR 24873-N."

Issued also in microfiche. [s.l., 1976] 1 sheet (AD-B011100L).

596

United States foreign policy objectives and overseas military installations; prepared for the Committee on Foreign Relations, United States Senate, by the Foreign Affairs and National Defense Division, Congressional Research Service, Library of Congress. Washington, for sale by the Supt. of Docs., U.S. Govt. Print. Off., 1979. 207 p. maps.

DLC

At head of title: 96th Congress, 1st session. Committee print.

Chapter on American political, economic, and military objectives in sub-Saharan Africa, by Raymond W. Copson, p. 122–133.

597

Vance, Cyrus R. The Secretary: issues facing the United States in Africa. *In* U.S. *Dept. of State.* The Department of State bulletin, v. 78, no. 2016, July 1978: 29–31. JX232.A33 v. 78

Statement by the Secretary of State before the Subcommittee on African Affairs, Committee on Foreign Relations, Senate, May 12, 1978.

598

—— U.S. relations with Africa. *In* U.S. *Dept. of State.* The Department of State bulletin, v. 78, no. 2017, Aug. 1978: 10–13. JX232.A33 v. 78

Address by the Secretary of State to the annual meeting of the U.S. Jaycees, Atlantic City, N.J., June 20, 1978.

599

—— The United States and Africa: building positive relations. *In* U.S. *Dept. of State.* The Department of State bulletin, v. 77, no. 1989, Aug. 8, 1977: 165–170. JX232.A33 v. 77

Address by the Secretary of State to the annual convention of the National Association for the Advancement of Colored People, St. Louis, July 1, 1977.

Main themes are American assistance programs, the promotion of human rights, and the questions of conditions in Namibia, Rhodesia, and South Africa.

Policies of Communist Nations

600

U.S. *Congress. House. Committee on International Relations. Subcommittee on Europe and the Middle East.* United States-Soviet relations, 1978: hearings, Ninety-fifth Congress, second session. Washington, U.S. Govt. Print. Off., 1978. 208 p.

KF27.I54916 1978e
J74.A23 95th Cong.,
House Comm. Inter.
Rel., v. 108

Lee H. Hamilton, chairman.
Hearings held Aug. 9–Sept. 26, 1978.

600 (cont.)

Topic is "Soviet Union and the Third World," with occasional references to Africa.

601

U.S. *Information Agency. Office of Research.* External cultural and information activities of East Germany (GDR) in non-Communist countries. Washington, 1978. 20 p.   DD261.4.U528   1978

"R-3-78."

Programs in sub-Saharan Africa are covered on p. 15–17.

602

———— Overview of external information and cultural activities of Communist countries in 1976. [Washington?], 1977. 33 p.

"R-15-77."

Africa is covered on p. 8–11.

Examined in the U.S. Information Agency, Washington, D.C.

603

U.S. *International Communication Agency.* External cultural and information activities and themes of Communist countries in 1977. Washington, 1978. 53 p.   AMAU

Activities of Communist nations in Africa south of the Sahara are covered on p. 17–28.

Held also by the U.S. Information Agency Library, Washington, D.C.

604

U.S. *Library of Congress. Congressional Research Service. Senior Specialists Division.* The Soviet Union and the Third World: a watershed in great power policy?; report to the Committee on International Relations, House of Representatives; prepared by Joseph Whelan and William B. Inglee. Washington, U.S. Govt. Print. Off., 1977. xvii, 186 p. 1 fold. leaf of plates., illus.

D849.U56   1977

At head of title: 95th Congress, 1st session. Committee print.

"The study seeks only to suggest the main thrust and broad lines of Soviet policy and activity in the Third World, concentrating mainly on the 'national liberation zone' of Asia and Africa."—p. 1.

605

Activities of Soviets, Cubans, East Germans in Africa reported. *In* U.S. *Joint Publications Research Service.* JPRS 71816. [Springfield, Va., National Technical Information Service, 1978] (Translations on Sub-Saharan Africa, no. 1988) p. 1–7.

Translation of articles in *Le Figaro*, Paris, Aug. 3, 1978.

Microfiche. [Washington, Supt. of Docs., U.S. Govt. Print. Off., 1978]

DLC-Micro JPRS 71816

606

Albright, David E. Gauging Soviet success in Africa and the Middle East: a commentary. Carlisle Barracks, Pa., Strategic Studies Institute, U.S. Army War College, 1980. 7 p. (Strategic issues research memorandum)

Microfiche. [s.l., Defense Technical Information Center, 1980] 1 sheet.

DLC-Sci RR AD-A087573

607

———— Soviet policy. Problems of Communism, v. 27, Jan./Feb. 1978: 2039. illus.

HX1.P75 v. 27

Issued by the U.S. Information Agency.

A review of the priorities and objectives of Soviet policy in Africa.

608

The Anti-Soviet dynamic: the basis of present Chinese African policy; special report. Ft. Wadsworth, N.Y., 432d Military Intelligence Detachment (Strategic), 1978. 8 p.

At head of title: Strategic Studies Institute, U.S. Army War College, Carlisle Barracks, Pa.

Microfiche. [s.l., Defense Documentation Center, 1979] 1 sheet.

DLC-Sci RR AD-A073104

609

Baudis, Dominique. Text of Castro interview in Italian weekly. *In* U.S. *Joint Publications Research Service.* JPRS 71489. [Springfield, Va., National Technical Information Service, 1978] (Translations on Sub-Saharan Africa, no. 1962) p. 2–6.

Translation of interview with President Fidel Castro on Cuban intervention in Africa, in *Epoca*, Milan, June 21, 1978, p. 40–41.

Microfiche. [Washington, Supt. of Docs., U.S. Govt. Print. Off., 1978]

DLC-Micro JPRS 71489

610

Bauman, Robert E. The Cuban connection. Congressional record, 95th Congress, 1st session, v. 123, Sept. 23, 1977: 30720–30722.   J11.R5 v. 123

Extension of remarks in the U.S. House of Representatives.

Includes text of report by the Education and Research Institute, American Conservative Union, on Cuban involvement in Africa.

611

Burk, Henry J., *and* Martin A. Hyman. Past Chinese-African involvement; special report. Ft. Wadsworth, N.Y., 432d Military Intelligence Detachment (Strategic), 1978. 13 p.

At head of title: Strategic Studies Institute, U.S. Army War College, Carlisle Barracks, Pa.

Microfiche. [s.l., Defense Documentation Center, 1979] 1 sheet.   DLC-Sci RR AD-A068793

612

Butler, Shannon R. Brotherhood-in-arms: East German foreign policy in Africa. [Monterey, Calif.], Naval Postgraduate School, 1980. 100 p.

Bibliography: p. 87–95.

Thesis (M.A.)—Naval Postgraduate School.

Microfiche. [s.l., Defense Technical Information Center, 1981] 2 sheets.

DLC-SCI RR AD-A092402

613

Chairoff, Patrick. Expose of Soviet strategy in Africa. *In* U.S. *Joint Publications Research Service.* JPRS 69029. [Springfield, Va., National Technical Information Service, 1977] (Translations on Sub-Saharan Africa, no. 1741) p. 1–7.

Translation of article in *Africa*, Dakar, Mar. 1977, p. 29–32.

Microfiche. [s.l., 1977]

DLC-Micro JPRS 69029

614

Colm, Peter W., *and* Karl F. Spielmann. Sino-Soviet involvement in sub-Saharan Africa: the element of mutual competition. Arlington, Va., International and Social Studies Division, Institute for Defense Analyses, 1977. 120 p.

"Paper P-1350."

Microfiche. [s.l., Defense Documentation Center, 1979] 2 sheets (DLC-Sci RR AD-A064185); issued in microfilm by University Publications of America (cited in its *Africa: Special Studies, 1962–1980*, p. 4).

615

Cook, Bruce C. Soviet involvement in Africa—a descriptive and quantitative analysis. Monterey, Calif., Naval Postgraduate School, 1978. 246 leaves. maps (FAR 29189-N)

Bibliography: leaves 237–245.

Thesis—Naval Postgraduate School.

Examined in the former Foreign Affairs Research Documentation Center, U.S. Dept. of State.

Issued also in microfiche. [s.l., Defense Documentation Center, 1978] 3 sheets (AD-B027850L).

616

Copson, Raymond W. The Soviet and Cuban role in Africa. *In* The U.S. role in a changing world political economy: major issues for the 96th Congress: a compendium of papers submitted to the Joint Economic Committee, Congress of the United States. Washington, U.S. Govt. Print. Off., 1979. p. 565–575.   HF1455.U54

617

Cuban foreign policy: implications for U.S. security interests. Carlisle Barracks, Pa., Army War College, Strategic Studies Institute, 1978. 65 p.   AMAU

Africa is covered on p. 29–32.

618

Cuban presence in Africa. Cockpit intelligence, June 1978: 15–18.   AMAU

Issued by the Deputy Chief of Staff Operations and Intelligence, U.S. Air Force, Europe.

619

Daily, Fred. *Jeune Afrique* survey shows rising concern about Soviet intervention in Africa and rising social inequalities. Washington, Office of Research, International Communication Agency, 1980. 3 leaves.   DLC

"Foreign opinion note N-26-80."

620

Fejto, François. Senghor discusses Soviet penetration in Africa. *In* U.S. *Joint Publications Research Service.* JPRS 72503. [Springfield, Va., National Technical Information Service, 1978] (Translations on Sub-Saharan Africa, no. 2043) p. 111–115.

Translation of interview with Léopold Senghor in *Il Gornale*, Rome, Oct. 20, 1978, p. 3.

Microfiche. [Washington, Supt. of Docs., U.S. Govt. Print. Off., 1979?]

DLC-Micro JPRS 72503

621

Fichet, Michel. Cuban subversion in Africa. *In* U.S. *Joint Publications Research Service.* JPRS 68215. [Springfield, Va., National Technical Information Service, 1976] (Translations on Sub-Saharan Africa, no. 1689) p. 3–10.

Translation of article in *Est et Ouest*, Paris, Oct. 1, 1976, p. 14–19.

Microfiche. [s.l., 1976]

DLC-Micro JPRS 68215

622

Franklin, Lawrence A. China's approach to Africa: revolutionary model and institutional framework. Ft. Wadsworth, N.Y., 432d Military Intelligence Detachment (Strategic), 1977. 10 p.

622 (cont.)

At head of title: Strategic Studies Institute, U.S. Army War College, Carlisle Barracks, Pa.

Microfiche. [s.l., Defense Documentation Center, 1979] 1 sheet.   DLC-Sci RR AD-A067862

623

Hill, Karen D. Soviet penetration in sub-Saharan Africa: case studies on Somalia and Guinea. Monterey, Calif., [Naval Postgraduate School], 1977. 414 p.   AMAU

Thesis—Naval Postgraduate School.

624

Hoche, Christian. About fifteen countries coming under Soviet influence. *In* U.S. *Joint Publications Research Service.* JPRS 68990. [Springfield, Va., National Technical Information Service, 1977] (Translations on Sub-Saharan Africa, no. 1739) p. 1–5.

Translation of article on Soviet influence in Africa and the Middle East, in *L'Express*, Paris, Mar. 21/27, 1977, p. 99, 101–103.

Microfiche. [s.l., 1977]

DLC-Micro JPRS 68990

625

Implications of Soviet and Cuban activities in Africa for U.S. policy, by Michael A. Samuels [and others] Washington, Center for Strategic and International Studies, Georgetown University, c1979. 73 p. (Significant issues series, v. 1, no. 5)

JX1428.A34I47

"This report was sponsored by the Office of the Assistant Secretary of Defense (International Security Affairs), under contract MDA 903-79-C-0168."

626

Increasing Communist influence in Africa. *In* U.S. *Joint Publications Research Service.* JPRS 69238. [Springfield, Va., National Technical Information Service, 1977] (Translations on Sub-Saharan Africa, no. 1758) p. 1–5. map.

Translation of article on Soviet influence, in *El Siglo*, Bogota, Apr. 10, 1977, p. 8–9.

Microfiche. [s.l., 1977]

DLC-Micro JPRS 69238

627

Interview with the President; remarks at a question-and-answer session with representatives of the Hispanic media. *In* U.S. *President.* Public papers of the Presidents of the United States. Jimmy Carter. 1978. Washington, U.S. Govt. Print. Off., 1979. p. 903–909.   J80.A283   1978

At a meeting on May 12, 1978, Cuban involvement in Africa was a major topic.

Note: This issue was discussed further by President Carter during an interview with editors and news directors on May 19, 1978 (p. 940–941).

628

Laidi, Zaki. Limits to Soviet penetration discussed. *In* U.S. *Joint Publications Research Service.* JPRS 72565. [Springfield, Va., National Technical Information Service, 1979] (Translations on Sub-Saharan Africa, no. 2047) p. 8–11.

Translation of article on Soviet policy toward Africa in *Défense nationale*, Paris, Dec. 1978, p. 19–23.

Microfiche. [Washington, Supt. of Docs., U.S. Govt. Print. Off., 1979]

DLC-Micro JPRS 72565

629

Legum, Colin. The African environment. Problems of Communism, v. 27, Jan./Feb. 1978: 1–19. illus., map.   HX1.P75 v. 27

Issued by the U.S. Information Agency.

Explores the spectrum of African attitudes toward the Soviet Union.

630

———— Angola and the Horn of Africa. *In* Mailed fist, velvet glove: Soviet armed forces as a political instrument [by] Stephen S. Kaplan [and others] [Washington?], Brookings Institution, 1979. p. 13-1–13-103.

Study sponsored by the U.S. Defense Advanced Research Projects Agency.

Microfiche. [s.l., Defense Documentation Center, 1979]   DLC-Sci RR AD-A073950

631

Moreira, Neiva, *and* Beatriz Bissio. Cubans in Africa. *In* U.S. *Joint Publications Research Service.* JPRS 73472. [Springfield, Va., National Technical Information Service, 1979] 80 p. (Translations on Latin America, no. 1998)

Translation of article in *Cuadernos del Tercer Mundo*, Mexico City, Mar. 1979, p. 6–60.

Microfiche. [Washington, Supt. of Docs., U.S. Govt. Print. Off., 1979]

DLC-Micro JPRS 73472

632

Olds, Hugh. Communist international broadcasting to sub-Saharan Africa in 1979. Washington, Office of Research, International Communication Agency, 1980. [3] leaves.   DLC

"Briefing paper B-52-80."

633

Perceptions: relations between the United States and the Soviet Union [by] Committee on Foreign Relations, United States Senate; John Sparkman, chairman. Washington, The Committee: for sale by the Supt. of Docs., U.S. Govt. Print. Off., 1979. xv, 462 p. illus. E183.8.R9P37

A collection of essays "designed to explore Soviet interests, attitudes, objectives and capabilities and U.S. policy responses."—p. iv.

Soviet-African relations are covered in essays by Gerald J. Bender (p. 225–229), Chester A. Crocker (p. 233–240), William E. Griffith (p. 241–244), Richard L. Sklar (p. 255–258), John Stremlau (p. 259–263), and W. Scott Thompson (p. 264–268).

634

Political elite training in Cuba for thousands of African children. *In* U.S. *Joint Publications Research Service.* JPRS 75463. [Springfield, Va., National Technical Information Service, 1980] (Sub-Saharan Africa report, no. 2232) p. 1–4.

Translation of article on Cuban camps for the training of students primarily from Ethiopia, Angola, and Mozambique, in *Der Spiegel*, Hamburg, Mar. 3, 1980, p. 167–169, 172.

Microfiche. [s.l., 1980]

DLC-Micro JPRS 75463

635

The President's news conference of June 14, 1978. *In* U.S. *President.* Public papers of the Presidents of the United States. Jimmy Carter. 1978. Washington, U.S. Govt. Print. Off., 1979. p. 1091–1100.

J80.A283   1978

The President responds to questions on Cuban involvement in Angola and on Cuban and Soviet activities in Ethiopia.

636

Spiro, Herbert J. United States-Soviet detente: implications for Africa. Washington, Policy Planning Staff, U.S. Dept. of State, 1973. 22 leaves.

DLC

Prepared for the Third International Congress of Africanists, Addis Ababa, 1973.

637

Wang, Peter. Application of graphic multivariate techniques in the policy sciences. Stanford, Calif., Dept. of Statistics, Stanford University, 1978. 61 p. map.

Prepared for the U.S. Office of Naval Research.

Bibliography: p. 59–61.

Includes an analysis of Soviet foreign policy

toward 25 African countries during the period 1964–75.

Abstract in *Government Reports Announcements & Index*, Mar. 31, 1978, p. 31.

Microfiche. [s.l., Defense Documentation Center, 1978] 1 sheet. DLC-Sci RR AD-A048792

638

Yu, George T. China's impact. Problems of Communism, v. 27, Jan./Feb. 1978: 40–50. illus.

HX1.P75 v. 27

Issued by the U.S. Information Agency.

An examination of Sino-Soviet rivalry in Africa.

Policies of Other Nations

639

Bernetel, Paul. De Guiringaud describes French African policy. *In* U.S. *Joint Publications Research Service.* JPRS 70696. [Springfield, Va., National Technical Information Service, 1978] (Translations on Sub-Saharan Africa, no. 1885) p. 4–10.

Translation of interview with Louis de Guiringaud, Minister of Foreign Affairs of France, in *Demain l'Afrique*, Paris, Jan. 5, 1978, p. 26–28.

Microfiche. [Washington, Supt. of Docs., U.S. Govt. Print. Off., 1978]

DLC-Micro JPRS 70696

640

Evolution of French-African relations examined. *In* U.S. *Joint Publications Research Service.* JPRS 73635. [Springfield, Va., National Technical Information Service, 1979] (Translations on Sub-Saharan Africa, no. 2116) p. 6–10.

From article in *West Africa*, London, May 14, 1979, p. 841–843.

Microfiche. [Washington, Supt. of Docs., U.S. Govt. Print. Off., 1979]

DLC-Micro JPRS 73635

641

France and the Third World. *In* U.S. *Joint Publications Research Service.* JPRS 73776. [Springfield, Va., National Technical Information Service, 1979] (Translations on Sub-Saharan Africa, 2126) p. 7–16.

From article in *West Africa*, London, May 28, 1979, p. 920–925.

Microfiche. [Washington, Supt. of Docs., U.S. Govt. Print. Off., 1979]

DLC-Micro JPRS 73776

642

Hammad, Majdī. Greater achievements seen in store for Arab-African dialogue. *In* U.S. *Joint Publi-*

642 (cont.)

cations Research Service. JPRS 69051. [Springfield, Va., National Technical Information Service, 1977] (Translations on Sub-Saharan Africa, no. 1743) p. 1–8.

Translation of article in *al-Ahrām*, Cairo, Mar. 4, 1977, p. 6.

Microfiche. [s.l., 1977]

DLC-Micro JPRS 69051

643

Kweyu, Dorothy. Agenda for Commonwealth heads of government meeting noted. *In* U.S. *Joint Publications Research Service.* JPRS 73803. [Springfield, Va., National Technical Information Service, 1979] (Sub-Saharan Africa report, 2128) p. 11–16.

Interview with Shridath Ramphal, Commonwealth Secretary-General, reported in *Sunday Nation*, Nairobi, June 10, 1979, p. 12.

Microfiche. [Washington, Supt. of Docs., U.S. Govt. Print. Off., 1979]

DLC-Micro JPRS 73803

644

Legum, Colin. Afro-Arab politico-military relations. [s.l., 1980?] 10 leaves.   DLC

On cover: "This paper was prepared for the Department of State as part of its external research program."

645

LeVine, Victor T., *and* Timothy Luke. Dimensions of African-Arab relations, emphasis on the post Six-Day War period. St. Louis, Washington University, 1977. [113] leaves. (FAR 27481-S)

Prepared for the Office of External Research, U.S. Dept. of State.

Examined in the former Foreign Affairs Research Documentation Center, U.S. Dept. of State.

646

Lewis, William H. Conference on African-Arab relations, May 2–3, 1980: general report. [s.l.], 1980. 22 leaves.   DLC

On cover: "This paper was prepared for the Department of State as part of its external research program."

Abstract in *Government Reports Announcements & Index*, Jan. 2, 1981, p. 26.

Issued also in microfiche. [s.l., Defense Technical Information Center, 1980] 1 sheet.

DLC-Sci RR AD-A089014

647

—— Interregional security issues. [s.l., 1980?] 14 leaves.   DLC

On cover: "This paper was prepared for the

Department of State as part of its external research program."

Prepared for the Dept. of State's Conference on Afro-Arab Relations, May 2–3, 1980

648

Malet, Roland, *and* Claude Feuillet. Growth of African-Arab cooperation. *In* U.S. *Joint Publications Research Service.* JPRS 72632. [Springfield, Va., National Technical Information Service, 1979] (Translations on Sub-Saharan Africa, no. 2051) p. 8–30.

Translation of article in *Demain l'Afrique*, Dec. 4, 1978, p. 44–62.

Microfiche. [Washington, Supt. of Docs, 1979]

DLC-Micro-JPRS 72632

649

Permanent Commission for Afro-Arab Cooperation meets in Niamey. *In* U.S. *Joint Publications Research Service.* JPRS 71513. [Springfield, Va., National Technical Information Service, 1978] (Translations on Sub-Saharan Africa, no. 1965) p. 1–5.

Translation of article in *Le Sahel*, Niamey, June 8, 1978, p. 2, 8.

Microfiche. [Washington, Supt. of Docs., U.S. Govt. Print. Off., 1978]

DLC-Micro JPRS 71513

650

President Numayri talks to "SUNA" about African and Arab unity. *In* U.S. *Joint Publications Research Service.* JPRS 71176. [Springfield, Va., National Technical Information Service, 1978] (Translations on Near East and North Africa, no. 1799) p. 120–127.

Translation of article in *al-Ṣaḥāfah*, Khartoum, Mar. 29, 1978, p. 3.

Microfiche. [Washington, Supt. of Docs., U.S. Govt. Print. Off., 1978]

DLC-Micro JPRS 71176

651

Rondos, Alex. Independence of francophone Africa examined. *In* U.S. *Joint Publications Research Service.* JPRS 76456. [Springfield, Va., National Technical Information Service, 1980] (Sub-Saharan Africa report, no. 2294) p. 33–37.

Article on general conditions in French-speaking nations and on their relations with France, in *West Africa*, London, Sept. 1, 1980, p. 1644–1647.

Microfiche. [s.l., 1980]

DLC-Micro JPRS 76456

652

—— Rondos reports on Nice conference. *In* U.S.

652 (cont.)

Joint Publications Research Service. JPRS 75862. [Springfield, Va., National Technical Information Service, 1980] (Sub-Saharan Africa report, no. 2256) p. 21–26.

Article on a meeting to consider the creation of a "francophone commonwealth", in *West Africa*, London, May 19, 1980, p. 865, 867–869.

Microfiche. [s.l., 1980]

DLC-Micro JPRS 75862

653

Wai, Dunstan M. African-Arab relations in a universe of conflict: an African perspective. [s.l., 1980?] 33 leaves.　　　　　　　　　　　　　　DLC

On cover: "This paper was prepared for the Department of State as part of its external research program."

"Selected bibliography on African-Arab relations": leaves 26–33.

654

Weinstein, Brian. Evolving Franco-African relations. [Washington?], 1975. 7 leaves. (FAR 22618-S)

Presented at the Symposium on Cameroon Politics, sponsored by the U.S. Dept. of State, July 1975.

Examined in the former Foreign Affairs Research Documentation Center, U.S. Dept. of State.

655

West German interest in Africa examined. *In* U.S. *Joint Publications Research Service.* JPRS 76716. [Springfield, Va., National Technical Information Service, 1980] (Sub-Saharan Africa report, no. 2318) p. 6–17.

Article in *West Africa*, London, Oct. 6, 1980, p. 1959, 1961, 1963, 1965, 1967–1969.

Microfiche. [s.l., 1980]

DLC-Micro JPRS 76716

656

Zayn, Ilyas. Arabs seen losing ground in Africa. *In* U.S. *Joint Publications Research Service.* JPRS 65444. [Springfield, Va., National Technical Information Service, 1975] (Translations on Africa, no. 1608) p. 1–10.

Translation of article in *al-Hawadith*, Beirut, June 13, 1975, p. 39–41.

Microfiche. [s.l., 1975]

DLC-Micro JPRS 65444

657

Zellers, Joanne M. Recent Afro-Libyan relations; a selected list of references. Washington, African Section, Library of Congress, 1981. (Africana directions, AD 81-1)　　　　　　　DLC

"Compiled from Western language sources, the list is divided into three main sections: recent sources on Afro-Arab relations, general Afro-Libyan relations since 1976, and Libyan relations with selected African countries."

658

Zoghby, Samir M. Arab-African relations, 1973–1975: a guide. Washington, African Section, Library of Congress, 1976. 26 p. (Maktaba Afrikana series)　　　　　　　　　　Z3013.Z63

150 entries, primarily citations to periodical articles.

Geography and Maps

659

[U.S. *Central Intelligence Agency*] Africa, population density. [Washington, 1979] col. map.

G8201.E2　1979.U5

Scale ca. 1 : 48,000,000.

"504280 10-79."

660

——— Africa: vegetation. 11–73. [Washington, 1973] col. map.　　　　　　　G8201.D2　1973.U5

Scale ca. 1 : 48,000,000.

"502060."

661

——— Maps of the world's nations. Washington, for sale by the Supt. of Docs., U.S. Govt. Print. Off., 1976–77. chiefly col. maps.　　G1021.U5　1976

Partial contents: v. 2. Africa (53 p.)

661a

U.S. *Dept. of State. Office of the Geographer.* Sudan-Zaire boundary. [Washington], 1978. 8 p. (*Its* International boundary study, no. 106 rev.)

DLC-G & M

662

Library of Congress. *Geography and Map Division.* Africa in maps: an exhibit of maps and atlases displayed in the Geography and Map Division of the Library of Congress from December 1, 1976 through February 28, 1977. [Washington], 1976. [21] leaves.

DLC-G & M

Typescript; consists of photocopies of the captions and citations used for the exhibit.

663

Mohr, Paul A. Mapping of the major structures of the African rift system. Cambridge, Mass., Smithsonian Institution, Astrophysical Observatory, 1974. 70 p., 8 leaves of plates, maps. (Smithsonian

663 (cont.)

Institution. Astrophysical Observatory. SAO special report, no. 361)

TL796.S6 no. 361

Bibliography: p. 59–70.
Abstract in English, French, and Russian.

Geology, Hydrology, and Mineral Resources

664

U.S. *Bureau of Mines.* Mineral industries of Africa. [Washington, 1976] 115 p. illus., maps.

HD9506.A382U54 1976

Prepared by the staff, Bureau of Mines; coordinated by the Bureau's Africa and Middle East Area Office, International Data and Analysis.

For each country, there are brief notes on the contribution of mineral industries to the gross domestic product, mineral exports, mineral industry organization, mineral industry labor, transportation (including pipelines), energy, and "trends and issues."

Issued also in microfiche (Springfield, Va., National Technical Information Service, [1976?] 2 sheets). DLC-Sci RR PB265549

665

U.S. *Congress. House. Committee on Interior and Insular Affairs. Subcommittee on Mines and Mining.* Sub-Sahara Africa: its role in critical mineral needs of the Western World; a report. Washington, U.S. Govt. Print. Off., 1980. 29 p. maps. DLC

Jim Santini, chairman.

At head of title: 96th Congress, 2d session. Committee print. no. 8.

Focus is on Zaire, South Africa, and Zimbabwe.

666

Ambrosio, Suzann C. The mineral industry of other East Africa countries. *In* Minerals yearbook, v. 3, 1980. [Washington, for sale by the Supt. of Docs., U.S. Govt. Print. Off., 1982] p. 1169–1184.

TN23.U612 1980, v. 3

Prepared by the U.S. Bureau of Mines.

Covers Burundi, Djibouti, Ethiopia, Lesotho, Malawi, Mauritius, Comoros, Réunion, Rwanda, Seychelles, Somalia, Swaziland, and Uganda.

667

Analysis of "Revelle" polders development scheme and design for a long range Lake Chad basin study. Cambridge, Mass., Meta Systems, inc., 1974. 224 p.

Prepared for the U.S. Agency for International Development.

Bibliography. p. 213–224.
Examined in the Development Information Center, AID, Washington, D.C.

668

Black Africa: a source of essential materials for the Unitd States, [by] John J. Nash [et al.] [Ft. Wadsworth, N.Y., 432d Military Intelligence Detachment (Strategic)], 1977. [44] p.

At head of title: Strategic Studies Institute, U.S. Army War College, Carlisle Barracks, Pa.

"The paper includes a comprehensive listing of mineral resources currently known to exist in each sub-Sahara African country, the relative abundance of each mineral, the amount produced and a comparison to world production and availability."—p. v.

Abstract in *Government Reports Announcements & Index,* Aug. 31, 1979, p. 102.

Microfiche. [s.l., Defense Documentation Center, 1979] 1 sheet (DLC-Sci RR AD-A067533); issued in microfilm by University Publications of America (cited in its *Africa: Special Studies, 1962–1980,* p. 5).

669

The Continental margin off Western Africa: Angola to Sierra Leone, [by] K. O. Emery [et al.] Woods Hole, Mass., Woods Hole Oceanographic Institution, 1974. 152 p. maps.

"Unpublished manuscript."

"Technical report, prepared for the International Decade of Ocean Exploration, National Science Foundation Grant GX-28193."

Issued in cooperation with the Centre national pour l'exploitation des oceans, Brest, France.

Microfiche. [Springfield, Va.; National Technical Information Service, 1975] 2 sheets.

DLC-Sci RR PB245408

Note: Issued also in the *AAPG Bulletin,* issued by the American Association of Petroleum Geologists, Dec. 1975, p. 2209–2265 (TN860.A3 v. 59).

670

Digest of African mining resources, potential. *In* U.S. *Joint Publications Research Service.* JPRS 75138. [Springfield, Va., National Technical Information Service, 1980] (Sub-Saharan Africa report, no. 2214) p. 12–15.

Article in *Afrique défense,* Paris, Jan. 1980.
Microfiche. [s.l., 1980]

DLC-Micro JPRS 75138

671

Ely, Northcutt. Summary of mining and petro-

671 (cont.)

leum laws of the world (in five parts) 4. Africa. [Washington], U.S. Bureau of Mines; [for sale by the Supt. of Docs., U.S. Govt. Print. Off., 1974] 205 p. (U.S. Bureau of Mines. Information circular, 8610)   TN295.U4 no. 8610

672

Frey, Herbert. Martian canyons and African rifts: structural comparisons and implications. Greenbelt, Md., Goddard Space Flight Center, 1978. 22 p. illus., maps. (U.S. National Aeronautics and Space Administration. NASA technical memorandum 79548)

Microfiche. [s.l., 1978] 1 sheet.
     DLC-Sci RR N78-24024

673

Jolly, Janice L. W. The mineral industry of Angola, Mozambique, and Guinea Bissau. *In* Minerals yearbook, v. 3, 1974. [Washington, for sale by the Supt. of Docs., U.S. Govt. Print. Off., 1977] p. 85–98.   TN23.U612 1974, v. 3

Prepared by the U.S. Bureau of Mines.

Includes also brief notes on the Cape Verde Islands and São Tomé and Principe.

674

——— The mineral industry of Angola, Mozambique, and Portuguese Guinea. *In* Minerals yearbook, v. 3, 1973. [Washington, For sale by the Supt. of Docs., U.S. Govt. Print. Off., 1976] p. 77–91.   TN23.U612 1973, v. 3

Prepared by the U.S. Bureau of Mines.

675

The Mineral industry of other African areas. *In* Minerals yearbook, v. 3, 1972. [Washington, For sale by the Supt. of Docs., U.S. Govt. Print. Off., 1974] p. 987–1043.   TN23.U612 1972, v. 3

Prepared by the U.S. Bureau of Mines.

Covers Botswana, Burundi, Cameroon, Central African Republic, Chad, Congo, Dahomey, Equatorial Guinea, Ethiopia, French Territory of the Afars and Issas, Gambia, Guinea, Ivory Coast, Lesotho, Malagasy Republic, Malawi, Mali, Mauritania, Mauritius, Niger, Rwanda, Senegal, Somalia, Southern Rhodesia, Spanish Sahara, Sudan, Swaziland, Togo, and Upper Volta.

676

The Mineral industry of other African areas. *In* Minerals yearbook, v. 3, 1973. [Washington, For sale by the Supt. of Docs., U.S. Govt. Print. Off., 1976] p. 1061–1126.   TN23.U612 1973, v. 3

Prepared by the U.S. Bureau of Mines.

Covers Botswana, Burundi, Cameroon, Central African Republic, Chad, Congo, Dahomey, Equatorial Guinea, French Territory of the Afars and Issas, Gambia, Guinea, Ivory Coast, Lesotho, Malagasy Republic, Malawi, Mali, Mauritania, Mauritius, Niger, Rwanda, Senegal, Somalia, Southern Rhodesia, Spanish Sahara, Sudan, Swaziland, Togo, and Upper Volta.

677

The Mineral industry of other areas of Africa. *In* Minerals yearbook, v. 3, 1974. [Washington, For sale by the Supt. of Docs., U.S. Govt. Print. Off., 1977] p. 1147–1210.   TN23.U612 1974, v. 3

Prepared by the U.S. Bureau of Mines.

Covers Botswana, Burundi, Cameroon, Central African Republic, Chad, Congo, Dahomey, Equatorial Guinea, Ethiopia, French Territory of the Afars and Issas, The Gambia, Guinea, Ivory Coast, Lesotho, Malagasy Republic, Malawi, Mauritania, Mauritius, Niger, Rwanda, Senegal, Somalia, Southern Rhodesia, Spanish Sahara, Sudan, Swaziland, Togo, and Upper Volta.

678

The Mineral industry of other areas of Africa. *In* Minerals yearbook, v. 3, 1975. [Washington, For sale by the Supt. of Docs., U.S. Govt. Print. Off., 1978] p. 1117–1174   TN23.U612 1975, v. 3

Prepared by the U.S. Bureau of Mines.

Covers Botswana, Burundi, Cameroon, Cape Verde Islands, Central African Republic, Chad, Congo, Dahomey, Equatorial Guinea, Ethiopia, French Territory of the Afars and Issas, The Gambia, Guinea, Guinea-Bissau, Ivory Coast, Lesotho, Malagasy Republic, Malawi, Mali, Mauritania, Mauritius, Niger, Rwanda, São Tomé and Principe, Senegal, Somalia, Spanish Sahara, Sudan, Swaziland, Togo, and Upper Volta.

679

The Mineral industry of other areas of Africa. *In* Minerals yearbook, v. 3, 1976. [Washington, For sale by the Supt. of Docs., U.S. Govt. Print. Off., 1980] p. 1225–1274.   TN23.U612 1976, v. 3

Prepared by the U.S. Bureau of Mines.

Covers the Territory of Afars and Issas, Benin, Botswana, Burundi, Cameroon, Cape Verde Islands, Central African Empire, Chad, Comoros, Equatorial Guinea, Ethiopia, The Gambia, Guinea, Guinea Bissau, Ivory Coast, Lesotho, Malawi, Mali, Mauritania, Mauritius, Niger, Réunion, Rwanda, São Tomé and Principe, Senegal, Seychelles, Somalia, Sudan, Swaziland, Togo, Uganda, and Upper Volta.

680

The Mineral industry of other areas of Africa. *In*

680 (cont.)

Minerals yearbook, v. 3, 1977. [Washington, For sale by the Supt. of Docs., U.S. Govt. Print. Off., 1981] p. 1101–1130.　　TN23.U612　1977, v. 3

Prepared by the U.S. Bureau of Mines.

Covers Benin, Burundi, Cameroon, Cape Verde Islands, Central African Empire, Chad, Comoros, Congo, Djibouti, Equatorial Guinea, Ethiopia, The Gambia, Guinea, Guinea Bissau, Ivory Coast, Lesotho, Malawi, Mali, Mauritius, Niger, Réunion, Rwanda, São Tomé e Principe, Senegal, Seychelles, Somalia, Swaziland, Togo, Uganda, and Upper Volta.

681

Morgan, George A. The mineral industry of other Central Africa countries. *In* Minerals yearbook, v. 3, 1980. [Washington, for sale by the Supt. of Docs., U.S. Govt. Print. Off., 1982] p. 1157–1168.　　　　　　TN23.U612　1980, v. 3

Prepared by the U.S. Bureau of Mines.

Covers Cameroon, Central African Republic, Chad, Congo, Equatorial Guinea, and São Tomé and Principe.

682

Nicholson, Sharon E. A climatic chronology for Africa: synthesis of geological, historical, and meteorological information and data. Madison, University of Wisconsin, 1976. xx, 324 leaves.

Dissertation—University of Wisconsin-Madison.

Supported in part by the U.S. Air Force and National Science Foundation.

Microfiche. [Sahel Documents and Disserations. Ann Arbor, Mich., University Microfilms International, 1980] 7 sheets.

DLC-Micro 5357 AS039

683

Schreiber, Joseph F., *and* W. Gerald Matlock. The phosphate rock industry in North and West Africa. Tucson, University of Arizona, 1978. 21 p.

Publication supported in part through a grant from the Office of Science and Technology, U.S. Agency for International Development.

"The topics discussed in this report include mining and exploration, mining methods, processing, production and trade, and the use of phosphates as fertilizer."—Abstract.

Abstract in *A.I.D. Research and Development Abstracts*, July 1978, p. 35.

Microfiche. [Washington, U.S. Agency for International Development, 1978?] 1 sheet.

DLC-Sci RR PN-AAF-347

684

Van Alstine, Ralph E., *and* Paul G. Schruben. Fluor-

spar resources of Africa. [Reston, Va.], U.S. Geological Survey; for sale by the Supt. of Docs., U.S. Govt. Print. Off., Washington, D.C., 1980. 25 p. illus., 1 fold. map (in pocket) (U.S. Geological Survey. Bulletin, 1487)　　QE75.B9 no. 1487

Bibliography: p. 21–25.

685

White, Gilbert F. Interdisciplinary studies of large reservoirs in Africa. *In* Conference on Interdisciplinary Analysis of Water Resources Systems. Proceedings. New York, American Society of Civil Engineers, [1975] p. 63–104.

"The conference on which these proceedings are based was supported in part by funds provided by the United States Department of the Interior, Office of Water Research and Technology."

Microfiche. [Springfield, Va., National Technical Information Service, 1976]

DLC-Sci RR PB248596

Health and Nutrition

686

U.S. *Congress. House. Committee on Foreign Affairs. Subcommittee on International Economic Policy and Trade.* Marketing and promotion of infant formula in developing countries: hearings, Ninety-sixth Congress, second session, January 30 and February 11, 1980. Washington, U.S. Govt. Print. Off., 1980, i.e. 1981. 184 p.

KF27.F6465　1980g
J74.A23 96th
Cong., House Comm.
For. Aff., v. 147

Jonathan B. Bingham, chairman.

Includes occasional references to sub-Saharan Africa.

687

U.S. *Congress. Senate. Committee on Human Resources. Subcommittee on Health and Scientific Research.* Marketing and promotion of infant formula in the developing nations, 1978: hearing, Ninety-fifth Congress, second session ... May 23, 1978. Washington, U.S. Govt. Print. off., 1978. 1498 p. illus.　　　　　　　KF26.H845　1978k
J74.A23 95th
Cong., Sen. Comm.
Human Res., v. 129

Edward M. Kennedy, chairman.

Includes a table on infant mortality rates in selected African countries, including Madagascar, Mauritius, Nigeria, Senegal, and South Africa: p. 1489–1490.

688

U.S. *Navy. Naval Medical Research Unit No. 5.* Medical research activities; cumulative report for period ending 31 December 1975. [Addis Ababa?, 1976?] 28 p.

The Unit's publications are listed on p. 25–28.

Microfiche. [s.l., 1976] 1 sheet.

DLC-Sci RR AD A026508

Note: The Unit, established in 1965, "is responsible for conducting research and development on infectious diseases of military importance in sub-sahara [sic] Africa."—p. 1.

689

U.S. *Public Health Service.* Program concerning Africa. [Washington?, 1977?]

Source: Duffy. *Survey.*

690

A.I.D. integrated low cost health delivery projects, [by] Naomi Baumslag [et al.] [Washington], Office of International Health, U.S. Dept. of Health, Education, and Welfare, 1978. 2 v.

Content: v. 1. Project summaries.—v. 2. Analysis.

In vol. 1, Africa is covered on p. 1–97 with specific reference to Cameroon, Cape Verde, Central African Empire, Ghana, Lesotho, Liberia, Mail, Niger, Senegal, Sudan, Tanzania, and Zaire.

Abstracts of both volumes in *A.I.D. Research & Development Abstracts*, v. 9, no. 3, 1981, p. 42.

Microfiche. [Washington, U.S. Agency for International Development, 1978?] (v. 1. PN-AAH-444; v. 2. PN-AAH-445) 6 sheets; held by Development Information Center, AID, Washington, D.C.

691

AID-supported primary health care projects: summary reviews. Washington, International Health Programs, American Public Health Association, 1981. 1 v. (looseleaf)

Pt. 3 includes brief descriptions of U.S. Agency for International Development-supported projects in Botswana, Central African Republic, Kenya, Lesotho, Mali, Mauritania, Niger, Senegal, Sudan, Swaziland, Tanzania, and Zaire.

Examined in the Development Information Center, Agency for International Development, Washington, DLC.

692

African health development bibliography: selected references pertinent to AID health, nutrition, and population program development. Rockville, Md., Office of International Health, U.S. Public Health Service, 1980. 30 leaves.

Prepared for the U.S. Agency for International Development.

96 entries.

Abstract in *Government Reports Announcements & Index*, Aug. 29, 1980, p. 3530.

Microfiche. [Springfield, Va., National Technical Information Service, 1980] 1 sheet (DLC-Sci RR PB80-182934); and [Washington, U.S. Agency for International Development, 1980?] 1 sheet (DLC-Sci RR PN-AAJ-158).

693

African Health Training Institutions Project. End of project report. Chapel Hill, Carolina Population Center, University of North Carolina at Chapel Hill, 1979. 84 p.   DLC

Report submitted to the U.S. Agency for International Development.

Photocopy supplied by the Program for International Training in Health, University of North Carolina at Chapel Hill.

Note: The duration of the project was July 1973–August 1979.

694

———— A manual of case studies in family health: nursing and midwifery; Elisabeth M. Edmands, editor; Sandy Mills, asst. editor. Chapel Hill, Carolina Population Center and Office of Medical Studies, University of North Carolina, 1979. 181 p.

Held by the Health Sciences Library, University of North Carolina, Chapel Hill.

695

———— Quarterly report. Chapel Hill, Carolina Population Center, University of North Carolina at Chapel Hill.

Supported by the U.S. Agency for International Development.

Report for July/Sept. 1978 in microfiche. [Washington, U.S. Agency for International Development, 1978?] 1 fiche.

DLC-Sci RR PN-AAG-312

696

———— A topical outline for the teaching of family health: a life-cycle approach. Chapel Hill, Carolina Population Center and Mecial School, Office of Medical Studies, University of North Carolina, 1977. 2 v.

Content: [v. 1] Medicine.—[v. 2] Nursing and midwifery.

Publication supported by the Bureau for Population and Humanitarian Assistance, U.S. Agency for International Development.

Held by the Health Science Library, University of North Carolina, Chapel Hill.

697

American Public Health Association. Phase II SHDS project; World Health Association comments, 31 March 1977. Washington, [1977] 57 p.

Prepared for the U.S. Agency for International Development under contract AID/afr-C-1178.

SHDS: Strengthening health delivery systems.

Review by the World Health Organization, Regional Office for Africa, Brazzaville, of a project to improve health training facilities, immunization programs, and health care at the village level in Central and West Africa.

Microfiche. [Washington, U.S. Agency for International Development, 1977?] 1 sheet.

DLC-Sci RR PN-AAG-087

698

Anglim, Patricia A. The urban bias in African health policies: some issues for research. Washington, TEMPO Center for Advanced Studies, General Electric, 1975. 25 p. (FAR 27542-N)

Prepared for the U.S. Agency for International Development.

Examined in the former Foreign Affairs Research Documentation Center, U.S. Dept. of State.

699

Barnum, Howard N. Background information for the formulation of a policy to combat childhood communicable diseases in sub-Saharan Africa. Washington, One America, inc., 1980. [72] leaves (in verious foliations)

Prepared for the Bureau for Africa, U.S. Agency for International Development.

Examined in the Documentation Center, Sahel Development Program, AID, Washington, D.C.

700

Bernard, Roger P., *and* David M. Potts. Evaluation report on African Health Training Institutions Project (UNC-AID/CM pha-C73-33) [Washington?] American Public Health Association, 1976. [52] leaves.

Prepared for the U.S. Agency for International Development.

Examined in the Development Information Center, AID, Washington, D.C.

701

Biomedical social science, unit II: health, culture and environment. Student text, part two: Africa. Rev. version. [Berkeley, Calif.], Biomedical Interdisciplinary Curriculum Project, 1975. 206 p. illus., maps.

Sponsored by the National Science Foundation.

An introduction to cultural, historical, and environmental issues in Africa, based on material originally developed by the American Universities Field Staff.

Abstract in *Resources in Education*, Dec. 1979, p. 134.

Microfiche. [Arlington, Va., ERIC Document Reproduction Service; prepared for Education Resources Information Center, National Institute of Education 1979] 3 sheets.

DLC-Micro ED174424

702

CARE Africa/Mideast Nutrition Planning Workshop, *Nairobi, 1975*. Final report. [New York], CARE, 1975. 26 p.

Supported by the U.S. Agency for International Development under grant AID/ta-G-1119.

Microfiche. [Washington, U.S. Agency for International Development, 1975?] 1 sheet.

DLC-Sci RR PN-AAF-100

703

Conde, Maryse. Children's position in society discussed. *In* U.S. *Joint Publications Research Service*. JPRS 75268. [Springfield, Va., National Technical Information Service, 1980] (Sub-Saharan Africa report, no. 2221) p. 4–7.

Translation of article on health problems of children in many African societies, in *Demain l'Afrique*, Paris, Jan. 28, p. 70–71.

Microfiche. [s.l., 1980]

DLC-Micro JPRS 75268

704

———— Lack of proper nutrition reported. *In* U.S. *Joint Publications Research Service*. JPRS 75520. [Springfield, Va., National Technical Information Service, 1980] (Sub-Saharan Africa report, no. 2236) p. 5–8.

Translation of article in *Demain l'Afrique*, Paris, Feb. 25, 1980, p. 76–77.

Microfiche. [s.l., 1980]

DLC-Micro JPRS 75520

705

Dalmat, Herbert T., John C. Eason, and A. E. Farwell. Report of Strategy Advisory Group on anti-malarial support strategy for tropical Africa; conclusions and recommendations of Strategy Advisory Group together with findings of Abidjan Workshop, March 27, 1980. [Washington?], American Public Health Association, 1980. [171] p.

Prepared for the Bureau for Africa, U.S. Agency for International Development.

Abstract in *A.I.D. Research & Development Abstracts*, v. 9, no. 4, 1981, p. 44.

705 (cont.)

Microfiche. [Washington, U.S. Agency for International Development, 1980?] 2 sheets.

DLC-Sci RR PN-AAJ-100

706

Field, Augusta N. Nutrition programs for children in developing countries; a report to the Presidential Commission on World Hunger. [s.l., 1980] 40 p.

DLC

Bibliography: p. 39–40.
Includes frequent references to Africa.

707

Furst, Barbara G. Traditional medicine and indigenous practitioners. Washington, Division of International Health Programs, American Public Health Association, 1974. 120 leaves.

Bibliography: leaves 116–120.
Prepared for the U.S. Agency for International Development under contract AID/csd-3423.
Medicine in Africa: leaves 10–42.
Examined in the Development Information Center, AID, Washington, D.C.

708

George, Emmett. Famine strikes again in Africa; by the thousands, African people are falling victim to malnutrition and starvation. Agenda, June 1980: 5–8. illus.   HC59.7.A742   1980

Issued by the U.S. Agency for International Development.

709

Giddings, L. E. Remote sensing for control of tsetse flies. Houston, Life Sciences Application Dept., Lockheed Electronics Co., 1976. [35] p. illus., map.

Prepared for the Bioengineering Systems Division, National Aeronautics and Space Administration, Lyndon B. Johnson Space Center, Houston, Tex.

Microfiche. [s.l., 1977] 1 sheet.

DLC-Sci RR N-7713491

710

Graham, Bettie J. Malaria eradication/control programs in sub-Saharan Africa. [Bethesda, Md.], National Institutes of Health, 1979. 270 p. maps.

Prepared for the U.S. Agency for International Development.

Microfiche. [Washington, U.S. Agency for International Development, 1979?] 3 sheets (PN-AAJ-407); examined in the Development Information Center, AID, Washington, D.C.

711

Health in Africa. [Washington], Sector /Problem Analysis Division, Bureau for Africa, Agency for International Development, 1975. 95 p.

"The background paper is designed to present an overview of the existing health problems in Africa, and of the various factors which impinge on or relate to developing solutions to these problems."

Abstract in *A.I.D. Research and Development Abstracts*, Apr. 1978, p. 29.

Microfiche. [Washington, U.S. Agency for International Development, 1975?] 1 sheet.

DLC-Sci RR PN-AAE-198

712

Herrin, Charles S., *and* Vernon J. Tipton. Ectoparasites of African mammals; final scientific report. Provo, Utah, Center for Health and Environmental Studies, Brigham Young University, 1976. 8 p.

"Supported by U.S. Army Research and Development Command . . . contract no. DADA 17-73-C-3042."

Report covers period Sept. 1970 – July 1976.

Abstract in *Government Reports Announcements & Index*, Mar. 18, 1977, p. 44–45.

Microfiche. [s.l., 1977] 1 sheet.

DLC-Sci RR AD-A033941

713

Hoogstraal, Harry. The epidemiology of tick-borne Crimean-Congo hemorrhagic fever in Asia, Europe, and Africa. Journal of medical entomology, v. 15, May 22, 1979: 307–417.   RA639.5.J6 v. 15

Study supported by the National Naval Medical Center, Bethesda, Md.; publication of article supported by the National Library of Medicine.

Issued also in microfiche. [s.l., Defense Technical Information Center, 1980] 2 sheets.

DLC-Sci RR AD-A086235

714

Immunity to the African trypanosomes; annual report. College Station, Dept. of Biology, Texas A&M University.

Supported by the U.S. Army Medical Research and Development Command.

Report for 1975 prepared by John R. Seed.

Report for 1975 issued in microfiche. [s.l., 1975] 1 sheet (AD-B007388L).

715

International Center for Health Sciences, Meharry Medical College, Nashville, Tennessee. [Nashville, 197–?] 15 p. illus., map.   DLC

The Center is funded in part by an institutional grant from the U.S. Agency for International Development.

Includes brief descriptions of the Center's pro-

715 (cont.)

grams in Africa with specific reference to the USAID/Botswana/Meharry Project.

716

International Conference on Health Problems of Black Populations, *1st, Washington*, 1975. Report. [Washington, 1975?] 2 v. (looseleaf) DLC

Conference held at the Pan American Health Organization, Feb. 3–7, 1975 under the sponsorship of the Howard University College of Medicine and the African-American Scholars Council with the support of the U.S. Agency for International Development.

Includes numerous contributions on sub-Saharan Africa.

717

International Conference on Programmatic and Research Strategy for the Control of Major Endemic Diseases in Africa, *Washington, D.C.*, 1977. Report. [Washington] 1977. 145 p.

Prepared for the U.S. Agency for International Development under grant AID/afr-G-1076.

Microfiche. [Washington, U.S. Agency for International Development, 1977?] 2 sheets (PN-AAH-415); examined in the Development Information Center, AID, Washington, D.C.

718

Jett, Joyce. The role of traditional midwives in the modern health sector in West and Central Africa. [s.l.], 1977. [147] p.

Prepared for the U.S. Agency for International Development under contract REDSO/WA-76-81.

Focus is on Senegal, Mali, Niger, Upper Volta, and Cameroon.

Abstract in *A.I.D. Research and Development Abstracts*, v. 7, no. 1, 1979, p. 17.

Microfiche. [Washington, U.S. Agency for International Development, 1977?] 2 sheets (DLC-Sci RR PN-AAG-344), and [Sahel Documents and Dissertations. Ann Arbor, Mich., University Microfilms International, 1980] 2 sheets (DLC-Micro 5357 AS 272).

719

Kovatch, Robert M., Bruce T. Wellde, *and* Wayne T. Hockmeyer. Research on immunization against African sleeping sickness. Nairobi, U.S. Army Medical Research Unit, Kenya, 1978. [15] p.

Microfiche. [s.l., Defense documentation Center, 1978] 1 sheet. DLC-Sci RR AD-A056458

720

Kuttler, K. L. East Coast fever (Theileriasis, Theileriosis, Rhodesian tick fever, Rhodesian red water)

[College Station, Texes A&M University, Institute of Tropical Veterinary Medicine, 1973] 13, 5 p.

Includes bibliographical references.

Microfiche. [Washington, U.S. Agency for International Development, 1973?] 1 sheet.

DLC-Sci RR PN-AAA-681

721

Low-cost extrusion cookers: second international workshop proceedings, Hotel Kilimanjaro, Dar es Salaam, Tanzania, January 15–18, 1979; David E. Wilson, editor; R. E. Tribelhorn, technical editor; sponsors, Agency for International Development, Development Support Bureau, Office of Nutrition, and United States Department of Agriculture, Office of International Cooperation and Development, Nutrition and Agribusiness Group. Ft. Collins, Colo., Available from Dept. of Agricultural and Chemical Engineering, Colorado State University, 1979. 288 p. illus. (LEC report, 7)

TP373.L68

"Co-hosts: Colorado State University, Department of Agricultural and Chemical Engineering, Department of Food Science and Nutrition, Fort Collins, Colorado, U.S.A. and National Milling Corporation, Dar es Salaam, Tanzania."

"Thanks to the recent development of the Brady low-cost extrusion cooker (LEC) and its accompanying technology, consumers in developing countries are beginning to have access to nutritious foods, particularly vitamin-rich foods for infants and young children, which can be processed locally at low cost from locally produced raw foods. These LEC-processed foods have included vitamin-enriched corn-soy-milk (CSM) baby food products marketed under the name "Lisha" (Tanzania)."—Abstract.

Abstract in *A.I.D. Research & Development Abstracts*, v. 9, no. 3, 1981, p. 57–58.

Issued also in microfiche. [Washington, U.S. Agency for International Development, 1979?] 3 sheets (PN-AAJ-326); held by the Development Information Center, AID, Washington, D.C.

722

McCook, Anne S. Report on child health in sub-Saharan Africa, with particular reference to EPI and diarrheal diseases. Washington, One America, inc., 1980. [106] leaves.

Prepared for the Bureau for Africa, U.S. Agency for International Development.

Examined in the Documentation Center, Sahel Development Program, AID, Washington, D.C.

723

Mecklenburg, Robert. Evaluation report, USAID grant no. AID/afr-G-1163, Dental Health Inter-

723 (cont.)

national, inc. [Improvement of oral hygiene and dental care among rural populations] Washington, U.S. Public Health Service, 1976. 31 p.

Concerns Cameroon, Lesotho, and Rwanda.

Examined in the Development Information Center, Agency for International Development, Washington, D.C.

724

Medicine and public health: a listing of U.S. non-profit organizations in medical and public health assistance abroad. New York, Technical Assistance Information Clearing House, American Council of Voluntary Agencies for Foreign Service, 1979. 168 p. DLC

"The Technical Assistance Information Clearing House (TAICH) has been operated by the Council since 1955 with support from the U.S. Government, currently a grant from the Agency for International Development."

Cites many organizations that offer assistance to African countries.

725

Meharry Medical College. *Maternal and Child Health/Family Planning, Training and Research Center.* Semi-annual report. 1st+ [1971?]+ [Nashville, Tenn.]

Prepared for the U.S. Agency for International Development.

A report on instructional programs for participants from Africa.

11th report (July/Dec. 1976) examined in the Development Information Center, AID, Washington, D.C.

726

Mothers, babies, and health: clinics, dispensaries bring care—and learning—to remote areas. Agenda, Feb. 1978: 8–14. illus.

HC59.7.A742 1978

Issued by the U.S. Agency for International Development.

Focus is on sub-Saharan Africa.

727

Munstermann, Leonard E. Report of possible relationships between reptilian malaria and aedes aegypti (L.) [Notre Dame, Ind.], University of Notre Dame, 1973. 7 p.

Study supported in part by the U.S. Agency for International Development under contract AID/csd-3159.

Microfiche. [Washington, U.S. Agency for International Development, 1973?] 1 sheet.

DLC-Sci RR PN-AAE-547

728

Nutrition planning; an international journal of abstracts about food and nutrition policy, planning and programs. v. 1+ Feb. 1978+ [Ann Arbor, Community Systems Foundation] quarterly.

TX359.N88

Prepared under a grant from the Office of Nutrition, U.S. Agency for International Development.

Includes abstracts to books and periodical articles on Africa.

L.C. has Feb. 1978+

729

Peters, Wallace. Chemotherapy of Leishmaniasis; final technical report. Liverpool, Dept. of Parasitology, Liverpool School of Tropical Medicine, 1977. [60] p. illus.

Sponsored by the U.S. Army Medical Research and Development Command.

Includes report on African *Leishmania*.

Microfiche. [s.l., Defense Documentation Center, 1978] 1 sheet.

DLC-Sci RR AD-A047617

730

Pielemeier, Nancy R., Edna M. Jones, *and* Sara J. Munger. Use of the child's growth chart as an educational tool. Allison Park, Pa., Synectics Corporation, 1978. 121 p.

Study submitted to the Office of Nutrition, U.S. Agency for International Development, under contract AID/ta-C-1231.

Concerns studies carried out in Ghana and Lesotho on educating mothers concerning the nutritional needs of their children.

Microfiche. [Washington, U.S. Agency for International Development, 1978?] 2 sheets (PN-AAH-387); examined in the Development Information Center, AID, Washington, D.C.

731

Programmatic and research strategy for the control of major endemic diseases in Africa. [Washington], Bureau for Africa, U.S. Agency for International Development, 1978. 51 p.

Microfiche. [Washington, U.S. Agency for International Development, 1978?] 1 sheet (PN-AAH-416); examined in the Development Information Center, AID, Washington, D.C.

732

Reaching out. v. 1, no. 1+ Apr. 1980+ Nashville, International Center for Health Sciences, Meharry Medical College. DLC

The Center is funded in part by an institutional grant from the U.S. Agency for International Development.

732 (cont.)

Includes information on the Center's programs in Africa.

L.C. has Apr. 1980.

733

Rosenfield, Patricia L., *and* Phyllis J. Gestrin. Socioeconomic analysis of impact of water projects on schistosomiasis; final report. Washington, Resources for the Future, inc., 1978. [146] p. maps.

Prepared for the U.S. Agency for International Development under contract AID/ta-C-1465

"A methodology for integrating a schistosomiasis transmission model and associated economic analysis into water resources project planning is described and applied to an area of small-scale water activities (furrow irrigation, cattle watering in ponds) in Misungwi, Tanzania where schistosomiasis control efforts were underway from 1967 to 1973."—p. ii.

Abstract in *A.I.D. Research and Development Abstracts*, Apr. 1979, p. 28.

Microfiche. [Washington, U.S. Agency for International Development, 1978?] 2 sheets.

DLC-Sci RR PN-AAG-137

A *Preliminary Report* (Washington, Resources for the Future, inc., 1978. [102] p.) is also available in microfiche. [Washington, U.S. Agency for International Development, 1978?] 2 sheets.

DLC-Sci RR PN-AAG-056

734

The Sahel epidemiological and environmental assessment studies. [Washington?], International Health Program Staff, American Public Health Association, 1977. 3v.

Prepared for the Office of Development Resources, Bureau for Africa, U.S. Agency for International Development under contract AID/afr-C-1253.

Although the focus of the studies is on the Sahelian countries, other areas of sub-Saharan Africa are also covered.

The major endemic diseases considered in the studies are filariasis, malaria, onchocerciasis, schistosomiasis, and trypanosomiasis.

Contents: v. 1. Studies on the prevalence and incidence of five major endemic diseases in eight African states [Liberia, Swaziland, Chad, Upper Volta, Niger, Benin, Mali, and Cameroon].—v. 2. Documentation of five major endemic diseases in ten African states [Benin, Cameroon, Chad, Liberia, Mali, Niger, Senegal, Swaziland, Upper Volta, and Zaire].—v. 3. Assessment team reports [covering the Lake Chad basin, Chad, Liberia, Niger, Senegal, Sudan, Swaziland, Upper Volta, and Zaire].

Microfiche. [Washington, U.S. Agency for International Development, 1977?] (PN-AAH-679–PN-AAH-691); examined in the Development Information Center, AID, Washington, D.C.

735

Seed, John R. Active immunization against *trypanosoma gambiense* with a partially purified protective antigen; final report (for the period 1 Nov. 1971 to 31 Dec. 1974). New Orleans, Tulane University, 1975. 23 p.

Research supported by the U.S. Army Medical Research and Development Command, Office of the Surgeon General, in cooperation with the Commission on Parasitic Diseases of the Armed Forces Epidemiological Board, contract no. DADA 17-72-C-2058.

Microfiche. [s.l., 1975] 1 sheet (AD-B003094L).

736

Shafer, Michael. Tsetse fly eradication and its implications. [Washington, Agency for International Development], 1977. [73] p. (in various pagings) maps.

Bibliography: p. 50–54.

Abstract in *A.I.D. Research and Development Abstracts*, Oct. 1978, p. 35.

Microfiche. [Washington, U.S. Agency for International Development, 1977?] 1 sheet; examined in the Development Information Center, AID, Washington, D.C.

737

Smith, Deborah T. Challenging the tsetse fly. War on hunger, Apr. 1977: 8–11, 14–15.

HD9000.1.W37 1977

Issued by the U.S. Agency for International Development.

738

The State of the art of delivering low-cost health services in developing countries: a summary study of 180 health projects. Washington, American Public Health Association, 1977. 62 p. illus., map.

Prepared for the Office of Health, U.S. Agency for International Development.

Barry Karlin, project director.

Includes references to African projects.

Microfiche. [Springfield, Va., National Technical Information Service, 1977?] 2 sheets.

DLC-Sci RR PB270038

739

Studies in the intermediate snail hosts of oriental and African schistosomiasis; annual progress report. Ann Arbor, Museum of Zoology, University of Michigan.

739 (cont.)

Supported by the U.S. Army Medical Research and Development Command.

Report for 1974/75 prepared by Henry Van der Schalie.

Report for 1974/75 issued in microfiche. [s.l., 1976] 1 sheet (AD-B008690L).

740

Study of African trypanosomiasis; final report. Nairobi, [U.S. Army Medical Research Unit-Government of Kenya], 1978. [24] p.

Supported by the U.S. Army Medical Research and Development Command under grant DAMD 17-77-G-9433.

Microfiche. [s.l., Defense Documentation Center, 1978] 1 sheet.   DLC-Sci RR AD-A057502

741

Studies on African trypanosomiasis; final report (for the period 1 September 1974 to 31 August 1975), [by] I. Muriithi [et al.] Nairobi, U.S. Army Medical Research Unit-Kenya, 1975. [28] p.

Supported by the U.S. Army Medical Research and Development Command under contract DAMD 17-75-G-9398.

Microfiche. [s.l., Defense Documentation Center, 1978] 1 sheet.   DLC-Sci RR AD-A047618

742

Syncrisis: the dynamics of health; an analytic series on the interactions of health and socioeconomic development [by] P. O. Woolley, Jr. [et al.] Washington, Division of Program Analysis, U.S. Public Health Service, 1970+ maps. (DHEW publication)   RA418.S98

Includes bibliographies.

Vols. 1–12 issued by the Division of Planning and Evaluation, Office of International Health; vols. 13–15 issued by the Division of Program Analysis, Office of International Health.

"The primary purpose of these studies is to provide a concise and up-to-date introduction to the health situation in a country, for use by AID and throughout the international health community." —v. 19, p. v.

Volumes in this series on individual African countries or regions are entered separately in this guide; they can be identified by consulting the index under *Syncrisis: the Dynamics of Health.*

743

Tsetse and trypanosomiasis control: a strategy for the future of Africa; based on the deliberations of an international task force under the auspices of IBAR and sponsored by USAID. [New York, Rockefeller Foundation, 1979] 51 p. illus.

IBAR: Interafrican Bureau for Animal Resources. Abstract in *A.I.D. Research and Development Abstracts*, Feb. 1981, p. 52.

Microfiche. [Washington, U.S. Agency for International Development, 1979?] 1 sheet.   DLC-Sci RR PN-AAH-531

744

Vaccine development in trypanosomiasis; final report, 1976–1977. Kabete, U.S. Army Medical Research Unit-Kenya, [1977?] [23] p.

Supported by the U.S. Army Medical Research and Development Command under grant DAMD 17-76-G-9421.

Microfiche. [s.l., Defense Documentation Center, 1978] 1 sheet.   DLC-Sci RR AD-A049582

745

Waife, Ronald S., *and* Marianne C. Burkhart. The nonphysician & family health in sub-Saharan Africa. [Boston], Pathfinder Fund, [1980] 141 p. illus., maps.

Proceedings of a conference held in Freetown, sierra Leone, Sept. 1–4, 1980.

Abstract in *A.I.D. Research & Development Abstracts*, v. 9, no. 4, 1981, p. 47.

Microfiche. [Washington, U.S. Agency for International Development, 1980?] 2 sheets.   DLC-Sci RR PN-AAJ-882

Housing and Urban Development

746

U.S. *Agency for International Development. Office of Housing.* Current research in building materials and low-cost housing in sub-Sahara Africa. Washington, [1977?] [110] leaves in various foliations.   TA404.2.U54   1977

Includes bibliographical references and indexes.

Abstract in *A.I.D. Research and Development Abstracts*, Jan. 1978, p. 34–35.

Issued also in microfiche. [Washington, U.S. Agency for International Development, 1977?] 2 sheets.   DLC-Sci RR PN-AAE-085

747

U.S. *General Accounting Office.* The challenge of meeting shelter needs in less developed countries: report to the Congress by the Comptroller General of the United States. Washington, 1977. 124 p. illus.   HD7391.U54   1977

"ID-77-39."

"Assistance from international agencies is discussed and recommendations, principally to the

747 (cont.)

U.S. Agency for International Development, are made to help them improve shelter assistance to the less developed countries."

Includes several specific references to conditions in sub-Saharan Africa.

Abstract in *Selected Appropriate Technologies for Developing Countries*, no. 1, p. 105.

Issued also in microfiche. [Springfield, Va., National Technical Information Service, 1977] 2 sheets.   DLC-Sci RR PB 273572

748

Anglim, Patricia A. The public management of African squatter settlements; the case of housing policy: a research formulation, Washington, Population Studies Unit, General Electric-TEMPO Center for Advanced Studies, [1975?] 20 leaves.
                              (FAR 27022-N)

Apparently prepared under a U.S. Government contract.

Examined in the former Foreign Affairs Research Documentation Center, U.S. Dept. of State.

The following items (entries 749–753) are listed in chronological order:

749

Conference on USAID Housing Guaranty Programs, *Abidjan*, 1973. Report. [Washington?], Agency for International Development, [1975?] 20 p.

In English and French.

Examined in the Development Information Center, AID, Washington, D.C.

750

Conference on Housing in Africa, *2d, Kinshasa*, 1975. [Report] [Washington?], Office of Housing, Agency for International Development, [1975?] 53 p. illus.

Examined in the Development Information Center, AID, Washington, D.C.

751

Conference on Housing in Africa, *3d, Nairobi*, 1976. Third Conference on Housing in Africa; sponsor, United States Agency for International Development; hosts, Kenya National Housing Corporation, Ministry of Housing and Social Services, Nairobi City Council. Washington, Office of Housing, Agency for International Development, 1976. 139 p. illus.   HD7286.C48 1976

The theme of the conference was the question of providing housing for lower-income groups.

Abstract in *A.I.D. Research and Development Abstracts*, Apr. 1978, p. 34.

Issued also in microfiche. [Washington, U.S.

Agency for International Development, 1976?] 2 sheets.   DLC-Sci RR PN-RAB-689

752

Conference on Housing in Africa, *5th, Monrovia*, 1978. [Proceedings] [Washington?, 1978] 212 p. illus.

Sponsored by the U.S. Agency for International Development.

Issued also in French.

Abstract in *A.I.D. Research and Development Abstracts*, v. 7, no. 2, 1979, p. 11.

Microfiche. [Washington, U.S. Agency for International Development, 1978?] 3 sheets.
                              DLC-Sci RR PN-AAG-675

753

Conference on Housing in Africa, *6th, Rabat*, 1979. [Proceedings] [Washington?, 1979?] 336 p.

Conference sponsored by the Government of Morocco and the Office of Housing, U.S. Agency for International Development.

Microfiche. [Washington, U.S. Agency for International Development, 1979?] 4 sheets (PN-AAJ-224); examined in the Development Information Center, Agency for International Development, Washington, D.C.

754

Kerst, Erna W., *and* Donald R. Mackenzie. Housing in developing countries: an annotated bibliography. [Charlottesville, Va.], 1976. 279 leaves.
                              Z7164.H8K47

Includes numerous references to Africa.

Abstract in *A.I.D. Research and Development Abstracts*, Oct. 1977, p. 35.

Issued also in microfiche. [Washington, U.S. Agency for International Development, 1976?] 3 sheets.   DLC-Sci RR PN-AAD-023

755

Van Huyck, Alfred P. African Development Bank: shelter sector policy considerations. [Washington?], Office of Housing, Agency for International Development, 1977. 52, 50 p.   HD7372.A3V34

Considers whether the Bank should undertake activities in support of the housing sector in Africa.

Abstracts in *A.I.D. Research and Development Abstracts*, Apr. 1978, p. 34–35, and *American Statistics Index*, 1978, Abstracts, p. 664.

Issued also in microfiche. [Washington, U.S. Agency for International Development, 1977?] 2 sheets (DLC-Sci RR PN-RAB-688), and [Washington, Congressional Information Service, 1977?] 2 sheets (DLC-Micro RR ASI:78 7208-13).

Human Rights

756

U.S. *Congress. House. Committee on Foreign Affairs. Subcommittee on Africa.* Human rights in Africa: hearing before the Subcommittees on Africa and on International Organizations of the Committee on Foreign Affairs, House of Representatives, Ninety-sixth Congress, first session, October 31, 1979. Washington, U.S. Govt. Print. Off.; for sale by the Supt. of Docs., U.S. Govt. Print. Off., 1980. 93 p.   KF27.F625 1979j

Stephen J. Solarz, chairman, Subcommittee on Africa.

Don Bonker, chairman, Subcommittee on International Organizations.

Among the appendixes is the following:

Appendix 3. A report on the United Nations Seminar on the Establishment of Regional Commissions on Human Rights with Specific Reference to Africa. p. 71–89.

757

U.S. *Congress. House. Committee on International Relations. Subcommittee on International Organizations.* Human rights and United States foreign policy: a review of the administration's record: hearing, Ninety-fifth Congress, first session, October 25, 1977. Washington, U.S. Govt. Print. Off., 1978. 74 p.   KF27.I5494 1977o
J74.A23 95th Cong.,
House Comm. Inter. Rel.,
v. 53

Donald M. Fraser, chairman.

Includes numerous references to Africa.

758

U.S. *Congress. Senate. Committee on Foreign Relations. Subcommittee on Foreign Assistance.* Human rights: hearings, Ninety-fifth Congress, first session … March 4 and 7, 1977. Washington, U.S. Govt. Print. Off., 1977. 104 p.
KF26.F6357   1977a
J74.A23 95th
Cong., Sen. Comm.
For. Rel., v. 11

Hubert H. Humphrey, chairman.

Includes occasional references to Africa.

759

U.S. *Dept. of State.* Country reports on human rights practices. 1978+ Washington, for sale by the Supt. of Docs., U.S. Govt. Print. Off., annual.
JC571.U48a

At head of title, 1978– : Joint committee print.

"Report submitted to the Committee on Foreign Affairs, U.S. House of Representatives and Committee on Foreign Relations, U.S. Senate by the Department of State in accordance with sections 116(d) and 502B(b) of the Foreign Assistance Act of 1961, as amended."

Report for 1979 includes specific information on human rights conditions in each sub-Saharan country plus tables on grants and loans from the United States and from international agencies for the period 1977–79 (p. 7–237).

L.C. has 1978+ (1978 held only in microfiche; DLC-Micro CIS78 S382-5).

760

————— Human rights practices in countries receiving U.S. security assistance; report, submitted to the Committee on International Relations, House of Representatives by the Department of State, in accordance with section 502B(b) of the Foreign Assistance Act, as amended. Washington, U.S. Govt. Print. Off., 1977. 137 p.   K3240.4.U54

At head of title: 95th Congress. 1st session. Committee print.

Africa is covered on p. 83–100 with specific reference to Botswana, Cameroon, Ethiopia, Gabon, Ghana, Kenya, Lesotho, Liberia, Nigeria, Senegal, Sudan, Swaziland, and Zaire.

761

————— Human right reports prepared by the Department of State in accordance with section 502(B) of the Foreign Assistance Act, as amended; submitted to the Subcommittee on Foreign Assistance of the Committee on Foreign Relations, United States Senate. Washington, for sale by the Supt. of Docs., U.S. Govt. Print. Off., 1977. 143 p.
JC571.U48   1977

At head of title: 95th Congress, 1st session. Committee print.

Africa is covered on p. 87–105 with specific reference to Botswana, Cameroon, Ethiopia, Gabon, Ghana, Kenya, Lesotho, Liberia, Nigeria, Senegal, Sudan, Swaziland, and Zaire.

762

————— Report on human rights practices in countries receiving U.S. aid: report, submitted to the Committee on Foreign Relations, U.S. Senate, and Committee on Foreign Affairs, U.S. House of Representatives, by the Department of State. Washington, for sale by the Supt. of Docs., U.S. Govt. Print. Off., 1979. 706 p.   JC571.U48   1979

At head of title: 96th Congress, 1st session. Joint committee print.

Africa is covered on p. 9–205, with specific references to Benin, Botswana, Burundi, Cameroon, Cape Verde, Central African Empire, Chad,

762 (cont.)

Comoros, Congo, Djibouti, Ethiopia, Gabon, The Gambia, Ghana, Guinea, Guinea-Bissau, Ivory Coast, Kenya, Lesotho, Liberia, Madagascar, Malawi, Mali, Mauritania, Mauritius, Mozambique, Niger, Rwanda, São Tomé and Principe, Senegal, Seychelles, Sierra Leone, Somalia, Sudan, Swaziland, Tanzania, Togo, Upper Volta, Zaire, and Zambia.

Among the appendixes are the following:

Appendix 1. Freedom House ratings of political rights and civil liberties for 1978. p. 659–665.

Countries are rated on a scale of one to seven of factors of political rights and civil liberties.

Appendix 2. The world socio-economic situation in 1976. p. 666–673.

For each country, there is a physical quality of life index and a figure indicating the percentage of "absolute poor," i.e., those whose per capita income is below the level at which it is possible to secure the "minimum requirements of life."

763

U.S. *Library of Congress. Foreign Affairs and National Defense Division.* Human rights conditions in selected countries and the U.S. response, prepared for the Subcommittee on International Organizations of the Committee on Internationl Relations, U.S. House of Representatives, by the Foreign Affairs and National Defense Division, Congressional Research Service, Library of Congress. Washington, for sale by the Supt. of Docs., U.S. Govt. Print. Off., 1978. 372 p.

JC571.U5   1978

Prepared by Brenda Branaman, and others.

At head of title: 95th Congress, 2d session.

Includes bibliographical references.

Chapters on Africa: "Human Rights Conditions in Namibia 1977" (p. 171–183) and "Human Rights Conditions in South Africa" (p. 238–260), both by Brenda Branaman, and "Zaire" (p. 332–340), by William N. Raiford.

764

Amnesty International on African human rights violations. *In* U.S. *Joint Publications Research Service.* JPRS 70667. [Springfield, Va., National Technical Information Service, 1978] (Translations on Sub-Saharan Africa, no. 1882) p. 1–3.

Article in *West Africa*, London, Jan. 16, 1978, p. 100–101.

Microfiche. [Washington, Supt. of Docs., U.S. Govt. Print. Off., 1978]

DLC-Micro JPRS 70667

765

Derian, Patricia M. Human rights in South Africa. Washington Bureau of Public Affairs, U.S. Dept. of State, 1980. [4] p. (U.S. Dept. of State. Current policy, no. 181)   DLC

Statement by the Assistant Secretary of State for Human Rights and Humanitarian Affairs before the Subcommittees on Africa and International Organizations of the Committee on Foreign Affairs, U.S. House of Representatives, May 13, 1980.

766

Mbaye, Keba. Human rights in Africa reviewed. *In* U.S. *Joint Publications Research Service.* JPRS 76584. [Springfield, Va., National Technical Information Service, 1980] (Sub-Saharan Africa report, no. 2304) p. 1–6.

Translation of article in *Africa*, Dakar, June–July 1980, p. 13–15, 98.

Microfiche. [s.l., 1980]

DLC-Micro JPRS 76584

767

Weinstein, Warren, Lisa Jones, *and* Frank McCoy. African perspectives on human rights. Washington, Council for Policy and Social Research, 1980. [238] p. (in various pagings)   DLC

On cover: Department of State contract no. 1722-920096.

Appendices: 1. Human rights provisions in African constitutions.—2. Human rights international instruments; African signatories, ratifications, accessions, etc. as of 1 January 1979; List of participants at African human rights meetings; Conclusions of conferences and colloquia on human rights in Khartoum (1975), Dar es Salaam (1976), Freetown (1978), Butare (1978), and Dakar (1978).

Labor

768

U.S. *Agency for International Development.* Evaluation of the union-to-union activities in Africa of the International Federation of Petroleum and Chemical Workers (IFPCW) [Washington?], 1973. 14 p.

Issued as a supplement to the *Report on the Evaluation of the Program of the African-American Labor Center.*

Examined in the Development Information Center, AID, Washington, D.C.

769

Fiks, Alfred, Rey Hill, *and* Peter Cannon. Evaluation study of selected labor development activities in

769 (cont.)

Ghana, Togo, and Kenya. Alexandria, Va., Group Seven Associates, inc., 1979. 109 leaves.

Study submitted to the Bureau for Africa, U.S. Agency for International Development, under contract AID/otr-C-1387.

Microfiche. [Washington, U.S. Agency for International Development, 1980] 2 sheets (PN-AAG-517); held by the Development Information Center, AID, Washington, D.C.

770

Mironov, V. Mironov attacks AFL-CIO activity in Africa. *In* U.S. *Joint Publications Research Service.* JPRS 66130. [Springfield, Va., National Technical Information Service, 1975] (Translations on Sub-Saharan Africa, no. 1625) p. 1–5.

Translation of article in *Aziya i Afrika Segodnya*, Moscow, no. 8, 1975, p. 46–47.

AFL-CIO: American Federation of Labor-Congress of Industrial Organizations.

Microfiche. [s.l., 1975]

DLC-Micro JPRS 66130

771

Person, Yves. Report on trade unions in Black Africa. *In* U.S. *Joint Publications Research Service.* JPRS 76456. [Springfield, Va., National Technical Information Service, 1980] (Sub-Saharan Africa report, no. 2294) p. 10–32.

Translation of article in *Le Mois en Afrique*, Paris, Apr. – May 1980, p. 22–26.

Microfiche. [s.l., 1980]

DLC-Micro JPRS 76456

Language and Languages

772

Center for Applied Linguistics. A survey of materials for the study of uncommonly taught languages [by] Dora E. Johnson [and others] Arlington, Va., c1976. 8 v.   Z7001.C45   1976

Prepared for the U.S. Office of Education under contract no. OEC-300-75-0201.

"A revision of A provisional survey of materials for the study of the neglected languages which the Center for Applied Linguistics published in 1969."

Partial contents: v. 6. Languages of Sub-Saharan Africa.

Abstract of volume 6 in *Resources in Education*, July 1979, p. 92.

Volume 6 issue also in microfiche. [Arlington, Va., ERIC Document Reproduction Service; prepared for Educational Resources Information Center, National Institute of Education, 1979] 1 sheet.

DLC-Micro ED166949

773

Conference on African Linguistics, *6th, Ohio State University*, 1975. Proceedings; edited by Robert K. Herbert. Columbus, Dept. of Linguistics, Ohio State University, 1975. 299 p. (Ohio. State University, Columbus. Dept. of Linguistics. Working papers in linguistics, no. 20)

Abstract in *Resources in Education*, July 1978, p. 84.

Microfiche. [Arlington, Va., ERIC Document Reproduction Service; prepared for Educational Resources Information Center, National Institute of Education, 1978] 4 sheets.

DLC-Micro ED150854

774

Fontaine, André. Senghor notes gap between French-English-speaking Africa. *In* U.S. *Joint Publications Research Service.* JPRS 71348. [Springfield, Va., National Technical Information Service, 1978] (Translations on Sub-Saharan Africa, no. 1951) p. 77–88.

Translation of interview with President Senghor which included a wide-ranging discussion with some emphasis on the need to learn European languages for international communication, in *Le Monde*, Paris, May 17, 18, 1978.

Microfiche. [Washington, Supt. of Docs., U.S. Govt. Print. Off., 1978]

DLC-Micro JPRS 71348

775

Herbert, Robert K. Patterns of language, culture, and society: sub-Saharan Africa. Columbus, Dept. of Linguistics, Ohio State University, 1975. [215] p. (Ohio. State University, Columbus. Dept. of Linguistics. Working papers in linguistics, no. 19)

On cover: Proceedings of the Symposium on African Language, Culture, and Society, held at Ohio State University, Columbus, April 11, 1975.

Abstract in *Resources in Education*, July 1978, p. 87.

Microfiche. [Arlington, Va., ERIC Document Reproduction Service; prepared for Educational Resources Information Center, National Institute of Education, 1978] 3 sheets.

DLC-Micro ED150872

776

Hodge, Carleton T. Reconsideration of language priorities: Africa. [s.l., 1974?] 79 p.

Bibliography: p. 63–79.

Paper presented at the Columbia Conference on Material Development Needs in the Uncommonly Taught Languages: Priorities for the 70's, 1974.

A revision of the Fife-Nielsen report (1961) listing African languages in priority order.

776 (cont.)

Abstract in *Resources in Education*, Oct. 1975, p. 102.

Microfiche. [Arlington, Va., ERIC Document Reproduction Service; prepared for Educational Resources Information Center, National Institute of Education, 1975] 1 sheet.

DLC-Micro ED107130

777

Petrov, Julia A., *and* John P. Brosseau. Foreign language, area, and other international studies: a bibliography of research and instructional materials completed under the National Defense Education Act of 1958, title VI, section 602: list no. 9, compiled by Julia A. Petrov; edited by John Brosseau. [Washington], U.S. Dept. of Education; [for sale by the Supt. of Docs., U.S. Govt. Print. Off., 1980] 79 p.   Z5818.L35P47 1980

892 entries, including citations to publications on African languages.

A cumulative guide, updating a publication with the same title (list no. 8), issued in 1976 by the U.S. Office of Education (Z5818.L35P47 1976).

778

Ruchti, James R. The US Government requirements for foreign languages. *In* President's Commission on Foreign Language and International Studies: background papers and studies. Washington, for sale by the Supt. of Docs., U.S. Govt. Print. Off., 1979. p. 197–220.   P57.U7P7

A list of the foreign languages required by various Federal Government agencies, together with an indication of the number of employees proficient in these languages, is given on p. 210–220.

Libraries and Library Resources

779

U.S. *Library of Congress*. LC acquisition trends. no. 1-11 July 1977–Apr. 1982. [Washington] semiannual.   Z733.U585a

"Replacing the National Program for Acquisitions and Cataloging progress report (issued September 1966–February 1977) and the Special Foreign Acquisitions Program newsletter (issued August 1974–February 1977)."

Includes reports on acquisition survey trips in Africa undertaken by Library representatives.

L.C. has July 1977–Apr. 1982.

780

The African Section in the Library of Congress.

[Rev. ed. Washington, African Section, Library of Congress, 1981] folder ([5] p.)   DLC

List of Library of Congress publications on Africa, 1965–1981: p. [2–5].

781

Africana in the Library of Congress. [Washington, African Section, Library of Congress, 1977] folder ([5] p.)   DLC

"The African Section has prepared this brief introductory guide to assist its readers in locating material pertinent to their work."

782

Larby, Patricia M. Materials for African studies: the contribution of SCOLMA. Overseas universities, Sept. 1974: 26–28.

LB2331.5.094 1974

SCOLMA: Standing Conference on Library Materials on Africa.

Issued also in microfiche. [Arlington, Va., ERIC Document Reproduction Service; prepared for Educational Resources Informational Center, National Institute of Education, 1975] 1 sheet.

DLC-Micro ED098961

783

Mascarenhas, O. C. Africa Bibliographic Centre (ABC): an experiment in African documentation and library resource sharing. [s.l.], 1977. 12 p.

Paper prepared for the 1977 IFLA-UNESCO Pre-Session Seminar on Resource Sharing of Libraries in Developing Countries.

Abstract in *Resources in Education*, 1980 annual cumulation, p. 299.

Microfiche. [Arlington, Va., ERIC Document Reproduction Service; prepared for Educational Resources Information Center, National Institute of Education, 1980] 1 sheet.

DLC-Micro ED176753

784

Meeting of experts on planning documentation and library networks in Africa (NATIS), Brazzaville, 5–10 July 1976. [Paris, United Nations Educational, Scientific, and Cultural Organization], 1976. 36 p.

"CC-76/CONF.610/3."

NATIS: National information system.

Includes reports on the current state of documentation and library services in 32 sub-Saharan countries.

Abstract in *Resources in Education*, Mar. 1978, p. 107.

Microfiche. [Arlington, Va., ERIC Document Reproduction Service; prepared for Educational

784 (cont.)

Resources Information Center, National Institute of Education, 1978] 1 sheet.

DLC-Micro ED145814

785

Obi, Dorothy S. Education for library, archive, and information science in sub-Saharan Africa: a blueprint for regional planning. [s.l.], 1974. 49 p. map.

Paper presented at the General Council Meeting of the International Federation of Library Associations, 1974.

Abstract in *Resources in Education*, Aug. 1975, p. 120.

Microfiche. [Arlington, Va., ERIC Document Reproduction Service; prepared for Educational Resources Information Center, National Institute of Education, 1975] 1 sheet.

DLC-Micro ED104446

786

Ogunṣheye, F. Adetowun. Library education and manpower planning in Africa. [s.l., 1974?] 33 p.

Paper presented at the General Council Meeting of the International Federation of Library Associations, 1974.

Abstract in *Resources in Education*, Sept. 1975, p. 111–112.

Microfiche. [Arlington, Va., ERIC Document Reproduction Service; prepared for Educational Resources Information Center, National Institute of Education, 1975] 1 sheet.

DLC-Micro ED105826

787

Pankhurst, Rita. The Standing Conference of African University Libraries—"SCAUL" Overseas universities, Sept. 1974: 22–25. illus.

LB2331.5.O94 1974

Issued also in microfiche. [Arlington, Va., ERIC Document Reproduction Service; prepared for Educational Resources Information Center, National Institute of Education, 1975] 1 sheet.

DLC-Micro ED098961

788

Widenmann, Elizabeth A. Africa, south of the Sahara. *In* American Library Association. Resources and Technical Services Division. Cataloging and Classification Section. Subject Analysis Committee. Ad Hoc Subcommittee on Subject Analysis of African and Asian Materials. Final report. [s.l.], 1978. p. 34–40.

Microfiche. [Arlington, Va., ERIC Document Reproduction Service; prepared for Educational Resources Information Center, National Institute of Education, 1980] DLC-Micro ED175391

789

Witherell, Julian W. Africana in Great Britain and the Netherlands: report of a publication survey trip, March–April 1977. [Washington], African Section, Library of Congress, 1977. 51 p. DLC

List of papers delivered at the Progress in African Bibliography Conference, London, Mar. 17–18, 1977: p. 37–38.

Military Affairs

790

U.S. *Arms Control and Disarmament Agency*. World military expenditures and arms transfers. 1965/74+ [Washington, for sale by the Supt. of Docs., U.S. Govt. Print. Off.] annual. (U.S. Arms Control and Disarmament Agency. Publication)

JX1974.A1U52

Continues the Agency's *World Military Expenditures and Arms Trade*.

Each vol. covers a 10-year period (e.g., 1970/79). Includes statistical data on sub-Saharan Africa.

791

U.S. *Congress. House. Committee on Armed Services*. Report of the delegation to the Middle East and Africa, February 6, 1978. Washington, U.S. Govt. Print. Off., 1978. 38 p. DLC-LL

J74.A23
95th Cong.
House. Comm.
Armed Serv.,
v. 51

"H.A.S.C. no. 95-51."

Melvin Price, chairman of delegation.

The delegation, which conducted its visit in Nov. 1977, sought to gain information on the conflict in the Horn of Africa, Soviet influence in Africa, and the flow of arms to African countries; sub-Saharan countries visited were Kenya, Somalia, Zambia, Zaire, and Ivory Coast.

792

U.S. *Congress. House. Committee on Armed Services. Delegation to Africa*. Report of the delegation to Africa: report to the Committee on Armed Services, House of Representatives, Ninety-sixth Congress, first session March 4, 1980. Washington, U.S. Govt. Print. Off., 1980. 29 p.

DT30.U58 1980

Melvin Price, chairman of delegation.

At head of title: 96th Congress, 1st session. Committee print.

The delegation visited Nigeria, South Africa, Zimbabwe, Tanzania, and Sudan in the period Nov. 17–26, 1979. Its primary purpose was to

792 (cont.)

obtain "an updated view of the strategic situation on the African continent and particularly on the prospects for avoiding further warfare in the southern half of Africa."—p. 1.

793

U.S. *Congress. House. Committee on the International Relations.* International Security Assistance Act of 1976: hearings, Ninety-fourth Congress, on H. R. 11963 ... Washington, U.S. Govt. Print. Off., 1976. 973 p.   KF27.I549 1975i
J74.A23 94th
Cong., house Comm.
Inter. Rel., v. 46

Thomas E. Morgan, chairman.

Hearings held Nov. 6, 1975–Feb. 19, 1976.

Includes occasional references to political and military situations in African states, with particular reference to Angola, Ethiopia, and Zaire.

794

U.S. *Congress. Senate. Committee on Foreign Relations.* The International Security Assistance and Arms Export Control Act of 1977; report (to accompany S. 1160) [Washington, U.S. Govt. Print. Off., 1977] 62 p.   DLC-LL

Report submitted by Senator John Sparkman.

At head of title: 95th Congress, 1st session. Senate. Report no. 95–195.

"Calendar no. 169."

Includes occasional references to Africa.

795

U.S. *General Accounting Office.* Military sales: an increasing U.S. role in Africa: report. [Washington] 1978. 35 p. map.

          HD9743.U6U59   1978

Cover title.

"ID-77-61."

"B-165731."

"This report to the Departments of State and Defense reviews military sales to Morocco, Ethiopia, Zaire, Kenya, and Nigeria."

Abstracts in *Government Reports Announcements & Index*, July 21, 1978, p. 33, and *American Statistics Index*, 1978, Abstracts, p. 1015.

Issued also in microfiche. [Springfield, Va., National Technical Information Service, 1978] sheet, (DLC-Sci RR PB 279481), and [Washington, Congressional Information Service, 1978?] 1 sheet (DLC-Micro ASI: 78 26108-619).

796

U.S. *Library of Congress. Foreign Affairs Division.* Means of measuring naval power with special reference to U.S. and Soviet activities in the Indian Ocean. Prepared for the Subcommittee on the Near East and South Asia of the Committee on Foreign Affairs. Washington, U.S. Govt. Print. Off., 1974. 16 p. maps.   V25.U54   1974

At head of title: Committee print. 93d Congress, 2d session.

Includes bibliographical references.

Table (p. 6) indicates calls by U.S. and Soviet naval ships at Indian Ocean ports in the period 1968–73, including ports in Ethiopia, Kenya, Malagasy Republic, Mauritius, Seychelles, Somalia, Sudan, and Tanzania.

797

Badara, Ali. African naval capability assessed. *In* U.S. *Joint Publications Research Service.* JPRS 73519. [Springfield, Va., National Technical Information Service, 1979] (Translations on Sub-Saharan Africa, no. 2109) p. 4–8.

Translation of article in *Revue africaine de strategie*, Paris, Apr.–June 1979, p. 41–45.

Microfiche. [Washington, Supt. of Docs., U.S. Govt. Print. Off., 1979]

          DLC-Micro JPRS 73519

798

Bonker, Don. The return of the mercenaries. Congressional record, 94th Congress, 2d session, v. 122, Aug. 5, 1976: 26064–26066.   J11.R5 v. 122

Extension of remarks in the U.S. House of Representatives.

Includes article from *Africa Report*.

799

Chaplin, Dennis. France—military involvement in Africa. Military review, Jan. 1979: 44–47. illus.

          Z6723.U35   1979

Published by the U.S. Army Command and General Staff College, Ft. Leavenworth, Kansas.

800

Civil-military roles of indigenous armed forces. Ft. Monroe, Va., Headquarters, U.S. Army Training and Doctrine Command; distributed by the National Technical Information Service, Springfield, Va., 1974. 3 v.

"Completed by 354th Civil Affairs, Area B, USAR [Riverdale, Md.], July 1974."

Includes occasional references to the political, economic, public service, and security roles of armed forces of African nations.

Contents: v. 1. Executive summary.—v. 2. Main report.—v. 3. Appendixes.

Microfiche. [Springfield, Va., National Technical Information Service, 1974?] 4 sheets.

          DLC-Sci RR AD-A009190

801
The Cuban military in Africa and the Middle East: from Algeria to Angola. Arlington, Va., U.S. Center for Naval Analyses, 1977. 1 v.   AMAU
"Professional paper, no. 201."

802
Darcourt, Pierre. Extensive Soviet military involvement in Africa described. *In* U.S. *Joint Publications Research Service*. JPRS 72271. [Springfield, Va., National Technical Information Service, 1978] (Translations on Sub-Saharan Africa, no. 2025) p. 27–31.
Translation of article in *Africa*, Dakar, Oct. 1978, p. 43–46.
Microfiche. [Washington, Supt. of Docs., U.S. Govt. Print. Off., 1978]
DLC-Micro JPRS 72271

803
Dawson, Charles H. Civil-military relations in Nigeria, Zaire and Ethiopia and their impact on U.S. national security interests. Carlisle Barracks, Pa., 1974. 46 p. (U.S. Army War College. Student research report)   AMAU

804
Durch, William J. Revolution from a F.A.R.—the Cuban armed forces in Africa and the Middle East. [Arlington, Va.], Center for Naval Analyses, [1977] 16 p. map. (Center for Naval Analyses. Professional paper, no. 199)
Microfiche. [s.l., Defense Documentation Center, 1977] 1 sheet   DLC-Sci RR AD-A046268

804a
Factors affecting the role and employment of peacekeeping forces in Africa south of the Sahara: final report. Urbana, University of Illinois, 1982. 199 leaves. maps.   IU
Prepared for the U.S. Defense Intelligence Agency under contract no. MDA 908-82-C-0174.
Principal researcher: Morris Davis.

805
Increased military spending reported. *In* U.S. *Joint Publications Research Service*. JPRS 74107. [Springfield, Va., National Technical Information Service, 1979] (Sub-Saharan Africa report, no. 2147) p. 8–11.
Translation of article on the military expenditures of African nations in *Europe Outre-Mer*, Paris, May 1979, p. 11, 12.
Microfiche. [Washington, Supt. of Docs., U.S. Govt. Print. Off., 1979]
DLC-Micro JPRS 74107

806
Itemized review of African defense forces. *In* U.S. *Joint Publications Research Service*. JPRS 75138. [Springfield, Va., National Technical Information Service, 1980] (Sub-Saharan Africa report, no. 2214) p. 16–23.
Translation of article in *Afrique défense*, Paris, Jan. 1980.
Microfiche. [s.l., 1980]
DLC-Micro JPRS 75138

807
McIlroy, John J., Leo Hazlewood, *and* Margaret D. Hayes. Developmental methodologies for medium- and long-range estimates; interim technical report. Arlington, Va., CACI Inc.-Federal, 1976. [110] p. (in various pagings)
"Rept. no. CAC-259."
Study sponsored by the Defense Advanced Research Projects Agency.
Concerns the use of military forces in several regions, including Africa.
Microfiche. [Springfield, Va.?, National Technical Information Service, 1976] 2 sheets.
DLC-Sci RR AD-A031466

808
OAU military strength reviewed. *In* U.S. *Joint Publications Research Service*. JPRS 73988. [Springfield, Va., National Technical Information Service, 1979] (Sub-Saharan Africa report, no. 2141) p. 4–13.
Translation of an overall review of the armed forces of Organization of African Unity member nations in *Afrique défense*, Paris, July 1979, p. 42–44.
Microfiche. [Washington, Supt. of Docs., U.S. Govt. Print. Off., 1979]
DLC-Micro JPRS 73988

809
Ojokojo, James S. The Organization of African Unity and peacekeeping: the Pan-African Defense Force. Ft. Leavenworth, Kan., Army Command and General Staff College, 1981. 94 p.
Thesis (M.A.)—U.S. Army Command and General Staff College.
Cited by the Defense Technical Information Center and an "unclassified report."

810
Pelletier, Renée. Larger African armies not always effective. *In* U.S. *Joint Publications Research Service*. JPRS 75373. [Springfield, Va., National Technical Information Service, 1980] (Sub-Saharan African report, no. 2226) p. 5–11.
Translation of article in *Africa*, Dakar, Feb. 1980, p. 37–41.

810 (cont.)
Microfiche. [s.l., 1980]
DLC-Micro JPRS 75373

811
Price, Melvin. House Armed Services Committee delegation visit to Africa. Congressional record [daily ed.], 96th Congress, 1st session, v. 125, Nov. 28, 1979: H11317–H11318.   J11.R7 v. 125
Remarks in the U.S. House of Representatives.
Includes report on the factfinding mission undertaken during the period Nov. 17–25, 1979.

812
Ra'anan, Gavriel D. The evolution of the Soviet use of surrogates in military relations with the Third World, with particular emphasis on Cuban participation in Africa. [Santa Monica, Calif., Rand Corporation], 1979. 97 p.
"P-6420."
Microfiche. [s.l., Defense Technical Information Center, 1981] 2 sheets.
DLC-Sci RR AD-A095442

813
Reportage on OAU defense force concept, needs. *In* U.S. *Joint Publications Research Service*. JPRS 74754. [Springfield, Va., National Technical Information Service, 1979] (Sub-Saharan Africa report, no. 2188) p. 14–25.
Translation of article commenting on the July 1979 report of the Defense Commission of the Organization of African Unity, in *Afrique défense*, Paris, Sept. 1979, p. 49, 50, 52, 54, and 55.
Microfiche. [s.l., 1980]
DLC-Micro JPRS 74754

814
Stitt, Wilbert. The African officer and the Command and General Staff College experience. [Ft. Leavenworth, Kan., U.S. Army Command and General Staff College, 1975. [25] leaves.
Presented at annual meeting of the African Studies Association, 1975.
Microfilm. [African Studies Association. Papers presented as the annual meeting. Chicago]
DLC-Micro Microfilm 03782 DT 1975, reel 2

Politics and Government

815
U.S. *Central Intelligence Agency*. Annotated bibliography on transnatonal and international terrorism. [Washington], 1976. 225 p.
Z7164.T3U54   1976

"PR 76 10073U."
Prepared by Edward F. Mickolus.
Citations on Africa: p. 123–124.

816
U.S. *Central Intelligence Agency. National Foreign Assessment Center*. Chiefs of state and cabinet members of foreign government. Oct. 1977+ [Washington] monthly. (*Its* Reference aid)
JF37.U5
Continues: *Chiefs of State and Cabinet Members of Foreign Governments* (L.C. has 1972–77), issued by the U.S. Central Intelligence Agency.
Prepared for the use of U.S. Government officials.
Includes all sub-Saharan nations.
L.C. has Oct. 1977+
Note: Microfilm of this publication for the period Aug. 1962–Dec. 1980 is available from the Photoduplication Service, Library of Congress, Washington, D.C. 20540

817
Bates, Robert H. The issue basis of rural politics in Africa. Comparative politics, Apr. 1978: 345–360.
JA3.C67   1978
"Expenses were deferred by NIH Grant (HD 05707-03)."—p. 357.
Issued also as Social Science Working Paper no. 102 of the Division of the Humanities and Social Sciences, California Institute of Technology.

818
Byrd, Harry F., Jr. The status of democracy in sub-Saharan Africa. Congressional record, 96th Congress, 1st session, v. 125, Mar. 27, 1979: 6388–6389.
J11.R5 v. 125
Remarks in the U.S. Senate.
Includes text of a survey prepared by the Library of Congress.

819
Clark, Dick. African concerns. Congressional record, 95th Congress, 2d session, v. 124, Mar. 13, 1978: 6611–6616.   J11.R5 v. 124
Remarks in the U.S. Senate on the death of Steve Biko and on the rebirth of democracy in Nigeria.
Includes text of Donald Woods' testimony before the Subcommittee on Africa and articles from the *Washington Post, New York Times*, and *Baltimore Sun*.

820
Collins, James L. Civil-military relations in Nigeria and Tanzania: a study of the success and failure of civil leadership in Africa. Ft. Leavenworth, Kan., U.S. Army Command and General Staff College, 1977. 122 p.

820 (cont.)

Bibliography: p. 117–122.

Thesis—U.S. Army Command and General Staff College.

Abstract in *Government Reports Announcements & Index*, Nov. 11, 1977, p. 24.

Microfiche. [s.l., Defense Documentation Center, 1977] 2 sheets.

DLC-Sci RR AD-A043725

821

Conclusion of sixth UPA meeting reported. *In* U.S. *Joint Publications Research Service*. JPRS 74452. [Springfield, Va., National Technical Information Service, 1979] (Sub-Saharan Africa report, no. 2170) p. 7–11.

Translation of article on the results of a meeting of the African Parliamentary Union, in *L'Observateur*, Ouagadougou, Sept. 17, 1979, p. 7, 9, and 10.

Microfiche. [Washington, Supt. of Docs., U.S. Govt. Print. Off., 1979]

DLC-Micro JPRS 74452

822

Critical situations: 1976–1977. Vienna, Va., BMD Corporation, [1975] [356] p. maps.

Prepared for the U.S. Assistant Secretary of Defense (International Security Affairs).

A study to determine "plausible developments having a high potential for becoming critical situations in the time period 1976–1977," including Ethiopia, Kenya, and Angola.

Microfiche. [Springfield, Va., National Technical Information Service, [1975] 4 sheets.

DLC-Sci RR AD-A017933

823

Dent, Martin. Three African constitutions compared. *In* U.S. *Joint Publications Research Service*. JPRS 74754. [Springfield, Va., National Technical Information Service, 1979] (Sub-Saharan Africa report, no. 2188) p. 1–5.

Article in *West Africa*, London, Nov. 26, 1979, p. 2173, 2175, and 2176, comparing the draft constitution of Zimbabwe with the constitutions of Ghana and Nigeria.

Microfiche. [s.l., 1980]

DLC-Micro JPRS 74754

824

Final declaration of fifth conference of MPJ. *In* U.S. *Joint Publications Research Service*. JPRS 74422. [Springfield, Va., National Technical Information Service, 1979] (Sub-Saharan Africa report, no. 2168) p. 6–13.

Translation of text of declaration of the Pan-

African Youth Movement conference held in Brazzaville, Aug. 9–14, 1979, recorded in *Etumba*, Brazzaville, Aug. 25, 1979, p. 6, 10.

Microfiche. [Washington, Supt. of Docs., U.S. Govt. Print. Off., 1979]

DLC-Micro JPRS 74422

825

Foltz, William J. Political boundaries and political competition in tropical Africa. [s.l., 1973?] [41] leaves. (FAR 17139-S)

Presented at the Conference on African Trends Through the 70's, Apr. 1973.

Examined in the former Foreign Affairs Research Documentation Center, U.S. Dept. of State.

826

Kafleche, Jean–Marc. New African divide: Congo to Ethiopia. *In* U.S. *Joint Publications Research Service*. JPRS 73489. [Springfield, Va., National Technical Information Service, 1979] (Translations on Sub-Saharan Africa, no. 2107) p. 18–21.

Translation of article in *Le Figaro*, Paris, Mar. 5, 1979, p. 16, concerning political conditions in Congo and Ethiopia.

Microfiche. [Washington, Supt. of Docs., U.S. Govt. Print. Off., 1979]

DLC-Micro JPRS 73489

827

McDonald, Larry. Conor Cruise O'Brien: still destabilizing pro-Western African governments. Congressional record [daily ed.], 96th Congress, 2d session, v. 126, Feb. 21, 1980: E737-E739.

J11.R7 v. 126

Extension of remarks in the U.S. House of Representatives.

Includes a biographical sketch of Mr. O'Brien.

828

McGovern, George S. Problems of Africa. Congressional record [daily ed.], 96th Congress, 2d session, v. 16, June 11, 1980: S6671-S6678.

J11.R7 v. 126

Remarks in the U.S. Senate.

Includes article, "The fire to come in South Africa," by David Halberstam in *Atlantic*, and "Reporting from Africa: modern impulses and the attractions of the bush," by Michael Kaufman in *Harper's*, which emphasizes political change in eastern Africa.

829

——— Revolution into democracy: Portugal after the coup: a report by Senator George McGovern to the Committee on Foreign Relations, United

829 (cont.)

States Senate. Washington, U.S. Govt. Print. Off., 1976. 111 p. map.   DP680.M23

At head of title: 9th Congress, 2d session. Committee print.

Includes frequent references to the effects of the 1974 revolution on Portuguese Africa.

830

Newsom, David D. Communism in Africa. Washington, Bureau of Public Affairs, U.S. Dept. of State, 1979. 6 p. (U.S. Dept. of State. Current policy, no. 99)   DLC

Statement by the Under Secretary of State for Political Affairs before the Subcommittee on Africa, Committee on Foreign Affairs, U.S. House of Representatives, Oct. 18, 1979.

831

Pfaltzgraff, Robert L., *and* Geoffrey Kemp. U.S. maritime interests in the South Atlantic. Appendix. [Cambridge, Mass., Institute for Foreign Policy Analysis, inc., 1977?] 2 v.

Distribution controlled by the U.S. Navy.

Partial contents: I-A-1. West, Robert L. Major regional powers in the South Atlantic area: Nigeria and its economic potential.—I-C-1. Crocker, Chester A. South Africa: its strategic perspectives and capabilities.—II-A-1. Major regional powers and their interests, geostrategic perspectives and capabilities: Nigeria.—II-C-1. Major regional powers and their interests, geostrategic perspectives and capabilities: South Africa.

Microfiche. [s.l., Defense Documentation Center, 1978] 4 sheets (AD-B025005L-AD-B025006L).

832

Popov, Milored. Soviet opportunities in the Third World: Communist parties, indigenous insurgent groups and international labor groups in sub-Saharan Africa. *In* Background studies: Soviet opportunities in the Third World. Arlington, Va., Strategic Studies Center, Stanford Research Institute, 1976. p. 145–190.

Prepared for the office of the Deputy Chief of Staff for Operations and Plans, U.S. Army.

Microfiche. [s.l., Defense Documentation Center, 1980]   DLC-Sci RR AD-A079603

833

President discusses African, scientific socialism. *In* U.S. *Joint Publications Research Service.* JPRS 68829. [Springfield, Va., National Technical Information Service, 1977] (Translations on Sub-Saharan Africa, no. 1726) p. 8–13.

Translation of interview with President Mathieu

Kérékou, in *Ehuzu*, Cotonou, Feb. 15, 1977, p. 1, 3, 6.

Microfiche. [s.l., 1977]
DLC-Micro JPRS 68829

834

Schneider, Michael J. Perspectives on symbolic leadership and political fragmentation in sub-Saharan Africa. [s.l., 1977] 32 p.

On cover: "Competitive paper submitted to the Commission on International and Intercultural Communication for the Speech Communication Association meeting in Washington, D.C., December 1977."

Abstract in *Resources in Education*, Apr. 1979, p. 47.

Microfiche. [Arlington, Va., ERIC Document Reproduction Service; prepared for Educational Resources Information Center, National Institute of Education, 1979] 1 sheet.
DLC-Micro ED162359

835

Snow, Donald M. Social origins of African revolutionaries: a statistical profile and analysis of the men who have led radical movements in sub-Saharan Africa since 1945. [Washington?], 1973. 39 leaves. (FAR 17509-S)

Cited in *Foreign Affairs Research Special Papers Available: Africa, Sub-Saharan, 1976*, p. 19, as prepared for the U.S. Dept. of State.

Examined in the former Foreign Affairs Research Documentation Center, U.S. Dept. of State.

836

Von der Mehden, Fred R. Communalism, bureaucracy, and access to public services in Afro-Asia: an overview. Houston, Tex., Program of Development Studies, William March Rice University, 1978. 29 p. (William March Rice University. Program of Development Studies. Paper no. 89)

Research supported by the U.S. Agency for International Development under contract AID/otr-C-1394.

Paper originally prepared for the annual meeting of the American Political Science Association, 1978.

Microfiche. [Washington, U.S. Agency for International Development, 1978?] 1 sheet.
DLC-Sci RR PN-AAG-228

Population Studies

837

U.S. *Agency for International Development. Office of Population.* Information package on current status

837 (cont.)

of population and family planning policies and grograms in sub-Saharan Africa. [Washington?], 1977. 27 p.

Examined in the Development Information Center, AID, Washington, D.C.

838

U.S. *Congress. House. Committee on Science and Technology. Subcommittee on Domestic and International Scientific Planning, Analysis and Cooperation.* Report of the honorable James H. Scheuer on the growing awareness of population and health issues in Africa, Ninety-fifth Congress, second session. Washington, for sale by the Supt. of Docs., U.S. Govt. Print. Off., 1978. 125 p. illus. maps.

HB3661.A3U54 1978

At head of title: Committee print.

"Serial BB."

A report on national family planning programs in six African nations: Kenya, Tanzania, Zaire, Nigeria, Ghana, and Senegal.

839

U.S. *Congress. House. Select Committee on Population.* Population and development: hearings, Ninety-fifth Congress, second session. Washington, U.S. Govt. Print. Off., 1978. 3 v. illus.

KF27.5.P67 1978b
J74.A23 95th
Cong., House Sel.
Comm. Pop., v. 6–8

James H. Scheuer, chairman.

Hearings held Apr. 18–May 4, 1978.

"No. 6-8."

Contents: v. 1. Overview of trends, consequences, perspectives, and issues.—v. 2. Status and trends of family planning/population programs in developing countries.—v. 3. Research in population and development needs and capacities.

Statement of Mr. Louis Gardella, Acting Director, Africa Division, Office of Population, Agency for International Development. v. 2, p. 100–111.

The following are selections of prepared statements in the Appendix to vol. 2:

Ravenholt, R. T. Population program assistance, U.S. Agency for International Development, 1965–1978. p. 195–268.

Sai, Fred T. Family planning in Africa—an overview. p. 421–436.

Kanani, S. Kenya's maternal, child health/family planning (MCH/FP) program: a summary. p. 447–461.

Gardella, Louis. Case study Kenya. p. 468–498.

840

U.S. *Congress. Senate. Committee on Foreign Relations.* World population trends: hearings, Ninety-sixth Congress, second session ... April 29 and June 5, 1980. Washington, U.S. Govt. Print. Off., 1980. 346 p.

KF26.F6 1980r

Frank Church, chairman.

Africa is covered specifically on p. 212–228 with testimony by Goler T. Butcher, Assistant Administrator, Bureau for Africa, U.S. Agency for International Development.

841

Bongaarts, John. The fertility impact of traditional and changing childspacing practices in tropical Africa. New York, Population Council, 1979. 27 p. (Population Council, New York. Center for Policy Studies. Working papers, no. 42)

HB1071.A3B65

Prepared for the U.S. Agency for International Development under contract AID/pha-C-1199.

Abstract in *A.I.D. Research & Development Abstracts*, July 1981, p. 56.

Issued also in microfiche. [Washington, U.S. Agency for International Development, 1979?] 1 sheet. DLC-Sci RR PN-AAH-321

841a

Demographic estimates for countries with a population of 10 million or more, 1981. Washington, U.S. Dept. of Commerce, Bureau of the Census; [for sale by the Supt. of Docs., U.S. Govt. Print. Off.], 1981. 169 p. maps.

HA155.D45 1981

Includes demographic data for Ethiopia, Ghana, Kenya, Mozambique, Nigeria, South Africa, Sudan, Tanzania, Uganda, and Zaire.

842

Family planning in five continents: Africa, America, Asia, Europe, Oceania. [London, International Planned Parenthood Federation] annual.

Vol. for 1976 issued in microfiche. [Arlington, Va., ERIC Document Reproduction Service; prepared for Educational Resources Information Center, National Institute of Education, 1977] 1 sheet.

DLC-Micro ED141076

Note: L.C. has also vols. for 1968 (HQ766.I52 1968) and 1970 (HQ766.I52 1970).

843

Family planning statistics, 1965 to 1973: Africa, Asia, and Latin America, [by] William O'Leary [et al.] Washington, International Statistical Programs Center, Bureau of the Census, 1975. 74 p.

Abstract in *American Statistics Index*, 1975, Abstracts, p. 194.

843 (cont.)

Microfiche. [Washington, Congressional Information Service, 1975?] 1 sheet.

DLC-Micro ASI:75 2328-8

844

Farley, Rawle. Professional migration: the brain drain from the West Indies and Africa. *In* Bryce-Laporte, Roy S., and Delores M. Mortimer. Caribbean immigration to the United States. Washington, Smithsonian Institution, Research Institute on Immigration and Ethnic Studies, 1976. (RIIES occasional papers, no. 1) p. 169–181.   DSI

Abstract in *American Statistics Index*, 1978. Abstracts, p. 881.

Issued also in microfiche. [Washington, Congressional Information Service, 1976?]

DLC-Micro ASI:78 9776-2.1

845

Ferry, B., *and* P. Cantrelle. ORSTOM population research in Africa: scope and prospects. *In* Population dynamics research in Africa: proceedings of workshop/seminar 4, 30 July – 3 August 1973, Lome, Togo, [by] Francis Olu. Okedeji, editor; co-sponsored by Council for the Development of Economic and Social Research in Africa, [and] Interdisciplinary Communications Program, Smithsonian Institution. [Washington, Interdisciplinary Communications Program, 1975] p. 97–116.

HB850.5.A35P66

"Contract no. AID/csd-3598."

ORSTOM: Office de la recherche scientifique et technique outre-mer.

846

Final report to Agency for International Development, Division of Population, contract number AID/CM/pha-C-73-18, "African data for decision making," [by] Hilary Whittaker [et al.] [s.l.], Data Use and Access Laboratories, 1976. [91] leaves.

A program consisting of projects in Yaoundé, Cameroon, and Nairobi, Kenya, "to demonstrate the feasibility of introducing easy access computer software systems and training African government planners to use computerized data in planning, especially in population-related activities."—p. 1.

Examined in the Development Information Center, AID, Washington, D.C.

847

Gachuhi, J. Mugo. African youths: their knowledge, attitudes and practice of family planning. *In* Population dynamics research in Africa: proceedings of workshop/seminar 4, 30 July – 3 August 1973, Lome, Togo, [by] Francis Olu. Okedeji, editor; co-sponsored by Council for the Development of

Economic and Social Research in Africa, [and] Interdisciplinary Communications Program, Smithsonian Institution. [Washington, Interdisciplinary Communications Program, 1975] p. 199–211.

HB850.5.A35P66

"Contract no. AID/csd-3598."

848

George, Emmett. Africa's population problem. War on hunger, Mar. 1977: 13–14. illus.

HD9000.1.W37   1977

Issued by the U.S. Agency for International Development.

849

International Demographic Data Center (U.S.) International population dynamics, 1950–79: demographic estimates for countries with a population of 5 million or more [by] Bureau of the Census, International Demographic Data Center. Washington, The Bureau: for sale by the Supt. of Docs., U.S. Govt. Print. Off., 1980. 258 p.

HA155.I57   1980

Edited by Ellen Jamison, with the assistance of James F. Spitler.

Includes bibliographies.

Includes data for the following sub-Saharan countries: Angola, Cameroon, Ethiopia, Ghana, Guinea, Ivory Coast, Kenya, Madagascar, Malawi, Mali, Mozambique, Niger, Nigeria, Senegal, South Africa, Sudan, Tanzania, Uganda, Upper Volta, Zaire, Zambia, and Zimbabwe.

849a

Janowitz, Barbara, *and* D. J. Nichols. The determinants of contraceptive use, reproductive goals and birth spacing in relation to mortality, breast-feeding and previous contraceptive behavior. [s.l.], International Fertility Research Program, 1980. 117 p.

Prepared for the U.S. Agency for International Development.

Abstract in *A.I.D. Research & Development Abstracts*, v. 10, no. 1/2, 1982, p. 60.

"A study was made of 20,000 women who delivered at selected hospitals in Iran, Egypt, the Sudan, and Nigeria."—Abstract.

850

Kpedekpo, G. M. K. The evaluation of some aspects of research methodologies and problems in African demographic analysis. *In* Population dynamics research in Africa: proceedings of workshop/seminar 4, 30 July – 3 August 1973, Lome, Togo, [by] Francis Olu. Okedeji, editor; co-sponsored by Council for the Development of Economic and Social Research in Africa, [and] Interdisciplinary

850 (cont.)

Communications Program, Smithsonian Institution. [Washington, Interdisciplinary Communications Program, 1975] p. 117–130.

HB850.5.A35P66

"Contract no. AID/csd-3598."

851

LeVine, Robert A., Suzanne Dixon, *and* Sarah LeVine. High fertility in Africa: a consideration of causes and consequences. [s.l.] 1976. 18 leaves.

Research supported by a grant from the National Science Foundation.

Presented at annual meeting of the African Studies Association, 1976.

Microfilm. [African Studies Association. Papers presented at the annual meeting. Chicago]

DLC-Micro 03782 DT
1976, reel 1

852

McHale, Magda C., John McHale, *and* Guy F. Streatfeild. Children in the world. Washington, Population Reference Bureau, 1979. 62 p. maps.

HQ767.9.M3

"Publication of this chartbook in observance of the International Year of the Child 1979 was made possible by a special grant from the U.S. Agency for International Development."

Includes numerous statistical charts and other demographic information on sub-Saharan Africa.

853

Population dynamics research in Africa: proceedings of workshop/seminar 4, 30 July – 3 August 1973, Lome, Togo, [by] Francis Olu. Okedeji, editor; co-sponsored by Council for the Development of Economic and Social Research in Africa, [and] Interdisciplinary Communications Program, Smithsonian Institution. [Washington, Interdisciplinary Communications Program, 1975] xvii, 295 p.

HB850.5.A35P66

"Contract no. AID/csd-3598."

Includes contributions on Benin, Cameroon, Ghana, Kenya, Nigeria, Sierra Leone, Togo, Zaire, and Zambia.

Selected other contributions are cited separately in this guide under their personal authors; these can be identified by consulting the index under the heading *Population Dynamics Research in Africa*.

854

Population Reference Bureau, *Washington, D.C.* World population growth and response, 1965–1975: a decade of global action. Washington, 1976. 271 p. illus. HB871.P672 1976

Prepared under U.S. Agency for International Development contract no. AID/pha-C-1096.

Africa is covered on p. 27–64.

Abstract in *A.I.D. Research and Development Abstracts*, Apr. 1978, p. 32.

Issued also in microfiche ([Washington, U.S. Agency for International Development, 1976?] 3 sheets). DLC-Sci RR PN-AAB-996

855

Wolfe, Bernard. Anti-contraception laws in sub-Saharan Francophone Africa: sources and ramifications. [Medford, Mass., Fletcher School of Law and Diplomacy, Tufts University], 1973. 40 p. (Law and population growth series. Monograph, no. 15) MMeT-F

Cited in *A.I.D. Research and Development Abstract*, v. 7, no. 2, 1979, p. 22, as being supported by the U.S. Agency for International Development.

856

World fertility survey. 1972/75+ Voorburg, Neth., International Statistical Institute. annual.

HB903.F4W67a

Financed by the United Nations Funds for Population Activities and the U.S. Agency for International Development.

Title varies: 1972/75, *The World Fertility Survey: the First Three Years, January 1972 – January 1975*.

Includes brief notes on fertility surveys in several sub-Saharan African countries.

L.C. has 1972/75+

857

World population: recent demographic estimates for the countries and regions of the world. [Washington], Bureau of the Census; [for sale by the Supt. of Docs., U.S. Govt. Print. Off.] biennial.

HB848.W67

Includes bibliographies.

Prepared by the International Demographic Data Center.

In 1979 vol., African countries are covered on p. 45–165.

L.C. has 1973, 1975, and 1979.

Note: In the introduction to the 1979 vol., it is reported that three African countries—Chad, Ethiopia, and Guinea—have never taken a census.

Refugees

858

U.S. *Congress. House. Committee on Foreign Affairs. Subcommittee on International Organizations.* Briefing on the growing refugee problem: implications for international organizations: hearing, Ninety-

858 (cont.)

sixth Congress, first session, June 5, 1979. Washington, U.S. Govt. Print. Off., 1979. 70 p.

KF27.F648   1979b
J74.A23 96th
Cong., House Comm.
For. Aff., v. 26

Don Bonker, chairman.

Among the appendixes is *1979 World Refugee Assessment*, prepared by the Office of the United States Coordinator for Refugee Affairs, which includes a section (p. 43–47) on those African countries with significant refugee settlements—Angola, Botswana, Djibouti, Ethiopia, Kenya, Mozambique, Namibia, Rhodesia, Sudan, Tanzania, Zaire, and Zambia, plus those that have large numbers of exiles living outside their borders—such as Equatorial Guinea and Zaire. Refugee problems resulting from the conflict in the western Sahara are covered on p. 49–50.

859

U.S. *Library of Congress. Congressional Research Service.* World refugee crisis: the international community's response: report prepared at the request of Senator Edward M. Kennedy, chairman, Committee on the Judiciary, United States Senate by the Congressional Research Service, Library of Congress, Ninety-sixth Congress, first session. Washington, U.S. Govt. Print. Off.; for sale by the Supt. of Docs., U.S. Govt. Print. Off., 1979. xxvi, 323 p. maps.   HV640.U57   1979

"Committee print."

Africa is covered on p. 40–118, with specific reference to refugees from Angola, Burundi, Equatorial Guinea, Ethiopia, Guinea, Kenya, Malawi, Namibia, Rhodesia, Rwanda, South Africa, Sudan, Uganda, and Zaire.

860

Clark, G. Edward, Jesse L. Snyder, *and* Karl O. Kohler. An assessment of the refugee situation in southern, central and eastern Africa. [Washington?, Robert Nathan Associates], 1977. 111 leaves. maps.

Prepared for the U.S. Agency for International Development under contract AID/otc-C-1380.

"Assesses new and chronic refugee problems in Southern, Central, and Eastern Africa and reviews American relief programs in order to develop a broad assistance strategy for helping refugees and host countries. The team conducted its field survey from August 8 to September 24, 1977. Visits were made to Botswana, Lesotho, Swaziland, Mozambique, Zambia, Zaire, Kenya, Sudan, and Djibouti."—Abstract.

Abstract in *A.I.D. Research and Development Abstracts*, July 1978, p. 31–32.

Microfiche. [Washington, U.S. Agency for International Development, 1977?] 2 sheets.

DLC-Sci RR PN-AAF-149

861

Kennedy, Edward M. Pan-African Conference on Refugees. Congressional record, 96th Congress, 1st session, v. 125, June 12, 1979: 14416–14419.

J11.R5 v. 125

Remarks in the U.S. Senate on the May 1979 conference held in Arusha, Tanzania.

Includes text of remarks by President Julius K. Nyerere of Tanzania and Frank Sieverts, Deputy Secretary of State for Refugee and Migration Affairs.

Religion

862

Emmons, Marian. Black tribal African religion with some emphasis on Christianity and Islam in Africa. Dayton, Ohio, Public Education Religion Studies Center, Wright State University, [1976] 25 p.

Supported by the National Endowment for the Humanities.

On cover: "Prepared for Sixth Grade Social Studies."

Prepared for the Teacher Education Institute on the Religious Dimension of World Cultures, 1976–77.

Abstract in *Resources in Education*, Nov. 1978, p. 189.

Microfiche. [Arlington, Va.; ERIC Document Reproduction Service; prepared for Educational Resources Information Center, National Institute of Education, 1978] 1 sheet.

DLC-Micro ED156606

863

M'Bokolo, Elikia. The Black Africa of the Prophet. *In* U.S. *Joint Publications Research Service.* JPRS 73060. [Springfield, Va., National Technical Information Service, 1979] (Translations on Sub-Saharan Africa, no. 2079) p. 2–8.

Translation of article on Islam in sub-Saharan Africa in *Demain l'Afrique*, Paris, Feb. 12, 1979, p. 26–28.

Microfiche. [Washington, Supt. of Docs., U.S. Govt. Print. Off., 1979]

DLC-Micro JPRS 73060

864

Nicolas, Guy. Islamic structures in sub-Saharan Africa studied. *In* U.S. *Joint Publications Research*

864 (cont.)

Service. JPRS 74987. [Springfield, Va., National Technical Information Service, 1980] (Sub-Saharan Africa report, no. 2203) p. 1–16.

Translation of article in *Revue française d'études politiques africaines*, Sept.–Oct. 1979, p. 86–107.

Microfiche. [s.l., 1980]

DLC-Micro JPRS 74987

865

—— Relationships of sub-Saharan African societies, Islam examined. *In* U.S. *Joint Publications Research Service.* JPRS 76526. [Springfield, Va., National Technical Information Service, 1980] (Sub-Saharan Africa report, no. 2300) p. 1–6.

Translation of article in *Le Mois en Afrique*, Paris, Apr.–May 1980, p. 47–64.

Microfiche. [s.l., 1980]

DLC-Micro JPRS 76526

866

Zoghby, Samir M. Islam in sub-Saharan Africa: a partially annotated guide. Washington, African Section, Library of Congress; for sale by the Supt. of Docs., U.S. Govt. Print. Off., 1978, 318 p.

Z7835.M6Z63
Z663.285.I84

2,682 entries.

Science and Technology

867

U.S. *Congress. House. Committee on Science and Technology. Subcommittee on Domestic and International Scientific Planning, Analysis, and Cooperation.* Appropriate technology: hearings, Ninety-fifth Congress, second session, July 25, 26, 27, 1978. Washington, U.S. Govt. Print. Off., 1978. 1289 p. illus.

KF27.S3927 1978e
J74.A23 95th Cong.,
House Comm. Sci. &
Tech., v. 6

James H. Scheuer, chairman.

In his opening remarks, Chairman Scheuer states "The Appropriate Technology (AT) 'movement' has emerged to provide alternatives to reliance on massive transfers of advanced technology for growth in the developing world to address the needs of the major portion of the population of the less developed countries who have heretofore been unable to reap the benefits of high technology."—p. 2–3.

Among the appendixes is the following:

Bulfin, Robert L., *and* Harry L. Weaver. Appropriate technology for natural resources development: an overview, annotated bibliography, and a guide to sources of information (Tucson, University of Arizona, 1977). p. 504–674.

868

Analysis of explosion generated surface waves in Africa, results from the discrimination experiment and summary of current research; quarterly technical report. Jan./Mar. 1978?+ La Jolla, Calif., Systems, Science and Software.

Sponsored by the Advanced Research Projects Agency, U.S. Dept. of Defense.

Report for Jan./Mar. 1978 issued in microfiche. [s.l., Defense Documentation Center, 1979] 2 sheets.

DLC-Sci RR AD-A061005

869

California. University. *Scripps Institution of Oceanography, La Jolla.* Initial reports of the Deep Sea Drilling Project: a project planned by and carried out with the advice of the Joint Oceanographic Institutions for Deep Sea Sampling. Washington, National Science Foundation; for sale by the Supt. of Docs., U.S. Govt. Print. Off., 1969+ illus., maps.

QE39.C3

"Prepared for the National Science Foundation, National Ocean Sediment Coring Program, under contract C-482."

Includes bibliographic references.

Covers the cruises of the drilling vessel "Glomar Challenger."

The following volumes relating to sub-Saharan Africa have been identified:

v.2. Hoboken, N.J. to Dakar, Senegal, Oct.–Nov. 1968.

v.3. Dakar, Senegal to Rio de Janeiro, Brazil, Dec. 1968–Jan. 1969.

v. 23. Colombo, Ceylon to Djibouti, F.T.A.I., Mar–May 1972.

v. 24. Djibouti, F.T.A.I. to Port Louis, Mauritius, May–June 1972.

v. 26. Durban, South Africa to Fremantle, Australia, Sept.–Oct. 1972.

v. 39. Amsterdam, Netherlands to Cape Town, South Africa, Oct.–Dec. 1974.

v. 40. Cape Town, South Africa to Abidjan, Ivory Coast, Dec. 1974–Feb. 1975.

v. 41. Abidjan, Ivory Coast to Malaga, Spain, Feb.–Apr. 1975.

870

Intermediate technology organizations in Africa and the Indian sub-continent. [s.l., Intermediate Technology Development Group (United Kingdom), 1976] [94] p.

Issued as an appendix to *Proposal for a Program in Appropriate Technology, Transmitted by the*

870 (cont.)

Agency for International Development, Pursuant to Section 107 of the Foreign Assistance Act. (Washington, U.S. Govt. Print. Off., 1977. 382 p. HC60.U6I48 1977).

The term "intermediate technology organizations" is defined as "organizations whose *principal* objectives are to mobilize knowledge on appropriate technologies, promote relevant r. and a. work and get field-tested information on technologies into the hands of people who can use them."—p. 2.

Abstract in *A.I.D. Research and Development Abstracts*, Apr. 1978, p. 37.

Microfice. [Washington, U.S. Agency for International Development, 1977?] 1 sheet.

DLC-Sci RR PN-AAE-699

871

Nimira, J. K. Comparison of estimated and observed values of solar radiation at the surface of the African continent. Silver Spring, Md., National Oceanic and Atmospheric Administration, 1980. 43 p. maps.

Abstract in *Government Reports Announcements & Index*, Aug. 1, 1980, p. 3027.

Microfiche. [Springfield, Va., National Technical Information Service, 1980] 1 sheet.

DLC-Sci RR PB 80-180417

872

Smithsonian Science Information Exchange. Information services on research in progress: a worldwide inventory. Services d'information concernant les recherches en cours: répertoire mondial; edited by the Smithsonian Science Information Exchange, and compiled in cooperation with Unesco. Springfield, Va., distribution by National Technical Information Service, 1978. xix, 432 p.

Q179.96.S63   1978

"NTIS PB 282025."

Bibliography: p. 39–46.

For sub-Saharan Africa, it describes programs of the following services: Centre d'études africaines, Paris, France; Joint EAAFRO/EAVRO Library, East African Agriculture and Forestry Research Organisation/East African Veterinary Research Organisation, Nairobi, Kenya; Council for Scientific and Industrial Research, Accra, Ghana; National Research Council Secretariat, Lilongwe, Malawi; Centre national de documentation scientifique et technique, Dakar, Senegal; National Council for Research, Khartoum, Sudan; and National Research Council, Kampala, Uganda.

Women

873

U.S. *Congress. House. Committee on International Relations. Subcommittee on Africa.* Minority and small business contracting policies of the Agency for International Development's Africa Bureau: hearing, Ninety-fifth congress, first session, September 27, 1977. Washington, U.S. Govt. Print. Off., 1978. 150 p.

KF27.I54914   1977g
J74.A23 95th Cong.,
House Comm. Int. Rel.,
v. 48

Charles C. Diggs, Jr., chairman.

Appendix: Problems and potentials of minorities and women as AID/AFR contractors and grantees—Volume 1. Report findings, analysis, and recommentations, submitted by the MATCH Institution. p. 95–150.

874

Dixon, Ruth B. Assessing the impact of development projects on women. [Washington], Office of Women in Development, U.S. Agency for International Development, 1980. 105 p. (A.I.D. program evaluation discussion paper, no. 8)   DLC

Bibliography: p. 101–105.

Issued in cooperation with the Agency's Office of Evaluation.

Many of the examples used to illustrate the author's comments are taken from sub-Saharan Africa.

875

Germain, Adrienne, *and* Audrey Smock. The status and roles of Ghanaian and Kenyan women: implications for fertility behavior. [s.l.], 1974. [46] p.

Bibliography: p. [42–46].

Paper presented at annual meeting of the American Psychological Association, 1974.

Abstract in *Resources in Education*, Apr. 1975, p. 35.

Microfiche. [Arlington, Va., ERIC Document Reproduction Service; prepared for Educational Resources Information Center, National Institute of Education, 1975] 1 sheet.

DLC-Micro ED098485

876

Illustrative statistics on women in development in selected developing countries. Washington, U.S. Bureau of the Census; [for sale by the Supt. of Docs., U.S. Govt. Print. Off., 1980]. 24 p.   DLC

Prepared for the Office of Women in Development, U.S. Agency for International Development.

876 (cont.)

Sub-Saharan African countries covered are Cameroon, Ghana, Kenya, Senegal, and Tanzania.

877

Mickelwait, Donald R., Mary Ann Riegelman, *and* Charles F. Sweet. Women in rural development; a survey of the roles of women in Ghana, Lesotho, Kenya, Nigeria, Bolivia, Paraguay , and Peru. Boulder, Colo., Westview Press, 1976. xvii, 224 p.   HN777.M5

Prepared for the Office of Development Administration, Bureau for Technical Asistance, U.S. Agency for International Development, under contract AID/CM/ta-C-73-41.

Issued also in microfiche. [Washington, U.S. Agency for International Development, 1976?] 3 sheets.   DLC-Sci RR PN-AAB-211

878

Pala, Achola O. African women in rural development: research trends and priorities. [Washington?] Overseas Liaison Committee, American Council on Education, 1976. 35 p. (American Council on Education. Overseas Liaison Committee. OLC paper, no. 12)   HQ1815.5.P43

Activities of the Overseas Liaison Committee are supported in part through a contract with the U.S. Agency for International Development.

Abstract in *A.I.D. Research and Development Abstracts*, Apr. 1978, p. 3–4.

Issued also in microfiche. [Washington, U.S. Agency for International Development, 1976?] 1 sheet.   DLC-Sci RR PN-AAE-750

879

Pan-African Women's Organization congress in Madagascar. *In U.S. Joint Publications Research Service.* JPRS 72497. [Springfield, Va., National Technical Information Service, 1978] (Translations on Sub-Saharan Africa, no. 2042) p. 1–7.

Translation of article in *Madagascar-Matin*, Antananarivo, Nov. 7, 1978, p. 1, 3.

Microfiche. [Washington, Supt. of Docs., U.S. Govt. Print. Off., 1978] DLC-Micro JPRS 72497

880

Phillips, Beverly. Women in rural development: a bibliography. Madison, Land Tenure Center Library, University of Wisconsin-Madison, 1979. 45 p. illus. (Wisconsin. University-Madison. Land Tenure Center. Training & methods series, no. 29)

Africa is specifically covered on p. 10–22.

Abstract in *A.I.D. Research and Development Abstracts*, Feb. 1981, p. 31.

Microfiche. [Washington, U.S. Agency for International Development, 1979?] 1 sheet.   DLC-Sci RR PN-AAH-331

881

Pre-feasibility study for providing assistance to African women small entrepreneurs. Washington, International Affairs Division, National Association of Negro Business and Professional Women's Clubs, 1977. 96 p.

Prepared for the U.S. Agency for International Development under grant AID/afr-G-1317.

Covers Senegal, The Gambia, Sierra Leone, Cameroon, and Malawi.

Abstract in *A.I.D. Research and Development Abstracts*, Oct. 1978, p. 26–27.

Microfiche. [Washington, U.S. Agency for International Development, 1977?] 1 sheet (PN-AAF-594); examined in the Development Information Center, Agency for International Development, Washington, D.C.

882

Riegelman, Mary Ann, *and* Keith M. Moore. A seven country survey on the roles of women in rural development. Washington, Development Alternatives, inc., 1974. [274] p. (in various pagings)

Prepared for the U.S. Agency for International Development under contract AID/CM/ta-C-73-41.

Bibliography: p. E-1 – E-7.

Includes data on development projects in Ghana, Nigeria, Kenya, Lesotho, Bolivia, Peru, and The Gambia.

Microfiche. [Washington, U.S. Agency for International Development, 1974?] 3 sheets.

DLC-Sci RR PN-AAB-211

883

Rural development, women's roles and fertility in developing countries: review of the literature [by] Gloria W. Javillonar [et al.] [s.l.], Research Triangle Institute, 1979, 298 p.

Prepared for the Office of Rural Development and Development Administration, U.S. Agency for International Development.

Issued in cooperation with the South East Consortium for International Development.

Africa is specifically covered on p. 32–75.

Abstract in *A. I. D. Research & Development Abstracts*, v. 9, no. 3, 1981, p. 27.

Microfiche. [Washington, U.S. Agency for International Development, 1979?] 4 sheets.

DLC-Sci RR PN-AAG-908

884

Vavrus, Linda G., *and* Ron Cadieux. Women in development: a selected annotated bibliography and resource guide. East Lansing, Non-Formal Education Information Center, Michigan State University, 1980. 69 p. (Michigan. State University. Non-Formal Education Information Center. Annotated bibliography, no. 1)   DLC

Published in cooperation with the U.S. Agency for International Development.

Works specifically on Africa and the Middle East are cited on p. 27–35.

885

Women in Africa: what is the impact of development? Agenda, Feb. 1978: 1–7. illus.

HC59.7.A742   1978

Issued by the U.S. Agency for International Development.

"The international donor community has begun taking a closer look at ways to integrate women into their planning projects. Among these are the Agency for International Development, which is reassessing its programs to make sure that the needs of women are considered from the very conception of a project."

886

Women in development: a roster of specialists. Washington, New Transcentury Foundation, 1979. 240 p.

Prepared for the Office of Women in Development, U.S. Agency for International Development, under contract AID/otr-C-1674.

Biographical sketches of specialists on sub-Saharan Africa: p. 151–210.

Examined in the Documentation Center, Sahel Development Program, AID, Washington, D.C.

887

Women in development: 1980 report to the Committee on Foreign Relations, United States Senate, and the Committee on Foreign Affairs, United States House of Representatives. Washington, Office of Women in Development, Agency for International Development, [1981?] [408] p. (in various pagings)   DLC

List of "Women in Development" publications: p. [399–405].

Updates report submitted in 1978.

Africa is covered on p. 96–130.

888

Women in migration: a Third World focus, [by] Nadia Youssef [et al.] Washington, International Center for Research on Women, 1979. [171] p.

DLC

Prepared for the Office of Women in Develop-

ment, U.S. Agency for International Development, under grant AID/otr-G-1592.

Bibliography: p. [155–171].

Includes frequent references to African conditions with statistical tables by country.

889

[Women in rural development program in Africa] Annual report. 1st+ 1975/76+ [Washington?] National Council of Negro Women, inc., International Division.

Prepared for the U.S. Agency for International Development.

Report for 1975/76 examined in the Development Information Center, AID, Washington, D.C.

Other Subjects

890

U.S. *Information Agency*. USIA activities in Africa. [Washington?, 197–?]

Source: Duffy. *Survey*.

891

U.S. *Naval Weather Service Detachment*. Climatic summaries for major Indian Ocean ports and waters. Washington, published by direction of the Commander, Naval Weather Service Command, 1974. 53 p., 36 leaves of plates, illus., maps.

QC994.5U54   1974

"NAVAIR 50-1C-63."

Bibliography: p. 8–9.

Includes data on ports of Sudan, Ethiopia, French Territory of the Afars and Issas, Somalia, Kenya, Tanzania, Mozambique, South Africa, Madagascar, Mauritius, and Seychelles.

892

—— Summary of synoptic meteorological observations (SSMO): West African and selected island coastal marine areas; prepared by the Naval Weather Service Detachment, Asheville, N.C., for the Director, Naval Oceanography and Meteorology. Asheville, N.C., The Detachment; obtainable from the National Technical Information Service, Springfield, Va., [1976?] 3 v.

QC994.2.U5   1976

Contents: v. 1. Area 1: Azores. Area 2: Madeira Islands. Area 3: Casablanca, SW. Area 4: Canary Islands. Area 5: Central Spanish Sahara. Area 6: Cape Blanc. Area 7: Cape Verde Islands. Area 8: Dakar.—v. 2. Area 9: Conakry. Area 10: Monrovia. Area 11: Ivory Coast. Area 12: Accra. Area 13: Gulf of Guinea, East. Area 14: Luanda, NW. Area 15: Lobito.—v. 3. Area 16: Skeleton Coast. —Area 17: Walvis Bay, SW. Area 18: Alexander

892 (cont.)
Bay. Area 19: Cape Town. Area 20: Port Elizabeth. Area 21. East London. Area 22: Durban.

893
U.S. *Social Security Administration*. Programs concerning Africa. [Washington?, 1977?]
"Unpublished document."
Source: Duffy. *Survey*.

894
Ahua, Bernard. Final report on African cultural renaissance meeting. *In* U.S. *Joint Publications Research Service*. JPRS 72390. [Springfield, Va., National Technical Information Service, 1978] (Translations on Sub-Saharan Africa, no. 2034) p. 6–16.
Translation of article reporting a meeting on the "specifics and dynamics of African cultures" in *Fraternité-Matin*, Abidjan, Oct. 24, 1978, p. 8–9.
Microfiche. [Washington, Supt. of Docs., U.S. Govt. Print. Off., 1978]
DLC-Micro JPRS 72390

895
Bates, Robert H. Ethnic competition and modernization in contemporary Africa. Contemporary political studies, Jan. 1974: 457–484.
JA3.C65 1974
Although there is no indication in the article of U.S. Government sponsorship, the Millikan Library of California Institute of Technology has indicated that this study had official U.S. support.
An earlier version, "Ethnicity and Modernization in Contemporary Africa," was issued as Social Science Working Paper no. 16 of the Division of the Humanities and Social Sciences, California Institute of Technology.

896
Beers, H. Dwight. African names and naming practices: a selected list of references in English. [Washington], African Section, [Library of Congress, [1977] [2] p.   DLC
Reprinted from the *Library of Congress Information Bulletin*, v. 36, Mar. 2, 1977, p. 206–207.

897
Burress, James R., *and* Leonard G. Perlman. Developments in services to handicapped people: Africa. Washington, People-to-People Committee for the Handicapped, 1980. 218 p.
Bibliography: p. 202–203.
Funded in part by the National Institute for Handicapped Research, U.S. Dept. of Health, Education, and Welfare.
Abstracts in *Resources in Education*, Feb. 1981,

p. 78–79, and *Government Reports Announcements & Index*, Oct. 24, 1980, p. 4649.
Microfiche. [Arlington, Va., ERIC Document Reproduction Service; prepared for Educational Resources Information Center, National Institute of Education, 1981] 3 sheets (DLC-Micro ED192493), and [Springfield, Va., National Technical Information Service, 1980] 3 sheets (DLC-Sci RR PB 80-201676).

898
The Celebration of death: two folk tales about death. New York, School Services Division, African-American Institute, [1976] 8 p.
Describes folk tales from Uganda and Zaire.
Microfiche. [Arlington, Va., ERIC Document Reproduction Service; prepared for Educational Resources Information Center, National Institute of Education, 1977] 1 sheet.
DLC-Micro ED132087

899
Coughlan, Margaret N. Folklore from Africa to the United States: an annotated bibliography. Washington, Library of Congress; for sale by the Supt. of Docs., U.S. Govt. Print Off., 1976. 161 p. illus.   Z5984.A35C68
Z663.292.C69
190 entries.
Abstract in *Resources in Education*, Aug. 1977, p. 57.
Issued also in microfiche. [Arlington, Va., ERIC Document Reproduction Service; prepared for Educational Resources Information Center, National Institute of Education, 1977] 2 sheets.
DLC-Micro ED136289

900
Edgar, Robert W. Harambee, Africa, and the Law of the Sea. Congressional record, 95th Congress, 1st session, v. 123, May 18, 1977: 15462–15464.
J11.R5 v. 123
Extension of remarks in the U.S. House of Representatives.
Includes text of address by John J. Logue, Director, World Order Research Institute, Villanova University, at the University of Nairobi, Jan. 19, 1977.

901
Field data collection in the social sciences: experiences in Africa and the Middle East; edited by Bryant Kearl, editorial committee: Salem Gafsi [and others] New York, Agricultural Development Council, c1976. xxiv, 200 p.   H61.F47
"Based on a conference ... held in Beirut, Lebanon, in December 1974."

901 (cont.)

Bibliography: p. 118–192.

The Research and Training Network of the Agricultural Development Council, which organized the conference, is funded through a contract with the U.S. Agency for International Development.

Abstract in *A.I.D. Research and Development Abstracts*, July 1976, p. 28.

Issued also in microfiche. [Washington, U.S. Agency for International Development, 1976?] 3 sheets.   DLC-Sci RR PN-AAB-723

902

Henry, Bernard. Witchcraft in Africa studied. *In* U.S. *Joint Publications Research Service*. JPRS 76803. [Springfield, Va., National Technical Information Service, 1980] (Sub-Saharan Africa report, no. 2318) p. 1–4.

Translation of article in *Spécial l'éventail*, Brussels, Sept. 26—Oct. 2, 1980, p. 21–23.

Microfiche. [s.l., 1980]
              DLC-Micro JPRS 76803

903

Hill, Kim Q., *and* Fred R. Von der Mehden. Data reliability in cross-national research; a test employing black Africa country experts. Houston, Program of Development Studies, Rice University, 1978. 28 p. ([William Marsh Rice University, Houston, Tex.] Program of Development Studies. Discussion paper series, no. 83)   TxHR

Research supported by the U.S. Agency for International Development under contract AID/otr-C-1394.

Abstract in *A.I.D Research and Development Abstracts*, Jan. 1979, p. 31.

Issued also in microfiche. [Washington, U.S. Agency for International Development, 1978?] (PN-AAF-004).

904

Hill, Robert A. Afro-American linkages with Africa in transnational perspective. Denver, Center for Teaching International Relations, University of Denver, 1976. [59] p.

Sponsored in part by the U.S. Office of Education.

Bibliography: p. [57–59].

Abstract in *Resources in Education*, Dec. 1979, p. 148.

Microfiche. [Arlington, Va., ERIC Document Reproduction Service; prepared for Education Resources Information Center, National Institute of Education, 1979] 1 sheet.
              DLC-Micro ED174527

905

International Working Conference on Stored-Product Entomology, *2d, Ibadan, Nigeria*, Sept. 10–16, 1978. Proceedings. Savannah, Ga., 1979. 455 p. illus.

Supported by a U.S. Agency for International Development grant.

Abstract in *A.I.D. Research and Development Abstracts*, v. 7, no. 3, 1980, p. 2.

Microfiche. [Washington, U.S. Agency for International Development, 1979?] 5 sheets.
              DLC-Sci RR PN-AAG-694

906

Jochmans, Robert P. Littérature néo-africaine de langue française pour les élèves de français de 4e année des écoles secondaires. [s.l.], 1973. 54 p. map.

Text in English or French.

Covers the literatures of Haiti, Guadeloupe, Martinique, French Guiana, Senegal, Ivory Coast, and Congo.

Abstract in *Resources in Education*, Sept. 1975, p. 95–96.

Microfiche. [Arlington, Va., ERIC Document Reproduction Service; prepared for Educational Resources Information Center, National Institute of Education, 1975] 1 sheet.   DLC- ED105707

907

Lamb, Peter J. Variations in general circulation and climate over the tropical Atlantic and Africa: weather anomalies in the subsaharan region. [Madison], University of Wisconsin-Madison, 1976. 113 leaves.

Dissertation—University of Wisconsin-Madison.

Study supported by the National Science Foundation.

Microfiche. [Sahel Documents and Dissertations. Ann Arbor, Mich., University Microfilms International, 1980] 2 sheets (DLC-Micro Microfiche 5357 AS 355); and [Ann Arbor, University Microfilms International, 1976] (DLC-Micro 76-15996).

908

McDonald, Larry. American Committee on Africa: transnational support for terrorism. Congressional record, 95th Congress, 1st session, v. 123, Sept. 9, 1977: 28601–18604.   J11.R5 v. 123

Extension of remarks in the U.S. House of Representatives.

Representative McDonald contends that the Committee "has for more than two decades served as the principal U.S. support group for Marxist terrorists movements on the African continent."

909

——— The National Council of Churches and Africa: accomodating terrorists. Congressional record, 95th Congress, 1st session, v. 123, Apr. 21, 1977: 11809–11812.   J11.R5 v. 123

Extension of remarks in the U.S. House of Representatives concerning the Council's "Conference on the Church and Southern Africa," Mar. 1977.

910

Mauro, Charles T. Indications and warning in Africa: evaluation of a quantitative model. Monterey, Calif., Naval Postgraduate School, 1980. 178 p.

Thesis (M.A.)—Naval Postgraduate School.

Cited by the Defense Technical Information Center as an "unclassified report" with distribution limited to U.S. Government agencies. "Other requests for this document must be referred to Superintendent, Naval Postgraduate School, attn: Code 012, Monterey, Ca 933940."

An examination of a test case involving the use of the daily reports of the Foreign Broadcast Information Service as an aid in intelligence analysis.

911

Murphy, E. Jefferson. The African mythology: old and new. Storrs, World Education Project, School of Education, University of Connecticut, 1973. 11 p.

Abstract in *Research in Education*, Sept. 1974, p. 132.

Microfiche. [Arlington, Va., ERIC Document Reproduction Service; prepared for Educational Resources Information Center, National Institute of Education, 1974] 1 sheet.

DLC-Micro ED091305

912

National Climatic Center. Summary of synoptic meteorological observations: East African and selected island coastal marine areas. [Washington], U.S. Naval Weather Service Command; [obtainable from the National Technical Information Service, Springfield, Va.], 1974. 5 v.

QC991.E3N37   1974

"Prepared under the direction of the U.S. Naval Weather Service Command."

Contents: v. 1. Area 1: Kuria Muria Islands. Area 2: West Arabian Sea. Area 3: Qamr Bay. Area 4: Socotra Island. Area 5. Gulf of Aden, NE. Area 6: Gulf of Aden, NW—v. 2. Area 7: Red Sea South. Area 8: Red Sea South Central. Area 9: Red Sea Central. Area 10: Red Sea North Central. Area 11: Red Sea North. Area 12: Gulf of Suez.—v. 3. Area 13: Gulf of Aden, SW. Area 14. Gulf of Aden, SE. Area 15: Somali coast, NE. Area 16: Somali

coast east. Area 17: Somali coast, SE. Area 18: Somali coast south.—v. 4. Area 19: Kenya coast. Area 20: Zanzibar. Area 21: Tanzania coast, SE. Area 22: Porto Amelia. Area 23: Lumbo. Area 24: Mozambique Channel NW. Area 25: Mozambique Channel SW.—v. 5. Area 26: Lourenco Marques. Area 27: Tulear. Area 28: Mozambique Channel SE. Area 29: Mozambique Channel NE. Area 30: Diego Garcia. Area 31. Gan. Area 32. Minicoy Island.

913

Pratt, Corny. The reportage and images of Africa in six U.S. news and opinion magazines: a comparative study. [s.l., 1977] 39 p.

Paper presented at the convention of the Association for Education in Journalism, 1977.

Journals covered are *Time, Newsweek*, *U.S. News and World Report*, *Nation*, *New Republic*, and *National Review*.

Abstract in *Resources in Education*, May 1978, p. 62.

Microfiche. [Arlington, Va., ERIC Document Reproduction Service; prepared for Educational Resources Information Center, National Institute of Education, 1978] 1 sheet.

DLC-Micro ED147855

914

Report of the AID remote sensing team. [Washington, U.S. Agency for International Development], 1975. 1 v. (various pagings)

A review of remote sensing projects in Africa.

Examined in the Development Information Center, AID, Washington, D.C.

915

Role of African intellectuals discussed. *In* U.S. *Joint Publications Research Service*. JPRS 75241. [Springfield, Va., National Technical Information Service, 1980] (Sub-Saharan Africa report, no. 2219) p. 10–27.

Translation of article on a roundtable discussion in Paris by francophone African scholars, in *Africa*, Dakar, Jan. 1980, p. 37–46.

Microfiche. [s.l., 1980]

DLC-Micro JPRS 75241

916

Ryan, James G., *and* K. V. Subrahmanyam. An analysis of average annual rainfall zones in the semiarid tropics of India, Africa and Brazil. [Begumpet, Hyderabad, India], International Crops Research Institute for the Semiarid Tropics, [1975] 8 p.

916 (cont.)

Microfiche. [Washington, U.S. Agency for International Development, 1975?] 1 sheet.

DLC-Sci RR PN-AAE-780

917

Scudder, Thayer. What it means to be dammed: the anthropology of large-scale development projects in the tropics and subtropics. Engineering and science, Apr. 1981: 9–15. illus.

T171.C217 1981

Information from the California Institute of Technology indicates that this study was supported in part by the National Science Foundation and the U.S. Agency for International Development.

Includes examples from sub-Saharan Africa.

918

Seyni, Bory. Aim, organization of CASA reported. *In* U.S. *Joint Publications Research Service.* JPRS 72773. [Springfield, Va., National Technical Information Service, 1979] (Translations on Sub-Saharan Africa, no. 2061)

Translation of article on the African Council of Sociologists and Anthropologists, in *Le Sahel*, Niamey, Jan. 5, 1979, p. 3, 8.

Microfiche. [Washington, Supt. of Docs., U.S. Govt. Print. Off., 1979]

DLC-Micro JPRS 72773

919

Thompson-Clewry, Pamela. Africa regional meeting report, Accra, Ghana, Apr. 11–19, 1976. [Washington?], American Home Economics Association, [1976?] 57 p.

Prepared for the U.S. Agency for International Development.

Examined in the Development Information Center, AID, Washington, D.C.

920

Underwood, Willard A., *and* Ralph E. Ferguson. Changing urbanization trends and human needs in developing African nations. [s.l.], 1976. [17] p.

Prepared for the Western Regional Meeting, World Population Society, 1976.

"The purpose of this paper is to analyse the increasing migration of African tribal members to urban centers and the resulting redefinition of cultural norms, social pressures, and human needs." Abstract.

Abstract in *Resources in Education*, Aug. 1976, p. 195.

Microfiche. [Arlington, Va., ERIC Document Reproduction Service; prepared for Educational Resources Information Center, National Institute of Education, 1976] 1 sheet.

DLC-Micro ED121694

921

Von der Mehden, Fred R., and Kim Q. Hill. Area experts' images of African nations; a test of a reputational measurement approach. Houston, Program of Development Studies, Rice University, 1978. 33 p. ([William March Rice University, Houston, Tex.] Program of Development Studies. Discussion paper series, no. 83)   TxHR

Abstract in *A.I.D. Research and Development Abstracts*, Jan. 1979, p. 31.

Issued also in microfiche. [Washington, U.S. Agency for International Development, 1978?] (PN-AAF-005)

922

Wekerle, Anton. Expulsion of aliens in selected French-speaking African countries south of the Sahara. [Washington], Library of Congress, Law Library, Library of Congress, 1975. [18] leaves. (Library of Congress. Law Library. Law Library studies, no. 75-1082 LL)   DLC-LL

Covers Burundi, Guinea, Malagasy Republic, Mali, Rwanda, Senegal, Somalia, and Zaire.

923

———— Guide to the text of the criminal law and criminal procedure codes of Cameroon and Togo. Washington, Library of Congress, 1976. 27 p. (Library of Congress. Law Library. Law Library studies, no. 76-10 LL)   DLC-LL

924

———— Modern African criminal law and procedure codes. *In* U.S. *Library of Congress.* Quarterly journal, v. 35, Oct. 1978: 282–287.

Z881.U49A3 v. 35

Central Africa

925

U.S. *Agency for International Development.* Annual budget submission: Cameroon and Central African Republic. [Washington]

Vol. for 1978 examined in the Development Information Center, AID, Washington, D.C.

926

—— Annual budget submission: USAIDS [sic] Cameroon and Gabon. [Washington]

Vol. for 1979 examined in the Development Information Center, AID, Washington, D.C.

927

—— Annual budget submission: Yaounde. [Washington?]

Covers various AID programs in Cameroon, Central African Republic, and Gabon.

Vol. for 1977 examined in the Development Information Center, AID, Washington, D.C.

928

[U.S. *Central Intelligence Agency*] Rwanda and Burundi. [Washington, 1975] col. map.

G8430 1975.U51

Scale ca. 1 : 1,000,000.
Relief shown by shading.
"Base 502629 6-75."

929

Jellema, B. M. Improvement of cereal production and marketing in the Central African region. Ibadan, International Institute of Tropical Agriculture, 1973. 100 p.   MiEM

Prepared under a U.S. Agency for International Development contract.

930

Jolly, Janice L. W. The mineral industry of other Central African countries. *In* Minerals yearbook, v. 3, 1978–79. [Washington, U.S. Govt. Print. Off., 1981] p. 1077–1084.

TN23.U612   1978–79, v. 3

Prepared by the U.S. Bureau of Mines.

Covers Cameroon, Chad, Central African Republic, Congo, Equatorial Guinea, and São Tomé and Principe.

931

Malékou, Paul. Central Africa problems discussed. *In* U.S. *Joint Publications Research Service.* JPRS 75009. [Springfield, Va., National Technical Information Service, 1980] (Sub-Saharan Africa report, no. 2204) p. 1–5.

Translation of article in *Africa*, Dakar, Dec. 1979, p. 17–19.

Microfiche. [s.l., 1980]

DLC-Micro JPRS 75009

932

Meier, Uwe H. Regional Textbook Center, Yaounde, United Republic of Cameroon; final report, project no. 625-11-691-329. [Yaoundé?, 1976?] [31] leaves. illus.   DLC

On cover: Contract no. AID-afr-C-73-16.

"The Regional Textbook Center was created on August 10, 1961 through an agreement between the Government of the United Republic of Cameroon and U.N.E.S.C.O. for the purpose of publishing, printing and the distribution of textbooks and related educational materials for Central West Africa."—p. [1]

The Center was established to serve Cameroon, Gabon, Chad, and the Central African Empire.

933

Wekerle, Anton. Guide to the text of the criminal law and criminal procedure codes of Burundi, Rwanda, and Zaire. [Washington], Library of Congress, Law Library, 1975. 38 p. (U.S. Library of Congress. Law Library. Law Library studies, no. 75-1 LL)

DLC-LL

Bibliography: p. iv–v.

Burundi

934

U.S. *Agency for International Development*. Annual budget submission: Burundi. Washington, U.S. International Development Cooperation Agency.

Vols. for 1979+ examined in the Development Information Center, AID, Washington, D.C.

935

—— Country development strategy statement: Burundi. [Washington] annual?

Vol. for 1981 examined in the Development Information Center, AID, Washington, D.C.

936

U.S. *Dept. of State*. Post report. Burundi. [Washington?], 1978. [21] p. illus., map.

JX1705.A286 Spec. Format

L.C. has also report issued in 1975.

Note: The "official post report," prepared periodically by most U.S. diplomatic missions in Africa, is primarily intended for the use of U.S. Government employees and their families newly assigned to the post. Background information is given on the geography and climate, politics and government, communications, economic conditions, health and educational facilities, and social life and customs of the country, together with notes on living conditions in the capital.

937

U.S. *Dept. of State. Bureau of Public Affairs*. Background notes. Burundi. [Washington, for sale by the Supt. of Docs., U.S. Govt. Print. Off.], 1980. 4 p. maps. (U.S. Dept. of State. Department of State publication 8084)   G59.U5

L.C. retains only the latest revision.

Note: The *Background Notes* for each country includes information on its people, land, history, government, politics, economy, foreign relations, and on current U.S. policy, together with brief travel notes, a list of principal government officials, and a reading list. Reprints are included in *Africa, Problems and Prospects: A Bibliographic Survey* (entry 18), and in *Countries of the World and Their Leaders*, 5th ed. (Detroit, Gale Research Co., c1979. 1180 p. Gl.C87).

938

U.S. *Dept. of State. Office of the Geographer*. Burundi: administrative divisions. [Washington], 1975. 2 p.

AMAU

"Geographic note GE-135."

939

Achour, Mouloud. Burundi described by Algerian journalist. *In* U.S. *Joint Publications Research Service*. JPRS 74295. [Springfield, Va., National Technical Information Service, 1979] (Sub-Saharan Africa report, no. 2159) p. 34–41.

Translation of article in *el Moudjahid*, Algiers, Aug. 9–11, 1979.

Microfiche. [Washington, Supt. of Docs., U.S. Govt. Print. Off., 1979]

DLC-Micro JPRS 74295

940

Africa: Burundi. Selected statistical data by sex. Washington, 1981. 31, 17 p.   DLC

Study supported by the U.S. Agency for International Development's Office of Women in Development and Office of Population.

Data assembled by the International Demographic Data Center, U.S. Bureau of the Census.

Among the tables, all based on 1970–71 data, are the following: unadjusted population by age and sex; population by province; life expectancy; population by marital status, age, and sex; number of households; number of economically active persons by age, sex, and urban/rural residence; economically active population by occupation status, sex, and urban/rural residence.

941

Arnould, Eric J. Draft environment profile of Burundi. [Tucson, Arid Lands Information Center, Office of Arid Lands Studies, University of Arizona], 1981. 157 p. illus., maps.   DLC

On cover: "AID RSSA SA/TOA 1-77 National Park Service Contract No. CX-0001-0-0003 with the U.S. Man and the Biosphere Secretariat, Department of State, Washington, D.C."

941a

Burundi health sector assessment and strategy, [by] John Kennedy [et al.] [s.l.], Dimpex Associates, inc., 1981. 288 p.

Prepared for the U.S. Agency for International Development under contract AID/afr-C-1701.

Issued also in French.

Abstract in *A.I.D. Research & Development Abstracts*, v. 10, no. 1/2, 1982, p. 46–47.

942

Chrétien, Jean-Pierre. Dialogue between authorities and rural masses. *In* U.S. *Joint Publications Research Service.* JPRS 68680. [Springfield, Va., National Technical Information Service, 1977] (Translations on Sub-Saharan Africa, no. 171) p. 4–9.

Translation of article in *Le Monde diplomatique*, Paris, Dec. 1976, p. 17.

Microfiche. [s.l., 1977]

DLC-Micro JPRS 68680

943

Decraene, Philippe. President Bagaza speaks about inter-African, international relations. *In* U.S. *Joint Publications Research Service.* JPRS 71662. [Springfield, Va, National Technical Information Service, 1978] (Translations on Sub-Saharan Africa, no. 1976) p. 12–16.

Translation of interview with Jean-Baptiste Bagaza, in *Le Monde diplomatique*, Paris, July 1978, p. 21, 23.

Microfiche. [Washington, Supt. of Docs., U.S. Govt. Print. Off., 1978]

DLC-Micro JPRS 71662

944

Foreign economic trends and their implications for the United States. Burundi. 1969+ Washington, for sale by the Supt. of Docs., U.S. Govt. Print. Off. annual. (International marketing information series) HC10.E416

Prepared by the U.S. Embassy, Bujumbura.

Vols. for 1969–77 distributed by the U.S. Bureau of International Commerce; vol. for 1978 by the U.S. Industry and Trade Administration; vols. for 1979 (i.e., FET 80-002)– by the U.S. International Trade Administration.

The following issues for the period 1973–81 have been identified in L.C.:

ET 73-044. 1973. 10 p.
ET 74-091. 1974. 9 p.
FET 75-042. 1975. 7 p.
FET 76-100. 1976. 8 p.
FET 77-111. 1977. 10 p.
FET 78-121. 1978. 5 p.
FET 80-002. 1980. 7 p.
FET 81-061. 1981. 19 p.

945

Mandi, Stanislas. Minister interviewed on provisional census results. *In* U.S. *Joint Publications Research Service.* JPRS 75359. [Springfield, Va., National Technical Information Service, 1980] (Sub-Saharan Africa report, no. 2225) p. 13–24.

Translation of interview with Stanislas Mandi, Minister of the Interior, in *Le Renouveau de Burundi*, Bujumbura, Nov. 12, 14, 1979.

Microfiche. [s.l., 1980]

DLC-Micro JPRS 75359

946

Technical Assistance Information Clearing House. Development assistance programs for Burundi; American Council of Voluntary Agencies for Foreign Service. New York, TAICH, 1974. 11 p.

HC557.B8T4 1974

The Clearing House is operated by the Council under a grant from the U.S. Agency for International Development.

947

—— Development assistance programs of U.S. non-profit organizations: Burundi. [New York] American Council of Voluntary Agencies for Foreign Service, 1979. 15 p. (TAICH country report) HC880.A1T42a

The Council operates the Clearing House under a grant from the U.S. Agency for International Development.

Cameroon

General

948

U.S. *Dept. of State*. Post report. Cameroon. [Washington?], 1975. 20 p. illus., map.

    Source: *Month. Cat.*, 1979, 79-2803.

    For a description of the contents of this publication, see the note to entry 936.

949

U.S. *Dept. of State. Bureau of Public Affairs*. Background notes. Cameroon. [Washington, for sale by the Supt. of Docs., U.S. Govt. Print. Off.] 1980. 6 p. illus., maps. (U.S. Dept. of State. Department of State publication 8010)   G59.U5

    L.C. retains only the latest revision.

    For a description of the contents of this publication, see the note to entry 937.

950

Draft environmental profile on United Republic of Cameroon. Tucson, Arid Lands Information Center, Office of Arid Lands Studies, University of Arizona, 1981. 79 p.   AzU

    Funded by the Office of Science and Technology, U.S. Agency for International Development.

    "National Park Service contract no. CX-0001-00003 in cooperation with U.S. Man and the Biosphere Secretarist, Department of State, Washington, D.C."

    Abstract in *A.I.D. Research & Development Abstracts*, v. 9, no. 4, 1981, p. 42.

    Issued also in microfiche. [Washington, U.S. Agency for International Development, 1981?] 1 sheet.   DLC-Sci RR PN-AAJ-626

Agriculture

951

Christy, Ralph D. Potentials for Cameroon's agriculture in economic development. Baton Rouge,

Unemployment and Underemployment Institute, Southern University and A&M College, [1976] 4, [4] p. (Staff papers series, no. 106-76)

                     HD2139.5.C47

    "International Economic Development Program."

    Bibliography: p. [8].

    Funds for the Institute provided by the U.S. Agency for International Development.

952

DeLancey, Mark W. Cameroon national food policies. [s.l., 1980] 17, xii p. maps.   DLC

    Paper presented at a Symposium on Cameroon Society, U.S. Dept. of State, Washington, D.C., June 11, 1980.

953

Goldman, Richard M. Structure of cocoa farms in the Lekie Division. Cameroon: a physical and financial evaluation. [Ithaca, N.Y., Cornell University] 1975. 150 p.

    Study funded by the U.S. Agency for International Development.

    Bibliography: p. 148–150.

    Thesis (M.S.)—Cornell University.

    Examined in the Development Information Center, AID, Washington, D.C.

954

Hoben, Allen. Social soundness analysis of the West Benoue integrated rural development proposal, and suggestions for alternative interventions in Margui-Wandala. [s.l.], 1976. 73 p. maps.

    Prepared for the U.S. AID Mission to Cameroon.

    Microfiche. [Washington, U.S. Agency for International Development, 1976?] 1 sheet.

               DLC-Sci RR PN-AAE-960

955

Resource inventory of North Cameroon, Africa, [by] Donald H. Fulton [et al.] [Washington?], Soil

955 (cont.)

Conservation Service, U.S. Dept. of Agriculture, [1978?] 189 p. illus., maps (part fold.)   DLC

Issued with the Fonds d'aide et de coopération of France in cooperation with the U.S. Agency for International Development.

Held also by DNAL.

956

Scott, William E. Development in the western highlands, United Republic of Cameroon, for United States Agency for International Development, Office of Agricultural and Rural Development, Cameroon. [Yaoundé?], 1980. [93] p. (in various pagings) maps.   DLC

Includes bibliography.

957

Scott, William E., *and* Miriam G. Mahaffey. Executive summary: agricultural marketing in the Northwest Province, United Republic of Cameroon. [Yaounde?], Office of Agricultural & Rural Development, U.S.A.I.D./Cameroon, 1980. [90] p. (in various pagings) maps.   DLC

958

A study of the development of the University Center for Agriculture at Dschang, Cameroon: agricultural manpower needs assessment and implications for participatory development, [by] Larry Busch [et al.] [Ithaca, N.Y.], Dept. of Agricultural Economics, Cornell University, 1979. 100 p.

Study conducted at the request of the U.S. Agency for International Development by the Rural Development Committee, Cornell University, in cooperation with the Ecole nationale supérieure agronomique, Cameroon.

Abstract in *A.I.D. Research and Development Abstracts*, v. 9, no. 3, 1981, p. 1.

Microfiche. [Washington, U.S. Agency for International Development, 1979?] 2 sheets.
DLC-Sci RR PN-AAH-055

959

University of Yaoundé. *National Advanced School of Agriculture.* Program of work: Southern University AID contract Afr-750. Yaoundé, 1973. 34 leaves.   HD1410.6.C27U54 1973

"The Department of Rural Economy was established in May 1971, at the National Advanced School of Agriculture (NASA), by Southern University (SU)/Cameroon Project acting under Contract Agreement effective November 4, 1970, between the Government of the United Republic of Cameroon and the United States Government, through the Agency for International Development (AID)."—p. [1].

960

Watts, Sherry R. The Mandara Mountains market system; report on the agricultural crops and traditional markets of the Mandara Mountains region. [Yaoundé?], 1979. 131 p.

Prepared for the U.S. AID Mission to Cameroon.

In English or French.

Microfiche. [Washington, U.S. Agency for International Development, 1979?] 2 sheets (PN-AAH-438); examined in the Development Information Center, Agency for International Development, Washington, D.C.

Assistance Programs

961

U.S. *Agency for International Development.* Annual budget submission: Cameroon. Washington, U.S. International Development Cooperation Agency.

Vols. for 1980+ examined in the Development Information Center, AID, Washington, D.C.

962

——— Country development strategy statement: Cameroon. Washington, U.S. International Development Cooperation Agency. annual.

Vols. for 1981+ examined in the Development Information Center, AID, Washington, D.C.

Abstract of 1981 vol. in *Government Reports Announcements & Index*, Oct. 12, 1979, p. 32.

Vol. for 1981 issued in microfiche. [Springfield, Va., National Technical Information Service, 1979] 1 sheet.   DLC-Sci RR PB298120

963

U.S. *Peace Corps. Cameroon.* Peace Corps volunteer health manual. [Yaoundé], Peace Corps, 1978. 50 p.
DPC

964

Cameroon. [*Treaties, etc. United States, 1978 May 18*] Project grant agreement between the United Republic of Cameroon and the United States of America for North Cameroon livestock and agriculture development. Accord de subvention au projet entre la République unie du Cameroun et les Etat-Unis d'Amerique pour le projet de développement intégre de l'élevage et de l'agriculture au Nord-Cameroun. *In* U.S. *Treaties.* United States treaties and other international agreements, v. 30, 1978–79. [Washington, Dept. of State; for sale by the Supt. of Docs., U.S. Govt. Print. Off., 1981] p. 4547–4568. ([Treaties and other international acts series, 9477])   JX231.A34 v. 30

964 (cont.)

A U.S. Agency for International Development grant; signed at Yaoundé May 18, 1978.

965

Cameroon. [*Treaties, etc. United States, 1978 Aug. 30*] Project loan agreement between the United Republic of Cameroon and the United States of America for Transcameroon Railroad III (Douala to Edea and Mandjab Station). Accord de prêt pour projet entre la République unie du Cameroun et les Etat-Unis d'Amerique pour Transcamerounais III (Douala-Edea et Gare Mandjab) *In* U.S. *Treaties, etc.* United States treaties and other international agreements, v. 30, 1978–79 [Washington, Dept. of State; for sale by the Supt. of Docs., U.S. Govt. Print. Off., 1981] p. 5031–5053. ([Treaties and other international acts series, 9497])

JX231.A34 v. 30

Concerns a U.S. Agency for International Development project.

966

Cameroon. [*Treaties, etc. United States, 1980 June 19*]. International military education and training (IMET). Agreement between the United States of America and Cameroon effected by exchange of notes dated at Yaounde March 3 and June 19, 1980. [Washington, Dept. of State; for sale by the Supt. of Docs., U.S. Govt. Print. Off., 1981] 4 p. (Treaties and other international acts series, 9862)

DLC

Concerns the "provision of training related to defense articles under the United States International Military Education and Training Program."

967

Cummings, Deborah. International technical assistance in Cameroun [*sic*] Yaoundé, U.S. Peace Corps, 1973. 39 p. map. DPC

968

Fikry, Mona, *and* François Tchala-Abina. People and water: social soundness analysis for the Mandara Mountains Water Resources Project for USAID-Yaoundé. [Yaoundé?], 1978. 71 leaves. maps.

Bibliography: p. 69–71.

Examined in the Documentation Center, Sahel Development Program, Agency for International Development, Washington, D.C.

969

Mahon, Dean. Peace Corps volunteers in cooperative development in Cameroon: mid-service conference. [Yaoundé, U.S. Peace Corps], 1977. 28 p.

DPC

970

Novick, Gary. Peace Corps volunteers in Cameroon inland fisheries: mid-service conference. [Yaoundé, U.S. Peace Corps] 1977. 16 p. DPC

971

Technical Assistance Information Clearing House. Development assistance programs of U.S. non-profit organizations: Cameroon. [New York], American Council of Voluntary Agencies for Foreign Service, 1977. 19 p. (TAICH country report) HC557.C3R4a

The Council operates the Clearing House under a grant from the U.S. Agency for International Development.

971a

Vlinski, C. A. Capital saving technology in the U.S. foreign assistance program in Cameroon; a field survey. [s.l.], 1980. 37 p.

Prepared for the U.S. Agency for International Development under contract AID/afr-C-1618.

Abstract in *A.I.D. Research & Development Abstracts*, v. 10, no. 1/2, 1982, p. 23–24.

Commerce

972

Market share reports. Country series: Cameroon, 1971–75 [Washington], U.S. Dept. of Commerce; for sale by the National Technical Information Service, Springfield, Va., [1977] 62 p.

Indicates the United States share of the market in Cameroon for various products compared to the shares for Belgium-Luxemburg, France, Federal Republic of Germany, Great Britain, Italy, Netherlands, Sweden, and Japan.

Microfiche. [Washington, Congressional Information Service, 1977?]

DLC-Micro ASI:77 2016-1.40

973

Market share reports. Country series: Cameroon, 1975–79. [Washington] International Trade Administration, U.S. Dept. of Commerce; for sale by the National Technical Information Service, Springfield, Va., [1979] 66 p.

Includes same comparative data as in *Market Share Reports. Country Series: Cameroon, 1971–75* (entry 972).

Microfiche. [Washington, Congressional Information Service, 1979?]

DLC-Micro ASI: 81 2046.2.37

974

Michelini, Philip. Marketing in Cameroon. [Wash-

974 (cont.)
ington] U.S. Dept. of Commerce, Domestic and International Business Administration; [for sale by the Supt. of Docs., U.S. Govt. Print. Off.], 1977. 25 p. (Overseas business reports. OBR 77-48)

HF91.U482 1977, no. 48
International marketing information series.

Superseded by the author's *Marketing in Cameroon* (Overseas business reports. OBR 80-26; entry 975).

Issued also in microfiche. [Washington, Congressional Information Service, 1977?] 1 sheet.

DLC-Micro ASI:77 2026-5.52

975
———— Marketing in Cameroon. [Washington], U.S. Dept. of Commerce, International Trade Administration; [for sale by the Supt. of Docs., U.S. Govt. Print. Off.] 1980. 33 p. (Overseas business reports. OBR 80-26)   HF91.U482   1980, no. 26
International marketing information series.

Supersedes the author's *Marketing in Cameroon* (Overseas business reports. OBR 77-48; entry 974).

Issued also in microfiche. [Washington, Congressional Information Service, 1980?]

DLC-Micro ASI: 80 2046-6.21

Economic Conditions

976
Ahidjo, Ahmadou. President outlines fourth development plan. *In* U.S. *Joint Publications Research Service.* JPRS 68023. [Springfield, Va., National Technical Information Service, 1976] (Translations on Sub-Saharan Africa, no. 1681) p. 9–25.

Translation of text of presidential address to the National Assembly recorded in *Cameroon Tribune*, Yaoundé, Aug. 26, 1976, p. 1, 3–5.

Microfiche. [s.l., 1976]

DLC-Micro JPRS 68023

977
Austin, Ralph A. Precolonial and colonial Cameroon: the political economy of development/underdevelopment. [s.l., 1979] 8 leaves. (FAR 22617-N)

Prepared for the Symposium on Cameroon Politics, sponsored by the U.S. Dept. of State, July 1975.

Examined in the former Foreign Affairs Research Documentation Center, U.S. Dept. of State.

978
Bolap, Henry P., *and* Essola N. Bidjeck. Douala port expansion planned to meet current, future needs. *In* U.S. *Joint Publications Research Service.* JPRS

68329. [Springfield, Va., National Technical Information Service, 1976] (Translations on Sub-Saharan Africa, no. 1694) p. 7–10.

Translation of article in *Cameroon Tribune*, Yaoundé, Oct. 24–25, 1976, p. 7.

Microfiche. [s.l., 1976]

DLC-Micro JPRS 68329

979
Bryson, Judy C. Women and economic development in Cameroon. [Washington?, Agency for International Development?], 1979. 153 p. map.

HQ1809.5.B79
"Prepared under Contract no. RDO 78/8 with USAID/Yaounde."

Annotated bibliography: p. 95–147.

980
Clignet, Remi, *and* Joyce Sween. Some prerequisties to the planning of modernization processes. [s.l., 1975] 55 leaves. (FAR 23009-N)

Research in West Cameroon supported by the U.S. National Institute of Mental Health.

Examined in the former Foreign Affairs Research Documentation Center. U.S. Dept. of State.

981
Ekoola, Jean–Paul. Expansion of Douala port half completed; details given. *In* U.S. *Joint Publications Research Service.* JPRS 71743. [Springfield, Va., National Technical Information Service, 1978] (Translations on Sub-Saharan Africa, no. 1982) p. 6–10.

Translation of article in *Cameroon Tribune*, Yaoundé, June 18/19, 1978, p. 3.

Microfiche. [Washington, Supt. of Docs., U.S. Govt. Print. Off., 1978]

DLC-Micro JPRS 71743

982
Foreign economic trends and their implications for the United States. Cameroon. 1969+ Washington, for sale by the Supt. of Docs., U.S. Govt. Print. Off. annual. (International marketing information series)

HC10.E416
Prepared by the U.S. Embassy, Yaoundé.

Vols. for 1969–78 distributed by the U.S. Bureau of International Commerce; vols. for 1978–79 by the U.S. Industry and Trade Administration; vols. for 1981–   by the U.S. International Trade Administration.

Not published in 1974.

The following issues for the period 1973–81 have been identified in L.C.:

ET 73-125. 1973. 10 p.

ET 75-027. 1975. 10 p.

FET 76-005. 1976. 9 p.

982 (cont.)
    FET 77-012. 1977. 9 p.
    FET 78-001. 1978. 10 p.
    FET 79-001. 1979. 11 p.
    FET 79-129. 1979. 11 p.
    FET 81-010. 1981. 14 p.

983
Kebzabo, Saleh. Finance minister interviewed on national economy. *In* U.S. *Joint Publications Research Service*. JPRS 73005. [Springfield, Va., National Technical Information Service, 1979] (Translations on Sub-Saharan Africa, no. 2075) p. 33–36.

    Translation of interview with Marcel Yonde, Minister of Finance, in *Demain l'Afrique*, Paris, Jan. 29, 1979, p. 48–50.

    Microfiche. [Washington, Supt. of Docs., U.S. Govt. Print. Off., 1979]

                 DLC-Micro JPRS 73005

984
Mundi, E. K. Construction and building materials industry in the United Republic of Cameroon. [Vienna?], United Nations Industrial Development Organization, [1978?] 20 p.

    Prepared for the International Forum on Appropriate Industrial Technology, New Delhi/Anand, India, Nov. 20–30, 1978. Workshop Group No. 5, Appropriate Technology for the Production of Cement and Building Materials.

    Abstract in *Government Reports Announcements & Index*, Sept. 28, 1979, p. 25.

    Microfiche. [Springfield, Va., National Technical Information Service, 1979] 1 sheet.

                 DLC-Sci RR PB-297258

985
Pabum, Anthony S. Engle's law: the case of Cameroon, West Africa. Baton Rouge, La., Southern University and A & M College, [1976] 12, [3] p.

                 HC557.C33C626

    Prepared as part of the activities of the University's Unemployment and Underemployment Institute, funded by the U.S. Agency for International Development.

    At head of title: International Economic Development Program. Series no. 146–76.

    Issued also in microfiche. [Washington, U.S. Agency for International Development, 1976?] 1 sheet.   DLC-Sci RR PN-AAE-512

Geography and Maps

986
[U.S. *Central Intelligence Agency*] Cameroon. [Washington, 1975] col. map.   G8730   1975.U5

Scale ca. 1 : 6,000,000.
"502437 2-75."

987
———— Cameroon. [Washington, 1975] col. map.
                 G8730   1975.U51
Scale ca. 1 : 6,000,000.
Relief shown by shading.
"502438 2-75."

Health and Nutrition

988
Catholic Relief Services. Basic rural health education/community health system in Cameroon: quarterly report. [Yaoundé?]

    Prepared for the U.S. Agency for International Development.

    Title supplied from "Bibliographic imput sheet."

    Report for Apr./June 1976 issued in microfiche. [Washington, U.S. Agency for International Development, 1976?] 1 sheet.

              DLC-Sci RR PN-AAF-372

989
Henn, Albert E. Planning for project re-review: University Center for Health Services, Yaoundé, Cameroun. [Washington?], American Public Health Services, Yaoundé, Cameroun. [Washington?], American Public Health Association, [1973?] [10] leaves.   DLC

    Prepared for the U.S. Agency for International Development under contract no. AID/csd 2604.

990
United Republic of Cameroon national nutrition survey, undertaken by the Government of Cameroon: final report. [Washington, Office of Nutrition, Agency for International Development], 1978. 387 p. maps.

    Prepared with the assistance of the UCLA Nutrition Assessment Unit, Division of Population, Family and International Health, School of Public Health, University of California, Los Angeles, in cooperation with the U.S. Agency for International Development.

    Bibliography: p. 382–387.

    Abstract in *A.I.D. Research and Development Abstracts*, v. 7, no. 3, 1980, p. 7.

    Microfiche. [Washington, U.S. Agency for International Development, 1978?] 5 sheets (DLC-Sci RR PN-AAG-664); and [Washington, Congressional Information Service, 1978?] 5 sheets (DLC-Micro ASI:80 7206-8.6).

991

University Center for Health Sciences, Yaounde, Cameroon: evaluation. [by] Herman L. Myers [et al.] [s.l.] 1977. 50 p.

Prepared for the U.S. Agency for International Development.

Examined in the Development Information Center, AID, Washington, D.C.

Politics and Government

992

Ahidjo, Amadou. President speaks out against fraud, corruption. *In* U.S. *Joint Publications Research Service*. JPRS 72764. [Springfield, Va., National Technical Information Service, 1979] (Translations on Sub-Saharan Africa, no. 2060) p. 7–11.

Translation of President's speech of Dec. 31, 1978 reported in *Cameroon Tribune*, Yaoundé, Jan. 1–2, 1979, p. 3.

Microfiche. [Washington, Supt. of Decs., U.S. Govt. Print. Off., 1979]

DLC-Micro JPRS 72764

993

DeLancey, Mark W. Federation and unity in Cameroon: ethnocentrism and integration in western Cameroon: [s.l.], 1975. 32 leaves. (FAR 22619-S)

Prepared for the Symposium on Cameroon Politics, sponsored by the U.S. Dept. of State, July 1975.

Examined in the former Foreign Affairs Research Documentation Center, U.S. Dept. of State.

994

Johnson, Willard R. Historical political development of Cameroon: enduring legacies and persistent patterns. [s.l., 1980?] 11 leaves. DLC

On cover: "Prepared for the State Department Colloquium on Cameroon, June 11, 1980."

995

Kofele-Kale, Ndiva. Cameroon's foreign relations. [s.l., 1980?] 26 p. DLC

Paper prepared for the U.S. Dept. of State.

On cover: "Prepared for delivery at the Colloquium on Cameroon for Ambassador Hume Horan, Department of State, Washington, D.C. June 11, 1980."

996

LeVine, Victor T. Cameroon politics in comparative perspective. [s.l., 1975] 7 leaves. (FAR 22588-S)

Presented at the Symposium on Cameroon Politics, sponsored by the U.S. Dept. of State, 1975.

Examined in the former Foreign Affairs Research Documentation Center, U.S. Dept. of State.

997

—— Perspectives on contemporary politics in Cameroon. [s.l., 1980?] [14] leaves. DLC

Paper prepared for the U.S. Dept. of State.

On cover: "Briefing for Ambassador-Designate Hume Horan, at the Department of State, Washington, D.C., June 11, 1980."

998

Shillinglaw, G. M. Role, structure, and functioning of the Department of Cooperation and Mutuality. [s.l.], Experience, inc., 1979. 82 p.

Microfiche. [Washington, U.S. Agency for international Development, 1979?] 1 sheet. (PN-AAH-495); examined in the Development Information Center, AID, Washington, D.C.

999

Weiss, Danielle. Premier notes nation's political, economic prospects. *In* U.S. *Joint Publications Research Service*. JPRS 66570. [Springfield, Va., National Technical Information Service, 1976] (Translations on Sub-Saharan Africa, no. 1633) p. 19–27.

Translation of interview with Paul Biya, Prime Minister, in *Europe Outremer*, Paris, Sept. 1975, p. 14–18.

Microfiche. [s.l., 1976]

DLC-Micro JPRS 66570

Population Studies

1000

Africa: Cameroon. Selected statistical data by sex. Washington, 1981. 31, 17 p. DLC

Study supported by the U.S. Agency for International Development's Office of Women in Development and Office of Population.

Data assembled by the International Demographic Data Center, U.S. Bureau of the Census.

Among the tables, all based on 1976 data, are the following: unadjusted population by age, sex, and urban/rural residence; population by province, sex, and urban/rural residence; population by nationality, sex, and urban/rural residence; life expectancy; urban and rural populations by marital status, age, and sex; number of households; number of literate persons by age, sex, and urban/rural residence; number of persons enrolled in school by age, sex, and urban/rural residence; and economically active population by occupational status, sex, and urban/rural residence.

1001

Clignet, Remi, *and* Joyce Sween. Plural marriage and family planning in West Cameroon. [s.l., 1978] [76] leaves. (FAR 23034-N)

Research supported by the National Institute of Mental Health.

Examined in the former Foreign Affairs Research Documentation Center, U.S. Dept. of State.

1002

———— Urbanization, plural marriage, and family size in two African cities. American ethnologist, v. 1, no. 1, May 1974: 221–242.

GN1.A53   1974

Research supported by a grant from the National Institute of Mental Health.

Analysis based on materials included in the census of Douala and Yaoundé.

1003

Gwan, Emmanuel A. Types, processes, and policy implications of various migrations in Western Cameroon. *In* The Dynamics of migration: internal migration and fertility; investigators: Emmanuel Achu Gwan [and others] Washington, Interdisciplinary Communications Program, Smithsonian Institution, 1976. (Interdisciplinary communications program. Occasional monograph series, no. 5 v. 1) p. 1–40.   HB1951.D96

"ICP work agreement reports."

Bibliography: p. 36–40.

Prepared for the U.S. Agency for International Development under contract AID/csd-3598.

Issued also in microfiche. [Washington, U.S. Agency for International Development, 1976?] 4 sheets.   DLC-Sci RR PN-AAG-398

1004

Mitchell, Joseph R., *and* Saul Helfenbein. Project design for a reproductive health program in Cameroon. [Washington?], American Public Health Association, [1978] 111 p.

Supported by the Office of Population, U.S. Agency for International Development, under contract AID/pha/C-1100.

Concerns family planning.

Microfiche. [Washington, U.S. Agency for International Development, 1978?] 2 sheets.

DLC-Sci RR PN-AAF-497

1005

Profiles of Sahelian countries: Cameroon. Washington, Socio-Economic Analysis Staff, International Statistical Programs Center, U.S. Bureau of the Census, 1974. [41] leaves (in various foliations)

Prepared at the request of the U.S. Agency for International Development.

Concerns demographic projections.

Examined in the Documentation Center, Sahel Development Program, AID, Washington, D.C.

1006

Schor, Sigmund. Consultant report on publication of census data, Government of Cameroon. [Washington?], American Public Health Association, 1977. 72 p.

Prepared for the U.S. Agency for International Development.

In English and French.

Examined in the Development Information Center, AID, Washington, D.C.

Refugees

1007

Bandolo, Henri. Cameroon faces burden of providing for Chadian refugees. *In* U.S. *Joint Publications Research Service.* JPRS 77115. [Springfield, Va., National Technical Information Service, 1981] (Sub-Saharan Africa report, no. 2340) p. 9–12.

Translation of article in *Africa*, Dakar, Nov. 1980, p. 20–21.

Microfiche. [s.l., 1981]

DLC-Micro JPRS 77115

1008

Ebongue, Ebwele. Situation of Chadian refugees in Cameroon explored. *In* U.S. *Joint Publications Research Service.* JPRS 76932. [Springfield, Va., National Technical Information Service, 1980] (Sub-Saharan Africa report, no. 2328) p. 13–19.

Translation of article in *Cameroon Tribune*, Yaoundé, Sept. 3, 4, 5, 1980.

Microfiche. [s.l., 1980]

DLC-Micro JPRS 76932

Other Subjects

1009

U.S. *Agency for International Development. Office of Housing.* Cameroon shelter sector analysis. [Washington], 1974. 96 p.

Microfiche. [Washington, U.S. Agency for International Development, 1974?] 2 sheets.

DLC-Sci RR PN-AAB-514

1010

U.S. *Information Agency. Research Service.* Preliminary audience estimate for Cameroon. [Washington?] 1976. [2] leaves.   DLC

"Research memorandum M-7-76."

1010 (cont.)

An estimate of the audience for Voice of America broadcasts.

1011

——— VOA audience estimate for urban Cameroon, 1974. [Washington?], 1976. 25 p.   DLC "E-22-76."

Issued also in microfiche. [Washington, Congressional Information Service, 1976?] 1 sheet.

DLC-Micro ASI: 77 9856-2.63

1012

Armed forces celebrate 20th anniversary. *In* U.S. *Joint Publications Research Service.* JPRS 76157. [Springfield, Va., National Technical Information Service, 1980] (Sub-Saharan Africa report, no. 2274) p. 17–33.

Translation of article in *Afrique défense*, Paris, June 1980, p. 68, 70–71, 76–78.

Microfiche. [s.l., 1980]

DLC-Micro JPRS 76157

1013

Clignet, Remi, *and* Joyce Sween. Some prerequisites to the planning of modernization processes in rural and urban units: West Cameroon. [s.l., 1975?] [23] leaves. (FAR 23035-N)

Research supported by the National Institute of Mental Health.

Examined in the former Foreign Affairs Research Documentation Center, Dept. of State.

1014

Fleming, A. F., *and* S. R. Lynch. Major causes of anemia in childhood and pregnancy: a report on selected provinces of Cameroon. [Washington], American Public Health Association, 1980. 60 p.

Prepared for the U.S. Agency for International Development.

Microfiche. [Washington, U.S. Agency for International Development, 1980?] 1 sheet (PN-AAJ-237); examined in the Development Information Center, AID, Washington, D.C.

1015

Franklin, Tom. Cameroon: rural water sector—a preliminary study. [Yaoundé?], U.S. AID/Cameroon, 1979. 62 p.

Microfiche. [Washington, U.S. Agency for International Development, 1979?] 1 sheet (PN-AAG-703); examined in the Development Information Center, Agency for International Development, Washington, D.C.

1016

Kendrick, Robin. A survey of labor relations in Cameroon. Ann Arbor, Center for Research on Economic Development, University of Michigan, 1976. 39 p. (Michigan. University. Center for Research on Economic Development. Discussion paper, no. 50)

Bibliography: p. 38–39.

Abstract in *A.I.D. Research and Development Abstracts*, Oct. 1976, p. 21.

Microfiche. [Washington, U.S. Agency for International Development, 1976?] 1 sheet.

DLC-Sci RR PN-AAC-127

1017

Lallez, Raymond. An experiment in the ruralization of education :IPAR and the Cameroonian reform; study prepared for the International Bureau of Education. Paris, Unesco Press, 1974. 113 p. (Experiments and innovations in education, 8)

LC5148.C2L34

Bibliography: p. 110–113.

IPAR: Institut de pédagogie appliquée à vocation rurale.

Abstract in *Resources in Education*, Sept. 1977, p. 131.

Issued also in microfiche. [Arlington, Va., ERIC Document Reproduction Service; prepared for Education Resources Information Center, National Institute of Education, 1977] 2 sheets.

DLC-Micro ED138402

1018

Lowenthal, James B. Report on the Program Design Workshop, Douala, Republique unie du Cameroun, Oct. 21–31, 1975. [s.l.], Associates for Planned Change, inc., 1975. 38 p.

Study conducted under U.S. Agency for International Development contract AID/afr-C-1187.

Examined in the Development Information Center, AID, Washington, D.C.

1019

Nkwi, Paul N., Bayie Kamanda, *and* Saibou Nassourou. Margui-Wandala Division (North Cameroon): an annotated bibliography. Yaoundé, Dept. of Sociology, University of Yaoundé, 1979. 79 p.

60 entries.

Abstract in *A.I.D. Research and Development Abstracts*, Feb. 1981, p. 64.

Microfiche. [Washington, U.S. Agency for International Development, 1979?] 1 sheet.

DLC-Sci RR PN-AAH-469

1020

Steedman, Charles. Cameroon renewable energy: project possibilities; a report to the U.S. Agency for International Development identifying actions

1020 (cont.)

required to develop an assessment of Cameroon's energy needs. Ann Arbor, Mich., 1979. 57 p.

Prepared under contract AID/afr-C-1542.

Emphasis is on solar and wind energy.

Abstract in *A.I.D. Research and Development Abstracts*, v. 8, no. 2, 1980, p. 24.

Microfiche. [Washington, U.S. Agency for International Development, 1979?] 1 sheet.

DLC-Sci RR PN-AAH-100

1021

Sween, Joyce, *and* Remi Clignet. Type of marriage and residential choice in urban Africa. [Chicago?, 1975?] [37] leaves. (FAR 23010-N)

Research supported by a grant from the U.S. Dept. of Health, Education, and Welfare.

Focus is on residential choices of families in Yaoundé.

Examined in the former Foreign Affairs Research Documentation Center, U.S. Dept of State.

1022

Ware, Helen R. E. Language problems in demographic field work in Africa: the case of the Cameroon fertility survey. Voorburg, Netherlands, International Statistical Institute, 1977. 48 p. map.

(International Statistical Institute. Scientific reports, no. 2) HB1075.4.A3W37

Issued in cooperation with the World Fertility Survey, London.

Abstract in *Resources in Education*, Sept. 1978, p. 68.

Issued also in microfiche. [Arlington, Va., ERIC Document Reproduction Service; prepared for Educational Resources Information Center, National Institute of Education, 1978] 1 sheet.

DLC-Sci RR ED153450

1023

Yaounde household and housing characteristics. [Yaoundé], Urban and Rural Lands Development Authority, Ministry of Equipment and Housing, 1978. 154 p. illus.

Prepared in cooperation with USAID Mission to Cameroon.

Abstract in *A.I.D. Research & Development Abstracts*, v. 9, no. 3, 1981, p. 66.

Microfiche. [Washington, U.S. Agency for International Development, 1978?] 2 sheets (PN-AAH-448); held by the Development Information Center, Agency for International Development, Washington, D.C.

Central African Republic

Note: From December 1976 to September 1979 called Central African Empire.

General

1024
U.S. *Dept. of State.* Post report. Central African Republic. [Washington?], 1974. 15 p. illus., map.
JX1705.A286 Spec. Format
For a description of the contents of this publication, see the note to entry 936.

1025
U.S. *Dept. of State. Bureau of Public Affairs.* Background notes. Central African Republic. [Washington, for sale by the Supt. of Docs., U.S. Govt. Print. Off.], 1980. 7 p. illus., maps. (U.S. Dept. of State. Department of State publication 7970)
G59.U5
L.C. retains only the latest revision.
For a description of the contents of this publication, see the note to entry 937.

1026
The Peace Corps in Central African Republic. [Washington, U.S. Govt. Print. Off., 1980] [6] p. illus., map. DLC
"ACTION 4200.76."
An introduction to the country for volunteers.

Assistance Programs

1027
U.S. *Agency for International Development.* Annual budget submission: Central African Republic. [Washington]
Title varies: 1979?–81?, *Annual Budget Submission: Central African Empire.*
On cover, 1979: RDO Yaounde.
Vols. for 1979–80 examined in the Development Information Center, AID, Washington, D.C.

1028
Dougherty, F. M. Central African Republic seed project; report to USAID/Yaounde and AID/W.

[s.l.], Seed Technology Laboratory, Mississippi State University, 1976. 32 p.
Microfiche. [Washington, U.S. Agency for International Development, 1976?] 1 sheet (PN-AAG-407); examined in the Development Information Center, Agency for International Development, Washington, D.C.

1029
Duncan, B. L. Review of Peace Corps fisheries program in the Central African Republic. Auburn, Ala., International Center for Aquaculture, Auburn University, 1975. 16 p.
Sponsored by the U.S. Agency for International Development.
Microfiche. [Washington, U.S. Agency for International Development, 1975?] 1 sheet.
DLC-Sci RR PN-AAF-065

1030
Foreign aid appropriations, 1979. Congressional record, 95th Congress, 2d session, v. 124, Aug. 14, 1978: 25916–25972. J11.R5 v. 124
Remarks in the U.S. House of Representatives, including questions on U.S. assistance to the Central African Empire (p. 25197–25920).

1031
Jeffries, Leonard, *and* Arlene Mitchell. Peace Corps Central African Empire: country program evaluation. [Washington?], 1979. [68] p. DPC
Prepared for the Division of Evaluation, Office of Policy and Planning, Action.

1032
Leiberg, Leon, *and* Paul Smith. Peace Corps Central African Empire: country program evaluation. [Washington?, Social, Educational Research and Development, inc., 1977] [55] p. DPC
Prepared for the Division of Evaluation, Office of Policy and Planning, Action.

1033
Technical Assistance Information Clearing House.

1033 (cont.)

Development assistance programs of U.S. non-profit organizations: Central African Republic. [New York], American Council of Voluntary Agencies for Foreign Service, 1976. 9 p. (TAICH country report)   HC547.C4T43a

The Council operates the Clearing House under a grant from the U.S. Agency for international Development.

Politics and Government

1034

Andresso, Simon. Political agitation, economic problems continuing. *In* U.S. *Joint Publications Research Service.* JPRS 74926. [Springfield, Va., National Technical Information Service, 1980] (Sub-Saharan Africa report, no. 2198) p. 10–13.

Translation of article in *Demain l'Afrique*, Paris, Nov. 1979, p. 40–41.

Microfiche. [s.l., 1980]

DLC-Micro JPRS 74926

1035

Bilinga, Jean. Country seen on way to rehabilitation following Bokassa. *In* U.S. *Joint Publications Research Service.* JPRS 75722. [Springfield, Va., National Technical Information Service, 1980] (Sub-Saharan Africa report, no. 2248) p. 22–33.

Translation of article in *L'Union*, Libreville, Mar. 20–25, 1980.

Microfiche. [s.l., 1980]

DLC-Micro JPRS 75722

1036

Decraene, Philippe. Post-Bokassa political, economic conditions noted. *In* U.S. *Joint Publications Research Service.* JPRS 75474. [Springfield, Va., National Technical Information Service, 1980] (Sub-Saharan Africa report, no. 2233) p. 8–17.

Translation of article in *Le Monde*, Paris, Feb. 23–25, 1980.

Microfiche. [s.l., 1980]

DLC-Micro JPRS 75474

1037

Duquesne, Jacques. France trying to drop Bokassa. *In* U.S. *Joint Publications Research Service.* JPRS 73803. [Springfield, Va., National Technical Information Service, 1979] (Sub-Saharan Africa report, 2128) p. 41–49.

Translation of article in *Le Point*, Paris, May 28, 1979, p. 70–75.

Microfiche. [Washington, Supt. of Docs., U.S. Govt. Print. Off., 1979]

DLC-Micro JPRS 73803

1038

Duteil, Mireille. France trying to get rid of Bokassa, keep CAE as ally. *In* U.S. *Joint Publications Research Service.* JPRS 74413. [Springfield, Va., National Technical Information Service, 1979] (Sub-Saharan Africa report, no. 2167) p. 25–28.

Translation of article in *Demain l'Afrique*, Paris, Sept. 10, 1979, p. 66–67.

CAE: Central African Empire.

Microfiche. [Washington, Supt. of Docs., U.S. Govt. Print. Off., 1979]

DLC-Micro JPRS 74413

1039

Prince George Bokassa discusses explusion from CAE. *In* U.S. *Joint Publications Research Service.* JPRS 72398. [Springfield, Va., National Technical Information Service, 1978] (Translations on Sub-Saharan Africa, no. 2035) p. 17–20.

Translation of interview in *Africa*, Dakar, Nov. 1978, p. 33–35.

CAE: Central African Empire.

Microfiche. [Washington, Supt. of Docs., U.S. Govt. Print. Off., 1978]

DLC-Micro JPRS 72398

Other Subjects

1040

U.S. *Dept. of State. Office of the Geographer.* Central African Empire: new political status for Central African Republic. Washington, 1976. 1 p.

AMAU

"Geographic note GE-165."

1041

U.S. *Peace Corps. Central African Empire.* Fiches d'éducation sanitaire. Bangui, Peace Corps, 1978. 61 p.   DPC

1042

—— Peace Corps volunteer health manual for the Central African Empire. [Bangui?], 1978. 50 p. illus.   DPC

1043

Cordell, Dennis D. A history of the Central African Republic. [Bangui?], Peace Corps, 1975. 27 p.

1044

Barber, Kenneth B., Stuart A. Buchanan, *and* Peter F. Galbreath. An ecological survey of the St. Floris National Park, Central African Republic. Washington, International Park Affairs Division, National Park Service, 1980. 161 p. illus., maps (part fold.)   DLC

1045

Earth Satellite Corporation. Training on satellite imagery and its use in resources development (Central African Republic); final report. [Washington?], 1974. 1 v. (various pagings)

Prepared for the U.S. Agency for International Development under contract AID/afr-C-1051.

Examined in the Development Information Center, AID, Washington, D.C.

1046

Eason, John C., John L. Lucas, *and* Janet Anderson. Feasibility study, rural health delivery service, République centrafricaine. [Washington?], American Public Health Association, 1975. 68 p.

Prepared for the U.S. Agency for International Development under the Development and Evaluation of Integrated Delivery Systems (DEIDS) program.

Microfiche. [Washington, U.S. Agency for International Development, 1975?] 1 sheet.

DLC-Sci RR PN-AAB-564

1047

Foreign economic trends and their implications for the United States. Central African Republic. 1969+ Washington, for sale by the Supt. of Docs., U.S. Govt. Print. Off. annual. (International marketing information series)   HC10.E416

Prepared by the U.S. Embassy, Bangui.

Vols. for 1969–77 distributed by the U.S. Bureau of International Commerce; vols. for 1978–79 by the U.S. Industry and Trade Administration; vols. for 1980– by the U.S. International Trade Administration.

Title varies: 1977–79, *Foreign Economic Trends and Their Implications for the United States. Central African Empire.*

The following issues for the period 1973–80 have been identified in L.C.:

ET 73-081. 1973. 11 p.
ET 74-071. 1974. 13 p.
FET 75-043. 1975. 8 p.
FET 76-042. 1976. 10 p.
FET 77-058. 1977. 11 p.
FET 78-066. 1978. 11 p.
FET 79-052. 1979. 12 p.
FET 80-080. 1980. 12 p.

1048

Marsh, Bruce D. On the origins of the Bangui magnetic anomaly, Central African Empire. Baltimore, Dept. of Earth and Planetary Sciences, Johns Hopkins University, [1977?] 58 p. maps.

"Submitted to the National Aeronautics and Space Administration Center under grant NSG-5090 to The Johns Hopkins University."

Microfiche. [s.l., 1977] 1 sheet.

DLC-Sci RR N77 25703

1049

Our people at the embassy in Bangui. *In* U.S. *Dept. of State.* Newsletter, no. 217, Nov. 1979: 32–35. illus., maps.   JX1.U542   1979

Primarily illustrations of activities of U.S. Embassy personnel.

1050

Regan, R. D. The Bangui magnetic anomaly, Central African Republic; final trip report. [Washington?. 1976?] 25 p. fold. maps in pocket.   DLC

"CAR-1."

"Prepared in cooperation with the National Aeronautics and Space Administration on behalf of the Central African Republic."

1051

Survey of foreign trade in 1976. *In* U.S. *Joint Publications Research Service.* JPRS 70796. [Springfield, Va., National Technical Information Service, 1978] (Translations on Sub-Saharan Africa, no. 1895) p. 10–14.

Translation of article in *Bulletin de l'Afrique noire*, Paris, Feb. 1, 1978, p. 18442–18444.

Microfiche. [Washington, Supt. of Docs., U.S. Govt. Print. Off., 1978]

DLC-Micro JPRS 70796

Congo

General

1052

U.S. *Dept. of State. Bureau of Public Affairs.* Background notes. Congo. [Washington, for sale by the Supt. of Docs., U.S. Govt. Print. Off.], 1980. [4] p. maps. (U.S. Dept. of State. Department of State publication 7986)   G59.U5

    L.C. retains only the latest revision.

    For a description of the contents of this publication, see the note to entry 937.

Agriculture

1053

Dumnov, D., *and* V. Lyusov. Development of agriculture in Congo described. *In* U.S. *Joint Publications Research Service*. JPRS 70364. [Springfield, Va., National Technical Information Service, 1977] (Translations on sub-Saharan Africa, no. 1854) p. 47–54.

    Translation of article in *Ekonomika Sel'skogo Khozyaystva*, Moscow, Sept. 1977, p. 112–115.

    Microfiche. [s.l., 1977]

                 DLC-Micro JPRS 70364

1054

Pre-project assessment of the agriculture and rural development sector in the People's Republic of the Congo. Final report, [by] Gregory N. Hung [et al.] Arlington, Va., Development Associates, 1980. xx, [267] p. (in various pagings) maps.

    Prepared for the U.S. Agency for International Development.

    Bibliography: p. [263–267].

    Abstract in *A.I.D. Research & Development Abstracts*, v. 9, no. 4, p. 6.

    Microfiche. [Washington, U.S. Agency for International Development, 1980?] 4 sheets.

               DLC-Sci RR PN-AAJ-230

Economic Conditions

1055

Conclusions, recommendations of state enterprises meeting. *In* U.S. *Joint Publications Research Service*. JPRS 75418. [Springfield, Va., National Technical Information Service, 1980] (Sub-Saharan Africa report, no. 2228) p. 34–41.

    Translation of article in *Etumba*, Brazzaville, Feb. 14, 1980, p. 4, 6.

    Microfiche. [s.l., 1980]

               DLC-Micro JPRS 75418

1056

Foreign economic trends and their implications for the United States. People's Republic of the Congo. 1978?+ Washington, for sale by the Supt. of Docs., U.S. Govt. Print. Off. annual. (International marketing information series)   HC10.E416

    Prepared by the U.S. Embassy, Brazzaville.

    Vols. for 1978–79 distributed by the U.S. Industry and Trade Administration; vols. for 1981– by the U.S. International Trade Administration.

    The following issues have been identified in L.C.:

    FET 78-123. 1978. 7 p.

    FET 79-128. 1979. 8 p.

    FET 81-019. 1981. 9 p.

1057

Problems confronting various state enterprises noted. *In* U.S. *Joint Publications Research Service*. JPRS 75971. [Springfield, Va., National Technical Information Service, 1980] (Sub-Saharan Africa report, no. 2261) p. 31–35.

    Translation of article in *Mweti*, Brazzaville, May 1, 1980, p. 3.

    Microfiche. [s.l., 1980]

               DLC-Micro JPRS 75971

Finance

1058

Goma, Louis-Sylvain. Premier gives details of budget

1058 (cont.)

for fiscal year 1981. *In* U.S. *Joint Publications Research Service*. JPRS 77115. [Springfield, Va., National Technical Information Service, 1981] (Sub-Saharan Africa report, no. 2340) p. 28–33.

Translation of address by the Prime Minister to the People's National Assembly, recorded in *Etumba*, Brazzaville, Nov. 24, 1980, p. 1, 7, 9.

Microfiche. [s.l., 1981]

DLC-Micro JPRS 77115

1059

Minister of Finance discusses 1979 budget. *In* U.S. *Joint Publications Research Service*. JPRS 72886. [Springfield, Va., National Technical Information Service, 1979] (Translations on Sub-Saharan Africa, no. 2069) p. 11–16.

Translation of interview with Henri Lopes, Minister of Finance, reported in *Etumba*, Brazzaville, Jan. 13, 1979, p. 6, 11.

Microfiche. [Washington, Supt. of Docs., U.S. Govt. Print. Off., 1979]

DLC-Micro JPRS 72886

Politics and Government

1060

Bertrand, Hugues. Regime said to have no choice but to govern by fear. *In* U.S. *Joint Publications Research Service*. JPRS 71230. [Springfield, Va., National Technical Information Service, 1978] (Translations on Sub-Saharan Africa, no. 1940) p. 29–33.

Translation of article in *Le Monde diplomatique*, Paris, Apr. 1978, p. 16.

Microfiche. [Washington, Supt. of Docs., U.S. Govt. Print. Off., 1978]

DLC-Micro JPRS 71230

1061

Debato, Pierre. President plants to accelerate revolutionary process. *In* U.S. *Joint Publications Research Service*. JPRS 74043. [Springfield, Va., National Technical Information Service, 1979] (Sub-Saharan Africa report, no. 2144) p. 16–20.

Translation of interview with President Denis Sassou-Nguesso in *Demain l'Afrique*, Paris, July 2, 1979, p. 33–35.

Microfiche. [Washington, Supt. of Docs., U.S. Govt. Print. Off., 1979]

DLC-Micro JPRS 74043

1062

Gomez Tello, J. L. Revolution expected to move to

center. *In* U.S. *Joint Publications Research Service*. JPRS 69301. [Springfield, Va., National Technical Information Service, 1977] (Translations on Sub-Saharan Africa, no. 1763) p. 16–24.

Translation of article in *Africa*, Madrid, May 1977, p. 2–6.

Microfiche. [s.l., 1977]

DLC-Micro JPRS 69301

1063

Organization, functioning of PCT entities noted. *In* U.S. *Joint Publications Research Service*. JPRS 76157. [Springfield, Va., National Technical Information Service, 1980] (Sub-Saharan Africa report, no. 2274) p. 40–49.

Translation of article on the Parti congolais du travail, in *Etumba*, Brazzaville, June 16, 1980, p. 3, 7–8.

Microfiche. [s.l., 1980]

DLC-Micro JPRS 76157

1064

Ouassa, Miche. President discusses decisions of PCT congress. *In* U.S. *Joint Publications Research Service*. JPRS 75058. [Springfield, Va., National Technical Information Service, 1980] (Sub-Saharan Africa report, no. 2209) p. 8–11.

Translation of interview with President Denis Sassou-Nguesso concerning political and economic issues, in *Ehuza*, Brazzaville, Dec. 14, 1979, p. 3–8.

PCT: Parti congolais du travail.

Microfiche. [s.l., 1980]

DLC-Micro JPRS 75058

1065

Ratsimbazafy, Aristide. Political, economic difficulties citied. *In* U.S. *Joint Publications Research Service*. JPRS 69918. [Springfield, Va., National Technical Information Service, 1977] (Translations on Sub-Saharan Africa, no. 1811) p. 16–19.

Translation of article in *Remarques africaines*, Brussels, July 15/31, 1977, p. 30–31.

Microfiche. [s.l., 1977]

DLC-Micro JPRS 69918

1066

Regime forced to make compromises in radicalizing revolution. *In* U.S. *Joint Publications Research Service*. JPRS 67146. [Springfield, Va., National Technical Information Service, 1976] (Translations on Sub-Saharan Africa, no. 1645) p. 2–10.

Translation of article in *Le Monde*, Paris, Mar. 21/22–23, 1976.

Microfiche. [s.l., 1976]

DLC-Micro JPRS 67146

Other Subjects

1967

U.S. *President, 1974–1977 (Ford)* Withdrawal of designation of the Congo as beneficiary developing country: communication from the President of the United States. Washington, U.S. Govt. Print. Off., 1977. 2 p. ([U.S. Congress. House] 95th Congress, 1st session. House doc. no. 95-59)   DLC-LL
  Issued Jan. 20, 1977.

1068

Final communique of CSC confederal council published. *In* U.S. *Joint Publications Research Research Service*. JPRS 75051. [Springfield, Va., National Technial Information Service, 1980] (Sub-Saharan Africa report, no. 2208) p. 11–16.
  Translation of article on the Confédération syndicate congolaise, in *Etumba*, Brazzaville, Dec. 18, 1979, p. 6, 7.
  Microfiche. [s.l., 1980]
                    DLC-Micro JPRS 75051

1069

[People's Republic of the Congo—diplomatic relations and recognition] *In* Boyd, John A. Digest of United States practice in international law. 1977. [Washington], Office of the Legal Adviser, Dept. of State; [for sale by the Supt. of Docs., U.S. Govt. Print. Off., 1979] (Department of State publication, 8960) p. 21–22.   JX21.R68 1977
  Concerns resumption of full diplomatic relations.

1070

Results of Sendji, Yanga drilling described. *In* U.S. *Joint Publications Research Service*. JPRS 74585. [Springfield, Va., National Technical Information Service, 1979] (Sub-Saharan Africa report, no. 2178) p. 18–28.
  Translation of article describing petroleum drilling operations off the coast of the Republic of Congo, in *Bulletin quotidien de l'ACI*, Brazzaville, Oct. 5, 1979, p. 5–6.
  Microfiche. [s.l., 1979]
                    DLC-Micro JPRS 74585

Equatorial Guinea

General

1071

U.S. *Dept. of State. Bureau of Public Affairs.* Background notes. Equatorial Guinea. [Washington, for sale by the Supt. of Docs., U.S. Govt. Print. Off.], 1977. 4 p. maps. (U.S. Dept. of State. Department of State publication 8025, rev.)

L.C. retains only the latest revision.

For a description of the contents of this publication, see the note to entry 937.

1072

Chipeaux, Françoise. Conditions following coup d'etat described. *In* U.S. *Joint Publications Research Service.* JPRS 74354. [Springfield, Va., National Technical Information Service, 1979] (Sub-Saharan Africa report, no. 2162) p. 12–22.

Translation of article in *Le Monde*, Paris, Aug. 29, 1979, p. 1, 4.

Microfiche. [Washington, Supt. of Docs., U.S. Govt. Print. Off., 1979]

DLC-Micro JPRS 74354

1073

Emane, Obame, *and* Jean Bilinga. Conditions on eve of twelfth anniversary of independence noted. *In* U.S. *Joint Publications Research Service.* JPRS 76857. [Springfield, Va., National Technical Information Services, 1980] (Sub-Saharan Africa report, no. 2322) p. 5–11.

Translation of article in *L'Union*, Libreville, Oct. 6–8, 10, 11–12, 1980.

Microfiche. [s.l., 1980]

DLC-Micro JPRS 76857

Economic Conditions

1074

Fraguas, Rafael. Nation has resources to become rich in a few years. *In* U.S. *Joint Publications Research Service.* JPRS 75138. [Springfield, Va., National Technical Information Service, 1980] (Sub-Saharan Africa report, no. 2214) p. 35–38.

Translation of article in *El Pais*, Madrid, Dec. 12, 1979, p. 7.

Microfiche. [s.l., 1980]

DLC-Micro JPRS 75138

1075

Nguema, Mba. Economy said to be far from recovery. *In* U.S. *Joint Publications Research Service.* JPRS 75551. [Springfield, Va., National Technical Information Service, 1980] (Sub-Saharan Africa report, no. 2239) p. 14–16.

Translation of article in *L'Union*, Libreville, Feb. 14, 1980, p. 1, 5.

Microfiche. [s.l., 1980]

DLC-Micro JPRS 75551

Foreign Relations

1976

Bilinga, Jean. Soviet, Spanish, Moroccan relations noted. *In* U.S. *Joint Publications Research Service.* JPRS 74789. [Springfield, Va., National Technical Information Service, 1979] (Sub-Saharan Africa report, no. 2191) p. 10–14.

Translation of article on Equatorial Guinea's foreign relations in *L'Union*, Libreville, Oct. 18–21, 1979.

Microfiche. [s.l., 1980]

DLC-Micro JPRS 74789

1077

Dorrego, Juan F. President expresses appreciation for Spanish cooperation. *In* U.S. *Joint Publications Research Service.* JPRS 75884. [Springfield, Va., National Technical Information Service, 1980] (Sub-Saharan Africa report, no. 2257) p. 26–30.

Translation of interview with President Teodoro Obiang Nguema Mbasogo, in *Madrid ABC*, Madrid, Apr. 27, 1980, p. 22–23.

1077 (cont.)

Microfiche. [s.l., 1980]

DLC-Micro JPRS 75884

1078

Thibaut, Jean. Cubans preventing any attempt at rebellion. *In* U.S. *Joint Publications Research Service.* JPRS 71270. [Springfield, Va., National Technical Information Service, 1978] (Translations on Sub-Saharan Africa, no. 1944] p. 56–58.

Translation of article in *France Eurafrique*, Paris, Mar. 1978, p. 21–22.

Microfiche. [Washington, Supt. of Docs., U.S. Govt. Print. Off., 1978]

DLC-Micro JPRS 71270

Human Rights

1079

Ashbrook, John M. Human rights violations: Africa. Congressional record, 95th Congress, 1st session, v. 123, Nov. 4, 1977: 37413-37414.

J11.R5 v. 123

Extension of remarks in the U.S. House of Representatives.

Includes article on Equatorial Guinea from the *Washington Post*.

1080

Heras, Jesus de las. Terror alleged in Equatorial Guinea. *In* U.S. *Joint Publications Research Service.* JPRS 68287. [Springfield, Va., National Technical Information Service, 1976] (Translations on Sub-Saharan Africa, no. 1693) p. 12–20.

Translation of interview with Donato F. Ndongo-Biyongo of ANRD, in *El Pais Semanal*, Madrid, Oct. 24, 1976, p. 7–12.

Microfiche. [s.l., 1976]

DLC-Micro JPRS 68287

1081

McDonald, Larry. Will the human rights advocates condemn slavery. Congressional record, 95th Congress, 1st session, v. 123, Apr. 21, 1977: 11806–11808. J11.R5 v. 123

Extension of remarks in the U.S. House of Representatives.

Includes article from the *Review of the News* on charges by the Anti-Slavery Society for the Protection of Human Rights concerning reports of slavery in Equatorial Guinea.

Politics and Government

1082

Biarnes, Pierre. Survey of political, economic conditions one year after coup. *In* U.S. *Joint Publications Research Service.* JPRS 76526. [Springfield, Va., National Technical Information Service, 1980] (Sub-Saharan Africa report, no. 2300) p. 43–47.

Translation of article in *Le Monde*, Paris, Aug. 20, 1980, p. 7.

Microfiche. [s.l., 1980]

DLC-Micro JPRS 76526

1083

Lagarde, Dominique. Uncertainty exists concerning Mbazogo's program. *In* U.S. *Joint Publications Research Service.* JPRS 74340. [Springfield, Va., National Technical Information Service, 1979] (Sub-Saharan Africa report, no. 2161) p. 18–21.

Translation of article in *Demain l'Afrique*, Paris, Aug. 27, 1979, p. 22, 24.

Microfiche. [Washington, Supt. of Docs., U.S. Govt. Print. Off., 1979]

DLC-Micro JPRS 74340

1084

Sese, Sinori. ANRD organized to combat Machias regime. *In* U.S. *Joint Publications Research Service.* JPRS 67709. [Springfield, Va., National Technical Information Service, 1976] (Translations on Sub-Saharan Africa, no. 1666) p. 16–18.

Translation of article in *Croissance des jeunes nations*, Paris, July/Aug. 1976, p. 11–12.

ANRD: Alianza Nacional de Restauración Democrática.

Microfiche. [s.l., 1976]

DLC-Micro JPRS 67709

Gabon

General

1085

U.S. *Dept. of State.* Post report. Gabon. [Washington, Dept. of State, Publishing Services Division; for sale by the Supt. of Docs., U.S. Govt. Print. Off.] 1980. 12 p. illus., map. (*Its* Department and Foreign Service series, 188)

JX1705.A286 Spec. Format

Department of State publication, 9129.

For a description of the contents of this publication, see the note to entry 936.

1086

U.S. *Dept. of State. Bureau of Public Affairs.* Background notes. Gabon. [Washington, for sale by the Supt. of Docs., U.S. Govt. Print. Off.], 1980. 4 p. illus., maps. (U.S. Dept. of State. Department of State publication, 7968)   G59.U5

L.C. retains only the latest revision.

For a description of the contents of this publication, see the note to entry 937.

Assistance Programs

1087

U.S. *Peace Corps. Gabon.* Peace Corps volunteer health manual for Gabon. [Libreville?] 1978. 50 p. illus.   DPC

1088

Gabon. [*Treaties, etc. United States, 1976 Feb. 21*] Loan agreement (Gabon access roads) between the Government of Gabon and the United States of America. *In* U.S. *Treaties, etc.* United States treaties and other international agreements, v. 28, 1976–77. [Washington, Dept. of State; for sale by the Supt. of Docs., U.S. Govt. Print. Off., 1978] p. 5041–5080. ([Treaties and other international acts series, 8612])   JX231.A34 v. 28

Signed at Libreville Feb. 21, 1976.

Concerns a U.S. Agency for International De-

velopment loan for the construction of roads and bridges.

1089

Hishmeh, Marylinda, Frederick B. Williams, *and* Paul Smith. Peace Corps/Gabon: country program evaluation. [Washington], Social, Educational Research and Development, inc., 1977. [91] leaves (in various foliations)   DPC

Evaluation conducted jointly by the Division of Evaluation, Office of Policy and Planning, Action, and its contractor, Social, Educational Research and Development, inc.

1090

Technical Assistance Information Clearing House. Development assistance programs of U.S. nonprofit organizations: Gabon. [New York], American Council of Voluntary Agencies for Foreign Service, 1978. 9 p. map. (TAICH country report)   DLC

"1st edition."

"Since 1955, the Council has operated the Technical Assistance Information Clearing House under contract with the U.S. Agency for International Development [and its predecessors]."—p. 3.

Commerce

1091

Market share reports. Country series: Gabon, 1971–75. [Washington], U.S. Dept. of Commerce; for sale by the National Technical Information Service, Springfield, Va., [1977] 61 p.

Indicates the United States share of the market in Gabon for various products compared to the shares for Belgium-Luxemburg, France, Federal Republic of Germany, Great Britain, Italy, Netherlands, Sweden, and Japan.

Microfiche. [Washington, Congressional Information Service, 1977?]

DLC-Micro ASI:77 2016-1.51

1092

Market share reports. Country series: Gabon, 1975–79. [Washington], International Trade Administration, U.S. Dept. of Commerce; for sale by the National Technical Information Service, Springfield, Va., [1979] 63 p.

Includes same comparative data as in *Market Share Reports. Country Series: Gabon, 1971–75* (entry 1091).

Microfiche. [Washington, Congressional Information Service, 1979?]

DLC-Micro ASI:81 2046-2.49

1093

Michelini, Philip. Marketing in Gabon. [Washington], U.S. Dept. of Commerce, Domestic and International Business Administration; [for sale by the Supt. of Docs., U.S. Govt. Print. Off.], 1976. 17 p. (Overseas business reports. OBR 76-20)

HF91.U482 1976, no. 20

International marketing information series.

Superseded by the author's *Marketing in Gabon* (Overseas business reports. OBR 78-43; entry 1094).

Abstract in *American Statistics Index*, 1976, Abstracts, p. 168.

Issued also in microfiche. [Washington, Congressional Information Service, 1976?] 1 sheet.

DLC-Micro ASI:76 2026-5.14

1094

——— Marketing in Gabon. [Washington], U.S. Dept. of Commerce, Industry and Trade Administration; [for sale by the Supt. of Docs., U.S. Govt. Print. Off.] 1978. 23 p. map. (Overseas business reports. OBR 78-43)

HF91.U482 1978, no. 43

International marketing information series.

Supersedes the author's *Marketing in Gabon* (Overseas business reports. OBR 76-20; entry 1093).

Economic Conditions

1095

Bongo, Omar. Bongo invites comparison between our economy, others. *In* U.S. *Joint Publications Research Service*. JPRS 75020. [Springfield, Va., National Technical Information Service, 1980] (Sub-Saharan Africa report, no. 2205) p. 26–32.

Translation of speech by President Bongo recorded in *L'Union*, Libreville, Nov. 17–19, 1979, p. 4, 5.

Microfiche. [s.l., 1980]

DLC-Micro JPRS 75020

1096

——— President's speech reviews general economic policy. *In* U.S. *Joint Publications Research Service*. JPRS 72198. [Springfield, Va., National Technical Information Service, 1978] (Translations on Sub-Saharan Africa, no. 2020) p. 15–23.

Translation of speech recorded in *L'Union*, Libreville, Aug. 23, 1978, p. 2–3.

Microfiche. [Washington, Supt. of Docs., U.S. Govt. Print. Off., 1978]

DLC-Micro JPRS 72198

1097

Economic development traceable essentially to oil. *In* U.S. *Joint Publications Research Service*. JPRS 68431. [Springfield, Va., National Technical Information Service, 1976] (Translations on Sub-Saharan Africa, no. 1700) p. 9–56.

Translation of articles in *Europe Outremer*, Paris, May 1976.

Microfiche. [s.l., 1976]

DLC-Micro JPRS 68431

1098

Foreign economic trends and their implications for the United States. Gabon. 1969?+ Washington, for sale by the Supt. of Docs., U.S. Govt. Print Off., annual. (International marketing information series)

HC10.E416

Continues *Economic Trends and Their Implications for the United States. Gabon.*

Prepared by the U.S. Embassy, Libreville.

Vols. for 1969?–78 distributed by the U.S. Bureau of International Commerce; vol. for 1979 by the U.S. Industry and Trade Administration; vols. for 1980– by the U.S. International Trade Administration.

The following issues for the period 1973–80 have been identified in L.C.:

ET 73-005. 1973. 11 p.
ET 74-118. 1974. 11 p.
FET 75-141. 1975. 11 p.
FET 75-141a. 1975. 11 p.
FET 76-126. 1976. 11 p.
FET 78-008. 1978. 10 p.
FET 79-126. 1979. 11 p.
FET 80-098. 1980. 10 p.

1099

Importance of oil to Gabonese economy discussed. *In* U.S. *Joint Publications Research Service*. JPRS 68097. [Springfield, Va., National Technical Information Service, 1976] (Translations on Sub-Saharan Africa, no. 1684) p. 15–18.

Translation of article in *Afrique industrie infrastructures*, Paris, Sept. 1, 1976, p. 29–31.

Microfiche. [s.l., 1976]

DLC-Micro JPRS 68097

1100

Organization of banks reported. *In* U.S. *Joint Publications Research Service.* JPRS 68841. [Springfield, Va., National Technical Information Service, 1977] (Translations on Sub-Saharan Africa, no. 1727) p. 12–16.

Translation of article in *Afrique industrie infrastructures*, Paris, Feb. 15, 1977, p. 69–70.

Microfiche. [s.l., 1977]

DLC-Micro JPRS 68841

Geology, Hydrology, and Mineral Resources

1101

Ampamba-Gouerangue, Paulin. Ore deposits evaluated, expansion planned. *In* U.S. *Joint Publications Research Services.* JPRS 70815. [Springfield, Va., National Technical Information Service, 1978] (Translations on Sub-Saharan Africa, no. 1898) p. 3–6.

Translation of article in *Afrique industrie infrastructures*, Paris, Jan. 15, 1978, p. 40–41.

Microfiche. [Washington, Supt. of Docs., U.S. Govt. Print. Off., 1978]

DLC-Micro JPRS 70815

The following items (entries 1102–1108) are listed in chronological order:

1102

Stipp, Henry E. The mineral industry of Gabon. *In* Minerals yearbook, v. 3, 1973. [Washington, for sale by the Supt. of Docs., U.S. Govt. Print. Off., 1976) p. 317–320.   TN23.U612   1973, v. 3

Prepared by the U.S. Bureau of Mines.

1103

Jolly, Janice L. W. The mineral industry of Gabon. *In* Minerals yearbook, v. 3, 1974. [Washington, for sale by the Supt. of Docs., U.S. Govt. Print. Off., 1977] p. 343–349.   TN23.U612   1974, v. 3

Prepared by the U.S. Bureau of Mines.

1104

———— The mineral industry of Gabon. Minerals yearbook, v. 3, 1975. [Washington, for sale by the Supt. of Docs., U.S. Govt. Print. Off., 1978] p. 393–398.   TN23.U612   1975, v. 3

Prepared by the U.S. Bureau of Mines.

1105

Stevens, Candice. The mineral industry of Gabon. *In* Minerals yearbook, v. 3, 1976. [Washington, for

sale by the Supt. of Docs., U.S. Govt. Print. Off., 1980] p. 411–418.   TN23.U612   1976, v. 3

Prepared by the U.S. Bureau of Mines.

1106

———— The mineral industry of Gabon. *In* Minerals yearbook, v. 3, 1977. [Washington, for sale by the Supt. of Docs., U.S. Govt. Print. Off., 1981] p. 341–346.   TN23.U612   1977, v. 3

Prepared by the U.S. Bureau of Mines.

1107

———— The mineral industry of Gabon. *In* Minerals yearbook, v. 3, 1978–79. [Washington, U.S. Govt. Print. Off., 1981] p. 361–366.

TN23.U612   1978–79, v. 3

Prepared by the U.S. Bureau of Mines.

1108

Clarke, Peter J. The mineral industry of Gabon. *In* Minerals yearbook, v. 3, 1980. [Washington, for sale by the Supt. of Docs., U.S. Govt. Print. Off., 1982] p. 361–368.   TN23.U612   1980, v. 3

Prepared by the U.S. Bureau of Mines.

Politics and Government

1109

Bongo, Omar. Bongo at PDG anniversary reviews accomplishments, mistakes. *In* U.S. *Joint Publications Research Service.* JPRS 73268. [Springfield, Va., National Technical Information Service, 1979] (Translations on Sub-Saharan Africa, no. 2092)

Translation of speech of President Bongo reported in *L'Union*, Libreville, Mar. 14, 1979, p. 4, 5.

PDG: Parti démocratique gabonais.

Microfiche. [Washington, Supt. of Docs., U.S. Govt. Print. Off., 1979]

DLC-Micro JPRS 73268

1110

Carvalho, Augusto de. Speculation on Gabon's motives towards Sao Tome. *In* U.S. *Joint Publications Research Service.* JPRS 70987. [Springfield, Va., National Technical Information Service, 1978] (Translations on Sub-Saharan Africa, no. 1915) p. 3–6.

Translation of article in *Expresso*, Lisbon, Feb. 25, 1978, p. 4R.

Microfiche. [Washington, Supt. of Docs., U.S. Govt. Print. Off., 1978]

DLC-Micro JPRS 70987

1111

Vermel, Pierre. African roots of PDG as sole party

1111 (cont.)

institution analyzed. *In* U.S. *Joint Publications Research Service.* JPRS 76693. [Springfield, Va., National Technical Information Service, 1980] (Sub-Saharan Africa report, no. 2311) p. 13–18.

Translation of article on the Parti démocratique gabonais in *Le Mois en Afrique*, Paris, Aug–Sept. 1980, p. 11, 13–19.

Microfiche. [s.l., 1980]

DLC-Micro JPRS 76693

Other Subjects

1112

U.S. *Agency for International Development. Office of Housing.* Shelter sector analysis, Gabon, 1973. [Washington], 1973. 135 p. map.

HD7375.9.A3U53   1973

On cover: Gabon shelter sector analysis.

Abstract in *A.I.D. Research and Development Abstracts*, Apr. 1976, p. 12.

Issued also in microfiche. [Washington, U.S. Agency for International Development, 1973?] 2 sheets.   DLC-Sci RR PN-AAB-511

1113

Berger (Louis) inc. Prefeasibility study of the forestry feeder road system associated with the Transgabonese railway: economic and engineering report and annexes [by] Louis Berger International, inc. Abidjan, Ivory Coast; East Orange, N.J., L. Berger International, 1975. 111 leaves in various foliations. illus.   TE229.5.B47   1975

At head of title: United States of America, Agency for International Development.

Includes bibliographical references.

1114

Craddock, John L. Report on tourism strategy; Republic of Gabon. [s.l.], 1974. 1 v. (various pagings)

Prepared for the U.S. Agency for International Development.

Examined in the Development Information Center, AID, Washington, D.C.

1115

Gabon's goal is to satisfy nation's food needs. *In* U.S. *Joint Publications Research Service.* JPRS 66792. [Springfield, Va., National Technical Information Service, 1976] (Translations on Sub-Saharan Africa, no. 1638) p. 16–19.

Translation of interview with Simon Essimengane, Minister of State for Agriculture and Rural Development, in *Afrique agriculture*, Paris, Jan. 1976, p. 42–44.

Microfiche. [s.l., 1976]

DLC-Micro JPRS 66792

1116

Profiles of Sahelian [sic] countries: Gabon. Washington, Socio-Economic Analysis Staff, International Statistical Programs Center, U.S. Bureau of the Census, 1974. [41] leaves (in various foliations)

Prepared at the request of the U.S. Agency for International Development.

Concerns demographic projections.

Examined in the Documentation Center, Sahel Development Program, AID, Washington, D.C.

Rwanda

1117

U.S. *Agency for International Development*. Annual budget submission: Rwanda. Washington, U.S. International Development Cooperation Agency.

Vols. for 1977, 1979+ examined in the Development Information Center, AID, Washington, D.C.

1118

—— Country development strategy statement: Rwanda. Washington, U.S. International Development Cooperation Agency. annual.

Vols. for 1981+ examined in the Development Information Center, AID, Washington, D.C.

1119

U.S. *Agency for International Development. Office of the Foreign Disaster Relief Coordinator*. Case report: Rwanda-floods-crop losses, October, 1974. [3] p. map.   DLC

A summary of U.S. Government disaster relief.

1120

U.S. *Dept. of State*. Post report. Rwanda. [Washington, Dept. of State, Bureau of Administration; for sale by the Supt. of Docs., U.S. Govt. Print. Off.] 1980. 12 p. illus., map. (*Its* Department and Foreign Service series, 172)

JX1705.A286 Spec. Format

Department of the State publication, 8998.

L.C. has also report issued in 1974.

For a description of the contents of this publication, see the note to entry 936.

1121

U.S. *Dept. of State. Bureau of Public Affairs*. Background notes. Rwanda. [Washington, for sale by the Supt. of Docs., U.S. Govt. Print. Off.], 1980. 4 p. illus., maps. (U.S. Dept. of State. Department of State publication 7916)   G59.U5

L.C. retains only the latest revision.

For a description of the contents of this publication, see the note to entry 937.

1122

Africa: Rwanda. Selected statistical data by sex. Washington, 1981. 31, 17 p.

Study supported by the U.S. Agency for International Development's Office of Women in Development and Office of Population.

Data assembled by the International Demographic Data Center, U.S. Bureau of the Census.

Among the tables, all based on 1970 data, are the following: unadjusted population by age, sex, and urban/rural residence; population by province, sex, and urban/rural residence; population by ethnic group, sex, and urban/rural residence; population by religion, sex, and urban/rural residence; life expectancy; urban and rural populations by marital status, age, and sex; number of households; number of economically active persons by age, sex, and urban/rural residence.

1123

Bigelow, Charles D. Integrated economic, social, environmental development; alternatives for tourism in Rwanda. [Menlo Park, Calif., Bigelow Associates], 1973. 64 p. map.

Prepared for the U.S. Agency for International Development under contract AID/CM/AFR-C-73-17.

Microfiche. [Washington, U.S. Agency for International Development, 1973?] 1 sheet.

DLC-Sci RR PN-AAE-729

1124

Burke, Robert, *and* Harry B. Pfost. Design and operation of community grain storages in Rwanda. Manhattan, Food and Feed Grain Institute, Kansas State University, [1976] 57 p. (Grain storage, processing and marketing, research report 11)

DLC

Prepared for the U.S. Agency for International Development under contract AID/ta-C-1162.

1125

Draft environmental profile on Rwanda. [Tucson, Arid Lands Information Center, Office of Arid

1125 (cont.)

Lands Studies, University of Arizona], 1981. 180 p. illus., maps.   DLC

On cover: "AID, Office of Forestry, Environment, and Natural Resources RSSA SA/TOA 1-77 with U.S. Man and the Biosphere Program of Department of State, Washington, D.C., National Park Service Contract No. CX-0001-0-0003."

1126

Food storage and marketing project in Rwanda; monthly report. [Nairobi?], Regional Economic Development Services Office/East Africa, Agency for International Development.

Dec. 1975 issue examined in the Development Information Center. AID, Washington, D.C.

1127

Foreign economic trends and their implications for the United States. Rwanda. 1969+ Washington, for sale by the Supt. of Docs., U.S. Govt. Print. Off. annual (International marketing information series)   HC10.E416

Prepared by the U.S. Embassy, Kigali.

Vols. for 1969–77 (i.e., through FET 78-002) distributed by the U.S. Bureau of International Commerce; vols. for 1978–79 by the U.S. Industry and Trade Administration; vols. for 1980– by the U.S. International Trade Administration.

Apparently not published in 1973.

The following issues for the period 1974–81 have been identified in L.C.:

FET 74-103. 1974. 10 p.
FET 76-131. 1976. 7 p.
FET 78-002. 1978. 8 p.
FET 78-142. 1978. 7 p.
FET 79-125. 1979. 9 p.
FET 80-115. 1980. 12 p.
FET 81-136. 1981. 9 p.

1128

General census decreed. *In* U.S. *Joint Publications Research Service*. JPRS 70287. [Springfield, Va., National Technical Information Service, 1977] (Translations on Sub-Saharan Africa, no. 1845) p. 58–62.

Translation of text of presidential decree, in *Journal officiel de la République rwandaise*, Kigali, Aug. 15, 1977, p. 382–385.

Microfiche. [s.l., 1977]
                                    DLC-Micro JPRS 70287

1128a

A Report on assistance to develop a national maternal and child health and family planning program in Rwanda, [by] W. H. Boyton [et al.] [Washington?] American Public Health Association, 1981. 234 p.

Prepared for the U.S. Agency for International Development.

Abstract in *A.I.D. Research & Development Abstracts*, v. 10, no. 1/2, 1982, p. 62.

1129

Rwanda. [*Treaties, etc. United States, 1974 Dec. 20*] Rwanda; Peace Corps. Agreement effected by exchange of notes signed at Kigali December 20, 1974; entered into force December 20, 1974. *In* U.S. *Treaties, etc.* United States treaties and other international agreements, v. 25, 1974. [Washington, Dept. of State; for sale by the Supt. of Docs., U.S. Govt. Print. Off., 1975] p. 3387–3393. ([Treaties and other international acts series, 7992])
                                    JX231.A34 v. 25

In English and French.

1130

Rwanda. [*Treaties, etc. United States, 1977 Apr. 26*] Rwanda; agricultural commodities: transfers under Title II. Agreement signed at Washington April 26 and 29, 1977; entered into force April 29, 1977. *In* U.S. *Treaties, etc.* United States treaties and other international and other international agreements, v. 29, 1976–77. [Washington, Dept. of State; for sale by the Supt. of Docs., U.S. Govt. Print. Off., 1975] p. 5269–5270. ([Treaties and other international acts series, 9102])   JX231.A34 v. 29

1131

Stallings, James L. A state-of-the-arts paper (SOAP) on techniques of enumeration of intercropping and associated cultivation and livestock numbers and products in subsistance agriculture in LDC's. [Auburn University, Ala., Dept. of Agricultural Economics, Auburn University, 1980] 54 p.

Prepared for the U.S. Agency for International Development under contract AID/afr-C-1607.

Bibliography: p. 51–54.

Emphasis is on Rwanda.

Abstract in *A.I.D. Research & Development Abstracts*, v. 10, no. 1/2, 1982, p. 1.

Microfiche. [Washington, U.S. Agency for International Development, 1980?] 1 sheet (PN-AAH-956); examined in the Development Information Center, AID, Washington, D.C.

1132

Technical Assistance Information Clearing House. Development assistance programs of U.S. non-profit organizations, Rwanda. [New York], American Council of Voluntary Agencies for Foreign Service, 1976. 13 p. map. (TAICH country report)
                                    HC557.R8T42a

The Clearing House operates under a contract with the U.S. Agency for International Development.

São Tomé e Principe

1133

U.S. *Dept. of State. Bureau of Public Affairs.* Background notes. Sao Tome and Principe. [Washington, for sale by the Supt. of Docs., U.S. Govt. Print. Off.] 1978. 4 p. maps. (U.S. Dept. of State. Department of State publication 8871, rev.)

G59.U5

L.C. retains only the latest revision.

For a description of the contents of this publication, see the note to entry 937.

1134

Africa: Sao Tome and Principe. Selected statistical data by sex. Washington, 1981. 31, 17 p.　DLC

Study supported by the U.S. Agency for International Development's Office of Women in Development and Office of Population.

Data assembled by the International Demographic Data Center, U.S. Bureau of the Census.

Among the tables are the following: unadjusted population by age, sex, and urban/rural residence (1960), population by province, sex, and urban/rural residence (1970), infant mortality (1973), and number of persons enrolled in school by sex (1972–73)

1135

Coordinating council, political bureau communiques. *In* U.S. *Joint Publications Research Service.* JPRS 76377. [Springfield, Va., National Technical Information Service, 1980] (Sub-Saharan Africa report, no. 2289) p. 63–66.

Text of communiques issued by the coordinating council and the political bureau of the Movimento de Libertação de São Tomé e Principe, in *Revolução*, São Tomé, June 13, 1980, p. 1, 4.

Microfiche. [s.l., 1980]

DLC-Micro JPRS 76377

1136

Ferreira, Luis A. Da Costa interviewed on Trovoada, foreign relations. *In* U.S. *Joint Publications Research Service.* JPRS 74663. [Springfield, Va.,

National Technical Information Service, 1979] (Sub-Saharan Africa report, no. 2183) p. 122–125.

Translation of interview with President Manuel P. da Costa of São Tomé and Principe concerning the case of former Prime Minister Miguel Trovoada and the country's foreign policy, in *Expresso*, Lisbon, Oct. 27, 1979, p. 6-R.

Microfiche. [s.l., 1979]

DLC-Micro JPRS 74663

1137

———— President voices views on national goals, Cuban assistance. *In* U.S. *Joint Publications Research Service.* JPRS 75884. [Springfield, Va., National Technical Information Service, 1980] (Sub-Saharan Africa report, no. 2257) p. 114–119.

Translation of interview with President Manuel Pinto de Costa, in *O Jornal*, Lisbon, May 16–22, 1980, p. 28.

Microfiche. [s.l., 1980]

DLC-Micro JPRS 75884

1138

Government establishes priorities. *In* U.S. *Joint Publications Research Service.* JPRS 67124. [Springfield, Va., National Technical Information Service, 1976] (Translations on Sub-Saharan Africa, no. 1644) p. 23–28.

Translation of interview with Leonel D'Alva, Minister of Foreign Affairs, in *O Seculo*, Lisbon, Mar. 12, 1976, p. 1, 4.

Microfiche. [s.l., 1976]

DLC-Micro JPRS 67124

1139

Ondo, Ngong, *and* Jean Bilinga. Foreign ties of islands surveyed. *In* U.S. *Joint Publications Research Service.* JPRS 71449. [Springfield, Va., National Technical Information Service, 1978] (Translations on Sub-Saharan Africa, no. 1959) p. 116–118.

Translation of article in *L'Union*, Libreville, Apr. 14, 1978, p. 2.

1139 (cont.)

Microfiche. [Washington, Supt. of Docs., U.S. Govt. Print. Off., 1978]

DLC-Micro JPRS 71449

1140

Regulations of foreign investments published. *In* U.S. *Joint Publications Research Service*. JPRS 76649. [Springfield, Va., National Technical Information Service, 1980] (Sub-Saharan Africa report, no. 2308) p. 85–94.

Translation of text of decrees published in *Diário da República*, São Tomé, Aug. 5, 1980, p. 264–267.

Microfiche. [s.l., 1980]

DLC-Micro JPRS 76649

1141

Report on former Prime Minister's dismissal, arrest. *In* U.S. *Joint Publications Research Service*. JPRS 74563. [Springfield, Va., National Technical Information Service, 1979] (Sub-Saharan Africa report, no. 2176) p. 94–96.

Translation of report on the arrest of Miguel Trovoada, former Prime Minister of São Tomé and Príncipe, in *Journal de Angola*, Luanda, Oct. 18, 1979, p. 1, 6.

Microfiche. [Washington, Supt. of Docs., U.S. Govt. Print. off., 1979]

DLC-Micro JPRS 74563

Zaire

General

1142

U.S. *Dept. of State.* Post report. Zaire. [Washington, Dept. of State, Publishing Service Division; for sale by the Supt. of Docs., U.S. Govt. Print. Off.], 1980. 28 p. illus., maps. (*Its* Department and Foreign Service series, 179)

JX1705.A286 Spec. Format

Department of State publication, 9116.

Includes information on Kinshasa, Bukavu, and Lubumbashi.

L.C. has also report issued in 1977.

For a description of the Contents of this publication, see the note to entry 936.

1143

U.S. *Dept. of State. Bureau of Public Affairs.* Background notes. Zaire. [Washington, for sale by the Supt. of Docs., U.S. Govt. Print. Off.], 1981. 8 p. maps. (U.S. Dept. of State, Department of State publication 7793, rev.) G59.U5

L.C. retains only the latest revision.

For a description of the contents of this publication, see the note to entry 937.

1144

American University, *Washington, D.C. Foreign Area Studies.* Zaire, a country study; edited by Irving Kaplan. 3d ed. Washington; for sale by the Supt. of Docs., U.S. Govt. Print. Off., c1979. xxi, 332 p. illus., maps. (Area handbook series)

DT644.A75 1979

"DA pam 550-67."

Written by H. M. Roth and others.

Bibliography: p. 297–314.

Supersedes the 1971 ed. prepared by Gordon C. McDonald and others, and issued under title: *Area Handbook for the Democratic Republic of the Congo (Congo Kinshasa).*

Issued also in microfiche. [s.l., Defense Documentation Center, 1979] 4 sheets.

DLC-Sci RR AD-A069322

1145

Henderson, Faye. Zaire, a country profile; prepared for the Office of U.S. Foreign Disaster Assistance, Bureau for Private and Development Cooperation, Agency for International Development, Department of State by Evaluation Technologies, Inc., under contract AID/SOD/PDC-C-0284; research and written by Faye Henderson. Washington, The Office, 1981. 65 p., 2 leaves of plates.

DT644.H46.

"July 1981."

"June 1981"—Cover.

Bibliography: p. 62–65.

A general introduction, with emphasis on political structure, population, health and nutrition, economics, agriculture, housing, economic conditions, geography, transportation, power, and communications.

1146

Natali, J. B. Deterioration resulting from Mobutu's despotism described. *In* U.S. *Joint Publications Research Service.* JPRS 75775. [Springfield, Va., National Technical Information Service, 1980] (Sub-Saharan Africa report, no. 2251) p. 113–120.

Translation of article in *Fôlha de São Paulo*, São Paulo, Apr. 13, 1980, p. 18.

Microfiche. [s.l., 1980]

DLC-Micro JPRS 75775

1147

Zaire: a country profile. Arlington, Va., Evaluation Technologies, inc., 1977. 58 leaves. DPC

Prepared for the Office of U.S. Foreign Disaster Assistance, U.S. Agency for International Development.

Agriculture

1148

Cardwell, Lucy, *and* James L. McCabe. Transport cost and other determinants of the intensity of cultivation in rural Zaire. New Haven, Economic

1148 (cont.)
Growth Center, Yale University, 1975. 35 p.
(Center discussion paper, no. 227)

HD2135.5.C37

"Portions of this research were financed by funds provided by the Agency for International Development under contract CSD/2492."

Abstract in *A.I.D. Research and Development Abstracts*, Sept. 1975, p. 17.

Issued also in microfiche. [Washington, U.S. Agency for International Development, 1975?] 1 sheet. DLC-Sci RR PN-AAB-149

1149
Green, H. Albert. An approach for assessing rural development projects. Washington, International Statistical Programs Center, Bureau of the Census, 1976–77. [140] p. (in various pagings)

Pt. 2, "An Illustrative Application," concerns the North Shaba (Zaire) Maize Production Project (58 p.).

Abstract in *A.I.D. Research and Development Abstracts*, July 1977, p. 3.

Microfiche. [Washington, U.S. Agency for International Development, 1977?] 2 sheets.

DLC-Sci RR PN-AAC-951

1150
Harms, Robert. Land tenure and agricultural development in Zaire, 1895–1961. Madison, Land Tenure Center, University of Wisconsin, 1974. 26 p. illus. (Wisconsin. University. Land Tenure Center. LTC, no. 99) HD1001.H37

Bibliography: p. 24–26.

Abstract in *A.I.D. Research and Development Abstracts*, July 1975, p. 30–31.

Issued also in microfiche. [Washington, U.S. Agency for International Development, 1974?] 1 sheet. DLC-Sci RR PN-AAB-065

1151
Lindblad, Carl. Grain storage: report and recommendations for Project North Shaba. Washington, Development Alternatives, 1979. 55 p.

Apparently prepared for the U.S. Agency for International Development.

Issued also in French.

Examined in the Development Information Center, AID, Washington, D.C.

1152
Linsenmeyer, Dean A. An economic analysis of maize production in the Kasai Oriental region of Zaire: a research proposal. East Lansing, Dept. of Agricultural Economics, Michigan State University, 1974. 53 p. maps. (African Rural Employment Research Network. Working paper, no. 2)

Bibliography: p. 49–53.

Microfiche. [Washington, U.S. Agency for International Development, 1974?] 1 sheet.

DLC-Sci RR PN-AAA-882

1153
North Shaba integrated maize production—Zaire—report on "Office des Routes." New York, Frederic R. Harris, inc., 1976. 24 leaves.

Prepared for the U.S. Agency for International Development under contract AID/otr-C-1298.

An analysis of rural road conditions.

Examined in the Development Information Center, AID, Washington, D.C.

1154
Schatzberg, Michael G. Blockage points in Zaire: the flow of budgets, bureaucrats, and beer. *In* Southall, Aidan. Small urban centers in rural development in Africa. Madison, African Studies Program, University of Wisconsin-Madison, 1979. p. 297–312.

Bibliography: p. 310–312.

A grant from the Office of Urban Development, U.S. Agency for International Development, assisted in the preparation for publication of the papers collected in the study.

Microfiche. [Washington, U.S. Agency for International Development, 1980?] (PN-AAJ-064); examined in the Development Information Center, AID, Washington, D.C.

1155
Sorenson, L. Orlo, John R. Pedersen, *and* Norton C. Ives. Maize marketing in Zaire, prepared for Agency for International Development, United States Department of State at the Food and Feed Grain Institute, Kansas State University. Manhattan, Kan., The Institute, 1975. 262 p. illus. (Grain storage, processing and marketing report, no. 51)

HD9049.C8Z347

Bibliography: p. 151–152.

Abstract in *A.I.D. Research and Development Abstracts*, July 1978, p. 10.

Issued also in microfiche. [Washington, U.S. Agency for International Development, 1977?] 3 sheets. DLC-Sci RR PN-AAC-916

1156
Steiner, Herbert H. Zaire ups food imports to offset declining domestic production. Foreign agriculture, Feb. 26, 1979: 8–9. illus.

HD1401.F65 1979

Issued by the U.S. Foreign Agricultural Service.

1157
Stern, Walter A. Zaire to import tobacco even if self-

1157 (cont.)

sufficient. Foreign agriculture, Jan. 20, 1975: 10–11, 14. illus.   HD1401.F65 1975

Issued by the U.S. Foreign Agricultural Service.

1158

Supplying fertilizers for Zaire's agricultural development, [by] R. B. Diamond [et al.] [Muscle Shoals, Ala., National Fertilizer Development Center, 1975?] 83 p. illus., maps.

Prepared for the U.S. Agency for International Development.

Examined in the Development Information Center, AID, Washington, D.C.

1159

Tollens, Eric F. Problems of micro-economic data collection on farms in northern Zaire. East Lansing, Dept. of Agricultural Economic, Michigan State University, 1975. 41 leaves. (African Rural Employment Research Network. Working paper, no. 7)
HD2140.T65

"AID 211(d) grant and an AID research contract (AID/csd 3625)"

Bibliography: leaves 38–39.

Issued also in microfiche. [Washington, U.S. Agency for International Development, 1975?] 1 sheet.   DLC-Sci RR PN-AAB-247

1160

Williams, T. T. Summary of Zaire's agricultural sector. [Baton Rouge, Unemployment and Underemployment Institute, Southern University and A & M College, 1976?] 11 leaves. (Staff papers series, no. 154–76)

Sponsored by the U.S. Agency for International Development.

Examined in the Development Information Center, AID, Washington, D.C.

Fisheries

1161

An Evaluation of proposed USAID project for improvement of Lake Tanganyika's fishery resources in Zaire, [by] Gordon E. Hall [et al.] Rev. ed. [Auburn, Ala., Dept. of Fisheries and International Center for Aquaculture, Auburn University], 1975. 69 p. illus.   DLC

Survey conducted at the request of the U.S. Agency for International Development.

Abstract in *A.I.D. Research and Development Abstracts*, July 1976, p. 4–5.

Issued also in microfiche. [Washington, U.S. Agency for International Development, 1975?] 1 sheet.   DLC-Sci RR PN-AAB-592

1162

Gregory, Steven. Freshwater fisheries: program planning. [Washington?], Office of Multilateral & Special Programs, Peace Corps, 1977. 72 p.

Includes a feasibility study of inland fisheries in the Bandundu region, Zaire, p. 6–27.

Abstract in *Selected Appropriate Technologies for Development Countries*, no. 1, p. 101.

Microfiche. [Springfield, Va., National Technical Information Service, 1977] 1 sheet.
DLC-Sci RR PB268987

1163

Hall, Calvert B. Inland fisheries feasibility survey, 7 April–28 May 1973, Bandundu Region, Republic of Zaire. [s.l., 1973?] 17 leaves. map.   DPC

Prepared by a U.S. Peace Corps Inland Fisheries Consultant.

Assistance Programs

1164

U.S. *Agency for International Development*. Annual budget submission: Zaire. Washington, U.S. International Development Cooperation Agency.

Vols. for 1978+ examined in the Development Information Center, AID, Washington, D.C.

1165

———— Loan paper; Zaire—commodity financing—standard procedures. [Washington?], 1976. 105 p.

Examined in the Development Information Center, AID, Washington, D.C.

1166

U.S. *Congress. House. Committee on International Relations.* International Security Assistance Act of 1977: report, together with supplemental and additional views on H. R. 6884. Washington, U.S. Govt. Print Off., 1977. 52 p.   DLC-LL

Clement J. Zablocki, chairman.

At head of title: 95th Congress, 1st session. House of Representatives. Report no. 95–274.

Includes brief references to African countries, particularly Zaire.

1167

U.S. *Congress. Senate. Committee on Banking, Housing, and Urban Affairs. Subcommittee on International Finance.* U.S. loans to Zaire: hearing, Ninety-sixth Congress, first session ... May 24, 1979. Washington, U.S. Govt. Print. Off., 1979. 68 p. 1 fold. leaf of plates, map.

KF26.B2946 1979c
J74.A23 96th Cong.,
Sen. Comm. Bank., v. 25

1167 (cont.)

Adlai E. Stevenson, chairman; Paul E. Tsongas, presiding officer.

Concerns an Export-Import Bank credit to Zaire for further construction of the Inga-Shaba power transmission line.

1168

U.S. *Congress. Senate. Committee on Foreign Relations. Subcommittee on African Affairs.* Security supporting assistance for Zaire: hearing before the Subcommittee on African Affairs and the Subcommittee on Foreign Assistance of the Committee on Foreign Relations, United States Senate, Ninety-fourth Congress, first session ... October 24, 1975. Washington, U.S. Govt. Print. Off., 1975. 49 p.   KF26.F625 1975
                                        J74.A23 94th
                                        Cong., Sen. Comm.
                                        For. Rel., v. 12

Dick Clark, chairman, Subcommittee on African Affairs.

Hubert H. Humphrey, chairman, Subcommittee on Foreign Assistance.

1169

U.S. *General Accounting Office.* Search for options in the troubled food-for-peace program in Zaire; report to the Subcommittee on Africa, House Committee on Foreign Affairs by the Comptroller General of the United States. [Washington], 1980. 35 p.   DLC

"ID-80-25, Feb. 22, 1980."

"Providing food to Zaire has been an important part of U.S. assistance to this economically troubled country since 1976. From the beginning of the program, monitoring and controlling food distribution—especially rice—has been a problem."—cover.

Issued also in microfiche. [Washington, U.S. Agency for International Development, 1980?] 1 sheet (PN-AAH-634); examined in the Development Information Center, AID, Washington, D.C.

1170

U.S. [*Treaties, etc. Zaire, 1976 Mar. 25*] Agreement between the Government of the United States of America and the Government of the Republic of Zaire for sales of agricultural commoditites. *In* U.S. *Treaties, etc.* United States treaties and other international agreements, v. 27, 1976. [Washington, Dept. of State; for sale by the Supt. of Docs., U.S. Govt. Print. Off., 1977] p. 3841–3865. ([Treaties and other international acts series, 8403])
                                        JX231.A34 v. 27
Signed at Kinshasa Mar. 25, 1976; amending agreement signed at Kinshasa Apr. 28, 1976.

1171

U.S. [*Treaties, etc. Zaire, 1976 June 29*] Loan agreement between the United States of America and the Republic of Zaire (FY 1976 commodity import program). *In* U.S. *Treaties, etc.* United States treaties and other international agreements, v. 28, 1976–77. [Washington, Dept. of State; for sale by the Supt. of Docs., U.S. Govt. Print. Off., 1978] p. 4501–4545. ([Treaties and other international acts series, 8604])
                                        JX231.A34 v. 28
Signed at Kinshasa June 29, 1976.
In English and French.
Concerns a U.S. Agency for International Development loan.

1172

U.S. [*Treaties, etc. Zaire, 1976 Dec. 7*] Zaire: agricultural commodities. Agreement amending the agreement of March 25, 1976, as amended; effected by exchange of notes dated at Kinshasa August 23 and December 7, 1976. *In* U.S. *Treaties, etc.* United States treaties and other international agreements, v. 28, 1976–77. [Washington, Dept. of State; for sale by the Supt. of Docs., U.S. Govt. Print. Off., 1978] p. 1299–1371. ([Treaties and other international acts series, 8507])   JX231.A34 v. 28
In English and/or French.
Concerns the sale of agricultural products to Zaire.

1173

U.S. [*Treaties, etc. Zaire, 1977 Jan. 27*] Project loan agreement between the Republic of Zaire and the United States of America for North Shaba rural development. *In* U.S. *Treaties, etc.* United States treaties and other international agreements, v. 29, 1976–77. [Washington, Dept. of State; for sale by the Supt. of Docs., U.S. Govt. Print. Off., 1979] p. 4961–5041. ([Treaties and other international acts series, 9090])   JX231.A34 v. 29
English and French.
Signed at Kinshasa, Jan. 27, 1977.
At head of title: A.I.D. project no. 660-0059.

1174

U.S. [*Treaties, etc. Zaire, 1977 May 24*] Agreement between the Government of the United States of America and the Government of the Republic of Zaire for the sale of agricultural commodities under the P.L. 480, Title I program. *In* U.S. *Treaties, etc.* United States treaties and other international agreements, v. 29, 1976–77. [Washington, Dept. of State; for sale by the Supt. of Docs., U.S. Govt. Print. Off., 1979] p. 287–296. ([Treaties and other international acts series, 8813])   JX231.A34 v. 29

1174 (cont.)

Signed at Kinshasa May 24, 1977, with memorandum of understanding, and amending agreements effected by exchange of notes signed at Kinshasa Aug. 15 and 19, 1977; entered into force Aug. 19, 1977; and exchange of notes signed at Kinshasa Sept. 19 and 20, 1977; entered into force Sept. 20, 1977.

In English and French.

1175

U.S. [*Treaties, etc. Zaire, 1978, July 7*] Agricultural commodities: agreement between the United States of America and Zaire amending the agreement of May 24, 1977, as amended, effected by exchange of notes dates at Kinshasa July 7, 1978. *In* U.S. *Treaties, etc.* United States treaties and other international agreements, v. 30, 1978–79. [Washington, Dept. of State; for sale by the Supt. of Docs., U.S. Govt. Print. Off., 1980] p. 1535–1537. ([Treaties and other international acts series, 9262])

JX231.A34 v. 30

1176

U.S. [*Treaties, etc. Zaire, 1978 Aug. 25*] Agreement between the Government of the United States of America and the Government of the Republic of Zaire for the sale of agricultural commodities under the P. L. 480 Title I program. *In* U.S. *Treaties, etc.* United States treaties and other international agreements, v. 30, 1978–79. [Washington, Dept. of State; for sale by the Supt. of Docs., U.S. Govt. Print. Off., 1980] p. 1521–1534. ([Treaties and other international acts series, 9261])

JX231.A34 v. 30

Signed at Kinshasa Aug. 25, 1978 with memorandum of understanding signed at Kinshasa Aug. 17, 24, and 25, 1978, and amending agreement effected by exchange of notes dated at Kinshasa Dec. 27, 1978 and Jan. 3, 1979.

1177

Action (Service Corps). *Division of Evaluation.* Peace Corps/Zaire; country program evaluation. [Washington] 1976. 79 p. (in various pagings)

DPC

Prepared by Joseph Beausoleil, Galen Hull, and Sally Cameron.

1178

American ORT Federation. Training for road construction repairs and maintenance: final report, Republic of Zaïre, Office des routes. [Geneva, 1975?] 53, [35] p. TE191.A63 1975

Project undertaken through a loan from the U.S. Agency for International Development.

1179

Hull, Galen. Is AID/ZAIRE living up to the new directions mandate? [s.l.], 1979. 9 p. DLC

On cover: "Prepared ... for Colloquium on Zaire for Ambassador Robert S. Oakley, October 25, 1979, Bureau of Intelligence/Research, Department of State."

1180

Proxmire, William. Inga-Shaba extra high voltage direct current transmission project in Zaire. Congressional record [daily ed.], 96th Congress, 1st session, v. 125, May 10, 1979: S5628–S5629.

J11.R7 v. 125

Remarks in the U.S. Senate.

Includes Export-Import Bank proposal for a loan to assist in completing the project.

1181

Technical Assistance Information Clearing House. Development assistance programs of U.S. non-profit organizations in Zaire. New York, American Council of Voluntary Agencies for Foreign Service, 1974. 33 p. (TAICH country report)'

HC591.C6T43 1974

The Clearing House is operated by the Council under a grant from the U.S. Agency for International Development.

1182

—— Development assistance programs of U.S. non-profit organizations: Zaire. [New York] American Council of Voluntary Agencies for Foreign Service, 1979. 47 p. maps. (TAICH country report) DLC

"2d edition."

Commerce

1183

Hauser, Timothy P. The market for water transport equipment in Zaire. Kinshasa, American Embassy, 1978. 27 p.

Prepared for the Industry and Trade Administration, U.S. Dept. of Commerce.

Abstract in *Government Reports Announcements & Index*, June 8, 1979, p. 28.

Microfiche. [Springfield, Va., National Technical Information Service, 1979] 1 sheet.

DLC-Sci RR DIB-79-05-501

1184

Karaer, Arma J. The market for aircraft in Zaire. Kinshasa, American Embassy, 1978. 22 p.

Prepared for the Industry and Trade Administration, U.S. Dept. of Commerce.

1184 (cont.)

Abstract in *Government Reports Announcements & Index*, Apr. 27, 1979, p. 18.

Microfiche. [Springfield, Va., National Technical Information Service, 1979] 1 sheet.

DLC-Sci RR DIB-79-03-508

1185

Market for agro-industrial equipment in Zaire. Kinshasa, Economic and Commercial Section, American Embassy, 1977. 35 p.

Prepared for Market Research Division, Office of International Marketing, U.S. Dept. of Commerce.

Abstract in *Government Reports Announcements & Index*, Mar. 3, 1978, p. 20.

Microfiche. [Springfield, Va., National Technical Informatio Service, 1978] 1 sheet.

DLC-Sci RR DIB-78-02-501

1186

The Market for railroad transportation equipment in Zaire. Kinshasa, American Embassy, 1979. 17 p.

Prepared for the Industry and Trade Administration, U.S. Dept. of Commerce.

Microfiche. [Springfield, Va., National Technical Information Service, 1979] 1 sheet.

DLC-Sci RR DIB-79-07-510

1187

Market share reports. Country series: Zaire, 1971–75. [Washington], U.S. Dept. of Commerce; for sale by the National Technical Information Service, Springfield, Va., [1977] 66 p.

Indicates the United States share of the market in Zaire for various products compared to the shares for Belgium-Luxemburg, France, Federal Republic of Germany, Great Britain, Italy, Netherlands, Sweden, and Japan.

Microfiche. [Washington, Congressional Information Service, 1977?]

DLC-Micro ASI: 77 2016-1.87

1188

Market share reports. Country series: Zaire, 1975–79. [Washington], International Trade Administration, U.S. Dept. of Commerce; for sale by the National Technical Information Service, Springfield, Va., [1979] 65 p.

Includes same comparative data as in *Market Share Reports. Country Series: Zaire, 1971–75* (entry 1187).

Microfiche. [Washington, Congressional Information Service, 1979?]

DLC-Micro ASI: 79 2046-2.87

1189

Michelini, Philip. Marketing in Zaire. [Washington], U.S. Dept. of Commerce, Domestic and International Business Administration; [for sale by the Supt. of Docs., U.S. Govt. Print. Off.], 1977. 27 p. (Overseas business reports. OBR 77-23)

HF91.U482   1977, no. 23

International marketing information series.

Supersedes *Marketing in Zaire* (Overseas business reports. OBR74-23), by Frank A. Ocwieja.

Issued also in microfiche. [Washington, Congressional Information Service, 1977?] 1 sheet.

DLC-Micro ASI-77 2026-5.29

1190

——— Marketing in Zaire. [Washington], U.S. Dept. of Commerce, Industry and Trade Administration; [for sale by the Supt. of Docs., U.S. Govt. Print. Off.] 1979. 39 p. (Overseas business reports. OBR79-44)   HF91.U482   1979, no. 44

International marketing information series.

Supersedes the author's *Marketing in Zaire* (entry 1189).

Issued also in microfiche. [Washington, Congressional Information Service, 1979?] 1 sheet.

DLC-Micro ASI: 80 2046-6.7

1191

Williams, John A. U.S. flour mill in Zaire accelerates use of U.S. wheat. Foreign agriculture, Nov. 7, 1977: 10–11. illus.

HD1401.F65   1977

Issued by the U.S. Foreign Agricultural Service.

1192

Zaire grain marketing paper. Minneapolis, Experience Incorporated, 1977. 187 p.

Prepared for the U.S. Agency for International Development under contract AID/afr-C-1130.

At head of title: Draft.

Microfiche. [Washington, U.S. Agency for International Development, 1977?] 2 sheets.

DLC-Sci RR PN-AAG-015

Economic Conditions

1193

Development of rail system continues. *In* U.S. *Joint Publications Research Service.* JPRS 69189. [Springfield, Va., National Technical Information Service, 1977] (Translations on Sub-Saharan Africa, no. 1754) p. 78–83. map.

Translation of article in *La Vie du rail outremer*, Paris, Apr. 1977, p. 27–29.

Microfiche. [s.l., 1977]

DLC-Micro JPRS 69189

1194

Foreign economic trends and their implications for the United States. Zaire. 1969+ Washington, for sale by the Supt. of Docs., U.S. Govt. Print. Off. (International marketing information series)

HC10.E416

Semiannual, 1969–72; annual, 1973–

Continues *Economic Trends and Their Implications for the United States. Democratic Republic of the Congo.*

Title varies: 1969–71, *Foreign Economic Trends and Their Implications for the United States. Democratic Republic of the Congo.*

Prepared by the U.S. Embassy, Kinshasa.

Vols. for 1969–77 distributed by the U.S. Bureau of International Commerce; vols. for 1978–79 by the U.S. Industry and Trade Administration; vols. for 1980– by the U.S. International Trade Administration.

Not published in 1975.

The following issues for the period 1973–81 have been identified in L.C.:

ET 73-054. 1973. 9 p.
FET 74-068. 1974. 10 p.
FET 76-082. 1976. 7 p.
FET 77-060. 1977. 7 p.
FET 78-063. 1978. 7 p.
FET 79-058. 1979. 7 p.
FET 80-074. 1980. 7 p.
FEt 81-143. 1981. 8 p.

1195

GECAMINES output for 1980 estimated. *In* U.S. *Joint Publications Research Service*. JPRS 76157. [Springfield, Va., National Technical Information Service, 1980] (Sub-Saharan Africa report, no. 2274) p. 128–132.

Translation of article in *Mjumbe*, Lubumbashi, May 3–4, 1980.

Gecamines: Générale des carrières et des mines du Zaire.

Microfiche. [s.l., 1980]

DLC-Micro JPRS 76157

1196

McCabe, James L. Distribution of labor incomes in urban Zaire. [New Haven], Economic Growth Center, Yale University, 1973. 28 p.

Microfiche. [Washington, U.S. Agency for International Development, 1973?] 1 sheet.

DLC-Sci RR PN-AA-695

1197

Mobutu Sese Seko. Mobutu presents economic recovery program for 1977. *In* U.S. *Joint Publications Research Service*. JPRS 68680. [Springfield, Va., National Technical Information Service, 1977]

(Translations on Sub-Saharan Africa, no. 1715) p. 53–63.

Translation of speech recorded in *Elima*, Kinshasa, Dec. 22, 1976, p. 1, 5, 7.

Microfiche. [s.l., 1977]

DLC-Micro JPRS 68680

Education

1198

Rideout, William M. A school system for an indigenous religious minority: the Kimbanguists in Zaire. [Tallahassee?], Florida State University, 1974. 24 p.

Prepared for the annual conference of the Comparative and International Education Society, 1974.

Microfiche. [Washington, U.S. Agency for International Development, 1974?] 1 sheet.

DLC-Sci RR PN-AAC-495

1199

——— An organizational model for the Centre de recherches interdisciplinaires pour le développement de l'éducation. Tallahassee, Center for Educational Technology, Florida State University, [1974] 15 p.

"The Center for Interdisciplinary Research for Educational Development (CRIDE) was founded in March, 1972, as an integral part of the Faculty of Education at the Kisangani Campus of the National University of Zaire (UNIZA)."

Microfiche. [Washington, U.S. Agency for International Development, 1974?] 1 sheet.

DLC-Sci RR PN-AAC-492

1200

——— The reorganization of higher education in Zaire. [Washington, Overseas Liaison Committee, American Council on Education, 1974] 25 p. (American Council on Education. Overseas Liaison Committee. OLC paper, no. 5)

Funding for Overseas Liaison Committee programs provided in part through a contract with the U.S. Agency for International Development.

Microfiche. [Arlington, Va., ERIC Document Reproduction Service, 1974] 1 sheet.

DLC-Sci RR ED 09326

Issued also in microfiche by the U.S. Agency for International Development ([Washington, 1974?]). 1 sheet. DLC-Sci RR PN-AAC-493

1201

Shapiro, David. Problems in human resource development: education in Zaire. [s.l.], 1979. 15 p.

DLC

1201 (cont.)

On cover: "This paper was prepared for the Department of State as part of its external research program."

Finance

1202

U.S. [*Treaties, etc. Zaire, 1977 Aug. 30*] Agreement between the United States of America and the Republic of Zaire regarding the consolidation and rescheduling of certain debts owed to, guaranteed by or insured by the United States Government and its agencies. *In* U.S. *Treaties, etc.* United States treaties and other international agreements, v. 28, 1976–77. [Washington, Dept. of State; for sale by the Supt. of Docs., U.S. Govt. Print. Off., 1978] p. 7593–7623. ([Treaties and other international acts series, 8731]) JX231.A34 v. 28

Signed at Washington June 17, 1977; entered into force Aug. 30, 1977.

In English and French.

1203

U.S. [*Treaties, etc. Zaire, 1978 July 19*] Zaire, finance: consolidation and rescheduling of certain debts. Agreement signed at Washington July 19, 1978; entered into force July 19, 1978. *In* U.S. *Treaties, etc.* United States treaties and other international agreements, v. 30, 1978–79. [Washington, Dept. of State; for sale by the Supt. of Docs., U.S. Govt. Print. Off., 1978] p. 3511–3525. ([Treaties and other international acts series, 9405]) JX231.A34, v. 30

In English and French.

1204

U.S. [*Treaties, etc. Zaire, 1979 Feb. 7*] Agreement between the United States of America and the Republic of Zaire regarding the consolidation and rescheduling of certain debts owed to, guaranteed by or insured by the United States Government and its agencies. *In* U.S. *Treaties, etc.* United States treaties and other international agreements, v. 30, 1978–79. [Washington, Dept. of State; for sale by the Supt. of Docs., U.S. Govt. Print. Off., 1980] p. 3601–3619. ([Treaties and other international acts series, 9416]) JX231.A34, v. 30

Signed at Washington Feb. 7, 1979.

In English and French.

1205

U.S. [*Treaties, etc. Zaire, 1979 Aug. 1*] Agreement between the United States of America and the Republic of Zaire regarding the consolidation and rescheduling of payments due under PL 480 Title I agricultural commodity agreements. *In* U.S. *Treaties, etc.* United States treaties and other international agreements, v. 30, 1978–79. [Washington, Dept. of State; for sale by the Supt. of Docs., U.S. Govt. Print. Off., 1980] p. 6279–6291. ([Treaties and other international acts series, 9553]) JX231.A34, v. 30

Signed at Washington Aug. 1, 1979.

1206

U.S. [*Treaties, etc. Zaire, 1980 Oct. 20*] Agreement between the United States of America and the Republic of Zaire regarding the consolidation and rescheduling of certain debts owed to, guaranteed or insured by the United States Government and its agencies. [Washington, Dept. of State; for sale by the Supt. of Docs., U.S. Govt. Print. Off., 1981] 36 p. (Treaties and other international acts series, 9907) DLC

Signed at Kinshasa July 28, 1980; entered into force Oct. 20, 1980.

Foreign Relations

1207

U.S. *President, 1977–1981 (Carter)* Meeting with President Mobutu Sese Seko of Zaire. White House statement, September 11, 1979. *In* U.S. *President.* Public papers of the Presidents of the United States. Jimmy Carter. 1979. [Washington, Office of the Federal Register, National Archives and Records Service; for sale by the Supt. of Docs., U.S. Govt. Print. Off., 1980] p. 1627–1628.

J80.A283 1979

1208

Bonker, Don. Our nation's growing involvement with the Government of Zaire. Congressional record, 95th Congress, 1st session, v. 123, May 11, 1977: 14403–14405. J11.R5 v. 123

Remarks in the U.S. House of Representatives.

1209

Delarue, Maurice. French accusations of Belgian negligence in Zaire refuted. *In* U.S. *Joint Publications Research Service.* JPRS 71425. [Springfield, Va., National Technical Information Service, 1978] (Translations on Sub-Saharan Africa, no. 1957) p. 127–132.

Translation of interview with Henri Simonet, Minister of Foreign Affairs of Belgium, in *Le Monde*, Paris, May 30, 1978, p. 3.

Microfiche. [Washington, Supt. of Docs., U.S. Govt. Print. Off., 1978]

DLC-Micro JPRS 71425

1210

Findley, Paul. President flunks first war powers test in Zaire. Congressional record, 95th Congress, 2d session, v. 124, Aug. 10, 1978: 25563–25566.

J11.R5 v. 124

Remarks in the House of Representatives concerning "the actions of the U.S. Armed Forces in Zaire in May and June of this year."

1211

Haskell, Floyd K. The need for more debate on our policy toward Zaire. Congressional record, 95th Congress, 1st session, v. 123, May 12, 1977: 14549–14552.   J11.R5 v. 123

Remarks in the U.S. Senate.

Includes articles from the *New Republic.*

1212

Mobutu wishes detente with Belgium. *In* U.S. *Joint Publications Research Service.* JPRS 71836. [Springfield, Va., National Technical Information Service, 1978] (Translations on Sub-Saharan Africa, no. 1990) p. 69–72.

Translation of article in *Le Soir*, Brussels, Aug. 4, 1978, p. 5.

Microfiche. [Washington, Supt. of docs., U.S. Govt. Print. Off., 1978]

ADLC-Micro JPRS 71836

1213

Moose, Richard M. Africa: U.S. policy toward Zaire. *In* U.S. *Dept. of State.* The Department of State bulletin, v. 79, no. 2026, May 1979: 42–44.

JX232.A33 v. 79

Statement by the Assistant Secretary of State for African Affairs before the Subcommittee on Africa, Committee on Foreign Affairs, House of Representatives, Mar. 5, 1979.

1214

Ugeux, Etienne. No privileges, discrimination, for Belgians in Zaire. *In* U.S. *Joint Publications Research Service.* JPRS 71836. [Springfield, Va., National Technical Information Service, 1978] (Translations on Sub-Saharan Africa, no. 1990) p. 73–77.

Translation of interview with Henri Simonet, Minister of Foreign Affairs of Belgium, in *Le Soir*, Brussels, Aug. 4, 1978, p. 1, 4.

Microfiche. [Washington, Supt. of Docs., U.S. Govt. Print. Off., 1978]

DLC-Micro JPRS 71836

1215

Walker, Lannon. U.S. policy toward Zaire. *In* U.S.

Dept. of State. The Department of State bulletin, v. 80, no. 2041, Aug. 1980: 46–48.

JX232.A33 v. 80

Geology, Hydrology, and Mineral Resources

The following items (entries 1216–1223) are listed in chronological order:

1216

Schroeder, Harold J. The mineral industry of Zaire. *In* Minerals yearbook, v. 3, 1972. [Washington, for sale by the Supt. of Docs., U.S. Govt. Print. Off., 1974] p. 893–901.   TN23.U612 1972, v. 3

Prepared by the U.S. Bureau of Mines.

1217

———— The mineral industry of Zaire. *In* Minerals yearbook, v. 3, 1973. [Washington, for sale by the Supt. of Docs., U.S. Govt. Print. Off., 1976] p. 959–964.   TN23.U612 1973, v. 3

Prepared by the U.S. Bureau of Mines.

1218

Coakley, George J. The mineral industry of Zaire. *In* Minerals yearbook, v. 3, 1974. [Washington, for sale by the Supt. of Docs., U.S. Govt. Print. Off., 1977] p. 1041–1046.   TN23.U612 1974, v. 3

Prepared by the U.S. Bureau of Mines.

1219

Ellis, Miller W. The mineral industry of Zaire. *In* Minerals yearbook, v. 3, 1975. [Washington, for sale by the Supt. of Docs., U.S. Govt. Print. Off., 1978] p. 1101–1105.   TN23.U612 1975, v. 3

Prepared by the U.S. Bureau of Mines.

1220

———— The mineral industry of Zaire. *In* Minerals yearbook, v. 3, 1976. [Washington, for sale by the Supt. of Docs., U.S. Govt. Print. Off., 1980] p. 1207–1213.   TN23.U612 1976, v. 3

Prepared by the U.S. Bureau of Mines.

1221

———— The mineral industry of Zaire. *In* Minerals yearbook, v. 3, 1977. [washington, for sale by the Supt. of Docs., U.S. Govt. Print. Off., 1981] p. 1087–1092.   TN23.U612 1977, v. 3

Prepared by the U.S. Bureau of Mines.

1222

———— The mineral industry of Zaire. *In* Minerals

1222 (cont.)

yearbook, v. 3, 1978–79. [Washington, U.S. Govt. Print. Off., 1981] p. 1061–1066.

TN23.U612   1978–79, v. 3

Prepared by the U.S. Bureau of Mines.

1223

———— The mineral industry of Zaire. *In* Minerals yearbook, v. 3, 1980. [Washington, for sale by the Supt. of Docs., U.S. Govt. Print. Off., 1982] p. 1129–1136.   TN23.U612   1980, v. 3

Prepared by the U.S. Bureau of Mines.

Health and Nutrition

1224

Adelman, Carol. Health/nutrition survey: Kinshasa, June 19–July 20, 1974. [s.l., 1974?] [43] p.

Survey organized and conducted with the support of the U.S. Agency for International Development.

Microfiche. [Washington, U.S. Agency for International Development, 1974?] 1 sheet.

DLC-Sci RR PN-AAD-498

1225

Brooks, G. D., *and* J. K. Shisler. The feasibility of a recommendation for anti-larval measures against vector anophelines in Zaire. [Washington, American Public Health Association], 1980. [32] p. maps.

Study supported by the U.S. Agency for International Development.

Microfiche. [Washington, U.S. Agency for International Development, 1980?] 1 sheet (PN-AAJ-239); examined in the Development Information Center, AID, Washington, D.C.

1226

Development of a maternal and child health/family planning program in Zaire; progress report. 1st–6th?; May 1973/Jan. 1974–Apr./Sept. 1976? [Geneva, Organization for Rehabilitation through Training] semiannual (irregular)

Apparently prepared for the U.S. Agency for International Development.

No more published?

1st–6th reports examined in the Development Information Center, AID, Washington, D.C.

1227

Guidelines for task-specific curriculum development for maternal and child health training. [Geneva] Organization for Rehabilitation through Training, [1977] 79 p.

On cover: "Based on the training program devel-

oped for the MCH Centers, Kinshasa, Republic of Zaire."

Abstract in *A.I.D Research and Development Abstracts*, Jan. 1979, p. 26.

Microfiche. [Washington, U.S. Agency for International Development, 1977?] 1 sheet.

DLC-Sci RR PN-AAF-494

1228

Lashman, Karen E. Zaire. Washington, Division of Program Analysis, Office of International Health; [for sale by the Supt. of Docs., U.S. Govt. Print. Off.], 1975. 178 p. map. (Syncrisis: the dynamics of health; an analytic series on the interactions of health and socioeconomic development, v. 14)

RA418.S98 v. 14

Bibliography: p. 172–178.

Abstract in *A.I.D Research and Development Abstracts*, Oct. 1976, p. 27.

Issued also in microfiche. [Washington, U.S. Agency for International Development, 1975?] 2 sheets.

DLC-Sci RR PN-AAB-997

1229

Maternal and child health care centers, Kinshasa, Republic of Zaire; operational program. [Geneva?], Organization for Rehabilitation through Training, [1977] 75 p.

Prepared for the U.S. Agency for International Development.

Abstract in *A.I.D Research and Development Abstracts*, Jan. 1979, p. 26.

Microfiche. [Washington, U.S. Agency for International Development, 1977?] 2 sheets.

DLC-Sci RR PN-AAF-493

1230

Maternal and child health/family planning program, Kinshasa, Republic of Zaire; final report. [Geneva] Organization for Rehabilitation through Training, [1977] [28] p.

Prepared for the U.S. Agency for International Development.

Microfiche. [Washington, U.S. Agency for International Development, 1977?] 1 sheet.

DLC-Sci RR PN-AAF-495

1231

Project for reform of medical action in rural areas of Zaire. Washington, U.S. Army Medical Intelligence and Information Agency, 1978. 18 p.

Translation of *Projet de reforme de l'action medicale dans les zones de développement rural au Zaire*.

Microfiche. [s.l., Defense Documentation Center, 1979] 1 sheet.   DLC-Sci RR AD-A062135

1232

Roots, Logan H. Measles immunization in city [sic], Kinshasa, Zaire. [Washington?], 1974. 4 p.

Consultation carried out under U.S. Agency for International Development contract AID/csd 3432.

Microfiche. [Washington, U.S. Agency for International Development, 1974?] 1 sheet.

DLC-Sci RR PN-AAB-546

Politics and Government

1233

Conference report on S.2009, Central Idaho Wilderness Act of 1980. Congressional record [daily ed.], 96th Congress, 2d session, v. 126, June 30, 1980: H5888-H5899. J11.R7 v. 126

In debate in the U.S. House of Representatives on the mining of cobalt, Representative Steven D. Symms comments on unrest in Zaire, America's primary supplier of cobalt (H5890-H5893).

Includes articles, "Unrest in Zaire: anti-Mobutu feeling swells among masses living in destitution," and "African tragedy: Zaire's rich soil feeds few because farming roads are primitive," from the *Wall Street Journal.*

1234

McClure, James A. How did we ever become so vunerable? Congressional record [daily ed.], 96th Congress, 2d session, v. 126, June 27, 1980: S8669-S8671. J11.R7 v. 126

Remarks in the U.S. Senate.

Includes article from the *Wall Street Journal* on unrest in Zaire.

1235

Mobutu Sese Seko. Mobutu addresses legislative council on state of nation. *In* U.S. *Joint Publications Research Service.* JPRS 75116. [Springfield, Va., National Technical Information Service, 1980] (Sub-Saharan Africa report, no. 2213) p. 69–96.

Translation of a French language broadcast from Kinshasa, Feb. 4, 1980.

Microfiche. [s.l. 1980]

DLC-Micro JPRS 75116

1236

Monheim, Francis. Measure taken of Mobutu's popularity. *In* U.S. *Joint Publications Research Service.* JPRS 69169. [Springfield, Va., National Technial Information Service, 1977] (Translations on Sub-Saharan Africa, no. 1753) p. 70–73.

Translation of article in *Spécial*, Brussels, Apr. 27, 1977, p. 35–36.

Microfiche. [s.l. 1977]

DLC-Micro JPRS 69169

1237

Newbury, Catherine. Political and economic crisis in Zaire: the view from below. [s.l., 1979?] 12 p.

DLC

On cover: "This paper was prepared for the Department of State as part of its external research program."

1238

Nzongola-Ntalaja. The Zairian political system: obstacles to reform. [Washington?], 1979. 14 p.

DLC

On cover: "Colloquium on Zaire for Ambassador Robert B. Oakley, U.S. Department of State, Washington, D.C., October 25, 1979."

1239

Papandropoulos, A. Interview with Mula Biondo. *In* U.S. *Joint Publications Research Service.* JPRS 74232. [Springfield, Va., National Technical Information Service, 1979) (Sub-Saharan Africa report, no. 2156) p. 44–51.

Translation of interview with the foreign minister of the Zairian exile organization, Front de libération nationale du Congo, in *O Oikonomikos Takhyromos*, Athens, Aug. 9, 1979, p. 13, 14.

Microfiche. [Washington, Supt. of Docs., U.S. Govt. Print. Off., 1979]

DLC-Micro JPRS 74232

1240

Reorganization of security services. *In* U.S. *Joint Publications Research Service.* JPRS 75862. [Springfield, Va., National Technial Information Service, 1980] (Sub-Saharan Africa report, no. 2256) p. 180–186.

Translation of a presidential ordinance reorganizing both the external and internal security forces of Zaire, in *Elima*, Kinshasa, Apr. 23–27, 1980.

Microfiche. [s.l. 1980]

DLC-Micro JPRS 75862

1241

Rideout, William M. The politics of national planning: the case of Zaire. [Tallahassee], Center for Educational Technology, Florida State University, 1974. 35 p. map.

Prepared for the annual conference of the International Society of Educational Planners, 1974.

Abstract in *A.I.D. Research and Development Abstracts*, Apr. 1977, p. 38–39.

Microfiche. [Washington, U.S. Agency for International Development, 1974?] 1 sheet.

DLC-Sci RR PN-AAC-494

1242

Schatzberg, Michael G. Aspects of local-level administration in Zaire. [s.l.], 1979. 10 p.   DLC

On cover: "Paper prepared for delivery at a colloquium on Zairian politics, U.S. Department of State, Washington, D.C. 25 October, 1979."

Shaba Conflict (1977–78)

Note: The following items (entries 1243–1254) concern armed conflicts over control of mineral-rich Shaba Province between forces loyal to the Zairian Government and rebel troops who mounted invasions from Angola in March–April 1977 and again in May 1978.

1243

U.S. *Congress. House. Committee on International Relations. Subcommittee on International Security and Scientific Affairs.* Congressional oversight of war powers compliance: Zaire airlift: hearing, Ninety-fifth Congress, second session, August 10, 1978. Washington, U.S. Govt. Print. Off., 1978. 38 p.   KF27.I5495   1978c
                          J74.A23 95th Cong.,
                          House Comm. Inter.
                          Re., v. 109

Clement J. Zablocki, chairman.

Witnesses are Representative Paul Findley and Herbert J. Hansell, Legal Adviser, U.S. Dept. of State.

A review of the implications of the War Powers Resolution (Public Law 93-148) relating to the American airlift of foreign military personnel and equipment in Zaire, May–June 1978.

1244

Davister, Pierre. Commentary on Mobutu plan. *In* U.S. *Joint Publications Research Service.* JPRS 70866. [Springfield, Va., National Technical Information Service, 1978] (Translations on Sub-Saharan Africa, no. 1903) p. 97–101.

Translation of article in *Spécial*, Brussels, Jan. 11, 1978, p. 4–5.

Microfiche. [Washington, Supt. of Docs., U.S. Govt. Print. Off., 1978]

DLC-Micro JPRS 70866

1245

Depoorter, Henri J. G. Kolwezi. Military review, Sept. 1979: 29–35. illus., map.

Z6723.U35   1979

Published by the U.S. Army Command and General Staff College, Ft. Leavenworth, Kansas.

A chronological account of military action in Shaba Province, May 16–22, 1978.

1246

Diop, Mouhamadou M. First-hand account of Senegalese in Shaba given. *In* U.S. *Joint Publications Research Service.* JPRS 71763. [Springfield, Va., National Technical Information Service, 1978] (Translations on Sub-Saharan Africa, no. 1983) p. 112–125.

Translation of article on a Senegalese military contingent in the Pan-African force assisting the Mobutu government in Shaba, in *Le Soleil*, Dakar, July 10–13, 1978.

Microfiche. [Washington, Supt. of Docs., U.S. Govt. Print. Off., 1978]

DLC-Micro JPRS 71763

1247

Emmanuel, Paul. Europeans want to remain. *In* U.S. *Joint Publications Research Service.* JPRS 71574. JPRS 71574. [Springfield, Va., National Technical Information Service, 1978] (Translations on Sub-Saharan Africa, no. 1969) p. 67–72.

Translation of article concerning European residents of Kolwezi, Zaire, in *Spécial*, Brussels, June 14, 1978, p. 50–53.

Microfiche. [Washington, Supt. of Docs., U.S. Govt. Print. Off., 1978]

DLC-Micro JPRS 71574

1248

Essolomma N. Linganga. Aggression in Shaba repulsed. *In* U.S. *Joint Publications Research Service.* JPRS 71449. [Springfield, Va., National Technical Information Service, 1978] (Translations on Sub-Saharan Africa, no. 1959) p. 157–160.

Translation of article in *Elima*, Kinshasa, May 21–22, 1978, p. 1, 3.

Microfiche. [Washington, Supt. of Docs., U.S. Govt. Print. Off., 1978]

DLC-Micro JPRS 71449

1249

Eyenga Sana. Aggressors attack Shaba again. *In* U.S. *Joint Publications Research Service.* JPRS 71449. [Springfield, Va., National Technical Information Service, 1978] (Translations on Sub-Saharan Africa, no. 1959) p. 157–160.

Translation of article in *Zaïre*, Kinshasa, May 22, 1978, p. 16–19.

Microfiche. [Washington, Supt. of Docs., U.S. Govt. Print. Off., 1978]

DLC-Micro JPRS 71449

1250

Katangan mercenary prisoner talks of Soviet's Shaba role. *In* U.S. *Joint Publications Research Service.* JPRS 69326. [Springfield, Va., National Technical

1250 (cont.)

Information Service, 1977] (Translations on Sub-Saharan Africa, no. 1765) p. 107–110.

Translation of article in *Elima*, Kinshasa, May 8, 1977, p. 6.

Microfiche. [s.l., 1977]

DLC-Micro JPRS 69326

1251

Langellier, Jean-Pierre. Multifaceted survey after Shaba war. *In* U.S. *Joint Publications Research Service.* JPRS 69331. [Springfield, Va., National Technical Information Service, 1977] (Translations on Sub-Saharan Africa, no. 1766) p. 59–80.

Translation of article in *Le Monde*, Paris, June 7–10, 1977.

Microfiche. [s.l., 1977]

DLC-Micro JPRS 69331

1252

McGovern, George. The lessons of Shaba. Congressional record, 95th Congress, 2d session, v. 124, Aug. 16, 1978: 26429-26431.   J11.R5 v. 124

Remarks in the U.S. Senate.

Includes article from the *New York Times*.

1253

Monheim, Francis. General Mobutu inspects front with press. *In* U.S. *Joint Publications Research Service.* JPRS 69189. [Springfield, Va., National Technical Information Service, 1977] (Translations on Sub-Saharan Africa, no. 1754) p. 68–74.

Translation of article in *Spécial*, Brussels, May 4, 1977, p. 30–32.

Microfiche. [s.l., 1977]

DLC-Micro JPRS 69189

1254

Pomonti, Jean-Claude. Regardless of outcome Africa seen losing from Shaba invasion. *In* U.S. *Joint Publications Research Service.* JPRS 69128. [Springfield, Va., National Technical Information Service, 1977] (Translations on Sub-Saharan Africa, no. 1749) p. 1–4.

Translation of article in *Le Monde*, Paris, Apr. 20, 1977, p. 1, 2.

Microfiche. [s.l., 1977]

DLC-Micro JPRS 69128

Other Subjects

1255

U.S. *Agency for International Development. Office of Housing.* Zaire shelter sector analysis. [Washington] 1975. 111 p.

Microfiche. [Washington, U.S. Agency for Inter-national Development, 1975?] 2 sheets.

DLC-Sci RR PN-AAB-510

1256

U.S. *Central Intelligence Agency.* Zaire. [Washington], for sale by the Supt. of Docs., U.S. Govt. Print. Off., [1979] map.

Scale 1 : 5,000,000.

Cover title: Map of Zaire.

Relief shown by shading and spot heights.

Includes location and comparative area map and maps of "Population," "Agriculture," "Vegetation," and "Minerals and industry."

Source: *Month. Cat.*, 1980, no. 80-10683.

1257

U.S. *Information Agency.* VOA-CAAP audience estimate for Kinshasa, Zaire. [Washington] 1974. 17 p.

"E-16-74."

VOA-CAAP: Voice of America Continuing Audience Analysis Program.

Microfiche. [Washington, Congressional Information Service, 1974?] 1 sheet.

DLC-Micro ASI:77 9856-2:62

1258

U.S. [*Treaties, etc. Zaire, 1975 Jan. 31*] Zaire remote sensing: acquisition of satellite data. Memorandum of understanding signed at Washington January 6, 1975 and at Kinshasa January 31, 1975; entered into force January 31, 1975. *In* U.S. *Treaties, etc.* United States treaties and other international agreements, v. 26, 1975. [Washington, Dept. of State; for sale by the Supt. of Docs., U.S. Govt. Print. Off., 1976] p. 1699–1704. ([Treaties and other international acts series, 8129])

JX231.A34 v. 26

1259

U.S. [*Treaties, etc. Zaire, 1978, Aug. 9*] Acquisition of excess property: agreement between the United States of America and Zaire, signed at Washington and Kinshasa July 10 and August 9, 1978. *In* U.S. *Treaties, etc.* United States treaties and other international agreements, v. 30, 1978–79. [Washington, Dept. of State; for sale by the Supt. of Docs., U.S. Govt. Print. Off., 1980] p. 1819–1824. (Treaties and other international acts series, 9292)

JX231.A34, v. 30

Concerns the transfer of U.S. Government-owned property to the Zairian National Transportation Office.

1260

Africa: Zaire. Selected statistical data by sex. Washington, 1981. 31, 17 p.   DLC

1260 (cont.)

Study supported by the U.S. Agency for International Development's Office of Women in Development and Office of Population.

Data assembled by the International Demographic Data Center, U.S. Bureau of the Census.

Most of the statistical tables are based on figures for the 1955–57 period.

1261

Decree announces results of 1974 census. *In* U.S. *Joint Publications Research Service.* JPRS 69095. [Springfield, Va., National Technical Information Service, 1977] (Translation on Sub-Saharan Africa, no. 1747) p. 54–71.

Includes translation of statistical tables on the census from the *Journal officiel de la République du Zaïre*, Kinshasa, Mar. 15, 1976, p. 248–267.

Microfiche. [s.l., 1977]

DLC-Micro JPRS 69095

1262

Hazelwood, Peter. Phase I environmental profile of the Republic of Zaire. Washington, Science and Technology Division, Library of Congress, 1980. [87] p. (in various pagings) maps.

On cover: "AID contract no. SA/TOA 1-77 with the U.S. Man and the Biosphere Secretariat, Department of State, Washington, D.C."

A "status of the environment" report with emphasis on water and soil conditions, forests, wildlife, and industrial pollution.

Abstract in *A.I.D. Research & Development Abstracts*, July 1981, p. 38.

Microfiche. [Washington, U.S. Agency for International Development, 1980?] 1 sheet.

DLC-Sci RR PN-AAJ-206

1263

Kiekie M. Ngebay. Zaire energy policy outlined. *In* U.S. *Joint Publications Research Service.* JPRS 75932. [Springfield, Va., National Technical Information Service, 1980] (Sub-Saharan Africa report, no. 2259) p. 107–110.

Translation of article in *Elima*, Kinshasa, May 18–19, 1980, p. 11.

Microfiche. [s.l. 1980]

DLC-Micro JPRS 75932

1264

Law governing organization of armed forces command. *In* U.S. *Joint Publications Research Service.* JPRS 69774. [Springfield, Va., National Technical Information Service, 1977] (Translations on Sub-Saharan Africa, no. 1799) p. 42–49.

Translation of text of law in *Journal officiel de la République du Zaïre*, no. 12, Jan. 15, 1976, p. 631–634.

Microfiche. [s.l., 1977]

DLC-Micro JPRS 69774

1265

Law on personal names promulgated by Presidency. *In* U.S. *Joint Publications Research Service.* JPRS 68342. [Springfield, Va., National Technical Information Service, 1976] (Translations on Sub-Saharan Africa, no. 1695) p. 48–51.

Translation of decree in *Journal officiel de la République du Zaïre*, Kinshasa, Nov. 15, 1975, p. 1405–1406.

Microfiche. [s.l., 1976]

DLC-Micro JPRS 68342

1266

Railroad, history, activities, future investment reviewed. In U.S. *Joint Publications Research Service.* JPRS 72192. [Springfield, Va., National Technical Information Service, 1978] (Translations on Sub-Saharan Africa, no. 2019) p. 185–195.

Translation of article in *Demain l'Afrique*, Paris, Sept. 1978, p. 94–98.

Microfiche. [Washington, Supt. of Docs., U.S. Govt. Print. Off., 1978].

DLC-Micro JPRS 72192

1267

Turner, Thomas. Problems of the Zairian military. [s.l.], 1979. 44 p.   DLC

On cover: "This paper was prepared for the Department of State as part of its external research program."

1268

U.S. Ztate [*sic*] Dept. people in Zaire. *In* U.S. *Dept. of State.* Newsletter, no. 226, Aug.–Sept. 1980: 44-48. illus.   JX1.U542   1980

Mostly illustrations of activities of U.S. Embassy personnel in Kinshasa.

1269

Wagoner, Fred E. Dragon rouge: the rescue of hostages in the Congo. Washington, Research Directorate, National Defense University; [for sale by the Supt. of Docs., U.S. Govt. Print. Off.], 1980. 219 p. illus., maps.

Bibliography: p. 217–219.

Concerns operations in and around Stanleyville in 1964.

Microfiche. [s.l., Defense Technical Information Center, 1981] 3 sheets.

DLC-Sci RR AD-A094969

1270

Wilson, Alton E. An assessment of population/family planning program activities in Zaire. [Washington], American Public Health Association, 1979. [31] p. maps.

Supported by the Office of Population, U.S. Agency for International Development.

Microfiche. [Washington, U.S. Agency for International Development, 1979?] 1 sheet (PN-AAH-707); examined in the Development Information Center, AID, Washington, D.C.

1271

Le Zaire: deuxième pays francophone du monde? [by] Sully Faïk [et al.] Québec, Centre international de recherche sur le bilingualisme, 1977. 34 p. (International Center for Research on Bilingualism. Publication B-61)

Abstract in *Resources in Education*, 1980 annual cumulation, p. 635.

Microfiche. [Arlington, Va., ERIC Document Reproduction Service; prepared for Educational Resources Information Center, National Institute of Education, 1980] 1 sheet.

DLC-Micro ED179081

Eastern Africa

General

1272

Howell, John B. East African Community: subject guide to official publications. Washington, Library of Congress; [for sale by the Supt. of Docs., U.S. Govt. Print. Off.] 1976. xvi, 272 p.   Z3582.H69
    Prepared in the Library's African Section.
    1,812 entries.

1273

Philippi, Thomas, *and* Cecily Mango. East Africa: a regional profile. Washington, Office of U.S. Foreign Disaster Assistance, Agency for International Development, 1981. xv, 322 p., 15 leaves of plates.
                                        DT365.18.P45
    "Prepared for the Office of U.S. Foreign Disaster Assistance, Bureau for Private and Development Cooperation, Agency for International Development, Department of State by Thomas Philippi and Cecily Mango of Evaluation Technologies, inc., under contract AID/SOD/PDC-C-0283."— p. i.
    Bibliography: p. 316–322.
    Covering Djibouti, Ethiopia, Kenya, Somalia, Sudan, Tanzania, and Uganda, the study attempts to determine the countries' vunerability to natural disaster and how well they are prepared to deal with the consequences. Its focus is on such topics as nutrition and food shortages.
    Issued also in microfiche. [Washington, U.S. Agency for International Development, 1981?] 4 sheets (PN-AAJ-519); examined in the Development Information Center, AID, Washington, D.C.

Agriculture

1274

U.S. *Congress. House. Committee on Foreign Affairs. Subcommittee on Africa.* Food needs in East Africa: hearing, Ninety-sixth Congress, second session, June 19, 1980. Washington, U.S. Govt. Print. Off., 1980. 51 p.   KF27.F625   1980a
                                    J74.A23 96th
                                    Cong., House Comm.
                                    For. Aff., v. 107
    Stephen J. Solarz, chairman.
    An examination of the problems of famine and food shortages in East Africa, particularly in Uganda.

1275

Connolly, Gerald E., *and* Helen A. Edwards. East Africa—blueprint for progress: report of a regional workshop on rural development. [s.l.], American Freedom from Hunger Foundation, 1976. 32 p.
    Funded by the U.S. Agency for International Development.
    Examined in the Development Information Center, AID, Washington, D.C.

1276

Jacobs, Alan H. Pastoral Maasai and tropical rural development. *In* Agricultural development in Africa: issues of public policy; edited by Robert H. Bates [and] Michael F. Lofchie. [New York], Praeger, 1980. p. 275–300.   HD2117.A35
    Publication supported in part by the National Science Foundation.
    "This chapter is concerned with the problem of planned development among the Pastoral Maasai of Kenya and Tanzania, an unusually self-reliant people whose traditional way of life and uniquely rich widelife environment have been the object of perennial debates and conflicting theories as to the proper course for development."—p. 275.

1277

Sperow, Charles B., *and* Robert F. Keefer. An introduction to soil science, applied to East Africa. [Morgantown], West Virginia University, [1975] 231 p. illus.   S591.S786
    "The first draft of this volume was written while the senior author was serving as lecturer at Bukalasa Agricultural College, Bombo, Uganda. . . . We

1277 (cont.)
also want to recognize the help and inspiration provided by our assignments to Bukalasa Agricultural College and Makerere University, Kampala, Uganda in fulfillment of West Virginia University/ United State Agency for International Development contracts."—Preface.

1278
Treakle, H. Charles. Desert locust outbreak spreading in East Africa. Foreign agriculture, July 17, 1978: 2-3. illus.   HD1401.F65 1978
    Issued by the U.S. Foreign Agricultural Service.

1279
Trends and interrelationships in food, population, and energy in eastern Africa: a preliminary analysis. Worcester, Mass., Program for International Development, Clark University, 1980. 3 v. maps. ([Eastern Africa regional studies]. Regional paper, no. 4–6)   DLC
    "Eastern Africa Regional Papers are prepared on behalf of the United States Agency for International Development."
    Contents: v. 1. Overview, [by] B. L. Turner [et al.].—v. 2. Background papers, [by] Leonard Berry [et al.].—v. 3. Literature summaries and reviews [by] Anwar Abdu [et al.].

1280
Turner, B. L. Agricultural livelihoods in Eastern Africa: classification and distribution; a first approximation. Worcester, Mass., Program for International Development, Clark University, 1980. 22 p. (Eastern Africa regional studies. Regional paper, no. 1)   DLC
    Bibliography: p. 18–22.
    "Eastern Africa Regional Studies are prepared on behalf of the United States Agency for International Development."

Assistance Programs

1281
U.S. *Agency for International Development.* Annual budget submission: East Africa regional program. [Washington]
    Vols. for 1977–79 examined in the Development Information Center, AID, Washington, D.C.

1282
An Annotated bibliography of the sociology and political economy of Somalia, Sudan, and Tanzania, [by] Patrick Fleuret [et al.] Binghamton, N.Y., Institute for Development Anthropology, inc., 1979. 30 p.

Prepared for the U.S. Agency for International Development under contract AID/afr-C-1504.
    "This bibliography is prepared as a guide, to assist development officers and contractor personnel in the identification, design, implementation, and assessment of socially sound programs and projects which better benefit low income populations...."
    Abstract in *A.I.D. Research and Development Abstracts*, Feb. 1981, p. 65.
    Microfiche. [Washington, U.S. Agency for International Development, 1979?] 1 sheet.
          DLC-Sci RR PN-AAH-474

1283
Development assistance program: East African Community, FY 1975–77. [Nairobi], Regional Development Office for East Africa, Agency for International Development, 1974. 29 p.
    Examined in the Development Information Center, AID, Washington, D.C.

1284
East African Food Crops Research Project. Report. [s.l.], 1975. 173 p.
    Prepared for the U.S. Agency for International Development under contract AID/afr-C-1114.
    J. Clark Ballard, Team Leader, Food Crops Study Team.
    Research project designed to provide assistance to member states of the East African Community.
    Microfiche. [Washington, U.S. Agency for International Development, 1975?] 2 sheets.
          DLC-Sci RR PN-AAE-761

1285
Evaluation of the Masai Livestock and Range Management Project, USAID project no. 621-11-130-093. [s.l.], 1976. 82 leaves.
    Study undertaken by a Utah State University team under U.S. Agency for International Development contract AID/afr-C-1207.
    Examined in the Development Information Center, AID, Washington, D.C.

1286
Sutinen, J. G., *and* W. D. Davies. An evaluation of USAID technical assistance to the EAFFRO Lake Victoria fisheries project. Narrangansett, Marine Advisory Service, University of Rhode Island, Narrangansett Bay Campus, 1975. 23 p. illus. (International Center for Marine Resource Development. Marine memorandum, 37)
    Evaluation undertaken at the request of the Regional Economic Development Services Office, East Africa, U.S. Agency for International Development.

1286 (cont.)

EAFFRO: East Africa Freshwater Fisheries Organization.

Held by the Library, International Center for Marine Resource Development, University of Rhode Island, Kingston.

Abstract in *A.I.D. Research and Development Abstracts*, Apr. 1977. p. 9–10.

Issued also in microfiche. [Washington, U.S. Agency for International Development, 1975?] 1 sheet.　　　　DLC-Sci RR PN-AAC-165

Economic Conditions

1287

Kantarelis, Demetrius, *and* Frank Puffer. Employment in Eastern Africa. Worcester, Mass., Program for International Development, Clark University, 1980. 72 p. (Eastern Africa regional studies. Regional paper, no. 2)　　　　DLC

Bibliography: p. 69–72.

"Eastern Africa Regional Studies are prepared on behalf of the United States Agency for International Development."

1288

Lake Victoria coffee smuggling operations described. *In*. U.S. *Joint Publications Research Service*. JPRS 69326. [Springfield, Va., National Technical Information Service, 1977] (Translations on Sub-Saharan Africa, no. 1765) p. 96–99.

Article in *Voice of Uganda*, Kampala, June 7, 1977, p. 4.

Microfiche. [s.l., 1977]

DLC-Micro JPRS 69326

1289

Mbogoro, D. A. K. East African Community's political, economic failure outlined. Economic failure. *In* U.S. *Joint Publications Research Service*. JPRS 72657. [Springfield, Va., National Technical Information Service, 1979] (Translations on Sub-Saharan Africa, no. 2052) p. 16–29.

Translation of article in *Revue française d'études politiques africaines*, Paris, Nov. 1978, p. 31–48.

Microfiche. [Washington, Supt. of Docs., U.S. Govt. Print. Off., 1979]

DLC-Micro JPRS 72657

1290

Porter, Richard C. Measuring the cost of granting tariff preferences. Ann Arbor, Center for Research on Economic Development, University of Michigan, 1974. 44 p. (Michigan. University. Center for Research on Economic Development. Discussion paper, no. 38)

The techniques developed in the paper are applied to the preferences accorded in 1971 by the East African Community to certain of its imports from the European Economic Community.

Microfiche. [Washington, U.S. Agency for International Development, 1974?] 1 sheet.

DLC-Sci RR PN-AAB-124

Foreign Relations

1291

Bonker, Don. U.S. policy in Horn of Africa. Congressional record, 95th Congress, 1st session, v. 123, Mar. 23, 1977: 8895-8896.　　　　J11.R5 v. 123

Extension of remarks in the U.S. House of Representatives.

Includes testimony by Assistant Secretary of State William Schaufele before the Subcommittee on African Affairs, Committee on Foreign Relations, U.S. Senate, Aug. 6, 1976 concerning American relations with Ethiopia, Somalia, Kenya, and Sudan.

1292

Calestous Juma. Ethiopian-Kenyan amity treaty renewed. *In U.S.* Joint Publications Research Service. JPRS 73197. [Springfield, Va., National Technical Information Service, 1979] (Translations on Sub-Saharan Africa, no. 2087) p. 1–5.

From article in *Ethiopian Herald*, Addis Ababa, Mar. 18, 1979, p. 2, 5.

Microfiche. [Washington, Supt. of Docs., U.S. Govt. Print. Off., 1979]

DLC-Micro JPRS 73197

1293

Cross, Richard W. Sino-Soviet competition in East Africa; a report submitted to the faculty. Maxwell Air Force Base, Ala., Air University, Air War College, 1976. 83 leaves.　　　　AMAU

"Professional study, no. 5880."

Bibliography: p. 80–83.

Focuses on Somalia and Tanzania.

Issued also in microfiche. [s.l., 1976] 1 sheet (AD-B011350L).

1294

Guillerez, Bernard. Horn of Africa: toward Ethiopian hegemony. *In U.S.* Joint Publications Research Service. JPRS 75997. [Springfield, Va., National Technical Information Service, 1980] (Sub-Saharan Africa report, no. 2264) p. 8–11.

Translation of article in *Défense nationale*, Paris, May 1980, p. 175–178.

Emphasis is on Ethiopia's relations with Sudan.

1294 (cont.)

Microfiche. [s.l., 1980]

DLC-Micro JPRS 75997

1294a

Henze, Paul B. Arming the Horn, 1960–1980. [Washington, International Security Studies Program, The Wilson Center], 1982. 34 p.   DLC

"Working papers. No. 43."

"The first draft of this study was presented to the VIIth International Conference on Ethiopian Studies at the University of Lund, Sweden, 26–29 April 1982."

Focus is on military expenditures, arms imports and military aid in Ethiopia, Kenya, Somalia, and Sudan.

1295

Moose, Richard M. Horn of Africa. *In* U.S. *Dept. of State.* The Department of State bulletin, v. 79, no. 2025, Apr. 1979: 12–13.   JX232.A33 v. 79

Statement by the Assistant Secretary of State for African Affairs before the Subcommittee on Africa, Committee on Foreign Affairs, House of Representatives, Feb. 28, 1979.

Focus is on Ethiopia, Djibouti, Somalia, and Kenya.

1296

Numayri's summit with Mengistu of Ethiopia described. *In* U.S. *Joint Publications Research Service.* JPRS 73193. [Springfield, Va., National Technical Information Service, 1979] (Translations on Near East and North Africa, no. 1940) p. 67–72.

Translation of article on meeting between President Gaafar Nimeiri of Sudan and Lt. Col. Mengistu Haile-Mariam, Chairman of the Provisional Military Administrative Council of Ethiopia, in *al-Mustaqbal*, Paris, Mar. 3, 1979, p. 23–25.

Microfiche. [Washington, Supt. of Docs., U.S. Govt. Print. Off., 1979]

DLC-Micro JPRS 73193

1297

Nurthen, William A. Soviet strategy in the Red Sea basin. Monterey, Calif., Naval Postgraduate School, 1980. 238 p.

Bibliography: p. 227–235.

Thesis (M.A.)—Naval Postgraduate School.

An analysis of Soviet policy in Ethiopia, Somalia, and the southwestern Arabian peninsula.

Microfiche. [s.l., Defense Technical Information Center, 1980] 3 sheets.

DLC-Sci RR AD-A086568

1298

Remnek, Richard. Soviet policy in the Horn of Africa: the decision to intervene. Alexandria, Va., Institute of Naval Studies, Center for Naval Analyses, 1980. 60 p.

"Rept. no. CNA-PP-270."

"Professional paper."

Microfiche. [s.l., Defense Documentation Center, 1980] 1 sheet.   DLC-Sci RR AD-A081195

1299

Rivière, Jean-Philippe. French diplomacy in East Africa examined. *In* U.S. *Joint Publications Research Service.* JPRS 73268. [Springfield, Va., National Technical Information Service, 1979] (Translations on Sub-Saharan Africa, no. 2092) p. 26–29.

Translation of article in *Demain l'Afrique*, Paris, Mar. 26, 1979, p. 40–42.

Microfiche. [Washington, Supt. of Docs., U.S. Govt. Print. Off., 1979]

DLC-Micro JPRS 73268

1300

Schaufele, William E. Department discusses U.S. policy toward countries in the horn of Africa. *In* U.S. *Dept. of State.* The Department of State bulletin, v. 75, no. 1940, Aug. 30, 1976: 300–303.

JX232.A33 v. 75

Statement by the Assistant Secretary of State for African Affairs before the Subcommittee on African Affairs, Committee on Foreign Relations, Senate, Aug. 6, 1976.

1301

Shaver, William G. United States involvement in the Horn of Africa. Maxwell Air Force Base, Ala., Air University, Air Command and Staff College, 1979. 69 p.   AMAU

"Research study."

1302

Soviet policy in the Horn of Africa: the decision to intervene. Carlisle Barracks, Pa., Strategic Studies Institute, Army War College, 1980. 25 p. AMAU

1303

Sudan-Ethiopia committee reaches agreements, mutual understanding. *In* U.S. *Joint Publications Research Service.* JPRS 76205. [Springfield, Va., National Technical Information Service, 1980] (Near East /North Africa report, no. 2162) p. 53–58.

Translation of article in *al-Ayyām*, Khartoum, May 13, 1980, p. 3.

Microfiche. [s.l., 1980]

DLC-Micro JPRS 76205

1304

Sudan seen mediating between Addis Ababa and Washington. *In* U.S. *Joint Publications Research Service.* JPRS 76221. [Springfield, Va., National Technical Information Service, 1980] (Near East/North Africa report, no. 2164) p. 99–102.

Translation of article in *al-Mustaqbal*, Paris, May 31, 1980, p. 32–33.

Includes notes on recommendations of the Sudanese Government for a peaceful settlement of the Eritrean question.

Microfiche. [s.l., 1980]

DLC-Micro JPRS 76221

Ethiopian-Somali Conflict

1305

U.S. *Congress. Senate. Committee on Foreign Relations. Subcommittee on African Affairs.* Ethiopia and the Horn of Africa: hearings, Ninety-fourth Congress, second session ... August 4, 5, and 6, 1976. Washington, U.S. Govt. Print. Off., 1976. 138 p.   KF26.F625   1976b

Dick Clark, chairman.

In his initial remarks, chairman Clark notes "we start with the premise that a radically altered situation requires a fundamental reassessment of American policies. Not only has the stability of Ethiopia's internal life collapsed, so too has the stability of Ethiopia's relations with her neighbors."—p. 1.

1306

U.S. *Factfinding Mission to Egypt, Sudan, Ethiopia, Somalia, and Kenya.* War in the Horn of Africa: a firsthand report on the challenges for United States policy: report of a Factfinding Mission to Egypt, Sudan, Ethiopia, Somalia, and Kenya, December 12 to 22, 1977, to the Committee on International Relations, U.S. House of Representatives. Washington, U.S. Govt. Print. Off., 1978. 51 p.

DT367.8.U54   1978

Report submitted by Representatives Don Bonker of the Committee on International Relations and Paul Tsongas of the Committee on Banking, Finance and Urban Affairs, who undertook the mission.

1307

Barre, Mohamed Siad. President cautions Ethiopia's supporters not to interfere. *In* U.S. *Joint Publications Research Service.* JPRS 70051. [Springfield, Va., National Technical Information Service, 1977] (Translations on Sub-Saharan Africa, no. 1824) p. 45–49.

Translation of speech recorded in *al-Ṭalī'ah*, Mogadishu, Sept. 16, 1977, p. 1, 2.

Microfiche. [s.l., 1977]

DLC-Micro JPRS 70051

1308

Brisset, Claire. Reportage on refugees in the Horn of Africa. *In* U.S. *Joint Publications Research Service.* JPRS 73553. [Springfield, Va., National Technical Information Service, 1979] (Translations on Sub-Saharan Africa, no. 2111) p. 1–8.

Translation of article in *Le Monde*, Paris, Apr. 26, 1979, p. 8.

Concerns refugees from the conflict in Ethiopia residing in Djibouti, Somalia, and Sudan.

Microfiche. [Washington, Supt. of Docs., U.S. Govt. Print. Off., 1979]

DLC-Micro JPRS 73553

1309

Eagleton, Thomas F. The Horn of Africa. Congressional record, 95th Congress, 2d session, v. 124, Feb. 8, 1978: 2664–2668.   J11.R5 v. 124

Remarks in the U.S. Senate on United States policy in the region, especially in relation to the conflict between Ethiopia and Somalia.

Includes articles from *Newsweek* and the *Washington Post*.

1310

——— The Horn of Africa. Congressional record, 95th Congress, 2d session, v. 124, Mar. 1, 1978: 5123–5128.   J11.R5 v. 124

Remarks in the U.S. Senate on Soviet and Cuban intervention in the Ethiopian-Somali conflict.

1311

Editorial questions Soviet relations with Somali [sic], Ethiopia. *In* U.S. *Joint Publications Research Service.* JPRS 69498. [Springfield, Va., National Technical Information Service, 1977] (Translations on Sub-Saharan Africa, no. 1778) p. 43–49.

Translation of editorial in *al-Ṭalī'ah*, Mogadishu May 27, 1977, p. 1, 4.

Microfiche. [s.l., 1977]

DLC-Micro JPRS 69498

1312

Ethiopia-Somalia ground forces comparison study. Arlington, Va., Intelligence and Threat Analysis Center, Army Intelligence and Security Command, U.S. Army, 1977. 1 v.   AMAU

1313

Ethiopian-Somali conflict manipulated by west. *In* U.S. *Joint Publications Research Service.* JPRS

1313 (cont.)

70931. [Springfield, Va., National Technical Information Service, 1978] (Translations on Sub-Saharan Africa, no. 1909) p. 44–48.

Translation of article in *Prisma del Meridiano*, Havana, Jan. 1–15, 1978, p. 2–4.

Microfiche. [Washington, Supt. of Docs., U.S. Govt. Print. Off., 1978]

DLC-Micro JPRS 70931

1314

Ferguson, Michael M. The Horn of Africa: historical patterns of conflict and strategic considerations. Monterey, Calif., Naval Postgraduate School, 1978. 156 p. maps.

Bibliography: p. 144–153.

Thesis (M.A.)— Naval Postgraduate School.

Abstract in *Government Reports Announcements & Index*, Mar. 16, 1979, p. 25.

Microfiche. [s.l., Defense Documentation Center, 1979] 2 sheets.   DLC-Sci RR AD-A061019

1315

Gawido, Abdi. The prospects in the Horn of Africa: a Somali's perception. Ottawa, Ontario, Operational Research and Analysis Establishment, Dept. of National Defence, 1978. 25 p.

Concerns Ethiopia and Somalia.

Microfiche. [s.l., Defense Documentation Center, 1979] 1 sheet.   DLC-Sci RR AD-A067328

1316

Liberation fronts report Russian, Cuban, Ethiopian casualties. *In* U.S. *Joint Publications Research Service.* JPRS 71417. [Springfield, Va., National Technical Information Service, 1978] (Translations on Sub-Saharan Africa, no. 1956) p. 85-89.

Articles reporting statements by the Western Somali Liberation Front and the Somali Abo Liberation Front, in *Danab*, Mogadishu, June 1978 (various dates).

Microfiche. [Washington, Supt. of Docs., U.S. Govt. Print. Off., 1978]

DLC-Micro JPRS 71417

1317

Lochstoer, Catherine. Western Somali liberation leader interviewed. *In* U.S. *Joint Publications Research Service.* JPRS 70157. [Springfield, Va., National Technical Information Service, 1977] (Translations on Sub-Saharan Africa, no. 1833) p. 47–50.

Translation of interview with Abdullahi Hassan, leader of the Western Somalia Liberation Front, in *Aftenposten*, Oslo, Oct. 20, 1977, p. 9.

Microfiche. [s.l., 1977]

DLC-Micro JPRS 70157

1318

Mengistu Haile-Mariam. Mengistu addresses cadets, warns Somali rulers. *In* U.S. *Joint Publications Research Service.* JPRS 72680. [Springfield, Va., National Technical Information Service, 1979] (Translations on Sub-Saharan Africa, no. 2054) p. 20–24.

From article in *Ethiopian Herald*, Addis Ababa, Jan. 2, 1979, p. 1, 5.

Microfiche. [Washington, Supt. of Docs., U.S. Govt. Print. Off., 1979]

DLC-Micro JPRS 72680

1319

——— Mengistu discusses war in Ogaden, pledges no expansionist aims. *In* U.S. *Joint Publications Research Service.* JPRS 70782. [Springfield, Va., National Technical Information Service, 1978] (Translations on Sub-Saharan Africa, no. 1894) p. 40–51.

Text of radio-television address recorded in *Granma*, Havana, Feb. 19, 1978, p. 2–5.

Microfiche. [Washington, Supt. of Docs., U.S. Govt. Print. Off., 1978]

DLC-Micro JPRS 70782

1320

Plight of refugees in Horn of Africa described. *In* U.S. *Joint Publications Research Service.* JPRS 72632. [Springfield, Va., National Technical Information Service, 1979] (Translations on Sub-Saharan Africa, no. 2051) p. 1–7.

From article in *West Africa*, London, Dec. 18, 1978, p. 2520, 2521, 2523, 2524.

Microfiche. [Washington, Supt. of Docs., U.S. Govt. Print. Off., 1979]

DLC-Micro JPRS 72632

1321

Pomonti, Jean-Claude. Ethiopia, Somalia bogged down in the Ogaden. *In* U.S. *Joint Publications Research Service.* JPRS 70218. [Springfield, Va., National Technical Information Service, 1977] (Translations on Sub-Saharan Africa, no. 1839) p. 1–5.

Translation of article in *Le Monde*, Paris, Nov. 6/7, 1977, p. 6.

Microfiche. [s.l., 1977]

DLC-Micro JPRS 70218

1322

Reasons for Kenya's support of Ethiopia analyzed.

1322 (cont.)

In U.S. *Joint Publications Research Service.* JPRS 71148. [Springfield, Va., National Technical Information Service, 1978] (Translations on Sub-Saharan Africa, no. 1930) p. 80–83.

Translation of article in *al-Ṭali'ah*, Mogadishu, Apr. 7, 1978, p. 1, 2.

Microfiche. [Washington, Supt. of Docs., U.S. Govt. Print. Off., 1978]

DLC-Micro JPRS 71148

1323

Somalia would be ready to go to war over Djibouti. *In* U.S. *Joint Publications Research Service.* JPRS 69354. [Springfield, Va., National Technical Information Service, 1977] (Translations on Sub-Saharan Africa, no. 1767) p. 64–67.

Article in *Events*, Beirut, June 3, 1977, p. 28, 29.

Microfiche. [s.l., 1977]

DLC-Micro JPRS 69354

1324

Soviets warned of what they will lose for supporting Ethiopia. *In* U.S. *Joint Publications Research Service.* JPRS 69498. [Springfield, Va., National Technical Information Service, 1977] (Translations on Sub-Saharan Africa, no. 1778) p. 50–60.

Translation of editorial in *al-Ṭalī'ah*, Mogadishu, June 3, 1977, p. 1, 3, 4, 5.

Microfiche. [s.l., 1977]

DLC-Micro JPRS 69473

1325

WSLF appeals to OAU labor commission session. *In* U.S. *Joint Publications Research Service.* JPRS 73528. [Springfield, Va., National Technical Information Service, 1979] (Translations on Sub-Saharan Africa, no. 2110) p. 6–9.

From article in *Danab*, Mogadiscio, Apr. 28, 1979, p. 1–9.

WSLF: Western Somali Liberation Front; OAU: Organization of African Unity.

An appeal for support against Ethiopian "imperialism."

Microfiche. [Washington, Supt. of Docs., U.S. Govt. Print. Off., 1979]

DLC-Micro JPRS 73528

1326

WSLF official stresses need for Arab unity. *In* U.S. *Joint Publications Research Service.* JPRS 75487. [Springfield, Va., National Technical Information Service, 1980] (Sub-Saharan Africa report, no. 2234) p. 125–129.

Interview with Abdullahi Mohamed Hassan, secretary-general of the Western Somali Liberation Front, in *Heegan*, Mogadishu, Mar. 7, 1980, p. 3. Microfiche. [s.l., 1980]

DLC-Micro JPRS 75487

1327

Weiss, Kenneth G. The Soviet involvement in the Ogaden war. Alexandria, Va., Institute of Naval Studies, Center for Naval Analyses, [1980] 42 p. (Center for Naval Analyses. Professional paper, 269)

Microfiche. [s.l., Defense Technical Information Center, 1980] 1 sheet.

DLC-Sci RR AD-A082219

Geography and Maps

1328

[U.S. *Central Intelligence Agency*] Horn of Africa. [Washington, 1977] col. map.

G8320   1977.U5

Scale 1 : 4,000,000.

"503443 11-77 (543299)."

Includes inset showing radial distances from Cape of Good Hope with comparative area map and inset of "administrative divisions."

1329

U.S. *Dept. of State. Office of the Geographer.* Djibouti-Somalia boundary. Washington, 1979. 5 p. col. map (*Its* International boundary study, no. 87 rev.)

DLC-G&M

First issued in 1968.

1330

—— Ethiopia-French Territory of the Afars and Issas boundary. [Washington?], 1976. 15 p. col. map. (*Its* International boundary study, no. 154)

DLC-G&M

1331

—— Ethiopia-Kenya boundary. Washington, 1975. 7 p. fold. col. map. (*Its* International boundary study, no. 152)

DLC-G&M

1332

—— Ethiopia-Somalia boundary. Washington, 1975. 12 p. (*Its* International boundary study, no. 123)

DLC-G&M

Bibliography: p. 11–12.

1333

—— Maritime boundary: Kenya-Tanzania. Washington, 1981. 6 p. fold. col. map (in pocket) (*Its* Limits in the seas, no. 92)

DLC-G&M

Geology, Hydrology, and Mineral Resources

1334

Burroughs, Richard H. Structural and sedimentological evolution of the Somali basin: paleo-oceanographic interpretations. Woods Hole, Mass., Woods Hole Oceanographic Institution, 1977. [288] p. maps.

Prepared for the Office of Naval Research under contract N00014-66-C-0241 and for the National Science Foundation under grant 27516.

Dissertation—Massachusetts Institute of Technology and Woods Hole Oceanographic Institution.

Abstract in *Government Reports Announcements & Index*, Oct. 28, 1977, p. 114.

Microfiche. [s.l., Defense Documentation Center, 1977] 4 sheets.

DLC-Sci RR AD-A043200

1335

Deutsch, Morris. East African Seminar and Workshop on Remote Sensing of Natural Resources and Environment, held at Nairobi, Kenya, March 31–April 3, 1974. Reston, Va., U.S. Geological Survey, 1975. [195] p. (in various pagings) illus.

Prepared for the Office of Science and Technology, U.S. Agency for International Development, in cooperation with the Government of Kenya.

Abstract in *A.I.D. Research and Development Abstract*, Sept. 1975, p. 21.

Microfiche. [Washington, U.S. Agency for International Development, 1975?] 3 sheets.

DLC-Sci RR PN-AAB-164

1336

——— East African seminar/workshop trip report. [Reston, Va., 1974] 17 p. illus. (U.S. Geological Survey. [Reports—Open file series, no. 74–193])

DI-GS

1337

Morse, David E. The mineral industry of other East African countries. *In* Minerals yearbook, v. 3, 1978–79. [Washington, U.S. Govt. Print. Off., 1981] p. 1085–1091.

TN23.U612   1978–79 v. 3

Prepared by the U.S. Bureau of Mines.

Covers Burundi, Djibouti, Ethiopia, Lesotho, Malawi, Mauritius, Comoros, Réunion, Rwanda, Seychelles, Somalia, Swaziland, and Uganda.

The following items (entries 1338–1341) are listed in chronological order:

1338

Reed, Avery H., *and* Robert G. Clarke. The mineral industry of Kenya, Tanzania, and Uganda. *In* Minerals yearbook, v. 3, 1972. [Washington, for sale by the Supt. of Docs., U.S. Govt. Print. Off., 1974] p. 503–511.

TN23.U612   1972, v. 3

Prepared by the U.S. Bureau of Mines.

1339

——— The mineral industry of Kenya, Tanzania, and Uganda. *In* Minerals yearbook, v. 3, 1973. [Washington, for sale by the Supt. of Docs., U.S. Govt. Print. Off., 1976] p. 533–545.

TN23.U612   1973, v. 3

Prepared by the U.S. Bureau of Mines.

1340

——— The mineral industry of Kenya, Tanzania, and Uganda. *In* Minerals yearbook, v. 3, 1974. [Washington, for sale by the Supt. of Docs., U.S. Govt. Print. Off., 1977] p. 565–575.

TN23.U612   1974, v. 3

Prepared by the U.S. Bureau of Mines.

1341

Jolly, Janice L. W., *and* David G. Willard. The mineral industry of Kenya, Tanzania, and Uganda. *In* Minerals yearbook, v. 3, 1975. [Washington, for sale by the Supt. of Docs., U.S. Govt. Print. Off., 1978] p. 597–614.   TN23.U612   1975, v.3

Prepared by the U.S. Bureau of Mines.

Politics and Government

1342

Bailey, Richard C. Pacific settlement of disputes in the East African Community. Maxwell Air Force Base, Ala., 1977. 34 p.   AMAU

"Air University. Air Command and Staff College. Research study."

1343

Barkan, Joel D. Bringing home the pork: legislator behavior, rural development and political change in East Africa. [Iowa City, Comparative Legislative Research Center, University of Iowa], 1975. [39] p. (Iowa. University. Comparative Legislative Research Center. Occasional paper, no. 9)

The Center is supported in part by a grant from the U.S. Agency for International Development.

Examined in the Development Information Center, AID, Washington, D.C.

1344

Constantin, François. East African Community's

1344 (cont.)

political, economic failure outlined. Political failure. *In* U.S. *Joint Publications Research Service.* JPRS 72657. [Springfield, Va., National Technical Information Service, 1979] (Translations on Sub-Saharan Africa, no. 2052) p. 1–15.

Translation of article in *Revue française d'études politiques africaines*, Paris, Nov. 1978, p. 12–30.

Microfiche. [Washington, Supt. of Docs., U.S. Govt. Print. Off., 1979]

DLC-Micro JPRS 72657

1345

Lechini, Gladys T. East African Community's political, economic failure outlined. *In* U.S. *Joint Publications Research Service.* JPRS 72657. [Springfield, Va., National Technical Information Service, 1979] (Translations on Sub-Saharan Africa, no. 2052) p. 29–44.

Translation of article in *Revue française d'études politiques africaines*, Paris, Nov. 1978, p. 49–67.

Microfiche. [Washington, Supt. of Docs., U.S. Govt. Print. Off., 1979]

DLC-Micro JPRS 72657

1346

Young, Robert A. Quantitative methods for long-range environmental forecasting; interim technical report, no. 2. Arlington, Va., Consolidated Analysis Centers, inc., 1973. 398 p.

Sponsored by the U.S. Advanced Research Projects Agency (ARPA order no. 2067).

Covers the period Feb. 1972–Jan. 1973.

Analyses and predictions concerning economic and political developments in certain Indian Ocean countries, including Ethiopia, Somalia, Kenya, and Tanzania.

Microfiche. [s.l., 1973] 5 sheets (AD-907247L).

Other Subjects

1347

U.S. *Congress. House. Committee on Government Operations. Legislation and National Security Subcommittee.* U.S. mission and office operations—East Africa: hearing before a subcommittee of the Committee on Government Operations, House of Representatives, Ninety-sixth Congress, second session, February 13, 1980. Washington, U.S. Govt. Print. Off., 1980. 72 p.

KF27.G6676   1980f
J74.A23 96th
Cong., House Comm.
Govt. Oper., v. 74

Jack Brooks, chairman.
Hearing held in Nairobi, Kenya.

Representative Brooks, in his opening statement, indicates that the "emphasis ... is on internal management."

Includes statements and testimony by officials of U.S. embassies and Agency for International Development missions.

1348

Abdulaziz, Mohamed H., *and* Melvin J. Fox. Evaluation report on survey of language use and language teaching of eastern Africa. [New York, Ford Foundation], 1978. [162] p.

Survey conducted in Kenya, Tanzania, Uganda, and Zambia.

Abstract in *Resources in Education*, 1980 annual cumulation, p. 463.

Microfiche. [Arlington, Va., ERIC Document Reproduction Service; prepared for Educational Resources Information Center, National Institute of Education, 1980] 2 sheets.

DLC-Micro ED177903

1349

Anglophone East African Working Party, *Nairobi, Kenya*, 29th November–8th December 1973. Report. [London?, 1973?] 80 p.

On cover: USAID grant no. CSD 3411.

At head of title: International Confederation of Midwives.

Issued in cooperation with the Joint Study Group of the International Confederation of Midwives and the International Federation of Gynaecology and Obstetrics.

Microfiche. [Washington, U.S. Agency for International Development, 1973?] 1 sheet.

DLC-Sci RR PN-AAF-532

1350

Dean, John. A regional library science program for Eastern Africa; a report prepared for the Standing Conference of African University Librarians (Eastern Africa) Perth, Australia, 1974. 64 p.

Abstract in *Resources in Education*, Nov. 1978, p. 117.

Microfiche. [Arlington, Va., ERIC Document Reproduction Service; prepared for Educational Resources Information Center, National Institute of Education, 1978] 1 sheet.

DLC-Micro ED156113

1351

Defense Mapping Agency. *Hydrographic Center.* Sailing directions (enroute) for East Africa and the South Indian Ocean. 1st ed. Washington, 1978. 531 p. maps. (Defense Mapping Agency, Hydrographic Center. Publication, 171)

VK887.D43   1978

1352

—— Sailing directions (enroute) for the Red Sea and Persian Gulf. 1st ed. Washington, 1978. 412 p. illus., maps. (*Its* Publication, 172)

VK895.D43   1978

Loose-leaf for updating.

Includes information on the harbors and coasts of Sudan, Ethiopia, Djibouti, and Somalia.

1353

Fuelwood and energy in Eastern Africa: an assessment of the environmental impact of energy uses. Worcester, Mass., Eastern Africa Environmental Trends Project, Program for International Development, Clark University, [1978] [158] p. illus.

"A draft report prepared on behalf of AID Contract no. AID/afr-G-1356."

Abstract in *A.I.D. Research & Development Abstracts*, July 1981, p. 41.

Microfiche. [Washington, U.S. Agency for International Development, 1978?] 2 sheets.

DLC-Sci RR PN-AAH-464

1354

Herman, Barry. Multinational oligopoly in poor countries: how East Africa got its petroleum refineries. Ann Arbor, Center for Research on Economic Development, University of Michigan, 1974. 32 p. (Michigan. University. Center for Research on Economic Development. Discussion paper, no. 39)

Abstract in *A.I.D. Research and Development Abstracts*, Sept. 1975, p. 12.

Microfiche. [Washington, U.S. Agency for International Development, 1974?] 1 sheet.

DLC-Sci PN-AAB-123

1355

International Conference on Marine Resources Development in Eastern Africa, *University of Dar es Salaam*, 1974. International Conference on Marine Resources Development in Eastern Africa, the University of Dar es Salaam, Dar es Salaam, Tanzania, April 4–9, 1974; editors, A. D. Msangi [and] J. J. Griffin. Dar es Salaam, The University, [1975?] 130 p. illus., map.   SH312.A42I57   1974

Publication of proceedings supported by grants from the U.S. Agency for International Development.

On cover: "In cooperation with the International Center for Marine Resource Development of the University of Rhode Island, USA."

Abstract in *A.I.D. Research and Development Abstracts*, Oct. 1976, p. 5–6.

Issued also in microfiche. [Washington, U.S.

Agency for International Development, 1975?] 2 sheets.

DLC-Sci RR PN-AAB-918

1356

Lachner, Ernest A., *and* Susan J. Karnella. Fishes of the genus Eviota of the Red Sea with descriptions of three new species (Teleostei, Gobiidae). Washington, Smithsonian Institution Press, 1978. 23 p. illus. (Smithsonian Institution. Smithsonian contributions to zoology, no. 286)

QL1.S54 no. 286

1357

Lindfors, Bernth. East African popular literature in English. [Austin?], University of Texas, 1976. [26] leaves.

Field research supported by the National Endowment for the Humanities.

Presented at annual meeting of the African Studies Association, 1976.

Microfilm. [African Studies Association. Papers presented at the annual meeting.]

DLC-Micro Microfilm 03782 DT 1976 reel 1

1358

Mohr, Paul. 1974 Ethiopian rift geodimeter survey. Cambridge, Mass., Smithsonian Institution, Astrophysical Observatory, 1977. [159] p. map. (Smithsonian Institution. Astrophysical Observatory. SAO special report, no. 376)

Microfiche. [s.l., 1977] 2 sheets.

DLC-Sci RR N77-25706

1359

Munroe, Ruth H., *and* Robert L. Munroe. Infant care and childhood performance in East Africa. [s.l.], 1975. [15] p.

Paper presented at the biennial meeting of the Society for Research in Child Development, 1975.

On cover: "Draft copy."

Abstract in *Resources in Education*, Apr. 1976, p. 130–131.

Microfiche. [Arlington, Va., ERIC Document Reproduction Service; prepared for Educational Resources Information Center, National Institute of Education, 1976] 1 sheet.

DLC-Sci RR ED115369

1360

O'Reilly, M. P. The compaction of soils and stabilized bases on roads in East Africa. Crowthorne, Eng., Overseas Unit, Transport and Road Research Laboratory, 1974, 71 p.

Abstract in *Selected Appropriate Technologies for Developing Countries*, no. 1, p. 76.

1360 (cont.)

Microfiche. [Springfield, Va., National Technical Information Service, 1974] 1 sheet.

DLC-Sci RR PB231391

1361

Pemberton, Robert W. Exploration for natural enemies of *hydrilla verticillata* in eastern Africa; final report. Gainesville, Fla., Agricultural Research Service, Southern Region, U.S. Dept. of Agriculture, 1980. 30, [22] p. maps. (U.S. Waterways Experiment Station, Vicksburg, Miss. Miscellaneous paper, A-80-1)

Prepared for the Chief of Engineers, U.S. Army.

Monitored by the Environmental Laboratory, U.S. Army Engineers Waterways Experiment Station, Vicksburg, Miss.

Issued also in microfiche. [s.l., Defense Documentation Center, 1980] 1 sheet.

DLC-Sci RR AD-A085875

1361a

Refugee movement within the Horn of Africa, by Susan Enea [et al.] Washington, International Demographic Data Center, U.S. Bureau of the Census, 1980. 204 leaves. DLC

Bibliography: leaves 197–204.

"This report attempts to estimate refugee movement within the Horn of Africa to the year 1980, to project alternative future refugee movement to the year 1983, and to discuss the demographic impact of this movement on the countries within the Horn

of Africa. Traditionally, the Horn is considered to be a region of East Africa bounded to the north by the Red Sea and to the east by the Indian Ocean and comprises the nations of Ethiopia, Djibouti, and Somalia. The Democratic Republic of the Sudan is also considered to be part of the Horn in this report, because the Sudan has been and continues to be integrally related to the culture and history of the region."—p. [1].

1362

Refugees in Eastern Africa: towards a policy formulation, [by] Philip O'Keefe [et al.] Worcester, Mass., Program for International Development, [Clark University], 1980. 25 p. (Eastern Africa regional studies. Regional paper, no. 3) DLC

Bibliography: p. 22–25.

"Eastern Africa Regional Studies are prepared on behalf of the United States Agency for International Development."

1363

Roper, D. Lee. The proud Maasai; illustrated by Eva K. Oemick. El Cajon, Calif., Roper, c1978. 91 p. illus. DT429.R67

Abstract in *Resources in Education*, Sept. 1979, p. 160.

Issued also in microfiche. [Arlington, Va., ERIC Document Reproduction Service; prepared for Educational Resources Information Center, National Institute of Education, 1979] 2 sheets.

DLC-Sci RR ED170233

Djibouti

General

1364

U.S. *Dept. of State.* Post report. Djibouti. [Washington, Dept. of State, Publishing Services Division; for sale by the Supt. of Docs., U.S. Govt. Print. Off.] 1981. 12 p. illus., map. (*Its* Department and Foreign Service series, 215)

JX1705.A286 Spec. Format

Department of State publication 9163.

For a description of the contents of this publication, see the note to entry 936.

1365

U.S. *Dept. of State. Bureau of Public Affairs.* Background notes. Djibouti. [Washington, for sale by the Supt. of Docs., U.S. Govt. Print. Off.], 1979. 4 p. maps. (U.S. Dept. of State. Department of State publication 8429, rev.)

G59.U5

L.C. retains only the latest revision.

For a description of the contents of this publication, see the note to entry 937.

1366

Berry, Leonard. Djibouti. Worcester, Mass., Program for International Development, Clark University, 1980. 43 p. maps. (Eastern Africa country profiles. Country profile no. 5) DLC

Bibliography: p. 42–43.

"This country profile of Djibouti is prepared as one in a series of Eastern African country profiles. They come in response to a request by the United States Agency for International Development to compile succinct statements of principal development issues along with an analysis of the distribution of poverty"—Foreword.

1367

Djibouti: a country profile. Arlington, Va., Evaluation Technologies, inc., 1979. 46 p. col. map.

DLC

Prepared for the Office of U.S. Foreign Disaster Assistance, U.S. Agency for International Development, under contract AID/otr-C-1553.

A general introduction, with emphasis on political structure, disaster preparedness, demography, health, nutrition, housing, economic conditions, agriculture, geography, transportation, and power.

Assistance Programs

1368

U.S. *Agency for International Development.* Annual budget submission: Djibouti. Washington, U.S. International Development Cooperation Agency.

Vols. for 1980+ examined in the Development Information Center, AID, Washington, D.C.

1369

——— Country development strategy statement: Djibouti. Small program statement. [Washington?] annual?

Vol. for 1982 examined in the Development Information Center, AID, Washington, D.C.

1370

U.S. *Agency for International Development. Office of Foreign Disaster Assistance.* Summary report: Djibouti floods I, October 1977; Djibouti floods II, February 1978. [Washington], 1979. [4] p. map.

Microfiche. [Washington, Congressional Information Service, 1978?]

DLC-Micro ASI: 79 7206-3.42

1371

Djibouti. [*Treaties, etc. United States, 1978 Jan. 9*] Djibouti, agricultural commodities: transfer under Title II. Agreement signed at Djibouti January 9, 1978; entered into force January 9, 1978. *In* U.S. *Treaties, etc.* United States treaties and other international agreements, v. 29, 1976–77. [Washington, Dept. of State; for sale by the Supt. of Docs., U.S. Govt. Print. Off., 1980] p. 5764–5767. ([Treaties and other international acts series, 9150])

JX231.A34 v. 29

1372

Shepard, James M. Field survey report: Djibouti, Sept. 18–20, 1975. [Addis Ababa, USAID Mission to Ethiopia], 1975. 3 leaves.

   Issued by the Mission's Drought Relief Division. Acquired by the Library of Congress Office, Nairobi.

Economic Conditions

1373

Briand, Pierre. Economy said devoid of real resources. *In* U.S. *Joint Publications Research Service.* JPRS 67366. [Springfield, Va., National Technical Information Service, 1976] (Translations on Sub-Saharan Africa, no. 1654) p. 30–38.

   Translation of article in *Revue française d'études politiques africaines*, Paris, Apr. 1976, p. 54–56.

   Microfiche. [s.l., 1976]

DLC-Micro JPRS 67366

1374

Decraene, Philippe. Foreign relations, economic situation noted. *In* U.S. *Joint Publications Research Service.* JPRS 76184. [Springfield, Va., National Technical Information Service, 1980] (Sub-Saharan Africa report, no. 2276) p. 29–38.

   Translation of article in *Le Monde*, Paris, July 4–5, 1980.

   Microfiche. [s.l., 1980]

DLC-Micro JPRS 76184

Finance

1375

Barkat, Gourad Hamadou. Prime Minister addresses National Assembly on 1980 budget. *In* U.S. *Joint Publications Research Service.* JPRS 75020. [Springfield, Va., National Technical Information Service, 1980] (Sub-Saharan Africa report, no. 2205) p. 14–17.

   Translation of article in *Le Reveil de Djibouti*, Djibouti, Nov. 22, 1979, p. 1, 3.

   Microfiche. [s.l., 1980]

DLC-Micro JPRS 75020

1376

Draft budget for 1979 discussed, compared to previous budgets. *In* U.S. *Joint Publications Research Service.* JPRS 72503. [Springfield, Va., National Technical Information Service, 1978] (Translations on Sub-Saharan Africa, no. 2043) p. 12–16.

   Translation of article in *Le Reveil de Djibouti*, Djibouti, Nov. 30, 1978, p. 1, 3.

Microfiche. [Washington, Supt. of Docs., U.S. Govt. Print. Off., 1979?]

DLC-Micro JPRS 72503

Politics and Government

1377

Abdallah Kamil address to Chamber of Deputies. *In* U.S. *Joint Publications Research Service.* JPRS 68457. [Springfield, Va., National Technical Information Service, 1977] (Translations on Sub-Saharan Africa, no. 1702) p. 8–16.

   Translation of speech by a member of the Council of Government recorded in *Le Reveil de Djibouti*, Djibouti, Dec. 4, 1976, p. 1, 3.

   Microfiche. [s.l., 1977]

DLC-Micro JPRS 68457

1378

Activities of ministries during first year of independence. *In* U.S. *Joint Publications Research Service.* JPRS 71600. [Springfield, Va., National Technical Information Service, 1978] (Translations on Sub-Saharan Africa, no. 1972) p. 10–22.

   Translation of excerpts of article in *Le Reveil de Djibouti*, Djibouti, June 29, July 6, 1978.

   Microfiche. [Washington, Supt. of Docs., U.S. Govt. Print. Off., 1978]

DLC-Micro JPRS 71600

1379

Basset, Robert. Chamber votes on censure motion. *In* U.S. Joint Publications Research Service. JPRS 67291. [Springfield, Va., National Technical Information Service, 1976] (Translations on Sub-Saharan Africa, no. 1651) p. 16–30.

   Translation of article in *Le Reveil de Djibouti*, Djibouti, Apr. 24, 1976, p. 1, 2, 14, 16.

   Microfiche. [s.l., 1976]

DLC-Micro JPRS 67291

1380

Country described as politically stable, dependent on foreign aid. *In* U.S. *Joint Publications Research Service.* JPRS 76437. [Springfield, Va., National Technical Information Service, 1980] (Sub-Saharan Africa report, no. 2293) p. 24–27.

   Translation of article in *Europe Outremer*, Paris, Mar. 1980, p. 37.

   Microfiche. [s.l., 1980]

DLC-Micro JPRS 76437

1381

Formation of RPP reported. *In* U.S. *Joint Publications Research Service.* JPRS 73365. [Springfield, Va., National Technical Information Service, 1979]

1381 (cont.)

(Translations on Sub-Saharan Africa, no. 2099) p. 8–11.

Translation of article on the Rassemblement populaire pour le progrès, in *Le Reveil de Djibouti*, Djibouti, Mar. 8, 1979, p. 1, 4.

Microfiche. [Washington, Supt. of Docs., U.S. Govt. Print. Off., 1979]

DLC-Micro JPRS 73365

1382

Hassan Gouled's opening address to parliament. *In* U.S. *Joint Publications Research Service.* JPRS 69169. [Springfield, Va., National Technical Information Service, 1977] (Translations on Sub-Saharan Africa, no. 1753) p. 13–18.

Translation of speech recorded in *Le Reveil de Djibouti*, Djibouti, May 14, 1977, p. 1, 11.

Microfiche. [s.l., 1977]

DLC-Micro JPRS 69169

1383

Large influx of refugees creates problems. *In* U.S. *Joint Publications Research Service.* JPRS 73365. [Springfield, Va., National Technical Information Service, 1979] (Translations on Sub-Saharan Africa, no. 2099) p. 17–21.

Translation of article in *Le Reveil de Djibouti*, Djibouti, Jan. 18, 1979, p. 5.

Microfiche. [Washington, Supt. of Docs., U.S. Govt. Print. Off., 1979)

DLC-Micro JPRS 73365

1384

Leymarie, Philippe. Analysis of African People's League for Independence. *In* U.S. *Joint Publications Research Service.* JPRS 67366. [Springfield, Va., National Technical Information Service, 1976] (Translations on Sub-Saharan Africa, no. 1654) p. 39–53.

Translation of article on the Ligue populaire africaine pour l'indépendance, in *Revue française d'études politiques africaines*, Paris, Apr. 1976, p. 91–108.

Microfiche. [s.l., 1976]

DLC-Micro JPRS 67366

1385

——— Leymarie discusses first year of Djibouti independence. *In* U.S. *Joint Publications Research Service.* JPRS 72510. [Springfield, Va., National Technical Information Service, 1978] (Translations on Sub-Saharan Africa, no. 2044) p. 27–40.

Translation of article in *Revue française d'études politiques africaines*, Paris, Oct. 1978, p. 43–59.

Microfiche. [Washington, Supt. of Docs., U.S. Govt. Print. Off., 1979?]

DLC-Micro JPRS 72510

1386

Official denounces exploitation of ethnic clashes. *In* U.S. *Joint Publications Research Service.* JPRS 65372. [Springfield, Va., National Technical Information Service, 1975] (Translations on Africa, no. 1606) p. 16–20.

Translation of unattributed article in *Le Reveil de Djibouti*, Djibouti, June 14, 1975, p. 1, 12.

Microfiche. [s.l., 1975]

DLC-Micro JPRS 65372

1387

Overseas secretary discusses independence, cooperation. *In* U.S. *Joint Publications Research Service.* JPRS 68366. [Springfield, Va., National Technical Information Service, 1976] (Translations on Sub-Saharan Africa, no. 1696) p. 10–19.

Translation of interview with Olivier Stirn, Secretary of State for Overseas Departments and Territories of France, in *Le Reveil de Djibouti*, Djibouti, Nov. 23, 1976, p. 2, 3.

Microfiche. [s.l., 1976]

DLC-Micro JPRS 68366

1388

Questions about RPP given. *In* U.S. *Joint Publications Research Service.* JPRS 73365. [Springfield, Va., National Technical Information Service, 1979] (Translations on Sub-Saharan Africa, no. 2099) p. 12–16.

Translation of article in *Le Reveil de Djibouti*, Mar. 8, 1979, p. 3.

Microfiche. [Washington, Supt. of Docs., U.S. Govt. Print. Off., 1979]

DLC-Micro JPRS 73365

1389

Report on municipalities in Djibouti. *In* U.S. *Joint Publications Research Service.* JPRS 75020. [Springfield, Va., National Technical Information Service, 1980] (Sub-Saharan Africa report, no. 2205) p. 18–25.

Translation of article in *Le Reveil de Djibouti*, Djibouti, Nov. 15, 1979, p. 1, 5.

Microfiche. [s.l., 1980]

DLC-Micro JPRS 75020

1390

Ṣāliḥ, Najīb. President discusses Red Sea security, Djibouti independence. *In* U.S. *Joint Publications Research Service.* JPRS 68710. [Springfield, Va., National Technical Information Service, 1977]

1390 (cont.)

(Translations on Sub-Saharan Africa, no. 1717) p. 101–105.

Translation of interview with President Mohamed Siad Barre, in *al-Ra'y al-'āmm*, Kuwait, Jan. 21, 1977, p. 14.

Microfiche. [s.l., 1977]

DLC-Micro JPRS 68710

1391

Vazeilles, Benoît. Political development since 1967 reviewed. *In* U.S. *Joint Publications Research Service.* JPRS 67366. [Springfield, Va., National Technical Information Service, 1976] (Translations on Sub-Saharan Africa, no. 1654) p. 16–29.

Translation of article in *Revue française d'études politiques africaines*, Paris, Apr. 1976, p. 36–53.

Microfiche. [s.l., 1976]

DLC-Micro JPRS 67366

1392

al-Wayshī, Ibrāhīm. Premier stresses nonalignment, asks for money. *In* U.S. *Joint Publications Research Service.* JPRS 76917. [Springfield, Va., National Technical Information Service, 1980] (Sub-Saharan Africa report, no. 2326) p. 14–19.

Translation of interview with Prime Minister Gourad Hamadou Barkat, in *al-Qabas*, Kuwait, Oct. 5, 1980, p. 9.

Microfiche. [s.l., 1980]

DLC-Micro JPRS 76917

1393

———— President gives views on international, domestic issues. *In* U.S. *Joint Publications Research Service.* JPRS 76917. [Springfield, Va., National Technical Information Service, 1980] (Sub-Saharan Africa report, no. 2326) p. 6–13.

Translation of interview with President Gouled A. Hassan, in *al-Qabas*, Kuwait, Oct. 4, 1980, p. 1, 9.

Microfiche. [s.l., 1980]

DLC-Micro JPRS 76917

Other Subjects

1394

Africa: Djibouti. Selected statistical data by sex. Washington, 1981. 31, 17 p.   DLC

Study supported by the U.S. Agency for International Development's Office of Women in Development and Office of Population.

Data assembled by the International Demographic Data Center, U.S. Bureau of the Census.

Only one table, "unadjusted population," based on 1960–61 data is completed; for other headings, there is a notation of "search conducted but data not found."

1395

Broadnax, Madison, J. K. McDermott, and Claudio Shuftans. Survey of Djibouti's agricultural development. [Washington, Office of Eastern Africa Affairs, Bureau for Africa, Agency for International Development], 1977. 35 p.

Abstract in *A.I.D. Research and Development Abstracts*, Oct. 1978, p. 4.

Microfiche. [Washington, U.S. Agency for International Development, 1977?] 1 sheet (PN-AAF-584); examined in the Development Information Center, AID, Washington, D.C.

1396

[Djibouti—diplomatic relations and recognition] *In* Boyd, John A. Digest of United States practice in international law. 1977. [Washington] Office of the Legal Adviser, Dept. of State; [for sale by the Supt. of Docs., U.S. Govt. Print. Off., 1979] (Department of State publication, 8960) p. 15–16.

JX21.R68   1977

1397

Djibouti: newly independent state. [Washington] Office of the Geographer, U.S. Dept. of State, 1977. 2 p. maps.   DLC-G&M

"Geographic note. GE-173."

1398

Duteil, Mireille. Port to play growing role in transit activities. *In* U.S. *Joint Publications Research Service.* JPRS 75920. [Springfield, Va., National Technical Information Service, 1980] (Sub-Saharan Africa report, no. 2258) p. 41–44.

Translation of article on the port of Djibouti, in *Demain l'Afrique*, Paris, Feb. 11, 1980, p. 48–49.

Microfiche. [s.l., 1980]

DLC-Micro JPRS 75920

1399

Small-scale fisheries in Djibouti. Los Altos, Calif., Resources Development Associates, 1978. 97 p. illus., maps.

Prepared for the Industry and Trade Administration, U.S. Dept. of Commerce.

Microfiche. [Springfield, Va., National Technical Information Service, 1979] 2 sheets.

DLC-Sci RR DIB-79-10-500

Ethiopia

General

1400

U.S. *Dept. of State.* Post report. Ethiopia. [Washington?], 1978. 20 p. illus., map.

Examined in the Foreign Service Institute Library, Rosslyn, Va.

L.C. has report issued in 1972 (JX1705.A286 Spec. Format).

For a description of the contents of this publication, see the note to entry 936.

1401

U.S. *Dept. of State. Bureau of Public Affairs.* Background notes. Ethiopia. [Washington, for sale by the Supt. of Docs., U.S. Govt. Print. Off.], 1981. 7 p. illus., maps. (U.S. Dept. of State. Department of State publication 7785)   G59.U5

L.C. retains only the latest revision.

For a description of the contents of this publication, see the note to entry 937.

1402

Berry, Leonard. Ethiopia. Worcester, Mass., Program for International Development, Clark University, 1980. 29 p. maps. (Eastern Africa country profiles. Country profile no. 7)   DLC

"This country profile of Ethiopia is prepared as one in a series of Eastern African country profiles. . . . They come in response to a request by the United States Agency for International Development to compile succinct statements of principal development issues along with an analysis of the distribution of poverty."—Preface.

1403

Ethiopia, a country study. 3d ed., edited by Harold D. Nelson and Irving Kaplan. Washington, American University, Foreign Area Studies; [for sale by the Supt. of Docs., U.S. Govt. Print. Off.], 1981. xxix, 366 p. illus., maps.

DT378.E73   1981

"DA pam; 550–29."

Revision of *Area Handbook for Ethiopia*, [by] Irving Kaplan [et al.], 1971.

Bibliography: p. 319–344.

Contents: Historical setting, [by] Richard P. Stevens.—The society and its environment, [by] Irving Kaplan.—The economy, [by] Donald P. Whitaker.—Government and politics, [by] Harold D. Nelson.—National security, [by] Robert Rinehart.

Among the appendixes are the following:

Table 13. Survey of opposition groups, 1980. p. 310–311.

Tables 14–17. Major military weapons, defense expenditures, and manpower levels. p. 312–318.

1404

Pastorett, Tomma N. Ethiopia: selected unclassified references. Maxwell Air Force Base, Ala., Air University Library, 1977. 23 p.   DLC

1405

Philippi, Thomas. Ethiopia, a country profile; prepared for the Office of U.S. Foreign Disaster Assistance, Bureau for Private and Development Cooperation, Agency for International Development, Department of State by Evaluation Technologies, Inc., under contract AID/SOD/PDC-C-0283; written and researched by Thomas Philippi. Washington, The Office, 1978. 79 p., 2 leaves of plates.

DT373.P39

"December 1978."

Bibliography: p. 76–78.

A general introduction, with emphasis on political structure, disaster preparedness, demography, health, nutrition, housing, economic conditions, agriculture, geography, transportation, power, and communications.

Agriculture

1406

Betru Gebregziabher. Integrated development in rural Ethiopia: an evaluative study of the Chilalo Agri-

1406 (cont.)

cultural Development Unit. [Bloomington, Documentation and Analysis Center, International Development Research Center, Indiana University, c1975] [79] p. map.

"The Chilalo Agricultural Development Unit (CADU) is a research and demonstration organization developed by Sweden and jointly financed by Sweden and Ethiopia."—Abstract.

Abstract in *A.I.D. Research and Development Abstracts*, Apr. 1976, p. 28.

Microfiche. [Washington, U.S. Agency for International Development, 1975?] 1 sheet.

DLC-Sci RR PN-AAB-461

1407

Directives on cooperatives explained by experts. *In* U.S. *Joint Publications Research Service.* JPRS 73895. [Springfield, Va., National Technical Information Service, 1979] (Sub-Saharan Africa report, 2135) p. 9–13.

Concerns new guidelines for agricultural cooperatives in Ethiopia; from *Ethiopian Herald*, Addis Ababa, June 28, 1979, p. 1, 4, 6.

Microfiche. [Washington, Supt. of Docs., U.S. Govt. Print. Off., 1979]

DLC-Micro JPRS 73895

1408

Hendrix, J. Walter. Preliminary report on Ethiopian ergot infestation: field site consulation, May 6–May 15, 1978. [Addis Ababa, USAID Mission to Ethiopia], 1978. 5 leaves.

Acquired by the Library of Congress Office, Nairobi.

1409

Hoben, Allen. Social soundness analysis of agrarian reform in Ethiopia. [s.l.], 1976. 145 p. maps.

Prepared for the U.S. AID Mission to Ethiopia.

Abstract in *A.I.D. Research and Development Abstracts*, Apr. 1979, p. 9.

Microfiche. [Washington, U.S. Agency for International Development, 1976?] 2 sheets.

DLC-Sci RR PN-AAE-958

1410

Holmberg, Johan, *and* J. M. Cohen. Small farmer credit in Ethiopia. Washington, Agency for International Development, 1973. 165 p. (Spring review of small farmer credit, 1973. v. 8, no. SR 108)

DPC

Held also by MiEM.

Abstract in *A.I.D. Research Abstracts*, v. 1, Oct. 1973, p. 5.

Issued also in microfiche. [Washington, U.S. Agency for International Development, 1973?]

2 sheets (PN-AAA-129); examined in the Development Information Center, AID, Washington, D.C.

1411

Lulseged Asfaw. The role of state domain lands in Ethiopia's agricultural development. Madison, Land Tenure Center, University of Wisconsin, 1975. 36 p. (Wisconsin. University. Land Tenure Center. LTC no. 106) HD979.L84

"This paper was written in December 1973, as part of the author's training at the Land Tenure Center during the period September–December 1973, under a contract between the Center and USAID/Ethiopia."

Issued also in microfiche. [Washington, U.S. Agency for International Development, 1975?] 1 sheet. DLC-Sci RR PN-AAB-352

1412

Manig, Winfried. Marketing of selected agricultural commodities in the Baco area, Ethiopia. [Ithaca, N.Y.?], Dept. of Agricultural Economics, Cornell University, 1973. 79 p. NIC

"Employment and Income Distribution Project. Occasional paper, no. 66."

Preparation of report supported in part by the U.S. Agency for International Development.

Bibliography: p. 71–72.

Issued also in microfiche. [Washington, U.S. Agency for International Development, 1973?] 1 sheet. DLC-Sci RR PN-AAA-579

1413

Melaku Worede. Genetic improvement of quality and agronomic characteristics of durum wheat for Ethiopia. Lincoln, Dept. of Agronomy, University of Nebraska, 1974. 141 p.

The author's graduate studies were supported by the U.S. Agency for International Development under contract AID/csd-1208.

Thesis (Ph.D.)—University of Nebraska.

Abstract in *A.I.D. Research and Development Abstracts*, Jan. 1976, p. 9.

Microfiche. [Washington, U.S. Agency for International Development, 1974?] 2 sheets.

DLC-Sci RR PN-AAB-328

Microfilm, [Ann Arbor, Mich., University Microfilms International, 1975?]

DLC-Micro 75-03456

1414

Mellor, John W. Report on rural development issues in Ethiopia—problems and prescriptions with special reference to EPID and the ADA project. [Ithaca, N.Y., Dept. of Agricultural Economics, Cornell University], 1974. 30 p.

1414 (cont.)

Abstract in *A.I.D. Research and Development Abstracts*, Jan. 1976, p. 30.

Microfiche. [Washington, U.S. Agency for International Development, 1974?] 1 sheet.

DLC-Sci RR PN-AAB-284

1415

Spencer, Dunstan S. C. Proposed five year evaluation of the socio-economic impact of the Ada District Development Project (ADDP) in Ethiopia; consultant's report. East Lansing, Dept. of Agricultural Economics, Michigan State University, 1973. 23 p.

Microfiche. [Washington, U.S. Agency for International Development, 1973?] 1 sheet.

DLC-Sci RR PN-RAA-526

1416

Stavis, Benedict. Social soundness analysis of Ethiopia's minimum package program II. Ithaca, N.Y., Center for International Studies, Cornell University, 1977. 121 leaves.   HD2124.5.S73

Prepared in association with Pacific Consultants, Washington, D.C.

"A report to the U.S. Agency for International Development."

Concerns a nationwide agricultural extension program.

1417

Tecle, Tesfai. The evolution of alternative rural development strategies in Ethiopia: implications for employment and income distribution. East Lansing, Dept. of Agricultural Economics, Michigan State University, 1975. 113 p. (African rural employment paper, no. 12)

HN789.Z9C67

At head of title: African Rural Employment Research Network.

Bibliography: p. 109–113.

"This paper has been published as part of a study of rural employment problems in Ethiopia which was initially financed under an Agency for International Development contract (AID/csd 3625) and subsequently financed by the U.S.A.I.D. Mission to Ethiopia contract with the Institute of Development Research (IDR), Addis Ababa University, and an IDR sub-contract with Michigan State University."

Abstracts in *A.I.D. Research and Development Abstracts*, Apr. 1976, p. 16, and *Appropriate Technical Information for Developing Countries*, 2d ed., 1979, p. 197.

Issued also in microfiche. [Washington, U.S. Agency for International Development, 1975?] 2 sheets (DLC-Sci RR PN-AAB-425), and [Spring-

field, Va., National Technical Information Service, 1979] 2 sheets (DLC-Sci RR PB 294095).

1418

Treakle, H. Charles, *and* Lawrence A. Witucki. War conditions imperil Ethiopia's food supply. Foreign agriculture, Oct. 10, 1977: 9–10.

HD1401.F65   1977

Issued by the U.S. Foreign Agricultural Service.

Land Tenure and Reform

1419

Alemseged Tesfai. Communal land ownership in northern Ethiopia and its implications for government development policies. Madison, Land Tenure Center, University of Wisconsin-Madison, 1973. 30 p. (Wisconsin. University-Madison. Land Tenure Center. LTC paper, no. 88)

Microfiche. [Washington, U.S. Agency for International Development, 1973?] 1 sheet.

DLC-Sci RR PN-AAA-915

1420

Cohen, John M., Arthur A. Goldsmith, *and* John W. Mellor. Revolution and land reform in Ethiopia: peasant associations, local government and rural development. [Ithaca, N.Y.], Rural Development Committee, Center for International Studies, Cornell University, 1976. 133 p. (Cornell University. Rural Development Committee. Rural development occasional paper, no. 6)   NIC

Abstract in *A.I.D. Research and Development Abstract*, Apr. 1977, p. 39.

Issued also in microfiche. [Washington, U.S. Agency for International Development, 1976?] 2 sheets.

DLC-Sci RR PN-AAC-184

1421

Hailu W. Emmanuel. Land tenure, land-use, and development in the Awash Valley—Ethiopia. Madison, Land Tenure Center, University of Wisconsin, 1975. 40 p. maps. (Wisconsin. University-Madison. Land Tenure Center. LTC no. 105)

"This paper was written in December 1973, as part of the author's training at the Land Tenure Center during the period September–December 1973, under a contract between the Center and USAID/Ethiopia."

Abstract in *A.I.D. Research and Development Abstracts*, Jan. 1976, p. 31.

Microfiche. [Washington, U.S. Agency for International development, 1975?] 1 sheet.

DLC-Sci RR PN-AAB-353

1422

Mellor, John W. Post land reform and rural development issues in Ethiopia. [Ithaca, N.Y.], Cornell University, 1975. 34 p.

Prepared for the U.S. Agency for International Development under contract AID/afr-C-1105.

Examined in the Development Information Center, Agency for International Development, Washington, D.C.

1423

Parsons, Kenneth H. Consultant's report: On the incorporation of land tenure problems in a research programme in the Ada District. [East Lansing, Dept. of Agricultural Economics, Michigan State University], 1974. 14 p.

"This paper has been developed as part of a three year study of rural employment problems in Africa which is being financed under an AID/Washington contract (AID/csd 3625) with the Department of Agricultural Economics at Michigan State University."

Microfiche. [Washington, U.S. Agency for Inter-Development, 1974?] 1 sheet.

DLC-Sci RR PN-RAA-522

1424

Proclamation on land nationalization. *In* U.S. *Joint Publications Research Service.* JPRS 65419. [Springfield, Va., National Technical Information Service, 1975] (Translations on Africa, no. 1607) p. 21–35.

Translation of radio broadcast, Addis Ababa, July 26, 1975.

Michrofiche. [s.l., 1975]

DLC-Micro JPRS 65419

Assistance Programs

1425

U.S. *AID Mission to Ethiopia.* Assessment of effectiveness of economic assistance. Addis Ababa, 1978.

Cited in *Ethiopia: A Country Profile* (entry 1405).

1426

———— The United States Agency for International Development assistance program to Ethiopia: past, present and planned activities, 1951 through September 30, 1978. [Addis Ababa, 1978] 8 leaves.

Acquired by the Library of Congress Office, Nairobi.

1427

U.S. *AID Mission to Ethiopia. Office of the Con-troller.* Program operations status report. [Addis Ababa?] annual?

HC591.A3U52a

L.C. has 1969 and volume covering the transitional quarter, July–Sept. 1976.

1428

U.S. *AID Mission to Ethiopia. Program Office.* The AID program in Ethiopia. [Addis Ababa?], 1975. [14] leaves. HC591.A3U52 1975

1429

U.S. *Agency for International Development.* Annual budget submission: Ethiopia. [Washington?]

Vols. for 1977–81 examined in the Development Information Center, AID, Washington, D.C.

1430

———— Assistance strategy for Ethiopia. [Washington?] annual?

Vol. for 1977/78 examined in the Development Information Center, AID, Washington, D.C.

1431

———— Disaster relief, case report: Ethiopia-drought, 1974–1975. Washington, [1976?] 8 p. illus., map.

Microprint. [New York, Readex Microprint, 1980]

DLC-Micro U.S. G.P.O. Month. Cat. 78-5229

1432

———— Examination of agricultural sector activities in Ethiopia. [s.l.], 1975. 27 p.

Prepared by the Area Auditor General-Africa.

Examined in the Development Information Center, AID, Washington, D.C.

1433

U.S. *Congress. House. Committee on International Relations. Subcommittee on International Resources, Food, and Energy.* Food problems of developing countries: implications for U.S. policy: hearings, Ninety-fourth Congress, first session, May 21, June 3 and 5, 1975. Washington, for sale by the Supt. of Docs., U.S. Govt. Print. Off., 1975. 355 p. illus.

KF27.I54947 1975a
J74.A23 94th
Cong., House Comm.
Inter. Rel., v. 18

Charles C. Diggs, Jr., chairman.

Among the appendixes is the following: Appendix 9. Letter and report on Ethiopian drought relief from the Inspector General of Foreign Assistance, Department of State dealing with spoiled grain shipped under the Public Law 480 program. p. 176–187.

1434

Bonner, Margaret. Trip report: Dire Dawa, Dega-habur, 8/25–8/27, 1976. [Addis Ababa, U.S. AID Mission to Ethiopia], 1976. 4 leaves.   DLC

    Caption title.

    Memorandum.

    Cyclostyled.

    Primary purpose of trip was to investigate relief centers in Ogaden and to view initial attempts at resettlement.

1435

——— Trip report: Kelafo-Gode, 9/22–9/23, 1976. [Addis Ababa, Drought Relief Division, U.S. AID Mission to Ethiopia], 1976. 3 leaves, [1] leaf of plates. map.   DLC

    Caption title.

    Memorandum.

    Cyclostyled.

    An investigation of "the extent to which relief camps are still operating and the status of Gode resettlement schemes."

1436

Dahlstedt, Anne L. Trip report to the Ogaden, March 15–17, 1976. [Addis Ababa, U.S. AID Mission to Ethiopia], 1976. 4 leaves.   DLC

    Caption title.

    Memorandum.

    Cyclostyled.

    Purpose of trip was to observe grain storage stocks, conditions at relief shelters, and to inspect resettlement sponsored by the U.S. Agency for International Development.

1437

Emiru Woldeyes. Trip report: Awassa (3/31–4/1/76). [Addis Ababa, Drought Relief Division, U.S. AID Mission to Ethiopia] 1976. 5 leaves.   DLC

    Caption title.

    Memorandum.

    Cyclostlyed.

    An assessment of relief grain distribution in Sidamo Province.

1438

Ethiopia. [*Treaties, etc. United States, 1974 July 1*] Ethiopia, military assistance; payments under Foreign Assistance Act of 1973. Agreement effected by exchange of notes dated at Addis Ababa May 13 and June 26, 1974; entered into force July 1, 1974. *In* U.S. *Treaties, etc.* United States treaties and other international agreements, v. 25, 1974. [Washington, Dept. of State; for sale by the Supt. of Docs., U.S. Govt. Print. Off., 1975] p. 1437–1439. ([Treaties and other international acts series, 7872])   JX231.A34 v. 25

1439

Ethiopia. [*Treaties, etc. United States, 1975 Feb. 20*] Ethiopia drought recovery program grant agreement between the Government of Ethiopia and the United States of America. *In* U.S. *Treaties, etc.* United States treaties and other international agreements, v. 26, 1975. [Washington, Dept. of State; for sale by the Supt. of Docs., U.S. Govt. Print. Off., 1976] p. 1617–1629. ([Treaties and other international acts series, 8121])   JX231.A34 v. 26

    Signed at Addis Ababa Feb. 20, 1975; amending agreement signed at Addis Ababa Apr. 17, 1975.

1440

Ethiopia. [*Treaties, etc. United States, 1975 Sept. 26*] Loan agreement between the Government of Ethiopia and the United States of America for malaria control program—phase IV. *In* U.S. *Treaties, etc.* United States treaties and other international agreements, v. 28, 1976–77. [Washington, Dept. of State; for sale by the Supt. of Docs., U.S. Govt. Print. Off., 1978] p. 27–56. ([Treaties and other international acts series, 8463])

             JX231.A34 v. 28

    Signed at Addis Ababa Sept. 26, 1975.

    "This agreement provides that AID [U.S. Agency for International Development] will lend the Government of Ethiopia up to $7.2 million to assist the Government of Ethiopia in carrying out its Malaria Control Program."—p. 28.

1441

Ethiopia. [*Treaties, etc. United States, 1976 June 15*] Agreement between the Government of the United States of America and the Provisional Military Government of Socialist Ethiopia for sales of agricultural commodities. *In* U.S. *Treaties, etc.* United States treaties and other international agreements, v. 28, 1976–77. [Washington, Dept. of State; for sale by the Supt. of Docs., U.S. Govt. Print. Off., 1978] p. 7345–7369. ([Treaties and other international acts series, 8715])

             JX231.A34 v. 28.

    Signed at Addis Ababa June 15, 1976.

1442

Ethiopia. [*Treaties, etc. United States, 1976 June 30*] Ethiopia: nutrition/health warning system and access road construction. Ethiopia recovery and rehabilitation grant agreement between Government of Ethiopia and United States of America. *In* U.S. *Treaties, etc.* United States treaties and other international agreements, v. 27, 1976. [Washington, Dept. of State; for sale by the Supt. of Docs., U.S. Govt. Print. Off., 1977] p. 2658–2666. ([Treaties and other international acts series, 8337])

             JX231.A34 v. 27

1442 (cont.)

Signed at Addis Ababa June 30, 1976

Concerns a U.S. Agency for International Development grant for the establishment and operation of a national food and nutrition surveillance system and the construction of roads in southern Gemu Gofa Province to facilitate famine relief efforts.

1443

Ethiopia. [*Treaties, etc. United States, 1978 Sept. 22*] Ethiopia, agricultural commodities: transfer under Title II. Agreement signed at Addis Ababa September 22, 1978; entered into force September 22, 1978. *In* U.S. *Treaties, etc.* United States treaties and other international agreements, v. 30, 1978–79. [Washington, Dept. of State; for sale by the Supt. of Docs., U.S. Govt. Print Off., 1980] p. 3149–3151. ([Treaties and other international acts series, 9386])   JX231.A34 v. 30

1444

Fraenkel, Peter L. Food from windmills: a report on the wind mill [*sic*] irrigation project initiated by the American Presbyterian Mission at Omo Station in Ethiopia; for the Intermediate Technology Development Group Ltd. London, Intermediate Technology Publications Ltd., 1975. 5, 56, xix p. illus., map.   TC927.F7

Bibliography: p. xviii–xix.

Concerns the use of windmills for irrigation.

Abstract in *Appropriate Technical Information for Developing Countries*, 2d ed., 1979, p. 220.

Issued also in microfiche. [Springfield, Va., National Technical Information Service, 1979] 1 sheet.   DLC-Sci RR PB-297559

1445

Heckman, James R. Guide for the establishment of a school repair project. Addis Ababa, [Peace Corps] 1975. 23 leaves.   DPC

1446

——— Peace Corps Ethiopia school repair projects in 1975: final report. [Addis Ababa, Peace Corps] 1975. 21 leaves.   DPC

1447

Makonnen Desta. The history of Peace Corps Ethiopia, 1962–1975. [Addis Ababa, U.S. Peace Corps, 1976] 133 p.   DPC

1448

Olnick, Norman, *and* Edwin K. Fox. "Management team" report on drought-related PL 480 Title II assistance to Ethiopia. [Washington?], Agency for International Development, 1974. 10 p.

Examined in the Development Information Center, AID, Washington, D.C.

1449

Pavich, Frank R. Field survey report: Bale Province (Goba, Malka Odu, Raitu, Malka-Sungota, Harujilo, Shakisa, Kere, El-Medu, Cheretti, Hurgele, Afker, Barey, Dolo Baye), August 25 to 30, 1975. 14 leaves. illus., map.

Prepared by the Mission's Drought Relief Division.

Acquired by the Library of Congress Office, Nairobi.

Note: Additional trip reports by the Mission's Drought Relief Division are cited in Accessions List, Eastern Africa (entry 19), v. 11, no. 6, Nov. 1978, p. 202–205.

1450

——— Field survey report: Gemu Gofa Province (Gato River, Konso, Waito River, Arbore, Omo Raate), February 10–16, 1976. Addis Ababa, USAID Mission to Ethiopia, 1976. 5 leaves.   DLC

Caption title.

Memorandum.

Cyclostyled.

A survey of drought-affected areas of southern Gemu Gofa Province.

1451

——— Field trip, Gemu Gofa 10/18/76–11/9/76. [Addis Ababa, Drought Relief Division, U.S. AID Mission to Ethiopia, 1976] 10 leaves, [1] leaf of plates. map.   DLC

Caption title.

Memorandum.

"Annex B."

Cyclostyled.

Stated purpose of trip was "to accompany the Southern Gemu Gofa Area Rehabilitation Project design team to the project area for a physical reconnaissance of the project areas and to conduct interviews with local government officials and members of peasants associations."

1452

——— Field trip, Gemu Gofa, 3/8/77–3/17/77. [Addis Ababa, USAID Mission to Ethiopia], 1977. 4 leaves. illus., map.

Prepared by the Mission's Arid Lands Division.

Acquired by the Library of Congress Office, Nairobi.

Note: Additional field trip reports sponsored by the Mission's Arid Lands Division in 1977–78 are cited in Accessions List, Eastern Africa (entry 19), v. 11, no. 6, Nov. 1978, p. 210–202.

1453

―――― Ogaden floods over-flight, May 22, 1976. [Addis Ababa, Drought Relief Division, U.S. AID Mission to Ethiopia] 1976. 5 leaves, [1] leaf of plates. map.   DLC

Caption title.
Memorandum.
Cyclostyled.

1454

Peace Corps Ethiopia: preparation manual for pre-service training and in-service training, summer 1975. Addis Ababa, Training Center, Alem Public Relations Consultants, 1975. 2 v.   DPC

1455

Peace Corps Ethiopia training program, summer 1974, final in-country training report. Addis Ababa, Alem Public Relations Consultants, 1974. 199 p.   DPC

1456

Potts, H. C., *and* James M. Beck. Seed program/ industry development in Ethiopia; technical aspects of a project paper. Report to USAID/Ethiopia, AID/W and ESC/MOA. [s.l.], Seed Technology Laboratory, Mississippi State University, 1979. 69 p.   MsSM

Issued also in microfiche. [Washington, U.S. Agency for International Development, 1979?] 1 sheet (PN-AAG-708); examined in the Development Information Center, Agency for International Development, Washington, D.C.

1457

Purifoy, Leroy. Trip report: Sidamo surface water development project grant no. 663-F-601, activity, E-1. [Addis Ababa, Drought Relief Division, U.S. AID Mission to Ethiopia], 1976. 3 leaves.
                                        DLC

Caption title.
Memorandum.
Cyclostyled.

1458

The Role of women in Ethiopian development; ad hoc review of USAID's program in relation to the Percy Amendment, [by] Yeshi-Emebet Imagnu [et al.] [s.l.], 1974. 66 leaves.   DPC

1459

United States arms policies in the Persian Gulf and Red Sea areas: past, present, and future: report of a staff survey mission to Ethiopia, Iran and the Arabian peninsula, pursuant to H. Res. 313. Washington, U.S. Govt. Print. Off., 1977. 181 p. maps.   UA853.P47U54

At head of title: 95th Congress, 1st session. Committee print.

"Printed for the use of the Committee on International Relations."

In Oct. – Nov. 1976, George R. Berdes, Michael H. Van Dusen, and Richard M. Preece visited Ethiopia, Yemen Arab Republic, Saudi Arabia, Oman, Bahrain, United Arab Emirates, and Iran.

The section on Ethiopia (p. 167–169) includes information on the composition of the armed forces.

Commerce

1460

Market share reports. Country series: Ethiopia, 1971– 75. [Washington], U.S. Dept. of Commerce; for sale by the National Technical Information Service, Springfield, Va., [1977] 60 p.

Indicates the United States share of the market in Ethiopia for various products compared to the shares for Belgium-Luxembourg, France, Federal Republic of Germany, Great Britain, Italy, Netherlands, Sweden, and Japan.

Microfiche. [Washington, Congressional Information Service, 1977?]
                    DLC-Micro ASI:77 2016-1:50

1461

Market share reports. Country series: Ethiopia, 1975– 79. [Washington], International Trade Administration, U.S. Dept. of Commerce; for sale by the National Technical Information Service, Springfield, Va., [1979] 61 p.

Includes same comparative data as in *Market Share Reports. Country Series: Ethiopia, 1971–75* (entry 1460).

Microfiche. [Washington, Congressional Information Service, 1979?]
                    DLC-Micro ASI:81 2046-2.48

Communications and Transporation

1462

Ethiopia road maintenance study. [New York], Frederic R. Harris, inc., 1973. 2 v. maps.

Study financed in part by the U.S. Agency for International Development.

Microfiche. [Washington, U.S. Agency for International Development, 1973?] 8 sheets (PN-AAJ-294); examined in the Development Information Center, AID, Washington, D.C.

1463

Kurzman, Harold. Ethiopian rural roads projects; consultant's design report. [s.l.], Louis Berger International, 1976. 15 p.

Prepared for the U.S. Agency for International Development under contract AID/afr-C-1132.

Examined in the Development Information Center, AID, Washington, D.C.

Economic Conditions

1464

Babu, S. K. Mineral assets related to industrial development. *In* U.S. *Joint Publications Research Service.* JPRS 75487. [Springfield, Va., National Technical Information Service, 1980] (Sub-Saharan Africa report, no. 2234) p. 8–12.

Article in *Ethiopian Herald*, Addis Ababa, Mar. 18, 1980, p. 2, 4.

Michrofiche. [s.l., 1980]

DLC-Micro JPRS 75487

1465

Foreign economic trends and their implications for the United States. Ethiopia. 1969+ Washington, for sale by the Supt. of Docs., U.S. Govt. Print. Off. (International marketing information series)

HC10.E416

Semiannual, 1969; annual, 1970+

Continues *Economic Trends and Their Implications for the United States. Ethiopia.*

Prepared by the U.S. Embassy, Addis Ababa.

Vols. for 1969–77 distributed by the U.S. Bureau of International Commerce; vol. for 1979 by the U.S. Industry and Trade Administration; vols. for 1981– by the U.S. International Trade Administration.

Not published in 1978, 1980.

The following issues for the period 1973–81 have been identified in L.C.:

ET 73-016. 1973. 8 p.
ET 74-013. 1974. 8 p.
ET 75-057. 1975. 8 p.
FET 76-050. 1976. 8 p.
FET 77-071. 1977. 10 p.
FET 79-137. 1979. 11 p.
FET 81-075. 1981. 10 p.

1466

Girma Begashaw. The economic role of traditional savings and credit institutions in Ethiopia. [Columbus?], Dept. of Agricultural Economics and Rural Sociology, Ohio State University, 1978. 24 p.

"Economics and sociology occasional paper, no. 456."

Abstract in *A.I.D. Research and Development Abstracts*, Apr. 1979, p. 25.

Microfiche. [Washington, U.S. Agency for International Development, 1978?] 1 sheet (PN-AAG-276); examined in the Development Information Center, AID, Washington, D.C.

1467

Mengistu Haile-Mariam. Mengistu speaks on economic development campaign. *In* U.S. *Joint Publications Research Service.* JPRS 72839. [Springfield, Va., National Technical Information Service, 1979] (Translations on Sub-Saharan Africa, no. 2065) p. 24–32.

Translation of broadcast speech by the Chairman of the Provisional Military Administrative Council, Feb. 3, 1979.

Microfiche. [Washington, Supt. of Docs., U.S. Govt. Print. Off., 1979]

DLC-Micro JPRS 72839

Education

1468

Ato Bekele Getahun. Innovative reform in Ethiopia. *In* Educational reforms and innovations in Africa: studies prepared for the Conference of Ministers of Education of African Member States of Unesco. Paris, Unesco, 1978. 77 p. (Experiments and innovations in education, no. 34) LA1500.E38

Issued also in microfiche. [Arlington, Va., ERIC Document Reproduction Service; prepared for Educational Resources Information Center, National Institute of Education, 1978] 1 sheet.

DLC-Micro ED160036

1469

McDivit, Virginia A. African values and American teachers in Ethiopia: a cross-cultural experience. [s.l., 1976] 15 p.

Abstract in *Resources in Education*, May 1978, p. 187.

Microfiche. [Arlington, Va., ERIC Document Reproduction Service; prepared for Educational Resources Information Center, National Institute of Education, 1978] 1 sheet.

DLC-Micro ED148743

1470

Wagaw, Teshome G. Appraisal of adult literacy program in Ethiopia. [s.l., 1977] 14 p.

Paper presented at the annual meeting of the International Reading Association, 1977.

Abstract in *Resources in Education*, Jan. 1978, p. 43.

Microfiche. [Arlington, Va., ERIC Document

1470 (cont.)

Reproduction Service; prepared for Educational Resources Information Center, National Institute of Education, 1978] 1 sheet.

DLC-Micro ED142934

1471

——— Education in Ethiopia: prospect and retrospect. Ann Arbor, University of Michigan Press, 1979. xv, 256 p. map. LA1316.W33

Study supported in part by the U.S. AID Mission to Ethiopia.

Bibliography: p. 217–251.

Foreign Relations

1472

Abebe Worku. U.S. foreign policy said to oppose human rights. *In* U.S. *Joint Publications Research Service.* JPRS 76884. [Springfield, Va., National Technical Information Service, 1980] (Sub-Saharan Africa report, no. 2323) p. 19–22.

Article with an emphasis on United States relations with Ethiopia, in *Ethiopian Herald,* Addis Ababa, Oct. 31, 1980, p. 2.

Microfiche. [s.l., 1980]

DLC-Micro JPRS 76884

1473

Ethiopia embattled—a chronology of events in the Horn of Africa, 1 July 1977–30 March 1978. [Washington?], Directorate for Intelligence Research, Defense Intelligence Agency, 1978. 117 p.

AMAU

"DDB 2200-44."

1474

Ethiopia: principal aspects of relations of the United States with Ethiopia; the question of providing United States military equipment to Ethiopia; interests of the United States in the former Italian colony of Eritrea. *In* U.S. *Dept. of State.* Foreign relations of the United States. 1951, v. 5. Washington, U.S. Govt. Print. Off., 1982. p. 1237–1265. (U.S. Dept. of State. Department of State publication 9114) JX233.A3 1951, v. 5

Includes "Memorandum by the Acting Deputy Director, International Security Affairs (Ohly) to the Director, Office of Military Assistance, Department of Defense (Scott), Jan. 11, 1951."

1475

Ford, Gerald R. Statement on the death of Emperor Haile Selassie of Ethiopia. *In* U.S. *President.* Public papers of the Presidents of the United States.

Gerald R. Ford. 1975. Washington, U.S. Govt. Print. Off., 1976. p. 1244–1245.

J80.A283 1975

1476

Mulcahy, Edward W. Department discusses developments in Ethiopia. *In* U.S. *Dept. of State.* The Department of State bulletin, v. 72, no. 1865, Mar. 24, 1975: 383–386. JX232.A33 v. 72

Statement by the Acting Assistant Secretary of State for African Affairs before the Subcommittee on International Political and Military Affairs, Committee on Foreign Affairs, House of Representatives, Mar. 5, 1975.

Health and Nutrition

1477

Aklilu Lemma, Donald Heyneman, *and* Helmut Kloos. Studies on molluscicadal and other properties of the Endod plant, *Phytolacca dodencandra,* with special emphasis on the epidemiology of schistosomiasis in Ethiopia and the possibility of localized control using Endod as a molluscicide on a community self-help basis. Final report. [s.l.], 1979. 522 p. illus., maps.

Prepared for the U.S. Office of Naval Research.

Includes bibliographies.

Microfiche. [s.l., Defense Documentation Center, 1980] 6 sheets.

DLC-Sci RR AD-A080030

1478

Armstrong, J. C. Susceptibility to vivax malaria in Ethiopia. *In* Royal Society of Tropical Medicine and Hygiene, *London.* Transactions. v. 72, no. 4, 1978. p. 342–344. RC960.R6 v. 72

Study supported by the U.S. Navy.

Issued also in microfiche. [s.l., Defense Documentation Center, 1979] 1 sheet.

DLC-Sci RR AD-A062893

1479

Britanak, Rose A., Joe H. Davis, *and* John A. Daly. Ethiopia. Washington, Division of Planning and Evaluation, Office of International Health; for sale by the Supt. of Docs., U.S. Govt. Print. Off., 1974. 109 p. maps. (Syncrisis: the dynamics of health; an analytic series on the interactions of health and socioeconomic development, v. 8)

RA418.S98 v. 8

Abstracts in *A.I.D. Research and Development Abstracts,* Oct. 1976, p. 25; *Government Reports Announcements & Index,* Aug. 17, 1979, p. 65; and *American Statistics Index,* 1974, Abstracts, p. 278–279.

1479 (cont.)

Issued also in microfiche. [Washington, U.S. Agency for International Development, 197–?] 2 sheets (DLC-Sci RR PN-AAB-971); and [Washington, Congressional Information Service, 197–?] 2 sheets (DLC-Micro ASI:74 4006-1.8).

1480

Clinical and epidemiological studies on rickettsial infections; annual report. 1975?+ Baltimore, Dept. of Microbiology, University of Maryland.

Prepared under contract for the U.S. Office of Naval Research.

Title varies: 1975–77, *Clinical and Epidemiological Studies on Rickettsial Infections in Ethiopia.*

Report for 1978 focuses on Ethiopia and Burma.

Ethiopian field operations for the project were terminated in 1977.

Vols. for 1975–78 issued in microfiche ([s.l., Defense Documentation Center]) and are held by DLC-Sci RR under the following identification numbers:

1975: AD-A019033
1976: AD-A033083
1977: AD-A047946
1978: AD-A061952

1481

Cross, Edward B., *and* Norman E. Holly. Review of the health sector of the Ethiopian fourth five year plan: an analysis for the USAID Mission in Ethiopia. [s.l.], 1973. 61 leaves.   RA395.E8C76

1482

Krafsur, E. S., *and* J. C. Armstrong. An integrated view of entomological and parasitological observations on falciparum malaria in Gambela, western Ethiopian lowlands. *In* Royal Society of Tropical Medicine and Hygiene, *London*. Transactions. v. 72, no. 4, 1978. London, 1979. p. 348–356.
          RC960.R6 v. 72

Study supported by the U.S. Navy.

Issued also in microfiche. [s.l., Defense Documentation Center, 1979] 1 sheet.
          DLC-Sci RR AD-A062871

1483

Sholdt, L. Lance, Marvin L. Holloway, *and* W. Don Fronk. The epidemiology of human pediculosis in Ethiopia. Jacksonville, Fla., Navy Disease Vector Ecology and Control Center, Naval Air Station, 1979. 150 p. illus., map. (Navy Disease Vector Ecology and Control Center. Special publication)
          RL764.P4S56

"From a dissertation submitted by the senior author to the academic faculty of Colorado State University."

Bibliography: p. 145–150.

"Our initial objective was to gather basic epidemiological information on the distribution and density of human louse infestations within the environment of a rural developing country. The investigation was later expanded to include a description of the various physical, behavioral, cultural, and physiological factors which may influence pediculosis and louse-borne diseases."—vii.

Issued also in microfiche. [s.l., Defense Documentation Center, 1979] 2 sheets.
          DLC-Sci RR AD-A074088

Human Rights

1484

Amnesty allegations dismissed as baseless. *In* U.S. *Joint Publications Research Service.* JPRS 73098. [Springfield, Va., National Technical Information Service, 1979] (Translations on Sub-Saharan Africa, no. 2082) p. 46–51.

From article in *Ethiopian Herald*, Addis Ababa, Mar. 6, 1979, p. 1, 5.

Text of article denouncing Amnesty International for its allegations concerning human rights in Ethiopia.

Microfiche. [Washington, Supt. of Docs., U.S. Govt. Print. Off., 1979]
          DLC-Micro JPRS 73098

1485

Aspin, Les. Ethiopia continues to intern political prisoners without prospect of fair trial. Congressional record, 94th Congress, 2d session, v. 122, Aug. 24, 1976: 27522-27523.   J11.R5 v. 122

Remarks in the U.S. House of Representatives.

Representative Aspin includes text of his correspondence on this issue plus relevant journal articles.

1486

Damblain, Jean-Marie. Eyewitness account of Red Terror. *In* U.S. *Joint Publications Research Service.* JPRS 71356. [Springfield, Va., National Technical Information Service, 1978] (Translations on Sub-Saharan Africa, no. 1952) p. 33–37.

Translation of article in *France Eurafrique*, Paris, Mar. 1978, p. 6–7.

Microfiche. [Washington, Supt. of Docs., U.S. Govt. Print. Off., 1978]
          DLC-Micro JPRS 71356

1487

Duteil, Mireille. Details on Red Terror in Addis Ababa. *In* U.S. *Joint Publications Research Service.* JPRS 71043. [Springfield, Va., National Tech-

1487 (cont.)

nical Information Service, 1978] (Translations on Sub-Saharan Africa, no. 1920) p. 20–24.

Translation of article in *Demain l'Afrique*, Paris, Mar. 7, 1978, p. 18–20.

Microfiche. [Washington, Supt. Of Docs., U.S. Govt. Print. Off., 1978]

DLC-Micro JPRS 71043

1488

Gaudio, Attilio. Repression, torture, suppression of liberties described. *In* U.S. *Joint Publications Research Service*. JPRS 73934. [Springfield, Va., National Technical Information Service, 1979] (Sub-Saharan Africa report, 2137) p. 25–29.

Translation of article in *Africa*, Dakar, June–July 1979, p. 37–39.

Microfiche. [Washington, Supt. of Docs., U.S. Govt. Print. Off., 1979]

DLC-Micro JPRS 73934

Politics and Government

1489

U.S. *Central Intelligence Agency*. Profile of violence: an analytical model. [Washington], 1976. 55 p. illus. (*Its* Research project)

JC32816.U55   1976

"PR 76 10025."

Includes bibliographical references.

The Ethiopian situation in the period November 1974 to June 1975 is one of the crises analyzed.

1490

Chaliand, Gérard. Situation in Ethiopia discussed. *In* U.S. *Joint Publications Research Service*. JPRS 69654. [Springfield, Va., National Technical Information Service, 1977] (Translations on Sub-Saharan Africa, no. 1787) p. 19–27.

Translation of article in *Le Monde diplomatique*, Paris, July 1977, p. 6.

Microfiche. [s.l., 1977]

DLC-Micro JPRS 69654

1491

Cohen, John M. Local government reform in Ethiopia: an analysis of the problems and prospects of the Awraja self development proposal, with particular emphasis on rural change, local participation, and potential areas of external assistance. Washington, U.S. Agency for International Development, Dept. of State, 1974. xxiii, 167, [80] p. map.   JS7755.3.A2   1974

"Produced at the request of the Ethiopian Mission of USAID."—p. i.

1492

Cuban rationale for revolution, its objectives. *In* U.S. *Joint Publications Research Service*. JPRS 70782. [Springfield, Va., National Technical Information Service, 1978] (Translations on Sub-Saharan Africa, no. 1894) p. 23–39.

Article on the background and progress of the Ethiopian revolution, in *Granma Weekly Review*, Havana, Feb. 1978 (various dates).

Microfiche. [Washington, Supt. of Docs., U.S. Govt. Print. Off., 1978]

DLC-Micro JPRS 70782

1493

Degorce, Brigette N. Domestic opposition to regime, government reforms evaluated. *In* U.S. *Joint Publications Research Service*. JPRS 71348. [Springfield, Va., National Technical Information Service, 1978] (Translations on Sub-Saharan Africa, no. 1951) p. 16–37.

Translation of article in *Revue française d'études politiques africaines*, Paris, Apr. 1978, p. 20–53.

Microfiche. [Washington, Supt. of Docs., U.S. Govt. Print. Off., 1978]

DLC-Micro JPRS 71348

1494

Doubts regarding Mengistu's survival as ruler of Ethiopia. *In* U.S. *Joint Publications Research Service*. JPRS 75359. [Springfield, Va., National Technical Information Service, 1980] (Sub-Saharan Africa report, no. 2225) p. 29–33.

Translation of article in *al-Ḥawādith*, London, Dec. 28, 1979, p. 25, 27.

Microfiche. [s.l., 1980]

DLC-Micro JPRS 75359

1495

Duties of peasant's association detailed. *In* U.S. *Joint Publications Research Service*. JPRS 71102. [Springfield, Va., National Technical Information Service, 1978] (Translations on Sub-Saharan Africa, no. 1926) p. 52–57.

Article on the proposed All Ethiopia Peasants' Association, in *Ethiopian Herald*, Addis Ababa, Apr. 25, 1978, p. 1, 4, 6.

Microfiche. [Washington, Supt. of Docs., U.S. Govt. Print. Off., 1978]

DLC-Micro JPRS 71102

1496

Ethiopian leaders in North America reaffirm solidarity. *In* U.S. *Joint Publications Research Service*. JPRS 73967. [Springfield, Va., National Technical Information Service, 1979] (Sub-Saharan Africa report, 2139) p. 22–26.

Article in *Ethiopian Observer*, Addis Ababa, July

1496 (cont.)

11, 1979, p. 1, 2, 4; based on interviews with leaders of the United Progressive Ethiopian Students' Union in North America-Bolshevik (UPESUNA) who express support for the Ethiopian revolution.

Microfiche. [Washington, Supt. of Docs., U.S. Govt. Print. Off., 1979]

DLC-Micro JPRS 73967

1497

Felleke Gedle-Giorgis. Ethiopian Foreign Minister Felleke addresses OAU summit. *In* U.S. *Joint Publications Research Service.* JPRS 73993. [Springfield, Va., National Technical Information Service, 1979] (Sub-Saharan Africa report, no. 2142) p. 1–11.

Text of address before the Organization of African Unity in *Ethiopian Herald*, Addis Ababa, July 21, 1979, p. 1, 6, 7.

Microfiche. [Washington, Supt. of Docs., U.S. Govt. Print. Off., 1979]

DLC-Micro JPRS 73993

1498

Guillebaud, Jean-Claude. An inside look at enigmatic Ethiopia. *In U.S. Joint Publications Research Service.* JPRS 68596. [Springfield, Va., National Technical Information Service, 1977] (Translations on Sub-Saharan Africa, no. 1710) p. 8–13.

Translation of article in *Le Monde*, Paris, Dec. 30, 1976, p. 1, 3.

Microfiche. [s.l., 1977]

DLC-Micro JPRS 68596

1499

——— Reportage on situation in Ethiopia. *In* U.S. *Joint Publications Research Service.* JPRS 65278. [Springfield, Va., National Technical Information Service, 1975] (Translations on Africa, no. 1604) p. 5–16.

Translation of article in *Le Monde*, Paris, June 5–7, 1975.

Microfiche. [s.l., 1975]

DLC-Micro JPRS 65278

1500

Harbeson, John W. Reform, revolution and military leadership in contemporary Ethiopia. [s.l., 1976] [14] leaves. (FAR 25494-S)

Paper presented at the Colloquium on Ethiopia, sponsored by the U.S. Dept. of State, Oct. 1976.

Examined in the former Foreign Affairs Research Documentation Center, Dept. of State.

1501

Henze, Paul P. Communism and Ethiopia. Problems

of Communism, v. 30, May/June 1981: 55–74. illus., maps. HX1.P75 v. 30

Issued by the U.S. International Communications Agency.

1502

Lefort, René. Internal contradictions place future of revolution in doubt. *In* U.S. *Joint Publications Research Service.* JPRS 71489. [Springfield, Va., National Technical Information Service, 1978] (Translations on Sub-Saharan Africa, no. 1962) p. 35–43.

Translation of article in *Le Monde diplomatique*, Paris, June 1978, p. 2–3.

Microfiche. [Washington, Supt. of Docs., U.S. Govt. Print. Off., 1978]

DLC-Micro JPRS 71489

1503

Madhun, Raba'i. Mengistu discusses Havana conference, local political, economic issues. *In* U.S. *Joint Publications Research Service.* JPRS 74827. [Springfield, Va., National Technical Information Service, 1979] (Sub-Saharan Africa report, no. 2193) p. 14–17.

Translation of interview with Mengistu Haile Mariam, Chairman of the Provisional Military Administrative Council, in *al-Ḥurrīyah*, Beirut, Nov. 12, 1979, p. 34–35.

Microfiche. [s.l., 1980]

DLC-Micro JPRS 74827

1504

Mann, Harry A. The rise and fall of Haile Selassie. Maxwell Air Force Base, Ala., Air War College, Air University, 1975. 78 leaves. (FAR 18308-N)

"Professional study, no. 5680."

Bibliography: leaves 76–78.

Examined in the former Foreign Affairs Research Documentation Center, U.S. Dept. of State.

Issued also in microfiche. [s.l., 1976] 1 sheet (AD-B011106L).

1505

Mulcahy, Edward W. Recent developments in Ethiopia. [Washington], Bureau of Public Affairs, Dept. of State, 1975. 3 p. (U.S. Dept. of State. Department of State news release, Mar. 5, 1975)

DLC

Statement by the Acting Assistant Secretary of State for African Affairs before the Subcommittee on Political and Military Affairs, Committee on Foreign Affairs, House of Representatives.

1506

PMAC Secretary-General calls for purge of reactionary groups. *In* U.S. *Joint Publications Research*

1506 (cont.)

Service. JPRS 71049. [Springfield, Va., National Technical Information Service, 1978] (Translations on Sub-Saharan Africa, no. 1921) p. 49–58.

Article reporting statement by Fikre-Selassie Wogderes of the Provisional Military Administrative Council (Dergue), in *Ethiopian Herald*, Addis Ababa, Apr. 8, 1978, p. 1, 3, 4.

Microfiche. [Washington, Supt. of Docs., U.S. Govt. Print. Off., 1978]

DLC-Micro JPRS 71049

1507

Pomonti, Jean-Claude. Report on progress of Ethiopian revolution. *In* U.S. *Joint Publications Research Service*. JPRS 74789. [Springfield, Va., National Technical Information Service, 1979] (Sub-Saharan Africa report, no. 2191) p. 15–22.

Translation of article in *Le Monde*, Paris, Nov. 6, 7, 1979.

Microfiche. [s.l., 1980]

DLC-Micro JPRS 74789

1508

Revolution and Development Committees established. *In* U.S. *Joint Publications Research Service*. JPRS 69084. [Springfield, Va., National Technical Information Service, 1977] (Translations on Sub-Saharan Africa, no. 1746) p. 20–27.

Article on the inauguration of "Revolution and Development Committees with broad mandates to help expedite the progress of the ongoing revolution in urban and rural areas and to crush anti-revolutionary and anti-unity forces," in *Ethiopian Herald*, Addis Ababa, Apr. 22, 1977, p. 1, 3.

Microfiche. [s.l., 1977]

DLC-Micro JPRS 69084

1509

Schatten, Fritz. Ethiopian state's church policy, persecutions reported. *In* U.S. *Joint Publications Research Services*. JPRS 73115. [Springfield, Va., National Technical Information Service, 1979] (Translations on Sub-Saharan Africa, no. 2083) p. 15–18.

Translation of article in *Deutsche Zeitung*, Feb. 9, 1979, p. 13.

Microfiche. [Washington, Supt. of Docs., U.S. Govt. Print. Off., 1979]

DLC-Micro JPRS 73115

1510

Witness reports widespread dissatisfaction with Mengistu regime. *In* U.S. *Joint Publications Research Service*. JPRS 70608. [Springfield, Va., National Technical Information Service, 1978] (Translations on Sub-Saharan Africa, no. 1876) p. 21–29.

Translation of article in *al-Ṣaḥāfah*, Khartoum, Dec. 5, 1977, p. 3–7.

Microfiche. [Washington, Supt. of Docs., U.S. Govt. Print. Off., 1978]

DLC-Micro JPRS 70608

Eritrean Conflict

1511

Bitterlin, Lucien. Eritrea compared to Palestine. *In* U.S. *Joint Publications Research Service*. JPRS 66363. [Springfield, Va., National Technical Information Service, 1975] (Translations on Sub-Saharan Africa, no. 1630) p. 16–20.

Translation of article in *France-Pays Arabes*, Paris, Oct. 1975, p. 6–8.

Microfiche. [s.l., 1975]

DLC-Micro JPRS 66363

1512

al-Dabbās, Aḥmad. Jordanian correspondent tours 'Eritrean front.' *In* U.S. *Joint Publications Research Service*. JPRS 72904. [Springfield, Va., National Technical Information Service, 1979] (Translations on Sub-Saharan Africa, no. 2070) p. 44–67.

Translation of article in *al-Dustūr*, Amman, Nov. 29 – Dec. 6, 1978.

Microfiche. [Washington, Supt. of Docs., U.S. Govt. Print. Off., 1979]

DLC-Micro JPRS 72904

1513

Dirani, Salih. Eritrean official discusses military situation, peace. *In* U.S. *Joint Publications Research Service*. JPRS 72414. [Springfield, Va., National Technical Information Service, 1978] (Translations on Sub-Saharan Africa, no. 2036) p. 33–36.

Translation of interview with 'Uthmān Abū-Bakr, aide to the Secretary-General, Eritrean Liberation Front-People's Liberation Forces, in *al-Waṭan al-'Arabī*, Paris, Oct. 21–27, 1978, p. 33.

Microfiche. [Washington, Supt. of Docs., U.S. Govt. Print. Off., 1978?]

DLC-Micro JPRS 72414

1514

ELF-PLF chairman Osman Saleh Sabbe interviewed. *In* U.S. *Joint Publications Research Service*. JPRS 74978. [Springfield, Va., National Technical Information Service, 1980] (Sub-Saharan Africa report, no. 2202) p. 17–21.

Article in *Heegan*, Mogadishu, Dec. 28, 1979, p. 3.

1514 (cont.)

ELF-PLF: Eritrean Liberation Front-People's Liberation Forces.
Microfiche. [s.l., 1980]
DLC-Micro JPRS 74978

1515

ELF Secretary General seeks increased international support. *In* U.S. *Joint Publications Research Service.* JPRS 65717. [Springfield, Va., National Technical Information Service, 1975] (Translations on Africa, no. 1612) p. 1–8.

Translation of interview with Osman Saleh Sabbe of the Eritrean Liberation Front-Popular Liberation Forces, in *al-'Alam*, Rabat, July 19, 1975, p. 5.
Microfiche. [s.l., 1975]
DLC-Micro JPRS 65717

1516

Eritrea and the Soviet-Cuban connection, [by] Daniel S. Papp. Carlisle Barracks, Pa., Strategic Studies Institute, U.S. Army War College, 1978. 24 p. (Military issues research memorandum)
AMAU

Abstract in *Government Reports Announcements & Index*, June 8, 1979, p. 34.

Issued also in microfiche. [s.l., Defense Documentation Center, 1979] 1 sheet (DLC-Sci RR AD-A063938); issued in microfilm by University Publications of America (cited in its *Africa: Special Studies, 1962–1980*, p. 8).

1517

The Eritrean insurgency. Washington, Directorate for Intelligence, U.S. Defense Intelligence Agency, 1977. 36 p.   AMAU
"DDI no. 2310-1."

1518

Eritrean Liberation Front's organizational structure outlined. *In* U.S. *Joint Publications Research Service.* JPRS 71246. [Springfield, Va., National Technical Information Service, 1978] (Translations on Sub-Saharan Africa, no. 1941) p. 87–96.

Translation of article in *al-Thawrah al-Irītrīyah*, Beirut, 1977, p. 51–62.
Microfiche. [Washington, Supt. of Docs., U.S. Govt. Print. Off., 1978]
DLC-Micro JPRS 71246

1519

Famil, Silmi. Eritrean revolutionary leaders discuss status of struggle. *In* U.S. *Joint Publications Research Service.* JPRS 70080. [Springfield, Va., National Technical Information Service, 1977]

(Translations on Sub-Saharan Africa, no. 1826) p. 12–18.

Translation of article in *al-Ba'th*, Damascus, Sept. 26, 1977, p. 4, 11.
Microfiche. [s.l., 1977]
DLC-Micro JPRS 70080

1520

al-Furzuli, Sulayman. Eritrean leader decries U.S.-Soviet concurrence in support of Ethiopia. *In* U.S. *Joint Publications Research Service.* JPRS 74681. [Springfield, Va., National Technical Information Service, 1979] (Sub-Saharan Africa report, no. 2184) p. 34–42.

Translation of interview with Osman Saleh Sabbe, secretary-general of the Eritrean Liberation Front-Popular Liberation Forces, in *al-Ḥawādith*, London, Oct. 12, 1979, p. 22–24.
Microfiche. [s.l., 1979]
DLC-CNP RR JPRS 74681

1521

Gaudio, Attilio. EPLF representative criticizes repression, foreign dependence. *In* U.S. *Joint Publications Research Service.* JPRS 70677. [Springfield, Va., National Technical Information Service, 1978] (Translations on Sub-Saharan Africa, no. 1883) p. 34–37.

Report on an interview with Nafi H. Kurdi, representative of the Eritrean People's Liberation Front in France, in *Africa*, Dakar, Jan. 1978, p. 55–56.
Microfiche. [Washington, Supt. of Docs., U.S. Govt. Print. off., 1978]
DLC-Micro JPRS 70677

1522

Guillebaud, Jean-Claude. Reasons given for Eritrean's success. *In* U.S. *Joint Publications Research Service.* JPRS 70379. [Springfield, Va., National Technical Information Service, 1977] (Translations on Sub-Saharan Africa, no. 1855) p. 16–20.

Translation of article in *Le Monde*, Paris, Nov. 16, 1977, p. 3.
Microfiche. [s.l., 1977]
DLC-Micro JPRS 70379

1523

Hamdi, Mahir. ELF officials Nasir, Yasin affirm commitment to peaceful settlement. *In* U.S. *Joint Publications Research Service.* JPRS 71774. [Springfield, Va., National Technical Information Service, 1978] (Translations on Sub-Saharan Africa, no. 1984) p. 4–16.

Translation of interview with Ahmad M. Nasir, chairman of ELF, and Zayn-al-'Abidin Yasin, in *al-Hurrīyah*, Beirut, July 17, 1978, p. 30–34.

1523 (cont.)

Microfiche. [Washington, Supt. of Docs., U.S. Govt. Print. Off., 1978]

DLC-Micro JPRS 71774

1524

Haydar, As'ad. Eritrean leaders discuss differences, unity. *In* U.S. *Joint Publications Research Service.* JPRS 70114. [Springfield, Va., National Technical Information Service, 1977] (Translations on Sub-Saharan Africa, no. 1830) p. 3–11.

Translation of interview with Osman Saleh Sabbe, Ibrahim Tutil, and Heruy T. Bairu, in *al-Mustaqbal*, Paris, Oct. 8, 1977, p. 20–22.

Microfiche. [s.l., 1977]

DLC-Micro JPRS 70114

1525

al-Khafaji, Azhar. Causes of rift between Eritrean liberation factions discussed. *In* U.S. *Joint Publications Research Service.* JPRS 77005. [Springfield, Va., National Technical Information Service, 1980] (Sub-Saharan Africa report, no. 2333) p. 16–21.

Translation of article in *al-Qabas*, Kuwait, Oct. 10, 1980, p. 5.

Microfiche. [s.l., 1980]

DLC-Micro JPRS 77005

1526

Khuri, Rajih. ELF leader speaks out about Eritrean revolution. *In* U.S. *Joint Publications Research Service.* JPRS 67124. [Springfield, Va., National Technical Information Service, 1976] (Translations on Sub-Saharan Africa, no. 1644) p. 3–8.

Translation of interview with Osman Saleh Sabbe, in *al-Ḥawādith*, Beirut, Mar. 5, 1976, p. 24, 25.

Microfiche. [s.l., 1976]

DLC-Micro JPRS 67124

1527

—— Osman Saleh Sabbe discusses difficulties facing Eritrean rebels. *In* U.S. *Joint Publications Research Service.* JPRS 69417. [Springfield, Va., National Technical Information Service, 1977] (Translations on Sub-Saharan Africa, no. 1772) p. 5–10.

Translation of article in *al-Ḥawādith*, Beirut, May 6, 1977, p. 20, 21.

Microfiche. [s.l., 1977]

DLC-Micro JPRS 69417

1528

—— Report on parties, attitudes in the war in Eritrea. *In* U.S. *Joint Publications Research Service.* JPRS 71449. [Springfield, Va., National Technical

Information Service, 1978] (Translations on Sub-Saharan Africa, no. 1959) p. 12–16.

Translation of article in *al-Ḥawādith*, Beirut, May 26, 1978, p. 32, 33.

Microfiche. [Washington, Supt. of Docs., U.S. Govt. Print. Off., 1978]

DLC-Micro JPRS 71449

1529

LeBrun, Olivier. Resistance by EPLF to Ethiopian offensive described. *In* U.S. *Joint Publications Research Service.* JPRS 73820. [Springfield, Va., National Technical Information Service, 1979] (Sub-Saharan Africa report, 2129) p. 21–31.

Translation of article in *Le Monde*, Paris, May 26–28, 1979.

EPLF: Eritrean Peoples Liberation Front.

Microfiche. [Washington, Supt. of Docs., U.S. Govt. Off., 1979]

DLC-Micro JPRS 73820

1530

Michler, Walter. EPLF official Haile Menkerios describes present situation in Eritrea. *In* U.S. *Joint Publications Research Service.* JPRS 74043. [Springfield, Va., National Technical Information Service, 1979] (Sub-Saharan Africa report, no. 2144) p. 21–25.

Translation of article in *Frankfurter Rundschau*, July 6, 1979, p. 13.

Microfiche. [Washington, Supt of Docs., U.S. Govt. Print. Off., 1979]

DLC-Micro JPRS 74043

1531

Moves made to solve Eritrean problem peacefully. *In* U.S. *Joint Publications Research Service.* JPRS 71786. [Springfield, Va., National Technical Information Service, 1978] (Translations on Sub-Saharan Africa, no. 1985) p. 15–18.

Translation of article in *al-Nahār al-'Arabī wa al-duwalī*, Paris, July 8, 1978, p. 10.

Microfiche. [Washington, Supt. of Docs., U.S. Govt. Print. Off., 1978]

DLC-Micro JPRS 71786

1532

Nouaille-Degorge, Brigitte. Islamic factors in Eritrean conflict discussed. *In* U.S. *Joint Publications Research Service.* JPRS 65710. [Springfield, Va., National Technical Information Service, 1975] (Translations on Africa, no. 1602) p. 14–24.

Translation of article in *Revue française d'études politiques africaines*, Paris, May 1975, p. 65–78.

Microfiche. [s.l., 1975]

DLC-Micro JPRS 65710

1533

Pomonti, Jean-Claude. Writer reports on life behind lines in Eritrean conflict. *In* U.S. *Joint Publications Research Service.* JPRS 74519. [Springfield, Va., National Technical Information Service, 1979] (Sub-Saharan Africa report, no. 2174) p. 32–39.

Translation of article in *Le Monde*, Paris, Oct. 4–5, 1979.

Microfiche. [s.l., 1979]

DLC-Micro JPRS 74519

1534

Reuss, Henry. The United States and the Ethiopian civil war—a new approach. Congressional record, 94th Congress, 2d session, v. 122, July 19, 1976: 22530-22535.   J11.R5 v. 122

Remarks in the U.S. House of Representatives.

Includes texts of his correspondence with the U.S. Dept. of State and the Eritrean People's Liberation Front.

1535

Sabbe discusses political settlement efforts, military situation. *In* U.S. *Joint Publications Research Service.* JPRS 71895. [Springfield, Va., National Technical Information Service, 1978] (Translations on Sub-Saharan Africa, no. 1996) p. 16–22.

Translation of interview with Osman Saleh Sabbe of ELF-PLF, in *al-Dustūr*, London, June 12–18, 1978, p. 15–17.

Microfiche. [s.l., 1978]

DLC-Micro JPRS 71895

1536

Virtanen, Pauli. Liberation factions threaten unity of Eritrean independence struggle. *In* U.S. *Joint Publications Research Service.* JPRS 70051. [Springfield, Va., National Technical Information Service, 1977] (Translations on Sub-Saharan Africa, no. 1824) p. 19–26.

Translation of article in *Suomen Kuvalehti*, Helsinki, Sept. 30. 1977, p. 14–21.

Microfiche. [s.l., 1977]

DLC-Micro JPRS 70051

1537

Wood, Richard E. Ethiopia: Soviet penetration and the Eritrean conflict. Maxwell Air Force Base, Ala., Air Command and Staff College, Air University, 1979. 62 p.   AMAU

"Research report."

Other Subjects

1538

Africa: Ethiopia. Selected statistical data by sex. Washington, 1981. 31, 17 p.   DLC

Study supported by the U.S. Agency for International Development's Office of Women in Development and Office of Population.

Data assembled by the International Demographic Data Center, U.S. Bureau of the Census.

Among the tables, all based on 1970 data (unless noted), are the following: unadjusted population by age, sex, and urban/rural residence (1977); rural population by marital status, age, and sex; number of households; number of literate persons by age, sex, and urban/rural residence; number of economically active persons by age, sex, and urban/rural residence; economically active population by occupational status, sex, and urban/rural residence.

1539

Ash, John S. Bird-ringing in Ethiopia; report no. 5, 1969–1975. New York, U.S. Naval Medical Research Unit No. 5, APO New York, 1976. 17 p. (U.S. Office of Naval Research. Technical report, no. 1)

Prepared for the U.S. Office of Naval Research.

Issued in cooperation with the Smithsonian Institution.

Microfiche. [s.l., 1976] 1 sheet.

DLC-Sci RR AD A029421

1540

Bale relief and rehabilitation; request for assistance to African refugees and dislocated persons, by Anita Mackie [et al.] [Addis Ababa?], USAID/Ethiopia, 1979. 36 leaves. map.

Examined in the Development Information Center, AID, Washington, D.C.

1541

Daniel Haile, *and* Erku Yimer. Law and population growth in Ethiopia. Medford, Mass., Law and Population Programme, Fletcher School of Law and Diplomacy, 1976. 52 p. (Law and population monograph series, no. 35)   DLC-LL

Includes bibliographical references.

"The Law and Population Programme and its field work are supported in part by the International Planned Parenthood Federation, the United Nations Fund for Population Activities, and the U.S. Agency for International Development."

1542

Ecological relationships between arboviruses, ectoparasites, and vertebrates in Ethiopia. Annual report. no. [1]+ [1971/72?]+ New York, NAMUR-5, Ethiopia, APO New York.

Prepared for the U.S. Office of Naval Research.

Reports for 1973/74–1974/75 prepared by George E. Watson and John S. Ash.

Reports for 1973/74–1974/75 issued in micro-

1542 (cont.)

fiche. [Springfield, Va., National Technical Information Service, 1974–75] 2 sheets.

DLC-Sci RR AD-787611
AD-A017364

1542a

Gazetteer of Ethiopia: names approved by the United States Board on Geographic Names; prepared and published by the Defense Mapping Agency. Washington, Defense Mapping Agency, 1982. xxii, 663 p. maps.   DLC-G&M

Transliteration system for Amharic: p. xix–xxi.

1543

Gebrehiwet Zere. Economics and water development on government lands in Southern and Southeastern Ethiopia. [Tucson], Dept. of Watershed Management, University of Arizona, 1973. 120 p.

Research supported in part by the U.S. Agency for International Development under contract AID/csd-2457.

Thesis (Ph.D.)—University of Arizona.

Microfiche. [Washington, U.S. Agency for International Development, 1973?] 2 sheets.

DLC-Sci RR PN-AAA-552

Microfilm. [Ann Arbor, Mich., University Microfilms International, 1973]

DLC-Micro 73-28783

1544

Leslau, Wolf. English-Amharic context dictionary. Wiesbaden, Otto Harrassowitz, 1973. xviii, 1503 p.

PJ9237.E7L43

"The research reported herein was performed pursuant to a contract with the United States Department of Health, Education, and Welfare, Office of Education, Institute of International Studies."

1545

Macomber, William F. A catalogue of Ethiopia manuscripts microfilmed for the Ethiopian Manuscript Microfilm Library, Addis Ababa, and for the Monastic Manuscript Microfilm Library, Collegeville. Collegeville, Minn., Monastic Manuscript Microfilm Library, St. John's Abbey and University, 1975–81? [6] v. illus.

Z6605.E8M32

Supported by the National Endowment for the Humanities.

Vol. 4 by Getatchew Haile.

Vol. 6 by Getatchew Haile and William F. Macomber.

Vols. 3–6 issued by the Hill Monastic Manuscript Library, St. John's Abbey and University, and distributed by University Microfilms International, Ann Arbor, Mich.

1546

Obeck, Douglas K., *and* Gera Michael Berhanu. Leptospirosis survey of rodents and domestic animals in Ethiopia. New York, Naval Medical Research Unit no. 5, APO New York, 1976. 12 p. map. (U.S. Navy. Naval Medical Research Unit No. 5. Technical report, no. 12)

Abstract in *Government Reports Announcements & Index*, Mar. 18, 1977, p. 45.

Microfiche. [Springfield, Va.?, National Technical Information Service, 1977] 1 sheet.

DLC-Sci RR AD-A033991

1547

Watson, George E., John S. Ash, *and* Owen L. Wood. Ecological relationships between arboviruses, ectoparasites and vertibrates in Ethiopia. Final technical report, September 1, 1971 through June 30, 1978. Washington, Dept. of Vertibrate Zoology, National Museum of Natural History, Smithsonian Institution, 1978. 156 p. map.

Prepared for the Microbiology Program, U.S. Office of Naval Research.

Abstract in *Government Reports Announcements & Index*, Feb. 2, 1979, p. 66.

Microfiche. [s.l., Defense Documentation Center, 1978] 2 sheets.

DLC-Sci RR AD-A059961

Kenya

General

1548

U.S. *Dept. of State.* Post report. Kenya. [Washington?] 1978. [21] p. illus., map.

JX1705.A286 Spec. Format

For a description of the contents of this publication, see the note to entry 936.

1549

U.S. *Dept. of State. Bureau of Public Affairs.* Background notes. Kenya. [Washington, for sale by the Supt. of Docs., U.S. Govt. Print. Off.], 1980. 7 p. illus., maps. (U.S. Dept. of State. Department of State publication 8024) G59.U5

L.C. retains only the latest revision.

For a description of the contents of this publication, see the note to entry 937.

1550

Howell, John B. Kenya: subject guide to official publications. Washington, Library of Congress; [for sale by the Supt. of Docs., U.S. Govt. Print. Off.] 1978. xix, 423 p. Z3587.H68

Prepared in the Library's African Section.

3, 048 entries.

1551

Kaplan, Irving. Area handbook for Kenya; coauthors, Irving Kaplan [with] Margarita K. Dobert [et al.] 2d. Washington, for sale by the Supt. of Docs., U.S. Govt. Print. Off., 1976. 472 p. illus., maps (part fold.) DT433.5.K36 1976

"DA Pam 550-56."

"One of a series of handbooks prepared by Foreign Area Studies (FAS) of the American University."

Bibliography: p. 423–451.

1552

The Peace Corps in Kenya. [Washington, U.S. Govt. Print. Off., 1980] 1 fold sheet (6 p.) illus., map.

DLC

"ACTION 4200.52."

An introduction to the country for Volunteers.

1553

The Republic of Kenya, [by Leonard] Berry [et al.] Worcester, Mass., Program for International Development, Clark University, 1980. 139 p. maps. (Eastern Africa country profiles. [Country profile no. 3]) DLC

Bibliography: p. 137–139.

Apparently prepared at the request of the U.S. Agency for International Development.

Agriculture

1554

Agricultural horticulturalists training program: evaluation report. Nairobi, Technical Consultants International, 1977. [150] leaves. DPC

Prepared under Action contract 76-042-1012.

1555

Axinn, George H., James W. Birkhead, *and* Allan W. Sudholt. Evaluation of the Kenya national range and range development project (AID project no. 615-0157) [Washington, Devres, inc.], 1979. 179 leaves.

Prepared for the U.S. Agency for International Development under contract AID/afr-C-1558.

Examined in the Development Information Center, AID, Washington, D.C.

1556

Berry, Leonard. Environmental issues and prospects for rural progress in Kenya. Worcester, Mass., Clark University, 1975. [49] leaves. maps.

DLC

Apparently prepared for the U.S. Agency for International Development.

1557

Desrosiers, Russell, Tim Rose, *and* James Matata. Agricultural research in Kenya; review and assess-

1557 (cont.)
ment of the agricultural research capabilities and effectiveness of the Scientific Research Division. McLean, Va., American Technical Assistance Corporation, 1977. 84 p.

"Report CR-A-201."

Submitted to the U.S. AID Mission to Kenya and to the Government of Kenya; prepared under U.S. Agency for International Development contract AID/afr-C-1142.

Concerns the Division of Scientific Research, Ministry of Agriculture, Government of Kenya.

Abstract in *A.I.D. Research and Development Abstracts*, July 1978, p. 1–2.

Microfiche. [Washington, U.S. Agency for International Development, 1977?] 1 sheet.

DLC-Sci RR PN-AAF-264

1558
Dunmore, John C. Kenyan pastoralists enter 20th century. Foreign agriculture, Jan. 3, 1978: 10-11. illus.   HD1401.F65   1975

Issued by the U.S. Foreign Agricultural Service.

1559
Durr, G., *and* G. Lorenzl. Potato production and utilization in Kenya. Lima, Peru, Centro Internacional de la Papa, 1980. 133 p. maps.

Issued in cooperation with the Dept. of Agricultural Economics, University of Nairobi, and the Institute of Socio-Economics of Agricultural Development, Technical University, Berlin.

Abstract in *A.I.D. Research & Development Abstracts*. v. 9, no. 4, p. 7.

Microfiche. [Washington, U.S. Agency for International Development, 1980?] 2 sheets.

DLC-Sci RR PN-AAJ-221

1560
Dworkin, David M. Kenya rural water supply: programs, progress, prospects. [Washington?], U.S. Agency for International Development, 1980. [35] p. (in various pagings) (A.I. D. project impact evaluation report, no. 5)   DLC

Abstract in *A.I.D. Research & Development Abstracts*, July 1981, p. 6.

Issued also in microfiche. [Washington, U.S. Agency for International Development, 1980?] 1 sheet.   DLC-Sci RR PN-AAH-724

1561
Garst, Ronald D. Spatial diffusion in rural Kenya: the impact of infrastructure and centralized decision making. [Columbus?], Dept. of Geography, Ohio State University, [1976?] 35 leaves. maps. (Studies in the diffusion of innovation. Discussion paper, no. 17)

FAR 26645-N.

Study supported by the National Science Foundation.

A review of the impact of government decisions on the diffusion of agricultural innovations.

Examined in the former Foreign Affairs Research Documentation Center, U.S. Dept. of State.

1561a
George, Emmett. At home on the range in Kenya: with AID's help, Kenya is improving its beef production as well as the lives of the nomads who depend on their cattle for existence. Agenda, May 1978: 16–20. illus.   HC59.7.A742   1978

Issued by the U.S. Agency for International Development.

1562
Gerhart, John. The diffusion of hybrid maize in western Kenya; abridged by CIMMYT. Mexico, Centro Internacional de Mejoramiento de Maiz y Trigo, 1975. 57 p.

Abstract in *A.I.D. Research and Development Abstracts*, Apr. 1977, p. 3.

Microfiche. [Washington, U.S. Agency for International Development, 1975?] 1 sheet.

DLC-Sci RR PN-AAC-547

1563
Ingle, M.D., *and* A. M. Lago. Rural development data gathering and analysis methods; Kenya rural roads evaluation design: consultancy report. [Washington, Practical Concepts, inc.], 1978. 85 p.

Prepared for the U.S. Agency for International Development under contract AID/ta-C-1469.

Concerns in part a rural access roads program.

Abstract in *A.I.D. Research and Development Abstracts*, Oct. 1978, p. 24.

Examined in the Development Information Center, AID, Washington, D.C.

1564
Is small beautiful? The organizational conditions for effective small-scale self-help development projects in rural Kenya, [by] Joel D. Barkan [et al.] [Iowa City, Comparative Legislative Research Center, University of Iowa], 1979. 35, 4 p. (Iowa. University. Comparative Legislative Research Center. Occasional paper, no. 15)   DLC

"A paper delivered at the 22nd annual meeting of the African Studies Association, Los Angeles, November 2, 1979, and at a seminar at the Agency for International Development, Washington, November 19, 1979."

1565
Kabwegyere, T. B. Small urban centers and the

1565 (cont.)

growth of underdevelopment in rural Kenya. *In* Southall, Aidan. Small urban centers in rural development in Africa. Madison, African Studies Program, University of Wisconsin-Madison, 1979. p. 36–44.

A grant from the Office of Urban Development, U.S. Agency for International Development, assisted in the preparation for publication of the papers collected in the study.

Microfiche. [Washington, U.S. Agency for International Development, 1980?] (PN-AAJ-064); examined in the Development Internation Center, AID, Washington, D.C.

1566

Kenya national crop storage study. Manhattan, Kan., Development Planning & Research Associates, inc., 1980. [267] p. (in various pagings) illus., map.

Prepared for the U.S. Agency for International Development under contract AID/afr-C-1562.

Abstract in *A.I.D. Research & Development Abstracts*, v. 10, no. 1/2, 1982, p. 2.

Microfiche. [Washington, U.S. Agency for International Development, 1980?] 3 sheets (PN-AAJ-658); examined in the Development Information Center, AID, Washington, D.C.

1567

Kitale maize: the limits of success, [by] Charles W. Johnson [et al.] [Washington?], Agency for International Development, 1979. [54] p. (in various pagings) (A.I.D. project impact evaluation report, no. 2)   DLC

Bibliography: Appendix E (9 p.).

"Ninety percent of Kenya's people depend on maize as their staple food. This report examines the impacts of A.I.D.'s support to maize breeding projects in Kenya."—Abstract.

Abstract in *A.I.D. Research & Development Abstract*, July 1981, p. 2.

Microfiche. [Washington, U.S. Agency for International Development, 1979?] 1 sheet.

DLC-Sci RR PN-AAH-723

1568

Mass, Frederick H. Summary of work performed and recommendations pertaining to Northeastern Province portion of USAID/Kenya national range and ranch development project. Falls Church, Va., 1974. 21 p.

Prepared for the U.S. Agency for International Development under contract AID/afr-C-1062.

Microfiche. [Washington, U.S. Agency for International Development, 1974?] 1 sheet.

DLC-Sci RR PN-AAF-370

1568a

Moland, John, *and* T. T. Williams. Societal views and perceived social integration with emphasis on the farmer's cooperatives in Kenya. [Baton Rouge?], Unemployment-Underemployment Institute, Southern University, 1979. 23 p.

Prepared for the U.S. Agency for International Development under contract AID/csd-3414.

Cited in list prepared by the Development Information Center, AID; not examined.

1569

Parkin, David. Along the line of road: expanding rural centers in Kenya's Coast Province. *In* Southall, Aidan. Small urban centers in rural development in Africa. Madison, African Studies Program, University of Wisconsin-Madison, 1979. p. 56–68.

A grant from the Office of Urban Development, U.S. Agency for International Development, assisted in the preparation for publication of the papers collected in the study.

Microfiche. [Washington, U.S. Agency for International Development, 1980?] (PN-AAJ-064); examined in the Development Information Center, Agency for International Development, Washington, D.C.

1570

Pfost, Donald L., *and* Dale G. Anderson. Smallholder grain storage in Kenya: problems and proposed solutions. Manhattan, Food and Feed Grain Institute, Kansas State University, [1978] 55 p. (Grain storage, processing and marketing, report no. 72)   DLC

Prepared for the U.S. Agency for International Development under contract AID/ta-C-1162.

1571

Pre-investment study of agricultural potential of selected marginal semi-arid lands in Kenya, [by] William Johnson [et al.] [Nairobi], U.S. AID Mission to Kenya, 1975. 35 p.

Issued in cooperation with the University of Arizona.

Examined in the Development Information Center, Agency for International Development, Washington, D.C.

1572

Professional and subprofessional agricultural manpower in Kenya (demand, supply, education and utilization), [by] Kurt Hecht [et al.] McLean, Va., American Technical Assistance Corporation, 1978. 159 p.

"Report CR-A-210."

Submitted to the U.S. AID Mission to Kenya and the Government of Kenya; prepared under

1572 (cont.)

U.S. Agency for International Development contract AID/afr-C-1142.

Abstract for report and its appendixes in *A.I.D. Research and Development Abstracts*, July 1978, p. 4–5.

Microfiche. [Washington, U.S. Agency for International Development, 1978?] 2 sheets.

DLC-Sci RR PN-AAF-265

1573

———— Appendices A thru F & H. McLean, Va., American Technical Assistance Corporation, 1978. [140] p. (in various pagings)

"Report CR-A-210."

Bibliography: p. H-1—H-6.

Submitted to the U.S. AID Mission to Kenya and the Government of Kenya; prepared under U.S. Agency for International Development contract AID/afr-C-1142.

Microfiche. [Washington, U.S. Agency for International Development, 1978?] 2 sheets.

DLC-Sci RR PN-AAF-266

1574

———— Appendices G1 & G2. McLean, Va., American Technical Assistance Corporation, 1978. [189] p.

"Report CR-A-210."

Submitted to the U.S. AID Mission to Kenya and the Government of Kenya; prepared under U.S. Agency for International Development contract AID/afr-C-1142.

Microfiche. [Washington, U.S. Agency for International Development, 1978?] 2 sheets.

DLC-Sci RR PN-AAF-267

1575

Small farmers on the move: results of a panel study in rural Kenya, [by] Fred W. Chege [et al]. [s.l., 1976] 39 p.

Paper presented at the Fourth World Congress of Rural Sociology, 1976.

Abstract in *Resources in Education*, Apr. 1977, p. 115.

Microfiche. [Arlington, Va., ERIC Document Reproduction Service; prepared for Educational Resources Information Center, National Institute of Education, 1977] 1 sheet.

DLC-Micro ED131984

1576

Stringham, Glen E. Agricultural engineering expansion program at Egerton College, Njoro, Kenya. [Logan?, Utah State University], 1978. 94 p.

Prepared for the U.S. Agency for International Development under contract AID/afr-C-1140.

Abstract in *A.I.D. Research and Development Abstract*, Jan. 1979, p. 1.

Economic Aspects

1577

Avidor, Abraham. Kenya's farm problems retard economic growth. Foreign agriculture, Mar. 1981: 19–20. illus.   HD1401.F65   1981

Issued by the U.S. Foreign Agricultural Service.

1578

Brokensha, David, *and* Bernard W. Riley. Introduction of cash crops in a marginal area of Kenya. *In* Agricultural development in Africa: issues of public policy; edited by Robert H. Bates [and] Michael F. Lofchie. [New York], Praeger, 1980. p. 244–274. map.   HD2117.A35

Publication supported in part by the National Science Foundation.

1579

Browne, Glenn G. Kenya agricultural credit evaluation. [s.l.], Dimpex Associates, 1977. 46 p.

Prepared for the U.S. Agency for International Development under contract AID/afr-C-1269.

Examined in the Development Information Center, AID, Washington, D.C.

1580

Rose, Irene. Ecology fears boost Kenyan pyrethrum exports. Foreign agriculture, Jan. 26, 1976: 9–10. illus.   HD1401.F65   1976

Issued by the U.S. Foreign Agricultural Service.

1581

———— Kenya's tea output, usage, exports on general uptrend. Foreign agriculture, May 17, 1976: 10–11. illus.   HD1401.F65   1976

Issued by the U.S. Foreign Agricultural Service.

1582

Rusch, William H. *and* Tim H. Rose. Kenya-smallholders production services and credit project baseline survey, agricultural year 1975–1976; executive summary and analysis. McLean, Va., American Technical Assistance Corporation, 1977. 179 p.

Prepared for the U.S. Agency for International Development under contract AID/afr-C-1213.

"This is a survey of 778 farmers in the Eastern, Western, and South Nyanza provinces of Kenya."— p. 1.

Abstract in *A.I.D. Research & Development Abstracts*, v. 9, no. 3, 1981, p. 31.

Microfiche. [Washington, U.S. Agency for International Development, 1977?] 2 sheets (PN-AAG-

1582 (cont.)

805), held by the Development Information Center, Agency for International Development, Washington, D.C.

1583

Small farmer credit in Kenya. Washington, Agency for International Development, 1973. 207 p. (Spring review of small farmer credit, 1973. v. 7, no. SR 107)

　Microfiche. [Springfield, Va., National Technical Information Service, 1973?] 3 sheets.
　　　　　　　　DLC-Sci RR PN-AAA-128

1584

Witucki, Lawrence A. Agricultural development in Kenya since 1967. Washington, U.S. Dept. of Agriculture, Economic Research Service, 1976. 12 p. map. (Foreign agricultural economic report, no. 123)　　　　　　HD1411.F59 no. 123

1585

——— Kenya's tea exports, output boomed in '77. Foreign agriculture, Feb. 6, 1978: 6–7. illus.
　　　　　　　　HD1401.F65　1978
Issued by the U.S. Foreign Agricultural Service.

Assistance Programs

1586

U.S. *AID Mission to Kenya*. Country development strategy statement: 1981–1985. [Nairobi?], 1979. 54 p.

　Abstract in *Appropriate Technical Information for Developing Countries*, 2d ed., 1979, p. 224.

　Microfiche. [Springfield, Va., National Technical Information Service. 1979] 1 sheet.
　　　　　　　　DLC-Sci RR PB 298092

1587

U.S. *Agency for International Development*. Annual budget submission: Kenya. Washington, U.S. International Development Cooperation Agency.

　Vols. for 1977+ examined in the Development Information Center, AID, Washington, D.C.

1588

——— Country development strategy statement: Kenya. Washington, U.S. International Development Cooperation Agency. annual.

　Vols. for 1981+ examined in the Development Information Center, AID, Washington, D.C.

1589

——— Review of USAID/Kenya procurement practices. [Washington], 1980. 32 p.

"Audit report 3-615-80-9."
Prepared by the Area Auditor General-Africa.
Examined in the Development Information Center, AID, Washington, D.C.

1590

Bender, Stephen, *and* Barbara Wilson. An evaluation of Peace Corps/Kenya's Harambee school project. Washington, Evaluation Division, Office of Policy and Planning, Action, 1977. 46 p. (in various pagings)　　　　　　　　DLC

　"The Government of Kenya has long considered formal education as a top priority and presently devotes a full third of its annual budget to the education sector. The informal secondary education system consists of what are known as Harambee schools."

1591

Biggs, Huntley, *and* John R. Schott. An evaluation of CARE-assisted village water development activites in Kenya, for U.S. AID Mission to Kenya as Work Order No. 8 of AID/otr-C-1379. [Nairobi?] 1976. 34 leaves.　　　DLC

　Evaluation performed by the American Technical Assistance Corporation.

1592

Kenya. [*Treaties, etc. 1974 Sept. 11*] Loan agreement among the Republic of Kenya and the Agricultural Finance Corporation and the United States of America for Kenya livestock development. *In* U.S. *Treaties, etc.* United States treaties and other international agreements, v. 28, 1976–77. [Washington, Dept. of State; for sale by the Supt. of Docs., U.S. Govt. Print. Off., 1978] p. 5617–5669 ([Treaties and other international acts series, 8650])
　　　　　　　　JX231.A34 v. 28
　Signed at Nairobi Sept. 11, 1974; amending agreement signed at Nairobi July 20, 1977.

1593

Kenya. [*Treaties, etc. United States, 1975 Nov. 10*] Loan agreement (agricultural sector loan) between the Republic of Kenya and the United States of America. *In* U.S. *Treaties, etc.* United States treaties and other international agreements, v. 28, 1976–77. [Washington, Dept. of State; for sale by the Supt. of Docs., U.S. Govt. Print. Off., 1978] p. 266–310. ([Treaties and other international acts series, 8470])　　　　　JX231.A34 v. 28
　Signed at Nairobi Nov. 10, 1975.

　"This agreement provides that AID [U.S. Agency for International Development] will lend the Government of Kenya up to $13.5 million to finance certain U.S. dollar and local currency costs of agricultural development activities."—p. 266.

1594

Kenya. [*Treaties, etc. United States, 1976 June 30*]
Kenya rural planning project. Agreement signed at
Nairobi June 30, 1976; entered into force June 30,
1976. *In* U.S. *Treaties, etc.* United States treaties
and other international agreements, v. 28, 1976–77.
[Washington, Dept. of State; for sale by the Supt.
of Docs., U.S. Govt. Print. Off., 1978] p. 1563–
1579. ([Treaties and other international acts series,
8520])   JX231.A34 v. 28
   Concerns a U.S. Agency for International Development grant for the purpose of implementing
and evaluating agricultural and rural development
policies and programs.

1595

Kenya. [*Treaties, etc. United States, 1976 Aug. 24*]
Kenya: military assistance; eligibility requirements
pursuant to the International Security Assistance
and Arms Export Control Act of 1976. *In* U.S.
Treaties, etc. United States treaties and other inter-
national agreements, v. 28, 1976–77. [Washington,
Dept. of State; for sale by the Supt. of Docs., U.S.
Govt. Print. Off., 1978] p. 2468–2471. ([Treaties
and other international acts series, 8568])
                          JX231.A34 v. 28
   Agreement effected by exchange of notes dates
at Nairobi Aug. 10 and 24, 1976; entered into force
Aug. 24, 1976.

1596

Kenya. [*Treaties, etc., United States, 1977 Mar. 25*]
Kenya; social security. Agreement effected by exchange of notes dated at Nairobi January 31 and
March 21, 1977; entered into force March 25,
1977. *In* U.S. *Treaties, etc.* United States treaties
and other international agreements, v. 29, 1976–
77. [Washington, Dept. of State; for sale by the
Supt. of Docs., U.S. Govt. Print. Off., 1979]
p. 678–683. ([Treaties and other international acts
series, 8847])   JX231.A34 v. 29
   Concerns the enrollment of certain employees of
the U.S. Government in Kenya in the National
Social Security Fund of Kenya.

1597

Kenya. [*Treaties, etc. United States, 1977 July 1*]
Project agreement between the Republic of Kenya
("The Government") and the United States of
America acting through Agency for International
Development ("A.I.D"), road gravelling project.
In U.S. *Treaties, etc.* United States treaties and
other international agreements, v. 29, 1976–77.
[Washington, Dept. of State; for sale by the Supt.
of Docs., U.S. Govt. Print. Off., 1979] p. 2510–
2550. ([Treaties and other international acts series,
8954])   JX231.A34, v. 29

Signed at Nairobi July 1, 1977.
   For the purpose of upgrading to all-weather
standard approximately 800 miles of roads in
Western and Nyanza provinces.

1598

Kenya. [*Treaties, etc. United States, 1977 Sept. 30*]
Project agreement between the Republic of Kenya
("The Government") and the United States of
America acting through Agency for International
Development ("A.I.D."), rural roads system pro-
ject. *In* U.S. *Treaties, etc.* United States treaties
and other international agreements, v. 29, 1976–77.
[Washington, Dept. of State; for sale by the Supt. of
Docs., U.S. Govt. Print. Off., 1979] p. 3498–3536.
([Treaties and other international acts series, 9025])
                          JX231.A34 v.29
   Signed at Nairobi, Sept. 30, 1977.
   Project for the construction or improvement of
all-weather access roads in Western and Nyanza
provinces.

1599

Kenya. [*Treaties, etc. United States, 1978 Aug. 29*]
Project agreement between the Republic of Kenya
and the United States of America acting through
the Agency for International Development; agricultural systems support project. *In* U.S. *Treaties,
etc.* United States treaties and other international
agreements, v. 30, 1978–79. [Washington, Dept. of
State; for sale by the Supt. of Docs., U.S. Govt.
Print. Off., 1981] p. 4967–4991]. ([Treaties and
other international acts series, 9495])
                          JX231.A34 v. 30
   The project consisted of five components: increased trained agricultural manpower through
expansion of Egerton College; range research system support; credit system support; cooperation
system support; and storage and marketing system
support.

1600

Kenya. [*Treaties, etc. United States, 1980 Mar. 6*]
Agreement between the Government of the United
States and the Government of the Republic of
Kenya for sales of agricultural commodites. [Wash-
ington, Dept. of State; for sale by the Supt. of
Docs., U.S. Govt. Print. Off., 1980] 21 p. (Treaties
and other international acts series, 9735)
                                       DLC
   Signed at Nairobi, Mar. 6, 1980.

1601

Kenya. [*Treaties, etc. United States, 1980 May 15*]
Agreement between the United States of America
and Kenya amending the agreement of March 6,
1980; effected by exchange of notes dated at Nairobi

1601 (cont.)

May 15, 1980. [Washington, Dept. of State; for sale by the Supt. of Docs., U.S. Govt. Print. Off., 1981] 5 p. (Treaties and other international acts series, 9815)   DLC

1602

Kenya. [*Treaties, etc. United States, 1980 Dec. 31*] Agreement between the Government of the United States of America and the Government of the Republic of Kenya for sales of agricultural commodities. [Washington, Dept. of State; for sale by the Supt. of Docs., U.S. Govt. Print. Off., 1981] 13 p. (Treaties and other international acts series, 9969)   DLC

Signed at Nairobi Dec. 31, 1980 and Jan. 7, 1981; entered into force Dec. 31, 1980.

1603

Sternin, Jerry, John Hatch, *and* Carol Tuxson. Peace Corps/Kenya country program evaluation. [Washington], Evaluation Division, Office of Policy and Planning, Action, 1976. [87] leaves (in various foliations)   DPC

1604

Technical Assistance Information Clearing House. Development assistance programs of U.S. non-profit organizations in Kenya. [New York], American Council of Voluntary Agencies for Foreign Service, 1976. 41 p. (TAICH country report)   DLC

The Council operates the Clearing House with funding by the U.S. Agency for International Development.

1605

———— Development assistance of U.S. non-profit organizations: Kenya. [New York], American Council of Voluntary Agencies for Foreign Service, 1980. 59 p. map. (TAICH country report)   DLC

"2d edition."

1606

Two views of 'liberation': a Kenyan and a Black American work on village water project. Agenda, Feb. 1978: 19-22. illus.   HC59.7.A742 1978

Issued by the U.S. Agency for International Development.

Describes the roles of two CARE representatives in western Kenya.

1607

Young, Andrew. Atlantans help the blind in Kenya.

Congressional record, 94th Congress, 2d session, v. 122, Mar. 3, 1976: 5270-5272.

     J11.R5 v. 122

Extension of remarks in the U.S. House of Representatives.

Includes article from the magazine of the *Atlanta Journal and Constitution* concerning a program of the International Eye Foundation.

Commerce

1608

Manley, Mary L. Marketing in Kenya. [Washington] U.S. Dept. of Commerce, Domestic and International Business Administration; [for sale by the Supt. of Docs., U.S. Govt. Print. Off.] 1977. 39 p. (Overseas business reports. OBR 77-22)

     HF91.U482 1977, no. 22

International marketing information series.

Supersedes *Marketing in Kenya* (Overseas business reports. OBR 74-53), by Sally K. Miller and Thomas A. Forbord.

1609

Market share reports. Country series: Kenya, 1971–75. [Washington], U.S. Dept. of Commerce; for sale by the National Technical Information Service, Springfield, Va., [1977] 67 p.

Indicates the United States share of the market in Kenya for various products compared to the shares for Belgium-Luxemburg, France, Federal Republic of Germany, Great Britain, Italy, Netherlands, Sweden, and Japan.

Microfiche. [Washington, Congressional Information Service, 1977?]

     DLC-Micro ASI:77 2016-1.62

1610

Market share reports. Country series: Kenya, 1975–79. [Washington], International Trade Administration, U.S. Dept. of Commerce; for sale by the National Technical Information Service, Springfield, Va., [1979] 66 p.

Includes same comparative data as in *Market Share Reports. Country Series: Kenya, 1971–75* (entry 1609).

Microfiche. [Washington, Congressional Information Service, 1979?]

     DLC-Micro ASI:81 2046-2.60

Economic Conditions

1611

Esibi, John. Commercial bank chairman discusses economic trends. *In* U.S. *Joint Publications Re-*

1611 (cont.)

search Service. JPRS 75241. [Springfield, Va., National Technical Information Service, 1980] (Sub-Saharan Africa report, no. 2219) p. 57–63.

Interview with Philip Ndegwa, chairman of the Kenya Commercial Bank, in *Sunday Nation,* Nairobi, Feb. 3, 1980, p. 5.

Microfiche. [s.l., 1980]

DLC-Micro JPRS 75241

1612

—— Minister discusses minimum wage policy, Kenyanization. *In* U.S. *Jont Publications Research Service.* JPRS 75463. [Springfield, Va., National Technical Information Service, 1980] (Sub-Saharan Africa report, no. 2232) p. 37–42.

Interview with W. Elijah Mwangale, Minister of Labor, in *Sunday Nation,* Nairobi, Mar. 16, 1980, p. 4.

Microfiche. [s.l., 1980]

DLC-Micro JPRS 75463

1613

Foreign economic trends and their implications for the United States. Kenya. 1969+ Washington, for sale by the Supt. of Docs., U.S. Govt. Print. Off. annual. (International marketing information series) HC10.E416

Prepared by the U.S. Embassy, Nairobi.

Vols. for 1969–77 distributed by the U.S. Bureau of International Commerce; vols. for 1978–79 by the U.S. Industry and Trade Administration; vols. for 1980– by the U.S. International Trade Administration.

The following issues for the period 1973–80 have been identified in L.C.:

ET 73-078. 1973. [20] p.
ET 74-080. 1974. 11 p.
FET 75-095. 1975. 9 p.
FET 76-092. 1976. 11 p.
FET 77-121. 1977. 12 p.
FET 78-100. 1978. 14 p.
FET 79-083. 1979. 12 p.
FET 80-089. 1980. 10 p.

1614

Household income distributions for Nairobi and income estimates for other municiplties in Kenya. Chicago, Real Estate Research Corporation, 1976. 31 p.

Prepared for the U.S. Agency for International Development.

Examined in the Development Information Center, AID, Washington, D.C.

1615

Kibaki, Mwai. Kibaki notes 1979's economic high-

lights, 1980 outlook. *In* U.S. *Joint Publications Research Service.* JPRS 76009. [Springfield, Va., National Technical Information Service, 1980] (Sub-Saharan Africa report, no. 2265) p. 58–64.

Extracts of remarks by the Kenyan Vice-President and Minister for Finance reported in *Daily Nation,* Nairobi, June 20, 1980, p. 12.

Microfiche. [s.l., 1980]

DLC-Micro JPRS 76009

1616

Pack, Howard. Employment and productivity in Kenyan manufacturing. New Haven, Economic Growth Center, Yale University, 1974. 41 p. (Center discussion paper, no. 196)

"Portions of this research were financed by funds provided by the Agency for International Development under contract CSD/2492."

Abstract in *A.I.D. Research and Development Abstracts,* July 1978, p. 34.

Microfiche. [Washington, U.S. Agency for International Development, 1974?] 1 sheet.

DLC-Sci RR PN-AAE-517

1617

Porter, Richard C. Some doubts about Kenya's future as an exporter of manufactures. Ann Arbor, Center for Research on Economic Development, University of Michigan, 1973. 28 p. (Michigan. University. Center for Research on Economic Development. Discussion paper, no. 31)

Microfiche. [Washington, U.S. Agency for International Development, 1973?] 1 sheet.

DLC-Sci RR PN-AAA-455

1618

Positive developments brighten Kenyan scene as regional ties fade. Commerce America, Sept. 12, 1977: 22-28. HF1.C38

Issued by the U.S. Dept. of Commerce.

Education

1619

Anderson, John E. Organization and financing of self-help education in Kenya. Paris, UNESCO, International Institute for Educational Planning, 1973. 70 p. (Financing educational systems: special case studies, 4) LB2970.K4A5

Includes bibliographical references.

Label mounted on t.p.: UNIPUB Inc., New York.

"IIEP 72/VIb.4/A."

Abstract in *Research in Education,* Feb. 1974, p. 63–64.

Issued also in microfiche. [Bethesda, Md., ERIC

1619 (cont.)

Document Reproduction Service; prepared for Educational Resources Information Center, U.S. Office of Education, 1974] 1 sheet.

DLC-Micro ED082336

1620

Esibi, John. Minister of Basic Education discusses duties, plans. *In* U.S. *Joint Publications Research Service.* JPRS 75314. [Springfield, Va., National Technical Information Service, 1980] (Sub-Saharan Africa report, no. 2223) p. 66–71.

Interview with Moses B. Mundavadi, Minister of Basic Education, in *Sunday Nation*, Nairobi, Feb. 17, 1980, p. 5.

Microfiche. [s.l. 1980]

DLC-Micro JPRS 75314

1620a

An Evaluation of cooperative education and training in Kenya with recommendations for improvements, [by] James Bell [et al.] [s.l.], Agricultural Cooperative Development International, 1980. [106] p. (in various pagings) illus.

Studies submitted to the Ministry of Cooperative Development, Government of Kenya, and the U.S. AID Mission to Kenya.

Concerns cooperative movements in agriculture, credit and banking, and consumer activities.

Microfiche. [Washington, U.S. Agency for International Development, 1980?] 2 sheets (PN-AAJ-787); examined in the Development Information Center, AID, Washington, D.C.

1621

Godfrey, E. M. Technical and vocational training in Kenya and the Harambee Institutes of Technology. [Nairobi], Institute for Development Studies, University of Nairobi, 1973. [58] p. (Nairobi. University. Institute for Development Studies. Discussion paper, no. 169)

Abstract in *Resources in Education*, Sept. 1975, p. 37.

Microfiche. [Arlington, Va., ERIC Document Reproduction Service; prepared for Educational Resources Information Center, National Institute of Education, 1975] 1 sheet.

DLC-Micro ED105266

1622

Kinyanjui, Peter E., *and* Ben K. Gitau. Distance teaching and mass education, Kenya. *In* Educational reforms and innovations in Africa: studies prepared for the Conference of Ministers of Education of African Member States of Unesco. Paris, Unesco, 1978. p. 65–72. (Experiments and innovations in education, no. 34)   LA1500.E38

Issued also in microfiche. [Arlington, Va., ERIC Document Reproduction Service; prepared for Educational Resources Information Center, National Institute of Education, 1978] 1 sheet.

DLC-Micro ED160036

1622a

Lindahl, Thomas, J., Wayne Robinson, *and* M.J. Guderyon. Cooperative College in Kenya: feasibility study for expansion. [s.l.], Agricultural Cooperative Development International, [1980] 53 p.

Study submitted to the Ministry of Cooperative Development, Government of Kenya, and the U.S. AID Mission to Kenya.

Microfiche. [Washington, U.S. Agency for International Development, 1980?] 1 sheet (PN-AAJ-789); examined in the Development Information Center, AID, Washington, D.C.

1623

Mook, Byron T. *and* J. C. P. Oxenham. Qualification and selection in educational systems: a programme of research. Pt. 2: Job-seekers and job placement services. [Brighton, Institute of Development Studies, University of Sussex], 1975. 13 p. (Institute of Development Studies. IDS discussion paper, no. 71)   HD6276.K4M66

Kenya and Sri Lanka are used as examples.

Abstract in *Resources in Education*, Mar. 1978, p. 64.

Issued also in microfiche. [Arlington, Va., ERIC Document Reproduction Service; prepared for Educational Resources Information Center, National Institute of Education, 1978] 1 sheet.

DLC-Micro ED145508

Note: L.C. has also pt. 1, *How Employers Use Qualifications and How Qualifications Affect Schools*, ([Brighton, Institute of Development Studies, University of Sussex, 1975]) in microfiche. [Arlington, Va., ERIC Document Reproduction Service; prepared for Educational Resources Information Center, National Institute of Education, 1978] 1 sheet. DLC-Sci RR ED145507.

1624

Technical Consultants International. Harambee IV secondary school teachers, special education teachers, special education teachers, coop volunteers, final (training) report and evaluation. Nairobi, 1978. [250] leaves.   DPC

Prepared under Action contract 76-042-1012.

Foreign Relations

1625

U.S. *President, 1977–1981 (Carter)* Visit of President Daniel T. arap Moi of Kenya; remarks at the welcoming ceremony, February 20, 1980. *In* U.S. *President.* Public papers of the Presidents of the

1625 (cont.)

United States. Jimmy Carter. 1980–81. [Washington, Office of the Federal Register, National Archives and Records Service; for sale by the Supt. of Docs., U.S. Govt. Print. Off., 1981] p. 352–353.
J80.A283   1980–81

These remarks are followed by a White House statement on the visit (p. 354–355).

1626

Hirtzel, Richard D. The relations of Kenya with its bordering states. Carlisle Barracks, Pa., U.S. Army War College, 1976. 24 p.

At head of title: USAWC essay.

Concerns Kenya's relations with Sudan, Tanzania, Ethiopia, Somalia, and Uganda.

Abstract in *Government Reports Announcements & Index*, May 13, 1977, p. 27.

Microfiche. [s.l., 1977] 1 sheet.
DLC-Sci RR AD-A036227

1627

Kennedy, Edward M. Arms sales to Africa. Congressional record, 94th Congress, 2d session, v. 122, Aug. 6, 1976: 26264-26266.   J11.R5 v. 122

Remarks in the U.S. Senate with emphasis on sales of American weapons to Kenya.

Includes report prepared by the Washington Office on Africa.

Geology, Hydrology, and Mineral Resources

1628

Jolly, Janice L. W. The mineral industry of Kenya. *In* Minerals yearbook, v. 3, 1976. [Washington, for sale by the Supt. of Docs., U.S. Govt. Print. Off., 1980] p. 645–655.   TN23.U612   1976, v. 3

Prepared by the U.S. Bureau of Mines.

1629

—— The mineral industry of Kenya. *In* Minerals yearbook, v. 3, 1977. [Washington, for sale by the Supt. of Docs., U.S. Govt. Print. Off., 1981] p. 561–567.   TN23.U612   1977, v. 3

Prepared by the U.S. Bureau of Mines.

1630

—— The mineral industry of Kenya. *In* Minerals yearbook, v. 3, 1978–79. [Washington, U.S. Govt. Print. Off., 1981] p. 567–576.
TN23.U612   1978–79, v. 3

Prepared by the U.S. Bureau of Mines.

1631

Swarzanski, Wolfgang V., *and* Maurice J. Mundorff. Geohydrology of North Eastern Province, Kenya; prepared in cooperation with the Water Department, Kenya Ministry of Agriculture under the auspices of the U.S. Agency for International Development. Washington, [for sale by the Supt. of Docs.], U.S. Govt. Print. Off., 1977. 68 p. maps (5 fold. in pocket) (U.S. Geological Survey. Water-supply paper, 1757-N)   TC801.U2 no. 1757-N

Contributions to the hydrology of Africa and the Mediterranean region.

Bibliography: p. 44–45.

"The Government of Kenya, with international assistance, has been engaged since 1968 in a long-term project to develop the livestock resources of the country. Under the first phase of the project, a cooperative agreement between Kenya's Ministry of Agriculture and the U.S. Agency for International Development provided for a survey to evaluate the water resources of the North Eastern Province and for the development of plans for the optimum utilization of range lands and available water resources in selected areas of the province. The present report, largely concerned with ground water, is based on the findings of the water-resources investigation undertaken under Phase I (1968–1973) of the project."—Abstract.

Health and Nutrition

1632

U.S. *AID Mission to Kenya.* Rural health/maternal and child health/family planning: staff paper. [Nairobi], 1976. 54 p.

Examined in the Development Information Center, Agency for International Development, Washington, D.C.

1633

Anderson, Mary Ann, *and* Tina Grewal. Nutrition planning in the developing world; proceedings of regional workshops held by CARE in India, Kenya, and Colombia, 1976. [New York, CARE, inc., 1977] 267 p.

"The preparation of this book was co-sponsored by the Office of Nutrition, Technical Assistance Branch, Agency for International Development."

Microfiche. [Washington, U.S. Agency for International Development, 1977?] 3 sheets.
DLC-Sci RR PN-AAD-741

1634

Barnum, Howard N. Cost effectiveness of programs to combat communicable childhood diseases in Kenya. Washington, One America, 1980. 32 leaves.

1634 (cont.)

Prepared for the Bureau for Africa, U.S. Agency for International Development.

Examined in the Documentation Center, Sahel Development Program, AID, Washington, D.C.

1635

Barrett, Fred F. Review of feasibility of alternatives for the school milk and school lunch feeding programs in Kenya. [Washington?], Nutrition and Agricbusiness Group, Office of International Cooperation and Development, U.S. Dept. of Agriculture, 1980. [24] p.   DNAL

Prepared for the U.S. Agency for International Development.

Abstract in *A.I.D. Research & Development Abstracts*, v. 9, no. 3, 1981, p. 51–52.

Microfiche. [Washington, U.S. Agency for International Development, 1980?] 1 sheet.

DLC-Sci RR PN-AAJ-348

1636

Berndtson, B. E. Planning for the audio visual equipment and commodity needs, Kenya Ministry of Health. [s.l.], 1977. 82 p.

Prepared for the U.S. Agency for International Development under contract AID/pha-C-1100.

Examined in the Development Information Center, AID, Washington, D.C.

1637

Byerly, Elizabeth L. Kenya health education project consultant's report for Action (Peace Corps) [s.l.], 1974. 25 leaves.   DPC

1638

Eighmy, Thomas H. An analysis of pilot study survey data in three countries. Washington, Checchi and Co., 1977. 108 p.

Prepared for the Office of Nutrition and the Office of Development Program Review and Evaluation, U.S. Agency for International Development.

Kenya, Colombia, and Philippines were included in the survey.

Issued as chapter four of *Evaluation Methods for Child Feeding Projects in Developing Countries; Final Report.*

Microfiche. [Washington, U.S. Agency for International Development, 1977?] 2 sheets.

DLC-Sci RR PN-AAE-07611

1639

George, Emmett. Better vision for Kenya; a roving eye clinic brings the gift of a lifetime of sight to thousands of Kenyans each year. Agenda, July/Aug. 1978: 1-4. illus.   HC59.7.A742   1978

Issued by the U.S. Agency for International Development

1640

Kaminsky, Donald C. Preventive medicine in tropical Africa (Peace Corps Kenya health handbook). [Nairobi, Peace Corps, 197?] 55 p.   DPC

1641

Perry, Cynthia S. Medical education training program, Peace Corps/Kenya, fall 1975. [Nairobi], Peace Corps Kenya, 1976. 100 p.   DPC

1642

Qureshi, Iqbal. Installation of audiovisual equipment in the Health Education Division/Nairobi. [s.l.], American Public Health Association, 1979. 21 p.

Prepared for the U.S. Agency for International Development under contract AID/pha-C-1100.

Examined in the Development Information Center, AID, Washington, D.C.

1643

Technical Consultants International pre-service training for medical education volunteers, Kenya; final report and evaluation. Nairobi, 1977. [250] leaves.   DPC

Prepared under Action contract 76-042-1012.

Housing and Urban Development

1644

Caminos, Horacio, Reinhard Goethert, *and* Tara S. Chana. Dwellings and land: urbanization in developing countries; case studies in Nairobi, Kenya, urban settlement design program. [Cambridge, School of Architecture and Planning, Massachusetts Institute of Technology, 1973] 95 p. illus., maps.

Supported in part by the U.S. Agency for International Development.

Held by the School of Architecture and Planning, Massachusetts Institute of Technology, Cambridge, Mass.

Issued also in microfiche. [Washington, U.S. Agency for International Development, 1973?] 1 sheet   DLC-Sci RR PN-AAA-742

1645

Gattoni, George, *and* Pratful Patel. Residential land utilization case study: Nairobi, Kenya. Cambridge, School of Architecture and Planning, Massachu-

1645 (cont.)

setts Institute of Technology, 1973. 130 p. illus., maps.

Study prepared as part of a project on "Development of Basic Performance Standards for Urbanization and Housing Technologies through Testing of Models, in Nairobi, Kenya," supported in part by the U.S. Agency for International Development.

Held by the School of Architecture and Planning, Massachusetts Institute of Technology, Cambridge, Mass.

Issued also in microfiche. [Washington, U.S. Agency for International Development, 1973?] 2 sheets.   **DLC-Sci RR PN-AAA-744**

1646

Implications of providing single-family versus multi-family housing in Nairobi, Kenya. [Chicago, Real Estate Research Corporation], 1976/ 17 leaves.

Prepared for the Office of Housing, U.S. Agency for International Development.

Examined in the Development Information Center, AID, Washington, D.C.

1647

Interim urbanization project: Dandora, Nairobi, Kenya, [by] Horacio Caminos [et al.] Cambridge, School of Architecture and Planning, Massachusetts Institute of Technology, 1973. [47] p. illus., maps.

Study prepared as part of a project on "Development of Basic Performance Standards for Urbanization and Housing Technologies through Testing of Models, in Nairobi, Kenya," supported in part by the U.S. Agency for International Development.

Study conducted in the Ruaraka/Dandora sector of Nairobi.

Held by the School of Architecture and Planning, Massachusetts Institute of Technology, Cambridge, Mass.

Issued also in microfiche. [Washington, U.S. Agency for International Development, 1973?] 1 sheet.   **DLC-Sci RR PN-AAA-743**

1648

Kenya shelter sector study and AID's experience [by] Nils O. Jorgensen [et al.] [Washington], Office of Housing, Agency for International Development, 1979, 243 p. map.

Abstract in *A.I.D. Research and Development Abstracts*, Feb. 2981, p. 67.

Microfiche. [Washington, U.S. Agency for International Development, 1979?] 3 sheets.
     DLC-Sci RR PN-AAH-491

1649

Muga, Erasto. Socio-economic conditions which pertain to cost of construction and operation of water and sewage treatment facilities and quality of water consumption in Kenya. [Norman?], Bureau of Water and Environmental Resources Research, University of Oklahoma, 1976. 288 p.

Research supported in part by the U.S. Agency for International Development.

Abstract in *A.I.D. Research and Development Abstracts*, Oct. 1977, p. 26.

Microfiche. [Washington, U.S. Agency for International Development, 1976?] 4 sheets.
     DLC-Sci RR PN-AAD-290

1650

Review of tenant purchase selection criteria and procedures for the low-income housing project of the City Council of Nairobi, Kenya. [Chicago, Real Estate Research Corporation], 1975. [20] leaves.

Prepared for the Office of Housing, U.S. Agency for International Development.

Examined in the Development Information Center, AID, Washington, D.C.

Politics and Government

1651

Barkan, Joel D., *and* John J. Okumu. Political linkage in Kenya: citizens, local elites, and legislators. [Iowa City, Comparative Legislative Research Center, University of Iowa], 1974. [28] p. (Iowa. University. Comparative Legislative Research Center. Occasional paper, no. [1])   **IaU**

Research supported in part by the U.S. Agency for International Development.

1652

Corruption described as 'way of life in Kenya.' *In* U.S. *Joint Publications Research Service*. JPRS 74699. [Springfield, Va., National Technical Information Service, 1979] (Sub-Saharan Africa report, no. 2185) p. 39–43.

From *Uganda Times*, Kampala, Oct. 15, 1979, p. 4.

Microfiche. [s.l. 1979]
     DLC-Micro JPRS 74699

1653

Full text of KANU manifesto published. *In* U.S. *Joint Publications Research Service*. JPRS 74492. [Springfield, Va., National Technical Information Service, 1979] (Sub-Saharan Africa report, no. 3173) p. 22–27.

Text of the election manifesto of the Kenya

1653 (cont.)

African National Union, in *Daily Nation*, Nairobi, Oct. 5–6, 1979.

Microfiche. [s.l. 1979]

DLC-Micro JPRS 74492

1654

Huntington, Samuel P., *and* Joan M. Nelson. Socioeconomic change and political participation; report to the Civic Participation Division of the Agency for International Development. [Cambridge, Mass.?], Center for International Affairs, Harvard University, 1973. [87] p. (in various pagings)

Prepared under research grant AID/csd-2502.

A discussion of the effects of economic and social modernization on patterns of political participation in four countries—Colombia, Kenya, Pakistan, and Turkey.

Microfiche. [Washington, U.S. Agency for International Development, 1973?] 3 sheets.

DLC-Sci RR PN-AAA-601

1655

Legislatures and social change: a cross-national study of Kenya, Korea, and Turkey, [by] Chong Lim Kim [et al.] [Iowa City, Comparative Legislative Research Center, University of Iowa], 1979. 25 p. (Iowa. University. Comparative Legislative Research Center. Occasional paper, no. 14)

Available from the Center, Iowa City, Iowa.

Examined in the Development Information Center, Agency for International Development, Washington, D.C.

1656

Magazine article sums up Moi's first 2 years. *In* U.S. *Joint Publications Research Service*. JPRS 76857. [Springfield, Va., National Technical Information Service, 1980] (Sub-Saharan Africa report, no. 2322) p. 20–25.

Article in *The Weekly Review*, Nairobi, Oct. 10, 1980, p. 4–6, 9, 11, 12, 15, 17.

Microfiche. [s.l. 1980]

DLC-Micro JPRS 76857

1657

Moi, Daniel T. arap. Moi addresses nation, stresses unity. *In* U.S. *Joint Publications Research Service*. JPRS 76803. [Springfield, Va., National Technical Information Service, 1980] (Sub-Saharan Africa report, no. 2318) p. 20–23.

Article in *Daily Nation*, Nairobi, Oct. 21, 1980, p. 1, 4.

Microfiche. [s.l. 1980]

DLC-Micro JPRS 76803

1658

Nyamboki, Cornelius. Report reveals shortcomings in local administration. *In* U.S. *Joint Publications Research Service*. JPRS 75862. [Springfield, Va., National Technical Information Service, 1980] (Sub-Saharan Africa report, no. 2256) p. 87–90.

Article in *Daily Nation*, Nairobi, May 23, 1980, p. 1, 3, 6.

Microfiche. [s.l. 1980]

DLC-Micro JPRS 75862

1659

Struggles for influence expected to follow 'Mzee's' death. *In* U.S. *Joint Publications Research Service*. JPRS 71950. [Springfield, Va., National Technical Information Service, 1978] (Translations on Sub-Saharan Africa, no. 2000) p. 56–59.

Translation of article on the potential for political conflict in Kenya following the death of Jomo Kenyatta, in *Spécial*, Brussels, Aug. 30, 1978, p. 35, 36.

Microfiche. [s.l. 1978]

DLC-Micro JPRS 71950

Population Studies

1660

U.S. *Bureau of the Census*. Country demographic profiles: Kenya. [Washington, for sale by the Supt. of Docs., U.S. Govt. Print. Off.] 1978. 17 p. (ISP-DP-11)

DLC

"This profile of the population of Kenya contains tables of selected demographic information, including size of population, and estimates of fertility and mortality. Specifically, annual estimates of total population are shown beginning in 1950. An adjusted distribution of the population by age and sex is given for the latest census year, as well as for 1976."

Data was obtained primarily from the Aug. 24–25, 1969 population census.

1661

Africa: Kenya. Selected statistical data by sex. Washington, 1981. 32, 17 p.

DLC

Study supported by the U.S. Agency for International Development's Office of Women in Development and Office of Population.

Data assembled by the International Demographic Data Center, U.S. Bureau of the Census.

Among the tables, all based on 1969 data (unless noted), are the following: unadjusted population by age, sex, and urban/rural residence; population by province, sex, and urban/rural residence; population by ethnic group, sex, and urban/rural residence; population by nationality (including Asians

1661 (cont.)

and Europeans); life expectancy; number of economically active persons by age and sex (1980).

1662

Black, Timothy R. L., *and* Philip D. Harvey. A report on a contraceptive social marketing experiment in rural Kenya. Studies in family planning, v. 7, Apr. 1976: 101–108.

                               HQ763.S8

Project supported by the U.S. Agency for International Development.

1663

Dow, Thomas E., *and* Alvan O. Zarata. Evaluation of the Population Studies and Research Institute, University of Nairobi. [s.l., 1978?] 96 p.

Prepared under the auspices of the American Public Health Association, with support from the Office of Population, U.S. Agency for International Development.

Some pages illegible in microfiche copy examined.

Microfiche. [Washington, U.S. Agency for International Development, 1978?] 2 sheets.

                   DLC-Sci RR PN-AAG-311

1664

Henin, Roushi A. District population profiles. [Nairobi], Population Studies and Research Institute, University of Nairobi, [1979] [71] p.

Cover title: Population profiles for the districts of Kenya.

Abstract in *A.I.D. Research and Development Abstracts*, v. 7, no. 2, 1979, p. 7.

Microfiche. [Washington, U.S. Agency for International Development, 1979] 1 sheet.

                   DLC-Sci RR PN-AAG-870

1665

———— Recent demographic trends in Kenya and their implication for economic and social development. [Nairobi, Population Studies and Research Institute, University of Nairobi, 1979] 41 p.

Abstract in *A.I.D. Research and Development Abstracts*, v. 7, no. 2, 1979, p. 7.

Microfiche. [Washington, U.S. Agency for International Development, 1979?] 1 sheet.

                   DLC-Sci RR PN-AAG-871

1666

Herz, Barbara K. Demographic pressure and economic change: the case of Kenyan land reforms. Washington, Office of Policy Development and Analysis, Agency for International Development, 1974. 329 p.   HD989.K4H47 1974

Originally presented as the author's thesis, Yale University.

Bibliography: p. 323–329.

Abstract in *A.I.D. Research and Development Abstracts*, July 1977, p. 28.

Issued also in microfiche. [Washington, U.S. Agency for International Development, 1974?] 4 sheets.   DLC-Sci RR PN-AAC-823

1667

Horsley, Kathryn. Population studies in Kenyan secondary schools. *In* Cultural factors and population in developing countries; investigators: Somjit Supannatas [et al.] Washington, Interdisciplinary Communications Program, Smithsonian Institution, 1976. (Interdisciplinary Communications Program. Occasional monograph series, no. 6) p. 81–127.   HQ766.7.C84

"ICP work agreement reports."

'WAM-206-76."

Bibliography: p. 125–127.

Issued also in microfiche. [Washington, U.S. Agency for International Development, 1976?] 2 sheets   DLC-Sci RR PN-AAD-329

1668

The Kenya fertility survey, 1978: a summary of findings. Voorburg, Netherlands, International Statistical Institute; London, World Fertility Survey, [1978?] [14] p. (World Fertility Survey, no. 26)

                   HB1072.5.A3K46

Abstract in *A.I.D. Research & Development Abstracts*, July 1981, p. 54–55.

Issued also in microfiche. [Washington, U.S. Agency for International Development, 1978?] 1 sheet.   DLC-Sci RR PN-AAJ-146

1669

Kibaki, Mwai. Family planning: footnote or theme? Agenda, Nov. 1981: 14–17. illus.

                  HC59.7.A742 1981

Issued by the U.S. Agency for International Development.

Adapted from remarks by the Vice President of Kenya at the Parliamentary Conference on Population and Development, Nairobi, July 1981.

1670

Provincial Planning Seminar on the Use of Population Data in Economic and Social Planning, *1st, Kericho, Kenya,* Aug. 16–19, 1978. Proceedings. [Nairobi], Population Studies and Research Institute, University of Nairobi, [1979] 77 p.

Abstract in *A.I.D. Research and Development Abstract*, v. 7, no. 2, 1979, p. 12.

1670 (cont.)

Microfiche. [Washington, U.S. Agency for International Development, 1979?] 1 sheet.

DLC-Sci RR PN-AAG-869

1671

Rierson, Michael. Country report: Kenya. [Washington], Interdisciplinary Communications Program, Smithsonian Institution, 1976. [30] p.

Prepared for the U.S. Agency for International Development under contract AID/csd-3598.

Includes bibliographical references.

Concerns population policy.

Examined in the Development Information Center, AID, Washington, D.C.

1672

Uche, U. U. Law and population growth in Kenya: background paper for Workshop on the Teaching of Population Dynamics in Law Schools, University of Nairobi, November 24–30, 1974. Medford, Mass., Law and Population Programme, Fletcher School of Law and Diplomacy, Tufts University, 1974. 40 p. (Law and population monograph series, no. 22) DLC-LL

Includes bioliographical references.

"The Law and Population Programme and its field work are supported in part by the International Planned Parenthood Federation, the United Nations Fund for Population Activities, and the U.S. Agency for International Development."

Issued also in microfiche. [Washington, U.S. Agency for International Development, 1974?] 1 sheet. DLC-Sci RR PN-AAF-169

Women

1673

Abbott, Susan. Full-time farmers and week-end wives: an analysis of altering conjugal roles. [s.l., 1974] [18] p.

Paper presented at the annual meeting of the American Anthropological Association.

A study of family life among rural Kikuyu.

Abstract in *Resources in Education*, Aug. 1975, p. 143.

Microfiche. [Arlington, Va., ERIC Document Reproduction Service; prepared for Educational Resources Information Center, National Institute of Education 1975] 1 sheet.

DLC-Micro ED104593

1674

Kanyua, Nguru. Role of women in Kenya's development. [Nairobi], USAID/Kenya, 1974. 8 p.

Examined in the Development Information Center, Agency for International Development, Washington, D.C.

1674a

Village women: their changing lives and fertility: studies in Kenya, Mexico, and the Philippines, [by] Priscilla Reining [et al.] Washington, American Association for the Advancement of Science, c1977. 273 p. (AAAS publication, no. 77-6)

Q181.A1A68 no. 77-6

Project funded by the U.S. Agency for International Development.

Kenya is covered on p. 11–110.

1675

The Women sing of Harambee: used to hard and long work, they strive for a better life. Agenda, v. 1, no. 2, Feb. 1978: 15–18. illus.

HC59.7.A742 1978

Issued by the U.S. Agency for International Development.

Concerns rural Kenya.

Other Subjects

1676

U.S. *Central International Agency*. Kenya. 1–74. [Washington, 1974] col. map.

G8410 1974.U5

Scale 1 : 2,37000.

Relief shown by shading and spot heights.
"501721."

1677

U.S. *Information Agency*. VOA-CAAP audience estimate for Kenya, 1973. [Washington], 1974. 19 p.

"E-12-74."

VOA-CAAP: Voice of America Continuing Audience Analysis Program.

Microfiche. [Washington, Congressional Information Service, 1974?] 1 sheet.

DLC-Micro ASI:77 9856-2.61

1678

U.S. *Information Agency. Office of Research*. Relevance of the American experience to Kenya audiences. [Washington?], 1976. 79 leaves.

"R-7-76."

Based on interviews in 1975 to determine how Kenyans "perceive American institutions and achievement as being relevant to Kenya's most pressing problems."

Abstract in *American Statistics Index*, 1977, Abstracts, p. 914.

1678 (cont.)

Microfiche. [Washington, Congressional Information Service, 1976?] 1 sheet.

DLC-Micro ASI:77 9856-2:30

1679

Hutchinson, P. William. Theatre safari in East Africa: an exploration of theatre in Kenya. [s.l., 1977] [16] p.

Paper presented at the annual meeting of the American Theatre Association, 1977.

Abstract in *Resources in Education*, June 1978, p. 61.

Microfiche. [Arlington, Va., ERIC Document Reproduction Service; prepared for Educational Resources Information Center, National Institute of Education, 1978] 1 sheet.

DLC-Micro ED149409

1680

An Introduction to the arts of Kenya. Washington, Museum of African Art, Smithsonian Institution [c1979] [37] p. illus., map.   DLC

1681

Jones, T. E. Axle-loads on paved roads in Kenya. Crowthorne, Eng., Overseas Unit, Transport and Road Research Laboratory, 1977. [28] p. illus. (Transport and Road Research Laboratory. TRRL laboratory report, 763)

Microfiche. [Springfield, Va., National Technical Information Service, 1978] 1 sheet.

DLC-Sci RR PB280874

1682

Kitui District environmental assessment report. Nairobi, National Environment Secretariat, Ministry of Environment and Natural Resources, 1981. 117 p. maps.   DLC

Prepared in cooperation with Clark University, Worcester, Mass., and the U.S. Agency for International Development.

1683

Lubin, David, *and* Beatrice B. Whiting. Learning techniques of persuasion: an analysis of sequences of interaction. [s.l.] 1977. 26 p.

Study sponsored in part by the National Institute of Mental Health.

Paper presented at the biennial meeting of the Society for Research in Child Development, 1977.

"This research describes how 24 male and 24 female Kikuyu children ages two through nine years attempt to persuade other Kikuyu children and adults to comply with their demands."—Abstract.

Abstract in *Resources in Education*, Aug. 1977, p. 144.

Microfiche. [Arlington, Va., ERIC Document Reproduction Service; prepared for Educational Resources Information Center, National Institute of Education, 1977] 1 sheet.

DLC-Micro ED136943

1684

Roberts, Betty Jean. "Kikuyu lifestyles;" an instructional unit for intermediate, elementary grades. Urbana, African Studies Program, University of Illinois, [1977] 34p.

Report developed as part of an interdisciplinary workshop project in African curriculum development funded by the National Endowment for the Humanities.

Abstract in *Resources in Education*, 1980 annual cumulation, p. 2122.

Microfiche. [Arlington, Va., ERIC Document Reproduction Service; prepared for Educational Resources Information Center, National Institute of Education, 1980] 1 sheet.

DLC-Micro ED188992

1685

Scotton, James F. Kenya's maligned African press: a reassessment. [s.l., 1974] 35 p.

Prepared for presentation at the annual meeting of the Association for Education in Journalism, 1974.

Abstract in *Resources in Education*, Feb. 1975, p. 45.

Microfiche. [Arlington, Va., ERIC Document Reproduction Service; prepared for Educational Resources Information Center, National Institute of Education, 1975] 1 sheet.

DLC-Micro ED096679

1686

The Structure of infant-adult social reciprocity; a cross cultural study of face to face interaction: Gusii infants and mothers, [by] Constance H. Keefer [et al.] [Boston, Child Development Unit, Children's Hospital Medical Center, 1977] 14 p.

Sponsored in part by the National Science Foundation.

Paper presented at the biennial meeting of the Society for Research in Child Development, 1977.

Abstract in *Resources in Education*, Feb. 1978, p. 133.

Microfiche. [Arlington, Va., ERIC Document Reproduction Service; prepared for Educational Resources Information Center, National Institute of Education, 1978] 1 sheet.

DLC-Micro ED144701

1687

Super, Charles M. Infant care and motor development in rural Kenya: some preliminary data on precocity and deficit. [Nairobi?, 1973?] [9] p.

"Presented at the regional meeting of the International Association for Cross-Cultural Psychology, Ibadan, Nigeria, Arpil 2–6, 1973."

Abstract in *Research in Education*, Oct. 1974, p. 114.

Microfiche. [Arlington, Va., ERIC Document Reproduction Service; prepared for the Educational Resources Information Center, National Institute of Education, 1974] 1 sheet.

DLC-Micro ED093388

1688

TRSB microwave landing system demonstration program at Nairobi, Kenya; final report. [Atlantic City, N.J., National Aviation Facilities Experimental Center]; available from National Technical Information Service, Springfield, Va., 1978. [39] p. (in various pagings) illus.

Prepared for Systems Research & Development Service, U.S. Federal Aviation Administration.

"Report no. FAA-RD-78-22."

TRSB: Time Reference Scanning Beam.

Microfiche. [s.l., Defense Documentation Center, 1978] 1 sheet.

DLC-Sci RR AD-A054646

1689

Watts, Ronald A. Country labor profile: Kenya. [Washington], Bureau of International Labor Affairs, U.S. Dept. of Labour; [for sale by the Supt. of Docs., U.S. Govt. Print. Off.], 1980. 7 p. maps. DLC

Cited in the Dept. of Labor Library as "no. 29."

Issued also in *International Labor Profiles: Com-prehensive Reports on the Labor Forces of 40 Key Nations, Including Data on Wage and Hour Standards, Labor Organizations, Social Benefit Programs, Governmental Regulations, and Other Labor-Related Topics*. 1st ed. (Detroit, Grand River Books, 1981) p. 164–171. HD4901.I56

1690

Whiting, Beatrice B. The effect of modernization on socialization. [s.l., 1974?] 11 p.

Paper presented at the annual meeting of the Society for Cross Cultural Research, 1974.

"This paper reviews evidence obtained from an analysis of the behavior of 3 to 11 year olds as observed in natural settings in the six culture study and preliminary findings from observing the behavior of mothers and children in a variety of settings in Kenya."

Abstract in *Resources in Education*, Sept. 1975, p. 194.

Microfiche. [Arlington, Va., ERIC Document Reproduction Service, Educational Resources Infromation, Center, National Institute of Education, 1975] 1 sheet. DLC-Micro ED106402

1691

Wolff, William A. OTEC thermal resource report for Mombasa. Monterey, Calif., Ocean Data Systems, inc., 1979. [41] p. (in various pagings) maps.

Prepared for the Division of Central Solar Technology, Dept. of Energy, under contract no. ET-78-C-01-2898.

Bibliography: p. R-1–R-4.

OTEC: Ocean Thermal Energy Conversion.

Microfiche. [s.l, Technical Information Center, Dept. of Energy, 1979] 1 sheet.

DLC-Sci RR HCP/T2898-01/4

Somalia

General

1692

U.S. *Dept. of State.* Post report. Somalia. [Washington?], 1976. 24 p. illus., map.

Examined in the Foreign Service Institute Library, Rosslyn, Va.

L.C. has report issued in 1974 (JX1705.A286 Spec. Format).

For a description of the contents of this publication, see the note to entry 936.

1693

U.S. *Dept. of State. Bureau of Public Affairs.* Background notes. Somalia. [Washington, for sale by the Supt. of Docs., U.S. Govt. Print. Off.], 1981. 7 p. illus., maps. (U.S. Dept. of State. Department of State publication 7881)   G59.U5

L.C. retains only the latest revision.

For a description of the contents of this publication, see the note to entry 937.

1694

Azzam, Henry T. Economic, human resources examined. *In* U.S. *Joint Publications Research Service.* JPRS 74200. [Springfield, Va., National Technical Information Service, 1979] (Sub-Saharan Africa report, no. 2154) p. 42–57.

From article in *al-Nahar Arab Report & Memo,* Paris, Aug. 20, 27, 1979.

An analysis of Somalia's resources, economic development planning, labor force, demographic characteristics, and educational programs.

Microfiche. [Washington, Supt. of Docs., U.S. Govt. Print. Off., 1979]

DLC-Micro JPRS 74200

1695

Berry, Leonard, T. Taurus, *and* Richard B. Ford. The Republic of Somalia. Worcester, Mass., Program for International Development, Clark University, 1980. 119 p. maps. (Eastern Africa country profiles. Country profile no. 4)   DLC

Bibliography: p. 116–119.

"This country profile of Somalia is prepared as one in a series of Eastern African country profiles. They come in response to a request by the United States Agency for International Development to compile succinct statements of principal development issues along with an analysis of the distribution of poverty."—Foreword.

1696

Kaplan, Irving. Area handbook for Somalia; coauthors, Irving Kaplan [et al.] 2d ed. Washington, for sale by the Supt. of Docs., U.S. Govt. Print. Off., 1977. xvi, 392 p. maps.   DT401.K33 1977

"DA pam 550-86."

"Prepared by Foreign Area Studies (FAS) of The American University."

Bibliography: p. 351–372.

Superseded by *Somalia, A Country Study* (entry 1698).

Abstract in *Government Reports Announcements & Index,* Oct. 1, 1977, p. 28.

Issued also in microfiche. [s.l., 1977] 5 sheets.

DLC-Sci RR AD-A041791

1697

Mango, Cecily. Somalia: a country profile; prepared for the Office of U.S. Foreign Disaster Assistance, Bureau for Private and Development Cooperation, Agency for International Development, Department of State by Evaluation Technologies, Inc., under contract AID/SOD/PDC-C-0283. 2d ed., Washington, The Office, 1980. 51 p., 1 leaf of plates.

DT401.5.M364 1980

Bibliography: p. 49–51.

A general introduction, with emphasis on political structure, disaster preparedness, demography, health, nutrition, housing, economic conditions, agriculture, geography, transportation, power, and communications.

1698

Somalia, a country study; edited by Harold D. Nelson. [Washington, for sale by the Supt. of Docs., U.S.

1698 (cont.)

Govt. Print. Off., 1982] xxvii, 346 p. illus., maps.
DT401.5.S68   1982

"DA pam 550-86."

"Research completed October 1981."

Prepared by Foreign Area Studies, The American University.

Bibliography: p. 301–327.

Supersedes *Area Handbook for Somalia* (entry 1696).

1699

Technical proposal for the construction of the Merca Port. [s.l.], U.S. Army Engineer Division, Middle East, 1979. [79] leaves. illus., maps (part fold.)

Prepared for the State Planning Commission of Somalia and the Saudi Arabia Development Fund.

Includes a general survey of the geography, resources, economy, and transportation system of Somalia.

Examined in the Development Information Center, Agency for International Development, Washington, D.C.

Assistance Programs

1700

U.S. *Agency for International Development.* Annual budget submission: Somalia. Washington, U.S. International Development Cooperation Agency.

Vols. for 1980+ examined in the Development Information Center, AID, Washington, D.C.

1701

——— Country development strategy statement: Somalia. Washington, U.S. International Development Cooperation Agency.

Vols. for 1978, 1981+ examined in the Development Information Center, AID, Washington, D.C.

1702

——— Disaster relief, case report: Somalia—drought, 1974–1975. Washington, Agency for International Development, [1976?] [9] p. illus., map.

Microprint. [New York, Readex Microprint, 1980]

DLC-Micro U.S. G.P.O. Month. Cat., 78-5253

1703

U.S. *Agency for International Development. Regional Inspector General for Audit.* An assessment of AID's Public Law 480 Title II assistance for Somalia refugee relief. [Washington?], 1981. 16 p.

"Audit report no. 81-46."

Examined in the Development Information Center, AID, Washington, D.C.

1704

U.S. *Congress. House. Committee on Foreign Affairs. Subcommittee on Africa.* Reprograming of military aid to Somalia: hearing, Ninety-sixth Congress, second session, August 26, 1980. Washington, U.S. Govt. Print. Off., 1980. 35 p. maps.
KF27.F625 1980b
J74.A23 96th
Cong., House Comm.
For. Aff., v. 108

Stephen J. Solarz, chairman.

Testimony by representatives of the Dept. of Defense and the Dept. of State.

1705

Andrianov, Vasiliy. Soviet assistance helps Somalia on independent path. *In* U.S. *Joint Publications Research Service.* JPRS 66130. [Springfield, Va., National Technical Information Service, 1975] (Translations on Sub-Saharan Africa, no. 1625) p. 64–71.

Translation of article in *Za Rubezhom*, Moscow, no. 29, Sept. 19–25, 1975, p. 12.

Microfiche. [s.l., 1975]
DLC-Micro JPRS 66130

1706

Somalia. [*Treaties, etc. United States, 1976 June 7*] Somalia; agricultural commodities: transfer under Title II. *In* U.S. *Treaties, etc.* United States treaties and other international agreements, v. 29, 1976–77. [Washington, Dept. of State; for sale by the Supt. of Docs., U.S. Govt. Print. Off., 1979] p. 998–1000. ([Treaties and other international acts series, 8859])
JX231.A34 v. 29

Signed at Mogadishu June 7, 1976.

Under Title II, Public Law 480, the Commodity Credit Corporation was authorized to transfer and deliver food to Somalia.

1707

Somalia. [*Treaties, etc. United States, 1977 Dec. 18*] Somalia; agricultural commodities: transfers under Title II; agreement signed at Mogadiscio December 18, 1977; entered into force December 18, 1977. *In* U.S. *Treaties, etc.* United States treaties and other international agreements, v. 29, 1976–77. [Washington, Dept. of State; for sale by the Supt. of Docs., U.S. Govt. Print. Off., 1980] p. 5297–5299. ([Treaties and other international acts series, 9109])
JX231.A34 v. 29

1708

Somalia. [*Treaties, etc. United States, 1978 Mar. 20*] Agreement between the Government of the United States of America and the Government of the Somali Democratic Republic for sales of agricul-

1708 (cont.)

tural commodities. *In* U.S. *Treaties, etc.* United States treaties and other international agreements, v. 30, 1978–79. [Washington, Dept. of State; for sale by the Supt. of Docs., U.S. Govt. Print. Off., 1980] p. 828–843. ([Treaties and other international acts series, 9222])   JX231.A34 v. 30

     Signed at Mogidishu, Mar. 20, 1978.

1109

Somalia. [*Treaties, etc. United States, 1978 Apr. 29*] Furnishing of defense articles and services. Agreement between the United States of America and Somalia effected by exchanges of letters signed at Mogadiscio March 22 and 23 and April 19 and 29, 1978. [Washington, Dept. of State; for sale by the Supt. of Docs., U.S. Govt. Print. Off., 1981] 6 p. (Treaties and other international acts series, 9794)   DLC

1710

Somalia. [*Treaties, etc. United States, 1978 Aug. 10*] Agricultural commodities. Agreement between the United States of America and Somalia amending the agreement of March 20, 1978 effected by exchange of notes signed at Mogadiscio July 18 and August 10, 1978. *In* U.S. *Treaties, etc.* United States treaties and other international agreements, v. 30, 1978–79. [Washington, Dept. of State; for sale by the Supt. of Docs., U.S. Govt. Print. Off., 1980] p. 2351–2353. ([Treaties and other international acts series, 9342])   JX231.A34 v. 30

1711

Somalia. [*Treaties, etc. United States, 1980 June 25*] Agreement between the Government of the United States of America and the Government of the Somalia [sic] Democratic Republic for the sale of agricultural commodities under Public Law 480, Title I program. [Washington, Dept. of State; for sale by the Supt. of Docs., U.S. Govt. Print. Off., 1981] 13 p. (Treaties and other international acts series, 9833)   DLC

     Signed at Mogadishu June 25, 1980, and amending agreement effected by exchange of letters signed at Mogadishu Aug. 14 and 17, 1980; entered into force Aug. 17, 1980.

1712

Somalia. [*Treaties, etc. United States, 1981 Jan. 12*] Agricultural commodities; agreement between the United States of America and Somalia, signed at Mogadishu, January 12, 1981. [Washington, Dept. of State; for sale by the Supt. of Docs., U.S. Govt. Print. Off., 1981] 9 p. (Treaties and other international acts series, 10065)   DLC

1713

Technical Assistance Information Clearing House. Development assistance programs of U.S. non-profit organizations in Somalia. [New York], American Council of Voluntary Agencies for Foreign Service, 1976. 7 p. (TAICH country report)   DLC

     The Clearing House is operated by the Council under a grant from the U.S. Agency for International Development.

1714

———— Development assistance programs of U.S. non-profit organizations: Somalia. [New York] American Council of Voluntary Agencies for Foreign Service, 1981. 17 p. (TAICH country report)   DLC

Foreign Relations

1715

U.S. *Congress. Senate. Committee on Appropriations. Subcommittee on Military Construction.* Visit to the Democratic Republic of Somalia: report to the Committee on Appropriations, U.S. Senate by members of the fact-finding team sent to Somalia at the invitation of the President of Somalia. Washington, U.S. Govt. Print. Off., 1975. 40 p. map.   UA770.U62 1975

     Mike Mansfield, chairman.

     Report of an investigation of allegations that Soviet naval and air facilities were under construction in Berbera, Somalia.

1716

Akdogan, Lutfi. President Siad: Somalia wants 150,000 Turkish workers and peasants. *In* U.S. *Joint Publications Research Service.* JPRS 72192. [Springfield, Va., National Technical Information Service, 1978] (Translations on Sub-Saharan Africa, no. 2019) p. 174–177.

     Translation of interview with President Siad Barre Mohamed and other Somali political leaders, in *Turcüman*, Istanbul, Aug. 12, 1978, p. 1, 3.

     Microfiche. [Washington, Supt. of Docs., U.S. Govt. Print. Off., 1978]

     DLC-Micro JPRS 72192

1717

al-Maghribī, 'Umar. Growing cooperation between Libya, Somalia cited. *In* U.S. *Joint Publications Research Service.* JPRS 65956. [Springfield, Va., National Technical Information Service, 1975] (Translation on Sub-Saharan Africa, no. 1621) p. 37–40.

     Translation of article in *al-Fajr al-Jadid*, Tripoli, Sept. 6, 1975, p. 5.

1717 (cont.)

Microfiche. [s.l., 1975]

DLC-Micro JPRS 65956

1718

——— Somali minister outlines foreign policy. *In* U.S. *Joint Publications Research Service.* JPRS 65755. [Springfield, Va., National Technical Information Service, 1975] (Translations on Africa, no. 1616) p. 25–30.

Translation of interview with Foreign Minister Omar A. Ghalib, in *al-Fajr al-Jadīd*, Tripoli, Aug. 28, 1975, p. 5, 6.

Microfiche. [s.l., 1975]

DLC-Micro JPRS 65755

1719

Nimetz, Matthew. Somalia and the U.S. security framework. *In* U.S. *Dept of State.* The Department of State bulletin, v. 80, no. 2045, Dec. 1980: 22–26.

JX232.A33 v. 80

Statement by the Under Secretary of State for Security Assistance, Science, and Technology, before the Subcommittee on Foreign Operations, Committee on Appropriations, House of Representatives, Sept. 16, 1980.

1720

Payton, Gary D. Soviet military presence abroad: the lessons of Somalia. Military review, Jan. 1979: 67–77. illus., maps. Z6723.U35 1979

Published by the U.S. Army Command and General Staff College, Ft. Leavenworth, Kansas.

1721

Phillips, Heidi S. Host press coverage of Soviet naval visits to Islamic countries, 1968–73. Arlington, Va., Institute of Naval Studies, Center for Naval Analyses, 1976. 30 p.

Prepared for the Office of Naval Research and the Office of the Chief of Naval Operations.

Include press coverage from Somalia, p. 19–22.

Abstract in *Government Reports Announcements & Index*, Apr. 15, 1977, p. 25.

Microfiche. [s.l., 1977] 1 sheet.

DLC-Sci RR AD-A035255

1722

al-Sharqawi, Bakr. Controversy over Soviet military base in Berbera resolved. *In* U.S. *Joint Publications Research Service.* JPRS 65629. [Springfield, Va., National Technical Information Service, 1975] (Translations on Africa, no. 1613) p. 32–37.

Translation of article in *al-Usbū 'al-'Arabī*, Beirut, July 7, 1975, p. 18–21.

Microfiche. [s.l., 1975]

DLC-Micro JPRS 65629

1723

Simon, Paul. Staying out of Somalia. Congressional record [daily ed.], 96th Congress, 2d session, v. 126, July 23, 1980 E3522-E3523. J11.R7 v. 126

Extension of remarks in the U.S. House of Representatives.

Includes article by Representative Stephen J. Solarz in the *New York Times*.

1724

Somalis urged to rely on themselves, Arabs, and not on Soviets. *In* U.S. *Joint Publications Research Service.* JPRS 70235. [Springfield, Va., National Technical Information Service, 1977] (Translations on Sub-Saharan Africa, no. 1841) p. 11–14.

Translation of editorial in *al-Tali'ah*, Mogadishu, Oct. 28, 1977, p. 1, 4.

Microfiche. [s.l., 1977]

DLC-Micro JPRS 70235

Refugees

1725

Decraene, Philippe. Reportage on refugee situation in various camps. *In* U.S. *Joint Publications Research Service.* JPRS 76157. [Springfield, Va., National Technical Information Service, 1980] (Sub-Saharan Africa report, no. 2274) p. 113–118.

Translation of article in *Le Monde*, Paris, June 27, 1980, p. 7.

Microfiche. [s.l., 1980]

DLC-Micro JPRS 76157

1726

Dornan, Robert K. Tragedy in the Horn of Africa. Congressional record [daily ed.], 96th Congress, 2d session, v. 126, Nov. 12, 1980: E4905-E4906.

J11.R7 v. 126

Extension of remarks in the U.S. House of Representatives on the Ethiopian-Somali conflict.

Includes text of a sermon by Father Elwood P. Kaiser who had examined conditions among refugees in Somalia.

1727

George, Emmett. Flight from fear and famine:— refugees in Somalia. Agenda, July–Aug. 1980: 2–6. illus. HC59.7.A742 1980

Issued by the U.S. Agency for International Development.

1728

Kennedy, Edward M. Refugee crisis in Somalia. Congressional record [daily ed.], 96th Congress, 1st session, v. 125, Dec. 5, 1979: S17890-S17891.

J11.R7 v. 125

1728 (cont.)

Remarks in the U.S. Senate.

Includes report, "Somalia: a tragedy beyond Cambodia's," by Kevin M. Cahill, which appeared in the *New York Daily News.*

1729

Maguire, Andrew. A resolution for the Somali refugees. Congressional record [daily ed.], 96th Congress, 2d session, v. 126, Aug. 25, 1980: E3997-E3998.　　　　　　　　　　　J11.R7 v. 126

Extension of remarks in the U.S. House of Representatives.

Includes text of H. Con. Res. 415, "that the United States should provide immediate humanitarian assistance to Somalia in order to help that nation cope with the massive influx of refugees."

1730

Plight of refugees discussed. *In* U.S. *Joint Publications Research Service.* JPRS 74391. [Springfield, Va., National Technical Information Service, 1979] (Sub-Saharan Africa report, no. 2162) p. 37–41.

Translation of article in *Najmat-Aktubar,* Mogadishu, Sept. 11, 1979, p. 1, 6.

Microfiche. [Washington, Supt. of Docs., U.S. Govt. Print. Off., 1979]

DLC-Micro JPRS 74391

1731

Rousseau, Rudolph, *and* James Fox. An assessment of the refugee situation in Somalia: a staff report prepared for the Committee on Foreign Relations, United States Senate. Washington, U.S. Govt. Print. Off., 1980. 19 p. map.

HV640.4.S58R68

At head of title: 96th Congress, 2d session. Committee print.

Includes tables indicating food contributions by the United States and other nations.

Other Subjects

1732

Abdirahman, Salah. Agricultural self-sufficiency policies discussed. *In* U.S. *Joint Publications Research Service.* JPRS 69918. [Springfield, Va., National Technical Information Service, 1977] (Translations on Sub-Saharan Africa, no. 1811) p. 134–141.

Article in *Halgan,* Mogadisnu, Aug. 1977, p. 6–9, 14.

Microfiche. [s.l., 1977]

DLC-Micro JPRS 69918

1733

Africa: Somali Republic. Selected statistical data by sex. Washington, 1981. 31, 17 p.　　　　　DLC

Study supported by the U.S. Agency for International Development's Office of Women in Development and Office of Population.

Data assembled by the International Demographic Data Center, U.S. Bureau of the Census.

The several statistical tables presented are based on data from the 1963–70 period.

1734

Carver, H. E. The Serum and Vaccine Institute, Mogadiscio, Somalia. [Washington?], Agency for International Development, 1979. [26] p.

Includes a review of the livestock situation in Somalia.

Microfiche. [Washington, U.S. Agency for International Development, 1979?] 1 sheet.

DLC-Sci RR PN-AAG-336

1735

Dahir, Osman J., *and* Muse H. Askar. Introduction of the written Somali language. *In* Educational reforms and innovations in Africa: studies prepared for the Conference of Ministers of Education of African Member States of Unesco. Paris, Unesco, 1978. (Experiments and innovations in education, no. 34) p. 58–64.　　LA1500.E38

Issued also in microfiche. [Arlington, Va., ERIC Document Reproduction Service; prepared for Educational Resources Information Center, National Institute of Education, 1978] 1 sheet.

DLC-Sci RR ED160036

1736

Decraene, Philippe. Developments in Somali socialism reviewed. *In* U.S. *Joint Publications Research Service.* JPRS 69381. [Springfield, Va., National Technical Information Service, 1977] (Translations on Sub-Saharan Africa, no. 1977) p. 52–72.

Translation of article in *Revue française d'études politiques africaines,* Paris, May 1977, p. 54–78.

Microfiche. [s.l., 1977]

DLC-Micro JPRS 69381

1737

Foreign economic trends and their implications for the United States. Somalia. 1969+ Washington, for sale by the Supt. of Docs., U.S. Govt. Print. Off. annual. (International marketing information series)　　　　　　　　　　　HC10.E416

Continues *Economic Trends and Their Implications for the United States. Somali Republic.*

Title varies slightly.

Prepared by the U.S. Embassy, Mogadishu.

Vols. for 1969–76 distributed by the U.S. Bureau

1737 (cont.)

of International Commerce; vols. for 1980– by the U.S. International Trade Administration.

Apparently not published in 1973 or in the period 1977–79.

The following issues for the period 1973–81 have been identified in L.C.:

ET 74-003. 1973 [sic] 7 p.

FET 75-153. 1975. 13 p.

FET 76-132. 1976. 9 p.

FET 80-006. 1980. 7 p.

FET 81-008. 1981. 9 p.

1737a

Gazetteer of Somalia: names approved by the United States Board on Geographic Names. Washington, Defense Mapping Agency, 1982. 231 p. map.

DLC-G&M

1738

Somalia's mass literacy campaign: the people carried the message. Development communication report, no. 30, Apr. 1980: 8-9, 12. illus.　　　DLC

Issued by the Clearinghouse on Development Communication with support from the U.S. Agency for International Development.

Sudan

General

1739

U.S. *Dept. of State.* Post report. Sudan. [Washington?] 1978. 19 p. illus., map.

JX1705.A286 Spec. Format

L.C. has also report issued in 1976.

For a description of the contents of this publication, see the note to entry 936.

1740

U.S. *Dept. of State. Bureau of Public Affairs.* Background notes. Sudan. [Washington, for sale by the Supt. of Docs., U.S. Govt. Print. Off.], 1982. 7 p. illus., maps (U.S. Dept. of State. Department of State publication 8022)   G59.U5

L.C. retains only the latest revision.

For a description of the contents of this publication, see the note to entry 937.

1741

Eastern African country profiles: the Republic of Sudan, by [Leonard] Berry [et al.] Worcester, Mass., Program for International Development, Clark University, 1979. 121 p. maps.   MWC

Bibliography: p. 120–121.

Apparently prepared for the U.S. Agency for International Development.

Photocopy examined in L.C.

1742

Selim, George D. American doctoral dissertations on the Arab world, 1883–1974. 2d ed. Washington, Near East Section, Library of Congress; [for sale by the Supt. of Docs., U.S. Govt. Print. Off.], 1976. xviii, 173 p.   Z3013.S43   1976

First ed. published in 1970 under title: *American Doctoral Dissertations on the Arab World, 1883–1968.*

Dissertations specifically on Sudan can be identified through the Index.

Agriculture

1743

'Abd-al-'Aziz, Usamah S. Problems faced in establishing energy sources reported. *In* U.S. *Joint Publications Research Service.* JPRS 71244. [Springfield, Va., National Technical Information Service, 1978] (Translations on Near East and North Africa, no. 1804) p. 59–64.

Translation of article in *al-Ayyām*, Khartoum, Apr. 5, 1978, p. 5, concerning the use of nuclear energy in the fields of agriculture, geology, and medicine.

Microfiche. [Washington, Supt. of Docs., U.S. Govt. Print. Off., 1978]

DLC-Micro JPRS 71244

1744

'Abd-al-Salam, Yusuf. Arab strategy to make Sudan breadbasket of Arab world. *In* U.S. *Joint Publications Research Service.* JPRS 76198. [Springfield, Va., National Technical Information Service, 1980] (Near East/North Africa report, no. 2161) p. 94–98.

Translation of article in *al-Ṣaḥāfah*, Khartoum, May 20, 1980, p. 6.

Microfiche. [s.l., 1980]

DLC-Micro JPRS 76198

1745

Abou-Bakr, Ahmed. Arab money to vitalize agriculture in Sudan. Foreign agriculture, July 18, 1977: 2-4, 11. illus.   HD1401.F65   1977

Issued by the U.S. Foreign Agricultural Service.

1746

Abu-Hajj, Zayn-al-'Abidin. Governor discusses southern Kordofan's agricultural development. *In* U.S. *Joint Publications Research Service.* JPRS 77434. [Springfield, Va., National Technical Information Service, 1981] (Near East/North Africa report, no. 2270) p. 94–99.

Translation of article in *al-Ṣaḥāfah*, Khartoum Nov. 19, 1980, p. 3.

1746 (cont.)

Microfiche. [s.l., 1981]

DLC-Micro JPRS 77434

1747

Ahmed, Abdel G., *and* Mustafa Abdel Rahman. Small urban centers: vanguards of exploitation— two cases from Sudan. *In* Southall, Aidan. Small urban centers in rural development in Africa. Madison, African Studies Program, University of Wisconsin-Madison, 1979. p. 101–117. maps.

Concerns Radoam and Kongor.

A grant from the Office of Urban Development, U.S. Agency for International Development, assisted in the preparation for publication of the papers collected in the study.

Microfiche. [Washington, U.S. Agency for International Development, 1980?] (PN-AAJ-064); examined in the Development Information Center, AID, Washington, D.C.

1748

Bashiri, Mahjub 'Umar. Irrigation organization provides key to development. *In* U.S. *Joint Publications Research Service.* JPRS 73107. [Springfield, Va., National Technical Information Service, 1979] (Translations on Near East and North Africa, no. 1931) p. 59–62.

Translation of article in *al-Ṣaḥāfah*, Khartoum, Khartoum, Jan. 21, 1979, p. 8.

Microfiche. [Washington, Supt. of Docs., U.S. Govt. Print. Off., 1979]

DLC-Micro JPRS 73107

1749

George, Emmett. Rituals of life yield to change: big business slowly eases out Sudan's small farmers. Agenda, July–Aug. 1979: 5-7. illus.

HC59.7.A742 1979

Issued by the U.S. Agency for International Development.

1750

Gezira scheme being restructed. *In* U.S. *Joint Publications Research Service.* JPRS 75777. [Springfield, Va., National Technical Information Service, 1980] (Near East/North Africa report, no. 2122) p. 316–329. map.

Article in *Sudanow*, Khartoum, Mar. 1980, p. 33–38, 42–46.

Microfiche. [s.l., 1980]

DLC-Micro JPRS 75777

1751

Mina, Amal. Causes in drop in al-Jezira project output reviewed. *In* U.S. *Joint Publications Research Service.* JPRS 74345. [Springfield, Va., National Technical Information Service, 1979] (Near East/ North Africa report, no. 2030)

Translation of article in *al-Ayyam*, Khartoum, Aug. 1, 1979, p. 3.

Microfiche. [Washington, Supt. of Docs., U.S. Govt. Print. Off., 1979]

DLC-Micro JPRS 74345

1752

Murdock, Muneera S. The impact of agricultural development on a pastoral society: the Shukriya of the eastern Sudan. Binghamton, Dept. of Anthropology, State University of New York, 1979. 57 p.

Report submitted to the U.S. Agency for International Development.

Bibliography: p. 56–57.

Issued in cooperation with the Institute for Development Anthropology.

Abstracts in *A.I.D. Research and Development Abstracts*, v. 8, no. 2, 1980, p. 3.

Microfiche. [Washington, U.S. Agency for International Development, 1979?] 1 sheet.

DLC-Sci RR PN-AAH-053

1753

Voll, Sarah P. Development in the African Sahel: the Gazirah [sic] perspective. [s.l., 1978] [27] leaves. (FAR 28782-N)

Prepared for the Conference on the Sudan, sponsored by the U.S. Dept. of State, July 1978.

Examined in the former Foreign Affairs Research Documentation Center, Dept. of State.

Aquatic Weed Control

1754

Aquatic weed management: integrated central techniques for the Gezira irrigation scheme; report of a workshop, 3–6 December 1978. Wad Medani, Sudan, University of Gezira, 1979. 96 p.

Cosponsored by the Board on Science and Technology for International Relations, National Academy of Sciences-National Research Council of the United States.

Microfiche. [Washington, U.S. Agency for International Development, 1979?] 1 sheet.

DLC-Sci RR PN-AAG-923

1755

Workshop on Aquatic Weed Management and Utilization, *Khartoum, Sudan, 1975.* Aquatic weed management: some prospects for the Sudan and the Nile basin: report of a workshop held 24–29 November 1975, Khartoum, Sudan. Cosponsors: National Council for Research, Agricultural Research Council, Democratic Republic of the Sudan

1755 (cont.)

[and] National Academy of Sciences, United States of America. Khartoum, Agricultural Research Council, [1975?] 57 p. illus., map.

SB615.W3W67 1975

Includes bibliographies.

Abstract in *Government Reports Announcement & Index*, Mar. 4, 1977, p. 84.

Issued also in microfiche. [Springfield, Va., National Technical Information Service, 1977] 1 sheet. DLC-Sci RR PB 259990

1756

———— Aquatic weeds in the Sudan with special reference to water hyacinth: background for the problem in the Sudan, prepared for the Workshop on Aquatic Weed Management and Utilization; organized by the National Council for Research, Sudan, and National Academy of Sciences, U.S.A., Khartoum, 24–29 November, 1975; edited by Mohammed Obeid. Khartoum, Agricultural Research Council, National Council for Research, 1975. 150 p., 7 leaves of plates. maps.

SB615.W3W67 1975a

Abstract in *A.I.D. Research and Development Abstracts*, July 1977, p. 14.

Issued also in microfiche. [Washington, U.S. Agency for International Development, 1977?] 2 sheets. DLC-Sci RR PN-AAC-696

1757

———— Staff summary report. Washington, 1975. 26 leaves. DLC

Sponsored by National Council for Research-Agricultural Research Council, Sudan, and National Academy of Sciences-National Research Council, U.S.A.

1758

Yeo, Richard R., *and* William Bailey. Report of travel to Egypt-Sudan, May 20 through June 4, 1976 [Washington, Commission on International Relations, National Academy of Sciences, 1976] [46] p. illus.

"Report to the Board on Science and Technology for International Development (BOSTID), Commission on International Relations, National Academy of Sciences, of advisory activities resulting from the Regional Workshop on Aquatic Weed Control and Management, held in Khartoum, Sudan, November 24–29, 1975."

Travel funds provided by the Office of Science and Technology, Bureau for Technical Assistance, U.S. Agency for International Development.

Microfiche. [Washington, U.S. Agency for International Development, 1976?] 1 sheet.

DLC-Sci RR PN-AAC-700

Assistance Programs

1759

U.S. *Agency for International Development*. Annual budget submission: Sudan. Washington, U.S. International Development Cooperation Agency.

Vols. for 1980+ examined in the Development Information Center, AID, Washington, D.C.

1760

———— Country development strategy statement: Sudan. Washington, U.S. International Development Cooperation Agency. annual.

Vols for 1981+ examined in the Development Information Center, AID, Washington, D.C.

Vol. for 1981 abstracted in *Government Reports Announcements & Index*, Oct. 12, 1979, p. 31.

Vol. for 1981 issued also in microfiche. [Springfield, Va., National Technical Information Service, 1979] 1 sheet. DLC-Sci RR PB298086

1761

———— Disaster relief, case report: Sudan—floods, September, 1975. Washington, [1976] [4] p. illus., map.

Microprint. [New York, Readex Microprint, 1980]

DLC-Micro U.S. G.P.O. Month. Cat., 78-5236

1762

Bonker, Don. Aid to Sudan. Congressional record, 95th Congress, 1st session, v. 123, Apr. 20, 1977: 11468-11470. J11.R5 v. 123

Remarks in the U.S. House of Representatives.

1763

Cramer, Ray D. Memorandum report on USAID/Sudan non-project assistance. Nairobi, Area Auditor General, East Africa, U.S. Agency for International Development, 1980. 12 leaves.

Concerns food assistance programs.

Examined in the Development Information Center, AID, Washington, D.C.

1764

Massive aid needed to save regime. *In* U.S. *Joint Publications Research Service*. JPRS 74202. [Springfield, Va., National Technical Information Service, 1979] (Near East/North Africa report, no. 2019) p. 152–155.

From article in *al Nahar Arab Report & Memo*, Paris, Aug. 20, 1979, p. 1–2.

Microfiche. [Washington, Supt. of Docs., U.S. Govt. Print. Off., 1979]

DLC-Micro JPRS 74202

1765

Mickelwait, Donald R., Craig V. Olson, *and* Eric W. Crawford. Strategies for the reintroduction of development assistance to the Sudan; a seminar held under the auspices of the Office of Eastern and Southern Africa Affairs, Bureau for Africa, Agency for International Development, October 18 and 19, 1976. Washington, Development Alternatives, inc., [1976?] 121 p.

    Abstract in *A.I.D. Research and Development Abstracts*, Oct. 1977, p. 13.

    Microfiche. [Washington, U.S. Agency for International Development, 1976?] 2 sheets.

                 DLC-Sci RR PN-AAC-993

1766

Sudan. [*Treaties, etc. United States, 1974 May 8*] Agreement between the Government of the United States and the Government of the Democratic Republic of the Sudan for the sale of agricultural commodities. *In* U.S. *Treaties, etc*. United States treaties and other international agreements, v. 25, 1974. [Washington, Dept. of State; for sale by the Supt. of Docs., U.S. Govt. Print. Off., 1975] p. 844–849. ([Treaties and other international acts series, 7827])   JX231.A34 v. 25

1767

Sudan. [*Treaties, etc. United States, 1977 May 12*] Agreement between the Government of the United States of America and the Government of the Democratic Republic of the Sudan for Sudan quelea bird research project. *In* U.S. *Treaties, etc*. United States treaties and other international agreement, v. 29, 1976–77. [Washington, Dept. of State; for sale by the Supt. of Docs., U.S. Govt. Print. Off., 1979] p. 297–303. ([Treaties and other international acts series, 8814])

                 JX231.A34 v. 29

Signed at Khartoum May 12, 1977.

1768

Sudan. [*Treaties, etc. United States, 1977 July 7*] Agreement between the Government of the United States of America and the Government of the Sudan for sales of agricultural commodities. *In* U.S. *Treaties, etc*. United States treaties and other international agreements, v. 29, 1976–77. [Washington, Dept. of State; for sale by the Supt. of Docs., U.S. Govt. Print. Off., 1979] p. 967–977. ([Treaties and other international acts series, 8856])   JX231.A34 v. 29

Signed at Khartoum Feb. 21, 1977; entered into force July 7, 1977.

1769

Sudan. [*Treaties, etc. United States, 1977 Dec. 24*] Agreement between the Government of the United States of America and the Government of the Democratic Republic of the Sudan for sales of agricultural commodities. *In* U.S. *Treaties, etc*. United States treaties and other international agreements, v. 29, 1976–77. [Washington, Dept. of State; for sale by the Supt. of Docs., U.S. Govt. Print. Off., 1980] p. 5874–5892. ([Treaties and other international acts series, 9157])

                 JX231.A34 v. 29

Signed at Khartoum Dec. 24, 1977.

1770

Sudan. [*Treaties, etc. United States, 1978 Aug. 30*] Project grant agreement between the Democratic Republic of the Sudan and the United States of America for southern manpower development project. *In* U.S. *Treaties, etc*. United States treaties and other international agreements, v. 30, 1978–79. [Washington, Dept. of State; for sale by the Supt. of Docs., U.S. Govt. Print. Off., 1981] p. 5205–5246. ([Treaties and other international acts series, 9503])   JX231.A34 v. 30

Signed at Khartoum Aug. 30, 1978.

A U.S. Agency for International Development project to assist Sudan "to increase the quantity and quality of trained agricultural personnel working with the small-holder farmer in the Southern Region of the Sudan."—p. 5208.

1771

Sudan. [*Treaties, etc. United States, 1979 Dec. 31*] Grant agreement between the United States of America and the Democratic Republic of Sudan for commodity imports. [Washington, Dept. of State; for sale by the Supt. of Docs., U.S. Govt. Print. Off., 1980] 23 p. (Treaties and other international acts series, 9674)   DLC

Signed at Khartoum, Dec. 31, 1979.

Concerns a U.S. Agency for International Development grant "for the foreign exchange costs of commodities and commodity-related services."—p. 5.

1772

Sudan. [*Treaties, etc. United States, 1980 June 19*] Sudan, finance: consolidation and rescheduling of certain debts. Agreement signed at Khartoum May 17, 1980, entered into force for the 1979/1980 debt June 19, 1980; entered into force for the 1980/1981 debt April 14, 1981; and agreement signed at Khartoum August 18, 1980, entered into force for the 1979/1980 debt August 18, 1980, entered into force for the 1980/1981 debt April 14, 1981. [Washington, Dept. of State; for sale by the Supt. of Docs., U.S.

1772 (cont.)

Govt. Print. Off., 1981] 26 p. (Treaties and other international acts series, 9952)   DLC

1773

Sudan-AID involvement in traditional agriculture, [by] Leonard Kornfeld [et al.], McLean, Va., American Technical Assistance Corporation, 1977. 2 v.

"Report CR-A-183."

Prepared for the Office of Development Resources, U.S. Agency for International Development, under contract AID/afr-C-1147.

Examined in the Development Information Center, AID, Washington, D.C.

1774

Sudan seeks monetary assistance. *In* U.S. *Joint Publications Research Service.* JPRS 72571. [Springfield, Va., National Technical Information Service, 1979] (Translations on Near East and North Africa, 1890) p. 76–79.

Translation of article in *al-Mustaqbal*, Paris, Oct. 28, 1978, p. 45–46.

Microfiche. [Washington, Supt. of Docs., U.S. Govt. Print. Off., 1979]

DLC-Micro JPRS 72571

1775

Technical Assistance Information Clearing House. Development assistance programs of U.S. non-profit organizations; Sudan. [New York], American Council of Voluntary Agencies for Foreign Service, 1979. 29 p. maps. (TAICH country report)   DLC

The Clearing House is operated by the Council under a grant from the U.S. Agency for International Development.

1776

Western support may enable Nimeiri to save economy. *In* U.S. *Joint Publications Research Service.* JPRS 76243. [Springfield, Va., National Technical Information Service, 1980] (Near East/North Africa report, no. 2166] p. 63–66.

Translation of article in *al-Ra'y al-'amm*, Kuwait, June 3, 1980, p. 17.

Microfiche. [s.l., 1980]

DLC-Micro JPRS 76243

Commerce

1777

Aḥmad, 'Abdallah S. State of Sudanese exports reported. *In* U.S. *Joint Publications Research Service.* JPRS 70717. [Springfield, Va., National

Technical Information Service, 1978] (Translations on Near East and North Africa, no. 1765) p. 95–100.

Translation of article in *al-Ayyām*, Khartoum, Jan. 9, 1978, p. 6.

Microfiche. [Washington, Supt. of Docs., U.S. Govt. Print. Off., 1978]

DLC-Micro JPRS 70717

1778

American businessman's handbook; contact & information list. Khartoum, Economic/Commercial Section, U.S. Embassy, 1981. 36 p.   DLC

1779

Manley, Mary L. Marketing in the Sudan. [Washington], U.S. Dept. of Commerce, Domestic and International Business Administration; [for sale by the Supt. of Docs., U.S. Govt. Print. Off.], 1975. 30 p. (Overseas business reports. OBR 75-56)

HF91.U482   1975, no. 56

Superseded by the author's *Marketing in the Sudan* (Overseas business reports. OBR 77-52; entry 1780).

1780

——— Marketing in the Sudan. [Washington], U.S. Dept. of Commerce, Bureau of International Commerce; [for sale by the Supt. of Docs., U.S. Govt. Print. Off.], 1977. 32 p. (Overseas business reports. OBR 77-52)   HF91.U482   1977, no. 52

International marketing information series.

Supersedes the author's *Marketing in the Sudan* (Overseas business reports. OBR 75-56; entry 1779).

Issued also in microfiche. [Washington, Congressional Information Service, 1977?]

DLC-Micro ASI:77 2026-5.59

1781

Manley, Mary L., *and* Freddie L. Stokelin. Marketing in the Sudan. Washington, U.S. Dept. of Commerce, International Trade Administration; [for sale by the Supt. of Docs., U.S. Govt. Print. Off.] 1981. 22 p. (Overseas business reports. OBR 81-30)

HF91.U482   1981, no. 30

International marketing information series.

1782

Problems in marketing cotton explored. *In* U.S. *Joint Publications Research Service.* JPRS 73752. [Springfield, Va., National Technical Information Service, 1979] (Translations on Near East and North Africa, 1987) p. 88–94.

Translation of article in *al-Ṣaḥāfah*, Khartoum, Apr. 11, 1979, p. 5.

1782 (cont.)

Microfiche. [Washington, Supt. of Docs., U.S. Govt. Print. Off., 1979]

DLC-Micro JPRS 73752

1783

Treakle, H. Charles. Rising nonfarm imports put Sudan trade in red. Foreign agriculture, July 25, 1977: 6-8. illus.　　　HD1401.F65　1977

Issued by the U.S. Foreign Agricultural Service.

Communications and Transportation

1784

'Abd-al-Raḥmān, Ja'far, *and* Bābakr 'Isá. Efforts to enhance telecommunications stressed. *In* U.S. *Joint Publications Research Service.* JPRS 70615. [Springfield, Va., National Technical Information Service, 1978] (Translations on Near East and North Africa, no. 1759) p. 89–94.

Translation of article in *al-Ayyām*, Khartoum, Nov. 29, 1977, p. 5.

Microfiche. [Washington, Supt. of Docs., U.S. Govt. Print. Off., 1978]

DLC-Micro JPRS 70615

1785

——— Transportation minister discusses growth of services. *In* U.S. *Joint Publications Research Service.* JPRS 70671. [Springfield, Va., National Technical Information Service, 1978] (Translations on Near East and North Africa, no. 1762) p. 112–118.

Translation of article in *al-Ayyām*, Khartoum, Dec. 21, 1977, p. 5.

Microfiche. [Washington, Supt. of Docs., U.S. Govt. Print. Off., 1978]

DLC-Micro JPRS 70671

1786

George, Emmett. The road to Juba: a 300-mile highway, long a symbol of need, portends progress in Southern Sudan. Agenda, July–Aug. 1979: 3-4. illus.　　　HC59.7.A742　1979

Issued by the U.S. Agency for International Development.

1787

al-Rih, 'Abd-al-Rahim. National Research Council outlines transport problems. *In* U.S. *Joint Publications Research Service.* JPRS 70358. [Springfield, Va., National Technical Information Service, 1977] (Translations on Near East and North Africa, no. 1741) p. 64–69.

Translation of article by a staff member of the

National Council for Economic and Social Research, in *al-Ṣaḥāfah*, Khartoum, Oct. 18, 1977, p. 4.

Microfiche. [s.l., 1977]

DLC-Micro JPRS 70358

1788

Shabshah, al-Tayyib. Freedom of the press defined by Numayri. *In* U.S. *Joint Publications Research Service.* JPRS 71794. [Springfield, Va., National Technical Information Service, 1978] (Translations on Near East and North Africa, no. 1837) p. 45–53.

Translation of article in *al-Ayyām*, Khartoum, June 9, 1978, p. 3.

Microfiche. [Washington, Supt. of Docs., U.S. Govt. Print. Off., 1978]

DLC-Micro JPRS 71794

1789

Shanab, Mirghani A. Status of broadcasting in nation reviewed. *In* U.S. *Joint Publications Research Service.* JPRS 69355. [Springfield, Va., National Technical Information Service, 1977] (Translations on Near East and North Africa, no. 1674) p. 78–82.

Translation of interview with Muhammad K. Salihin, director of broadcasting, in *al-Ayyām*, Khartoum, Apr. 26, 1977, p. 9.

Microfiche. [s.l., 1977]

DLC-Micro JPRS 69355

1790

'Sudanow' reports on four development projects. *In* U.S. *Joint Publications Research Service.* JPRS 76069. [Springfield, Va., National Technical Information Service, 1980]. (Sub-Saharan Africa report, no. 2149) p. 43–51.

Article in *Sudanow*, Khartoum, June 1980, on projects for the development of oil pipelines, port facilities at Port Sudan, road transport, and river transport.

Microfiche. [s.l., 1980]

DLC-Micro JPRS 76069

1791

Zarūq, 'Abd al-Raḥmān. Jonglei canal project defended, progress reviewed. *In* U.S. *Joint Publications Research Service.* JPRS 73516. [Springfield, Va., National Technical Information Service, 1979] (Translations on Near East and North Africa, no. 1956) p. 75–80.

Translation of interview with Dr. Qama Ḥasan, General Commissioner of the Jonglei Canal Project, in *al-Ayyām*, Khartoum, Apr. 18, 1979, p. 3.

Microfiche. [Washington, Supt. of Docs., U.S. Govt. Print. Off., 1979]

DLC-Micro JPRS 73516

Economic Conditions

1792

Faraḥ, 'Abd al-'Azīz Muḥammad. Development problems in nation aired, assayed. *In* U.S. *Joint Publications Research Service.* JPRS 68651. [Springfield, Va., National Technical Information Service, 1977] (Translations on Near East and North Africa, no. 1615) p. 104–107.

Translation of article in al-Ayyām, Khartoum, Oct. 2, 1976, p. 7.

Microfiche. [s.l., 1977]

DLC-Micro JPRS 68651

1793

Foreign economic trends and their implications for the United States. Sudan. 1969+ Washington, for sale by the Supt. of Docs., U.S. Govt. Print. Off. annual. (International marketing information series) HC10.E416

Prepared by the U.S. Embassy, Khartoum.

Vols. for 1969–77 distributed by the U.S. Bureau of International Commerce; vols. for 1980– by the U.S. International Trade Administration.

Not published, 1978–79.

The following issues for the period 1973–81 have been identified in L.C.:

ET 73-004. 1973. 10 p. map.
ET 74-004. 1974. 9 p.
FET 75-055. 1975. 8 p.
FET 76-066. 1976. 8 p.
FET 77-059. 1977. 8 p.
FET 80-076. 1980. 10 p.
FET 81-102. 1981. 12 p.

1794

Mashal, Muhammad U. Role of merchant marine in bolstering economy praised. *In* U.S. *Joint Publications Research Service.* JPRS 76759. [Springfield, Va., National Technical Information Service, 1980] (Near East/North Africa report, no. 2215) p. 71–74.

Translation of article in *al-Ayyām*, Khartoum, Aug. 29, 1980, p. 4.

Microfiche. [s.l., 1980]

DLC-Micro JPRS 76759

1795

al-Junayd Sugar Mill faces crisis. *In* U.S. *Joint Publications Research Service.* JPRS 70971. [Springfield, Va., National Technical Information Service, 1978] (Translations on Near East and North Africa, no. 1783) p. 86–94.

Translation of article in *al-Ṣaḥāfah*, Khartoum, Feb. 4, 1978, p. 3.

Microfiche. [Washington, Supt. of Docs., U.S. Govt. Print. Off., 1978]

DLC-Micro JPRS 70971

1796

al-Malik, Muḥammad. An account of Sudan's economic progress during the 70's. *In* U.S. *Joint Publications Research Service.* JPRS 76249. [Springfield, Va., National Technical Information Service, 1980] (Near East/North Africa report, no. 2167) p. 122–131.

Translation of article in *al-Ṣaḥāfah*, Khartoum, May 25, 1980, p. 17.

Microfiche. [s.l., 1980]

DLC-Micro JPRS 76249

1797

al-Marāghī, Maḥmūd. President discusses causes of economic problems. *In* U.S. *Joint Publications Research Service.* JPRS 73523. [Springfield, Va., National Technical Information Service, 1979] (Translations on Near East and North Africa, no. 1967) p. 121–127.

Translation of article in *Rūz al-Yūsuf*, Cairo, Apr. 9, 1979, p. 6–9, on President Nimeiri's comments concerning Sudan's economic condition.

Microfiche. [Washington, Supt. of Docs., U.S. Govt. Print. Off., 1979]

DLC-Micro JPRS 73523

1798

Muḥammad, Ḥasan. Industrial problems enumerated, solutions proposed. *In* U.S. *Joint Publications Research Service.* JPRS 70717. [Springfield, Va., National Technical Information Service, 1978] (Translations on Near East and North Africa, no. 1765) p. 106–112.

Translation of article in *al-Ayyām*, Khartoum, Jan. 8, 1978, p. 6.

Microfiche. [Washington, Supt. of Docs., U.S. Govt. Print. Off., 1978]

DLC-Micro JPRS 70717

1799

Mauri, Arnaldo, *and* Paulo Mottura. Mobilization of rural savings: the case of the Sudanese Savings Bank. [s.l.], 1979. [21] p. (International Conference on Rural Finance Research Issues, *2d.* Paper no. 11)

Conference supported in part by the U.S. Agency for International Development.

Abstract in *A.I.D. Research & Development Abstracts*, Feb. 1981.

Microfiche. [Washington, U.S. Agency for International Development, 1979?] 1 sheet.

DLC-Sci RR PN-AAH-356

1800

Sulaymān, Badr al-Dīn. Finance minister presents 1980–1981 national budget proposal. *In* U.S. *Joint Publications Research Service.* JPRS 76169. [Springfield, Va., National Technical Information Service, 1980] (Near East/North Africa report, no. 2159) p. 124–134.

Article in *SUNA Bulletin*, Khartoum, June 19, 1980, p. 5–19.

Microfiche. [s.l., 1980]

DLC-Micro JPRS 76169

1801

al-Ṭayyib, Aḥmad al-Ballāl. Status of development projects in provinces reported. *In* U.S. *Joint Publications Research Service.* JPRS 71176. [Springfield, Va., National Technical Information Service, 1978] (Translations on Near East and North Africa, no. 1799) p. 128–132.

Translation of article in *al-Ayyām*, Khartoum, Apr. 3, 1978, p. 7.

Microfiche. [Washington, Supt. of Docs., U.S. Govt. Print. Off., 1978

DLC-Micro JPRS 71176

Foreign Relations

1802

Ayyūb, Usāmah. Egypt, Sudan integration achievements to be reviewed. *In* U.S. *Joint Publications Research Service.* JPRS 70829. [Springfield, Va., National Technical Information Service, 1978] (Translations on Near East and North Africa, no. 1773) p. 92–98.

Translation of article in *Uktūbar*, Cairo, Jan. 22, 1978, p. 33–34.

Microfiche. [Washington, Supt. of Docs., U.S. Govt. Print. Off., 1978]

DLC-Micro JPRS 70829

1803

Barbier de Fodor, Marienne, *and* Jean Wolf. Numayri discusses position on Eritrea. *In* U.S. *Joint Publications Research Service.* JPRS 69600. [Springfield, Va., National Technical Information Service, 1977] (Translations on Near East and North Africa, no. 1622) p. 43–55.

Translation of interview with the Sudanese President in *Remarques africaines*, Brussels, June 1977, p. 84–86.

Microfiche. [Washington, Supt. of Docs., U.S. Govt. Print. Off., 1977]

DLC-Micro JPRS 69600

1804

Bonker, Don. Sudan and the United States. Congressional record, 95th Congress, 1st session, v. 123, Feb. 24, 1977: 5419–5420.   J11.R5 v. 123

Extension of remarks in the U.S. House of Representatives.

Includes articles from the *Washington Post*.

1805

Egypt: interest of the United States in Anglo-Egyptian negotiations over the future of the Suez Canal Zone and the Sudan; concern of the United States over Egyptian abrogation of the 1936 Anglo-Egyptian Defense Treaty and the 1899 condominium agreement regarding Sudan. *In* U.S. *Dept. of State.* Foreign relations of the United States. 1951, v. 5. Washington, U.S. Govt. Print. Off., 1982. p. 343–444 (U.S. Dept. of State. Department of State publication 9114)   JX233.A3 1951, v. 5

1806

Hafiz, Sahah. Numayri explains Egypt-Sudan integration, other policies. *In* U.S. *Joint Publications Research Service.* JPRS 71363. [Springfield, Va., National Technical Information Service, 1978] (Translations on Near East and North Africa, no. 1811) p. 106–113.

Translation of interview with President Numayri, in *Rūz al-Yūsuf*, Cairo, May 8, 1978, p. 6–12.

Microfiche. [Washington, Supt. of Docs., U.S. Govt. Print. Off., 1978]

DLC-Micro JPRS 71363

1807

———— Unification between Egypt, Sudan seen possible but elusive. *In* U.S. *Joint Publications Research Service.* JPRS 71818. [Springfield, Va., National Technical Information Service, 1978] (Translations on Near East and North Africa, no. 1838) p. 1–12.

Translation of article in *Rūz al-Yūsuf*, Cairo, July 10, 17, 1978.

Microfiche. [Washington, Supt. of Docs., U.S. Govt. Print. Off., 1978]

DLC-Micro JPRS 71818

1808

Information minister discusses Sudan's position on Arab cause. *In* U.S. *Joint Publications Research Service.* JPRS 74288. [Springfield, Va., National Technical Information Service, 2979] (Near East/North Africa report, no. 2025) p. 64–68.

Translation of interview with Ali Shumo, Minister of Information of Sudan, in *al-Rāyah*, Qatar, July 30, 1979, p. 3.

Microfiche. [Washington, Supt. of Docs., U.S. Govt. Print. Off., 1979]

DLC-Micro JPRS 74288

1809

Matar, Fuʿad. President discusses relations with Egypt, Ethiopia, other nations. *In* U.S. *Joint Publications Research Service*. JPRS 69459. [Springfield, Va., National Technical Information Service, 1977] (Translations on Near East and North Africa, no. 1681) p. 70–77.

Translation of article in *al-Nahār al-ʿArabī wa al-duwalī*, Paris, May 14, 1977, p. 10, 11.

Microfiche. [s.l., 1977]

DLC-Micro JPRS 69459

1810

Numayri views Camp David accords as best possible current solution. *In* U.S. *Joint Publications Research Service*. JPRS 72491. [Springfield, Va., National Technical Information Service, 1978] (Translations on Near East and North Africa, no. 1884) p. 96–106.

Translation of interview with President Nimeiri in *al-Mustaqbal*, Paris, Nov. 11, 1978, p. 18–21.

Microfiche. [Washington, Supt. of Docs., U.S. Govt. Print. Off., 1979?]

DLC-Micro JPRS 72491

1811

President Numaryi on foreign, domestic issues. *In* U.S. *Joint Publications Research Service*. JPRS 71677. [Springfield, Va., National Technical Information Service, 1978] (Translations on Near East and North Africa, no. 1830) p. 57–61.

Article in *SUNA Daily Bulletin*, Khartoum, July 5, 1978, p. 5–10.

Microfiche. [Washington, Supt. of Docs., U.S. Govt. Print. Off., 1978]

DLC-Micro JPRS 71677

1812

Sudanese-Egyptian military pact denounced. *In* U.S. *Joint Publications Research Service*. JPRS 69213. [Springfield, Va., National Technical Information Service, 1977] (Translations on Sub-Saharan Africa, no. 1756) p. 13–16.

Article in *Ethiopian Herald*, Addis Ababa, May 14, 1977, p. 2, 4.

Microfiche. [s.l., 1977]

DLC-Micro JPRS 69213

1813

Support for Sadat dooms Numayri regime. *In* U.S. *Joint Publications Research Service*. JPRS 73935. [Springfield, Va., National Technical Information Service, 1979] (Near East/North Africa report, 2002) p. 149–153.

Translation of article in *al-Dustūr*, London, June 4–10, 1979, p. 18–19.

Microfiche. [Washington, Supt. of Docs., U.S. Govt. Print. Off., 1979]

DLC-Micro JPRS 73935

1814

al-Tawīlah, ʿAbd al-Sattār. Lack of funds hampers Egyptian-Sudanese interdependence. *In* U.S. *Joint Publications Research Service*. JPRS 73107. [Springfield, Va., National Technical Information Service, 1979] (Translations on Near East and North Africa, no. 1931) p. 63–66.

Translation of article in *Rūz al-Yūsuf*, Cairo, Jan. 22, 1979, p. 6–7.

Microfiche. [Washington, Supt. of Docs., U.S. Govt. Print. Off., 1979]

DLC-Micro JPRS 73107

Geology, Hydrology, and Mineral Resources

1815

ʿAbd al-ʿAzīz, Usāmah S. New oil finds described. *In* U.S. *Joint Publications Research Service*. JPRS 74345. [Springfield, Va., National Technical Information Service, 1979] (Near East/North Africa report, no. 2030) p. 61–65.

Translation of article in *al-Ayyām*, Khartoum, July 18, 1979, p. 5.

Microfiche. [Washington, Supt. of Docs., U.S. Govt. Print. Off., 1979]

DLC-Micro JPRS 74345

The following items (entries 1816–1819) are listed in chronological order:

1816

ʿArafat, Abu. Mining foundation director general discusses future of mining. *In* U.S. *Joint Publications Research Service*. JPRS 70679. [Springfield, Va., National Technical Information Service, 1978] (Translations on Near East and North Africa, no. 1763) p. 105,–110.

Translation of article in *al-Ṣaḥāfah*, Khartoum, Jan. 2, 1978, p. 5.

Microfiche. [Washington, Supt. of Docs., U.S. Govt. Print. Off., 1978]

DLC-Micro JPRS 70679

1817

Stevens, Candice. The mineral industry of Sudan. *In* Minerals yearbook, v. 3, 1977. [Washington, for sale by the Supt. of Docs., U.S. Govt. Print. Off., 1981] p. 873–877.   TN23.U612 1977, v. 3

Prepared by the U.S. Bureau of Mines.

1818

Shekarchi, E. The mineral industry of Sudan. *In* Minerals yearbook, v. 3, 1978–79. [Washington, U.S. Govt. Print. Off., 1981] p. 867–872.

TN23.U612   1978–79, v. 3

Prepared by the U.S. Bureau of Mines.

1819

———— The mineral industry of Sudan. *In* Minerals yearbook, v. 3, 1980. [Washington, for sale by the Supt. of Docs., U.S. Govt. Print. Off., 1982] p. 907–912.   TN23.U612   1980, v. 3

Prepared by the U.S. Bureau of Mines.

1819a

Makki, Ba-Bakr Hasan. Energy minister discusses oil finds. *In* U.S. *Joint Publications Research Service.* JPRS 76311. [Springfield, Va., National Technical Information Service, 1980] (Near East/North Africa report, no. 2171) p. 124–127.

Translation of interview with Muhammad Sharif al-Tuhami, Minister of Energy and Mining, in *al-Siyāsah*, Kuwait, July 14, 1980, p. 15.

Microfiche. [s.l., 1980]

DLC-Micro JPRS 76311

1820

Tambal, Sharif. Energy minister discusses new finds. *In* U.S. *Joint Publications Research Service.* JPRS 76211. [Springfield, Va., National Technical Information Service, 1980] (Near East/North Africa report, no. 2163) p. 89–103.

Article on a discussion led by Muhammad Sharīf al-Tuhāmī, Minister of Energy and Mining, in *al-Ṣaḥāfah*, Khartoum, May 14, 1980, p. 4–6.

Microfiche. [s.l., 1980]

DLC-Micro JPRS 76211

Health and Nutrition

1821

Aḥmad, Bā-Bakr ʿIsá. New program aims at upgrading public health drastically. *In* U.S. *Joint Publications Research Service.* JPRS 68651. [Springfield, Va., National Technical Information Service, 1977] (Translations on Near East and North Africa, no. 1615) p. 108–111.

Translation of article in *al-Ṣaḥāfah*, Khartoum, Oct. 3, 1976, p. 5.

Microfiche. [s.l., 1977]

DLC-Micro JPRS 68651

1822

Chin, James. Selected bibliographies and state-of-the-art review for disease control. Rockville, Md., Office of International Health, Public Health Ser-

vice, [1979] 71 p. (International health planning reference series)

Study financed by the U.S. Agency for International Development.

Among the "health planning methods" examined is that of Sudan.

Abstract in *A.I.D. Research and Development Abstracts*, v. 8, no. 2, 1980, p. 14.

Microfiche. [Washington, U.S. Agency for International Development, 1979] 1 sheet.

DLC-Sci RR PN-AAH-121

1823

Cross, Edward B. Health sector report—Sudan. [Washington?], Bureau for Africa, Agency for International Development, 1976. 22 p.

Examined in the Development Information Center, AID, Washington, D.C.

1824

Health Sector Assessment Team, Sudan. Report, [by] Edward Cross [et al.] Arlington, Va., Medical Service Consultants, 1977. [372] p. (in various pagings) map.

Prepared for the U.S. Agency for International Development.

"The purpose of the A.I.D. health sector assessment team visit to the Sudan was to review the recently formulated National Health Plan, to assess the resources and needs of the program, and to develop a strategy for possible A.I.D. assistance that would help the Government of Sudan (GOS) achieve its goal of strengthening delivery of rural health services over the next seven year development period."—Abstract.

Abstract in *A.I.D. Research and Development Abstracts*, Oct. 1978, p. 33.

Examined in the Development Information Center, AID, Washington, D.C.

1825

Lambrecht, Frank. International health program: diseases of the arid regions of the world: Sudan (Africa) [Tucson, International Health Program, University of Arizona, 1976] [37] leaves. maps.

Prepared for the U.S. Agency for International Development.

Examined in the Development Information Center, AID, Washington, D.C.

1826

Sulaymān, Fārūq. Comprehensive health program to be launched. *In* U.S. *Joint Publications Research Service.* JPRS 77378. [Springfield, Va., National Technical Information Service, 1981] (Near East/North Africa report, no. 2265) p. 51–58.

1826 (cont.)

Translation of article in *al-Ṣaḥāfah*, Khartoum, Nov. 22, 1980, p. 3.

Microfiche. [s.l., 1981]

DLC-Micro JPRS 77378

Housing and Urban Development

1827

Housing sector said facing shortages, high prices. *In* U.S. *Joint Publications Research Service.* JPRS 73059. [Springfield, Va., National Technical Information Service, 1979] (Translations on the Near East and North Africa, no. 1926) p. 108–114.

Translation of article in *al-Ṣaḥāfah*, Khartoum, Jan. 15, 1979, p. 3.

Microfiche. [Washington, Supt. of Docs., U.S. Govt. Print. Off., 1979]

DLC-Micro JPRS 73059

1828

Sudan shelter sector assessment, [by] Axel Jerome [et al.] [Washington], Office of Housing, Agency for International Development, [1978] [208] p.

Study prepared by Louis Berger International at the request of the Government of the Sudan and under the auspices of the U.S. Agency for International Development.

Abstract in *A.I.D. Research and Development Abstracts*, v. 7, no. 1, 1979, p. 14.

Microfiche. [Washington, U.S. Agency for International Development, 1978?] 3 sheets.

DLC-Sci RR PN-AAG-514

Language and Languages

1829

Chernush, Kay. Starting with ABC: linguists help Sudan record—and learn—its many languages. Agenda, Dec. 1979: 5-7. illus.

HC59.7.A742 1979

Issued by the U.S. Agency for International Development.

1830

English language teaching profile: Sudan. London, English-Teaching Information Centre, 1977. 12 p.

Abstract in *Resources in Education*, May 1978, p. 105.

Microfiche. [Arlington, Va., ERIC Document Reproduction Service; prepared for Educational Resources Information Center, National Institute of Education, 1978] 1 sheet.

DLC-Sci RR ED148175

Politics and Government

1831

Ahmad, ʻAbdallah S. al-Ṣādiq al-Mahdī airs views on national policies. *In* U.S. *Joint Publications Research Service.* JPRS 70990. [Springfield, Va., National Technical Information Service, 1978] (Translations on Near East and North Africa, no. 1784) p. 116–123.

Translation of article in *al-Ayyām*, Khartoum, Mar. 2, 1978, p. 6–7.

Microfiche. [Washington, Supt. of Docs., U.S. Govt. Print. Off., 1978]

DLC-Micro JPRS 70990

1832

ʻAql, Pierre. Opposition leader pledges continued resistance. *In* U.S. *Joint Publications Research Service.* JPRS 76436. [Springfield, Va., National Technical Information Service, 1980] (Near East/North Africa report, no. 2182) p. 133–141.

Translation of interview with al-Sharīf al-Hindī in *al-Dustūr*, London, June 30–July 6, 1980, p. 8–11.

Microfiche. [s.l., 1980]

DLC-Micro JPRS 76436

1833

al-Dirani, Sulayman. Communist leader foresees decisive developments in near future. *In* U.S. *Joint Publications Research Service.* JPRS 74543. [Springfield, Va., National Technical Information Service, 1979] (Near East/North Africa report, no. 2042) p. 58–63.

Translation of interview with Ibrahim Zakariya, member of the central committee of the Sudanese Communist Party, in *al-Nidāʼ al-Usbūʻi*, Beirut, Sept. 16, 1979, p. 12.

Microfiche. [Washington, Supt. of Docs., U.S. Govt. Print. Off., 1979]

DLC-Micro JPRS 74543

1834

Hashk, Muhammed A. Numayri retained as president; accomplishments cited. *In* U.S. *Joint Publications Research Service.* JPRS 69556. [Springfield, Va., National Technical Information Service, 1977] (Translations on Near East and North Africa, no. 1688) p. 80–84.

Translation of article in *al-Ayyām*, Khartoum, May 30, 1977, p. 5.

Microfiche. [s.l., 1977]

DLC-Micro JPRS 69556

1835

al-Hindī, al-Sharīf Ḥusayn. Exiled opposition leader attacks Numayri. *In* U.S. *Joint Publications Re-*

1835 (cont.)

search Service. JPRS 75614. [Springfield, Va., National Technical Information Service, 1980] (Near East/North Africa report, no. 2108) p. 84–94.

Translation of article by the leader of the Sudanese National Front, in *al-Dustūr*, London, Mar. 3–9, 1980, p. 9–12.

Microfiche. [s.l., 1980]

DLC-Micro JPRS 75614

1836

—— Opposition leader urges anti-Nimeiri Arab stance. *In* U.S. *Joint Publications Research Service.* JPRS 75777. [Springfield, Va., National Technical Information Service, 1980] (Near East/North Africa report, no. 2122) p. 300–308.

Translation of article in *al-Dustūr*, London, Mar. 3–9, 1980, p. 9–12.

Microfiche. [s.l., 1980]

DLC-Micro JPRS 75777

1837

—— Opposition leader urges neutral Arab stand on Sudan. *In* U.S. *Joint Publications Research Service.* JPRS 75777. [Springfield, Va., National Technical Information Service, 1980] (Near East/North Africa report, no. 2122) p. 290–299.

Translation of article in *al-Dustūr*, London, Mar. 17–23, 1980, p. 4–7.

Microfiche. [s.l., 1980]

DLC-Micro JPRS 75777

1838

Idrīs, Maḥmūd. People's assembly deliberations detailed. *In* U.S. *Joint Publications Research Service.* JPRS 72987. [Springfield, Va., National Technical Information Service, 1979] (Translations on Near East and North Africa, no. 1922) p. 129–135.

Translation of article in *al-Madīnah*, Jiddah, Dec. 24, 1978, p. 11.

Microfiche. [Washington, Supt. of Docs., U.S. Govt. Print. Off., 1979]

DLC-Micro JPRS 72987

1839

al-Kafrī, 'Abd al-Ra'uf. Opposition leader says revolution against Numayri imminent. *In* U.S. *Joint Publications Research Service.* JPRS 74517. [Springfield, Va., National Technical Information Service, 1979] (Near East/North Africa report, no. 2041) p. 112–122.

Translation of interview with Ḥusayn 'Uthmān Manṣūr, leader of the Democratic Unionist Party of Sudan, in *al-Ba'th*, Damascus, Sept. 2, 6, 1979.

Microfiche. [Washington, Supt. of Docs., U.S. Govt. Print. Off., 1979]

DLC-Micro JPRS 74517

1840

—— Radical leader gives press conference in Syria. *In* U.S. *Joint Publications Research Service.* JPRS 74854. [Springfield, Va., National Technical Information Service, 1980] (Near East/North Africa report, no. 2063) p. 113–121.

Report on statements by Husayn 'Uthman Mansur, secretary-general of the Sudanese National Democratic Front and the Democratic Federation Party, in *al-Ba'th*, Damascus, Nov. 20, 1979, p. 3.

Microfiche. [s.l., 1980]

DLC-Micro JPRS 74854

1841

Karkutī, Muṣṭafá. Opposition leader rejects compromise with Numayri. *In* U.S. *Joint Publications Research Service.* JPRS 74612. [Springfield, Va., National Technical Information Service, 1979] (Near East/North Africa report, no. 2047) p. 134–140.

Translation of interview with al-Sharīf al-Hindī, leader of the Sudanese Democratic Federation, in *al-Safīr*, Beirut, Sept. 25, 1979, p. 10.

Microfiche. [s.l., 1979]

DLC-Micro JPRS 74612

1842

—— Opposition leader reviews domestic, regional issues. *In* U.S. *Joint Publications Research Service.* JPRS 72917. [Springfield, Va., National Technical Information Service, 1979] (Translations on Near East and North Africa, no. 1917) p. 53–62.

Interview with al-Ṣādiq al-Mahdī, in *al-Safīr*, Beirut, Jan. 28, 1979, p. 11.

Microfiche. [Washington, Supt. of Docs., U.S. Govt. Print. Off., 1979]

DLC-Micro JPRS 72917

1843

Kasfir, Nelson. Rhetorical socialism and the Sudan: the military regime of Ja'afer Nimeiri. [s.l.], 1978. 7 leaves. (FAR 28921-N)

Paper presented at the Conference on the Sudan, sponsored by the U.S. Dept. of State, July 1978.

Examined in the former Foreign Affairs Research Documentation Center, Dept. of State.

1844

Lofgren, William W. Sudanese Communism: a blow to Soviet military objectives in seeking Third World leadership. Maxwell Air Force Base, Ala., Air Command and Staff College, Air University, 1972. 112 p. (U.S. Air Command and Staff College. Research study. Report no. 1,05-72)

Bibliography: p. 105–112.

Thesis—Auburn University.

Microfiche. [s.l., 1973] 2 sheets (AD-910031L).

1845

Mattar, Fu'ad. Sudan said to face diverse dangers. *In* U.S. *Joint Publications Research Service.* JPRS 73580. [Springfield, Va., National Technical Information Service, 1979] (Translations on Near East and North Africa, no. 1971) p. 40–46.

Translation of interview with President Gaafar Nimeiri in *al-Mustaqbal*, Paris, Mar. 17, 24, 1979.

Microfiche. [Washington, Supt. of Docs., U.S. Govt. Print. Off., 1979]

DLC-Micro JPRS 73580

1846

Mīnā, Amal. Returnees express satisfaction with national reconciliation. *In* U.S. *Joint Publications Research Service.* JPRS 72973. [Springfield, Va., National Technical Information Service, 1979] (Translations on Near East and North Africa, no. 1921) p. 103.–107.

Translation of interviews with political refugees who returned to Sudan following a general amnesty, in *al-Ayyām*, Khartoum, Dec. 17, 1978, p. 4.

Microfiche. [Washington, Supt. of Docs., U.S. Govt. Print. Off., 1979]

DLC-Micro JPRS 72973

1847

Nimeiri, Gaafar M. Numayri reviews current issues. *In* U.S. *Joint Publications Research Service.* JPRS 73080. [Springfield, Va., National Technical Information Service, 1979] (Translations on Near East and North Africa, no. 1928)

Excerpts from article in *SUNA Bulletin*, Khartoum, Feb. 27, 1979, p. 13–39.

Microfiche. [Washington, Supt. of Docs., U.S. Govt. Print. Off., 1979]

DLC-Micro JPRS 73080

1848

Numayri's religious mood linked to health, domestic turmoil. *In* U.S. *Joint Publications Research Service.* JPRS 77173. [Springfield, Va., National Technical Information Service, 1981] (Near East/North Africa report, no. 2247) p. 96–101.

Translation of article in *al-Mustaqbal*, Paris, Nov. 15, 1980, p. 26–29.

Microfiche. [s.l., 1981]

DLC-Micro JPRS 77173

1849

Party congress issues administrative, economic, political recommendations. *In* U.S. *Joint Publications Research Service.* JPRS 75427. [Springfield, Va., National Technical Information Service, 1980] (Near East/North Africa report, no. 2097) p. 155–162.

Translation of article on the third national congress of the Sudanese Socialist Union, in *al-Qūwat al-musallaḥah*, Khartoum, Feb. 7, 1980, p. 4.

Microfiche. [s.l., 1980]

DLC-Micro JPRS 75427

1850

Possibilities of change in country explored. *In* U.S. *Joint Publications Research Service.* JPRS 74787. [Springfield, Va., National Technical Information Service, 1979] (Near East/North Africa report, no. 2059) p. 94–97.

Translation of article in *al-Nahār al-'Arabi wa al-duwalī*, Paris, Nov. 5–11, 1979, p. 30.

Microfiche. [s.l., 1980]

DLC-Micro JPRS 74787

1851

al-Sadiq al-Mahdi discusses national reconciliation, relations with Egypt. *In* U.S. *Joint Publications Research Service.* JPRS 76495. [Springfield, Va., National Technical Information Service, 1980] (Near East/North Africa report, no. 2187) p. 168–178.

Translation of interview with a leader of the Umma Party, in *al-Siyāsah*, Kuwait, July 9, 1980, p. 12, 15.

Microfiche. [s.l., 1980]

DLC-Micro JPRS 76495

1852

'al-Safir' analyzes Sudanese internal, external problems. *In* U.S. *Joint Publications Research Service.* JPRS 71587. [Springfield, Va., National Technical Information Service, 1978] (Translations on Near East and North Africa, no. 1823) p. 51–55.

Translation of article in *al-Safīr*, Beirut, June 9, 1978, p. 9.

Microfiche. [Washington, Supt. of Docs., U.S. Govt. Print. Off., 1978]

DLC-Micro JPRS 71587

1853

Shuwayri, Yusuf. Opposition leader given reasons for regime's impending collapse. *In* U.S. *Joint Publications Research Service.* JPRS 73523. [Springfield, Va., National Technical Information Service, 1979] (Translations on Near East and North Africa, no. 1967) p. 111–120.

Translation of article in *al-Dustūr*, London, Mar. 26–Apr. 1, 1979, p. 13–16.

Microfiche. [Washington, Supt. of Docs., U.S. Govt. Print. Off., 1979]

DLC-Micro JPRS 73523

1854

Sudan Communist Party declaration reissued. *In* U.S. *Joint Publications Research Service.* JPRS

1854 (cont.)

72949. [Springfield, Va., National Technical Information Service, 1979] (Translations on Near East and North Africa, no. 1919) p. 75–79.

Translation of statement in *al-Nidā' al-Usbū'*, Beirut, Jan. 14, 1979, p. 7.

Microfiche. [Washington, Supt. of Docs., U.S. Govt. Print. Off., 1979]

DLC-Micro JPRS 72949

1855

Voll, John. Local and cosmopolitan poles in Sudanese orientations. [s.l., 1978] [10] leaves. (FAR 28920-N)

Prepared for the Conference on the Sudan, sponsored by the U.S. Dept. of State, July 1978.

Examined in the former Foreign Affairs Research Documentation Center, Dept. of State.

Southern Region

1856

Government tries to exert control of turbulent, arming south. *In* U.S. *Joint Publications Research Service.* JPRS 76137, [Springfield, Va., National Technical Information Service, 1980] (Near East/North Africa report, no. 2156) p. 98–101.

Article in *Sudanow*, Khartoum, July 1980, p. 9–14.

Microfiche. [s.l., 1980]

DLC-Micro JPRS 76137

1857

al-Husaynī, Hudá. Joseph Lagu on opposition in south, inter-African affairs. *In* U.S. *Joint Publications Research Service.* JPRS 72987. [Springfield, Va., National Technical Information Service, 1979] (Translation on Near East and North Africa, no. 1922) p. 123–128.

Translation of interview with General Lagu, President of the High Executive Council of Sudan's southern region, in *al-Nahār al-'Arabī wa al-duwalī*, Paris, Jan. 1, 1979, p. 7.

Microfiche. [Washington, Supt. of Docs., U.S. Govt. Print. Off., 1929]

DLC-Micro JPRS 72987

1858

Power struggle in south ends with Alier on top. *In* U.S. *Joint Publications Research Service.* JPRS 76069. [Springfield, Va., National Technical Information Service, 1980] (Near East/North Africa report, no. 2149) p. 36–42.

Article on political developments in the Southern Region and the success of Abel Alier, President,

High Executive Council for the Southern Region, in *Sudanow*, Khartoum, June 1980, p. 10–11, 15.

Microfiche. [s.l., 1980]

DLC-Micro JPRS 76069

1859

Southern political situation discussed. *In* U.S. *Joint Publications Research Service.* JPRS 76520. [Springfield, Va., National Technical Information Service, 1980] (Near East/North Africa report, no. 2190) p. 94–101.

Article on the politics of the Southern Region, in *Sudanow*, Khartoum, Aug. 1980, p. 13–17, illus.

Microfiche. [s.l., 1980]

DLC-Micro JPRS 76520

1860

Southern regional government reshuffled. *In* U.S. *Joint Publications Research Service.* JPRS 73080. [Springfield, Va., National Technical Information Service, 1979] (Translations on Near East and North Africa, no. 1928) p. 66–69.

Text of article in *SUNA Bulletin*, Khartoum, Feb. 25, 1979, p. 9–13.

Microfiche. [Washington, Supt. of Docs., U.S. Govt. Print. Off., 1979]

DLC-Micro JPRS 73080

Religion

1861

'Ajūbah, Mukhtār. Islam plays vital role in development of society. *In* U.S. *Joint Publications Research Service.* JPRS 74429. [Springfield, Va., National Technical Information Service, 1979] (Near East/North Africa report, no. 2035) p. 45–53.

Translation of article in *al-Ayyām*, Khartoum, July 29, 1979, p. 3.

Microfiche. [Washington, Supt. of Docs., U.S. Govt. Print. Off., 1979]

DLC-Micro JPRS 74429

1862

al-Jirah, Mahmūd. Political, social ramifications of return to Islam discussed. *In* U.S. *Joint Publications Research Service.* JPRS 73516. [Springfield, Va., National Technical Information Service, 1979] (Translations on Near East and North Africa, no. 1966) p. 67–74.

Translation of interview with Hasan A. al-Turabi of the Sudanese Socialist Union in *al-Sahāfah*, Khartoum, Apr. 18, 1979, p. 3.

Microfiche. [Washington, Supt. of Docs., U.S. Govt. Print. Off., 1979]

DLC-Micro JPRS 73516

1863

al-Khifājī, Azjar. Leader of Sudanese Muslim Brotherhood talks about his movement. *In* U.S. *Joint Publications Research Service.* JPRS 75967. [Springfield, Va., National Technical Information Service, 1980] (Near East/North Africa report, no. 2142) p. 185–191.

Translation of interview with Ḥasan A. al-Turabi, Attorney General of Sudan and leader of the Muslim Brotherhood, in *al-Qabas*, Kuwait, June 9, 1980, p. 23.

Microfiche. [s.l., 1980]

DLC-Micro JPRS 75967

Other Subjects

1864

U.S. *Dept. of State. Office of the Geographer.* Sudan: administrative divisions. Washington, 1975. 1 p.

AMAU

"Geographic note GE-132."

1865

U.S. *International Communication Agency. Office of Research and Evaluation.* Listening to international radio stations, including VOA, and perceptions and interests of radio audiences in urban Sudan. [Washington?], 1978. 23 p. DLC

"Research report: E-17-78."

1866

Africa: Sudan. Selected statistical data by sex. Washington, 1981. 31, 17 p. DLC

Study supported by the U.S. Agency for International Development's Office of Women in Development and Office of Population.

Data assembled by the International Demographic Data Center, U.S. Bureau of the Census.

Among the tables, all based on 1973 data, are the following: unadjusted population by age, sex, and urban/rural residence; population by province, sex, and urban/rural residence; life expectancy; urban and rural populations by marital status; number of households; heads of household by age, sex, and urban/rural residence; number of literate persons by age, sex, and urban/rural residence; number of persons enrolled in school by age, sex, and urban/rural residence; number of economically active persons by age, sex, and urban/rural residence; and economically active population by occupational status, sex, and urban/rural residence.

1867

Bates, Robert H. The preservation of order in stateless societies: a reinterpretation of Evans-

Pritchard's *The Nuer: Frontiers of Economics.* [Pasadena, California Institute of Technology], 1979. 26 p. (California Institute of Technology. Social science working paper, no. 112) CPT

Cited by the Millikan Library, California Institute of Technology, as a study supported by the U.S. Government.

Held by the Institute's Munger Library.

1868

Development of education, 1974–1976. National report presented to the XXXVIth session of the International Conference on Education, Geneva, 30 August – 8 September 1977. Khartoum, Documentation and Research Centre, Ministry of Education, [1977] 52 p.

Abstract in *Resources in Education*, Feb. 1978, p. 165.

Microfiche. [Arlington, Va., ERIC Document Reproduction Service; prepared for Educational Resources Information Center, National Institute of Education, 1978] 1 sheet.

DLC-Micro ED144902

1869

Hashal, Muḥammad U. U.S. equipment helps water projects in Red Sea province. *In* U.S. *Joint Publications Research Service.* JPRS 70717. [Springfield, Va., National Technical Information Service, 1978] (Translations on Near East and North Africa, no. 1765) p. 90–94.

Translation of article on improvements in water resources, in *al-Ayyām*, Khartoum, Jan. 5, 1978, p. 5.

Microfiche. [Washington, Supt. of Docs., U.S. Govt. Print. Off., 1978]

DLC-Micro JPRS 70717

1870

Ihrāhīm, 'Abd al-Rahmān. Refugee commissioner discusses Sudan's approach to refugee program. *In* U.S. *Joint Publications Research Service.* JPRS 76111. [Springfield, Va., National Technical Information Service, 1980] (Near East/North Africa report, no. 2154) p. 201–205.

Translation of interview with Aḥmad 'Abd al-Wadūd Kararawī, Assistant Refugee Commissioner, in *al-Ṣaḥāfah*, Khartoum, May 7, 1980, p. 6.

Microfiche. [s.l., 1980]

DLC-Micro JPRS 76111

1871

Nation's purported fuel shortage reviewed. *In* U.S. *Joint Publications Research Service.* JPRS 72819. [Springfield, Va., National Technical Information

1871 (cont.)

Service, 1979] (Translations on Near East and North Africa, no. 1910) p. 84–90.

Translation of article in *al-Ṣaḥāfah*, Khartoum, Dec. 4, 1978, p. 5.

Microfiche. [Washington, Supt. of Docs., U.S. Govt. Print. Off., 1979]

DLC-Micro JPRS 72819

1872

New efforts undertaken against smuggling at Port Sudan. *In* U.S. *Joint Publications Research Service.* JPRS 76049. [Springfield, Va., National Technical Information Service, 1980] (Near East/ North Africa report, no. 2147) p. 136–141.

Article in *Sudanow*, Khartoum, June 1980, p. 25–27.

Microfiche. [s.l., 1980]

DLC-Micro JPRS 76049

1873

Sanyal, Bikas C., *and* El Sammani A. Yacoub. Higher education and employment in the Sudan. Paris, International Institute for Educational Planning, c1975. 263 p. illus. (Higher education and employment; case studies, 1)   LA1813.S26

Bibliography: p. 260–263.

Abstract in *Resources in Education*, Aug. 1977, p. 111.

Issued also in microfiche. [Arlington, Va., ERIC Document Reproduction Service; prepared for Educational Resources Information Center, National Institute of Education, 1977] 3 sheets.

DLC-Micro ED136709

1874

Standardization and measurement services in the Sudan, [by] H. Steffen Peiser [et al.] [Washington], National Bureau of Standards, U.S. Dept. of Commerce, [1980] 84 p.   DLC

"NBSIR 80-2020."

Prepared for the U.S. Agency for International Development.

Based on a survey by an international team advisory to the Government of Sudan.

Issued also in microfiche. [Springfield, Va.,

National Technical Information Service, 1981] 1 sheet.   DLC-Sci RR PB81-151425

1875

Sudan. [*Treaties, etc. United States, 1977 Sept. 23*] Agreement on procedures for mutual assistance between the United States Department of Justice and the Attorney General's chambers of the Democratic Republic of the Sudan, in connection with matters relating to the Boeing Company. *In* U.S. *Treaties, etc.* United States treaties and other international agreements, v. 28, 1976–77. [Washington, Dept. of State; for sale by the Supt. of Docs., U.S. Govt. Print. Off., 1978] p. 7482–7487. ([Treaties and other international acts series, 8723])

JX231.A34 v. 28

Signed at Washington Sept. 23, 1977.

Concerns "alleged illicit acts pertaining to the sales activities in The Sudan of The Boeing Company, and its subsidiaries and affiliates."—p. 7483.

1876

Sudan Symposium and Workshop on Remote Sensing, Oct. 10–11, 1979. Proceedings, [by] A. S. Andrawis [and] M. O. Khidir. [Brookings?], Remote Sensing Institute, South Dakota State University, 1980. 2 v.

Issued for the U.S. Agency for International Development under contract AID/ta-C-1468.

Abstract in *A.I.D. Research & Development Abstracts*, v. 10, no. 1/2, 1982, p. 65.

1877

Tawir, Nur. Conference explores hopes, fears of Sudanese women. *In* U.S. *Joint Publications Research Service.* JPRS 73446. [Springfield, Va., National Technical Information Service, 1979] (Translations on Near East and North Africa, no. 1961) p. 49–57.

Translation of article in *al-Ṣaḥāfah*, Khartoum, Mar. 10, 1979, p. 5, concerning a conference, "The Changing Status of Sudanese Women," held Feb. 23 – Mar. 1, 1979.

Microfiche. [Washington, Supt of Docs., U.S. Govt. Print. Off., 1979]

DLC-Micro JPRS 73446

Tanzania

General

1878

U.S. *Dept. of State.* Post report. Tanzania. [Washington, Dept. of State, Publishing Services Division; for sale by the Supt. of Docs., U.S. Govt. Print. off., 1980] 16 p. illus., map. (*Its* Department and Foreign Service series, 211)

JX1705.A286 Spec. Format
Department of State publication, 9158.

L.C. has also reports issued in 1973 and 1977.

For a description of the contents of this publication, see the note to entry 936.

1879

U.S. *Dept. of State. Bureau of Public Affairs.* Background notes. Tanzania. [Washington, for sale by the Supt. of Docs., U.S. Govt. Print. Off., 1979] 8 p. illus., maps. (U.S. Dept. of State. Department of State publication 8097)   G59.U5

L.C. retains only the latest revision.

For a description of the contents of this publication, see the note to entry 937.

1880

American University, *Washington, D.C. Foreign Area Studies.* Tanzania: a country study. Edited by Irving Kaplan. [Washington, for sale by the Supt. of Docs., U.S. Govt. Print. Off., c1978] xix, 344 p. illus., maps.   DT438.A46   1978

"DA Pam 550-62."

"Research completed January 1978."

Bibliography: p. 299–319.

Supersedes the 1968 ed. by Allison B. Herrick and others, published under title: *Area Handbook for Tanzania* (DT438.H4).

Issued also in microfiche. [s.l., Defense Documentation Center, 1979] 4 sheets.

DLC-Sci RR AD-A064121

1881

The Environmental context of development in Tanzania: a map of environmental pressure points. Worcester, Mass., Program for International Development, Clark University, [1977] [11] leaves. col. map.   DLC

"This map was prepared as part of an AID project (Contract AID/afr-C-1223) to analyze environmental trends in Ethiopia, Tanzania, Kenya, Zambia, Malawi, and Botswana."

1882

The Peace Corps in Tanzania. [Washington, U.S. Govt. Print. Off., 1980] 1 fold. sheet (6 p.) illus., map.   DLC

"ACTION 4200.70."

An introduction to the country for volunteers.

Agriculture

1883

Berry, Leonard. Environmental impact of agricultural development in Tanzania. [Worcester, Mass.?, Clark University?], 1975. [57] p. (in various pagings) maps.   DLC

Apparently prepared for the U.S. Agency for International Development.

Appendix:

"Siasa ni Kilimo;" TANU party guidelines on modern agriculture. [8] p.

1884

Due, Jean M. Agricultural credit in Tanzania. [Urbana], Dept of Agricultural Economics, University of Illinois at Urbana-Champaign, 1977–78. 3 v. (Illinois agricultural economics staff paper, 77 E-2 & 15, 78 E-38)   IU

Research supported in part by the U.S. AID Mission to Tanzania.

Part II, also by Wayne Miller, covers only Iringa region.

1885

——— The allocation of credit to Ujamaa villages and to small private farmers in Tanzania. [s.l., 1977] [28] leaves. (FAR 27797-N)

1885 (cont.)

Research supported in part by the U.S. AID Mission to Tanzania.

Examined in the former Foreign Affairs Research Documentation Center, U.S. Dept. of State.

1886

Dworkin, Daniel. Rural water projects in Tanzania: technical, social, and administrative issues. [Washington?], U.S. Agency for International Development, 1980. [25] p. (in various pagings) (A.I.D. evaluation special study, no. 3)   DLC

Abstract in *A.I.D. Research & Development Abstracts*, July 1981, p. 7–8.

Issued also in microfiche. [Washington, U.S. Agency for International Development, 1980?] 1 sheet.   DLC-Sci RR PN-AAH-974

1887

Evaluation team report on AID agricultural marketing development project no. 621-11-150-099, Tanzania. Washington, 1976. 78 leaves.

Examined in the Development Information Center, AID, Washington, D.C.

1888

Fortmann, Louise. Observations on the Mbulu small farmer food crop loan program. [s.l.], 1978. 29 p.

Prepared for the U.S. AID Mission to Tanzania.

Examined in the Development Information Center, AID, Washington, D.C.

1889

——— Peasants, officials and participation in rural Tanzania: experience with villagization and decentralization. [Ithaca, N.Y.], Rural Development Committee, Center for International Studies, Cornell University, 1980. [149] p. maps. (Special series on rural location organization, RLO no. 1)

Bibliography: p. 137–148.

"This report examines Tanzania's colonial and post-independence bureaucracies in relation to rural development's two conflicting driving forces: the need for genuine local decisionmaking to ensure a commitment to development programs and the need for central control to allocate scarce resources in a coherent nation-building strategy."—p. [149].

Abstract in *A.I.D. Research & Development Abstracts*, v. 9, no. 3, 1981, p. 22.

Microfiche. [Washington, U.S. Agency for International Development, 1980?] 2 sheets.
          DLC-Sci RR PN-AAJ-632

1890

Gunter, Jock. Tanzanian campaigns achieve popular participation. Development communication report, no. 17, Jan. 1977: 1, 4-5.   DLC

Issued by the Clearinghouse on Development Communication with support from the U.S. Agency for International Development.

Concerns rural development.

1891

Hyden, Goran. The resilience of the peasant mode of production: the case of Tanzania. *In* Agricultural development in Africa: issues of public policy; edited by Robert H. Bates [and] Michael F. Lofchie. [New York], Praeger, 1980, p. 218–243.
          HD2117.A35

Publication supported in part by the National Science Foundation.

1892

Jacobs, Alan H. A final report of development in Tanzania Maasailand: the perspective over 20 years, 1957–1977. [Dar es Salaam?], 1978. [59] p. (in various pagings)   IEN

Prepared for the U.S. AID Mission to Tanzania under contract AID/afr-C-1279.

Abstract in *A.I.D. Research and Development Abstracts*, Oct. 1978, p. 4.

Issued also in microfiche. [Washington, U.S. Agency for International Development, 1978?] 1 sheet.   DLC-Sci RR PN-AAF-553

1893

Kocher, James E., *and* Beverly Fleischer. A bibliography on rural development in Tanzania. East Lansing, Dept. of Agricultural Economics, Michigan State University, 1979. 77 p. (MSU rural development paper, no. 3)   Z7164.C842K6

"Prepared and published under Agency for International Development contract AID/ta-CA-3."

761 entries.

Abstracts in *Resources in Education*, Oct. 1979, p. 157, and *A.I.D. Research and Development Abstracts*, v. 8, no. 2, 1980, p. 7.

Issued also in microfiche. [Arlington, Va., ERIC Document Reproduction Service; prepared for Educational Resources Information Center, National Institute of Education, 1979] 1 sheet (DLC-Micro ED171495); and [Washington, U.S. Agency for International Development, 1979?] 1 sheet (DLC-Sci RR PN-AAG-938).

1894

Maro, Paul S., *and* Wilfred F. I. Mlay. Decentralization and the organization of space in Tanzania. *In* Southall, Aidan. Small urban centers in rural development in Africa. Madison, African Studies Program, University of Wisconsin-Madison, 1979. p. 274–285. maps.

A grant from the Office of Urban Development,

1894(cont.)

U.S. Agency for International Development, assisted in the preparation for publication of the papers collected in the study.

Microfiche. [Washington, U.S. Agency for International Development, 1980?] (PN-AAJ-064); examined in the Development Information Center, AID, Washington, D.C.

1895

Miller, S. F., *and* L. C. Burrill. Weed control problems in Tanzania; a review team report. Corvallis, International Plant Protection Center, Oregon State University, 1980. 42 p. DLC

Prepared for the U.S. Agency for International Development under contract AID/ta-C-1303.

Abstract in *A.I.D. Research & Development Abstracts*, July 1981, p. 15.

Issued also in microfiche. [Washington, U.S. Agency for International Development, 1980?] 1 sheet (PN-AAH-969); examined in the Development Information Center, AID, Washington, D.C.

1896

Report on progress of ujamaa villages. *In* U.S. *Joint Publications Research Service.* JPRS 71133. [Springfield, Va., National Technical Information Service, 1978] (Translations on Sub-Saharan Africa, no. 1929) p. 115–119.

Translation of article in *Neue Zürcher Zeitung*, Zurich, Apr. 20, 1978, p. 5.

Microfiche. [Washington, Supt. of Docs., U.S. Govt. Print. Off., 1978]

DLC-Micro JPRS 71133

1897

Tanzania agricultural manpower project; progress report. 1975?–78? Morgantown, Office of International Programs, West Virginia University. Annual. DLC

Prepared under U.S. Agency for International Development contract AID/afr-C-1067.

No more published?

L.C. has 1975–76; more complete holdings in WvU.

1898

West Virginia University. Program proposal for a Department of Agricultural Education & Extension and a Center for Continuing Education in Agriculture at the Faculty of Agriculture & Forestry at Morogoro, Tanzania. [Morgantown?, 1975?] 37 p. illus. ([West Virginia University. Office of International Programs. Report] no. 43) DLC

Issued in cooperation with North Carolina Agricultural and Technical State University,

Greensboro, under U.S. Agency for International Development contract AID/afr-C-1067.

"Prepared for the Faculty of Agriculture and Forestry, University of Dar es Salaam; Ministry of Agriculture, Manpower Division; the Ministry of Education, Secondary and Technical Division, [and] USAID/Tanzania."

1899

Witucki, Lawrence A. Tanzania boosts food output, cuts imports. Foreign agriculture, Jan. 16, 1978: 10-11. HD1401.F65 1978

Issued by the U.S. Foreign Agricultural Service.

Grain and Grain Storage

1900

An analysis of the Tanzanian food-crop subsector by the University of Missouri at Columbia; final report, contract no. AID/CM/Afr-C-73-11, [by] Melvin Blase [et al.] [Columbia?, 1975] 241 p.

"The purpose of the paper is to provide guidelines on alternative approaches to the development of the basic food crop sector using Tanzania as a case study. The paper covers a range of policy choices and project activities considered as alternative strategies to increase cereal production in the short, medium, and long run."—Foreword.

Microfiche. [Washington, U.S. Agency for International Development, 1975?] 3 sheets.

DLC-Sci RR PN-AAF-351

1901

Chung, Do Sup. Review of on-farm grain storage in Tanzania; prepared for the Agency for International Development, United States Department of State. Manhattan, Food and Feed Grain Institute, Kansas State University, 1975. 67 p. (Grain storage, processing and marketing; report no. 49)

SB190.C57

"Contract number: AID/ta-C-1162."

Bibliography: p. 43–44.

Abstract in *A.I.D. Research and Development Abstracts*, July 1976, p. 3.

Issued also in microfiche. [Washington, U.S. Agency for International Development, 1975?] 1 sheet. DLC-Sci RR PN-AAB-644

1902

Colegrave, Michael. Termination report of Maize Agronomist for the Tanzanian maize and grain legume research program, October 1973 – October 1975. [Mexico City?], International Maize and Wheat Improvement Center, [1975?] 20 p.

Prepared for the U.S. Agency for International Development.

1902 (cont.)

Examined in the Development Information Center, AID, Washington, D.C.

1903

Fortmann, L. P. An evaluation of the progress of the national maize project at the end of one cropping season in Morogoro and Arusha regions. [Dar es Salaam], USAID/Tanzania, 1976, 40 p.

Examined in the Development Information Center, Agency for International Development, Washington, D.C.

1904

Seed multiplication project in Tanzania: evaluation report, [by] Irving H. Licht [et al.] [Washington], Agency for International Development, 1975. 27 p.

Prepared under contract with Experience, inc.

Examined in the Development Information Center, AID, Washington, D.C.

1905

Tanzania seed industry survey: report of evaluations and recommendations, [by] Albert R. Hagan [et al.] [Columbia?, University of Missouri], 1979. 167 p. map.   MoU

Sponsored by the U.S. Agency for International Development under contract AID/afr-C-1139.

Abstract in *A.I.D. Research & Development Abstracts*, July 1981, p. 13.

Issued also in microfiche. [Washington, U.S. Agency for International Development, 1979?] 2 sheets.   DLC-Sci RR PN-AAH-870

Livestock and Range Management

1906

George, Emmett. Modernizing the Masai: Tanzania's cattlemen cling to tradition as civilization forces changes in their nomadic life. Agenda, Mar. 1978: 12–16. illus.   HC59.7.A742   1978

Issued by the U.S. Agency for International Development.

1907

Hess, Oleen. The establishment of cattle ranching associations among the Masai of Tanzania. [Ithaca, N.Y.?], Rural Development Committee, Cornell University, [1976?] 57 p.   DLC

"Occasional paper no. 7."

Apparently funded by the U.S. Agency for International Development.

1908

Hoben, Allen. Social soundness of the Masai Live-

stock and Range Management Project. [s.l.], 1976. 86 p.

Prepared for the U.S. AID Mission to Tanzania.

Abstract in *A.I.D. Research and Development Abstracts*, Apr. 1979, p. 9.

Microfiche. [Washington, U.S. Agency for International Development, 1976?] 1 sheet.   DLC-Sci RR PN-AAE-959

1909

Johnston, Larry D. Livestock marketing and development project (Tanzania); final report. College Station, Office of International Programs, Texas A&M University, 1982. [167] leaves (in various foliations)   DLC

Prepared under U.S. Agency for International Development contract AID/afr-C-1095.

The reports covers the project's progress in the period 1974–81.

1910

Tanzania livestock marketing and development project—an evaluation, [by] David B. Dorsey [et al.] [s.l.], Al L. Nellum and Associates, 1979, 96 p.

Report submitted to the U.S. Agency for International Development.

An evaluation of a Texas A&M University project.

Examined in the Development Information Center, AID, Washington, D.C.

1911

Tanzanian livestock-meat subsector. [College Station?], International Programs, Texas A&M University, 1976. 4 v.

Issued in cooperation with the U.S. Agency for International Development under contract AID/afr-C-1095.

Contents: v. 1. Consultants' report.—v. 2. Livestock survey data and marketing model.—v. 3. Regional and district survey data: Mara Region, Mwanza Region, Shinyanga Region, Tabora Region.—v. 4. Regional livestock survey data: Singida Region, Dodoma Region, Arusha Region.

Microfiche. [Washington, U.S. Agency for International Development, 1976?] (PN-AAK-420-PN-AAK-423); examined in the Development Information Center, AID, Washington, D.C.

Assistance Programs

1912

U.S. *Agency for International Development*. Annual budget submission: Tanzania. Washington, U.S. International Development Cooperation Agency.

1912 (cont.)

Vols. for 1979+ examined in the Development Information Center, AID, Washington, D.C.

1913

——— Country development strategy statement: Tanzania. Washington, U.S. International Development Cooperation Agency.

Vols. for 1982+ examined in the Development Information Center, AID, Washington, D.C.

Vol. for 1981 abstracted in *Government Reports Announcements & Index*, Oct. 12, 1979, p. 31.

Vol. for 1981 issued in microfiche. [Springfield, Va., National Technical Information Service, 1979] 1 sheet.   DLC-Sci RR PB298038

1914

U.S. *Agency for International Development. Office of the Auditor General.* Appraisal report of the AID program in Tanzania. [Washington?], 1977. 66 p.

Examined in the Development Information Center, AID, Washington, D.C.

1915

Agricultural research project, IITA/USAID-Tanzania contract; annual progress report. 1973?+ [s.l.]

IITA: International Institute of Tropical Agriculture.

Report for 1977 issued in microfiche. [Washington, U.S. Agency for International Development, 1978?] 1 sheet.
    DCL-Sci RR PN-AAG-288

Note: The project was established in 1973 with the objective of aiding the Tanzanian Ministry of Agriculture in the development of a food crops research program.

1916

Checchi and Company, *Washington, D.C.* Final report for administrator's evaluation review on rural poverty, prepared for Agency for International Development under contract no. AID/CM/otr-C-73-199 (work order no. 7) [Washington], 1975. 189 p.   HC190.P6C48 1975

A study of social and economic conditions in Brazil and Tanzania with specific reference to the rural poor.

Abstract in *A.I.D. Research and Development Abstracts*, Jan. 1976, p. 30.

Issued also in microfiche. [Washington, Agency for International Development, 1975?] 3 sheets.
    DLC-Sci RR PN-AAB-334

1917

——— Summary issues paper for administrator's evaluation review seminar, March 4–5, 1975. Washington, 1975. 126 p.

Prepared for the U.S. Agency for International Development.

Microfiche. [Washington, U.S. Agency for International Development, 1975?] 2 sheets.
    DLC-Sci RR PN-AAC-027

1918

——— Summary of AID inputs and socio-economic conditions in: Brazil and Tanzania. Washington, 1975. [68] p.

Prepared for the U.S. Agency for International Development.

Microfiche. [Washington, U.S. Agency for International Development, 1975?] 1 sheet.
    DLC-Sci RR PN-AAC-028

1919

A Conceptual framework for USAID agricultural assistance in Tanzania, [by] Edmond C. Hutchinson [et al.] [s.l.], American Technical Assistance Corporation, 1976. 58 p.

Prepared for the U.S. Agency for International Development under contract AID/afr-C-1142.

Examined in the Development Information Center, AID, Washington, D.C.

1920

Cramer, Ray D. Memorandum report on review of USAID/Tanzania cash management operations. [Nairobi], Area Auditor General, East Africa, Agency for International Development, 1980. 6 p.

"Audit report no. 3-621-80-15."

Examined in the Development Information Center, AID, Washington, D.C.

1921

Evaluation of the Masai livestock and range management project, USAID project no. 621-11-130-093, performed by a Utah State University team together with officials and representatives of USAID/Washington under contract no. AID afr-C-1207. [s.l.], 1976. 82 leaves.

Examined in the Development Information Center, Agency for International Development, Washington, D.C.

1922

Evaluation team report on AID agricultural marketing development project, Tanzania, [by] Edwin W. Lofthouse [et al.] [s.l.], 1977. 78 p.

Prepared for the U.S. Agency for International Development.

Examined in the Development Information Center, AID, Washington, D.C.

1923

Fox, Edwin K., *and* Harry M. Houck. Management [of the P. L. 480 Program] and the drought/famine situation in Tanzania. Evaluation of contractor's (Catholic Relief Services) performance. [Washington?], Office of Food for Peace, U.S. Agency for International Development, 1974. 12 p.

Prepared for the Government of Tanzania and the U.S. AID Mission to Tanzania.

Examined in the Development Information Center, AID, Washington, D.C.

1924

McDermott, J. K. Program strategy considerations for USAID/Tanzania. [s.l.], 1978, 55 p.

Microfiche. [Washington, U.S. Agency for International Development, 1978?] 1 sheet.

DLC-Sci RR PN-AAG-653

1925

Memorandum report on the USAID/Tanzania participant training program. [Nairobi], Area Auditor General, East Africa, Agency for International Development, 1980. 8 p.

"Audit report no. 3-621-80-25."

Examined in the Development Information Center, AID, Washington, D.C.

1926

Mudge, James, Michael Crosswell, *and* Kwan Kim. Tanzanian development performance and implications for development assistance. Washington, Agency for International Development, 1980. 230 p.

Microfiche. [Washington, U.S. Agency for International Development, 1980?] 3 sheets (PN-AAJ-279) held by the Development Information Center, AID, Washington, D.C.

1927

Pendelton, Roger L. Tanzania: a model for Chinese aid in Africa in the 1980's. Carlisle Barracks, Pa., U.S. Army War College, 1975. 26 p.

Microfiche. [s.l., 1975?] 1 sheet.

DLC-Sci RR AD A012621

1928

Tanzania. [*Treaties, etc. United States, 1975 May 23*] Agreement between the Government of the United States of America and the Government of the United Republic of Tanzania for the sale of agricultural commodities. *In* U.S. *Treaties, etc.* United States treaties and other international agreements, v. 26, 1975. [Washington, Dept. of State; for sale by the Supt. of Docs., U.S. Govt. Print. Off., 1976] p. 2291–2304. ([Treaties and other international

acts series, 81581]) JX231.A34 v. 26

Signed at Dar es Salaam May 23, 1975.

1929

Tanzania. [*Treaties, etc. United States, 1975 Aug. 13*] Tanzania; drought assistance in Arusha region. Agreement signed at Dar es Salaam August 12 and 13, 1975; entered into force August 13, 1975. *In* U.S. *Treaties, etc.* United States treaties and other international agreements, v. 29, 1976–77. [Washington, Dept. of State; for sale by the Supt. of Docs., U.S. Govt. Print. Off., 1979] p. 9–21. ([Treaties and other international acts series, 8786]) JX231.A34 v. 29

1930

Tanzania. [*Treaties, etc. United States, 1976 Apr. 13*] Tanzania; agricultural commodities: transfer under Title II; agreement signed at Dar es Salaam April 13, 1976; entered into force April 13, 1976. *In* U.S. *Treaties, etc.* United States treaties and other international agreements, v. 29, 1976–77. [Washington, Dept. of State; for sale by the Supt. of Docs., U.S. Govt. Print. Off., 1979] p. 1003–1005. ([Treaties and other international acts series, 8861]) JX231.A34 v. 29

Under Title II, Public Law 480, the Commodity Credit Corporation was authorized to transfer and deliver food grain to the Government of Tanzania.

1931

Tanzania. [*Treaties, etc. United States, 1976 June 15*] Agreement between the Government of the United States of America and the Government of the United Republic of Tanzania for the sale of agricultural commodities. *In* U.S. *Treaties, etc.* United States treaties and other international agreements, v. 27, 1976. [Washington, Dept. of State; for sale by the Supt. of Docs., U.S. Govt. Print. Off., 1977] p. 2314–2328. ([Treaties and other international acts series, 8310]) JX231.A34 v. 27

Singed at Dar es Salaam June 15, 1976.

1932

Tanzania. [*Treaties, etc. United States, 1977 Mar. 19*] Agreement between the Government of the United States of America and the Government of the United Republic of Tanzania for the sale of agricultural commodities under the Public Law 480 Title I program. *In* U.S. *Treaties, etc.* United States treaties and other international agreements, v. 29, 1976–77. [Washington, Dept. of State; for sale by the Supt. of Docs., U.S. Govt. Print. Off., 1979] p. 1–5. ([Treaties and other international acts series, 8784]) JX231.A34 v. 29

Agreement signed at Dar es Salaam Mar. 19, 1977.

1933

Tanzania. [*Treaties, etc. United States, 1977 Aug. 15*] Tanzania; agricultural commodities: transfer under Title II. Agreement signed at Dar es Salaam August 15, 1977; entered into force August 15, 1977. *In U.S. Treaties, etc.* United States treaties and other international agreements, v. 29, 1976–77. [Washington, Dept. of State; for sale by the Supt. of Docs., U.S. Govt. Print. Off., 1980] p. 5276–5278. ([Treaties and other international acts series, 9104])   JX231.A34 v. 29

1934

Tanzania. [*Treaties, etc. United States, 1977, Dec, 28*] Project agreement between the Department of State, Agency for International Development (AID), an agency of the Government of the United States of America, and the Treasury, an agency of the Government of the United Republic of Tanzania. *In U.S. Treaties, etc.* United States treaties and other international agreements, v. 29, 1976–77. [Washington, Dept. of State; for sale by the Supt. of Docs., U.S. Govt. Print. Off., 1980] p. 5589–5598. ([Treaties and other international acts series, 9132])   JX231.A34 v. 29

Agreement signed at Dar es Salaam, Dec. 28 and 29, 1977; entered into force, Dec. 19, 1977.

An agricultural research project "directed toward developing an effective agricultural research system in Tanzania with emphasis on food crops grown by small farmers."—p. 5591.

1935

Tanzania. [*Treaties, etc., United States, 1978 Apr. 28*] Agreement between the Government of the United States of America and the Government of the United Republic of Tanzania for the sale of agricultural commodities under the Public Law 480 Title I program. *In U.S. Treaties, etc.* United States treaties and other international agreements, v. 29, 1976–77. [Washington, Dept. of State; for sale by the Supt. of Docs., U.S. Govt. Print. Off., 1980] p. 6078–6081. ([Treaties and other international acts series, 9170])   JX231.A34 v. 29

Signed at Dar es Salaam Apr. 28, 1978.

1936

Tanzania. [*Treaties, etc. United States, 1978 July 6*] Training of maternal and child health aides. Agreement between the United States of America and Tanzania, signed at Dar es Salaam July 6, 1978. *In U.S. Treaties, etc.* United States treaties and other international agreements, v. 30, 1978–79. [Washington, Dept. of State; for sale by the Supt. of Docs., U.S. Govt. Print. Off., 1981] p. 4622–4625. ([Treaties and other international acts series, 9482])   JX231.A34 v. 30

Agreement for U.S. Agency for International Development assistance to the Ministry of Health for the training of aides for assignment to rural health facilities.

1937

Tanzania. [*Treaties, etc. United States, 1979 Jan. 9*] Tanzania, Peace Corps. Agreement effected by exchange of letters signed at Dar es Salaam January 9, 1979; entered into force January 9, 1979. *In U.S. Treaties, etc.* United States treaties and other international agreements, v. 30, 1978–79. [Washington, Dept. of State; for sale by the Supt. of Docs., U.S. Govt. Print. Off., 1980] p. 3486–3492. ([Treaties and other international acts series, 9402])   JX231.A34 v. 30

1938

Tanzania. [*Treaties, etc. United States, 1980 Mar. 19*] Agreement between the Government of the United States of America and the Government of the United Republic of Tanzania for the sale of agricultural commodities under the Public Law 480 Title I program. [Washington, Dept. of State; for sale by the Supt. of Docs., U.S. Govt. Print. Off., 1980] 8 p. (Treaties and other international acts series, 9736)]   DLC

Signed at Dar es Salaam Mar. 19, 1980.

1939

Tanzania agricultural sector manpower study: the demand, supply, education, and utilization of professional and technical agricultural personnel, 1979–1986. Washington, Agency for International Development, 1980. 494 p. (in various pagings)

Issued in cooperation with the Ministry of Agriculture and Ministry of Manpower Development of Tanzania, the Office of International Programs, West Virginia University, and the U.S. AID Mission to Tanzania.

Microfiche. [Washington, U.S. Agency for International Development, 1980?] 6 sheets (PN-AAH-516); examined in the Development Information Center, AID, Washington, D.C.

1940

Technical Assistance Information Clearing House. Development assistance programs of U.S. non-profit organizations in Tanzania. New York, American Council of Voluntary Agencies for Foreign Service, 1974. 33 p. (TAICH country report)   HC557.T3T4 1974

The Council operates the Clearing House under a grant from the U.S. Agency for International Development.

1941

Development assistance programs of U.S. non-profit organizations: Tanzania. [New York] 1979. 36 p. maps. (TAICH country report)

DLC

1942

Texas A & M University, *College Station. International Programs.* Semi-annual report on the technical assistance by Texas A & M Univeristy in the development of an effective livestock marketing system in Tanzania. Dec. 1974/May 1975?+ College Station.

Prepared for the U.S. Agency for International Development under contract AID/afr-C-1095.

Vol. for Dec. 1975/May 1976 examined in the Development Information Center, AID, Washington, D.C.

Commerce

1943

Market share reports. Country series: Tanzania, 1971–75. [Washington], U.S. Dept. of Commerce; for sale by the National Technical Information Service, Springfield, Va., [1977] 60 p.

Indicates the United States share of the market in Tanzania for various products compared to the shares for Belgium-Luxemburg, France, Federal Republic of Germany, Great Britain, Italy, Netherlands, Sweden, and Japan.

Microfiche. [Washington, Congressional Information Service, 1977?]

DLC-Micro ASI:77 2016-1.80

1944

Market share reports. Country series: Tanzania, 1975–79. [Washington], International Trade Administration, U.S. Dept. of Commerce; for sale by the National Technical Information Service, Springfield, Va., [1979] 63 p.

Includes same comparative data as in *Market Share Reports. Country Series: Tanzania, 1971–75* (entry 1943).

Microfiche. [Washington, Congressional Information Service, 1979?]

DLC-Micro ASI:81 2046-2.80

1945

Pfund, Leona, *and* Temple Cole. Marketing in Tanzania. [Washington], U.S. Dept. of Commerce, Domestic and International Business Administration; [for sale by the Supt. of Docs., U.S. Govt.

Print. Off.], 1977, 17 p. (Overseas business reports, OBR 77-09)   HF91.U482   1977, no. 9

International marketing information series.

Communications and Transportation

1946

Bhandari, Anil, *and* Fredric Berger. The highway cost model: application to the Dar es Salaam-Morogoro section of the Tanzania-Zambia highway; draft report. [Cambridge?], Program for Transportation Planning in Developing Countries, Massachusetts Institute of Technology, 1975. [95] p. (in various pagings)

Prepared for the Office of Science and Technology, U.S. Agency for International Development.

Abstract in *A.I.D. Research and Development Abstracts*, Oct. 1976, p. 31–32.

Microfiche. [Washington, U.S. Agency for International Development, 1975?] 2 sheets.

DLC-Sci RR PN-AAC-180

1947

Economic and technical feasibility study, Bukombe-Isaka road link, Tanzania; final report. East Orange, N.J., Louis Berger International, 1981. [208] p. (in various pagings) map.

Prepared for the U.S. Agency for International Development under contract AID/otr-C-1788.

Abstract in *A.I.D. Research & Development Abstracts*, v. 9, no. 4, p. 69.

Microfiche. [Washington, U.S. Agency for International Development, 1981?] 3 sheets.

DLC-Sci RR PN-AAJ-434

Economic Conditions

1948

Blue, Richard N., *and* James H. Weaver. A critical assessment of the Tanzanian model of development. [Washington, Development Studies Program, Agency for International Development, 1977] [82] p. (U.S. Agency for International Development. Development Studies Program. Occasional paper, no. 1)

Abstract in *A.I.D. Research and Development Abstracts*, Oct. 1977, p. 13.

Microfiche. [Washington, U.S. Agency for International Development, 1977?] 1 sheet.

DLC-Sci RR PN-AAC-993

1948 (cont.)

Note: The Development Studies Program was established in 1975 to help the Agency improve its capability to carry out programs in rural development.

1949

Foreign economic trends and their implications for the United States. Tanzania. 1969?+ Washington, for sale by the Supt. of Docs., U.S. Govt. Print. Off. annual. (International marketing information series)   HC10.E416

Prepared by the U.S. Embassy, Dar es Salaam.

Vols. for 1969?–77 distributed by the U.S. Bureau of International Commerce; vol. for 1978 by the U.S. Industry and Trade Administration; vols. for 1980– by the U.S. International Trade Adminstration.

Not published in 1979.

Vol. for 1980 (FET 80-050) "replaces FET 80-003 which was not issued."

The following issues for the period 1973–81 have been identified in L.C.:

ET 73-095. 1973. 9 p.
ET 74-094. 1974. 11 p.
FET 75-134. 1975. 9 p.
FET 76-114. 1976. 7 p.
FET 77-117. 1977. 11 p.
FET 78-139. 1978. 8 p.
FET 80-050. 1980. 9 p.
FET 81-012. 1981. 9 p.

Education

1950

Gillette, Arthur. Beyond the non-formal fashion: towards educational revolution in Tanzania. Amherst, Center for International Education, University of Massachusetts, c1977. 321 p.
                  LA1841.G5

Bibliography: p. 313–321.

Abstract in *Resources in Education*, Feb. 1978, p. 64.

Issued also in microfiche. [Arlington, Va., ERIC Document Reproduction Service; prepared for Educational Resources Information Center, National Institute of Education, 1978] 4 sheets.
                  DLC-Micro ED144206

1951

Grenholm, Lennart H. Radio study group campaigns in the United Republic of Tanzania. Paris, United Nations Educational, Scientific, and Cultural Organization, 1975. 51 p. (Experiments and innovations in education, no. 15)

Abstract in *Resources in Education*, Sept. 1976, p. 117.

Microfiche. [Arlington, Va., ERIC Document

Reproduction Service; prepared for Educational Resources Information Center, National Institute of Education, 1976] 1 sheet.
                  DLC-Micro ED122755

1952

Hall, Budd L. Participation and education in Tanzania. Brighton, Eng., Institute of Development Studies at the University of Sussex, 1975. 29 p. (Institute of Development Studies. I. D. S. Discussion paper, no. 86)   LA1841.H34

Abstract in *Resources in Education*, Feb. 1978, p. 60.

Issued also in microfiche. [Arlington, Va., ERIC Document Reproduction Service; prepared for Educational Resources Information Center, National Institute of Education, 1978] 1 sheet.
                  DLC-Micro ED144173

1953

——— The structure of adult education and rural development in Tanzania. Brighton, Eng., Institute of Development Studies, University of Sussex, 1975. 13, 4 p. illus. (Institute of Development Studies. I.D.S. discussion paper, no. 67)
                  LC5163.T34H34

Abstract in *Resources in Education*, July 1978, p. 4.

Microfiche. [Arlington, Va., ERIC Document Reproduction Service; prepared for Educational Resources Information Center, National Institute of Education, 1978] 1 sheet.
                  DLC-Micro ED150284

1954

Kinunda, M. J. Experience in Tanzania in identifying and satisfying local needs in education. Paris, International Institute for Educational Planning, c1975. 26 p. (International Institute for Educational Planning. IIEP seminar paper, 14)

On cover: "A contribution to the IIEP Seminar on 'The planning of learning arrangements of all kinds of local communities,' 9–17 December 1974."

Abstract in *Resources in Education*, June 1977, p. 68.

Microfiche. [Arlington, Va., ERIC Document Reproduction Service; prepared for Educational Resources Information Center, National Institute of Education, 1977] 1 sheet.
                  DLC-Micro ED133859

1955

———The place of evaluation in the Tanzanian system of education: a contribution to the IIEP Seminar on "The Evaluation of the Qualitative Aspects of Education, 30 September – 4 October

1955 (cont.)

1974." Paris, International Institute for Educational Planning, c1975. 22 p. (International Institute for Educational Planning. IIEP seminar paper, 6)   LA1841.K56

Issued also in microfiche. [Arlington, Va., ERIC Document Reproduction Service; prepared for Educational Resources Information Center, National Institute of Education, 1977] 1 sheet.

DLC-Micro ED141374

1956

Mitande, P. K., *and* R. Z. Mwajombe. Mass education linked to development: Tanzanian experience. *In* Educational reforms and innovations in Africa: studies prepared for the Conference of Ministers of Education of African Member States of Unesco. Paris, Unesco, 1978. (Experiments and innovations in education, no. 34) p. 25–30.

LA1500.E38

Issued also in microfiche. [Arlington, Va., ERIC Document Reproduction Service; prepared for Educational Resources Information Center, National Institute of Education, 1978]

DLC-Micro ED160036

1957

Samoff, Joel. Education in Tanzania: class formation and reproduction. [Ann Arbor], Center for Afro-american and African Studies, Dept. of Political Science, University of Michigan, c1976. 36 p.

Paper presented at the annual meeting of the American Political Science Association, 1976.

Discusses the link between education and class situation in northern Tanzania near Mt. Kilimanjaro.

Abstract in *Resources in Education*, Aug. 1977, p. 183.

Microfiche. [Arlington, Va., ERIC Document Reproduction Service; prepared for Educational Resources Information Center, National Institute of Education, 1977] 1 sheet.

DLC-Micro ED137201

1958

Schoeneberger, Mary M., *and* E. S. Odynak. Tanzania Project: a case study of an international teacher education program. [Edmonton], Dept. of Elementary Education, Faculty of Education, University of Alberta, 1974. 119 leaves.

LB2286.C2S36

The Tanzania Project was established and administered by the Faculty of Education, University of Alberta and the Canadian International Development Agency.

Bibliography: leaves 118–119.

Abstract in *Resources in Education*, Nov. 1975, p. 189.

Issued also in microfiche. [Arlington, Va., ERIC Document Reproduction Service; prepared for Educational Resources Information Center, National Institute of Education, 1975] 2 sheets.

DLC-Sci RR ED109065

1959

Siwale, Edmond W., *and* Mohamed M. Sefu. The development of primary education in Tanzania. St. Catherines, Ont., Brock University, 1977. 64 p.

Abstract in *Resources in Education*, Dec. 1977, p. 114.

Microfiche. [Arlington, Va., ERIC Document Reproduction Service; prepared for Educational Resources Information Center, National Institute of Education, 1977] 1 sheet.

DLC-Sci RR ED142280

1960

Sorenson, Donald A. Final report on primary school vocationalization project. Arusha, Tanzania, 1977. [53] leaves (in various foliations)

Prepared for the Ministry of National Education of Tanzania and the U.S. Agency for International Development.

Examined in the Development Information Center, AID, Washington, D.C.

1961

Ta-ngoc-Chau, *and* Françoise Caillods. Educational policy and its financial implications in Tanzania. Paris, Unesco Press, 1975. 137 p. illus. (Financing educational systems. Country case studies, 4)

LB2970.T3T36

At head of title: International Institute for Educational Planning.

Includes bibliographical references.

Abstract in *Resources in Education*, June 1977, p. 69.

Issued also in microfiche. [Arlington, Va., ERIC Document Reproduction Service; prepared for Educational Resources Information Center, National Institute of Education, 1977] 2 sheets.

DLC-Micro ED133866

Energy Resources— Production & Consumption

1962

Fleuret, Patrick, *and* Anne Fleuret. Fuelwood use in a peasant community; a Tanzanian case study. [Los Angeles, California State University, 1977?] [19] leaves.

1962 (cont.)

Based on fieldwork in Lushoto, Tanzania, 1975–77, supported in part by the National Science Foundation of the United States.

Examined in the National Science Foundation, Washington, D.C.

1963

Workshop on Solar Energy for the Villages of Tanzania, *Dar es Salaam, 1977.* [Report] [Dar es Salaam], Tanzania National Scientific Research Council, 1978. 167 p. illus.

Jointly sponsored by the Tanzania National Scientific Research Council and the Board on Science and Technology for International Development, Commission on International Relations, National Academy of Sciences-National Research Council of the United States.

Abstract in *A.I.D. Research and Development Abstracts*, July 1978, p. 39, and *Government Reports Announcements & Index*, Oct. 13, 1978, p. 162.

Microfiche. [Washington, U.S. Agency for International Development, 1978?] 2 sheets (DLC-Sci RR PN-AAF-415); and [Springfield, Va., National Technical Information Service, 1978] 2 sheets (DLC-Sci RR PB 282941).

1964

————Staff summary report. [Washington], National Academy of Sciences, National Research Council, Board on Science and Technology for International Development, 1977. 49 p.

DNAS-NAE

Abstract in *A.I.D. Research and Development Abstracts*, Apr. 1978, p. 38–39.

Issued also in microfiche. [Washington, U.S. Agency for International Development, 1977?] 1 sheet.　　　DLC-Sci RR PN-AAE-792

Foreign Relations

1965

Dash, Michael E. Inroads into East Africa: the PRC and Tanzania. Military review, Apr. 1976: 58–64. illus., map.　　　Z6723.U35　1976

Published by the U.S. Army Command and General Staff College, Ft. Leavenworth, Kansas.

1966

Nyerere, Julius K. Nyerere speaks about Amin in Tanzanian anniversary speech. *In* U.S. *Joint Publications Research Service.* JPRS 72555. [Springfield, Va., National Technical Information Service, 1979] (Translations on Sub-Saharan Africa, no. 2046) p. 168–172.

Translation of radio report of speech in Swahili, Dec. 9, 1978.

Microfiche. [Washington, Supt. of Docs., U.S. Govt. Print. Off., 1979]

DLC-Micro JPRS 72555

1967

Visit of President Nyerere of Tanzania. Remarks to reporters following the President's departure, August 5, 1977. *In* U.S. *President.* Public papers of the Presidents of the United States. Jimmy Carter. 1977. Washington, U.S. Govt. Print. Off., [1978] p. 1433–1434.　　　J80.A283　1977

President Carter is questioned by reporters concerning the visit.

1968

Visit of President Nyerere of Tanzania. White House statement issued following the conclusion of the meetings between the President and President Nyerere. August 5, 1977. *In* U.S. *President.* Public papers of the Presidents of the United States. Jimmy Carter. 1977. Washington, U.S. Govt. Print. Off., [1978] p. 1434–1435.

J80.A283　1977

Geology, Hydrology, and Mineral Resources

The following items (entries 1969–1972) are listed in chronological order:

1969

Morse, David E. The mineral industry of Tanzania. *In* Minerals yearbook, v. 3, 1976. [Washington, for sale by the Supt. of Docs., U.S. Govt. Print. Off., 1980] p. 1019–1025.

TN23.U612 1976, v. 3

Prepared by the U.S. Bureau of Mines.

1970

————The mineral industry of Tanzania. *In* Minerals yearbook, v. 3, 1977. [Washington, for sale by the Supt. of Docs., U.S. Govt. Print. Off., 1981] p. 919–924.　　　TN23.U612 1977, v. 3

Prepared by the U.S. Bureau of Mines.

1971

————The mineral industry of Tanzania. In Minerals yearbook, v. 3, 1978–79. [Washington, U.S. Govt. Print. Off., 1981] p. 915–920.

TN23.U612 1978–79, v. 3

Prepared by the U.S. Bureau of Mines.

1972

Ambrosio, Suzann C. The mineral industry of Tanzania. *In* Minerals yearbook, v. 3, 1980. [Washington, for sale by the Supt. of Docs., U.S. Govt. Print. Off., 1982] p. 953–957.

TN23.U612 1980, v. 3

Prepared by the U.S. Bureau of Mines.

1972a

Potential groundwater and land resource analysis for planning and development, Arusha region, United Republic of Tanzania. [Washington?], Earth Satellite Corporation, 1975. 243 p.

Prepared for the U.S. Agency for International Development under contract AID/afr-C-1119.

Cited in list prepared by the Development Information Center, AID; not examined.

Health and Nutrition

1973

Hall, Budd L. Mtu ni Afya: Tanzania's health campaign. Washington, Clearinghouse on Development Communication, 1978. 74 p. (Clearinghouse on Development Communication. Information bulletin, no. 9)   DLC

"This study was made possible through financial support from: the Swedish International Development Authority, the Institute of Development Studies, University of Sussex, [and] the International Council for Adult Education."

"The U.S. Agency for International Development has funded the editing, printing, and distribution of this document through a contract between the Office of Education & Human Resources of the Development Support Bureau of AID and the Academy for Educational Development."

Issued also in microfiche. [Washington, U.S. Agency for International Development, 1978?] 1 sheet (PN-AAJ-501); examined in the Development Information Center, AID, Washington, D.C.

1974

Henn, Albert E. Tanzania health sector strategy. Dar es Salaam, Office of Health, Nutrition, and Population, USAID/Tanzania, 1980. [149] p. (in various pagings)

Annex II: A review of Zanzibar's health sector (43 p.).

Abstract in *A.I.D. Research & Development Abstracts*, v. 10, no. 1/2, 1982, p. 45.

Examined in the Development Information Center, Agency for International Development, Washington, D.C.

1975

Lewis, Charles E. Consultant report on the health sector of Tanzania. Los Angeles, Division of General Internal Medicine and Health Services Research, Dept. of Medicine, University of California, 1976. [88] p.

Abstract in *A.I.D. Research and Development Abstracts*, Jan. 1979, p. 27.

Microfiche. [Washington, U.S. Agency for International Development, 1976?] 1 sheet (PN-AAF-646), examined in the Development Information Center, AID, Washington, D.C.

1976

Olson, Howard C., Ronald A. Ward, *and* Earl W. Kerhberg. Considerations in the design of a field trial for tsetse fly control; final report. McLean, Va., American Technical Assistance Corporation, 1974. 81 p. maps. (Contract report OAD-CR-89)

"This report is submitted to fulfill the requirements for the study 'Redesign Field Trial for Tsetse Fly Control,' Work Order No. 11 of Contract no.AII.D/CM/otr-C-73-198, undertaken for the Agency for International Development, through the Office of Agriculture, Technical Assistance Bureau."

Emphasis is on Tanzania.

Microfiche. [Washington, U.S. Agency for International Development, 1974?] 1 sheet.

DLC-Sci RR PN-AAB-245

1977

Rosenfield, Patricia L., *and* Phyllis J. Gestrin. Socio-economic analysis of impact of water projects on schistosomiasis; final report. Washington, Resources for the Future, 1978. [146] p. (in various pagings) maps.

Prepared for the U.S. Agency for International Development.

"A methodology for integrating a schistosomiasis transmission model and associated economic analysis into water resources project planning is described and applied to an area of small-scale water activities (furrow irrigation, cattle watering in ponds) in Misungwi, Tanzania. "—p. ii.

Microfiche. [Washington, U.S. Agency for International Development, 1978?] 2 sheets.

DLC-Sci RR PN-AAG-137

1978

————Socio-economic analysis of impact of water projects on schistosomiasis; results of cost-effective analysis. Washington, Resources for the Future, 1978. [20] p.

Prepared for the U.S. Agency for International Development under contract 931-1133.

1978 (cont.)

Concerns data from Tanzania.

Abstract in *A.I.D. Research and Development Abstracts*, Jan. 1979, p. 30.

Microfiche. [Washington, U.S. Agency for International Development, 1978] 1 sheet.

DLC-Sci RR PN-AAG-057

1979

The Tsetse Research Project; an environmental assessment. [Washington, Office of Agriculture, Bureau for Development Support, Agency for International Development], 1977. [152] p. (in various pagings)

Report prepared by the Environmental Assessment Team, Tsetse Research Project, Tanga, Tanzania.

"This report assesses a project jointly sponsored by A.I.D. and the United Republic of Tanzania to determine the effect of the sterile insect release method on the tsetse fly population of Tanga, Tanzania."—Abstract.

Abstract in *A.I.D. Research and Development Abstracts*, Apr. 1978, p. 30–31.

Microfiche. [Washington, U.S. Agency for International Development, 1977?] 2 sheets.

DLC-Sci RR PN-AAE-794

1980

Williamson, D. Leroy. Report on tsetse research project, Tanga, Tanzania. July/Dec. 1974?+ [s.l.] semiannual.

Prepared under an agreement between the Government of Tanzania and the U.S. Agency for International Development.

L.C. has July/Dec. 1974–Jan./June 1975 in microfiche. [Washington, U.S. Agency for International Development, 1975?] 2 sheets.

DLC-Sci RR PN-AAB-643
PN-AAC-769

Libraries and Library Resources

1981

Munn, Robert F. Improving agricultural library services in Tanzania. [Morgantown?, 1976?] 8 p. illus. ([West Virginia University]. Office of International Programs. Report, no 55)   WvU

Issued in cooperation with North Carolina Agricultural and Technical State University, Greensboro, under U.S. Agency for International Development contract AID/afr-C-1067.

Prepared in conjunction with the Tanzania Agricultural Manpower Project.

1982

Tawete, Felix K. The need for resource sharing among libraries in Tanzania. [s.l.], 1977. 17 p.

Paper prepared for the 1977 IFLA-UNESCO Pre-Session Seminar on Resource Sharing of Libraries in Developing Countries.

Abstract in *Resources in Education*, 1980 annual cumulation, p. 300.

Microfiche. [Arlington, Va., ERIC Document Reproduction Service; prepared for Educational Resources Information Center, National Institute of Education, 1980] 1 sheet.

DLC-Micro ED176760

Politics and Government

1983

Boutta, Djamel. Reality said to contrast flagrently with written reports. *In* U.S. *Joint Publications Research Service*. JPRS 69828. [Springfield, Va., National Technical Information Service, 1977] (Translations on Sub-Saharan Africa, no. 1804) p. 144–153.

Translation of article on the progress of socialism in Tanzania, in *Révolution africaine*, Algiers, Aug. 3–9, 1977, p. 24–31.

Microfiche. [s.l., 1977]

DLC-Micro JPRS 69828

1984

Langellier, Jean-Pierre. Successes, failures of Nyerere's political, economic policies. *In* U.S. *Joint Publications Research Service*. JPRS 76923. [Springfield, Va., National Technical Information Service, 1980] (Sub-Saharan Africa report, no. 92–102.

Translation of article in *Le Monde*, Paris, Oct. 21, 22, 23, 1980.

Microfiche. [s.l., 1980]

DLC-Micro JPRS 76923

1985

Pomonti, Jean-Claude. "Human socialism" losing ground. *In* U.S. *Joint Publications Research Service*. JPRS 68795. [Springfield, Va., National Technical Information Service, 1977] (Translations on Sub-Saharan Africa, no. 1723) p. 29–37.

Translation of article in *Le Monde*, Paris, Feb. 8, 9, 1977.

Microfiche. [s.l., 1977]

DLC-Micro JPRS 68795

Bibliographies

1986

Howell, John B. Tanganyika African National Union: a guide to publications by and about TANU. Washington, General Reference and Bibliography Division, Reader Services Dept., Library of Congress, 1976. 52 p. (Maktaba Afrikana series)

Z7165.T3H68

Compiled in the African Section.

234 entries.

1987

————Zanzibar's Afro-Shirazi Party, 1957–1977: a bibliography. Washington, Library of Congress, 1978. 20 p. (Maktaba Afrikana series)

Z7164.P8H68
Z663.285.Z36

Compiled in the African Section.

85 entries.

Population Studies

1987a

Africa: Tanzania. Selected statistical data by sex. Washington, 1981. 32, 17 p.

Study supported by the U.S. Agency for International Development's Office of Women in Development and Office of Population.

Data assembled by the International Demographic Data Center, U.S. Bureau of the Census.

Among the tables, all based on 1967 data, are the following: unadjusted population by age, sex, and urban/rural residence; population by region, sex, and urban/rural residence; population by ethnic group, sex, and urban/rural residence; population by nationality, sex, and urban/rural residence; urban and rural populations by marital status, age, and sex; number of households; number of literate persons by age, sex, and urban/rural residence; number of persons enrolled in school by age, sex, and urban/rural residence; number of economically active persons by age, sex, and urban/rural residence; economically active population by occupational status, sex, and urban/rural residence.

1988

Country report: Tanzania. [Washington], Interdisciplinary Communications Program, Smithsonian Institution, 1976. [23] p.

Prepared for the U.S. Agency for International Development under contract AID/csd-3598.

Research on the analysis of population problems.

Microfiche. [Washington, U.S. Agency for International Development, 1976?] 1 sheet (PN-AAF-

566); examined in the Development Information Center, AID, Washington, D.C.

1988a

Johnston, Alan. Population profile of the Arusha region. [Dar es Salaam, U.S. AID Mission to Tanzania, 1980] 161 p.

Cited in list prepared by the Development Information Center, U.S. Agency for International Development; not examined.

1989

Kocher, James E. Rural development and demographic change in northeastern Tanzania. *In* New perspectives on the demographic transition; investigators: Robert W. Morgan [and others] Washington, Interdisciplinary Communications Program, Smithsonian Institution, 1976. (Interdisciplinary Communications Program. Occasional monograph, series, no. 4) p. 53–93.

HB871.N47

"ICP work agreement reports."

Prepared for the U.S. Agency for International Development under contract AID/csd-3598.

Issued also in microfiche. [Washington, U.S. Agency for International Development, 1976?] 3 sheets.

DLC-Sci RR PN-AAG-397

1990

————Rural development and fertility change in tropical Africa: evidence from Tanzania. East Lansing, Dept. of Agricultural Economics, Michigan State University, 1979. 95 p. (African rural economy paper, no. 19)

HB1072.9.A3K6

Prepared and published under U.S. Agency for International Development contract AID/afr-C-1261.

Bibliography: p. 92–95.

Abstract in *A.I.D. Research and Development Abstracts*, v. 7, no. 3, 1980, p. 7.

Issued also in microfiche. [Washington, U.S. Agency for International Development, 1979?] 2 sheets.

DLC-Sci RR PN-AAG-633

1991

———— Rural development, health, mortality and fertility in rural northeastern Tanzania. [s.l.] Harvard Institute for International Development, 1980. 123 p.

Prepared for the U.S. Agency for International Development under grant AID/otr-G-1671.

Abstract in *A.I.D. Research & Development Abstracts*, v. 9, no. 3, 1981, p. 54.

Microfiche. [Washington, U.S. Agency for International Development, 1980?] 2 sheets.

DLC-Sci RR PN-AAJ-458

Women

1992

Reynolds, D. R. An appraisal of rural women in Tanzania. [Nairobi], Regional Economic Development Services Office/East Africa, [U.S. Agency for International Development], 1975. 46 p.

Bibliography: p. 44–46.

Examined in the Development Information Center, AID, Washington, D.C.

1993

Stanley, Joyce, *and* Alisa Lundeen. Audio cassette listening forums: a participatory women's development project. [Dar es Salaam?, U.S. AID Mission, 1978?] [110] p. (in various pagings) illus., maps.   DLC

Bibliography: p. 90–92.

The project, focusing on women in the Majengo and Kimundo regions of northern Tanzania, "was an attempt to provide a development program that enabled women to recognize the importance of their role and at the same time encouraged implementation of self-determined action plans primarily related to health and nutrition."—p. ii.

Other Subjects

1994

The American team in Tanzania. *In* U.S. *Dept. of State*. Newsletter, no. 202, June 1978: 36–41. illus.
    JX1.U542 1978

Mainly illustrations of activities of U.S. Embassy personnel in Dar es Salaam.

1995

Bueneman, Ervan. Special report on techniques of aided self-help housing ... some examples of U.S. and overseas experience. [Washington?], Office of International Affairs, Dept. of Housing and Urban Development, [1973?] 24 p. (FAR 17771-N)

Tanzania is covered on p. 13–15.

Examined in the former Foreign Affairs Research Documentation Center, U.S. Dept. of State.

1996

Hawkinson, Annie K. Tanzanian Swahili. Brattleboro, Vt., Experiment in International Living, for ACTION/Peace Corps, 1979. 4 v. illus. (Peace Corps language handbook series)   DPC

Contents: [1] Communications and culture handbook.—[2] Grammar handbook.—[3] Teacher's handbook.—[4] Special skills handbook.

Uganda

General

1997

U.S. *Dept. of State. Bureau of Public Affairs.* Background notes. Uganda. [Washington, for sale by the Supt. of Docs., U.S. Govt. Print. Off.], 1978. 5 p. illus., maps. (U.S. Dept. of State. Department of State publication 7958, rev.)   G59.U5

    L.C. retains only the latest revision.

    For a description of the contents of this publication, see the note to entry 937.

1998

Berry, Leonard, *and* Ellen Huges-Cromwick. Uganda. Worcester, Mass., Program for International Development, Clark University, 1980. 112 p. maps. (Eastern Africa country profiles. Country profile no. 6)   DLC

    Bibliography: p. 110–112.

    "This country profile of Uganda is prepared as one in a series of Eastern African country profiles. They come in response to a request by the United States Agency for International Development to compile succinct statements of principal development issues along with an analysis of the distribution of proverty."—Foreword.

Bibliographies

1999

Gray, Beverly A. Uganda: subject guide to official publications. Washington, Library of Congress, 1977. 271 p.   Z3586.G7

    Compiled in the African Section.

    2,442 entries.

2000

Hoben, Susan J. A select annotated bibliography on social science material for Uganda, followed by an expanded bibliography. [Washington, U.S. Agency for International Development], 1979. [53] p. (in various pagings)

    "The purpose of this bibliography is to identify available, clearly written, non-technical publications in the social sciences that will help USAID personnel and contractors in the Uganda program to plan and implement development assistance programs and projects adapted to the distinctive socio-economic institutions, the culture, and the historic setting of that country."

    Abstract in *A.I.D. Research and Development Abstracts*, Feb. 1981, p. 63–64.

    Microfiche. [Washington, U.S. Agency for International Development, 1979?] 1 sheet.

    DLC-Sci RR PN-AAH-226

2001

Pastorett, Tomma N. Uganda: selected references. Maxwell Air Force Base, Ala., Air University Library, 1977. 18 p.   DLC

Assistance Programs

2002

U.S. *Agency for International Development.* Annual budget submission: Uganda. Washington, U.S. International Development Cooperation Agency.

    Vols. for 1981, 1983 examined in the Development Information Center, AID, Washington, D.C.

2003

——— Country development strategy statement: Uganda. Washington, U.S. International Development Cooperation Agency. annual?

    Vol. for 1982 examined in the Development Information Center, AID, Washington, D.C.

2004

Planning minister expresses disappointment on foreign aid. *In* U.S. *Joint Publications Research Service.* JPRS 74407. [Springfield, Va., National Technical Information Service, 1979] (Sub-Saharan Africa report, no. 2166) p. 117–120.

    Translation of interview with Anthony Ocaya, Minister of Planning and Economic Development

2004 (cont.)
of Uganda, in *Tempo*, Maputo, Sept. 9, 1979, p. 44–47.
Microfiche. [Washington, Supt. of Docs., U.S. Govt. Print. Off., 1979]
DLC-Micro JPRS 74407

2005
Presidential authority re Uganda. Congressional record [daily ed.], 96th Congress, 1st session, v. 125, May 21, 1979; H3476-H3479.
J11.R7 v. 125
Debate in the U.S. House of Representatives on H.R.3897, a bill to enable the President to waive prohibitions on assistance to Uganda "if he determines that the Government of Uganda does not engage in a consistant pattern of gross violations of internationally recognized human rights and that such assistance would further the foreign policy interests of the United States."—p. H3476.

Commerce

2006
Bretton Woods Agreement Act amendments of 1978. Congressional record, 95th Congress, 2d session, v. 124, July 28, 1978: 23229–23269.
J11.R5 v. 124
Debate in U.S. Senate includes extensive comments on American trade with Uganda and an amendment to impose a trade embargo against that country (p. 23245–23255).

2007
Market share reports. Country series: Uganda, 1971–75. [Washington], U.S. Dept. of Commerce; for sale by the National Technical Information Service, Springfield, Va., [1977] 58 p.
Indicates the United States share of the market in Uganda for various products compared to the shares for Belgium-Luxemburg, France, Federal Republic of Germany, Great Britain, Italy, Netherlands, Sweden, and Japan.
Microfiche. [Washington, Congressional Information Service, 1977?]
DLC-Micro ASI:77 2016-1.82

2008
Market share reports. Country series: Uganda, 1975 79. [Washington], International Trade Administration, U.S. Dept. of Commerce; for sale by the National Technical Information Service, Springfield, Va., [1979] 55 p.
Includes same comparative data as in *Market Share Reports. Country Series: Uganda, 1975–79* (entry 2007).

Microfiche. [Washington, Congressional Information Service, 1979?]
DLC-Micro ASI:81 2046-2.82

2009
The Ugandan connection. Congressional record, 95th Congress, 2d session, v. 124, May 3, 1978: 12311–12316.
J11.R5 v. 124
Remarks, primarily by Senator Frank Church, in U.S. Senate on American trade with Uganda.
Includes an article on this issue from the *New York Times*.

Economic Conditions

2010
Country's economic recovery problems detailed. *In* U.S. *Joint Publications Research Service*. JPRS 75680. [Springfield, Va., National Technical Information Service, 1980] (Sub-Saharan Africa report, no. 2246) p. 87–91.
Article in *The Star*, Johannesburg, Apr. 8, 1980, p. 23.
Microfiche. [s.l., 1980]
DLC-Micro JPRS 75680

2011
Rukandema, F. M. Prices and cotton supply analysis in Uganda. Ithaca, New York State College of Agriculture and Life Sciences, Cornell University, [1973] 35 p. (Cornell international agriculture mimeograph 43)
Bibliography: p. 34–35.
Microfiche. [Washington, U.S. Agency for International Development, 1973?] 1 sheet.
DLC-Sci RR PN-AAA-703

2012
Schultheis, Michael J. Economics and economic research in Uganda during the Amin period. Ithaca, Dept. of Agricultural Economics, New York State College of Agriculture and Life Sciences, Cornell University, 1974. 32 p. (Cornell agricultural economics staff paper, no. 74-27)
Research supported in part by the U.S. Agency for International Development.
Microfiche. ([Washington, U.S. Agency for International Development, 1974?] 1 sheet)
DLC-Sci RR PN-AAB-485

2013
Turner, John A. Child quality and income distribution in a less developed country. [Washington, Population Studies Unit, Center for Advanced Studies, General Electric-TEMPO], 1975. 21 leaves. (FAR 27024-N)

2013(cont.)

Prepared for the U.S. Agency for International Development.

Focus is on male secondary school graduates in Uganda.

Examined in the former Foreign Affairs Research Documentation Center, U.S. Dept. of State.

Education

2014

Gould, W. T. S. Planning the location of schools: Ankole District, Uganda. Paris, UNESCO, International Institute for Educational Planning, 1973. 88 p.

Abstract in *Research in Education*, July 1974, p. 51.

Microfiche. [Arlington, Va., ERIC Document Reproduction Service; prepared for Educational Resources Information Center, National Institute of Education, 1974] 1 sheet.

DLC-Micro ED088190

Issued also as part of the author's *Movement to School in Ankole, Uganda* (LA1569.A54G68).

2015

Heyneman, Stephen P. Influences on academic achievement: a comparison of results from Uganda and more industrialized societies. Washington, Social Research Group, The George Washington University, [1975?] 20 p.

Paper presented at the annual meeting of the American Education Research Association, 1975.

Abstract in *Resources in Education*, Aug. 1975, p. 170.

Microfiche. [Arlington, Va., ERIC Document Reproduction Service; prepared for Educational Resources Information Center, National Institute of Education, 1975] 1 sheet.

DLC-Micro ED104764

Foreign Relations

2016

U.S. *Congress. House. Committee on Foreign Affairs. Subcommittee on Africa.* U.S. policy toward Uganda: hearing, Ninety-sixth Congress, first session, April 26, 1979. Washington, U.S. Govt. Print. Off., 1979. 22 p.　　KF27.F625　1979
J74.A23　96th
Cong., House Comm.
For. Aff., v. 18

Stephen J. Solarz, chairman.

A review of the relationship between the United States and Uganda in the wake of the downfall of Idi Amin.

2017

U.S. *Congress. House. Committee on International Relations. Subcommittee on Africa.* United States-Uganda relations: hearings before the Subcommittees on Africa, International Organizations, and International Economic Policy and Trade of the Committee on International Relations, House of Representatives, Ninety-fifth Congress, second session. Washington, U.S. Govt. Print. Off., 1978. 343 p.　　KF27.I54914　1978
J74.A23 95th
Cong., House Comm.
Inter. Rel., v. 68

Charles C. Diggs, Jr., chairman, Subcommittee on Africa.

Donald M. Fraser, chairman, Subcommittee on International Organizations.

Jonathan B. Bingham, chairman, Subcommittee on International Economic Policy and Trade.

Hearings held Feb. 1 – Apr. 26, 1978.

Among the prepared statements and material submitted for the record are the following:

Comparison of United States policies toward Uganda and South Africa, submitted by the Department of State. p. 73–75.

Mazrui, Ali A. Violation of human rights in Uganda: is it a case for international sanctions? p. 192–207.

Among the appendixes is the following:

Appendix 4. Imports of Ugandan coffee by company, in pounds and dollar amounts, for 1975 and 1976 combined. p. 310–311.

2018

Uganda: US policy. [Washington], Bureau of Public Affairs, Dept. of State, 1978. [2] p.　　DLC

At head of title: Gist—a quick reference aid on U.S. foreign relations primarily for Government use.

United States—Economic Sanctions

2019

Aid to Uganda. Congressional record [daily ed.], 96th Congress, 1st session, v. 125, May 7, 1979: S5395-5418.　　J11.R7 v. 125

Consideration in the U.S. Senate of S.1019 to amend the International Development and Food Assitance Act of 1978 and the Foreign Assistance and Related Appropriations Act, 1979, by striking out certain prohibitions relating to Uganda.

2020

S.1018—repeal of certain provisions relating to the Republic of Uganda. Congressional record, 96th Congress, 1st session, v. 125, Apr. 26, 1979: 8767-8769.   J11.R5 v. 125

Remarks in the U.S. Senate, primarily by Senator Mark O. Hatfield, calling for the removal of United States trade sanctions.

Entebbe Raid (1976)

2021

Congress should take a strong position in support of the Israeli rescue mission at Entebbe Airport and a new treaty more effectively limiting terrorism. Congressional record, 94th Congress, 2d session, v. 122, Aug. 3, 1976: 25342-25349.

J11.R5 v. 122

Remarks in the U.S. House of Representatives. Includes text of H. Con. Res. 700 commending the Israeli action.

2022

Pastorett, Tomma N. The Entebbe Raid: selected references. Maxwell Air Force Base, Ala., Air University Library, 1977. 3 p.   DLC

2023

U.S. gives views in Security Council debate on Israeli rescue of hijacking victims at Entebbe Airport. *In* U.S. *Dept. of State.* The Department of State bulletin, v. 75, no. 1936, Aug. 2, 1976: 181-186.

JX232.A33 v. 75

Statements by U.S. Representatives William W. Scranton, July 12, 1976, and W. Tapley Bennett, Jr., July 14, 1976.

Health and Nutrition

2024

McGovern, George. Hunger in Africa. Congressional record, [daily ed.], 96th Congress, 2d session, v. 126, June 11, 1980: S6684-S6687.

J11.R7 v. 126

Remarks in the U.S. Senate with emphasis on Uganda.

Includes article from the *Washington Post.*

2025

Solarz, Stephen J. Five hundred a day die from hunger in Uganda. Congressional record [daily ed.], 96th Congress, 2d session, v. 126, June 11, 1980: E2895-E2897.   J11.R7 v. 126

Extension of remarks in the U.S. House of Representatives.

Includes articles from the *Washington Post.*

Human Rights

2026

U.S. *Congress. House. Committee on International Relations.* Condemning violations of human rights by the Government of Uganda, May 31, 1978: report together with supplementary views (to accompany H. Con. Res 612) [Washington, U.S. Govt. Print. Off., 1978] 10 p.   DLC-LL

Report submitted by Representative Charles C. Diggs, Jr.

At head of title: 95th Congress, 2d session. House of Representatives. Report no. 95-1233.

2027

U.S. *Congress. Senate. Committee on Foreign Relations.* Recent deaths in Uganda: report together with additional views (to accompany S. Res. 175). [Washington, 1977] 8 p.   DLC-LL

Report submitted by Senator John Sparkman.

At head of title: 95th Congress, 1st session. Senate. Report no. 95-222.

The purpose of the resolution was "to express the sense of the Senate that the actions of the current regime in Uganda violating the human rights of its citizens and residents deserve condemnation of the world community and by the Organization of African Unity."

Includes "additional views" of Senator Clifford P. Case.

2028

U.S. *Congress. Senate. Committee on Foreign Relations. Subcommittee on Foreign Economic Policy.* Uganda: the human rights situation: hearings, Ninety-fifth Congress, second session ... June 15, 21, 26, 1978. Washington, U.S. Govt. Print. Off., 1978. 129 p.   KF26.F6364   1978a

J74.A23 95th

Cong., Sen. Comm.

For. Rel., v. 55

Frank Church, chairman.

In his opening remarks, Chairman Church indicates that the purpose of the hearings is "to look into the human rights policies of Uganda and what role the United States and American companies have played in maintaining the regime of Idi Amin in power."—p. 1.

2029

Clark, Dick. Ugandan atrocities. Congressional record, 95th Congress, 1st session, v. 123, Sept. 13,

2029 (cont.)

1977: 29117–29119.   J11.R5 v. 123
Remarks in the U.S. Senate.
Includes article from the *New York Times*.

2030

Condemning violations of human rights by the Government of Uganda. Congressional record, 95th Congress, 2d session, v. 124, June 12, 1978: 17174–17180.   J11.R5 v. 124
Remarks in the U.S. House of Representatives.

2031

Hatfield, Mark O. Atrocities in Uganda. Congressional record, 95th Congress, 2d session, v. 124, Apr. 6, 1978: 8973–8974.   J11.R5 v. 124
Remarks in the U.S. Senate.

2032

———— Uganda. Congressional record, 95th Congress, 2d session, v. 124, Apr. 3, 1978: 8368–8369.   J11.R5 v. 124
Remarks in the U.S. Senate on repression in Uganda and on the need for the United States to lead a boycott by western nations of Ugandan products, especially coffee.

2033

Human rights in Uganda. Memorandum on the normalization of U.S.-Ugandan trade relations. *In* U.S *President*. Public papers of the Presidents of the United States. Jimmy Carter. 1979. Washington, U.S. Govt. Print. Off., [1980] p. 867.
          J80.A283   1979
States that the "Government of Uganda is no longer committing a consistent pattern of gross violations of human rights."

2034

McDonald, Larry. African atrocity: the tyrant of Uganda. Congressional record, 94th Congress, 2d session, v. 122, Sept. 14, 1976: 30349–30351.
          J11.R5 v. 122
Extension of remarks in the U.S. House of Representatives.
Includes article from *New York Review*.

2035

Pease, Donald J. The case against Idi Amin. Congressional record, 95th Congress, 2d session, v. 124, Feb. 21, 1978: 4024–4026.   J11.R5 v. 124
Extension of remarks in the U.S. House of Representatives.
Includes text of his testimony during a House hearing on United States policy toward Uganda.

2036

Reed, W. Cyrus. The political context of human rights in Uganda. Notre Dame, Ind., University of Notre Dame, 1977. [32] leaves. (FAR 28005-N)
Prepared for the Area Studies Program, University of Notre Dame.
Presented at the U.S. Naval Academy Foreign Affairs Conference, Annapolis, Md., 1977.
Examined in the former Foreign Affairs Research Documentation Center, U.S. Dept. of State.

2037

Stone, Richard B. Down with Amin. Congressional record, 95th Congress, 1st session, v. 123, June 17, 1977: 19637–19639.   J11.R5 v. 123
Remarks in the U.S. Senate.
Includes editorial from the *Washington Post* and a statement by Senator Clifford P. Case, "With Respect to the Recent Deaths in Uganda."

Politics and Government

2038

Binaisa, Godfrey. President addresses rally marking UNLF anniversary. *In* U.S. *Joint Publications Research Service*. JPRS 75545. [Springfield, Va., National Technical Information Service, 1980] (Sub-Saharan Africa report, no. 2238) p. 72–76.
Speech by the President of Uganda on the first anniversary of the Ugandan National Liberation Front, broadcast on the Kampala Domestic Service, Mar. 25, 1980.
Microfiche. [s.l., 1980]
          DLC-Micro JPRS 75545.

2039

Constitution of Uganda People's Congress published. *In* U.S. *Joint Publications Research Service*. JPRS 76932. [Springfield, Va., National Technical Information Service, 1980] (Sub-Saharan Africa report, no. 2328) p. 46–54.
Article in *Uganda Times*, Kampala, Oct. 30, 31, and Nov. 1, 1980.
Microfiche. [s.l., 1980]
          DLC-Micro JPRS 76932

2040

Defense minister: army to be demobilized, reorganized. *In* U.S. *Joint Publications Research Service*. JPRS 74407. [Springfield, Va., National Technical Information Service, 1979] (Sub-Saharan Africa report, no. 2166) p. 113–116.
Translation of interview with Yoweri Museveni, Minister of Defense of Uganda, in *Tempo*, Maputo, Sept. 9, 1979, p. 47–49.

2040 (cont.)

Microfiche. [Washington, Supt. of Docs., U.S. Govt. Print. Off., 1979]

DLC-Micro JPRS 74407

2041

Langellier, Jean-Pierre. Chaos, disillusion 6 months after Amin's fall. *In* U.S. *Joint Publications Research Service.* JPRS 74608. [Springfield, Va., National Technical Information Service, 1979] (Sub-Saharan Africa report, no. 2179) p. 60–64.

Translation of article in *Le Monde*, Paris, Oct. 7–8, 1979, p. 1, 3.

Microfiche. [s.l., 1979]

DLC-Micro JPRS 74608

2042

Manifesto of Democratic Party published. *In* U.S. *Joint Publications Research Service.* JPRS 77053. [Springfield, Va., National Technical Information Service, 1980] (Sub-Saharan Africa report, no. 2336) p. 49–54.

Article in *The Citizen*, Kampala, Nov. 18, 24, 1980.

Microfiche. [s.l., 1981]

DLC-Micro JPRS 77053

2043

Memorandum outlines overthrow of Ugandan regime. *In* U.S. *Joint Publications Research Service.* JPRS 68710. [Springfield, Va., National Technical Information Service, 1977] (Translations on Sub-Saharan Africa, no. 1717) p. 127–139.

The alleged text of a statement by Milton Obote, broadcast over the Kampala domestic service, Feb. 16, 1977.

Microfiche. [s.l., 1977]

DLC-Micro JPRS 68710

2044

Ndonzuau Nzonzila. Zairian reports on trip to Uganda. *In* U.S. *Joint Publications Research Service.* JPRS 70987. [Springfield, Va., National Technical Information Service, 1978] (Translations on Sub-Saharan Africa, no. 1915) p. 101–108.

Translation of article in *Elima*, Kinshasa, Feb. 25, 1978, p. 3.

Microfiche. [Washington, Supt. of Docs., U.S. Govt. Print. Off., 1978]

DLC-Micro JPRS 70987

2045

UNLF political manifestio published. *In* U.S. *Joint Publications Research Service.* JPRS 74537. [Springfield, Va., National Technical Information Service, 1979] (Sub-Saharan Africa report, no. 2175) p. 81–87.

From *Uganda Times*, Kampala, Oct. 12, 1979, p. 4–5.

Microfiche. [Washington, Supt. of Docs., U.S. Govt. Print. Off., 1979]

DLC-Micro JPRS 74537

Other Subjects

2046

Adams, Bert N., Cecil Pereira, *and* Mike Bristow. Ugandan Asians in exile: household and kinship in the resettlement crisis. [s.l.], 1975. 17 leaves. (FAR 23002-N)

Research supported by the National Science Foundation.

Paper presented at the annual meeting of the American Sociological Association, 1975.

Examined in the former Foreign Affairs Research Documentation Center, U.S. Dept. of State.

2047

Ferguson, Donald S., *and* Thomas T. Poleman. Modernizing African animal production: the Uganda tick control project. Ithaca, Dept. of Agricultural Economics, New York State College of Agriculture and Life Sciences, Cornell University, 1973. 139 p. maps. (Cornell international agriculture mimeograph 42)

Microfiche. [Washington, U.S. Agency for International Development, 1973?] 2 sheets.

DLC-Sci RR PN-RAA-407

2048

Kiapi, Abraham. Law and population in Uganda. Medford, Mass., Law and Population Programme, Fletcher School of Law and Diplomacy, Tufts University, 1977. 53 p. (Law and population monograph series, no. 42) DLC-LL

"The Law and Population Programme and its field work are supported in part by the International Planned Parenthood Federation, the United Nations Fund for Population Activities, and the U.S. Agency for International Development."

Issued also in microfiche. [Washington, U.S. Agency for International Development, 1977?] 1 sheet. DLC-Sci RR PN-AAF-172

2049

Pollnac, Richard B. Cognitive variability and its sociocultural correlates among the Baganda. Ethos, v. 3, spring 1975: 22–40. GN270.E85

Based on field research supported in part by a grant from the U.S. Office of Education.

Abstract in *A.I.D. Research and Development Abstracts*, Oct. 1976, p. 36.

Issued also in microfiche. [Washington, U.S.

2049 (cont.)
Agency for International Development, 1975?]
1 sheet.   DLC-Sci RR PN-AAC-191

2050
——— Intra-cultural variability in the structure of
the subjective color lexicon in Buganda. American
ethnologist, v. 2, Feb. 1975: 89–109.
GN1.A53
Based on field research supported in part by a
grant from the U.S. Office of Education.
Abstract in *A.I.D. Research and Development
Abstracts*, Apr. 1977, p. 36.

Issued also in microfiche. [Washington, U.S.
Agency for International Development, 1975?]
1 sheet.   DLC-Sci RR PN-AAC-194

2051
Rudran, Rasanayagam. Socioecology of the blue
monkeys (cercopithecus mitis stuhlmanni) of the
Kibale Forest, Uganda. Washington, Smithsonian
Institution Press, 1978. 88 p. illus. (Smithsonian
Institution. Smithsonian contributions to zoology,
no. 249)   QL1.S54 no. 249
Bibliography: p. 86–88.

Southern Africa

General

2052

U.S. *Agency for International Development*. A report to the Congress on development needs and opportunities for cooperation in southern Africa. [Washington], 1979. 162 p. map.

An overview of conditions in southern Africa, emphasizing demography, economic development, education, agriculture, transportation, communications, mining, manufacturing, health, labor migration, and the refugee problem, followed by individual reports on Botswana, Lesotho, Swaziland, Zambia, Malawi, Mozambique, Angola, Namibia, and Zimbabwe.

Abstract in *A.I.D. Research and Development Abstracts*, v. 8, no. 2, 1980, p. 25.

Microfiche. [Washington, U.S. Agency for International Development, 1979?] 2 sheets.

DLC-Sci RR PN-AAH-150

Note: Annex A of this report consists of separate volumes on the development needs and potential of the emerging nations of southern Africa; these volumes are entered in this bibliography under each country, as follows: Angola (entry 2165), Botswana (entry 2345), Lesotho (entry 2395), Malawi (entry 2445), Mozambique (entry 2467), Nambia (entry 2551), Swaziland (entry 2801), Zambia (entry 2833), and Zimbabwe (entry 2896). Annex B consists of separate volumes on major topics; these are entered as follows: Agriculture (entry 2062), Health (entry 2131), Labor Migration (entry 2135), Manpower (entry 2160), Manufacturing (entry 2082), Mining (entry 2128), Refugees (entry 2155), Transport/Telecommunications (entry 2081), and Urban and Shelter Needs (entry 2159).

2053

U.S. *Agency for International Development. Southern Africa Task Force*. A framework for U.S. assistance in southern Africa: country resource papers, submitted by the Office of Eastern and Southern Africa Affairs, Bureau for Africa, Agency for International Development; prepared by Southern Africa Task Force. Washington, 1977. 9 v. maps.

HC900.U54 1977

Includes bibliographies.

Added t.p. has title: Transition in Southern Africa.

Prepared under contract AID/afr-C-1142, etc., by Tim Rose and others.

On cover: "This paper was prepared to provide background information on the issues and opportunities for economic assistance to the countries of Southern Africa thru and following the periods of transition in Zimbabwe and Nambia. It includes social, geographic, economic, and political information."

Contents: [1] Angola [by] Joseph Miller.—[2] Botswana [by] Gerald A. Epstein.—[3] Lesotho [by] Tim Rose.—[4] Malawi [by] Philip W. Moeller. [5] Mozambique [by] Harry Carr.—[6] Namibia [by] Stephen C. Wilcox.—[7] Rhodesia [by] Margarita K. Dobert, Stanislaw Wellisz, and Stephen C. Wilcox.—[8] Swaziland [by] Tim Rose.—[9] Zambia [by] Roger A. Sedjo.

Abstracts of each number in *A.I.D. Research and Development Abstracts*, July 1978, p. 29–31.

Issued also in microfiche. [Washington, U.S. Agency for International Development, 1977?]

[1] Angola. 2 sheets (DLC-Sci RR PN-AAF-090);

[2] Botswana. 2 sheets (DLC-Sci RR PN-AAF-096);

[3] Lesotho. 2 sheets (DLC-Sci RR PN-AAF-092);

[4] Malawi. 2 sheets (DLC-Sci RR PN-AAF-093);

[5] Mozambique. 2 sheets (DLC-Sci RR PN-AAF-095);

[6] Namibia. 2 sheets (DLC-Sci RR PN-AAF-098);

[7] Rhodesia. 2 sheets (DLC-Sci RR PN-AAF-094);

[8] Swailand. 2 sheets (DLC-Sci RR PN-AAF-091);

[9] Zambia. 2 sheets (DLC-Sci RR PN-AAF-097)

2054

Baker, Donald G. Zimbabwe and Namibia. [s.l.], 1977. [123] p. (in various pagings) (Transition problems in a developing nation [Namibia] Occasional paper, no. 9)

Prepared for the African-American Scholars

2054 (cont.)

Council and the U.S. Agency for International Development under subcontract AID/afr-C-1254.

Contents: [1] Namibia: an overview.—[2] Zimbabwe and Namibia: development problems and prospects.—[3] Zimbabwe, Namibia and external links: independence and interdependence.

Abstract in *A.I.D. Research and Development Abstracts*, Oct. 1978, p. 38.

Microfiche. [Washington, U.S. Agency for International Development, 1977?] 2 sheets.

DLC-Sci RR PN-AAF-263

2055

Bryant, Coralie, Richard N. Blue, *and* Tom De Gregori. Planning, budgeting, and management issues in Zambia, Malawi, and Swaziland. [Washington, Agency for International Development] 1979. [71] p. (U.S. Agency for International Development. Development Studies Program. Case studies in development assistance, no. 4)

Prepared for the Southern Africa Development Analysis Program.

Microfiche. [Washington, U.S. Agency for International Development, 1979?] 1 sheet.

DLC-Sci RR PN-AAG-901

2056

Southern Africa Project. Anticipation of economic and humanitarian needs: transition problems of developing nations in southern Africa: final report [by] Samuel C. Adams, Jr., project director; sponsored by the African-American Scholars Council under contract with the Agency for International Development (contract number C-1254). [Washington], The Council, 1977. 338, [165] leaves. maps.

HC517.S7S66   1977

At head of title: Zimbabwe, Namibia.

Bibliography: leaves [12]–[30] (3d group).

Introductory chapters on both Zimbabwe and Namibia cover historical and political background, economic factors, and human resources. These are followed by chapters outlining transition and development problems with sections on "possible U.S. response to development assistance" needs. The appendices consist of statistical tables and maps on population, language usage, migration, and education, plus an annotated bibliography on Southern Africa, financial data on international assistance to Zimbabwe and Namibia, and a list of institutions with research, education and training capabilities related to the region. Information is also given on Zimbabwean and Namibian refugees/exiles, indicating numbers and locations, and the number of students from these two states in other countries.

Abstract in *A.I.D. Research and Development Abstracts*, Oct. 1978, p. 24.

Issued also in microfiche. [Washington, U.S. Agency for International Development, 1977?] 6 sheets.   DLC-Sci RR PN-AAF-099

Bibliographies

2057

AFRIECON/SADAP accessions bulletin. no. 1-18/19. May 30, 1978–Feb. 28, 1979. Washington, African Bibliographic Center. biweekly.

"A bi-weekly listing of recent acquisitions by the African Bibliographic Center (ABC) of publications relevant to the Southern Africa Development Analysis Project (SADAP) of the U.S. Agency for International Development."—Feb. 28, 1979 issue.

Superseded by *SADEX* (entry 2059).

Complete set of issues examined in the African Bibliographic Center, Washington, D.C.

2058

Goshen, Carolyn J. Southern Africa: a select bibliography of bibliographies for development. [Washington], African Bibliographic Center, [1979] 8 leaves.

DLC

"Produced for the Southern Africa Development Analysis Project under the U.S. Agency for International Development contract number AID/afr-C-1421."

2059

SADEX. v. 1+ June/July 1979+ Washington, African Bibliographic Center. bimonthly.

HC900.A1S23

Supersedes *AFRIECON/SADAP Accessions Bulletin* (entry 2057).

"*SADEX* is produced in conjunction with the Southern Africa Development Information/Documentation Exchange (SADEX) project under a contract from the Africa Bureau of the U.S. Agency for International Development (AID) to the African Bibliographic Center."—June/July 1979, p. i.

Designed as an "information and documentation guide" including bibliographic references focusing on the nine nations that participate in the Southern African Development Coordination Conference—Angola, Botswana, Lesotho, Malawi, Mozambique, Swaziland, Tanzania, Zambia, and Zimbabwe.

L.C. has June/July 1979+

Agriculture

2060

Anderson, Dale G., *and* Donald Jack. Grain storage problems and needs in Lesotho and Botswana.

2060 (cont.)

[Manhattan, Food and Feed Grain Institute, Kansas State University], 1978. 102 p. illus., maps. (Grain storage, processing, and marketing report, no. 73)   DNAL

Cited in a publications list prepared by the Food and Feed Grain Institute as printed under contract for the U.S. Agency for international Development.

Held by DNAL's District of Columbia Branch.

2061

Doggett, Clinton L. Land tenure and agricultural development in Lesotho and Swaziland: a comparative analysis. [Washington?], Agriculture/Rural Development Division, Bureau for Africa, [Agency for International Development], 1980. 62 p.

Bibliography: p. 57–62.

Abstract in *A.I.D. Research & Development Abstracts*, v. 10, no. 1/2, 1982, p. 1.

Examined in the Development Information Center, AID, Washington, D.C.

2062

Jansma, J. Dean. Regional overview of development concerns in the agricultural sector of southern Africa. [Washington?], South-East Consortium for International Development, [1979] 48 p.

Issued in cooperation with the U.S. Dept. of Agriculture.

Cover title: *A Report to the Congress on Development Needs and Opportunities for Cooperation in Southern Africa. Annex B: Agriculture.*

Prepared at background material for a U.S. Agency for International Development-sponsored Colloquium on Development Issues and Opportunities for Cooperation in Southern Africa, Jan. 8–10, 1979.

Abstract in *A.I.D. Research and Development Abstracts*, v. 8, no. 2, 1980, p. 26.

Microfiche. [Washington, U.S. Agency for International Development, 1979?] 1 sheet.
                                    DLC-Sci RR PN-AAH-160

2063

Johnson, Robert W. Tobacco production and trade in southern Africa. [Washington] U.S. Dept. of Agriculture, Foreign Agricultural Service, 1975. 11 p. (U.S. Foreign Agricultural Service. FAS-M, 263)   S21.Z2383 no. 263

Covers Rhodesia, Malawi, Zambia, Tanzania, Uganda, Kcnya, Malagasy Republic, Zaire, South Africa, Mozambique, and Angola.

Abstract in *American Statistical Index*, 1975, Abstracts, p. 137.

Issued also in microfiche. [Washington, Congressional Information Service, 1975?]
                                    DLC-Micro ASI:75   1926-1.61

2064

Regional overview of development concerns in the agricultural sector of southern Africa. [s.l., 1979?] 68 leaves.

Apparently issued for the U.S. Agency for International Development.

Examined in the Development Information Center, AID, Washington, D.C.

2065

Southern hemisphere citrus production up in 1980; northern hemisphere also rose in 1979/80. Washington, U.S. Dept. of Agriculture, Foreign Agricultural Service, 1980. 21 p. (Foreign agriculture circular. Fresh and processed citrus fruits, FCF 2-80)   S21.F615

Includes information on citrus production in southern Africa.

Note: Additional reports and statistics on citrus production in Africa are given in other numbers in the Fresh and Processed Citrus Fruit subseries of the Foreign Agriculture Circular.

Assistance Programs

2066

U.S. *Agency for International Development.* Annual budget submission: Southern Africa regional. Washington, U.S. International Development Cooperation Agency.

Vols. for 1977–79, 1982+ examined in the Development Information Center, AID, Washington, D.C.

2067

——— Southern Africa regional country development strategy statement. Washington, U.S. International Development Cooperation Agency. annual?

Vols. for 1982+ examined in the Development Information Center, AID, Washington, D.C.

2068

U.S. *Agency for International Development. Bureau for Africa. Office of Eastern and Southern Africa Affairs.* A framework for United States assistance programs in Southern Africa. [Washington?], 1977. 88 p. maps.

A summary of findings on Angola, Botswana, Lesotho, Malawi, Mozambique, Namibia, Rhodesia, Swaziland, and Zambia.

Abstract in *A.I.D. Research and Development Abstracts*, July 1978, p. 29.

2068 (cont.)

Microfiche. [Washington, U.S. Agency for International Development, 1977?] 2 sheets.

DLC-Sci RR PN-AAF-100

2068a

U.S. *General Accounting Office.* Meeting U.S. political objects through economic aid in the Middle East and southern Africa: report to the Congress, by the Comptroller General of the United States. Washington, 1979. 42 p. maps.

HC415.15.U54 1979

"ID-79-23."

"B-125029."

2069

African Bibliographic Center. Proceedings of the Agency for International Development colloquium "Development needs and opportunities for cooperation in southern Africa." Washington, [1979] 204 leaves.

Colloquium held in the U.S. Dept. of State, Jan. 8–10, 1979.

Examined in the African Bibliographic Center, Washington, D.C.

2070

Association of Black Foundation Executives. Report of the ABFE Task Force visit to Southern Africa: Zambia, Botswana, and Lesotho, July 6–July 30, 1977. [Washington, 1977?] 48 p.

Prepared for the Bureau of Educational and Cultural Affairs, Office of African Programs, U.S. Dept. of State.

Report initiated "to help create, in the philanthropic community, a climate for increasing and improving foundation giving in Africa."

Cited in *AFRIECON/SADAP Accessions Bulletin*, no. 1, May 30, 1978, p. 3.

2071

Correl, Frank, D., Joseph Kovach, *and* William J. Siffin. Southern Africa Development Personnel and Training Project (SADPT); mid-project evaluation. [Washington?], Agency for International Development, 1976. 54 p.

Project focusing on Botswana, Lesotho, and Swaziland to train local personnel to replace expatriate advisors.

Examined in the Development Information Center, AID, Washington, D.C.

2072

Diggs, Charles C. Southern African cooperation: an opportunity for the West. Congressional record [daily ed.], 96th Congress, 1st session, v. 125, Sept. 19, 1979: H8202–H8203. J11.R7 v. 125

Remarks in the U.S. House of Representatives concerning the first Southern African Development Coordination Conference, July 3–4, 1979, Arusha, Tanzania.

Includes text of address to the Conference by Sir Seretse Khama, President of Botswana.

2073

Foreign assistance appropriations, 1977. Congressional record, 94th congress, 2d session, v. 122, Sept. 1, 1976: 29487–29489. J11.R5 v. 122

U.S. Senate discussion of aid to southern Africa; appended is report, *Botswana: A Summary of Development Priorities, Constraints, and Prospects.*

2074

International Development Cooperation Act of 1979. Congressional record, 96th Congress, 1st session, v. 125, Apr. 9, 1979: 7750–7750.

J11.R5 v. 125

Debate in the U.S. House of Representatives regarding assistance to Mozambique, Angola, Tanzania, and Zambia.

2075

International Security Assistance Act of 1977. Congressional record, 95th Congress, 1st session, v. 123, May 24, 1977: 16171–16186. J11.R5 v. 123

Includes debate in the U.S. House of Representatives on assistance to southern African nations and the question of majority rule in Rhodesia.

2076

International Security Assistance and Arms Export Control Act of 1977. Congressional record, 95th Congress, 1st session, v. 123, June 15, 1977: 19289–19298. J11.R5 v. 123

Debate in the U.S. Senate on assistance to southern Africa.

2077

Kornegay, Francis A. Information & documentation for development in Southern Africa: a Southern African technical and scientific information and documentation network. Washington, African Bibliographic Center, 1978. 28 leaves. (AFRIECON/SADAP information memorandum) DLC

Findings of an acquisition trip and survey of information/documentation, research, and publishing activities on Southern Africa prepared under contract to the Bureau for Africa, U.S. Agency for International Development. Based on findings in Kenya, Zambia, Botswana, Lesotho, South Africa, Great Britain, Netherlands, Federal Republic of Germany, Sweden, and Brazil.

2078

———— Southern Africa: a guide to selected information & documentation resource centers for development. Washington, African Bibliographic Center, 1979. 11 p.   DLC

Produced for the Southern Africa Development Analysis Project (SADAP) of the U.S. Agency for International Development.

Communications and Transporation

2079

[U.S. *Central Intelligence Agency*] Principal railroads and ports of Southern Africa. [Washington, 1977] col. map.   G8481.P3   1977.U5

Scale ca. 1 : 7,500,000.

"503386 8-77 (542522)."

2080

Cannell, Roger S., *and* William R. Thomas. A program for planning: regional transportation in Southern Africa. East Orange, N.J., Louis Berger International, 1976.

Prepared for the Office of East and Southern African Affairs, Bureau for Africa, U.S. Agency for International Development.

Covers Zambia, Botswana, Malawi, Rhodesia, and Namibia.

Cited in *AFRIECON/SADAP Accessions Bulletin*, no. 1, May 30, 1978, p. 2.

2081

Le Bel, Allen, *and* Philip W. Moeller. Transportation and telecommunications in the Southern Africa region. [s.l.], Pacific Consultants, [1979?] 450 leaves. maps.

Prepared for the U.S. Agency for International Development under contract AID/afr-C-1424.

Bibliography: p. 431–440.

Cover title: *A Report to the Congress on Development Needs and Opportunities for Cooperation in Southern Africa. Annex B: Transport/ Telecommunications.*

Abstract in *A.I.D. Research and Development Abstracts*, v. 8, no. 2, 1980, p. 29.

Microfiche. [Washington, U.S. Agency for International Development, 1979?] 5 sheet.

DLC-Sci RR PN-AAH-176

Economic Conditions

2082

Manufacturing in the southern Africa region. [s.l.], Pacific Consultants, 1978. 241 p.

Prepared for the U.S. Agency for International Development under contract AID/afr-C-1424.

Cover title: *A Report to the Congress on Development Needs and Opportunities for Cooperation in Southern Africa. Annex B: Manufacturing.*

Abstract in *A.I.D. Research and Development Abstracts*, v. 8, no. 2, 1980, p. 28.

Microfiche. [Washington, U.S. Agency for International Development, 1978?] 3 sheets.

DLC-Sci RR PN-AAH-173

2083

U.S. business involvement in Southern Africa. *In* Rovine, Arthur W. Digest of United States practice in international law. 1973. [Washington], Office of the Legal Adviser, Dept. of State; [for sale by the Supt. of Docs., U.S. Govt. Print. Off., 1974] (Department of State publication, 8756) p. 420–422.   JX21.R68   1973

Excerpts of a statement by David D. Newsom, Assistant Secretary of State for African Affairs, before the Subcommittee on Africa, Committee on Foreign Affairs, House of Representatives, Mar 27, 1973.

Education

2084

Smythe, Mabel M. The education of refugees in Zimbabwe and Namibia. New York, Phelps Stokes, 1977. 19 p. (Transition problems in a developing nation [Namibia] Occasional paper, no. 8).

Prepared for the African-American Scholars Council and the U.S. Agency for International Development under subcontract AID/afr-C-1254.

Abstract in *A.I.D. Research and Development Abstracts*, Oct. 1978, p. 30.

Microfiche. [Washington, U.S. Agency for International Development, 1977?] 1 sheet.

DLC-Sci RR PN-AAF-262

2085

University of Botswana, Lesotho, and Swaziland. Report of a working party on a regional school certicate examination. [s.l.], 1975. 104 p.

Funded in part by the U.S. Agency for International Development.

Bibliography: p. 103–104.

Examined in the Development Information Center, AID, Washington, D.C.

Energy Resources

2086

Cavan, Ann. Energy resources in southern Africa: a select bibliography. Washington, African Bibliog-

2086 (cont.)

raphic Center, 1981. 65 p.　　Z5853.P83C38

"A publication of the Southern Africa Development Information/Documentation Exchange (SADEX) project."

473 entries.

2087

Straaten, J. F. van. Solar energy research and application with special reference to solar water heating in southern Africa. *In* Southeastern Conference on Application of Solar Energy, *2d, Baton Rouge, La., 1976.* Proceedings. p. 252–257. illus.

Conference sponsored by the U.S. Energy Research and Development Administration.

Microfiche. [s.l., 1976] sheet 3 of 6

DLC-Sci RR CONF-760423

Foreign Relations

2088

U.S. *Congress. House. Committee on International Relations. Subcommittee on Africa.* United States policy toward southern Africa: hearing, Ninety-fifth Congress, first session, March 3, 1977. Washington, U.S. Govt. Print. Off., 1977. 52 p.

KF27.I54914　1977a
J74.A23 95th
Cong., House Comm.
Inter. Rel., v. 3

Charles C. Diggs, Jr., chairman.

Principal witnesses are Philip C. Habib, Under Secretary of State for Political Affairs, and William E. Schaufele, Jr., Assistant Secretary of State for African Affairs. Included in Mr. Schaufele's testimony is a statement on the Zimbabwe Development Fund (p. 32–33).

Among the appendixes are the following:

Appendix 1. Bonker, Don. U.S. relations with South Africa. p. 45–47.

Appendix 2. Questions submitted by Subcommittee Chairman Diggs and responses of the Development of State. p. 48–52.

2089

U.S. *Congress. Senate. Committee on Foreign Relations. Subcommittee on African Affairs.* U.S. policy toward Africa: hearings before the Subcommittee on African Affairs and the Subcommittee on Arms Control, International Organizations and Security Agreements, and the Committee on Foreign Relations, United States Senate, Ninety-fourth Congress, second session. Washington, U.S. Govt. Print. Off., 1976. 336 p.

KF26.F625　1976a
J74.A23 94th
Cong., Sen. Comm.
For. Rel., v. 17

Dick Clark, chairman, Subcommittee on African Affairs.

Stuart Symington, chairman, Subcommittee on Arms Control, International Organizations and Security Agreements.

John Sparkman, chairman, Committee on Foreign Relations.

Hearings held Mar. 5–May 27, 1976.

Emphasis is on proposals "for bringing greater nonviolent pressure to bear for change in southern Africa."—p. 2.

2090

—— U.S. policy toward southern Africa: hearings, Ninety-fourth Congress, first session. Washington, for sale by the Supt. of Docs., U.S. Govt. Print. Off., 1976. 527 p. maps.

KF26.F625　1975a
J74.A23 94th
Cong., Sen. Comm.
For. Rel., v. 16

Dick Clark, chairman.

Hearings held June 11–July 29, 1975.

Focus is on Mozambique, Angola, Rhodesia, South Africa, and Namibia.

Appendix:

Barton, Robert. Southern Africa—self-rule or self-destruction: a trip report, April 12–May 5, 1975. p. 503–527.

2091

Angola-South Africa negotiations: comments on 'last chance.' *In* U.S. *Joint Publications Research Service.* JPRS 76377. [Springfield, Va., National Technical Information Service, 1980] (Sub-Saharan Africa report, no. 2289) p. 1–4.

Translation of article in *Le Monde*, Paris, Aug. 3–4, 1980, p. 3.

Microfiche. [s.l., 1980]

DLC-Micro JPRS 76377

2092

Carter, Jimmy. Interview with the Magazine Publishers Association, June 10, 1977. *In* U.S. *President.* Public papers of the Presidents of the United States. Jimmy Carter. 1977. [Washington, Office of the Federal Register, National Archives and Records Service; for sale by the Supt. of Docs., U.S. Govt. Print. Off., 1977] p. 1087–1097.

J80.A283　1977

During the interview, President Carter discusses U.S. policy toward Africa with an emphasis on the southern region.

2093

Christopher, Warren. Africa: peaceful solutions to conflicts in Namibia and Southern Rhodesia. *In* U.S. *Dept. of State.* The Department of State bulletin, v. 78, no. 2019, Oct. 1978: 15–16.

JX232.A33 v. 78

Address by the Deputy Secretary of State before the litigation section of the American Bar Association, New York, Aug. 9, 1978.

2094

Clark, Dick. Africa: report to the Committee on Foreign Relations, United States Senate, by Dick Clark, Chairman, Subcommittee on African Affairs, Committee on Foreign Relations, United States Senate. Washington, U.S. Govt. Print. Off., 1977. 43 p. DT746.C57

At head of title: 95th Congress, 1st session. Committee print.

Emphasis is on southern Africa.

2095

———— Sensible African policy. Congressional record, 94th Congress, 2d session, v. 122, Mar. 31, 1976: 8815–8817. J11.R5 v. 122

Remarks in the U.S. Senate.

Includes articles, "African policy starts in Havana," and "No Rhodesia again?", both from the *Economist.*

2096

Department discusses situation in South Africa and Namibia. *In* U.S. *Dept of State.* The Department of State bulletin, v. 73, no. 1887, Aug. 25, 1975: 269–273. JX232.A33, v. 73

Statements by Nathaniel Davis, Assistant Secretary of State for African Affairs, and William B. Buffum, Assistant Secretary of State for International Organization Affairs, before the Subcommittee on African Affairs, Committee on Foreign Relations, Senate, July 24, 1975.

2097

Duncan, Robert. Report of a study mission to Africa. Washington, U.S. Govt. Print. Off., 1979. 13 p.

DT746.D86

At head of title: 96th Congress, 1st session. Committee print.

"Printed for the use of the Committee on Appropriations."

A special mission focusing primarily on problems in Rhodesia, Namibia, and South Africa.

2098

———— The trouble in South Africa and what we can do to help. Congressional record, 95th Congress, 1st session, v. 125, Apr. 30, 1979: 9085–9089.

J11.R5 v. 125

Remarks in the U.S. House of Representatives. Primarily a report on his trip to southern Africa.

2099

Goldwater, Barry. South Africa. Congressional record, 95th Congress, 2d session, v. 124, Apr. 13, 1978: 10070–10073. J11.R5 v. 124

Remarks in the U.S. Senate.

Includes article, "Why does the U.S. advocate terrorism in southern Africa?," from the *Government Executive.*

2100

Gorman, Thomas P. The potential for insurgency and great power conflict in southern Africa. Carlisle Barracks, Pa., U.S. Army War College, 1974. 19 p.

Microfiche. [Springfield, Va., National Technical Information Service, 1974?] 1 sheet.

DLC-Sci RR AD-A009949

2101

Habib, Philip C. Southern Africa in the global context. *In* U.S. *Dept. of State.* The Department of State bulletin, v. 76, no. 1971, Apr. 4, 1977: p. 318–321. JX232.A33 v. 76

Statement by the Under Secretary of State for Political Affairs before the Subcommittee on Africa, Committee on International Relations, House of Representatives, Mar. 3, 1977.

Concerns primarily American policy on Rhodesia and Namibia.

2102

Hamilton, Lee H. U.S. foreign policy in southern Africa. Congressional record, 94th Congress, 2d session, v. 122, Mar. 30, 1976: 8739–8740.

J11.R5 v. 122

Extension of remarks in the U.S. House of Representatives.

Representative Hamilton includes his exchange of letters with the U.S. Dept. of State concerning "present and future U.S. policy in Southern Africa."

2103

Hatfield, Mark O. U.S. military action against Cuba. Congressional record, 94th Congress, 2d session, v. 122, Mar. 29, 1976: 8331–8333.

J11.R5 v. 122

Remarks in the U.S. Senate concerning U.S. policy toward southern Africa in view of Cuban intervention there.

2104

Kissinger, Henry A. Press conference, September 11, 1976. [Washington], Office of Media Services, Bureau of Public Affairs, Dept. of State, [1976] 7 p.   DLC

Major topics are Southern Africa and Lebanon.

2105

—— Secretary discusses southern Africa in interview for NBC "Today" show. *In* U.S. *Dept. of State.* The Department of State bulletin, v. 75, no. 1948, Oct. 25, 1976: 528–531.

JX232.A33 v. 75

Transcript of an interview with the Secretary of State by Tom Brokaw and Richard Valeriani recorded on Sept. 27 and broadcast Sept. 28, 1976.

2106

—— Southern Africa and the United States: an agenda for cooperation. [Washington], Office of Media Services, Bureau of Public Affairs, U.S. Dept. of State, 1976. 7 p.   DLC

Text of remarks in Lusaka, Zambia, Apr. 27, 1976.

2107

—— The challenges of Africa *In* U.S. *Dept. of State.* The Department of State bulletin, v. 75, no. 1943, Sept. 20, 1976: 349–357.

JX232.A33 v. 75

Address by the Secretary of State before the conventions of the Opportunities Industralization Centers, Philadelphia, Aug. 31, 1976.

Presents an analysis of American policy, with an emphasis on southern Africa.

2108

—— United States policy on southern Africa. *In* U.S. *Dept. of State.* The Department of State bulletin, v. 74, no. 1927, May 31, 1976: 672–679.

JX232.A33 v. 74

Address by the Secretary of State at a luncheon hosted by President Kenneth Kaunda of Zambia, Lusaka, Apr. 27, 1976.

2109

McDonald, Larry. Soviet aggression in southern Africa—part I. Congressional record [daily edition], 96th Congress, 2d session, v. 126, Sept. 29, 1980: E4625–E4627.   J11.R7 v. 126

Extension of remarks in the U.S. House of Representatives.

Includes text of a paper, *Democracy Against Socialism*, by Igor Glagoler.

2110

McGovern, George S. Impressions of southern Africa: a report to the Committee on Foreign Relations, United States Senate, December 1979 Washington, U.S. Govt. Print. Off., 1979. 38 p.

DT747.U6M33

At head of title: 96th Congress, 1st session. Committee print.

Concerns the senator's trip to Mozambique, Zambia, Rhodesia, South Africa, and Angola, Nov. 21–Dec. 14, 1979.

2111

Moose, Richard M. The U.S. role in southern Africa. *In* U.S. *Dept. of State.* The Department of State bulletin, v. 79, no. 2031, Oct. 1979: 20–23.

JX232.A33 v. 79

Address by the Assistant Secretary of State for African Affairs before the Southern Africa Research Program Symposium on Race Conflict in Southern Africa, Yale University, Apr. 18, 1979.

2112

Papp, Daniel S. The Soviet Union and Southern Africa. Carlisle Barracks, Pa., Strategic Studies Institute, U.S. Army War College, 1980. 28 p.

"Strategic issues research memorandum."

Microfiche. [s.l., Defense Technical Information Center, 1980] 1 sheet.

DLC-Sci RR AD-A089399

2113

Percy, Charles H. The United States and southern Africa: a report by Senator Charles H. Percy to the Committee on Foreign Relations, United States Senate, on his study mission to southern Africa conducted between April 13 and April 25, 1976. Washington, U.S. Govt. Print. Off., 1976. 33 p.

DT747.U6P47

At head of title: 94th Congress, 2d session. Committee print.

Report of a study mission to Tanzania, Zambia, Mozambique, Namibia, South Africa, and Botswana.

2114

Rogers, William D. The search for peace in southern Africa. *In* U.S. *Dept. of State.* The Department of State bulletin, v. 75, no. 1948, Oct. 25, 1976: 532–537.   JX232.A33 v. 75

Statement by the Under Secretary of State for Economic Affairs before the Subcommittee on African Affairs, Committee on Foreign Relations, Senate, Sept 30, 1976.

2115

Sakaike, Tonic. Kaunda expresses willingness to cooperate with Zimbabwe. *In* U.S. *Joint Publications Research Service.* JPRS 75551. [Springfield, Va.,

2115 (cont.)

National Technical Information Service, 1980] (Sub-Saharan Africa report, no. 2239) p. 4–8.

Interview with President Kaunda in *The Herald*, Salisbury, Apr. 8, 1980, p. 5.

Microfiche. [s.l., 1980]

DLC-Micro JPRS 75551

2116

Schaufele, William E. United States relations in southern Africa. *In* U.S. *Dept. of State*. The Department of State bulletin, v. 76, no. 1976, May 9, 1977: 464–471.   JX232.A33 v. 76

Statement by the Assistant Secretary of State for African Affairs before the American Academy of Political and Social Science, Philadelphia, Apr. 16, 1977.

2117

Secretary Kissinger discusses southern African issues with African and British officials. *In* U.S. *Dept. of State*. The Department of State bulletin, v. 75, no. 1948, Oct. 25, 1976: 511–527.

JX232.A33 v. 75

A collection of statements and news conferences concerning the Secretary of State's visit to Tanzania, Zambia, South Africa, Zaire, Kenya, and the United Kingdom, Sept. 14–24, 1976.

2118

Secretary Kissinger's news conference at Philadelphia, August 31. *In* U.S. *Dept. of State*. The Department of State bulletin. v. 75, no. 1943, Sept. 20, 1976: 358–362.   JX232.A33 v. 75

Questions to the Secretary of State concern conditions in southern Africa.

2119

Southern Africa: US policy. [Washington], Bureau of Public Affairs, Dept. of State, 1976. 2 p. DLC

At head of title: Gist—a quick reference aid on U.S. foreign relations primarily for Government use.

2120

Symms, Steven D. American policy in Africa. Congressional record, 94th Congress, 2d session, v. 122, Mar. 11, 1976: 6321–6323.   J11.R5 v. 122

Extension of remarks in the U.S. House of Representatives.

Includes article, "War clouds over southern Africa," in *Wall Street Journal*.

2121

United States reiterates support for the independence of Namibia and Zimbabwe at Maputo conference.

In U.S. *Dept. of State*. The Department of State bulletin, v. 77, no. 1985, July 11, 1977: 55–66.

JX232.A33 v. 77

Statements by Andrew Young, U.S. Representative to the United Nations and Charles W. Maynes, Assistant Secretary of State for International Organization Affairs, at the International Conference in Support of the Peoples of Zimbabwe and Namibia, May 16–21, 1977; also includes text of the final declaration and program of action.

2122

Van Meter, Karl M. South Atlantic and Southern Africa: from Kissinger to Carter. *In* U.S. *Joint Publications Research Service*. JPRS 70667. [Springfield, Va., National Technical Information Service, 1978] (Translations on Sub-Saharan Africa, no. 1882) p. 63–77.

Translation of article in *Revue française d'études politiques africaines*, Paris, Dec. 1977, p. 59–75.

Microfiche. [Washington, Supt. of Doc., U.S. Govt. Print Off., 1978]

DLC-Micro JPRS 70667

2123

Ward, Jennifer C. U.S. policy toward Southern Africa. *In* The U.S. role in a changing world political economy: major issues for the 96th Congress: a compendium of papers submitted to the Joint Economic Committee, Congress of the United States. Washington, U.S. Govt. Print. Off., 1979. p. 576–596.   HF1455.U54

Bibliography: p. 595–596.

Geography and Maps

2124

[U.S. *Central Intelligence Agency*] Southern Africa. [Washington, 1977] col. map.

G8480 1977.U5

Scale 1 : 5,000,000.

Relief shown by shading and spot heights.

"503340 8-77 (543275)."

Includes inset showing radial distances from Cape of Good Hope with comparative area map and inset of "administrative divisions."

Includes Angola, Botswana, Comoros, Lesotho, Madagascar, Malawi, Mozambique, Namibia, South Africa, Southern Rhodesia, Swaziland, and Zambia.

2125

———— Southern Africa. [Washington, 1977] col. map.   G8480 1977.U52

Scale 1 : 5,500,000.

"Sinusoidal equal-area projection."

2125 (cont.)

Relief shown by shading

"503383 9-77 (543397)."

Geology, Hydrology, and Mineral Resources

2126

Byrd, Harry F., Jr. Southern Africa and world strategy. Congressional record, 96th Congress, 1st session, v. 125, Jan. 29, 1979: 1258–1260.

J11.R5 v. 125

Remarks in the U.S. Senate on strategic materials from the region and the importance of maritime routes there.

2127

Continental margin off Western Africa: Cape St. Francis (South Africa) to Walvis Ridge (South-West Africa), [by] K. O. Emery [et al.] *In* American Association of Petroleum Geologists. AAPG bulletin, v. 59, no. 1, Jan. 1975: 3–59. illus.

TN860.A3 v. 59

"The Eastern Atlantic Continental Margin Program was funded by National Science Foundation Grant GX-28193 as part of the International Decade of Ocean Exploration."—p. 3.

2128

Dean, Robert M. Mining in the southern Africa region. [s.l.], Robert Dean Consultants, 1978. 57 p.

Prepared for the U.S. Agency for International Development under contract AID/afr-C-1424.

Cover title: *A Report to the Congress on Development Needs and Opportunities for Cooperation in Southern Africa. Annex B: Mining.*

Microfiche. [Washington, U.S. Agency for International Development, 1978?] 1 sheet.

DLC-Sci RR PN-AAH-174

2129

Scrutton, Roger A. Geophysical study of the continental margin of southern Africa. *In* Geological Society of America. Bulletin, v. 89, May 1978: 791–794. illus., maps. QE1.G2 v. 89

Work supported by a National Science Foundation grant and a Office of Naval Research contract.

Issued also in microfiche. [s.l., Defense Documentation Center, 1979] 1 sheet.

DLC-Sci RR AD-A062181

2130

Thurmond, Strom. The importance of southern Africa, the "Persian Gulf of Minerals," to the

United States. Congressional record [daily ed.], 96th Congress, 1st session, v. 125, Sept. 5, 1979: S11795–S11797. J11.R7 v. 125

Remarks in the U.S. Senate.

Health and Nutrition

2131

Bicknell, William J. A review of health issues in southern Africa: an approach for developing country-specific health strategies. Washington, Family Health Care, inc., 1979. 92 p. (Health and development in southern Africa, v. 10)

Submitted to the Southern Africa Development Analysis Program, U.S. Agency for International Development.

Issued in cooperation with Africare.

Cover title: *A Report to the Congress on Development Needs and Opportunities for Cooperation in Southern Africa. Annex B: Health.*

Abstract in *A.I.D. Research and Development Abstracts*, v. 8, no. 2, 1980, p. 27.

Microfiche. [Washington, U.S. Agency for International Development, 1979?] 1 sheet.

DLC-Sci RR PN-AAH-170

2132

Pielemeier, Nancy R. Botswana, Lesotho, and Swaziland. Washington, Division of Program Analysis, Office of International Health; [for sale by the Supt. of Docs., U.S. Govt. Print. Off.], 1975. 136 p. maps. (Syncrisis: the dynamics of health; an analytic series on the interactions of health and socioeconomic development, v. 13)

RA418.S98 v. 13

Abstract in *A.I.D. Research and Development Abstracts*, Oct. 1976, p. 27.

Issued also in microfiche. [Washington, U.S. Agency for International Development, 1975?] 2 sheets. DLC-Sci RR PN-AAB-976

Labor Migration

2133

Contract workers to South Africa: who and why. *In* U.S. *Joint Publications Research Service.* JPRS 75551. [Springfield, Va., National Technical Information Service, 1980] (Sub-Saharan Africa report, no. 2239) p. 65–68.

Translation of article in *Tempo*, Maputo, Mar. 16, 1980, p. 29–33.

Microfiche. [s.l., 1980]

DLC-Micro JPRS 75551

2134

Discussion on southern Africa's migratory labor reviewed. *In* U.S. *Joint Publications Research Service.* JPRS 76908. [Springfield, Va., National Technical Information Service, 1980] (Sub-Saharan Africa report, no. 2325) p. 6–12.

Translation of article on the migration of workers to South African mines, in *Notícias*, Maputo, Oct. 23, 24, 1980.

Microfiche. [s.l., 1980]

DLC-Micro JPRS 76908

2135

Walker, Gary A., *and* William Lovelace. Labor migration in southern Africa and possible supplier state alternatives. [s.l.], Pacific Consultants, 1978. 184 leaves. DLC

Prepared for the U.S. Agency for International Development under contract AID/afr-C-1424.

Bibliography: leaves 171–175.

Cover title: *A Report to the Congress on Development Needs and Opportunities for Cooperation in Southern Africa. Annex B: Labor Migration.*

A study of conditions for foreign migrant workers in South Africa, particularly in the mining industry, together with an analysis of South African policy toward labor migration. "Supplier states" include Botswana, Lesotho, Malawi, Mozambique, Namibia, Swaziland, and Zimbabwe-Rhodesia.

Abstract in *A.I.D. Research and Development Abstracts*, v. 8, no. 2, 1980, p. 27–28.

Issued also in microfiche. [Washington, U.S. Agency for International Development, 1978?] 3 sheets. DLC-Sci RR PN-AAH-171

Military Affairs

2136

U.S. *Congress. House. Committee on International Relations. Special Subcommittee on Investigations.* Mercenaries in Africa: hearing, Ninety-fourth Congress, second session, August 9, 1976. Washington, U.S. Govt. Print. Off., 1976. 75 p.

KF27.I5498 1976
J74.A23 94th
Cong., House. Comm.
Inter. Rel., v. 82

Lee H. Hamilton, chairman.

Focus is on mercenary activities in Angola and Rhodesia.

Among the appendixes is the following:

Appendix 3. Foreign assistance in the Angola civil war: chronology of reported events, 1957–76, by Mark M. Lowenthal, Analyst in National Defense, Foreign Affairs and National Defense Division, Congressional Research Service, Library of Congress. p. 36–69.

2137

Adelman, Kenneth L., *and* John Seiler. Alternative futures in Southern Africa. Arlington, Va., SRI International, Strategic Studies Center, 1979. 107 p.

Prepared under contract to the Office of the Assistant Secretary of Defense for International Security Affairs.

Cited in *SADEX*, v. 1, no. 3, Nov./Dec. 1979, p. 53.

2138

Bissell, Richard E. Southern Africa and the future of American naval power. [Washington, Center for Strategic and International Studies, Georgetown University, 1980] [18] p.

Issued as Appendix C of the *Conference Report on the Future of Maritime Strategy (April 1, 1980) and Geopolitics and Maritime Power (September 17, 18, 1980).*

Microfiche. [s.l., Defense Technical Information Center, 1981] 3 sheets.

DLC-Sci RR AD-A101012

2139

Brewer, Jerry D. South African and Rhodesian close air support capability and counterinsurgency; a research report submitted to the faculty. Maxwell Air Force Base, Ala., Air Command and Staff College, Air University, 1978. 66 leaves (FAR 29115-N) AMAU

"Air Command and Staff College. Research report 0235-78."

Bibliography: leaves 64–66.

Copy examined in the former Foreign Affairs Research Documentation Center, U.S. Dept. of State.

Issued also in microfiche. [s.l., Defense Documentation Center, 1978] 1 sheet (AD-B028379L)

2140

Roberts, Kenneth E. U.S. defense and the South Atlantic. Carlisle Barracks, Pa., Strategic Studies Institute, U.S. Army War College, 1976. 25 p. (Military issues research memorandum)

Considers American and Soviet policies in the South Atlantic, including southern Africa.

Abstract in *Government Reports Announcements & Index*, Apr. 15, 1977, p. 25.

Microfiche. [Springfield, Va.?, National Technical Information Service, 1977] 1 sheet.

DLC-Sci RR AD-A035153

2141

Stein, Edward J. The compelling strategic area of southern Africa. Maxwell Air Force Base, Ala., 1977. 65 p. (U.S. Air University. Air War College. Research report)   AMAU

2142

Winkelman, Alton B. Conflict in southern Africa: a warning to the U.S. Maxwell Air Force Base, Ala., 1974. 65 p. (U.S. Air University. Air Command and Staff College. Research study)
                                        AMAU

Abstract in *Air University Abstracts of Research Reports*, 1974, no. 419.

Politics and Government

2143

U.S. *Congress. Senate. Committee on Foreign Relations. Subcommittee on Foreign Assistance.* The political and economic crisis in southern Africa: a staff report to the Subcommittee on Foreign Assistance of the Committee on Foreign Relations, United States Senate [written by Frank Ballance and Constance Freeman] Washington, U.S. Govt. Print. Off., 1976. 52 p. maps.

DT746.U54   1976

Hubert H. Humphrey, chairman.

At head of title: 94th Congress, 2nd session. Committee print.

"Following Secretary Kissinger's trip to Africa in April, 1976 and his major policy statement in Lusaka, Zambia, the Subcommittee requested that the staff undertake a study of the economic and political conditions in southern Africa to assist it in making informed judgments regarding the possible provision of assistance to countries of the region."
— p. v.

The report, was based on the three-week trip in May 1976 to Zambia, Mozambique, South Africa, Tanzania, and Zaire.

2144

Christopher, Warren. Peaceful solutions. [Washington], Office of Public Communication, Bureau of Public Affairs, Dept. of State, 1978. 4 p. (U.S. Dept. of State. Current policy, no. 28)   DLC

Remarks by the Deputy Secretary of State at a meeting of the American Bar Association, New York, Aug. 9, 1978, includes statements on Namibia and Rhodesia.

2145

International Security Assistance and Arms Export Control Act of 1976–77. Congressional record,

94th Congress, 2d session, v. 122, June 11, 1976: 17668–17673.   J11.R5 v. 122

Remarks in the U.S. Senate.

Debate focuses on the situations in Mozambique and Rhodesia; includes articles from *U.S. News & World Report*, *Wall Street Journal*, and *Washington Post*, and a statement by the Rhodesian Information Office.

2146

Lagarde, Dominique. Destabilization of southern Africa claimed. *In* U.S. *Joint Publications Research Service.* JPRS 74967. [Springfield, Va., National Technical Information Service, 1980] (Sub-Saharan Africa report, no. 2201) p. 1–5.

Translation of article on the impact of raids by Rhodesian and South African forces into neighboring countries, especially Zambia and Mozambique, in *Demain l'Afrique*, Paris, Dec. 17, 1979, p. 38–39.

Microfiche. [s.l., 1980]

DLC-Micro JPRS 74967

2147

Legum, Colin. "National liberation" in southern Africa. Problems of Communism, v. 24, Jan./Feb. 1975: 1–20. illus., maps.   HX1.P75 v. 24

Issued by the U.S. Information Agency.

2148

McClelland, Charles A., Patrick J. McGowan, *and* Wayne R. Martin. Threat, conflict, and commitment. Final report, 1976; Threat Recognition & Analysis Project. [Los Angeles?], International Relations Research Institute, School of International Relations, University of Southern California, 1976. [266] p. (in various pagings)

"This research was supported by the Advanced Research Projects Agency of the Department of Defense."

"TR&A technical report, no. 39."

Partial contents: Pt. 2. McGowan, Patrick J. Threat recognition and analysis in a regional subsystem: the case of Southern Africa since January 1973.

Microfiche. [s.l., 1976] 3 sheets.

DLC-Sci RR AD A031438

2149

McGovern, George S. Flora Lewis on Africa issues. Congressional record, 96th Congress, 1st session, v. 125, Jan. 23, 1979: 841–844.   J11.R5 v. 125

Remarks in the U.S. Senate.

Includes articles from the *New York Times* concerning Southern Africa, particularly political issues and American policy toward the region.

2150

Moose, Richard M. Southern Africa: four years later. *In* U.S. *Dept. of State.* The Department of State bulletin, v. 81, no. 2046, Jan. 1981: 8–11.
JX232.A33 v. 81

Statement by the Assistant Secretary of State for African Affairs before the African Studies Symposium of the Black Studies Program, Pennsylvania State University, University Park, Oct. 13, 1980.

2151

Rotberg, Robert I. Change, conflict, and liberation in Southern Africa. [s.l.], 1973. 6 leaves. (FAR 17137-S)

Prepared for the Conference on African Trends through the 70's, sponsored by the U.S. Dept. of State, Apr. 1973.

Examined in the former Foreign Affairs Research Documentation Center, Dept. of State.

Refugees

2152

Kennedy, Edward M. Refugee crisis in Southern Africa. Congressional record, 95th Congress, 2d session, v. 124, Sept. 15, 1978: 29685–29686.
J11.R5 v. 124

Remarks in the U.S. Senate.

Includes article from the *Wall Street Journal.*

2153

Mullane, Lee. The unnoticed refugees: while the plight of the boat people captures headlines, little public attention has yet focused on Southern Africa's million homeless. Agenda, Sept. 1979: 11–13. map.   HC59.7.A742   1979

Issued by the U.S. Agency for International Development.

2154

Van Egmond, Alan. Report on the status of refugees in Botswana, Lesotho, and Swaziland with guidelines for U.S. assistance. [Washington?], Robert R. Nathan Associates, 1977. 61 p.

Prepared for the U.S. Agency for International Development under contract AID/afr-C-1134.

Examined in the Development Information Center, AID, Washington, D.C.

2155

Walker, Gary A. Refugees in Southern Africa. [s.l.], Pacific Consultants, 1978. 136 leaves.   DLC

Prepared for the U.S. Agency for International Development under contract no. AID/afr-C-1424.

Bibliography: leaves 127–128.

Cover title: *A Report to the Congress on Development Needs and Opportunities for Cooperation in Southern Africa. Annex B: Refugees.*

"At the end of 1978, there were approximately 200,000 refugees in Southern Africa. More than 80% of these had fled from white minority-ruled countries (70% from the Republic of South Africa alone) to majority-ruled states, principally Mozambique (with 40% of all refugees) and Zambia (30%)."—Abstract.

Abstract in *A.I.D. Research and Development Abstracts*, v. 8, no. 2, 1980, p. 29.

Issued also in microfiche. [Washington, U.S. Agency for International Development, 1978?] 2 sheets.   DLC-Sci RR PN-AAH-175

Other Subjects

2156

Derian, Patricia M. Human rights: the role of law and lawyers. [Washington], Bureau of Public Affairs, Office of Public Communication, Dept. of State, 1978. 5 p.   DLC

Speech on human rights in South Africa and Namibia, with special reference to the trial of Rev. Theo Kotze, by the Assistant Secretary for Human Rights and Humanitarian Affairs before the Lawyers' Committee for Civil Rights Under Law and Division V of the D.C. Bar Association.

2157

Ebert, James I. Comparability between hunter-gatherer groups in the past and present: modernization versus explanation. Botswana notes and records, v. 10, [1978]: 19–26. map.
DT790.B67   1978

"Many of the ideas included in this paper are the direct result of fieldwork conducted by the University of New Mexico Kalahari Project in Botswana's Central District, under the support of the U.S. National Science Foundation (Grant SOC75-02253)."—p. 25.

2158

Goshen, Carolyn J., *and* Philip Musser. Southern Africa: a select guide to U.S. organizational interests. [Washington], African Bibliographic Center, 1979. 74 p.   DT729.9.U6G67

"Produced for the Southern Africa Development Analysis Project under the U.S. Agency for International Development contract number AID/afr-C-1421."

Includes the names, addresses, and brief statements of purpose of various organizations in the United States with an interest in Southern Africa, among them business groups, church affiliated or-

2158 (cont.)

ganizations, consultants, groups concerned with specific issues (e.g., education, health, nutrition, housing), and liberation movements and their support groups.

2159

Settlement patterns, urbanization, and shelter in Southern Africa. Washington, Rivkin Associates, inc., 1979. 110 p. illus., maps.

Prepared for the Office of Housing and the Southern Africa Development Analysis Project, U.S. Agency for International Development.

Cover title: *A Report to the Congress on Development Needs and Opportunities for Cooperation in Southern Africa. Annex B: Urban and Shelter Needs.*

Abstract in *A.I.D. Research and Development Abstracts*, v. 8, no. 2, 1980, p. 29–30.

Microfiche. [Washington, U.S. Agency for International Development, 1979?] 2 sheets.

DLC-Sci RR PN-AAH-117

2160

Walker, Gary A. Manpower in Southern Africa: a summary: and synthesis of manpower findings from SADAP sector analyses and an assessment of manpower opportunities and constraints. [s.l.], Pacific Consultants, 1978. 222 leaves. DLC

Prepared for the U.S. Agency for International Development under contract AID/afr-C-1424.

Bibliography: leaves 211–222.

SADAP: Southern Africa Development Analysis Project.

Cover title: *A Report to the Congress on Development Needs and Opportunities for Cooperation in Southern Africa: Annex B: Manpower.*

Abstract in *A.I.D. Research and Development Abstracts*, v. 8, no. 2, 1980, p. 28.

Issued also in microfiche. [Washington, U.S. Agency for International Development, 1978?] 3 sheets. DLC-Sci RR PN-AAH-172

2161

Wilmsen, Edwin N. Seasonal effects of dietary intake on Kalahari San. Ann Arbor, Museum of Anthropology, University of Michigan, 1977. [27] leaves.

Paper delivered at a symposium, "Contribution of Anthropology to the Assessment of Nutritional Status," Chicago, 1977.

Research supported in part by the National Science Foundation.

Examined in the National Science Foundation, Washington, D.C.

2162

——— Summary report of research on Basarwa in western Ngamiland. Ann Arbor, Museum of Anthropology, University of Michigan, [1976?] [46] leaves.

Research supported in part by the National Science Foundation.

Examined in the National Science Foundation, Washington, D.C.

2163

Yale-Wesleyan Southern African Research Program. Newsletter. [no.] 1+ Nov. 1977+ [New Haven, Yale University] semiannual. DLC

"The Southern African Research Program, located at Yale University, is a joint program of Yale and Wesleyan Universities supported by major grants from the National Endowment for the Humanities and the Ford Foundation for an initial period of July 1977 through June 1980.... The program is devoted to scholarly research into the causes and consequences of racial and ethnic conflict in Southern Africa since 1652."—no. 1, p. 3.

L.C. has Nov. 1977.

2164

Yates, Leslie M. Integration of women in development in Southern Africa; an evaluation with recommendations for USAID programs in Botswana, Lesotho, and Zambia. SADEX; the Southern Africa Development Information/Documentation Exchange, v. 1, Nov./Dec. 1979: 1–15.

DLC

Bibliography: p. 11–15.

Angola

General

2165

U.S. *Agency for International Development.* A report to the Congress on development needs and opportunities for cooperation in Southern Africa. Annex A: Angola. [Washington], 1979. 115 p.

Bibliography: p. 113–115.

A background statement, including a note on United States-Angolan relations, is followed by chapters on economic conditions, political structure, agriculture, health, education, housing, industry, mining, energy, transportation, communications, and foreign assistance programs.

Microfiche. [Washington, U.S. Agency for International Development, 1979?] 2 sheets.

DLC-Sci RR PN-AAH-151

2166

U.S. *Dept. of State. Bureau of Public Affairs.* Background notes. Angola. [Washington, for sale by the Supt. of Docs., U.S. Govt. Print. Off.], 1979. 7 p. maps. (U.S. Dept. of State. Department of State publication 7975, rev.) G59.U5

L.C. retains only the latest revision.

For a description of the contents of this publication, see the note to entry 937.

2167

American University, *Washington, D.C. Foreign Area Studies.* Angola, a country study; edited by Irving Kaplan. 2d ed. Washington, for sale by the Supt. of Docs., U.S. Govt. Print. Off., c1979. xxiii, 286 p. illus., maps. (Area handbook series)

DT611.H47 1979

First ed., by Allison B. Herrick and others, published in 1967 under title: *Area Handbook for Angola* (DT611.H47).

"Research completed October 1978."

"DA pam 550-59."

Bibliography: p. 259–274.

2168

Essential objectives, tasks of Angolan reconstruction. [Springfield, Va., National Technical Information Service, 1978] 99 p. (U.S. Joint Publications Research Service. JPRS 70891)

Translations on Sub-Saharan Africa, no. 1905.

Translation of *Os Objetivos e as Tarefas Essenciais da Fase de Reconstrução Nacional* (Luanda, 1977), p. 3–76.

An MPLA document outlining basic objectives in such fields as economic development, education, health, and judicial reform.

Microfiche. [Washington, Supt. of Docs., U.S. Govt. Print. Off., 1978]

DLC-Micro JPRS 70891

2169

Grimm, Don A. Angola—an analysis; a research report submitted to the faculty. Maxwell Air Force Base, Ala., Air War College, Air University, 1976. 78 leaves. (FAR 24774-N)

"Professional study, no. 5928."

"The history of the country, its national liberation movements and natural resources are reviewed as a background for analyzing the interests of the outside states involved."

Examined in the former Foreign Affairs Research Documentation Center, U.S. Dept. of State.

Issued also in microfiche. [s.l., 1976] 1 sheet (AD-B011132L).

2170

Situation in Mocamedes Province unsatisfactory, plans drawn. *In* U.S. *Joint Publications Research Service.* JPRS 74663. [Springfield, Va., National Technical Information Service, 1979] (Sub-Saharan Africa report, no. 2183) p. 16–20.

Translation of article describing general conditions in the province, in *Jornal de Angola,* Luanda, Oct. 26, 1979, p. 1, 7.

Microfiche. [s.l., 1979]

DLC-Micro JPRS 74663

Agriculture

2171

Augusto, Manuel. Officials categorically deny food-stuffs shortage rumor. *In* U.S. *Joint Publications Service.* JPRS 77433. [Springfield, Va., National Technical Information Service, 1981] (Sub-Saharan Africa report, no. 2363) p. 9–12.

Translation of article in *Jornal de Angola,* Luanda, Nov. 28, 1980, p. 3.

Microfiche. [s.l., 1981]

DLC-Micro JPRS 77433

2172

Development of cooperatives facing difficulties. *In* U.S. *Joint Publications Research Service.* JPRS 69029. [Springfield, Va., National Technical Information Service, 1977] (Translations on Sub-Saharan Africa, no. 1741) p. 21–25.

Translation of article in *Jornal de Angola,* Luanda, Mar. 27, 1977, p. 5.

Microfiche. [s.l., 1977]

DLC-Micro JPRS 69029

2173

Foy, Colin. Survey of agricultural, industrial conditions. *In* U.S. *Joint Publications Research Service.* JPRS 76456. [Springfield, Va., National Technical Information Service, 1980] (Sub-Saharan Africa report, no. 2294) p. 40–43.

Article in *West Africa,* London, Aug. 11 and Aug. 18, 1980.

Microfiche. [s.l., 1980]

DLC-Micro JPRS 76456

2174

Neto, Agostinho. Neto declares 1978 year of agriculture. *In* U.S. *Joint Publications Research Service.* JPRS 70600. [Springfield, Va., National Technical Information Service, 1978] (Translations on Sub-Saharan Africa, no. 1874) p. 25–29.

Translation of speech recorded in *Jornal de Angola,* Luanda, Jan. 1, 1978, p. 1, 2.

Microfiche. [Washington, Supt. of Docs., U.S. Govt. Print. Off., 1978]

DLC-Micro JPRS 70600

2175

—— Neto urges reform in agriculture, industry, government. *In* U.S. *Joint Publications Research Service.* JPRS 70663. [Springfield, Va., National Technical Information Service, 1978] (Translations on Sub-Saharan Africa, no. 1880) p. 14–17.

Translation of speech recorded in *Jornal de Angola,* Luanda, Jan. 10, 1978, p. 1, 6.

Microfiche. [Washington, Supt. of Docs., U.S. Govt. Print. Off., 1978]

DLC-Micro JPRS 70663

2176

Peasant association to raise productivity, political awareness. *In* U.S. *Joint Publications Research Service.* JPRS 70663. [Springfield, Va., National Technical Information Service, 1978] (Translations on Sub-Saharan Africa, no. 1880) p. 10–13.

Translation of article in *Jornal de Angola,* Luanda, Dec. 24, 1977, p. 1, 6.

Microfiche. [Washington, Supt. of Docs., U.S. Govt. Print. Off., 1978]

DLC-Micro JPRS 70663

2177

Profiteering on agricultural products defies regulations. *In* U.S. *Joint Publications Research Service.* JPRS 72555. [Springfield, Va., National Technical Information Service, 1979] (Translations on Sub-Saharan Africa, no. 2046) p. 47–50.

Translation of article in *Semanario,* Luanda, no. 39, Nov. 11, 1978, p. 24–27.

Microfiche. [Washington, Supt. of Docs., U.S. Govt. Print Off., 1979]

DLC-Micro JPRS 72555

2178

Santos, José E. dos. Dos Santos exhorts peasants to increase production. *In* U.S. *Joint Publications Research Service.* JPRS 75451. [Springfield, Va., National Technical Information Service, 1980] (Sub-Saharan Africa report, no. 2231) p. 9–13.

Translation of speech by President Dos Santos in Malange Province, recorded in *Jornal de Angola,* Luanda, Feb. 27, 1980, p. 1, 3.

Microfiche. [s.l., 1980]

DLC-Micro JPRS 75451

2179

Steiner, Herbert H. Angola's agricultural economy in brief. [Washington] U.S. Dept. of Agriculture, Economic Research Service, [1977] 40 p. maps. (Foreign agricultural economic report, no. 139)

DNAL

Bibliography: p. 39–40.

Fisheries

2180

Fishing industry almost at a standstill. *In* U.S. *Joint Publications Research Service.* JPRS 69029. [Springfield, Va., National Technical Information Service, 1977] (Translations on Sub-Saharan Africa, no. 1741) p. 26–30.

2180 (cont.)

Translation of article in *Jornal de Angola*, Luanda, Mar. 31, 1977, p. 4.

Microfiche. [s.l., 1977]

DLC-Micro JPRS 69029

2181

Mocamedes fishing sector reviewed, low production analyzed. *In* U.S. *Joint Publications Research Service.* JPRS 74699. [Springfield, Va., National Technical Information Service, 1979] (Sub-Saharan Africa report, no. 2185) p. 16–19.

Translation of article in *Jornal de Angola*, Luanda, Oct. 28, 1979, p. 1, 11.

Microfiche. [s.l., 1979]

DLC-Micro JPRS 74699

Assistance Programs

2182

U.S. *Congress. House. Committee on International Relations. Subcommittee on International Resources, Food, and Energy.* Disaster assistance in Angola: hearings, Ninety-fourth Congress, November 5, 1975, February 26, and March 10, 1976. Washington, U.S. Govt. Print. Off., 1976. 207 p.

KF27.I54947 1975b
J74.A23 9TH Cong.
House Comm. Inter.
Rel., v. 66

Charles C. Diggs, Jr., Chairman.

In his introduction, Chairman Diggs indicated the purpose of the hearings: "The nature and status of U.S. efforts to provide disaster assistance in Angola; the efforts made by the international community, including individual states and international organizations, with respect to disaster assistance, and, the impact of the war in Angola on the civilian population."—p. 1.

Among the appendixes are the following:

Appendix 5. Statement by Gulf Oil on Gulf's operations in Angola. p. 160–161.

Appendix 6. Perry, Moses. Report of Library of Congress Congressional Research Service on "An international law analysis of certain questions relating to South Africa and Angola." p. 162–171.

Appendix 13. Browne, Robert S. Report of a seminar between a group of Americans and an official delegation of the People's Republic of Angola, held in Havana, Cuba, February 26–29, 1976. p. 190–198.

Appendix 14. Houser, George M. Report of the Havana seminar, February 26–29, 1976. p. 199–203.

2183

U.S. *Congress. Senate. Committee on Foreign Relations.* Restrictions on assistance to Angola: report (to accompany S. J. Res. 156) [Washington?, 1975?] 6 p. J66 Serial 13096-9

Report submitted by Senator John Sparkman.

At head of title: 94th Congress, 1st session. Senate. Report no. 94–584.

The purpose of the resolution was "to prohibit any type of assistance which might involve the United States more deeply in the civil war in Angola."

2184

U.S. *President, 1974–1977 (Ford)* Remarks on Senate action to prohibit United States assistance to Angola, December 19, 1975. *In* U.S. *President.* Public papers of the Presidents of the United States. Gerald R. Ford. 1975. [Washington, Office of the Federal Register, National Archives and Records Service; for sale by the Supt. of Docs., U.S. Govt. Print. Off., 1977] p. 1981.

J80.A283 1975

2185

Braeckman, Colette. Angolans hoping for Belgian reconstruction assistance. *In* U.S. *Joint Publications Research Service.* JPRS 72175. [Springfield, Va., National Technical Information Service, 1978] (Translations on Sub-Saharan Africa, no. 2018) p. 4–7.

Translation of article in *Le Soir*, Brussels, Sept. 12, 1978.

Microfiche. [Washington. Supt. of Docs., U.S. Govt. Print. Off., 1978]

DLC-Micro JPRS 72175

2186

Mulcahy, Edward W. Department testifies on Angolan disaster assistance. *In* U.S. *Dept. of State.* The Department of State bulletin, v. 73, no. 1901, Dec. 1, 1975: 800–802. JX232.A33 v. 73

Statement by the Acting Assistant Secretary of State for African Affairs before the Subcommittee on International Resources, Food, and Energy, Committee on International Relations, House of Representatives, Nov. 5, 1975.

2187

Schaufele, William E. Humanitarian aid to Angola discussed by Department. *In* U.S. *Dept. of State.* The Department of State bulletin, v. 74, no. 1917, Mar. 22, 1976: 375–376. JX232.A33 v. 74

Statement by the Assistant Secretary of State for African Affairs before the Subcommittee on International Resources, Food, and Energy of the

2187 (cont.)

Committee on International Relations, House of Representatives, Feb. 26, 1976.

2188

———— U.S. disaster assistance to Angola. Washington, 1976. 2 p. (U.S. Dept. of State. Bureau of Public Affairs. Office of Media Services. News release)   DLC

2189

Technical Assistance Information Clearing House. Development assistance programs of U.S. non-profit organizations, Angola. [New York], American Council of Voluntary Agencies for Foreign Service, 1980. 11 p. maps. (TAICH country report)
DLC

The Clearing House is operated by the Council under a grant from the U.S. Agency for International Development.

Communications and Transportation

2190

Construction, transportation plans discussed. *In* U.S. *Joint Publications Research Service.* JPRS 68009. [Springfield, Va., National Teachnical Information Service, 1976] (Translations on Sub-Saharan Africa, no. 1680) p. 18–36.

Translation of interview with Manuel Rezende de Oliveira, Minister of Public Works, Housing, and Transportation, in *Jornal de Angola*, Luanda, Sept. 7–8, 1976.

Microfiche. [s.l., 1976]

DLC-Micro JPRS 68009

2191

Reopening of vital Benguela Railroad discussed. *In* U.S. *Joint Publications Research Service.* JPRS 74295. [Springfield, Va., National Technical Information Service, 1979] (Sub-Saharan Africa report, no. 2159) p. 4–8. map.

Translation of article in *Demain l'Afrique*, Paris, Aug. 1979, p. 50–51.

Microfiche. [Washington, Supt. of Docs., U.S. Govt. Print. Off., 1979]

DLC-Micro JPRS 74295

Economic Conditions

2192

Details given on multinational companies. *In* U.S. *Joint Publications Research Service.* JPRS 64468.

[Springfield, Va., National Technical Information Service], 1975. (Translations on Africa, no. 1576) p. 7–22.   AS36.U57 JPRS 64468

Translation of article in *Eurafrica*, Brussels, Feb. 1975, p. 52–61.

Emphasis is on the major multinational companies operating in Angola, such as Companhia do Caminho de Ferro de Benguela (Benguela Railway Company), Companhia de Diamantes de Angola (DIAMANG), Companhia Mineira do Lobito, Cabinda Gulf Oil Company, Companhia de Petróleos de Angola (PETERANGOL), Companhia do Manganês de Angola, and Banco Comercial de Angola.

2193

Details of law on foreign investments disclosed. *In* U.S. *Joint Publications Research Service.* JPRS 74107. [Springfield, Va., National Technical Information Service, 1979] (Sub-Saharan Africa report, no. 2147) p. 39–49.

Translation of the text of the law given in *Jornal de Angola*, Luanda, July 6, 1979, p. 1, 6.

Microfiche. [Washington, Supt. of Docs., U.S. Govt. Print. Off., 1979]

DLC-Micro JPRS 74107

2194

Guidelines for economic, social development until 1980. *In* U.S. *Joint Publications Research Service.* JPRS 70364. [Springfield, Va., National Technical Information Service, 1977] (Translations on Sub-Saharan Africa, no. 1854) p. 27–33.

Translation of article in *Jornal de Angola*, Luanda, Nov. 23, 1977, p. 5.

Microfiche. [s.l., 1977]

DLC-Micro JPRS 70364

2195

Minister discusses orientation of national economy. *In* U.S. *Joint Publications Research Service.* JPRS 67366. [Springfield, Va., National Technical Information Service, 1976] (Translations on Sub-Saharan Africa, no. 1654) p. 5–9.

Translation of interview with Carlos Rocha, Minister of Planning, in *Jornal de Angola*, Luanda, Mar. 26, 1976, p. 1, 6.

Microfiche. [s.l., 1976]

DLC-Micro JPRS 67366

2196

Neto, Agostinho. Neto stresses peace, regional economic ties at Ceausescu reception. *In* U.S. *Joint Publications Research Service.* JPRS 73673. [Springfield, Va., National Technical Information Service, 1979] (Translations on Sub-Saharan Africa, no. 2119) p. 5–8.

2196 (cont.)

Translation of speech by President Neto, delivered at a reception for visiting Romanian President Nicolae Ceauşescu, reported in *Jornal de Angola*, Luanda, Apr. 15, 1979, p. 1, 6.

Microfiche. [Washington, Supt. of Docs., U.S. Govt. Print. Off., 1979]

DLC-Micro JPRS 73673

2197

————President warns against petit bourgeois ambition. *In* U.S. *Joint Publications Research Service.* JPRS 74213. [Springfield, Va., National Technical Information Service, 1979] (Sub-Saharan Africa report, no. 2155) p. 16–19.

Translation of article in *Jornal de Angola*, Luanda, Aug. 23, 1979, p. 1, 4.

Microfiche. [Washington, Supt. of Docs., U.S. Govt. Print. Off., 1979]

DLC-Micro JPRS 74213

2198

Organization, management of state companies spelled out. *In* U.S. *Joint Publications Research Service.* JPRS 70184 [Springfield, Va., National Technical Information Service, 1977] (Translations on Sub-Saharan Africa, no. 1836) p. 12–16.

Translation of article in *Jornal de Angola*, Luanda, Oct. 16, 1977, p. 1, 9.

Microfiche. [s.l., 1977]

DLC-Micro JPRS 70184

2199

Price stabilization of certain essential products. *In* U.S. *Joint Publications Research Service.* JPRS 69814. [Springfield, Va., National Technical Information Service, 1977] (Translations on Sub-Saharan Africa, no. 1803) p. 2–6.

Translation of article in *Jornal de Angola*, Luanda, Aug. 14, 1977, p. 1, 6.

Microfiche. [s.l., 1977]

DLC-Micro JPRS 69814

2200

Problems, solutions for nationalized factory discussed. *In* U.S. *Joint Publications Research Service.* JPRS 70696. [Springfield, Va., National Technical Information Service, 1978] (Translations on Sub-Saharan Africa, no. 1885) p. 13–16.

Translation of article on a nationalized rubber factory, in *Jornal de Angola*, Luanda, Jan. 5, 1978, p. 6.

Microfiche. [Washington, Supt. of Docs., U.S. Govt. Print. Off., 1978]

DLC-Micro JPRS 70696

2201

Rocha, Carlos. Minister discusses political aspects of economy. *In* U.S. *Joint Publications Research Service.* JPRS 67596. [Springfield, Va., National Technical Information Service, 1976] (Translations on Sub-Saharan Africa, no. 1661) p. 6–13.

Translation of article in *Diario de Luanda*, Luanda, June 21, 1976, p. 7–9,

Microfiche. [s.l., 1976]

DLC-Micro JPRS 67596

Education

2202

Details on educational reform. *In* U.S. *Joint Publications Research Service.* JPRS 70337. [Springfield, Va., National Technical Information Service, 1977] (Translations on Sub-Saharan Africa, no. 1850) p. 23–27.

Translation of article in *Jornal de Angola*, Luanda, Oct. 28, 1977, p. 2, 6.

Microfiche. [s.l., 1977]

DLC-Micro JPRS 70337

2203

Marxism-Leninism to be taught at university. *In* U.S. *Joint Publications Research Service.* JPRS 71133. [Springfield, Va., National Technical Information Service, 1978] (Translations on Sub-Saharan Africa, no. 1929) p. 22–28.

Translation of article in *Jornal de Angola*, Luanda, Apr. 21, 1978, p. 1, 6.

Microfiche. [Washington, Supt. of Docs., U.S. Govt. Print. Off., 1978]

DLC-Micro JPRS 71133

Foreign Relations

2204

U.S. *Information Agency. Office of Research.* Communist propaganda activities in sub-Saharan Africa and the implications of Angola. [Washington?], 1976. 27 p.   DLC

"R-21-76."

"This report reviews and compares information and cultural activities of selected Communist countries in sub-Saharan Africa between 1973 and early 1976 with emphasis on the period from Angolan independence in November 1975 to April 1976. Communist propaganda themes and the impact of events in Angola are also discussed."—cover.

2205

Bartlett, Dewey F. Angola. Congressional record, 94th Congress, 2d session, v. 122, Jan. 28, 1976: 1237–1238.   J11.R5 v. 122

   Remarks in the U.S. Senate.

   Emphasis is on policies of the United States and the Soviet Union.

2206

Bingham, Jonathan B. President Kaunda's statement on Angola. Congressional record, 94th Congress, 2d session, v. 122, Feb. 3, 1976: 2198–2200.
                    J11.R5 v. 122

   Extension of remarks in the U.S. House of Representatives.

   Includes statement by the Zambian President before the Organization of African Unity, Jan. 12, 1976.

2207

Brazilian ambassador stresses ties with Africa. *In* U.S. *Joint Publications Research Service.* JPRS 73227. [Springfield, Va., National Technical Information Service, 1979] (Translations on Sub-Saharan Africa, no. 2089) p. 27–33.

   Translation of interview with Rodolfo de Sousa Dantas, Ambassador of Brazil to Angola, in *Jornal de Angola*, Luanda, Mar. 10, 1979, p. 1, 4, 6.

   Microfiche. [Washington, Supt. of Docs., U.S. Govt. Print. Off., 1979]

                    DLC-Micro JPRS 73227

2208

Kissinger, Henry A. The global significance of events in Angola. *In* U.S. *Dept. of State.* Newsletter, no. 176, Feb. 1976: 4–9.   JX1.U542 1976

   Testimony by the Secretary of State before the Subcommittee on African Affairs, Committee on Foreign Relations, U.S. Senate, Jan. 29, 1976.

2209

Neto, Agostinho. Neto comments on relations with Portugal. *In* U.S. *Joint Publications Research Service.* JPRS 70913. [Springfield, Va., National Technical Information Service, 1978] (Translations on Sub-Saharan Africa, no. 1908) p. 14–18.

   Translation of speech recorded in *Jornal de Angola*, Luanda, Feb. 14, 1978, p. 4.

   Microfiche. [Washington, Supt. of Docs., U.S. Govt. Print. Off., 1978]

                    DLC-Micro JPRS 70913

2210

—— Neto on Namibia, stresses training, national realities. *In* U.S. *Joint Publications Research Service.* JPRS 73060. [Springfield, Va., National Tech-

nical Information Service, 1979] (Translations on Sub-Saharan Africa, no. 2079] p. 49–55.

   Text of speech recorded in *Jornal de Angola*, Luanda, Feb. 5, 1979, p. 1, 3.

   Wide-ranging review focusing on the situation in Namibia and on the training of technicians to meet Angola's agricultural and industrial needs.

   Microfiche. [Washington, Supt. of Docs., U.S. Govt. Print. Off., 1979]

                    DLC-Micro JPRS 73060

2211

—— Neto stresses socialist aid, rejects foreign copies. *In* U.S. *Joint Publications Research Service.* JPRS 74281. [Springfield, Va., National Technical Information Service, 1979] (Sub-Saharan Africa report, no. 2158] p. 12–16.

   Translation of text of address recorded in *Jornal de Angola*, Luanda, Aug. 21, 1979, p. 1, 4.

   Microfiche. [Washington, Supt. of Docs., U.S. Govt. Print. Off., 1979]

                    DLC-Micro JPRS 74281

2212

Report on foreign involvement in Angolan affairs. *In* U.S. *Joint Publications Research Service.* JPRS 69659. [Springfield, Va., National Technical Information Service, 1977] (Translations on Sub-Saharan Africa, no. 1788) p. 1–5.

   Translation of article in *Expresso*, Lisbon, July 9, 1977. p. 8R–9R.

   Microfiche. [s.l., 1977]

                    DLC-Micro JPRS 69659

2213

Rodriques, Miguel U. Dos Santos on relations with S. Africa, Portugal. *In* U.S. *Joint Publications Research Service.* JPRS 77396. [Springfield, Va., National Technical Information Service, 1981] (Sub-Saharan Africa report, no. 2360) p. 9–13.

   Translation of interview with President José Eduardo dos Santos, in *Jornal de Angola*, Luanda, Dec. 17, 1980, p. 3.

   Microfiche. [s.l., 1981]

                    DLC-Micro JPRS 77396

2214

Schaufele, William E. The African dimension of the Angolan conflict. *In* U.S. *Dept. of State.* The Department of State bulletin, v. 74, no. 1914, Mar. 1, 1976: 278–283.   JX232.A33 v. 74

   Statement by the Assistant Secretary of State for African Affairs before the Subcommittee on African Affairs, Committee on Foreign Relations, U.S. Senate, Feb. 6, 1976.

2215

Watson, Thomas H. The Angolan affair, 1974–1976. Maxwell Air Force Base, Ala., Air War College, Air University, 1977. 99 leaves. maps. (U.S. Air War College. Research report, no. 257)

DT611.75.W37

Bibliography: leaves 98–99.

Discusses foreign involvement in Angola during this period, particularly by the Sovient Union, Cuba, United States, and South Africa.

Issued also in microfiche. [s.l., Defense Documentation Center, 1977] 2 sheets (AD-B020760L).

United States

2216

U.S. *Congress. House. Committee on Foreign Affairs. Subcommittee on Africa.* United States policy toward Angola—update: hearings, Ninety-sixth Congress, second session, September 17 and 30, 1980. Washington, U.S. Govt. Print. Off., 1980. 76 p. map.

KF27.F625   1980e
J74.A23 96th
Cong., House Comm.
For. Aff., v. 118

Stephen J. Solarz, chairman.

The appendix (p. 75–76) includes tables, arranged by African country, of "Communist economic technicians in subsaharan Africa—1978," "Communist military personnel in subsaharan Africa—1978," and "French military troops in Africa (as of September 1979)."

2217

U.S. *Congress. House. Committee on International Relations.* United States policy on Angola: hearing, Ninety-fourth Congress, second session, January 26, 1976. Washington, U.S. Govt. Print. Off., 1976. 45 p.

KF27.I549   1976h
J74.A23   94th
Cong., House Comm.
Inter. Rel., v. 82

Thomas E. Morgan, chairman.

Chronology of events relating to Angola (April 25, 1974–January 29, 1976): p. 37–45.

Witnesses are William E. Schaufele, Jr., Assistant Secretary of State for African Affairs, and Edward W. Mulcahy, Deputy Assistant Secretary of State for African Affairs.

2218

U.S. *Congress. House. Committee on International Relations. Subcommittee on Africa.* United States-Angolan relations: hearings, Ninety-fifth Congress, second session, May 25, 1978. Washington, U.S. Govt. Print. Off., 1978. 55 p.

KF27.I54914   1978a
J74.A23 95th Cong.,
House Comm. Inter. Rel.,
v. 81

Charles C. Diggs, Jr., chairman.

Testimony by Gerald J. Bender, University of California, San Diego, and John Stockwell, former chief, Angola Task Force, Central Intelligence Agency.

Statement of Gulf Oil Corporation on its activities in Angola. p. 37–39.

2219

U.S. *Congress. Senate. Committee on Foreign Relations. Subcommittee on African Affairs.* Angola: hearings, Ninety-fourth Congress, second session, on U.S. involvement in civil war in Angola. Washington, U.S. Govt. Print. Off., 1976. 212 p.

KF26.F625   1976
J74.A23 94th
Cong., Sen. Comm.
For. Rel., v. 15

Dick Clark, chairman.

Prepared statement of Henry A. Kissinger, Secretary of State: p. 14–21.

2220

Angola—watershed of American foreign policy. Congressional record, 94th Congress, 2d session, v. 122, Jan. 22, 1976: 608–610.   J11.R5 v. 122

Remarks in the U.S. Senate, primarily by Sen. Dewey F. Bartlett.

2221

The Angolan adventure. Congressional record, 96th Congress, 1st session, v. 125, Mar. 7, 1979: 4075–4076.   J11.R5 v. 125

Remarks in the U.S. Senate by Senators Paul Tsongas and George McGovern concerning United States policy.

222

Bartlett, Dewey, F. An African doctrine: the missing chapter in American foreign policy. Congressional record, 94th Congress, 2d session, v. 122, Mar. 11, 1976: 6176–6177.   J11.R5 v. 122

Remarks in the U.S. Senate on United States policy toward Angola.

2223

Bell, Alphonzo. Angola's strategic implications for the United States. Congressional record, 94th Congress, 2d session, v. 122, Feb. 19, 1976: 3954–3956.   J11.R5 v. 122

Extension of remarks in the U.S. House of Representatives.

2224

Bonker, Don. Introduction of resolution on Angola. Congressional record, 94th Congress, 2d session, v. 122, Jan. 26, 1976: 893–894.

J11.R5 v. 122

Remarks in the U.S. House of Representatives. Resolution advises the President "to refrain from aiding factions in Angola unless and until Congress explicitly approves;" includes list of cosponsors.

2225

———— Tunney amendment. Congressional record, 94th Congress, 2d session, v. 122, Feb. 4, 1976: 2427–2428.
J11.R5 v. 122

Extension of remarks in the U.S. House of Representatives.

Concerns the use of U.S. Government funds in Angola.

2226

Conference report on H. R. 9861, Department of Defense appropriations, fiscal year 1976. Congressional record, 94th Congress, 2d session, v. 122, Jan. 27, 1976: 1035–1057.
J11.R5 v. 122

Remarks in the U.S. House of Representatives.

Includes debate on the question of providing funds "for any activities involving Angola other than intelligence gathering."

2227

Ford, Gerald R. President Ford reiterates U.S. objective in Angola. *In* U.S. *Dept. of State.* The Department of State bulletin, v. 74, no. 1912, Feb. 16, 1976: 182–183.
JX232.A33 v. 74

Text of a letter to Carl Albert, Speaker of the House of Representatives, Jan. 27, 1976.

2228

Griffin, Robert P. Secretary Kissinger's statement on Angola. Congressional record, 94th Congress, 2d session, v. 122, Jan. 29, 1976: 1506–1509.
J11.R5 v. 122

Remarks in the U.S. Senate.

Includes text of the Secretary of State's testimony before the Subcommittee on African Affairs, Committee on Foreign Relations, U.S. Senate, Jan. 29, 1976, and a list of Congressional briefings on Angola; (see also entry 2233).

2229

Heinz, John. Need to move with caution on Angola. Congressional record [daily ed.], 96th Congress, 2d session, v. 126, June 27, 1980: S8561–S8563.
J11.R7 v. 126

Remarks in the U.S. Senate.

2230

Humphrey, Hubert H. U.S. involvement in Angola must end. Congressional record, 94th Congress, 2d session, v. 122, Jan. 22, 1976: 639–641.
J11.R5 v. 122

Remarks in the U.S. Senate.

2231

International Security and Development Cooperation Act of 1980. Congressional record [daily ed.], 96th Congress, 2d session, v. 126, June 17, 1980: S7149–S7194.   J11.R7 v. 126

Includes discussion on U.S. policy toward Angola (S7180–S7184).

2232

Kemp, Jack F. Detente and Angola. Congressional record, 94th Congress, 2d session, v. 122, Jan. 21, 1976: 530–532.   J11.R5 v. 122

Remarks in the U.S. House of Representatives. Concerns American policy.

2233

Kissinger, Henry A. Implications of Angola for future U.S. foreign policy. *In* U.S. *Dept. of State.* The Department of State bulletin, v. 74, no. 1912, Feb. 16, 1976: 174–182.   JX232.A33 v. 74

Statement by the Secretary of State before the Subcommittee on African Affairs, Committee on Foreign Relations, U.S. Senate, Jan. 29, 1976; (see also entry 2228).

2234

Moose, Richard M. The United States and Angola. *In* U.S. *Dept. of State.* The Department of State bulletin, v. 80, no. 2045, Dec. 1980: 28–31.
JX232.A33. v. 80

Statement by the Assistant Secretary of State for African Affairs before the Subcommittee on Africa, Committee on Foreign Affairs, House of Representatives, Sept. 30, 1980.

2235

Moynihan, Daniel P. U.S. discusses Angola in U.N. General Assembly. *In* U.S. *Dept. of State.* The Department of State bulletin, v. 74, no. 1908, Jan. 19, 1976: 80–84.   JX232.A33 v. 74

Statement made in plenary session of the U.N. General Assembly on December 8 during the debate on proposed amendments to a resolution recommended by the Special Political Committee under agenda item 53, Policies of Apartheid of the Government of South Africa.

2236

Rangel, Charles B. Congressional Black Caucus calls for halt to U.S. intervention in Angola. Congres-

2236 (cont.)
sional record, 94th Congress, 2d session, v. 122, Jan. 21, 1976: 577–578.   J11.R5 v. 122
    Extension of remarks in the U.S. House of Representatives.
    Includes the press release issued by the Caucus on Dec. 17, 1975.

2237
Santos, José E. dos. Dos Santos: U.S. goal is direct intervention. *In* U.S. *Joint Publications Research Service.* JPRS 75528. [Springfield, Va., National Technical Information Service, 1980] (Sub-Saharan Africa report, no. 2237) p. 22–26.
    Translation of speech by the President of Angola during a visit to Cuba, recorded in *Jornal de Angola*, Luanda, Mar. 19, 1980, p. 1, 7.
    Microfiche. [s.l., 1980]
                        DLC-Micro JPRS 75528

2238
Wheeler, Douglas L. U.S. policy toward Angola: some modest proposals for the future. [s.l.], 1978. 12 leaves. (FAR 28039-S)
    Presented at the Conference on Angola and the United States, sponsored by the U.S. Dept. of State, Feb. 1978.
    Examined in the former Foreign Affairs Research Documentation Center, Dept. of State.

Cuba

2239
Ambassador Young and the double standard. Congressional record, 95th Congress, 1st standard, v. 123, Feb. 7, 1977: 3752–3755.
                        J11.R5 v. 123
    Remarks in the U.S. Senate, by Senators Howard H. Baker, Jr. and Jesse A. Helms, with press reports, concerning the Angolan situation and the statement by Andrew Young, U.S. Ambassador to the United Nations, that Cuban presence there brought "a certain stability and order."

2240
Bell, Alphonzo. Cuba's intervention in Angola. Congressional record, 94th Congress, 2d session, v. 122, Feb. 18, 1976: 3702–3704.
                        J11.R5 v. 122
    Extension of remarks in the U.S. House of Representatives.
    Includes article, "Cuban intervention in Angola intrigues world capitals," from the *Washington Post*.

2241
"Che" Guevara brigade to Angola. *In* U.S. *Joint Publications Research Service.* JPRS 70973. [Springfield, Va., National Technical Information Service, 1978] (Translations on Sub-Saharan Africa, no. 1914) p. 7–12.
    Translation of article on the "'Che' Guevara Internationalist Teachers Brigade," in *Juventud Rebelde*, Havana, Mar. 14, 1978, p. 6.
    Microfiche. [Washington, Supt. of Docs., U.S. Govt. Print. Off., 1978]
                        DLC-Micro JPRS 70973

2242
Dominguez, Jorge I. The Cuban operation in Angola, costs and benefits for the Angolan armed forces. [Cambridge, Mass.?], Harvard University, 1977. 21 leaves. (FAR 27906-N)
    The author's research on Cuban foreign military policy was supported at the University of Pittsburgh through the Project on the Role of Cuba in Hemispheric and World Affairs funded by the U.S. Dept. of State.
    Examined in the former Foreign Affairs Research Documentation Center, U.S. Dept. of State.

2243
Durch, William J. The Cuban military in Africa and the Middle East: from Algeria to Angola. Arlington, Va., Center for Naval Analyses, 1977. 67 p. maps. (Center for Naval Analyses. Professional paper, no. 201)
    Cuban involvement in Angola is covered on p. 39–52.
    Microfiche. [s.l., Defense Documentation Center, 1977] 1 sheet.   DLC-Sci RR AD-A045675

2244
Garcia Marquez, Gabriel. Gabriel Garcia Marquez writes on Cuba's intervention in Angola. *In* U.S. *Joint Publications Research Service.* JPRS 68689. [Springfield, Va., National Technical Information Service, 1977] (Translations on Sub-Saharan Africa, no. 1716) p. 7–24.
    Translation of article in *La Prensa*, Lima, Jan. 1977 (various dates).
    Microfiche. [s.l., 1977] DLC-Micro JPRS 68689

2245
Johansson, Anders. Cubans find gratitude for aid, but fail to overcome suspicions. *In* U.S. *Joint Publications Research Service.* JPRS 71200. [Springfield, Va., National Technical Information Service, 1978] (Translations on Sub-Saharan Africa, no. 1937) p. 7–14.
    Translation of article in *Dagens Nyheter*, Stockholm, Apr. 4, 7, 1978.

2245 (cont.)

Microfiche. [Washington, Supt. of Docs., U.S. Govt. Print. Off., 1978]

DLC-Micro JPRS 71200

2246

Jorge on relations with Brazil, Cuban presence. *In* U.S. *Joint Publications Research Service.* JPRS 76163. [Springfield, Va., National Technical Information Service, 1980] (Sub-Saharan Africa report, no. 2275) p. 1–6.

Translation of interview of Paulo T. Jorge, Minister of Foreign Affairs, by Brazilian journalists, in *Jornal de Angola*, Luanda, June 15, 1980, p. 1, 10.

Microfiche. [s.l., 1980]

DLC-Micro JPRS 76163

2247

McDonald, Larry. Cubans build a U.S. support apparat [sic] for Soviet puppets in Angola. Congressional record, 94th Congress, 2d session, v. 122, Mar. 11, 1976: 6354–6356.

J11.R5 v. 122

Extension of remarks in the U.S. House of Representatives.

Cites American groups that support the MPLA.

2248

Marcella, Gabriel. Cuba and the regional balance of power. Carlisle Barracks, Pa., Strategic Studies Institute, Army War College, 1977. 27 p. (Military issues research memo)

"The objective of this memorandum is to survey the dynamics of the new Cuban role in the Caribbean environment in view of Angola, Cuba's larger international role, institutional developments within Cuba, Soviet-Cuban relations, and interactions with a number of Caribbean countries."—Foreword.

Microfiche. [s.l., 1977] 1 sheet.

DLC-Sci RR AD-A047576

2249

Mota, Santana. Cuban role in economy discussed. *In* U.S. *Joint Publications Research Service.* JPRS 67855. [Springfield, Va., National Technical Information Service, 1976] (Translations on Sub-Saharan Africa, no. 1672) p. 17–20.

Translation of article on the economic and military situation in Angola, in *O Estado de São Paulo*, Aug. 3, 1976, p. 13.

Microfiche. [s.l., 1976]

DLC-Micro JPRS 67855

2250

Neto receives credentials from Cuban ambassador. *In* U.S. *Joint Publications Research Service.* JPRS

69835. [Springfield, Va., National Technical Information Service, 1977] (Translations on Sub-Saharan Africa, no. 1805) p. 3–8.

Translation of article quoting from speeches delivered on the occasion of the presentation of credentials of Manuel Agramont, Ambassador of Cuba, in *Jornal de Angola*, Luanda, Aug. 13, 1977, p. 1, 6.

Microfiche. [s.L., 1977]

DLC-Micro JPRS 69835

Soviet Union

2251

Brezhnev sends solidarity message to President Neto. *In* U.S. *Joint Publications Research Service.* JPRS 69530. [Springfield, Va., National Technical Information Service, 1977] (Translations on Sub-Saharan Africa, no. 1780) p. 1–11.

Translation of article in *Jornal de Angola*, Luanda, June 24, 1977, p. 1–2.

Microfiche. [s.l., 1977]

DLC-Micro JPRS 69530

2252

Kanet, Roger E. The Soviet Union and Angola: a new phase in the U.S.S.R.'s African policy? [s.l.], 1978. 10 leaves. (FAR 28045-S)

Paper presented at the Conference on Angola, sponsored by the U.S. Dept. of State, Feb. 1978.

Examined in the former Foreign Affairs Research Documentation Center, U.S. Dept. of State.

2253

Kemp, Jack F. Détente: the testing of a policy. Congressional record, 94th Congress, 2d session, v. 122, Jan. 29, 1976: 1650–1652.

J11.R5 v. 122

Remarks in the U.S. House of Representatives.

Concerns Soviet policy in Angola.

2254

Kissinger, Henry A. The permanent challenge to peace: U.S. policy toward the Soviet Union. *In* U.S. *Dept. of State.* The Department of State bulletin, v. 74, no. 1913, Feb. 23, 1976: 201–212.

JX232.A33 v. 74

Address by the Secretary of State before the Commonwealth Club of San Francisco and the World Affairs Council of Northern California, San Francisco, Feb. 3, 1976.

Includes a statement on the Soviet Union and Angola (p. 209–211).

2255
Klinghoffer, Arthur J. The Soviet Union and Angola. Carlisle Barracks, Pa., Strategic Studies Institute, U.S. Army War College, 1980. 28 p. (Strategic studies research memorandum)

Microfiche. [s.l., Defense Technical Information Center, 1980] 1 sheet (DLC-Sci RR AD-A088004); issued in microfilm by University Publications of America (cited in its *Africa: Special Studies*, 1962–1980, p. 7).

2256
McConnell, Robert B. Conventional military force and Soviet foreign policy. [Monterey, Calif.], Naval Postgraduate School, 1978, 158 p.

Bibliography: p. 151–156.

Thesis: Naval Postgraduate School.

Includes a section on Soviet support of the Movimento Popular de Libertação de Angola (MPLA).

Microfiche. [s.l., Defense Documentation Center, 1978] 2 sheets.

DLC-Sci RR AD-A057259

2257
Secretary Kissinger interviewed by panel in Los Angeles. *In* U.S. *Dept. of State*. The Department of State bulletin, v. 74, no. 1914, Mar. 1, 1976: 263–274.　　　　JX232.A33 v. 74

Includes comments of the Secretary of State on Soviet and Cuban involvement in Angola (p. 265–266).

Geography and Maps

2258
[U.S. *Central Intelligence Agency*] Angola. [Washington, 1975] col. map.　　G8649 1975.U5

Scale ca. 1 : 8,500,000.

"502866 12-75."

2259
———Angola. [Washington, 1975] col. map.
G8640 1975.U51

Scale ca. 1 : 8,500,000.

"502867 12-75."

Relief shown by shading.

2260
U.S. *Dept. of State. Office of the Geographer*. Angola: newly independent state. Washington, 1975. 1 p.
AMAU

"Geographic note GE-131."

Geology, Hydrology, and Mineral Resources

2261
Diamang activities report for 1979. *In* U.S. *Joint Publications Research Service*. JPRS 75971. [Springfield, Va., National Technical Information Service, 1980] (Sub-Saharan Africa report, no. 2261) p. 4–15.

Translation of article on the 1979 report of the Companhia de Diamantes de Angola, in *Jornal de Angola*, Luanda, May 15, 1980.

Microfiche. [s.l., 1980]

DLC-Micro JPRS 75971

2262
Jolly, Janice L. W. The mineral industry of Angola. Minerals yearbook, v. 3, 1975. [Washington, for sale by the Supt. of Docs., U.S. Govt. Print. Off., 1978] p. 101–105.　　TN23.U612　1975, v. 3

Prepared by the U.S. Bureau of Mines.

2263
——— The mineral industry of Angola. *In* Minerals yearbook, v. 3, 1976. [Washington, for sale by the Supt. of Docs., U.S. Govt. Print. Off., 1980] p. 93–97.　　TN23.U612　1976, v. 3

Prepared by the U.S. Bureau of Mines.

2264
——— The mineral industry of Angola. *In* Minerals yearbook, v. 3, 1977. [Washington, for sale by the Supt. of Docs., U.S. Govt. Print. Off., 1981] p. 63–67.　　TN23.U612　1977, v. 3

Prepared by the U.S. Bureau of Mines.

2265
——— The mineral industry of Angola. *In* Minerals yearbook, v. 3, 1978–79. [Washington, U.S. Govt. Print. Off., 1981] p. 65–70.
TN23.U612　1978–79, v. 3

Prepared by the U.S. Bureau of Mines.

2266
Morgan, George A. The mineral industry of Angola. In Minerals yearbook, v. 3. 1980. [Washington, for sale by the Supt. of Docs., U.S. Govt. Print. Off., 1982] p. 65–67.　　TN23.U612　1980, v. 3

Prepared by the U.S. Bureau of Mines.

2267
Lack of trained personnel hampers DIAMANG operations. *In* U.S. *Joint Publications Research Service*. JPRS 72414. [Springfield, Va., National

2267 (cont.)

Technical Information Service, 1978] (Translations on Sub-Saharan Africa, no. 2036) p. 26–29.

Translation of article in *Jornal de Angola*, Nov. 8, 1978, p. 3, 6.

Microfiche. [Washington, Supt. of Docs., U.S. Govt. Print. Off., 1978]

DLC-Micro JPRS 72414

2268

Minister reviews national petroleum sector. *In* U.S. *Joint Publications Research Service*. JPRS 73005. [Springfield, Va., National Technical Information Service, 1979] (Translations on Sub-Saharan Africa, no. 2075) p. 25–29.

Translation of article in *Jornal de Angola*, Luanda, Feb. 1, 1979, p. 1, 6.

Microfiche. [Washington, Supt. of Docs., U.S. Govt. Print. Off., 1979]

DLC-Micro JPRS 73005

2269

Morais, Jorge A. de. Oil minister provides explanation of contract awards. *In* U.S. *Joint Publications Research Service*. JPRS 75418. [Springfield, Va., National Technical Information Service, 1980] (Sub-Saharan Africa report, no. 2228) p. 23–28.

Translation of speech by the Minister of Petroleum in *Jornal de Angola*, Luanda, Jan. 16, 1980, p. 1, 7.

Microfiche. [s.l., 1980]

DLC-Micro JPRS 75418

2270

Neto, Agostinho. Neto: DIAMANG authority will be curbed. *In* U.S. *Joint Publications Research Service*. JPRS 72555. [Springfield, Va., National Technical Information Service, 1979] (Translations on Sub-Saharan Africa, no. 2046) p. 35–39.

Translation of speech recorded in *Jornal de Angola*, Luanda, Nov. 17, 1978, p. 1, 3.

Microfiche. [Washington, Supt. of Docs., U.S. Govt. Print. Off., 1979]

DLC-Micro JPRS 72555

Labor

2271

Duties, rights of cooperants detailed. *In* U.S. *Joint Publications Research Service*. JPRS 70931. [Springfield, Va., National Technical Information Service, 1978] (Translations on Sub-Saharan Africa, no. 1909) p. 6–17.

Translation of decree, "Statute of the Cooperant," concerning foreign workers in Angola,

recorded in *Jornal de Angola*, Luanda, Feb. 23, 1978, p. 1, 6.

Microfiche. [Washington, Supt. of Docs., U.S. Govt. Print. Off., 1978]

DLC-Micro JPRS 70931

2272

Neto, Agostinho. Neto's May Day speech stresses need to improve workers' lot. *In* U.S. *Joint Publications Research Service*. JPRS 73647. [Springfield, Va., National Technical Information Service, 1979] (Translations on Sub-Saharan Africa, no. 2117) p. 12–16.

Translation of President Neto's speech reported in *Jornal de Angola*, Luanda, May 2, 1979, p. 1, 4.

Microfiche. [Washington, Supt. of Docs., U.S. Govt. Print. Off., 1979]

DLC-Micro JPRS 73647

Military Affairs

2273

Bonker, Don. Angola and the mercenary issue. Congressional record, 94th Congress, 2d session, v. 122, July 2, 1976: 22476–22479.

J11.R5 v. 122

Remarks in the U.S. House of Representatives.

Representative Bonker includes correspondence with the Dept. of State, Dept. of Justice, and the Central Intelligence Agency on this question.

2274

Carreira, Henrique T. No draft exemptions, some soldiers may have international mission. *In* U.S. *Joint Publications Research Service*. JPRS 71246. [Springfield, Va., National Technical Information Service, 1978] (Translations on Sub-Saharan Africa, no. 1941) p. 22–27.

Translation of speech by the Minister of Defense recorded in *Jornal de Angola*, Luanda, Mar. 21, 1978, p. 1, 6.

Microfiche. [Washington, Supt. of Docs., U.S. Govt. Print. Off., 1978]

DLC-Micro JPRS 71246

2275

Defense minister discusses FAPLA. *In* U.S. *Joint Publications Research Service*. JPRS 68400. [Springfield, Va., National Technical Information Service, 1976] (Translations on Sub-Saharan Africa, no. 1698) p. 6–10.

Translation of interview with Henrique T. Carreira, in *Jornal de Angola*, Luanda, Nov. 11, 1976, p. 24–25.

Microfiche. [s.l., 1976]

DLC-Micro JPRS 68400

2276

Details on Cahama military maneuvers published. *In* U.S. *Joint Publications Research Service.* JPRS 74563. [Springfield, Va., National Technical Information Service, 1979] (Sub-Saharan Africa report, no. 2176) p. 10–13.

Translation of article on a military exercise in Cunene Province, Angola, in *Jornal de Angola*, Luanda, Sept. 27, 1979, p. 1, 7.

Microfiche. [Washington, Supt. of Docs., U.S. Govt. Print. Off., 1979]

DLC-Micro JPRS 74563

2277

Lara, Lúcio. Lara discusses army deficiencies, rectification campaign. *In* U.S. *Joint Publications Research Service.* JPRS 70832. [Springfield, Va., National Technical Information Service, 1978] (Translations on Sub-Saharan Africa, no. 1899) p. 19–31.

Translation of remarks by the Secretary-General of MPLA in *Jornal de Angola*, Luanda, Feb. 3, 1978, p. 4–5.

Microfiche. [Washington, Supt. of Docs., U.S. Govt. Print. Off., 1978]

DLC-Micro JPRS 70832

2278

Nascimento, Lopo F. F. do. Prime Minister stresses political character of army. *In* U.S. *Joint Publications Research Service.* JPRS 71043. [Springfield, Va., National Technical Information Service, 1978] (Translations on Sub-Saharan Africa, no. 1920) p. 10–14.

Translation of speech to political commissars of FAPLA, recorded in *Jornal de Angola*, Luanda, Mar. 29, 1978, p. 3.

Microfiche. [Washington, Supt. of Docs., U.S. Govt. Print. Off., 1978]

DLC-Micro JPRS 71043

2279

Neto, Agostinho. Neto to armed forces: fight, study, teach, produce. *In* U.S. *Joint Publications Research Service.* JPRS 69756. [Springfield, Va., National Technical Information Service, 1977] (Translations on Sub-Saharan Africa, no. 1797) p. 1–13.

Translation of speech recorded in *Jornal de Angola*, Luanda, Aug. 2, 1977, p. 4–5, 7.

Microfiche. [s.l., 1977]

DLC-Micro JPRS 69756

2280

Rivera, Armando L. Defense minister terms FAPLA a 'new army.' *In* U.S. *Joint Publications Research Service.* JPRS 69841. [Springfield, Va., National

Technical Information Service, 1977] (Translations on Sub-Saharan Africa, no. 1806) p. 1–6.

Translation of interview with Henrique T. Carreira, in *Verde Olivo*, Havana, Aug. 7, 1977, p. 56–57.

Microfiche. [s.l., 1977]

DLC-Micro JPRS 69841

Politics and Government

2281

Alves, Nito. Nito Alves addresses the nation on elections. *In* U.S. *Joint Publications Research Service.* JPRS 67504. [Springfield, Va., National Technical Information Service, 1976] (Translations on Sub-Saharan Africa, no. 1658) p. 1–6.

Translation of speech by the Minister of Internal Administration recorded in *Diario de Luanda*, Luanda, June 4, 1976, p. 3–4.

Microfiche. [s.l., 1976]

DLC-Micro JPRS 67504

2282

Bailey, Norman A. Alternative futures in Angola. [s.l.], 1975. 26 leaves. (FAR 22550-S)

"Submitted ... in fulfillment of the terms of Department of State contract 1722-520042 entitled 'The Future Political Development of Angola'."

Examined in the former Foreign Affairs Research Documentation Center, U.S. Dept. of State.

2283

Begonha, Manuel B. de. Naval officer favorably assesses political, economic situation. *In* U.S. *Joint Publications Research Service.* JPRS 71264. [Springfield, Va., National Technical Information Service, 1978] (Translations on Sub-Saharan Africa, no. 1943) p. 2–16.

Translation of article in *Anais do Clube Militar Naval*, Lisbon, Jan.–Mar. 1978, p. 125–142.

Microfiche. [Washington, Supt. of Docs., U.S. Govt. Print. Off., 1978]

DLC-Micro JPRS 71264

2284

Branquinho, J. Lara comments on various aspects of national situation. *In* U.S. *Joint Publications Research Service.* JPRS 77005. [Springfield, Va., National Technical Information Service, 1980] (Sub-Saharan Africa report, no. 2333) p. 2–11.

Translation of interview with Lúcio Lara of the Movimento Popular de Libertação de Angola-Partido de Trabalho (MPLA-PT), in *Notícias*, Maputo, Nov. 11, 12, 1980.

Microfiche. [s.l., 1980]

DLC-Micro JPRS 77005

2285

Carvalho, Augusto de. Possible reasons for government reshuffle contemplated. *In* U.S. *Joint Publications Research Service*. JPRS 72706. [Springfield, Va., National Technical Information Service, 1979] (Translations on Sub-Saharan Africa, no. 2056) p. 8–11.

Translation of article in *Expresso*, Lisbon, Dec. 16, 1978, p. 9.

Microfiche. [Washington, Supt. of Docs., U.S. Govt. Print. Off., 1979]

DLC-Micro JPRS 72706

2286

Castro, Raúl. Cuba's Raul Castro addresses MPLA congress. *In* U.S. *Joint Publications Research Service*. JPRS 70509. [Springfield, Va., National Technical Information Service, 1978] (Translations on Sub-Saharan Africa, no. 1866) p. 17–21.

Translation of speech recorded in *Jornal de Angola*, Luanda, Dec. 6, 1977, p. 4, 5.

Microfiche. [Washington, Supt. of Docs., U.S. Govt. Print. Off., 1978]

DLC-Micro JPRS 70509

2287

Cuban roundup of attempted coup in Luanda. *In* U.S. *Joint Publications Research Service*. JPRS 69450. [Springfield, Va., National Technical Information Service, 1977] (Translations on Sub-Saharan Africa, no. 1774) p. 11–17.

Translation of article on an attempted coup by dissident members of the ruling MPLA on May 27, 1977, in *Verde Olivo*, Havana, June 12, 1977, p. 6–11.

Microfiche. [s.l., 1977]

DLC-Micro JPRS 69450

2288

Details of new judicial system explained. *In* U.S. *Joint Publications Research Service*. JPRS 71356. [Springfield, Va., National Technical Information Service, 1978] (Translations on Sub-Saharan Africa, no. 1952) p. 16–19.

Translation of article in *Semanário*, Luanda, May 27–june 2, 1978, p. 4–7.

Microfiche. [Washington, Supt. of Docs., U.S. Govt. Print. Off., 1978]

DLC-Micro JPRS 71356

2289

Draft statutes of MPLA-Labor Party. *In* U.S. *Joint Publications Research Service*. JPRS 70364. [Springfield, Va., National Technical Information Service, 1977] (Translations on Sub-Saharan Africa, no. 1854) p. 3–26.

Translation of text of statutes in *Jornal de Angola*, Luanda, Nov. 23, 1977.

Microfiche. [s.l., 1977]

DLC-Micro JPRS 70364

2290

First year of self-government reviewed. *In* U.S. *Joint Publications Research Service*. JPRS 68388. [Springfield, Va., National Technical Information Service, 1976] (Translations on Sub-Saharan Africa, no. 1697) p. 2–16.

Translation of interview with Prime Minister Lopo F. F. do Nascimento, in *Jornal de Angola*, Luanda, Nov. 11, 1976, p. 9, 13, 15.

Microfiche. [s.l., 1976]

DLC-Micro JPRS 68388

2291

Goldwater, Barry. Angola. Congressional record, 95th Congress, 2d session, v. 124, Apr. 11, 1978: 9603–9614.   J11.R5 v. 124

Remarks in the U.S. Senate.

Includes series of articles from the *Pretoria News*.

2292

Information on Angolan personalities. *In* U.S. *Joint Publications Research Service*. JPRS 76065. [Springfield, Va., National Technical Information Service, 1980] (Sub-Saharan Africa report, no. 2269) p. 5–9.

Translation of extracts from *Journal de Angola*, Luanda, including brief notes on Angolan political and industrial leaders.

Microfiche. [s.l., 1980]

DLC-Micro JPRS 76065

2293

Lara, Lúcio. Lara comments on MPLA founding, ideology. *In* U.S. *Joint Publications Research Service*. JPRS 74247. [Springfield, Va., National Technical Information Service, 1979] (Sub-Saharan Africa report, no. 2157) p. 6–9.

Translation of article on the Movimento Popular de Libertação de Angola in *Jornal de Angola*, Luanda, Sept. 5, 1979, p. 3, 4.

Microfiche. [Washington, Supt. of Docs., U.S. Govt. Print. Off., 1979]

DLC-Micro JPRS 74247

2294

—— Lara discusses provincial problems, Zairian refugees. *In* U.S. *Joint Publications Research Service*. JPRS 70170. [Springfield, Va., National Technical Information Service, 1977] (Translations on Sub-Saharan Africa, no. 1834) p. 10–13.

Translation of article by the Secretary-General

2294 (cont.)
of the MPLA in *Jornal de Angola*, Luanda, Oct. 11, 1977, p. 1, 6.
Microfiche. [s.l., 1977]
DLC-Micro JPRS 70170

2295
Legislation governing People's Revolutionary Courts. *In* U.S. *Joint Publications Research Service*. JPRS 71586. [Springfield, Va., National Technical Information Service, 1978] (Translations on Sub-Saharan Africa, no. 1971) p. 1–12.
Translation of text of law reprinted in *Jornal de Angola*, Luanda, June 22, 1978, p. 2, 6.
Microfiche. [Washington, Supt. of Docs., U.S. Govt. Print. Off., 1978]
DLC-Micro JPRS 71586

2296
Miller, Robert C. Angola—portent of the future. Maxwell Air Force Base, Ala., 1979. 64 p. (U.S. Air University. Air Command and Staff College. Research study) AMAU

2297
Neto, Agostinho. Neto emphasizes work to achieve development and effect change. *In* U.S. *Joint Publications Research Service*. JPRS 70711. [Springfield, Va., National Technical Information Service, 1978] (Translations on Sub-Saharan Africa, no. 1887) p. 1–6.
Translation of speech recorded in *Jornal de Angola*, Luanda, Jan. 15, 1978, p. 1, 6.
Microfiche. [Washington, Supt. of Docs., U.S. Govt. Print. Off., 1978]
DLC-Micro JPRS 70711

2298
———— Neto New Year message: state must be subordinated to party. *In* U.S. *Joint Publications Research Service*. JPRS 72773. [Springfield, Va., National Technical Information Service, 1979] (Translations on Sub-Saharan Africa, no. 2061) p. 17–20.
Translation of speech recorded in *Jornal de Angola*, Luanda, Jan. 3, 1979, p. 1, 5.
Microfiche. [Washington, Supt. of Docs., U.S. Govt. Print. Off., 1979]
DLC-Micro JPRS 72773

2299
New legal measures will serve class struggle. *In* U.S. *Joint Publications Research Service*. JPRS 70600. [Springfield, Va., National Technical Information Service, 1978] (Translations on Sub-Saharan Africa, no. 1874) p. 16–20.

Translation of article in *Jornal de Angola*, Luanda, Dec. 30, 1977, p. 2.
Microfiche. [Washington, Supt. of Docs., U.S. Govt. Print. Off., 1978]
DLC-Micro JPRS 70600

2300
Police will help with revolution. *In* U.S. *Joint Publications Research Service*. JPRS 70677. [Springfield, Va., National Technical Information Service, 1978] (Translations on Sub-Saharan Africa, no. 1883) p. 8–11.
Translation of article, in *Jornal de Angola*, Luanda, Jan. 3, 1978, p. 9.
Microfiche. [Washington, Supt. of Docs., U.S. Govt. Print. Off., 1978]
DLC-Micro JPRS 70677

2301
Political deficiencies of civil service noted. *In* U.S. *Joint Publications Research Service*. JPRS 70279. [Springfield, Va., National Technical Information Service, 1977] (Translations on Sub-Saharan Africa, no. 1844) p. 20–23.
Translation of article in *Jornal de Angola*, Luanda, Oct. 25, 1977, p. 1, 2.
Microfiche. [s.l., 1977]
DLC-Micro JPRS 70279

2302
Report of MPLA central committee to first congress. *In* U.S. *Joint Publications Research Service*. JPRS 70530. [Springfield, Va., National Technical Information Service, 1978] (Translations on Sub-Saharan Africa, no. 1868) p. 15–61.
Translation of special undated supplement to *Jornal de Angola*, Luanda, p. 4–11.
Microfiche. [Washington, Supt. of Docs., U.S. Govt. Print. Off., 1978]
DLC-Micro JPRS 70530

2303
Santos, José E. dos. Dos Santos: politics above technology, skin color unimportant. *In* U.S. *Joint Publications Research Service*. JPRS 74563. [Springfield, Va., National Technical Information Service, 1979] (Sub-Saharan Africa report, no. 2176) p. 6–9.
Translation of speech by the President of Angola recorded in *Jornal de Angola*, Luanda, Oct. 18, 1979, p. 1, 6.
Microfiche. [Washington, Supt. of Docs., U.S. Govt. Print. Off., 1979]
DLC-Micro JPRS 74563

2304

—— Dos Santos repudiates "black socialism" theory. *In* U.S. *Joint Publications Research Service.* JPRS 77011. [Springfield, Va., National Technical Information Service, 1980] (Sub-Saharan Africa report, no. 2334) p. 22–25.

Translation of speech rejecting the "Black Socialist Republic" views of Jonas Savimbi, recorded in *Jornal de Angola*, Luanda, Oct. 29, 1980, p. 3.

Microfiche. [s.l., 1980]

DLC-Micro JPRS 77011

2305

—— President assesses national achievements, challenges. *In* U.S. *Joint Publications Research Service.* JPRS 77433. [Springfield, Va., National Technical Information Service, 1981] (Sub-Saharan Africa report, no. 2363) p. 4–8.

Translation of excerpts of speech recorded in *Jornal de Angola*, Luanda, Dec. 11, 1980, p. 3, 10.

Microfiche. [s.l., 1981]

DLC-Micro JPRS 77433

2306

Text of constitution published. *In* U.S. *Joint Publications Research Service.* JPRS 70812. [Springfield, Va., National Technical Information Service, 1978] (Translations on Sub-Saharan Africa, no. 1897) p. 2–13.

Translation of text published in *Jornal de Angola*, Luanda, Feb. 18, 1978, p. 4–5.

Microfiche. [Washington, Supt. of Docs., U.S. Govt. Print. Off., 1978]

DLC-Micro JPRS 70812

Cabinda

2307

Cabinda situation discussed. *In* U.S. *Joint Publications Research Service.* JPRS 67833. [Springfield, Va., National Technical Information Service, 1976] (Translations on Sub-Saharan Africa, no. 1671) p. 4–8.

Translation of article in *Jornal de Angola*, Luanda, July 29, 1976, p. 1, 7.

Microfiche. [s.l., 1976]

DLC-Micro JPRS 67833

2308

FLEC's position paper on Cabinda. *In* U.S. *Joint publications Research Service.* JPRS 70572. [Springfield, Va., National Technical Information Service, 1978] (Translations on Sub-Saharan Africa, no. 1871) p. 16–31.

Translation of article in *Revue française d'études politiques africaines*, Paris, Oct. 1977, p. 84–110.

FLEC: Frente de Libertação do Enclave de Cabinda.

Microfiche. [Washington, Supt. of Docs., U.S. Govt. Print. Off., 1978]

DLC-Micro JPRS 70572

2309

Lara, Lúcio. Lara press conference on Cabinda situation. *In* U.S. *Joint Publications Research Service.* JPRS 65889. [Springfield, Va., National Technical Information Service, 1975] (Translations on Sub-Saharan Africa, no. 1619) p. 5–10.

Translation of article in *O Comercio*, Luanda, Aug. 28, 1975, p. 1–2.

Microfiche. [s.l., 1975]

DLC-Micro JPRS 65889

2310

Rivera, Armando L. Angolan claim to Cabinda reiterated. *In* U.S. *Joint Publications Research Service.* JPRS 69789. [Springfield, Va., National Technical Information Service, 1977] (Translations on Sub-Saharan Africa, no. 1801) p. 1–6.

Translation of article in *Verde Olivo*, Havana, June 19, 1977, p. 34–39.

Microfiche. [s.l., 1977]

DLC-Micro JPRS 69789

2311

Sigaud, Paul. French newsman reports on FLEC activities. *In* U.S. *Joint Publications Research Service.* JPRS 75009. [Springfield, Va., National Technical Information Service, 1980] (Sub-Saharan Africa report, no. 2204) p. 12–16.

Translation of article in *Le Figaro Magazine*, Paris, Dec. 8, 1979, p. 66–72.

Microfiche. [s.l., 1980]

DLC-Micro JPRS 75009

Civil War

2312

Ashbrook, John M. Angola, another American embarrassment. Congressional record, 96th Congress, 1st session, v. 125, June 22, 1979: 16240–16243. 		J11.R5 v. 125

Extension of remarks in the U.S. House of Representatives.

Includes article, "Angola—a call for courage," from the *Free Trade Union News*, on the civil war and United States policy toward the conflict.

2313

Barroqueiro, Silverio. Angola: a revolution in transition. Washington, Defense Intelligence School, 1976. 62 p.   AMAU

"Intelligence research paper."

2314

Benguela affected by drought, shortages, guerrillas. *In* U.S. *Joint Publications Research Service.* JPRS 71246. [Springfield, Va., National Technical Information Service, 1978] (Translations on Sub-Saharan Africa, no. 1941) p. 63–67.

Translation of interview with Garcia Vaz Contreiras, provincial commissioner of Benguela Province, in *Jornal de Angola*, Luanda, Apr. 15, 1978, p. 1, 6.

Microfiche. [Washington, Supt. of Docs., U.S. Govt. Print. Off., 1978]

DLC-Micro JPRS 71246

2315

Branquinho, J. FAPLA, South African, UNITA war activities detailed. *In* U.S. *Joint Publications Research Service* JPRS 76526. [Springfield, Va., National Technical Information Service, 1980] (Sub-Saharan Africa report, no. 2300) p. 20–33.

Translation of article in *Notícias*, Maputo, Aug. 17, 24, and 27, 1980.

FAPLA: Forças Armadas Populares de Libertação de Angola.

UNITA: União Nacional para a Independência Total de Angola.

Microfiche. [s.l., 1980]

DLC-Micro JPRS 76526

2316

Damage UNITA has inflicted on Huambo detailed. *In* U.S. *Joint Publications Research Service.* JPRS 71270. [Springfield, Va., National Technical Information Service, 1978] (Translations on Sub-Saharan Africa, no. 1944) p. 10–16.

Translation of interview with Pedro M. Tonha, provincial commissioner of Huambo, in *Jornal de Angola*, Luanda, May 11, 1978, p. 3, 6.

Microfiche. [Washington, Supt. of Docs., U.S. Govt. Print. Off., 1978]

DLC-Micro JPRS 71270

2317

Davis, Nathaniel. Department discusses situation in Angola. *In* U.S. *Dept of State.* The Department of State bulletin, v. 73, no. 1885, Aug. 11, 1975: 212–213.   JX232.A33 v. 73

Statement by the Assistant Secretary of State for African Affairs before the Subcommittee on African Affairs, Committee on Foreign Relations, U.S. Senate, July 14, 1875.

2318

Derwinski, Edward J. Angola. Congressional record [daily ed.], 96th Congress, 2d session, v. 126, Mar. 28, 1980: E1635–E1636.   J11.R7 v. 126

Extension of remarks in the U.S. House of Representatives.

Includes text of statement by Jonas Savimbi during his Nov. 1979 visit to the United States.

2319

Dessart, Francis. Exclusive interview with Holden Roberto. *In* U.S. *Joint Publications Research Service.* JPRS 68414. [Springfield, Va., National Technical Information Service, 1976] (Translations on Sub-Saharan Africa, no. 1699) p. 1–5.

Translation of interview with the president of FNLA, in *Remarques africaines*, Brussels, Dec. 1, 1976, p. 56–57.

Microfiche. [s.l., 1976]

DLC-Micro JPRS 68414

2320

Dia, Mam L. 'Le Soleil' interviews UNITA leader. *In* U.S. *Joint Publications Research Service.* JPRS 66226. [Springfield, Va., National Technical Information Service, 1975] (Translations on Sub-Saharan Africa, no. 1628) p. 1–6.

Translation of interview with Jonas Savimbi in *Le Soleil*, Dakar, Oct. 27, 1975, p. 7.

Microfiche. [s.l., 1975]

DLC-Micro JPRS 66226

2321

FAPLA political cadres outline goals. *In* U.S. *Joint Publications Research Service.* JPRS 67291. [Springfield, Va., National Technical Information Service, 1976] (Translations on Sub-Saharan Africa, no. 1651) p. 1–6.

Translation of article in *Diario de Luanda*, Mar. 29, 1976, p. 3–4.

Microfiche. [s.l., 1976]

DLC-Micro JPRS 67291

2322

Garcia Marquez, Gabriel. Columbian journalist tells of situation in Angola. *In* U.S. *Joint Publications Research Service.* JPRS 69654. [Springfield, Va., National Technical Information Service, 1977] (Translations on Sub-Saharan Africa, no. 1787) p. 5–13.

Translation of article in *Oiga*, Lima, July 15, 1977, p. 18–21, 24.

Microfiche. [s.l., 1977]

DLC-Micro JPRS 69654

2323

Garn, Jake. Angola: the black struggle against Communism. Congressional record, 95th Congress, 2d session, v. 124, May 23, 1978: 15024–15027.

J11.R5 v. 124

Remarks in the U.S. Senate.

Includes article from the *Sunday Telegraph* (London) describing Cuban military activity in Angola.

2324

Humbert, Michel. Newsman meets Savimbi, reports on successful Benguela sabotage. *In* U.S. *Joint Publications Research Service*. JPRS 73489. [Springfield, Va., National Technical Information Service, 1979] (Translations on Sub-Saharan Africa, no. 2107) p. 25–28.

Translation of article in *Le Figaro*, Paris, Mar. 2–4, 1979.

Microfiche. [Washington, Supt. of Docs., U.S. Govt. Print. Off., 1979]

DLC-Micro JPRS 73489

2325

International Security and Development Cooperation Act of 1980. Congressional record [daily ed.], 96th Congress, 2d session, v. 126, Dec. 3, 1980: S15312– S15317. J11.R7 v. 126

Debate in the U.S. Senate includes remarks by Senator Jesse Helms on the civil war in Angola, with particular reference to the role of Jonas Savimbi (S15314– S15316).

2326

Kavutirwaki, Kambale. Liberation front spokesman discusses Angola. *In* U.S. *Joint Publications Research Service*. JPRS 65787. [Springfield, Va., National Technical Information Service, 1975] (Translations on Africa, no. 1617) p. 1–5.

Translation of press conference held by Moneiro Barreto of FNLA, in *Zaïre*, Kinshasa, Aug. 18, 1975, p. 34–35.

Microfiche. [s.l., 1975]

DLC-Micro JPRS 65787

2327

Lefort, René. Struggle continues on morrow of victory. *In* U.S. *Joint Publications Research Service*. JPRS 67984. [Springfield, Va., National Technical Information Service, 1976] (Translations on Sub-Saharan Africa, no. 1679) p. 8–16.

Translation of article in *Le Monde*, Paris, Sept. 2, 3, 4, 1976.

Microfiche. [s.l., 1976]

DLC-Micro JPRS 67984

2328

MPLA powers diagramed. *In* U.S. *Joint Publications Research Service*. JPRS 68284. [Springfield, Va., National Technical Information Service, 1976] (Translations on Sub-Saharan Africa, no. 1692) p. 7–12.

Translation of article in *Jornal de Angola*, Luanda, Nov. 6, 1976, p. 5.

Microfiche. [s.l., 1976]

DLC-Micro JPRS 68284

2329

Macho, Juan. Guerrilla warfare against Cubans in Angola described. *In* U.S. *Joint Publications Research Service*. JPRS 70254. [Springfield, Va., National Technical Information Service, 1977] (Translations on Sub-Saharan Africa, no. 1842) p. 8–11.

Translation of article in *Gente*, Lima, Oct. 12, 1977, p. 3–7.

Microfiche. [s.l., 1977]

DLC-Micro JPRS 70254

2330

Neto, Agostinho. Neto speech emphasizes traitorous UNITA role. *In*. U.S. *Joint Publications Research Service*. JPRS 73439. [Springfield, Va., National Technical Information Service, 1978] (Translations on Sub-Saharan Africa, no. 2040) p. 1–10.

Translation of speech recorded in *Jornal de Angola*, Luanda, Nov. 12, 1978, p. 1, 3–4.

Michrofiche. [Washington, Supt. of Docs., U.S. Govt. Print. Off., 1978]

DLC-Micro JPRS 72478

2331

Official admits losses, stresses defense capability improvement. *In* U.S. *Joint Publications Research Service*. JPRS 73439. [Springfield, Va., National Technical Information Service, 1979] (Translations on Sub-Saharan Africa, no. 2103) p. 5–11.

Translation of interview with Henrique T. Carreira, Minister of Defense of Angola, in *Jornal de Angola*, Luanda, Apr. 12, 1979, p. 1, 6.

Microfiche. [Washington, Supt. of Docs., U.S. Govt. Print. Off., 1979]

DLC-Micro JPRS 73439

2332

Official communique on leaders' summit meeting in Nakuru. *In* U.S. *Joint Publications Research Service*. JPRS 65210. [Springfield, Va., National Technical Information Service, 1975] (Translations on Africa, no. 1602) p. 1–11.

Translation of communique issued at end of meeting of leaders of MPLA, FNLA, and UNITA,

2332 (cont.)
in Nakuru, Kenya, June 16–21, 1975; broadcast over Luanda radio, June 22, 1975.
Microfiche. [s.l., 1975]
DLC-Micro JPRS 65210

2333
Puku, Mariano. Angolans in south support MPLA against UNITA. *In* U.S. *Joint Publications Research Service*. JPRS 70051. [Springfield, Va., National Technical Information Service, 1977] (Translations on Sub-Saharan Africa, no. 1824) p. 1–6.
Translation of statement by the provincial commissioner of Kuando-Kubango, in *Jornal de Angola*, Luanda, Sept. 29, 1977, p. 1, 6.
Microfiche. [s.l., 1977]
DLC-Micro JPRS 70051

2334
Rafael, Pedro. Disarmament of Angolan liberation movement urged. *In* U.S. *Joint Publications Research Service*. JPRS 65042. [Springfield, Va., National Technical Information Service], 1975. (Translations on Africa, no. 1598) p. 7–16.
AS36.U57 JPRS 65042
Translation of interview with José Campelo, a former Portuguese official in Angola, in *Diario de Notícias*, Lisbon, May 19, 1975, p. 7, 10.

2335
Refuge's allegations in South Africa vehemently denied; editorial attacks South Africa. *In* U.S. *Joint Publications Research Service*. JPRS 72773. [Springfield, Va., National Technical Information Service, 1979] (Translations on Sub-Saharan Africa, no. 2061) p. 25–28.
Translation of editorial in *Jornal de Angola*, Jan. 15, 1979, p. 1.
Microfiche. [Washington, Supt. of Docs., U.S. Govt. Print. Off., 1979]
DLC-Micro JPRS 72773

2336
Reichle, Denis. FRG journal reports on guerrilla warfare. *In* U.S. *Joint Publications Research Service*. JPRS 76222. [Springfield, Va., National Technical Information Service, 1980] (Sub-Saharan Africa report, no. 2279) p. 11–14.
Translation of article in *Der Spiegel*, Hamburg, Aug. 4, 1980, p. 101–104.
Microfiche. [s.l., 1980]
DLC-Micro JPRS 76222

2337
Rodrigues, Luiz. Reporter relates experiences with UNITA unit. *In* U.S. *Joint Publications Research*

Service. JPRS 69095. [Springfield, Va., National Technical Information Service, 1977] (Translations on Sub-Saharan Africa, no. 1747) p. 3–11.
Translation of article in *Expresso*, Lisbon, Apr. 1, 1977, p. 16, 17.
Microfiche. [s.l., 1977]
DLC-Micro JPRS 69095

2338
Santos, José E. dos. Dos Santos: clemency measures do not include 'false leaders.' *In* U.S. *Joint Publications Research Service*. JPRS 75528. [Springfield, Va., National Technical Information Service, 1980] (Sub-Saharan Africa report, no. 2237) p. 31–34.
Translation of speech by the President of Angola recorded in *Jornal de Angola*, Luanda, Mar. 9, 1980, p. 1, 10.
Microfiche. [s.l., 1980]
DLC-Micro JPRS 75528

2339
Semprum, Alfredo. FNLA official interviewed on military situation. *In* U.S. *Joint Publications Research Service*. JPRS 71463. [Springfield, Va., National Technical Information Service, 1978] (Translations on Sub-Saharan Africa, no. 1960) p. 1–4.
Translation of interview with unidentified FNLA official, in *ABC*, Madrid, May 23, 1978, p. 27.
Microfiche. [Washington, Supt. of Docs., U.S. Govt. Print. Off., 1978]
DLC-Micro JPRS 71463

2340
UNITA official interviewed. *In* U.S. *Joint Publications Research Service*. JPRS 66399. [Springfield, Va., National Technical Information Service, 1975] (Translation on Sub-Saharan Africa, no. 1631) p. 3–7.
Translation of interview with Jorge Sangumba, UNITA's secretary for foreign affairs, in *Jornal do Brasil*, Rio de Janeiro, Nov. 9, 1975, p. 1.
Microfiche. [s.l., 1975]
DLC-Micro JPRS 66399

Refugees

2341
Political education underway for Zairian refugees. *In* U.S. *Joint Publications Research Service*. JPRS 70955. [Springfield, Va., National Technical Information Service, 1978] (Translations on Sub-Saharan Africa, no. 1912) p. 25–29.
Translation of article in *Jornal de Angola*, Luanda, Feb. 21, 1978, p. 3.

2341 (cont.)

Microfiche. [Washington, Supt. of Docs., U.S. Govt. Print. Off., 1978]

DLC-Micro JPRS 70955

2342

Zairian refugees, other problems in Lunda province. *In* U.S. *Joint Publications Research Service.* JPRS 70955. [Springfield, Va., National Technical Information Service, 1978] (Translations on Sub-Saharan Africa, no. 1912) p. 21–24.

Translation of article on the refugee situation and on education and health conditions, in *Jornal de Angola*, Luanda, Feb. 26, 1978, p. 1, 6.

Microfiche. [Washington, Supt. of Docs., U.S. Govt. Print. Off., 1978]

DLC-Micro JPRS 70955

Other Subjects

2343

Carp, Carol. A review of health care in Angola: issues, analyses, and recommendations. Washing-ton, Family Health Care, inc., 1978. [89] p. (Health and development in Southern Africa, v. 5)

Submitted to the Southern Africa Development Analysis Program, U.S. Agency for International Development.

Bibliography: p. [87–89].

Issued in cooperation with Africare.

Microfiche. [Washington, U.S. Agency for International Development, 1979?] 1 sheet.

DLC-Sci RR PN-AAH-165

2344

Women's emancipation part of class struggle. *In* U.S. *Joint Publications Research Service.* JPRS 67901. [Springfield, Va., National Technical Information Service, 1976] (Translations on Sub-Saharan Africa, no. 1673) p. 6–10.

Translation of article in *Journal de Angola*, Luanda, Aug. 15, 1976, p. 1, 7.

Microfiche. [s.l., 1976]

DLC-Micro JPRS 67901

Botswana

General

2345

U.S. *Agency for International Development*. A report to the Congress on development needs and opportunities for cooperation in Southern Africa. Annex A: Botswana. [Washington], 1979. 170 p.

Bibliography: p. 164–170.

An introduction to the economic situation and potential of Botswana, with sections on its dependence on South Africa, agriculture, mining, industry, commerce, transportation, education, housing, health conditions, development planning, and foreign assistance programs.

Microfiche. [Washington, U.S. Agency for International Development, 1979?] 2 sheets.

DLC-Sci RR PN-AAH-152

2346

U.S. *Dept. of State*. Post report. Botswana. [Washington, Dept. of State, Publishing Services Division; for sale by the Supt. of Docs., U.S. Govt. Print. Off., 1980] 16 p. illus., map. (*Its* Department and Foreign Service series, 189)

JX1705.A286 Spec. Format

Department of State publication, 9130.

L.C. has also report issued in 1974; report for 1977 examined in the Foreign Service Institute Library, Rosslyn, Va.

For a description of the contents of this publication, see the note to entry 936.

2347

U.S. *Dept. of State. Bureau of Public Affairs*. Background notes. Botswana. [Washington, for sale by the Supt. of Docs., U.S. Govt. Print. Off.], 1980. 4 p. maps. (U.S. Dept. of State. Department of State publication 8046)

G59.U5

L.C. retains only the latest revision.

For a description of the contents of this publication, see the note to entry 937.

2348

Dale, Richard. Prospects for Botswana in the 1970's [s.l.], 1974. 14 leaves. (FAR 19858-N)

Prepared for the Colloquium on Botswana, Lesotho, and Swaziland, sponsored by the U.S. Dept. of State, Feb. 1974.

Examined in the former Foreign Affairs Research Documentation Center, Dept. of State.

2349

The Peace Corps in Botswana. [Washington?, ACTION; U.S. Govt. Print. Off., 1980] folder ([6] p.) illus., map.

An introduction to the country for volunteers.

Agriculture

2350

Agricultural sector assessment: Botswana, [by] Joseph Motheral [et al.] [s.l.], 1978. 68 p.

A sector assessment undertaken in conjunction with the Southern Africa Development Analysis Project, U.S. Agency for International Development.

Prepared for the Southern Africa Development Assistance Project.

Microfiche. [Washington, U.S. Agency for International Development, 1978?] 1 sheet

DLC-Sci RR PN-AAH-178

2351

Fortmann, Louise. Women's involvement in high risk arable agriculture: the Botswana case. [Washington, distributed by Office of Women in Development, Agency for International Development, International Development Cooperation Agency, 1980] 27, 5 p.   HQ1803.F67

Bibliography: p. [29–32].

"Prepared for presentation at Ford Foundation Workshop on Women in Agriculture in Eastern and Southern Africa, Nairobi, 9–11 April 1980."

2352

Mochudi tool bar (Makgonatsotlhe). Mochudi, Botswana, Mochudi Farmers Brigade, [1975] 53 p. illus.

Concerns the development of a multi-purpose farming implement.

Abstract in *Government Reports Announcements & Index*, Oct. 12, 1979, p. 8.

Microfiche. [Springfield, Va., National Technical Information Service, 1979] 1 sheet.

DLC-Sci RR PB-297144

2353

Odell, Marcia. Planning for agriculture in Botswana: a report on the arable lands survey. [s.l.], Institute of Development Management, 1980. [162] p. (in various pagings)

"Research paper no. 7."

Study supported in part by the U.S. Agency for International Development.

Microfiche. [Washington, U.S. Agency for International Development, 1980?] 2 sheets (PN-AAJ-794); examined in the Development Information Center, AID, Washington, D.C.

2354

Roe, Emery. Development of livestock, agriculture and water supplies in Botswana before independence: a short history and policy analysis. [Ithaca, N.Y., Rural Development Committee, Cornell University, 1980] 56 p.   DLC

"Occasional paper no. 10."

Bibliography: p. 53–56.

Abstract in *A.I.D. Research & Development Abstracts*, v. 9, no. 3, 1981, p. 6.

Issued also in microfiche. [Washington, U.S. Agency for International Development, 1980?] 1 sheet.   DLC-Sci RR PN-AAJ-639

Bibliographies

2355

Eicher, Shirley F. Rural development in Botswana: a select bibliography, 1966–1980. Washington, African Bibliographic Center, 1981. 145 p.

Z7164.C842E37

"This is a publication of the Southern Africa Development Information/Documentation Exchange (SADEX) project, which is funded by the Agency for International Development."

Partly annotated, the guide includes citations to monographs, official documents, and periodical articles.

Abstract in *A.I.D. Research & Development Abstracts*, v. 9, no. 3, 1981, p. 25.

Issued also in microfiche. [Washington, U.S.

Agency for International Development, 1981?] 2 sheets.   DLC-Sci RR PN-AAJ-699

2356

Kjaer-Olsen, Pia. A preliminary bibliography on rural development in Botswana. Gaberone, 1979. 25 p.

Prepared for the U.S. AID Mission to Botswana.

Cited in *Rural Development in Botswana: A Select Bibliography, 1966–1980*, p. 57.

Assistance Programs

2357

U.S. *Agency for International Development*. AID development assistance program: Botswana. [Washington?], 1975. 39 p.

Examined in the Development Information Center, AID, Washington, D.C.

2358

———— Annual budget submission: Botswana. Washington, U.S. International Development Cooperation Agency.

Vols. for 1981+ examined in the Development Information Center, AID, Washington, D.C.

2359

———— Country development strategy statement: Botswana. Washington, U.S. International Development Cooperation Agency. annual?

Vol. for 1982 examined in the Development Information Center, AID, Washington, D.C.

2360

Botswana. [Treaties, etc. United States, 1975 Sept. 19] Loan agreement between the Government of Botswana and the United States of America for the northern abattoir. *In* U.S. *Treaties, etc.* United States treaties and other international agreements, v. 28, 1976–77. [Washington, Dept. of State; for sale by the Supt. of Docs., U.S. Govt. Print. Off., 1978] p. 791–808. ([Treaties and other international acts series, 8481])   JX231.A34 v. 28

Signed at Gaberone Sept. 19, 1975.

Concerns U.S. Agency for International Development support for constructing and equipping an abattoir, with access roads, in Dukwe, Botswana.

2361

Botswana. [*Treaties, etc. United States, 1980 Feb. 26*] International military education and training (IMET) agreement between the United States of America and Botswana by exchange of notes dated at Gaberone February 26 and March 21, 1980. [Washington, Dept. of State; for sale by the Supt.

2361 (cont.)

of Docs., U.S. Govt. Print. Off., 1980] 3 p. (Treaties and other international acts series, 9742)

DLC

Agreement to permit the training of members of the Botswana Defense Force in the United States.

2362

Vermeer, Donald E. National development and integration in Botswana: perspectives, prospects, and projects; a discussion paper. [Washington], Development Studies Program, Agency for International Development, 1977. 13 p. maps.

Examined in the Development Information Center, AID, Washington, D.C.

Commerce

2363

Chittum, J. Marc. Marketing in Botswana. [Washington], U.S. Dept. of Commerce, Domestic and International Business Administration; [for sale by the Supt. of Docs., U.S. Govt. Print. Off.], 1977. 19 p. (Overseas business reports. OBR 77-26)

HF91.U482   1977, no. 26

International marketing information series.

Issued also in microfiche. [Washington, Congressional Information Service, 1977?]

DLC-Micro ASI:7 2026-5.32

2364

Miller, Sally K. Marketing in Botswana. Washington, U.S. Dept. of Commerce, Domestic and International Business Administration; [for sale by the Supt. of Docs., U.S. Govt. Print. Off.], 1975. 17 p. (Overseas business reports. OBR 75-51)

HF91.U482   1975, no. 51

Abstract in *American Statistics Index*, 1975, Abstracts, p. 147.

Issued also in microfiche. [Washington, Congressional Information Service, 1975?]

DLC-Micro ASI:75 2026-4.51

Economic Conditions

2365

Adams, John. Economic stability and growth in Botswana. College Park, Dept. of Economics, University of Maryland, 1978. 71 leaves. (FAR 28872-S)

"A study prepared for the Department of State under its External Research Program."

Examined in the former Foreign Affairs Research Documentation Center, U.S. Dept. of State.

2366

Foreign economic trends and their implications for the United States. Botswana. 1973?+ Washington, for sale by the Supt. of Docs., U.S. Govt. Print. Off. annual? (International marketing information series)

HC10.E416

Prepared by the U.S. Embassy, Gaberone.

Vol. for 1973 distributed by the U.S. Bureau of International Commerce; vol. for 1978 by the U.S. Industry and Trade Administration.

Apparently not published in 1974–77.

The following issues have been identified in L.C.:

ET 73-039. 1973. 14 p.

FET 78-064. 1978. 9 p.

Education

2367

Botswana. National policy on education: approved by the National Assembly, August 1977, Gaberone, Republic of Botswana. [Gaberone], 1977. 18 p. (Botswana. Government paper, 1977, no. 1)

LA1601.B62   1977

Abstract in *Resources in Education*, Oct. 1978, p. 60.

Issued also in microfiche. [Arlington, Va., ERIC Document Reproduction Service; prepared for Educational Resources Information Center, National Institute of Education, 1978] 1 sheet.

DLC-Micro ED154521

2368

Botswana. *National Commission on Education.* Kagisano ka thuto. Education for kagisano: report of the National Commission on Education. Gaberone, 1977. 2 v. illus.

LA1601.B63   1977

Volume 2 has also special title: Annexes.

In English.

Includes a bibliography.

"This report presents the findings and recommendations of Botswana's National Commission on Education, based on the commission's 15-month review of Botswana's education system and its goals and major problems."—Abstract.

Abstract in *Resources in Education*, Oct. 1978, p. 60–61.

Issued also microfiche. [Arlington, Va., ERIC Document Reproduction Service; prepared for Educational Resources Information Center, National Institute of Education, 1978] 4 sheets.

DLC-Micro ED154522

2369

Correa, Hector, *and* Larry Fisher. Decision model for planning technologically assisted education: with application to Botswana. [s.l., 1973] 17 p.

Abstract in *Research in Education*, Apr. 1974, p. 50.

Microfiche. [Bethesda, Md., ERIC Document Reproudction Service; prepared for Educational Resources Information Center, U.S. Office of Education, 1974] 1 sheet.

DLC-Micro ED084677

Ethnology

2370

Crowell, Aron L., *and* Robert K. Hitchcock. Basarwa ambush hunting in Botswana. Botswana notes and records, v. 10, [1978]: 37–51. illus.

DT790.B67   1978

"We would like to thank the U.S. National Science Foundation for support of the research upon which this paper is based."—p. 50.

2371

Ebert, Melinda C. Patterns of manufacture and use of baskets among Basarwa of the Nata River region. Botswana notes and records, v. 9, [1977]: 69–83. illus.   DT790.B67   1977

Research supported by a grant from the U.S. National Science Foundation.

2372

Gelburd, Diane J. Indicators of culture change among the Dobe !Kung San. Botswana notes and records, v. 10, [1978]: 27–36.

DT790.B67   1978

Research supported by a grant from the U.S. National Science Foundation.

2373

Sero-genetic studies on the 'Masarwa' of northeastern Botswana, [by] W. J. Chasko [et al.] Botswana notes and records, v. 11, [1979]: 15–19.

DT790.B67   1980

Research supported in part by a grant from the U.S. National Science Foundation.

Geology, Hydrology, and Mineral Resources

2374

Jolly, Janice L. W. The mineral industry of Botswana. *In* Minerals yearbook, v. 3, 1977. [Washington,

for sale by the Supt. of Docs., U.S. Govt. Print. Off., 1981] p. 151–154.

TN23.U612   1977, v. 3

Prepared by the U.S. Bureau of Mines.

2375

——— The mineral industry of Botswana. *In* Minerals yearbook, v. 3, 1978–79. [Washington, U.S. Govt. Print. Off., 1981] p. 161–166.

TN23.U612   1978–79, v. 3

Prepared by the U.S. Bureau of Mines.

2376

Morgan, George A. The mineral industry of Botswana. *In* Minerals yearbook, v. 3, 1980. [Washington, for sale by the Supt. of Docs., U.S. Govt. Print. Off., 1982] p. 159–161.

TN23.U612   1980, v. 3

Prepared by the U.S. Bureau of Mines.

Health and Nutrition

2377

Continuities between the practices of traditional and scientific Botswana health care practitioners. Washington, African-American Scholars Council, 1977. [88] p.

Prepared in collaboration with the U.S. Agency for International Development.

Abstract in *A.I.D. Research and Development Abstracts*, Oct. 1978, p. 34.

Microfiche. [Washington, U.S. Agency for International Development, 1977?] 1 sheet (PN-AAF-590); examined in the Development Information Center, AID, Washington, D.C.

2378

Filling in for doctors: too few physicians, so nurses and midwives learn to detect and treat disease in Botswana. Agenda, Sept. 1979: 18–19. illus.

HC59.7.A742   1979

Issued by the U.S. Agency for International Development.

2379

LaGrone, Don. Medical handbook. [Gaberone, Peace Corps, 1978?] 43 leaves.   DPC

2380

Meriwether, Delano. A review of health care in Botswana: issues, analyses, and recommendations. Washington, Family Health Care, inc., 1978. 168 p. (Health and development in Southern Africa, v. 8)

2380 (cont.)

Submitted to Southern Africa Development Analysis Program, U.S. Agency for International Development.

Issued in cooperation with Africare.

Microfiche. [Washington, U.S. Agency for International Development, 1978?] 2 sheets.

DLC-Sci RR PN-AAH-168

Housing and Urban Development

2381

U.S. *Agency for International Development.* Project paper: Republic of Botswana—housing guaranty program. [Washington?], 1976. 61 p.

Examined in the Development Information Center, AID, Washington, D.C.

2382

U.S. *Agency for International Development. Office of Housing.* Botswana shelter sector analysis. [Washington], 1976. [96] leaves (in various foliations) illus., map.

Examined in the Development Information Center, AID, Washington, D.C.

2383

DeVoy, Robert S. Botswana shelter sector assessment. [s.l.], DeVoy Associates, 1979. [153] p. illus., maps.

Prepared for the Office of Housing, U.S. Agency for International Development.

Abstract in *A.I.D. Research & Development Abstracts*, v. 9, no. 3, 1981, p. 47.

Microfiche. [Washington, Congressional Information Service, 1979?] 2 sheets (DLC-Micro ASI:80 7206-5.21); and [Washington, U.S. Agency for International Development, 1979?] 2 sheets (PN-AAH-739), examined in the Development Information Center, AID, Washington, D.C.

2384

Mansion in the sky: a lesson in self-help housing from Gaberone, Botswana. [s.l.], International Program, Foundation for Cooperative Housing, [1979] 36 p. illus., map.

Study supported by the U.S. Agency for International Development.

Microfiche. [Washington, U.S. Agency for International Development, 1979?] 1 sheet (PN-AAJ-746); examined in the Development Information Center, AID, Washington, D.C.

Other Subjects

2835

U.S. *Bureau of the Census.* Country demographic profiles: Botswana. [Washington, Data User Services Division, Bureau of the Census], 1981. 41 p. map. DLC

"ISP-DP-27."

Prepared by the agency's International Demographic Data Center.

Based primarily on the national censuses of 1964 and 1971.

2386

Africa: Botswana. Selected statistical data by sex. Washington, 1981. 31, 17 p. DLC

Study supported by the U.S. Agency for International Development's Office of Women in Development and Office of Population.

Data assembled by the International Demographic Data Center, U.S. Bureau of the Census.

Among the tables, all based on 1971 data, are the following: unadjusted population by age and sex; population by district, sex, and urban/rural residence; life expectancy; total population by marital status, age, and sex; number of literate persons by sex; number of persons enrolled in school by age and sex; number of economically active persons by age and sex.

2387

Botswana. [*Treaties, etc. United States, 1978 Nov. 7*] Alien amateur radio operators agreement between the United States of America and Botswana effected by exchange of notes dated at Gaberone November 7, 1978 and September 26, 1979. [Washington, Dept. of State; for sale by the Supt. of Docs., U.S. Govt. Print. Off., 1980] 3 p. (Treaties and other international acts series, 9776) DLC

2388

Botswana. [*Treaties, etc. United States, 1980 Mar. 28*] Telecommunications; Voice of America radio relay facility. Agreement between the United States of America and Botswana, signed at Gaberone March 28, 1980. [Washington, Dept. of State; for sale by the Supt. of Docs., U.S. Govt. Print. Off., 1980] 10 p. (Treaties and other international acts series, 9741) DLC

Agreement enabling the United States to construct, operate, and maintain radio transmitters at Selebi-Phikwe, Botswana.

2389

Busse, Curt. Leopard and lion predation upon Chacma baboons living in the Moremi Wildlife

2389 (cont.)

Reserve. Botswana notes and records, v. 12, 1980: 15–21.   DT790.B67   1980

Research funded by the U.S. National Institutes of Health.

2390

Hardpacked and fast: the BotZam Road cuts days off the trip from Botswana to Zambia and opens a frontier for development. Agenda, Sept. 1979: 14–17. illus., map.   HC59.7.A742   1979

Issued by the U.S. Agency for International Development.

Concerns an AID-financed road from the Zambian border to central Botswana.

2391

Hitchcock, Robert K., Bryan A. Marozas, *and* James I. Ebert. Analogy and the archaeology of hunters and gatherers. Albuquerque, Dept. of Anthropology, University of New Mexico, [1975?] [16] leaves. (New Mexico. University. Kalahari Project Anthropology Series. Contribution, no. 1)

"Concepts and ideas presented herein were developed from studies supported by National Science Foundation Grant SOC75-02253."

Concerns the Kalahari region of Botswana.

Examined in the National Science Foundation, Washington, D.C.

2392

Hopkins, David B. Setswana. Brattleboro, Vt., Experiment in International Living, for ACTION/ Peace Corps, 1979. 4 v. illus. (Peace Corps language handbook series)   DPC

Contents: [1] Communication and culture handbook.—[2] Grammar handbook.—[3] Teacher's handbook.—[4] Special skills handbook.

2393

Human resources development study for Botswana; final report, [by] Thomas R. Collins [et al.] Research Triangle Park, N.C., Research Triangle Institute, 1976. 118 p.

Prepared for the Bureau for Africa, U.S. Agency for International Development.

Examined in the Development Information Center, AID, Washington, D.C.

2394

Simon, Paul. Botswana: a beacon of freedom and good sense. Congressional record, 95th Congress, 2d session, v. 124, Jan. 19, 1978: 163–164.

J11.R5 v. 125

Extension of remarks in the U.S. House of Representatives.

Includes article, "Letter from Botswana: Texas-size country in southern Africa enjoys tranquillity and true democracy," from the *Washington Post*.

Lesotho

General

2395

U.S. *Agency for International Development.* A report to the Congress on development needs and opportunities for cooperation in Southern Africa. Annex A: Lesotho. [Washington], 1979. 107 p.

An overview of economic conditions, including factors impeding growth, an analysis of government development planning, and the role of foreign assistance.

Microfiche. [Washington, U.S. Agency for International Development, 1979?] 2 sheets.

DLC-Sci RR PN-AAH-153

2396

U.S. *Dept. of State.* Post report. Lesotho. [Washington?], 1979. 16 p. illus., map.

Examined in the Foreign Service Institute Library, Rosslyn, Va.

For a description of the contents of this publication, see the note to entry 936.

2397

U.S. *Dept. of State. Bureau of Public Affairs.* Background notes. Lesotho. [Washington, for sale by the Supt. of Docs., U.S. Govt. Print. Off.], 1979. 6 p. illus., maps. (U.S. Dept. of State. Department of State publication 8091, rev.)   G59.U5

L.C. retains only the latest revision.

For a description of the contents of this publication, see the note to entry 937.

2398

[The Peace Corps in Lesotho] Washington, U.S. Govt. Print. Off., 1980] 1 fold. sheet (6 p.)

DLC

"ACTION 4200.53."

An introduction to the country for Volunteers.

Agriculture

2399

Agricultural sector assessment: Lesotho, [by] Eugene Mathia [et al.] [s.l., 1978] [73] p. map.

Prepared for the Southern Africa Development Analysis Project, U.S. Agency for International Development.

Microfiche. [Washington, U.S. Agency for International Development, 1979?] 1 sheet.

DLC-Sci RR PN-AAH-182

2400

Eckert, Jerry B. Rainfall oscillations in Lesotho and the possible impact of drought in the 1980's. [Ft. Collins], Dept. of Economics, Colorado State University, 1980. 25 p. (Lesotho Agricultural Sector Analysis Project. LASA discussion paper, no. 10)

Abstract in *A.I.D. Research & Development Abstracts*, July 1981, p. 27.

Microfiche. [Washington, U.S. Agency for International Development, 1980?] 1 sheet.

DLC-Sci RR PN-AAH-923

2401

An Exploratory study of the food system of Lesotho; a report to the Lesotho Food and Nutrition Council, [by] Charles Slater [et al.] [s.l.], 1978. 118 p.

On cover: "For the Kingdom of Lesotho in cooperation with Planning Assistance, inc."

Abstract in *A.I.D. Research and Development Abstracts*, Jan. 1979, p. 14.

Microfiche. [Washington, U.S. Agency for International Development, 1978?] 2 sheet.

DLC-Sci RR PN-AAG-018

2402

Lesotho Agricultural Sector Analysis Project. Annual administrative report. 1976/77+ [Ft. Collins], Dept. of Economics, Colorado State University.

DLC

Prepared for the U.S. Agency for International Development.

2402 (cont.)

L.C. has 1979/80; more complete holdings in CoFS.

Vol. for 1977/78 issued also in microfiche. [Washington, U.S. Agency for International Development, 1978?] 2 sheets.

DLC-Sci RR PN-AAG-217

2403

Ntsane, Chaka, *and* Jerry B. Eckert. Lesotho's agriculture; a review of existing information. [Ft. Collins], Dept. of Economics, Colorado State University, 1978. 180 p. (Lesotho Agricultural Sector Analysis Project. LASA research report, no. 2)

Prepared for the U.S. Agency for International Development.

Abstract in *A.I.D. Research and Development Abstracts*, Apr. 1979, p. 7.

Microfiche. [Washington, U.S. Agency for International Development, 1978] 2 sheets (PN-AAG-325); examined in the Development Information Center, AID, Washington, D.C.

2404

To save a scarred land: Lesotho struggles to restore fertility to fields ravaged by runoff. Agenda, Sept. 1979: 3–6. illus. HC59.7.A742

Issued by the U.S. Agency for International Development.

2405

Wilken, Gene C. Agroclimatology of Lesotho. [Ft. Collins, Engineering Research Center, Colorado State University], 1978. 36 p. (Lesotho Agricultural Sector Analysis Project. LASA discussion paper, no. 1.)

Prepared for the U.S. Agency for International Development.

Abstract in *A.I.D. Research and Development Abstracts*, Oct. 1978, p. 14.

Microfiche. [Washington, U.S. Agency for International Development, 1978] 1 sheet (PN-AAF-576); examined in the Development Information Center, AID, Washington, D.C.

2406

Wilken, Gene C., *and* M. H. Fowler. Profiles of Basotho farmers. [Ft. Collins], Dept. of Economics, Colorado State Unifersity, 1979. 51 p. map. (Lesotho Agricultural Sector Analysis Project. LASA discussion paper, no. 8)

Bibliography: p. 46–51.

Study financed by the U.S. Agency for International Development.

Abstract in *A.I.D. Research & Development Abstracts*, July 1981, p. 1.

Microfiche. [Washington, U.S. Agency for International Development, 1979?] 1 sheet.

DLC-Sci RR PN-AAH-351

Bibliographies

2407

Catalog of holdings and other references in the Lesotho MOA/LASA Library, [by] Gene C. Wilken [et al.] Maseru, Lesotho Agricultural Sector Analysis Project, Ministry of Agriculture, 1980. 1 v. (various pagings) (Lesotho Agricultural Sector Analysis Project. LASA research report, no. 5) DLC

A list of monographs and periodical articles held by the LASA centers in Maseru, Lesotho, and/or Ft. Collins, Colorado or by selected libraries in Great Britain and the United States (e.g., National Agricultural Library, Beltsville, Maryland).

Abstract in *A.I.D. Research & Development Abstracts*, July 1981, p. 2.

Issued also in microfiche. [Washington, U.S. Agency for International Development, 1980?] 4 sheets. DLC-Sci RR PN-AAH-529

2408

Eckert, Jerry B. Lesotho's land tenure: an analysis and annotated bibliography. [Ft. Collins], Dept. of Economics, Colorado State University, 1980. 58 p. (Lesotho Agricultural Sector Analysis Project. LASA special bibilography, no. 2)

Prepared for the U.S. Agency for International Development.

Microfiche. [Washington, U.S. Agency for International Development, 1980] 1 sheet (PN-AAJ-258); examined in the Development Information Center, AID, Washington, D.C.

2409

Leathers, Roxanna M., *and* Matsaba J. Leballo. Extension in Lesotho: bibliography of materials available in Maseru. [Ft. Collins, Dept. of Economics, Colorado State University], 1979. 10 p. (Lesotho Agricultural Sector Analysis Project. LASA special bibliography, no. 1) CoFS

Prepared for the U.S. Agency for International Development.

Economic Aspects

2410

Eckert, Jerry B. Quantitative analyses of Lesotho's official yield data for maize and sorghum. [Ft. Collins], Dept. of Economics, Colorado State Uni-

2410 (cont.)

versity, 1980. 35 p. (Lesotho Agricultural Sector Analysis Project. LASA research report, no. 8)

Prepared with the support of the U.S. Agency for International Development under cooperative agreement AID/ta-Ca-1.

Issued in cooperation with the Ministry of Agriculture of Lesotho.

Abstract in *A.I.D. Research and Development Abstracts*, July 1981, p. 3.

Microfiche. [Washington, U.S. Agency for International Development, 1980?] 1 sheet.
DLC-Sci RR PN-AAH-922

2411

——— The supply of data for agricultural administration and development planning. [Ft. Collins], Dept. of Economics, Colorado State University, 1978. 32 p. (Lesotho Agricultural Sector Analysis Project. LASA discussion paper, no. 2)

Prepared for the U.S. Agency for International Development.

Issued for the Workshop on Minimum Information Systems for Agricultural Development, Agricultural Development Council, 1976.

Microfiche. [Washington, U.S. Agency for International Development, 1978?] 1 sheet (PN-AAF-439); examined in the Development Information Center, AID, Washington, D.C.

2412

Eckert, Jerry B., *and* Joseph N. Mohapi. The future environment for agricultural planning, 1980–2000 A.D. [Ft. Collins], Dept. of Economics, Colorado State University, 1980. 30 p. (Lesotho Agricultural Sector Analysis Project. LASA discussion paper, no. 9)

Bibliography: p. 28–29.

Study financed by the U.S. Agency for International Development.

Issued in cooperation with the Ministry of Agriculture of Lesotho.

Abstract in *A.I.D. Research & Development Abstracts*, July 1981, p. 26.

Microfiche. [Washington, U.S. Agency for International Development, 1980?] 1 sheet.
DLC-Sci RR PN-AAH-920

2413

Nobe, K. C., *and* D. W. Seckler. An economic and policy analysis of soil-water problems in the Kingdom of Lesotho. [Ft. Collins], Dept. of Economics, Colorado State University, 1979. 209 p. (Lesotho Agricultural Sector Analysis Project. LASA research report, no. 3)

Prepared for the U.S. Agency for International Development under contract AID/afr-C-1387.

Microfiche. [Washington, U.S. Agency for International Development, 1979] 3 sheets (PN-AAH-005); examined in the Development Information Center, AID, Washington, D.C.

2414

Wykstra, Ronald A. Farm labor in Lesotho: scarcity or surplus? Ft. Collins, Dept. of Economics, Colorado State University, 1978. 42 p. (Lesotho Agricultural Sector Analysis Project. LASA discussion paper, no. 5) CoFS

Prepared with partial support of the U.S. Agency for International Development.

Issued in cooperation with the Ministry of Agriculture of Lesotho.

Abstract in *A.I.D. Research and Development Abstracts*, v. 7, no. 1, 1979, p. 4.

Issued also in microfiche. [Washington, U.S. Agency for International Development, 1978?] 1 sheet.
DLC-Sci RR PN-AAG-511

Assistance Programs

2415

U.S. *Agency for International Development*. AID development assistance program: Lesotho. [Washington?], 1975. 48 p.

Examined in the Development Information Center, AID, Washington, D.C.

2416

——— Annual budget submission: Lesotho. Washington, U.S. International Development Cooperation Agency.

Vols. for 1981+ examined in the Development Information Center, AID, Washington, D.C.

2417

——— Country development strategy statement: Lesotho. Washington, U.S. International Development Cooperation Agency. annual.

Vols. for 1982+ examined in the Development Information Center, AID, Washington, D.C.

2418

Hartman, L. M. Towards an integrated perspective on development planning in Lesotho. [Ft. Collins], Dept. of Economics, Colorado State University, 1977. 31 p. (Lesotho Agricultural Sector Analysis Project. LASA discussion paper, no. 3)

Financed by the U.S. Agency for International Development.

Issued in cooperation with the Ministry of Agriculture of Lesotho.

Examined in the Development Information Center, AID, Washington, D.C.

2419

Lesotho. [*Treaties, etc. United States, 1978 Aug. 31*] Project grant agreement between Lesotho and the United States of America for Southern Africa manpower development. *In* U.S. *Treaties, etc.* United States treaties and other international agreements, v. 30, 1978–79. [Washington, Dept. of State; for sale by the Supt. of Docs., U.S. Govt. Print. Off., 1980] p. 5441–5469. ([Treaties and other international acts series, 9510]) JX231.A34 v. 30
Signed at Maseru Aug. 31, 1978.
A U.S. Agency for International Development project to assist Lesotho "in alleviating critical manpower shortages which exist in the public sector."—p. 5445.

2420

Peace Corps/Lesotho country program evaluation, [by] Jon A. Leeth [et al.] [Washington?], Social, Educational Research and Development, inc., 1977. [88] p. (in various pagings) DPC
Study conducted in cooperation with the Evaluation Division of Action.

2421

Pellish, David M., and Robert V. Shoemaker. An economic and technical appraisal of the funding request by the Architectural and Construction Society of Lesotho (ACSL) [Washington], Agency for International Development, 1974. 66 p.
Examined in the Development Information Center, AID, Washington, D.C.

2422

Pieces from Peace Corps Lesotho. Dec. 1975+ [Maseru, U.S. Peace Corps] irregular. DPC

2423

Wilson, John R. Lesotho donors conference, agricultural sector, Maseru, Lesotho, 1980; USAID position paper and review of conference. [s.l.], 1980. 122 p.
Prepared for the U.S. Agency for International Development under contract AID/afr-C-1703.
Microfiche. [Washington, U.S. Agency for International Development, 1980] 2 sheets (PN-AAJ-220); held by the Development Information Center, AID, Washington, D.C.

Economic Conditions

2424

Eckert, Jerry B., *and* Ronald A. Wykstra. South African mine wages in the seventies and their effects on Lesotho's economy. [Ft. Collins], Dept. of Economics, Colorado State University, 1980. 25 p.

(Lesotho Agricultural Sector Analysis Project. LASA research report, no. 7)
Issued in cooperation with the Ministry of Agriculture of Lesotho.
Abstract in *A.I.D. Research & Development Abstracts,* July 1981, p. 25.
Microfiche. [Washington, U.S. Agency for International Development, 1980?] 1 sheet.
DLC-Sci RR PN-AAH-871

2425

Foreign economic trends and their implications for the United States. Kingdom of Lesotho. 1979?+ Washington, for sale by the Supt. of Docs., U.S. Govt. Print. Off. annual. (International marketing information series) HC10.E416
Prepared by the U.S. Embassy, Maseru.
Vol. for 1979 distributed by the U.S. Industry and Trade Administration; vols. for 1981– by the U.S. International Trade Administration.
Not published in 1980.
The following issues have been identified in L.C.:
FET 79-019. 1979. 6 p.
FET 81-086. 1981. 5 p.

2426

Human resources development study for Lesotho. Final report, [by] Paul F. Mulligan [et al.] Research Triangle Park, N.C., Research Triangle Institute, 1976. 135 p. DLC
"FR21 U-1216."
Prepared for the U.S. Agency for International Development.
"The impetus for the study was the widely held opinion that the scarcity of a wide variety of manpower skills was the major constraint to achievement of national development goals."—p. iii.

2427

Mohair: industry on the rise; women in Lesotho spin Mohari yarn, boosting income and a vital national industry. Agenda, Sept. 1979: 7–10. illus.
HC59.7.A742 1979
Issued by the U.S. Agency for International Development.

2428

Wagner, William E. The spatial context for integrated development strategy in Lesotho. Ft. Collins, Dept. of Economics, Colorado State University, 1978. 25 p. (Lesotho Agricultural Sector Analysis Project. LASA discussion paper, no. 4) CoFS
Bibliography: p. 23–25.
Abstract in *A.I.D. Research and Development Abstracts*, July 1978, p. 8.

2428 (cont.)

Issued also in microfiche. [Washington, U.S. Agency for International Development, 1978?] 1 sheet   DLC-Sci RR PN-AAF-349

2429

Wilken, Gene C., *and* Carolyn F. Amiet. Bibliography for planning and development in Lesotho. [Ft. Collins], Dept. of Economics, Colorado State University, 1977. 1 v. (various pagings) (Lesotho Agricultural Sector Analysis Project. LASA research report, no. 1)   CoFS

Prepared for the U.S. Agency for International Development.

Copy examined in the Development Information Center, AID, Washington, D.C.

Education

2430

Cain, Bonnie J., *and* Francis J. Method. Nonformal education activities at Lesotho Distance Teaching Centre; evaluation report. [s.l.], Creative Associates, 1979. 106 p.

Prepared under U.S. Agency for International Development contract AID/ocr-C-1729.

Microfiche. [s.l., 1979] 2 sheets (PN-AAG-862); examined in the Development Information Center, AID, Washington, D.C.

2431

Joyner, Orville. Project planning study for Lesotho Instructional Materials Resource Center; trip report, June 18–July 24, 1976. [s.l.], Academy for Educational Development, 1976. 1 v. (various pagings)

Prepared for the U.S. Agency for International Development.

Examined in the Development Information Center, AID, Washington, D.C.

2432

Kotsokoane, Joseph R. L. Education minister attempts to dispel misconceptions. *In* U.S. *Joint Publications Research Service.* JPRS 70887. [Springfield, Va., National Technical Information Service, 1978] (Translations on Sub-Saharan Africa, no. 1904) p. 16–19.

Translation of article in *Remarques africaines,* Brussels, Feb. 1978, p. 10, 11.

Microfiche. [Washington, Supt. of Docs., U.S. Govt. Print. Off., 1978]

DLC-Micro JPRS 70887

2433

McQueen, F. T., *and* Robert A. Cox. A feasibility

study of the proposed instructional materials center, National Teacher Training College, Maseru, Lesotho, Africa. [s.l., 1976?] 81 p.

Prepared for the U.S. Agency for International Development.

Examined in the Development Information enter, AID, Washington, D.C.

Health and Nutrition

2434

Anderson, Jim. Resources guide for nutrition planning in Lesotho. Maseru, Lesotho, Ministry of Agriculture, 1978. 41 p. (Lesotho Agricultural Sector Analysis Project. LASA discussion paper, no. 6)

"Prepared with partial support of the United States Agency for International Development."

Issued in cooperation with the Dept. of Economics, Colorado State University.

Abstract in *A.I.D. Research and Development Abstracts,* Apr. 1979, p. 20–21.

Microfiche. [Washington, U.S. Agency for International Development, 1978?] 1 sheet.

DLC-Sci RR PN-AAG-324

2434a

Franks, James A., *and* Robert L. Minnis. Maternal and child health/family planning project for the Kingdom of Lesotho, Southern Africa. Final report (March 31, 1977) Santa Cruz, University of California Extension, 1977. [457] p. (in various pagings)   DLC

Prepared pursuant to an agreement with the Ministry of Health of Lesotho.

"The University of California Extension/Santa Crus became involved in developing a Maternal and Child Health/Child Spacing project through the invitation of USAID."—Introduction, p. 2.

2435

A Review of the health sector of Lesotho, [by] Oscar Gish [et al.] [Washington?], American Public Health Association, [1975?] [65] p.

Prepared for the U.S. Agency for International Development under the Development and Evaluation of Integrated Delivery Systems (DEIDS) program.

Microfiche. [Washington, U.S. Agency for International Development, 1975?] 1 sheet.

DLC-Sci RR PN-AAB-551

2436

A Review of health care in Lesotho: issues, analyses, and recommendations, [by] Kevin Lowther [et al.]

2436 (cont.)

Washington, Family Health Care, inc., 1978. 78 p. (Health and development in Southern Africa, v. 3)

Submitted to the Southern Africa Development Analysis Program, U.S. Agency for International Development.

Issued in cooperation with Africare.

Microfiche. [Washington, U.S. Agency for International Development, 1979?] 1 sheet

DLC-Sci RR PN-AAH-163

Housing and Urban Development

2437

DeVoy, Robert S. Lesotho shelter sector assessment. [s.l.], DeVoy Collaborative, 1978. [129] p. illus.

Prepared for the U.S. Agency for International Development under contract AID/otr-C-1634.

Abstract in *A.I.D. Research & Development Abstracts*, v. 9, no. 3, 1981, p. 47.

Microfiche. [Washington, U.S. Agency for International Development, 1978?] 2 sheets (DLC-Sci RR PN-AAH-737); and [Washington, Congressional Information Service, 1978?] 2 sheet (DLC-Micro ASI:80 7206-5.20).

2438

Lesotho shelter sector study. [s.l.], Foundation for Cooperative Housing, 1976. 85 p.

Prepared under the auspices of the Office of Housing, U.S. Agency for International Development.

Examined in the Development Information Center, AID, Washington, D.C.

Labor

2439

Eckert, Jerry B., *and* Ronald A. Wykstra. Lesotho's employment challenge: alternative scenarios, 1980–2000 A.D. [Ft. Collins], Dept. of Economics, Colorado State University, 1979. [32] p. (Lesotho Agricultural Sector Analysis Project. LASA discussion paper, no. 7).

Prepared for the U.S. Agency for International Development.

Issued in cooperation with the Ministry of Agriculture of Lesotho.

Abstract in *A.I.D. Research & Development Abstracts*, July 1981, p. 23–24.

Microfiche. [Washington, U.S. Agency for International Development, 1979?] 1 sheet.

DLC-Sci RR PN-AAH-330

2440

Nchapi, M'ampiti F. A critical analysis of manpower utilization issues in Lesotho. [Ft. Collins], Dept. of Economics, Colorado State University, [1980] 47 p. (Lesotho Agricultural Sector Analysis Project. LASA research report, no. 9)

Bibliography: p. 46–47.

Prepared for the U.S. Agency for International Development.

Issued in cooperation with the Ministry of Agriculture of Lesotho.

Abstract in *A.I.D. Research & Development Abstracts*, July 1981, p. 26.

Microfiche. [Washington, U.S. Agency for International Development, 1980] 1 sheet.

DLC-Sci RR PN-AAH-921

2441

Wykstra, Ronald A., *and* Jerry B. Eckert. Manpower vs. machinery: a case study of conservation works in Lesotho. [Ft. Collins], Dept. of Economics, Colorado State University, 1980. 24 p. (Lesotho Agricultural Sector Analysis Project. LASA research report, no. 6)

Prepared for the U.S. Agency for International Development.

Issued in cooperation with the Ministry of Agriculture of Lesotho.

"This paper propounds the use of labor-intensive over capital-intensive methods in conservation and other public works as a way of providing domestic employment."—Abstract.

Abstract in *A.I.D. Research & Development Abstracts*, July 1981, p. 25.

Microfiche. [Washington, U.S. Agency for International Development, 1980?] 1 sheet.

DLC-Sci RR PN-AAH-742

2442

——— The future of Basotho migration to the Republic of South Africa. [Ft. Collins], Dept. of Economics, Colorado State University, 1979. 25 p. (Lesotho Agricultural Sector Analysis Project. LASA research report, no. 4)

Bibliography: p. 22–24.

Prepared for the U.S. Agency for International Development under cooperative agreement AID/ta-CA-1.

Issued in cooperation with the Ministry of Agriculture of Lesotho.

Abstract in *A.I.D. Research & Development Abstracts*, July 1981, p. 23.

Microfiche. [Washington, U.S. Agency for International Development, 1979?] 1 sheet.

DLC-Sci RR PN-AAH-103

Other Subjects

2443

Africa: Lesotho. Selected statistical data by sex. Washington, 1981. 31, 17 p.   DLC

Study supported by the U.S. Agency for International Development's Office of Women in Development and Office of Population.

Data assembled by the International Demographic Data Center, U.S. Bureau of the Census.

Among the tables, based on 1966 data (unless noted), are the following: unadjusted population (1972); population by province, sex, and urban/rural residence (1976); population by ethnic group; population by religion; population by marital status, age, and sex; number of persons enrolled in school by age, sex, and urban/rural residence; number of economically active persons by age, sex, and urban/rural residence; economically active population by occupational status, sex, and urban/rural residence.

2444

Sherer, Albert W. U.S. joins Security Council appeal for assistance to Lesotho. *In* U.S. *Dept. of State.* The Department of State bulletin, v. 76, no. 1960, Jan. 17, 1977: 51–52.   JX232.A33 v. 76

Statement by the U.S. Representative in the United Nations Security Council, Dec. 22, 1976, together with text of a resolution adopted by the Council.

Concerns the restriction of movement of people between Lesotho and Transkei.

Malawi

General

2445

U.S. *Agency for International Development.* A report to the Congress on development needs and opportunities for cooperation in Southern Africa. Annex A: Malawi. [Washington], 1979. 93 p.

A general background statement, followed by sections on economic conditions, commerce, agriculture, transportation, manufacturing, health, education, and labor.

Microfiche. [Washington, U.S. Agency for International Development, 1979?] 1 sheet.

DLC-Sci RR PN-AAH-154

2446

U.S. *Dept. of the State.* Post report. Malawi. [Washington, Dept. of State, Publishing Services Division; for sale by the Supt. of Docs., U.S. Govt. Print. Off.], 1980. 12 p. illus., map. (*Its* Department and Foreign Service series, 177)

JX1705.A286 Spec. Format

Department of State publication, 9111.

L.C. has also reports issued in 1972 and 1977.

For a description of the contents of this publication, see the note to entry 936.

2447

U.S. Dept. of State. Bureau of Public Affairs. Background notes. Malawi. [Washington, for sale by the Supt. of Docs., U.S. Govt. Print. Off., 1981] 4 p. maps. (U.S. Dept. of State. Department of State publication 7790) G59.U5

L.C. retains only the latest revision.

For a description of the contents of this publication, see the note to entry 937.

2448

Aradoum, Fassil. University of Malawi publications: a guide. Washington, Library of Congress, 1979. 41 p. (Maktaba Afrikana series) Z3577.A72

Compiled in the African Section.

185 entries.

2448a

The Peace Corps in Malawi. [Washington, U.S. Govt. Print Off., 1980] 1 fold. sheet (6 p.) illus., map. DLC

"ACTION 4200.78."

An introduction to the country for Volunteers.

Assistance Programs

2449

U.S. *Agency for International Development.* Annual budget submission: Malawi. Washington, U.S. International Development Cooperation Agency.

Vols. for 1981+ examined in the Development Information Center, AID, Washington, D.C.

2450

——— Country development strategy statement: Malawi. Washington, U.S. International Development Cooperation Agency. annual.

Vols. for 1982+ examined in the Development Information Center, AID, Washington, D.C.

2451

Malawi. [*Treaties, etc. United States, 1976 Apr. 29*] Malawi; Bunda College of Agriculture, agreement signed at Lilongwe April 29, 1976; entered into force April 29, 1976. *In* U.S. *Treaties, etc.* United States treaties and other international agreements, v. 29, 1976–77. [Washington, Dept. of State; for sale by the Supt. of Docs., U.S. Govt. Print. Off., 1979] p. 5245–5262. ([Treaties and other international acts series, 9099]) JX231.A34 v. 29

An Agency for International Development agreement to increase the number of agricultural technicians in Malawi by extending the capacity of the Bunda College of Agriculture.

2452

Malawi. [*Treaties, etc. United States, 1980 Mar. 20*] International military education and training (IMET) agreement between the United States of America and Malawi effected by exchange of notes

2452 (cont.)
dated at Lilongwe March 20 and May 1, 1980. [Washington, Dept. of State; for sale by the Supt. of Docs., U.S. Govt. Print. Off., 1981] 3 p. (Treaties and other international acts series, 9744)

DLC

Concerns the training of a member of the Malawi armed forces in the United States.

2453
Technical Assistance Information Clearing House. Development assistance programs of U.S. non-profit organizations: Malawi. Nov. 1977. [New York], American Council of Voluntary Agencies for Foreign Service, 1977. 19 p. maps. (TAICH country report)   HC517.M3T4a

The Clearing House is operated by the Council under a grant from the U.S. Agency for International Development.

Communications and Transportation

2454
Daniel, Mann, Johnson & Mendenhall. Technical & economic feasibility, Chikwawa-Bangula Road, Malawi. Washington, 1973. 80, [52] p. map.

TE119.M3D36   1973

"Report ... submitted in accordance with Article III B on contract no. AID/C-M/afr-C-73-1 dated October 10, 1972 between the U.S. Agency for International Development and Daniel, Mann, Johnson, & Mendenhall."

Includes bibliographical references.

2455
Fouracre, P. R., *and* I. A. Sayer. Travel characteristics of road users in Malawi. Crowthorne, Berks., England, Overseas Unit, Transport and Road Research Laboratory, 1977. [29] p. map.

Microfiche. [Springfield, Va., National Technical Information Service, 1978] 1 sheet.

DLC-Sci RR PB276835

Economic Conditions

2456
Foreign economic trends and their implications for the United States. Malawi. 1969+ Washington, for sale by the Supt. of Docs., U.S. Govt. Print. Off. annual. (International marketing information series)   HC10.E416

Prepared by the U.S. Embassy, Lilongwe (formerly in Blantyre).

Vols. for 1969–77 (i.e., including FET 78-003) distributed by the U.S. Bureau of International Commerce; vol. for 1978 by the U.S. Industry and Trade Administration; vols. for 1979 (i.e., FET 80-002)- by the U.S. International Trade Administration.

The following issues for the period 1973–80 have been identified in L.C.:
ET 73-073. 1973. [8] p.
ET 74-084. 1974. 8 p.
FET 74-085. 1975. 6 p.
FET 76-090. 1976. 7 p.
FET 78-003. 1978. 7 p.
FET 78-097. 1978. 7 p.
FET 80-022. 1980. 10 p.
FET 80-120. 1980. 14 p.

2457
Moeller, Philip W. Country resource paper: Malawi; a framework for U.S. assistance in Southern Africa. [s.l.], American Technical Assistance Corporation, 1977. [107] p. (in various pagings)

Bibliography: p. B-1–B-6.

Prepared for the U.S. Agency for International Development under contract AID/afr-C-1142.

Examined in the Development Information Center, AID, Washington, D.C.

Geography and Maps

2458
[U.S. *Central Intelligence Agency*] Malawi. [Washington, 1975] col. map.

G8610   1975.U5

Scale ca. 1 : 4,000,000.
"502844 11–75."
Includes location map and comparative area map.

2459
U.S. *Dept. of State. Office of the Geographer.* Malawi: new national capital. Washington, 1975. 1 p.

AMAU

"Geographic note GE-140."

Other Subjects

2460
Africa: Malawi. Selected statistical data by sex. Washington, 1981. 31, 17 p.   DLC

Study supported by the U.S. Agency for International Development's Office of Women in Development and Office of Population.

Data assembled by the International Demographic Data Center, U.S. Bureau of the Census.

2460 (cont.)

Among the tables are the following: unadjusted population by sex and urban/rural residence (1977); population by province, sex, and urban/rural residence (1977); population by ethnic group (i.e., "African," "Asiatic," "European") (1966), sex and urban/rural residence; population by nationality, sex, and urban/rural residence (1966); population by language, sex, and urban/rural residence (1966); life expectancy (1970–72); urban and rural populations by marital status, age, and sex (1970–72); heads of households by age, sex, and urban/rural residence (1970–72); number of literate persons by age, sex, and urban/rural residence (1966); number of persons enrolled in school by age, sex, and urban/rural residence (1966); and number of economically active persons by age, sex, and urban/rural residence (1975).

2461

An Agricultural sector assessment of Malawi. [s.l.], South-East Consortium for International Development, Malawi Agricultural Sector Assessment Team, 1978. 151 p.

Prepared for the Southern Africa Development Analysis Project, U.S. Agency for International Development.

Bibliography: p. 150–151.

Microfiche. [Washington, U.S. Agency for International Development, 1979?] 2 sheets.

DLC-Sci RR PN-AAH-179

2462

Beck, Glenn H., Harold S. Kugler, *and* Allan L. Pitcher. Requirements analysis for developing the University of Malawi Bunda College of Agriculture 1975–80. [Washington?], 1974. 62 p.

S539.M35B862

"Sponsored by USAID—Washington, D.C."

2463

Mughogho, Spider K. Organic phosphorus studies in some soils of Malawi.

[Ithaca, N.Y.?], 1975. 107 p.

Thesis (M.S.)—Cornell University.

Microfiche. [Washington, U.S. Agency for International Development, 1975?] 2 sheets.

DLC-Sci RR PN-AAA-954

2464

Nathan (Robert R.) Associates, *Washington, D.C.* Shelter sector assessment for the Government of Malawi: submitted to Office of Housing, Agency for International Development. Washington, 1978. 149 p. illus., maps.

HD7375.A3N37 1978

Abstract in *A.I.D. Research and Development Abstracts*, Jan. 1979, p. 22.

Issued also in microfiche. [Washington, U.S. Agency for International Development, 1978?] 2 sheets. DLC-Sci RR PN-AAG-016

2465

Nicholas, David D., Alan W. Fairbank, *and* Alameda Harper. A review of health care in Malawi: issues, analyses, and recommendations. Washington, Family Health Care, inc., 1978. 123 p. (Health and development in Southern Africa, v. 4)

Submitted to the Southern Africa Development Analysis Program, U.S. Agency for International Development.

Bibliography: p. 119–120.

Issued in cooperation with Africare.

Microfiche. [Washington, U.S. Agency for International Development, 1979?] 2 sheets.

DLC-Sci RR PN-AAH-164

2466

Report of an engineering manpower survey of Malawi. [s.l.], Louis Berger International, inc., 1979. 124 p.

Prepared for the U.S. Agency for International Development under contract AID/afr-C-1132.

Abstract in *A.I.D. Research & Development Abstracts*, v. 10, no. 1/2, 1982, p. 37.

Mozambique

General

2467

U.S. *Agency for International Development*. A report to the Congress on development needs and opportunities for cooperation in Southern Africa. Annex A: Mozambique. [Washington], 1979. 103 p.

An overview of the country's situation, including reports on agriculture, health, education, transportation, industry, labor, finance, and development planning.

Microfiche. [Washington, U.S. Agency for International Development, 1979?] 2 sheets.

DLC-Sci RR PN-AAH-155

2468

U.S. *Congress. House. Committee on International Relations. Subcommittee on Africa*. Perspectives on Mozambique: hearing ... Ninety-fifth Congress, second session, May 16, 1978. Washington, U.S. Govt. Print. Off., 1978. 71 p.

KF27.I54914　1978c
J74.A23 95th
Cong., House Comm.
Inter. Rel., v. 83

Charles C. Diggs, Jr., chairman.

Witnesses include Richard M. Moose, Assistant Secretary of State for African Affairs, other representatives of the Dept. of State, and Allen Isaacman, Dept. of History, University of Minnesota. Prepared statement by Prof. Isaacman: p. 32–59.

2469

U.S. *Dept. of State*. Post report. Mozambique. [Washington?], 1978. 16 p. illus., map.

JX1705.A286 Spec. Format

L.C. has also report issued in 1974.

For a description of the contents of this publication, see the note to entry 936.

2470

U.S. *Dept. of State. Bureau of Public Affairs*. Background notes. Mozambique. [Washington, for sale by the Supt. of Docs., U.S. Govt. Print. Off.], 1980. 6 p. illus., maps. (U.S. Dept. of State. Department of State publication 7965)　G59.U5

L.C. retains only the latest revision.

For a description of the contents of this publication, see the note to entry 937.

2471

Kaplan, Irving. Area handbook for Mozambique; coauthors, Irving Kaplan [et al.] 2d ed. Washington, for sale by the Supt. of Docs., U.S. Govt. Print. Off., 1977. xx, 240 p. maps.　DT453.K36

Bibliography: p. 215–228.

"Supersedes DA pam 550–64, February 1969."

"This volume is one of a series of handbooks prepared by Foreign Area Studies (FAS) of the American University."

Abstract in *Government Reports Announcements & Index*, Mar. 31, 1978, p. 30.

Issued also in microfiche. [s.l., 1977?] 3 sheets.

DLC-Sci RR AD-A048572

Assistance Programs

2472

U.S. *Agency for International Development*. Annual budget submission: Mozambique. Washington, U.S. International Development Cooperation Agency.

Vol. for 1982 examined in the Development Information Center, AID, Washington, D.C.

2473

Allen, James B. No aid for Marxist regime in Mozambique. Congressional record, 94th Congress, 2d session, v. 122, Aug. 26, 1976: 27922–27924.　J11.R5 v. 122

Remarks in the U.S. Senate.

2474

Mozambique. [*Treaties, etc. United States, 1976 Sept. 14*] Mozambique; agricultural commodities:

2474 (cont.)

transfers under Title II. Agreement signed at Maputo September 14, 1976; entered into force September 14, 1976, with related note. *In* U.S. *Treaties, etc.* United States treaties and other international agreements, v. 28, 1976–77. [Washington, Dept. of State; for sale by the Supt. of Docs., U.S. Govt. Print. Off., 1978] p. 7165–7168. ([Treaties and other international acts series, 8711])

JX231.A34 v. 28

2475

Mozambique. [*Treaties, etc. United States, 1977 Dec. 2*] Mozambique; agricultural commodities: transfer under Title II. Agreement signed at Maputo December 2, 1977; entered into force December 2, 1977. *In* U.S. *Treaties, etc.* United States treaties and other international agreements, v. 29, 1976–77. [Washington, Dept. of State; for sale by the Supt. of Docs., U.S. Govt. Print. Off., 1980] p. 5294–5296. ([Treaties and other international acts series, 9108])   JX231.A34 v. 29

2476

Mozambique. [*Treaties, etc. United States, 1979 June 28*] Agreement between the Government of the United States of America and the Government of the People's Republic of Mozambique for sales of agricultural commodities. [Washington, Dept. of State; for sale by the Supt. of Docs., U.S. Govt. Print. Off., 1980] 43 p. (Treaties and other international acts series, 9635)   DLC

Signed at Maputo June 28, 1979 with agreed minute.

In English and Portuguese.

2477

Mozambique. [*Treaties, etc. United States, 1980 June 23*] Mozambique, agricultural commodities. Agreement signed at Maputo June 23, 1980; entered into force June 23, 1980. With agreed minutes of negotiations. And amending agreement effected by exchange of notes, signed at Maputo July 24, 1980; entered into force July 24, 1980. [Washington, Dept. of State; for sale by the Supt. of Docs., U.S. Govt. Print. Off., 1981] 23 p. (Treaties and other international acts series, 9857)   DLC

In English and Portuguese.

2478

Technical Assistance Information Clearing House. Development assistance programs of U.S. nonprofit organizations: Mozambique. 1st ed. [New York], American Council of Voluntary Agencies for Foreign Service, 1976. 11 p. map. (TAICH country report)   HC578.M6T4 1976

The Clearing House is operated by the Council

under a grant from the U.S. Agency for International Development.

Crime and Criminals

2479

Director of police discusses crime, its causes. *In* U.S. *Joint Publications Research Service.* JPRS 70750. [Springfield, Va., National Technical Information Service, 1978] (Translations on Sub-Saharan Africa, no. 1891) p. 24–28.

Translation of press conference held by Raposo Pereira, director of the criminal investigation police, in *Notícias*, Maputo, Jan. 20, 1978, p. 2.

Microfiche. [Washington, Supt. of Docs., U.S. Govt. Print. Off., 1978]

DLC-Micro JPRS 70750

2480

FRELIMO intensifies combat against crime. *In* U.S. *Joint Publications Research Service.* JPRS 67901. [Springfield, Va., National Technical Information Service, 1976] (Translations on Sub-Saharan Affrica, no. 1673) p. 28–34.

Translation of article in *Notícias*, Maputo, Aug. 12, 1976, p. 3.

Microfiche. [s.l., 1976]

DLC-Micro JPRS 67901

Economic Conditions

2481

Additional banknotes issued, reasons given. *In* U.S. *Joint Publications Research Service.* JPRS 72324. [Springfield, Va., National Technical Information Service, 1978] (Translations on Sub-Saharan Affrica, no. 2030) p. 55–59.

Translation of interview with Candida Perestrelo, an administrator with the Banco de Moçambique, in *Notícias*, Maputo, Oct. 9, 1978, P. 2.

Microfiche. [Washington, Supt. of Docs., U.S. Govt. Print. Off., 1978]

DLC-Micro JPRS 72324

2482

David, Luis. Evolution of salary policy in national socialist economy reviewed. *In* U.S. *Joint Publications Research Service.* JPRS 76094. [Springfield, Va., National Technical Information Service, 1980] (Sub-Saharan Africa report, no. 2271) p. 60–70.

Translation of article in *Tempo*, Maputo, May 25, June 1–8, 1980.

Microfiche. [s.l., 1980]

DLC-Micro JPRS 76094

2483

—— Slow progress, indifference of production councils cited. *In* U.S. *Joint Publications Research Service.* JPRS 77005. [Springfield, Va., National Technical Information Service, 1980] (Sub-Saharan Africa report, no. 2333) p. 56–59.

Translation of article in *Tempo*, Maputo, Oct. 26, 1980, p. 22–27.

Microfiche. [s.l., 1980]
DLC-Micro JPRS 77005

2484

Development ministry issues 1978 government program guidelines. *In* U.S. *Joint Publications Research Service.* JPRS 70379. [Springfield, Va., National Technical Information Service, 1977] (Translations on Sub-Saharan Africa, no. 1855) p. 34–43.

Translation of article in *Notícias*, Maputo, Oct. 26, 1977, p. 2, 4.

Microfiche. [s.l., 1977]
DLC-Micro JPRS 70379

2485

Dukes, James. Institutional changes needed in the Mozambique economy. [s.l., 1974] 7 leaves. (FAR 20602-N)

Prepared for the Colloquium on Portuguese Africa, sponsored by the U.S. Dept. of State, Oct. 1974.

Examined in the former Foreign Affairs Research Documentation Center, Dept. of State.

2486

Economic sabotage widespread, costly. *In* U.S. *Joint Publications Research Service.* JPRS 70364. [Springfield, Va., National Technical Information Service, 1977] (Translations on Sub-Saharan Africa, no. 1834) p. 81–90.

Translation of article in *Notícias*, Maputo, Oct. 1977 (various dates).

Microfiche. [s.l., 1977]
DLC-Micro JPRS 70364

2487

Foreign economic trends and their implications for the United States. Mozambique. 1969+ Washington, for sale by the Supt. of Docs., U.S. Govt. Print. Off. annual. (International marketing information series) HC10.E416

Vols. for 1969–74 prepared by the U.S. Consulate General, Lourenço Marques; vol. for 1975 by the U.S. Embassy, Lourenço Marques; vols. for 1977?- by the U.S. Embassy, Maputo.

Vols. for 1969–78 distributed by the U.S. Bureau of International Commerce; vol. for 1979 by the U.S. Industry and Trade Administration;

vols. for 1980- by the U.S. International Trade Administration.

Apparently not published in 1973 or 1976.

The following issues for the period 1974–80 have been identified in L.C.:
ET 74-089. 1974. 8 p.
FET 75-136. 1975. 11 p.
FET 77-110. 1977. 10 p.
FET 78-011. 1978. 12 p.
FET 79-030. 1979. 7 p.
FET 80-026. 1980. 9 p.

2488

Import-export state enterprises organized. *In* U.S. *Joint Publications Research Service.* JPRS 67525. [Springfield, Va., National Technical Information Service, 1976] (Translations on Sub-Saharan Africa, no. 1659) p. 14–22.

Translation of article in *Notícias*, Maputo, June 9, 1976, p. 3.

Microfiche. [s.l., 1976]
DLC-Micro JPRS 67525

2489

Long-term electricity supply, development reviewed. *In* U.S. *Joint Publications Research Service.* JPRS 75884. [Springfield, Va., National Technical Information Service, 1980] (Sub-Saharan Africa report, no. 2257) p. 85–88.

Translation of article in *Tempo*, Maputo, May 11, 1980, p. 19–22.

Microfiche. [s.l., 1980]
DLC-Micro JPRS 75884

2490

Machel, Samora M. General conditions in Beira under fire by Machel. *In* U.S. *Joint Publications Research Service.* JPRS 75138. [Springfield, Va., National Technical Information Service, 1980] (Sub-Saharan Africa report, no. 2214) p. 82–87.

Translation of speech recorded in *Notícias*, Maputo, Jan. 18, 1980, p. 3, 4.

Microfiche. [s.l., 1980]
DLC-Micro JPRS 75138

2491

—— President Machel stresses importance of central planning. *In* U.S. *Joint Publications Research Service.* JPRS 77396. [Springfield, Va., National Technical Information Service, 1981] (Sub-Saharan Africa report, no. 2360) p. 30–35.

Translation of excerpts of speech recorded in *Notícias*, Maputo, Dec. 19, 1980, p. 3.

Microfiche. [s.l., 1981]
DLC-Micro JPRS 77396

2492

Machel speech covers every facet of economy. *In* U.S. *Joint Publications Research Service*. JPRS 74151. [Springfield, Va., National Technical Information Service, 1979] (Sub-Saharan Africa report, no. 2149) p. 41–53.

Translation of speech by President Machel reported in *Notícias*, Maputo, Aug. 5, 1979, p. 3–5.

Microfiche. [Washington, Supt. of Docs., U.S. Govt. Print. Off., 1979]

DLC-Micro JPRS 74151

2493

Official comments on salary regulations, application to foreigners. *In* U.S. *Joint Publications Research Service*. JPRS 76649. [Springfield, Va., National Technical Information Service, 1980] (Sub-Saharan Africa report, no. 2308) p. 66–70.

Translation of interview with Rui B. D. Alves, Minister of Finance, in *Notícias*, Maputo, Sept. 18, 1980, p. 3.

Microfiche. [s.l., 1980]

DLC-Micro JPRS 76649

2494

Santos, Marcelino dos. Dos Santos discusses regional planning problems. *In* U.S. *Joint Publications Research Service*. JPRS 70608. [Springfield, Va., National Technical Information Service, 1978] (Translations on Sub-Saharan Africa, no. 1876) p. 52–61.

Translation of speech by the Minister of Planning recorded in *Notícias*, Maputo, Dec. 25, 1977, p. 2, 8.

Microfiche. [Washington, Supt. of Docs., U.S. Govt. Print. Off., 1978]

DLC-Micro JPRS 70608

2495

——— Dos Santos discusses shortages, plans to organize economy. *In* U.S. *Joint Publications Research Service*. JPRS 71246. [Springfield, Va., National Technical Information Service, 1978] (Translations on Sub-Saharan Africa, no. 1941) p. 120–128.

Translation of speech by the Minister for Development and Economic Planning recorded in *Notícias*, Maputo, Apr. 20, 1978, p. 2, 4.

Microfiche. [Washington, Supt. of Docs., U.S. Govt. Print. Off., 1978]

DLC-Micro JPRS 71246

2496

——— Dos Santos speech at FRELIMO economic policy meeting. *In* U.S. *Joint Publications Research Service*. JPRS 76293. [Springfield, Va., National

Technical Information Service, 1980] (Sub-Saharan Africa report, no. 2283) p. 22–26.

Translation of speech by the secretary for economic policy of the Frente de Libertação de Moçambique recorded in *Notícias*, Maputo, July 8, 1980, p. 3.

Microfiche. [s.l., 1980]

DLC-Micro JPRS 76293

2497

Simmons, Richard L. Mozambique: an economic base study with emphasis on agriculture. [s.l.], 1978. 112 p. maps.

Bibliography: p. 111–112.

On cover: "This sector assessment was undertaken in conjunction with the Southern Africa Development Analysis Project."

Microfiche. [Washington, U.S. Agency for International Development, 1978?] 2 sheets. (PN-AAH-185); examined in the Development Information Center, AID, Washington, D.C.

Finance

2498

Details given on budget priorities. *In* U.S. *Joint Publications Research Service*. JPRS 70887. [Springfield, Va., National Technical Information Service, 1978] (Translations on Sub-Saharan Africa, no. 1904) p. 44–49.

Translation of article, in *Notícias*, Maputo, Feb. 22, 1978, p. 7.

Microfiche. [Washington, Supt. of Docs., U.S. Govt. Print. Off., 1978]

DLC-Micro JPRS 70887

2499

Details on new fiscal policy reported. *In* U.S. *Joint Publications Research Service*. JPRS 70887. [Springfield, Va., National Technical Information Service, 1978] (Translations on Sub-Saharan Africa, no. 1904) p. 53–56.

Translation of article in *Notícias*, Maputo, Feb. 18, 1978, p. 1.

Microfiche. [Washington, Supt. of Docs., U.S. Govt. Print. Off., 1978]

DLC-Micro JPRS 70887

2500

Magide, Osman. Finance ministry restructuring, priorities discussed. *In* U.S. *Joint Publications Research Service*. JPRS 70750. [Springfield, Va., National Technical Information Service, 1978] (Translations on Sub-Saharan Africa, no. 1891) p. 16–23.

Translation of article in *Notícias*, Maputo, Jan. 31, 1978, p. 2, 4.

2500 (cont.)
Microfiche. [Washington, Supt. of Docs., U.S. Govt. Print. Off., 1978]
DLC-Micro JPRS 70750

Foreign Relations

2501
Cuba, Mozambique issue joint communique. *In* U.S. *Joint Publications Research Service*. JPRS 69029. [Springfield, Va., National Technical Information Service, 1977] (Translations on Sub-Saharan Africa, no. 1741) p. 48–54.
Text of communique issued on the occasion of an official visit to Mozambique by President Fidel Castro, in *Notícias*, Maputo, Mar. 24, 1977, p. 5.
Microfiche. [s.l., 1977]
DLC-Micro JPRS 69029

2502
Davis, Nathaniel. Department testifies on U.S. policy toward Mozambique. *In* U.S. *Dept. of State*. The Department of State bulletin, v. 73, no. 1882, July 21, 1975: 103–105.
JX232.A33 v. 73
Statement by the Assistant Secretary of State for African Affairs.

2503
Ford, Gerald R. Letter to President Samora Machel on United States recognition of Mozambique. June 25, 1975. *In* U.S. *President*. Public papers of the Presidents of the United States. Gerald R. Ford. 1975. [Washington, Office of the Federal Register, National Archives and Records Service; for sale by the Supt. of Docs., U.S. Govt. Print. Off., 1977] p. 878. J80.A283 1975

2504
Foreign policy, economy, relations with Brazil discussed. *In* U.S. *Joint Publications Research Service*. JPRS 76035. [Springfield, Va., National Technical Information Service, 1980] (Sub-Saharan Africa, no. 2267) p. 63–74.
Translation of interview with Sérgio Vieira, Governor of the Banco de Moçambique, in *Notícias*, Maputo, June 13, 1980, p. 3.
Microfiche, [s.l., 1980]
DLC-Micro JPRS 76035

2505
Joint communique with Hungary issued. *In* U.S. *Joint Publications Research Service*. JPRS 76744. [Springfield, Va., National Technical Information Service, 1980] (Sub-Saharan Africa report, no. 2315) p. 31–38.
Translation of statement issued on the occasion of the visit of President Pál Losonczi of Hungary to Mozambique, in *Notícias*, Maputo, Sept. 25, 1980, p. 4.
Microfiche. [s.l., 1980]
DLC-Micro JPRS 76744

2506
Joint resolution published on Machel visit to USSR. *In* U.S. *Joint Publications Research Service*. JPRS 77145. [Springfield, Va., National Technical Information Service, 1981] (Sub-Saharan Africa report, no. 2343) p. 32–35.
Translation of the text of an official "assessment" of President Machel's visit to the Soviet Union on Nov. 17–22, 1980, in *Notícias*, Maputo, Dec. 5, 1980, p. 3.
Microfiche. [s.l., 1981]
DLC-Micro JPRS 77145

2507
Thom, William G. Military assistance to the Mozambique Liberation Front (FRELIMO) [Washington?], Dept. of Defense, 1975. [11] leaves.
Presented at annual meeting of the African Studies Association, 1975.
Microfilm. [African Studies Association. Papers presented at the annual meeting]
DLC-Micro Microfilm 03782 DT 1975, reel 2

Geology, Hydrology, and Mineral Resources

The following items (entries 2508–12) are listed in chronological order:

2508
Morse, David E. The mineral industry of Mozambique. *In* Minerals yearbook, v. 3, 1975. [Washington, for sale by the Supt. of Docs., U.S. Govt. Print. Off., 1978] p. 703–708.
TN23.U612 1975, v. 3
Prepared by the U.S. Bureau of Mines.

2509
—— The mineral industry of Mozambique. *In* Minerals yearbook, v. 3, 1976. [Washington, for sale by the Supt. of Docs., U.S. Govt. Print. Off., 1980] p. 751–754. TN23.U612 1976, v. 3
Prepared by the U.S. Bureau of Mines.

2510

—— The mineral industry of Mozambique. *In* Minerals yearbook, v. 3, 1977. [Washington, for sale by the Supt. of Docs., U.S. Govt. Print. Off., 1981] p. 661–663.   TN23.U612   1977, v. 3
Prepared by the U.S. Bureau of Mines.

2511

Ellis, Miller W. The mineral industry of Mozambique. *In* Minerals yearbook, v. 3, 1978–79. [Washington, U.S. Govt. Print. Off., 1981] p. 663–666.   TN23.U612   1978–79, v. 3
Prepared by the U.S. Bureau of Mines.

2512

—— The mineral industry of Mozambique. *In* Minerals yearbook, v. 3, 1980. [Washington, for sale by the Supt. of Docs., U.S. Govt. Print. Off., 1982] p. 691–695.   TN23.U612   1980, v. 3
Prepared by the U.S. Bureau of Mines.

2513

Optimistic prospects for coal mining. *In* U.S. *Joint Publications Research Service.* JPRS 68122. [Springfield, Va., National Technical Information Service, 1976] (Translations on Sub-Saharan Africa, no. 1686) p. 8–13.
Translation of article in *Notícias*, Maputo, Sept. 29, 1976, p. 2.
Microfiche. [s.l., 1976]
                    DLC-Micro JPRS 68122

Health and Nutrition

2514

Carp, Carol. A review of health care in Mozambique: issues, analyses, and recommendations. Washington, Family Health Care, inc., 1978. 101 p. (Health and development in Southern Africa, v. 6)
Submitted to the Southern Africa Development Analysis Program, U.S. Agency for International Development.
Bibliography: p. 97–101.
Issued in cooperation with Africare.
Microfiche. [Washington, U.S. Agency for International Development, 1979?] 2 sheets.
                    DLC-Sci RR PN-AAH-166

2515

Machel, Samora M. Machel speech at opening of WHO regional meeting. *In* U.S. *Joint Publications Research Service.* JPRS 74407. [Springfield, Va., National Technical Information Service, 1979] (Sub-Saharan Africa report, no. 2166) p. 31–40.
Translation of speech on Mozambique's health policy at the opening of the meeting of the World

Health Organization Regional Committee on Africa, Maputo, Sept. 19, 1979, recorded in *Notícias*, Maputo, Sept. 20, 1979, p. 3, 4.
Microfiche. [Washington, Supt. of Docs., U.S. Govt. Print. Off., 1979]
                    DLC-Micro JPRS 74407

2516

—— Machel speech on hospitals condemns excesses in egalitarianism. *In* U.S. *Joint Publications Research Service.* JPRS 74987. [Springfield, Va., National Technical Information Service, 1980] (Sub-Saharan Africa report, no. 2203) p. 75–90.
Translation of article in *Notícias*, Maputo, Dec. 9, 1979, p. 3–6.
Microfiche. [s.l., 1980]
                    DLC-Micro JPRS 74987

2517

—— President stresses need for collectivizing, democratizing health services. *In* U.S. *Joint Publications Research Service.* JPRS 68184. [Springfield, Va., National Technical Information Service, 1976] (Translations on Sub-Saharan Africa, no. 1688) p. 43–63.
Translation of statement recorded in *Notícias*, Maputo, Oct. 8, 1976, p. 6–8.
Microfiche. [s.l., 1976]
                    DLC-Micro JPRS 68184

Military Affairs

2518

Explanation provided for creation of military ranks. *In* U.S. *Joint Publications Research Service.* JPRS 76768. [Springfield, Va., National Technical Information Service, 1980] (Sub-Saharan Africa report, no. 2316) p. 84–88.
Translation of article in *Notícias*, Maputo, Sept. 23, 1980, p. 3.
Microfiche. [s.l., 1980]
                    DLC-Micro JPRS 76768

2519

Lopes, Arlindo. General staff chief on military operations, maneuvers. *In* U.S. *Joint Publications Research Service.* JPRS 76526. [Springfield, Va., National Technical Information Service, 1980] (Sub-Saharan Africa report, no. 2300) p. 81–85.
Translation of interview with Sebastião M. Mobote, chief of staff of the Forças Populares da Libertação de Moçambique, in *Tempo*, Maputo, Aug. 24, 1980, p. 26–29.
Microfiche. [s.l., 1980]
                    DLC-Micro JPRS 76526

Politics and Government

2520

All-encompassing party role defined. *In* U.S. *Joint Publications Research Service.* JPRS 72369. [Springfield, Va., National Technical Information Service, 1978] (Translations on Sub-Saharan Africa, no. 2033) p. 32–35.

Translation of article in *Notícias*, Maputo, Nov. 14, 1978, p. 2.

Concerns an expanded role for the Frente de Libertação de Moçambique (FRELIMO).

Microfiche. [Washington, Supt. of Docs., U.S. Govt. Print. Off., 1978]

DLC-Micro JPRS 72369

2521

Carvalho, Augusto de. FRELIMO opposition analyzed. *In* U.S. *Joint Publications Research Service.* JPRS 68965. [Springfield, Va., National Technical Information Service, 1977] (Translations on Sub-Saharan Africa, no. 1737) p. 12–20.

Translation of article in *Expresso*, Lisbon, Mar. 11, 1977, p. 14.

Microfiche. [s.l., 1977]

DLC-Micro JPRS 68965

2522

Crime, aggression practiced against Mozambican people; infiltrators admit Rhodesian training. *In* U.S. *Joint Publications Research Service.* JPRS 72749. [Springfield, Va., National Technical Information Service, 1979] (Translations on Sub-Saharan Africa, no. 2059) p. 51–54.

Translation of article in *Notícias*, Maputo, Jan. 10, 1979, p. 1.

Microfiche. [Washington, Supt. of Docs., U.S. Govt. Print. Off., 1979]

DLC-Micro JPRS 72749

2523

Document sets forth recommendations for political-ideological training. *In* U.S. *Joint Publications Research Service.* JPRS 77396. [Springfield, Va., National Technical Information Service, 1981] (Sub-Saharan Africa report, no. 2360) p. 36–41.

Translation of text of a FRELIMO document, in *Notícias*, Maputo, Dec. 14, 1980, p. 5.

Microfiche. [s.l., 1981]

DLC-Micro JPRS 77396

2524

Electoral law for the first general elections. *In* U.S. *Joint Publications Research Service.* JPRS 69835. [Springfield, Va., National Technical Information Service, 1977] (Translations on Sub-Saharan Africa, no. 1805) p. 47–57.

Translation of article in *Notícias*, Maputo, Sept. 2, 1977, p. 7, 8, 13.

Microfiche. [s.l., 1977]

DLC-Micro JPRS 69835

2525

Filho, Artur P. Editor of Portuguese weekly interviews President Machel. *In* U.S. *Joint Publications Research Service.* JPRS 69733. [Springfield, Va., National Technical Information Service, 1977] (Translations on Sub-Saharan Africa, no. 1794) p. 29–42.

Translation of interview, in *Notícias*, Maputo, July 12, 1977, p. 6–7.

Microfiche. [s.l., 1977]

DLC-Micro JPRS 69733

2526

Hoff, Arve. Discussion of Mozambique since independence. *In* U.S. *Joint Publications Research Service.* JPRS 70036. [Springfield, Va., National Technical Information Service, 1977] (Translations on Sub-Saharan Africa, no. 1828) p. 34–45.

Translation of article in *Aftenposten*, Oslo, Sept. 22, 23, 26, and 28, 1977.

Microfiche. [s.l., 1977]

DLC-Micro JPRS 70036

2527

Independence compared and contrasted: the United States and Mozambique. New York, School Services Division, African-American Institute, 1976. 7 p.

Abstract in *Resources in Education*, Apr. 1977, p. 130.

Microfiche. [Arlington, Va., ERIC Document Reproduction Service; prepared for Educational Resources Information Center, National Institute of Education, 1977] 1 sheet.

DLC-Micro ED132091

2528

Lagarde, Dominique. Rural areas visited, national difficulties, hopes reported. *In* U.S. *Joint Publications Research Service.* JPRS 72680. [Springfield, Va., National Technical Information Service, 1979] (Translations on Sub-Saharan Africa, no. 2054) p. 83–86.

Translation of article in *Demain l'Afrique*, Paris, no. 16, Dec. 18, 1978, p. 32, 34.

Microfiche. [Washington, Supt. of Docs., U.S. Govt. Print. Off., 1979]

DLC-Micro JPRS 72680

2529

Lang, Nicolas. Divisiveness plagues Machel regime. *In* U.S. *Joint Publications Research Service.* JPRS 68184. [Springfield, Va., National Technical Information Service, 1976] (Translations on Sub-Saharan Africa, no. 1688) p. 27–31.

Translation of article in *Est et Ouest*, Paris Sept. 16–30, 1976, p. 10–13.

Microfiche. [s.l., 1976]

DLC-Micro JPRS 68184

2530

Langellier, Jean-Pierre. French newsman considers country's theory, reality. *In* U.S. *Joint Publications Research Service.* JPRS 77084. [Springfield, Va., National Technical Information Service, 1980] (Sub-Saharan Africa report, no. 2338) p. 16–26.

Translation of article in *Le Monde*, Paris, Dec. 2, 3, 4, 1980.

Microfiche. [s.l., 1981]

DLC-Micro JPRS 77084

2531

Lefott, René. Political, economic, ideological difficulties explored. *In* U.S. *Joint Publications Research Service.* JPRS 68689. [Springfield, Va., National Technical Information Service, 1977] (Translations on Sub-Saharan Africa, no. 1716) p. 45–51.

Translation of article in *Le Monde*, Paris, Jan. 27, 28, 1977.

Microfiche. [s.l., 1977]

DLC-Micro JPRS 68689

2532

Machel, Samora M. Machel discusses domestic achievements, foreign policy. *In* U.S. *Joint Publications Research Service.* JPRS 70696. [Springfield, Va., National Technical Information Service, 1978] (Translations on Sub-Saharan Africa, no. 1885) p. 30–36.

Translation of speech recorded in *Notícias*, Maputo, Jan. 7, 1978, p. 2.

Microfiche. [Washington, Supt. of Docs., U.S. Govt. Print. Off., 1978]

DLC-Micro JPRS 70696

2533

—— Machel discusses reorganization of district administration. *In* U.S. *Joint Publications Research Service.* JPRS 76857. [Springfield, Va., National Technical Information Service, 1980] (Sub-Saharan Africa report, no. 2322) p. 33–43.

Translation of speech recorded in *Notícias*, Maputo, Oct. 9, 1980, p. 3–4.

Microfiche. [s.l., 1980]

DLC-Micro JPRS 76857

2534

—— Machel: former prisoners to be resettled in Niassa Province. *In* U.S. *Joint Publications Research Service.* JPRS 74663. [Springfield, Va., National Technical Information Service, 1979] (Sub-Saharan Africa report, no. 2183) p. 49–65.

Translation of excerpts of speech by President Machel denouncing Portuguese colonialism and western imperialism, in *Notícias*, Maputo, Oct. 28, 1979, p. 3–8.

Microfiche. [s.l., 1979]

DLC-Micro JPRS 74663

2535

Machel message to FPLM on 25 September. *In* U.S. *Joint Publications Research Service.* JPRS 74563. [Springfield, Va., National Technical Information Service, 1979] (Sub-Saharan Africa report, no. 2176) p. 63–69.

Translation of text of speech by President Samora Machel to the Forças Populares da Libertação de Moçambique, Sept. 25, 1979, recorded in *Notícias*, Maputo, Sept. 25, 1979, p. 3, 4.

Microfiche. [s.l., 1979]

DLC-Micro JPRS 74563

2536

Monteiro, Caceres. Visits to reeducation centers, communal villages recounted. *In* U.S. *Joint Publications Research Service.* JPRS 75775. [Springfield, Va., National Technical Information Service, 1980] (Sub-Saharan Africa report, no. 2251) p. 68–73.

Translation of article in *O Jornal*, Lisbon, Apr. 23–29, 1980.

Microfiche. [s.l., 1980]

DLC-Micro JPRS 75775

2537

Monteiro, José Oscar. Monteiro discusses new organization of state. *In* U.S. *Joint Publications Research Service.* JPRS 70608. [Springfield, Va., National Technical Information Service, 1978] (Translations on Sub-Saharan Africa, no. 1876) p. 52–61.

Translation of speech by the Minister of State for the Presidency recorded in *Notícias*, Maputo, Dec. 26, 1977, p. 4.

Microfiche. [Washington, Supt. of Docs., U.S. Govt. Print. Off., 1978]

DLC-Micro JPRS 70608

2538

Officials comment on electoral process. *In* U.S. *Joint Publications Research Service.* JPRS 70254. [Springfield, Va., National Technical Information

2538 (cont.)

Service, 1977] (Translations on Sub-Saharan Africa, no. 1842) p. 60–64.

Translation of article in *Notícias*, Maputo, Oct. 12, 1977, p. 3, 5.

Microfiche. [s.l., 1977]

DLC-Micro JPRS 70254

2539

President discusses domestic problems. *In* U.S. *Joint Publications Research Service.* JPRS 65479. [Springfield, Va., National Technical Information Service, 1975] (Translations on Africa, no. 1609) p. 27–30.

Translation of article relating to a speech by Samora Machel, in *Expresso*, Lisbon, July 26, 1975, p. 7.

Microfiche. [s.l., 1975]

DLC-Micro JPRS 65479

2540

Provincial meetings register successes, failures. *In* U.S. *Joint Publications Research Service.* JPRS 76649. [Springfield, Va., National Technical Information Service, 1980] (Sub-Saharan Africa report, no. 2308) p. 55–58.

Translation of article in *Notícias*, Maputo, Sept. 21, 1980, p. 1–2.

Concerns meetings of provincial bodies of Maputo, Niassa, and Tete.

Microfiche. [s.l., 1980]

DLC-Micro JPRS 76649

2541

Publication of Mondlane letter sheds new light on FRELIMO history. *In* U.S. *Joint Publications Research Service.* JPRS 68869. [Springfield, Va., National Technical Information Service, 1977] (Translations on Sub-Saharan Africa, no. 1729) p. 39–43.

Translation of article in *Diario de Notícias*, Lisbon, Feb. 25, 1977, p. 19.

Microfiche. [s.l., 1977]

DLC-Micro JPRS 68869

2542

The Revolution in Mozambique moves steadily forward. *In* U.S. *Joint Publications Research Service.* JPRS 69473. [Springfield, Va., National Technical Information Service, 1977] (Translations on Sub-Saharan Africa, no. 1776) p. 36–39.

Translation of article in *Tap Chi Cong San*, Hanoi, June 1977, p. 75–77.

Microfiche. [s.l., 1977]

DLC-Micro JPRS 69473

2543

Text of resolution issued by central committee's eighth session. *In* U.S. *Joint Publications Research Service.* JPRS 77279. [Springfield, Va., National Technical Information Service, 1981] (Sub-Saharan Africa report, no. 2351) p. 78–89.

Translation of text of FRELIMO resolution, in *Notícias*, Maputo, Dec. 20, 1980, p. 3, 4.

Microfiche. [s.l., 1981]

DLC-Micro JPRS 77279

Other Subjects

2544

Africa: Mozambique. Selected statistical data by sex. Washington, 1981. 31, 17 p.　　　　DLC

Study supported by the U.S. Agency for International Development's Office of Women in Development and Office of Population.

Data assembled by the International Demographic Data Center, U.S. Bureau of the Census.

Among the tables, all based on 1970 data, are the following: unadjusted population by age and sex; population by province, sex, and urban/rural residence; population by ethnic group and sex; population by religion and sex; population by nationality ("foreign population"); population by marital status, age, and sex; number of households; number of literate persons by age, sex, and urban/rural residence; number of economically active persons by age, sex, and urban/rural residence; economically active population by occupational status and sex.

2545

Alves, Rui Baltazar dos Santos. Justice minister discusses concept, function of justice. *In* U.S. *Joint Publications Research Service.* JPRS 71246. [Springfield, Va., National Technical Information Service, 1978] (Translations on Sub-Saharan Africa, no. 1941) p. 129–138.

Translation of speech recorded in *Notícias*, Maputo, Apr. 19, 1978, p. 2, 4.

Microfiche. [Washington, Supt. of Docs., U.S. Govt. Print. Off., 1978]

DLC-Micro JPRS 71246

2546

Machel, Samora M. Problems of women in Mozambique discussed. *In* U.S. *Joint Publications Research Service.* JPRS 67246. [Springfield, Va., National Technical Information Service, 1976] (Translations on Sub-Saharan Africa, no. 1649) p. 24–33.

Translation of speech recorded in *Notícias*, Maputo, Apr. 1, 1976, p. 3, 6.

2546 (cont.)

Microfiche. [s.l., 1976]

DLC-Micro JPRS 67246

2547

President calls for restructuring of prison system. *In* U.S. *Joint Publications Research Service.* JPRS 67525. [Springfield, Va., National Technical Information Service, 1976] (Translations on Sub-Saharan Africa, no. 1659) p. 9–13.

Translation of article in *Notícias*, Maputo, June 1, 1976, p. 3.

Microfiche. [s.l., 1976]

DLC-Micro JPRS 67525

2548

Public works sector problems, outlook. *In* U.S. *Joint Publications Research Service.* JPRS 70608. [Springfield, Va., National Technical Information Service, 1978] (Translations on Sub-Saharan Africa, no. 1876) p. 62–71.

Translation of article in *Notícias*, Maputo, Dec. 22, 1977, p. 2, 4

Microfiche. [Washington, Supt. of Docs., U.S. Govt. Print. Off., 1978]

DLC-Micro JPRS 70608

2549

Robinson, Howard T. Mozambique: a unique potential. [Washington], Senior Seminar in Foreign Policy, U.S. Dept. of State, [1975?] 15 p. maps. (FAR 22727-S)

A study of Mozambique's transportation infrastructure.

Examined in the former Foreign Affairs Research Documentation Center, Dept. of State.

2550

Steiner, Herbert H. Mozambique's agricultural economy in brief. Washington, Economic Research Service, U.S. Dept. of Agriculture, 1976. 27 p. map. (Foreign agricultural economic report, no. 116)

HD1411.F59 no. 116

Namibia

Note: Until the late 1970s, the country was called South-West Africa (sometimes printed as Southwest Africa) in most U.S. Government documents.

General

2551

U.S. *Agency for International Development.* A report to the Congress on development needs and opportunities for cooperation in Southern Africa. Annex A: Namibia. [Washington], 1979. 129 p.

An overview of the country is followed by sections on the socio-economic effects of South Africa's policies, education, labor, health, mining, fisheries, agriculture, manufacturing, transportation, communications, and foreign assistance needs.

Microfiche. [Washington, U.S. Agency for International Development, 1979?] 2 sheets.

DLC-Sci RR PN-AAH-156

2552

U.S. *Dept. of State. Bureau of Public Affairs.* Background notes. Namibia (South-West Africa) [Washington, for sale by the Supt. of Docs., U.S. Govt. Print. Off.], 1980. 7 p. illus., maps. (U.S. Dept. of State. Department of State publication 8168)   G59.U5

L.C. retains only the latest revision.

For a description of the contents of this publication, see the note to entry 937.

2553

Rotberg, Robert I. Namibia: politics, ecology, and society. Cambridge, Dept. of Political Science, Massachusetts Institute of Technology, 1977. 62 p. (Transition problems in a developing nation [Namibia] Occasional paper, no. 2)

Prepared for the African-American Scholars Council and the U.S. Agency for International Development under subcontract AID/afr-C-1254.

Abstract in *A.I.D. Research and Development Abstracts*, Oct. 1978, p. 37.

Microfiche. [Washington, U.S. Agency for International Development, 1977?] 1 sheet.

DLC-Sci RR PN-AAF-256

Foreign Relations

2554

U.S. *Congress. House. Committee on Foreign Affairs. Subcommittee on Africa.* Namibia update: hearing, Ninety-sixth Congress, second session, September 9, 1980. Washington, U.S. Govt. Print. Off., 1981. 35 p. map.   KF27.F625 1980h
                                  J74.A23 96th
                         Cong., House Comm.
                             For. Aff., v. 133

Stephen J. Solarz, chairman.

Chairman Solarz introduced the hearing by noting that it would cover "the current situation in Namibia and the ongoing efforts on the part of five Western powers and the Secretary General [of the United Nations] to find a basis for a solution to the Namibian problem that will be acceptable to South Africa, the parties within the territory, SWAPO, and the frontline states."—p. 1.

Witness is Donald F. McHenry, U.S. Permanent Representative to the United Nations.

Appendix: Statement by members of the Council of Ministers of the Territory of South-West Africa. p. 25–35.

2555

———— The current situation in Namibia: hearing, Ninety-sixth Congress, first session, May 7, 1979. Washington, U.S. Govt. Print. Off., 1979. 36 p.
                         KF27.F625 1979a
                             J74.A23 96th
                         Cong., House Comm.
                             For. Aff., v. 21

Stephen J. Solarz, chairman.

Testimony by Donald F. McHenry, Deputy U.S. Ambassador to the United Nations.

2556

U.S. *Congress. House. Committee on International Relations. Subcommittee on International Organizations.* Namibia, the United Nations and U.S. policy: hearings, Ninety-fourth Congress, second

2556 (cont.)

session, August 24 and 27, 1976. Washington, for sale by the Supt. of Docs., U.S. Govt. Print. Off., 1976. 258 p. map.

> KF27.I5494   1976l
> J74.A23 94th Cong.,
> House Comm. Inter.
> Rel., v. 105

Donald M. Fraser, chairman.

In his opening statement, Chairman Fraser states that "the purpose of our hearings is to examine U.S. policy options and the role of the United Nations in the face of South Africa's continued illegal occupation of territory known both as Namibia and South-West Africa."—p. 1.

Among the appendixes are the following:

Appendix 1. Security Council resolutions concerning Namibia (1973–1976), voting record of United States, United Kingdom, and France. p. 91–125.

Appendix 6. Document of the International Conference on Namibia and Human Rights, International Institute of Human Rights, "Human rights in Namibia," by Elizabeth S. Landis, held in Dakar, January 5–8, 1976. p. 151–223.

2557

U.S. *Congress. Senate. Committee on Foreign Relations. Subcommittee on African Affairs.* Namibia: hearing, Ninety-sixth Congress, first session on the current situation in Namibia, June 25, 1979. Washington, U.S. Govt. Print. Off., 1979. 50 p.

> KF26.F625 1979
> J74.A23 96th
> Cong., Sen. Comm.
> For. Rel., v. 18

George McGovern, chairman.

Testimony by Donald F. McHenry, Deputy U.S. Representative to the United Nations.

Appendix: Letter to Senator McGovern from W. R. Retief, Minister, Embassy of South Africa, dated June 22, 1979, with attachments concerning background on issues of disagreement between South Africa and the Secretary-General of the United Nations. p. 23–50.

2558

Africa: Secretary Vance discusses Namibia with South African officials. *In* U.S. *Dept. of State.* The Department of State bulletin, v. 78, no. 2021, Dec. 1978: 21–25.   JX232.A33 v. 78

Text of the Secretary of State's statements, Oct. 19, 1978.

2559

Bonker, Don. American/Angolan diplomacy in Southern Africa promising. Congressional record,

95th Congress, 2d session, v. 124, July 25, 1978: 22725–22727.   J11.R5 v. 124

Extension of remarks in the U.S. House of Representatives.

Includes articles on Namibia and on American policy regarding Cubans in Africa.

2560

Butcher, Goler T. U.S. policy choices in Namibia. Washington, White, Fine, and Verville, 1977. [94] p. (in various pagings) (Transition problems in a developing nation [Namibia] Occasional paper, no. 1)

Prepared for the African-American Scholars Council and the U.S. Agency for International Development under subcontract AID/afr-C-1254.

Abstract in *A.I.D. Research and Development Abstracts*, Oct. 1978, p. 25–26.

Microfiche. [Washington, U.S. Agency for International Development, 1977?] 1 sheet.

> DLC-Sci RR PN-AAF-255

2561

Davis, Nathaniel. Department summarizes U.S. policy toward Namibia. *In* U.S. *Dept. of State.* The Department of State bulletin, v. 73, no. 1880, July 7, 1975: 36–39.   JX232.A33 v. 73

Statement by the Assistant Secretary of State for African Affairs before the Subcommittee on International Resources, Food, and Energy, Committee on International Relations, House of Representatives, June 10, 1975.

2562

[Economic sanctions—Namibia] *In* Rovine, Arthur W. Digest of United States practice in international law. 1974. [Washington], Office of the Legal Adviser, Dept. of State; [for sale by the Supt. of Docs., U.S. Govt. Print. Off., 1975] (Department of State publication, 8809) p. 598–601.

> JX21.R68   1975

U.S. compliance with international legal obligations.

2563

Goldwater, Barry. Report on Senator Goldwater's trip. Congressional record, 95th Congress, 2d session, v. 124, Apr. 17, 1978: 10238–10240.

> J11.R5 v. 124

Remarks in the U.S. Senate.

Senator Goldwater reports on his recent trip to South Africa and Namibia; emphasis of remarks is on the South West Africa People's Organization.

2564

Namibia. [Washington], Bureau of Public Affairs, Dept. of State, 1979. [2] p.   DLC

2564 (cont.)

At head of title: Gist: a quick reference aid on U.S. foreign relations.

2565

Scali, John A. U.S. vetoes resolution on Namibia in U.N. Security Council. *In* U.S. *Dept. of State.* The Department of State bulletin, v. 73, no. 1880, July 7, 1975: 42–46.   JX232.A33 v. 73

Statements by the U.S. Representative on June 3 and June 6, 1975, together with the text of the draft resolution.

2566

Status of talks analyzed. *In* U.S. *Joint Publications Research Service.* JPRS 69503. [Springfield, Va., National Technical Information Service, 1977] (Translations on Sub-Saharan Africa, no. 1779) p. 72–75.

Translation of article on negotiations between South Africa and the western powers on the future of Namibia, in *Die Suidwester*, Windhoek, June 10, 1977, p. 4.

Microfiche. [s.l., 1977]
DLC-Micro JPRS 69503

2567

Text of Bundstag debate about Windhoek consulate. *In* U.S. *Joint Publications Research Service.* JPRS 69554. [Springfield, Va., National Technical Information Service, 1977] (Translations on Sub-Saharan Africa, no. 1782) p. 67–77.

Text of a debate in the West German parliament over the issue of closing the German consultate in Windhoek, in *Allgemeine Zeitung*, Windhoek, June 30, July 1, 1977.

Microfiche. [s.l., 1977]
DLC-Micro JPRS 69554

2568

Top secret frontline states minutes said leaked by SA [South Africa] *In* U.S. *Joint Publications Research Service.* JPRS 73971. [Springfield, Va., National Technical Information Service, 1979] (Sub-Saharan Africa report, no. 2140) p. 2–8.

Record of a summit meeting of Mar. 3–4, 1979, Lusaka, Zambia, seeking a solution to the Namibian problem.

From *Windhoek Observer*, Windhoek, July 14, 1979, p. 22–23.

Microfiche. [Washington, Supt. of Docs., U.S. Govt. Print. Off., 1979]
DLC-Micro JPRS 73971

2569

U.S. deplores continued occupation of Namibia by South Africa. *In* U.S. *Dept. of State.* The Depart-ment of State bulletin, v. 72, no. 1858, Feb. 3, 1975: 161–163.   JX232.A33 v. 72

Statement by U.S. Representative John A. Scali to the United Nations Security Council, Dec. 17, 1974, together with the text of a resolution adopted by the Council.

2570

U.S. reaffirms commitment to self-determination and independence for Namibia. *In* U.S. *Dept. of State.* The Department of State bulletin, v. 76, no. 1960, Jan. 17, 1977: 43–48.   JX232.A33 v. 76

Statements in Committee IV (Trusteeship) of the United Nations General Assembly by U.S. Representative William W. Scranton, Dec. 2, 1976, and U.S. Representative Stephen Hess, Dec. 10, 1976, together with the texts of two resolutions adopted by the General Assembly on Dec. 20.

2571

U.S. supports U.N. resolutions on situation in Namibia. *In* U.S. *Dept. of State.* The Department of State bulletin, v. 74, no. 1913, Feb. 23, 1976: 243–246.   JX232.A33 v. 74

Includes statements by Daniel P. Moynihan, U.S. Representative to the United Nations in the U.N. Security Council, Jan. 29 and 30, 1976, and the text of a resolution adopted by the Council on Jan. 30, 1976.

2572

White, Barbara M. Self-determination for Namibia urged by United States. *In* U.S. *Dept. of State.* The Department of State bulletin, v. 73, no. 1899, Nov. 17, 1975: 715–717.   JX232.A33 v. 73

Statement by the U.S. Representative to Committee IV (Trusteeship) of the United Nations General Assembly.

Geography and Maps

2573

[U.S. *Central Intelligence Agency*] Namibia. [Washington, 1978] col. map.
G8621.G6   1978.U5

Scale ca. 1 : 5,200,000.
"503615 2-78."
Relief shown by shading.
Shows "homelands" (Basterland (Rehoboth), Bushmanland, Damaraland, Hercroland, Kaoko-veld, Namaland, Tswanaland) and "homelands" granted self-rule (Caprivi, Kavangoland, and Ovamboland).

2574
——— Namibia and Walvis Bay/Central Intelligence Agency. [Washington, 1978] col. map.
G8620   1978.U51
Scale 1 : 4,000,000.
"Lambert conformal conic projection, standard parallels 6° and 30°."
Relief shown by shading and spot heights.

2575
——— South-West Africa (Namibia) [Washington, 1976] col. map.   G8620   1976.U5
Scale ca. 1 : 9,500,000.
"568922 3-76."

2576
U.S. *Dept. of State. Office of the Geographer.* Southwest Africa: U.S. implementation of Namibia as official country name. Washington, 1977. 1 p.
AMAU

"Geographic note GE-166."

Geology, Hydrology, and Mineral Resources

2577
Conyers, John. The exploitation of Namibia. Congressional record [daily ed.], 96th Congress, 2d session, v. 126, Nov. 18, 1980: E4991–E4992.
J11.R7 v. 126
Extension of remarks in the U.S. House of Representatives.
Includes article, "Uranium colony: the illegal exploitation of Namibia," from the *Nation*.

The following items (entries 2578–85) are listed in chronological order:

2578
Jolly, James H. The mineral industry of the Territory of South-West Africa. *In* Minerals yearbook, v. 3, 1972. [Washington, for sale by the Supt. of Docs., U.S. Govt. Print. Off., 1974] p. 723–730.
TN23.U612   1972, v. 3
Prepared by the U.S. Bureau of Mines.

2579
——— The mineral industry of the Territory of South-West Africa. *In* Minerals yearbook, v. 3, 1973. [Washington, for sale by the Supt. of Docs., U.S. Govt. Print. Off., 1976] p. 771–778.
TN23.U612   1973, v. 3
Prepared by the U.S. Bureau of Mines.

2580
——— The mineral industry of the Territory of South-West Africa. *In* Minerals yearbook, v. 3, 1974. [Washington, for sale by the Supt. of Docs., U.S. Govt. Print. Off., 1977] p. 817–823.
TN23.U612   1974, v. 3
Prepared by the U.S. Bureau of Mines.

2581
Stevens, Candice. The mineral industry of the Territory of South-West Africa. *In* Minerals yearbook, v. 3, 1975. [Washington, for sale by the Supt. of Docs., U.S. Govt. Print. Off., 1978] p. 875–884.   TN23.U612   1975, v. 3
Prepared by the U.S. Bureau of Mines.

2582
——— The mineral industry of the Territory of South-West Africa. *In* Minerals yearbook, v. 3, 1976. [Washington, for sale by the Supt. of Docs., U.S. Govt. Print. Off., 1980] p. 943–949.
TN23.U612   1976, v. 3
Prepared by the U.S. Bureau of Mines.

2583
——— The Mineral industry of the Territory of South-West Africa. *In* Minerals yearbook, v. 3, 1977. [Washington, for sale by the Supt. of Docs., U.S. Govt. Print. Off., 1981] p. 849–853.
TN23.U612   1977, v.3
Prepred by the U.S. Bureau of Mines.

2584
Ellis, Miller W., *and* Candice Stevens. The mineral industry of the Territory of South-West Africa. *In* Minerals yearbook, v. 3, 1978–79. [Washington, U.S. Govt. Print. Off., 1981] p. 847–851.
TN23.U612   1978–79, v. 3
Prepared by the U.S. Bureau of Mines.

2585
Ellis, Miller W. The mineral industry of Namibia (Territory of South-West Africa) *In* Minerals yearbook, v. 3, 1980. [Washington, for sale by the Supt. of Docs., U.S. Govt. Print. Off., 1982] p. 697–701.
TN23.U612   1980, v. 3
Prepared by the U.S. Bureau of Mines.

Health and Nutrition

2586
Cohn, Helen. A review of health care in Namibia: issues, analyses, and recommendations. Washington, Family Health Care, inc., 1978. 56 p. (Health and development in Southern Africa, v. 9)
Submitted to the Southern Africa Development

2586 (cont.)

Analysis Program, U.S. Agency for International Development.

Bibliography: p. 55–56.

Issued in cooperation with Africare.

Microfiche. [Washington, U.S. Agency for International Development, 1979?] 1 sheet.

DLC-Sci RR PN-AAH-169

2587

Watson, James C. Health consequences of transition in Namibia. [Houston, Tex.?] 1977. 50 p. (Transition problems in a developing nation [Namibia] Occasional paper, no. 7)

Prepared for the African-American Scholars Council and the U.S. Agency for International Development under subcontract AID/afr-C-1254.

Abstract in *A.I.D. Research and Development Abstracts*, Oct. 1978, p. 33–34.

Microfiche. [Washington, U.S. Agency for International Development, 1977?] 1 sheet.

DLC-Sci RR PN-AAF-261

Military Affairs

2588

Goff, Walter M. Namibia: another Angola?; a research report submitted to the faculty. Maxwell Air Force Base, Ala., Air War College, Air University, 1978. 50 p.   AMAU

U.S. Air War College. Research report, no. 348.

Bibliography: p. 46–50.

An examination of the guerrilla war in Namibia.

Issued also in microfiche. [s.l., Defence Documentatition Center, 1978] 1 sheet (AD-B029187L).

2589

Goldwater, Barry. South African action. Congressional record, 95th Congress, 2d session, v. 124, May 15, 1978: 13742–13743.

J11.R5 v. 124

Remarks in the U.S. Senate.

Includes a statement by the South African Government on its "preemtive action" against SWAPO bases.

2590

McCrary, Michael S. Guerrilla warfare in Namibia and associated implications for external military involvement. [Monterey, Calif.], Naval Postgraduate School, 1979. 269 p. maps.

Bibliography: p. 262–267.

Thesis (M.A.)—Naval Postgraduate School.

Microfiche. [s.l., Defense Documentation Center, 1979] 3 sheets.

DLC-Sci RR AD-A070220

2591

Roux, André le. General updates information on forces engaged in border war. *In* U.S. *Joint Publications Research Service*. JPRS 75066. [Springfield, Va., National Technical Information Service, 1980] (Sub-Saharan Africa report, no. 2210) p. 6–10.

Translation of interview with Major General Jan J. Geldenhuys, commander of South African forces in South-West Africa (Namibia), in *Die Transvaler*, Johannesburg, Dec. 31, 1979, p. 4.

Microfiche. [s.l., 1980]

DLC-Micro JPRS 75066

2592

Walvis Bay military base described. *In* U.S. *Joint Publications Research Service*. JPRS 69530. [Springfield, Va., National Technical Information Service, 1977] (Translations on Sub-Saharan Africa, no. 1780) p. 35–42. illus.

Translation of article in *Die Suidwester*, Windhoek, June 21, 1977, p. 6, 7.

Microfiche. [s.l., 1977]

DLC-Micro JPRS 69530

Politics and Government

2593

U.S. *Congress. House. Committee on International Relations. Subcommittee on International Resources, Food, and Energy.* Resources in Namibia: implications for U.S. policy: hearings, Ninety-fourth Congress, June 10, 1975 and May 13, 1976. Washington, U.S. Govt. Print. Off., 1976. 165 p.

KF27.I54947 1976d
J74.A23 94th
Cong., House Comm.
Inter. Rel., v. 106

Charles C. Diggs, Jr., chairman.

Includes bibliographical references.

In his opening remarks, Chairman Diggs states that "Independence in Namibia is now inevitable and the implications of the prospect for long-term U.S. access to resources in Namibia, which include diamonds, lead, zinc, copper, vanadium, and manganese, are clear. Certainly, a majority-ruled independent Namibia would be mindful of what action the United States is taking now to expedite progress toward independence in their country."— p. 1.

Among the appendixes are the following:

Appendix 1. Statement of the South-West Africa People's Organization (SWAPO) of Namibia presented by Sam Numoja, President of SWAPO to the U.N. Security Council, N.Y., May 30, 1975. p. 95–99.

2593 (cont.)

Appendix 7. Discussion paper entitled "The constitution of independent Namibia," by SWAPO. p. 143–152.

2594

Coetzer, Piet. Dirk Mudge seen mainstay of Turnhalle Conference. *In* U.S. *Joint Publications Research Service.* JPRS 68710. [Springfield, Va., National Technical Information Service, 1977] (Translations on Sub-Saharan Africa, no. 1717) p. 50–53'

Translation of article in *Die Transvaler*, Johannesburg, Dec. 4, 1976, p. 4.

Microfiche. [s.l., 1977]

DLC-Micro JPRS 68710

2595

Federal Party analyzes political situation. *In* U.S. *Joint Publications Research Service.* JPRS 70863. [Springfield, Va., National Technical Information Service, 1978] (Translations on Sub-Saharan Africa, no. 1902) p. 193–200.

Translation of article in *Allgemeine Zeitung*, Windhoek, Feb. 10, 17, 1978.

Microfiche. [Washington, Supt. of Docs., U.S. Govt. Print. Off., 1978]

DLC-Micro JPRS 70863

2596

Forret, David. Viljoen speaks out on future of South-West Africa. *In* U.S. *Joint Publications Research Service.* JPRS 74585. [Springfield, Va., National Technical Information Service, 1979] (Sub-Saharan Africa report, no. 2178) p. 54–58.

From interview with Gerrit Viljoen, administrator-general of South-West Africa, in *Rand Daily Mail*, Johnnesburg, Oct. 25, 1979, p. 13.

Microfiche. [s.l., 1979]

DLC-Micro JPRS 74585

2597

Gaudio, Attilio. Obstacles in path of independence discussed. *In* U.S. *Joint Publications Research Service.* JPRS 77222. [Springfield, Va., National Technical Information Service, 1981] (Sub-Saharan Africa report, no. 2348) p. 48–53.

Translation of article in *Africa*, Dakar, Nov. 1980, p. 52–54, 110.

Microfiche. [s.l., 1981]

DLC-Micro JPRS 77222

2598

Germans reconciled to Black control after independence. *In* U.S. *Joint Publications Research Service.* JPRS 70887. [Springfield, Va., National Technical Information Service, 1978] (Translations on Sub-Saharan Africa, no. 1904) p. 104–108.

Translation of article on the outlook for Germans in South-West Africa, in *Zeit Magazin*, Hamburg, Feb. 17, 1978, p. 4–10.

Microfiche. [Washington, Supt. of Docs., U.S. Govt. Print. Off., 1978]

DLC-Micro JPRS 70887

2599

Kennedy, Edward M. Progress in Namibia. Congressional record [daily ed.], 96th Congress, 2d session, v. 126, Dec. 12, 1980: S16461–S16462.

J11.R7 v. 126

Remarks in the U.S. Senate.

Includes article from the *Christian Science Monitor*.

2600

Mbitiru, Chege. Kenyan reporter gives first-hand account on elections. *In* U.S. *Joint Publications Research Service.* JPRS 72555. [Springfield, Va., National Technical Information Service, 1979] (Translations on Sub-Saharan Africa, no. 2046) p. 138–141.

From report in *Daily Nation*, Nairobi, Dec. 11, 1979, p. 6.

Microfiche. [Washington, Supt. of Docs., U.S. Govt. Print. Off., 1979]

DLC-Micro JPRS 72555

2601

Namibia National Front plan for territory published. *In* U.S. *Joint Publications Research Service.* JPRS 71133. [Springfield, Va., National Technical Information Service, 1978] (Translations on Sub-Saharan Africa, no. 1929) p. 96–99.

Article in *Windhoek Advertiser*, Windhoek, Apr. 21, 1978, p. 6.

Microfiche. [Washington, Supt. of Docs., U.S. Govt. Print. Off., 1978]

DLC-Micro JPRS 71133

2602

Nujoma: SWAPO victory assured in free elections. *In* U.S. *Joint Publications Research Service.* JPRS 73060. [Springfield, Va., National Technical Information Service, 1979] (Translations on Sub-Saharan Africa, no. 2079) p. 186–189.

Translation of interview with Sam Nujoma, President of the South West Africa People's Organization, in *Tempo*, Maputo, Feb. 4, 1979, p. 39–41.

Microfiche. [Washington, Supt. of Docs., U.S. Govt. Print. Off., 1979]

DLC-Micro JPRS 73060

2603

O'Linn, Bryan. South-West African political situation analyzed. *In* U.S. *Joint Publications Research Service.* JPRS 70184. [Springfield, Va., National Technical Information Service, 1977] (Translations on Sub-Saharan Africa, no. 1836) p. 91–99.

Translation of article in *Allgemeine Zeitung,* Windhoek, Oct. 13–14, 1977.

Microfiche. [s.l., 1977]

DLC-Micro JPRS 70184

2604

Press opinion on Namibia settlement given. *In* U.S. *Joint Publications Research Service.* JPRS 71816. [Springfield, Va., National Technical Information Service, 1978] (Translations on Sub-Saharan Africa, no. 1988) p. 76–83.

Article in *South African Digest,* Pretoria, July 21, July 28, and Aug. 4, 1978.

Microfiche. [Washington, Supt. of Docs., U.S. Govt. Print. Off., 1978]

DLC-Micro JPRS 71816

2605

Roux, André le. Interview of Namibia Administrator-General Viljoen. *In* U.S. *Joint Publications Research Service.* JPRS 74537. [Springfield, Va., National Technical Information Service, 1979] (Sub-Saharan Africa report, no. 2175) p. 41–47.

Translation of article in *Die Transvaler,* Johannesburg, Sept. 10–11, 1979.

Microfiche. [s.l., 1979]

DLC-Micro JPRS 74537

2606

SWA 36 Battalion working to integrate Bushmen. *In* U.S. *Joint Publication Research Service.* JPRS 76213. [Springfield, Va., National Technical Information Service, 1980] (Sub-Saharan Africa report, no. 2277) p. 54–57.

Article in *Windhoek Advertiser,* Windhoek, July 5, 1980, p. 24.

Microfiche. [s.l., 1980]

DLC-Micro JPRS 76213

2607

Shack, William A. The multi-ethnic factor in Namibia. Berkeley, Dept. of Anthropology, University of California, 1977. 65 p. maps. (Transition problems in a developing nation [Namibia] Occasional paper, no. 5)

Prepared for the African-American Scholars Council and the U.S. Agency for International Development under subcontract AID/afr-C-1254.

Abstract in *A.I.D. Research and Development Abstracts,* Oct. 1978, p. 37–38.

Microfiche. [Washington, U.S. Agency for International Development, 1977?] 1 sheet.

DLC-Sci RR PN-AAF-259

2608

Short, Joseph N. Politics in Namibia: final report. [Washington, African-American Scholars Council], 1977. 35 leaves. (Transition problems in a developing nation [Namibia] Occasional paper, no. 3)   DT714.S5

"Subcontract AID/afr-C-1254 for African-American Scholars Council, inc. and the Agency for International Development."

Abstract in *A.I.D. Research and Development Abstracts,* Oct. 1978, p. 37.

Issued also in microfiche. [Washington, U.S. Agency for International Development, 1977?] 1 sheet.   DLC-Sci RR PN-AAF-257

2609

Simon, Mary. South-West African People's Organization leader expresses views. *In* U.S. *Joint Publications Research Service.* JPRS 70931. [Springfield, Va., National Technical Information Service, 1978] (Translations on Sub-Saharan Africa, no. 1909) p. 132–138.

Translation of interview with Sam Nujoma, in *Prisma del Meridiano,* Havana, Jan. 1–15, 1978, p. 16–19.

Microfiche. [Washington, Supt. of Docs., U.S. Govt. Print. Off., 1978]

DLC-Micro JPRS 70931

2610

Spence, Floyd. Political situation in South West Africa/Namibia. Congressional record [daily ed.], 96th Congress, 2d session, v. 126, Dec. 5, 1980: E5287–E5289.   J11.R7 v. 126

Extension of remarks in the U.S. House of Representatives.

Includes text of a "statement of the Council of Ministers of South West Africa/Namibia."

2611

Steyn gives views on December election. *In* U.S. *Joint Publications Research Service.* JPRS 72503. [Springfield, Va., National Technical Information Service, 1978] (Translations on Sub-Saharan Africa, no. 2043) p. 35–42.

Translation of interview with Administrator-General Marthinus J. Steyn, in *Allgemeine Zeitung,* Windhoek, Nov. 6–7, 1978.

Microfiche. [Washington, Supt. of Docs., U.S. Govt. Print. Off., 1978]

DLC-Micro JPRS 72503

2612

Stone, David M. Namibia 1979: another Angola? [Monterey, Calif.], Naval Postgraduate School, 1979. 167 p. maps.

Thesis (M.A.)—Naval Postgraduate School.

Bibliography: p. 162–167.

"This thesis examines the complex factors involved in Namibia's transition process. The roles of the various actors are described and the similarities to the Angola crisis of 1975 analyzed. Particular attention is paid to recent Soviet-Cuban activities in the region."—Abstract.

Microfiche. [s.l., Defense Documentation Center, 1979] 2 sheets (DLC-Sci RR AD-A071080); issued also in microfilm by University Publications of America (cited in its *Africa: Special Studies 1962–1980*, p. 11).

2613

Ugoani, Anene. 'Golden Harvest' ship's Namibia mission questioned. *In* U.S. *Joint Publications Research Service.* JPRS 72304. [Springfield, Va., National Technical Information Service, 1978] (Translations on Sub-Saharan Africa, no. 2028) p. 3–6.

Article in *Daily Times*, Lagos, Oct. 30, 1978, p. 17, concerning a Nigerian investigation of the crew of the ship *Golden Harvest* en route to Namibia with a shipment of books for the South West African People's Organization of Namibia and other liberation groups.

Microfiche. [Washington, Supt. of Docs., U.S. Govt. Print. Off., 1978]

DLC-Micro JPRS 72304

Other Subjects

2614

Anschel, Kurt R., *and* Russell H. Brannon. The agricultural sector of Namibia: a brief assessment. [s.l.], 1978. 60 p.

"Prepared in cooperation with the Southeast Consortium for International Development (SECID), the U.S. Department of Agriculture, and the U.S. Agency for International Development."

Microfiche. [Washington, U.S. Agency for International Development, 1979?] 1 sheet.

DLC-Sci RR PN-AAH-180

2615

Foreign assistance appropriations, 1980. Congressional record [daily ed.], 96th Congress, 1st session, v. 125, Oct. 12, 1979: S14463–S14479.

J11.R7 v. 125

Includes remarks in U.S. Senate, primarily by Senators Jesse A. Helms and Daniel K. Inouye, on Amendment no. 512 to H.R. 4473 that would "prohibit funding for the Institute for Namibia." Supporting documents cover SWAPO, the United Nations Council for Namibia, and the Institute for Namibia (p. S14465–S14471).

2616

Kornicker, Louis S. Myodocopid Ostracoda from Southern Africa. Washington, Smithsonian Institution Press, 1976. 39 p. illus. (Smithsonian contributions to zoology, no. 214)

QL1.S54 no. 214

2617

Namibia: economic growth, structure, and prospects, [by] Elliot Berg [et al.] Ann Arbor, Center for Research on Economic Development, University of Michigan, 1977. 62 p. (Transition problems in a developing nation [Namibia] Occasional paper, no. 4)

Prepared for the African-American Scholars Council and the U.S. Agency for International Development under subcontract AID/afr-C-1254.

Abstract in *A.I.D. Research and Development Abstracts*, Oct. 1978, p. 29.

Microfiche. [Washington, U.S. Agency for International Development, 1977?] 1 sheet.

DLC-Sci RR PN-AAF-258

2618

Scranton, Mary I., *and* John W. Farrington. Methane production in the waters off Walvis Bay. Journal of geophysical research, v. 82, Oct. 20, 1977: 4947–4953. maps.

Study supported by a National Science Foundation grant and by Office of Naval Research contracts.

Issued also in microfiche. [s.l., Defense Documentation Center, 1979] 1 sheet.

DLC-Sci RR AD-A061195

2619

Wilks, Brian S. An analysis of the main aspects of manpower and education needs for Namibia in a situation of transition to majority rule. Houston, Tex., Center for International Education, University of Houston, 1977. 33 p. (Transition problems in a developing nation [Namibia] Occasional paper, no. 6)

Prepared for the African-American Scholars Council and the U.S. Agency for International Development under subcontract AID/afr-C-1254.

Abstract in *A.I.D. Research and Development Abstracts*, Oct. 1978, p. 30.

Microfiche. [Washington, U.S. Agency for International Development, 1977?] 1 sheet.

DLC-Sci RR PN-AAF-260

South Africa

General

2620

U.S. *Congress. House. Committee on Foreign Affairs. Subcommittee on International Economic Policy and Trade.* U.S. policy toward South Africa: hearings before the Subcommittees on International Economic Policy and Trade, on Africa, and on International Organizations of the Committee on Foreign Affairs, House of Representatives, Ninety-sixth Congress, second session. Washington, for sale by the Supt. of Docs., U.S. Govt. Print. Off., 1980. 912 p. map.   KF27.F6465 1980b
                              J74.A23 96th
                              Cong., House Comm.
                              For. Aff., v. 113

Jonathan B. Bingham, chairman, Subcommittee on International Economic Policy and Trade.

Stephen J. Solarz, chairman, Subcommittee on Africa.

Don Bonker, chairman, Subcommittee on International Organizations.

Hearings held Apr. 30–June 10, 1980.

Includes bibliographical references.

Each hearing is devoted to a particular topic, e.g., South African reform; homelands policy and the prospects for political change; human rights; U.S. corporate involvement in South Africa; and options for U.S. policy.

Among materials submitted for the record:

Ciskei Commission report, appendix 12, Black attitudes survey, February 1980. p. 210–258. illus.

Survey of attitudes among the peoples of Ciskei toward independence.

Prepared statement of Chester A. Crocker, Director of African Studies, Center for Strategic and International Studies, Georgetown University. p. 664–709.

2621

U.S. *Dept. of State.* Post report. South Africa. [Washington?], 1979. 35 p. illus., maps.
                              JX1705.A286 Spec. Format

Includes reports on Pretoria, Cape Town, Durban, and Johannesburg.

L.C. has also report issued in 1976.

For a description of the contents of this publication, see the note to entry 936.

2622

U.S. *Dept. of State. Bureau of Public Affairs.* Background notes. South Africa. [Washington, for sale by the Supt. of Docs., U.S. Govt. Print. Off.], 1980. 8 p. illus., maps. (U.S. Dept. of State. Department of State publication 8021)   G59.U5

L.C. retains only the latest revision.

For a description of the contents of this publication, see the note to entry 937.

2623

South Africa: a country study; edited by Harold D. Nelson. [Washington, for sale by the Supt. of Docs., U.S. Govt. Print. Off., c1981] xxix, 464 p. illus., maps.   DT753.S57 1981

Area handbook series. DA Pam 550-93.

Bibliography: p. 403–438.

"Supersedes 1971 edition."

"Research completed December 1980."

Among the appendixes are the following:

Table 5. Black population estimates by official ethnolinguistic categories, 1979. p. 379.

Table 10, Enrollment in universities by race, 1979. p. 381.

Table 12. Production of selected minerals, 1972–78, p. 382.

Table 14. Destination of exports. 1975–79. p. 383.

Table 17. Sources of imports, 1975–79. p. 386.

Table 20. Foreign investment by geographic source, end of 1978. p. 390–391.

Table 21. Employment by racial group in selected industry divisions, selected years, 1970–78. p. 392–393.

Table 22. Average annual earnings by racial group in nonagricultural sectors, 1977. p. 394.

Table 25. Principal newspapers, 1980. p. 396.

2623 (cont.)

Indicates circulation figures and political orientation.

Tables 26–29. Lists of military manpower and equipment, indicating country of origin of various weapons. p. 399–402.

Agriculture

2624

[U.S. *Central Intelligence Agency*] South Africa; agriculture. [Washington, 1978] col. map.

G8501.K1   1978.U5

Scale ca. 1 : 6,000,000.

"503620 3-78."

2625

——— South Africa; agriculture and mining. [Washington, 1977] col. map.

G8501.J1   1977.U5

Scale ca. 1 : 10,000,000.

"503202 1-77 (543001)."

2626

U.S. *Foreign Agricultural Service.* Report on world sugar supply and demand, 1980 and 1985. [Washington], Foreign Agricultural Service, United States Department of Agriculture, [1977] 303 p.

HD9100.4.U54   1977

South Africa is covered on p. 153–161.

2627

Canned deciduous fruit: production and trade statistics in selected countries. Washington, U.S. Dept. of Agriculture, Foreign Agricultural Service, 1980. 54 p. (Foreign agriculture circular. FCAN 1-80)

S21.F615

Includes data on South African exports.

2628

Deciduous fruit: world production and trade statistics. Washington, Foreign Agricultural Service, U.S. Dept. of Agriculture, 1978. 79 p. (Foreign agriculture circular. Fresh deciduous fruits and grapes. FDAP 2-78)

S21.F615

Includes statistics on South Africa, primarily for the period 1971–76.

2629

Howard, James O. South African corn—I. Proper stimulus could send exports soaring in decade. Foreign agriculture, Feb. 1981: 7–9. illus.

HD1401.F65   1981

Issued by the U.S. Foreign Agricultural Service.

2630

——— South African corn—II. Port facility growth needed for South Africa to meet corn export potential in 15 years. Foreign agriculture, Mar. 1981: 9–11. illus.

HD1401.F65   1981

Issued by the U.S. Foreign Agricultural Service.

2631

Livestock statistics in selected countries, 1960–1975. Washington, Foreign Agricultural Service, U.S. Dept. of Agriculture, 1978. 73 p. (Foreign agriculture circular. Livestock and meat. FLM 10–78)

S21.F615

Includes statistics for South Africa.

2632

McDonald, Roy E. South Africa's citrus industry focuses on export markets. Foreign agriculture, May 29, 1978: 6–8. illus.

HD1401.F65   1978

Issued by the U.S. Foreign Agricultural Service.

2633

Murray, Kenneth L. South Africa anticipates record harvests and exports of grain. Washington, Foreign Agricultural Service, U.S. Dept. of Agriculture, 1974. 4 p. (Foreign agriculture circular. Grain. FG 4-74)

S21.F615

2634

Smith, Samuel D. Cotton in South Africa. Washington, Foreign Agricultural Service, U.S. Dept. of Agriculture, 1980. 11 p. (Foreign agriculture circular. Cotton. FC6-80)

S21.F615

2635

Witucki, Lawrence A. New role seen for South African agriculture. Foreign agriculture, Nov. 22, 1976: 2–4, 15. illus.

HD1401.F65   1976

Issued by the U.S. Foreign Agricultural Service.

Commerce

2636

U.S. *Congress. House. Committee on Banking, Finance, and Urban Affairs. Subcommittee on International Trade, Investment, and Monetary Policy.* Export-Import Bank and trade with South Africa: hearing, Ninety-fifth Congress, second session, February 9, 1978. Washington, U.S. Govt. Print. Off., 1978. 130 p. illus.

KF27.B577   1978b
J74.A23 95th
Cong., House Comm.
Bank., v. 45

Stephen L. Neal, chairman.

2637

U.S. *President, 1977–1981 (Carter)* Export controls for foreign policy purposes. Letter to the Speaker of the House and the President of the Senate. December 29, 1979. *In* U.S. *President.* Public papers of the Presidents of the United States. Jimmy Carter. 1979. [Washington, Office of the Federal Register, National Archives and Records Service; for sale by the Supt. of Docs., U.S. Govt. Print. Off., 1980] p. 2290–2297.

J80.A283   1979

Includes examples of the effects on American companies of the prohibition of the export of virtually all items to military and police forces in South Africa (p. 2293–2294).

2638

Dreyer, Lynette. Commercial relations with neighboring nations. *In* U.S. *Joint Publications Research Service.* JPRS 74852. [Springfield, Va., National Technical Information Service, 1980] (Sub-Saharan Africa report, no. 2194) p. 139–142.

Translation of article in *Die Transvaler*, Johannesburg, Nov. 27, 1979, p. 10.

Microfiche. [s.l., 1980]

DLC-Micro JPRS 74852

2639

Gibson, Urath. Marketing in South Africa. Washington, U.S. Dept. of Commerce, International Trade Administration; [for sale by the Supt. of Docs., U.S. Govt. Print. Off.], 1981. 36 p. (Overseas business repors. OBR 81-03)

HF91.U482   1981, no. 3

International marketing information series.

2640

Human rights policy affects export controls: South Africa is current case in point. Commerce America, June 5, 1978: 7–8.   HF1.C38

Issued by the U.S. Dept. of Commerce.

"In a recent precedent-setting action, the Department of Commerce has imposed far-reaching controls on the exports of goods or technical data for use by the police or military forces of the South African government."

The regulations were published in *Export Administration Bulletin*, no. 175, Feb. 16, 1978.

2641

Library of Congress. *Congressional Research Service.* Imports of minerals from South Africa by the United States and the OECD countries; prepared for the Subcommittee on African Affairs of the Committee on Foreign Relations, United States

Senate. Washington, U.S. Govt. Print. Off., 1980, xviii, 46 p.

HD9506.S72L52   1980

Includes bibliographical references.

At head of title: 96th Congress, 2d session. Committee print.

"September 1980."

2642

Market share reports. Country series: South Africa, 1971–75. [Washington], U.S. Dept. of Commerce; for sale by the National Technical Information Service, Springfield, Va., [1977] 70 p.

Indicates the United States share of the market in South Africa for various products compared to the shares for Belgium-Luxemburg, France, Federal Republic of Germany, Great Britain, Italy, Netherlands, Sweden, and Japan.

Microfiche. [Washington, Congressional Information Service, 1977?]

DLC-Micro ASI:77 2016-1.78

2643

Market share reports. Country series: South Africa, 1975–79. [Washington], International Trade Administration, U.S. Dept. of Commerce; for sale by the National Technical Information Service, Springfield, Va., [1979] 70 p.

Includes same comparative data as in *Market Share Reports. Country Series: South Africa, 1971–75* (entry 2642).

Microfiche. [Washington, Congressional Information Service, 1979?]

DLC-Micro ASI:81 2046-2.78

2644

Market survey of communications equipment and systems: South Africa. Maidenhead, Berkshire, England, Alan Stratford & Associates, 1975. [111] p.

Prepared for the Domestic and International Business Administration, U.S. Dept. of Commerce.

Cited, with annotation, in *Government Reports Announcement & Index*, June 11, 1976, p. 20.

Microfiche. [Springfield, Va.], National Technical Information Service, [1976] 2 sheets.

DLC-Sci RR DIB-76-04-504

2645

Survey of the market for medical equipment in South Africa. Johannesburg, Markct Rescarch Africa Pty., ltd., 1976. 218 p.

Prepared for Domestic and International Business Administration, U.S. Dept. of Commerce.

Abstract in *Government Reports Announcements & Index*, May 13, 1977, p. 20.

2645 (cont.)
Microfiche. [Springfield, Va., National Technical Information Service, 1977] 3 sheets.
DLC-Sci RR DIB-77-04-506

2646
Walker, Libby J. Market factors in South Africa. [Washington], U.S. Dept. of Commerce, Domestic and International Business Administration; [for sale by the Supt. of Docs., U.S. Govt. Print. Off.] 1977. 32 p. (Overseas business reports. OBR 77-08)
HF91.U482   1977, no. 8
International marketing information series.
Supersedes *Market Factors in South Africa* (Overseas business reports. OBR 74-57), by Sally K. Miller.

Economic Conditions

2647
[U.S. *Central Intelligence Agency*] South Africa; industry. [Washington, 1978] col. map.
G8501.M1   1978.U5
Scale ca. 1 : 6,000,000.
"503622 3-78."

2648
Clark, Dick. U.S. corporate interests in South Africa: report to the Committee on Foreign Relations, United States Senate, by Senator Dick Clark, Iowa, chairman, Subcommittee on African Affairs of the Committee on Foreign Relations, United States Senate. Washington, U.S. Govt. Print. Off., 1978. 232 p.   HD2922.C53
At head of title: 95th Congress, 2d session. Committee print.
Bibliography: p. 76–79.
Includes a summary, prepared by Susan M. Mowle, of hearings on South Africa held before the Subcommittee on African Affairs in September 1976 (see entry 2653).
Among the appendixes is the following:
Appendix B. U.S. *Consulate General, Johannesburg.* American firms, subsidiaries and affiliates—South Africa, May 1976. p. 133–164.

2649
Foreign economic trends and their implications for the United States. Republic of South Africa. 1969+ Washington, For sale by the Supt. of Docs., U.S. Govt. Print. Off. semiannual. (International marketing information series)
HC10.E416
Continues *Economic Trends and Their Implications for the United States. South Africa.*
Title varies slightly.

Prepared by the U.S. Embassy, Pretoria.
Vols. for 1969–77 distributed by the U.S. Bureau of International Commerce; vols. for 1978–79 by the U.S. Industry and Trade Administration; vols for 1980– by the U.S. International Trade Administration.
The following issues for the period 1973–81 have been identified in L.C.:
ET 73-066. 1973. [12] p.
ET 73-134. 1973. 11 p.
ET 74-063. 1974. 11 p.
FET 75-011. 1975. 7 p.
FET 75-078. 1975. 8 p.
FET 76-109. 1976. 11 p.
FET 77-004. 1977. 11 p.
FET 77-082. 1977. 13 p.
FET 77-158. 1977. 12 p.
FET 78-078. 1978. 13 p.
FET 78-138. 1978. 11 p.
FET 79-068. 1979. 13 p.
FET 80-029. 1980. 12 p.
FET 80-065. 1980. 13 p.
FET 81-002. 1981. 14 p.
FET 81-091. 1981. 10 p.

2650
Kling, Gordon. Economic indicators for 1980 reported. *In* U.S. *Joint Publications Research Service.* JPRS 77253. [Springfield, Va., National Technical Information Service, 1981] (Sub-Saharan Africa report, no. 2349) p. 83–89.
Article in *The Cape Times*, Cape Town, Dec. 31, 1980, p. 9.
Microfiche. [s.l., 1981]
DLC-Micro JPRS 77253

United States Investments

2651
U.S. *Congress. House. Committee on International Relations. Subcommittee on Africa.* United States private investment in South Africa: hearings before the Subcommittees on Africa and on International Economic Policy and Trade of the Committee on International Relations, House of Representatives, Ninety-fifth Congress, second session. Washington, U.S. Govt. Print. Off., 1978. 641 p.
KF27.I54914   1978d
J74.A23 95th
Cong., House Comm.
Inter. Rel., v. 107
Charles C. Diggs, Jr., chairman, Subcommittee on Africa.
Jonathan B. Bingham, chairman, Subcommittee on International Economic Policy and Trade.
Hearings held June 27-Sept. 7, 1978.

2651 (cont.)

In his introductory remarks, Chairman Diggs notes that the purpose of the hearings is to examine "our economic relationship with the Republic of South Africa. Specifically, we shall examine the role of foreign investment and particularly that of U.S. corporations."—p. i–ii.

Among the appendixes are statements of representatives of American corporations.

2652

U.S. *Congress. House. Committee on International Relations. Subcommittee on International Resources, Food, and Energy*. Resource development in South Africa and U.S. policy: hearings, Ninety-fourth Congress, second session, May 25, June 8 and 9, 1976. Washington, for sale by the Supt. of Docs., U.S. Govt. Print. Off., 1976. 443 p.

> KF27.I54947 1976e
> J74.A23 94th Cong.,
> House Comm. Inter. Rel.,
> v. 98

Charles C. Diggs, Jr., chairman.

In his opening remarks, Chairman Diggs states that the purpose of the hearings are to examine the "full range and status of development of resources in South Africa, the role of the U.S. Government, American corporations, and private institutions and groups in developing these resources, and the implications of U.S. policy for continued U.S. access to resources in South Africa, including the way in which U.S. relations with the peoples and states of the area may affect such access."—p. 1.

The hearing on June 8, 1976 focused on the issue of the exchange and transfer of nuclear materials and technology to South Africa from the Arms Control and Disarmament Agency and the Energy Research and Development Administration. p. 49–88.

Among the appendixes are the following:

Appendix 1. Agreements between the United States, South Africa, and the International Atomic Energy Agency. p. 207–234.

Appendix 2. Responses by the Department of State to additional questions submitted in writing by Congressman Diggs. p. 235–253.

Appendix 3. Responses by the Export-Import Bank to additional questions submitted in writing by Congressman Diggs. p. 254–269.

> Includes tables on the Bank's authorizations in Africa, FY 1971–1976.

Appendix 6. Responses by the Energy Research and Development Administration to additional questions submitted in writing by Congressman Diggs. p. 293–327.

Appendix 7. Letter from J. Robert Vastine, Department of the Treasury, dated August 25, 1976, enclosing responses to additional questions submitted in writing by Congressman Diggs. p. 328–395.

> Includes *American Firms, Subsidiaries and Affiliates Operating in the Republic of South Africa*. p. 335–360.

Appendix 11. Responses to additional questions submitted in writing by Congressman Diggs to the Department of Commerce. p. 411–442.

> Includes list of U.S. exports to Africa, 1966–75 (p. 416–425), and U.S. general imports from Africa, 1966–75 (p. 426–435).

2653

U.S. *Congress. Senate. Committee on Foreign Relations. Subcommittee on African Affairs*. South Africa: hearings, Ninety-fourth Congress, second session, on South Africa-U.S. policy and the role of U.S. corporations. Washington, for sale by the Supt. of Docs., U.S. Govt. Print. Off., 1977. 792 p. illus.

> KF26.F625 1976c
> J74.A23 94th
> Cong., Sen. Comm.
> For. Rel., v. 49

Dick Clark, chairman.

Hearings held Sept. 8–30, 1976.

A review of American policy and the "nature and role of U.S. business in South Africa in an effort to determine whether it is consonant with U.S. policy."

Among the insertions for the record are *The Oil Conspiracy: An Investigation into How Multinational Oil Companies Provide Rhodesia's Oil Needs* (p. 299–350), a 1976 study by the Center for Social Action, United Church of Christ; a report on this document by the Mobil Oil Corporation (p. 357–377); and a memorandum on "the position of the Bantu in our economy" by the Transvaal Chamber of Industries (p. 467–504).

Among the appendixes is *Employment Practices of U.S. Firms in South Africa* (p. 768–780), prepared by the U.S. Dept. of State, Bureau of African Affairs.

Note: A summary of these hearings appears in *U.S. Corporate Interests in South Africa* (entry 2648).

2654

Goldwater, Barry. Investment in South Africa. Congressional record, 95th Congress, 2d session, v. 124, Apr. 12, 1978: 9834–9835.

> J11.R5 v. 124

Remarks in the U.S. Senate.

Includes text of documents, *Investment in South Africa*, prepared by the South African Embassy.

2655

Gray, William H. Sullivan's principles at work in South Africa. Congressional record, [daily ed.], 96th Congress, 2d session, v. 126, May 20, 1980: E2489–E2490.   J11.R7 v. 126

Extension of remarks in the U.S. House of Representatives.

Includes testimony before the Subcommittee on Africa, House Committee on Foreign Affairs, by Rev. Leon Sullivan, author of a fair employment code for American companies in South Africa.

Note: Representative Gray includes additional comments on Rev. Sullivan's assessment of the fair employment code in the *Congressional Record* of May 21, 1980 (p. E2527–E2529).

2656

Report on portfolio companies with operations in South Africa. [Cambridge, Mass.?], Advisory Committee on Shareholder Responsibility, Harvard University, 1979. 40 p.

A. Michael Spence, chairman.

Abstract in *Resources in Education*, 1980 annual cumulation, p. 481.

Microfiche. [Arlington, Va., ERIC Document Reproduction Service; prepared for Educational Resources Information Center, National Institute of Education, 1980] 1 sheet.

DLC-Micro ED178016

2657

Report with respect to South African shareholder responsibility. [Cambridge, Mass.?], Advisory Committee on Shareholder Responsibility, Harvard University, 1978. 52 p.

Henry B. Reiling, chairman.

Abstract in *Resources in Education*, 1980 annual cumulation, p. 481.

Microfiche. [Arlington, Va., ERIC Document Reproduction Service; prepared for Educational Resources Information Center, National Institute of Education, 1980] 1 sheet.

DLC-Micro ED178015

2658

Solarz, Stephen J. Solarz testimony on H.R. 12463. Congressional record, 95th Congress, 2d session, v. 124, June 26, 1978: 19066–19068.

J11.R5 v. 124

Extension of remarks in the U.S. House of Representatives.

Includes remarks on the Representative's testimony regarding H.R. 12463 and H.R. 12464, bills which would "end all new American investment in South Africa and require U.S. corporations there to engage in a fair employment code of conduct."

2659

South Africa divestiture: target report no. 11. Washington, United States Student Association, 1979. 18 p.

Prepared by the South Africa Catalyst Project.

Focus is on student anti-apartheid activities in the United States.

Abstract in *Resources in Education*, Nov. 1979, p. 110.

Microfiche. [Arlington, Va., ERIC Document Reproduction Service; prepared for Educational Resources Information Center, National Institute of Education, 1979] 1 sheet.

DLC-Micro ED172623

2660

Symms, Steven D. Address by the Honourable R. F. Botha, Minister of Foreign Affairs of the Republic of South Africa: Seminar: "Why Invest in South Africa," New York, 20 June 1977. Congressional record, 95th Congress, 1st session, v. 123, June 24, 1977: 20744–20747.   J11.R5 v. 123

Remarks in the U.S. House of Representatives.

Includes text of the Foreign Minister's address.

2661

Tsongas, Paul. University divestiture. Congressional record [daily ed.], 96th Congress, 1st session, v. 125, May 9, 1979: S5550–S5552.   J11.R7 v. 125

Remarks in the U.S. Senate on university investments in companies doing business in South Africa.

Education

2662

Muller, Freda. A remedial school for a changing world. [s.l., 1978] 12 p.

Paper presented at the World Conference on Future Special Education, 1978.

"The paper discusses the educational system in South Africa, with emphasis on private remedial schools for the learning disabled student."—Abstract.

Abstract in *Resources in Education*, Dec. 1978, p. 72.

Microfiche. [Arlington, Va., ERIC Document Reproduction Service; prepared for Educational Resources Information Center, National Institute of Education, 1978] 1 sheet.

DLC-Micro ED157350

2663

Phasha, G. M. Programming handicapped children for the future. [s.l., 1978] 15 p.

2663 (cont.)
Paper presented at the World Conference on Future Special Education, 1978.
Concerns special education for Blacks in South Africa.
Abstract in *Resources in Education*, Dec. 1978, p. 74.
Microfiche. [Arlington, Va., ERIC Document Reproduction Service; prepared for Educational Resources Information Center, National Institute of Education, 1978] 1 sheet.
DLC-Micro ED157364

2664
Robertson, Neville L., *and* Barbara L. Robertson. Education in South Africa. Bloomington, Ind., Phi Delta Kappa Educational Foundation, c1977. 37 p. illus (Phi Delta Kappa. Educational Foundation. Fastback, 90)   LA1536.R6
Abstract in *Resources in Education*, Oct. 1977, p. 142.
Issued also in microfiche. [Arlington, Va., ERIC Document Reproduction Service; prepared for Educational Resources Information Center, National Institute of Education, 1977] 1 sheet.
DLC-Micro ED139698

2665
Van den Berg, D. J. The training of mathematics teachers in the Republic of South Africa and in some western countries. Pretoria, South African Human Sciences Research Council, 1976. 353 p. (Human Sciences Research Council. Institute for Educational Research. Report no. 0–39)
QA14.S6V36
Summary in Afrikaans.
Abstract in *Resources in Education*, Jan. 1979, p. 148.
Issued also in microfiche. [Arlington, Va., ERIC Document Reproduction Service; prepared for Educational Resources Information Center, National Institute of Education, 1979] 4 sheets.
DLC-Micro ED159021

"Homelands"

2666
Brazelle, R. R., *and* I. Van Rooyen. Forecasts of primary and secondary school enrolment in Bophuthatswana, 1979–1983 and the implications thereof for the provision of teachers and classrooms and for government expenditure. Bloemfontein, Research Unit for Education System Planning, University of the Orange Free State, 1978. 34 p.

Abstract in *Resources in Education*, 1980 annual cumulation, p. 431.
Microfiche. [s.l., 1980]
DLC-Micro ED177677

2667
Mdluli, S. B. A description of the educational system of Kwazulu with emphasis on pupil repetition. Bloemfontein, University of the Orange Free State, 1980. 277 p.
Dissertation—University of the Orange Free State.
Microfiche. [Arlington, Va., ERIC Document Reproduction Service; prepared for Educational Resources Information Center, National Institute of Education, 1981] 3 sheets.
DLC-Micro ED198058

Energy Resources— Production & Consumption

2668
Carter, Tim Lee. Coal gasification. Congressional record, 95th Congress, 1st session, v. 123, Oct. 17, 1977: 34045–34046; 34129–34130.
J11.R5 v. 123
Extension of remarks in the U.S. House of Representatives.
Includes report, "Oil from coal—an energy alternative," on coal gasification research in South Africa with emphasis on the South African Coal, Oil and Gas Corporation, ltd (Sasol).

2669
Ford, Wendell H. South Africa is doing it with U.S. technology. Congressional record, 96th Congress, 1st session, v. 125, Apr. 30, 1979: 8902–8904.
J11.R5 v. 125
Remarks in the U.S. Senate.
Includes articles from the *Washington Post* and *Coal Daily* on South Africa's program of converting coal to oil.

2669a
South Africa: future energy prospects with emphasis on shale oil as an energy resource; special report. Ft. Wadsworth, N.Y., 432d Military Intelligence Detachment (Strategic), Ft. Wadsworth USAR Center, 1976. 24 p.   DLC
At head of title: Strategic Studies Institute, US Army War College, Carlisle Barracks, Pa. 17013.
On cover: "Approved for public release; distribution unlimited."

Atomic Energy

2670

U.S. *Congress. House. Committee on International Relations. Subcommittee on Africa.* United States-South Africa relations—nuclear cooperation: hearings, Ninety-fifth Congress, first session, June 30 and July 12, 1977. Washington, U.S. Govt. Print. Off., 1978. 83 p.   KF27.I54914 1977l
J74.A23 95th Cong.,
House Comm. Inter.
Rel., v. 62

Charles C. Diggs, Jr., chairman.

In his introductory remarks, Chairman Diggs notes that the hearings are being held to examine specific points: (1) the legal basis for U.S.-South African nuclear cooperation; (2) the status of South Africa's capability to develop nuclear weapons; (3) the application and reliability of safeguards; (4) trade in nuclear materials and technology; (5) political, economic, and military incentives for South African development of a nuclear weapon; (6) implications for both Americans and Africans of South Africa's nuclear weapons capability; (7) recommentations for U.S. policy.

Appendix: Pertinent data submitted by the U.S. Energy Research and Development Administration. p. 71–83.

2671

U.S. *Congress. Senate. Committee on Foreign Relations. Subcommittee on Arms Control, International Organizations and Security Agreements.* Nonproliferation issues: hearings, Ninety-fourth Congress, first and second sessions. Washington, U.S. Govt. Print. Off., 1977. 426 p.
KF26.F628 1975a
J74.A23 94th Cong.,
Sen. Comm. For. Rel.,
v. 49

Stuart Symington, chairman.
Hearings held Mar. 19, 1975 – Nov. 8, 1976.
Includes bibliographical references and index.
Includes brief references to South Africa.

2672

Conyers, John. Plutonium and racism do not mix. Congressional record, 95th Congress, 1st session, v. 123, Mar. 2, 1977: 6033–6034.
J11.R5 v. 123
Extension of remarks in the U.S. House of Representatives.
Includes article, "South Africa, with U.S. aid, near A-Bomb," from the *Washington Post.*

2673

International Atomic Energy Agency. [*Treaties, etc. 1974 June 28*] Agreement to amend the agreement of 26 July 1967 between the International Atomic Energy Agency, the Government of the Republic of South Africa and the Government of the United States of America for the application of safeguards. *In* U.S. *Treaties, etc.* United States treaties and other international agreements, v. 25, 1974. [Washington, Dept. of State; for sale by the Supt. of Docs., U.S. Govt. Print. Off., 1975] p. 1175–1177. ([Treaties and other international acts series, 7848])   JX231.A34 v. 25

Signed at Vienna June 20, 1974; entered into force June 28, 1974.

2674

South Africa. [*Treaties, etc. United States, 1974 July 28*] Amendment to agreement for cooperation between the Government of the United States of America and the Government of the Republic of South Africa concerning the civil uses of atomic energy. *In* U.S. *Treaties, etc.* United States treaties and other international agreements, v. 25, 1974. [Washington, Dept. of State; for sale by the Supt. of Docs., U.S. Govt. Print. Off., 1975] p. 1158–1169. ([Treaties and other international acts series, 7845])   JX231.A34 v. 25

Agreement amending and extending the agreement of July 8, 1957, as amended and extended; signed at Washington May 22, 1974; entered into force July 28, 1974 with exchange of notes.

Foreign Relations

2675

U.S. *Congress. House. Committee on Government Operations. Subcommittee on Government Information and Individual Rights.* Discriminatory overseas assignment policies of Federal agencies: hearings, Ninety-fourth Congress, first and second sessions, April 8, 9, 1975 and July 27, 1976. Washington, U.S. Govt. Print. Off., 1976. 319 p.
KF27.G6628 1975f
J74.A23 94th
Cong., House Comm.
Govt. Oper., v. 74

Bella S. Abzug, chairwoman.

Includes brief reference to the assignment of Black foreign service personnel to South Africa (p. 204–206).

2676

U.S. *Congress. House. Committee on International Relations. Subcommittee on Africa.* United States policy toward South Africa: hearing before the

2676 (cont.)

Subcommittees on Africa and on International Organizations of the Committee on International Relations, House of Representatives, Ninety-fifth Congress, second session, January 31, 1978. Washington, U.S. Govt. Print. Off., 1978. 21 p.

> KF27.I54914 1978b
> J74.A23 95th Cong.,
> House Comm. Inter.
> Rel., v. 61

Charles C. Diggs, Jr., chairman, Subcommittee on Africa.

Donald M. Fraser, chairman, Subcommittee on International Organizations.

Witness is Donald Woods, exiled editor of the *Daily Dispatch*, East London, South Africa.

2677

———— United States-South African relations: South Africa's visa policy: hearing before the Subcommittees on Africa and International Organizations of the Committee on International Relations, House of Representatives, Ninety-fifth Congress, first session, May 26, 1977. Washington, U.S. Govt. Print. Off., 1978. 45 p.

> KF27.I54914 1977i
> J74.A23 95th Cong.,
> House. Comm. Inter.
> Rel., v. 85

Charles C. Diggs, Jr., chairman, Subcommittee on Africa.

Donald M. Fraser, chairman, Subcommittee on International Organizations.

Among the witnesses are representatives of the Dept. of State, the African-American Institute, and the Lawyer's Committee for Civil Rights Under Law.

2678

Anderson, John B. The African-American Conference. Congressional record, 95th Congress, 1st session, v. 123, Jan. 19, 1977: 1850–1853.

> J11.R5 v. 123

Extension of remarks in the U.S. House of Representatives.

Includes text of Representative Anderson's remarks to a conference held in Maseru, Lesotho, Nov. 29 – Dec. 2, 1976; title of remarks: "Carter, Congress, and morality in foreign policy: with a view to U.S.-South African relations."

2679

Byrd, Harry F., Jr. U.S. policy toward Southern Africa. Congressional record, 95th Congress, 1st session, v. 123. Oct. 7, 1977: 32950–32953.

> J11.R5 v. 123

Remarks in the U.S. Senate, with emphasis on South Africa.

Includes article by George W. Ball in *Atlantic Monthly*.

2680

Goldwater, Barry. South Africa. Congressional record, 95th Congress, 2d session, v. 124: 9493–9599.

> J11.R5 v. 124

Remarks in the U.S. Senate.

Includes text of a paper, *Strangulation with Finesse: U.S. Policy toward SA*, by D. S. Prinsloo.

2681

Lake, Anthony. Africa: U.S. policy toward South Africa. *In* U.S. *Dept. of State*. The Department of State bulletin, v. 79, no. 2022, Jan. 1979: 18–20.

> JX232.A33 v. 79

Address by the Director of Policy Planning Staff, Dept. of State, before the Conference on U.S. Foreign Policy in Africa, San Francisco, Oct. 31, 1978.

2682

Moose, Richard M. U.S. policy toward South Africa. *In* U.S. *Dept. of State*. The Department of State bulletin, v. 80, no. 2040, July 1980: 20–21.

> JX232.A33 v. 80

Statement by the Assistant Secretary of State for African Affairs before the Subcommittee on Africa, Committee on Foreign Affairs, House of Representatives, Apr. 30, 1980.

2683

Secretary Kissinger meets with South African Prime Minister at Zurich and confers with British, French, and German leaders. *In* U.S. *Dept. of State*. The Department of State bulletin, v. 75, no. 1944, Sept. 27, 1976: 377–385.

> JX232.A33 v. 75

Transcripts of news conferences.

Transcript of Sept. 6, 1976 conference concerns the Secretary's meeting with Prime Minister Vorster.

2684

Snodgrass, Charles G. The Republic of South Africa and United States foreign policy. Maxwell Air Force Base, Ala., 1979. 76 p. (Air University. Air Command and Staff College. Research study)

> AMAU

2685

Solarz, Stephen J., *and* Benjamin S. Rosenthal. South Africa, change and confrontation: report of a study mission to South Africa, July 3–11, 1980, to the Committee on Foreign Affairs, U.S. House of

2685 (cont.)

Representatives. Washington, U.S. Govt. Print.
Off., 1981. 29 p.   DT763.S562

At head of title: 96th Congress, 2d session.
Committee print.

Purpose of study mission was "to get a better
understanding of South Africa's policies and to
reexamine existing United States policy toward
South Africa."

2686

Union of South Africa: principal policies and prob-
lems in relations with the Union of South Africa.
In U.S. *Dept. of State.* Foreign relations of the
United States. 1951, v. 5. Washington, U.S. Govt.
Print. Off., 1982. p. 1427–1464. (U.S. Dept. of
State. Department of State publication 9114)
                                  JX233.A3   1951, v. 5

2687

Vice President Mondale visits Europe and meets with
South African Prime Minister Vorster. *In* U.S.
Dept. of State. The Department of State bulletin,
v. 76, no. 1982, June 20, 1977: 659–666.
                                  JX232.A33 v. 76

Statement by President Carter announcing the
trip and statements and the transcript of a news
conference by the Vice President during his trip.

Geology, Hydrology, and Mineral Resources

2688

[U.S. *Central Intelligence Agency*] South Africa; minerals. [Washington, 1978] col. map.
                                  G8501.H1   1978.U5

Scale ca. 1 : 6,000,000.
"503621 3-78."

*The following items (entries 2689–95) are listed in
chronological order:*

2689

Jolly, James H. The mineral industry of the Republic
of South Africa. *In* Minerals yearbook, v. 3, 1973.
[Washington, for sale by the Supt. of Docs., U.S.
Govt. Print. Off., 1976] p. 745–769.
                                  TN23.U612   1973, v. 3
Prepared by the U.S. Bureau of Mines.

2690

Jolly, James H., *and* Charles W. Sweetwood. The
mineral industry of the Republic of South Africa.
In Minerals yearbook, v. 3, 1974. [Washington,

for sale by the Supt. of Docs., U.S. Govt. Print.
Off., 1977] p. 791–815.
                                  TN23.U612   1974, v. 3

2691

Ellis, Miller W., *and* Charles W. Sweetwood. The
mineral industry of the Republic of South Africa.
In Minerals yearbook, v. 3, 1975. [Washington,
for sale by the Supt. of Docs., U.S. Govt. Print.
Off., 1978] p. 845–865.
                                  TN23.U612   1975, v. 3
Prepared by the U.S. Bureau of Mines.

2692

—— The mineral industry of the Republic of
South Africa. *In* Minerals yearbook, v. 3, 1976.
[Washington, for sale by the Supt. of Docs., U.S.
Govt. Print. Off., 1980] p. 923–941.
                                  TN23.U612   1976, v. 3
Prepared by the U.S. Bureau of Mines.

2693

—— The mineral industry of the Republic of
South Africa. *In* Minerals yearbook, v. 3, 1977.
[Washington, for sale by the Supt. of Docs., U.S.
Govt. Print. Off., 1981] p. 825–847.
                                  TN23.U612   1977, v. 3
Prepared by the U.S. Bureau of Mines.

2694

—— The mineral industry of the Republic of
South Africa. *In* Minerals yearbook, v. 3, 1978–79.
[Washington, U.S. Govt. Print. Off., 1981] p. 823–
845.   TN23.U612   1978–79, v. 3
Prepared by the U.S. Bureau of Mines.

Note: Production and sales statistics for South African
minerals are occasionally cited in *Mineral Trade Notes*
(TN1.U62), a monthly publication of the U.S. Bureau of Mines.

2695

Ellis, Miller W. The mineral industry of the Republic
of South Africa. *In* Minerals yearbook, v. 3, 1980.
[Washington, for sale by the Supt. of Docs., U.S.
Govt. Print. Off., 1982] p. 859–886.
                                  TN23.U612   1980, v. 3
Prepared by the U.S. Bureau of Mines.

2696

Thurmond, Strom. Articles on South Africa. Congressional record [daily ed.], 96th Congress, 2d
session, v. 126, July 22, 1980: S9547–S9549.
                                  J11.R7 v. 126

Remarks in the U.S. Senate.

Includes articles from the *Augusta Chronicle*
(Augusta, Ga.) with emphasis on South Africa's
minerals and its conversion of coal to oil.

Human Rights

2697

U.S. *Congress. House. Committee on Foreign Affairs. Subcommittee on Africa.* Current situation in South Africa: hearing, Ninety-sixth Congress, first session, September 6, 1979. Washington, U.S. Govt. Print. Off., 1979. 37 p.

> KF27.F625   1979e
> J74.A2 96th Cong.,
> House Comm. for. Aff.,
> v. 37

Stephen J. Solarz, chairman.

Witness is Rev. Jesse L. Jackson, President, Operation PUSH, who had recently visited South Africa.

2698

U.S. *Congress. House. Committee on International Relations.* Expressing concern abou the recent acts of repression by the government of the Republic of South Africa: report (to accompany H. Con. Res. 388). [Washington, U.S. Govt. Print. Off.] 1977. 5 p.   DLC-LL

Report submitted by Representative Charles C. Diggs, Jr.

At head of title: 95th Congress, 1st session. House of Representatives. Report no. 95–779.

The resolution notes that the circumstances surrounding the death of Steve Biko "have aroused deep concern among Americans and within the world community" and "that the actions taken by the South African Government on October 19, 1977, to close newspapers, to outlaw peaceful religious and social groups, to detain and ban South African white and black citizens who oppose apartheid, represent serious violations of human rights."—p. [1]

2699

U.S. *Congress. House. Committee on International Relations. Subcommittee on Africa.* Resolutions to investigate Steve Biko's death and to condemn the government of South Africa for massive violations of the civil liberties of the people of South Africa: hearing, Ninety-fifth Congress, first session, on H. Res. 809 and H. Con. Res. 398, October 26, 1977. Washington, U.S. Govt. Print. Off., 1978. 50 p.

> KF27.I54914   1977c
> J74.A23 95th Cong.,
> House Comm. Inter.
> Rel., v. 54

Charles C. Diggs, Jr. chairman.

List of treaties and agreements between the United States and South Africa. p. 36–39.

2700

U.S. *Congress. Senate. Committee on Foreign Relations. Subcommittee on African Affairs.* Conditions in South Africa: hearing, Ninety-fifth Congress, second session, on February 3, 1978. Washington, U.S. Govt. Print. Off., 1978. 24 p.

> KF26.F625   1978
> J74.A23 95th
> Cong., Sen. Comm.
> For. Rel., v. 38

Dick Clark, chairman.

Witness is Donald Woods, editor of the *Daily Dispatch* (East London, South Africa).

2701

ANC spokesman interviewed. *In* U.S. *Joint Publications Research Service.* JPRS 70572. [Springfield, Va., National Technical Information Service, 1978] (Translations on Sub-Saharan Africa, no. 1871) p. 1–4.

Translation of interview with Sindelo Thami, representative of the African National Congress in Algiers, in *Témoignages*, St. Denis, Dec. 8, 1977, p. 2.

Microfiche. [Washington, Supt. of Docs., U.S. Govt. Print. Off., 1978]

> DLC-Micro JPRS 70572

2702

Bonker, Don. Repression in South Africa: Congressional action still needed. Congressional record, 95th Congress, 2d session, v. 124, Apr. 11, 1978: 9707–9709.   J11.R5 v. 124

Extension of remarks in the U.S. House of Representatives.

Includes text of article, "Excerpts from a letter to the Ad Hoc Monitoring Group on South Africa from Amnesty International, March 24, 1978," in the *London Observer*.

2703

——— U.S. relations with South Africa. Congressional record, 95th Congress, 1st session, v. 123, May 9, 1977: 14059–14060.   J11.R5 v. 123

Extension of remarks in the U.S. House of Representatives.

Includes documents by the U.S. Dept. of State on American policy regarding the apartheid issue.

2704

Brown, Trevor. Did anybody know his name? Coverage of Steven Biko and the Black Conciousness Movement in South Africa by the New York *Times* and the Washington *Post*, 1969–1977. [Bloomington?], School of Journalism, Indiana University, [1978] 24 p.

Paper presented to the Mass Communications

2704 (cont.)

and Society Division, Association for Education in Journalism, 1978.

Abstract in *Resources in Education*, Feb. 1979, p. 63.

Microfiche. [Arlington, Va., ERIC Document Reproduction Service; prepared for Educational Resources Information Center, National Institute of Education, 1979]   DLC-Micro ED159724

2705

Clark, Dick. Statement by Senator Clark on South Africa and the Biko death. Congressional record, 95th Congress, 1st session, v. 123, Nov. 4, 1977: 37327–37328.   J11.R5 v. 123

Remarks in the U.S. Senate.

2706

Congressman Downey announces initiation of political prisoner project. Congressional record [daily ed.], 96th Congress, 2d session, v. 126, Mar. 24, 1980: H2076–H2079.   J11.R7 v. 126

Remarks in the U.S. House of Representatives, primarily by Representative Thomas J. Downey, on the Congressional Ad Hoc Monitoring Group on Southern Africa (established in Oct. 1977) and on the human rights record of South Africa.

2707

Developments concerning apartheid. *In* U.S. *Dept. of State.* The Department of State bulletin, v. 77, no. 1997, Oct. 3, 1977: 446–451.   JX232.A33 v. 77

Statement by Andrew Young, U.S. Ambassador to the United Nations, at the World Conference for Action Against Apartheid, Lagos, Aug. 25, 1977, together with the text of the Declaration of Action Against Apartheid.

2708

Dornan, Robert K. Breaking the color barrier. Congressional record, 95th Congress, 2d session, v. 124, May 8, 1978: 12941–12942.

J11.R5 v. 124

Extension of remarks in the U.S. House of Representatives.

Includes text of report on the "progress that the Republic of South Africa is making on the integration of its athletic teams."

2709

Emmanuel, Paul. Abuse, repression of Blacks described. *In* U.S. *Joint Publications Research Service.* JPRS 69756. [Springfield, Va., National Technical Information Service, 1977] (Translations on Sub-Saharan Africa, no. 1797) p. 44–48.

Translation of article on the treatment of Black

mental patients in South Africa, in *Spécial*, Brussels, July 20, 1977, p. 24–26.

Microfiche. [s.l., 1977]

DLC-Micro JPRS 69756

2710

Expressing concern about the recent acts of repression by the Government of the Republic of South Africa. Congressional record, 95th Congress, 1st session, v. 123, Oct. 31, 1977: 35965–35975.

J11.R5 v. 123

Debate in the House of Representatives on H. Con. Res. 388; the vote on the resolution is given on p. 35981.

2711

Ferguson, Clarence Clyde. The United States, the United Nations and the struggle against racial apartheid. [s.l.], 1978. 14 leaves. (FAR 29064-N)

"One of a collection of essays prepared for a workshop held at the University of South Carolina. Partial support for the workshop was provided by a grant from the Department of State as part of its external research program."

Examined in the former Foreign Affairs Research Documentation Center, U.S. Dept. of State.

2712

First anniversary of the tragic death of Steve Biko. Congressional record, 95th Congress, 2d session, v. 124, Sept. 12, 1978: 29030–29036.

J11.R5 v. 124

Remarks in the U.S. House of Representatives.

2713

Foltz, William J. The growing confrontation in South Africa: a conference report. [s.l.], 1977. 5 p. (FAR 27464-S)

Summary report of the Conference on Urban Conflict and Change in South Africa, sponsored by the U.S. Dept. of State, Apr. 1977.

Examined in the former Foreign Affairs Research Documentation Center, U.S. Dept. of State.

2714

—— Urban conflict and change in South Africa. [s.l.], 1977. 17 leaves. (FAR 27073-S)

Report based on the Conference on Urban Conflict and Change in South Africa, sponsored by the U.S. Dept. of State, Apr. 1977.

Examined in the former Foreign Affairs Research Documentation Center, U.S. Dept. of State.

2715

Goldwater, Barry. South Africa. Congressional record, 95th Congress, 1st session, v. 123, Nov. 2, 1977: 36433–36435.   J11.R5 v. 123

2715 (cont.)

Remarks in the U.S. Senate opposing resolutions that express concern about South African human rights practices.

2716

Greenberg, Stanley B. Public disorder and business response, 1960 and 1976. [s.l., 1977] [16] leaves. (FAR 26983-S)

Paper presented at the Conference on Urban Conflict and Change in South Africa, sponsored by the U.S. Dept. of State, Apr. 1977.

Examined in the former Foreign Affairs Research Documentation Center, U.S. Dept. of State.

2717

Hachten, William A. The Black journalist in South Africa. [s.l.], 1979. 20 p.

Paper presented at the annual meeting of the Association for Education in Journalism, 1979.

Abstract in *Resources in Education*, 1980 annual cumulation, p. 42.

Microfiche. [Arlington, Va., ERIC Document Reproduction Service; prepared for Educational Resources Information Center, National Institute of Education, 1980] 1 sheet.

DLC-Micro ED175018

2718

History of Soweto students movement featured. *In* U.S. *Joint Publications Research Service*. JPRS 69654. [Springfield, Va., National Technical Information Service, 1977] (Translations on Sub-Saharan Africa, no. 1787) p. 37–42.

Article in *Weekend World*, Johannesburg, July 31, 1977, p. B2, B3.

Microfiche. [s.l., 1977]

DLC-Micro JPRS 69654

2719

Interview with ANC president Oliver Tambo. *In* U.S. *Joint Publications Research Service*. JPRS 67596. [Springfield, Va., National Technical Information Service, 1976] (Translations on Sub-Saharan Africa, no. 1661) p. 35–40.

Translation of interview in *Diario de Luanda*, Luanda, June 19, 1976, p. 11.

Microfiche. [s.l., 1976]

DLC-Micro JPRS 67596

2720

Karis, Thomas. South African Black organizations and their demands and aims. [s.l.], 1977. 21 leaves. (FAR 26603-S)

Paper presented at the Conference on Urban Conflict and Change in South Africa, sponsored by the U.S. Dept. of State.

Examined in the former Foreign Affairs Research Documentation Center, U.S. Dept. of State.

2721

List of banned, jailed published. *In* U.S. *Joint Publications Research Service*. JPRS 71688. [Springfield, Va., National Technical Information Service, 1978] (Translations on Sub-Saharan Africa, no. 1978) p. 50–56.

Article in *The Star*, Johannesburg, July 21, 1978, p. 8.

Microfiche. [Washington, Supt. of Docs., U.S. Govt. Print. Off., 1978]

DLC-Micro JPRS 71688

2722

McDonald, Larry. An apologist for terrorism visits Capitol Hill. Congressional record, 95th Congress, 2d session, v. 124, Feb. 7, 1978: 2636–2637.

J11.R5 v. 124

Extension of remarks in the U.S. House of Representatives concerning the visit of Donald Woods to the Capitol.

Includes text of statement by the African National Congress and excerpts from a House staff study.

2723

—— The Steve Biko case: has our government backed another African terrorist movement? Congressional record, 95th Congress, 1st session, v. 123, Oct. 21, 1977: 34845–34849.

J11.R5 v. 123

Extension of remarks in the U.S. House of Representatives.

2724

Magalhaes, Fernando. ANC leader discusses struggle for majority rule. *In* U.S. *Joint Publications Research Service*. JPRS 69598. [Springfield, Va., National Technical Information Service, 1977] (Translations on Sub-Saharan Africa, no. 1785) p. 19–25.

Translation of interview with Oliver Tambo, president of ANC, in *Diario de Notícias*, Lisbon, July 8, 1977, p. 17, 19.

Microfiche. [s.l., 1977]

DLC-Micro JPRS 69598

2725

Merrick, Walter F. Black South Africans against apartheid: a continuing struggle. [Washington], Defense Intelligence School, 1977. 173 p.

Bibliography: p. 161–173.

Thesis (M.S.)—Defense Intelligence School.

Microfiche. [s.l., Defense Documentation Center, 1979] 2 sheets (DLC-Sci RR AD-A065635);

2725 (cont.)

issued in microfilm by University Publications of America (cited in its *Africa: Special Studies 1962–1980*, p. 13).

2726

Mitchell, Clarence M. U.S. discusses human rights in South Africa. *In* U.S. *Dept. of State.* The Department of State bulletin, v. 73, no. 1905, Dec. 29, 1975: 935–944.   JX232.A33 v. 73

Statement by the U.S. Representative to the United Nations General Assembly, Nov. 28, 1975.

2727

——— United States reiterates opposition to apartheid. *In* U.S. *Dept. of State.* The Department of State bulletin, v. 73, no. 1899, Nov. 17, 1975: 717–719.   JX232.A33 v. 73

Statement by the U.S. Representative to the Special Political Committee, United Nations General Assembly, Oct. 23, 1975.

2728

Moose, Richard M. Concern expressed on recent events in South Africa. *In* U.S. *Dept. of State.* The Department of State bulletin, v. 77, no. 2008, Dec. 19, 1977: 897–899.   JX232.A33 v. 77

Statement by the Assistant Secretary of State for African Affairs before the Subcommittee on Africa, Committee on International Relations, House of Representatives, Oct. 26, 1977.

Concerns the action taken by the South African Government on Oct. 19, 1977 placing certain Black leaders in preventive detention, banning organizations, and closing publishing offices.

2729

One-year anniversary of death of Steven Biko. Congressional record, 95th Congress, 2d session, v. 124, Sept. 12, 1978: 29026–29030.

J11.R5 v. 124

Remarks in the U.S. House of Representatives.

2730

Onum, Nduka. PAC official discusses Azania liberation. *In* U.S. *Joint Publications Research Service.* JPRS 71867. [Springfield, Va., National Technical Information Service, 1978] (Translations on Sub-Saharan Africa, no. 1993) p. 139–143.

Interview with Mike Sibeko, Secretary for Foreign Affairs of the Pan Africanist Congress of Azania, in *The Punch*, Ikeja, Aug. 23, 1978, p. 7.

Microfiche. [s.l., 1978]

DLC-Micro JPRS 71867

2731

Racial violence in South Africa. Congressional re-

cord [daily ed.], 96th Congress, 2d session, v. 126, June 18, 1980: H5208–H5218.   J11.R7 v. 126

Remarks in the U.S. House of Representatives, primarily by Representatives Thomas J. Downey, Howard Wolpe, and Charles B. Rangel.

Includes articles from the *New York Times* and *Atlantic Monthly*.

2732

Salvador, Joaquim. ANC activist interviewed on Botha 'liberalization' policy. *In* U.S. *Joint Publications Research Service.* JPRS 75920. [Springfield, Va., National Technical Information Service, 1980] (Sub-Saharan Africa report, no. 2258) p. 137–143.

Translation of interview with Joe Slovo, an "ANC activist," in *Notícias*, Maputo, Apr. 15–16, 1980.

Microfiche. [s.l., 1980]

DLC-Micro JPRS 75920

2733

Senate Concurrent Resolution 60—submission of a concurrent resolution relating to South Africa. Congressional record, 95th Congress, 1st session, v. 123, Oct. 31, 1977: 36097–36100.

J11.R5 v. 123

Resolution, introduced by Senator Dick Clark, denounces repressive measures by the South African Government.

2734

Smit, P. Increasing black commuters, visitors pose problem. *In* U.S. *Joint Publications Research Service.* JPRS 72175. [Springfield, Va., National Technical Information Service, 1978] (Translations on Sub-Saharan Africa, no. 2018) p. 119–123.

Translation of article, "Newcastle's grumbling about 'open' post office; this is undoubtedly a problem elsewhere too," in *Die Transvaler*, Johannesburg, Sept. 11, 1978, p. 11.

Microfiche. [Washington, Supt. of Docs., U.S. Govt. Print. Off., 1979]

DLC-Micro JPRS 72175

2735

Stewart, Bennett M. South Africa's racial policies. Congressional record [daily ed.], 96th Congress, 2d session, v. 126, Sept. 8, 1980: H8683–H8686

J11.R7 v. 126

Remarks in the U.S. House of Representatives.

Includes text of a memorandum, "A comparison of the racial situation in South Africa and the United States with particular attention to the causes of the Miami, Florida riots," by Brenda Branaman, Congressional Research Service, Library of Congress.

2736

Tambo, Oliver. Continuing struggle in South Africa discussed. *In* U.S. *Joint Publications Research Service.* JPRS 71399. [Springfield, Va., National Technical Information Service, 1978] (Translations on Sub-Saharan Africa, no. 1955) p. 64–78.

Translation of speech by the president of the African National Congress and of subsequent discussion with other members of ANC, in *Tricontinental*, Havana, Jan. 1978, p. 38–58.

Microfiche. [Washington, Supt. of Docs., U.S. Govt. Print. Off., 1978]

DLC-Micro JPRS 71399

2737

Tsongas, Paul E. An act of political repression. Congressional record [daily ed.], 96th Congress, 2d session, v. 126, Mar. 6, 1980: S2290–S2291.

J11.R7 v. 126

Remarks in the U.S. Senate concerning South Africa's revocation of the passport of Bishop Desmond Tutu.

2738

——— Betrayal of hope in South Africa. Congressional record [daily ed.], 96th Congress, 2d session, v. 126, July 2, 1980: S9282–S9284.

J11.R7 v. 126

Remarks in the U.S. Senate on South Africa's policy concerning the issuance of passports to dissidents, its stand on Namibia, and the enactment of anti-apartheid legislation.

2739

——— Political prisoners in South Africa. Congressional record [daily ed.], 96th Congress, 2d session, v. 126, Mar. 20, 1980: S2697–S2700.

J11.R7 v. 126

Remarks in the U.S. Senate announcing the political prisoner project of the Congressional Ad Hoc Monitoring Group on Southern Africa, "a bicameral, bipartisan congressional organization devoted to the promotion of political, social, and economic justice in Southern Africa. Forty-eight Members of Congress are members of the group."

2740

U.N. Security Council condemns South Africa's apartheid policy and imposes a mandatory arms embargo. *In* U.S. *Dept. of State.* The Department of State bulletin, v. 77, no. 2007, Dec. 12, 1977: 859–866. map. JX232.A33 v. 77

Includes statements by Andrew Young, U.S. Ambassador to the United Nations, made in the Security Council, Oct. 31, 1977 and Nov. 4, 1977, together with texts of two resolutions adopted by the Council on those dates.

2741

Whalen, Charles W. Steve Biko. Congressional record, 95th Congress, 1st session, v. 123, Nov. 15, 1977: 37747–37749. J11.R5 v. 123

Extension of remarks in the U.S. House of Representatives.

Includes text of an interview with Mr. Biko which appeared in the *Christian Science Monitor.*

2742

Young, Andrew. Hour of crisis for South Africa. Congressional record, 94th Congress, 2d session, v. 122, Apr. 29, 1976: 11930–11934.

J11.R5 v. 122

Remarks in the U.S. House of Representatives. Includes text of speech by Chief Gatsha Buthelezi of KwaZulu.

Labor

2743

U.S. *Congress. House. Committee on Foreign Affairs. Subcommittee on Africa.* Labor situation in South Africa—fall 1980; hearing, Ninety-sixth Congress, second session, November 13, 1980. Washington, U.S. Govt. Print. Off., 1981. 21 p.

KF27.F625 1980g
J74.A23 96th
Cong., House Comm.
For. Aff., v. 139

Stephen J. Solarz, chairman.

Focus is on "the current labor situation in South Africa, particularly among the more that 2 million black and colored urban workers, and its implications for political developments in that important and troubled country."—p. 1.

Witness is Tozamile Botha, self-exiled South African labor leader.

2744

Black trade unionist interviewed on clashes with whites. *In* U.S. *Joint Publications Research Service.* JPRS 68505. [Springfield, Va., National Technical Information Service, 1977] (Translations on Sub-Saharan Africa, no. 1704) p. 37–40.

Translation of interview with Drake Koka, in *Frankfurter Rundschau*, Frankfurt, Jan. 4, 1977, p. 10.

Microfiche. [s.l., 1977]

DLC-Micro JPRS 68505

2745

Breitenstein, Gerhart. BAWU official interviewed. *In* U.S. *Joint Publications Research Service.* JPRS 70913. [Springfield, Va., National Technical In-

2745 (cont.)

formation Service, 1978] (Translations on Sub-Saharan Africa, no. 1908) p. 49–54.

Translation of interview with Thamsanga Fane-kiso, exilted deputy secretary general of the Black Allied Workers Union, concerning South African refugees in Botswana, in *Informations Dienst Südliches Afrika*, Bonn, Jan. 1978, p. 17–19.

Microfiche. [Washington, Supt. of Docs., U.S. Govt. Print. Off., 1978]

DLC-Micro JPRS 70913

2746

Brewer, James C. Country labor profile: South Africa. [Washington], Bureau of International Labor Affairs, U.S. Dept. of Labor; for sale by the Supt. of Docs., U.S. Govt. Print. Off.] 1980. 7 p. map.

DLC

Issued also in *International Labor Profiles: Comprehensive Reports on the Labor Forces of 40 Key Nations, Including Data on Wage and Hour Standards, Labor Organizations, Social Benefit Programs, Governmental Regulations, and Other Labor-Related Topics*. 1st ed. (Detroit, Grand River Books, 1981) p. 251–258. map.

HD4901.I56

2747

Scholtz, Leopold. Analysis of dangerous black unemployment situation. *In* U.S. *Joint Publications Research Service*. JPRS 74472. [Springfield, Va., National Technical Information Service, 1979] (Sub-Saharan Africa report, no. 2172) p. 127–134.

Translation of article in *Die Burger*, Cape Town, Sept. 12–13, 1979.

Microfiche. [Washington, Supt. of Docs., U.S. Govt. Print. Off., 1979]

DLC-Micro JPRS 74472

2748

South Africa: South African trade unions and the demands of economic rationalization in an industrializing society: a critique of some "conventional wisdom:" special report. Ft. Wadsworth, N.Y., 432d Military Intelligence Detachment (Strategic), Ft. Wadsworth USAR Center, 1976. 29 p.

DLC

At head of title: Strategic Studies Institute, U.S. Army War College, Carlisle Barracks, Pennsylvania 17013.

On cover: "Approved for public release; distribution unlimited."

An introduction to the problem of apartheid policies as they affect South Africa's labor force.

Language and Languages

2749

Hauptfleisch, T. Language loyalty in South Africa. Pretoria, Institute for Languages, Literature and Arts, South African Human Sciences Research Council, 1977–78. 2 v.   P115.5.S6H3

Concerns South Africa's official languages, Afrikaans and English.

Contents: Vol. 1. Bilingual policy in South Africa—opinions of white adults in urban areas.—Vol. 2. Using and improving usage in the second language—some opinions of white adults in urban areas.

Abstracts of both volumes in *Resources in Education*, Sept. 1978, p. 73–74 (vol. 1) and Nov. 1978, p. 93 (vol. 2).

Issued also in microfiche. [Arlington, Va., ERIC Document Reproduction Service; prepared for Educational Resources Information Center, National Institute of Education, 1978] 4 sheets.

DLC-Micro ED153482
ED155924

2750

Schuring, G. K. A multilingual society: English and Afrikaans amongst Blacks in the RSA. [Pretoria], Human Sciences Research Council, [1979] 78 p.

"Report no. TLK/L-7."

Abstract in *Resources in Education*, 1980 annual cumulation, p. 2041.

Microfiche. [Arlington, Va., ERIC Document Reproduction Service; prepared for Educational Resources Information Center, National Institute of Education, 1980] 1 sheet

DLC-Sci RR ED188456

Military Affairs

2751

U.S. *Congress. House. Committee on International Relations. Subcommittee on Africa*. United States-South Africa relations: arms embargo implementation: hearings, Ninety-fifth Congress, first session, July 14 and 20, 1977. Washington, U.S. Govt. Print. Off., 1978. 67 p.   KF27.I54914 1977k
J74.A23 95th Cong.
House Comm. Inter.
Rel., v. 61

Charles C. Diggs, Jr., chairman.

Includes bibliographical references.

2752

Groesbeck, Wesley A. Transkei—key to US naval strategy in the Indian Ocean. Military review, June 1976: 18–24. illus., map.   Z6723.U35 1976

2752 (cont.)

Published by the U.S. Army Command and General Staff College, Ft. Leavenworth, Kansas.

Considers the strategic importance of a seaport at Port St. Johns.

2753

Latour, Charles. South Africa: NATO's unwelcome ally. Military review, Feb. 1977: 84–93. illus., map.
Z6723.U35 1977

Published by the U.S. Army Command the General Staff College, Ft. Leavenworth, Kansas.

A look at South Africa's strategic position and its armed forces.

2754

[Military sanctions—arms embargo—South Africa] *In* Boyd, John A. Digest of United States practice in international law. 1977. [Washington] Office of the Legal Adviser, Dept. of State; [for sale by the Supt. of Docs., U.S. Govt. Print. Off., 1979] (Department of State publication, 8960) p. 934–936.
JX21.R68 1977

2755

Pinson, James W. The emergence of the Republic of South Africa as a regional power. [Maxwell Air Force Base, Ala.?, 1974?] 37 p.   AMAU

Abstract in *Air University Abstracts of Research Reports*, 1974, no. 458.

2756

Pretorius, P. Botha's "total onslaught" warning discussed. *In* U.S. *Joint Publications Research Service.* JPRS 74608. [Springfield, Va., National Technical Information Service, 1979] (Sub-Saharan Africa report, no. 2179) p. 32–35.

Translation of article on warnings by Prime Minister Botha of South Africa's security problems, in *Die Vaterland*, Johannesburg, Oct. 2, 1979, p. 12.

Microfiche. [s.l., 1979]
DLC-Micro JPRS 74608

2757

Scible, Robert H. The strategic significance of South Africa: an analysis. Maxwell Air Force Base, Ala., Air Command and Staff College, 1974. 37 leaves. (FAR 21829-N)

"A research study submitted to the faculty."
Examined in the former Foreign Affairs Research Documentation Center, U.S. Dept. of State.

2758

South Africa: South African sea lanes, shipping, and marine orientation in U.S. strategic considerations; special report, [by] Henry Jacobson [et al.]

Ft. Wadsworth, N.Y., 432d Military Intelligence Detachment (Strategic), 1976. 33 p. map.
AMAU

At head of title: Strategic Studies Institute, U.S. Army War College, Carlisle Barracks, Pa.

Examines the strategic significance of the Cape of Good Hope route and the rising naval and maritime capabilities of South Africa.

Issued also in microfiche. [s.l., 1977] 1 sheet (AD-B01884L).

2759

Viviers, Jack. Botha's achievements as defense minister reviewed. *In* U.S. *Joint Publications Research Services.* JPRS 76637. [Springfield, Va., National Technical Information Service, 1980] (Sub-Saharan Africa report, no. 2307) p. 57–60.

Translation of article in *Die Burger*, Cape Town, Aug. 29, 1980, p. 21.

Microfiche. [s.l., 1980]
DIC-Micro JPRS 76637

Politics and Government

2760

U.S. *Congress. House. Committee on International Relations. Subcommittee on Africa.* United States-South Africa relations: internal change in South Africa: hearing, Ninety-fifth Congress, first session, June 3, 1977. Washington, U.S. Govt. Print. Off., 1978. 42 p.   KF27.I54914 1977d
J74.A23 95th Cong.,
House Comm. Inter
Rel., v. 74

Charles C. Diggs, Jr., chairman.

The current situation and prospects for change in South Africa are examined by the subcommittee's witnesses: Colin Legum of the *London Observer* and *Africa Contemporary Record*, John Chettle of the South African Foundation, and David Sibeko of the Pan-Africanist Congress of Azania.

2761

Botha, Andries. Discussion on National Party policy reported. *In* U.S. *Joint Publications Research Service.* JPRS 71010. [Springfield, Va., National Technical Information Service, 1978] (Translations on Sub-Saharan Africa, no. 1917) p. 96–103.

Translation of two articles in *Die Transvaler*, Johannesburg, Mar. 9, 10, 1978.

Microfiche. [Washington, Supt. of Docs., U.S. Govt. Print. Off., 1978]
DLC-Micro JPRS 71010

2762

Botha, Pieter W. Botha discusses domestic, international status. *In* U.S. *Joint Publications Research Service.* JPRS 75051. [Springfield, Va., National Technical Information Service, 1980] (Sub-Saharan Africa report, no. 2208) p. 64–67.

Translation of article in *Le Figaro,* Paris, Dec. 18, 1979, p. 1, 5.

Microfiche. [s.l., 1980]

DLC-Micro JPRS 75051

2763

Diouf, Bara. South African opposition leader interviewed. *In* U.S. *Joint Publications Research Service.* JPRS 70024. [Springfield, Va., National Technical Information Service, 1977] (Translations on Sub-Saharan Africa, no. 1822) p. 63–71.

Translation of interview with Colin W. Eglin, parliamentary leader of the Progressive Federal Party, in *Le Soleil,* Dakar, Sept. 19, 1977, p. 13, 14.

Microfiche. [s.l., 1977]

DLC-Micro JPRS 70024

2764

Future constitutional arrangement for South Africa discussed. *In* U.S. *Joint Publications Research Service.* JPRS 74452. [Springfield, Va., National Technical Information Service, 1979] (Sub-Saharan Africa report, no. 2170) p. 109–112.

Translation of interview with Prof. Hennis C. O. Krause, in *Die Vaterland,* Johannesburg, Sept. 5, 1979, p. 14.

Microfiche. [Washington, Supt. of Docs., U.S. Govt. Print. Off., 1979]

DLC-Micro JPRS 74452

2765

Hatch, Orrin G. "South Africa: what is Black?." by Xan Smiley. Congressional record [daily ed.], 96th Congress, 1st session, v. 125, May 3, 1979: S5283–S5286.   J11.R7 v. 125

Remarks in the U.S. Senate.

Includes article from the *New York Review of Books* on the Pan Africanist Congress and the African National Congress.

2766

Klerk, Willem de. De Klerk envisions constitutional changes. *In* U.S. *Joint Publications Research Service.* JPRS 75520. [Springfield, Va., National Technical Information Service, 1980] (Sub-Saharan Africa report, no. 2236) p. 80–84.

Translation of article in *Die Transvaler,* Johannesburg, Feb. 13, 1980, p. 10.

Microfiche. [s.l., 1980]

DLC-Micro JPRS 75520

2767

—— Political choices at a crossroads. *In* U.S. *Joint Publications Research Service.* JPRS 74884. [Springfield, Va., National Technical Information Service, 1980] (Sub-Saharan Africa report, no. 2195) p. 146–149.

Translation of article in *Die Transvaler,* Johannesburg, Nov. 14, 1979, p. 8.

Microfiche. [s.l., 1980]

DLC-Micro JPRS 74884

2768

—— U.S. views on South Africa rejected. *In* U.S. *Joint Publications Research Service.* JPRS 69450. [Springfield, Va., National Technical Information Service, 1977] (Translations on Sub-Saharan Africa, no. 1774). p. 36–39.

Translation of article in *Die Transvaler,* Johannesburg, June 17, 1977, p. 10.

Microfiche. [s.l., 1977]

DLC-Micro JPRS 69450

2769

—— Willem de Klerk comments on Botha's 12-point plan. *In* U.S. *Joint Publications Research Service.* JPRS 74754. [Springfield, Va., National Technical Information Service, 1979] (Sub-Saharan Africa report, no. 2188) p. 147–159.

Translation of article on the Prime Minister's political program, in *Die Transvaler,* Johannesburg, Oct. 15–19, 1979.

Microfiche. [s.l., 1980]

DLC-Micro JPRS 74754

2770

Lagarde, Dominique. Activities of BOSS described. *In* U.S. *Joint Publications Research Service.* JPRS 70287. [Springfield, Va., National Technical Information Service, 1977] (Translations on Sub-Saharan Africa, no. 1845) p. 70–76.

Translation of article on the Bureau of State Security, in *Demain l'Afrique,* Paris, Nov. 1977, p. 24–27.

Microfiche. [s.l., 1977]

DLC-Micro JPRS 70287

2771

PFP announces constitutional proposals. *In* U.S. *Joint Publications Research Service.* JPRS 72324. [Springfield, Va., National Technical Information Service, 1978] (Translations on Sub-Saharan Africa, no. 2030) p. 112–119.

Translation of article in *Die Transvaler,* Johannesburg, Oct. 27, 1978, p. 4, 12.

PFP: Progressive Federal Party.

2771 (cont.)

Microfiche. [Washington, Supt. of Docs., U.S. Govt. Print. Off., 1978]

DLC-Micro JPRS 72324

2772

Reis, Alf. Prime Minister Botha interviewed on national policy. *In* U.S. *Joint Publications Research Service*. JPRS 76157. [Springfield, Va., National Technical Information Service, 1980] (Sub-Saharan Africa report, no. 2274) p. 120–123.

Translation of article in *Die Burger*, Cape Town, June 18, 1980, p. 11.

Microfiche. [s.l., 1980]

DLC-Micro JPRS 76157

2773

United States urges peaceful change in South Africa. *In* U.S. *Dept. of State*. The Department of State bulletin, v. 76, no. 1960, Jan. 17, 1977: 48–51.

JX232.A33 v. 76

Statements in the U.N. General Assembly by U.S. Representative Stephen Hess, Nov. 3, 1976, and U.S. Representative Robert P. Hupp, Nov. 9, 1976.

2774

Vorster reviews 30 years of Nationalist Party rule. *In* U.S. *Joint Publications Research Service*. JPRS 71513. [Springfield, Va., National Technical Information Service, 1978] (Translations on Sub-Saharan Africa, no. 1965) p. 123–126.

Translation of interview with Prime Minister Balthazar J. Vorster, in *Die Suidwester*, Windhoek, May 25, 1978, p. 7.

Microfiche. [Washington, Supt. of Docs., U.S. Govt. Print. Off., 1978]

DLC-Micro JPRS 71513

2775

Young, Andrew. In support for a change in South Africa. Congressional record, 94th Congress, 2d session, v. 122, Aug. 31, 1976: 28706–28708.

J11.R5 v. 122

Extension of remarks in the U.S. House of Representatives.

Includes articles from the *New York Times*.

"Homelands"

2776

[U.S. *Central Intelligence Agency*] Bophuthatswana. [Washington, 1977] col. map.

G8503.B6   1977.U5

Scale ca. 1 : 3,400,000.
Includes location map.

2777

——— South Africa; homelands. [Washington, 1977] col. map.   G8501.G6   1977.U5

Scale ca. 1 : 10,000,000.
"503537 11-77 (543001)."

Indicates Basotho Qwa Qwa, Bophuthatswana, Ciskei, Gazankulu, Kwa Zulu, Lebowa, South Ndebele, Swazi, Transkei, and Venda.

2778

——— South Africa; homelands. [Washington, 1978] col. map.   G8501.G6   1978.U5

Scale ca 1 : 6,000,000.
"503628 3-78."

Indicates the boundaries and administrative centers of Bophuthatswana, Ciskei, Gazankulu, Kwazulu, Lebowa, Qwa, Qwa, South Ndebele, Swazi, Transkei, and Venda.

2779

——— South Africa; homelands. Scale [ca. 1 : 10,000,000] [Washington, 1980] col. map.

G8501.G6   1980.U5

"504631 10-80 (543001)."

Indicates the boundaries and seats of government of Bophuthatswana, Ciskei, Gazankulu, Kangwane (former Swazi), Kwandebele (former South Ndebele), Kwa Zulu, Lebowa, Qwa Qwa, Transkei, and Venda.

2780

U.S. *Congress. House. Committee on International Relations*. Urging the President not to extend diplomatic or other recognition to the Transkei Territory. [Washington?], 1976. 7 p. map.

DLC-LL

At head of title: 94th Congress, 2d session. House of Representatives. Report no. 94–1463.

Submitted by Representative Stephen J. Solarz.

2781

McClure, James A. Transkei looks for recognition. Congressional record, 95th Congress, 1st session, v. 123, June 27, 1977: 21067–21069.

J11.R5 v. 123

Remarks in the U.S. Senate.
Includes article from *New Leader*.

2782

Solarz, Stephen J. Solarz urges President not to extend diplomatic recognition to the Transkei. Congressional record, 94th Congress, 2d session, v. 122, Sept. 14, 1976: 30262–30264.

J11.R5 v. 122

Remarks in the U.S. House of Representatives.
Includes text of report filed by the Committee on International Relations, U.S. House of Represen-

2782 (cont.)

tatives, and a relevant article from the *New York Times*.

2783

Urging President not to extend diplomatic or other recognition to the Transkei Territory. Congressional record, 94th Congress, 2d session, v. 122, Sept. 21, 1976: 31585–31592.   J11.R5 v. 122
Remarks in the U.S. House of Representatives on H. Res. 1509.

Population Studies

2784

[U.S. *Central Intelligence Agency*] South Africa; black population as a percentage of total population (by magisterial district). [Washington, 1978] col. map.   G8501.E1   1970.U5
Scale ca. 1 : 6,000,000.
"Source of data: South Africa, population census, 1970."
"503623 5-78."
Includes inset map of Johannesburg region.

2785

——— South Africa; Indian population as a percentage of total population (by magisterial district) [Washington, 1978] col. map.
          G8501.E1   1970.U53
"Source of data: South Africa, population census, 1970."
"503626 5-78."
Includes inset map of Johannesburg region.

2786

——— South Africa; white population as a percentage of total population (by magisterial district). [Washington, 1978] col. map.
          G8501.E1   1970.U51
Scale ca. 1 : 6,000,000.
"Source of data: South Africa, population census, 1970."
"503624 3-78."
Includes inset map of Johannesburg region.

2786a

Johnson, Peter D., *and* Paul R. Campbell. Detailed statistics on the population of South Africa, by race and urban/rural residence: 1950 to 2010. Washington, International Demographic Data Center, U.S. Bureau of the Census, 1982. 455 p.
          DLC
Bibliography: p. 445–455.
"This report on the Black, White, Coloured, and Asian populations of South Africa contains tables

of selected demographic information, including size of population, and estimates of fertility, mortality, and migration by race. Specifically, annual estimates of total population, by sex and race, are shown beginning in 1950. An adjusted distribution of the population, by age, sex, and race is given for the 1970 census year, as well as projections for selected years, 1980 to 2010."—p. 1.
Includes also statistics on life expectancies, infant mortality, "age-sex-specific migration rates for the international component," family planning, religion, school enrollment and completion, literacy, labor force by industry and occupation, gross national product, and number and size of households.

2787

Schoen, Robert. Rapid demographic change in an overseas Indian population: the case of South Africa. [Urbana], Dept. of Sociology, University of Illinois at Urbana-Champaign, 1975. 25 leaves. (FAR 22995-N)
"Working papers in applied social statistics, WP 7513."
Research supported in part by the National Science Foundation.
Presented at the annual meeting of the American Sociological Association, 1975.
Examined in the former Foreign Affairs Research Documentation Center, U.S. Dept. of State.

Other Subjects

2788

U.S. *Central Intelligence Agency*. South Africa. [Washington, 1979] col. map.
          G8500   1979.U5
Scale 1 : 4,250,000.
"Base 503972 4-79 (543840).'
"Lambert conformal conic projection, standard parallels 6° and 30°."

2789

U.S. *Information Agency. Office of Research.* VOA audience estimate for South Africa, 1976. [Washington?], 1978. 26 p.   DLC
"E-5-78."

2790

——— VOA audience estimate for the South African white population, 1976. [Washington?], 1976. 12 p.
          DLC
"E-26-76."
Issued also in microfiche. [Washington, Congressional Information Service, 1976?] 1 sheet.
          DLC-Micro ASI:77 9856-2.67

2791

U.S. *Information Agency. Research Service.* Preliminary VOA audience estimate for the South African black population. [Washington?], 1976. [3] leaves.
DLC

"Research memorandum M-34-76."

2792

U.S. *International Communication Agency. Office of Research and Evaluation.* Listening to international radio stations, including VOA, in South Africa (1977) [Washington?], 1978. 20 p.

"Research report, E-11-78."

Examined in the U.S. Information Agency, Washington, D.C.

2793

Dally, James W. Research in rock mechanics in South Africa. College Park, Photomechanical Laboratory, University of Maryland, 1977. 21 p.

Prepared for the National Science Foundation under grant NSF-APR 73-07908-A03.

Abstract in *Government Reports Announcements & Index*, Dec. 9, 1977, p. 112.

Microfiche. [Springfield, Va., National Technical Information Service, 1977] 1 sheet.
DLC-Sci RR PB 272275

2794

Nyquist, Thomas. Urban Africans in South Africa. [s.l.], 1977. [63] leaves. (FAR 18172-S)

Prepared for the Office of External Research, U.S. Dept. of State.

Examined in the former Foreign Affairs Research Documentation Center, U.S. Dept. of State.

2795

Orme, Antony R. Estuarine sedimentation along the Natal coast, South Africa. Los Angeles, Dept. of Geography, University of California, 1974. 53 p. illus., maps. (U.S. Office of Naval Research. Technical report, no. 5)

Prepared for the U.S. Office of Naval Research.
Microfiche. [Springfield, Va., National Technical Information Service, 1975] 1 sheet.
DLC-Sci RR AD-A007485

2796

——— Field studies and remote sensing along the Natal coast, South Africa. final report. Los Angeles, Dept. of Geography, University of California, 1974. 19 p.

Prepared for the U.S. Office of Naval Research.
Microfiche. [Springfield, Va., National Technical Information Service, 1975] 1 sheet.
DLC-Sci RR AD-A007285

2797

Orme, Antony R., *and* Larry L. Loeher. Remote sensing of subtropical coastal environments: Natal, South Africa. Los Angeles, Dept. of Geography; University of California; distributed by National Technical Information Service, Springfield, Va., 1974. 89 p. illus., maps. (U.S. Office of Naval Research. Technical report, no. 3)

Prepared for the U.S. Office of Naval Research.
Microfiche. [Springfield, Va., National Technical Information Service, 1974] 1 sheet.
DLC-Sci RR AD-A000280

2798

Pélissier, René. African area studies reviewed. *In* U.S. *Joint Publications Research Service.* JPRS 70665. [Springfield, Va., National Technical Information Service, 1978] (Translations on Sub-Saharan Africa, no. 1881) p. 21–28.

Translation of article on African studies in South Africa, in *Revue française d'études politiques africaines*, Paris, Dec. 1977, p. 76–96.

Microfiche. [Washington, Supt. of Docs., U.S. Govt. Print. Off., 1978]
DLC-Micro JPRS 70665

2799

Rossouw, S. F. On-line training in Africa. [s.l.], 1980. 16 p.

Paper presented at the National Online Information Meeting, New York, 1980.

"The background of online information retrieved at the Institute for Medical Literature (IML), South Africa's center for providing such services to the country's biomedical community, is briefly sketched."—Abstract.

Abstract in *Resources in Education*, Jan. 1981, p. 103.

Microfiche. [Arlington, Va., ERIC Document Reproduction Service; prepared for Educational Resources Information Center, National Institute of Education, 1980] 1 sheet.
DLC-Micro ED176638

2800

The Shaping of South African society, 1652–1820; edited by Richard Elphick and Hermann Giliomee. Cape Town, Longman, 1979. xvi, 415 p. illus., map. DT761.S5

"We are grateful to the Southern African Research Program (SARP), whose award of a fellowship to Hermann Giliomee in 1977–78 made possible the final editing of this book and the redrafting of the last chapter. SARP is funded by the National Endowment for the Humanities and the Ford Foundation, and is located at Yale University."—p. x.

Swaziland

General

2801

U.S. *Agency for International Development.* A report to the Congress on development needs and opportunities for cooperation in Southern Africa. Annex A: Swaziland. [Washington], 1979. 73 p.

Bibliography: p. 72–73.

An overview of the country's economic situation, emphasizing factors impeding development, government development planning, and the role of foreign assistance.

Microfiche. [Washington, U.S. Agency for International Development, 1979?] 1 sheet.

DLC-Sci RR PN-AAH-157

2802

U.S. *Dept. of State.* Post report. Swaziland. [Washington, for sale by the Supt. of Docs., U.S. Govt. Print. Off.], 1981. 16 p. illus., map. (U.S. Dept. of State. Department of State publication, 9206)

JX1705.A286 Spec. Format

Department and Foreign Service series, 253.

L.C. has also report issued in 1978.

For a description of the contents of this publication, see the note to entry 936.

2803

U.S. *Dept. of State. Bureau of Public Affairs.* Background notes. Swaziland. [Washington, for sale by the Supt. of Docs., U.S. Govt. Print. Off.], 1980. 6 p. maps. (U.S. Dept. of State. Department of State publication 8174, rev.) G59.U5

L.C. retains only the latest revision.

For a description of the contents of this publication, see the note to entry 937.

2804

Draft environmental profile of Swaziland. Washington, Science and Technology Division, Library of Congress, 1980. 97 p. maps.

Prepared under a U.S. Agency for International Development contract with the U.S. Man and the Biosphere Secretariat, U.S. Dept. of State.

Abstract in *A.I.D. Research & Development Abstracts*, July 1981, p. 32.

Microfiche. [Washington, U.S. Agency for International Development, 1980?] 2 sheets.

DLC-Sci RR PN-AAH-754

2805

The Peace Corps in Swaziland. [Washington, U.S. Govt. Print. Off., 1980] 1 fold. sheet (6 p.) illus., map. DLC

"ACTION 4200.69."

An introduction to the country for Volunteers.

Agriculture

2806

Agricultural assessment: Swaziland, [by] James Stallings [et al.] [s.l., 1978] 125 p. map.

Prepared for the Southern Africa Development Assistance Project, U.S. Agency for International Development.

Bibliography: p. 119–121.

Microfiche. [Washington, U.S. Agency for International Development, 1979?] 2 sheets.

DLC-Sci RR PN-AAH-183

2807

Allred, Keith R., William F. Farnsworth, *and* John D. Downes. Swaziland cropping systems research and extension training design study. Logan, Utah State University, 1980. 118 p.

"Report submitted to USAID/Swaziland."

Issued in cooperation with Texas Tech University, Lubbock, with both universities representing the Consortium for International Development.

Abstract in *A.I.D. Research & Development Abstracts*, v. 9, no. 4, 1981, p. 4.

Microfiche. [Washington, U.S. Agency for International Development, 1981?] 2 sheets.

DLC-Sci RR PN-AAJ-121

2808

Rural development in Swaziland; an evaluation report, [by] John L. Fischer [et al.], [Tucson?], 1974. 34 p.

Prepared for the U.S. Agency for International Development under contract AID/afr-C-1078.

Examined in the Development Information Center, AID, Washington, D.C.

2809

Swaziland water and related land resources framework plan. [Omaha, Neb.?], Omaha District Corps of Engineers, Dept. of the Army, 1981. [448] p. (in various pagings)

Prepared for the Government of Swaziland; funded by the U.S. Agency for International Development.

Abstract in *A.I.D. Research & Development Abstracts*, v. 9, no. 4, 1981, p. 12.

Microfiche. [Washington, U.S. Agency for International Development, 1981?] 5 sheets.

DLC-Sci RR PN-AAJ-560

Assistance Programs

2810

U.S. *Agency for International Development.* Annual budget submission: Swaziland. Washington, U.S. International Development Cooperation Agency.

Vols. for 1981+ examined in the Development Information Center, AID, Washington,D.C.

2811

——— Country development strategy statement: Swaziland. Washington, U.S. International Development Cooperation Agency. annual.

Vols. for 1982+ examined in the Development Information Center, AID, Washington, D.C.

2812

AID development assistance program: Swaziland. [Washington?], 1974. 3 v.

Contents: [Main report]—[Annex A] Agricultural sector assessment.—Annex B. Education and human resources development sector assessment.

Examined in the Development Information Center, U.S. Agency for International Development, Washington, D.C.

2813

Duff, William. Southern Africa academic and skills training. [Greeley, Colo.?, 1978] [16] p.

Prepared for the U.S. Agency for International Development under contract AID/afr-C-1461.

"The objective of this contract was to assist the [Swaziland] Ministry of Education in the analysis

and preliminary implementation of the Third National Development Plan."

Microfiche. [Washington, U.S. Agency for International Development, 1978] 1 sheet.

DLC-Sci RR PN-AAG-185

2814

Incwadzi yetfu; Volunteer newsletter, Peace Corps Swaziland. Oct. 1974+ [Mbabane?] irregular?

DPC

2815

Russin, Antoinette, Jack Colburn, *and* Lester Feldmann. Peace Corps/Swaziland: country program evaluation. [Washington], Social, Educational Research and Development, inc., 1977. [102] p. (in various pagings) DPC

Prepared jointly with the Division of Evaluation, Action (Service Corps).

2816

Sebenta National Institute. Final report, July education programme, 1976, submitted to Peace Corps/Swaziland. [s.l., 1976?] 25 leaves. DPC

"This report deals with the 1976 July (Summer) Education Training Programme for 39 new [Peace Corps] volunteers."—leaf 1.

2817

Swaziland. [*Treaties, etc. United States, 1978 Aug. 31*] Project grant agreement between Swaziland and the United States of America for Southern Africa manpower development. *In* U.S. *Treaties, etc.* United States treaties and other international agreements, v. 30, 1978–79. [Washington, Dept. of State; for sale by the Supt. of Docs., U.S. Govt. Print. Off., 1980] p. 5471–5492. ([Treaties and other international acts series, 9511]

JX231.A34 v. 30

A U.S. Agency for International Development project to assist Swaziland "in alleviating critical manpower shortages which exist in the public sector."—p. 5475.

2818

Technical Assistance Information Clearing House. Development assistance programs of U.S. nonprofit organizations in Swaziland. [New York], American Council of Voluntary Agencies for Foreign Service, 1976. 9 p. maps. (TAICH country report) HC517.S9T4a

The Clearing House is operated by the Council under a grant from the U.S. Agency for International Development.

Commerce

2819

Chittum, J. Marc. Marketing in Swaziland. [Washington], U.S. Dept. of Commerce, Domestic and International Business Administration; [for sale by the Supt. of Docs., U.S. Govt. Print. Off.] 1977. 21 p. (Overseas business reports. OBR 77-36)

HF91.U482   1977, no. 36

International marketing information series.

Issued also in microfiche. [Washington, Congressional Information Service, 1977?] 1 sheet.

DLC-Micro ASI:77 2026-5.42

2820

Miller, Sally K. Marketing in Swaziland. Washington, U.S. Dept. of Commerce, Domestic and International Business Administration; [for sale by the Supt. of Docs., U.S. Govt. Print. Off.], 1975. 19 p. (Overseas business reports. OBR 75-55)

HF91.U482   1975, no. 55

Health and Nutrition

2821

U.S. *Peace Corps. Swaziland.* Medical handbook. [Mbabane, 1978?] 52 leaves.   DPC

2822

Boostrom, Eugene R. Report on planning activities for the health manpower training institution, Swaziland. [Washington?], American Public Health Association, 1975. [8] p.

Prepared for the U.S. Agency for International Development under contract no. AID/csd 3423.

Microfiche. [Washington, U.S. Agency for International Development, 1975?] 1 sheet.

DLC-Sci RR PN-AAB-562

2823

Carp, Carol. A review of health care in Swaziland: issues, analyses, and recommendations. Washington, Family Health Care, inc., 1978. [126] p. (in various pagings), map. (Health and development in Southern Africa, v. 1)

A sector assessment undertaken in conjuction with the Southern Africa Development Analysis Project, U.S. Agency for International Development.

Issued in cooperation with Africare.

Abstract in *A.I.D. Research and Development Abstracts*, v. 8, no. 2, 1980, p. 26.

Microfiche. [Washington, U.S. Agency for International Development, 1979?] 2 sheets.

DLC-Sci RR PN-AAH-161

2824

Gish, Oscar. Planning the health services of Swaziland. [Washington], American Public Health Association, [1974?] 49 leaves.

Prepared under an agreement with the U.S. Agency for International Development.

Examined in the Development Information Center, AID, Washington, D.C.

2825

Yergen, Laura H. Report on visit to Swaziland. [Washington?], American Public Health Association, 1975. [32] p. (in various pagings)

Prepared for the U.S. Agency for International Development under the Development and Evaluation of Integrated Delivery Systems (DEIDS) project.

An overview of health manpower training.

Microfiche. [Washington, U.S. Agency for International Development, 1975?] 1 sheet.

DLC-Sci RR PN-AAB-563

Language and Languages

2826

Corum, Claudia W. An introduction to the Swazi (siSwati) language. Bloomington, African Studies Program, Indiana University, [1978] [278] p. (in various pagings)   InU

Prepared under contract for the U.S. Office of Education.

Abstract in *Resources in Education*, Oct. 1978, p. 78.

Issued also in microfiche. [Arlington, Va., ERIC Document Reproduction Service; prepared for Educational Resources Information Center, National Institute of Education, 1978] 3 sheets.

DLC-Micro ED154644

2827

———— Siswati. Brattleboro, Vt., Experiment in International Living, for ACTION/Peace Corps, [1980] [4] v. illus. (Peace Corps language handbook series)   DLC

Partial contents: Special skills handbook.

Other Subjects

2828

Africa: Swaziland. Selected statistical data by sex. Washington, 1981. 31, 17 p.   DLC

Study supported by the U.S. Agency for International Development's Office of Women in Development and Office of Population.

2828 (cont.)

Data assembled by the International Demographic Data Center, U.S. Bureau of the Census.

Among the titles, all based on 1966 data (unless noted), are the following: unadjusted population by age, sex, and urban/rural residence; population by district, sex and urban/rural residence; population by ethnic group, sex, and urban/rural residence; number of persons enrolled in school, by age, sex, and urban/rural residence (1976); number of economically active persons by age, sex, and urban/rural residence.

2829

Cook, Paul F. Swaziland curriculum and educational materials development: final report. Washington, American Institutes for Research, 1975. [119] p. (in various pagings)

Prepared for the U.S. Agency for International Development under contract AID/afr 668.

Covers the period Apr. 1973–Aug. 1975.

"This is the final report of a project to assist the Kingdom of Swaziland to plan and implement a reform in its primary school curriculum."—p. i.

Microfiche. [Arlington, Va., ERIC Document Reproduction Service; prepared for Educational Resources Information Center, National Institute of Education, 1977] 2 sheets.

DLC-Micro ED134323

2830

Foreign economic trends and their implications for the United States. Swaziland. 1975+ Washington, for sale by the Supt. of Docs., U.S. Govt. Print.

Off. annual? (International marketing information series)   HC10.E416

Prepared by the U.S. Embassy, Mbabane.

Vol. for 1975 distributed by the U.S. Bureau of International Commerce; vols. for 1981– by the U.S. International Trade Administration.

Not published, 1976–80.

The following issues have been identified in L.C.:

FET 75-076. 1975. 8 p.

FET 81-113 1981. 12 p.

2831

Human resources development study for Swaziland; final report, [by] Thomas R. Collins [et al.] Research Triangle Park, N.C., Research Triangle Institute, 1976. 113 p.

Prepared for the Bureau for Africa, U.S. Agency for International Development.

Examined in the Development Information Center, AID, Washington, D.C.

2832

Rivkin Associates Inc. Swaziland shelter sector assessment, prepared for the Government of Swaziland and USAID by Rivkin Associates, inc., in association with Carl House. Washington, Agency for International Development, Office of Housing, 1978. [277] p. (in various pagings) illus., maps.   HD7374.8.A3R58 1978

Includes bibliographical references.

Abstract in *A.I.D. Research and Development Abstracts*, v. 7, no. 1, 1979, p. 15.

Zambia

General

2833

U.S. *Agency for International Development.* A report to the Congress on development needs and opportunities for cooperation in Southern Africa. Annex A: Zambia. [Washington] 1979. 137 p.

Bibliography: p. 131–137.

An overview of economic conditions, emphasizing government development policies, the role of foreign assistance, and problems of development in such fields as agriculture, health, labor, manufacturing, mining, transportation, and housing.

Microfiche. [Washington, U.S. Agency for International Development, 1979?] 2 sheets.

DLC-Sci RR PN-AAH-158

2834

U.S. *Dept. of State.* Post report. Zambia. [Washington, for sale by the Supt. of Docs., U.S. Govt. Print. Off.], 1982. 16 p. illus., map. (U.S. Dept. of State. Department of State publication 9283)

DLC

Department and Foreign service series 316.

For a description of the contents of this publication, see the note to entry 936.

L.C. has also the 1979 edition (JX1705.A286 Spec. Format).

2835

U.S. *Dept. of State. Bureau of Public Affairs.* Background notes. Zambia. [Washington, for sale by the Supt. of Docs., U.S. Govt. Print. Off.], 1979. 5 p. illus., maps. (U.S. Dept. of State. Department of State publications 7841, rev.) G59.U5

L.C. retains only the latest revision.

For a description of the contents of this publication, see the note to entry 937.

2836

Zambia, a country study; edited by Irving Kaplan. 3d ed. Washington, American University, Foreign Area Studies; for sale by the Supt. of Docs., U.S. Govt. Print. Off., 1979. xxv, 308 p. illus., maps. (Area handbook series) DT963.K26 1979

"DA pam 550-75."

Includes bibliographies and index.

"This volume is one of a continuing series of books written by Foreign Area Studies, The American University, under the Area Handbook Program."

Second ed., 1974, by Irving Kaplan and others, published under title: *Area Handbook for Zambia* (DT963.K26 1974)

Agriculture

2837

Bates, Robert H. Rural development in Kasumpa Village, Zambia. Journal of African studies, Fall 1975: 333–362. DT1.J653 1975–76

"This study was supported by the Division of Humanities and Social Sciences of the California Institute of Technology and by grant no. HD 05707-01-01/02 from the Public Health Service of the Department of Health, Education, and Welfare.—p. 333.

Issued also as Social Science Working Paper no. 34 of the Division of the Humanities and Social Sciences, California Institute of Technology.

2838

Far-reaching measures to end Namboard's problems planned. *In* U.S. *Joint Publications Research Service.* JPRS 72175. [Springfield, Va., National Technical Information Service, 1978] (Translations on Sub-Saharan Africa, no. 2018) p. 147–150.

Article on the National Agricultural Marketing Board of Zambia in *Zambia Daily Mail*, Lusaka, Oct. 16, 1978, p. 1.

Microfiche. [Washington, Supt. of Docs, U.S. Govt. Print. Off., 1978]

DLC-Micro JPRS 72175

2839

Mann, Robert D. Rural Africa development project: a survey technique for identifying the needs of small farmers, and an example of its use in Zambia. London, Intermediate Technology Publications Ltd., [1974] [50] p. map.

Microfiche. [Springfield, Va., National Technical Information Service, 1980] 1 sheet.

DLC-Sci RR PB 80-145733

2840

—— Rural Africa development project: identifying the problems of small farmers; a farm-level survey technique to identify labour, machinery, and other input requirements, with an example of its use in Zambia. Rev. ed., rev. by John Boyd. London, Intermediate Technology Publications, 1976. 49 p. maps.   HD1476.Z35M35   1976

Bibliography: p. 48–49.

Primarily concerns the Southern Province of Zambia.

Abstract in *Appropriate Technology Information for Developing Countries*, 2d ed., 1979, p. 221–222.

Issued also in microfiche. [Springfield, Va., National Technical Information Service, 1979] 1 sheet.   DLC-Sci RR PB-297785

2841

Siegel, Brian. Centers on the periphery: rural development in Ndola rural center. *In* Southall, Aidan. Small urban centers in rural development in Africa. Madison, African Studies Program, University of Wisconsin-Madison, 1979, p. 69–89.

A grant from the Office of Urban Development, U.S. Agency for International Development, assisted in the preparation for publication of the papers collected in the study.

Microfiche. [Washington, U.S. Agency for International Development, 1980?] (PN-AAJ-064); examined in the Development Information Center, AID, Washington, D.C.

2842

Tuthill, Dean F. Agricultural sector assessment: Zambia. [s.l.], 1978. [139] p.

Prepared for the Southern Africa Development Assistance Project, U.S. Agency for International Development.

Microfiche. [Washington, U.S. Agency for International Development, 1979?] 2 sheets.

DLC-Sci RR PN-AAH-181

Assistance Programs

2843

U.S. *Agency for International Development.* Annual budget submission: Zambia. Washington, U.S. International Development Cooperation Agency.

Vols. for 1980+ examined in the Development Information Center, AID, Washington, D.C.

2844

—— Country development strategy statement: Zambia. Washington, U.S. International Development Cooperation Agency. annual.

Vols. for 1982+ examined in the Development Information Center, AID, Washington, D.C.

2845

U.S. *Agency for International Development. Office of U.S. Foreign Disaster Assistance.* Summary report: Zambia floods, February 1978. [Washington], 1979. 2 p. map.

Microfiche. [Washington, Congressional Information Service, 1979?]

DLC-Micro ASI:79 7206-3.47

2846

U.S. *General Accounting Office.* Meeting U.S. political objectives through economic aid in the Middle East and Southern Africa: report to the Congress by the Comptroller General of the United States. [Washington], 1979. 42 p. maps.

HC415.15.U54   1979

"ID-79-23."

"E-125029."

Emphasis is on the Middle East, with brief references to economic assistance to Southern African nations, especially Zambia.

2847

U.S. [*Treaties, etc. Zambia, 1976 Aug. 24*] Agreement between the Government of the United States of America and the Government of the Republic of Zambia for the sale of agricultural commodities. *In* U.S. *Treaties, etc.* United States treaties and other international agreements, v. 27, 1976. [Washington, Dept. of State; for sale by the Supt. of Docs., U.S. Govt. Print. Off., 1977] p. 3452–3466. ([Treaties and other international acts series, 8377])   JX231.A34 v. 27

Signed at Lusaka Aug. 24, 1976.

2848

U.S. [*Treaties, etc. Zambia, 1976 Dec. 3*] Loan agreement (Zambia program loan) between the Republic of Zambia and the United States of America. *In* U.S. *Treaties, etc.* United States treaties and other international agreements, v. 28, 1976–77. [Washington, Dept. of State; for sale by the Supt. of Docs., U.S. Govt. Print. Off., 1979] p. 8751–8786. ([Treaties and other international acts series, 8770])   JX231.A34 v. 28

2848 (cont.)

Signed at Lusaka Dec. 3, 1976.

Purpose of the loan was to assist Zambia "to alleviate balance of payments problems." — p. 8754.

2849

U.S. [*Treaties, etc. Zambia, 1978 Mar. 30*] Loan agreement (Zambia program loan) between the Republic of Zambia and the United States of America. *In* U.S. *Treaties, etc.* United States treaties and other international agreements, v. 30, 1978–79. [Washington, Dept. of State; for sale by the Supt. of Docs., U.S. Govt. Print. Off., 1980] p. 1889–1915. ([Treaties and other international acts series, 9299]) JX231.A34 v. 30

Concerns a U.S. Agency for International Development loan to finance the foreign exchange costs of certain commodities and commodity-related services.

2850

Technical Assistance Information Clearing House. Development assistance programs of U.S. non-profit organizations in Zambia. New York, American Council of Voluntary Agencies for Foreign Service, 1974. 23 p. (TAICH country report)
HC517.R42T4 1974

The Clearing House is operated by the Council under contract to the U.S. Agency for International Development.

2851

—— Development assistance programs of U.S. non-profit organizations: Zambia. Apr. 1978. [New York], American Council of Voluntary Agencies for Foreign Service, 1978. 27 leaves. maps. (TAICH country report) DLC

2852

U.S. *Agency for International Development.* Project paper—Zambia—commodity import loan. [s.l.], 1976. 30 p.

Examined in the Development Information Center, AID, Washington, D.C.

Commerce

2853

U.S. *Agency for International Development.* Zambia: FY 1980 commodity import loan paper 611-K-005. [Washington?, Agency for International Development, 1980] [85] p. (in various pagings) DLC

2854

Black market in essential commodities 'flourishing.'

In U.S. *Joint Publications Research Service.* JPRS 73439. [Springfield, Va., National Technical Information Service, 1979] (Translations on Sub-Saharan Africa, no. 2103) p. 87–90.

From article in *Zambia Daily Mail*, Lusaka, Apr. 12, 1979, p. 4.

Microfiche. [Washington, Supt. of Docs., U.S. Govt. Print Off., 1978] DLC-Micro JPRS 73439

2855

Lwenje, Patches. Smuggling described along Zambian-Zairian border. *In* U.S. *Joint Publications Research Service.* JPRS 68841. [Springfield, Va., National Technical Information Service, 1977] (Translations on Sub-Saharan Africa, no. 1727) p. 83–89.

Article in *Sunday Times of Zambia*, Lusaka, Mar. 6, 1977, p. 5.

Microfiche. [s.l., 1977]
DLC-Micro JPRS 68841

2856

Market share reports. Country series: Zambia, 1971–75. [Washington], U.S. Dept. of Commerce; for sale by the National Technical Information Service, Springfield, Va., [1977] 65 p.

Indicates the United States share of the market in Zambia for various products compared to the shares for Belgium-Luxemburg, France, Federal Republic of Germany, Great Britain, Italy, Netherlands, Sweden, and Japan.

Microfiche. [Washington, Congressional Information Service, 1977?]
DLC-Micro ASI:77 2016-1.88

2857

Market share reports. Country series: Zambia, 1975–79. [Washington], International Trade Administration, U.S. Dept. of Commerce; for sale by the National Technical Information Service, Springfield, Va., [1979] 64 p.

Includes same comparative data as in *Market Share Reports. Country Series: Zambia, 1971–75* (entry 2856).

Microfiche. [Washington, Congressional Information Service, 1979?]
DLC-Micro ASI:81 2046-2.88

2858

Michelini, Philip. Marketing in Zambia. [Washington], U.S. Dept. of Commerce, Industry and Trade Administration; [for sale by the Supt. of Docs., U.S. Govt. Print. Off.], 1978. 26 p. (Overseas business reports. OBR 78-24)
HF91.U482 1978, no. 24

International marketing information series.

Economic Conditions

2859

Bates, Robert H. Patterns of uneven development: causes and consequences in Zambia. Denver, University of Denver, [1974] 59 p. (Denver. University. Social Science Foundation. Monograph series in world affairs, v. 11, no. 3)

HC517.R42B38

"The research for this paper was conducted while Dr. Bates was an affiliate of the Institute for African Studies of the University of Zambia, and was supported by the Division of Humanities and Social Sciences of the California Institute of Technology and by the Public Health Service of the United States Department of Health, Education, and Welfare."

2860

———— Rural responses to industrialization: a study of village Zambia. New Haven, Yale University Press, 1976. 380 p. HN803.A8B37

"The study was financed with grants from the Joint Committee on African Studies of the Social Science Research Council, the National Institutes of Health (grant number HD 05707-01/03), and the Division of the Humanities and Social Sciences of the California Institute of Technology."—p ix.

2861

Beveridge, Andrew. Varieties of African businessmen in the emerging Zambian stratification system. [s.l.], 1973. 11 leaves. (FAR 19088-N)

Research supported in part by the National Institute of Mental Health.

Examined in the former Foreign Affairs Research Documentation Center, U.S. Dept. of State.

2862

Foreign economic trends and their implications for the United States. Zambia. 1969+ Washington, for sale by the Supt. of Docs., U.S. Govt. Print. Off. annual. (International marketing information series) HC10.E416

Prepared by the U.S. Embassy, Lusaka.

Vols. for 1969–77 distributed by the U.S. Bureau of International Commerce; vol. for 1979 by the U.S. Industry and Trade Administration; vols. for 1981– by the U.S. International Trade Administration.

Not published in 1978, 1980.

The following issues for the period 1973–81 have been identified in L.C.:

ET 73-103. 1973. 11 p.

ET 74-065. 1974. 10 p.
FET 75-109. 1975. 7 p.
FET 76-118. 1976. 7 p.
FET 77-094. 1977. 9 p.
FET 79-033. 1979. 11 p.
FET 81-122. 1981. 10 p.

2863

Kaunda, Kenneth D., President addresses assembly, declares war on poverty. *In* U.S. *Joint Publications Research Service.* JPRS 75058. [Springfield, Va., National Technical Information Service, 1980] (Sub-Saharan Africa report, no. 2209) p. 120–127.

Speech before the National Assembly recorded in *Zambia Daily Mail*, Lusaka, Jan. 12, 1980, p. 4, 5.

Microfiche. [s.l., 1980]

DLC-Micro JPRS 75058

2864

Lwenje, Patches. Poverty of Chama District described. *In* U.S. *Joint Publications Research Service.* JPRS 76213. [Springfield, Va., National Technical Information Service, 1980] (Sub-Saharan Africa report, no. 2277) p. 92–96.

Article in *Times of Zambia*, Lusaka, July 20, 1980, p. 3.

Microfiche. [s.l., 1980]

DLC-Micro JPRS 76213

2865

Seidman, Ann. Alternative development strategies in Zambia. Madison, Land Tenure Center, University of Wisconsin, 1973. 43 p. (Wisconsin. University-Madison. Land Tenure Center. LTC, no. 89)

Microfiche. [Washington, U.S. Agency for International Development, 1973?] 1 sheet.

DLC-Sci RR PN-AAA-407

Education

2866

Draisma, Tom. African socialism and educational practice. [s.l.], 1975. [73] p.

Prepared for the Education Division, Commonwealth Secretariat, London.

On cover: "Draft."

Special focus on Zambia.

Abstract in *Resources in Education*, Feb. 1976, p. 196.

Microfiche. [Arlington, Va., ERIC Document Reproduction Service, Educational Resources Information Center, National Institute of Education, 1976] 1 sheet. DLC-Micro ED113286

2867

Pritchard, Mervyn W. Primary school inspection in Zambia. Paris, International Institute for Educational Planning, c1975. 75 p. (International Institute for Educational planning. IIEP research report; 12)

On cover: "The organization and staffing of the primary school inspectorate: case studies-6."

Microfiche. [Arlington, Va., ERIC Document Reproduction Service; prepared for Educational Resources Information Center, National Institute of Education, 1977] 1 sheet.

DLC-Micro ED133864

2868

Scudder, Thayer, *and* Elizabeth Colson. Secondary education and the formation of an elite: the impact of education on Gwembe District, Zambia. New York, Academic Press, c1980. 190 p. map.

LA1599.G87S38

Not available for examination during this compilation; information from the California Institute of Technology indicates that the National Science Foundation was among the funding sources for this study.

Foreign Relations

2869

Africa: visit of Zambian president Kaunda. *In* U.S. *Dept. of State.* The Department of State bulletin, v. 78, no. 2016, July 1978: 33–34.

JX232.A33 v. 78

Exchange of toasts between President Jimmy Carter and President Kenneth D. Kaunda, Washington, May 17, 1978.

2870

Clark, Dick. Remarks of President of Zambia at National Press Club luncheon. Congressional record, 95th Congress, 2d session, v. 124, June 15, 1978: 17766–17767.   J11.R5 v. 124

Remarks in the U.S. Senate.

Includes text of statement by President Kaunda on May 18, 1978.

2871

President Kaunda of Zambia visits Washington. *In* U.S. *Dept. of State.* The Department of State bulletin, v. 72, no. 1872, May 12, 1975: 614–618.

JX232.A33 v. 72

Exchange of toasts between President Kaunda and President Gerald Ford at the White House, Apr. 19, 1975.

2872

Young, Andrew. Statement by Hon. Dr. Siteke G. Mwale, Minister of Foreign Affairs of the Republic of Zambia. Congressional record, 94th Congress, 2d session, v. 122, Aug. 5, 1976: 26043–26045.

J11.R5 v. 122

Extension of remarks in the U.S. House of Representatives.

Concerns Dr. Mwale's speech to the United Nations Security Council..

Geology, Hydrology, and Mineral Resources

The following items (entries 2873–78) are listed in chronological order:

2873

Greenspoon, Gertrude N. The mineral industry of Zambia. *In* Minerals yearbook, v. 3, 1974. [Washington, for sale by the Supt. of Docs., U.S. Govt. Print. Off., 1977] p. 1047–1054.

TN23.U612   1974, v. 3

Prepared by the U.S. Bureau of Mines.

2874

Ellis, Miller W. The mineral industry of Zambia. *In* Minerals yearbook, v. 3, 1975. [Washington, for sale by the supt. of Docs., U.S. Govt. Print. Off., 1978] p. 1107–115.   TN23.U612   1975, v. 3

Prepared by the U.S. Bureau of Mines.

2875

———— The mineral industry of Zambia. *In* Minerals yearbook, v. 3, 1976. Washington, for sale by the Supt. of Docs., U.S. Govt. Print. Off., 1980] p. 1215–1224.   TN23.U612   1976, v. 3

Prepared by the U.S. Bureau of Mines.

2876

———— The mineral industry of Zambia. *In* Minerals yearbook, v. 3, 1977. [Washington, for sale by the Supt. of Docs., U.S. Govt. Print. Off., 1981] p. 1093–1099.   TN23.U612   1977, v. 3

Prepared by the U.S. Bureau of Mines.

2877

———— The mineral industry of Zambia. *In* Minerals yearbook, v. 3, 1978–79. [Washington, U.S. Govt. Print. Off., 1981] p. 1067–1075.

TN23.U612   1978–79, v. 3

Prepared by the U.S. Bureau of Mines.

2878

——— The mineral industry of Zambia. *In* Minerals yearbook, v. 3, 1980. [Washington, for sale by the Supt. of Docs., U.S. Govt. Print. Off., 1982] p. 1137–1143.   TN23.U612 1980, v. 3

2879

Tembo, Franklin. Mining industry recruitment effort studied. *In* U.S. *Joint Publications Research Service.* JPRS 76213. [Springfield, Va., National Technical Information Service, 1980] (Sub-Saharan Africa report, no. 2277) p. 16–20.

Article on the employment of non-Zambians in Zambian mines, in *Times of Zambia*, Lusaka, July 20, 1980, p. 5.

Microfiche. [s.l., 1980]

DLC-Micro JPRS 76213

Health and Nutrition

2880

A Review of health care in Zambia: issues, analyses, and recommendations. Washington, Family Health Care, inc., 1978. 140 p. (Health and development in Southern Africa, v. 2)

Submitted to the Southern Africa Development Analysis Program, U.S. Agency for International Development.

Bibliography: p. 132–135.

Issued in cooperation with Africare.

Microfiche. [Washington, U.S. Agency for International Development, 1979?] 2 sheets.

DLC-Sci RR PN-AAH-162

2881

Woodville, Lucille. A report on the matron's seminar, University Teaching Hospital, Lusaka, Zambia, May 1974. [Washington?], American Public Health Association, 1974. [22] leaves.

DLC

Prepared for the U.S. Agency for International Development.

Housing and Urban Development

2882

U.S. *Agency for International Development.* Project paper; Zambia—housing investment guaranty. [Washington?], 1976. 40 p.

Examined in the Development Information Center, AID, Washington, D.C.

2883

Zambia home improvement revolving fund. [Washington], Robert S. DeVoy and Associates, 1977. 31 leaves.

Prepared for the Office of Housing, U.S. Agency for International Development, under contract AID/otr-C-1538.

Examined in the Development Information Center, AID, Washington, D.C.

Politics and Government

2884

Javits, Jacob. President Kaunda of Zambia. Congressional record, 94th Congress, 2d session, v. 122, Apr. 5, 1976: 9341–9344.

J11.R5 v. 122

Remarks in the U.S. Senate.

Includes article on the President by Colin Legum, from the *New York Times*.

2885

Lwenje, Patches, *and* Franklin Tembo. People shunning elections more and more. *In* U.S. *Joint Publications Research Service.* JPRS 69847. [Springfield, Va., National Technical Information Service, 1977] (Translations on Sub-Saharan Africa, no. 1807) p. 67–70.

Article in *Times of Zambia*, Lusaka, Sept. 4, 1977, p. 5.

Microfiche. [s.l., 1977]

DLC-Micro JPRS 69847

Other Subjects

2886

Africa: Zambia. Selected statistical data by sex. Washington, 1981. 31, 17 p.   DLC

Study supported by the U.S. Agency for International Development's Office of Women in Development and Office of Population.

Data assembled by the International Demographic Data Center, U.S. Bureau of the Census.

Among the tables, all based on 1969 data (unless noted) are the following: unadjusted population statistics (1975); population by province, sex, and urban/rural residence (1974); population by ethnic group (i.e., "African," "European," "Asian," "Coloured"), sex, and urban, rural residence; life expectancy; population by marital status, age, and sex; number of households; number of literate persons by age, sex and urban/rural residence; number of persons enrolled in school by age, sex, and urban/rural residence; number of economically active persons by age, sex, and urban/rural residence.

2887

Bates, Robert H., *and* Bruce W. Bennett. Determinants of the rural exodus in Zambia; a study of intercensal migration, 1963–1969. Cahiers d'études africaines, v. 14, 1974: 543–564.

DT1.C3   1974

"This article grows out of a broader study of Zambia, the costs of which are defrayed in part by grant no. 1 RO HD050707-01 from the National Institutes of Health."—p. 543.

Issued also as Social Science Working paper no. 22 of the Division of the Humanities and Social Sciences, California Institute of Technology.

2888

Colson, Elizabeth, *and* Thayer Scudder. Long-term research in Gwembe Valley, Zambia. In Long-term field research in social anthropology; edited by George M. Foster [et al.] New York, Academic Press, c1979. p. 227–254.

GN345.L66

Not available for examination during this compilation; information from the California Institute of Technology indicates that the National Science Foundation was among the funding sources for this study.

2889

——— Old age in Gwembe District, Zambia. *In* Other ways of growing old: anthropological perspectives, edited by Pamela T. Amoss and Stevan Harrell. Stanford, Calif., Stanford University Press, 1981. p. 125–153.   GN485.083

Study supported in part by the National Science Foundation under grant no. GS-3295.

2890

Goldberg, Susan. A study of mother-infant interaction in Zambia: personal dilemmas. [s.l.], 1974. 19 p.

Bibliography: p. 18–19.

A review of research methodology.

Abstract in *Research in Education*, July 1976, p. 191.

Microfiche. [Arlington, Va., ERIC Document Reproduction Service; prepared for Educational Resources Information Center, National Institute of Education, 1976] 1 sheet.

DLC-Micro ED120038

2891

Hansen, Art. Once the running stops: assimilation of Angolan refugees into Zambian border villages. Gainesville, University of Florida, [1976?] 21 leaves. (FAR 27639-N)

Paper delivered at the symposium, "Involuntary Migration and Resettlement: the Problems and Responses of Dislocated Peoples," at the annual meeting of the American Anthropological Association, Washington, D.C., Nov. 18, 1976.

"The field research upon which this report is based was funded by a grant from the Training Program in Anthropology of the National Institutes of Health (NIH MS-1256) to the Department of Anthropology of Cornell University."

Examined in the former Foreign Affairs Research Documentation Center, U.S. Dept. of State.

2892

Jules-Rosette, Bennetta. From art to manufacture: some aspects of contemporary art production in urban Africa. [s.l., 1976?] 79 leaves. (FAR 25292-N)

Research in Lusaka, Zambia supported in part by the National Institute of Mental Health.

The focus of the study is on Lusaka.

Examined in the former Foreign Affairs Research Documentation Center, U.S. Dept. of State.

2893

Moeller, Philip W. Field report: an assessment of transport infrastructure relative to Zambian coastal linkage. [Lusaka], USAID/Lusaka, 1980. 216 p. illus., maps.

"Contract no. AID-611-002-T."

Abstract in *A.I.D. Research & Development Abstracts*, v. 9, no. 4, 1981, p. 65.

Microfiche. [Washington, U.S. Agency for International Development, 1980?] 3 sheets.

DLC-Sci RR PN-AAH-729

2894

Need for revision of social security laws noted. *In* U.S. *Joint Publications Research Service*. JPRS 72398. [Springfield, Va., National Technical Information Service, 1978] (Translations on Sub-Saharan Africa, no. 2035) p. 177–181.

Article in *Times of Zambia*, Lusaka, Nov. 13, 1978, p. 4.

Microfiche. [Washington, Supt. of Docs., U.S. Govt. Print. Off., 1978]

DLC-Micro JPRS 72398

2895

Simuchoba, Arthur. Unemployed youth rate increases. *In* U.S. *Joint Publications Research Service*. JPRS 75058. [Springfield, Va., National Technical Information Service, 1980] (Sub-Saharan Africa report, no. 2209) p. 135–139.

Article in *Times of Zambia*, Lusaka, Jan. 13, 1980, p. 3.

Microfiche. [s.l., 1980]

DLC-Micro JPRS 75058

Zimbabwe

Note: Until 1979, the country was called Rhodesia in most publications, although it was established in the Library of Congress as Southern Rhodesia (cataloged under Rhodesia, Southern); for an explanation of the U.S. Government's position on the official name during the 1965–79 period, see The United States and Africa; Guide to U.S. Official Documents and Government-Sponsored Publications of Africa, 1785–1975 *(Z3501.W57), p. 566, note under "Southern Rhodesia." For simplicity, Rhodesia is used in the text of the present guide. In June 1979, in the wake of an internal settlement and general elections, the name Zimbabwe-Rhodesia was adopted. After a constitutional conference in London, it reverted temporarily to colonial status in December 1979 as Southern Rhodesia. Following successful all-party general elections in February 1980, the independent nation of Zimbabwe was proclaimed on April 18, 1980.*

General

2896

U.S. *Agency for International Development.* A report to the Congress on development needs and opportunities for cooperation in Southern Africa. Annex A: Zimbabwe. [Washington], 1979. 115 p.

Bibliography: p. 115–116.

An overview of the country's economic situation with an emphasis on the impact of the protracted conflict in Rhodesia-Zimbabwe, the development needs of the emerging nation, and implications for foreign assistance.

Microfiche. [Washington, U.S. Agency for International Development, 1979?] 2 sheets.

DLC-Sci RR PN-AAH-159

2897

U.S. *Dept. of State. Bureau of Public Affairs.* Background notes. Zimbabwe. [Washington, for sale by the Supt of Docs., U.S. Govt. Print. Off.], 1982. 7 p. maps. (U.S. Dept. of State. Department of State publication 8104)　　　　G59.U5

L.C. retains only the latest revision.

For a description of the contents of this publication, see the note to entry 937.

2898

Haywood, Willie M. Southern Rhodesia: a society in transition. Carlisle Barracks, Pa., U.S. Army War College, 1975. 18 p. map.

At head of title: USAWC essay.

Microfiche. [s.l., 1976] 1 sheet.

DLC-Sci RR AD A021849

2899

Rotberg, Robert I. Zimbabwe, anticipation of economic and humanitarian needs: Rhodesia. [Washington, African-American Scholars Council], 1977. 21 p. (Transition problems in a developing nation; consultant [occasional] paper, no. 4)

Prepared for the U.S. Agency for International Development under contract AID/afr-C-1154.

"This occasional paper gives an overview of Rhodesia as it prepares to change to majority rule, and it covers history, geography, ethnicity and sectionalism, the administration of Africans, and the administrative reservoir; it also covers the neighboring countries and foreign relations, industrial and consumer markets, transportation, politics, and the liberation struggle."—Abstract.

Abstract in *A.I.D. Research and Development Abstracts*, Oct. 1978, p. 25.

DLC-Sci RR PN-AAF-241

2900

Solarz, Stephen J. Old myths and new realities in Southern Africa. Congressional record, 94th Congress, 2d session, v. 122, Aug. 4, 1976: 25482–25485.　　　　J11.R5 v. 122

Remarks in the U.S. House of Representatives, with emphasis on Rhodesia.

Agriculture

2901

Bratton, Michael. Land and agriculture: policy issues in the transition to Zimbabwe. [s.l.], 1979. [25] p.

DLC

On cover: "Paper presented at the Conference on Zimbabwe-Rhodesia and U.S. Policy, U.S. Department of State, Washington, D.C., July 12–13, 1979."

2902

Ikiara, G. K. Establishment of cooperatives studied. *In* U.S. *Joint Publications Research Service.* JPRS 76584. [Springfield, Va., National Technical Information Service, 1980] (Sub-Saharan Africa report, no. 2304) p. 120–123.

Article in *The Herald-Business Herald*, Salisbury, Sept. 25, 1980, p. 3.

Concerns agricultural cooperatives.

Microfiche. [s.l., 1980]

DLC-Micro JPRS 76584

2903

Langellier, Jean-Pierre. Redistribution of land discussed. *In* U.S. *Joint Publications Research Service.* JPRS 75663. [Springfield, Va., National Technical Information Service, 1980] (Sub-Saharan Africa report, no. 2245) p. 94–97.

Translation of article in *Le Monde*, Paris, Feb. 27, 1980, p. 1, 8.

Microfiche. [s.l., 1980]

DLC-Micro JPRS 75663

2904

McCloskey, Paul N. Repeal of the Rhodesian Land Tenure Act of 1969. Congressional record, 96th Congress, 1st session, v. 125, June 11, 1979: 16154–16155.   J11.R5 v. 125

Extension of remarks in the U.S. House of Representatives.

Includes text of a paper by John Payton on the land tenure situation.

2905

Nziramasanga, Mudziviri. The agricultural sector in Rhodesia. Ann Arbor, Center for Research on Economic Development, University of Michigan, 1977. 41 p. (Transition problems in a developing nation. Occasional paper, no. 7)

Michigan. University. Center for Research on Economic Development. Paper, no. 2.

Prepared for the African-American Scholars Council and the U.S. Agency for International Development under subcontract AID/afr-C-1254.

Abstract in *A.I.D. Research and Development Abstracts*, Oct. 1978, p. 1.

Microfiche. [Washington, U.S. Agency for International Development, 1977?] 1 sheet.

DLC-Sci RR PN-AAF-244

2906

Robbins, Richard D. The agricultural sector of Zimbabwe. [s.l.], 1978. 98 p. map.

Study undertaken in conjunction with the Southern Africa Development Analysis Project, U.S. Agency for International Development.

Bibliography: p. 96–98.

Microfiche. [Washington, U.S. Agency for International Development, 1979?] 2 sheets.

DLC-Sci RR PN-AAH-184

2907

Roder, Wolf. White and black irrigation in Rhodesia. Ann Arbor, Center for Research on Economic Development, 1977. 69 p. maps. (Transition problems in a developing nation. Occasional paper, no. 8)

Michigan. University. Center for Research on Economic Development. paper, no. 3.

Prepared for the African-American Scholars Council and the U.S. Agency for International Development under subcontract AID/afr-C-1254.

Abstract in *A.I.D. Research and Development Abstracts*, Oct. 1978, p. 18.

Microfiche. [Washington, U.S. Agency for International Development, 1977?] 1 sheets.

DLC-Sci RR PN-AAF-245

2908

Shack, William A. Land reform in Zimbabwe: problems and prospects. Berkeley, Dept. of Anthropology, University of California, 1977. 63 p. map. (Transition problems in a developing nation. Occasional paper, no. 15)

Prepared for the African-American Scholars Council and the U.S. Agency for International Development under subcontract AID/afr-C-1254.

Abstract in *A.I.D. Research and Development Abstracts*, Oct. 1978, p. 1.

Microfiche. [Washington, U.S. Agency for International Development, 1977?] 1 sheet.

DLC-Sci RR PN-AAF-252

Economic Aspects

2909

Beef industry decline deplored. *In* U.S. *Joint Publications Research Service.* JPRS 72444. [Springfield, Va., National Technical Information

2909 (cont.)

Service, 1978] (Translations on Sub-Saharan Africa, no. 2038) p. 27–30.

Article in *The Herald*, Salisbury, Nov. 30, 1978, p. 16.

Microfiche. [Washington, Supt. of Docs., U.S. Govt. Print. Off., 1978]

DLC-Micro JPRS 72444

2910

Haresnape, Robert E. Rhodesia's political change may alter tobacco trade. Foreign agriculture, Apr. 25, 1977: 2–4.　　HD1401.F65　1977

Issued by the U.S. Foreign Agricultural Service.

2911

Howard, James O. Zimbabwe's tobacco growers weather a difficult year ... better times ahead? Foreign agriculture, Apr. 1981: 14–16, 35.

HD1401.F65　1981

Issued by the U.S. Foreign Agricultural Service.

2912

Wilson, John H. An independent Zimbabwe moving to reclaim its farm trade position. Foreign agriculture, June 1980: 7–9, 21.　　HD1401.F65　1980

Issued by the U.S. Foreign Agricultural Service.

Includes statistics on production of major agri-culutral commodities for the period 1961–79 and on agricultural exports for 1964–79.

2913

Zimbabwe tobacco industry still intact after sixteen years of sanctions. Washington, U.S. Dept. of Agriculture, Foreign Agricultural Service, 1980. [8] p. (Foreign agriculture circular. Tobacco. FT 10-80)　　S21.F615

Note: Additional reports and statistics on tobacco produc-tion in Africa are given in other numbers in the Tobacco subseries of the Foreign Agriculture Circular.

Assistance Programs

2914

U.S. *Agency for International Development*. Annual budget submission: Zimbabwe. 1983?+ Wash-ington, U.S. International Development Coopera-tion Agency.

Vol. for 1983 issued in Jan. 1981.

Vol. for 1983 examined in the Development Information Center, AID, Washington, D.C.

2915

——— Country development strategy statement: Zimbabwe. 1983?+ Washington, U.S. Interna-tional Development Cooperation Agency.

Vol. for 1983 issued in Feb. 1981.

Vol. for 1983 examined in the Development Information Center, AID, Washington, D.C.

2916

U.S. *Congress. House. Committee on Foreign Affairs. Subcommittee on Africa.* Aid to Zimbabwe: hear-ing, Ninety-sixth Congress, second session, September 23, 1980. Washington, U.S. Govt. Print. Off., 1980. 20 p.　　KF27.F625　1980d

J74.A23 96th

Cong., House Comm.

For. Aff., v. 109

Stephen J. Solarz, chairman.

Witnesses are Cyrus R. Vance, former Secretary of State, and W. Averell Harriman, former gover-nor of New York.

2917

U.S. *Congress. Senate. Committee on Foreign Relations. Subcommittee on Foreign Assistance.* Security assistance authorization: hearings before the Subcommittee on Foreign Assistance, Subcommittee on Africa, and Subcommittee on Arms Control, Oceans, and International Environment of the Committee on Foreign Relations, United States Senate, Ninety-fifth Congress, first session, on S. 1160. Washington, U.S. Govt. Print. Off., 1977., 265 p.

KF26.F6357　1977d

J74.A23 95th Cong.,

Sen. Comm. For. Rel.,

v. 9

Hubert H. Humphrey, chairman, Subcommit-tee on Foreign Assistance.

Dick Clark, chairman, Subcommittee on Africa.

Claiborne Pell, chairman, Subcommittee on Arms Control, Oceans, and International Environment.

Hearings held Apr. 21 – May 2, 1977.

Hearing on Apr. 28, 1977 focused on the Zimbabwe Development Fund; principal witness was William E. Schaufele, Assistant Secretary of State for African Affairs (p. 187–214).

2918

U.S. [*Treaties, etc. Zimbabwe, 1980 Sept. 25*] Agriculture, science and technology. Memo-randum of understanding between the United States of America and Zimbabwe, signed at Salisbury, September 25, 1980. [Washington, Dept. of State; for sale by the Supt. of Docs., U.S. Govt. Print. Off., 1981] 4 p. (Treaties and other international acts series, 10054)　　DLC

2919

Gran, Guy. Anticipated U.S. legislative require-ments for effective U.S. response to a Zimbabwe transition situation. [s.l.], 1977. 94 p. (Transition problems in a developing nation. Occasional paper, no. 3)

Prepared for the African-American Scholars Council and the U.S. Agency for International Development under subcontract AID/afr-C-1254.

Abstract in *A.I.D. Research and Development Abstracts*, Oct. 1978, p. 25.

Microfiche. [Washington, U.S. Agency for International Development, 1977] 2 sheets.

DLC-Sci RR PN-AAF-240

2920

U.S. aid to Zimbabwe; Department statement, Apr. 14, 1980. *In* U.S. *Dept. of State.* The Depart-ment of State bulletin, v. 80, no. 2039, June 1980: 19–20. JX232.A33 v. 80

Read to news correspondents by Department spokesman Hodding Carter.

Commerce

2921

Gibson, Urath C. Marketing in Zimbabwe. Wash-ington, U.S. Dept. of Commerce, International Trade Administration; [for sale by the Supt. of Docs., U.S. Govt. Print. Off.], 1981. 15 p. (Overseas business reports. OBR 81-21)

HF91.U482 1981, no. 21

International marketing information series.

2922

Market share reports. Country series: Rhodesia, 1971–75. [Washington], U.S. Dept. of Commerce; for sale by the National Technical Information Service, Springfield, Va., [1977] 41 p.

Indicates the United States share of the market in Rhodesia for various products compared to the shares for Belgium-Luxemburg, France, Federal Republic of Germany, Great Britain, Italy, Netherlands, Sweden, and Japan.

For most countries, figures not available.

Microfiche. [Washington, Congressional Infor-mation Service, 1977?]

DLC-Micro ASI:77 2016-1.75

2923

Market share reports. Country series: Rhodesia, 1975–79. [Washington], International Trade Administration, U.S. Dept. of Commerce; for sale by the National Technical Information Service, Springfield, Va., [1979] 35 p.

Includes same comparative data as in *Market*

Share Reports. Country Series: Rhodesia, 1971–75 (entry 2922).

For most countries, figures not available.

Microfiche. [Washington, Congressional Infor-mation Service, 1979?]

DLC-Micro ASI:81 2046-2.75

Communications and Transportation

2924

BBC recommendations for ZBC detailed. *In* U.S. *Joint Publications Research Service.* JPRS 76035. [Springfield, Va., National Technical Information Service, 1980] (Sub-Saharan Africa report, no. 2267) p. 125–129.

Article in *The Herald*, Salisbury, June 26, 1980, p. 11.

BBC: British Broadcasting Corporation.

ZBC: Zimbabwe Broadcasting Corporation.

Microfiche. [s.l., 1980]

DLC-Micro JPRS 76035

2925

Humphreys, Isabel. Transportation system potential discussed. *In* U.S. *Joint Publications Research Service.* JPRS 75976. [Springfield, Va., National Technical Information Service, 1980] (Sub-Saharan Africa report, no. 2262) p. 161–166.

Article in *The Herald-Business Herald*, Salis-bury, June 12, 1980, p. 4, 9, 11.

Microfiche. [s.l., 1980]

DLC-Micro JPRS 75976

2926

Pinckney, Annette. Survey of the transport-communications sector. Ann Arbor, Center for Research on Economic Development, University of Michigan, 1977. 13 p. (Transition problems in a developing nation. Occasional paper, no. 12)

Prepared for the African-American Scholars Council and the U.S. Agency for International Development under subcontract AID/afr-C-1254.

Abstract in *A.I.D. Research and Development Abstracts*, Oct. 1978, p. 27.

Microfiche. [Washington, U.S. Agency for International Development, 1977?] 1 sheet.

DLC-Sci RR PN-AAF-249

Economic Conditions

2927

U.S. *Congress. House. Committee on Interna-tional Relations. Subcommittee on International*

2927 (cont.)

Resources, Food, and Energy. Resources in Rhodesia: implications for U.S. policy: hearings, Ninety-fourth Congress, second session, April 13 and May 6, 1976. Washington, U.S. Govt. Print. Off., 1976. 88 p.   KF27.I54947 1976c

Charles C. Diggs, Jr., chairman.

2928

Ashbrook, John M. Rhodesia is thriving. Congressional record, 94th Congress, 2d session, v. 122, Jan. 27, 1976: 1211–1212.

J11.R5 v. 122

Extension of remarks in the U.S. House of Representatives.

Includes article from *Wall Street Journal.*

2929

Berg, Elliot. Growth structure and prospects of the Zimbabwe economy. Ann Arbor, Center for Research on Economic Development, University of Michigan, 1977. [33] p. (Transition problems in a developing nation. Occasional paper, no. 6)

Michigan. University. Center for Research on Economic Development. Paper, no. 1.

Prepared for the African-American Scholars Council and the U.S. Agency for International Development under subcontract AID/afr-C-1254.

Abstract in *A.I.D. Research and Development Abstracts*, Oct. 1978, p. 27.

Microfiche. [Washington, U.S. Agency for International Development, 1977?] 1 sheet.

DLC-Sci RR PN-AAF-243

2930

Broomfield, William S. The U.S. interest in Rhodesia. Congressional record, 95th Congress, 2d session, v. 124, Mar. 10, 1978: 6509–6510.

J11.R5 v. 124

Extension of remarks in the U.S. House of Representatives.

Includes article, "Black Rhodesian workers hope white employers will not flee," from *New York Times.*

2931

Foreign economic trends and their implications for the United States. Zimbabwe. 1981+ Washington, for sale by the Supt. of Docs., U.S. Govt. Print. Off. annual. (International marketing information series)   HC10.E416

Prepared by the U.S. Embassy, Salisbury.

Vols. for 1981- distributed by the U.S. International Trade Administration.

The following issue has been identified in L.C.: FET 81-040. 1981. 11 p.

2932

Nziramasanga, Mudziviri. The manufacturing sector in Rhodesia, 1975–77. [s.l.], 1979. [11] p.

DLC

On cover: "Paper presented at the Conference on Zimbabwe-Rhodesia and U.S. Policy, U.S. Department of State, Washington, D.C., July 12–13, 1979."

2933

Porter, Richard C., *and* Jacqueline R. Sherman. Rhodesian manufacturing and UDI. Ann Arbor, Center for Research on Economic Development, University of Michigan, 1977. 24 p. (Transition problems in a developing nation. Occasional paper, no. 10)

Michigan. University. Center for Research on International Development. Paper, no. 5.

Prepared for the African-American Scholars Council and the U.S. Agency for International Development under subcontract AID/afr-C-1254.

UDI: Unilateral declaration of independence.

Abstract in *A.I.D. Research and Development Abstracts*, Oct. 1978, p. 28.

Microfiche. [Washington, U.S. Agency for International Development, 1977?] 1 sheet.

DLC-Sci RR PN-AAF-247

2934

Rhodesian economy—investing into the 1980s. *In* U.S. *Joint Publication Research Service.* JPRS 75241. [Springfield, Va., National Technical Information Service, 1980] (Sub-Saharan Africa report, no. 2219) p. 83–86.

Article in *The Financial Gazette*, Salisbury, Feb. 8, 1980, p. 17, 18.

Microfiche. [s.l., 1980]

DLC-Micro JPRS 75241

2935

Verblow, Jack. Survey of top industries, companies published. *In* U.S. *Joint Publications Research Service.* JPRS 76157. [Springfield, Va., National Technical Information Service, 1980] (Sub-Saharan Africa report, no. 2274) p. 145–160.

Article in *The Financial Gazette*, Salisbury, July 4, 1980.

Microfiche. [s.l., 1980]

DLC-Micro JPRS 76157

2936

Wolgin, Jerome. Zimbabwe: current economic conditions. [Washington], Economic Development Division, Bureau for Program and Policy Coordination, U.S. Agency for International Development, 1981. 35 p.

2936 (cont.)

Abstract in *A.I.D. Research & Development Abstracts*, v. 10, no. 1/2, 1982, p. 33.

Education

2937

Orbell, S. F. W., D. J. Freer, *and* Elizabeth Hendrikz. Pre-school opportunity and sex differences as factors affecting educational progress. Salisbury, University of Rhodesia, 1973. 30 p. (Series in education; occasional paper, no. 2)　　　LB1140.2.O72

Abstract in *Resources in Education*, Feb. 1976, p. 157.

Microfiche. [Arlington, Va., ERIC Document Reproduction Service; prepared for Educational Resources Information Center, National Institute of Education, 1976] 1 sheet.

DLC-Micro ED113027

2938

Report of an investigation into the possibilities for educational development in Rhodesia-Zimbabwe after a political settlement. Salisbury, 1978. [74] p.

Apparently prepared by the Faculty of Education, University of Rhodesia.

Abstract in *Resources in Education*, May 1979, p. 71.

Microfiche. [Arlington, Va., ERIC Document Reproduction Service; prepared for Educational Resources Information Center, National Institute of Education, 1979] 1 sheet.

DLC-Micro ED163645

2939

Smith, G. A. A report on literacy and development in the Rhodesian Tribal Trust Lands. [Salisbury?] Institute of Adult Education, University of Rhodesia, [1973] 35 p.

Bibliography: p. 33–35.

Abstract in *Research in Education*, Jan. 1974, p. 17.

Microfiche. [Bethesda, Md., ERIC Document Reproduction Service; prepared for Educational Resources Information Center, U.S. Office of Education, 1973] 1 sheet.

DLC-Micro ED080884

2940

Zimbabwe, anticipation of economic and humanitarian needs: educational and training opportunities with Zimbabwe and in neighboring countries during and after transition. [Washington, African-American Scholars Council], 1977. 74 p. (Transition problems in a developing nation; consultant [occasional] paper, no. 17)

Abstract in *A.I.D. Research and Development Abstracts*, Oct. 1978, p. 29–30.

Microfiche. [Washington, U.S. Agency for International Development, 1977?] 1 sheet (PN-AAF-254).

Foreign Relations

2941

Mugomba, Agrippah T. The international dimensions of the Zimbabwe conflict: a position paper. [s.l.], 1979. 17 p.　　　DLC

On cover: "Paper presented at the Conference on Zimbabwe-Rhodesia and U.S. Policy, U.S. Department of State, Washington, D.C. July 12–13, 1979."

2942

Onum, Nduka. Mugabe discusses relationship with Cuba. *In* U.S. *Joint Publications Research Service*. JPRS 71878. [Springfield, Va., National Technical Information Service, 1978] (Translations on Sub-Saharan Africa, no. 1994) p. 104–110.

Interview with Robert Mugabe of ZANU, in *The Punch*, Ikeja, Aug. 22, 1978, p. 12, 13, 18.

Microfiche. [s.l., 1978]

DLC-Micro JPRS 71878

2943

Rhodesia—proposals for a settlement. *In* U.S. *Dept. of State*. The Department of State bulletin, v. 77, no. 1997, Oct. 3, 1977: 417–439.

JX232.A33 v. 77

Joint news conference by British Foreign Secretary David Owen and U.S. Ambassador to the United Nations Andrew Young, London, Sept. 2, 1977, plus the texts of proposals for establishing majority rule in Zimbabwe presented to the British Parliament on Sept. 1 by Secretary Owen.

United States

2944

U.S. *Congress. House. Committee on Foreign Affairs. Subcommittee on Africa.* Review of President Carter's first report to Congress on Rhodesia: hearing, Ninety-sixth Congress, first session, July 25, 1979. Washington, U.S. Govt. Print. Off., 1979. 29 p.　　　KF27.F625　1979c

J74.A23 96th
Cong., House Comm.
For. Aff., v. 34

Stephen J. Solarz, chairman.

Principal witness is Richard M. Moose, Assistant Secretary of State for African Affairs.

2945

U.S. *Congress. House. Committee on International Relations. Subcommittee on Africa.* United States policy toward Rhodesia: a report on the new Anglo-American initiative: hearing, Ninety-fifth Congress, first session, September 7, 1977. Washington, U.S. Govt. Print. Off., 1977. 20 p.

> KF27.I54914 1977e
> J74.A23 95th
> Cong., House Comm.
> Inter. Rel., v. 60

Charles C. Diggs, Jr., chairman.

Witnesses are Andrew Young, U.S. Ambassador to the United Nations, and Richard Moose, Assistant Secretary of State for African Affairs.

2946

U.S. *Congress. Senate. Committee on Foreign Relations.* Rhodesia: hearings, Ninety-sixth Congress, first session ... March 5 and 7, 1979. Washington, U.S. Govt. Print. Off., 1979. 131 p.

> KF26.F6 1979b
> J74.A23 96th
> Cong., Sen. Comm.
> For. Rel., v. 3

Frank Church, chairman.

Hearings, presided over by Sen. George McGovern, focused on the course of the war in Rhodesia, U.S. policy toward the situation, the sanctions issue, and the question of sending observers to monitor the April 1979 Rhodesian election.

2947

U.S. *Congress. Senate. Committee on Foreign Relations. Subcommittee on African Affairs.* Recent developments in Rhodesia: hearing, Ninety-sixth Congress, first session ... July 23, 1979. Washington, U.S. Govt. Print. Off., 1979. 18 p.

> KF 26.F627 1979
> J74.A23 96th
> Cong., Sen. Comm.
> For. Rel., v. 21

George S. McGovern, chairman.

Testimony by Richard M. Moose, Assistant Secretary of State for African Affairs, responding to questions on the Administration's current policy.

2948

U.S. *President, 1977–1981 (Carter)* Meeting with Prime Minister Abel Tendekai Muzorewa of Rhodesia. White House statement. July 11, 1979. *In* U.S. *President.* Public papers of the Presidents of the United States. Jimmy Carter. 1979. [Washington, Office of the Federal Register,

National Archives and Records Service; for sale by the Supt. of Docs., U.S. Govt. Print. Off., 1980] p. 1230.   J80.A283 1979

2949

——— Meeting with Prime Minister Robert Mugabe of Zimbabwe; remarks at a White House reception, August 27, 1980. *In* U.S. *President.* Public papers of the Presidents of the United States. Jimmy Carter. 1980–81. [Washington, Office of the Federal Register, National Archives and Records Service; for sale by the Supt. of Docs., U.S. Govt. Print. Off.] 1982. p. 1579–1584.

> J80.A283   1980–81

Remarks by President Carter and Prime Minister Mugabe, followed by a White House statement, "Meeting with Prime Minister Mugabe of Zimbabwe," (p. 1584–1585).

2950

Africa: Secretary Vance and British Foreign Secretary Owen discuss Rhodesia. *In* U.S. *Dept. of State.* The Department of State bulletin, v. 78, no. 2018, Sept. 1978: 17–18.   JX232.A33 v. 78

Briefing in London, July 20, 1978.

2951

Barber, James. British and American policy and current developments in Zimbabwe-Rhodesia. [s.l.], 1978. 9 p.   DLC

On cover: "Paper presented at the Conference on Zimbabwe-Rhodesia and U.S. Policy, U.S. Department of State, Washington, D.C., July 12–13, 1979."

2952

Blake, James. Southern Rhodesia developments reviewed by Department. *In* U.S. *Dept. of State.* The Department of State bulletin, v. 74, May 3, 1976: 590–592.   JX232.A33 v. 74

2953

Bowman, Larry W. U.S. policy toward Zimbabwe-Rhodesia: regional and international perspectives. [s.l.], 1979. 10 leaves.   DLC

On cover: "Presented to the Department of State Conference on Zimbabwe-Rhodesia and U.S. Policy."

2954

Butcher, Goler T. U.S. policy choices in Zimbabwe. Washington, White, Fine & Verville, 1977. 83, 30 p. (Transition problems in a developing nation. Occasional paper, no. 2)

Prepared for the African-American Scholars Council and the U.S. Agency for International Development under subcontract AID/afr-C-1254.

2954 (cont.)

Appendix: UDI and the impact of sanctions. 30 p.

Abstract in *A.I.D. Research and Development Abstracts*, Oct. 1978, p. 24.

Microfiche. [Washington, U.S. Agency for International Development, 1977?] 2 sheets.

DLC-Sci RR PN-AAF-239

2955

Collins, Cardiss. Testimony on Rhodesia before joint hearing of House Foreign Affairs Subcommittees on Africa and International Organizations. Congressional record [daily ed.], 95th Congress, 1st session, v. 125, May 21, 1979: H3540-H3542.

J11.R7 v. 125

Remarks in the U.S. House of Representatives presenting views of the Congressional Black Caucus concerning United States policy toward Rhodesia.

2956

Crane, Philip M. Kissinger's dangerous plan to crush Rhodesia. Congressional record, 94th Congress, 2d session, v. 122, May 5, 1976: 12730–12732.

J11.R5 v. 122

Extension of remarks in the U.S. House of Representatives.

Includes article, "Kissinger outlines plan to crush Rhodesia," from *Human Events*.

2957

Department discusses situation in Southern Rhodesia. *In* U.S. *Dept. of State*. The Department of State bulletin, v. 73, no. 1855, Aug. 11, 1975: 209–212. JX232.A33 v. 73

Statements by Nathaniel Davis, Assistant Secretary of State for African Affairs, and William B. Buffum, Assistant Secretary of State for International Organization Affairs, before the Subcommittee on African Affairs, Committee on Foreign Relations, U.S. Senate, July 10, 1975.

2958

Dole, Robert J. The Rhodesian visas. Congressional record, 95th Congress, 2d session, v. 124, Oct. 4, 1978: 33430–33431. J11.R5 v. 124

Remarks in the U.S. Senate calling for the approval of visas for Ian D. Smith and Ndabaningi Sithole.

Includes articles from the *Washington Post* and *Washington Star*.

2959

Fraser, Donald M. United States reaffirms position on Southern Rhodesia. *In* U.S. *Dept. of State*. The Department of State bulletin, v. 73, no. 1899, Nov. 17, 1975: 714–715. JX232.A33 v. 73

Statement by Congressman Fraser, U.S. Representative to the United Nations General Assembly, made in Committee IV (Trusteeship), Oct. 9, 1975.

2960

Gann, Lewis H. American policy toward Zimbabwe-Rhodesia: a reappraisal. [s.l.], 1979. 16 p.

DLC

On cover: "Paper distributed at the conference on Zimbabwe-Rhodesia and U.S. Policy, U.S. Department of State, Washington, D.C., July 12–13, 1979."

2961

Helms, Jesse A. The State Department on Rhodesia and rebuttal by Bishop Muzorewa and Prime Minister Smith. Congressional record, 95th Congress, 2d session, v. 124, July 19, 1978: 21680–21684. J11.R5 v. 124

Remarks in the U.S. Senate.

Includes texts of a U.S. Dept. of State press briefing of July 17, Bishop Abel T. Muzorewa's speech at Georgetown University, and a press statement by Prime Minister Ian D. Smith.

2962

McDonald, Steven. United States policy in Zimbabwe/Rhodesia. [s.l.], 1979. 9 leaves. DLC

On cover: "Paper presented at the Conference on Zimbabwe-Rhodesia and U.S. Policy, U.S. Department of State, Washington, D.C., July 12–13, 1979."

2963

McGovern, George S. Ambassador Robert Keeley. Congressional record, [daily ed.], 96th Congress, 2d session, v. 126, June 11, 1980: S6679–S6681.

J11.R7 v. 126

Remarks in the U.S. Senate concerning Robert V. Keeley, the new U.S. Ambassador to Zimbabwe.

Includes article from the *Washington Post*.

2964

Moose, Richard M. Africa: report on Southern Rhodesia. *In* U.S. *Dept. of State*. The Department of State bulletin, v. 79, no. 2031, Oct. 1979: 18–19. JX232.A33 v. 79

Statement by the Assistant Secretary of State for African Affairs before the Subcommittee on African Affairs, Committee on Foreign Relations, U.S. Senate, July 23, 1979.

2965

—— Rhodesia. [Washington], Office of Public Communications, Bureau of Public Affairs, Dept. of State, 1979. 5 p. (U.S. Dept. of State. Current policy, no. 59)   DLC

Testimony before the Committee on Foreign Relations, U.S. Senate, Mar. 7, 1979.

2966

—— Southern Rhodesia: eve of independence. *In* U.S. *Dept. of State.* The Department of State bulletin, v. 80, no. 2039, June 1980: 18–19.

JX232.A33 v. 80

Statement by the Assistant Secretary of State for African Affairs before the Subcommittee on Africa, Committee on Foreign Affairs, U.S. House of Representatives, Mar. 27, 1980.

2967

New policy toward Rhodesia is doubly disastrous. Congressional record, 94th Congress, 2d session, v. 122, Apr. 29, 1976: 11919–11920.

J11.R5 v. 122

Remarks in the U.S. House of Representative.

Principal speakers are Representatives Steven D. Symms, Larry McDonald, and William L. Dickinson.

2968

Rhodesia: US policy. [Washington], Bureau of Public Affairs, U.S. Dept. of State, 1978. 2 p.

DLC

At head of title: Gist: a quick reference aid on U.S. foreign relations primarily for Government use.

2969

Rhodesia (Zimbabwe) [Washington], Bureau of Public Affairs, Dept. of State, 1980. [2] p.

DLC

At head of title: Gist: a quick reference aid on U.S. foreign relations.

2970

Samuels, Michael A. Zimbabwe Rhodesia: policy issues and implications. [s.l.], 1979. 8 p.   DLC

On cover: "Paper presented at the conference on Zimbabwe Rhodesia and U.S. Policy, U.S. Department of State, Washington, D.C., July 12–13, 1979."

2971

Senate Concurrent Resolution 69—submission of a concurrent resolution endorsing Rhodesian settlement. Congressional record, 95th Congress, 2d session, v. 124, Mar. 7, 1978: 5817–5818.

J11.R5 v. 124

Resolution, introduced by Senator Robert Dole, noting that the Mar. 3, 1978 internal agreement "relating to the transition to Majority Rule in Rhodesia, is a positive step towards settlement of internal differences" and recommends that the United States support efforts "toward gaining international recognition for the internal agreement."

2972

Solarz, Stephen J. Rhodesia, where do we go from here?: Report of a study mission to Rhodesia, Mozambique, Zambia, Tanzania, Botswana, and South Africa, April 13–20, 1979, to the Committee on Foreign Affairs, U.S. House of Representatives. Washington, U.S. Govt. Print. Off., 1979. 18 p.

DT962.8.S64

At head of title: 96th Congress, 1st session. Committee print.

Report submitted by Stephen J. Solarz, chairman of the Committee's Subcommittee on Africa, who conducted the study mission.

2973

U.S. reiterates support for negotiated solution in Rhodesia. *In* U.S. *Dept. of State.* The Department of State bulletin, v. 76, no. 1960, Jan. 17, 1977: 53–57.   JX232. A33 v. 76

Statements by William W. Scranton, U.S. Representative in Committee IV (Trusteeship) of the United Nations General Assembly, Dec. 13, 1976; by Richard Petree, U.S. Representative, on Dec. 14, 1976; and by Albert W. Sherer, U.S. Representative, on Dec. 20, 1976, plus the texts of two resolutions adopted by the Committee on Dec. 14 and by the General Assembly on Dec. 20.

2974

Zimbabwe. [Washington], Bureau of Public Affairs, Dept. of State, 1980. [2] p.   DLC

At head of title: Gist: a quick reference aid on U.S. foreign relations.

United States—Economic Sanctions

Note: The following items (entries 2975–3030), listed chronologically by year, concern the issue of economic sanctions by the United States against the minority-controlled government of Rhodesia (Zimbabwe-Rhodesia after the April 1979 elections). The issue of sanctions with respect to certain designated commodities, including chrome ore, had been a major concern of the U.S. Government since 1966; (see The United States and Africa: Guide to U.S. Official Documents and Government-Sponsored Publications on Africa, 1785–1975 *(Z3501.W57),*

2974 (cont.)

especially entries 6034–6107). Key dates in the continuing debate after 1975 are Mar. 18, 1977, when the United States reimposed the ban on the importation of Rhodesian chrome, and Dec. 16, 1979, when President Carter lifted them five days before an agreement was signed in London which introduced an interim British administration and paved the way for an independent Zimbabwe. For a chronological account of U.S. policy on this issue and Congressional debate and votes, see the Congressional Quarterly Almanac *(annual; JK1.C66).*

1975

2975

U.S. *Congress. House. Committee on International Relations. Subcommittee on International Organizations.* The Rhodesian sanctions bill: hearings before the Subcommittee on International Organizations of the Committee on Foreign Affairs, House of Representatives, Ninety-fourth Congress, first session. Washington, U.S. Govt. Print. Off., 1975. 2 v.   KF27.I5494 1975k

J74.A23 94th
Cong., House Comm.
Inter. Rel., v. 24

Donald M. Fraser, chairman.

Hearings in part 2 held before the Subcommittee on International Organizations of the Committee on International Relations, House of Representatives.

Hearings held Feb. 26 – June 19, 1975.

Includes bibliographical references.

Part 2 considers an amendment to H. R, 1287, "a bill to halt the importation of Rhodesian chrome and restore the United States to full compliance with United Nations trade sanctions against Southern Rhodesia."—p. 1.

2976

Department urges passage of bill reimposing full sanctions against Southern Rhodesia. *In* U.S. *Dept. of State.* The Department of State bulletin, v. 72, no. 1865, Mar. 24, 1975: 387–391.

JX232.A33 v. 72

Statements by Julius L. Katz, Deputy Assistant Secretary of State for Economic and Business Affairs, and James Blake, Deputy Assistant Secretary of State for African Affairs, before the Subcommittee on International Organizations and Movements, Committee on Foreign Affairs, House of Representatives, Feb. 26, 1975.

2977

[Economic sanctions—Southern Rhodesia] *In* McDowell, Eleanor C. Digest of United States

practice in international law. 1975. [Washington, Dept. of State; for sale by the Supt. of Docs., U.S. Govt. Print. Off., 1976] (Department of State publication, 8865) p. 693–694.   JX21.R68 1975

The Ford Administration supports H.R. 1287, a bill to halt the importation of Rhodesian chrome.

2978

James, Charles A. Repeal urged of Byrd Amendment on chrome from Southern Rhodesia. *In* U.S. *Dept. of State.* The Department of State bulletin, v. 73, no. 1882, July 21, 1975: 102–103.

JX232.A33 v. 73

Statement by the Deputy Assistant Secretary of State for African Affairs before the Subcommittee on International Organizations of the Committee on International Relations, House of Representatives, June 19, 1975.

1976

2979

Strack, Harry R. The influence of transnational actors on the enforcement of sanctions against Rhodesia. Naval War College review, v. 28, no. 4, spring 1976: 52–64.   V1.U48 1976

Issued by the U.S. Naval War College, Newport, R.I.

Excerpts from the author's *Sanctions: the Case of Rhodesia* (Syracuse, N.Y., Syracuse University Press, 1978. 296 p. DT962.62.S86).

2980

Tunney, John V. Importation of goods from Rhodesia—Senate Joint Resolution 191. Congressional record, 94th Congress, 2d session, v. 122, Apr. 28, 1976: 11495–11497.   J11.R5 v. 122

Remarks in the U.S. Senate.

Senator Tunney commends the Ford Administration for supporting the repeal of the "Byrd Amendment."

1977

2981

U.S. *Congress. House. Committee on International Relations.* Amending the United Nations Participation Act of 1945 to halt the importation of Rhodesian chrome: report together with additional, supplemental, minority, and dissenting views (to accompany H. R. 1746). [Washington, U.S. Govt. Print. Off.], 1977. 19 p.   DLC-LL

Report submitted by Representative Donald M. Fraser.

At head of title: 95th Congress, 1st session. House of Representatives. Report no. 95-59.

"The primary purpose of H. R. 1746 is to allow

2981 (cont.)

reimposition of the embargo on imports of chrome ore, ferrochrome, and nickel from Rhodesia and thus return the United States to full compliance with United Nations economic sanctions."

2982

U.S. *Congress. House. Committee on International Relations. Subcommittee on Africa.* The Rhodesian sanctions bill: hearings before the Subcommittees on Africa and International Organizations of the Committee on International Relations, House of Representatives, Ninety-fifth Congress, first session, on H.R. 1746, February 24, 1977. Washington, U.S. Govt. Print. Off., 1977. 68 p.

> KF27.I54914 1977
> J74.A23 95th
> Cong., House Comm.
> Inter. Rel., v. 2

Charles C. Diggs, Jr., chairman, Subcommittee on Africa.

Donald M. Frasesr, chairman, Subcommittee on International Organizations.

H.R. 1746: "A bill to amend the United Nations Participation Act or 1945 to halt the importation of Rhodesian chrome."

2983

—— United States policy toward Rhodesia: hearing, Ninety-fifth Congress, first session, June 8, 1977. Washington, U.S. Govt. Print. Off., 1978. 72 p.

> K27.I54914 1977m
> J74.A23 95th
> Cong., House Comm.
> Inter. Rel., v. 103

Charles C. Diggs, Jr., chairman.

Includes documentation on allegations that Mobil Oil Corporation's South African subsidiary was supplying petroleum products to Rhodesia in violation of sanctions regulations. p. 22–59.

2984

U.S. *Congress. Senate. Committee on Foreign Relations.* Rhodesian sanctions: report (to accompany S. 174) [Washington?, 1977] 13 p.   DLC-LL

Report submitted by Senator Dick Clark.

At head of title: 95th Congress, 1st session. Senate. Report no. 95-37.

The purpose of bill no. S. 174 was to amend the United Nations Participation Act of 1945 to halt the importation of Rhodesian chrome.

2985

U.S. *Congress. Senate. Committee on Foreign Relations. Subcommittee on African Affairs.* Rhodesian sanctions: hearings, Ninety-fifth Congress, first session on S. 174 . . . February 9 and

10, 1977. Washington, U.S. Govt. Print. Off., 1977. 81 p.

> KF26.F625 1977
> J74.A23 95th
> Cong., Sen. Comm.
> For. Rel., v. 17

Dick Clark, chairman.

Consideration of S. 174, a bill to amend the United Nations Participation Act of 1945 to halt the importation of Rhodesian chrome; among the witnesses were Cyrus R. Vance, Secretary of State, and Julius L. Katz, Assistant Secretary of State for Economic and Business Affairs.

2986

U.S. *General Accounting Office.* Implementation of economic sanctions against Rhodesia: report of the Comptroller General of the United States. [Washington], 1977. 41 p.

> HF1456.R5U52 1977

"ID-77-27."

"B-187410."

Report prepared at the request of Senator Edward M. Kennedy.

"The economic and political existence of Rhodesia for the past 11 years is evidence that the sanctions have not been completely effective. . . . The U.S. has established mechanisms to enforce the sanctions and has acted against some of its businesses and individuals and against firms in third countries.—cover.

2987

U.S. *President, 1977–1981 (Carter)* Rhodesian chrome bill. Remarks on signing H.R. 1746 into law. March 18, 1977. *In* U.S. *President.* Public papers of the Presidents of the United States. Jimmy Carter. 1977. [Washington, Office of the Federal Register, National Archives and Records Service; for sale by the Supt. of Docs., U.S. Govt. Print. Off., 1977] p. 451–453.

> J80.A283 1977

Measure restoring Executive authority to re-establish an embargo against the purchase of Rhodesian chrome.

2988

Amending United Nations Participation Act of 1945 to halt importation of Rhodesian chrome. Congressional record, 95th Congress, 1st session, v. 123, Mar 14, 1977: 7416–7448.

> J11.R5 v. 123

Remarks in the U.S. House of Representatives on H.R. 1746 calling for repeal of the "Byrd Amendment." The vote to pass the bill is given on p. 7448.

2989

Department urges passage of bill to halt the importation of Rhodesian chrome. *In* U.S. *Dept. of State.* The Department of State bulletin, v. 76, no. 1966, Feb. 28, 1977: 170–174.

JX232.A33 v. 76

Statements by Cyrus R. Vance, Secretary of State, and Julius L. Katz, Assistant Secretary of State for Economic and Business Affairs, before the Subcommittee on African Affairs, Committee on Foreign Relations, U.S. Senate, Feb. 10, 1977.

2990

The Hypocrisy of international politics surrounding the United Nations sanctions against Rhodesia. Congressional record, 95th Congress, 1st session, v. 123, Mar. 7, 1977: 6460–6464.

J11.R5 v. 123

Remarks in the U.S. House of Representatives, primarily by Representative Richard Ichord.

2991

Importation of Rhodesian chrome. Congressional record, 95th Congress, 1st session, v. 123, Mar. 11, 1977: 7336–7348. J11.R5 v. 123

Consideration in the U.S. Senate of S. 174, "to amend the United Nations Participation Act of 1945 to halt the importation of Rhodesian chrome."

2992

Importation of Rhodesian chrome. Congressional record, 95th Congress, 1st session, v. 123, Mar. 14, 1977: 7385–7403. J11.R5 v. 123

Continued consideration in the U.S. Senate of S. 174.

2993

Importation of Rhodesian chrome. Congressional record, 95th Congress, 1st session, v. 123, Mar. 15, 1977: 7604–7606. J11.R5 v. 123

Consideration in the U.S. Senate of H.R. 1746, a bill to halt the importation of Rhodesian chrome; the vote passing the bill is given on p. 7606.

2994

McDonald, Larry. Embargo on chrome: it puts the U.S. seal of approval on aggression. Congressional record, 95th Congress, 1st session, v. 123, Mar. 30, 1977: 9737–9739. J11.R5 v. 123

Extension of remarks in the U.S. House of Representatives.

Includes article from *Barron's.*

2995

Porter, Richard C. Economic sanctions: the theory and the evidence from Rhodesia. Ann Arbor,

Center for Research on Economic Development, University of Michigan, 1977 19 p (Michigan, University. Center for Research on Economic Development. Discussion paper, no. 68)

Abstract in *A.I.D. Research and Development Abstracts,* Jan. 1979, p. 16.

Microfiche. [Washington, U.S. Agency for International Development, 1977?] 1 sheet.

DLC-Sci RR PN-AAD-395

2996

———— The effectiveness of economic sanctions against Rhodesia. Ann Arbor, Center for Research on Economic Development, University of Michigan, 1977. 15 p. (Transition problems in a developing nation. Occasional paper, no. 9).

Michigan. University. Center for Research on Economic Development. Paper, no. 4.

Prepared for the African-American Scholars Council and the U.S. Agency for International Development under subcontract AID/afr-C-1254.

Abstract in *A.I.D. Research and Development Abstracts,* Oct. 1978, p. 27.

Microfiche. [Washington, U.S. Agency for International Development, 1977?] 1 sheet.

DLC-Sci RR PN-AAF-246

2997

Providing for consideration of H.R. 1746, United Nations Participation Act of 1945 to halt importation of Rhodesian chrome. Congressional record, 95th Congress, 1st session, v. 123, Mar. 14, 1977: 7410–7416. J11.R5 v. 123

Remarks in the U.S. House of Representatives.

2998

[Southern Rhodesia] *In* Boyd, John A. Digest of United States practice in international law. 1977. [Washington], Office of the Legal Adviser, Dept. of State; [for sale by the Supt. of Docs., U.S. Govt. Print. Off., 1979] (Department of State publication, 8960) p. 830–834, 392–896.

JX21.R68 1977

Brief references to the Rhodesian situation; additional references are indicated in the index.

2999

U.S. supports expansion of sanctions against Rhodesia. *In* U.S. *Dept. of State.* The Department of State bulletin, v. 77, no. 1985, July 11, 1977: 66–67. JX232.A33 v. 77

Statement by James F. Leonard, Acting U.S. Permanent Representative, in the United Nations Security Council, May 27, 1977, together with the text of a resolution adopted by the Council.

1978

3000

U.S. *Congress. House. Committee on Appropriations.*
International security assistance act of 1978; conference report (to accompany S. 3075) [Washing-
ton] 1978. 46 p.   DLC-LL

Report submitted by Representative Clement J.
Zablocki.

At head of title: 95th Congress, 2d session.
House of Representatives. Report no. 95-1546.

Section 27 concerns the Rhodesian embargo
(p. 17); the committee's action on this issue is
explained on p. 29–30.

3001

Byrd, Harry F., Jr. American policy in Rhodesia.
Congressional record, 95th Congress, 2d session,
v. 124, Feb. 2, 1978: 2143–2144.

J11.R5 v. 124

Extension of remarks in the U.S. Senate.

Includes articles from the *Richmond Times-
Dispatch* and *Washington Star.*

3002

Foreign Relations Authorization Act, 1979. Congressional record, 95th Congress, 2d session,
v. 124, June 28, 1978: 19211–19224.

J11.R5 v. 124

Debate in the U.S. Senate on the question of
lifting sanctions against Rhodesia.

Senator Jesse Helms introduces an amendment
lifting sanctions and includes documents relating
to the internal constitutional agreement of Mar. 3,
1978.

3003

Heinz, John. U.S. policy in Rhodesia. Congressional
record, 95th Congress, 2d session, v. 124, Aug. 23,
1978: 27492–27493.   J11.R5 v. 124

Remarks in the U.S. Senate.

3004

Helms, Jesse A. The Senate consensus on Rhodesia:
94 Senators. Congressional record, 95th Congress,
2d session, v. 124, Aug. 1, 1978: 23664–23666.

J11.R5 v. 124

Remarks in the U.S. Senate.

Includes articles from the *San Diego Union* and
Washington Star.

1979

3005

U.S. *Congress. House. Committee on Foreign Affairs.*
Rhodesian sanctions, should the United States lift
them? Hearing and markup before the Committee

on Foreign Affairs and its Subcommittees on
Africa and on International Organizations, House
of Representatives, Ninety-Sixth Congress, first
session on S. 2076, December 5 and 11, 1979.
Washington, U.S. Govt. Print. Off., 1980. 80 p.

KF27.F6   1979j
J74.A23
96th Cong.,
House Comm. For.
Aff., v. 58

Clement J. Zablocki, chairman.

Stephen J. Solarz, chairman, Subcommittee on
Africa.

Don Bonker, chairman, Subcommittee on
International Organizations.

S. 2076, introduced on Dec. 4, 1979, would require the President to terminate sanctions against
Zimbabwe-Rhodesia under certain circumstances.

3006

——— Zimbabwe-Rhodesia: the issue of sanctions;
report, together with supplemental views (to accompany H.R. 4439) [Washington], 1979. 13 p.

DLC-LL

Report submitted by Representative Stephen J.
Solarz.

At head of title: 96th Congress, 1st session.
House of Representatives. Report no. 96–283.

The purpose of H.R. 4439 was to direct the
President to terminate sanctions by Oct. 15, 1979
unless he determined that it would not be in the
national interest to do so.

Includes a legislative history of the sanctions
issue.

3007

U.S. *Congress. House. Committee on Foreign Affairs.
Subcommittee on Africa.* Economic sanctions
against Rhodesia: hearings before the Subcommittees on Africa and on International Organizations of the Committee on Foreign Affairs,
House of Representatives, Ninety-sixth Congress,
first session. Washington, U.S. Govt. Print. Off.,
1979. 475 p. illus., map.   KF27.F625   1970d

Stephen J. Solarz, chairman, Subcommittee on
Africa.

Don Bonker, chairman, Subcommittee on
International Organizations.

Hearings held Apr. 2–May 21, 1979.

Among the appendixes are the following:

Appendix 7. Report of American Security
Council's factfinding mission to Zimbabwe-
Rhodesia elections. p. 253–279.

Appendix 8. "Free and fair? The Rhodesian
election," a report by observers on behalf of the
British Parliamentary Human Rights Group—
May 1979. p. 280–347.

3007 (cont.)

Includes tables showing election results by province.

Appendix 9. Report of the Freedom House mission to observe the common roll election in Zimbabwe-Rhodesia—April 1979. p. 348–415.

Indicates, by province, the percentage of the vote won by each party.

Appendix 10. Report of the American Conservative Union Factfinding mission to Zimbabwe-Rhodesia elections along with biographical sketches of members. p. 416–466.

3008

——— United States policy toward Rhodesia: hearings, Ninety-sixth Congress, first session. Washington, U.S. Govt. Print. Off., 1979. 245 p.

> KF27.F625 1979b
> J74.A23 96th
> Cong., House Comm.
> For. Aff., v. 11

Stephen J. Solarz, chairman.

Hearings held Mar. 22 – Apr. 2, 1979.

In his opening statement, Chairman Solarz indicates the importance of laying "a firm foundation for the Congress before it proceeds to reach whatever decisions it ultimately decides to take in connection with sanctions or any other aspects of our foreign policy toward Rhodesia."—p. i.

3009

U.S *Congress. Senate. Committee on Foreign Relations.* A bill to terminate sanctions against Zimbabwe-Rhodesia under certain circumstances: report (to accompany S. 2076) [Washington, 1979] 9 p.   DLC-LL

Report submitted by Senator Claiborne Pell.

At head of title: 96th Congress, 1st session. Senate. Report no. 96-447.

Includes a background statement on Congressional action in the sanctions question.

"Calendar no. 480."

3010

——— Concurrent resolution to terminate sanctions against Zimbabwe-Rhodesia: report (to accompany S. Con. Res. 51) [Washington, 1979] 8 p.

> DLC-LL

Report submitted by Senator Claiborne Pell.

At head of title: 96th Congress, 1st session. Senate. Report no. 96-448.

"Calendar no. 481."

3011

——— Rhodesia: hearings, Ninety-sixth Congress, first session. Washington, U.S. Govt. Print. Off.,

1980. 59 p.

> KF26.F6 1979ab
> J74.A23 96th
> Cong., Sen. Comm.
> For. Rel., v. 26

Frank Church, chairman; George McGovern, presiding officer.

Concerns the question of lifting economic sanctions; principal witness is Richard M. Moose, Assistant Secretary of State for African Affairs.

3012

——— Trade sanctions against Rhodesia: hearing, Ninety-sixth Congress, first session, on President Carter's decision not to lift trade sanctions against Rhodesia, June 12, 1979. 35 p.

> KF26.F 1979o
> J74.A23 96th
> Cong., Sen. Comm.
> For. Rel., v. 15

Frank Church, chairman.

Witness is Cyrus R. Vance, Secretary of State.

Concerns the President's decision of June 7, 1979 not to lift the sanctions.

3013

U.S. *President, 1977–1981 (Carter)* Revoking Rhodesian sanctions. Executive Order 12183. December 16, 1979. *In* U.S. *President.* Public papers of the Presidents of the United States. Jimmy Carter. 1979. [Washington, Office of the Federal Register, National Archives and Records Service; for sale by the Supt. of Docs., U.S. Govt. Print. Off., 1980] p. 2251–2252.

> J80.A283 1979

3014

——— Settlement of conflict in Zimbabwe-Rhodesia. White House statement. December 17, 1979. *In* U.S. *President.* Public papers of the Presidents of the United States. Jimmy Carter. 1979. [Washington, Office of the Federal Register, National Archives and Records Service; for sale by the Supt. of Docs., U.S. Govt. Print. Off., 1980] p. 2262–2263.   J80.A283 1979

Concerns the final Lancaster House agreement.

3015

——— Trade sanctions against Rhodesia. Remarks announcing continuation of the U.S. sanctions. June 7, 1979. *In* U.S. *President.* Public papers of the Presidents of the United States. Jimmy Carter 1979. [Washington, Office of the Federal Register, National Archives and Records Service; for sale by the Supt. of Docs., U.S. Govt. Print. Off., 1980] p. 1012–1014.   J80.A283 1979

3016

———— Trade sanctions against Zimbabwe-Rhodesia. Memorandum from the President. November 14, 1979. *In* U.S. *President.* Public papers of the Presidents of the United States. Jimmy Carter. 1979. [Washington, Office of the Federal Register, National Archives and Records Service; for sale by the Supt. of Docs., U.S. Govt. Print. Off., 1980] p. 2120–2121.

J80.A283 1979

A memorandum for the Secretary of State stating that the President has determined "that it is in the national interest of the United States to continue sactions against Zimbabwe-Rhodesia at this time;" includes a statement justifying this action.

3017

Africa: decisions on Southern Rhodesia sanctions. *In* U.S. *Dept. of State.* The Department of State bulletin, v. 79, no. 2029, Aug. 1979: 25–30.

JX232.A33 v. 79

Remarks by President Jimmy Carter taken from the weekly compilation of presidential documents, June 11, 1979, and a White House press release of June 7, 1979, plus statement by Secretary of State Cyrus Vance before the Committee on Foreign Relations, Senate, and the Committee on Foreign Affairs, House of Representatives, June 12, 1979.

3018

Aid to Uganda. Congressional record [daily ed.], 96th Congress, 1st session, v. 125, May 7, 1979: S5359–S5418.

J11.R7 v. 125

Includes discussion in the U.S. Senate on sanctions against Rhodesia, plus text of an analysis of trade restrictions prepared by the Lawyers' Committee for Civil Rights under Law (p. S5399–S5417).

3019

Defense authorizations, 1980—conference report. Congressional record [daily ed.], 96th Congress, 1st session, v. 125, Oct. 23, 1979: S14922–S14926.

J11.R7 v. 125

Remarks in the U.S. Senate include Senator Jesse Helms' comments on the issue of lifting sanctions.

3020

Defense authorizations, 1980—conference report. Congressional record [daily ed.], 96th Congress, 1st session, v. 125, Oct. 24, 1979: S15074–S15080.

J11.R7 v. 125

In debate in the U.S. Senate, Senator Harry F. Byrd, Jr. calls attention to section 818 mandating the lifting of sanctions against Zimbabwe-Rhodesia (p. S15076–S15078).

3021

Department of Defense Authorization Act, 1980. Congressional record, 96th Congress, 1st session, v. 125, June 12, 1979: 14304–14354.

J11.R5 v. 125

Debate in the U.S. Senate include frequent remarks on Africa, especially the issue of sanctions against Rhodesia.

3022

Hatch, Orrin G. Economic sanctions against Zimbabwe-Rhodesia. Congressional record, 96th Congress, 1st session, v. 125, June 12, 1979: 14370–14371. J11.R5 v. 125

Remarks in the U.S. Senate.

Includes statement by Prime Minister Abel T. Muzorewa of Zimbabwe-Rhodesia.

3023

Sanctions on Zimbabwe-Rhodesia. Congressional record, 96th Congress, 1st session, v. 125, June 28, 1979: 17195–17225. J11.R5 v. 125

Debate in the U.S. House of Representatives on H. Res. 325 concerning the sanctions issue; it relates to H.R. 4439, a bill directing the President to terminate sanctions by Oct. 15, 1979.

3024

Senate Concurrent Resolution 25—submission of a concurrent resolution on the non-enforcement of sanctions against Zimbabwe Rhodesia. Congressional record, 96th Congress, 1st session, v. 125, Apr. 23, 1979: 8287–8288. J11.R5 v. 125

Introduced in the U.S. Senate by Senator Richard S. Schweiker.

3025

Senate Concurrent Resolution 51–submission of a concurrent resolution with respect to sanctions against Zimbabwe-Rhodesia. Congressional record, [daily ed.], 96th Congress, 1st session, v. 125, Nov. 14, 1979: S16636–S16638.

J11.R7 v. 125

Remarks in the U.S. Senate on a resolution introduced by Senator Jesse Helms.

3026

Solarz, Stephen J. Economic sanctions on Zimbabwe-Rhodesia. Congressional record, [daily ed.], 95th Congress, 1st session, v. 125, Sept. 14, 1979: E4519–E4520. J11.R7 v. 125

Extension of remarks in the U.S. House of Representatives.

Includes report from President Carter on political developments in that country for the period July–August 1979.

3027

——— Vance explains administration's Rhodesian policy. Congressional record, 96th Congress, 1st session, v. 125, June 22, 1979: 16211–16214.

J11.R5 v. 125

Extension of remarks in the U.S. House of Representatives.

Includes text of testimony by Secretary of State Cyrus R. Vance before the House Committee on Foreign Affairs concerning the maintenance of sanctions.

3028

Termination of sanctions against Zimbabwe-Rhodesia. Congressional record [daily ed.], 96th Congress, 1st session, v. 125, Dec. 6, 1979: S17900–S17909. J11.R7 v. 125

Debate in the U.S. Senate on S. 2076, a bill "to require the President to terminate sanctions against Zimbabwe-Rhodesia under certain circumstances."

3029

Thurmond, Strom. Rhodesian sanctions must be lifted. Congressional record [daily ed.], 96th Congress, 1st session, v. 125, May 9, 1979: S5543–S5547. J11.R7 v. 125

Remarks in the U.S. Senate.

Includes article, "Eyewitness report on the Rhodesian elections," from *Human Events.*

3030

Tsongas, Paul E. Senate Resolution 301—submission of a resolution with respect to sanctions against Rhodesia. Congressional record [daily ed.], 95th Congress, 1st session, v. 125, Dec. 5, 1979: S17874–S17875. J11.R7 v. 125

Remarks in the U.S. Senate.

Resolution states that "President Carter should remove the economic sanctions imposed on Rhodesia, and that such action should become effective on the date the British governor of Rhodesia arrives in Salisbury."

Geography and Maps

3031

[U.S. *Central Intelligence Agency*] Southern Rhodesia (U.K.) [Washington, 1976] col. map.

G8560 1976.U51

Scale ca. 1 : 5,500,000.

"Base 503025 7-76."

Relief shown by shading.

3032

——— Southern Rhodesia (U.K.) [Washington, 1979] col. map. G8650 1979.U5

Scale 1 : 2,170,000.

"503850 2-79 (543857)."

"Transverse Mercator projection."

Relief shown by shading and spot heights.

Includes maps of "Population," "Land apportionment," "Economic activity," "Mining," and "Vegetation," comparative area map, location map, and "Ethnolinguistic composition" diagr.

3033

——— Southern Rhodesia (U.K.) [Washington, 1979] col. map. G8560 1979.U51

Scale 1 : 2,170,000.

"Base 503381 2-79 (543857)."

"Transverse Mercator projection."

Geology, Hydrology, and Mineral Resources

3034

Black, R. Anthony. The mining sector of the Rhodesian economy. Ann Arbor, Center for Research on Economic Development, University of Michigan, 1977. 9 p. (Transition problems in a developing nation. Occasional paper, no. 14)

Prepared for the African-American Scholars Council and the U.S. Agency for International Development under subcontract AID/afr-C-1254.

Abstract in *A.I.D. Research and Development Abstracts*, Oct. 1978, p. 28.

Microfiche. [Washington, U.S. Agency for International Development, 1977?] 1 sheet.

DLC-Sci RR PN-AAF-251

3035

Jolly, Janice L. W. The mineral industry of Southern Rhodesia. *In* Minerals yearbook, v. 3, 1975. [Washington, for sale by the Supt. of Docs., U.S. Govt. Print. Off., 1978] p. 867–874.

TN23.U612 1975, v. 3

Prepared by the U.S. Bureau of Mines.

3036

——— The mineral industry of Southern Rhodesia. *In* Minerals yearbook, v. 3, 1976. [Washington, for sale by the Supt. of Docs., U.S. Govt. Print. Off., 1980] p. 883–891.

TN23.U612 1976, v. 3

Prepared by the U.S. Bureau of Mines.

3037

—— The mineral industry of Southern Rhodesia. *In* Minerals yearbook, v. 3, 1977. [Washington, for sale by the Supt. of Docs., U.S. Govt. Print. Off., 1981] p. 785–791.

TN23.U612   1977, v. 3

Prepared by the U.S. Bureau of Mines.

3038

—— The mineral industry of Southern Rhodesia. *In* Minerals yearbook, v. 3, 1978–79. [Washington, U.S. Govt. Print. Off., 1981] p. 785–792.

TN23.U612   1978–79, v. 3

Prepared by the U.S. Bureau of Mines.

3039

Morgan, George A. The mineral industry of Zimbabwe. *In* Minerals yearbook, v. 3, 1980. [Washington, for sale by the Supt. of Docs., U.S. Govt. Print. Off., 1982] p. 1145–1155.

TN23.U612   1980, v. 3

Prepared by the U.S. Bureau of Mines.

3040

Mining industry developments, outlook reported. *In* U.S. *Joint Publications Research Service.* JPRS 76456. [Springfield, Va., National Technical Information Service, 1980] (Sub-Saharan Africa report, no. 2294) p. 162–168.

Excerpts from series of articles in *The Herald-Business Herald*, Salisbury, Sept. 4, 1980, p. 3–12.

Microfiche. [s.l., 1980]

DLC-Micro JPRS 76456

Health and Nutrition

3041

Cohn, Helen. A review of health care in Rhodesia: issues, analyses, and recommendations. Washington, Family Health Care, inc., 1978. 94 p. (Health and development in Southern Africa, v. 7)

Submitted to the Southern Africa Development Analysis Program, U.S. Agency for International Development.

Bibliography: p. 91–94.

Issued in cooperation with Africare.

Microfiche. [Washington, U.S. Agency for International Development, 1979] 1 sheet.

DLC-Sci RR PN-AAH-167

3042

National health service plan discussed in Assembly. *In* U.S. *Joint Publications Research Service.* JPRS 76293. [Springfield, Va., National Technical Information Service, 1980] (Sub-Saharan Africa report, no. 2283) p. 44–47.

A parliamentary discussion of a planned free national health service, reported in *The Herald*, Salisbury, Aug. 14, 1980, p. 4.

Microfiche. [s.l., 1980]

DLC-Micro JPRS 76293

3043

Watson, James C. Health consequences of transition in Zimbabwe. [Houston, Tex.?], 1977. 101 p. (Transition problems in a developing country. Occasional paper, no. 16)

Prepared for the African-American Scholars Council and the U.S. Agency for International Development under subcontract AID/afr-C-1254.

Abstract in *A.I.D. Research and Development Abstracts*, Oct. 1978, p. 33.

Microfiche. [Washington, U.S. Agency for International Development, 1977?] 2 sheets.

DLC-Sci RR PN-AAF-253

Housing and Urban Development

3044

Wright, James, David Oakley, *and* Lee Baker. Zimbabwe shelter sector assessment. [s.l., PADCO], 1981. 99 p. illus., map.

Prepared for the Office of Housing, U.S. Agency for International Development.

PADCO: Planning and Development Cooperative.

Abstract in *A.I.D. Research & Development Abstracts*, v. 9, no. 3, 1981, p. 49.

Microfiche. [Washington, U.S. Agency for International Development, 1981] 2 sheets.

DLC-Sci RR PN-AAJ-277

3045

Zimbabwe shelter sector assessment: technical appendices. Washington, Office of Housing, Agency for International Development, 1981. 82 p. maps.

Microfiche. [Washington, U.S. Agency for International Development, 1981] 1 sheet (PN-AAJ-278); held by the Development Information Center, AID, Washington, D.C.

Politics and Government

3046

U.S. *Congress. House. Committee on International Relations. Subcommittee on Africa.* Political developments in Southern Rhodesia, fall, 1977: hearing, Ninety-fifth Congress, first session, October 4,

3046 (cont.)
1977. Washington, U.S. Govt. Print. Off., 1978.
63 p.   KF27.I54914 1977h
J74.A23 95th
Cong., House Comm.
Inter. Rel., v. 63
Charles C. Diggs, Jr., chairman.
Appendix: Testimony regarding the supply of oil to Rhodesia made before the Sanctions Committee of the United Nations Security Council by Bernard Rivers, representing the Haslemere Group, July 25, 1977. p. 31–63.

3047
U.S. *Congress. Senate. Committee on Foreign Relations.* A Rhodesian settlement? Analysis of an agreement signed by Prime Minister Ian Smith of Rhodesia, the Reverend Ndabaningi Sithole, Bishop Abel Muzorewa, and Senator Jerimiah Chirau on March 3, 1978: a staff report to the Committee on Foreign Relations, United States Senate. Washington, for sale by the Supt. of Docs., U.S. Govt. Print. Off., 1978. 15 p.
           DT962.75.U55 1978
John Sparkman, chairman.
At head of title: 95th Congress, 2d session. Committee print.
"This analysis of the Rhodesian internal agreement was made at the request of Senator Dick Clark, Chairman of the Subcommittee on African Affairs of the Foreign Relations Committee. It consists of a study of the provisions of the Rhodesian agreement signed on March 3, 1978, focusing on the strengths and weaknesses of the accord, the role of black public opinion, the kinds of decisions the settlement presents for the international community, and its significance for U.S. foreign policy.—p. iii.
Appendix: Text of Rhodesian agreement preparing the way for majority rule. p. 11–15.

3048
Ashbrook, John M. John Davenport on Rhodesia, Congressional record, 95th Congress, 2d session, v. 124, Apr. 19, 1978: 10874–10877.
           J11.R5 v. 124
Extension of remarks in the U.S. House of Representatives.
Includes article from the *National Review* on the politics and foreign relations of Rhodesia.

3049
Baker, Howard H. The role of Senator Helms at the London conference on Rhodesia. Congressional record [daily ed.], 96th Congress, 1st session, v. 125, Sept. 27, 1979: S13532–S13533.
           J11.R7 v. 125

Remarks in the U.S. Senate.
Includes article from the *Wall Street Journal.*

3050
Baker, Pauline H. The birth of Zimbabwe: a turning point for Southern Africa: a report to the Committee on Foreign Relations, United States Senate, May 1980. Washington, U.S. Govt. Print. Off., 1980. 21 p. illus.   DT962.8.B34
At head of title: 96th Congress, 2d session. Committee print.
Based on the author's trip to Zimbabwe, South Africa, Mozambique, and Great Britain; assesses the impact of the election of Robert G. Mugabe as Prime Minister of Zimbabwe on U.S. policy in Southern Africa.

3051
Bond, George C. Zimbabwe, anticipation of economic and humanitarian needs: local government and political integration. [Washington, African-American Scholars Council], 1977. 25 p. (Transition problems in a developing nation; consultant [occasional] paper, no. 1)
Prepared for the U.S. Agency for International Development under contract AID/afr-C-1254.
Abstract in *A.I.D. Research and Development Abstracts,* Oct. 1978, p. 36–37.
Microfiche. [Washington, U.S. Agency for International Development, 1977?] 1 sheet. (PN-AAF-238); examined in the Development Information Center, AID, Washington, D.C.

3052
Byrd, Harry F., Jr. Rhodesia and American security. Congressional record, 96th Congress, 1st session, v. 125, Feb. 8, 1979: 2128–2129.
           J11.R5 v. 125
Remarks in the U.S. Senate.
Includes editorial, "'Neo-Fascism' in Rhodesia," from the *Washington Post.*

3053
Duncan, Marion. Disillusionment of white Zimbabweans in SA. *In* U.S. *Joint Publications Research Service.* JPRS 76456. [Springfield, Va., National Technical Information Service, 1980] (Sub-Saharan Africa report, no. 2294) p. 3–8.
Article on reasons for the flight of whites from Zimbabwe to South Africa, in *The Star,* Johannesburg, Aug. 26, 1980, p. 24–25.
Microfiche. [s.l., 1980]
           DLC-Micro JPRS 76456

3054
Esibi, John. Minister says whites cooperating with new government. *In* U.S. *Joint Publications*

3054 (cont.)

Research Service. JPRS 75971. [Springfield, Va., National Technical Information Service, 1980] (Sub-Saharan Africa report, no. 2261) p. 105–111.

Interview with Richard Hove, Minister of Public Service, in *Sunday Nation*, Nairobi, June 1, 1980, p. 10.

Microfiche. [s.l., 1980]

DLC-Micro JPRS 75971

3055

Garfield Todd's suppressed speech published. *In* U.S. *Joint Publications Research Service.* JPRS 76266. [Springfield, Va., National Technical Information Service, 1980] (Sub-Saharan Africa report, no. 2282) p. 14–17.

After the former Prime Minister of Rhodesia was denied a South African visa, the text of his speech prepared for delivery at the University of the Witwatersrand was printed in the *Rand Daily Mail*, Johannesburg, July 25, 1980, p. 13; excerpts are reprinted by JPRS.

Microfiche. [s.l., 1980]

DLC-Micro JPRS 76266

3056

Garn, Jake. Rhodesia—responsible majority rule. Congressional record, 94th Congress, 2d session, v. 122, June 15, 1976: 18244–18246.

J11.R5 v. 122

Remarks in the U.S. Senate.

Includes text of Apr. 27, 1976 speech by Prime Minister Ian D. Smith of Rhodesia.

3057

Goldwater, Barry. In defense of Rhodesian constitutional agreement. Congressional record, 95th Congress, 2d session, v. 124, July 21, 1978: 22191–22202.   J11.R5 v. 124

Remarks in the U.S. Senate.

Includes text of a booklet, *In Defence of the Rhodesian Constitutional Agreement: A Power Promise*, by Ndabaningi Sithole.

3058

Helms, Jesse A. A telephone call from London. Congressional record [daily ed.], 96th Congress, 1st session, v. 125, Sept. 20, 1979: S13078–S13080.

J11.R7 v. 125

Remarks in the U.S. Senate concerning allegations that two of the Senator's associates had interfered in negotiations concerning Zimbabwe-Rhodesia.

Includes articles from the *Washington Post* and *New York Times*.

3059

——— The London conference on Zimbabwe-Rhodesia. Congressional record [daily ed.], 96th Congress, 1st session, v. 125, Sept. 10, 1979: S12332–S12335.   J11.R7 v. 125

Remarks in the U.S. Senate.

3060

——— Will justice prevail under Mugabe in Zimbabwe? Congressional record [daily ed.], 96th Congress, 2d session, v. 126, Aug. 6, 1980: S11029–S11030.   J11.R5 v. 126

Remarks in the U.S. Senate.

Includes articles from the *New York Times* and *Washington Post.*

3061

Humphrey, Muriel. Rhodesia—a comparison of the internal settlement and the Anglo-American proposal. Congressional record, 95th Congress, 2d session, v. 124, Mar. 23, 1978: 8314–8320.

J11.R5 v. 124

Remarks in the U.S. Senate.

Includes the texts of the documents, an analysis of the internal settlement by the Washington Office on Africa, and an article from the *New York Times.*

3062

International Security and Development Cooperation Act of 1980. Congressional record [daily ed.], 96th Congress, 2d session, v. 126, June 17, 1980: S7149–S7194.   J11.R7 v. 126

Debate in the U.S. Senate includes discussion of an amendment (no. 1168) introduced by Senator Jesse Helms stating that if Zimbabwe should receive American assistance, the President should be required to report regularly to Congress on that country's implementation of the Declaration of Rights drawn up at the Constitutional Conference on Southern Rhodesia, Dec. 22, 1979 (S7157–S7160).

Includes text of the Declaration of Rights.

3063

Kennedy, Edward M. Events in Southern Africa. Congressional record, 94th Congress, 2d session, v. 122, Mar. 23, 1976: 7603–7607.

J11.R5 v. 122

Remarks in U.S. Senate emphasizing situation in Rhodesia.

3064

McGovern, George S. Zimbabwe, Southern Africa, and the rise of Robert Mugabe. Congressional record [daily ed.], 96th Congress, 2d session, v. 126, July 1, 1980: S9159–S9165.   J11.R7 v. 126

Remarks in the U.S. Senate.

3064 (cont.)

Includes article by Xan Smiley in *Foreign Affairs.*

3065

Malate, Ricardo, *and* Joaqium Salvador. Mugabe stresses ZANU-ZAPU alliance despite differences. *In* U.S. *Joint Publications Research Service.* JPRS 75418. [Springfield, Va., National Technical Information Service, 1980] (Sub-Saharan Africa report, no. 2228) p. 92–98.

Translation of article in *Notícias,* Maputo, Mar. 2, 1980, p. 5.

ZANU: Zimbabwe African National Union.

ZAPU: Zimbabwe African People's Union.

Microfiche. [s.l., 1980]

DLC-Micro JPRS 75418

3066

Mugabe speaks on Zimbabwe's future. *In* U.S. *Joint Publications Research Service.* JPRS 75487. [Springfield, Va., National Technical Information Service, 1980] (Sub-Saharan Africa report, no. 2234) p. 116–122.

Interview with Robert G. Mugabe in *Sunday Nation,* Nairobi, Mar. 30, 1980, p. 10–11.

Microfiche. [s.l., 1980]

DLC-Micro JPRS 75487

3067

National unity government planned after April election. *In* U.S. *Joint Publications Research Service.* JPRS 72414. [Springfield, Va., National Technical Information Service, 1978] (Translations on Sub-Saharan Africa, no. 2036) p. 98–101.

Article in *The Herald,* Salisbury, Dec. 1, 1978, p. 1.

Microfiche. [Washington, Supt. of Docs., U.S. Govt. Print. Off., 1978]

DLC-Micro JPRS 72414

3068

Nkomo calls for retention of modified emergency powers. *In* U.S. *Joint Publications Research Service.* JPRS 76184. [Springfield, Va., National Technical Information Service, 1980] (Sub-Saharan Africa report, no. 2276) p. 112–115.

Statement by Joshua Nkomo in *The Herald,* Salisbury, July 24, 1980, p. 1, 2, 3.

Microfiche. [s.l., 1980]

DLC-Micro JPRS 76184

3069

O'Meara, Patrick. Zimbabwe Rhodesia, the internal settlement: a preliminary assessment. [s.l.], 1979. 11 p. DLC

On cover: "Paper presented at the conference on Zimbabwe Rhodesia and U.S. policy, U.S. Department of State, Washington, D.C., July 12–13, 1979."

3070

Onyeame, Dillibe. Mugabe on transition period. *In* U.S. *Joint Publications Research Service.* JPRS 74776. [Springfield, Va., National Technical Information Service, 1979] (Sub-Saharan Africa report, no. 2189) p. 54–57.

Interview with Robert G. Mugabe, in *West Africa,* London, Nov. 19, 1979, p. 2125–2126.

Microfiche. [s.l., 1980]

DLC-Micro JPRS 74776

3071

Prime Minister says he delivered promised peace. *In* U.S. *Joint Publications Research Service.* JPRS 74900. [Springfield, Va., National Technical Information Service, 1980] (Sub-Saharan Africa report, no. 2197) p. 60–63.

Interview with Bishop Abel T. Muzorewa, in *Sunday Mail,* Salisbury, Dec. 23, 1979, p. 6.

Microfiche. [s.l., 1980]

DLC-Micro JPRS 74900

3072

Short, Joseph N. Politics in Zimbabwe. [s.l.], 1977. 53 p. (Transition problems in a developing nation. Occasional paper, no. 5)

Prepared for the African-American Scholars Council and the U.S. Agency for International Development under subcontract AID/afr-C-1254.

Abstract in *A.I.D. Research and Development Abstracts,* Oct. 1978, p. 25.

Microfiche. [Washington, U.S. Agency for International Development, 1977?] 1 sheet.

DLC-Sci RR PN-AAF-242

3073

Simoko, Patu. Power struggle between Muzorewa, Sithole, and Chirau noted. *In* U.S. *Joint Publications Research Service.* JPRS 71257. [Springfield, Va., National Technical Information Service, 1978] (Translations on Sub-Saharan Africa, no. 1942) p. 55–58.

Article in *Daily Mail,* Lusaka, May 4, 1978, p. 4.

Microfiche. [Washington, Supt. of Docs., U.S. Govt. Print. Off., 1978]

DLC-Micro JPRS 71257

3074

Solarz, Stephen J. MacNeil/Lehrer interview with Robert Mugabe. Congressional record [daily ed.], 96th Congress, 2d session, v. 126, Apr. 30, 1980: E2153–E2155. J11.R7 v. 126

3074 (cont.)

Extension of remarks in the U.S. House of Representatives.

Includes text of interview on Mar. 24, 1980.

3075

————Statement of Robert Mugabe. Congressional record [daily ed.], 96th Congress, 2d session, v. 126, Apr. 24, 1980: E2037–E2038.   J11.R7 v. 126

Extension of remarks in the U.S. House of Representatives.

Includes text of an "address to the nation" by Prime Minister-Elect Mugabe on Mar. 4, 1980.

3076

Steinbauer, Wolf D., *and* Heinz P. Lohfeldt. Mugabe interviewed on domestic, foreign policy problems. *In* U.S. *Joint Publications Research Service.* JPRS 76124. [Springfield, Va., National Technical Information Service, 1980] (Sub-Saharan Africa report, no. 2272) p. 152–160.

Translation of interview with Prime Minister Mugabe in *Der Spiegel*, Hamburg, July 7, 1980, p. 105–110.

Microfiche. [s.l., 1980]
DLC-Micro JPRS 76124

3077

Thomas, David. Success of new parliament examined. *In* U.S. *Joint Publications Research Service.* JPRS 76908. [Springfield, Va., National Technical Information Service, 1980] (Sub-Saharan Africa report, no. 2325) p. 106–109.

Article in *The Star*, Johannesburg, Nov. 3, 1980, p. 18.

Microfiche. [s.l., 1980]
DLC-Micro JPRS 76908

3078

Tsongas, Paul E. Hope for peace in Zimbabwe. Congressional record [daily ed.], 96th Congress, 1st session, v. 125, Oct. 23, 1979: S14921–S14922.
J11.R7 v. 125

Remarks in the U.S. Senate.

Includes article, "Guerrillas agree to Rhodesian plan offered by Britain," from the *Washington Post.*

3079

Wright, Robin. Interview with Rhodesian Prime Minister by CBS TV reporter. *In* U.S. *Joint Publications Research Service.* JPRS 67940. [Springfield, Va., National Technical Information Service, 1976] (Translations on Sub-Saharan Africa, no. 1675) p. 29–35.

Text of interview with Ian Smith broadcast on Salisbury Domestic Service, Aug. 25, 1976.

Microfiche. [s.l., 1976]
DLC-Micro JPRS 67940

Civil War

3080

Alphin, Arthur B. The warrior heritage: a study of Rhodesia. [Houston, Rice University], 1980. 218 p. illus.

Bibliography: p. [200]–218.

Thesis (M.A.)—Rice University.

Concerns the military history of British occupation of Rhodesia and its lessons for the "anti-terrorist" war.

Microfiche. [s.l., Defense Technical Information Center, 1980] 3 sheets (DLC-Sci RR AD-A084916); issued also in microfilm by University Publications of America; cited in its *Africa: Special Studies 1962–1980*, p. 12.

3081

Ashbrook, John M. Maynard Jackson, Joshua Nkomo and the disgrace in Atlanta. Congressional record [daily ed.] 96th Congress, 1st session, v. 125, May 30, 1979: H3897–H3898.   J11.R7 v. 125

Remarks in the U.S. House of Representatives concerning the reception given to Joshua Nkomo by Mayor Jackson of Atlanta.

Includes articles from the *Atlanta Journal* and *Atlanta Constitution.*

3082

Brown, William J. Rhodesia: an analysis of the insurgency movement: a research study submitted to the faculty. Maxwell, Air Force Base, Ala., Air Command and Staff College, Air University, 1978. 51 leaves. map. (FAR 29126-N).

Bibliography: leaves 49–51.

Examined in the former Foreign Affairs Research Documentation Center, U.S. Dept. of State.

Issued also in microfiche. [s.l., Defense Documentation Center, 1978] 1 sheet (AD-B028899L)

3083

Bruton, James K. Counterinsurgency in Rhodesia. Military review, Mar. 1979: 26–39.
Z6723.U35 1979

Published by the U.S. Army Command and General Staff College, Ft. Leavenworth, Kansas.

3084

Garn, Jake. Killers in Rhodesia. Congressional record, 95th Congress, 2d session, v. 124, July 26, 1978: 22831–22833.   J11.R5 v. 124

3084 (cont.)

Remarks in the U.S. Senate.

Includes articles from the Rhodesian press describing guerrilla activities.

3085

Gomes, Alves, ZANU guerilla leader discusses Zimbabwe after ceasefire. *In* U.S. *Joint Publications Research Service.* JPRS 74725. [Springfield, Va., National Technical Information Service, 1979] (Sub-Saharan Africa report, no. 2186) p. 5–9.

Interview with Josiah Tongogara, commander of the Zimbabwe African National Liberation Army, in *Sunday Times of Zambia*, Lusaka, Nov. 11, 1979, p. 3.

Microfiche. [s.l., 1979]

DLC-Micro JPRS 74725

3086

Humphrey, Hubert H. Rhodesian raids on Mozambique. Congressional record, 95th Congress, 1st session, v. 123, Dec. 15, 1977: 39465–39470. J11.R5 v. 123

Remarks in the U.S. Senate.

Includes articles from the *New York Times* and *Washington Post*.

3087

Interview with ZANU's Robert Mugabe reported. *In* U.S. *Joint Publications Research Service.* JPRS 72414. [Springfield, Va., National Technical Information Service, 1978] (Translations on Sub-Saharan Africa, no. 2036) p. 102–105.

Translation of article in *Nin*, Belgrade, Nov. 19, 1978, p. 48–49.

Microfiche. [Washington, Supt. of Docs., U.S. Govt. Print. Off., 1978]

DLC-Micro JPRS 72414

3088

Kennedy, Edward M. Toward peace in Rhodesia. Congressional record, 95th Congress, 2d session, v. 124, Oct. 14, 1978: 37889–37890.

J11.R5 v. 124

Remarks in the U.S. Senate.

3089

McDonald, Larry. Rhodesian terrorists have U.S. branch. Congressional record, 94th Congress, 2d session, v. 122, Sept. 1, 1976: 28912–28913.

J11.R5 v. 122

Remarks in the U.S. House of Representatives.

Concerns American support for the Zimbabwe African National Union.

3090

MacNicoll, Donald C. The future of close air support in the Rhodesian war. Maxwell Air Force Base, Ala., Air Command and Staff College, 1978. 52 p.

AMAU

"Report no. ACSC-1515-78."

3091

Ratcliff, Spencer. Guerrilla attempts to stop building of fortresses described. *In* U.S. *Joint Publications Research Service.* JPRS 68965. [Springfield, Va., National Technical Information Service, 1977] (Translations on Sub-Saharan Africa, no. 1737) p. 38–41. illus.

Article in *Sunday Mail*, Salisbury, Mar. 27, 1977, p. 13.

Microfiche. [s.l., 1977]

DLC-Micro JPRS 68965

3092

Schutz, Barry M. The military dimension in Zimbabwe: some policy perspectives. [s.l.], 1979. 12 p.

On cover: "Paper presented at the Conference on Zimbabwe-Rhodesia and U.S. Policy, U.S. Department of State, Washington, D.C., July 12–13, 1979."

3093

Tsongas, Paul E. Interview of President Julius Nyerere of Tanzania. Congressional record, 96th Congress, 1st session, v. 125, Mar. 12, 1979: 4687–4689. J11.R5 v. 125

Remarks in the U.S. Senate.

Includes text of interview entitled "Next: race war in Africa," in *Washington Post*, primarily on the conflict in Rhodesia.

3094

ZANU's war activities from October 1977–January 1978. *In* U.S. *Joint Publications Research Service.* JPRS 71257. [Springfield, Va., National Technical Information Service, 1978] (Translations on Sub-Saharan Africa, no. 1942) p. 68–73.

Article in *Zimbabwe News*, Maputo, Jan.–Feb. 1978, p. 8–13.

Microfiche. [Washington, Supt. of Docs., U.S. Govt. Print. Off., 1978]

DLC-Micro JPRS 71257

Election—1979

3095

U.S. *Congress. Senate. Committee on Foreign Relations.* Impartial observers of the forthcoming

3095 (cont.)

election in Rhodesia; report (to accompany S. Con. Res. 8) [Washington], 1979. 19 p.

DLC-LL

At head of title: 96th Congress, 1st session. Senate. Report no. 96–41.

Report submitted by Senator Frank Church.

The committee reported favorably on a resolution to send a congressionally sponsored team of election observers to monitor the Rhodesian election.

3096

Bauman, Robert E. United States policy must change now; a report on elections held in Zimbabwe-Rhodesia. Congressional record, 96th Congress, 1st session, v. 125, Apr. 25, 1979: 8531–8533. J11.R5. v. 125

Remarks in the U.S House of Representatives.

Includes text of H. Con. Res. 110 calling for the lifting of economic sanctions and the granting of diplomatic recognition to Zimbabwe-Rhodesia, plus reports issued by an observer team from the American Conservative Union.

3097

Byrd, Harry F., Jr. Victory in Rhodesia. Congressional record, 96th Congress, 1st session, v. 125, Apr. 23, 1979: 8201–8203.

J11.R5 v. 125

Remarks in the U.S. Senate on the recent election.

Includes articles from the *Washington Post* and *Washington Star*.

3098

——— Zimbabwe Rhodesia and Mr. Andrew Young. Congressional record, 96th Congress, 1st session, v. 125, June 11, 1979: 14156–14159.

J11.R5 v. 125

Remarks in the U.S. Senate on the recent election and the question of continuing economic sanctions.

Includes newspaper accounts of these issues.

3099

Calvalho, Sol, *and* José Baptista. Mugabe speaks of strategies in face of forthcoming elections. *In* U.S. *Joint Publications Research Service.* JPRS 73365. [Springfield, Va., National Technical Information Service, 1979] (Translations on Sub-Saharan Africa, no. 2099) p. 47–52.

Translation of interview with Robert Mugabe in *Tempo*, Maputo, Apr. 1, 1979, p. 36–39.

Microfiche. [Washington, Supt. of Docs., U.S. Govt. Print. Off., 1979]

DLC-Micro JPRS 73365

3100

Foreign Relations Authorization Act, 1980 and 1981. Congressional record [daily ed.], 96th Congress, 1st session, v. 125, May 15, 1979: S5858–S5917. J11w v. 125

Includes debate in the U.S. Senate (S5858–S5910) on the lifting of sanctions against Rhodesia and a review of the recent elections.

Among the supporting documents are statements by election observers.

3101

Helms, Jesse A. Report of the British observer team. Congressional record, 96th Congress, 1st session, v. 125, June 11, 1979: 14198–14208.

J11.R5 v. 125

Remarks in the U.S. Senate.

Includes text of report of an official team of British observers of the Rhodesian election.

3102

——— Zimbabwe-Rhodesia: it is time to lift sanctions. Congressional record, 96th Congress, 1st session, v. 125, Apr. 24, 1979: 8437–8439.

J11.R5 v. 125

Senator Helms introduced S. 996, a bill designed to lift United States sanctions; the emphasis of his remarks is on the recent election.

3103

Impartial observers of the forthcoming election in Rhodesia. Congressional record, 96th Congress, 1st session, v. 125, Mar. 28, 1979: 6547–6562.

J11.R5 v. 125

Debate in the U.S. Senate on S. Con. Res. 8, a resolution to send an official United States observer team.

3104

Senate Concurrent Resolution 8—submission of a concurrent resolution providing for impartial observers of the forthcoming election in Rhodesia. Congressional record, 96th Congress, 1st session, v. 125, Mar. 22, 1979: 5943–5945.

J11.R5 v. 125

Resolution introduced in the U.S. Senate by Senators George McGovern and Samuel I. Hayakawa.

Includes article by former Senator Dick Clark in the *New York Times*.

3105

Symms, Steven D. The Rhodesian elections and the sanctions issues. Congressional record, 95th Congress, 1st session, v. 125, June 26, 1979: 16757–16759. J11.R5 v. 125

3105 (cont.)

Extension of remarks in the U.S. House of Representatives.

Includes sections of a study on the Rhodesian Constitution.

3106

Tsongas, Paul. The election in Rhodesia. Congressional record, 96th Congress, 1st session, v. 125, Mar. 22, 1979: 5943–5945.

J11.R5 v. 125

Remarks in the U.S. Senate.

Includes text of a letter to President Carter from "a large group of concerned citizens" opposed to sending election observers.

Election—1980

3107

U.S. *Congress. House. Committee on Foreign Affairs. Subcommittee on Africa.* Results of the recent elections in Zimbabwe: hearing, Ninety-sixth Congress, second session, March 27, 1980. Washington, U.S. Govt. Print. Off., 1980. 101 p.

KF27.F625 1980

Stephen J. Solarz, chairman.

Principal witness is Richard M. Moose, Assistant Secretary of State for African Affairs. The discussion concerns the Feb. 27–29, 1980 elections; the results, by electoral district, are given on p. 21–26.

Appendixes:

1. Report of the Freedom House mission to observe the common roll election in Southern Rhodesia (Zimbabwe), February 1980. p. 41–87.

2. Biographics [sic] of members of newly elected government. p. 88–95.

3. Additional questions asked of the Department of States and responses. p. 96–101.

3108

Dickinson, William L. The 1980 Zimbabwe-Rhodesian election: the West's dilemma. Congressional record [daily ed.], 96th Congress, 2d session, v. 126, Mar. 27, 1980: H2312–H2317.

J11.R7 v. 126

Remarks in the U.S. House of Representatives.

Includes report by Belden Bell to the Heritage Foundation.

3109

Helms, Jesse A. Rhodesia: hostage to terrorism. Congressional record [daily ed.], 96th Congress, 2d session, v. 126, Mar. 4, 1980: S2183–S2186.

J11.R7 v. 126

Remarks in the U.S. Senate.

Includes report on the Feb. 1980 election by a member of the Senator's staff and an article from the *Washington Post*.

3110

——— Will Mugabe be Zimbabwe's Castro? Congressional record [daily ed.], 96th Congress, 2d session, v. 126: Apr. 17, 1980: S3861–S3865.

J11.R7 v. 126

Remarks in the U.S. Senate.

Includes article by Andrew Young in the *Washington Post* and a report by Richard T. McCormick, *Elections: 1980, the Rhodesian Debacle.*

3111

LaFalce, John H. The effect of Mr. Mugabe's triumph. Congressional record [daily ed.], 96th Congress, 2d session, v. 126, Apr. 2, 1980: E1750–E1751.

J11.R7 v. 126

Extension of remarks in the U.S. House of Representatives.

Includes article from the *Manchester Guardian.*

3112

Tsongas, Paul E. Elections in Rhodesia. Congressional record [daily ed.], 96th Congress, 2d session, v. 126, Mar. 4, 1980: S2085–S2087.

J11.R7 v. 126

Remarks in the U.S. Senate.

Includes articles from the *Washington Post* on the findings of Commonwealth observers of the February 1980 election.

Other Subjects

3113

U.S. [*Treaties, etc. Zimbabwe, 1980 Sept. 25*] Zimbabwe, scientific and technical cooperation. Agreement signed at Salisbury September 25, 1980; entered into force September 25, 1980. [Washington, Dept. of State; for sale by the Supt. of Docs., U.S. Govt. Print. Off., 1981] 2 p. (Treaties and other international acts series, 9967)

DLC

3114

Details of Finance Minister Smith's speech reported. *In* U.S. *Joint Publications Research Service.* JPRS 69563. [Springfield, Va., National Technical Information Service, 1977] (Translations on Sub-Saharan Africa, no. 1783) p. 52–58.

Article on a speech by David C. Smith in *Rhodesian Herald*, Salisbury, July 15, 1977, p. 4, 5. Microfiche. [s.l., 1977]

DLC-Micro JPRS 69563

3115

Fasenfest, David. Observations on the labor force in Zimbabwe. Ann Arbor, Center for Research on Economic Development, 1977. 30 p. (Transition problems in a developing nation. Occasional paper, no. 11)

Prepared for the African-American Scholars Council and the U.S. Agency for International Development under subcontract AID/afr-C-1254.

Abstract in *A.I.D. Research and Development Abstracts*, Oct. 1978 p. 28.

Microfiche. [Washington, U.S. Agency for International Development, 1977?] 1 sheet.
DLC-Sci RR PN-AAF-248

3116

Kuimba, Giles. Historical role of venerated Shona prophets reviewed. *In* U.S. *Joint Publications Research Service*. JPRS 75884. [Springfield, Va., National Technical Information Service, 1980] (Sub-Saharan Africa report, no. 2257) p. 155–159.

Article in *The National Observer*, Salisbury, May 23, 1980, p. 2, 3.

Microfiche. [s.l., 1980]
DLC-Micro JPRS 75884

3117

Smith, G. A. A report on the Dulverton Pilot Scheme for Rural Libraries. [Salisbury?], Institute of Adult Education, University of Rhodesia, [1973] 23 p.

A project, financed by the Dulverton Trust, to provide reading material to adults in rural areas.

Abstract in *Research in Education*, Jan. 1974, p. 17.

Microfiche. [Bethesda, Md., ERIC Document Reproduction Service; prepared for Educational Resources Information Center, U.S. Office of Education, 1973] 1 sheet.   DLC-ED080883

3118

Wolff, Theodore. Electric energy and the transition. Ann Arbor, Center for Research on Economic Development, 1977. 8 p. map. (Transition problems in a developing nation. Occasional paper, no. 13)

Prepared for the African-American Scholars Council and the U.S. Agency for International Development under subcontract AID/afr-C-1254.

Concerns Zimbabwe.

Abstract in *A.I.D. Research and Development Abstracts*, Oct. 1978, p. 27–28.

Microfiche. [Washington, U.S. Agency for International Development, 1977?] 1 sheet.
DLC-Sci RR PN-AAF-250

West Africa

General

3119

Landsat related study for regional planning of onchocerciasis-free areas (Feb. 1978 to Jan. 1980) [s.l.], TAMS & EARTHSAT, [1980] [ca. 600] p.
MiEM

Financed by the U.S. Agency for International Development through the African Development Bank for agencies of the governments of Upper Volta, Ghana, and Benin.

"Includes chapters on climate, geology and mineral resources, hydrology and water resources, land use and land cover, human resources and infrastructure, agricultural potential, rangeland potential, forestry potential, wildlife areas and fisheries potential."—*Sahel Bibliographic Bulletin*, v. 5, no. 4, 1981, p. 183.

3120

University of Arizona. *Arid/Semi-Arid Natural Resources Program.* Annual report. 1974/75–1978/79. Tucson. maps.
AzU

Report submitted to the U.S. Agency for International Development.

Includes frequent references to Africa with a particular focus on West Africa.

Abstract of 1976/77 report in *A.I.D. Research and Development Abstracts*, July 1978, p. 40.

AzU has 1974/75–1978/79.

Vol. for 1976/77 issued also in microfiche. [Washington, U.S. Agency for International Development, 1977?] 2 sheets.
DLC-Sci RR PN-AAF-083

3121

West Africa Conference, *Tucson, Arizona*, Apr. 11–15, 1976. Proceedings; edited for publication by Patricia Paylore and Richard A. Haney, Jr. Tucson, University of Arizona, 1976. 315 p. illus., maps.
AzU

Co-sponsored by the Council for Scientific and Industrial Research of Ghana and the University of Arizona under the aegis of the U.S. Agency for International Development.

"Designed to discuss natural resources development and management in the arid and semi-arid countries of West Africa and the related social, economic, and political constraints."—p. i.

The sessions covered such topics as pastoral nomads in the Sahel; West African migration, urbanization and rural development; the Volta River basin; the issue of providing effective technical assistance; and the role of U.S. universities in West African development.

Issued also in microfiche. [Washington, U.S. Agency for International Development, 1976?] 4 sheets.
DLC-Sci RR PN-AAG-796

Agriculture

3122

Agricultural expansion in West Africa points to need for equipment. Commerce America, May 8, 1978: 13–14. illus.
HF1.C38

Issued by the U.S. Dept. of Commerce.

3123

An Assessment of animal traction in francophone West Africa, by Merritt W. Sargent [et al.] East Lansing, Dept. of Agricultural Economics, Michigan State University, 1981. 101 p. (African Rural Economy Program. Working paper, no. 34)
MiEM

"Prepared and published under West African Animal Traction Study Contract REDSO/WA 78–144 between the Regional Economic Development Services Office West Africa, Abidjan, Ivory Coast, and the Department of Agricultural Economics, Michigan State University, East Lansing, Michigan."

Bibliography: p. 95–101.

Abstract in *A.I.D. Research & Development Abstracts*, v. 10, no. 1/2, 1982, p. 11.

3124

Charreau, Claude. Soils of tropical dry and dry-wet climatic areas of West Africa and their use and management. Ithaca, N.Y., Dept. of Agronomy, Cornell University, 1974. 434 p. maps.

Based on a series of lectures; supported by the U.S. Agency for International Development.

"Agronomy mimeo 74–26."

Includes bibliographies.

At head of title: "Draft; not for publication."

Microfiche. [Sahel Documents and Disserations. Ann Arbor, Mich., University Microfilms International, 1980] 6 sheets (DLC-Micro Microfiche 5357 AS 311); and [Washington, U.S. Agency for International Development, 1974?] 5 sheets (DLC-Sci RR PN-RAA-542).

3125

Conseil de l'Entente. [*Treaties, etc. United States, 1976 Aug. 31*] Accord de subvention d'investissement entre l'Agence pour le développement international et le Fonds d'entraide et de garantie des emprunts du Conseil de l'Entente pour la production vivrière. Capital grant agreement between the Agency for International Development and the Mutual Aid and Loan Guaranty Fund of the Council of the Entente states for food production. *In* U.S. *Treaties, etc.* United States treaties and other international agreements, v. 28, 1976–77. [Washington, Dept. of State; for sale by the Supt. of Docs., U.S. Govt. Print. Off., 1979] p. 8807–8865. ([Treaties and other international acts series, 8773])   JX231.A34 v. 28

Signed Aug. 31, 1976.

3126

Delgado, Christopher L. An investigation of the lack of mixed farming in the West African savannah: a farming systems approach. *In* Shapiro, Kenneth H. Livestock production and marketing in the Entente states of West Africa: summary report. [Ann Arbor], Center for Research on Economic Development, University of Michigan, 1979. p. 70–143.

Study financed by the U.S. Agency for International Development under contract AID/afr-C-1169.

Issued also in microfiche. [Sahel Documents and Dissertations. Ann Arbor, Mich., University Microfilms International, 1980] (DLC-Micro Microfiche 5357 AS 162); and [Washington, U.S. Agency for International Development, 1979?] (PN-AAJ-217).

3127

Forbes, Terry R. A West African climosequence and some aspects of foodcrop potential. [Ithaca, N.Y.,

Dept. of Agronomy, Cornell University], 1975. 172 p.

Thesis (M.S.)—Cornell University.

"This work is supported in part by the Agency for International Development under the Cornell University grant AID/csd 2834."

Microfiche. [Washington, U.S. Agency for International Development, 1975?] 2 sheet.

DLC-Sci RR PN-AAB-600

3128

Kassam, A. H. Crops of the West African semi-arid tropics. Begumpet, Hyderabad, India, International Crops Research Institute for the Semi-Arid Tropics, [1976] 154 p.

Bibliography p. 129–153.

The Institute receives part of its support from the U.S. Agency for International Development.

Abstract in *A.I.D. Research and Development Abstracts*, Oct. 1977, p. 8.

Microfiche. [Washington, U.S. Agency for Interational Development, 1976?] 2 sheets.

DLC-Sci RR PN-AAD-120

3129

Klimaj, Andrzej. Fishery atlas of the northwest African shelf. (Atlas rybacki szelfu Afryki pólnocnozachodniej) Warsaw, Poland, Published for the National Marine Fisheries Service, U.S. Dept. of Commerce, and the National Science Foundation, Washington, D.C., by the Foreign Scientific Publications Dept. of the National Center for Scientific, Technical, and Economic Information; [available from the National Technical Information Service, U.S. Dept. of Commerce, Springfield, Va.], 1976. 221 p. illus., maps.

SH312.W47K5713

Translation of vols. 1–2 of *Atlas Rybacki Szelfu Afryki Pótnocno-Zachodniej.*

"TT 73-54097."

Covers the coast from Morocco to Sierra Leone.

3130

Koeppen, Robert C., *and* S. Blair Hutchison. The problem of unbalanced species utilization in the forests of Ghana and Nigeria. [Washington?], 1973. [27] p.

Prepared for the U.S. Agency for International Development.

Microfiche. [Washington, U.S. Agency for International Development, 1973?] 1 sheet.

DLC-Sci RR PN-AAD-450

3131

Lawani, S. M., *and* Jean de Chantel. Report of the meeting of West African agricultural librarians and documentalists, IITA, Ibadan, Nigeria, Jan.

3131 (cont.)

20 22, 1975. Compte rendu de la réunion des bibliothécaires et documentalistes de l'Afrique occidentale spécialises en agriculture, IITA, Ibadan, Nigeria, Jan. 20–22, 1975. [Ibadan], International Institute of Tropical Agriculture, [1975?] 16, 16 p.

Issued in cooperation with the International Development Research Centre of Canada.

Microfiche. [Washington, U.S. Agency for International Development, 1975?] 1 sheet.

DLC-Sci RR PN-AAC-761

3132

Moisture Utilization in Semi-Arid Tropics: Summer Rainfall Agriculture Project. Moisture Utilization in Semi-Arid Tropics, Summer Rainfall Agriculture (MUSAT:sra) Project: a bibliographic data base, compiled by the MUSAT:sra library staff under the direction of Gretchen Walsh, Project librarian. Boston, G. K. Hall, c1977. xxxiii, 401 p. (Bibliographies and guides in African studies)

Z5074.D8M64 1977

"In June 1974, the University of California, Riverside, received a 211(d) grant from the Agency for International Development (AID) to improve its institutional capacity to respond to the research and consultative needs of agricultural development in the semi-arid tropics."—p. ix.

A bibliography, including citations to monographs, journal articles, reports, maps, unpublished papers, and proceedings of conferences covering some 8,500 items in the MUSAT:sra data base. Its focus is on the semi-arid tropical regions of West Africa.

3133

Sargent, Merritt W. A provisional planning and implementation guide for the introduction and maintenance of animal traction. East Lansing, Dept. of Agricultural Economics, Michigan State University, 1979. 24 p.

Prepared for the U.S. Agency for International Development under contract AID/afr-C-1260.

Concerns French-speaking West Africa.

Microfiche. [Washington, U.S. Agency for International Development, 1979?] 1 sheet.

DLC-Sci RR PN-AAH-059

3134

—— A village level extension guide for the introduction and maintenance of animal traction. East Lansing, Dept. of Agricultural Economics, Michigan State University, 1979. 50 p.

Prepared for the U.S. Agency for International Development under contract AID/afr-C-1260.

Covers French-speaking West Africa.

Abstract in *A.I.D. Research & Development Abstracts*, v. 8, no. 2, 1980, p. 4.

Microfiche. [Washington, U.S. Agency for International Development, 1979?]

DLC-Sci RR PN-AAH-058

3135

—— Recommendations to national governments and international donors for the design and implementation of animal traction programs. East Lansing, Dept. of Agricultural Economics, Michigan State University, 1979. 13 p.

Prepared for the U.S. Agency for International Development under contract AID/afr-C-1260.

Abstract in *A.I.D. Research & Development Abstracts*, v. 8, no. 2, 1980, p. 4.

Microfiche. [Washington, U.S. Agency for International Development, 1979?] 1 sheet.

DLC-Sci RR PN-AAH-057

3136

Stockinger, Karl R. Major cereals project research review. [s.l., 1976?] 15 leaves (FAR 27084-N)

A project to study food crops in West Africa, financed by the U.S. Agency for International Development.

Examined in the former Foreign Affairs Research Documentation Center, U.S. Dept. of State.

3137

West Africa fertilizer study, [by] Ray B. Diamond [et al.] [Florence, Ala., International Fertilizer Development Center, 1976–78] 7 v. (International Fertilizer Development Center. Technical bulletin, no. T3–T9) AMuI

Prepared for the U.S. Agency for International Development under contract AID/afr-C-1176.

Issued also in French.

Contents: v. 1. Regional overview.—v. 2. Senegal.—v. 3. Mali.—v. 4. Upper Volta.—v. 5. Niger.—v. 6. Chad.—v. 7. Mauritania.

Abstract for each volume in *A.I.D. Research and Development Abstracts*, Apr. 1979, p. 15–16.

Issued also in microfiche. [Sahel Documents and Dissertations. Ann Arbor, Mich., University Microfilms International, 1980] 6 sheet.

DLC-Micro Microfiche 5357 AS 359

Vols. 2–7 issued also in microfiche by the U.S. Agency for International Development ([Washington, 1976–78]) as follows:

v. 2. Senegal. 1 sheet.

DLC-Sci RR PN-AAG-270

v. 3. Mali. 1 sheet.

DLC-Sci RR PN-AAG-081

v. 4. Upper Volta. 1 sheet.

DLC-Sci RR PN-AAG-082

3137 (cont.)
v. 5. Niger, 1 sheet.
DLC-Sci RR PN-AAG-271
v. 6. Chad. 1 sheet.
DLC-Sci RR PN-AAG-272
v. 7. Mauritania. 1 sheet.
DLC-Sci RR PN-AAG-273

3138
West African workshop: "The role of agricultural cooperation in development strategies," Accra, Ghana, March 24–30, 1974: final report. [s.l.] Agricultural Cooperative Development International, 1974. 1 v. (various pagings)
Study financed by the U.S. Agency for International Development.
Examined in the Development Information Center, AID, Washington, D.C.

Economic Aspects

3139
Hart, Keith. The development of commercial agriculture in West Africa. Ann Arbor, Dept. of Anthropology, University of Michigan, 1979, 357 p.
On cover: "Discussion paper prepared for the United States Agency for International Development under purchase order REDSO/WA/79/169."
Manuscript copy held by the Dept. of Anthropology Library, University of Michigan, Ann Arbor.

3139a
Michigan State University. *Dept. of Agricultural Economics.* Annual report of research on poor rural households, technical change and income distribution. 1976/77?–1977/78? East Lansing.
MiEM
Prepared for the U.S. Agency for International Development under contract AID/ta-C-1328.
No more published?
Focus is on Nigeria and Sierra Leone.
Reports for 1976/77–1977/78 examined in the Development Information Center, AID, Washington, D.C.

3140
Poor rural households, technical change, & income distribution in less developed countries: a summary report of findings from West Africa, Southeast Asia, and Brazil. [East Lansing], Dept. of Agricultural Economics, Michigan State University, 1980. 197 p.

Prepared for the U.S. Agency for International Development under contract AID/ta-C-1328.
Issued in cooperation with the Dept. of Agricultural Economics, Cornell University, and the Purdue Research Foundation.
Abstract in *A.I.D. Research & Development Abstracts*, v. 10, no. 1/2, 1982, p. 32.

3141
Poor rural households, technical change, and income distribution in developing countries: two case studies from West Africa, [by] Peter Matlon [et al.] East Lansing, Dept. of Agricultural Economics, Michigan State University, 1979. 190 p. (African rural economy program. Working paper, no. 29)
MiEM
Prepared for the U.S. Agency for International Development under contract AID/ta-C-1328.
Bibliography: p. 185–190.
Case studies are from Sierra Leone and Nigeria.
Annotation in *Sahel Bibliographic Bulletin*, v. 4, no. 1, 1980, p. 63.
Issued also in microfiche. [Washington, U.S. Agency for International Development, 1979?] 3 sheets (DLC-Sci RR PN-AAG-889); and [Sahel Documents and Dissertations. Ann Arbor, Mich., University Microfilms International, 1980] 3 sheets (DLC-Micro Microfiche 5357 AS 197).

3142
Sargent, Merritt W. A village level extension guide for the introduction of animal traction. East Lansing, Dept. of Agricultural Economics, Michigan State University, 1979. 50 p.
Prepared under U.S. Agency for International Development contract AID/afr-C-1260, "Agricultural Services in the Sahel."
Concerns French-speaking West Africa.
Microfiche. [Washington, U.S. Agency for International Development, 1979?] 1 sheet (DLC-Sci RR PN-AAH-058); and [Sahel Documents and Dissertations. Ann Arbor, Mich., University Microfilms International, 1980] 1 sheet (DLC-Micro Microfiche 5357 AS 356).

3143
—— Recommendations to national governments and international donors for the design and implementation of animal traction programs. East Lansing, Dept. of Agricultural Economics, Michigan State University, 1979. 13 p.
Prepared under U.S. Agency for International Development contract AID/afr-C-1260, "Agricultural Services in the Sahel."
Concerns French-speaking West Africa.
"Since 1960, over one hundred rural development projects which emphasize draft animal tech-

3143 (cont.)

nology have been financed in francophone West Africa. National governments and international donors continue to maintain a funding priority on animal traction (ANTRAC) projects. The recent Sahelian drought and the rise in petroleum product prices further reinforce arguments for this technology."—p. 1.

Microfiche. [Washington, U.S. Agency for International Development, 1979] 1 sheet.

DLC-Sci RR PN-AAH-057

3144

Zalla, Tom, Ray B. Diamond, *and* Mohinder S. Mudahar. Economic and technical aspects of fertilizer production and use in West Africa. Florence, Ala., International Fertilizer Development Center, 1977. (African Rural Economy Program. Working paper, no. 22) 118 p.

HD9483.A442Z34

"Prepared under a United States Agency for International Development contract (AID/afr-C-1260) with Michigan State University with the cooperation and assistance of the International Fertilizer Development Center of Florence, Alabama."

Bibliography: p. 112–118.

Abstract in *A.I.D. Research and Development Abstracts*, July 1978, p. 4.

Issued also in microfiche. [Sahel Documents and Dissertations. Ann Arbor, Mich., University Microfilms International, 1980] 2 sheets (DLC-Micro Microfiche 5357 AS 091); and [Washington, U.S. Agency for International Development, 1977?] 2 sheets (DLC-Sci RR PN-AAF-061).

Grain and Grain Storage

3145

Olson, R. V. Semiarid food grain research and development, West Africa: technical analysis, objectively verifiable indicators, training activities. [s.l.], 1976. 26 leaves.

Apparently prepared for the U.S. Agency for International Development.

Examined in the Development Information Center, AID, Washington, D.C.

3146

Stryker, Josiah Dirck. The potential for intra-regional cereals cooperation and trade in western Africa. [s.l.], 1976. 41 p.

Paper, presented at the annual meeting of the African Studies Association, 1976, was part of a research project financed by the U.S. Agency for International Development and carried out jointly

with the West Africa Rice Development Association and the Food Research Institute, Stanford University.

Microfiche. [Sahel Documents and Dissertations. Ann Arbor, Mich., University Microfilms International, 1980] 1 sheet.

DLC-Micro Microfiche 5357 AS 197

Livestock and Range Management

3147

U.S. *Agency for International Development. Regional Economic Development Services Office, West Africa.* REDSO livestock seminar, August 22–26, 1977, Abidjan, Ivory Coast. [Abidjan?, 1977?] 29 leaves.

Examined in the Documentation Center, Sahel Development Program, AID, Washington, D.C.

3148

Ariza-Niño, Edgar J., *and* Charles Steedman. Synthesis report. *In* Livestock and meat marketing in West Africa, [by] Edgar J. Ariza-Niño [et al.] v. 1. [Ann Arbor], Center for Research on Economic Development, University of Michigan, 1980. p. 1–33.

MiU

Prepared for the Regional Economic Development Services Office, West Africa, U.S. Agency for International Development, under contract REDSO/WA 77-105.

For information on abstracts/reviews of this report, see entry 3161.

Issued also in microfiche. [Washington, U.S. Agency for International Development, 1980?]

DLC-Sci RR PN-AAJ-212

3149

Ariza-Niño, Edgar J., *and* J. L. P. Griffith. Suppliers: Argentina, Australia, New Zealand. [Ann Arbor], Center for Research on Economic Development, University of Michigan, 1979. 239 p. maps.

MiU

Vol. 4 of *Livestock and Meat Marketing in West Africa* (entry 3161).

Prepared for the Regional Economic Development Services Office, West Africa, U.S. Agency for International Development, under contract REDSO/WA 77-105.

An examination of the role of non-African suppliers in the West African market.

For information on abstracts/reviews of this report, see entry 3161.

Issued also in microfiche. [Washington, U.S. Agency for International Development, 1979?] 3 fiche.

DLC-Sci RR PN-AAJ-215

3150

Ariza-Niño, Edgar J., D. W. Manly, *and* Kenneth H. Shapiro. The world meat economy: other supplier and consumer countries. [Ann Arbor], Center for Research on Economic Development, University of Michigan, 1980. 183 p.

Vol. 5 of *Livestock and Meat Marketing in West Africa* (entry 3161).

Prepared for the Regional Economic Development Services Office, West Africa, U.S. Agency for International Development, under contract REDSO/WA 77-105.

Includes chapters on Uruguay, France, and Denmark as suppliers of meat and meat products to West Africa, and market opportunities for Sahelian meat in the Near East and North Africa.

For information on abstracts/reviews of this report, see entry 3161.

Issued also in microfiche. [Washington, U.S. Agency for International Development, 1980?] 2 fiche.   DLC-Sci RR PN-AAJ-216

3151

Conseil de l'Entente. [*Treaties, etc. United States, 1976 Sept. 29*] Capital grant agreement between the Agency for International Development and the Mutual Aid and Loan Guaranty Fund of the Council of the Entente States for livestock production. *In* U.S. *Treaties, etc.* United States treaties and other international agreements, v. 28, 1976–77. [Washington, Dept. of State; for sale by the Supt. of Docs., U.S. Govt. Print. Off., 1979] p. 8637–8702. ([Treaties and other international acts series, 8766])   JX231.A34 v. 28

Signed Aug. 31 and Sept. 29, 1976; entered into force Sept. 29, 1976.

In English and French.

3152

Deboer, A. John. The short run and long run position of Australian beef supplies and the competitiveness of Australian beef in international trade. [Ann Arbor], Center for Research on Economic Development, University of Michigan, 1979. 50 p. (Livestock production and marketing in the Entente states of West Africa. Working paper, no. 5)   MiU

Prepared for the U.S. Agency for International Development under contract AID/afr-C-1169.

3153

Delgado, Christopher J., *and* John M. Staatz. Ivory Coast, Mali. [Ann Arbor], Center for Research on Economic Development, University of Michigan, 1980. 439 p.   MiU

Vol. 3 of *Livestock and Meat Marketing in West Africa* (entry 3161).

Prepared for the Regional Economic Development Services Office, West Africa, U.S. Agency for International Development, under contract REDSO/WA 77-105.

Bibliography: p. 431–439.

For information on abstracts/reviews of this report, see entry 3161.

Issued also in microfiche. [Washington, U.S. Agency for International Development, 1980?] 5 fiche.   DLC-Sci RR PN-AAJ-514

3154

Ergas, Aimée. Livestock production and marketing in the Entente states of West Africa: annotated bibliography. In Shapiro, Kenneth H. Livestock production and marketing in the Entente states of West Africa: summary report. [Ann Arbor], Center for Research on Economic Development, University of Michigan, 1979. p. 438–523.

MiU

Study financed by the U.S. Agency for International Development under contract AID/afr-C-1169.

Includes numerous citations to AID-sponsored research.

Issued also in microfiche. [Sahel Documents and Dissertations. Ann Arbor, Mich., University Microfilms International, 1980] (DLC-Micro Microfiche 5357 AS 162, sheets 6–7); and [Washington, U.S. Agency for International Development, 1979?] (PN-AAJ-217).

3155

Ferguson, Donald S. A conceptual framework for the evaluation of livestock production development projects and programs in sub-Saharan West Africa. [Ann Arbor], Center for Research on Economic Development, University of Michigan, 1979. xvii, 134 p. (Livestock production and marketing in the Entente states of West Africa. Working paper, no. 1)   MiU

Prepared for the U.S. Agency for International Development under contract AID/afr-C-1169.

Bound with Ferguson, Donald S., *and* Jonathan A. Sleeper. *A Select Bibliography of West African Livestock Development* (entry 3157).

Issued also in microfiche. [Washington, U.S. Agency for International Development, 1979?] 3 sheets (PN-AAH-775); examined in the Development Information Center, AID, Washington, D.C.

3156

——— Modernizing Entente region livestock production systems. [Ann Arbor], Center for Research on Economic Development, [1975] 128 p.

3156 (cont.)

Prepared for the U.S. Agency for International Development under contract AID/afr-C-1169.

Microfiche. [Washington, U.S. Agency for International Development, 1975?] 2 sheets (PN-AAJ-517); examined in the Development Information Center, Agency for International Development, Washington, D.C.

3157

Ferguson, Donald S., *and* Jonathan A. Sleeper. A select bibliography of West African livestock development. [Ann Arbor], Center for Research on Economic Development, University of Michigan, 1979. 49 p. (Livestock production and marketing in the Entente states of West Africa. Working paper, no. 1)   MiU

Prepared for the U.S. Agency for International Development under contract AID/afr-C-1169.

Bound with Ferguson, Donald S. *A Conceptual Framework for the Evaluation of Livestock Production Development Projects and Programs in Sub-Saharan West Africa* (entry 3155).

Issued also in microfiche. [Washington, U.S. Agency for International Development, 1979?] (PN-AAH-775); examined in the Development Information Center, AID, Washington, D.C.

3158

Fitzhugh, II. A., *and* Gordon E. Bradford. Hair sheep production systems, a survey of genetic resources; final project report. Morrilton, Ark., Winrock International Livestock Research and Training Center, 1979. 117 p. illus.

Study supported by the U.S. Agency for International Development.

Includes references to West Africa.

Abstract in *A.I.D. Research and Development Abstracts*, v. 8, no. 2, 1980, p. 3.

Microfiche. [Washington, U.S. Agency for International Development, 1979?] 2 sheets.
DLC-Sci RR PN-AAH-001

Note: Additional studies on this topic, prepared with partial financial support from AID, are published in *Hair Sheep of Western Africa and the Americas: A Genetic Resource for the Tropics*, edited by H. A. Fitzhugh and Gordon E. Bradford (Boulder, Colo., Westview Press, 1982. xv, 319 p. illus. SF373.H17H37 1982).

3159

Gray, Leo R., *and* Norman G. Paulhus. The economic feasibility of the West African regional poultry project. [Washington], Economic Research Service, U.S. Dept. of Agriculture, 1973. 30 p.

Issued in cooperation with the U.S. Agency for International Development.

Microfiche. [Washington, U.S. Agency for

International Development, 1973?] 1 sheet.
DLC-Sci RR PN-AAA-354

3160

Josserand, Henri, *and* Gregory Sullivan. Benin, Ghana, Liberia, Togo. [Ann Arbor], Center for Research on Economic Development, University of Michigan, 1979. 446 p. maps.   MiU

Vol. 2 of *Livestock and Meat Marketing in West Africa* (entry 3161).

Prepared for the Regional Economic Development Services Office, West Africa, U.S. Agency for International Development, under contract REDSO/WA 77-105.

Bibliography: p. 445–446.

For information on abstracts/reviews of this report, see entry 3161.

Issued also in microfiche. [Washington, U.S. Agency for International Development, 1979?] 5 fiche.   DLC-Sci RR PN-AAJ-213

3161

Livestock and meat marketing in West Africa, [by] Edgar J. Ariza-Niño [et al.] [Ann Arbor], Center for Research on Economic Development, University of Michigan, 1979–80. 5 v.   MiU

Prepared for the Regional Economic Development Services Office, West Africa, U.S. Agency for International Development, under contract REDSO/WA 77-105.

Abstracts in *A.I.D. Research & Development Abstracts*, v. 9, no. 4, 1981, p. 13–15; reviewed in *Sahel Bibliographic Bulletin*, v. 5, no. 3, 1981, p. 99–101.

Issued also in microfiche. [Washington, U.S. Agency for International Development, 1980?]
DLC-Sci RR PN-AAJ-212-PN-AAJ-216

Note: Each volume is entered separately in this guide under its personal authors; these volumes can be identified by consulting the index under the heading *Livestock and Meat Marketing in West Africa.*

3162

Livestock production in the subhumid zone of West Africa: a regional review. Addis Ababa, International Livestock Centre for Africa, 1979. 184 p. maps. (ILCA systems study, 2)

The Consultative Group on International Agricultural Research, which supports the activities and publications of the International Livestock Centre for Africa, is funded in part by the U.S. Government.

Bibliography: p. 145–175.

"A definition of the zone is given, followed by a brief description of the environment and the Fulani pastoralists who own most of the livestock. The fodder and animal resources of the zone are

3162 (cont.)

then described, followed by sections on tsetse-transmitted trypanosomiasis and other animal diseases, and concluding with an analysis of land-use and development strategies. The report is based largely on experience in Nigeria with ruminant livestock production."—Abstract.

Abstract in *A.I.D. Research and Development Abstracts*, Feb. 1981, p. 19–20.

Microfiche. [Washington, U.S. Agency for International Development, 1979?] 2 sheets.

DLC-Sci RR PN-AAH-564

3163

Porter, Richard C. The uses of economic models in analysis of the cattle sector. [Ann Arbor], Center for Research on Economic Development, University of Michigan, 1979. 23 leaves. (Livestock production and marketing in the Entente states of West Africa. Working paper, no. 6)   MiU

Prepared for the U.S. Agency for International Development under contract AID/afr-C-1169.

Copy examined in the Documentation Center, Sahel Development Program, AID, Washington, D.C.

3164

Shapiro, Kenneth H. Livestock production and marketing in the Entente states of West Africa: summary report. [Ann Arbor], Center for Research on Economic Development, University of Michigan, 1979. 528 p.   MiU

Study financed by the U.S. Agency for International Development under contract AID/afr-C-1169.

Issued also in microfiche. [Sahel Documents and Dissertations. Ann Arbor, Mich., University Microfilms International, 1980] 7 sheets (DLC-Micro 5357 Microfiche AS 162); and [Washington, U.S. Agency for International Development, 1979?] 6 sheets (PN-AAJ-217).

Note: Selected chapters of this study are entered under their personal authors; they can be identified by consulting the index under the heading *Livestock Production and Marketing in the Entente States of West Africa: Summary Report.*

3165

Sleeper, Jonathan A. Animal traction and small unit feeding in Central West Africa. [s.l.], 1978. 10 p.

"Presented at the Seminar on West African Livestock Production and Marketing Development, U.S. A.I.D., Department of State, June 2, 1978, for the Center for Research on Economic Development, University of Michigan."

Summary of the author's M.S. thesis, University of Maryland.

Microfiche. [Washington, U.S. Agency for International Development, 1978?] 1 sheet.

DLC-Sci RR PN-AAG-035

3166

——— An economic analysis of the role of ox-plowing and cattle-feeding in the stratification of West African livestock production. [Ann Arbor?], Center for Research on Economic Development, University of Michigan, 1979. 161 p. (Livestock production and marketing in the Entente states of West Africa. Working paper, no. 4)   MiU

Prepared for the U.S. Agency for International Development under contract AID/afr-C-1169.

Thesis (M.S.)—University of Maryland.

Abstract in *A.I.D. Research and Development Abstracts*, Jan. 1979, p. 10.

Issued also in microfiche. [Washington, U.S. Agency for International Development, 1979?] 2 sheets.   DLC-Sci RR PN-AAG-035

3167

Small ruminant production in the humid tropics. Addia Ababa, International Livestock Centre for Africa, 1979. [122] p. (ILCA systems study, 3)

The Consultative Group on International Agricultural Research, which supports the activities and publications of the International Livestock Centre for Africa, is funded in part by the U.S. Government.

Bibliography: p. 97–112.

Based on a 1978 survey of sheep and goat production in four West African countries—Ghana, Ivory Coast, Nigeria, and Togo.

Microfiche. [Washington, U.S. Agency for International Development, 1979?] 2 sheets.

DLC-Sci RR PN-AAH-563

3168

Swift, Jeremy. West African pastoral production systems. [Ann Arbor?], Center for Research on Economic Development, University of Michigan, 1979. [111] p. (Livestock production and marketing in the Entente states of West Africa. Working paper, no. 3)   MiU

Prepared for the U.S. Agency for International Development under contract AID/afr-C-1169.

Copy examined in the Documentation Center, Sahel Development Program, AID, Washington, D.C.

Rice

3169

An Evaluation of the West Africa Rice Development Association, [by] Robert Adams [et al.] [s.l., 1977?] 79 leaves.

3169 (cont.)

Prepared for the U.S. Agency for International Development.

Bibliography: leaves 76–79.

Includes list of WARDA publications: leaves 77–79.

Examined in the Documentation Center, Sahel Development Program, AID, Washington, D.C.

3170

George, Emmett. Filling West Africa's rice bowls. Agenda, Apr. 1978: 5–8. illus.

HC59.7.A742 1978

Issued by the U.S. Agency for International Development.

3171

Page, John M., *and* Josiah Dirck Stryker. Methodology for estimating comparative costs and incentives. *In* Pearson, Scott R. Rice in West Africa: policy and economics. Stanford, Calif., Stanford University Press, 1981. p. 435–454.

HD9066.A462P4

Publication results from a research project carried out jointly by the Food Research Institute, Stanford University, and the West Africa Rice Development Association and funded by the U.S. Agency for International Development (see more complete note in entry 3172).

3172

Pearson, Scott R., Charles P. Humphreys, *and* Eric A. Monke. A comparative analysis of rice policies in five West African countries. *In* Pearson, Scott R. Rice in West Africa: policy and economics. Stanford, Calif, Stanford University Press, 1981. p. 363–395.   HD9066.A462P4

Publication results from a research project, "The Political Economy of Rice in West Africa," carried out jointly by the Food Research Institute, Stanford University, and the West Africa Rice Development Association between June 1976 and Sept. 1979, and funded by the U.S. Agency for International Development under contract AID/afr-C-1235.

3173

A Review of the organization, administrative and financial management and programs of the West Africa Rice Development Association, [by] Lloyd E. Clyburn [et al.] Washington, U.S. Agency for International Development, 1973. 52 p.

Microfiche. [Washington, U.S. Agency for International Development, 1973?] 1 sheet.

DLC-Sci RR PN-AAB-268

3174

Stryker, Josiah Dirck. Comparative advantage and public policy in West African rice. *In* Pearson, Scott R. Rice in West Africa: policy and economics. Stanford, Calif., Stanford University Press, 1981. p. 396–431.   HD9066.A462P4

Publication results from a research project carried out jointly by the Food Research Institute, Stanford University, and the West Africa Rice Development Association and funded by the U.S. Agency for International Development (see more complete note in entry 3172).

3175

Stryker, Josiah Dirck, John M. Page, *and* Charles P. Humphreys. Shadow price information. *In* Pearson, Scott R. Rice in West Africa: policy and economics. Stanford, Calif., Stanford University Press, 1981. p. 455–482.   HD9066.A462P4

Publication results from a research project carried out jointly by the Food Research Institute, Stanford University, and the West Africa Rice Development Association and funded by the U.S. Agency for International Development (see more complete note in entry 3172).

Assistance Programs

3176

U.S. *Agency for International Development.* Annual budget submission: Africa regional Entente fund; Africa regional; Africa regional other. [Washington?]

Vol. for 1980 examined in the Documentation Center, Sahel Development Program, AID, Washington, D.C.

3177

——— Annual budget submission, Afr/SFWA—regional programs and summary. [Washington?]

SFWA: Sahel and Francophone West Africa.

Vol. for 1978 examined in the Documentation Center, Sahel Development Program, AID, Washington, D.C.

3178

——— Annual budget submission: Cape Verde/Guinea-Bissau. [Washington]

Title varies slightly.

Vols. for 1980–81 examined in the Development Information Center, AID, Washington, D.C.

3179

——— Annual budget submission: Dakar. [Washington?]

Title varies slightly.

Covers programs for The Gambia, Guinea, and Senegal.

3179 (cont.)

Vols. for 1977–79 examined in the Development Information Center, AID, Washington, D.C.

3180

—— Annual budget submission: Entente area. [Washington?]

Title varies: 1980, *Annual Budget Submission: Niger, Benin, Togo, Ivory Coast.*

Vols. for 1979, 1981 cover Benin, Ivory Coast, Niger, Togo, and Upper Volta.

Vols. for 1979–81 examined in the Development Information Center, AID, Washington, D.C.

3181

—— Annual budget submission: Togo/Benin. Washington, U.S. International Development Cooperation Agency.

Vols. for 1982+ examined in the Development Information Center, AID, Washington, D.C.

3182

—— Entente states: African enterprises II: proposal and recommendations for the review of the Development Loan Committee. Washington, 1975. [160] p.　　　　　　MiEM

3183

U.S. *Congress. House. Committee on Government Operations. Legislation and National Security Subcommittee.* U.S. mission and office operations— West Africa: hearing before a subcommittee of the Committee on Government Operations, House of Representatives, Ninety-sixth Congress, second session, Feb. 16, 1980. Washington, U.S. Govt. Print. Off., 1980. 75 p.　　KF27.G6676　1980j J74.A23 96th Cong., House Comm. Govt. Oper., v. 75

Jack Brooks, chairman.

Hearings held in Abidjan, Ivory Coast.

In reviewing the missions, the subcommittee concentrated its attention "on whether the programs currently in operation and our foreign policy objectives are receiving the optimum support possible under the existing circumstances."— p. 1.

Includes statements and testimony by officials of U.S. embassies and Agency for International Development missions.

3184

U.S. *Dept. of State. Inspector General of Foreign Assistance.* Selected PL 480, Title II programs in the Entente states of West Africa; inspection report. [Washington?], 1976. 14 p.

Examined in the Development Information Center, Agency for International Development, Washington, D.C.

3185

Chester, John C., *and* John H. Sullivan. The Peace Corps in West Africa, 1975: report of a staff survey team to the Committee on International Relations, U.S. House of Representatives. Washington, U.S. Govt. Print. Off., 1976. 28 p.　　HC60.5.C52

At head of title: 94th Congress, 2d session. Committee print.

The mission, conducted in the period Nov. 28 – Dec. 18, 1975, included visits to Sierra Leone, Ivory Coast, Upper Volta, Ghana, Nigeria, and Senegal. Its purpose was to evaluate specific Peace Corps programs, the qualification of volunteers, cooperation with host countries, and to review U.S.–supported aid programs in West Africa.

3186

Joyce, Charles L. Comparative evaluation of the regional institutions for the development of the Senegal River, Niger River and Lake Chad basins. Boston, 1978. 14 leaves.

Prepared for the U.S. Agency for International Development under contract AID/afr-C-1407.

Examined in the Documentation Center, Sahel Development Program, AID, Washington, D.C.

3187

—— Final report: technical support to the River Niger Commission. [Boston, 1974] 38 p.

Prepared for the River Niger Commission under contract AID/afr- 847 with the U.S. Agency for International Development.

A report on the transportation potential of the Niger basin.

Microfiche. [Washington, U.S. Agency for International Development, 1974?] 1 sheet.　　DLC-Sci PN-AAG-123

3188

McFarland, H. W., *and* J. K. Fordyce. Report on the SFWA-Field Planning Workshop. [s.l.], Action Programs International, [1976?] 98 leaves.

Prepared for the U.S. Agency for International Development under contract AID/afr-C-1245.

Examined in the Documentation Center, Sahel Development Program, AID, Washington, D.C.

3189

Sullivan, John H., *and* John C. Chester. U.S. development aid programs in West Africa: report of a staff survey mission. Washington, U.S. Govt. Print. Off., 1976. 56 p. maps.　　HC517.W5S9

At head of title: 94th Congress, 2d session. Committee print.

3189 (cont.)

"Printed for the use of the Committee on International Relations."

Contents: population planning activities.—The Senegal River Basin project.—Reimbursable development in Nigeria.

3190

Thompson-Clewry, Pamela. Report of activities of regional coordinator for West Africa, Jan.–Apr. 1976. [Washington?], American Home Economics Association, [1976?] 19 p.

Prepared for the U.S. Agency for International Development.

Examined in the Development Information Center, AID, Washington, D.C.

Economic Conditions

3191

BCEAO described as aiding West African development, anti-inflation drive. *In* U.S. *Joint Publications Research Service.* JPRS 73734. [Springfield, Va., National Technical Information Service, 1979] (Translations on Sub-Saharan Africa, no. 2123) p. '–6.

Translation of interview with Abdoulaye Fadiga, Governor of the Banque centrale des états de l'Afrique de l'Ouest, in *Demain l'Afrique*, Paris, May 21, 1979, p. 104–'06.

Microfiche. [Washington, Supt. of Docs., U.S. Govt. Print. Off., 1979]

DLC-Micro JPRS 73734

3192

Economic and social development in West Africa. [Abidjan], Regional Economic Development Services Office, West Africa, [Agency for International Development], 1979. 73 p.

Cited in list prepared by the Development Information Center, AID; not examined.

3193

Fordwor, Kwame D. Pragmatism needed in West African economic planning. *In* U.S. *Joint Publications Research Service.* JPRS 72454. [Springfield, Va., National Technical Information Service, 1978] (Translations on Sub-Saharan Africa, no. 2039) p. 10–17.

Article by the President, African Development Bank, in *West Africa*, London, Nov. 27, 1978, p. 2362–2369.

Microfiche. [Washington, Supt. of Docs., U.S. Govt. Print. Off., 1979?]

DLC-Micro JPRS 72454

3194

Liptako summit meeting communiques issued. *In* U.S. *Joint Publications Research Service.* JPRS 73528. [Springfield, Va., National Technical Information Service, 1979] (Translations on Sub-Saharan Africa, no. 2110) p. 1–5.

Translation of aritcle in *L'Observateur*, Ouagadougou, Apr. 12, 1979, p. 6–8.

Concerns a meeting of the chiefs of state of Mali, Niger, and Upper Volta to discuss the Liptako-Gourma regional development authority.

Microfiche. [Washington, Supt. of Docs., U.S. Govt. Print. Off., 1979]

DLC-Micro JPRS 73528

3195

1978—a lean year for French Africa. *In* U.S. *Joint Publications Research Service.* JPRS 74391. [Springfield, Va., National Technical Information Service, 1979] (Sub-Saharan Africa report, no. 2165) p. 2–5.

A review of the 1978 report of the central bank of the Union monétaire ouest africaine, in *West Africa*, London, Sept. 24, 1979, p. 1734–1736.

Microfiche. [Washington, Supt. of Docs., U.S. Govt. Print. Off., 1979]

DLC-Micro JPRS 74391

3196

Ondobo, Claude. River Niger development plan reported. *In* U.S. *Joint Publications Research Service.* JPRS 73044. [Springfield, Va., National Technical Information Service, 1979] (Translations on Sub-Saharan Africa, no. 2078) p. 27–30.

Translation of article in *Demain l'Afrique*, Paris, Feb. 12, 1979, p. 68–69.

Microfiche. [Washington, Supt. of Docs., U.S. Govt. Print. Off., 1979]

DLC-Micro JPRS 73044

3197

Riesman, Paul. The Fulani in the development context: the relevance of cultural traditions for coping with change and crisis. [s.l., 1979?] 90 p.

Prepared under contract to the Regional Economic Development Services Office/West Africa, U.S. Agency for International Development.

Bibliography: p. 86–90.

Microfiche. [Washington, U.S. Agency for International Development, 1979?] 1 sheet.

DLC-Sci RR PN-AAG-856

3198

Seminar on the Food Industry in West Africa, *University of Ghana, 1974.* Seminar on the Food Industry in West Africa. Legon, Dept. of Nutrition

3198 (cont.)
and Food Science, University of Ghana [1975]
143 p.   TP369.A44S45 1974
    Includes bibliographical references.
    "Publication costs were carried by the University of Ghana Publications Committee and in particular the United States Agency for International Development (A.I.D.) in Washington."—p. 2.
    Issued also in microfiche. [Washington, U.S. Agency for International Development, 1975?] 2 sheets.   DLC-Sci RR PN-AAD-439

3199
Wall, N. C. Stimulating the growth of small-scale industry; final report, year V. [Atlanta?], Office of International Programs, Georgia Institute of Technology, 1979. 144 p.
    Prepared for the U.S. Agency for International Development.
    Includes end-of-project report.
    Covers Brazil, Ghana, Korea, Nigeria, and the Philippines.
    Microfiche. [Washington, U.S. Agency for International Development, 1979] 2 sheets (PN-AAG-723); examined in the Development Information Center, AID, Washington, D.C.

Economic Community of West African States

3200
Achonu-Abidjan, E. Possibility of ECOWAS, CEAO merger considered. *In* U.S. *Joint Publications Research Service.* JPRS 74681. [Springfield, Va., National Technical Information Service, 1979] (Sub-Saharan Africa report, no. 2184) p. 2–5.
    From article on the Economic Community of West African States and the Communauté économique de l'Afrique de l'ouest, in *Business Times*, Lagos, Nov. 6, 1979, p. 7.
    Microfiche. [s.l., 1979]
                              DLC-Micro JPRS 74681

3201
Axline, W. Andrew. The Economic Community of West African States (ECOWAS) in comparative perspective: the lessons of Asian, Caribbean, and Latin American integration. [s.l.] 1980. 12 leaves.
                                                    DLC
    Paper prepared for the Conference on the Economic Community of West African States, U.S. Dept. of State, Washington, D.C., June 9, 1980.
    On cover: "This paper was prepared for the Department of State as part of its external research program."

Abstract in *Government Reports Announcements & Index*, Jan. 2, 1981, p. 26.
    Issued also in microfiche. [s.l., Defense Technical Information Center, 1980] 1 sheet.
                              DLC-Sci RR AD-A089017

3202
Diejomoah, V. P. New directions for ECOWAS discussed. *In* U.S. *Joint Publications Research Service.* JPRS 76075. [Springfield, Va., National Technical Information Service, 1980] (Sub-Saharan Africa report, no. 2270) p. 4–7.
    Article in *West Africa*, London, Jan. 30, 1980 p. 1168–1170.
    ECOWAS: Economic Community of West African States.
    Microfiche. [s.l., 1980]
                              DLC-Micro JPRS 76075

3203
Gamabari, A. Benefits, goals of ECOWAS should be reviewed. *In* U.S. *Joint Publications Research Service.* JPRS 71264. [Springfield, Va., National Technical Information Service, 1978] (Translations on Sub-Saharan Africa, no. 1943) p. 89–93.
    Article in *Daily Times*, Lagos, May 6, 1978, p. 19.
    Microfiche. [Washington, Supt. of Docs., U.S. Govt. Print. Off., 1978]
                              DLC-Micro JPRS 71264

3204
Jackson, Jeffrey L. Summary of a conference on ECOWAS, June 9, 1980, U.S. Department of State. [s.l.], 1980. 14 leaves.   DLC
    On cover: "This paper was prepared for the Department of State as part of its external research program."

3205
Ravenhill, John. ECOWAS and Lome. [s.l.], 1980. 13 leaves.   DLC
    On cover: "Paper prepared for a conference on the Economic Community of West African States, State Department, Washington, D.C., 9th June 1980."
    Abstract in *Government Reports Announcements & Index*, Jan. 2, 1981, p. 26.
    Issued also in microfiche. [s.l., Defense Documentation Center, 1980] 1 sheet.
                              DLC-Sci RR AD-A089016

3206
Renninger, John P. ECOWAS and other West African regional organizations. [s.l., 1980?] 5 leaves.   DLC

3206 (cont.)

Prepared for a U.S. Dept. of State conference on the Economic Community of West African States.

On cover: "This is an updated and revised version of material which first appeared in the author's *Multinational Cooperation for Development in West Africa* (Elmsford, Pergamon Press, 1979)."

Issued also in microfiche. [s.l., Defense Technical Information Center, 1981] 1 sheet.

DLC-Sci RR AD-A093660

3207

Tubman, Robert C. Scope, purpose and operation of the ECOWAS Fund. [s.l.], 1980. [12] leaves.

At head of title: Department of State. Conference on the Economic Community of West African States-ECOWAS.

Abstract in *Government Reports Announcements & Index*, Jan. 2, 1981, p. 25–26.

Microfiche. [s.l., Defense Technical Information Center, 1980] 1 sheet.

DLC-Sci RR AD-A089012

3208

Zormelo, Justice, *and* Jeffrey Jackson. ECOWAS: performance, promise, and problems. [s.l.], 1980. 33 leaves.   DLC

On cover: "This paper was prepared for the Department of State as part of its external research program."

Abstract in *Government Reports Announcements & Index*, Jan. 2, 1981, p. 26.

Issued also in microfiche. [s.l., Defense Documentation Center, 1980] 1 sheet.

DLC-Sci RR AD-089018

Education

3209

Bowers, John E. Test development and research: West African Examinations Council. Pittsburgh, American Institutes for Research, 1973. [108] p. (in various pagings)

Prepared for the U.S. Agency for International Development under contract AID/afr-595.

Report covers the Council's activities in the member countries (Nigeria, Ghana, Sierra Leone, The Gambia) for the period Jan. 1969–Aug. 1973.

Abstract in *Resources in Education*, Feb. 1978, p. 179.

Microfiche. [Arlington, Va., ERIC Document Reproduction Service; prepared for Educational Resources Information Center, National Institute of Education, 1978] 2 sheets.

DLC-Micro ED144998

3210

Edwards, Cecile H. Quality of life —family. [Washington?], Dept. of Home Economics, Howard University, 1973. [224] p. (in various pagings)

Prepared for the U.S. Agency for International Development.

Covers Sierra Leone, Ghana, Nigeria, Bahamas, and Trinidad and Tobago.

"The major objective of the Quality of Life—Family Project was to explore the feasibility of developing non-formal education programs to improve the quality of life in rural and urban family units, in their cultural context."

Microfiche. [Washington, U.S. Agency for International Development, 1973?] 3 sheets.

DLC-Sci RR PN-AAA-395

Fauna and Flora

3211

Korniker, Louis S., *and* Francisca E. Caraion. West African myodocopid ostracoda (Sarsiellidae, Rutidermatidae) Washington, Smithsonian Institution Press, 1978. 110 p. illus., map. (Smithsonian contributions to zoology, no. 250)

QL1.S54 no. 250

Describes crustacea near the coasts of Spanish Sahara and Mauritania.

3212

Manning, Raymond B., *and* L. B. Holthuis. West African brachyuran crabs (Crustacea: Decapoda) Washington, Smithsonian Institution Press, 1981. 379 p. illus. (Smithsonian contributions to zoology, no. 306)   QL1.S54 no. 306

Bibliography: p. 353–379.

Foreign Relations

3213

Agreements signed by Senegal-Republic of Cape Verde. *In* U.S. *Joint Publications Research Service.* JPRS 73044. [Springfield, Va., National Technical Information Service, 1979] (Translations on Sub-Saharan Africa, no. 2078) p. 31–36.

Translation of article in *Le Soleil*, Dakar, Jan. 31, 1979, p. 3.

Agreements were signed relating to telecommunications and maritime trade.

Microfiche. [Washington, Supt. of Docs., U.S. Govt. Print. Off., 1979]

DLC-Micro JPRS 73044

3214

Gerteiny, Alfred G. Trans-Saharan ties and tensions—the cases of Chad & Western Saharan. [s.l.], 1980. 15 leaves.   DLC

On cover: "This paper was prepared for the Department of State as part of its external research program."

At head of title: Conference on African-Arab Relations (May 2–3, 1980).

3215

Joint communique on official visit of Togolese president to Niger. *In* U.S. *Joint Publications Research Service.*. JPRS 73044. [Springfield, Va., National Technical Information Service, 1979] (Translations on Sub-Saharan Africa, no. 2078) p. 1–15.

Translation of article on the Jan, 9–12, 1979 visit of President Gnassingbé Eyadéma of Togo to President Seyni Kountché of Niger, in *Le Sahel*, Niamey, Jan. 15, 1979, p. 4, 8.

Microfiche. [Washington, Supt. of Docs. U.S. Govt. Print. Off., 1979]

DLC-Micro JPRS 73044

3216

Joint Nigerian-Beninese communique issued. *In* U.S. *Joint Publications Research Service.* JPRS 74340. [Springfield, Va., National Technical Information Service, 1979] (Sub-Saharan Africa report, no. 2161) p. 4–8.

Translation of statement on the Aug. 24, 1979 meeting of the heads of state of Benin and Nigeria, reported in *Ehuzu*, Cotonou, Aug. 27, 1979, p. 1, 4, 6.

Microfiche. [Washington, Supt. of Docs., U.S. Govt. Print. Off., 1979]

DLC-Micro JPRS 74340

3217

Senegalo-Gambian ministerial committee's joint communique. *In* U.S. *Joint Publications Research Service.* JPRS 72773. [Springfield, Va., National Technical Information Service, 1979] (Translations on Sub-Saharan Africa, no. 2061) p. 8–11.

Translation of report on the 13th session of the committee, held in Banjul, Dec. 14–16, 1978, in *Le Soleil*, Dakar, Dec. 28, 1978, p. 4.

Microfiche. [Washington, Supt. of Docs., U.S. Govt. Print. Off., 1979]

DLC-Micro JPRS 72773

Geography and Maps

3218

U.S. *Dept. of State. Office of the Geographer*. Ivory Coast-Mali. Washington, 1979. 4 p. col. map. (*Its*

International boundary study, no. 171)

DLC-G&M

3219

———— Ivory Coast-Upper Volta. Washington, 1979. 4 p. col. map. (*Its* International boundary study, no. 169)   DLC-G&M

3220

———— Maritime boundary: The Gambia-Senegal. [Washington?], 1979. 5 p. fold. col. map. (*Its* Limits in the seas, no. 85)   DLC-G&M

3221

———— Territorial sea and continental shelf boundary: Guinea-Bissau-Senegal. Washington, 1976. 4 p. (*Its* Limits in the seas, no. 68)   DLC-G&M

3222

Defense Mapping Agency. *Hydrographic Center.* Sailing directions (enroute) for the west coast of Europe and northwest Africa. 1st ed. Washington, 1976. 511 p. illus., maps. (*Its* Publication, 143)

VK876.D44   1976

Loose-leaf for updating.

Includes information on the harbors and coasts of Western Sahara, Mauritania, Cape Verde, Senegal, The Gambia, Guinea-Bissau, Guinea, Sierra Leone, and Liberia.

Geology, Hydrology, and Mineral Resources

3223

Forbes, Terry R. Ferrallitic and ferruginous tropical soils of West Africa. Ithaca, N.Y., Dept. of Agronomy, Cornell University, 1973. 36 p. (Agronomy mimeo 73–20)

"Supported by grant csd 2834 to Cornell University by the Agency for International Development."

A review of the literature on West African soils, particularly studies of the Office de la recherche scientifique et technique outre-mer (ORSTOM).

Microfiche. [Washington, U.S. Agency for International Development, 1973?] 1 sheet.

DLC-Sci RR PN-AAA-666

3224

Huvos, Joseph B. The mineral industry of other West African countries. *In* Minerals yearbook, v. 3, 1980. [Washington, for sale by the Supt. of Docs., U.S. Govt. Print. Off., 1982] p. 1185–1196.

TN23.U612 1980, v. 3

Prepared by the U.S. Bureau of Mines.

3224 (cont.)

Covers Benin, Cape Verde, The Gambia, Guinea, Guinea-Bissau, Ivory Coast, Mali, Niger, Senegal, Togo, and Upper Volta.

3225

Lyday, Phyllis A. The mineral industry of other West African countries. *In* Minerals yearbook, v. 3, 1978–79. [Washington, U.S. Govt. Print. Off., 1981] p. 1093–1110.

TN23.U612 1978–79, v. 3

Prepared by the U.S. Bureau of Mines.

Covers Benin, Cape Verde, The Gambia, Guinea, Guinea-Bissau, Ivory Coast, Mali, Niger, Senegal, Togo, and Upper Volta.

Health and Nutrition

3226

U.S. [*Treaties, etc. 1975 May 7*] Multilateral onchocerciasis fund. Agreement done at Washington May 7, 1975; entered into force May 7, 1975. *In* U.S. *Treaties, etc.* United States treaties and other international agreements, v. 26, 1975. [Washington, Dept. of State; for sale by the Supt. of Docs., U.S. Govt. Print. Off., 1976] p. 1343–1437. ([Treaties and other international acts series, 8117])   JX231.A34 v. 26

In English and French.

Annex two (p. 1361–1381): Agreement governing the operations of the onchocerciasis control programme in the Volta River Basin area.

3227

AID program in West Africa: cooperation brings success. War on hunger, v. 10, no. 1, Jan. 1976: 8–12. illus., map.   HD9000.1.W37   1976

Issued by the U.S. Agency for International Development.

A report on efforts to eradicate smallpox.

3228

Anglophone West African Working Party, *Accra, Ghana*, 7th–16th December 1972. Report. [London?, 1973] [57] p.

On cover: USAID grant no. CSD 3411.

At head of title: International Confederation of Midwives.

Issued in cooperation with the Joint Study Group of the International Confederation of Midwives and the International Federation of Gynaecology and Obstetrics.

Microfiche. [Washington, U.S. Agency for International Development, 1973?] 1 sheet.

DLC-Sci RR PN-AAF-535

3229

Francophone West African Working Party, *Dakar, Senegal*, 17th–23rd November, 1974. Report. [London?, 1974] 208 p.

On cover: USAID grant no. CSD 3411.

At head of title: International Confederation of Midwives. Role of the midwife in family planning.

Sponsored by the Joint Study Group of International Confederation of Midwives and the International Federation of Gynaecology and Obstetrics.

Microfiche. [Washington, U.S. Agency for International Development, 1974?] 3 sheets.

DLC-Sci RR PN-AAF-461

3229a

Franks, James A., Robert L. Minnis, *and* Paul E. Wilson. Maternal and child health/family planning project for the Republic of The Gambia and the People's Republic of Benin, West Africa, contract AID/afr-C-1295. Final report, February 29, 1980. [Santa Cruz], University of California Extension, 1980. 514 p.   DLC

Prepared under the auspices of the U.S. Agency for International Development.

3230

Hilbron, Elizabeth, *and* Walker Williams. Report of an evaluation of the maternal and child health extension project in The Gambia and Dahomey. [Washington?], American Public Health Association, 1975. [39] p. (in various pagings)

Prepared for the U.S. Agency for International Development under contract AID/csd 2604.

Abstract in *A.I.D. Research and Development Abstracts*, Apr. 1978, p. 30.

Microfiche. [Washington, U.S. Agency for International Development, 1975?] 1 sheet.

DLC-Sci RR PN-RAB-635

3231

Lambrecht, Frank L. Development and health in the tropics. Part 1: West Africa. Tucson, College of Medicine, University of Arizona, [1977] 163 p.

On cover: "Prepared for Arid Lands Studies Office, University of Arizona, A.I.D. Project 211(d)."

Abstract in *A.I.D. Research and Development Abstracts*, v. 8, no. 2, 1980, p. 13.

Microfiche. [Washington, U.S. Agency for International Development, 1977?] 2 sheets.

DLC-Sci RR PN-AAG-857

3232

Maternal and child health/family planning project for The Gambia, West Africa, and the People's Republic of Benin, West Africa; semiannual

3232 (cont.)

report. Jan./June 1977?+ Santa Cruz, University of California Extension, University of California-Santa Cruz.

Issued for the U.S. Agency for International Development under contract AID/afr-C-1295.

Report for July/Dec. 1977 prepared by James A. Franks and Robert L. Minnis.

Report for July/Dec. 1977 issued in microfiche. [Washington, U.S. Agency for International Development, 1978?] 2 sheets.

DLC-Sci RR PN-AAF-425

3233

A Preliminary examination of the delivery of pharmaceutical products and services in four nations in West and Central Africa [by] David M. Frence [et al.] Abidjan, Project for Strengthening Health Delivery Systems in Central and West Africa, [1979] [235] leaves (in various foliations)

Prepared for the U.S. Agency for International Development.

In English or French.

Covers Nigeria, Togo, Senegal, and Ivory Coast.

Microfiche. [Washington, U.S. Agency for International Development, 1979] 3 sheets (PN-AAH-782); held by the Development Information Center, AID, Washington, D.C.

3234

West Africa rural water supply and sanitation pre-project analysis. Washington, Pacific Consultants, 1978. [222] leaves (in various foliations), [156] p. (in various pagings)

Study sponsored by the Bureau for Africa, U.S. Agency for International Development.

Emphasis is on Chad, Togo, and Upper Volta.

Examined in the Documentation Center, Sahel Development Program, AID, Washington, D.C.

Language and Languages

3235

Akamba, Bawah, *and* A. Crakye Denteh. Spoken Hausa for non-Hausa beginners. Accra-North, Ghana, Pointer Ltd., [1974] 74 p.

Abstract in *Resources in Education*, Dec. 1977, p. 87.

Microfiche. [Arlington, Va., ERIC Document Reproduction Service; prepared for Educational Resources Information Center, National Institute of Education, 1977] 1 sheet.

DLC-Micro ED142070

3236

Bagari, Dauda M., William R. Leben, *and* Faye M.

Knox. Manual of Hausa idioms. [Stanford, Calif.] NDEA Center for African Language and Area Studies, Stanford University, 1976. 238 p.

Prepared under contract for the U.S. Office of Education.

Abstract in *Resources in Education*, Jan. 1978, p. 82.

Microfiche. [Arlington, Va., ERIC Document Reproduction Service; prepared for Educational Resources Information Center, National Institute of Education, 1978] 3 sheets.

DLC-Micro ED143223

3237

Bird, Charles S., *and* Mamadou Kanté. An ka bamanakan kalan: intermediate Bambara. Bloomington, Linguistics Club, Indiana University, 1976. 282 p. illus., maps.   InU

Prepared under contract with the U.S. Office of Education.

Abstract in *Resources in Education*, May 1977, p. 92.

Issued also in microfiche. [Arlington, Va., ERIC Document Reproduction Service; prepared for Educational Resources Information Center, National Institute of Education, 1977] 3 sheets.

DLC-Micro ED132856

3238

——— Bambara-English, English-Bambara student lexicon. Bloomington, Linguistic Club, Indiana University, 1977. [84] p.   InU

Sponsored by the U.S. Office of Education.

Abstract in *Resources in Education*, Aug. 1977, p. 96.

Issued also in microfiche. [Arlington, Va., ERIC Document Reproduction Service; prepared for Educational Resources Information Center, National Institute of Education, 1977]

DLC-Micro ED-136597

3239

Denteh, A. Crakye. Spoken Twi for non-Twi beginners. Accra-North, Ghana, Pointer Ltd., [1974] 68 p.

Abstract in *Resources in Education*, Nov. 1977, p. 103.

Microfiche. [Arlington, Va., ERIC Document Reproduction Service; prepared for Educational Resources Information Center, National Institute of Education, 1977] 1 sheet.

DLC-Micro ED140609

3239a

Hutchinson, John P., *and* Mamadou Kanté. An ka bamanankan kalan: Bambara text. Bamako, U.S. Peace Corps, 1973. 3 v.   DPC

3240

Maddieson, Ian. A possible new cause of tone-splitting—evidence from Cama, Yoruba, and other languages. [Los Angeles, Dept. of Linguistics, University of California, 1974] 18 p.

Bibliography: p. 13–18.

Abstract in *Resources in Education*, Apr. 1975, p. 77.

Microfiche. [Arlington, Va., ERIC Document Reproduction Service; prepared for Educational Resources Information Center, National Institute of Education, 1975] 1 sheet.

DLC-Micro ED098806

3241

Pelletier, Corinne A., *and* Neil A. Skinner. Adamawa Fulfulde: an introductory course. Madison, African Studies Program, University of Wisconsin, 1979. 441 p.   WU

Sponsored by the U.S. Office of Education.

Abstract in *Resources in Education*, 1980 annual cumulation, p. 806.

3242

Soninke [by] Martha B. Kendall [et al.] Brattleboro, Va., Experiment in International Living, for ACTION/Peace Corps, [1980] 4 v. illus. (Peace Corps language handbook series)   DPC

Contents: [1] Communication and culture handbook.—[2] Grammar handbook.—[3] Special skills handbook.—[4] Teacher's handbook.

Held also by CtY.

Libraries and Library Resources

3243

Gray, Beverly A. Report of a publication survey trip to West Africa. [Washington], African Section, Library of Congress, 1977. 57 p.   DLC

Covers The Gambia, Sierra Leone, Liberia, Ghana, Nigeria, and Upper Volta.

3244

Jusu-Sheriff, Gladys M. Resources sharing in West Africa: some implications for the development of national information policies [by] G. M. Sheriff. [s.l.] 1977. 14 p.

Paper prepared for the 1977 IFLA-UNESCO Pre-Session Seminar on Resource Sharing of Libraries in Developing Countries.

An examination of library cooperation in several anglophone and francophone West African countries.

Abstract in *Resources in Education*, 1980 annual cumulation, p. 300.

Microfiche. [Arlington, Va., ERIC Document Reproduction Service; prepared for Educational Resources Information Center, National Institute of Education, 1980] 1 sheet.

DLC-Micro ED176764

3245

Nyarko, K. Library literature in English-speaking West Africa; its achievements, problems and prospects. [s.l.], 1979. 15 p.

Paper presented at the 1979 conference of the International Federation of Library Associations.

A survey of "the development of librarianship in West Africa since 1954, focusing primarily on the production of professional library literature in Gambia, Ghana, Nigeria, Sierra Leone, and Liberia."—Abstract.

Abstract in *Resources in Education*, 1980 annual cumulation, p. 1670.

Microfiche. [Arlington, Va., ERIC Document Reproduction Service; prepared for Educational Resources Information Center, National Institute of Education, 1980] 1 sheet.

DLC-Micro ED186006

3246

Stutzman, Mary. The role and problems of libraries in developing countries: the West African experience. [Los Angeles?], 1978. 112 p.

Thesis (M.L.S.)—University of California at Los Angeles.

Abstract in *Resources in Education*, 1980 annual cumulation, p. 298.

Microfiche. [Arlington, Va., ERIC Document Reproduction Service; prepared for Educational Resources Information Center, National Institute of Education, 1980] 2 sheets.

DLC-Micro ED176744

3247

Zellers, Joanne M. Report of a publication survey trip to francophone and lusophone West Africa. [Washington], African Section, Library of Congress, 1980. 63 p.   DLC

Covers Senegal, Mauritania, Cape Verde, Guinea-Bissau, Guinea, Ivory Coast, Togo, Benin, Niger, Upper Volta, and Mali.

Military Affairs

3248

Gen. Eyadema discusses West African defense pact. *In* U.S. *Joint Publications Research Service*. JPRS 73268. [Springfield, Va., National Technical Infor-

3248 (cont.)
mation Service, 1979] (Translations on Sub-Saharan Africa, no. 2092) p. 15–24.

Translation of interview with President Gnassingbé Evadéma of Togo in *Revue africaine de strategie*, Paris, Jan./Mar. 1979, p. 7–11., concerning his proposal for a defense pact among West African nations.

Microfiche. [Washington, Supt. of Docs., U.S. Govt. Print. Off., 1979]

DLC-Micro JPRS 73268

3249
Hall, David K. Naval diplomacy in West African waters. *In* Mailed fist, velvet glove: Soviet armed forces as a political instrument [by] Stephen S. Kaplan [and others] [Washington?], Brookings Institution, 1979. p. 12-1–12-88.

Study sponsored by the U.S. Defense Advanced Research Projects Agency.

Concerns Ghana's seizure of two Soviet trawlers in 1968 and the appearance of Soviet naval vessels in West African waters following the Portuguese attack on Conakry, Guinea in 1970.

Microfiche. [s.l., Defense Documentation Center, 1979]   DLC-Sci RR AD-A073950

3250
Lestapis, J. de. Niger President Kountche explains ECOWAS defense pact. *In* U.S. *Joint Publications Research Service*. JPRS 73939. [Springfield, Va., National Technical Information Service, 1979] (Sub-Saharan Africa report, 2138) p. 1–5.

Translation of an interview with President Seyni Kountché in *Afrique défense*, Paris, July 1979, p. 38–39.

ECOWAS: Economic Community of West African States.

Microfiche. [Washington, Supt. of Docs., U.S. Govt. Print. Off., 1979]

DLC-Micro JPRS 73939

3251
Mitchell, Joseph R. Evolution of the military in West Africa. Maxwell Air Force Base, Ala., 1978. 70 p. (U.S. Air University. Air Command and Staff College. Research report)   AMAU

Politics and Government

3252
Debro, Julius. Return of civilian control: an aftermath of coup d'etat in Sub-Sahara [*sic*] Africa; individual research project. Carlisle Barracks, Pa., U.S. Army War College, 1975. 22 p.

Examines Ghana, Nigeria, and Sierra Leone.
Microfiche. [Springfield, Va.?, National Technical Information Service, 1975] 1 sheet.

DLC-Sci RR AD-A017114

3253
Johnson, Jeremy W. Political directions in former French (West) African colonies; special report. Ft. Wadsworth, N.Y., 432d Military Intelligence Detachment (Strategic), 1978. 9 p.

At head of title: Strategic Studies Institute, U.S. Army War College, Carlisle Barracks, Pa.

Emphasis is on Ivory Coast and Senegal.

Abstract in *Government Reports Announcements & Index*, Sept. 28, 1979, p. 26.

Microfiche. [s.l., Defense Documentation Center, 1979] 1 sheet.   DLC-Sci RR AD-A068698

3254
OAU secretary discusses Chad, Liberia situations, energy. *In* U.S. *Joint Publications Research Service*. JPRS 76035. [Springfield, Va., National Technical Information Service, 1980] (Sub-Saharan Africa report, no. 2267) p. 1–9.

Translation of interview with Edem Kodjo, Secretary-General of the Organization of African Unity, in *Le Soleil*, Dakar, May 24–26, 1980, p. 4.

Microfiche. [s.l., 1980]

DLC-Micro JPRS 76035

Population Studies

3255
Ewbank, Douglas C. Age misreporting and age-selective underenumeration: sources, patterns, and consequences for demographic analysis. Washington, National Academy Press, 1981. xv, 112 p. (National Research Council. Committee on Population and Demography. Report, no. 4)

HB1531.E94   1981

Bibliography: p. 105–112.

"This report reviews several studies on age misreporting (AM) and underenumeration (UE) conducted in Paraguay, Nigeria, South Korea, and other developing countries during 1966–80."—Abstract.

Among the tables are demographic statistics from The Gambia, Ghana, Liberia, Nigeria, and Senegal.

Abstract in *A.I.D. Research & Development Abstracts*, v. 9, no. 3, 1981, p. 55.

Issued also in microfiche. [Washington, U.S. Agency for International Development, 1981] 2 sheets.   DLC-Sci RR PN-AAJ-514

3256
Feasibility report on the historical role of migrations between Sahelian and coastal states of West Africa. Washington, 1977. 20 leaves.
    Apparently prepared for the U.S. Agency for International Development.
    Examined in the Documentation Center, Sahel Development Program, AID, Washington, D.C.

3257
Nason, Rachel C. IAW-GAW Seminar on Family Planning, Accra, 1974; a report. [Washington?], American Public Health Association, 1974. 18 leaves. illus.   DLC
    Published under an agreement with the U.S. Agency for International Development.
    IAW: International Alliance of Women.
    GAW: Ghana Assembly of Women.
    Participants were from Ghana, Nigeria, Sierra Leone, Liberia, Upper Volta, Dahomey, Togo, and Mali.

Religion

3258
Charney, Jean-Paul. Islam, stability in West Africa discussed. *In* U.S. *Joint Publications Research Service.* JPRS 77184. [Springfield, Va., National Technical Information Service, 1981] (Sub-Saharan Africa report, no. 2346) p. 2–9.
    Translation of article in *Défense nationale*, Paris, Nov. 1980, p. 107–118.
    Microfiche. [s.l., 1981]
             DLC-Micro JPRS 77184

3259
————— Reflections on West African Islam, negritude. *In* U.S. *Joint Publications Research Service.* JPRS 76932. [Springfield, Va., National Technical Information Service, 1980] (Sub-Saharan Africa report, no. 2328) p. 1–9.
    Translation of article in *Défense nationale, ernes*, Paris, 3d quarter, 1980, p. 3–16.
    Microfiche. [s.l., 1980]
             DLC-Micro JPRS 76932

Science and Technology

3260
Brief survey of potential for solar salt ponds in West Africa. Ann Arbor, Center for Research on Economic Development, University of Michigan, 1980. 31 p.   MiU-RE
    Prepared for the Regional Economic Development Support Office, West Africa, U.S. Agency for International Development, under contract REDSO/WA 77 105.

3261
Dalsted, K. J., *and* B. K. Worcester. Remote sensing for interpretations of soil-plant interactions as indicators of desertification in Western Africa. *In* International Arid Lands Conference on Plant Resources, *Texas Tech University*, 1978. Arid land plant resources: proceedings of the International Arid Lands Conference on Plant Resources, Texas Tech University; editors, J. R. Goodin [and] David K. Northington; sponsored by Committee on Deserts and Arid Zone Research, South-western and Rocky Mountain Division, American Association for the Advancement of Science [et al.] Lubbock, International Center for Arid and Semiarid Land Studies, Texas Tech University, 1979. p. 629–649. maps.   S612.2.I57 1978
    Study funded by the U.S. Agency for International Development.

3262
Duval, William P. Aircraft-observed winds over a coastal upwelling region. Tallahassee, Dept. of Meteorology, Florida State University, 1977. 120 p. maps. (Coastal upwelling ecosystems analysis. Technical report, 29)
    Sponsored by the National Science Foundation.
    At head of title: International Decade of Ocean Exploration.
    A study of the northwestern coast of Africa, including Mauritania and former Spanish Sahara.
    Microfiche. [Springfield, Va., National Technical Information Service, 1977] 2 sheets.
           DLC-Sci RR PB 267369

3263
Uhart, Michael S. A case study of a land-sea breeze phenomena over the Western African coast. Tallahassee, Dept. of Meteorology, Florida State University, 1976, 125 p. maps. (Coastal upwelling ecosystems analysis. Technical report, 28)
    Prepared for the National Science Foundation.
    At head of title: International Decade of Ocean Exploration.
    Microfiche. [Springfield, Va., National Technical Information Service, 1977] 2 fiche.
           DLC-Sci RR PB 261869

Women

3264
African women in development; final report. Falls Church, Va., Jeffalyn Johnson and Associates,

3264 (cont.)

inc., 1980. [125] leaves (in various foliations)

MiEM

Prepared for the Bureau for Africa, U.S. Agency for International Development.

A study of seven small-scale projects "involving vegetable production and women's workload in Senegal, day care in Ghana, the cloth industry in Sierra Leone, and studies of the vegetable tannin and silkworm industries and of the role of women in Upper Volta."—Abstract.

Abstract in *A.I.D. Research & Development Abstracts*, v. 10, no. 1/2, 1982, p. 31.

3265

Bilingual Regional Seminar: Increasing Women's Credit through Credit Unions in West Africa, *Dakar*, Mar. 2–6, 1981. Report, by Barbara M. Reno [et al.] Nairobi, Africa Co-operative Savings and Credit Association, 1981. [43] p. (in various pagings) illus.

Report prepared under a U.S. Agency for International Development grant.

Text in English or French.

Microfiche. [Washington, U.S. Agency for International Development, 1981?] 1 sheet (PN-AAJ-910); examined in the Development Information Center, AID, Washington, D.C.

3266

McCaffrey, Kathleen M. Images of women in the literatures of selected developing countries; (Ghana, Senegal, Haiti, Jamaica) Washington, Office of Women in Development, Agency for International Development, [1978?] 229 p.

PN849.U43M3

"Pacific Consultants contract Afr-C-1197, work order 36."

Bibliography: p. 217–229.

Ghana is covered specifically on p. 10–70, Senegal on p. 71–117.

Abstract in *A.I.D. Research and Development Abstracts*, July 1978, p. 37.

Issued also in microfiche. [Washington, U.S. Agency for International Development, 1978?] 3 sheets.　　　DLC-Sci RR PN-AAF-271

3267

North, Jeanne F. Women participants in the food marketing system in West Africa. *In* International Conference on Women and Food, *University of Arizona, Tucson*, Jan. 8–11, 1978. Proceedings and papers. v. 2. [Tucson?], 1978. p. 103–112.

Conference sponsored by the Consortium for International Development with the support of a U.S. Agency for International Development grant.

Microfiche. [Washington, U.S. Agency for International Development, 1978?]

DLC-Sci RR PN-AAG-530

Other Subjects

3268

U.S. *Information Agency. Office of Research.* Cultural centers in francophone Africa. [Washington?], 1974. 18 p. (FAR 21630-N)

"A survey conducted in Lome and Niamey (April–May 1973) examined the reach of and audience opinions on programs presented at foreign cultural centers."

Examined in the former Foreign Affairs Research Documentation Center, U.S. Dept. of State.

3269

U.S. *Information Agency. Research Service.* Readership and reactions to *Topic* and *Informations et documents* magazines in Ghana and Senegal. [Washington], 1973. 2 v. (FAR 19391-N)

Contents: Pt. 1. Findings.—Pt. 2. Appendices.

Examined in the former Foreign Affairs Research Documentation Center, U.S. Dept. of State.

3270

U.S. *International Communication Agency. Office of Research and Evaluation.* International radio listener discussion panels: final report and recommendations. [Washington?], 1978. 14 p.　DLC

"Research report: R-27–28."

Report summarizing the findings of a series of listener panels in five countries, including Nigeria and Ivory Coast.

3271

Bay, Edna G. Guidelines for developing an instructional unit on Africa: the Manding of West Africa. [s.l., 1980] 9 p.

"An earlier draft of these guidelines was written by Richard A. Corby and me as part of a special project on African curriculum development for public schools carried out at the University of Illinois from 1977–1980."—p. 2.

Abstract in *Resources in Education*, 1980 annual cumulation, p. 1106.

Microfiche. [Arlington, Va., ERIC Document Reproduction Service; prepared for Educational Resources Information Center, National Institute of Education, 1980] 1 sheet

DLC-Micro ED182227

3272

Berry, Sara. Rural class formation in West Africa. *In* Agricultural development in Africa: issues of public policy; edited by Robert H. Bates [and] Michael F. Lofchie. [New York], Praeger, 1980. p. 401–424.   HD2117.A35

Publication supported in part by the National Science Foundation.

3273

Hutchinson, Louise D. Out of Africa: from West African kingdoms to colonization. Washington, Smithsonian Institution Press; [for sale by the Supt. of Docs., U.S. Govt. Print. Off.], 1979. 223 p. illus., maps.   DT476.H87

Published by the Anacostia Neighborhood Museum of the Smithsonian Institution.

Bibliography: p. 208–216.

3274

Marriage in West Africa—a composite. New York, School Services Division, African-American Institute, [1976] 7 p. illus.

Abstract in *Resources in Education*, Apr. 1977, p. 129.

Microfiche. [Arlington, Va., ERIC Document Reproduction Service; prepared for Educational Resources Information Center, National Institute of Education, 1977] 1 sheet.

DLC-Micro ED132086

3275

Mills, William J. West Africa is emerging market for U.S. poultry. Foreign agriculture, Nov. 3, 1975: 10–11, 16.   HD1401.F65   1975

Issued by the U.S. Foreign Agricultural Service.

3276

Nikiema, Roger. CEAO working to coordinate energy programs. *In* U.S. *Joint Publications Research Service*. JPRS 71335. [Springfield, Va., National Technical Information Service, 1978] (Translations on Sub-Saharan Africa, no. 1950) p. 1–15.

Translation of article in *Le Sahel*, Niamey, May 26, 1978, p. 2.

CEAO: Communauté économique de l'Afrique de l'ouest.

Microfiche. [Washington, Supt. of Docs., U.S. Govt. Print. Off., 1978]

DLC-Micro JPRS 71335

3277

Parker, Letitia M. "The Akan and the Manding;" an instructional unit for third grade. Urbana, African Studies Program, University of Illinois, [1978] 31 p.

Bibliography: p. 29–31.

Report developed as part of an interdisciplinary workshop project in African curriculum development funded by the National Endowment for the Humanities.

Abstract in *Resources in Education*, 1980 annual cumulation, p. 2122.

Microfiche. [Arlington, Va., ERIC Document Reproduction Service; prepared for Educational Resources Information Center, National Institute of Education, 1980] 1 sheet.

DLC-Micro ED188990

3278

Spangler, Leandra. "Patterns in tie-dye and batik from West Africa;" an instructional unit for eighth and ninth grade art. Urbana, African Studies Program, University of Illinois, [1978] 36 p.

Report developed as part of an interdisciplinary workshop project in African curriculum development funded by the National Endowment for the Humanities.

Abstract in *Resources in Education*, 1980 annual cumulation, p. 2124.

Microfiche. [Arlington, Va., ERIC Document Reproduction Service; prepared for Educational Resources Information Center, National Institute of Education, 1980] 1 sheet.

DLC-Micro ED189001

3279

Thompson-Clewry, Pamela. Role of home economics in family planning, Ghana and the Ivory Coast. Report of a consultation, Dec. 14–18, 1975. [s.l., 1976?] 5 p.

Prepared for the U.S. Agency for International Development.

Examined in the Development Information Center, AID, Washington, D.C.

3280

Tourism development: Togo and Dahomey. [Ithaca, N.Y.?], School of Hotel Administration, Cornell University, 1973. 92 p.

Prepared for the U.S. Agency for International Development.

Examined in the Development Information Center, AID, Washington, D.C.

Sahel

Note: The following items (entries 3281–3485) are documents covering all or part of that region of West Africa known as the Sahel. Included are publications on two or more of the countries commonly identified with that region: Cape Verde, Chad, The Gambia, Mali, Mauritania, Niger, Senegal, and Upper Volta.

General

3281

Arid lands of sub-Saharan Africa. Washington, National Academy of Sciences, [1975] [431] p. (in various pagings)

Prepared by the staff of the Advisory Panel on Arid Lands of Sub-Saharan Africa, Board on Science and Technology for International Development, Commission on International Relations, National Academy of Sciences-National Research Council.

The Advisory Panel, established in 1973 with John J. McKelvey, Jr. as chairman, was supported by the Bureau for Africa, U.S. Agency for International Development, under contract no. AID/csd-2548.

Includes bibliographies.

Concerns long-term development in the Sahel.

Contents: Staff final report (36 p.). —Staff progress report, Sept. 1973–June 1974 (118 p.).—Appendices to the Staff Final Report, July 1974–Dec. 1974 (277 p.).

Abstracts of the reports and appendices in *Appropriate Technical Information for Developing Countries*, 2d ed., 1979, p. 114.

Microfiche. [Washington, Agency for International Development, 1975?] 5 sheets (DLC-Sci RR PN-AAB-332); and [Springfield, Va., National Technical Information Service, 1975] 6 sheets (DLC-Sci RR PB-245593-PB-245595).

3282

A Framework for evaluating long-term strategies for the development of the Sahel-Sudan region [by] William W. Seifert [and others] Cambridge, Center for Policy Alternatives, Massachusetts Institute of Technology, 1974. 12 v. maps.   HC591.S25F7

Includes bibliographies.

Supported by the U.S. Agency for International Development under contract AID-afr-C-1040.

Contents: v. 1. Summary report.—v. 2. A framework for agricultural development planning.—

annex 1. Economic considerations for long-term development. —annex 2. Health, nutrition, and population.—annex 3. Industrial and urban development.—annex 4. Sociopolitical factors in ecological reconstruction.—annex 5. A systems analysis of pastoralism in the West African Sahel.—annex 6. Technology, education, and institutional development.—annex 7. The role of transportation.—annex 8. An approach to water resource planning.—annex 9. Energy and mineral resources.—annex 10. Listing of project library holdings and organizations contacted.

Issued also in microfiche (Washington, U.S. Agency for International Development, [1975?])
     DLC-Sci RR PN-AAB-213—PN-AAB-224

3283

Remote sensing applications to resource management in the Sahel, [by] Jack B. Bale [et al.] Washington, Earth Satellite Corporation, 1974. 262 p. illus., maps.

Prepared for the U.S. Agency for International Development under contract AID/afr-C-1058.

Includes chapters on resource management, economic conditions, cartography, livestock, dune sands and dune migration, climatology, hydrology, agriculture, natural vegetation, and demography.

Abstract in *A.I.D. Research and Development Abstracts*, Jan. 1976, p. 27–28.

Microfiche. [Washington, U.S. Agency for International Development, 1974?] 3 sheets (DLC-Sci RR PN-AAB-243); and [Springfield, Va., National Technical Information Service, 1975] 3 sheets (DLC-Sci RR PB 239867).

3284

Skinner, Elliott P. A brief history of the Sahel. *In* Sahelian social development, edited by Stephen P. Reyna. Abidjan, Regional Economic Development Services Office, West Africa, U.S. Agency for International Development, 1980. p. 15–70.

Microfiche. [Washington, U.S. Agency for International Development, 1980?] (PN-AAH-

3284 (cont.)

943); examined in the Development Information Center, AID, Washington, D.C.

Bibliographies

3285

U.S. *Agency for International Development. Sahel Development Program. Documentation Center.* Accessions list. [Washington] monthly (irregular)
DLC

Scattered issues for 1980–81 held by the African and Middle Eastern Division.

3286

Kostinko, Gail A. A selected bibliography of Club du Sahel and CILSS documents. Washington, Koba Associates, 1979. 44 leaves.

"Work performed under contract AID/SOD-C-32."

CILSS: Comité permanent inter-états de lutte contre la sécheresse dans le Sahel.

Microfiche. [Sahel Documents and Dissertations. Ann Arbor, Mich., University Microfilms International, 1980] 1 sheet (DLC-Micro Microfiche 5357 AS 300); and [Washington, U.S. Agency for International Development, 1979?] 1 sheet (PN-AAH-197).

3287

Sahel bibliographic bulletin. Sahel bulletin bibliographique. v. 1+ 1977+ East Lansing, Sahel Documentation Center, Michigan State University Libraries. quarterly.   Z7165.S23S23

"The Sahel Documentation Center (SDC) was established in September 1976 within the Michigan State University Libraries as a joint project of the University Libraries, the African Studies Center through a grant from the U.S. Office of Education, and the Department of Agricultural Economics through AID contract no. AID/afr-G-1261."—v. 5, no. 3, 1981.

L.C. has v. 1, no. 1, 1977+

Agriculture

3288

U.S. *Agency for International Development.* Regional food crop protection (phase II); project 625–1928; project paper. [Washington?. 1979?] [107] p.

"The purpose of this project is to encourage and facilitate the extension of integrated pest management (IPM) concepts and techniques to small food crop farmers in the Sahel."

Covers Senegal, Mauritania, The Gambia, Cape Verde, Chad, Guinea-Bissau, and Cameroon.

Examined in the Documentation Center, Sahel Development Program, AID, Washington, D.C.

3289

U.S. *Agency for International Development. Bureau for Africa.* AID participation in the CILSS-sponsored plant protection program. Washington, 1977. 22 p.   MiEM

3290

U.S. *Agency for International Development. Sahel Development Program.* Review and analysis of forestry/ecology sector in the Sahel. [Washington?, 1979?] [40] p.   MiEM

3291

Barclay, A. H. Proposed strategy and framework for evaluating the Sahel Development Program: a report prepared for AID/AFR/SFWA. Washington, Development Alternatives, 1980. 68 p.
MiEM

3292

Besoins en formation des cadres des niveaux supérieur et moyen dans le domaine des activités rurales durant la période 1978–1982 pour les pays membres du CILSS. [s.l.], 1978. [10] v.

At head of title: Mission CILSS/USAID/BIT.

Contents: Presentation d'ensemble.—1. Cap Vert.—2. Gambie.—3. Haute-Volta.—4. Mali.—5. Mauritanie.—6. Niger.—7. Sénégal.—8. Tchad.—Présentation d'ensemble. Conclusions et recommandations.

Microfiche. [Sahel Documents and Dissertations. Ann Arbor, Mich., University Microfilms International, 1980] 11 sheets.
DLC-Micro 5357 AS 027

3293

Bloom, Roger. A review of technical evidence on the use of animal traction in Sahelian farming systems. [East Lansing], Dept. of Agricultural Economics, Michigan State University, 1980, 67 p.   MiEM

3294

Brokensha, David W., Michael M. Horowitz, *and* Thayer Scudder. The anthropology of rural development in the Sahel: proposals for research. Binghamton, N.Y., Institute for Development Anthropology, 1977. 157 p. maps. (Institute for Development Anthropology. Publications, 4 i.e. 3)
H62.5.S27B76

"Contract no. REDSO/WA-77-91, Agency for International Development."

Issued also in microfiche. [Sahel Documents and

3294 (cont.)

Dissertations. Ann Arbor, Mich., University Microfilms International, 1980] 2 sheets.

DLC-Micro Microfiche 5357 AS 015

3295

Colloquium on the Effects of Drought on the Productive Strategies of Sudano-Sahelian Herdsmen and Farmers, *Université de Niamey*, 1975. Report; edited by Michael M. Horowitz. Binghamton, N.Y., Institute for Development Anthropology, 1976. 96 p.

HC591.S253F325 1975

Sponsored jointly by the Regional Economic Development Services Office/West Africa of the U.S. Agency for International Development and the Institute de Recherches en Sciences Humaines of the Université de Niamey.

Colloquium held in Niamey, Niger, June 25–27, 1975.

Issued also in microfiche. [Sahel Documents and Dissertations. Ann Arbor, Mich., University Microfilms International, 1980] 2 sheets.

DLC-Micro Microfiche 5357 AS 044

3296

Cooley, Maurice E., *and* R. M. Turner. Applications of ERTS products in range and water management problems, Sahelian zone: Mali, Upper Volta, and Niger. [Reston, Va.], 1975. 68 p. illus., maps (part col., part in pocket) col. overlays (in pocket) (U.S. Geological Survey. [Reports—Open file series] no. 75–498)

DI-GS

Project report (IR) WA-4.

Prepared for the Office of Science and Technology, U.S. Agency for International Development.

Bibliography: p. 67–68.

ERTS: Earth Resources Technology Satellite.

Abstract in *A.I.D. Research and Development Abstracts*, Apr. 1976, p. 8–9.

Issued also in microfiche (without maps in pocket or color overlays in pocket) [Washington, U.S. Agency for International Development 1975?] 1 sheet. DLC-Sci RR PN-AAB-489

3297

Derman, Bill. Cooperatives, initiative, participation and socio-economic change in the Sahel. [East Lansing, Dept. of Agricultural Economics], Michigan State University, 1978. [76] p.

MiEM

Prepared for the U.S. Agency for International Development under contract AID/afr-C-1260.

Bibliography: p. [66–76].

Abstract in *A.I.D. Research and Development Abstracts*, Feb. 1981, p. 34.

Issued also in microfiche. [Washington, U.S. Agency for International Development, 1978?] 1 sheet. DLC-Sci RR PN-AAH-310

Issued also in *Sahelian Social Development*, edited by Stephen P. Reyna. Abidjan, Regional Economic Development Services Office, U.S. Agency for International Development, 1980. p. 605–702; microfiche (PN-AAH-943) examined in the Development Information Center, AID, Washington, D.C.

3298

Dommen, Arthur, J. Data considerations in agricultural project design in the Sahel. [s.l.], Intech, inc., 1975. 13 p. MiEM

Prepared for the U.S. Agency for International Development under contract AID/afr-147-8.

3299

Drought impact in the Sahelian-Sudanic zone of West Africa: a comparative analysis of 1910–15 and 1968–74, [by] Robert W. Kates [et al.] Worcester, Mass., Center for Technology, Environment, and Development, Clark University, 1981. 92 p. map. DLC

"Research for this paper was supported by contract (AID/otr 147-79006) with the Agency for International Development and a grant (ATM 77-15019) from the National Science Foundation. It was originally produced for the Agency for International Development's Office of Evaluation as Working Paper No. 32."

Bibliography: p. 78–82.

On cover: "Background paper no. 2."

3300

Felker, Peter. State of the art: *Acacia albida* as a complementary permanent intercrop with annual crops. Riverside, Dept. of Soil and Environmental Sciences, University of California, [1978] 133 p.

Prepared for the U.S. Agency for International Development.

"Acacia albida, a leguminous tree, has substantially increased the well-being of small farmers in the Sahelian desert region of West Africa by increasing soil fertility and crop yields and by providing pods for animal food."—Abstract.

Abstract in *A.I.D. Research & Development Abstracts*, v. 9, no. 3, 1981, p. 15.

Microfiche. [Washington, U.S. Agency for International Development, 1978?] 2 sheets.

DLC-Sci RR PN-AAH-147

3301

Humphreys, Charles P., *and* Scott R. Pearson. Choice of technique, natural protection, and efficient expansion of rice production in Sahelian

3301 (cont.)

countries. [Stanford, Calif.?], Food Research Institute, Stanford University, 1979. 109 p.

Report submitted to the U.S. Agency for International Development under contracts AID/afr-C-1503 and AID/afr-C-1506.

Examined in the Documentation Center, Sahel Development Program, AID, Washington, D.C.

Issued also in *Food Research Institute Studies*, v. 17, no. 3, 1979–80 (HD9000.1.S78).

3302

International Symposium on Rainfed Agriculture in Semi-Arid Regions, *Riverside, Calif.*, Apr. 17–22, 1977. Proceedings; edited for publication by Glen H. Cannell. [Riverside?, 1977] 703 p. illus., maps.

Organized with the assistance of the U.S. Agency for International Development.

The Symposium "evolved from linkages established between the University of California, Riverside (UCR), Oregon State University (OSU), and the Consortium for Arid Lands Institute."—p. i.

Emphasis is on the Sahel.

Microfiche. [Washington, U.S. Agency for International Development, 1977?] 8 sheets (DLC-Sci RR PN-AAG-338); and [Sahel Documents and Dissertations. Ann Arbor, Mich., University Microfilms International, 1980] 9 sheets (DLC-Micro Microfiche 5357 AS 211).

3303

Irrigation pilot projects for vegetable production in the Gambia River basin, [by] Alvin R. Hanson [et al.] Banjul, The Gambia, 1977. [124] leaves (in various foliations)

Prepared for the U.S. Agency for International Development.

On cover: Utah State University, Logan.

Examined in the Documentation Center, Sahel Development Program, AID, Washington, D.C.

3304

Joyce, Charles L. River basin development in Sahel. Boston, 1978. [54] leaves (in various foliations)

Prepared for the U.S. Agency for International Development under contract AID/afr-C-1407.

Includes studies of The Gambia and Senegal River basins.

Examined in the Documentation Center, Sahel Development Program, AID, Washington, D.C.

3305

Lowenthal, James B. Pre-project study for the proposed PAID/Sahel school; final report, November 1976-February 1977, submitted in partial fulfillment of contract no. AID/afr-C-1280. Nashville, Tenn., Associates for Planned Change, inc., 1977. 84 leaves.

Concerns management training in activities related to integrated rural development.

Examined in the Development Information Center, AID, Washington, D.C.

3306

McDonald, John W. Information activities for integrated pest management programme. Dakar, Club du Sahel, 1977. 13 p.   MiEM

Prepared under contract to the U.S. Agency for International Development.

3307

Michigan State University. *Dept. of Agricultural Economics.* Agricultural economic services in the Sahel; annual report. 1976/77?–1977/78? East Lansing.   MiEM

Prepared for the U.S. Agency for International Development under contract AID/afr-C-1260.

Title varies slightly.

No more published?

Vols. for 1976/77–1977/78 examined in the Development Information Center, AID, Washington, D.C.

3308

Morris, W. H. M. Progress report on contracts AID/AFR C-1257 and 1258: the costs and returns of sorghum and millet production in the Sahelian countries; the costs and benefits from small and medium sized irrigation perimeters in the Sahelian countries. Lafayette, Ind., West African Program, Dept. of Agricultural Economics, Purdue University, 1978. 135 p.   MiEM

Abstract in *A.I.D. Research and Development Abstracts*, Oct. 1978, p. 10.

Issued also in microfiche. [Sahel Documents and Dissertations. Ann Arbor, Mich., University Microfilms International, 1980] 2 sheets.

DLC-Micro Microfiche 5357 AS 218

3309

———— The food supply of the Sahelian countries. West Lafayette, Ind., Purdue University, [1976?] 14 leaves.

The paper, "a contribution to AID/SFWA contracts no. C 1257 and 1258 in Purdue University, Department of Agricultural Economics," was presented at the annual meeting of the African Studies Association, 1976.

AID/SFWA: Office of Sahel and Francophone West Africa Affairs, Bureau for Africa, U.S. Agency of International Development.

3309 (cont.)

Microfilm. [African Studies Association. Papers presented at the annual meeting.]

DLC-Micro Microfilm 03782 DT   1976, reel 1

3310

Nelson, Gary, *and* Fred M. Tileston. Irrigation: "a paradox for Sahelian development." [Abidjan?, Regional Economic Development Services Office, West Africa, U.S. Agency for International Development], 1977. 35 p.

Microfiche. [Sahel Documents and Dissertations. Ann Arbor, Mich., University Microfilms International, 1980]1 sheet.

DLC-Micro Microfiche 5357 AS 157

3311

Netting, Robert M., David Cleveland, *and* Frances Stier. The conditions of agricultural intensification in the West African savannah. *In* Sahelian social development, eidted by Stephen P. Reyna. Abidjan, Regional Economic Development Services Office, West Africa, U.S. Agency for International Development, 1980. p. 187–506.

Bibliography: p. 491–506.

Microfiche. [Washington, U.S. Agency for International Development, 1980?] (PN-AAH-943); held by the Development Information Center, AID, Washington, D.C.

3312

Newman, Mark D., *and* David C. Wilcock. Food self-sufficiency, marketing and reserves in the Sahel: a working bibliography. East Lansing, Dept. of Agricultural Economics, Michigan State University, 1976. 13 p. (African rural economy program. Working paper, no. 16)   MiEM

Issued in partial fulfillment of U.S. Agency for International Development contract AID/afr-C-1260.

Abstract in *A.I.D. Research and Development Abstracts*, Oct. 1977, p. 33.

Issued also in microfiche. [Washington, U.S. Agency for International Development, 1976?] 1 sheet (DLC-Sci RR PN-AAC-657); and [Sahel Documents and Dissertations. Ann Arbor, Mich., University Microfilms International, 1980] 1 sheet (DLC-Micro Microfiche 5357 AS 126).

3313

Plant protection in CILSS member countries. Dakar, Inter-States Permanent Committee for Drought Control in the Sahel, 1977. [275] p. maps.

Study supported in part by the U.S. Agency for International Development.

Issued in cooperation with the Club des Amis du Sahel.

Includes the following annexes: A. Strengthening of national plant protection services. B. Research on and development of integrated pest management for basic food crops in the Sahel. C. Proposals for a regional locust control programme in the Sudano-Sahelian zone. D. Proposals for regional projects on research and technical cooperation for protection of crops against grain eating birds. E. Proposals for an inter-country programme to improve post-harvest food protection in the Sahelian zone. F. Programme of research on improvement of control of rodent damage. G. Information activities for integrated pest management programme.

Examined in the Documentation Center, Sahel Development Program, AID, Washington, D.C.

3314

Pollaris, R. Review of food supply position in the Sahelian countries of West Africa (excluding Cabo Verde) [Washington?, U.S. Agency for International Development], 1978. 25 leaves.

Examined in the Documentation Center, Sahel Development Program, AID, Washington, D.C.

3315

Prospects for Sahel agricultural development, 1975–1990. *In* U.S. *Joint Publications Research Service*, JPRS 68097. [Springfield, Va., National Technical Information Service, 1976] (Translations on Sub-Saharan Africa, no. 1684) p. 1–5.

Translation of article in *Bulletin de l'Afrique noire*, Paris, Sept. 15, 1976, p. 17171–17173.

Microfiche. [s.l., 1976]

DLC-Micro JPRS 68097

3316

Quimby, Lucy G. The local-level dynamics of development in the Sahelian states. [s.l.], 1977. 120 p. maps.

Prepared for the U.S. Agency for International Development under contract AID/afr-C-1286.

"This paper discusses the social and cultural issues involved in local-level planning and implementation of agricultural development projects in the Sahel states."—p. [1].

Microfiche. [Sahel Documents and Dissertations. Ann Arbor, Mich., University Microfilms International, 1980] 2 sheets.

DLC-Micro Microfiche 5357 AS 163

3317

Rosenberg, Norman J. Report to USAID Technical Assistance Bureau/AGR on soils and climatic problems basic to medium and long term planning of Sahelian zone recovery and development with a discussion of program opportunities in the Sahel

3317 (cont.)

and a survey of sources of soils and climatic data. Lincoln, University of Nebraska, 1974. 34 p.

Microfiche. [Sahel Documents and Dissertations. Ann Arbor, Mich., University Microfilms International, 1980] 1 sheet.

DLC-Micro Microfiche 5357 AS 310

3318

Sahel Crop Pest Management Conference, *Washington*, 1974. Report. Berkeley, University of California, [1975?] 81 p.

Ray F. Smith and David E. Schlegel, rapporteurs.

Conference held at the invitation of the U.S. Agency for International Development; report prepared for AID under contract AID/csd-3296.

Issued also in French.

Microfiche. [Washington, U.S. Agency for International Development, 1974?] 1 sheet (DLC-Sci RR PN-AAB-094); and [Sahel Documents and Dissertations. Ann Arbor, Mich., University Microfilms International, 1980] 1 sheet (DLC-Micro Microfiche 5357 AS 254).

3319

Stryker, Josiah Dirck. Food security, self-sufficiency, and economic growth in the Sahelian countries of West Africa. Stanford, Calif., Food Research Institute, Stanford University, 1978. 60 p.

MiEM

Preliminary draft prepared for the U.S. Agency for International Development.

Abstract in *A.I.D. Research & Development Abstracts*, v. 10, no. 1/2, 1982, p. 6.

Issued also in microfiche. [Sahel Documents and Dissertations. Ann Arbor, Mich., University Microfilms International, 1980] 1 sheet.

DLC-Micro Microfiche 5357 AS 125

3320

Waldstein, Abraham S. Government sponsored agricultural intensification schemes in the Sahel: development for whom? [s.l.], 1978. 114 p.

"This paper has been prepared for USAID's 'Papers on Sahelian Social Development' series under contract REDSO/WA 78-139."—Cover.

Bibliography: p. 98–106.

Abstract in *A.I.D. Research & Development Abstracts*, v. 9, no. 3, 1981, p. 2.

Microfiche. [Sahel Documents and Dissertations. Ann Arbor, Mich., University Microfilms International, 1980] 2 sheets (DLC-Micro 5357 Microfiche AS 134); and [Washington, U.S. Agency for International Development, 1978?] 2

sheets; examined in the Development Information Center, AID, Washington, D.C.

Issued also in *Sahelian Social Development*, edited by Stephen P. Reyna. Abidjan, Regional Economic Development Services Office, U.S. Agency for International Development, 1980. p. 507–604; microfiche (PN-AAH-943) examined in the Development Information Center, AID, Washington, D.C.

3321

Weber, Fred R. Economic & ecologic criteria; proposed Club des Amis du Sahel forestry/anti-desertification program. [Washington?], 1977. [57] leaves. MiEM

Prepared for the Office of Sahel and Francophone West Africa, Bureau for Africa, U.S. Agency for International Development.

3322

Workshop on Sahelian Agriculture, [*1st*], *Purdue University*, Feb. 1–2, 1979. [Papers] [Lafayette, Ind.?, 1979] 1 v. (various pagings) InLP

Held at Purdue's Dept. of Agricultural Economics under U.S. Agency for International Development contracts AID/afr-C-1257 and AID/afr-C-1258.

Copy examined in the Documentation Center, Sahel Development Program, AID, Washington, D.C.; among the papers examined are the following:

Cohen, S. A. Dogon agriculture: a socioeconomic study; a preliminary report. 25 p.

Loose, Edna E. Women in rural Senegal: some economic and social observations. 25 p. map.

Marzouk, Yasmine. Socioeconomic study of agriculture in the lower Casamance. 27 leaves. maps.

Saunders, Margaret O. Social organization of farm families and implications for farm modeling. 17 p.

3323

Workshop on Sahelian Agriculture, *2d*, *Purdue University*, May 19–21, 1980. [Papers] [Lafayette, Ind.?], Dept. of Agricultural Economics, Purdue University, [1980] 1 v. (various pagings)

InLP

Prepared under U.S. Agency for International Development contracts AID/afr-C-1257 and AID/afr-C-1258.

Copy examined in the Documentation Center, Sahel Development Program, AID, Washington, D.C.

Papers prepared for the workshop are cited in the *Sahel Bibliographic Bulletin*, v. 5, no. 2, 1981.

Grain and Grain Storage

3324

Becker, John A. An analysis and forecast of cereals availability in the Sahelian Entente states of West Africa; final report. [s.l.], 1974. 184 p. maps.

Prepared for the U.S. Agency for International Development under contract no. AID/CM/afr-C-73-20.

Bibliography: p. [182]–184.

Abstract in *A.I.D. Research and Development Abstracts*, July 1978, p. 14.

Microfiche. [Washington, U.S. Agency for International Development, 1974?] 2 sheets (DLC-Sci RR PN-AAE-504); and [Sahel Documents and Dissertations. Ann Arbor, Mich., University Microfilms International, 1980] 3 sheets (DLC-Micro Microfiche 5357 AS 011).

3325

Cereals policy in Sahel countries. Acts of the Nouakchott Colloquy, 2–6 July 1979. [Ouagadougou?], Comité permanent inter-états du lutte contre la sécheresse dans le Sahel, [1979?] 474 p.

Publication financed in part by the U.S. Agency for International Development.

Issued with the Club du Sahel.

Examined in the Documentation Center, Sahel Development Program, AID, Washington, D.C.

3326

Etude sur le stockage des céréales dans les pays du Sahel. [s.l.], Arup Partners, 1978. 4 v.   MiEM

CILSS/Club du Sahel document financed by the Fond européen de développement and the U.S. Agency for International Development.

3327

Marketing, price policy and storage of food grains in the Sahel; a survey. [Ann Arbor], Center for Research on Economic Development, University of Michigan, 1977. 2 v. maps.   MiU

Study financed by the U.S. Agency for International Development.

Elliot J. Berg, project director.

At head of title: CILSS-Club du Sahel, Working Group on Marketing, Price Policy and Storage.

Issued also in French under title *Commersialisation, politique des prix et stockage des céréales au Sahel; étude diagnostique.*

Contents: v. 1. Synthesis with statistical compilation and annotated bibliography.—v. 2. Country studies.

Issued also in microfiche. [Sahel Documents and Dissertations. Ann Arbor, Mich., University Microfilms International, 1980] 15 sheets (DLC-Micro Microfiche 5357 AS 166); and [Washington, U.S. Agency for International Development, 1977?] 13 sheets (DLC-Sci RR PN-AAF-397; PN-AAF-399).

The country reports in vol. 2 are also issued separately in microfiche and are held by DLC-Sci RR under the following identification numbers:
Chad. PN-AAF-401
Gambia. PN-AAF-403
Mali. PN-AAF-405
Niger. PN-AAF-409
Senegal. PN-AAF-411
Upper Volta. PN-AAF-413

3328

Peek, L. Stanley. Guidelines for AFR/CWR strategy in assisting the Sahel states to increase cereal production. [Washington], Bureau for Africa, Agency for International Development, 1974. 28 p.

Examined in the Development Information Center, AID, Washington, D,C.

3329

Pinckney, Annette M. An analysis of grain storage in three interior Sahel countries. [Ann Arbor], Center for Research on Economic Development, [1979] 75 p. (Michigan. University. Center for Research on Economic Development. Discussion paper, no. 75)   MiU

Prepared for the U.S. Agency for International Development under contract AID/afr-C-1143.

Covers Mali, Niger, and Upper Volta.

Abstract in *A.I.D. Research & Development Abstracts*, v. 9, no. 4, 1981, p. 4–5.

Issued also in microfiche. [Sahel Documents and Dissertations. Ann Arbor, Mich., University Microfilms International, 1980] 1 sheet (DLC-Micro 5357 Microfiche AS 013); and [Washington, U.S. Agency for International Development, 1979?] 1 sheet (PN-AAG-167).

3330

Sargent, Merritt W. Institut de recherches d'agronomie tropicale (IRAT); research on cereal production technology in Senegal and Upper Volta. Washington, [U.S. Agency for International Development], 1974. 63 p.

An investigation of IRAT programs relating to cereal production.

Microfiche. [Sahel Documents and Dissertations. Ann Arbor, Mich., University Microfilms International, 1980] 1 sheet.

DLC-Micro Microfiche 5357 SG 068

3331

Study on storage of food grains in the Sahel: synthesis & The Gambia. [s.l.], Arup Partners, [1978?] [69] p.   MiEM

3331 (cont.)

CILSS/Club du Sahel document, financed in part by the U.S. Agency for International Development.

Apparently a summary of *Etude sur le stockage des céréales dans les pays du Sahel* (entry 3326).

3332

Wilcock, David C. The political economy of grain marketing and storage in the Sahel. East Lansing, Dept. of Agricultural Economics, Michigan State University, 1978. 308 p. illus. (African Rural Economy Program. Working paper, no. 24)

HD9047.S242W54

Published under terms of U.S. Agency for International Development contract AID/afr-C-1260.

Bibliography: p. 290–308.

Thesis (Ph.D.)—Michigan State University.

Abstract in *A.I.D. Research and Development Abstracts*, July 1978, p. 8.

Issued also in microfiche. [Washington, U.S. Agency for International Development, 1978?] 4 sheets (DLC-Sci RR PN-AAF-071); [Sahel Documents and Dissertations. Ann Arbor, Mich., University Microfilms International, 1980] 4 sheets (DLC-Micro 5357 Microfiche AS 194); and [Ann Arbor, Mich., University Microfilms International, 1978] (DLC-Micro 78-15181).

Livestock and Range Management

3333

Clyburn, Lloyd. Application of Loomis Processionally Articulated Structural Social Systems Model to change among Sahel-Sudan pastoral systems. [Washington?], Agency for International Development, 1975. 41 p.

Examined in the Development Information Center, AID, Washington, D.C.

3334

—— Grazing patterns in the Sahel-Sudan region. [Washington, Bureau for Africa, Agency for International Development], 1974. 11 p.

"An AID/AFR/CWR Technical Staff Paper."

Microfiche. [Sahel Documents and Dissertations. Ann Arbor, Mich., University Microfilms International, 1980] 1 sheet.

DLC-Micro Microfiche 5357 AS 135

3335

—— The process of change in certain livestock owner and operating groups in the West African Sahel. [Washington?], Agency for International Development, [1977?] 14 p.

Examined in the Development Information Center, AID, Washington, D.C.

3336

Moeller, Arnold N., *and* Frank Abercrombie. Utilization of grazing areas in the Sahelian countries of Africa; an analysis of development costs and impacts for alternate systems of utilization. [Washington, U.S. Agency for International Development, 1974] [19] leaves.

Microfiche. [Sahel Documents and Dissertations. Ann Arbor, Mich., University Microfilms International, 1980] 1 sheet.

DLC-Micro Microfiche 5357 AS 354

3337

Sahelian livestock industry status and development strategy. [Washington?], Sahel Development Program, U.S. Agency for International Development, 1980. 27 leaves.

Examined in the Documentation Center, Sahel Development Program, AID, Washington, D.C.

3338

Scope of work: Sahel livestock team—Senegal, Mali, Mauritania. [Washington?], U.S. Agency for International Development, 1974. [20] p. map.

MiEM

3339

Touré, Saydil M. Enquêtes sur les maladies du bétail dans la région de Sélibabi (République islamique de Mauritanie) et de la région de Bakel (République du Sénégal) Dakar-Hann, Laboratoire national de l'élevage et de recherches vétérinaires, 1976. 43 p. maps. MiEM

"Rapport relatif aux enquêtes effectuées conformément à la convention passée entre l'USAID de Nouakchott et l'Institut sénégalais de recherches agricoles: contrat USAID no. CDO/NKC-76-1 & Project PIO/T no. 682-201-3-505 02."

Summary in English.

Assistance Programs

3340

U.S. *Agency for International Development*. Administrator's visit to Sahel-West Africa, October 26–November 1, 1974. Washington, 1974. [90] p.

MiEM

"Briefing paper."

3341

—— Annual budget submission: Sahel regional. [Washington]

Vol. for 1981 examined in the Documentation Center, Sahel Development Program, AID, Washington, D.C.

3342

—— Country development strategy statement: Sahel Regional. Washington. annual?

Vol. for 1983 examined in the Documentation Center, Sahel Development Program, AID, Washington, D.C.

3343

—— Development assistance program. Section three: Senegal, Mali, Mauritania. [Washington] annual?

Vol. for 1975 issued in microfiche. [Sahel Documents and Dissertations. Ann Arbor, Mich., University Microfilms International, 1980] 3 sheets.

DLC-Micro Microfiche 5357 SG 036

3344

—— Development assistance program: Upper Volta & Niger. [Washington?] annual?

Vol. for 1975 issued in microfiche. [Sahel Documents and Dissertations. Ann Arbor, Mich., University Microfilms International, 1980] 3 sheets.

DLC-Micro Microfiche 5357 UV 044

3345

—— Draft evaluation of Sahel R & R procedures. Washington, [1975?] 89 p.   MiEM

An evaluation of the Sahel Relief and Recovery program, analyzing the mechanism for assistance in Niger and Chad and recommending methods for improvement.

Issued also in microfiche. [Sahel Documents and Dissertations. Ann Arbor, Mich., University Microfilms International, 1980]; 1 sheet.

DLC-Micro Microfiche 5357 AS 086

3346

—— Proposal for a long-term comprehensive development program for the Sahel. Washington, 1976. 2 v. maps.

At head of title: Report to the United States Congress.

Includes bibliography.

Contents: [pt. 1] Major findings and programs (28 p.).—Pt. 2. Technical background papers (306 p., in various pagings).

Abstract in *A.I.D. Research and Development Abstracts*, Apr. 1979, p. 21.

Microfiche. [Washington, U.S. Agency for International Development, 1976?] 5 sheets (DLC-Sci RR PN-AAC-843; PN-AAC-872); and [Sahel Documents and Dissertations. Ann Arbor, Mich., University Microfilms International, 1980] 4 sheets (DLC-Micro Microfiche 5357 AS 222).

Note: International relief efforts to alleviate the effects of severe drought conditions were initiated in 1972, and these programs pointed out basic development needs. The first Congressional appropriation to support long-term development in the Sahel came in Dec. 1973.

3347

—— Sahel recovery and rehabilitation program, regional proposal and recommendation. Washington, [1974] 1 v. (various pagings)

At head of title: Program assistance paper.

Examined in Documentation Center, Sahel Development Program, AID, Washington, D.C.

3348

—— United States response to the Sahel drought. [Washington], 1977. 43 p.   DLC

Issued as the Agency's 3d special report to the Congress.

Includes specific statements on Chad, Mauritania, Mali, Niger, Upper Volta, and Senegal.

Statistical tables indicate U.S. emergency food aid to the Sahel in the period 1973–76 and U.S. appropriations for the African drought, 1974–77.

Issued also in microfiche. [Washington, U.S. Agency for International Development, 1977?] 1 sheet (PN-AAA-153); examined in the Development Information Center, AID, Washington, D.C.

3349

U.S. *Agency for International Development. Office of the Foreign Disaster Relief Coordinator.* Disaster relief: case report, Sahel regional (Senegal, Mauritania, Mali, Upper Volta, Niger, and Chad) drought, 1972 to 1975. Washington, 1975. 24 p.

MiEM

3350

U.S. *Agency for International Development. Sahel Development Planning Team.* Sahel development program: U.S. and other donor support of priority sectors. Washington, 1978. 23 p.   MiEM

3351

U.S. *Agency for International Development. Sahel Development Program.* Annual report to the Congress. 1977+ Washington. illus., maps.   DLC

An overview of the operations of CILSS and the role of AID in its programs, plus statements on each country in the Sahel.

L.C. has 1978, 1981; more complete holdings in the Documentation Center, Sahel Development Program, AID, Washington, D.C.

Vol. for 1978 issued also in microfiche. [Sahel Documents and Dissertations. Ann Arbor, Mich., University Microfilms International, 1980] (DLC-Micro 5357 AS 279); and [Washington, U.S. Agency for International Development, 1977?] 1

3351 (cont.)

sheet (PN-AAG-490); examined in the Development Information Center, AID, Washington, D.C.

3552

——— Regional development strategy statement. Washington, 1979. 81 p.   MiEM

3353

U.S. *Congress. Senate. Committee on Appropriations.* Foreign assistance and related appropriations bill, 1980: report (to accompany H. R. 4473) [Washington?], 1979. 163 p.   DLC-LL

Report submitted by Senator Daniel K. Inouye. At head of title: 96th Congress, 1st session. Senate report no. 96–358.

The Committee's recommendations regarding the Sahel Development Program are given on p. 90–91.

3354

U.S. *Congress. Senate. Committee on Appropriations. Subcommittee on Foreign Operations.* Foreign assistance and related programs appropriations for fiscal year 1980: hearings before a subcommittee of the Committee on Appropriations, United States Senate, Ninety-sixth Congress, first session, on H. R. 4473. Washington, U.S. Govt. Print. Off., 1979. 2 v. illus.   KF26.A647 1979
J74.A23 96th
Cong., Sen. Comm.
Approp., v. 5

Daniel K. Inouye, chairman.

The Sahel Development Program, Agency for International Development, is discussed in part 1, p. 375–390; principal witness is Goler T. Butcher, the Agency's Assistant Administrator for Africa. In part 2, statistical tables indicate United States and multinational assistance to various African countries

3355

U.S. *Congress. Senate. Committee on Foreign Relations.* Foreign assistance authorization: hearings before the Committee on Foreign Relations and the Subcommittee on Foreign Assistance of the Committee on Foreign Relations, United States Senate, Ninety-fifth Congress, first session, on the International Development Assistance Act of 1977, March 23, 24, and 25, 1977. Washington, U.S. Govt. Print. Off., 1977. 260 p.   KF26.F6 1977c
J74.A23 95th
Cong., Sen. Comm.
For. Rel., v. 7

John Sparkman, chairman, Committee on Foreign Relations.

Hubert H. Humphrey, chairman, Subcommittee on Foreign Assistance.

Hearings on Mar. 25, 1977 focused on the Sahel programs of the Agency for International Development; principal witness was John J. Gilligan, the Agency's Administrator.

3356

U.S. *General Accounting Office.* Need for an international disaster relief agency, Department of State, Agency for International Development; report to the Congress by the Comptroller General of the United States. Washington, 1976. 58 p. illus.   HV553.U54 1976

"ID-76-15."

"B-159652."

"GAO's case study of worldwide relief effort in the Sahel region of Africa shows that the response to future disasters should be more timely and better managed."—cover.

Abstract in *American Statistics Index*, 1976, Abstracts, p. 1058.

Issued also in microfiche. [Washington, Congressional Information Service, 1976?] 1 sheet.   DLC-Micro ASI:76   26108-332

3357

——— The Sahel development program—progress and constraints. Report to the Congress by the Comptroller General of the United States. [Washington] 1978. 64 p. map.

"ID-78-18."

"This report outlines the United States' progress in helping eight central and west African countries achieve food self-sufficiency and economic growth through the international Club du Sahel. Some of the problems confronting the achievement of those goals are examined. The report contains a number of recommendations for improving the effect of the United States' participation in the internationally supported Sahel development process. "—p. [i]

Abstract in *Government Reports Announcements & Index*, July 7, 1978, p. 39.

Microfiche. [Springfield, Va., National Technical Information Service, 1978?] 1 sheet.   DLC-Sci RR PB278886

3358

——— U.S. development assistance to the Sahel: progress and problems. Report to the Congress of the United States by the Comptroller General. [Washington], 1979. 58 p.

"ID-79-9."

"This report discusses the problems encountered by the Agency for International Development and Action in planning, organizing, and implementing

3358 (cont.)

development activities in eight countries of Central and West Africa."—p. i.

Abstract in *Government Reports Announcements & Index*, July 20, 1979, p. 36.

Microfiche. [Springfield, Va., National Technical Information Service, 1979] 1 sheet.

DLC-Sci RR PB-293745

3359

U.S. *Peace Corps*. Report on Sahel Planning Workshop, October 22–26, 1978, Dakar, Senegal. Washington, [1978?] 142 p.

The workshop "was convened in Dakar ... as an active step in carrying out the Peace Corps' policies of allocating additional resources to the most needy countries of the Third World, and of systematically improving the quality and training of volunteers throughout its operations."—p. 1.

Examined in the Documentation Center, Sahel Development Program, Agency for International Development, Washington, D.C.

3360

AID/W-Field Sahel Planning Workshop, *5th, Bamako, Mali*, 1978. Final report. [s.l.], Action Programs International, [1978?] 25 leaves.

Prepared for the U.S. Agency for International Development under contract AID/afr-C-1245.

Examined in the Documentation Center, Sahel Development Program, AID, Washington, D.C.

3361

Beazer, William F., *and* Larry B. Pulley. Foreign aid and the domestic costs of Sahel development projects. [Ann Arbor], Center for Research on Economic Development, University of Michigan, 1978. 86, 12 p.

Prepared for the U.S. Agency for International Development.

Microfiche. [Sahel Documents and Dissertations. Ann Arbor, Mich., University Microfilms International, 1980] 2 sheets.

DLC-Micro Microfiche 5357 AS 127

3362

Bessis, Sophie. Food aid prolongs dependence of Sahel countries. *In* U.S. *Joint Publications Research Service*. JPRS 77279. [Springfield, Va., National Technical Information Service, 1981] (Sub-Saharan Africa report, no. 2351) p. 10–13.

Translation of article in *Le Monde*, Paris, Nov. 9, 1980, p. 15.

Microfiche. [s.l., 1981]

DLC-Micro JPRS 77279

3363

Bingen, R. James. Research/studies in Sahel francophone West Africa: regional; an inventory of research, studies, and reports sponsored by the U.S. Agency for International Development, 1977. [141] p.

Covers 108 projects undertaken in the period 1962–77.

Abstract for series on francophone West Africa and The Gambia in *A.I.D. Research and Development Abstracts*, Oct. 1977, p. 12–13.

Microfiche. [Washington, U.S. Agency for International Development, 1977?] 2 sheets.

DLC-Sci RR PN-AAD-519

3364

Brown, Barbara J. Making disaster relief more effective: lessons from the Sahel. [s.l.], 1976. 5 p. (FAR 26593)

"External research study, INR/XRS-4."

Examined in the former Foreign Affairs Research Documentation Center, U.S. Dept. of State.

3365

Brown, Barbara J., Janet C. Tuthill, *and* E. Thomas Rowe. International disaster response: the Sahelian experience. [Denver?], Graduate School of International Studies, University of Denver, 1976. [180] p. (in various pagings) map.

Research carried out under a U.S. Agency for International Development grant.

Microfiche. [Sahel Documents and Dissertations. Ann Arbor, Mich., University Microfilms International, 1980] 3 sheets (DLC-Micro 5357 Microfiche AS 152), and [s.l., Defense Technical Information Center, 1980] 3 sheets (DLC-Sci RR AD-A081200).

3366

Club du Sahel. Annual report to AID on the Club du Sahel and the CILSS. Paris.

Vol. for 1978 examined in the Documentation Center, Sahel Development Program, Agency for International Development, Washington, D.C.

3367

Colloquium "Toward a Rational U.S. Policy on River Basin Development in the Sahel," *Washington*, 1978. Proceedings. [Washington, 1978] 315 p. map.

On cover: "Prepared by Charles I. Joyce."

Sponsored by the U.S. Agency for International Development.

Microfiche. [Sahel Documents and Dissertations. Ann Arbor, Mich., University Microfilms International, 1980] 4 sheets.

DLC-Micro Microfiche 5357 AS 210

3368
Cook, Peter D. Issues paper on AID infrastructure policy with reference to the Sahel. [s.l.], Agency for International Development, [1978?] 15 p.

MiEM

3369
DeBenko, Eugene. Aid to the Sahel; report on a conference and acquisition trip. [East Lansing], Sahel Documentation Center, Michigan State University, 1978. [115] p. (In various pagings)　MiEM

Supported by the U.S. Agency for International Development.

Report on a November 1978 conference in Dakar sponsored by CILSS and the Institut du Sahel, plus comments on the acquisition of documents on socio-economic conditions in Senegal, Mali, Cape Verde, and The Gambia.

Issued also in microfiche. [Sahel Documents and Dissertations. Ann Arbor, Mich., University Microfilms International, 1980] 2 sheets.

DLC-Micro Microfiche 5357 AS 008

3370
Disaster relief in the Sahel. Development digest, v. 13, Apr. 1975: 62–69.　HC10.D44　1975

Prepared by the National Planning Association for the U.S. Agency for International Development.

3371
Fendrick, Daniel. Making disaster relief more effective: lessons from the Sahel. [Washington], U.S. Dept. of State, 1976. 5 p. (FAR 26593-S)

"External research study."

Examined in the former Foreign Affairs Research Documentation Center, U.S. Dept. of State.

3372
Improvements must be made in the Sahel regional development program. Washington, Regional Inspector General for Audit, U.S. Agency for International Development, 1981. 37 p. map.

"From 1974 to 1980, the international donor community committed about $7 billion for Sahel regional development. There is strong evidence the Sahelian states cannot effectively use this magnitude of assistance. The Agency should, through the CILSS and Club du Sahel, support a study which addresses realistic funding levels required for Sahel regional development."—Title-page.

Microfiche. [Washington, U.S. Agency for International Development, 1981?] 1 sheet (PN-AAK-426); examined in the Development Information Center.

3373
Infrastructure development in the Sahel in support of basic human needs assistance. [s.l., 1979] 29 p.

Apparently prepared by the U.S. Agency for International Development.

Microfiche. [Sahel Documents and Dissertations. Ann Arbor, Mich., University Microfilms International, 1980] 1 sheet.

DLC-Micro Microfiche 5357 AS 146

3374
International development strategies for the Sahel; a conference held at the Bellagio Study and Conference Center, Italy, October 1974. Summary, condensed transcript, abstracts of papers. [s.l.], 1975. 50 p.

Conference convened by the National Academy of Sciences with the support of the U.S. Agency for International Development and the Rockefeller Foundation.

Examined in the Documentation Center, Sahel Development Program, AID, Washington, D.C.

3375
Kissinger, Henry A. United States proposal for Sahel development. *In* U.S. *Dept. of State.* The Department of State bulletin, v. 74, no. 1927, May 31, 1976: 685–688.　JX232.A33 v. 74

Remarks at a luncheon hosted by Assane Seck, Minister of Foreign Affairs of Senegal, Dakar, May 1, 1976.

3376
Koehring, John W. Sahel regional aid coordinating and planning. [Washington? U.S. Agency for International Development], 1978. [116] leaves (in various foliations)

Concerns funding for the Sahel Regional Aid Coordination and Planning Project.

Examined in the Documentation Center, Sahel Development Program, AID, Washington, D.C.

3377
A Legislative history of U.S. aid to the Sahel: the Sahelian development program. Washington, Koba Associates, inc., 1979. [15] leaves.

Prepared for the U.S. Agency for International Development under contract AID/sod-C-32.

Traces the Congressional authorizations, appropriations, committee reports, and hearings leading to the establishment of the Sahel Development Program.

Microfiche. [Sahel Documents and Dissertations. Ann Arbor, Mich., University Microfilms International, 1980] 1 sheet.

DLC-Micro Microfiche 5357 AS 159

3378

Multi-year Sahelian planning paper. [s.l., U.S. Agency for International Development, 1974] [96] p.

Microfiche. [Sahel Documents and Dissertations. Ann Arbor, Mich., University Microfilms International, 1980] 2 sheets.

DLC-Micro Microfiche 5357 AS 173

3379

National Research Council. *Board on Science and Technology for International Development. Advisory Committee on the Sahel.* Sahel regional aid planning and coordination; semiannual management report. Aug. 1977/Feb. 1978?–Mar./Aug. 1979? Washington.

Prepared for the U.S. Agency for International Development under contract AID/afr-C-1354.

No more published?

Vol. for Mar./Aug. 1979 examined in the Development Information Center, AID, Washington, D.C.

Vols. for Aug. 1977/Feb. 1978–Mar./Aug. 1978 issued in microfiche. [Washington, U.S. Agency for International Development, 1978?] 1 sheet.

DLC-Sci RR PN-AAG-354

3380

New U.S. initiative on Sahel. War on hunger, v. 10, no. 8, 1976: 10–14.   HD9000.1.W37   1976

Issued by the U.S. Agency for International Development.

3381

Pitchford, Gerald E., Stephen D. Nelson, *and* Nathaniel Fields. U.S. assistance in the Sahel: report of a staff study mission to Niger, Upper Volta, Mali, and Senegal, October 26 – November 20, 1978, to the Committee on Foreign Affairs, U.S. House of Representatives. Washington, U.S. Govt. Print. Off., 1979. 64 p.   HC591.S25P49

At head of title: 96th Congress, 1st session. Committee print.

3382

SFWA-Field Planning Workshop, *3d, Ouagadougou,* Sept. 27 – Oct. 1, 1976. Report. [s.l.], Action Programs International, [1976?] 108 p.

Prepared for the U.S. Agency for International Development under contract AID/afr-C-1245.

"This Workshop was the third in a series begun in 1974. These annual workshops have been one means by which the Office of Sahelian and Francophone West Africa [SFWA] has developed a particularly strong Washington-field team with the capacity to manage this country's large and urgent commitments in the Sahel."—p. ii.

Microfiche. [Washington, U.S. Agency for International Development, 1976?] 2 sheets.

DLC-Sci RR PN-AAG-341

3383

SWFA-Field Planning Workshop, *4th, Washington,* 1977. Report. [Washington?], Action Programs International, [1977?] 113 p. map.

Examined in the Documentation Center, Sahel Development Program, AID, Washington, D.C.

3384

Shear, David. International long-term planning in the Sahel. [Washington?], Agency for International Development, 1976. 21 leaves.

Presented at annual meeting of the African Studies Association, 1976.

Microfilm. [African Studies Association. Papers presented at the annual meeting.]

DLC-Micro Microfilm 03782 DT 1976, reel 2

3385

Technical Assistance Information Clearing House. Development assistance programs of U.S. organizations in the Sahel. [New York], American Council of Voluntary Agencies for Foreign Service, 1978. 21 p.

The Clearing House is operated by the Council under a grant from the U.S. Agency for International Development.

Examined in the Development Information Center, AID, Washington, D.C.

3386

Ulinski, Carol A. U.S. forestry and ecology program in the Sahel. [Washington], 1978. 61 p.

Prepared for the U.S. Agency for International Development under contract AID/afr-C-1453.

Bibliography: p. 60–61.

A description of the forestry and ecology program of the Club du Sahel and the United States contribution to the effort to arrest and reverse the desertification in sub-Saharan Africa.

Abstract in *A.I.D. Research and Development Abstracts*, Apr. 1979, p. 17.

Microfiche. [Sahel Documents and Dissertations. Ann Arbor, Mich., University Microfilms International, 1980] (DLC-Micro Microfiche 5357 AS 351); and [Washington, U.S. Agency for International Development, 1978?] 1 sheet (PN-AAG-242).

3387

United Nations Development Programme. Development of the Gambia River basin; multidisciplinary multidonor mission. Final mission report. New York, 1980. 2 v. fold. col. maps.

3387 (cont.)

Study funded in part by the U.S. Agency for International Development.

Issued also in French.

Examined in the Development Information Center, AID, Washington, D.C.

3388

────── Development of the Gambia River basin; multidisciplinary mission, multi-donor mission, March–April 1977: programme of action. [s.l., 1977?] [273] leaves. fold. col. map.

Mission included representatives of the U.S. Agency for International Development.

On cover: "Draft."

Examined in the Documentation Center, Sahel Development Program, AID, Washington, D.C.

3389

Walton, Grant F. Strengthening Sahelian institutional capability (SSIC). Washington, Agency for International Development, 1978. [160] p.

MiEM

"Project paper."

3390

Weil, Peter M. Social conditions in the basin in relation to *Report on a Development Program for the Gambia River Basin: United Nations Multidonor Mission.* [s.l.], 1977. 29 leaves.

Apparently prepared for the U.S. Agency for International Development.

Examined in the Documentation Center, Sahel Development Program, AID, Washington, D.C.

3391

Whalen, Charles W. U.S. participation in the Sahel development program: report on study missions to the African Sahelian countries, submitted to the Committee on International Relations, U.S. House of Representatives. Washington, U.S. Govt. Print. Off., 1978. 22 p. HC591.S25W48

At head of title: 95th Congress, 2d session. Committee print.

Report on study missions in April 1977 and March–April 1978 to Mali, Niger, Upper Volta, The Gambia, Mauritania, and Senegal.

Among the appendixes is the following:

Appendix 2. 1978 report by the Gambian Ministry of Agriculture and National Resources on the drought situation—assessment of crop losses and impact on livestock. p. 17–21.

3392

Williams, Maurice J. Club du Sahel: a new framework

for development cooperation. War on hunger, v. 11, no. 1, Jan 1977: 1–3, 15–16. illus.

HD9000.1.W37 1977

Issued by the U.S. Agency for International Development.

Communications and Transportation

3393

Academy for Educational Development. Discussion paper on communication in development for the Sahel, submitted to the Club des Amis du Sahel. Ottawa, 1977. 6 p.

Prepared for the Office of Education and Human Resources, Bureau for Technical Assistance, U.S. Agency for International Development under contract AID/ta-BOA-1060.

Microfiche. [Washington, U.S. Agency for International Development, 1977?] 1 sheet.

DLC-Sci RR PN-RAB-677

3394

Etude diagnostique d'entretien routier au Sahel; esquisse du rapport final. [s.l.], Louis Berger International, inc., 1977. 9 v.

Study financed by the U.S. Agency for International Development.

Contents. v. 1. Synthèse régionale.—v. 2. Cap Vert.—v. 3. Gambie.—v. 4. Haute Volta.—v. 5. Mali.—v. 6. Mauritanie.—v. 7. Niger.—v. 8. Sénégal.—v. 9. Tchad.

Vol. 8 (Senegal) issued in microfiche. [Sahel documents and dissertations. Ann Arbor, Mich., University Microfilms International, 1980] 3 sheets. DLC-Micro Microfiche 5357 SG 048

3395

Hradsky, James A. USAID experience in policy formulation and project design in the transport sector of the Sahel: a personal opinion. [Washington?], 1978. [55] p.

Prepared for the U.S. Agency for International Development.

At head of title: "Draft."

Microfiche. [Sahel Documents and Dissertations. Ann Arbor, Mich., University Microfilms International, 1980] 1 sheet.

DLC-Micro Microfiche 5357 AS 352

3396

Hudson, Heather, *and* Allan Kulakow. Communications in development for the Sahel. [s.l.], Academy for Educational Development, 1977. [40] leaves (in various foliations)

3396 (cont.)

Prepared for the U.S. Agency for International Development under contract AID/ta-BOA-1377.

Concerns the use of radio in rural communications.

Examined in the Documentation Center, Sahel Development Program, AID, Washington, D.C.

3397

Inventory of data on the transport infrastructure of the Sahel: Senegal, The Gambia, Mauritania, Mali, Upper Volta, Niger, Chad, Cape Verde Islands. [Washington?], Louis Berger International, inc., 1977. 278 p.

Prepared for the Transport & Infrastructure Working Group of the Club des Amis du Sahel under a U.S. Agency for International Development contract.

Microfiche. [Sahel Documents and Dissertations. Ann Arbor, Mich., University Microfilms International, 1980] 5 sheets.

DLC-Micro Microfiche 5357 AS 156

3398

Kulakow, Allan M. Rural radio in the Sahel: a survey of six countries. [s.l.], Academy for Educational Development, 1979. 2 v.

Study funded by the Sahel Development Program, U.S. Agency for International Development.

Prepared for the CILSS secretariat, Bamako, Mali.

Covers Senegal, The Gambia, Mauritania, Niger, Upper Volta, and Mali.

Contents: v. 1. Overview and country profiles. —v. 2. Annex.

Examined in the Documentation Center, Sahel Development Program, AID, Washington, D.C.

3399

Matthews, Daniel G. Information and communications in the Sahelian development strategy. [Washington], BLK Group, 1978. 33 p.

Prepared for the U.S. Agency for International Development under contract AID/afr-C-1199.

Microfiche. [Sahel Documents and Dissertations. Ann Arbor, Mich., University Microfilms International, 1980] 1 sheet (DLC-Micro 5357 Microfiche AS 145); and [Washington, U.S. Agency for International Development, 1978?] 1 sheet, examined in the Development Information Center, AID, Washington, D.C.

3400

Philippi, Thomas. A Sahel transportation survey: a regional profile. Washington, Office of Foreign Disaster Assistance, Agency for International Development, 1979. 137 p.   HE286.5.A1P48

"Prepared for the Office of U.S. Foreign Disaster Assistance, Bureau for Private and Development Cooperation, Agency for International Development, Department of State by Evaluation Technologies, Inc. under contract AID-otr-C-1553."—p. i.

"Designed as a supplement to the series of country profiles developed in support of the planning, analysis and relief operations of the Office of U.S. Foreign Disaster Assistance (OFDA)."— p. ii.

Covers Chad, The Gambia, Mali, Mauritania, Niger, Senegal, and Upper Volta.

3401

Preliminary notes on transport system modelling and planning in the Sahel for USAID. [s.l.], Louis Berger International, inc., 1976. [17] leaves. map.

Issued als in French.

Examined in the Documentation Center, Sahel Development Program, AID, Washington, D.C.

3402

Road maintenance diagnostic study for the Sahel; draft final report. [s.l.], Louis Berger International, inc., 1977. [240] p.

Financed by the U.S. Agency for International Development.

Prepared in association with INGECOT, Abidjan, Ivory Coast.

Microfiche. [Sahel Documents and Dissertations. Ann Arbor, Mich., University Microfilms International, 1980] 3 sheets.

DLC-Micro Microfiche 5357 AS 268

3403

The Role of AID in the development of Sahel transportation infrastructure. Washington, Office of International Transportation Programs, U.S. Dept. of Transportation, 1978. 1 v. (various pagings)

"Preliminary draft report."

Examined in the Development Information Center, U.S. Agency for International Development, Washington, D.C.

3404

The Role of AID in the development of Sahel transportation infrastructure; a strategy proposed by the Office of International Transportation Programs. Washington, U.S. Dept. of Transportation, 1979. 2 v.

Prepared for the U.S. Agency for International Development.

Vol. 2 has title, *The Economy and Geography of the Sahel.*

Vol. 1–2 examined in the Documentation Center,

3404 (cont.)

Sahel Development Program, AID, Washington, D.C.

Vol. 1 issued also in microfiche. [Sahel Documents and Dissertations. Ann Arbor, Mich., University Microfilms International, 1980] 4 sheets.

DLC-Micro Microfiche 5357 AS 271

3405

Sahel diagnostic road maintenance study; interim report. Ouagadougou, Louis Berger International, inc., 1977. 1 v. (various pagings)

Financed by the U.S. Agency for International evelopment.

Prepared in association with INGECOT for the Transport and Infrastructure Working Group, Club des Amis du Sahel.

Microfiche. [Sahel Documents and Dissertations. Ann Arbor, University Microfilms International, 1980] 3 sheets.

DLC-Micro Microfiche 5357 AS 281

Economic Conditions

3406

Baier, Stephen, *and* David J. King. Drought and the development of Sahelian economies: a case study of Hausa-Tuareg interdependence. Madison, Land Tenure Center, University of Wisconsin, 1975. 11 p.

Focuses on Niger and northern Nigeria.

Abstract in *A.I.D. Research and Development Abstracts*, Sept. 1975, p. 35.

Microfiche. [Washington, U.S. Agency for International Development, 1975?] 1 sheet.

DLC-Sci RR PN-AAB-226

3407

Baker, Raymond W. Private sector involvement in Sahelian development. [Bethesda, Md.], 1979. [44] leaves (in various foliations)

Prepared for the U.S. Agency for International Development.

Examined in the Documentation Center, Sahel Development Program, AID, Washington, D.C.

3408

Berg, Elliot. The economic impact of drought and inflation in the Sahel. Ann Arbor, Center for Research on Economic Development, University of Michigan, 1976. 35 p. (Michigan. University. Center for Research on Economic Development. Discussion paper, no. 51)   MiU

"This paper is based on a report, *The Recent Economic Evolution of the Sahel*, prepared by the University of Michigan for AID."

Abstract in *A.I.D. Research and Development Abstracts*, Apr. 1979, p. 2.

Issued also in microfiche. [Washington, U.S. Agency for International Development, 1976?] 1 sheet.   DLC-Sci RR PN-AAC-740

3409

——— The recent economic evolution of the Sahel. Ann Arbor, Center for Research on Economic Development, University of Michigan, 1975. 247 p. illus.   HC591.S25B47

Prepared for the U.S. Agency for International Development under the "Sahel Economic Survey" contract.

Bibliography: p. 231–247.

Abstracts in *A.I.D. Research and Development Abstracts*, Apr. 1976, p. 13–14.

Issued also in microfiche. [Washington, U.S. Agency for International Development, 1975?] 3 sheets (DLC-Sci RR PN-AAB-423); and [Sahel Documents and Dissertations. Ann Arbor, Mich., University Microfilms International, 1980] 5 sheets (DLC-Micro Microfiche 5357 AS 247).

3410

George, Emmett. After the drought: a slow recovery. War on hunger, v. 11, no. 8, Aug. 1977: 12–17. illus.   HD9000.1.W37

Issued by the U.S. Agency for International Development.

3411

Horenstein, Nadine. Comparative analysis of national plans and budgets of the Sahelian countries. Washington, BLK Group, 1979. [188] p.

DLC

Prepared for the Sahel Development Program, U.S. Agency for International Development, under contract AID/afr-C-1199.

Covers The Gambia, Mali, Mauritania, Niger, Senegal, Upper Volta, Cape Verde, and Chad.

Abstract in *A.I.D. Research & Development Abstracts*, July 1981, p. 24–25.

Issued also in microfiche. [Washington, U.S. Agency for International Development, 1979?] (PN-AAH-371).

3412

Horowitz, Michael M., John V. Lewis, *and* Tom Painter. The sociology and political economy of the Sahel: an annotated bibliography. Binghampton, N.Y., Institute for Development Anthropology, inc., [1979?] 34 p.

Prepared for the U.S. Agency for International Development under contract AID/afr-C-1469.

On t.p.: Workshop on Social Analysis of De-

3412 (cont.)

velopment Programs and Projects, Nouakchott, Islamic Republic of Mauritania, April 4–7, 1979.

Abstract in *A.I.D. Research and Development Abstracts*, Feb. 1981, p. 65.

Microfiche. [Washington, U.S. Agency for International Development, 1979?] 1 sheet (DLC-Sci RR PN-AAH-473); and [Sahel Documents and Dissertations. Ann Arbor, Mich., University Microfilms International, 1980] 1 sheet (DLC-Micro 5357 AS 308).

3413

Opportunity for self-reliance: an overview of the Sahel development potential. Washington, Agency for International Development, [1976] 16 p. illus., maps.   DLC

"This overview sketches the nature of the Sahel's vulnerability and its potential for self-sufficiency and presents the concepts of the Sahel Development Program."

Issued also in microfiche. [Sahel Documents and Dissertations. Ann Arbor, Mich., University Microfilms International, 1980] 1 sheet (DLC-Micro Microfiche 5357 AS 185); and [Washington, U.S. Agency for International Development, 1976?] 1 sheet (PN-AAA-081).

Geology, Hydrology, and Mineral Resources

3414

Sahel water data network and water resources management project; final report. [Washington?], U.S. National Oceanic and Atmospheric Administration, 1975. [229] p. map.

Prepared for the U.S. Agency for International Development.

Microfiche. [Sahel Documents and Dissertations. Ann Arbor, Mich., University Microfilms International, 1980] 3 sheets.

DLC-Micro Microfiche 5357 AS 283

3415

Sahel water data network—625-0917 (amendment). Washington, U.S. Agency for International Development, 1978. [80] p.   MiEM

'Project paper.'

Health and Nutrition

3416

U.S. *Agency for International Development.* Report of at-risk team survey to Mauritania, Mali, Niger, and Upper Volta. [Washington, 1974?] 1 v. (various foliations of leaves) maps.

Helen Wilson and Raymond Fontaine, team leaders.

An investigation of the existance of "at-risk populations" as a result of drought conditions.

Examined in the Documentation Center, Sahel Development Program, AID, Washington, D.C.

3417

Barbiero, Victor K. Health impact guidelines for the design of development projects in the Sahel. Washington, Family Health Care, inc., 1979. 2 v.

Prepared for the U.S. Agency for International Development under contract AID/afr-C-1138.

Includes bibliography.

Contents: v. 1. Sector-specific reviews and methodology (133 p.).—v. 2. Reference manual (206 p.).

Abstracts of both vols. in *A.I.D. Research & Development Abstracts*, v. 9, no. 3, 1981, p. 44–45.

Microfiche. [Sahel Documents and Dissertations. Ann Arbor, Mich., University Microfilms International, 1980] 7 sheets.

DLC-Micro Microfiche 5357 AS 136

3418

Health impact guidelines for non-health development personnel in the Sahel: a total perspective approach. Dryland agriculture booklet. Washington, Family Health Care, inc., 1978. 63 p.

Prepared under U.S. Agency for International Development contract AID/afr-C-1138.

"Submitted in draft: October 3, 1978 to: Comité permanent inter-états de lutte contre la sécheresse dans le Sahel, Ouagadougou, Upper Volta."

"The main purpose of this document is to help non-health sector project officers identify the impact(s) their projects may have on human health. It is designed to increase the awareness of development personnel about the types and causes of health problems in the Sahel."—p. iv.

Examined in the Documentation Center, Sahel Development Program, AID, Washington, D.C.

The following additional booklets/manuals prepared by Family Health Care, inc. under the same AID contract have also been examined in the Sahel Development Program's Documentation Center:

Livestock development booklet. 1978. 66 p.
Transportation booklet. 1978. 66 leaves.
Tropical disease manual. 1979. 112 p.

3419

Joseph, Stephen C., *and* Stanley C. Scheyer. A strategy for health as a component of the Sahel development program. Washington, Family Health Care, inc., 1977. [128] p.

3419 (cont.)

Financed by the U.S. Agency for International Development under contract AID/atr-C-1138.

Bibliography: p. [124–128].

Prepared for CILSS and the Club des amis du Sahel.

Issued also in French.

Microfiche. [Washington, U.S. Agency for International Development, 1977?] 2 sheets (DLC-Sci RR PN-AAE-111); and [Sahel Documents and Dissertations. Ann Arbor, Mich., University Microfilms International, 1980] 2 sheets (DLC-Micro Microfiche 5357 AS 321)

3420

Nutrition strategy in the Sahel; final report. Silver Spring, Md., Intech, inc., 1977. 146 p. illus.

Prepared for the U.S. Agency for International Development under contract AID/ta-C-1214.

Covers Chad, Mali, Mauritania, Niger, Senegal, and Upper Volta.

Abstract in *A.I.D. Research and Development Abstracts*, Oct. 1977, p. 12.

Microfiche. [Washington, U.S. Agency for International Development, 1977?] 2 sheets (DLC-Sci RR PN-AAD-520); and [Sahel Documents and Dissertations. Ann Arbor, Mich., University Microfilms International, 1980] 2 sheets (DLC-Micro Microfiche 5357 AS 183).

3421

Nutritional surveillance in drought affected areas of West Africa (Mali, Mauritania, Niger, Upper Volta) August-September 1973. Atlanta, Center for Disease Control, U.S. Public Health Service, [1973] 37 p. maps.

Microfiche. [Sahel Documents and Dissertations. Ann Arbor, Mich., University Microfilms International, 1980] 1 sheet.

DLC-Micro Microfiche 5357 AS 184

3422

Progress report on the health/water/nutrition component of the Sahel Development Program. 1977?+ Washington, Family Health Care, inc. annual.

Prepared for the Sahel Development Program, U.S. Agency for International Development, under contract AID/afr-C-1138.

Vols. for 1977–78 examined in the Documentation Center, Sahel Development Program, AID, Washington, D.C.

3423

Sahel nutrition survey, 1974. Atlanta, Center for Disease Control, Bureau of Smallpox Eradication, [1974?] 65 leaves. map.

Examined in the Documentation Center, Sahel Development Program, U.S. Agency for International Development, Washington, D.C.

Bibliographies

3424

Bibliography of documents on health and diseases in the Sahel. [Washington], Documentation Center, Sahel Development Program, U.S. Agency for International Development, 1980. 6 leaves.

Examined in the Documentation Center, Sahel Development Program, AID, Washington, D.C.

3425

Bibliography of nutrition in the Sahel. Silver Spring, Md., Intech, inc., 1977. 484 p.

Prepared for the U.S. Agency for International Development under contract AID/ta-C-1214.

Issued as an annex to *Nutrition Strategy in the Sahel* (entry 3420).

Includes approximately 2,600 entries; partially annotated.

Abstract in *A.I.D. Research and Development Abstracts*, Oct. 1977, p. 33.

Microfiche. [Washington, U.S. Agency for International Development, 1977?] 5 sheets.

DLC-Sci RR PN-AAD-521

3426

Fikry, Mona. Traditional maternal and child health care and related problems in the Sahel; a bibliographic study. [s.l.], BLK Group, inc., 1977. 123 p.

"This report is prepared at the request of the Sahel Development Project-Health Sector, U.S.A.I.D."

Includes a 55-page essay and a 60-page annotated bibliography.

At head of title: Preliminary report.

Abstract in *A.I.D. Research and Development Abstracts*, Oct. 1977, p. 33–34.

Microfiche. [Washington, U.S. Agency for International Development, 1977?] 2 sheets (DLC-Sci RR PN-AAC-942); and [Sahel Documents and Dissertations. Ann Arbor, Mich., University Microfilms International, 1980] 2 sheets (DLC-Micro Microfiche 5357 AS 203).

Libraries and Library Resources

3427

DeBenko, Eugene. Documentation for development in the Sahel: report of an acquisitions tour. East

3427 (cont.)

Lansing, Sahel Documentation Center, Michigan State University Libraries, 1977. 37 p.   MiEM

Based on a report of travel to Chad, Niger, Upper Volta, Mali, Mauritania, and Senegal under U.S. Agency for International Development contract AID/afr-C-1261.

Issued also in microfiche. [Sahel Documents and Dissertations. Ann Arbor, Mich., University Microfilms International, 1980] 1 sheet.
DLC-Micro Microfiche 5357 AS 081

3428

—— Drought control in the Sahel; report on a conference and acquisitions trip. East Lansing, Sahel Documentation Center, Michigan State University Libraries, 1977. 20 p.

Report of a survey trip to France, Senegal, Upper Volta, Cape Verde, and The Gambia, Oct.–Nov. 1977, under U.S. Agency for International Development contract AID/afr-C-1261.

Microfiche. [Sahel Documents and Dissertations. Ann Arbor, Mich., University Microfilms International, 1980] 1 sheet.
DLC-Micro Microfiche 5357 AS 087

3429

Matthews, Daniel G. Documentation in the Sahelian development strategy: the Sahelian scientific and technical information and documentation network. [Washington], BLK Group, 1978. 119 p.

Prepared under U.S. Agency for International Development contract AID/afr-C-1199.

Prepared pursuant to a request by CILSS and the Sahel Development Program, AID, "to survey and ascertain both short-term and long-term documentation and information priorities."—p. 1.

Microfiche. [Sahel Documents and Dissertations. Ann Arbor, Mich., University Microfiche 5357 AS 082); and [Washington, U.S. Agency for International Development, 1978?] 2 sheets (PN-AAF-718), examined in the Development Information Center, AID, Washington, D.C.

3430

Walsh, Gretchen. Access to sources of information on agricultural development in the Sahel. East Lansing, Dept. of Agricultural Economics, Michigan State University, 1976. 25 p. (African Rural Economy Program. Working paper, no. 17)
MiEM

Prepared under U.S. Agency for International Development grant AID/afr-C-1261.

List of bibliographies: p. 22–25.

Paper presented at the annual meeting of the African Studies Association, 1976.

Abstract in *A.I.D. Research and Development Abstracts*, Jan. 1979, p. 24.

Issued also in microfiche. [Washington, U.S. Agency for International Development, 1976?] 1 sheet (DLC-Sci RR PN-AAF-491); and [Sahel Documents and Dissertations. Ann Arbor, Mich., University Microfilms International, 1980] 1 sheet (DLC-Micro Microfiche 5357 AS 002).

Population Studies

3431

Caldwell, John C. The Sahelian drought and its demographic implications. [Washington], Overseas Liaison Committee, American Council on Education, 1975. 88 p. map. (American Council on Education. Overseas Liaison Committee. OLC paper, no. 8)   HC591.S25F32

Activities of the Overseas Liaison Committee are funded in part through a contract with the U.S. Agency for International Development.

Bibliography: p. 77–87.

At head of title: Development from below.

Abstract in *A.I.D. Research and Development Abstracts*, Jan. 1978, p. 32.

Issued also in microfiche. [Washington, U.S. Agency for International Development, 1975?] 1 sheet (DLC-Sci RR PN-AAD-586); and [Sahel Documents and Dissertations. Ann Arbor, Mich., University Microfilms International, 1980] 2 sheets (DLC-Micro Microfiche 5357 AS 285).

3432

Colvin, Lucie G. Labor and migration in colonial Senegambia. *In* The Uprooted of the western Sahel: migrants' quest for cash in the Senegambia, [by] Lucie Gallistel Colvin [et al.] New York, Praeger, [1981] p. 58–80. maps.   HB2125.5.A3U67

"The U.S. Agency for International Development (AID) funded this research."—p. iii.

3433

—— Migration and public policy in the Senegambia. *In* The Uprooted of the western Sahel: migrants' quest for cash in the Senegambia, [by] Lucie Gallistel Colvin [et al.] New York, Praeger, [1981] p. 317–343. map.   HB2125.5.A3U67

"The U.S. Agency for International Development (AID) funded this research."—p. iii.

3434

—— Senegambia migration study; mid-term report. [s.l., 1978?] [39] p. map.

Prepared for the U.S. Agency for International Development under contract AID/afr-C-1363.

Microfiche. [Sahel Documents and Disserta-

3434 (cont.)

tions. Ann Arbor, Mich., University Microfilms International, 1980] 1 sheet.

DLC-Micro Microfiche 5357 SG 082

3435

Harris, Joseph E. Feasibility report on historical role of migration between Sahelian and coastal states of West Africa. [s.l.], BLK Group, inc., 1977. 15 p.

Prepared for the U.S. Agency for International Development under contract AID/afr-C-1199.

Examined in the Development Information Center, AID, Washington, D.C.

3436

An Inventory of demographic capabilities and activities in the Sahel. Washington, Family Health Care, inc., 1979. [174] p. (in various pagings)

Prepared for the U.S. Agency for International Development.

Issued in association with the Population Council, New York, and the Sahel Institute, Bamako.

Microfiche. [Washington, U.S. Agency for International Development, 1979?] 2 sheets.

DLC-Sci RR PN-AAG-799

3437

Need to consider population growth in Sahel development planning: a case study. *In* U.S. *General Accounting Office*. Reducing population growth through social and economic change in developing countries: a new direction for U.S. assistance: report to the Congress, by the Comptroller General of the United States. Washington, 1978. p. 58–70.

HC60.U6G4 1978a

"ID-78-6."

3438

An Operation strategy for a demographic program in the Sahel. Washington, Family Health Care, inc., 1979. [108] p.

Submitted to the Sahel Development Program, U.S. Agency for International Development, under contract AID/afr-C-1413.

Issued in cooperation with the Population Council, New York.

In English or French.

Microfiche. [Washington, U.S. Agency for International Development, 1979?] 2 sheets (PN-AAG-800); examined in the Development Information Center, AID, Washington, D.C.

3439

Sabagh, Georges. Consultant report on CILSS conference, Upper Volta—October 1977. [s.l., 1977?] 11 p.

Report prepared under the auspices of the American Public Health Association with support from the Office of Population, U.S. Agency for International Development.

Concerns demographic research.

Microfiche. [Washington, U.S. Agency for International Development, 1977?] 1 sheet.

DLC-Sci RR PN-AAG-086

3440

The Uprooted of the western Sahel: migrants' quest for cash in the Senegambia, [by] Lucie Gallistel Colvin [et al.] New York, Praeger, [1981] 385 p. illus., maps. HB2125.5.A3U67

"The U.S. Agency for International Development (AID) funded this research."—p. iii.

Bibliography: p. 344—385.

Note: Selected chapters of the study are cited individually in this guide under their personal authors; they can be identified through the index under *The Uprooted of the Western Sahel.*

Remote Sensing

3441

Grolier, Maurice J., R. W. Fary, *and* S. J. Gawarecki. The Sahelian zone remote sensing seminar/workshop at Bamako, Mali, West Africa, April 17–28, 1973. [Reston, Va., 1974] 32 leaves. (U.S. Geological Survey. [Reports—Open file series, no. 74-196]) DI-GS

3442

Jones, James R., *and* R. H. Miller. Application of ERTS technology in development programs for the Liptako-Gourma Authority countries (Mali, Niger, and Upper Volta) [Reston, Va.?], 1973. 16, 13 p. (U.S. Geological Survey. Interagency report. West Africa investigations, (IR) WA, no. 1)

DI-GS

Study requested by the U.S. Agency for International Development.

Issued also in microfiche. [Sahel Documents and Dissertations. Ann Arbor, Mich., University Microfilms International, 1980] 1 sheet.

DLC-Micro Microfiche 5357 UV 019

3443

Worcester, B. K., K. J. Dalsted, *and* D. G. Moore. Sahel-Sudano desertification study. Brookings, Remote Sensing Institute, South Dakota State University, 1978. 62 leaves. illus.

Prepared for the U.S. Agency for International Development.

"This study was initiated to evaluate the usefulness of Landsat data for monitoring the effects of desertification on arid and semi-arid lands. A

3443 (cont.)

study area was selected which encompasses parts of Mauritania, Mali, and Senegal."

Held by the Remote Sensing Institute, South Dakota State University, Brookings.

Senegal River Basin

3444

U.S. *Agency for International Development.* Annual budget submission: OMVS. [Washington]

Title varies slightly.

OMVS: Organisation pour la mise en valeur du fleuve Sénégal.

Covers Mali, Mauritania, and Senegal.

Vols. for 1977/78, 1980+ examined in the Development Information Center, AID, Washington, D.C.

3445

Assessment of environmental effects of proposed developments in the Senegal River basin; final report. [s.l.], Gannett, Fleming, Corddry, and Carpenter, inc., 1977. 2 v.

Contents: v. 1. Synthesis (209 p.).—v. 2. Plan of action (188 p.).

Microfiche. [Washington, U.S. Agency for International Development, 1977?] 5 sheets (PN-AAJ-571—PN-AAJ-572); examined in the Development Information Center, U.S. Agency for International Development, Washington, D.C.

3446

Assessment of environmental effects of proposed developments in the Senegalese River Basin: interim report: public health aspects. [Harrisburg, Pa.?], Gannett, Fleming, Corddry, and Carpenter, inc., [1980?] 2 v.   MiEM

Funded by the U.S. Agency for International Development.

Prepared for the Organisation pour la mise en veleur du fleuve Sénégal.

3447

Cost allocation alternatives for the Senegal River development program, by H. Paul Riley [et al.] Logan, Utah State University, 1978. 129 p. illus., maps. (Utah. Water Research Laboratory. Water resources planning series, P-78/06)   ULA

"Revised draft" (1977), funded by the U.S. Agency for International Development, examined in the Documentation Center, Sahel Development Program, AID, Washington, D.C.

3448

Development of irrigated perimeters in the Senegal River basin. [Washington?, U.S. Agency for International Development, 1977?] 15 p.

At head of title: Project review paper.

Microfiche. [Sahel Documents and Dissertations. Ann Arbor, Mich., University Microfilms International, 1980] 1 sheet.

DLC-Micro Microfiche 5357 SG 037

3449

Dudley, Earll D. A hydrologic review of the proposed Bakel-small perimeters, Senegal River basin. [Washington?] U.S. Bureau of Reclamation, 1976. 28 leaves. illus., maps.

Prepared for the U.S. Agency for International Development.

"The report recommends measures which should be taken to protect the irrigated perimeters from anticipated floods."

Examined in the Documentation Center, Sahel Development Center, AID, Washington, D.C.

3450

Environmental program for the integrated development of the Senegal River basin; terms of reference. [Washington?], U.S. Agency for International Development, 1975. 35 p.

At head of title: Organisation pour la mise en valeur du fleuve Sénégal (O.M.V.S.).

Microfiche. [Sahel Documents and Dissertations. Ann Arbor, Mich., University Microfilms International, 1980] 1 sheet.

DLC-Micro Microfiche 5357 SG 045

3451

Issues paper on "U.S. assistance to the OMVS and the Senegal River basin." [Washington?, 1978?] [69] leaves.

Apparently prepared by the U.S. Agency for International Development.

Examined in the Documentation Center, AID, Washington, D.C.

3452

Lubin, Samuel. Review of the Bureau of Reclamation *Senegal River Basin Water Resources Development Analysis.* [Washington? 1975] 21 p.

Review and summary of a report prepared by the U.S. Bureau of Reclamation for the U.S. Agency for International Development.

Microfiche. [Washington, U.S. Agency for International Development, 1975?] 1 sheet.

DLC-Sci RR PN-AAG-124

3453

May, Jacques M. Environmental program for the integrated development of the Senegal River basin. Annex C: Public health aspects. [Washington?],

3453 (cont.)

U.S. Agency for International Development, 1975 37 p.

At head of title: Organisation pour la mise en valeur du fleuve Sénégal (OMVS).

Microfiche. [Sahel Documents and Dissertations. Ann Arbor, Mich., University Microfilms International, 1980] 1 sheet.

DLC-Micro Microfiche 5357 SG 043

3454

OMVS/Senegal River basin hydrometeorological system and hydrogeologic investigations and evaluation: project review paper. [Washington?, Agency for International Development, 1976?] [69] leaves (in various foliations) map.

Examined in the Documentation Center, Sahel Development Program, AID, Washington, D.C.

3455

Organisation pour la mise en valeur du fleuve Sénégal. [*Treaties, etc. United States, 1976 Feb. 25*] Grant agreement for the environmental assessment of the Senegal River basin between the Agency for International Development and the Organisation pour la mise en valeur du fleuve Sénégal (O.M.V.S.). *In* U.S. *Treaties, etc.* United States treaties and other international agreements, v. 28, 1976–77. [Washington, Dept. of State; for sale by the Supt. of Docs., U.S. Govt. Print. Off., 1978] p. 5081–5107. ([Treaties and other international acts series, 8613])   JX231.A34 v. 28
Signed at Dakar Feb. 25, 1976.
In English and French.

3456

Organisation pour la mise en valeur du fleuve Sénégal. [*Treaties, etc. United States, 1976 Aug. 31*] Grant agreement for the O.M.V.S. Senegal River basin survey and mapping between the Agency for International Development ("A.I.D.") and the Organisation pour la mise en valeur du fleuve Senegal ("O.M.V.S."). *In* U.S. *Treaties, etc.* United States treaties and other international agreements, v. 28, 1976–77. [Washington, Dept. of State; for sale by the Supt. of Docs., U.S. Govt. Print. Off., 1979] p. 8985–9000. ([Treaties and other international acts series, 8779])
JX231.A34 v. 28
Signed at Dakar Aug. 31, 1976.
In English and French.

3457

Pierce, Phillip C. Environmental program for the integrated development of the Senegal River basin. Annex D. Plant and animal life aspects. Washing-ton, Office of the Chief of Engineers, U.S. Army Corps of Engineers, 1975. 53 p.

At head of title: U.S. Agency for International Development; Organisation pour la mise en valeur du fleuve Sénégal (OMVS).

Microfiche. [Sahel Documents and Dissertations. Ann Arbor, Mich., University Microfilms International, 1980] 1 sheet.

DLC-Micro Microfiche 5357 SG 044

3458

Problems involved in implementation of OMVS projects noted. *In* U.S. *Joint Publications Research Service.* JPRS 72680. [Springfield, Va., National Technical Information Service, 1979] (Translations on Sub-Saharan Africa, no. 2054) p. 10–14.

Translation of article in *Remarques Arabo-Africaines*, Brussels, Nov. 1978, p. 22–24.

Microfiche. [Washington, Supt. Of Docs., U.S. Govt. Print. Off., 1979]

DLC-Micro JPRS 72680

3459

Scherrer, J. Carole. Evaluation of the socio-economic studies. [Washington?], BLK Group, 1978. 16 p.

A review of a survey conducted in 1977–78 to gather recent data on traditional farming in the Senegal River basin before change was brought about through the introduction of irrigation.

Microfiche. [Sahel Documents and Dissertations. Ann Arbor, Mich., University Microfilms International, 1980] 1 sheet.

DLC-Micro Microfiche 5357 SG 053

3460

Senegal River basin preliminary basic data examination and suggested study program. [Washington?], U.S. Bureau of Reclamation, 1976. 195 p. maps.

Prepared for the U.S. Agency for International Development.

Microfiche. [Sahel Documents and Dissertations. Ann Arbor, Mich., University Microfilms International, 1980] 3 sheets.

DLC-Micro Microfiche 5357 SG 123

3461

Senegal River basin survey and mapping proposal and terms of reference. [Washington], Topographic Center, Defense Mapping Agency, [1976?] [98] leaves. maps.

Sponsored by the U.S. Agency for International Development.

Examined in the Documentation Center, Sahel Development Program, AID, Washington, D.C.

3462

Senegal River development programs discussed. *In* U.S. *Joint Publications Research Service.* JPRS 68571. [Springfield, Va., National Technical Information Service, 1977] (Translations on Sub-Saharan Africa, no. 1708) p. 51–60.

Translation of series of articles in *Europe Outremer*, Paris, Sept. 1976, p. 21–24.

Microfiche. [s.l., 1977]

DLC-Micro JPRS 68571

3463

A study of the OMVS organization and training program. [s.l.], Stevens, Thompson & Runyan, inc., 1975. 64 leaves. map.

Prepared for the U.S. Agency for International Development under contract AID/otr-C-1301.

On cover: Organisation pour la mise en valeur du fleuve Sénégal. Senegal-Mali-Mauritania.

Microfiche. [Washington, U.S. Agency for International Development, 1975?] 1 sheet.

DLC-Sci RR PN-RAB-608

3464

Traoré, Moussa. New OMVS head optimistic about future. *In* U.S. *Joint Publications Research Service.* JPRS 67767. [Springfield, Va., National Technical Information Service, 1976] (Translations on Sub-Saharan Africa, no. 1668) p. 3–7.

Translation of article in *Le Soleil*, Dakar, July 17, 1976, p. 3.

Microfiche. [s.l., 1976]

DLC-Micro JPRS 67767

Social Conditions

3465

U.S. *Agency for International Development. Sahel Development Program.* Infrastructure development in the Sahel in support of basic human needs assistance. [s.l.], 1979. 29 p.   MiEM

3466

——— Sahel development program projects which relate to the human resources sector. Washington, 1977. 13 p.   MiEM

3467

New adaptive social mechanisms evolving among three Sahelian populations affected by the drought: Senegal, Niger, Upper Volta, [by] Elliott P. Skinner [et al.] Washington, African-American Scholars Council, 1978. 423 p.

Issued for the U.S. Agency for International Development under contract AID/afr-G-1162 covering the period Aug. 1975–July 1978.

An investigation by four research teams of ways in which farmers and herders adapted to the 1966–73 drought.

Microfiche. [Sahel Documents and Dissertations. Ann Arbor, Mich., University Microfilms International, 1980] 5 sheets.

DLC-Micro Microfiche AS 174

3468

Sahelian social development, edited by Stephen P. Reyna. Abidjan, Regional Economic Development Services Office, West Africa, U.S. Agency for International Development, 1980. 702 p.

Includes bibliographies.

A compilation of papers "on social aspects of historial development and on social limitations of bilateral and multilateral development projects undertaken since independence." These papers are entered separately in this guide; entry numbers are given in the index under the heading *Sahelian Social Development.*

Abstract in *A.I.D. Research & Development Abstracts*, v. 9, no. 3, 1981, p. 66–67.

Microfiche. [Washington, U.S. Agency for International Development, 1980?] 8 sheets (PN-AAH-943); held by the Development Information Center, Agency for International Development, Washington, D.C.

3469

The Tuareg: nature changes life style. New York, School Services Division, African-American Institute, [1975] 7 p.

A brief outline of the effects of drought conditions.

Abstract in *Resources in Education*, Apr. 1977, p. 131.

Microfiche. [Arlington, Va., ERIC Document Reproduction Service; prepared for Educational Resources Information Center, National Institute of Education, 1977] 1 sheet.

DLC-Micro ED132094

Women

3470

Black Women's Community Development Foundation. Report. [s.l., 1975. 72 p.

Prepared for the U.S. Agency for International Development.

Concerns the Sahel region.

Microfiche. [Sahel Documents and Dissertations. Ann Arbor, Mich., University Microfirms International, 1980] 1 sheet.

DLC-Micro Microfiche 5357 AS119

3471

Cloud, Kathleen. Sex roles in food production and food distribution systems in the Sahel. Washington, Office of Women in Development, Agency for International Development, 1977. 20 leaves.

DLC

On cover: "This paper was prepared under contract for USAID, Bureau for Africa, AFR/SFWA Project Activity No. 625-11-625-0907, Order No. AFR-147-42."

Bibliography: leaves 19-20.

Abstract in *A.I.D. Research and Development Abstracts*, Oct. 1978, p. 6.

Issued also in microfiche in the *Proceedings* of the International Conference on Women and Food, University of Arizona, Tucson, Jan. 8–11, 1978, p. 62–89 ([Washington, U.S. Agency for International Development, 1978?] DLC-Sci RR PN-AAG-053).

3472

Dinnerstein, Myra, *and* Kathleen Cloud. Report of a fact-finding trip to Niger, Mali, Senegal, and Upper Volta. [s.l.], 1976. [10] p.

Sponsored by the U.S. Agency for International Development.

Expressed purpose of the trip was "to assess the degree of integration of women into development projects in these countries, with specific reference to the Niger Cereals Project and the Bakel Village Livestock Project."—title page.

Microfiche. [Sahel Documents and Dissertations. Ann Arbor, Mich., University Microfilms International, 1980] 1 sheet.

DLC-Micro Microfiche 5357 AS 252

3473

Dulansey, Maryanne. Women in development program concerns in francophone Sahel; report on a workshop, July 5–7, 1979, Bobo-Dioulasso, Upper Volta. Washington, Office of Women in Development, U.S. Agency for International Development, [1979?] 11 p.

DLC

3474

Examples of women in development programs in Sahel francophone West Africa. [Washington?, Office of Sahel & Francophone West Africa Affairs, Bureau for Africa, Agency for International Development], 1979. 27 p.

Microfiche. [Washington, U.S. Agency for International Development, 1979?] 1 sheet (PN-AAK-281); examined in the Development Information Center, AID, Washington, D.C.

3475

Non-formal education—women in Sahel. [Washing-

ton?, U.S. Agency for International Development, 1978] [23] leaves.

Examined in the Documentation Center, Sahel Development Program, AID, Washington, D.C.

Other Subjects

3476

Barbiero, Victor K. An ecological analysis of famine: the case of the Sahel drought. Baltimore, School of Hygiene and Public Health, Johns Hopkins University, 1977. 71 leaves.

Supported in part by the U.S. Agency for International Development.

Thesis (M.S.)—Johns Hopkins University.

Examined in the Documentation Center, Sahel Development Program, AID, Washington, D.C.

3477

Barry, Boubacar. Economic anthropology of precolonial Senegambia from the fifteenth through the nineteenth centuries. *In* The Uprooted of the western Sahel: migrants' quest for cash in the Senegambia, [by] Lucie Gallistel Colvin [et al.] New York, Praeger, [1981] p. 27–57. map.

HB2125.5.A3U67

"The U.S. Agency for International Development (AID) funded this research."—p. iii.

3478

Mortimer, Robert A. Trans-Saharan ties and tensions: Maghrebi policy in Sahelian West Africa. [s.l.], 1980. 14 leaves.
DLC

On cover: "A paper prepared for the Conference on African-Arab Relations, Department of State, May 2–3, 1980."

"This paper examines the policy of four North African states—Algeria, Morocco, Tunisia, and Libya—toward the Sahelian states stretching from Senegal and Mauritania to Chad."—p. 2.

Abstract in *Government Reports Announcements & Index*, Jan. 2, 1981, p. 26.

Issued also in microfiche. [s.l., Defense Documentation Center, 1980] 1 sheet.

DLC-Sci RR AD-A089015

3479

Reisman, Paul. The Fulani in a development context. *In* Sahelian social development, edited by Stephen P. Reyna. Abidjan, Regional Economic Development Services Office, West Africa, U.S. Agency for International Development, 1980. p. 71–186.

Bibliography: p. 181–186.

Microfiche. [Washington, U.S. Agency for International Development, 1980?] (PN-AAH-943); held

3479 (cont.)

by the Development Information Center, Agency for International Development, Washington, D.C.

3480

Resources for short-term skills training in the Sahel, [by] Allan M. Kulakow [et al.] Washington, Academy for Educational Development, inc., 1977. [230] p. (in various pagings)   DLC

Prepared for the U.S. Agency for International Development under contract AID/afr-C-1131.

Issued also in French under title *Ressourcement de la formation pratique a court terme pour les pays du Sahel*; microfiche held by DLC-Sci RR (PN-AAG-074 2 sheets).

3481

Rifkin, Norman. Human resources sector analysis. [Washington], Office of Sahel and Francophone West Africa, U.S. Agency for International Development, 1980. 25 p.

"To help identify the human resources needed for the Sahel's development over the next 20 years, this report analyzes three areas of education—formal (primary and secondary), technical and higher, and nonformal (NFE)—and suggests priority areas for A.I.D. support."—Abstract.

Abstract in *A.I.D. Research & Development Abstracts*, v. 10, no. 1/2, 1982, p. 38.

3482

The Sahel Development Program proposals for: energy supply/demand and development study, and management, planning and program assessment system design and implementation. Washington, 1978. [33] leaves.

Apparently prepared for the U.S. Agency for International Development.

Examined in the Documentation Center, Sahel Development Program, AID, Washington, D.C.

3483

Shaw, Margaret G. Administrative structures and civil service in the Sahel countries. [s.l.], 1979. [141] leaves.   DLC

Prepared for the U.S. Agency for International Development under contract AID/afr-C-1454.

Includes bibliographies.

For each Sahelian country—Cape Verde, Chad, Mali, Mauritania, Niger, Senegal, The Gambia, and Upper Volta—there is a list of government ministries, bureaus, and other agencies.

3484

Stavis, Ben. Institutions in the Sahel. East Lansing, Dept. of Agricultural Economics, Michigan State University, 1979. 29 p.   MiEM

Interim report to the Office of Sahel and Francophone West Africa Affairs, U.S. Agency for International Development.

3485

Workshop on Ecology and Environmental Programs in the Sahel, *Bamako, Mali*, Jan. 22–26, 1980. Staff summary report. Washington, Advisory Committee on the Sahel, Board on Science and Technology for International Development, National Academy of Sciences-National Research Council, 1980. 57 p.

"Participation of the National Academy of Sciences was made possible through funds provided by the Office of Sahel and Francophone West Africa Affairs, Bureau for Africa, Agency for International Development, under contract AID/afr-C-1354."

Abstract in *A.I.D. Research & Development Abstracts*, v. 9, no. 4, 1981, p. 40–41.

Microfiche. [Washington, U.S. Agency for International Development, 1980?] 1 sheet.

DLC-Sci RR PN-AAJ-889

Benin

General

3486

U.S. *Dept. of State*. Post report. Benin. [Washington, Dept. of State, Publishing Services Division; for sale by the Supt. of Docs., U.S. Govt. Print. Off], 1980. 12 p. illus., map.

JX1705.A286 Spec. Format

L.C. has also reports issued in 1971 and 1977.

For a description of the contents of this publication, see the note to entry 936.

3487

U.S. *Dept. of State. Bureau of Public Affairs*. Background notes. Benin. [Washington, for sale by the Supt. of Docs., U.S. Govt. Print. Off.], 1979. 4 p. maps. (U.S. Dept. of State. Department of State publication 8091, rev.)   G59.U5

L.C. retains only the latest revision.

For a description of the contents of this publication, see the note to entry 937.

3488

The Peace Corps in Benin. [Washington, U.S. Govt. Print. Off., 1980] 1 fold. sheet (6 p.) illus., map.

DLC

"ACTION 4200.39."

An introduction to the country for Volunteers.

Agriculture

3489

Dine, Saefoulaye. Cour d'agriculture spéciale à l'intention des volontaires du Corps de la Paix. Sekou, Dahomey, Peace Corps, 1974. 35 leaves.

DPC

3490

Nation aims to become self-sufficient in agriculture. *In* U.S. *Joint Publications Research Service*. JPRS 69563. [Springfield, Va., National Technical In-formation Service, 1977] (Translations on Sub-Saharan Africa, no. 1783) p. 1–5.

Translation of article in *Europe Outremer*, Paris, Mar. 1977, p. 20–23.

Microfiche. [s.l., 1977]

DLC-Micro JPRS 69563

3491

Sargent, Merritt W. The use of animal traction techniques in the Kouande and Kerou districts, Province de l'Atakora, Republique populaire du Benin; a preliminary report. East Lansing, Dept. of Agricultural Economics, Michigan State University, 1977. 10 p.

Prepared for the U.S. Agency for International Development under contract AID/afr-C-1260.

Microfiche. [Washington, U.S. Agency for International Development, 1977?] 1 sheet.

DLC-Sci RR PN-AAE-510

Assistance Programs

3492

U.S. *Agency for International Development*. Annual budget submission: Benin. [Washington]

Vols. for 1981+ examined in the Development Information Center, AID, Washington, D.C.

3493

——— Country development strategy statement: Benin. Washington, U.S. International Development Cooperation Agency. annual?

Vols. for 1982 examined in the Development Information Center, AID, Washington, D.C.

3494

——— Small program strategy statement: Benin, 1981–1985. [Washington] 1979. 19 p.

Examined in the Development Information Center, AID, Washington, D.C.

Politics and Government

3495

Benin's handling of current situation criticized. *In* U.S. *Joint Publications Research Service.* JPRS 70677. [Springfield, Va., National Technical Information Service, 1978] (Translations on Sub-Saharan Africa, no. 1883) p. 21–24.

Translation of article in *Afrique*, Dakar, Jan. 1978, p. 47–48.

Microfiche. [Washington, Supt. of Docs., U.S. Govt. Print. Off., 1978]

DLC-Micro JPRS 70677

3496

Bentsi-Enchill, Nii K. Publicity value of mercenary invasion emphasized. *In* U.S. *Joint Publications Research Service.* JPRS 70667. [Springfield, Va., National Technical Information Service, 1978] (Translations on Sub-Saharan Africa, no. 1882) p. 12–15.

Article on the Jan. 16, 1977 attack on Cotonou, in *West Africa*, London, Jan. 16, 1978, p. 92–93.

Microfiche. [Washington, Supt. of Docs., U.S. Govt. Print. Off., 1978]

DLC-Micro JPRS 70667

3497

CC member says 'imperialism' behind takeover attempt. *In* U.S. *Joint Publications Research Service.* JPRS 68800. [Springfield, Va., National Technical Information Service, 1977] (Translations on Sub-Saharan Africa, no. 1724) p. 5–9.

Translation of interview with Baba-Moussa Amidou, member of the central committee (CC) of the Parti de la révolution populaire du Bénin, reporting on the attack on Cotonou, Jan. 16, 1977, *Notícias*, Maputo, Feb. 22, 1977, p. 5.

Microfiche. [s.l., 1971]

DLC-Micro JPRS 68800

3498

CDR internal regulations published. *In* U.S. *Joint Publications Research Service.* JPRS 68457. [Springfield, Va., National Technical Information Service, 1977] (Translations on Sub-Saharan Africa, no. 1702) p. 1–5.

Translation of text of regulations establishing "revolutionary defense committees … in all public, semi-public and private firms and in all state and local collective services", in *Ehuzu*, Cotonou, Nov. 23, 1976, p. 3.

Microfiche. [s.l., 1977]

DLC-Micro JPRS 68457

3499

Kérékou, Mathieu. Kerekou explains reasons for socialist nation-building. *In* U.S. *Joint Publications Research Service.* JPRS 72565. [Springfield, Va., National Technical Information Service, 1979] (Translations on Sub-Saharan Africa, no. 2047) p. 38–48.

Translation of article in *Ehuzu*, Cotonou, Dec. 6, 1978, p. 1, 3, 5, 6.

Microfiche. [Washington, Supt. of Docs., U.S. Govt. Print. Off., 1979]

DLC-Micro JPRS 72565

3500

——— Kerekou urges Marxist-Leninist principles at command personnel seminar. *In* U.S. *Joint Publications Research Service.* JPRS 72497. [Springfield, Va., National Technical Information Service, 1978] (Translations on Sub-Saharan Africa, no. 2042) p. 12–18.

Translation of speech recorded in *Ehuzu*, Cotonou, Nov. 20, 1978, p. 1, 4, 5, 6.

Microfiche. [Washington, Supt. of Docs., U.S. Govt. Print. Off., 1979?]

DLC-Micro JPRS 72497

3501

——— President discusses nation's present situation, future priorities. *In* U.S. *Joint Publications Research Service.* JPRS 77184. [Springfield, Va., National Technical Information Service, 1981] (Sub-Saharan Africa report, no. 2346) p. 17–23.

Translation of speech recorded in *Ehuzu*, Cotonou, Nov. 13, 1980, p. 1, 3, 6.

Microfiche. [s.l., 1981]

DLC-Micro JPRS 77184

3502

——— President urges trainees to study Marxism-Leninism. *In* U.S. *Joint Publications Research Service.* JPRS 75971. [Springfield, Va., National Technical Information Service, 1980] (Sub-Saharan Africa report, no. 2261) p. 16–24.

Translation of speech recorded in *Ehuzu*, Cotonou, May 23, 1980, p. 1, 3, 6, 8.

Microfiche. [s.l., 1980]

DIC-Micro JPRS 75971

3503

New territorial districting reported. *In* U.S. *Joint Publications Research Service.* JPRS 72510. [Springfield, Va., National Technical Information Service, 1978] (Translations on Sub-Saharan Africa, no. 2044) p. 9–15.

Translation of article in *Ehuzu*, Cotonou, Nov. 30, 1978, p. 48–52.

3503 (cont.)

Microfiche. [Washington, Supt. of Docs., U.S. Govt. Print. Off., 1979?]

DLC-Micro JPRS 72510

3504

President closes third central committee meeting. *In* U.S. *Joint Publications Research Service*. JPRS 75051. [Springfield, Va., National Technical Information Service, 1980] (Sub-Saharan Africa report, no. 2208) p. 4–7.

Translation of report on remarks by President Mathieu Kérékou at meeting of the Parti de la révolution populaire du Bénin, in *Ehuzu*, Cotonou, Jan. 2, 1980, p. 1, 3.

Microfiche. [s.l., 1980]

DLC-Micro JPRS 75051

3505

Sanchez, Juan. Country said to have been victim of mercenary aggression. *In* U.S. *Joint Publications Research Service*. JPRS 68928. [Springfield, Va., National Technical Information Service, 1977] (Translations on Sub-Saharan Africa, no. 1733) p. 10–13.

Translation of article on the Jan. 16, 1977 attack on Cotonou, in *Bohemia*, Havana, Feb. 18, 1977, p. 62–65.

Microfiche. [s.l., 1977]

DLC-Micro JPRS 68928

3506

Senaux, François. Resentment against military dictatorship growing. *In* U.S. *Joint Publications Research Service*. JPRS 68474. [Springfield, Va., National Technical Information Service, 1977] (Translations on Sub-Saharan Africa, no. 1703) p. 10–13.

Translation of article in *Croissance des jeunes nations*, Paris, Dec. 1976, p. 8–10.

Microfiche. [s.l., 1977]

DLC-Micro JPRS 68474

3507

Sico, Euloge. Discontent with president spreading in Dahomey. *In* U.S. *Joint Publications Research Service*. JPRS 65372. [Springfield, Va., National Technical Information Service, 1975] (Translations on Africa, no. 1606) p. 8–11.

Translation of article in *Afrique nouvelle*, Dakar, June 11–17, 1975, p. 8, 9.

Microfiche. [s.l., 1975]

DLC-Micro JPRS 65372

3508

Zinsou, Emile D. Kerekou regime condemned. *In* U.S. *Joint Publications Research Service*. JPRS

66872. [Springfield, Va., National Technical Information Service, 1976] (Translations on Sub-Saharan Africa, no. 1639) p. 8–13.

Translation of article in *France Eurafrique*, Paris, Nov.–Dec. 1975, p. 39–41.

Microfiche. [s.l., 1976]

DLC-Micro JPRS 66872

Population Studies

3509

Africa: Benin. Selected statistical data by sex. Washington, 1981. 31, 17 p. DLC

Study supported by the U.S. Agency for International Development's Office of Women in Development and Office of Population.

Data assembled by the International Demographic Data Center, U.S. Bureau of the Census.

Among the tables, based on 1961 data (unless noted), are the following: unadjusted population by age, sex, and urban/rural residence (1979); population by ethnic group, sex, and urban/rural residence; population by religion, sex and urban/rural residence; population by nationality, sex and urban/rural residence; urban and rural populations by marital status, age, and sex; number of households; heads of households by age, sex and urban/rural residence; number of literate persons by age, sex, and urban/rural residence; number of persons enrolled in school by age, sex, and urban/rural residence; number of economically active persons by age, sex, and urban/rural residence; economically active population by occupational status, sex, and urban/rural residence.

3510

Profiles of Sahelian countries: Dahomey. Washington, Socio-Economic Analysis Staff, International Statistical Programs Center, U.S. Bureau of the Census, 1974. [41] leaves (in various foliations)

Prepared at the request of the U.S. Agency for International Development.

Concerns demographic projections.

Examined in the Documentation Center, Sahel Development Program, AID, Washington, D.C.

Other Subjects

3511

U.S. *Peace Corps. Dahomey*. Medical guide for Dahomey. [Cotonou, 197–?] 35 leaves. DPC

3512

Beninese-Czechoslovak joint communique released. *In* U.S. *Joint Publications Research Service*. JPRS

3512 (cont.)

72357. [Springfield, Va., National Technical Information Service, 1978] (Translations on Sub-Saharan Africa, no. 2032) p. 10–16.

Translation of text of communique in *Ehuzu*, Cotonou, Oct. 10, 1978, p. 3, 5.

Microfiche. [Washington, Supt. of Docs., U.S. Govt. Print. Off., 1978]

DLC-Micro JPRS 72357

Note: Similar communiques between Benin and Soviet-bloc nations (Poland, Hungary, Vietnam), all relating to common positions in international relations, are also recorded in JPRS 72357.

3513

Foreign economic trends and their implications for the United States. Benin. 1969+ Washington, for sale by the Supt. of Docs., U.S. Govt. Print. Off. annual. (International marketing information series) HC10.E416

Continues *Economic Trends and Their Implications for the United States. Dahomey.*

Prepared by the U.S. Embassy, Cotonou.

Vols. for 1974?–77 distributed by the U.S. Bureau of International Commerce; vols. for 1978–79 by the U.S Industry and Trade Administration.

Title varies: 1969–75, *Foreign Economic Trends and Their Implications for the United States. Dahomey.*

Apparently not published in 1973, 1976, 1979–80.

The following issues for the period 1973–81 have been identified in L.C.:

ET 74-010. 1974. 14 p.
FET 75-110. 1975. 8 p.
FET 77-105. 1977. 8 p.
FET 78-141. 1978. 7 p.
FET 81-030. 1981. 16 p.
FET 81-120. 1981. 12 p.

3514

Montilus, Guerin C. Africa in diaspora: the myth of Dahomey in Haiti. [s.l.] 1979. 23 p.

"Although many scholars have regarded Dahomey as the homeland of the Haitian people, this analysis may not withstand rigorous historical and linguistic scrutiny."—Abstract.

Abstract in *Resources in Education*, 1980 annual cumulation, p. 942.

Microfiche. [Arlington, Va., ERIC Document Reproduction Service; prepared for Educational Resources Information Center, National Institute of Education, 1980] 1 sheet.

DLC-Micro ED181159

3515

Pliya, Jean. The fundamental reform of education in Benin, with particular reference to basic education. *In* Educational reforms and innovations in Africa: studies prepared for the Conference of Ministers of Education of African Member States of Unesco. Paris, Unesco, 1978. (Experiments and innovations in education, no. 34) p. 31–37.

LA1500.E38

Issued also in microfiche. [Arlington, Va., ERIC Document Reproduction Service; prepared for Educational Resources Information Center, National Institute of Education, 1978] 1 sheet.

DLC-Micro ED160036

3516

Rural water resource development in Benin, Atacora and Borgou provinces. [s.l.], 1978. [210] p.

MiEM

Prepared for the U.S. Agency for International Development.

3517

Training of army officers reported. *In* U.S. *Joint Publications Research Service.* JPRS 72510. [Springfield, Va., National Technical Information Service, 1978] (Translations on Sub-Saharan Africa, no. 2044) p. 20–23.

Translation of article in *Ehuzu*, Cotonou, Dec. 4, 1978, p. 1, 6.

Microfiche. [Washington, Supt. of Docs., U.S. Govt. Print. Off., 1979?]

DLC-Micro JPRS 72510

Cape Verde

General

3518

U.S. *Dept. of State.* Post report. Cape Verde. [Washington?], 1979. 13 p. illus., map.

JX1705.A286 Spec. Format

For a description of the contents of this publication, see the note to entry 936.

3519

U.S. *Dept. of State. Bureau of Public Affairs.* Background notes. Cape Verde. [Washington, for sale by the Supt. of Docs., U.S. Govt. Print. Off.], 1981. 4 p. maps. (U.S. Dept. of State. Department of State publication 8874) G59.U5

L.C. retains only the latest revision.

For a description of the contents of this publication, see the note to entry 937.

3520

Draft environmental profile on Cape Verde. Tucson, Arid Lands Information Center, Office of Arid Lands Studies, University of Arizona, 1980. 51 p. maps. DLC

Sponsored by the U.S. Agency for International Development.

Bibliography: p. 44–50.

On cover: "National Park Service Contract No. CX-0001-0-0003 with U.S. Man and the Biosphere Secretariat, Department of State, Washington, D.C."

Abstract in *A.I.D. Research & Development Abstracts*, July 1981, p. 36.

Issued also in microfiche. [Washington, U.S. Agency for International Development, 1980?] 1 sheet. DLC-Sci RR PN-AAJ-201

3521

Henderson, Faye. Cape Verde, a country profile; prepared for the Office of U.S. Foreign Disaster Assistance, Bureau for Private and Development Cooperation, Agency for International Development, Department of State by Evaluation Technologies, Inc., under contract AID-otr-C-1533; researched and written by Faye Henderson. Washington, The Office, 1979. 55 p. 1 leaf of plates.

DT671.C215H46

"January 1979."

"February 1979"—Cover.

Bibliography: p. 54–55.

A general introduction, with emphasis on political structure, demography, health and sanitation, agriculture, nutrition, economic conditions, geography, power, and communications.

Agriculture

3522

Cabo Verde; estudo do sector agricola, [by] Peter H. Freeman [et al.] McLean, Va., General Research Corporation, 1978. 281 p. maps.

Submitted to the U.S. Agency for International Development under contract AID/afr-C-1142.

Apparently issued also in English.

Microfiche. [Washington, U.S. Agency for International Development, 1978?] (PN-AAG-960); examined in the Development Information Center, AID, Washington, D.C.

3523

Cape Verde: assessment of the agricultural sector; report. Appendices, [by] Peter H. Freeman [et al.] McLean, Va., General Research Corporation, 1978. 37 p.

Submitted to the U.S. Agency for International Development under contract AID/afr-C-1142.

Issued also in Portuguese?

Microfiche. [Washington, U.S. Agency for International Development, 1978?] 1 sheet (PN-AAG-961); examined in the Development Information Center, AID, Washington, D.C.

Assistance Programs

3524

U.S. *Agency for International Development.* Annual budget submission: Cape Verde. Washington, U.S. International Development Cooperation Agency.

Vols. for 1982+ examined in the Development Information Center, AID, Washington, D.C.

3525

———— Country development strategy statement: Cape Verde; small program statement. Washington, U.S. International Development Cooperation Agency. annual.

Vols. for 1982+ examined in the Development Information Center, AID, Washington, D.C.

3526

Cape Verde. [*Treaties, etc. United States, 1975 June 30*] Grant agreement between the Transitional Government of Cape Verde and the United States of America (food for work and distribution) *In* U.S. *Treaties, etc.* United States treaties and other international agreements, v. 28, 1976–77. [Washington, Dept. of State; for sale by the Supt. of Docs., U.S. Govt. Print. Off., 1978] p. 959–970. ([Treaties and other international acts series, 8487])

JX231.A34 v. 28

Signed at Mindelo June 30, 1975; and amending agreement signed at Praia Nov. 3, 1975.

Concerns a U.S. Agency for International Development grant for humanitarian and economic needs.

3527

Cape Verde. [*Treaties, etc. United States, 1975 June 30*] Loan agreement between the Transitional Government of Cape Verde and the United States of America for agricultural sector support (rural works). *In* U.S. *Treaties, etc.* United States treaties and other international agreements, v. 28, 1976–77. [Washington, Dept. of State; for sale by the Supt. of Docs., U.S. Govt. Print. Off., 1978] p. 2903–2923. ([Treaties and other international acts series, 8573]) JX231.A34 v. 28

Agreement signed at Mindelo June 30, 1975; and amending agreement signed at Abidjan and Praia Mar. 3 and 23, 1976.

3528

Cape Verde. [*Treaties, etc. United States, 1977 May 21*] Cape Verde; agricultural commodities: transfers under Title II Agreement signed May 21, 1977; entered into force May 21, 1977. *In* U.S. *Treaties, etc.* United States treaties and other international agreements, v. 29, 1976–77. [Washington, Dept. of State; for sale by the Supt. of Docs., U.S. Govt. print. Off., 1979] p. 335–341. ([Treaties and other international acts series, 8819])

JX231.A34 v. 29

In English and Portuguese.

Under Title II of Public Law 480, the Commodity Credit Corporation was authorized to transfer and deliver food to Cape Verde.

3529

Cape Verde. [*Treaties, etc. United States, 1978 May 22*] Cape Verde, agricultural commodities: transfer under title II; agreement signed May 22, 1978; entered into force May 22, 1978. *In* U.S. *Treaties, etc.* United States treaties and other international agreemens, v. 30, 1978–79. [Washington, Dept. of State; for sale by the Supt. of Docs., U.S. Govt. Print. Off., 1980] p. 3128–3131. ([Treaties and other international acts series, 9382])

JX231.A34 v. 30

Authorizes the Commodity Credit Corporation to transfer and deliver food grain to Cape Verde.

3530

Figueirido, Xavier de. Government, international aid fighting drought. *In* U.S. *Joint Publications Research Service.* JPRS 71270. [Springfield, Va., National Technical Information Service, 1978] (Translations on Sub-Saharan Africa, no. 1944) p. 32–35.

Translation of article in *Diario de Notícias*, Lisbon, Apr. 18, 1978, p. 7.

Microfiche. [Washington, Supt. of Docs., U.S. Govt. Print. Off., 1978]

DLC-Micro JPRS 71270

3531

Technical Assistance Information Clearing House. Development assistance programs of U.S. nonprofit organizations: Cape Verde. Feb. 1978. [New York], American Council of Voluntary Agencies for Foreign Service, inc., 1978. 11 leaves. (TAICH country report) HC578.C3T4a

The Clearing House is operated by the Council under a grant from the U.S. Agency for International Development.

3532

U.S provides assistance to Cape Verde. *In* U.S. *Dept. of State.* The Department of State bulletin, v. 73, no. 1885, Aug. 11, 1975: 215–216.

JX232.A33 v. 73

From U.S. Agency for International Development, Press Release 65, July 2, 1975.

Economic Conditions

3533

Foreign economic trends and their implications for the United States. Cape Verde. 1978?+ Washington, for sale by the Supt. of Docs., U.S. Govt. Print. Off. annual. (International marketing information series) HC10.E416

Prepared by the U.S. Embassy, Praia.

Vols. for 1978–79 distributed by the U.S. Industry and Trade Administration; vols. for 1981– by the U.S. International Trade Administration.

Not published in 1980.

The following issues have been identified in L.C.:

FET 78-057. 1978. 7 p.
FET 79-086. 1979. 7 p.
FET 81-037. 1981. 4 p.

3534

Mokdad, Halim. Pires reviews achievements, plans of Cape Verde. *In* U.S. *Joint Publications Research Service*. JPRS 66363. [Springfield, Va., National Technical Information Service, 1975] (Translations on Sub-Saharan Africa, no. 1630) p. 10–15.

Interview with the Prime Minister in *el Moudjahid*, Algiers, Oct. 28, 1975, p. 9.

Microfiche. [s.l., 1975]

DLC-Micro JPRS 66363

3535

Prime Minister elaborates on policy, objectives. *In* U.S. *Joint Publications Research Service*. JPRS 66226. [Springfield, Va., National Technical Information Service, 1975] (Translations on Sub-Saharan Africa, no. 1628) p. 7–14.

Translation of interview with Pedro Pires in *Notícias*, Lourenço Marques, Oct. 30, 1975, p. 5.

Microfiche. [s.l., 1975]

DLC-Micro JPRS 66226

Foreign Relations

3536

Cape Verde president interviewed: no Soviet bases. *In* U.S. *Joint Publications Research Service*. JPRS 72680. [Springfield, Va., National Technical Information Service, 1979] (Translations on Sub-Saharan Africa, no. 2054) p. 1–4.

Translation of interview with President Aristides Pereira in *No Pintcha*, Bissau, Nov. 25, 1978, p. 1, 4.

Microfiche. [s.l., 1978]

DLC-Micro JPRS 72680

3537

Pacheco, Fernando A. Pires on nation's future, relations with Portugal. *In* U.S. *Joint Publications Research Service*. JPRS 75775. [Springfield, Va., National Technical Information Service, 1980] (Sub-Saharan Africa report, no. 2251) p. 14–17.

Translation of interview with Pedro Pires, Prime Minister of Cape Verde, in *O Jornal*, Lisbon, Apr. 11, 1980, p. 23–24.

Microfiche. [s.l., 1980]

DLC-Micro JPRS 75775

Politics and Government

3538

McDonald, Larry. Red gains in Africa. Congressional record, 94th Congress, 2d session, v. 122, Feb. 24, 1976: 4234–4236. J11.R5 v. 122

Extension of remarks in the U.S. House of Representatives.

Includes article from *Review of the News* concerning Communist penetration of Cape Verde.

3539

Pereira, Aristides. President Aristides Pereira's year-end message. *In* U.S. *Joint Publications Research Service*. JPRS 68589. [Springfield, Va., National Technical Information Service, 1977] (Translations on Sub-Saharan Africa, no. 1709) p. 10–13.

Translation of article in *No Pintcha*, Bissau, Jan. 11, 1977, p. 1, 4, 8.

Microfiche. [s.l., 1977]

DLC-Micro JPRS 68589

3540

Pires, Pedro. Prime Minister analyzes first year of independence. *In* U.S. *Joint Publications Research Service*. JPRS 67833. [Springfield, Va., National Technical Information Service, 1976] (Translations on Sub-Saharan Africa, no. 1671) p. 25–29.

Translation of article in *No Pintcha*, Bissau, July 31, 1976, p. 1, 5, 8.

Microfiche. [s.l., 1976]

DLC-Micro JPRS 67833

3541

President grants exclusive interview to Angolan daily. *In* U.S. *Joint Publications Research Service*. JPRS 69774. [Springfield, Va., National Technical Information Service, 1977] (Translations on Sub-Saharan Africa, no. 1799) p. 3–12.

Translation of interview with President Aristides Pereira, in *Jornal de Angola*, Luanda, July 21, 1977, p. 4–5.

Microfiche. [s.l., 1977]

DLC-Micro JPRS 69774

Water Resources

3542

Cape Verde—desalination and power (Sal) [Washington], U.S. Agency for International Development, [1977] 2 v.

Richard R. Solem, project team leader.

Concerns specifically the Ilha do Sal.

Microfiche. [Sahel Documents and Dissertations. Ann Arbor, Mich., University Microfilms International, 1980] 4 sheets.

DLC-Micro Microfiche 5357 CV 004

3543

Dimanche, Pierre. Watershed management report. [s.l.], 1978. [51] p.

Prepared for the U.S. Agency for International Development.

Microfiche. [Sahel Documents and Dissertations. Ann Arbor, Mich., University Microfilms International, 1980] 1 sheet.

DLC-Micro Microfiche 5357 CV 017

3544

Hargreaves, George H. Water and conservation programs for Cape Verde. [Washington?], 1977. 56 p. illus.

Prepared for the U.S. Agency for International Development under contract AID/afr-C-1303.

Issued also in French.

Abstract in *A.I.D. Research and Development Abstracts*, v. 7, no. 1, 1979, p. 9.

Microfiche. [Washington, U.S. Agency for International Development, 1977?] 1 sheet (DLC-Sci RR PN-AAG-339); and [Sahel Documents and Dissertations. Ann Arbor, Mich., University Microfilms International, 1980] 1 sheet (DLC-Micro Microfiche 5357 CV 016).

Other Subjects

3545

U.S. *President, 1974–1977 (Ford)* Letter to President Aristides Pereira on United States recognition of the Republic of Cape Verde. *In* U.S. *President.* Public papers of the Presidents of the United States, containing the public messages, speeches and statements of the President. Gerald R. Ford. 1975. Washington, [Office of the Federal Register, National Archives and Records Service; for sale by the Supt. of Docs.], U.S. Govt. Print. Off., 1977. p. 992–993. J80.A283 1975

3546

Africa: Cape Verde. Selected statistical data by sex. Washington, 1981. 31, 17 p. DLC

Study supported by the U.S. Agency for International Development's Office of Women in Development and Office of Population.

Data assembled by the International Demographic Data Center, U.S. Bureau of the Census.

Among the tables, based on 1960 data (unless noted), are the following: unadjusted population by age, sex, and urban/rural residence (1970); population by ethnic group (e.g., "white," "black," "mixed") and sex; population by religion, sex, and urban/rural residence; population by nationality and sex; population by language and sex; population by marital status, age, and sex; number of literate persons by age, sex, and urban/rural residence; number of economically active persons by sex; economically active population by occupational status, sex, and urban/rural residence.

3547

Cape Verde. [*Treaties, etc. United States, 1976 Nov. 19*] Memorandum of agreement between the Federal Aviation Administration, Department of Transportation, United States of America, and the Director of Civil Aviation, Republic of Cape Verde. *In* U.S. *Treaties, etc.* Treaties and other international agreements, v. 28, 1976–77. [Washington, Dept. of State; for sale by the Supt. of Docs., U.S. Govt. Print. Off., 1978] p. 8086–8089. ([Treaties and other international acts series, 8742]) JX231.A34 v. 28

Agreement signed at Washington and Praia Oct. 13 and Nov. 19, 1976; entered into force Nov. 19, 1976.

Concerns a program of assistance by the Federal Aviation Administration to Cape Verde.

3548

Cape Verde. [*Treaties, etc. United States, 1977 Aug. 17*] Cape Verde, aviation: provision of services. Agreements amending and extending the memorandum of agreement of October 13 and November 19, 1976, signed at Washington and Praia August 17 and October 18, 1977, entered into force October 18, 1977; effective October 1, 1977, and signed at Washington and Praia March 10 and April 4, 1978, entered into force April 4, 1978, effective April 1, 1978. *In* U.S. *Treaties, etc.* United States treaties and other international agreements, v. 29, 1976–77. [Washington, Dept. of State; for sale by the Supt. of Docs., U.S. Govt. Print. Off., 1980] p. 5893–5896. ([Treaties and other international acts series, 9158]) JX 231.A34 v. 29

3549

Cape Verde: solar market conditions and potential. Washington, Systems Consultants, inc., 1981. 5 p.

DLC

On cover: Solar Energy Research Institute International Market Development Program (DOE).

Prepared under contract to the Solar Energy Research Institute, Golden, Colo., as part of the Export Information Task No. 1168.20 for the U.S. Dept. of Energy.

3550

Nyhan, Patricia, *and* Raymond A. Almeida. Nho lobo: folk tales of the Cape Verdean people. Boston, Tchuba-The American Committee for Cape Verde, inc. 1976. 27 p.   MiEM

Prepared under an Ethnic Heritage Studies Grant for the U.S. Office of Education.

3551

Trade union conference establishes sole trade union. *In* U.S. *Joint Publications Research Service*. JPRS 72175. [Springfield, Va., National Technical Information Service, 1978] (Translations on Sub-Saharan Africa, no. 2018) p. 15–21.

Translation of article in *Voz di Povo*, Praia, Sept. 23, 1978, p. 1, 4, 12.

Microfiche. [Washington, Supt. of Docs., U.S. Govt. Print. Off., 1978]

DLC-Micro JPRS 72175

Chad

General

3552

U.S. *Dept. of State.* Post report. Chad. [Washington?], 1976. 20 p. illus., map.

JX1705.A286 Spec. Format

For a description of the contents of this publication, see the note to entry 936.

3553

U.S. *Dept. of State. Bureau of Public Affairs.* Background notes. Chad. [Washington, for sale by the Supt. of Docs., U.S. Govt. Print. Off.], 1977. 4 p. map. (U.S. Dept. of State. Department of State publication 7669, rev.) G59.U5

L.C. retains only the latest revision.

For a description of the contents of this publication, see the note to entry 937.

3554

Chad: a country profile. Arlington, Va., Evaluation Technologies, inc., 1977. 39 p.

Prepared for the Office of U.S. Foreign Disaster Assistance, U.S. Agency for International Development.

Microfiche. Sahel Documents and Dissertations. [Ann Arbor, Mich., University Microfilms International, 1980] 1 sheet.

DLC-Micro 5357 CD 006

3555

Mango, Cecily, Chad, a country profile; prepared for the Office of U.S. Foreign Disaster Assistance, Bureau for Private and Development Cooperation, Agency for International Development, Department of State by Evaluation Technologies, Inc., under contract AID/SOD/PDC-C-0283. 2d ed; researched and written by Cecily Mango. Washington, The Office, 1980. 48 p., 2 leaves of plates. DT546.422.M36 1980

Bibliography: p. 46–48.

A general introduction, with emphasis on political structure, disaster preparedness, demography, health, nutrition, housing, economic conditions, agriculture, geography, transportation, power, and communications.

Agriculture

3556

Chad. [*Treaties, etc. United States, 1976 Aug. 30*] Chad; program to assist Sahel rural population. *In* U.S. *Treaties, etc.* United States treaties and other international agreements, v. 29, 1976–77. [Washington, Dept. of State; for sale by the Supt. of Docs., U.S. Govt. Print. Off., 1979] p. 1139–1187. ([Treaties and other international acts series, 8871]) JX231.A34 v. 29

Signed at N'Djamena Aug. 30, 1976.

Concerns U.S. Agency for International Development assistance to increase food production, improve livestock, promote public health facilities in rural areas, and develop agricultural education.

3557

Chad. [*Treaties, etc. United States, 1977 Jan. 25*] Chad; Lake Chad agriculture. Agreement signed at N'Djamena January 25, 1977; entered into force January 25, 1977; and amending agreements signed at N'Djamena August 30, 1977; entered into force August 30, 1977; and signed at N'Djamena September 28, 1977; entered into force September 28, 1977. *In* U.S. *Treaties, etc.* United States treaties and other international agreements, v. 29, 1976–77. [Washington, Dept. of State; for sale by the Supt. of Docs., U.S. Govt. Print. Off., 1979] p. 2581–2615. ([Treaties and other international acts series, 8959]) JX231.A34 v. 29

Concerns a U.S. Agency for International Development grant for the development of the polders area of Lake Chad for increased agricultural production through the use of irrigation systems.

3558

Chad. [*Treaties, etc. United States, 1978 Aug 15*] Chad, agricultural institutional development. Agreement signed at N'Djamena August 15, 1978; entered into force August 15, 1978. *In* U.S. *Treaties, etc.* United States treaties and other international agreements, v. 30, 1978–79. [Washington, Dept. of State; for sale by the Supt. of Docs., U.S. Govt. Print. Off., 1981] p. 4671–4698. ([Treaties and other international acts series, 9485])

JX231.A34 v. 30

In English and French.

Agreement for U.S. Agency for International Development funding of programs to assist the Ministry of Agriculture of Chad in planning, staff training, extension services, and the collection and analysis of statistics.

3559

Hill, Barry, Analysis of fisheries development potential in Chad. Washington, Multinational Agribusiness Systems, inc., 1976. 56 p. illus.

Prepared for the U.S. Agency for International Development under contract AID/afr-C-1149.

Abstract in *A.I.D. Research and Development Abstracts*, Apr. 1978, p. 16.

Microfiche. [Washington, U.S. Agency for International Development, 1976?] 1 sheet.

DLC-Sci RR PN-RAB-636

3560

King, Jack. Chad: economy and rural development. [s.l.] 1979. 18 p.   DLC

"A presentation for the Colloquium on Chad, October 29, 1979, Department of State."

3561

Sargent, Merritt W. Chad: Sategui-Deressia irrigation project. [s.l.], 1973. 27 p.

Prepared for the U.S. Agency for International Development under contract AID/CM/afr-C-73-30.

Microfiche. [Washington, U.S. Agency for International Development, 1973?] 1 sheet.

DLC-Sci RR PN-AAG-118

3562

Tandal Polder feasibility study. [s.l.], CHZM Hill, inc., 1978. 271 p. maps.

Prepared for the U.S. Agency for International Development.

Concerns an irrigation project in Bol, Chad, on the northern shore of Lake Chad.

Examined in the Documentation Center, Sahel Development Program, AID, Washington, D.C.

Grain and Grain Storage

3563

Borsdorf, Roe. Evaluation of proposed marketing interventions for Chad; prepared for Agency for International Development, United States Department of State. AID/ta-C-1162, technical assistance in grain storage, processing and marketing and agribusiness development. Manhattan, Food & Feed Grain Institute, Kansas State University, 1976. 35 p. (Grain storage, processing and marketing report, no. 62)   HD9017.C452B67

"The general objective of this report is to provide technical input concerning the marketing segment of the Agronomic Research, Seed Multiplication and Grain Marketing Project, USAID/Chad."—p. 1.

Abstracts in *A.I.D. Research and Development Abstracts*, Oct. 1977, p. 6.

Issued also in microfiche. [Washington, U.S. Agency for International Development, 1976?] 1 sheet (DLC-Sci RR PN-AAD-125); and [Sahel Documents and Dissertations. Ann Arbor, Mich., University Microfilms International, 1980] 1 sheet (DLC-Micro Microfiche 5357 CD 025).

3564

Chung, Do Sup. Evaluation of proposed "Rural Family Grain Storage Project" by CARE in Chad. Manhattan, Food & Feed Grain Institute, Kansas State University, 1977. 56 p. (Grain storage, processing and marketing report, no. 65)   DLC

Prepared for the U.S. Agency for International Development under contract AID/ta-C-1162.

3565

Graetz, H., *and* Richard Maxon. Grain marketing in Chad. Washington, Multinational Agribusiness Systems, inc., 1977. 74 p. map.

Prepared for the U.S. Agency for International Development under contract AID/afr-C-1149.

Microfiche. [Sahel Documents and Dissertations. Ann Arbor, Mich., University Microfilms International, 1980] 1 sheet.

DLC-Micro Microfiche 5357 CD 027

3566

Maxon, Richard. Analysis of grain marketing in Chad. Washington, Multinational Agribusiness Systems, inc., 1976. 79 p. map.

Prepared for the U.S. Agency for International Development under contract AID/afr-C-1149.

Microfiche. [Washington, U.S. Agency for International Development, 1976?] 1 sheet (DLC-

3566 (cont.)

Sci RR PN-AAG-115); and [Sahel Documents and Dissertations. Ann Arbor, Mich., University Microfilms International, 1980] 2 sheets (DLC-Micro Microfiche 5357 CD 003).

3567

Potts, Howard C. Agronomic research sub-project of the agronomic research, seed multiplication and grain marketing PRP for Chad. Mississippi State, Seed Technology Laboratory, Mississippi State University, [1976] 29 p.   MsSM

Prepared for the U.S. Agency for International Development under contract AID/ta-C-1219.

PRP: Project resource paper.

Issued also in microfiche. [Washington, U.S. Agency for International Development, 1976?] 1 sheet.   DLC-Sci RR PN-AAG-117

3568

Vaughan, Charles E. Report to USAID/Chad and AID/W on seed multiplication and distribution in Chad. Mississippi State, Seed Technology Laboratory, Mississippi State University, 1976. 28 p.

Prepared for the U.S. Agency for International Development under contract AID/ta-c-1219.

Abstract in *A.I.D. Research and Development Abstracts*, Jan. 1977, p. 4.

Microfiche. [Washington, U.S. Agency for International Development, 1976?] 1 sheet
DLC-Sci RR PN-AAC-600

Livestock and Range Management

3569

Magee, Charles, *and* Frederick H. Mass. Range development and grazing system plan for the Assale-Serbewel project area; guidelines & design. [N'Djamena?, 1975] [34] p.

Prepared for the U.S. AID Mission to Chad.

Microfiche. [Washington, U.S. Agency for International Development, 1975?] 1 sheet.
DLC-Sci RR PN-AAG-114

3570

Republic of Chad, multipurpose herder support project of the U.S.A.I.D. financed Chad Range and Livestock Development Project 201; implementing agency: the Livestock Service of the Chad Ministry of Agriculture. Edited by Richard Carron. N'Djamena, Country Development Office, USAID, 1976, 23 leaves.

Document acquired by the Library of Congress Office, Nairobi, Kenya.

Assistance Programs

3571

U.S. *Agency for International Development*. Annual budget submission: Chad. Washington, U.S. International Development Cooperation Agency.

Vols. for 1977+ examined in the Development Information Center, AID, Washington, D.C.

3572

———— Country development strategy statement: Chad. [Washington?] annual.

Vols. for 1979 and 1981 examined in the Development Information Center, AID, Washington, D.C.

3573

———— Sahel recovery and rehabilitation program: Chad, proposal and recommendations. Washington, [1974] [160] p.   MiEM

3574

U.S. *General Accounting Office*. Problems in managing U.S. food aid to Chad. [Report] by the Comptroller General of the United States. [Washington], 1975. 17 p.   DPC

Primarily a review of U.S. Agency for International Development records.

3575

Bingen, R. James. Research/studies in Sahel francophone West Africa: Chad; an inventory of research, studies, and reports sponsored by the U.S. Agency for International Development. Washington, Sahel Development Program, U.S. Agency for International Development, 1977. [55] p.

Covers 42 projects undertaken in the period 1962–77.

Abstract for series on francophone West Africa and The Gambia in *A.I.D. Research and Development Abstracts*, Oct. 1977, p. 12–13.

Microfiche. [Washington, U.S. Agency for International Development, 1977?] 1 sheet.
DLC-Sci RR PN-AAD-512

3576

Chad. [*Treaties, etc. United States, Aug. 25, 1977*] Chad, human resources development; agreement signed at N'Djamena August 25, 1977, entered into force August 25, 1977, and amending agreement signed at N'Djamena February 28, 1978. [Washington, Dept. of State; for sale by the Supt. of Docs., U.S. Govt. Print. Off., 1980] 69 p. (Treaties and other international acts series, 9594)
DLC

In English and French.

3576 (cont.)

Concerns U.S. Agency for International Development projects in educational reform, manpower training, and "improving efficiency" of Chadian management of development programs.

3577

Technical Assistance Information Clearing House. Development assistance programs of U.S. nonprofit organizations, Chad, September 1977. [New York], American Council of Voluntary Agencies for Foreign Service, inc., Technical Assistance Information Clearing House, 1977. 19 p. maps. (TAICH country report)   DLC

The Clearing House is operated by the Council under a grant from the U.S. Agency for International Development.

Politics and Government

3578

GUNT president's press conference. *In* U.S. *Joint Publications Research Service.* JPRS 74519. [Springfield, Va., National Technical Information Service, 1979] (Sub-Saharan Africa report, no. 2174) p. 19–25.

Text of the press conference of Weddeye Goukouni, President of the Gouvernement d'union nationale de transition, reported in *Info Tchad*, N'Djamena, Sept. 29, 1979, p. 1–9.

Microfiche. [s.l., 1979]

DLC-Micro JPRS 74519

3579

Independence said to rest on fragile basis. *In* U.S. *Joint Publications Research Service.* JPRS 74852. [Springfield, Va., National Technical Information Service, 1980] (Sub-Saharan Africa report, no. 2194) p. 18–22.

Article in *West Africa*, London, Dec. 10, 1979, p. 2269–2271.

Microfiche. [s.l., 1980]

DLC-Micro JPRS 74852

3580

Malloum, Habre interviewed by French television team. *In* U.S. *Joint Publications Research Service.* JPRS 71478. [Springfield, Va., National Technical Information Service, 1978] (Translations on Sub-Saharan Africa, no. 1961) p. 8–18.

Translation of interviews with President Félix Malloum N'gakoutou Bey-Ndi and Prime Minister Hissein Habré, in *Info Tchad*, N'Djamena, June 9, 1978, p. 1–16.

Microfiche. [Washington, Supt. of Docs., U.S.

Govt. Print. Off., 1978]

DLC-Micro JPRS 71478

Civil War

3581

Abba Siddick says demilitarization essential for peace. *In* U.S. *Joint Publications Research Service.* JPRS 76649. [Springfield, Va., National Technical Information Service, 1980] (Sub-Saharan Africa report, no. 2308) p. 18–26.

Translation of interview with the secretary-general of FROLINAT (Front de libération national du Tchad), in *Africa*, Dakar, June–July 1980, p. 53–56.

Microfiche, [s.l., 1980]

DLC-Micro JPRS 76649

3582

Boggio, Philippe. 'Le Monde' updates Chad war developments. *In* U.S. *Joint Publications Research Service.* JPRS 77053. [Springfield, Va., National Technical Information Service, 1980] (Sub-Saharan Africa report, no. 2336) p. 1–4.

Translation of article in *Le Monde*, Paris, Dec. 11, 1980, p. 1, 5.

Microfiche. [s.l., 1981]

DLC-Micro JPRS 77053

3583

Claude, Patrice. Conditions in Ndjamena, among refugees described. *In* U.S. *Joint Publications Research Service.* JPRS 76693. [Springfield, Va., National Technical Information Service, 1980] (Sub-Saharan Africa report, no. 2311) p. 8–12.

Translation of article in *Le Monde*, Paris, Sept. 17, 1980, p. 1, 8.

Microfiche. [s.l., 1980]

DLC-Micro JPRS 76693

3584

——— Special correspondent describes conditions in south. *In* U.S. *Joint Publications Research Service.* JPRS 76842. [Springfield, Va., National Technical Information Service, 1980] (Sub-Saharan Africa report, no. 2321) p. 21–27.

Translation of article in *Le Monde*, Paris, Oct. 11, 12, 1980.

Microfiche. [s.l., 1980]

DLC-Micro JPRS 76842

3585

Criton, Jean-Claude. President discusses rebellion, Libyan occupation. *In* U.S. *Joint Publications Research Service.* JPRS 69923. [Springfield, Va., National Technical Information Service, 1977]

3585 (cont.)

(Translations on Sub-Saharan Africa, no. 1812) p. 16–20.

Translation of interview with Félix Malloum N'gakoutou Bey-Ndi, in *Info Tchad*, N'Djamena, Aug. 23, 1977, p. 1–7.

Microfiche. [s.l., 1977]

DLC-Micro JPRS 69923

3586

Decraene, Philippe. Signs of deteriorating security noted. *In* U.S. *Joint Publications Research Service*. JPRS 72839. [Springfield, Va., National Technical Information Service, 1979] (Translations on Sub-Saharan Africa, no. 2065) p. 16–23.

Translation of article in *Le Monde*, Paris, Jan. 21/22 and 23, 1979.

Microfiche. [Washington, Supt. of Docs., U.S. Govt. Print. Off., 1979]

DLC-Micro JPRS 72839

3587

Doreinville, Roger. FAN chief discusses attitude toward Libya, France. *In* U.S. *Joint Publications Research Service*. JPRS 76890. [Springfield, Va., National Technical Information Service, 1980] (Sub-Saharan Africa report, no. 2324) p. 4–8.

Translation of interview with Hissein Habré in *Africa*, Dakar, Oct. 1980, p. 37–39.

FAN: Forces armées du nord.

Microfiche. [s.l., 1980]

DLC-Micro JPRS 76890

3588

Insurgency and Libyan involvement in Chad. Washington, Defense Intelligence Agency, 1978. 21 p.

AMAU

"DDN 2200-36."

3589

Junqua, Daniel. Chances for peace in Chad said to be slim. *In* U.S. *Joint Publications Research Service*. JPRS 66399. [Springfield, Va., National Technical Information Service, 1975] (Translations on Sub-Saharan Africa, no. 1631) p. 8–11.

Translation of article in *Le Monde*, Paris, Nov. 4, 1975, p. 1–2.

Microfiche. [s.l., 1975]

DLC-Micro JPRS 66399

3590

Kebzabo, Saleh. Nation undergoing most serious of its many crises. *In* U.S. *Joint Publications Research Service*. JPRS 75757. [Springfield, Va., National Technical Information Service, 1980] (Sub-Saharan Africa report, no. 2249) p. 20–24.

Translation of article in *Demain l'Afrique*, Paris, Apr. 7, 1980, p. 18–21.

Microfiche. [s.l., 1980]

DLC-Micro JPRS 75757

3591

—— Nation will survive only if leaders check ambitions. *In* U.S. *Joint Publications Research Service*. JPRS 74372. [Springfield, Va., National Technical Information Service, 1979] (Sub-Saharan Africa report, no. 2164) p. 5–8.

Translation of article in *Demain l'Afrique*, Paris, Aug. 21, 1979, p. 40–41.

Microfiche. [Washington, Supt. of Docs., U.S. Govt. Print. Off., 1979]

DLC-Micro JPRS 74372

3592

Kuntz, Joelle. Role of Goukouni, Habre, France, Libya noted. *In* U.S. *Joint Publications Research Service*. JPRS 75785. [Springfield, Va., National Technical Information Service, 1980] (Sub-Saharan Africa report, no. 2252) p. 54–57.

Translation of article on the positions and goals of Weddeye Goukouni, Hissein Habré and their supporters, in *Le Matin*, Paris, Apr. 7, 1980, p. 7.

Microfiche. [s.l., 1980]

DLC-Micro JPRS 75785

3593

Labertit, Guy. Peace described as fragile, future uncertain. *In* U.S. *Joint Publications Research Service*. JPRS 75622. [Springfield, Va., National Technical Information Service, 1980] (Sub-Saharan Africa report, no. 2243) p. 22–33.

Translation of article in *Le Monde diplomatique*, Mar. 1980, p. 20, 21.

Microfiche. [s.l., 1980]

DLC-Micro JPRS 75622

3594

Langellier, Jean-Pierre. Capital's demilitarization to text GUNT's cohesiveness. *In* U.S. *Joint Publications Research Service*. JPRS 74827. [Springfield, Va., National Technical Information Service, 1979] (Sub-Saharan Africa report, no. 2193) p. 10–13.

Translation of article in *Le Monde*, Paris, Nov. 14, 1979, p. 6.

Microfiche. [s.l., 1980]

DLC-Micro JPRS 74827

3595

Lemarchand, René. Chad: background to conflict. [s.l.], 1979. 11 p.   DLC

"A report to the State Department, Oct. 1979."

3596

Magassouba, Moriba. Premier notes objectives of his struggle. *In* U.S. *Joint Publications Research Service*. JPRS 73066. [Springfield, Va., National Technical Information Service, 1979] (Sub-Saharan Africa report, no. 2080) p. 26–29.

Translation of interview with Prime Minister Hissein Habré in *Demain l'Afrique* Paris, Feb. 26, 1979, p. 23–24.

Microfiche. [Washington, Supt. of Docs., U.S. Govt. Print. Off., 1979]

DLC-Micro JPRS 73066

3597

Malet, Roland. Solution to civil war not to be found in Sudan, Libya. *In* U.S. *Joint Publications Research Service*. JPRS 71449. [Springfield, Va., National Technical Information Service, 1978] (Translations on Sub-Saharan Africa, no. 1959) p. 1–8.

Translation of article in *Demain l'Afrique*, Paris, June 10, 1978, p. 31–33.

Microfiche. [Washington, Supt. of Docs., U.S. Govt. Print. Off., 1978]

DLC-Micro JPRS 71449

3598

Malloum discusses Frolinat, Claustre affair. *In* U.S. *Joint Publications Research Service*. JPRS 67353. [Springfield, Va., National Technical Information Service, 1976] (Translations on Sub-Saharan Africa, no. 1653) p. 15–19.

Translation of interview with President Félix Malloum N'gakoutou Bey-Ndi for French television concerning the current political situation in Chad and specifically the negotiations for release of Françoise Claustre, held hostage by rebel forces, recorded in *Info Tchad*, N'Djamena, Apr. 26, 1976, p. 1–7.

Microfiche. [s.l., 1976]

DLC-Micro JPRS 67353

3599

Miller, Richard P. International dimensions of the conflict in Chad. [s.l.] 1979. 23 p. maps.   DLC

"This paper was prepared for the Department of State as part of its external research program."

3600

Nigerian paper publishes text of Kano accord. *In* U.S. *Joint Publications Research Service*. JPRS 73299. [Springfield, Va., National Technical Information Service, 1979] (Translations on Sub-Saharan Africa, no. 2094) p. 5–8.

Agreement, signed in Kano, Nigeria, between factions in the Chadian civil war; recorded in *Daily Times*, Lagos, Mar. 21, 1979, p. 9.

Microfiche. [Washington, Supt. of Docs., U.S. Govt. Print. Off., 1979]

DLC-Micro JPRS 73299

3601

Njinta, Michel N. Solution to conflict appears impossible without Goukouni. *In* U.S. *Joint Publications Research Service*. JPRS 72390. [Springfield, Va., National Technical Information Service, 1978] (Translations on Sub-Saharan Africa, no. 2034) p. 28–31.

Translation of article on Chad politics in *Leader-Africain*, Paris, Oct. 1978, p. 10–11.

Microfiche. [Washington, Supt. of Docs., U.S. Govt. Print. Off., 1978]

DLC-Micro JPRS 72390

3602

President discusses rebellion, domestic program. *In* U.S. *Joint Publications Research Service*. JPRS 67984. [Springfield, Va., National Technical Information Service, 1976] (Translations on Sub-Saharan Africa, no. 1679) p. 30–34.

Translation of interview with Félix Malloum N'gakoutou Bey-Ndi, in *Info Tchad*, N'Djamena, July 27, 1976, p. 7–13.

Microfiche. [s.l., 1976]

DLC-Micro JPRS 67984

3603

Situation in Chad following Libyan capture of capital. *In* U.S. *Joint Publications Research Service*. JPRS 77370. [Springfield, Va., National Technical Information Service, 1981] (Sub-Saharan Africa report, no. 2359) p. 4–7.

Translation of article in *al-Majallah*, London, Dec. 27, 1980, p. 24, 27.

Microfiche. [s.l., 1981]

DLC-Micro JPRS 77370

3604

Thivent, Agnes. Results of French intervention 'difficult' to assess. *In* U.S. *Joint Publications Research Service*. JPRS 75622. [Springfield, Va., National Technical Information Service, 1980] (Sub-Saharan Africa report, no. 2243) p. 34–43.

Translation of article in *Le Monde diplomatique*, Paris, Mar. 1980, p. 21, 22.

Microfiche. [s.l., 1980]

DLC-Micro JPRS 75622

3605

Works, John A. Whither Chad? Scenarios and prospects. [s.l.], 1979. 13 p.

"A paper prepared for the Department of State, October 29, 1979."

Population Studies

3606

Africa: Chad. Selected statistical data by sex. Washington, 1981. 31, 17 p.　　　　　　　DLC

Study supported by the U.S. Agency for International Development's Office of Women in Development and Office of Population.

Data assembled by the International Demographic Data Center, U.S. Bureau of the Census.

Among the tables, all based on 1964 data, are the following: unadjusted population by age, sex, and urban/rural residence; population by prefecture, sex, and urban/rural residence; population by ethnic group, sex, and urban/rural residence; population by religion, sex, and urban/rural residence; life expectancy; urban and rural populations by marital status, age, and sex; number of literate persons by age, sex, and urban/rural residence; number of persons enrolled in school by sex; number of economically active persons by age, sex, and urban/rural residence; economically active population by occupational status, sex, and urban/rural residence.

3607

Profiles of Sahelian countries: Chad. Washington, Socio-Economic Analysis Staff, International Statistical Programs Center, U.S. Bureau of the Census, 1974. [41] leaves (in various foliations)

Prepared at the request of the U.S. Agency for International Development.

Concerns demographic projections.

Examined in the Documentation Center, Sahel Development Program, AID, Washington, D.C.

Other Subjects

3608

U.S. *Dept. of State. Office of the Geographer*. Chad-Libya boundary. Rev. Washington, 1978. 5 p. col. map. (*Its* International boundary study, no. 3)
　　　　　　　DLC-G&M

First issued in 1961.

3609

U.S. *Peace Corps. Chad*. Peace Corps volunteer health manual for Chad. [N'Djamena, Peace Corps], 1978. 50 p. illus.　　　　　DPC

3610

Bardinet, D., *and* J. M. Monget. LANCHAD: remote sensing of the N'Djamena area and the Logoni-Chari confluent. Washington, National Aeronautics and Space Administration, 1978. 149 p. illus.,

maps. (U.S. National Aeronautics and Space Administration. Technical memorandum 75087)

Translation of *Télédétection de la zone de N'Djamena et du confluent Logone-Chari* (Paris, 1977).

Microfiche. [s.l., 1978] 2 sheets.
　　　　　　　DLC-Sci RR N7821570

3611

Chad. [*Treaties, etc. United States, 1977 June 10*] Chad; agricultural commodities; transfer under Title II; entered into force June 10, 1977. *In* U.S. *Treaties, etc.* United States treaties and other international agreements, v. 29, 1976–77. [Washington, Dept. of State; for sale by the Supt. of Docs., U.S. Govt. Print. Off., 1980] p. 5741–5745. ([Treaties and other international acts series, 9146])
　　　　　　　JX231.A34 v. 29

3612

Chad. [*Treaties, etc. United States, 1978 June 2*] Chad, agricultural commodities: transfer under title II. Agreement signed at N'Djamena June 2, 1978; entered into force June 2, 1978. *In* U.S. *Treaties, etc.* United States treaties and other international agreements, v. 30, 1978–79. [Washington, Dept. of State; for sale by the Supt. of Docs., U.S. Govt. Print. Off., 1980] p. 3132–3137. ([Treaties and other international acts series, 9383])
　　　　　　　JX231.A34 v. 30

Authorizes the Commodity Credit Corporation to transfer and deliver food grain to Chad.

3613

Chad. [*Treaties, etc. United States, 1978 Aug. 30*] Chad, road maintenance; agreement signed at N'Djamena August 30, 1978; entered into force August 30, 1978. [Washington, Dept. of State; for sale by the Supt. of Docs., U.S. Govt. Print. Off., 1980] 52 p. (Treaties and other international acts series, 9596)　　　　　DLC

In English and French.

A U.S. Agency for International Development project "aimed at improving the efficiency of road maintenance operations, strengthen road maintenance and planning, and improve the operations of the trucking industry."—p. 2.

3614

Chipeaux, Françoise. Leaders say French cooperation must be preserved. *In* U.S. *Joint Publications Research Service*. JPRS 75775. [Springfield, Va., National Technical Information Service, 1980] (Sub-Saharan Africa report, no. 2251) p. 20–23.

Translation of article in *Le Monde*, Paris, Apr. 23, 1980, p. 1, 3.

3614 (cont.)

Microfiche. [s.l., 1980]

DLC-Micro JPRS 75775

3615

Comprehensive human resources development in Chad. Santa Monica, Calif., Action Programs International, [1976?] 3 v.   DLC

Prepared for the U.S. Agency for International Development under project AID/afr-667-0005.

Contents: Component 1. Support of the National Institute of Educational Sciences (INSE).— Component 2. Human resources planning.— Component 3. Project management training.

L.C. has Component 1.

3616

Foreign economic trends and their implications for the United States. Chad. 1969+ Washington, for sale by the Supt. of Docs., U.S. Govt. Print. Off. annual. (International marketing information series)   HC10.E416

Prepared by the U.S. Embassy, N'Djamena.

Vols. for 1969–77 distributed by the U.S. Bureau of International Commerce.

The following issues for the period 1973–80 have been identified in L.C.:

ET 73-115. 1973. 10 p.
ET 74-132. 1974. 19 p.
FET 75-118. 1975. 13 p.
FET 76-105. 1976. 11 p.
FET 77-146. 1977. 9 p.

3617

Malloum N'gakoutou Bey-Ndi, Félix. Malloum sees Chad as victim of religious imperialism. *In* U.S. *Joint Publications Research Service.* JPRS 71707. [Springfield, Va., National Technical Information Service, 1978] (Translations on Sub-Saharan Africa, no. 1980) p. 13–17.

Translation of speech recorded in *Info Tchad,* N'Djamena, July 15/16, 1978, p. 2–7, on religious liberty in Chad and on the anti-Christian statements of Libyan leader Mu'ammar Qadhafi.

Microfiche. [Washington, Supt. of Docs., U.S. Govt. Print. Off., 1978)

DLC-Micro JPRS 71707

3618

Smith, Douglas V. Photovoltaic power in less developed countries. Lexington, Lincoln Laboratory, Massachusetts Institute of Technology, 1977. 81 p. map.   DLC

Prepared for the U.S. Energy Research and Development Administration under contract no. EY-76-C-02-4094.

Includes data on the economic and technical viability of using solar cells to power irrigation pumps and for other village power-consuming needs in Chad.

Issued also in microfiche. [Washington?, Technical Information Center, Energy Research and Development Administration, 1977?] 1 sheet.

DLC-Sci RR COO-4094-1

The Gambia

Note: Cataloged in the Library of Congress as Gambia.

General

3619

U.S. *Dept. of State.* Post report. The Gambia. [Washington?], 1975. [13] p. illus., map.

Examined in the Foreign Service Institute Library, Rosslyn, Va.

For a description of the contents of this publication, see the note to entry 936.

3620

U.S. *Dept. of State. Bureau of Public Affairs.* Background notes. The Gambia. [Washington, for sale by the Supt. of Docs., U.S. Govt. Print. Off.], 1982. 4 p. maps. (U.S. Dept. of State. Department of State publication 8014)   G59.U5

L.C. retains only the latest revision.

For a description of the contents of this publication, see the note to entry 937.

3621

Draft environmental profile on The Gambia. Tucson, Arid Lands Information Center, Office of Arid Lands Studies, University of Arizona, 1981. 85 p. maps.   AzU

On cover: "National Park Service Contract No. CX-0001-0-0003 in cooperation with U.S. Man and the Biosphere Secretariat, Department of State, Washington, D.C. Funded by AID, Office of Science and Technology, under SA/TOA 1-77."

Bibliography: p. 73–85.

Abstract in *A.I.D. Research & Development Abstracts*, v. 9, no. 4, p. 41.

Issued also in microfiche. [Washington, U.S. Agency for International Development, 1981?] 1 sheet.   DLC-Sci RR PN-AAJ-396

3622

The Peace Corps in The Gambia. [Washington?], ACTION; U.S. Govt. Print. Off., 1980] folder ([6] p.) illus., map.   DLC

An introduction to the country for Volunteers.

Assistance Programs

3623

U.S. *Agency for International Development.* Annual budget submission: Gambia. Washington, U.S. International Development Cooperation Agency.

Vols. for 1980+ examined in the Development Information Center, AID, Washington, D.C.

3624

———— Country development small program statement: Gambia. [Banjul?] annual.

Title varies slightly.

Review of the nation's economic situation, development requirements, and AID assistance strategy.

Vols. for 1979, 1980, and 1982 examined in the Documentation Center, Sahel Development Program, AID, Washington, D.C.

3625

———— Development assistance program: The Gambia. [Washington?], 1977. [168] leaves (in various foliations)

Examined in the Development Information Center, AID, Washington, D.C.

3626

U.S. *Agency for International Development. Office of U.S. Foreign Disaster Assistance.* Summary report: Gambia power shortage, November 22, 1977 & June 25, 1978. [Washington], 1979. 3 p. map.

Microfiche. [Washington, Congressional Information Service, 1979?]

                   DLC-Micro ASI:79 7206-3.43

3627

U.S. *Peace Corps. Gambia.* In-country training, summer 1973. [Banjul, 1973] [200] p.   DPC

3628

———— Report on Peace Corps Gambia's all volunteer conference-seminar, April 1976. [Banjul, 1976] 15 leaves.   DPC

3629

Baer, Lillian. Evaluation of Peace Corps/The Gambia junior secondary schools—math/science teaching program; 1970–present or to 1977/8. [s.l.], Peace Corps, 1973. 13 leaves.   DPC

3630

Bingen, R. James. Research/studies in Sahel francophone [*sic*] West Africa: Gambia; an inventory of research, studies, and reports sponsored by the U.S. Agency for International Development. Washington, Sahel Development Program, U.S. Agency for International Development, 1977. [15] p.

Covers seven projects undertaken in the period 1962–77.

Abstract for series on francophone West Africa and The Gambia in *A.I.D. Research and Development Abstracts*, Oct. 1977, p. 12–13.

Microfiche. [Washington, U.S. Agency for International Development, 1977?] 1 sheet.

          DLC-Sci RR PN-AAD-513

3631

Cahill, Brian. Gambia in-country training, 1973: final report. Bathurst, Peace Corps, 1973. 52 leaves.

          DPC

3632

The Gambia. [*Treaties, etc. United States, 1977 Oct. 26*] The Gambia, agricultural commodities: transfer under Title II. Agreement signed at Banjul October 26 and 28, 1977; entered into force October 28, 1977. *In* U.S. *Treaties, etc.* United States treaties and other international agreements, v. 29, 1976–77. [Washington, Dept. of State; for sale by the Supt. of Docs., U.S. Govt. Print. Off., 1980] p. 5753–5755. ([Treaties and other international acts series, 9148])   JX231.A34 v. 29

3633

The Gambia. [*Treaties, etc. United States, 1978 Jan. 12*] The Gambia, agricultural commodities: transfers under Title II. Agreement signed at Banjul January 12 and February 20, 1978; entered into force February 20, 1978. *In* U.S. *Treaties, etc.* United States treaties and other international agreements, v. 29, 1976–77. [Washington, Dept. of State; for sale by the Supt. of Docs., U.S. Govt. Print. Off., 1980] p. 5772–5774. ([Treaties and other international acts series, 9152])   JX231.A34 v. 29

3634

Sternin, Jerry, *and* John Hatch. Peace Corps, The Gambia: country program evaluation. [Washing-ton], Evaluation Division, Office of Policy and Planning, Action, 1976. [48] p.   DPC

3635

Technical Assistance Information Clearing House. Development assistance programs of U.S. non-profit organizations: The Gambia. [New York], American Council of Voluntary Agencies for Foreign Service, inc., 1978. 15 p. (TAICH country report)   DLC

"1st edition"

The Clearing House is operated by the Council under a grant from the U.S. Agency for International Development.

Economic Conditions

3636

Drought causes decline in gross domestic product. *In* U.S. *Joint Publications Research Service*. JPRS 71807. [Springfield, Va., National Technical Information Service, 1978] (Translations on Sub-Saharan Africa, no. 1987) p. 4–7.

Article in *West Africa*, London, July 31, 1978, p. 1487–1488.

Microfiche. [Washington, Supt. of Docs., U.S. Govt. Print. Off., 1978]

          DLC-Micro JPRS 71807

3637

Foreign economic trends and their implications for the United States. Gambia. 1979+ Washington, for sale by the Supt. of Docs., U.S. Govt. Print. Off. annual. (International marketing information series)   HC10.E416

Prepared by the U.S. Embassy, Banjul.

Distributed by the U.S. Industry and Trade Administration.

The following issue has been identified in L.C.: FET 79-134. 1979. 10 p.

Population Studies

3638

Africa: The Gambia. Selected statistical data by sex. Washington, 1981. 31, 17 p.   DLC

Study supported by the U.S. Agency for International Development's Office of Women in Development and Office of Population.

Data assembled by the International Demographic Data Center, U.S. Bureau of the Census.

Among the tables, based on 1973 data (unless noted) are the following: unadjusted population by age, sex, and urban/rural residence; population by province, sex, and urban/rural residence;

3638 (cont.)

population by ethnic group, sex, and urban/rural residence; population by nationality, sex, and urban/rural residence; infant mortality rates; number of households; number of literate persons by sex (1962); number of persons enrolled in school by age, sex, and urban/rural residence.

3639

Colvin, Lucie G. The Gambia. *In* The Uprooted of the western Sahel: migrants' quest for cash in the Senegambia, [by] Lucie Gallistel Colvin [et al.] New York, Praeger, [1981] p. 287–313. illus., map.
HB2125.5.A3U67

"The U.S. Agency for International Development (AID) funded this research."—p. iii.

3640

Profiles of Sahelian countries: Gambia. Washington, Socio-Economic Analysis Staff, International Statistical Programs Center, U.S. Bureau of the Census, 1974. [41] leaves (in various foliations)

Prepared at the request of the U.S. Agency for International Development.

Concerns demographic projections.

Examined in the Documentation Center, Sahel Development Program, AID, Washington, D.C.

Other Subjects

3641

English language teaching profile: The Gambia. [London], English-Teaching Information Centre, 1978. [11] p.

Abstract in *Resources in Education*, Mar. 1979, p. 85.

Microfiche. [Arlington, Va., ERIC Document Reproduction Service; prepared for Educational Resources Information Center, National Institute of Education, 1979] 1 sheet.
DLC-Micro ED161286

3642

Harrell-Bond, B. E., *and* D. L. Harrell-Bond. 'Deleterious effects' of tourism on Gambian society noted. *In* U.S. *Joint Publications Research Service.* JPRS 72791. [Springfield, Va., National Technical Information Service, 1979] (Translations on Sub-Saharan Africa, no. 2062) p. 9–13.

From article in *West Africa*, London, Jan. 15, 1979, p. 77, 79–80.

Microfiche. [Washington, Supt. of Docs., U.S. Govt. Print. Off., 1979]
DLC-Micro JPRS 72791

3643

Reyna, Stephen P. Social soundness: The Gambia reforestation project (635-0205) Abidjan, Regional Economic Development Services Office, [U.S. Agency for International Development], 1979. 26 p.
MiEM

3644

Role of home economics in family planning, The Gambia. Report of a country survey, May 12–17, 1975, [by] Olive Andrews [et al.] [Washington], American Home Economics Association, [1975] 18 p.

Prepared for the U.S. Agency for International Development under contract AID/csd-3623.

Examined in the Development Information Center, AID, Washington, D.C.

3645

Workshop on Advanced Training in Communication for Social Development in The Gambia, *Banjul*, Feb. 26–Mar. 15, 1979. Final report. [Chicago?, 1979?] 62 p. illus.

Funded by the U.S. Agency for International Development.

Organized by Radio Gambia, The Gambia Family Planning Association, and the Community and Family Study Center, University of Chicago.

Microfiche. [Washington, U.S. Agency for International Development, 1979?] 1 sheet.
DLC-Sci RR PN-AAG-956

Ghana

General

3646

U.S. *Dept. of State.* Post report. Ghana. [Washington, for sale by the Supt. of Docs., U.S. Govt. Print. Off.], 1982. 20 p. illus., map. (Department of State publication, 9278)   DLC

Department and Foreign Service series, 313.

L.C. has also reports issued in 1972 and 1975 (JX1705.A286 Spec. Format); report for 1978 examined in the Foreign Service Institute Library, Rosslyn, Va.

For a description of the contents of this publication, see the note to entry 936.

3647

U.S. *Dept. of State. Bureau of Public Affairs.* Background notes. Ghana. [Washington, for sale by the Supt. of Docs., U.S. Govt. Print. Off.], 1981. 7 p. maps. (U.S. Dept. of State. Department of State publication 8089)   G59.U5

L.C. retains only the latest revision.

For a description of the contents of this publication, see the note to entry 937.

3648

The Peace Corps in Ghana. [Washington?, ACTION; U.S. Govt. Print. Off., 1980] folder ([6] p.) illus., map.   DLC

"ACTION 4200.47."

An introduction to the country for Volunteers.

3649

Turner, Sandra J. Draft environmental profile on Ghana. Tucson, Arid Lands Information Center, Office of Arid Lands Studies, University of Arizona, 1980. 172 p. maps.   DLC

Sponsored by the U.S. Agency for International Development.

Bibliography: p. 159–172.

On cover: "National Park Service Contract No. CX-0001-0-0003 with U.S. Man and the Biosphere

Secretariat, Department of State, Washington, D.C."

Abstract in *A.I.D. Research & Development Abstracts*, July 1981, p. 38.

Issued also in microfiche. [Washington, U.S. Agency for International Development, 1980?] 2 sheets.   DLC-Sci RR PN-AAJ-272

Agriculture

3650

Artisan fishery technology: Ghana, a case study of a West African fishery, [by] Matthew Caurie [et al.] [Kingston?], University of Rhode Island, 1979. [79] p. (in various pagings) illus., map.

Prepared by the International Center for Marine Resource Development, University of Rhode Island, in cooperation with the Food Research Institute of Ghana.

"This report is a case study of fish harvesting, handling, preparation, and marketing techniques, and, also, fish consumption patterns currently existing in Ghana."—Abstract.

Held by the Library, International Center for Marine Resource Development, University of Rhode Island.

Issued also in microfiche. [Washington, U.S. Agency for International Development, 1979?] 1 sheet.   DLC-Sci RR PN-AAG-674

3651

Bartlett, R. H. Field trip report—brief agriculture and food survey of the Northern, Upper and Volta regions, March 9–22, 1976. [Accra], USAID/Ghana, 1976. 19 p.

Examined in the Development Information Center, AID, Washington, D.C.

3652

Caurie, Matthew, Teng-ching Lee, *and* C. O. Chichester. Underutilization of food technology resulting in losses of available food in West Africa. Kingston, International Center for Marine Re-

3652 (cont.)

source Development, University of Rhode Island, 1977. 1 v. (various pagings)

Emphasis is on Ghana.

Abstract in *A.I.D. Research and Development Abstracts*, Apr. 1979, p. 18.

Held by the Library, International Center for Marine Resource Development, University of Rhode Island.

Issued also in microfiche. [Washington, U.S. Agency for International Development, 1977?] 2 sheets (PN-AAG-193); examined in the Development Information Center, AID, Washington, D.C.

3653

Ghana. [*Treaties, etc. United States, 1976 Sept. 29*] Ghana; small farmer development. Agreement signed at Accra September 29, 1976; entered into force September 29, 1976. *In* U.S. *Treaties, etc.* United States treaties and other international agreements, v. 29, 1976–77. [Washington, Dept. of State; for sale by the Supt. of Docs., U.S. Govt. Print. Off., 1979] p. 173–195. ([Treaties and other international acts series, 8804])

JX231.A34 v. 29

3654

Ghana. [*Treaties, etc. United States, 1978 Mar. 31*] Ghana, managed input delivery and agricultural services. Agreement signed at Accra March 31, 1978; entered into force March 31, 1978. *In* U.S. *Treaties, etc.* United States treaties and other international agreements, v. 30, 1978–79. [Washington, Dept. of State; for sale by the Supt. of Docs., U.S. Govt. Print. Off., 1981] p. 4534–4545. ([Treaties and other international acts series, 9476])

JX231.A34 v. 30

Agreement between the U.S. Agency for International Development and the Ministry of Economic Planning of Ghana to expand credit availability to small farmers and improve agricultural technical assistance programs.

3655

Grisso, Roberto D., *and* Darrell A. Russel. Ghana: progress in fertilizer production, marketing, education. [Muscle Shoals, Ala.], National Fertilizer Development Center, Tennessee Valley Authority, 1977. 50 p. AMuI

Prepared for the U.S. Agency for International Development.

Copy examined in the Development Information Center, AID, Washington, D.C.

3656

Hamilton, Lee H. Food problems in northern

Ghana. Congressional record, 95th Congress, 1st session, v. 123, Oct. 18, 1977: 34135–34136.

J11.R5 v. 123

Extension of remarks in the U.S. House of Representatives.

Representative Hamilton includes texts of his correspondence with the U.S. Agency for International Development and an article from the *Manchester Guardian.*

3657

Mughogho, Spider K. The effect of liming an [*sic*] ultisol in Ghana on maize (Zea mays L.) yield and some soil properties. [Ithaca, N.Y.?], Cornell University, 1977. 147 p.

Research funded in part by the U.S. Agency for International Development.

Thesis (Ph.D.)—Cornell University.

Abstract in *A.I.D. Research and Development Abstracts*, Apr. 1978, p. 12.

Microfiche. [Washington, U.S. Agency for International Development, 1977?] 2 sheets.

DLC-Sci RR PN-AAC-948

3658

Obeng, H. B. Soils data for agricultural development in Ghana. *In* Soil-resource data for agricultural development, edited by Leslie D. Swindale. Honolulu, Hawaii Agricultural Experiment Station, College of Tropical Agriculture, University of Hawaii, 1978. p. 143–154. maps.

S590.2.S63

"Funding for publication of this book was provided by the United States Agency for International Development (USAID) contract ta-C-1108, through the Benchmark Soils Project, Department of Agronomy and Soil Science, Hawaii Agricultural Experiment State, College of Tropical Agriculture, University of Hawaii, Honolulu, HI."

Issued also in microfiche. [Washington, U.S. Agency for International Development, 1978?] 4 sheets. DLC-Sci RR PN-AAG-179

3659

Russel, Darrell A., Robert D. Grisso, *and* Robert G. Lee. Fertilizer alternatives for Ghana. Muscle Shoals, Ala., National Fertilizer Development Center [197–?] 108 p. illus., maps. (National Fertilizer Development Center. Bulletin Y-56)

DLC

Prepared for the U.S. Agency for International Development.

3660

Seminar on the Joint CSIR/USAID/Northeast Ghana Savannah Research Project, *1st, Kumasi,*

3660 (cont.)

1976. [Report] Accra, Council for Scientific and Industrial Research, 1976. 121 p.

Study funded by the U.S. Agency for International Development.

Examined in the Development Information Center, AID, Washington, D.C.

3661

Testing of a delivery system to transfer agricultural technology to small farmers in LDC's; an interim report of the Ghana experience, [by] T.S. Harris [et al.] [Prairie View, Tex.?], Prairie View A & M University, 1979,. 21 p.

Prepared for the U.S. Agency for International Development.

Microfiche. [Washington, U.S. Agency for International Development, 1979?] 1 sheet (PN-AAG-884); examined in the Development Information Center, AID, Washington, D.C.

Economic Aspects

3662

Assessment of small farmer credit in Ghana, [by] Roger S. Karsk [et.al.] [s.l.], 1975. 84 p.

Prepared under the direction of the U.S. Agency for International Development and the U.S. AID Mission to Ghana.

Examined in the Development Information Center, AID, Washington, D.C.

3663

Brecher, Richard A., *and* Ian C. Parker. Cocoa, employment and capital in the Ghanaian economy: a theoretical and empirical analysis. New Haven, Economic Growth Center, Yale University, 1974. [53] p. (in various pagings) (Center discussion paper, no. 210)

Bibliography: p. R1–R3.

"Portions of this research were financed by funds provided by the Agency for International Development under contract CSD/2492."

Microfiche. [Washington, U.S. Agency for International Development, 1974?] 1 sheet.

DLC-Sci RR PN-AAA-698

3664

Feasibility study for implementation of a small farmer production credit program through the Ghana credit union movement. [s.l.], Credit Union National Association, inc., 1976. 321 p.

Prepared for the U.S. Agency for International Development.

Examined in the Development Information Center, AID, Washington, D.C.

3665

Ohene-Darko, Regina, *and* John Anim-Appiah. Supply responses of cotton farmers in Ghana: case study of northwestern Ghana. Petersburg, Bureau of Economic Research and Development, Virginia State University, [1979?] 42 p. map. (Virginia. State University, Petersburg. Bureau of Economic Research and Development. Monograph series, v. 6, no. 2)   DLC

Prepared for the U.S. Agency for International Development under contract AID/csd 3415.

3666

Prakah-Asante, Kwame. The cost-size relationships of food crop farms in the Mampong-Ejura Agricultural District of Ghana. Kumasi, Dept. of Agricultural Economics, University of Science and Technology, 1976. 102 p.

Study funded in part by the U.S. Agency for International Development.

Bibliography: p. 81–87.

Examined in the Development Information Center, AID, Washington, D.C.

3667

—— The input rates on Ghanaian food crop farms. Kumasi, Dept. of Agricultural Economics, University of Science and Technology, 1975. 99 p.

Study funded in part by the U.S. Agency for International Development.

Bibliography: p. 81–84.

Examined in the Development Information Center, AID, Washington, D.C.

3668

Virginia. State College, *Petersburg. Bureau of Economic Research and Development.* Annual report. 1st+ 1972/73+ Petersburg.

H67.V57A2

Prepared for the U.S. Agency for International Development.

Report of a project "to improve the competence of Virginia State College in analysing and contributing to the resolution of problems of low income farm and rural non-farm units in South Central Virginia and Ghana."—Abstract, 1976/77 report.

Abstract of 1976/77 report in *A.I.D. Research and Development Abstracts*, July 1978, p. 5.

L.C. has 1972/73.

Some reports issued also in microfiche (Washington, U.S. Agency for International Development) and are held in DLC-Sci RR under the following identification numbers:

1972/73: PN-AAC-118
1973/74: PN-AAC-119
1974/75: PN-RAB-383

3668 (cont.)
1975/76: PN-AAC-721
1976/77: PN-AAF-026

3669
Winch, Fred E. Costs and returns of alternative rice production systems in northern Ghana: implications for output, employment and income distribution. [East Lansing], Dept. of Agricultural Economics, Michigan State University, 1976. 195 p. map.   MiEM
Bibliography: p. 191–195.
Thesis (Ph.D.)—Michigan State University.
Abstract in *A.I.D. Research and Development Abstracts*, July 1976, p. 22.
Issued also in microfiche. [Washington, U.S. Agency for International Development, 1976?] 3 sheets.   DLC-Sci RR PN-AAB-649
Issued also in microfilm. [Ann Arbor, Mich., University Microfilms International, 1976]
                                          DLC-Micro 76-18687

Forests and Forestry

3670
Laundrie, James F. Ghanaian hardwood mixtures for pulp and paper. Madison, Wisc., Forest Products Laboratory, 1977. [22] p.
"AID report no. 7."
Issued in cooperation with the University of Wisconsin.
Abstract in *A.I.D. Research and Development Abstracts*, July 1977, p. 14.
Microfiche. [Washington, U.S. Agency for International Development, 1977?] 1 sheet.
                                          DLC-Sci RR PN-AAC-886

3671
Myers, Gary C. Hardboards from mixtures of Colombian and Ghanaian hardwoods. Madison, Wisc., Forest Products Laboratory, 1977. 12 p.
On cover: AID report no. 11.
"In cooperation with the University of Wisconsin."
Abstract in *A.I.D. Research and Development Abstracts*, Jan. 1978, p. 10–11.
Microfiche. [Washington, U.S. Agency for International Development, 1977?] 1 sheet.
                                          DLC-Sci RR PN-AAE-066

3672
Wahlgren, Harold E., *and* James F. Laundrie. Properties of 50 individual Philippine hardwood barks and mixtures of 22 Ghanaian and 18 Colombian hardwood barks. Madison, Wisc., Forest Products Laboratory, 1977. 14 p.

On cover: AID report no. 10.
"In cooperation with the University of Wisconsin."
Microfiche. [Washington, U.S. Agency for International Development, 1977?] 1 sheet.
                                          DLC-Sci RR PN-AAE-065

Assistance Programs

3673
U.S. *Agency for International Development*. Annual budget submission: Ghana. Washington, U.S. International Development Cooperation Agency.
Vols. for 1977+ examined in the Development Information Center, AID, Washington, D.C.

3674
—— Country development strategy statement: Ghana. Washington, U.S. International Development Cooperation Agency. annual.
Vols. for 1982+ examined in the Development Information Center, AID, Washington, D.C.
Abstract of vol. for 1981 in *Appropriate Technical Information for Developing Countries*, 2d ed., 1979, p. 224.
Vol. for 1981 issued also in microfiche. [Springfield, Va., National Technical Information Service, 1979] 1 sheet.   DLC-Sci RR PB-298083

3675
—— Development assistance program, FY 1976–FY 1980: Ghana. [Washington?], 1975. 3 pts.
Contents: Pt. 1. Overview.—Pt. 2. Strategy.—Pt. 3. Sector summaries and special statements.
Examined in the Development Information Center, AID, Washington, D.C.

3676
—— Development assistance program, FY 1976–FY 1980: Ghana. Annexes. [Washington?], 1975. 6 pts.
Contents: Annex A. Role of women.—Annex B. Health sector assessment (including nutrition)—Annex C. Population sector assessment.—Annex D. Agricultural sector assessment and supplement on role of women in Ghanaian agriculture.—Annex E. The guidelines for the five year development plan and U.S. assistance strategy; an overview.—Annex F. Women in national development in Ghana; study and annotated bibliography, [by] Jeanne North [et al.].
Examined in the Development Information Center, AID, Washington, D.C.
Annex F held by L.C.; issued also in microfiche (see entry 3780). The "annotated bibliography" in

3676 (cont.)

Annex F also issued separately in microfiche (see entry 3778).

3677

Boyle, Neil, Robert Blohm, *and* Charles Helfer. Peace Corps/Ghana country program evaluation. [Washington], Office of Policy and Planning, Evaluation Division, [Action], 1976. [77] p. (in various pagings) map.

Abstract in *Resources in Education*, Aug. 1977, p. 19.

Microfiche. [Arlington, Va., ERIC Document Reproduction Service; prepared for Educational Resources Information Center, National Institute of Education, 1977] 1 sheet.

DLC-Sci RR ED136008

3678

Finberg, Donald R. Review of AID program, Ghana. [Washington], Operations Appraisal Staff, Bureau for Program and Policy Coordination, Agency for International Development, 1978. 50 p.

Examined in the Development Information Center, AID, Washington, D.C.

3679

Ghana. [*Treaties, etc. United States, 1977 May 24*] Ghana; agricultural commodities: transfers under Title II. Agreement signed at Accra May 24, 1977; entered into force May 24, 1977. *In* U.S. *Treaties, etc.* United States treaties and other international agreements, v. 29, 1976–77. [Washington, Dept. of State; for sale by the Supt. of Docs., U.S. Govt. Print. Off., 1979] p. 342–344. ([Treaties and other international acts series, 8820])

JX231.A34 v. 29

Under Title II of Public Law 480, the Commodity Credit Corporation was authorized to transfer and deliver food to Ghana.

3680

Ghana. [*Treaties, etc. United States, 1979 Feb. 9*] Agreement between the Government of the United States of America and the Government of Ghana for sales of agricultural commodities. *In* U.S. *Treaties, etc.* United States treaties and other international agreements, v. 30, 1978–79. [Washington, Dept. of State; for sale by the Supt. of Docs., U.S. Govt. Print. Off., 1980] p. 3555–3584. ([Treaties and other international acts series, 9411])

JX231.A34 v. 30

Signed at Accra Feb. 9, 1979.

3681

Ghana. [*Treaties, etc. United States, 1980 Feb. 15*] Agreement between the Government of the United States of American and the Government of Ghana for sales of agricultural commodities. [Washington, Dept. of State; for sale by the Supt. of Docs., U.S. Govt. Print. Off., 1980] 20 p. (Treaties and other international acts series, 9738) DLC

Signed at Accra, Apr. 14, 1980 with agreed minutes and related letter signed at Accra, Feb. 15, 1980.

3682

Peace Corps Ghana in-country training program; introduction and general information, summer program 1974. Accra, Pointer Ltd., 1974. [118] p. (in various pagings) DPC

3683

Peace Corps Ghana in-country training; 1975 programme designs. Accra, Pointer Ltd., [1975?] 74 p. maps DPC

3684

Snead, Betty. Shirley Temple Black: a commitment for development. War on hunger, v. 11, no. 1, Jan. 1977: 4–7. HD9000.1.W37 1977

Issued by the U.S. Agency for International Development.

A review of development programs in Ghana, where Ambassador Black served as U.S. envoy.

3685

Talking drums. Jan. 1976+ Accra, U.S. Peace Corps. bimonthly. DPC

Supersedes the *Monthly Newsletter* of the U.S. Peace Corps, Ghana, issued during the period Jan. 1973–Nov. 1975.

3686

Technical Assistance Information Clearing House. Development assistance programs of U.S. non-profit organizations in Ghana. [New York], American Council of Voluntary Agencies for Foreign Service, inc., 1976. 31 p. maps. (TAICH country report) DLC

The Clearing House is operated by the Council under a grant from the U.S. Agency for International Development.

Commerce

3687

Crown, John R., *and* William T. Leasure. Marketing in Ghana. Washington, U.S. Dept. of Commerce, International Trade Administration; [for sale by the Supt. of Docs., U.S. Govt. Print. Off.], 1981. 13 p. (Overseas business reports. OBR 81-26)

HF91.U482 1981, no. 26

International marketing information series.

3687 (cont.)

Supersedes a publication with the same title issued in 1975 (HF91.U482 OBR 75-30).

3688

Franzel, Steven. Import substitution of food products in Ghana. Ithaca, Dept. of Agricultural Economics, New York State College of Agriculture and Life Sciences, Cornell University, 1974. 41 p. (Cornell agricultural economics staff paper, no. 74–9)

Bibliography: p. 39–41.

Abstract in *A.I.D. Research and Development Abstracts*, Jan. 1976, p. 23.

Microfiche. [Washington, U.S. Agency for International Development, 1974?] 1 sheet.

DLC-Sci RR PN-AAB-299

3689

Market share reports. Country series: Ghana, 1971–75. [Washington], U.S. Dept. of Commerce; for sale by the National Technical Information Service, Springfield, Va., [1977] 65 p.

Indicates the United States share of the market in Ghana for various products compared to the shares for Belgium-Luxemburg, France, Federal Republic of Germany, Great Britain, Italy, Netherlands, Sweden, and Japan.

Microfiche. [Washington, Congressional Information Service, 1977?]

DLC-Micro ASI:77   2016-1.53

3690

Market share reports. Country series: Ghana, 1975–79. [Washington], International Trade Administration, U.S. Dept. of Commerce; for sale by the National Technical Information Service, Springfield, Va., [1979] 65 p.

Includes same comparative data as in *Market Share Reports. Country Series: Ghana, 1971–75* (entry 3689).

Microfiche. [Washington, Congressional Information Service, 1979?]

DLC-Micro ASI:81   2046-2.51

3691

Moe, Lyle E. Ghana reduces farm imports to pay for its higher oil bills. Foreign agriculture, Sept. 22, 1975: 8–9. illus.   HD1401.F65   1975

Issued by the U.S. Foreign Agricultural Service.

Ecology

3692

Aziz, Mohammed A. Lake Volta: man-made lake in Ghana, Africa; annotated bibliography and

inventory. Washington, Office of Environmental Science, Smithsonian Institution, [1973] 73 p.

Microfiche. [Washington, U.S. Agency for International Development, 1973?] 1 sheet.

DLC-Sci RR PN-AAG-186

3693

Freeman, Peter H. The environmental impact of a large tropical reservoir: based upon a case study of Lake Volta, Ghana, in 1973 and 1974. Washington, Office of International and Environmental Programs, Smithsonian Institution, 1974. 86 p. illus., map.

"The guidelines and case study were prepared by the Smithsonian Instituiton for the Agency for International Development under A.I.D. contract csd-2608."—p. iii.

Bibliography: p. 78–82.

Abstracts in *Selected Appropriate Technologies for Developing Countries*, no. 1, p. 83, and in *A.I.D. Research and Development Abstracts*, Sept. 1975, p. 23.

Microfiche. [Washington, U.S. Agency for International Development, 1974?] 1 sheet (DLC-Sci RR PN-AAB-176); and [Springfield, Va., National Technical Information Service, 1976] 2 sheets (DLC-Sci RR PB247430).

3694

Matlock, W. Gerald, *and* Jack D. Johnson The northeast Ghana savannah project—a case study in project design. [s.l.], 1975. 25 p.

Project to study land degradation problems in northern Ghana; sponsored in part by the U.S. Agency for International Development.

Paper presented at the annual meeting of the American Society for Engineering Education, 1975.

Abstract in *Resources in Education*, June 1976, p. 166.

Microfiche. [Arlington, Va., ERIC Document Reproduction Service; prepared for Educational Resources Information Center, National Institute of Education, 1976] 1 sheet.

DLC-Micro ED118439

3695

Smithsonian Institution. *Office of International and Environmental Programs.* Environmental aspects of a large tropical reservoir: a case study of the Volta Lake, Ghana; a report for the Office of Science and Technology, Agency for International Development. Washington, 1974. xv, 340 p. illus., maps.   QH195.G53S64   1974

Edited by Peter H. Freeman.

"Contract no. AID/csd 2608."

"Annotated bibliography of the hydrobiology

3695 (cont.)

of Volta Lake, prepared by Dr. Mohammed A. Aziz": p. 275–326.

Bibliography: p. 252–263.

Abstracts in *Selected Appropriate Technologies for Developing Countries*, no. 1, p. 85, and in *Government Reports Announcements & Index*, Mar. 19, 1976, p. 131.

Issued also in microfiche. [Washington, U.S. Agency for International Development, 1974?] 4 sheets (DLC-Sci RR PN-RAB-300); and [Springfield, Va., National Technical Information Service, 1976] 4 sheets (DLC-Sci RR PB248630).

Economic Conditions

3696

Ayensu. Edward S. The role of science and technology in the economic development of Ghana. *In* Science, technology, and economic development: a historical and comparative study, edited by William Beranek, Jr., [and] Gustav Ranis. New York, Praeger Publishers, 1978. p. 288–340.

Q172.S33

Volume prepared under the auspices of the National Academy of Sciences; supported in part by the U.S. Agency for International Development and other U.S. Government agencies.

3697

Esseks, John D. The nationalization of the ownership of resources and of high-level employment in Ghana: continuity in policy objectives and instuments. [s.l.], 1974. [23] leaves. (FAR 20598-N)

Prepared for the Colloquium on Ghana, sponsored by the U.S. Dept. of State, Oct. 1974.

Examined in the former Foreign Affairs Research Documentation Center, U.S. Dept. of State.

3698

Foreign economic trends and their implications for the United States. Ghana. 1969+ Washington, for sale by the Supt. of Docs., U.S. Govt. Print. Off., (International marketing information series)

HC10.E416

Semiannual, 1969–70; annual, 1971+

Continues *Economic Trends and Their Implications for the United States. Ghana.*

Prepared by the U.S. Embassy, Accra.

Vols. for 1969–77 distributed by the U.S. Bureau of International Commerce; vols. for 1978–79 by the U.S. Industry and Trade Administration; vols. for 1980– by the U.S. International Trade Administration.

Not published in 1975.

The following issues for the period 1973–81 have been identified in L.C.:

ET 73-048. 1973. 8 p.
ET 74-087. 1974. 9 p.
FET 76-024. 1976. 9 p.
FET 77-051. 1977. 8 p.
FET 78-069. 1978. 11 p.
FET 79-074. 1979. 12 p.
FET 80-110. 1980. 9 p.
FET 81-111. 1981. 10 p.

3699

Fundamental difficulties affecting economy analyzed. *In* U.S. *Joint Publications Research Service.* JPRS 75241. [Springfield, Va., National Technical Information Service, 1980] (Sub-Saharan Africa report, no. 2219) p. 38–41.

Interview with Amon Nikoi, Minister of Finance and Economic Planning, in *West Africa*, London, Feb. 11, 1980, p. 243–245.

Microfiche. [s.l., 1980]

DLC-Micro JPRS 75241

3700

Killick, Tony. Development economics in action: a study of economic policies in Ghana. New York, St. Martin's Press, c1978. 392 p.

HC517.G6K54   1978

Bibliography: p. [361]–380.

Research at Harvard University supported in part by the U.S. Agency for International Development.

3701

——— The economic strategies of Nkrumah and his successors. Cambridge, Mass., Development Research Group, Center for International Affairs, Harvard University, 1973. 72 p.

"Portions of this research were supported by the Project for Quantitative Research in Economic Development through funds provided by the Agency for International Development under contract CSD-1543."

Microfiche. [Washington, U.S. Agency for International Development, 1973?] 1 sheet.

DLC-Sci RR PN-AAE-187

3702

Leith, J. Clark. Ghana's exchange control experience: an overview. [s.l.], 1973. 7 leaves (FAR 18557-S)

Prepared for presentation at the Ghana Colloquium, sponsored by the U.S. Dept. of State, Oct. 1973.

Examined in the former Foreign Affairs Research Documentation Center, U.S. Dept. of State.

3703

Lukey, F. W. Case study no. 1, Lab. Products Ltd. A case history of an attempt to use institutional support to create independent commercial manufacturing in Ghana. Kumasi, Ghana, Univeristy of Science and Technology, 1978. 31 p. illus.

At head of title: Technology Consultancy Centre.

Abstract in *Appropriate Technical Information for Developing Countries*, 2d ed., 1979, p. 208.

Microfiche. [Springfield, Va., National Technical Information Service, 1979] 1 sheet.

DLC-Sci RR PB-294762

3704

Merwin, Charles L. Ghana: financial developments since the advent of Acheampong. [s.l.], 1979. 9 leaves. DLC

Prepared for a conference on Ghana, sponsored by the U.S. Dept. of State, Oct. 1979.

3705

Pinder, Frank E. Assistance to the Ministry of Economic Planning, Government of Ghana. [s.l.], 1977. 44 p.

Prepared for the U.S. Agency for International Development.

Examined in the Development Information Center, AID, Washington, D.C.

3706

Stewart, William H. Developing the tourist industry in Ghana. Sarasota, Fla., [1974] [86] leaves. (FAR 21805)

Prepared for the U.S. AID Mission to Ghana and the Ghana Tourist Control Board.

Examined in the former Foreign Affairs Research Documentation Center, U.S. Dept. of State.

Education

3707

Bezanson, Keith A., *and* Nicolas Hawkes. Bilingual reading skills of primary schoolchildren in Ghana. [Toronto, Bilingual Education Project, Ontario Institute for Studies in Education, 1976] 32 p.

Bibliography: p. 28–32.

Abstract in *Resources in Education*, Feb. 1977, p. 76.

Microfiche. [Arlington, Va., ERIC Document Reproduction Service; prepared for Educational Resources Information Center, National Institute of Education, 1977] 1 sheet.

DLC-Micro ED129077

3708

Brown, W. C. An overview of the origin and administrative organization of Ghanaian higher education. [s.l., 1974] 16 p.

Abstract in *Resources in Education*, May 1975, p. 111.

Microfiche. [Arlington, Va., ERIC Document Reproduction Service; prepared for Educational Resources Information Center, National Institute of Education, 1975] 1 sheet.

DLC-Micro ED100244

3709

The *Densu Times*—self-made literacy. Development communication report, no. 21, Jan. 1978: 1, 3–4.

DLC

Issued by the Clearinghouse on Development Communications with support from the U.S. Agency for International Development.

Concerns the use of a school and community newspaper to combat illiteracy in Ghana.

3710

Development of education in Ghana, 1975 and 1976. Report to the 36th session of the International Conference on Education, Geneva, September 1977. [Accra?, Ministry of Education, 1977] [18] p.

Abstract in *Resources in Education*, Jan. 1978, p. 139.

Microfiche. [Arlington, Va., ERIC Document Reproduction Service; prepared for Educational Resources Information Center, National Institute of Education, 1978] 1 sheet.

DLC-Micro ED143617

3711

George, Betty G. S. Education in Ghana. Washington, U.S. Dept. of Health, Education, and Welfare, Office of Education; for sale by the Supt. of Docs., U.S. Govt. Print. Off., 1976. 288 p. illus. (U.S. Dept. of Health, Education, and Welfare. DHEW publication; no. (OE) 75-19119)

LA1625.G45

Bibliography: p. 287–288.

Issued also in microfiche. [Arlington, Va., ERIC Document Reproduction Service; prepared for Educational Resources Information Center, National Institute of Education, 1977] 4 sheets.

DLC-Micro ED131058

3712

Nonformal education in Ghana: a project report, edited by David C. Kinsey [and] John W. Bing. Amherst, Center for International Education, School of Education, University of Massachusetts, 1978. 203 p. LC45.8.G4N66

"The project was enabled by a 211(d) grant from

3712 (cont.)
USAID to the Center for International Education (CIE) at the University of Massachusetts for the purpose of improving competence and techniques in the field of non-formal education."—p. 3.

Abstract in *Resources in Education*, 1980 annual cumulation, p. 343.

Issued also in microfiche. [Arlington, Va., ERIC Document Reproduction Sercice; prepared for Educational Resources Information Center, National Institute of Education, 1980] 3 sheets.
DLC-Micro ED177052

Geology, Hydrology, and Mineral Resources

The following items (entries 3713–20) are listed in chronological order:

3713
Stipp, Henry E. The mineral industry of Ghana. *In* Minerals yearbook, v. 3, 1972. [Washington, for sale by the Supt. of Docs., U.S. Govt. Print. Off., 1974] pp. 347–351.   TN23.U612   1972, v. 3
Prepared by the U.S. Bureau of Mines.

3714
———— The mineral industry of Ghana. *In* Minerals yearbook, v. 3, 1973. [Washington, for sale by the Supt. of Docs., U.S. Govt. Print. Off., 1976] p. 363–368.   TN23.U612   1973, v. 3
Prepared by the U.S. Bureau of Mines.

3715
Jolly, Janice L. W. The mineral industry of Ghana. *In* Minerals yearbook, v. 3, 1974. [Washington, for sale by the Supt. of Docs., U.S. Govt. Print. Off., 1977] p. 393–400.   TN23.U612   1974, v. 3
Prepared by the U.S. Bureau of Mines.

3716
———— The mineral industry of Ghana. Minerals yearbook, v. 3, 1975. [Washington, for sale by the Supt. of Docs., U.S. Govt. Print. Off., 1978] p. 435–441.   TN23.U612   1975, v. 3
Prepared by the U.S. Bureau of Mines.

3717
———— The mineral industry of Ghana. *In* Minerals yearbook, v. 3, 1976. [Washington, for sale by the Supt. of Docs., U.S. Govt. Print. Off., 1980] p. 457–462.   TN23.U612   1976, v. 3
Prepared by the U.S. Bureau of Mines.

3718
Rowland, T. John. The mineral industry of Ghana. *In* Minerals yearbook, v. 3, 1977. [Washington, for sale by the Supt. of Docs., U.S. Govt. Print. Off., 1981] p. 389–392.   TN23.U612   1977, v. 3
Prepared by the U.S. Bureau of Mines.

3719
Jolly, Janice L. W. The mineral industry of Ghana. *In* Minerals yearbook, v. 3, 1978–79. [Washington, U.S. Govt. Print. Off., 1981] p. 409–414.
TN23.U612   1978–79, v. 3
Prepared by the U.S. Bureau of Mines.

3720
Morgan, George A. The mineral industry of Ghana. *In* Minerals yearbook, v. 3, 1980. [Washington, for sale by the Supt. of Docs., U.S. Govt. Print. Off., 1982] p. 407–410.   TN23.U612   1980, v. 3
Prepared by the U.S. Bureau of Mines.

3721
Tuffuor, Samuel. Optimal parameter identification of nonlinear, time-variant hydrologic system models. Ft. Collins, Colorado State University, 1973. 179 p. maps.

Research funded in part by the U.S. Agency for International Development and the National Science Foundation.

Thesis (Ph.D.)—Colorado State University.

Uses the Todzie River basin in Ghana as a case study.

Microfiche. [Washington, U.S. Agency for International Development, 1973?] 2 sheets.
DLC-Sci RR PN-AAA-802
Microfilm. [Ann Arbor, Mich., University Microfilms International, 1973]
DLC-Micro 73-29065

Health and Nutrition

3722
U.S. *Peace Corps. Ghana.* Ghana cookbook: a guide to the nutritional value and preparation of West African food. [Accra, 1977] 31 p.   DPC

3723
An Approach to planning the delivery of health care services. [Oakland], Kaiser Foundation International, 1979. [83] p.

"Health care services manual, no. 1."

Study supported in part by the U.S. Agency for International Development.

Issued in cooperation with the Ministry of Health of Ghana.

3723 (cont.)

Abstract in *A.I.D. Research & Development Abstracts*, v. 9, no. 3, 1981, p. 43–44.

Microfiche. [Washington, U.S. Agency for International Development, 1979?] 1 sheet.

DLC-Sci RR PN-AAJ-357

3724

Beamer, Lyndall, *and* Linda J. Gangloff. Ghana. Washington, Division of Planning and Evaluation, Office of International Health; for sale by the Supt. of Docs., U.S. Govt. Print. Off., 1974. 38a p. map. (Syncrisis: the dynamics of health; an analytic series on the interactions of health and socio-economic development, v. 10) RA418.S98 v. 10

DHEW publication no. (OS) 74-50006.

Bibliography: p. 37a–38a.

Includes tables on demographic and health statistics.

Abstracts in *A.I.D. Research and Development Abstracts*, Oct. 1976, p. 26; and *American Statistics Index*, 1974, Abstracts, p. 278–279.

Issued also in microfiche. [Washington, U.S. Agency for International Development, 197–?] 1 sheet (DLC-Sci RR PN-AAB-973); and [Washington, Congressional Information Service, 197–?] 1 sheet (DLC-Micro ASI:74 4006-1:10).

Note: The following items (entries 3725–34) concern the Danfa project, which focused on a region north of Accra. Funded in 1970 by the U.S. Agency for International Development through a contract with the University of California at Los Angeles, the project was completed in 1979. Additional titles prepared in connection with the contract are entered elsewhere in the Ghana section of this guide; these can be identified by consulting the index under Danfa Comprehensive Rural Health and Family Planning Project.

3725

Conducting a rural health survey: experience from the village health survey, Danfa Project, Ghana [by] D. W. Belcher [et al.] [Accra, University of Ghana Medical School], 1975. [78] p. (in various pagings) illus. (Danfa Comprehensive Rural Health and Family Planning Project, Ghana. Monograph series, no. 9) CLU

Issued in cooperation with the School of Public Health, University of California, Los Angeles, under a U.S. Agency for International Development grant.

Abstract in *A.I.D. Research and Development Abstracts*, Feb. 1981, p. 49–50.

Issued also in microfiche. [Washington, U.S. Agency for International Development, 1975?] 1 sheet. DLC-Sci RR PN-AAH-262

3726

The Danfa Comprehensive Rural Health and Family Planning Project, Ghana; final report. Los Angeles, Division of Population, Family and International Health, School of Public Health, University of California, 1979. [614] p. (in various pagings) illus., map. CLU

Issued in cooperation with the Dept. of Community Health, University of Ghana Medical School.

Issued also in microfiche. [Washington, U.S. Agency for International Development, 1979?] 7 sheets (PN-AAH-079); examined in the Development Information Center, AID, Washington, D.C.

3727

Danfa Comprehensive Rural Health and Family Planning Project, Ghana; proceedings of the annual review meeting. [1st] + [1970?]+ Accra, University of Ghana Medical School. CLU

Issued in cooperation with the School of Public Health, University of California, Los Angeles.

CLU has 5th (1974), 6th (1975), and 8th (1977) reports; 5th (1974)–7th (1976) reports examined in the Development Information Center, AID, Washington, D.C.

3728

Danfa Comprehensive Rural Health and Family Planning Project, Ghana; summary, conclusions and recommendations from the final report. [Los Angeles], School of Public Health, University of California, 1979. 88 p. illus., map. CLU

Issued in cooperation with the University of Ghana Medical School under a U.S. Agency for International Development contract.

Abstract in *A.I.D. Research and Development Abstracts*, v. 8, no. 2, 1980, p. 13–14.

Issued also in microfiche. [Washington, U.S. Agency for International Development, 1979?] 1 sheet. DLC-Sci RR PN-AAH-078

3729

Danfa Comprehensive Rural Health and Family Planning Project, Ghana; UCLA annual progress report. 1972?–77? Los Angeles. CLU

No more published?

CLU has 1972–77; vols. for 1972–77 examined in the Development Information Center, AID, Washington, D.C.

3730

An Evaluation of the Danfa Comprehensive Rural Health and Family Planning Project in Ghana, [by] Henry M. Gelfand [et al.] [Washington?], American Public Health Association, 1975. 96 p.

Prepared for the U.S. Agency for International Development.

3730 (cont.)

Examined in the Development Information Center, AID, Washington, D.C.

3731

Experience in selecting, training and supervising interviewers in a rural health project: Danfa Project, Ghana, [by] D. W. Belcher [et al.] [Accra, University of Ghana Medical School], 1976. [27] p. (Danfa Comprehensive Rural Health and Family Planning Project, Ghana. Monograph series, no. 11)   CLU

Issued in cooperation with the School of Public Health, University of California at Los Angeles, under a U.S. Agency for International Development contract.

Abstract in *A.I.D. Research and Development Abstracts*, v. 8, no. 2, 1980, p. 17, and Feb. 1981, p. 50.

Issued also in microfiche. [Washington, U.S. Agency for International Debelopment, 1976?] 1 sheet.   DLC-Sci RR PN-AAH-270

3732

Mapping and house-number methods in a rural health project: experience in the Danfa Project, Ghana, [by] D. W. Belcher [et al.] [Los Angeles, School of Public Health, University of California], 1976. 15 p. illus., maps. (Danfa Comprehensive Rural Health and Family Planning Project, Ghana. Monograph series, no. 10)   CLU

Prepared under a U.S. Agency for International Development contract.

Issued in cooperation with the University of Ghana Medical School.

Abstract in *A.I.D. Research and Development Abstracts*, v. 8, no. 2, 1980, p. 17.

Issued also in microfiche. [Washington, U.S. Agency for International Development, 1976?] 1 sheet.   DLC-Sci RR PN-AAH-269

3733

A Mass immunization campaign in rural Ghana; factors affecting participation, [by] D. W. Belcher [et al.] Public health reports, v. 93, no. 1, Jan./Feb. 1978: 170–176. illus.   RA11.B17

Issued by the Health Resource Administration, U.S. Public Health Service.

"All of the authors were working with the Danfa Comprehensive Rural Health and Family Planning Project in Ghana at the time of this study. The project is a collaborative effort of the University of Ghana Medical School, Ghana's Ministry of Health, and the University of California at Los Angeles School of Public Health."—p. 171.

3734

Report on examination of the management of rural health services project in Ghana. [Washington], Office of the Auditor General, U.S. Agency for International Development, 1976. 9 p.

Examined in the Development Information Center, AID, Washington, D.C.

3735

Health needs and health services in rural Ghana. Brighton, Eng., IDS Health Group, Institute of Development Studies, University of Sussex, 1978. 2 v.

Issued in collaboration with institutes of the University of Ghana under a grant from the Swedish International Development Authority and the Swedish Agency for Research Cooperation with Developing Countries.

Abstracts of the two volumes in *Appropriate Technical Information for Developing Countries*, 2d ed., 1979, p. 203–204.

Microfiche. [Springfield, Va., National Technical Information Service, 1979] 7 sheets.

DLC-Sci RR PB-294568, PB-294569

3736

Johnson, Olive G., Alfred K. Neumann, *and* S. Ofosu-Amaah. Health information system installation: principles and problems. Medical care, v. 14, Mar. 1976: 210–222.   R11.M519 v. 14

"This work is supported in part by the United States Agency for International Development Contract No. AID/afr-IDA-73-14."

Primarily concerns the Danfa Comprehensive Rural Health and Family Planning Project in Ghana.

Abstract in *Government Reports Announcements & Index*, Feb. 18, 1977, p. 47.

3737

Management of rural health services, Ghana; annual report. Oakland, Calif., Kaiser Foundation International.

Report submitted to the Ministry of Health, Ghana, and the U.S. Agency for International Development.

Abstract for 1977 report in *A.I.D. Research and Development Abstracts*, Jan. 1979, p. 27.

Vol. for 1977 examined in the Development Information Center, AID, Washington, D.C.

3738

Nutrition Training Seminar for Preschool Health Program Supervisors, *Accra*, Sept. 23–Oct. 4, 1974. [Accra?], Catholic Relief Services, [1974] 99 p.

3738 (cont.)

Supported by a grant from the U.S. Agency for International Development.

Microfiche. [Washington, U.S. Agency for International Development, 1975?] 2 sheets.

DLC-Sci RR PN-AAE-025

3739

Rice, Donald T. Ghana: DEIDS reconnaissance, March 19–23, 1973. [Washington, Division of International Health Programs, American Public Health Association, 1973] 18 p.

Prepared for the U.S. Agency for International Development.

DEIDS: Development and Evaluation of Integrated Delivery Systems.

Focus is on maternal and child health, family planning, and nutrition, especially in rural areas.

Microfiche. [Washington, U.S. Agency for Internalional Development, 1973?] 1 sheet.

DLC-Sci RR PN-AAB-565

Housing and Urban Development

3740

Development of low-cost roofing from indigenous materials in developing nations; final report, 18 May 1973 through 31 December 1977, [by] G. L. Ball [et al.] Dayton, Ohio, Dayton Laboratory, Monsanto Research Corporation, 1978. 417 p. illus.

"MRC-DA-751."

Prepared for the U.S. Agency for International Development.

Report on a research program in the Philippines, Jamaica, and Ghana.

Abstract in *A.I.D. Research and Development Abstracts*, July 1978, p. 38.

Microfiche. [Washington, U.S. Agency for International Development, 1978?] 5 sheets.

DLC-Sci RR PN-AAF-131

3741

Experimental derivation of a methodology for the reduction of the costs of public construction in developing countries. [s.l.], Arthur D. Little, inc., 1975. 1 v. (various pagings)

Prepared for the U.S. Agency for International Development.

Project incorporated three experiments in Colombia, the Philippines, and Ghana.

Examined in the Development Information Center, AID, Washington, D.C.

3742

Slingsby, Ernest, James Wright, *and* Marilyn Dawson. Ghana shelter sector: preliminary study. [Washington, Office of Housing, U.S. Agency for International Development], 1978. 124 leaves.

DPC

Abstract in *A.I.D. Research and Development Abstracts*, Oct. 1978, p. 40.

Issued also in microfiche. [Washington, U.S. Agency for International Development, 1978?] 2 sheets (PN-AAF-453); examined in the Development Information Center, AID, Washington, D.C.

Politics and Government

3743

Asante, Clement. Limann government pledges, activities reviewed. *In* U.S. *Joint Publications Research Service*. JPRS 74852. [Springfield, Va., National Technical Information Service, 1980] (Sub-Saharan Africa report, no. 2194) p. 27–30.

Article in *Ghanaian Times*, Accra, Nov. 26, 1979, p. 4.

Microfiche. [s.l., 1980]

DLC-Micro JPRS 74852

3744

Bennett, Valerie P. The return of military rule in Ghana: the Government of National Redemption. Cambridge, Mass., Energy Resources Co., 1974. 22 leaves. (FAR 20597)

Prepared for the Colloquium on Ghana, sponsored by the U.S. Dept. of State, Oct. 1974.

Examined in the former Foreign Affairs Research Documentation Center, U.S. Dept. of State.

3745

Comments on personalities, chances of political candidates. *In* U.S. *Joint Publications Research Service*. JPRS 73463. [Springfield, Va., National Technical Information Service, 1979] (Translations on Sub-Saharan Africa, no. 2105) p. 20–23.

From article in *Daily Graphic*, Accra, Mar. 23, 1979, p. 5.

Microfiche. [Washington, Supt. of Docs., U.S. Govt. Print. Off., 1979]

DLC-Micro JPRS 73463

3746

Gold Coast: interest of the United States in development in the Gold Coast. *In* U.S. *Dept. of State.* Foreign relations of the United States. 1951, v. 5. Washington, U.S. Govt. Print. Off., 1982. p. 1266–1273. (U.S. Dept. of State. Department of State publication 9114)   JX233.A3   1951, v. 5

3746 (cont.)

Includes remarks at an official Dept. of State luncheon in honor of Kwame Nkrumah, Gold Coast Leader of Government Business, June 8, 1951.

3747

Hayward, Fred M. Political attitudes and political culture in Ghana. [s.l., 1979?] 7 leaves.　　DLC

"This paper was prepared for the Department of State."

3748

Kraus, Jon. The political economy of political conflict in Ghana: group and popular demands and government capabilities. [s.l.], 1979. 25 leaves.　　DLC

"Prepared for Colloquium on Ghana, U.S. Department of State, October 11, 1979."

3749

Owusu, Maxwell. The Peoples National Party (P.N.P.) and the Nkrumah legacy. [s.l.], 1979. [12] leaves.　　DLC

"Paper presented at the Colloquium on Ghana, U.S. Department of State, Washington, D.C., October 11, 1979."

3750

Political personalities, parties, situation reviewed. *In* U.S. *Joint Publications Research Service.* JPRS 73098. [Springfield, Va., National Technical Information Service, 1979] (Translations on Sub-Saharan Africa, no. 2082) p. 64–67.

From article in *West Africa*, London, Mar. 12, 1979, p. 421, 424–425.

Microfiche. [Washington, Supt. of Docs., U.S. Govt. Print. Off., 1979]

DLC-Micro JPRS 73098

3751

Rawlings: disappointment over revolution's results. *In* U.S. *Joint Publications Research Service.* JPRS 75181. [Springfield, Va., National Technical Information Service, 1980] (Sub-Saharan Africa report, no. 2216) p. 19–22.

Interview with Jerry J. Rawlings, chairman of the former Armed Forced Revolutionary Council of Ghana, in *West Africa*, London, Feb. 4, 1980, p. 189, 191–192.

Microfiche. [s.l., 1980]

DLC-Micro JPRS 75181

3752

Reeck, Darrell. The castle and the umbrella: some religious dimensions of Kwame Nkrumah's rule in Ghana. [s.l.], 1975. 21 leaves.

"This study was undertaken with the help of a grant under the Summer Seminar for College Teachers program of the National Endowment for the Humanities."

Presented at annual meeting of the African Studies Association, 1975.

Microfilm. [African Studies Association. Papers presented at the annual meeting.]

DLC-Micro Microfilm 03732 DT　1975, reel 2

3753

Rothchild, Donald. The political-economy of instability: Ghana politics in the 1980's. [s.l., 1979?] 17 leaves.　　DLC

"This paper was prepared for the Department of State."

3754

Vichier-Guerre, Claude H. Nkrumahism—a reappraisal; a research report submitted to the faculty. Maxwell Air Force Base, Ala., Air Command and Staff College, Air University, 1974. 133 leaves. (FAR 21740)　　AMAU

"This study examines the potential for Communist inspired insurgency in West Africa using Ghana as an example of the area and the Nkrumah period as a forecast of possible future trends."—Abstract.

Population Studies

3755

U.S. *General Accounting Office.* Impact of population assistance to an African country, Department to State, Agency for International Development: report to the Congress, by the Comptroller General of the United States. [Washington], 1977. 65 p. illus.

HB3666.8.A3U54　1977

"ID-77-3."

"B-179421; B-156518."

"Ghana is one African country that has recognized its population problem, promulgated an official population policy, and established a family planning program. The United States has provided about 75 percent of the $15.9 million of population assistance to Ghana. Ghana's program, however, has reached only a small percentage of the population, primarily urban. GAO believes changes are needed if the population growth rate is to be lowered significantly and recommends actions the Agency [for International Development] should take, including integration of population and development assistance, to meet this object."—Cover.

3755 (cont.)

Abstract in *Government Reports Announcements & Index*, Oct. 28, 1977, p. 51.

Issued also in microfiche. [Springfield, Va., National Technical Information Service, 1977] 1 sheet (DLC-Sci RR PB 269743); issued also in microfilm by University Publications of America (cited in its *Africa: Special Studies 1962–1980*, p. 9).

3756

Africa: Ghana. Selected statistical data by sex. Washington, 1981. 31, 17 p.   DLC

Study supported by the U.S. Agency for International Development's Office of Women in Development and Office of Population.

Data assembled by the International Demographic Data Center, U.S. Bureau of the Census.

Among the tables, all based on 1970-71 data, are the following: adjusted population by age and sex, 1970; population by region, sex and urban/rural residence, 1970; population by nationality, sex and urban/rural residence, 1970; life expectancy; number of households; heads of households by age, sex and urban/rural residence; number of literate persons by age, sex and urban/rural residence, 1971; number of persons enrolled in school 6 to 24 years old by age, sex, and urban/rural residence, 1970; number of economically active persons by age, sex, and urban/rural residence; economically active population by occupational status, sex, and urban/rural residence.

3757

An Analysis of the characteristics of households, household size, household heads and the relationship within the households, [by] G. M. K. Kpedekpo [et al.] [Los Angeles, School of Public Health, University of California], 1975. 25 p. (Danfa Comprehensive Rural Health and Family Planning Project, Ghana. Monograph series, no. 8)   CLU

Prepared under a U.S. Agency for International Development contract.

Issued in cooperation with the University of Ghana Medical School.

Issued also in microfiche. [Washington, U.S. Agency for International Development, 1975?] 1 sheet.   DLC-Sci RR PN-AAH-261

3758

An Analysis of the marital status, education, ethnic, religious and occupational composition, [by] G. M. K. Kpedekpo [et al.] [Los Angeles, School of Public Health, University of California], 1975. 36 p. (Danfa Comprehensive Rural Health and

Family Planning Project, Ghana. Monograph series, no. 7)   CLU

Prepared under a U.S. Agency for International Development contract.

Issued in cooperation with the University of Ghana Medical School.

Abstract in *A.I.D. Research and Development Abstracts*, v. 8, no. 2, 1980, p. 16, and Feb. 1981, p. 58.

Issued also in microfiche. [Washington, U.S. Agency for International Development, 1975?] 1 sheet.   DLC-Sci RR PN-AAH-260

3759

An Analysis of the population size, age/sex distribution, [by] G. M. K. Kpedekpo [et al.] [Los Angeles, School of Public Health, University of California], 1975. 38 p. (Danfa Comprehensive Rural Health and Family Planning Project, Ghana. Monograph series, no. 6)   CLU

Prepared under a U.S. Agency for International Development contract.

Issued in cooperation with the University of Ghana Medical School.

Abstract in *A.I.D. Research and Development Abstracts*, v. 8, no. 2, 1980, p. 16.

Issued also in microfiche. [Washington, U.S. Agency for International Development, 1975?] 1 sheet.   DLC-Sci RR PN-AAH-259

3760

Bame, K. N. Some traditional and modern media for generating social change in rural Africa: a study of some traditional and modern media for communicating family planning in Ghana. [s.l.], 1976. 46 p.

Paper prepared for the Fourth World Congress of Rural Sociology, 1976.

Abstract in *Resources in Education*, May 1977, p. 130.

Microfiche. [Arlington, Va., ERIC Document Reproduction Service; prepared for Educational Resources Information Center, National Institute of Education, 1977] 1 sheet.   DLC-Micro ED133103

3761

Estimates of indices of fertility from registration data, [by] G. M. K. Kpedekpo [et al.] [Los Angeles, School of Public Health, University of California], 1975. 41 p. (Danfa Comprehensive Rural Health and Family Planning Project, Ghana. Monograph series, no. 3)   CLU

Issued in cooperation with the University of Ghana Medical School.

Issued also in microfiche. [Washington, U.S. Agency for International Development, 1975?] 1 sheet.   DLC-Sci RR PN-AAH-258

3762

Estimates of indices of mortality (infant, child and adult) from registration data, [by] G. M. K. Kpedekpo [et al.] [Los Angeles, School of Public Health, University of California], 1975. 28 p. (Danfa Comprehensive Rural Health and Family Planning Project, Ghana. Monograph series, no. 2)   CLU

Issued in cooperation with the University of Ghana Medical School.

Copy examined in the Development Information Center. AID, Washington, D.C.

3763

Ghana. Washington, U.S. Dept. of Commerce, Bureau of the Census, Population Division, 1977. 21 p. illus. (Country demographic profiles. ISP-DP-5)   DBC

Issued Sept. 1977.

Bibliograph: p. 20–21.

3764

Harper, Paul A. Consultant report on population dynamics programme, University of Ghana. [Washington?], American Public Health Association, 1976. 25 p.

Prepared for the U.S. Agency for International Development.

An evaluation of the population dynamics program administered by the University of North Carolina.

Examined in the Development Information Center, AID, Washington, D.C.

3765

Migration patterns, population growth and change in the project areas of Danfa. Los Angeles, School of Public Health, University of California, 1975. 28 p. ([Danfa Comprehensive Rural Health and Family Planning Project. Monograph series, no. 5])   CLU

Prepared for the U.S. Agency for International Development.

3766

Results of the analysis and evaluation of vital registration data from the four project areas. Los Angeles, School of Public Health, University of California, 1975. 34 p. ([Danfa Comprehensive Rural Health and Family Planning Project. Monograph series, no. 1])   CLU

Prepared under a U.S. Agency for International Development contract.

3767

Rierson, Michael. Country report: Ghana. [Washington], Interdisciplinary Communication Pro-gram, Smithsonian Institution, 1976. 32 p.

Prepared for the U.S. Agency for International Development under contract AID/csd-3598.

Concerns research on analyses of population problems.

Microfiche. [Washington, U.S. Agency for International Development, 1976?] 1 sheet (PN-AAF-570); examined in the Development Information Center, AID, Washington, D.C.

3768

Some results and problems on the estimation of vital rates in a rural Africa setting via multiple methods, [by] G. M. K. Kpedekpo [et al.] [s.l.], 1975. 27 p. (Danfa Comprehensive Rural Health and Family Planning Project, Ghana. Monograph series, no. 4)   CLU

Project supervised by the University of Ghana Medical School and the School of Public Health, University of California at Los Angeles, with financial support by the U.S. Agency for International Development.

Abstract in *A.I.D. Research and Development Abstracts*, v. 8, no. 2, 1980, p. 16, and Feb. 1981, p. 54–55.

Issued also in microfiche. [Washington, U.S. Agency for International Development, 1975?] 1 sheet.   DLC-Sci RR PN-AAH-268

3769

Turkson, Richard B. Law and population growth in Ghana. Medford, Mass., Law and Population Program, Fletcher School of Law and Diplomacy, 1975. 55 p. (Law and population monograph series, no. 33)   MMeT-F

"The Law and Population Programme and its field work are supported in part by the International Planned Parenthood Federation, the United Nations Fund for Population Activities, and the U.S. Agency for International Development, among others."

Issued also in microfiche. [Washington, U.S. Agency for International Development, 1975?] 1 sheet.   DLC-Sci RR PN-AAF-170

3770

Wilder, Frank. New directions in population communications in three developing countries. [Washington?], American Public Health Association, 1977. 64 p.

Prepared for the U.S. Agency for International Development under contract AID/pha-C-1100.

Concerns family planning in Ghana, Indonesia, and Thailand.

Microfiche. [Washington, U.S. Agency for International Development, 1977?] 1 sheet.

DLC-Sci RR PN-AAJ-311

Science and Technology

3771

Council for Scientific and Industrial Research (Ghana) *Joint Ad Hoc Committee for Scientific and Technical Cooperation. Report.* [Accra?], Council for Scientific and Industrial Research of Ghana, University of Ghana, and National Academy of Sciences of the United States, 1975. [120] p. (in various pagings)

The National Academy of Sciences participated through funds provided by the Office of Science and Technology, Bureau for Technical Assistance, U.S. Agency for International Development.

Summary report of a July 1974 meeting in Washington, D.C. to discuss proposals "aimed at relating science and technology more effectively in solving economic and social problems in Ghana."

Abstract in *Appropriate Technical Information for Developing Countries*, 2d ed., 1979, p. 112.

Microfiche. [Washington, U.S. Agency for International Development, 1975?] 2 sheets (DLC-Sci RR PN-AAC-410); and [Springfield, Va., National Technical Information Service, 1975] 2 sheets (DLC-Sci RR PB-243367).

3772

Koster, John R. Final scientific report: ionospheric research using satellites. The total electron content of the ionosphere over Legon for the year 1972. Legon, Dept. of Physics, University of Ghana, [1974] 86 p.

"This research has been sponsored in part by Air Force Cambridge Research Laboratories (CRPA), L. G. Hanscom Field, Bedford, Mass., through the European office of Aerospace Research, OAR, United States Air Force, under grant no. AFOSR-72-2258."

Microfiche. [Springfield, Va.?, National Technical Information Service, 1975] 1 sheet.

DLC-Sci RR AD-A000926

3773

Montgomery, John D., *and* Milton J. Esman. Science policy-making for development: reflections on five case studies. [Washington?], American Institutes for Research, 1974. 37 p.

"AIR-43500-6/74-FR."

Prepared for the Office of Science and Technology, U.S. Agency for International Development.

Case studies include Taiwan, Indonesia, Ghana, Colombia, and Brazil.

Microfiche. [Washington, U.S. Agency for International Development, 1974?] 1 sheet.

DLC-Sci RR PN-AAB-038

3774

Pyrolytic conversion of agricultural and forestry wastes in Ghana: a feasibility study, prepared for Agency for International Development, Office of Science and Technology by Tze I. Chiang [et al.] Atlanta, Economic Development Laboratory, Engineering Experiment Station, Georgia Institute of Technology, 1976. 39 leaves. illus.

TP360.P96

Prepared under contract AID/ta-C-1290.

A study demonstrating that wood, sawdust, ground nut shells, and rice straw can be converted to charcoal, oil, and gas by pyrolytic conversion.

Abstracts in *A.I.D. Research and Development Abstracts*, Apr. 1978, p. 39; and *Appropriate Technical Information for Developing Countries*, 2d ed., 1979, p. 141–142.

Issued also in microfiche. [Washington, U.S. Agency for International Development, 1976?] 1 sheet (DLC-Sci RR PN-AAE-557); and [Springfield, Va., National Technical Information Service, 1976] 1 sheet (DLC-Sci RR PB-271392).

3775

Scientific and technical information (STI) in Ghana: role of the CSIR in development of a national STI network; an action report by the Joint Consultative Committee of CSIR, U.S. National Academy of Sciences, International Development Research Center. Accra, Council for Scientific and Industrial Research, 1976. 82, 15 leaves.

DPC

3776

Workshop on the Role of the Council for Scientific and Industrial Research in Determining Science Policy and Research Priorities, *March 1973.* [Report] [Accra?], Council for Scientific and Industrial Research, [1973] 54 p.

Workshop sponsored in part by the National Academy of Sciences of the United States.

Microfiche. [Springfield, Va., National Technical Information Service, 1973] 1 sheet.

DLC-Sci RR PB-223310

Women

3777

Bryson, Judy C. Women in Ghanaian development projects. *In* International Conference on Women and Food, *University of Arizona, Tucson,* Jan. 8–11, 1978. Proceedings and papers. v. 3. [Tucson?], 1978. p. B21–B26.

Conference sponsored by the Consortium for International Development with the support of a U.S. Agency for International Development grant.

3777 (cont.)

Microfiche. [Washington, U.S. Agency for International Development, 1978?]
DLC-Sci RR PN-AAG-531

3778

Fuchs-Carsch, Marian. Women in Ghanaian development: an annotated bibliography. [Washington, Office of Central/West Africa Regional Affairs, Bureau for Africa, U.S. Agency for International Development], 1975. 69 p.

Prepared for the U.S. AID Mission to Ghana.

Issued as part of Annex F of the Agency's *Development Assistance Program, FY 1976-FY 1980: Ghana* (entry 3676).

Issued in microfiche. [Washington, U.S. Agency for International Development, 1975?] 1 sheet.
DLC-Sci RR PN-AAC-652

3779

Steel, William F. Report on research program for Ghana National Council of Women and Development. [Nashville], Vanderbilt University, 1976. 39 p.

Prepared for the U.S. Agency for International Development under contract AID/afr-C-1230.

Examined in the Development Information Center, AID, Washington, D.C.

3780

Women in national development in Ghana, [by] Jeanne North [et al.] [Washington?, U.S. Agency for International Development], 1975. [210] p. (in various pagings) DLC

Includes annotated bibliography.

Issued as Annex F of the Agency's *Development Assistance Program, FY 1976-FY 1980: Ghana* (entry 3676).

Abstract in *A.I.D. Research and Development Abstracts*, July 1976, p. 28.

Issued also in microfiche. [Washington, U.S. Agency for International Development, 1975?] 3 sheets. DLC-Sci RR PN-AAB-683

Other Subjects

3781

Allen, George E., *and* John Gaudet. Report on assessment of aquatic weed problems and the economic significance in Ghana. [Corvallis, Ore.?], International Plant Protection Center, 1978. [32] p. illus., maps. OrCS

Prepared for the U.S. Agency for International Development and the Ghana Water and Sewage Corporation.

Issued also in microfiche. [Washington, U.S.

Agency for International Development, 1978?] 1 sheet. DLC-Sci RR PN-AAG-635

3782

Baker, Patricia. "African art: adinkra cloth;" an instructional unit for seventh-ninth grade art. Urbana, African Studies Program, University of Illinois, [1978] 19 p.

Report developed as part of an interdisciplinary workshop project in African curriculum development funded by the National Endowment for the Humanities.

Abstract in *Resources in Education*, 1980 annual cumulation, p. 2123–2124.

Microfiche. [Arlington, Va., ERIC Document Reproduction Service; prepared for Educational Resources Information Center, National Institute of Education, 1980] 1 sheet.
DLC-Micro ED189000

3783

Bringing energy to the people: Washington, D.C. and Ghana; grades 6, 7. [Washington], National Science Teachers Association, 1978. 63 p. illus., maps.

Prepared for the Office of Education, Business and Labor Affairs, U.S. Dept. of Energy.

At head of title: Interdisciplinary student/teacher materials in energy, the environment, and the economy.

A comparison of Ghana and the Washington, D.C. area in terms of climate, geography, energy dependency, and public services.

Abstract in *Resources in Education*, Dec. 1978, p. 136.

Microfiche. [Arlington, Va., ERIC Document Reproduction Service; prepared for Educational Resources Information Center, National Institute of Education, 1978] 1 sheet.
DLC-Sci RR ED157817

3784

Brown, C. K. The Ghanaian rural youth: human resource or human burden. [s.l.] 1976. 29 p.

Paper presented at the Fourth World Congress of Rural Sociology, 1976.

Abstract in *Resources in Education*, Jan. 1977, p. 101.

Microfiche. [Arlington, Va., ERIC Document Reproduction Service; prepared for Educational Resources Information Center, National Institute of Education, 1977] 1 sheet.
DLC-Sci RR ED128118

3785

Cole, Herbert M., *and* Doran H. Ross. The arts of Ghana. Los Angeles, University of California,

3785 (cont.)

Museum of Cultural History, [c1977] 230 p. illus (part col.)   NX589.6.G5C64

"This exhibition and catalogue were organized by the Museum of Cultural History, University of California, Los Angeles, with the aid of a grant from the National Endowment for the Arts, Washington, D.C., a Federal Agency created by Act of Congress, 1963."

3786

Ghana. [*Treaties, etc. United States, 1977 Oct. 13*] Ghana; radio communications between amateur stations on behalf of third parties. Agreement effected by exchange of notes dated at Accra October 13 and 27, 1977; entered into force November 26, 1977. *In* U.S. *Treaties, etc.* United States treaties and other international agreements, v. 29, 1976-77. [Washington, Dept,. of State; for sale by the Supt. of Docs., U.S. Govt. Print. Off., 1979] p. 2787–2789. ([Treaties and other international acts series, 8975])   JX231.A34 v. 29

3787

Harris, Donald S. [Country labor profile]: Ghana. *In* International labor profiles: comprehensive reports on the labor forces of 40 key nations, including data on wage and hour standards, labor organizations, social benefit programs, government regulations, and other labor-related topics. 1st ed. Detroit, Grand River Books, 1981. p. 102–107. illus., map.   HD4901.I56

Report prepared by the Bureau of International Labor Affairs, U.S. Dept. of Labor.

3788

Hayward, Fred M. The growth and erosion of development potential: changing mass attitudes in three Ghanaian small urban centers. *In* Southall, Aidan. Small urban centers in rural development in Africa. Madison, African Studies Program, University of Wisconsin-Madison, 1979. p. 334–355.

Bibliography: p. 352–355.

A grant from the Office of Urban Development, U.S. Agency for International Development, assisted in the preparation for publication of the papers collected in the study.

Microfiche. [Washington, U.S. Agency for International Development, 1980?] (PN-AAJ-064); examined in the Development Information Center, Agency for International Development, Washington, D.C.

3789

Huber, Rosarita. "The Akan of Ghana;" an instructional unit for fourth grade. Urbana, African

Studies Program, University of Illinois, [1978] 27 p.

Report developed as part of an interdisciplinary workshop project in African curriculum development funded by the National Endowment for the Humanities.

Abstract in *Resources in Education*, 1980 annual cumulation, p. 2122.

Microfiche. [Arlington, Va., ERIC Document Reproduction Service; prepared for Educational Resources Information Center, National Institute of Education, 1980] 1 sheet.

DLC-Micro ED188991

3790

McJulien, Demetria H. Social security and national insurance trust of Ghana. Baton Rouge, Unemployment-Underemployment Institute, Southern University and A & M College, [1976] 13 p. (Staff papers series, no. 107–76)

Funds for the Institute provided by the U.S. Agency for International Development.

Abstract in *A.I.D. Research and Development Abstracts*, Oct. 1976, p. 21.

Microfiche. [Washington, U.S. Agency for International Development, 1976?] 1 sheet.

DLC-Sci RR PN-AAC-020

3791

Middleton, John. Home-town: a study of an urban centre in southern Ghana. *In* Southall, Aidan. Small urban centers in rural development in Africa Madison, African Studies Program, University of Wisconsin-Madison, 1979. p. 356–370. map.

Considers Akropong-Akwapim.

A grant from the Office of Urban Development, U.S. Agency for International Development, assisted in the preparation for publication of the papers collected in the study.

Microfiche. [Washington, U.S. Agency for International Development, 1980?] (PN-AAJ-064); examined in the Development Information Center, Agency for International Development, Washington, D.C.

3792

Njiiri, Ruth, *and* Matthew Roehrig. West Africa: an American heritage. Amherst, Center for International Education, University of Massachusetts, [1975] 83 p.

Sponsored by the U.S. Office of Education.

"This guide contains unit plans and learning activities designed to broaden elementary and secondary students' perception of Ghana."—Abstract.

Abstract in *Resources in Education*, July 1979, p. 171.

3792 (cont.)

Archival copy held by the Center for International Education, University of Massachusetts, Amherst.

3793

Scaife, Rugenal R. "A look at the literature of an African people: the Ashanti of Ghana;" an instructional unit for eleventh grade English. Urbana, African Studies Program, University of Illinois, [1978] 23 p.

Report developed as part of an interdisciplinary workshop project in African curriculum development funded by the National Endowment for the Humanities.

Abstract in *Resources in Education*, 1980 annual cumulation, p. 2124.

Microfiche. [Arlington, Va., ERIC Document Reproduction Service; prepared for Educational Resources Information Center, National Institute of Education, 1980] 1 sheet.

DLC-Sci RR ED189004

3794

Warren, Dennis M. Aspects of social change in Ghana. [s.l.], 1979. [20] p. (in various pagings)

DLC

Prepared for a briefing session sponsored by the U.S. Dept. of State.

Guinea

General

3795

U.S. *Dept. of State.* Post report. Guinea. [Washington?], 1976. 19 p. illus., map.

Examined in the Foreign Service Institute Library, Rosslyn, Va.

For a description of the contents of this publication, see the note to entry 936

3796

U.S. *Dept. of State. Bureau of Public Affairs.* Background notes. Guinea. [Washington, for sale by the Supt. of Docs., U.S. Govt. Print. Off.] 1980. 4 p. illus., map. (U.S. Dept. of State. Department of State publication 8057, rev.)　　G59.U5

L.C. retains only the latest revision.

For a description of the contents of this publication, see the note to entry 937.

3797

Touré, Ahmed Sékou. President's new year's message reported. *In* U.S. *Joint Publications Research Service.* JPRS 70665. [Springfield, Va., National Technical Information Service, 1978] (Translations on Sub-Saharan Africa, no. 1881) p. 9–13.

Translation of excepts of speech recorded in *Horoya*, Conakry, Jan. 1–7, 1978, p. 7–12.

Microfiche. [Washington, Supt. of Docs., U.S. Govt. Print. Off., 1978]

　　DLC-Micro JPRS 70665

Agriculture

3798

Fribourg, Henry A., *and* Jesse B. Williams. Guinea agricultural production capacity and training project. Ann Arbor, Center for Research on Economic Development, University of Michigan, 1977. [164] p. (in various pagings)　　MiU-RE

Prepared for the Bureau for Africa, U.S. Agency for International Development, under contract AID/afr-C-1143.

Issued also in microfiche. [Washington, U.S. Agency for International Development, 1977?] 2 sheets (PN-AAH-814); examined in the Development Information Center, AID, Washington, D.C.

3799

Guinea. [*Treaties, etc. United States, 1977 Sept. 27*] Project grant agreement between the Republic of Guinea and the United States of America for the Guinea agricultural production capacity and training project. *In* U.S. *Treaties, etc.* United States treaties and other international agreements, v. 29, 1976–77. [Washington, Dept. of State; for sale by the Supt. of Docs., U.S. Govt. Print. Off., 1980] p. 5043–5105. ([Treaties and other international acts series, 9091])　　JX231.A34 v. 29

Signed at Conakry Sept. 27, 1977 and amending agreement signed at Conakry Mar. 31, 1978.

In English and French.

At head of title: A.I.D. project no. 675-0201.

Assistance Programs

3800

U.S. *Agency for International Development.* Annual budget submission: Guinea. Washington, International Development Cooperation Agency.

Vols. for 1980+ examined in the Development Information Center, AID, Washington, D.C.

3801

—— Country development strategy statement: Guinea. Small program statement. Washington, U.S. International Development Cooperation Agency. annual.

Vols for 1982+ examined in the Development Information Center, AID, Washington, D.C.

3802

Guinea. [*Treaties, etc. United States, 1974 May 8*] Agreement between the Government of the United States of America and the Government of Guinea for sales of agricultural commodities. *In* U.S. *Treaties, etc.* United States treaties and other international agreements, v. 25, 1974. [Washington, Dept. of State; for sale by the Supt. of Docs., U.S. Govt. Print. Off., 1975] p. 917–923. ([Treaties and other international acts series, 7835])

JX231.A34 v. 25

Signed at Washington May 8, 1974; amending agreement effected by exchange of notes dated at Conakry May 24, 1974.

3803

Guinea. [*Treaties, etc. United States, 1974 June 14*] Agreement amending the agreement of May 8, 1974, as amended; effected by exchange of notes dated at Conakry June 13 and 14, 1974, entered into force June 14, 1974. *In* U.S. *Treaties, etc.* United States treaties and other international agreements, v. 25, 1974. [Washington, Dept. of State; for sale by the Supt. of Docs., U.S. Govt. Print. Off., 1975]) p. 1277–1279. ([Treaties and other international acts series, 7860])

JX231.A34 v. 25

In English and French.

3804

Guinea. [*Treaties, etc. United States, 1975 May 8*] Agreement between the Government of the United States of America and the Government of the Republic of Guinea for sales of agricultural commodities. *In* U.S. *Treaties, etc.* United States treaties and other international agreements, v. 27, 1976. [Washington, Dept. of State; for sale by the Supt. of Docs., U.S. Govt. Print. Off., 1977] p. 1474–1504. ([Treaties and other international acts series, 8258]) JX231.A34 v. 27

Signed at Conakry May 8, 1975, with memorandum of understanding signed at Conakry Oct. 7, 1975.

In English and French.

3805

Guinea. [*Treaties, etc. United States, 1976 Apr. 21*] Agreement between the Government of the United States of America and the Government of the Republic of Guinea for sale of agricultural commodities. *In* U.S. *Treaties, etc.* United States treaties and other international agreements, v. 27, 1976. [Washington, Dept. of State; for sale by the Supt. of Docs., U.S. Govt. Print. Off., 1977] p. 3468–3533. ([Treaties and other international acts series, 8378]) JX231.A34 v. 27

Signed at Conakry Apr. 21, 1976; entered into force Apr. 21, 1976 with memorandum of understanding.

In English and French.

3806

Guinea. [*Treaties, etc. United States, 1976 Sept. 22*] Agreement between the Government of the United States of America and the Government of the Republic of Guinea for the sale of agricultural commodities under the U.S. Food for Peace program PL 480 Title I. *In* U.S. *Treaties, etc.* United States treaties and other international agreements, v. 28, 1976–77. [Washington, Dept. of State; for sale by the Supt. of Docs., U.S. Govt. Print. Off., 1978] p. 3269–3292. ([Treaties and other international acts series, 8585]) JX231.A34 v. 28

Signed at Conakry Sept. 22, 1976.

In English and French.

3807

Guinea. [*Treaties, etc. United States, 1977 June 15*] Guinea; agricultural commodities: agreement amending the agreement of September 22, 1976; effected by exchange of notes dated at Conakry June 13 and 15, 1977; entered into force June 15, 1977. *In* U.S. *Treaties, etc.* United States treaties and other international agreements, v. 29, 1976–77. [Washington, Dept. of State; for sale by the Supt. of Docs., U.S. Govt. Print. Off., 1979] p. 1028–1030. ([Treaties and other international acts series, 8864]) JX231.A34 v. 29

In English and French.

3808

Guinea. [*Treaties, etc. United States, 1978 Apr. 14*] Guinea, agricultural commodities: transfer under Title II. Agreement signed at Washington and Conakry April 14 and June 5, 1978; entered into force June 5, 1978. *In* U.S. *Treaties, etc.* United States treaties and other international agreements, v. 29, 1976–77. [Washington, Dept. of State; for sale by the Supt. of Docs., U.S. Govt. Print. Off., 1980] p. 5756–5763. ([Treaties and other international acts series, 9149]) JX231.A34 v. 29

In English and French.

3809

Guinea. [*Treaties, etc. United States, 1980 May 22*] Agricultural commodities agreement between the United States of America and Guinea, signed at Conakry May 22, 1980 with memorandum of understanding signed at Conakry May 26, 1980. [Washington, Dept. of State; for sale by the Supt. of Docs., U.S. Govt. Print. Off., 1981] 36 p. (Treaties and other international acts series, 9779)

DLC

In English and French.

Economic Conditions

3810

Expanded foreign trade to boost economy. *In* U.S. *Joint Publications Research Service.* JPRS 66094. [Springfield, Va., National Technical Information Service, 1975] (Translations on Sub-Saharan Africa, no. 1624) p. 15–18.

Translation of article in *Le Moniteur africain*, Dakar, Sept. 12–17, 1975, p. 10–12.

Microfiche. [s.l., 1975]

DLC-Micro JPRS 66094

3811

Foreign economic trends and their implications for the United States. Guinea. 1975?+ Washington, for sale by the Supt. of Docs., U.S. Govt. Print. Off. annual. (International marketing information series)   HC10.E416

Prepared by the U.S. Embassy, Conakry.

Vols. for 1975–76 distributed by the U.S. Bureau of International Commerce; vols. for 1978–79 by the U.S. Industry and Trade Administration; vol. for 1980– by the U.S. International Trade Administration.

Not published in 1977.

The following issues have been identified in L.C.:

FET 75-032. 1975. 6 p.
FET 76-111. 1976. 10 p.
FET 78-033. 1978. 13 p.
FET 79-024. 1978 [sic] 15 p.
FET 80-045. 1980. 13 p.
FET 81-042. 1981. 12 p.

3812

Touré, Ahmed Sékou. President addresses economic development problems. *In* U.S. *Joint Publications Research Service.* JPRS 68474. [Springfield, Va., National Technical Information Service, 1977] (Translations on Sub-Saharan Africa, no. 1705) p. 16–27.

Translation of speech recorded in *Horoya*, Conakry, Dec. 5–11, 1976, p. 6–21.

Microfiche. [s.l., 1977]

DLC-Micro JPRS 68474

3813

—— Toure on private enterprise, foreign investments. *In* U.S. *Joint Publications Research Service.* JPRS 75920. [Springfield, Va., National Technical Information Service, 1980] (Sub-Saharan Africa report, no. 2258) p. 56–60.

Translation of article in *Horoya*, Conakry, Feb. 16, 1980, p. 12, 13, 19, 20.

Microfiche. [s.l., 1980]

DLC-Micro JPRS 75920

Politics and Government

3814

Comte, Gilbert. Sekou Toure: portrait of a despot. *In* U.S. *Joint Publications Research Service.* JPRS 68604. [Springfield, Va., National Technical Information Service, 1977] (Translations on Sub-Saharan Africa, no. 1711) p. 5–12.

Based on an interview with Jean-Paul Alata, author of *Prison d'Afrique*, in *Africa*, Dakar, Dec. 1976, p. 31–33.

Microfiche. [s.l., 1977]

DLC-Micro JPRS 68604

3815

Gaudio, Attilio. Eyewitness report praises Guinea today, details failings. *In* U.S. *Joint Publications Research Service.* JPRS 73060. [Springfield, Va., National Technical Information Service, 1979] (Translations on Sub-Saharan Africa, no. 2079) p. 97–103.

Translation of article in *Africa*, Dakar, Feb. 1979, p. 35–40.

Microfiche. [Washington, Supt. of Docs., U.S. Govt. Print. Off., 1979]

DLC-Micro JPRS 73060

3816

Touré, Ahmed Sékou. President scores fifth column, clarifies foreign policy. *IN* U.S. *Joint Publications Research Service.* JPRS 67945. [Springfield, Va., National Technical Information Service, 1976] (Translations on Sub-Saharan Africa, no. 1676) p. 22–26.

Translation of speech recorded in *Horoya*, Conakry, Aug. 29 – Sept. 4, 1976.

Microfiche. [s.l., 1976]

DLC-Micro JPRS 67945

3817

—— Sekou Toure speech opening party regional council session. *In* U.S. *Joint Publications Research Service.* JPRS 71111. [Springfield, Va., National Technical Information Service, 1978] (Translations on Sub-Saharan Africa, no. 1927) p. 16–27.

Translation of speech to the Parti démocratique de Guinée recorded in *Horoya*, Conakry, Mar. 19 / Apr. 1, 1978, p. 16–34.

Microfiche. [Washington, Supt. of Docs., U.S. Govt. Print. Off., 1978]

DLC-Micro JPRS 71111

3818

Warning sounded against internal enemies, counter-revolutionaries. *In* U.S. *Joint Publications Research Service*. JPRS 76499. [Springfield, Va., National Technical Information Service, 1980] (Sub-Saharan Africa report, no. 2296) p. 67–70.

Translation of article in *Horoya*, Conakry, June 18–23, 1980.

Microfiche. [s.l., 1980]

DLC-Micro JPRS 76499

Population Studies

3819

Africa: Guinea. Selected statistical data by sex. Washington, 1981. 31, 17 p.　　　　DLC

Study supported by the U.S. Agency for International Development's Office of Women in Development and Office of Population.

Data assembled by the International Demographic Data Center, U.S. Bureau of the Census.

Tables are based on 1954–55 data.

3820

Profiles of Sahelian countries: Guinea. Washington,

Socio-Economic Analysis Staff, International Statistical Programs Center, U.S. Bureau of the Census, 1974. [41] leaves (in various foliations)

Prepared at the request of the U.S. Agency for International Development.

Concerns demographic projections.

Examined in the Documentation Center, Sahel Development Program, AID, Washington, D.C.

Other Subjects

3821

Guinea: shelter sector assessment. [s.l., National Savings and Loan League], 1980. [91] p. (in various pagings) illus., maps.

Prepared for the Office of Housing, U.S. Agency for International Development, under contract AID/otr-C-1453.

Abstract in *A.I.D. Research & Development Abstracts*, v. 9, no. 4, 1981, p. 48–49.

Microfiche. [Washington, U.S. Agency for International Development, 1980?] 2 sheets.

DLC-Sci RR PN-AAJ-078

Guinea-Bissau

General

3822

U.S. *Dept. of State.* Post report. Guinea-Bissau. [Washington, Dept. of State, Publishing Services Division; for sale by the Supt. of Docs., U.S. Govt. Print. Off.], 1982. 8 p. illus., map. (*Its* Department and Foreign Service series, 286)

JX1705.A286 Spec. Format

Department of State publication 9247.

Report for 1979 examined in the Foreign Service Institute Library, Rosslyn, Va.

For a description of the contents of this publication, see the note to entry 936.

3823

U.S. *Dept. of State. Bureau of Public Affairs.* Background notes. Guinea-Bissau. [Washington, for sale by the Supt. of Docs., U.S. Govt. Print. Off.] 1979. 4 p. maps. (U.S. Dept. of State. Department of State publication 8988)   G59.U5

L.C. retains only the latest revision.

For a description of the contents of this publication, see the note to entry 937.

3824

Cabral, Luis de Almeida. President Cabral reviews events of 1977. *In* U.S. *Joint Publications Research Service.* JPRS 70682. [Springfield, Va., National Technical Information Service, 1978] (Translations on Sub-Saharan Africa, no. 1884) p. 55–61.

Translation of article in *No Pincha*, Bissau, Jan. 5, 1978, p. 1, 4, 8.

Microfiche. [Washington, Supt. of Docs., U.S. Govt. Print. Off., 1978]

DLC-Micro JPRS 70682

3825

Kamissoko, Gaoussou. Official discusses first year of independence. *In* U.S. *Joint Publications Research Service.* JPRS 66291. [Springfield, Va., National Technical Information Service, 1975] (Translations on Sub-Saharan Africa, no. 1629) p. 6–9.

Translation of interview with Manuel dos Santos, commissioner of information of Guinea-Bissau, in *Fraternité-Matin*, Abidjan, Oct. 21, 1975, p. 18.

Microfiche. [s.l., 1975]

DLC-Micro JPRS 66291

Assistance Programs

3826

U.S. *Agency for International Development.* Annual budget submission: Guinea-Bissau. Washington, U.S. International Development Cooperation Agency.

Vols. for 1982+ examined in the Development Information Center, AID, Washington, D.C.

3827

——— Country development strategy statement: Guinea-Bissau. Small program statement. Washington, U.S. International Development Cooperation Agency. annual.

Vols. for 1981+ examined in the Development Information Center, AID, Washington, D.C.

3828

Guinea-Bissau. [*Treaties, etc. United States, 1977 Nov. 10*] Guinea-Bissau; agricultural commodities: transfer under Title II. Agreement signed at Bissau November 10, 1977; entered into force November 10, 1977. *In* U.S. *Treaties, etc.* United States treaties and other international agreements, v. 29, 1976–77. [Washington, Dept. of State; for sale by the Supt. of Docs., U.S. Govt. Print. Off., 1980] p. 5289–5293. ([Treaties and other international acts series, 9107])   JX231.A34 v. 29

3829

Guinea-Bissau. [*Treaties, etc. United States, 1978 Jan. 28*] Guinea-Bissau, agricultural commodities: transfer under Title II; agreement signed at Bissau January 8, 1978; entered into force January 8, 1978. *In* U.S. *Treaties, etc.* United States treaties

3829 (cont.)

and other international agreements, v. 29, 1976–77. [Washington, Dept. of State; for sale by the Supt. of Docs., U.S. Govt. Print. Off., 1980] p. 5768–5771. ([Treaties and other international acts series, 9151]) JX231.A34 v. 29

3830

Technical Assistance Information Clearing House. Development assistance programs of U.S. non-profit organizations: Guinea-Bissau. [New York], American Council of Voluntary Agencies for Foreign Service, inc., 1978. 11 p. map. (TAICH country report) DLC

The Clearing House is operated by the Council under a grant from the U.S. Agency for International Development.

Economic Conditions

3831

Cabral, Luis de Almeida. Cabral emphasizes financial considerations in CNG opening speech. *In* U.S. *Joint Publications Research Service.* JPRS 73753. [Springfield, Va., National Technical Information Service, 1979] (Translations on Sub-Saharan Africa, no. 2124)

Translation of speech by President Cabral before the National Council of Guinea reported in *No Pintcha*, Bissau, May 5 and 8, 1979.

Microfiche. [Washington, Supt. of Docs., U.S. Govt. Print. Off., 1979]

DLC-Micro JPRS 73753

3832

Foreign economic trends and their implications for the United States. Guinea-Bissau. 1979+ Washington, for sale by the Supt. of Docs., U.S. Govt. Print. Off. annual. (International marketing information series) HC10.E416

Prepared by the U.S. Embassy, Bissau.

Vol. for 1979 distributed by the U.S. Industry and Trade Administration; vol. for 1981– by the U.S. International Trade Administration.

The following issues have been identified in L.C.:

FET 79-111. 1979. 10 p.

FET 81-041. 1981. 11 p.

3833

Trade balance for 1977 disclosed. *In* U.S. *Joint Publications Research Service.* JPRS 70364. [Springfield, Va., National Technical Information Service, 1977] (Translations on Sub-Saharan Africa, no. 1854) p. 56–59.

Translation of article in *No Pintcha*, Bissau, Nov. 12, 1977, p. 4, 5.

Microfiche. [s.l., 1977]

DLC-Micro JPRS 70364

Other Subjects

3834

Africa: Guinea-Bissau. Selected statistical data by sex. Washington, 1981. 31, 17 p. DLC

Study supported by the U.S. Agency for International Development's Office of Women in Development and Office of Population.

Data assembled by the International Demographic Data Center, U.S. Bureau of the Census.

Statistics are given for the following headings: unadjusted population by age and sex (1960); and population by administrative units, sex, and urban/rural residence (1970).

3835

Andrews, C. Hunter. Project paper (PP) review for seed laboratory, seed storage, and plant pathology in Guinea-Bissau. [s.l.], Seed Technology Laboratory, Mississippi State University, 1977. 27 p.

MsSM

Prepared for the U.S. Agency for International Development under contract AID/ta-C-1219.

Copy examined in the Development Information Center, AID, Washington, D.C.

3836

Cabral, Luis de Almeida. Cabral discusses third PAIGC congress: unity with Cape Verde. *In* U.S. *Joint Publications Research Service.* JPRS 69835. [Springfield, Va., National Technical Information Service, 1977] (Translations on Sub-Saharan Africa, no. 1805) p. 28–31.

Translation of excerpts of a statement by President Cabral recorded in *No Pintcha*, Bissau, Sept. 1, 1977, p. 5.

Microfiche. [s.l., 1977]

DLC-Micro JPRS 69835

3837

Interview with Director General of Department of Geology and Mines. *In* U.S. *Joint Publications Research Service.* JPRS 68045. [Springfield, Va., National Technical Information Service, 1976] (Translations on Sub-Saharan Africa, no. 1682) p. 30–37.

Translation of interview with Lorena Santos, in *No Pintcha*, Bissau, Aug. 17, 1976, p. 4, 5.

Microfiche. [s.l., 1976]

DLC-Micro JPRS 68045

3838
Office of health begins serious study of family planning. *In* U.S. *Joint Publications Research Service.* JPRS 67724. [Springfield, Va., National Technical Information Service, 1976] (Translations on sub-Saharan Africa, no. 1667) p. 13–18.

Translation of article in *No Pintcha*, Bissau, July 20, 1976, p. 4–5.

Microfiche. [s.l., 1976]

DLC-Micro JPRS 67724

3839
Reis, Daniel. Interview with education commissioner, *In* U.S. *Joint Publications Research Service.* JPRS 69238. [Springfield, Va., National Technical Information Sercice, 1977] (Translations on Sub-Saharan Africa, no. 1758) p. 30–34.

Translation of interview with Mário Cabral, Commissioner of National Education and Culture, in *No Pintcha*, Bissau, Apr. 28, 1977, p. 4–5.

Microfiche. [s.l., 1977]

DLC-Micro JPRS 69238

Ivory Coast

General

3840

U.S. *Dept. of State.* Post report. Ivory Coast. [Washington?], 1978. [29] p. illus., map.
JX1705.A286 Spec. Format
L.C. has also reports issued in 1971 and 1974.
For a description of the contents of this publication, see the note to entry 936.

3841

U.S. *Dept. of State. Bureau of Public Affairs.* Background notes. Ivory Coast. [Washington, for sale by the Supt. of Docs., U.S. Govt. Print. Off.] 1980. 7 p. illus., maps. (U.S. Dept. of State. Department of State publication 8119)
G59.U5
L.C. retains only the latest revision.
For a description of the contents of this publication, see the note to entry 937.

3842

The Peace Corps in Ivory Coast. [Washington?, ACTION; U.S. Govt. Print. Off., 1980] folder ([6] p.) illus., map.   DLC
An introduction to the country for Volunteers.

3843

Pomonti, Jean-Claude. Ivorian progress, development examined. *In* U.S. *Joint Publications Research Service.* JPRS 75441. [Springfield, Va., National Technical Information Service, 1980] (Sub-Saharan Africa report, no. 2229) p. 30–42.
Translation of article in *Le Monde*, Paris, Jan. 29–31, 1980.
Microfiche. [s.l., 1980]
DLC-Micro JPRS 75441

Agriculture

3844

Camara, Lanseille. Ivory Coast agricultural teachers total in-country training 1973: final report. Abidjan, Peace Corps, 1973. 11 leaves.   DPC

3845

Dougherty, George M., *and* G. Burns Welch. Preliminary report: M.S.U. consultation visit on soybean seed drying-processing-storage facilities in Ivory Coast. [Mississippi State, Miss.?], 1975.
MsSM
M.S.U.: Mississippi State University.
Issued also in microfiche. [Washington, U.S. Agency for International Development, 1975?] 1 sheet.   DLC-Sci RR PN-AAC-749

3846

Elliott, Howard J. C. *Animation rurale* and *Encadrement technique* in the Ivory Coast. Ann Arbor, Center for Research on Economic Development, University of Michigan, 1974. 33 p. (Michigan. University. Center for Research on Economic Development. Discussion paper, no. 40)
Bibliography: p. 32–33.
A discussion of Ivorian agricultural strategy based on the nation's experience with co-operatives.
Abstract in *A.I.D. Research and Development Abstracts*, Sept. 1975, p. 17.
Microfiche. [Washington, U.S. Agency for International Development, 1974?] 1 sheet.
DLC-Sci RR PN-AAB-146

3847

Thorbecke, Erik, *and* Gunars Dambe. Comparative analysis and typology of agricultural development performance and strategy. [Ames, Iowa State University], 1974. 29 p. (Iowa State University 211-d Grant Program. Occasional paper, no. 5)
Prepared for the U.S. Agency for International Development under grant 211-d.

3847 (cont.)

A study of agricultural unemployment and underemployment in selected countries, including Ivory Coast.

Microfiche. [Washington, U.S. Agency for International Development, 1974?] 1 sheet.

DLC-Sci RR PN-AAA-728

Economic Aspects

3848

Bessis, Sophie. Development plans described. *In* U.S. *Joint Publications Research Service.* JPRS 68450. [Springfield, Va., National Technical Information Service, 1977] (Translations on Sub-Saharan Africa, no. 1701) p. 27–39.

Translation of interview with Mohamed Diawara, Minister of Planning, in *Afrique agriculture*, Paris, Dec. 1976, p. 30–35.

Microfiche. [s.l., 1977]

DLC-Micro JPRS 68450

3849

Dambe, Gunars, *and* Erik Thorbecke. Agricultural production and employment in Ivory Coast. [Ames], Iowa State University, 1974. 17 leaves. (Iowa State University 211-d Grand Program. Occasional paper, no. 4)

Prepared for the U.S. Agency for International Development under grant 211-d.

One of a series of case studies by the authors published in *Comparative Analysis of Agricultural Development and Employment Performance and Planning* (Rome, Food and Agricultural Organization of the United Nations, 1974).

Abstract in *A.I.D. Research and Development Abstracts*, Jan. 1975, p. 24.

Microfiche. [Washington, U.S. Agency for International Development, 1975?] 1 sheet.

DLC-Sci RR PN-AAA-727

3850

Miracle, Marvin P., *and* Diane S. Miracle. Commercial links between Grand Bassam, Ivory Coast and rural populations in West Africa. *In* Southall, Aidan. Small urban centers in rural development in Africa. Madison, African Studies Program, University of Wisconsin-Madison, 1979. p. 175–198.

A grant from the Office of Urban Development, U.S. Agency for International Development, assisted in the preparation for publication of the papers collected in the study.

Microfiche. [Washington, U.S. Agency for International Development, 1980?] (PN-AAJ-064); examined in the Development Information Center, Agency for International Development, Washington, D.C.

3851

Staatz, John M. Cattle and beef marketing in Ivory Coast. [Ann Arbor, Center for Research on Economic Development, University of Michigan], 1977. 140 p.   MiU-RE

Report to the U.S. Agency for International Development under contract REDSO-WA 77-101.

3852

——— The economics of cattle and meat marketing in Ivory Coast. [Ann Arbor], Center for Research on Economic Development, University of Michigan, 1979. 589 p. (Livestock production and marketing in the Entente states of West Africa. Monograph, 2)   MiU

Financed by the U.S. Agency for International Development.

Issued also in microfiche. [Washington, U.S. Agency for International Development, 1979?] 7 sheets (PN-AAJ-218); examined in the Development Information Center, AID, Washington, D.C.

3853

——— The economics of cattle and meat marketing in Ivory Coast: a summary. *In* Shapiro, Kenneth H. Livestock production and marketing in the Entente states of West Africa: summary report. [Ann Arbor], Center for Research on Economic Development, University of Michigan, 1979. p. 144–231.   MiU

Study financed by the U.S. Agency for International Development under contract AID/afr-C-1169.

Issued also in microfiche. [Sahel Documents and Dissertations. Ann Arbor, Mich., University Microfilms International, 1980] (DLC-Micro 5357 AS 162); and [Washington, U.S. Agency for International Development, 1979?] (PN-AAJ-217).

Rice

3854

Humphreys, Charles P. Rice production in the Ivory Coast. *In* Pearson, Scott R. Rice in West Africa: policy and economics. Stanford, Calif., Stanford University Press, 1981. p. 61–105.

HD9066.A462P4

Publication results from a research project, "The Political Economy of Rice in West Africa," carried out jointly by the Food Research Institute,

3854 (cont.)

Stanford University, and the West Africa Rice Development Association between June 1976 and Sept. 1979, and funded by the U.S, Agency for International Development under contract AID/afr-C-1235.

3855

Humphreys, Charles P., *and* Patricia L. Rader. Rice policy in the Ivory Coast. *In* Pearson, Scott R. Rice in West Africa: policy and economics. Stanford, Calif., Stanford University Press, 1981. p. 15–60.
HD9066.A462P4

Publication results from a joint research project conducted by the Food Research Institute, Stanford University, and the West Africa Rice Development Association and funded by the U.S. Agency for International Development (see more complete note in entry 3854).

3856

Posner, Joshua L. Rice in the development of Ivory Coast agriculture. Ithaca, Dept. of Agricultural Economics, New York State College of Agriculture and Life Sciences, 1973. 43 p. maps. (Cornell agricultural economics staff paper, no. 73–6)

Bibliography: p. 41–43.

Microfiche. [Washington, U.S. Agency for International Development, 1973?] 1 sheet.
DLC-Sci RR PN-RAA-374

Assistance Programs

3857

U.S. *Peace Corps. Ivory Coast.* Training philosophy. [Abidjan, Peace Corps, 1975?] 6 leaves.   DPC

3858

The Jungle line. [Dec. 1976?]+ Abidjan, Peace Corps. monthly.   DPC

"Of, for, and by the Volunteers."

3859

Technical Assistance Information Clearing House. Development assistance programs of U.S. non-profit organizations, Ivory Coast. [New York], American Council of Voluntary Agencies for Foreign Service, 1977. 13 p. maps. (TAICH country report)   HC547.I8T4a

The Clearing House is operated by the Council under a grant from the U.S. Agency for International Development.

3860

United Nations-Ivorian projects outlined. *In* U.S.

Joint Publications Research Service. JPRS 72438. [Springfield, Va., National Technical Information Service, 1978] (Translations on Sub-Saharan Africa, no. 2037) p. 10–13.

Translation of article in *Fraternité-Matin*, Abidjan, Oct. 24, 1978, p. 19.

Concerns assistance by the United Nations Development Program.

Microfiche. [Washington, Supt. of Docs., U.S. Govt. Print. Off., 1978]
DLC-Micro JPRS 72438

Commerce

3861

Bassole, A. San Pedro port arrangements described. *In* U.S. *Joint Publications Research Service.* JPRS 75051. [Springfield, Va., National Technical Information Service, 1980] (Sub-Saharan Africa report, no. 2208) p. 20–23.

Translation of article in *Fraternité-Matin*, Abidjan, Dec. 5, 1979, p. 12.

Microfiche. [s.l., 1980]
DLC-Micro JPRS 75051

3862

Market share reports. Country series: Ivory Coast, 1971–75. [Washington], U.S. Dept. of Commerce; for sale by the National Technical Information Service, Springfield, Va., [1977] 66 p

Indicates the United States share of the market in Ivory Coast for various products compared to the shares for Belgium-Luxemburg, France, Federal Republic of Germany, Great Britain, Italy, Netherlands, Sweden, and Japan.

Microfiche. [Washington, Congressional Information Service, 1977?]
DLC-Micro ASI:77   2016-1.60

3863

Market share reports. Country series: Ivory Coast, 1975–79. [Washington], International Trade Administration, U.S. Dept. of Commerce; for sale by the National Technical Information Service, Springfield, Va., [1979] 67 p.

Includes same comparative data as in *Market Share Reports. Country series: Ivory Coast, 1971–75* (entry 3862).

Microfiche. [Washington, Congressional Information Service, 1979?]
DLC-Micro ASI:81   2046-2.58

3864

Market survey of communications equipment and systems: the Ivory Coast. Chobham, Surry,

3864 (cont.)

England, Alan Stratford and Associates, Ltd., 1980. 82 p.

Prepared for the International Trade Administration, U.S. Dept. of Commerce.

Microfiche. [Springfield, Va., National Technical Information Service, 1980] 1 sheet.

DLC-Sci RR DIB-80-04-505

3865

Michelini, Philip. Marketing in Ivory Coast. [Washington], U.S. Dept. of Commerce, Domestic and International Business Administration; [for sale by the Supt. of Docs., U.S. Govt. Print. Off.], 1976. 27 p. (Overseas business reports. OBR 76-50)

HF91.U482 1976, no. 50

International marketing information series.

Superseded by the author's *Marketing in Ivory Coast* (Overseas business reports. OBR 79-15; entry 3866).

Issued also in microfiche. [Washington, Congressional Information Service, 1976?]

DLC-Micro ASI:77 2026-5.31

3866

—— Marketing in Ivory Coast. [Washington], U.S. Dept. of Commerce, Industry and Trade Administration; [for sale by the Supt. of Docs., U.S. Govt. Print. Off.], 1979. 32 p. (Overseas business reports. OBR 79-15)

HF91.U482 1979, no. 15

International marketing information series.

Supersedes the author's *Marketing in Ivory Coast* (Overseas business reports. OBR 76-50; entry 3865).

Communications and Transportation

3867

Aye, Jean-Pierre. Efforts to improve domestic travel noted. *In* U.S. *Joint Publications Research Service*. JPRS 76791. [Springfield, Va., National Technical Information Service, 1980] (Sub-Saharan Africa report, no. 2317) p. 44–50.

Translation of article on improved roads and airline service, in *Fraternité-Matin*, Abidjan, Sept. 30, 1980, p. 8–9.

Microfiche. [s.l., 1980]

DLC-Micro JPRS 76791

3868

Boni, Desire. Minister of public works, transport discusses projects. *In* U.S. *Joint Publications Research Service*. JPRS 69455. [Springfield, Va.,

National Technical Information Service, 1977] (Translations on Sub-Saharan Africa, no. 1775) p. 18–24.

Translation of article in *Afrique industrie infrastructures*, Paris, June 1, 1977, p. 61–65.

Microfiche. [s.l., 1977]

DLC-Micro JPRS 69455

Economic Conditions

3869

Diallo, Lelouma. Economic, anti-inflationary measures in 1979 discussed. *In* U.S. *Joint Publications Research Service*. JPRS 73044. [Springfield, Va., National Technical Information Service, 1979] (Translations on Sub-Saharan Africa, no. 2078) p. 74–79.

Translation of article in *Africa*, Dakar, Feb. 1979, p. 25–27.

Microfiche. [Washington, Supt. of Docs., U.S. Govt. Print. Off., 1979]

DLC-Micro JPRS 73044

3870

Foreign economic trends and their implications for the United States. Ivory Coast. 1969+ Washington, for sale by the Supt. of Docs., U.S. Govt. Print. Off. (International marketing information series) HC10.E416

Semiannual, 1969–71; annual, 1972+

Continues *Economic Trends and Their Implications for the United States. Ivory Coast.*

Vols. for 1969–77 distributed by the U.S. Bureau of International Commerce; vols. for 1978–79 by the U.S. Industry and Trade Administration; vols. for 1980– by the U.S. International Trade Administration.

The following issues for the period 1973–81 have been identified in L.C.:

ET 73-031. 1973. 12 p.
ET 74-034. 1974. 11 p.
FET 75-067. 1975. 8 p.
FET 76-070. 1976. 10 p.
FET 77-108. 1977. 11 p.
FET 78-092. 1978. [14] p.
FET 79-077. 1979. 13 p.
FET 80-073. 1980. 9 p.
FET 81-101. 1981. 8 p.

3871

Montgomery, Barbara. The economic role of Ivorian women. Ann Arbor, Center for Research on Economic Development, University of Michigan, 1977. [49] p. (Michigan. University. Center for Research on Economic Development. Discussion paper, no. 61)

3871 (cont.)

Abstract in *A.I.D. Research and Development Abstracts*, Jan. 1978, p. 19–20.

Microfiche. [Washington, U.S. Agency for International Development, 1977?] 1 sheet.

DLC-Sci RR PN-AAD-388

3872

1976 economic, 1978 investment figures given. *In* U.S. *Joint Publications Research Service*. JPRS 70973. [Springfield, Va., National Technical Information Service, 1978] (Translations on Sub-Saharan Africa, no. 1914) p. 31–47.

Translation of article in *Bulletin de l'Afrique noire*, Paris, Feb. 22, 1978, p. 18497–19504.

Microfiche. [Washington, Supt. of Docs., U.S. Govt. Print. Off., 1978]

DLC-Micro JPRS 70973

3873

Operating budget for 1978 discussed. *In* U.S. *Joint Publications Research Service*. JPRS 70711. [Springfield, Va., National Technical Information Service, 1978] (Translations on Sub-Saharan Africa, no. 1887) p. 52–67.

Translation of article in *Bulletin de l'Afrique noire*, Paris, Jan. 4, 1978, p. 18368–18376.

Microfiche. [Washington, Supt. of Docs., U.S. Govt. Print. Off., 1978]

DLC-Micro JPRS 70711

3874

Rondos, Alex. State of Ivorian economy studied. *In* U.S. *Joint Publications Research Service*. JPRS 73489. [Springfield, Va., National Technical Information Service, 1979] (Translations on Sub-Saharan Africa, 2107) p. 34–44.

From article in *West Africa*, London, Apr. 16, 23, and 30, 1979.

Microfiche. [Washington, Supt. of Docs., U.S. Govt. Print. Off., 1979]

DLC-Micro JPRS 73489

3875

Rouze, Anne. Economic progress, 'success' discussed. *In* U.S. *Joint Publications Research Service*. JPRS 75823. [Springfield, Va., National Technical Information Service, 1980] (Sub-Saharan Africa report, no. 2253) p. 48–52.

Translation of article in *Africa*, Dakar, Apr. 1980, p. 23–25.

Microfiche. [s.l., 1980]

DLC-Micro JPRS 75823

3876

—— Impact of recession examined. *In* U.S. *Joint Publications Research Service*. JPRS 77258.

[Springfield, Va., National Technical Information Service, 1981] (Sub-Saharan Africa report, no. 2350) p. 49–54.

Translation of article in *Africa*, Dakar, Dec. 1980, p. 35–38.

Microfiche. [s.l., 1981]

DLC-Micro JPRS 77258

3877

Stryker, Richard E. "Trade-offs in development strategy: the Ivory Coast." [s.l.], 1979. 12 leaves.

DLC

On cover: "For U.S. Department of State Colloquium on the Ivory Coast for Ambassador Nancy V. Rawls, October 9, 1979."

Education

3878

Danière, André, *and* François Orivel. Post-primary options in the Ivory Coast. Washington, Academy for Educational Development, inc., 1977. 153 p.

Prepared for the U.S. Agency for International Development under contract AID/afr-C-1158.

Issued in cooperation with the Institute for Communication Research, Stanford University.

Abstracts in *Resources in Education*, Nov. 1979, p. 131, and *A.I.D. Research and Development Abstracts*, Feb. 1981, p. 45.

Microfiche. [Arlington, Va., ERIC Document Reproduction Service; prepared for Educational Resources Information Center, National Institute of Education, 1979] 3 sheets (DLC-Micro ED172750); and [Washington, U.S. Agency for International Development, 1977?] 2 sheets (DLC-Sci RR PN-AAG-840).

3879

Economic studies and out-of-school education program evaluation for the Ivory Coast: final report, [by] Stephen Grant [et al.] Washington, Academy for Educational Development, inc., 1978. 125 p.

Prepared for the U.S. Agency for International Development under contract AID/afr-C-1158.

Issued in cooperation with the Institute for Communication Research, Stanford University.

Bibliography: p. 105–108.

List of reports produced under the contract: p. [103–104].

Abstracts in *A.I.D. Research and Development Abstracts*, Jan. 1979, p. 20; and *Resources in Education*, Nov. 1979, p. 129.

Microfiche. [Arlington, Va., ERIC Document Reproduction Service; prepared for Educational Resources Information Center, National Institute of Education, 1979] 2 sheets (DLC-Micro

3879 (cont.)

ED172737); and [Washington, U.S. Agency for International Development, 1978?] 2 sheets (PN-AAF-007; examined in the Development Information Center, AID, Washington, D.C.).

3880

Hodges, Nora. Training program, Ivory Coast, 1975: TEFL, agricultural teachers, medical technologists. [Abidjan, Peace Corps, 1975] 11 leaves.

DPC

TEFL: Teaching English as a Foreign Language.

3881

McAnany, Emile G. Secondary school alternatives in the Ivory Coast: consideration. Stanford, Calif., Institute for Communication Research, Stanford University, 1976. [27] p.

Paper prepared for the Evaluation Unit, Ministry of Primary Education and Television, Abidjan.

Abstract in *Resources in Education*, Nov. 1979, p. 132.

Microfiche. [Arlington, Va., ERIC Document Reproduction Service; prepared for Educational Resources Information Center, National Institute of Education, 1979] 1 sheet.

DLC-Micro ED172755

3882

Wells, Stuart. Labor markets and the social demand for education: an analysis of the Ivory Coast. [Washington, Academy for Educational Development], 1977. 38 p.

"Research support of this project was provided by USAID through contracts with EDUTEL Communications and Development, Inc. and the Academy for Educational Development, Inc."

Abstract in *Resources in Education*, Nov. 1979, p. 130.

Microfiche. [Arlington, Va., ERIC Document Reproduction Service; prepared for Educational Resources Information Center, National Institute of Education, 1979] 1 sheet.

DLC-Micro ED172743

Educational Television

3883

Eicher, Jean-Claude, *and* François Orivel. Cost analysis of the primary instructional television program in the Ivory Coast. Washington, Academy for Educational Development, inc., 1977. 97 p.

Prepared for the U.S. Agency for International Development under contract AID/afr-C-1158.

Issued in cooperation with the Institute for Communication Research, Stanford University.

Abstract in *Resources in Education*, Nov. 1979, p. 129.

Microfiche. [Arlington, Va., ERIC Document Reproduction Service; prepared for Educational Resources Information Center, National Institute of Education, 1979] 2 sheets.

DLC-Micro ED172735

3884

Etaix, Mireille, *and* Frans Langlet. "Tele pour tous" in rural Ivory Coast: audience, impact, perceptions; report of two surveys conducted in January and April 1977. Washington, Academy for Educational Development, inc., 1977. [233] p. (in various pagings)

Prepared for the U.S. Agency for International Development under contract AID/afr-C-1158.

Bibliography: p. [231–233].

Issued in cooperation with the Institute for Communication Research, Stanford University.

Abstracts in *Resources in Education*, Nov. 1979, p. 132, and *A.I.D. Research and Development Abstracts*, Feb. 1981, p. 42.

Microfiche. [Arlington, Va., ERIC Document Reproduction Service; prepared for the Educational Resources Information Center, National Institute of Education, 1979] 3 sheets (DLC-Micro ED172757); and [Washington, U.S. Agency for International Development, 1977?] 3 sheets (DLC-Sci RR PN-AAG-833).

3885

Evaluation Unit of Educational Television Program, Republic of Ivory Coast; final report. Washington, Academy for Educational Development, inc., [1974] 24 p.

Prepared for the U.S. Agency for International Development under contract AID/afr-828.

Abstract in *A.I.D. Research and Development Abstracts*, Jan. 1978, p. 29.

Microfiche. [Washington, U.S. Agency for International Development, 1974?] 1 sheet.

DLC-Sci RR PN-AAD-858

3886

Evans, Stella, *and* Steven Klees. ETV program production in the Ivory Coast. Washington, Academy for Educational Development, inc., 1976. 73 p.

Prepared for the U.S. Agency for International Development under contract AID/afr-C-1158.

Issued in cooperation with the Institute for Communication Research, Stanford University.

ETV: Educational television.

Abstracts in *Resources in Education*, Nov. 1979,

3886 (cont.)

p. 129, and *A.I.D. Research and Development Abstracts*. Feb. 1981, p. 44–45.

Microfiche. [Arlington, Va., ERIC Document Reproduction Service; prepared for Educational Resources Information Center, National Institute of Education, 1979] 1 sheet (DLC-Micro ED172739); and [Washington, U.S. Agency for International Development, 1976?] 1 sheet (DLC-Sci RR PN-AAG-839).

3887

Grant, Stephen. An administrative history of out-of-school educational television in the Ivory Coast. Washington, Academy for Educational Development, inc., 1977. 100 p.

Prepared in cooperation with the Institute for Communication Research, Stanford University, under U.S. Agency for International Development contract AID/afr-C-1158.

Bibliography: p. 98–100.

Abstracts in *A.I.D. Research and Development Abstracts*, Feb. 1981, p. 44, and *Resources in Education*, Nov. 1979, p. 128.

Microfiche. [Washington, U.S. Agency for International Development, 1977?] 2 sheets (DLC-Sci RR PN-AAG-837), and [Arlington, Va., ERIC Document Reproduction Service; prepared for Educational Resources Information Center, National Institute of Education, 1979] 2 sheets (DLC-Micro ED 172730).

3888

——— On needs assessment of out-of school educational television in the Ivory Coast. Washington, Academy for Educational Development, 1978. 39 p.

Prepared for the U.S. Agency for International Development under contract AID/afr-C-1158.

Issued in cooperation with the Institute for Communication Research, Stanford University.

Abstract in *Resources in Education*, Nov. 1979, p. 130.

Microfiche. [Arlington, Va., ERIC Document Reporduction Service; prepared for Educational Resources Information Center, National Institute of Education, 1979] 1 sheet.

DLC-Micro ED172746

3889

Grant, Stephen, *and* Pierre T. Seya. Visits to twenty-three villages to determine the impàct of the water series produced by the out-of-school TV department. Washington, Academy for Educational Development, inc., 1975. 89 p.

Prepared for the U.S. Agency for International Development under contract AID/afr-C-1158.

Issued in cooperation with the Institute for Communication Research, Stanford University.

Water in its diverse forms in the Ivory Coast was the subject of a pilot adult education television series.

Abstracts in *Resources in Education*, Nov. 1979, p. 139, and *A.I.D. Research and Development Abstracts*, Feb. 1981, p. 41.

Microfiche. [Arlington, Va., ERIC Document Reproduction Service; prepared for Educational Resources Information Center, National Institute of Education, 1979] 2 sheets (DLC-Micro ED172760); and [Washington, U.S. Agency for International Development, 1975?] 1 sheet (DLC-Sci RR PN-AAG-832).

3890

Klees, Steven J. Cost analysis of non-formal ETV systems: a case study of the "extra-scolaire" system of the Ivory Coast. Washington, Academy for Educational Development, inc., 1977. 116 p.

Prepared for the U.S. Agency for International Development under contract AID/afr-C-1158.

Bibliography: p. 114–116.

Issued in cooperation with the Institute for Communication Research, Stanford University.

Abstracts in *Resources in Education*, Nov. 1979, p. 128, and *A.I.D. Research and Development Abstracts*, Feb. 1981, p. 43–44.

Microfiche. [Arlington, Va., ERIC Document Reproduction Service; prepared for Educational Resources Information Center, National Institute of Education, 1979] 1 sheet (DLC-Micro ED172734); and [Washington, U.S. Agency for International Development, 1977?] 2 sheets (DLC-Sci RR PN-AAG-836).

3891

Klees, Steven J., *and* Dean T. Jamison. A cost analysis of instructional television in the Ivory Coast. Washington, Academy for Educational Development, inc., 1976. 63 p.

Prepared in cooperation with the Institute for Communication Research, Stanford University, under U.S. Agency for International Development contract AID/afr-C-1158.

Bibliography: p. 62–63.

Abstract in *A.I.D. Research and Development Abstracts*, Feb. 1981, p. 44.

Microfiche. [Washington, U.S. Agency for International Development, 1976?] 1 sheet.

DLC-Sci RR PN-AAG-838

3892

Lenglet, Frans. The impact of 25 television programs on "water" produced and broadcast by the Ivorian out-of-school education project. Washington,

3892 (cont.)

Academy for Educational Development, 1976. [100] p. (in various pagings) map.

Prepared for the U.S. Agency for International Development under contract AID/afr-C-1158.

Issued in cooperation with the Institute for Communication Research, Stanford University.

Abstracts in *Resources in Education*, Nov. 1979, p. 130, and *A.I.D. Research and Development Abstracts*, Feb. 1981, p. 41.

Microfiche. [Arlington, Va., ERIC Document Reproduction Service; prepared for Educational Resources Information Center, National Institute of Education, 1979] 2 sheets (DLC-Micro ED172742); and [Washington, U.S. Agency for International Development, 1976?] 2 sheets (DLC-Sci RR PN-AAG-831)

3893

Seya, Pierre T. Communication and social change in Ivory Coast. A case study of radio and television. [Stanford, Calif.?], 1978.

Thesis (M.A.)—Institute for Communication Research, Stanford University.

Cited in a list prepared by the Institute as a study produced under contract for the U.S. Agency for International Development.

3894

Seya, Pierre T., *and* Faustin K. Yao. Television for the rural African village: studies of audiences and impact in the Ivory Coast. Stanford, Calif., Institute for Communication Research, Stanford University, 1977. [55] p.

Abstract in *Resources in Education*, Nov. 1979, p. 132.

Microfiche. [Arlington, Va., ERIC Document Reproduction Service; prepared for Educational Resources Information Center, National Institute of Education, 1979] 1 sheet.

DLC-Micro ED172758

3895

Silverman, L. Theresa. The reception and animation of out-of-school educational television programs in the Ivory Coast: a case study of four villages, by Annie Beneviste; an English summary. Washington, Academy for Educational Development, inc., [197–?] 40 p.

Prepared for the U.S. Agency for International Development under contract AID/afr-C-1158.

Issued in cooperation with the Institute for Communication Research, Stanford University.

Abstract in *A.I.D. Research and Development Abstracts*, Feb. 1981, p. 41.

Microfiche. [Washington, U.S. Agency for International Development, 197–?] 1 sheet.

DLC-Sci RR PN-AAG-835

3896

Yao, Faustin K. Learning with 'Tele pour tous.' An adult educational television program in rural Ivory Coast. [Stanford, Calif.?], 1978. 65 p.

Thesis (M.A.)—Institute for Communication Research, Stanford University.

Cited in a list prepared by the Institute as a study produced under contract for the U.S. Agency for International Development.

3897

——— Les causes de la faible participation des villageois aux émissions Télé pour Tous. Abidjan, Service d'Evaluation, 1976. 13 p.

Cited in a list prepared by the Institute for Communication Research, Stanford University, as a study produced under contract for the U.S. Agency for International Development.

Energy Resources—
Production & Consumption

3898

Aye, Jean-Pierre. Nation's electrification program to 1985 outlined. *In* U.S. *Joint Publications Research Service*. JPRS 76857. [Springfield, Va., National Technical Information Service, 1980] (Sub-Saharan Africa report, no. 2322) p. 14–19.

Translation of article in *Fraternité-Matin*, Abidjan, Sept. 29, 1980, p. 8–9.

Microfiche. [s.l., 1980]

DLC-Micro JPRS 76857

3899

Beyrard, Norbert. Nuclear? Thermal? Ivory Coast must choose new sources of energy to meet its needs in the year 2000. *In* U.S. *Joint Publications Research Service*. JPRS 72338. [Springfield, Va., National Technical Information Service, 1978] (Translations on Sub-Saharan Africa, no. 2031) p. 24–27.

Translation of article in *Eurafrique*, Paris, Sept./Oct. 1978, p. 36–37.

Microfiche. [Washington, Supt. of Docs., U.S. Govt. Print. Off., 1979?]

DLC-Micro JPRS 72338

3900

Mining minister discusses oil, iron, nickel prospects. *In* U.S. *Joint Publications Research Service*. JPRS 70682. [Springfield, Va., National Technical In-

3900 (cont.)
formation Service, 1978] (Translations on Sub-Saharan Africa, no. 1884) p. 67–73.

Translation of interview with Paul Gui-Dibo, Minister of Mines, in *Afrique industrie infrastructures*, Paris, Jan. 1, 1978, p. 82–85.

Microfiche. [Washington, Supt. of Docs., U.S. Govt. Print. Off., 1978]

DLC-Micro JPRS 70682

3901
Wolff, William A. OTEC thermal resource report for Ivory Coast. Monterey, Calif., Ocean Data Systems, inc., 1979. [31] p. (in various pagings) maps.

Prepared for the Division of Central Solar Technology, Dept. of Energy, under contract no. ET-78-C-01-2898.

Bibliography: p. R-1—R-4.

OTEC: Ocean Thermal Energy Conversion.

Microfiche. [s.l., Technical Information Center, Dept. of Energy, 1979] 1 sheet.

DLC-Sci RR HCP/T2898-01/1

Housing and Urban Development

3902
U.S. *Agency for International Development*. Ivory Coast—low income urban shelter program. [Washington], 1976. 33 p.

Examined in the Development Information Center, AID, Washington, D.C.

3903
Votaw, Albert N., *and* David Leibson. Ivory Coast shelter sector analysis. [Washington?], National Savings and Loan League, 1975. 242 p.

Study conducted for the U.S. Agency for International Development.

Issued in conjuction with the Foundation for Cooperative Housing.

Examined in the Development Information Center, AID, Washington, D.C.

Politics and Government

3904
Assembly approves municipal election reforms. *In* U.S. *Joint Publications Research Service*. JPRS 76923. [Springfield, Va., National Technical Information Service, 1980] (Sub-Saharan Africa report, no. 2327) p. 45–49.

Translation of article in *Fraternité-Matin*, Abidjan, Oct. 16, 1980, p. 3.

Microfiche. [s.l., 1980]

DLC-Micro JPRS 76923

3905
Ebony, Noel. Further report on presidential succession. *In* U.S. *Joint Publications Research Service*. JPRS 74926. [Springfield, Va., National Technical Information Service, 1980] (Sub-Saharan Africa report, no. 2198) p. 23–29.

Translation of article in *Demain l'Afrique*, Paris, Nov. 5, 1979, p. 37–39.

Microfiche. [s.l., 1980]

DLC-Micro JPRS 74926

3906
Houphouet in full control; President, party chairman. *In* U.S. *Joint Publications Research Service*. JPRS 76890. [Springfield, Va., National Technical Information Service, 1980] (Sub-Saharan Africa report, no. 2324) p. 19–25.

Translation of article in *Africa*, Dakar, Oct. 1980, p. 25–28.

Microfiche. [s.l., 1980]

DLC-Micro JPRS 76890

3907
Kabue, Buana. Political, economic problems threaten calm. *In* U.S. *Joint Publications Research Service*. JPRS 70191. [Springfield, Va., National Technical Information Service, 1977] (Translations on Sub-Saharan Africa, no. 1837) p. 16–22.

Translation of article in *Demain l'Afrique*, Paris, Sept. 1977, p. 26–29.

Microfiche. [s.l., 1977]

DLC-Micro JPRS 70191

3908
Malet, Roland. Political stability, economic changes described. *In* U.S. *Joint Publications Research Service*. JPRS 70679. [Springfield, Va., National Technical Information Service, 1978] (Translations on Sub-Saharan Africa, no. 1883) p. 40–50.

Translation of article in *Demain l'Afrique*, Paris, Jan. 5, 1978, p. 33–39.

Microfiche. [Washington, Supt. of Docs., U.S. Govt. Print. Off., 1978]

DLC-Micro JPRS 70679

3909
Manouan, Adonit. Foreign ministry official discusses diplomacy. *In* U.S. *Joint Publications Research Service*. JPRS 73357. [Springfield, Va., National Technical Information Service, 1979] (Translations on Sub-Saharan Africa, no. 2098) p. 20–38.

3909 (cont.)

Translation of article on Ivorian foreign policy in *Fraternité-Matin*, Abidjan, Mar. 29–31, 1979.

Microfiche. [Washington, Supt. of Docs., U.S. Govt. Print. Off., 1979]

DLC-Micro JPRS 73357

3910

New national assembly election law published. *In* U.S. *Joint Publications Research Service.* JPRS 76732. [Springfield, Va., National Technical Information Service, 1980] (Sub-Saharan Africa report, no. 2314) p. 18–29.

Translation of full text of the law in *Fraternité-Matin*, Abidjan, Sept. 15, 1980, p. 13–15.

Microfiche. [s.l., 1980]

DLC-Micro JPRS 76732

3911

Rondos, Alex. Factors in nation's political structure examined. *In* U.S. *Joint Publications Research Service.* JPRS 75775. [Springfield, Va., National Technical Information Service, 1980] (Sub-Saharan Africa report, no. 2251) p. 34–42.

Article in *West Africa*, London, Apr. 21 and Apr. 28, 1980.

Microfiche. [s.l., 1980]

DLC-Micro JPRS 75775

3912

——— Results of Democratic Party congress viewed. *In* U.S. *Joint Publications Research Service.* JPRS 76768. [Springfield, Va., National Technical Information Service, 1980] (Sub-Saharan Africa report, no. 2316) p. 47–52.

Article on the Parti démocratique de Côte d'Ivoire in *West Africa*, London, Oct. 13, 1980, p. 2001–2004.

Microfiche. [s.l., 1980]

DLC-Micro JPRS 76768

3913

Speculation voiced on choice of vice president. *In* U.S. *Joint Publications Research Service.* JPRS 77295. [Springfield, Va., National Technical Information Service, 1981] (Sub-Saharan Africa report, no. 2353) p. 26–29.

Translation of article in *Africa*, Dakar, Dec. 1980, p. 29, 31, 102.

Microfiche. [s.l., 1981]

DLC-Micro JPRS 77295

3913a

Staniland, Martin. Presidency, party, and administration in the Ivory Coast. Pittsburgh, University Center for International Studies, University of Pittsburgh, 1979. 12 leaves.   DLC

On cover: "Paper prepared for briefing of the United States Ambassador to the Ivory Coast, 9 October 1979."

Prepared for the U.S. Department of State.

3914

Yacé, Philippe. Party secretary general addresses political bureau meeting. *In* U.S. *Joint Publications Research Service.* JPRS 70343. [Springfield, Va., National Technical Information Service, 1977] (Translations on Sub-Saharan Africa, no. 1851) p. 37–42.

Translation of speech before the political bureau of the Parti démocratique de la Côte d'Ivoire recorded in *Fraternité-Matin*, Abidjan, Nov. 6, 1977, p. 6–7.

Microfiche. [s.l., 1977]

DLC-Micro JPRS 70343

Population Studies

3915

Africa: Ivory Coast. Selected statistical data by sex. Washington, 1981. 33, 17 p.   DLC

Study supported by the U.S. Agency for International Development's Office of Women in Development and Office of Population.

Data assembled by the International Demographic Data Center, U.S. Bureau of the Census.

Among the tables, all based on 1975 data, are the following: adjusted population by age and sex; population by province; population by ethnic group; population by nationality (i.e., "Ivorians," "foreigners"); number of literate persons by age, sex and urban/rural residence; number of economically active persons by age, sex, and urban/rural residence.

3916

Chegaray, Sophie. Demographic explosion in Ivory Coast. *In* U.S. *Joint Publications Research Service.* JPRS 73090. [Springfield, Va., National Technical Information Service, 1979] (Translations on Sub-Saharan Africa, no. 2081) p. 36–43.

Translation of article in *Fraternité-Matin*, Abidjan, Jan. 27–29, 1979.

Microfiche. [Washington, Supt. of Docs., U.S. Govt. Print. Off., 1979]

DLC-Micro JPRS 73090

3917

Profiles of Sahelian countries: Ivory Coast. Washington, Socio-Economic Analysis Staff, International Statistical Programs Center, U.S. Bureau of the Census, 1974. [41] leaves (in various foliations)

3917 (cont.)

Prepared at the request of the U.S. Agency for International Development.

Concerns demographic projections.

Examined in the Documentation Center, Sahel Development Program, AID, Washington, D.C.

Other Subjects

3918

U.S. *Information Agency. Office of Research.* 1975 VOA audience estimates for the Ivory Coast. [Washington?], 1976. 26 p. (FAR 25738-N)

Examined in the former Foreign Affairs Research Documentation Center, U.S. Dept. of State.

3919

U.S. *Information Agency. Research Service.* Preliminary VOA audience estimate for the Ivory Coast. [Washington?], 1976. [2] leaves.   DLC

"Research memorandum M-8-76."

3920

Charlick, Robert B. Students as an "Interest Group" in the Ivory Coast. [s.l., 1979] 14 p.   DLC

On cover: "This paper was prepared for the Department of State as part of its external research program."

3921

Kalil, Amoussa. Maraboutism in Ivory Coast examined. *In* U.S. *Joint Publications Research Service.* JPRS 74926. [Springfield, Va., National Technical Information Service, 1980] (Sub-Saharan Africa report, no. 2198) p. 30–41.

Translation of article in *Fraternité-Matin*, Abidjan, Oct. 15–19, 1979.

Microfiche. [s.l., 1980]

DLC-Micro JPRS 74926

3922

Kokora, Pascal D. Choice of national language dis-

cussed. *In* U.S. *Joint Publications Research Service.* JPRS 75859. [Springfield, Va., National Technical Information Service, 1980] (Sub-Saharan Africa report, no. 2255) p. 26–30.

Translation of article in *Fraternité-Matin*, Abidjan, May 6, 1980, p. 11.

Microfiche. [s.l., 1980]

DLC-Micro JPRS 75859

3923

Kokore, Koussi. 'Operation Merou' military maneuvers. *In* U.S. *Joint Publications Research Service.* JPRS 76124. [Springfield, Va., National Technical Information Service, 1980] (Sub-Saharan Africa report, no. 2272) p. 49–57.

Translation of article in *Fraternité-Matin*, Abidjan, June 25–26, 1980.

Microfiche. [s.l., 1980]

DLC-Micro JPRS 76124

3924

Korniker, Louis S. Ivory Coast ostracoda (Suborder Myodocopina) Washington, Smithsonian Institution Press, 1975. 46 p. illus. (Smithsonian contributions to zoology, no. 197)

QL1.S54 no. 197

3925

Monson, Terry D., *and* Garry Pursell. An evaluation of expatriate labor replacement in the Ivory Coast. Ann Arbor, Center for Research on Economic Development, University of Michigan, 1976. 75 p. illus. (Michigan. University. Center for Research on Economic Development. Discussion paper, no. 49)   HD8825.M66

Bibliography: p. 73–75.

Abstract in English and French; additional abstract in *A.I.D. Research and Development Abstracts*, Apr. 1977, p. 19.

Issued also in microfiche ([Washington, U.S. Agency for International Development, 1976?] 1 sheet).   DLC-Sci RR PN-AAC-128

Liberia

General

3926

U.S. *Dept. of State.* Post report. Liberia. [Washington?], 1978. 20 p. illus., map.

JX1705.A286 Spec. Format

For a description of the contents of this publication, see the note to entry 936.

3927

U.S. *Dept. of State. Bureau of Public Affairs.* Background notes. Liberia. [Washington, for sale by the Supt. of Docs., U.S. Govt. Print. Off.], 1979. 4 p. maps. (U.S. Dept. of State. Department of State publication 7991)   G59.U5

L.C. retains only the latest revision.

For a description of the contents of this publication, see the note to entry 937.

3928

Hazelwood, Peter T. Draft environmental report on Liberia. Washington, Science and Technology Division, Library of Congress, 1979. [45] p. maps.

Prepared under a U.S. Agency for International Development contract with the U.S. Man and the Biosphere Secretariat, U.S. Dept. of State.

Bibliography: p. [44–45].

Abstract in *A.I.D. Research & Development Abstracts*, July 1981, p. 29–30.

Microfiche. [Washington, U.S. Agency for International Development, 1979?] 1 sheet.

DLC-Sci RR PN-AAG-978

3929

The Peace Corps in Liberia. [Washington? ACTION; U.S. Govt. Print. Off., 1980] folder ([6] p.) illus., map.   DLC

An introduction to the country for Peace Corps Volunteers.

Agriculture

3930

U.S. *General Accounting Office.* AID must consider social factors in establishing cooperatives in developing countries: report to the Congress of the United States by the Comptroller General. Washington, for sale by the Supt. of Docs., U.S. Govt. Print. Off., 1980. 42 p.

HD3575.U54   1980

"ID-80-39."

On cover: "Political, economic and cultural factors play a large role in determining whether efforts by the Agency for International Development to establish cooperatives in developing countries succeed or fail. Yet, as the GAO review of AID-sponsored cooperatives in the Philippines, Paraguay, and Liberia demonstrates, AID often fails to consider these factors in planning and evaluating their projects."

Issued also in microfiche. [Washington, U.S. Agency for International Development, 1980] 1 sheet.   DLC-Sci RR PN-AAJ-137

3931

U.S. *Peace Corps. Liberia.* Ministry of Agriculture, Peace Corps/Liberia training program, June–August 1973. [Monrovia?], 1973. 1 v. (various pagings)   DPC

3932

Bong County integrated rural development project. Washington, Development Alternatives, inc., 1976. 1 v. (various pagings)

Apparently prepared for the U.S. Agency for International Development under contract AID/otr-C-1383.

Includes "issue papers" and "annexes."

Examined in the Development Information Center, AID, Washington, D.C.

3933

Classification and management of soils; a four year project design for technical assistance, agricultural sector, Liberia. [s.l.], Midamerica International Agricultural Consortium, 1976. 65 leaves.

Prepared for the U.S. Agency for International Development under contract AID/afr-C-1139.

Issued in cooperation with the University of Missouri.

Examined in the Development Information Center, AID, Washington, D.C.

3934

Contributions to the planning of the Bong County integrated rural development project. Washington, Development Alternatives, inc., [1976] [88] p. (in various pagings)

Prepared for the U.S. Agency for International Development under contract AID/otr-C-1383.

Examined in the Development Information Center, AID, Washington, D.C.

3935

Cory, Cynthia. The greening of Liberia: a vegetable gardening guide. Monrovia, U.S. Peace Corps, 1979. 49 p. illus.   DPC

3936

Environmental assessment: integrated rural development project, upper Bong County, Liberia. Dallas, Environmental Consultants, inc., [1976] [222] p. (in various pagings)

Prepared for the U.S. Agency for International Development under contract AID/otr-C-1519.

Examined in the Development Information Center, AID, Washington, D.C.

3937

Liberia. [*Treaties, etc. United States, 1977 Aug. 12*] Project grant agreement between the Republic of Liberia and the United States of America for agricultural cooperative development. *In* U.S. *Treaties, etc.* United States treaties and other international agreements, v. 29, 1976–77. [Washington, Dept. of State; for sale by the Supt. of Docs., U.S. Govt. Print. Off., 1979] p. 978–991. ([Treaties and other international acts series, 8857])

JX231.A34 v. 29

Signed at Monrovia Aug. 12, 1977.

Concerns a U.S. Agency for International Development grant to assist in the development of agricultural cooperatives.

3938

Liberia. [*Treaties, etc. United States, 1977 Aug. 12*] Project grant agreement between the Republic of Liberia and the United States of America for agri-

cultural sector analysis and planning. *In* U.S. *Treaties, etc.* United States treaties and other international agreements, v. 29, 1976–77. [Washington, Dept. of State; for sale by the Supt. of Docs., U.S. Govt. Print. Off., 1979] p. 2663–2675. ([Treaties and other international acts series, 8963])

JX231.A34 v. 29

Signed at Monrovia Aug. 12, 1977.

Concerns a U.S. Agency for International Development grant.

3939

Liberian plans to attain self-sufficiency in food production. *In* U.S. *Joint Publications Research Service.* JPRS 74754. [Springfield, Va., National Technical Information Service, 1979] (Sub-Saharan Africa report, no. 2188) p. 98–102.

From article in *West Africa*, London, Nov. 19, 1979, p. 2129–2130.

Microfiche. [s.l., 1980]

DLC-Micro JPRS 74754

3940

Nathan (Robert R.) Associates, *Washington, D.C.* Liberia's agricultural program development project: evaluation and recommended evolution. Washington, 1976. 55 leaves.

HD2147.5.N37 1976

"A report prepared for the USAID Mission in Liberia under AID/otr-1380, Work Order 3."

Bibliography: leaves 48–50; includes citations to reports prepared for the U.S. Agency for International Development and the U.S. AID Mission to Liberia.

Prepared by Richard G. Wheeler.

3941

Organization design applied: a case study of Bong County, Liberia. Annex H. *In* Project management for rural equality; organization design and information management for benefit distribution in less developed countries. Vol. 2. Theoretical, empirical, and case studies [by] George Honadle [and] Marcus Ingle. Syracuse, N.Y., 1976. p. 241–293.

Prepared for the Office of Development Administration, U.S. Agency for International Development, under contract AID/ta-C-1255.

Microfiche. [Washington, U.S. Agency for International Development, 1976?] 4 sheets.

DLC-Sci RR PN-AAD-821

3942

Rural development in action: Liberia. [Monrovia?], Rural Development Division, Ministry of Local Government, Rural Development and Urban Reconstruction, 1975. 36 p. illus.   DPC

3942 (cont.)

Prepared in cooperation with Peace Corps Volunteers.

Rice

3943

U.S. *Peace Corps. Liberia.* Staging handbook for volunteers preparing to live and work in Liberia as employees of (WARDA) West Africa Rice Development Association. Philadelphia, 1975. [50] leaves. map.   DPC

3944

Monke, Eric A. The economics of rice in Liberia. *In* Pearson, Scott R. Rice in West Africa: policy and economics. Stanford, Calif., Stanford University Press, 1981. p. 141–172.   HD9066.A462P4

Publication results from a research project, "The Political Economy of Rice in West Africa," carried out jointly by the Food Research Institute, Stanford University, and the West Africa Rice Development Association between June 1976 and Sept. 1979, and funded by the U.S. Agency for International Development under contract AID/afr-C-1235.

3945

——— Rice policy in Liberia. *In* Pearson, Scott R. Rice in West Africa: policy and economics. Stanford, Calif., Stanford University Press, 1981. p. 109–140. map.   HD9066.A462P4

Publication results from a research project carried out jointly by the Food Research Institute, Stanford University, and the West Africa Rice Development Association and funded by the U.S. Agency for International Development (see more complete note in entry 3944).

Assistance Programs

3946

U.S. *AID Mission to Liberia.* Development assistance plan (DAP) [Monrovia?], 1974. 204 p.   DLC

3947

U.S. *Agency for International Development.* Annual budget submission: Liberia. Washington, U.S. International Development Cooperation Agency.

Vols. for 1977+ examined in the Development Information Center, AID, Washington, D.C.

3948

——— Country development strategy statement: Liberia. Washington, U.S. International Development Cooperation Agency. annual.

Vols. for 1981+ examined in the Development Information Center, AID, Washington, D.C.

3949

——— Development assistance program: Liberia. [Washington?], 1978. [3] v.

Partial contents: v. 2. Sector assessment: health, population and nutrition.—v. 3. Sector assessment: education and human resources.

Vols. 2–3 examined in the Development Information Center, AID, Washington, D.C.

3950

U.S. *Agency for International Development. Office of U.S. Foreign Disaster Assistance.* Liberia fire, December 12, 1977. [Washington] 1979. 2 p. map.

Concerns a fire in the West Point neighborhood of Monrovia which left about 950 people homeless.

Microfiche. [Washington, Congressional Information Service, 1979?]

DLC-Micro ASI:79   7206-3.45

3951

U.S. *Peace Corps. Liberia.* Everything you've always wanted to know about Peace Corps/Liberia, but didn't know who to ask. [Monrovia?], 1975. 41 p.   DPC

3952

Action (Service Corps). *Division of Evaluation.* Peace Corps/Liberia. Country program evaluation. Washington, 1976. [36] p. (in various pagings)   DPC

3953

Kuman ju; the Volunteer's monthly. v. 1, no. 1+ [Apr. 1974?]+ Monrovia, Peace Corps. illus.   DPC

3954

Liberia. [*Treaties, etc. United States, 1980 Aug. 13*] Agricultural commodities. Agreement between the United States of America and Liberia, signed at Monrovia August 13, 1980. [Washington, Dept. of State; for sale by the Supt. of Docs., U.S. Govt. Print. Off., 1981] 25 p. (Treaties and other international acts series, 9841)   DLC

3955

Technical Assistance Information Clearing House. Development assistance programs of U.S. nonprofit organizations in Liberia. [New York], American Council of Voluntary Agencies for

3955 (cont.)

Foreign Service, 1976 25 p. maps. (TAICH country report)   HC591.L6T4a

The Clearing House is operated by the Council under a grant from the U.S. Agency for International Development.

Commerce

3956

Manley, Mary L. Marketing in Liberia. [Washington], U.S. Dept. of Commerce, Domestic and International Business Administration; [for sale by the Supt. of Docs., U.S. Govt. Print. Off.], 1977. 22 p. (Overseas business reports. OBR 77-11)
                    HF91.U482   1977, no. 11

International marketing information series.

Supersedes *Selling in Liberia* (Overseas business reports. OBR 72-036), by Joanne B. Kay (HF91.U482 OBR 72-036).

3957

Market share reports. Country series: Liberia, 1971–75. [Washington], U.S. Dept. of Commerce; for sale by the National Technical Information Service, Springfield, Va., [1977] 60 p.

Indicates the United States share of the market in Liberia for various products compared to the shares for Belgium-Luxemburg, France, Federal Republic of Germany, Great Britain, Italy, Netherlands, Sweden, and Japan.

Microfiche. [Washington, Congressional Information Service, 1977?]
                    DLC-Micro ASI:77   2016-1.65

3958

Market share reports. Country series: Liberia, 1975–79. [Washington], International Trade Administration, U.S. Dept. of Commerce; for sale by the National Technical Information Service, Springfield, Va., [1979] 62 p.

Includes same comparative data as in *Market Share Reports. Country series: Liberia, 1971–75.* (entry 3957).

Microfiche. [Washington, Congressional Information Service, 1979?]
                    DLC-Micro ASI:81   2046-2.63

Communications and Transportation

3959

U.S. *International Communication Agency. Office of Research and Evaluation.* International broadcast audiences, particularly VOA and BBC audiences, in Monrovia, Liberia (1977) [Washington?], 1978. 14 p.   DLC

"Research report: E-19-78."

3960

Checchi and Company, Washington, D.C. Liberia rural roads study: draft final report, by Checchi & Company, Lyon Associates, for the U.S. Agency for International Development. [s.l.], 1975. 3 v. illus., maps (3 fold. in pocket)
                    HE367.L512C45   1975

Includes bibliographical references.

Contents: v. 1. Feasibility reports.—v. 2. Socio-economic baseline report.—v. 3. Socio-economic baseline data.

3961

Liberia. [*Treaties, etc. United States, 1977 July 22*] Liberia; alien amateur radio operators: agreement effected by exchange of notes dated at Monrovia March 20, 1974 and July 22, 1977; entered into force July 22, 1977. *In* U.S. *Treaties, etc.* United States treaties and other international agreements, v. 29, 1976–77. [Washington, Dept. of State; for sale by the Supt. of Docs., U.S. Govt. Print. Off., 1979] p. 1494–1496. ([Treaties and other international acts series, 8892])   JX231.A34 v. 29

"An agreement for the reciprocal granting of authorizations or licenses to permit amateur radio operators of either country to operate stations in the other country."—p. 1494.

3962

Liberia. [*Treaties, etc. United States, 1978 Mar. 30*] Air transport agreement between the Government of the United States of America and the Government of the Republic of Liberia. *In* U.S. *Treaties, etc.* United States treaties and other international agreements, v. 29, 1976–77. [Washington, Dept. of State; for sale by the Supt. of Docs., U.S. Govt. Print. Off., 1979] p. 3063–3087. ([Treaties and other international acts series, 8997])
                    JX231.A34 v. 29

Signed at Monrovia, Mar. 30, 1978, with memorandum of understanding signed at Monrovia, Oct. 28, 1978.

Concerns commercial air service between the two countries.

3963

Liberia: rural roads, [by] Richard Cobb [et al.] [Washington], Agency for International Development, 1980. [50] p. (in various pagings) illus. (A.I.D. project impact evaluation report, no. 6)
                    DLC

3963 (cont.)

Abstract in *A.I.D. Research & Development Abstracts*, July 1981, p. 62.

Issued also in microfiche. [Washington, U.S. Agency for International Development, 1980?] 1 sheet.   DLC-Sci RR PN-AAH-750

3964

Liberia Rural Roads III: pre-project appraisal mission, March–April 1976, [by] M. Speers [et al.] [Washington], Agency for International Development, [1976] 1 v. (various pagings)

Examined in the Development Information Center, AID, Washington, D.C.

3965

Optimum Computer Systems. Evaluation of planned road construction in Liberia: quantitative analysis of socio-economic data; prepared for Agency for International Development. New York, OCS, 1976. 2 v. illus.   HE367.L512068   1976

Prepared by Charles E. Hansen.

Contents: v. 1. Report.—v. 2. Appendix.

Education

3966

New directions for education and training in Liberia; a preliminary survey. [Cambridge, Mass.], Institute for International Development, Harvard University, 1976. [145] leaves (in various foliations)

Study supported by the U.S. Agency for International Development.

Includes bibliographical references.

A study of the relationship between education and economic development.

Examined in the Development Information Center, AID, Washington, D.C.

3967

Reed, Rodney J. Characteristics of teachers: a survey tool for policy making; a descriptive study in Liberia. Berkeley, University of California, 1975. [216] p.

Study funded by the University's Program in International Education Finance, which is supported by the U.S. Agency for International Development.

Bibliography: p. 214–216.

Abstract in *Resources in Education*, Oct. 1976, p. 171.

Microfiche. [Arlington, Va., ERIC Document Reproduction Service; prepared for Educational Resources Information Center, National Institute of Education, 1976] 3 sheets.

DLC-Micro ED124535

Foreign Relations

3968

U.S. *President, 1977–1981 (Carter)* Meeting with President William R. Tolbert, Jr. of Liberia. White House statement. October 2, 1979. *In* U.S. *President*. Public papers of the Presidents of the United States. Jimmy Carter. 1979. [Washington, Office of the Federal Register, National Archives and Records Service; for sale by the Supt. of Docs., U.S. Govt. Print. Off., 1980] p. 1806–1807.

J80.A283   1979

3969

——— Remarks of President Carter and President William R. Tolbert, Jr., at the welcoming ceremony. April 3, 1978. *In* U.S. *President*. Public papers of the Presidents of the United States. Jimmy Carter. 1978. [Washington, Office of the Federal Register, National Archives and Records Service; for sale by the Supt. of Docs., U.S. Govt. Print. Off., 1979] p. 671–675.   J80.A283   1978

Note: Subsequent remarks by the two presidents at a working luncheon in Monrovia are given on p. 675–678.

3970

——— President's Commission on United States-Liberian Relations. *In* U.S. *President*. Public papers of the Presidents of the United States. Jimmy Carter. 1980–81. [Washington, Office of the Federal Register, National Archives and Records Service; for sale by the Supt. of Docs., U.S. Govt. Print. Off., 1981] p. 372–373.

J80.A283   1980–81

Text of Executive Order 12195, Feb. 22, 1980, establishing the commission "to review and recommend ways to improve United States-Liberian relations."

Note: The announcement of the establishment of the Commission and of the chair and vice chair is given on p. 373; the list of the 11 members is given on p. 508–509.

3971

Joint meeting of the House and Senate to hear an address by Dr. William R. Tolbert, Jr., President of the Republic of Liberia. Congressional record, 94th Congress, 2d session, v. 122, Sept. 23, 1976: 32082–32084.   J11.R5 v. 122

Includes text of President Tolbert's speech.

3972

Liberia: principal policies and problems in relations with Liberia. *In* U.S. *Dept. of State*. Foreign relations of the United States. 1951, v. 5. Washington, U.S. Govt. Print. Off., 1982. p. 1274–1312.

3972 (cont.)
(U.S. Dept. of State. Department of State publi cation 9114)   JX233.A3 1951, v. 5
Includes a Department of State policy statement (p. 1275–1281).

3973
Moose, Richard M. U.S. policy toward Liberia. *In* U.S. *Dept. of State.* The Department of State bulletin, v. 80, no. 2045, Dec. 1980: 26–28.
JX232.A33 v. 80
Statement by the Assistant Secretary of State for African Affairs before the Subcommittee on Foreign Operations, Committee on Appropriations, House of Representatives, Aug. 19, 1980.

Geology, Hydrology, and Mineral Resources

3974
Coonrad, Warren L. Mineral map of the Bopolu Quadrangle, Liberia. [Reston, Va.] U.S. Geological Survey, 1979. 25 p. fold. col. map (in pocket) (U.S. Geological Survey. Reports—Open file series, no. 79–1516)   DI-GS
Project report: Liberian investigations, (IR) LI-61E.
Prepared under the auspices of the Government of Liberia and the U.S. Agency for International Development.
Bibliography: p. 12–14.

3975
Force, Eric R., *and* H. M. Beikman. Geology of the Zwedru Quadrangle, Liberia. [Reston, Va], 1974. 12 leaves. fold. map (in pocket) (U.S. Geological Survey. [Reports—Open file series, no. 74–307])
DI-GS
Prepared under the auspices of the Government of Liberia and the U.S. Agency for International Development.

3976
Force, Eric R., *and* J. D. N. Dunbar. Geology of the Gbanka Quadrangle, Liberia. [Reston, Va., 1974] 14 leaves. fold. map (in pocket) (U.S. Geological Survey. [Reports—Open file series, no. 74–3061])
DI-GS
Prepared under the auspices of the Government of Liberia and the U.S. Agency for International Development.

3977
Force, Eric R., *and* J. W. Berge. Geology of the Sanokole Quadrangle. [Reston, Va.], 1974. 17 leaves. map (fold. in pocket) (U.S. Geological Survey. [Reports—Open file series, no. 74–304])
DI-GS
Prepared under the auspices of the Government of Liberia and the U.S. Agency for International Development.

3978
Geology of the Harper Quadrangle, Liberia, [by] Maurice R. Brock [et al.] [Reston, Va.], 1974. 12 leaves. fold. map (in pocket) (U.S. Geological Survey. [Reports—Open file series, no. 74–310]
DI-GS
Prepared under the auspices of the Government of Liberia and the U.S. Agency for International Development.

3979
Rosenblum, Sam, *and* S. P. Srivastava. The Bambuta phosphate deposit, Liberia—a reconnaissance report; an unusual deposit of iron and aluminum phosphates of at least 1.5 million tons containing 28 percent P05; prepared in cooperation with the Liberian Geological Survey under the sponsorship of the Agency for International Development, U.S. Department of State. Washington, [for sale by the Supt. of Docs.], U.S. Govt. Print. Off., 1979. 26 p. illus., maps. (U.S. Geological Survey. Bulletin, 1480)   QE75.B9 no. 1480

3980
Seitz, James F. Geology of the Voinjama Quadrangle, Liberia. [Reston, Va.], 1974. 16 leaves. fold. map in pocket. (U.S. Geological Survey. [Report—Open file series, no. 74–301])   DI-GS
Project report, Liberian investigations (IR) LI-68B.
Prepared under the auspices of the Government of Liberia and the U.S. Agency for International Development.

The following items (entries 3981–88) are listed in chronological order:

3981
Stipp, Henry E. The mineral industry of Liberia. In Minerals yearbook, v. 3, 1972. [Washington, for sale by the Supt. of Docs., U.S. Govt. Print. Off., 1974] p. 541–546.   TN23.U612 1972, v. 3
Prepared by the U.S. Bureau of Mines.

3982
———— The mineral industry of Liberia. *In* Minerals yearbook, v. 3, 1973. [Washington, for sale by the Supt. of Docs., U.S. Govt. Print. Off., 1976] p. 581–586.   TN23.U612 1973, v. 3
Prepared by the U.S. Bureau of Mines.

3983

Jolly, Janice L. W. The mineral industry of Liberia. *In* Minerals yearbook, v. 3, 1974. [Washington, for sale by the Supt. of Docs., U.S. Govt. Print. Off., 1977] p. 607–615.   TN23.U612 1974, v. 3
Prepared by the U.S. Bureau of Mines.

3984

―――― The mineral industry of Liberia. *In* Minerals yearbook, v. 3, 1975. [Washington, for sale by the Supt. of Docs., U.S. Govt. Print. Off., 1978] p. 647–654.   TN23.U612 1975, v. 3
Prepared by the U.S. Bureau of Mines.

3985

―――― The mineral industry of Liberia. *In* Minerals yearbook, v. 3, 1976. [Washington, for sale by the Supt. of Docs., U.S. Govt. Print. Off., 1980] p. 683–688.   TN23.U612 1976, v. 3
Prepared by the U.S. Bureau of Mines.

3986

―――― The mineral industry of Liberia. *In* Minerals yearbook, v. 3, 1977. [Washington, for sale by the Supt. of Docs., U.S. Govt. Print. Off., 1981] p. 595–602.   TN23.U612 1977, v. 3
Prepared by the U.S. Bureau of Mines.

3987

Lyday, Phyllis A. The mineral industry of Liberia. *In* Minerals yearbook, v. 3, 1978–79. [Washington, U.S. Govt. Print. Off., 1981] p. 603–608.
     TN23.U612 1978–79, v. 3
Prepared by the U.S. Bureau of Mines.

3988

Keyes, William F. The mineral industry of Liberia. *In* Minerals yearbook, v. 3, 1980. [Washington, for sale by the Supt. of Docs., U.S. Govt. Print. Off., 1982] p. 619–622.   TN23.U612 1980, v. 3
Prepared by the U.S. Bureau of Mines.

3989

Thorman, Charles H. A field trip in the vicinity of Monrovia, Liberia. Washington, U.S. Dept. of the Interior, Geological Survey, 1973. 14 leaves. maps (2 fold in pocket)   QE339.L5T46
"Project report Liberian investigations (IR) LI-81."
"Prepared under the auspices of the Agency for International Development, U.S. Department of State, and the Government of Liberia."
Bibliography: leaf 14.

3990

―――― Geological map of the Monrovia quadrangle, Liberia. [Reston, Va.], 1974. 18 leaves. map (fold. in pocket) (U.S. Geological Survey. [Reports—Open file series, no. 74–305])   DI-GS
Prepared for the Government of Liberia and the U.S. Agency for International Development.
Bibliography: leaves 17–18.

3991

Tysdal, Russell G. Geology of the Buchanan Quadrangle, Liberia; prepared in cooperation with the Liberian Geological Survey under the sponsorship of the Agency for International Development, U.S. Department of State. Washington, [for sale by the Supt. of Docs.], U.S. Govt. Print. Off., 1978. 31 p. maps. (U.S. Geological Survey. Bulletin, 1449)   QE75.B9 no. 1449
"This report describes the geology shown on U.S. Geological Survey Miscellaneous Investigations Map I-778-D."

3992

―――― Geology of the Juazohn Quadrangle, Liberia; prepared in cooperation with the Liberian Geological Survey under the sponsorship of the Agency for International Development, U.S. Department of State. Washington, [for sale by the Supt. of Docs.], U.S. Govt. Print. Off., 1978. 39 p. map. (U.S. Geological Survey. Bulletin, 1448)
     QE75.B9 no. 1448
"This report describes the geology shown on U.S. Geological Survey Miscellaneous Investigations Map I-799-D."

3993

Wallace, Robert M. Geology of the Bopolu Quadrangle, Liberia. [Reston, Va.], 1974. 13 leaves. map fold. in pocket. (U.S. Geological Survey. [Reports—Open file series, no. 74–302])
     DI-GS
Project report: Liberian investigations, (IR) LI-61B.
Prepared under the auspices of the Government of Liberia and the U.S. Agency for International Development.

Health and Nutrition

3994

Gaines, J. David. Preventive medicine in tropical Africa: Peace Corps Liberia handbook. [Washington], ACTION, 1974. 61 p.   DPC

3995

Gauldfeldt, Frank I., *and* Linda J. Gangloff. Liberia. Washington, Division of Planning and Evaluation, Office of International Health; for sale by the Supt. of Docs., U.S. Govt. Print. Off., 1973. 56 p.

3995 (cont.)

(Syncrisis: the dynamics of health; an analytic series on the interactions of health and socioeconomic development, v. 7) RA418.S98 v. 7
DHEW publication no. (OS) 74-50003.

Abstracts in *A.I.D. Research and Development Abstracts*, Oct. 1976, p. 25; and *American Statistics Index*, 1974, Abstracts, p. 278–279.

Issued also in microfiche. [Washington, U.S. Agency for International Development, 197–?] 1 sheet (DLC-Sci RR PN-AAB-970); and [Washington, Congressional Information Service, 197–?] 1 sheet (DLC-Micro ASI:74 4006-1.7)

3996

George, Emmett. Health center for a nation: Liberia's JFK Hospital could easily be taken for a Western World institution. Agenda, Jan. 1978: 9–11. illus.

Issued by the U.S. Agency for International Development.

3997

Liberia national nutrition survey (December 4, 1975 to March 25, 1976) Los Angeles, Nutrition Assessment Unit, School of Public Health, University of California, 1976. 139 p.

Prepared in cooperation with the U.S. Agency for International Development and the Ministry of Health and Social Welfare of Liberia.

"The main purpose of the survey is to provide a statistically valid assessment of the prevalence of acute, chronic protein-calorie malnutrition (PCM) and anemia in children 0–5 years old in the rural areas of Liberia."

Abstract in *A.I.D. Research and Development Abstracts*, Apr. 1979, p. 20.

Microfiche. [Washington, U.S. Agency for International Development 1976?] 2 sheets (DLC-Sci RR PN-AAE-026); and [Washington, Congressional Information Service, 1976?] (DLC-Micro ASI:79 7206-8.2).

3998

Liberia national nutrition survey (December 4, 1975 to March 25, 1976); subsample report. Los Angeles, Nutrition Assessment Unit, School of Public Health, University of California, 1976. 73 p.

Prepared in cooperation with the U.S. Agency for International Development and the Ministry of Health and Social Welfare of Liberia.

Abstract in *A.I.D. Research and Development Abstracts*, Apr. 1979, p. 20.

Microfiche. [Washington, U.S. Agency for International Development, 1976?] 1 sheet (DLC-Sci RR PN-AAE-027); and [Washington, Con-

gressional Information Service, 1976?] (DLC-Micro ASI:79 7206-8-2).

3999

Lofa County rural health project, Liberia, West Africa, [by] Thomas H. Hood [et al.] [Washington?], American Public Health Association, 1975. 1 v. (various pagings)

Prepared for the U.S. Agency for International Development under contract AID/csd-2604.

Examined in the Development Information Center, AID, Washington, D.C.

Politics and Government

4000

Bentsi-Enchill, Nii K. MOJA more threatening to status quo than PAL. *In* U.S. *Joint Publications Research Service.* JPRS 75268. [Springfield, Va., National Technical Information Service, 1980] (Sub-Saharan Africa report, no. 2221) p. 53–63.

From a two-part article in *West Africa*, London, Feb. 4 and 11, 1980.

MOJA: Movement for Justice in Africa.

PAL: Progressive Alliance of Liberia.

Microfiche. [s.l., 1980]

DLC-Micro JPRS 75268

4001

Bolta, Paul. Tolbert underestimated demands of people. *In* U.S. *Joint Publications Research Service.* JPRS 75785. [Springfield, Va., National Technical Information Service, 1980] (Sub-Saharan Africa report, no. 2252) p. 74–81.

Translation of article in *Le Monde*, Paris, Apr. 15–16, 1980.

Microfiche. [s.l., 1980]

DLC-Micro JPRS 75785

4002

Civil service development project, Government of Liberia: final report. [Sacramento], California State Personnel Board, 1979. 47 leaves. DLC

"A cooperative effort between the Civil Service Agency of the Republic of Liberia and the California State Personnel Board," under the auspices of the U.S. Agency for International Development.

Held also by the California State Library.

4003

Fahnballeh, H. Boima. MOJA member sets forth opposition viewpoint. *In* U.S. *Joint Publications Research Service.* JPRS 74827. [Springfield, Va., National Technical Information Service, 1979] (Sub-Saharan Africa report, no. 2193)

4003 (cont.)

Excerpts from addess by a member of the Movement for Justice in Africa, in *West Africa*, London, Dec. 3, 1979, p. 2221, 2223.

Microfiche. [s.l., 1980]

DLC-Micro JPRS 74827

4004

If avenues for peaceful change blocked, violence possible. *In* U.S. *Joint Publications Research Service*. JPRS 74754. [Springfield, Va., National Technical Information Service, 1979] (Sub-Saharan Africa report, no. 2188) p. 106–109.

Article on the mayoral election in Monrovia, in *West Africa*, Nov. 26, 1979, p. 2186–2188.

Microfiche. [s.l., 1980]

DLC-Micro JPRS 74754

4005

MOJA's anti-government press release denounced. *In* U.S. *Joint Publications Research Service*. JPRS 75528. [Springfield, Va., National Technical Information Service, 1980] (Sub-Saharan Africa report, no. 2237) p. 86–90.

Editorial in *The Liberian Age*, Mar. 21, 1980, p. 1, 2.

Microfiche. [s.l., 1980]

DLC-Micro JPRS 75528

4006

New York Liberians blast white citizenship proposal. *In* U.S. *Joint Publications Research Service*. JPRS 75181. [Springfield, Va., National Technical Information Service, 1980] (Sub-Saharan Africa report, no. 2216) p. 65–70.

Article in *The Voice of the Revolution*, Monrovia, Jan. 15, 1980, p. 4–9, includes text of a petition by the Liberian Community Association of New York calling on the Liberian legislature to reject President Tolbert's proposals for "non-negro citizenship."

Microfiche. [s.l., 1980]

DLC-Micro JPRS 75181

4007

Ormasa, Anthony J. Evaluation report: Institute of Public Administration project, Monrovia, Liberia. [s.l.], American Technical Assistance Corporation, 1975. 22 p.

Prepared for the U.S. Agency for International Development.

Examined in the Development Information Center, AID, Washington, D.C.

4008

Project for civil service development, Government of Liberia. Work plan and quarterly report. Sept.

1974–Feb. 1979. [Sacramento?], California State Personnel Board.   C

Prepared for the U.S. Agency for International Development under contract AID/afr-C-1008.

Issued in cooperation with the Civil Service Agency of Liberia.

Abstract of Apr.–June report in *A.I.D. Research and Development Abstracts*, v. 7, no. 1, 1979, p. 15.

The following reports are issued also in Microfiche: Oct.–Dec. 1977 [Washington, U.S. Agency for International Development, 1978?] 1 sheet (DLC-Sci RR PN-AAF-422); and Apr.–June 1978 (Washington, U.S. Agency for International Development, 1978?) 1 sheet (DLC-Sci RR PN-AAG-091).

4009

Regime denies opposition charges, notes achievements. *In* U.S. *Joint Publications Research Service*. JPRS 75474. [Springfield, Va., National Technical Information Service, 1980] (Sub-Saharan Africa report, no. 2233) p. 41–47.

Editorial in *The Liberian Age*, Monrovia, Mar. 18, 1980, p. 2, 7.

Microfiche. (s.l., 1980)

DLC-Micro JPRS 75474

Coup d'Etat–1980

4010

U.S. *Congress. House. Committee on Foreign Affairs. Subcommittee on Africa*. The situation in Liberia, spring 1980—update: hearing, 96th Congress, 2d session, April 29, 1980. Washington, U.S. Govt. Print. Off., 1980. 25 p.   KF27.F625   1980c
J74.A23 96th
Cong., House Comm.
For. Aff., v. 94

Stephen J. Solarz, chairman.

An inquiry into the recent military coup in Liberia and into "the extent to which any of the people who were executed 1 week ago either inquired about or applied for asylum from our Government and what the nature of our response was to that request [and in] trying to make some judgments, not only about the Liberian situation but also about our worldwide refuge and asylum policy, particularly insofar as the Liberian situation has focused attention on it."—p. 1.

Among the appendixes is the following:

Appendix 1. General economic policy statement by the Government of the People's Redemption Council, Republic of Liberia. p. 23–24.

4011

Biarnes, Pierre. New leaders unsuccessful in winning people's support. *In* U.S. *Joint Publications Research Service.* JPRS 76659. [Springfield, Va., National Technical Information Service, 1980] (Sub-Saharan Africa report, no. 2309) p. 26–30.

Translation of article in *Le Monde*, Paris, Sept. 4, 1980, p. 7.

Microfiche. [s.l., 1980]

DLC-Micro JPRS 76659

4012

Harrop, William C. Coup d'etat in Liberia. *In* U.S. *Dept. of State.* The Department of State bulletin, v. 80, no. 2040, July 1980: 18–19. map.

JX232.A33 v. 80

Statement by the Deputy Assistant Secretary of State for African Affairs before the Subcommittee on Africa, Committee on Foreign Affairs, House of Representatives, Apr. 29, 1980.

4013

Hayakawa, S. I. Senate Concurrent Resolution 89—submission of a concurrent resolution with regard to the overthrow of the Government of the Republic of Liberia. Congressional record [daily ed.], 96th Congress, 2d session, v. 126, Apr. 28, 1980: S4267-S4268. J11.R7 v. 126

Remarks in the U.S. Senate.

Includes articles from the *New York Times* and *Washington Star*.

4014

Members of military anxious to consolidate power. *In* U.S. *Joint Publications Research Service.* JPRS 75976. [Springfield, Va., National Technical Information Service, 1980] (Sub-Saharan Africa report, no. 2262) p. 71–75.

Article in *West Africa*, London, June 9, 1980, p. 1005–1009.

Microfiche. [s.l., 1980]

DLC-Micro JPRS 75976

4015

Pomonti, Jean-Claude. Many ambiguities apparent in post-coup situation. *In* U.S. *Joint Publications Research Service.* JPRS 75862. [Springfield, Va., National Technical Information Service, 1980] (Sub-Saharan Africa report, no. 2256) p. 96–99.

Translation of article in *Le Monde*, Paris, Apr. 29, 1980, p. 1, 8.

Microfiche. [s.l., 1980]

DLC-Micro JPRS 75862

4016

Post-coup political situation, relations with Soviet Union. *In* U.S. *Joint Publications Research*

Service. JPRS 76499. [Springfield, Va., National Technical Information Service, 1980] (Sub-Saharan Africa report, no. 2296) p. 88–90.

Translation of article in *Frankfurter allgemeine Zeitung*, Frankfurt, July 23, 1980, p. 3.

Microfiche. [s.l., 1980]

DLC-Micro JPRS 76499

Population Studies

4017

Africa: Liberia. Selected statistical data by sex. Washington, 1981. 31, 17 p. DLC

Study supported by the U.S. Agency for International Development's Office of Women in Development and Office of Population.

Data assembled by the International Demographic Data Center, U.S. Bureau of the Census.

Among the tables, based on 1974 data (unless other wise noted), are the following: unadjusted population by age, sex and urban/rural residence (1962); population by province, sex and urban/rural residence; population by ethnic group, sex and urban/rural residence; life expectancy (1971); urban and rural populations by marital status, age, and sex; number of households; heads of households; number of literate persons by age, sex and urban/rural residence; number of persons enrolled in school by age, sex and urban/rural residence; number of economically active persons by age, sex, and urban/rural residence; economically active population by occupational status, sex and urban/rural residence.

4018

Campbell, Paul R. Liberia. Washington, U.S. Dept. of Commerce, Bureau of the Census, 1982. 50 p. map. (Country demographic profiles. ISP-DP-28)

DBC

Issued March 1982.

Bibliography: p. 48–50.

Other Subjects

4019

Defense Mapping Agency. *Topographic Center.* Liberia: official standard names approved by the United States Board on Geographic Names. 2d ed., 1976. Washington, Dept. of the Interior, Board on Geographic Names, 1976. 167 p. map.

DT623.U53 1976

"Official standard names gazetteer."

"2924319."

4020

Foreign economic trends and their implications for the United States. Liberia. 1969+ Washington, for sale by the Supt. of Docs., U.S. Govt. Print. Off. (International marketing information series)
HC10.E416

Semiannual (irregular), 1969–72?; annual, 1974?+

Prepared by the U.S. Embassy, Monrovia.

Vols. for 1969–77 distributed by the U.S. Bureau of International Commerce; vols. for 1978–79 by the U.S. Industry and Trade Administration; vols. for 1981– by the U.S. International Trade Administration.

Not published in 1973?, 1980.

The following issues for the period 1974–81 have been identified in L.C.:

ET 74-024. 1974. 9 p.
FET 75-040. 1975. 6 p.
FET 76-035. 1976. 7 p.
FET 77-044. 1977. 7 p.
FET 78-049. 1978. 7 p.
FET 79-071. 1979. 7 p.
FET 81-081. 1981. 11 p.

4021

Liberia. [*Treaties, etc. United States, 1977 Mar. 17*] Liberia; military mission. Agreement amending and extending the agreement of January 11, 1951, as amended and extended, effected by exchange of notes signed at Monrovia May 2, 1975 and February 2, 4, and 16 and March 10 and 17, 1977; entered into force March 17, 1977, effective January 11, 1975. *In* U.S. *Treaties, etc.* United States treaties and other international agreements, v. 29, 1976–77. [Washington, Dept. of State; for sale by the Supt. of Docs., U.S. Govt. Print. Off., 1979] p. 668–677. ([Treaties and other international acts series, 8846])   JX231.A34 v. 29

Concerns the U.S. Military Mission to Liberia.

4022

Liberia. [*Treaties, etc. United States, 1978 Aug. 22*] Omega Navigation Station: agreement between the United States of America and Liberia amending the agreement of April 10 and 18, 1973, effected by exchange of notes dated at Monrovia March 22 and August 22, 1978. *In* U.S. *Treaties, etc.* United States treaties and other international agreements, v. 30, 1978–79. [Washington, Dept. of State: for sale by the Supt. of Docs., U.S. Govt. Print. Off., 1980] p. 1779–1785. ([Treaties and other international acts series, 9287])   JX231.A34 v. 30

4023

Liberia. [*Treaties, etc. United States, 1979 Jan. 15*] Shipping: jurisdiction over vessels in United States deepwater ports. Agreement between the United States of America and Liberia effected by exchange of notes signed at Washington October 27, 1978 and January 15, 1979. *In* U.S. *Treaties.* United States treaties and other international agreements, v. 30, 1978–79. [Washington, Dept. of State; for sale by the Supt. of Docs., U.S. Govt. Print. Off., 1980] p. 1706–1709. ([Treaties and other international acts series, 9279])   JX231.A34 v. 30

4024

Phoenix Housing Corporation. Republic of Liberia shelter sector analysis, January 24, 1977, [conducted by Phoenix Housing Corporation]. [Washington], Agency for International Development, Office of Housing, 1977. 75 leaves, [17] leaves of plates. illus., map (fold. in pocket)
HD7378.2.A3P5   1977

"The purpose of the study was to develop information and make recommendations relating to the shelter sector in Liberia and was in response to a request from the Government of Liberia."

Abstract in *A.I.D. Research and Development Abstracts*, Oct. 1977, p. 32.

Issued also in microfiche. [Washington, U.S. Agency for International Development, 1977?] 1 sheet.   DLC-Sci RR PN-AAD-067

4025

Workshop on Advanced Training in Communication for Social Development in Liberia, *Monrovia*, 1979. Final report. [Monrovia?], 1979. 73 p. illus.

Sponsored by the U.S. Agency for International Development.

"Organized by Ministry of Agriculture of the Republic of Liberia, Family Planning Association of Liberia, and the Community and Family Study Center, the University of Chicago."

Examined in the Development Information Center, AID, Washington, D.C.

Mali

General

4026

U.S. *Dept. of State.* Post report. Mali. [Washington?] 1978. 24 p. illus., map.

Examined in the Foreign Service Institute Library, Rosslyn, Va.

L.C. has report issued in 1973 (JX1705.A286 Spec. Format).

For a description of the contents of this publication, see the note to entry 936.

4027

U.S. *Dept. of State. Bureau of Public Affairs.* Background notes. Mali. [Washington, for sale by the Supt. of Docs., U.S. Govt. Print. Off.] 1981. 4 p. maps. (U.S. Dept. of State. Department of State publication 8056) G59.U5

L.C. retains only the latest revision.

For a description of the contents of this publication, see the note to entry 937.

4028

Grant, A. Paige, *and* Douglas F. Stotz. Draft environmental profile on Mali. Tucson, Arid Lands Information Center, Office of Arid Lands Studies, University of Arizona, 1980. 70 p. maps.

DLC

Sponsored by the U.S. Agency for International Development.

Bibliography: p. 57–70.

On cover: "National Park Service Contract No. CX-0001-00-0003 with U.S. Man and the Biosphere Secretariat, Department of State, Washington, D.C."

Abstract in *A.I.D. Research & Development Abstracts*, July 1981, p. 36.

Issued also in microfiche. [Washington, U.S. Agency for International Development, 1980?] 1 sheet   DLC-Sci RR PN-AAJ-202

4029

Mango, Cecily. Mali: a country profile; prepared for the Office of U.S. Foreign Disaster Assistance, Bureau for Private and Development Cooperation, Agency for International Development, Department of State by Evaluation Technologies, Inc., under contract AID/SOD/PDC-C-0283. 2d ed., researched and written by Cecily Mango. Washington, The Office, 1980. 47 p. col. map.

DT551.22.M36   1980

Bibliography: p. 45–47.

A general introduction, with emphasis on political structure, disaster preparedness, demography, health, nutrition, housing, economic conditions, agriculture, geography, transportation, power, and communications.

Note: An earlier edition (1978) was issued in microfiche. [Sahel Documents and Dissertations. Ann Arbor, Mich., University Microfilms International, 1980] 1 sheet (DLC-Micro Microfiche 5357 ML 045).

4030

The Peace Corps in Mali. [Washington?, ACTION; U.S. Govt. Print. Off., 1980] folder ([6] p.) illus., map.   DLC

"ACTION 4200.56."

An introduction to the country for Peace Corps Volunteers.

Agriculture

4031

Birnbaum, Philip. Mali crop production project. [Washington?], U.S. Agency for International Development, 1976. 33 p.   MiEM

4032

Eskelinen, Riitta K. Dogon agricultural systems: sociological aspects relating to development interventions. [s.l.], Research Foundation of State University of New York, 1977. [93] leaves.

Prepared for the U.S. Agency for International Development under contract AID/afr-C-1045.

Examined in the Development Information Center, AID, Washington, D.C.

4033

Khan, Akhter H. Rural development in Mali: a trip report, 5 April – 26 April 1978. East Lansing, Dept. of Agricultural Economics, Michigan State University, [1978?] 8 leaves.   MiEM

Apparently prepared for the U.S. Agency for International Development.

4034

Lewis, John V. Descendants and crops: two poles of production in a Malian peasant village. [New Haven, Yale University], c1978. 233 p.   CtY

Supported by U.S. Agency for International Development Contract AID/afr-C-1045.

Dissertation—Yale University

Copy examined in the Development Information Center, AID, Washington, D.C.

4035

Shaikh, Asif, *and* Patricia Larson. The economics of village-level forestry: a methodological framework. Washington, Sahel Development Program, U.S. Agency for International Development, [1981?] 73 p.   MiEM

Bibliography: p. 70–73.

Issued also in French.

Includes case studies from the Mopti region.

4036

Shulman, Robert. Strategy for the advancement of animal traction in Mali. Une strategie pour le progrès de la traction animale du Mali. Bamako, U.S.A.I.D., 1979. [60] p.   MiEM

Issued in cooperation with the Division du machinisme agricole of Mali.

4037

Temanson, Leslie. Peace Corps/Mali end of training report. Mali: pit silos. Bamako, [U.S. Peace Corps], 1974. [123] leaves (in various foliations)   DPC

Agricultural Education and Extension

4038

Howze, Glenn. Future manpower needs for CAA graduates and an evaluation of the present training program by employers of CAA graduates. [Tuskegee Institute. Ala., Center for Rural Development, Tuskegee Institute], 1980.   ATT

Cited in a list prepared by the Frissell Library, Tuskegee Institute, as researched and printed under a grant from the U.S. Agency for International Development.

Issued also in French.

4039

Howze, Glenn, *and* Cheickna Singaré. Junior level extension training in Mali: the third year. [Tuskegee Institute, Ala., Center for Rural Development, Tuskegee Institute], 1979.   ATT

Cited in a list prepared by the Frissell Library, Tuskegee Institute, as researched and printed under a grant from the U.S. Agency for International Development.

4040

———— Survey of second-year students at the three Centres d'apprentissage agricole in Mali; phase IV report. [Tuskegee Institute, Ala., Center for Rural Development, Tuskegee Institute], 1979. 83 p.   ATT

Prepared for the U.S. Agency for International Development.

Issued also in French.

Issued also in microfiche. [Sahel Documents and Dissertations. Ann Arbor, Mich., University Microfilms International, 1980] 1 sheet.

DLC-Micro Microfiche 5357 ML 091

4041

Mali. [*Treaties, etc. United States, 1977 May 13*] Project grant agreement between the Republic of Mali and the United States of America for improvement of agricultural officers training. *In* U.S. *Treaties, etc.* United States treaties and other international agreements, v. 29, 1976–77. [Washington, Dept. of State; for sale by the Supt. of Docs., U.S. Govt. Print. Off., 1979] p. 2306–2335. ([Treaties and other international acts series, 8940])

JX231.A34 v. 29

Signed at Bamako May 13, 1977.

In English and French.

Concerns a U.S. Agency for International Development grant to the Government of Mali to establish two agricultural apprenticeship centers.

4042

O'Sullivan, John M., Ngolo Coulibaly, *and* Glenn Howze. A survey of Malian farmers: views and recommendations concerning the training of *moniteurs* in the CAAs; phase V report. [Tuskegee Institute, Ala., Center for Rural Development, Tuskegee Institute], 1979. 30 p.   ATT

Prepared under U.S. Agency for International Development contract AID/ta-G-1452.

CAA: Centres d'apprentissage.

Issued also in microfiche. [Sahel Documents and Dissertations. Ann Arbor, Mich., University Microfilms International, 1980] 1 sheet.

DLC-Micro Microfiche 5357 ML 090

4043

Schoepf, Brooke, Glenn Howze, *and* Cheickna Singaré. Study of teachers in the CAA in the Republic of Mali, May 1979; phase III report. Tuskegee Institute, Ala., Tuskegee Institute, 1979. 47 p.   ATT

Prepared under U.S. Agency for International Development contract AID/ta-G-1452.

Issued also in French.

Issued also in microfiche. [Sahel Documents and Dissertations. Ann Arbor, Mich., University Microfilms International, 1980] 1 sheet.

DLC-Micro Microfiche 5357 ML 087

4044

Survey of Malian agricultural *moniteurs*, [by] Glenn Howze [et al.] [Tuskegee Institute, Ala., Center for Rural Development, Tuskegee Institute, 1979] 114 p.   ATT

Prepared for the U.S. Agency for International Development.

Issued also in microfiche. [Sahel Documents and Dissertations. Ann Arbor, Mich., University Microfilms International, 1980] 2 sheets.

DLC-Micro Microfiche 5357 ML 089

Economic Aspects

4045

Hopkins, Nicholas S. A comparison of the role of the small urban center in rural development: Kita (Mali) and Testour (Tunisia) *In* Southall, Aidan. Small urban centers in rural development in Africa. Madison, African Studies Program, University of Wisconsin-Madison, 1979. p. 21–35.

A grant from the Office of Urban Development, U.S. Agency for International Development, assisted in the preparation for publication of the papers collected in the study.

Microfiche. [Washington, U.S. Agency for International Development, 1980?] (PN-AAJ-064); examined in the Development Information Center, Agency for International Development, Washington, D.C.

4046

Lewis, John V. Exchange-labor and credit interventions in two Malian villages. Washington, U.S. Agency for International Development, [1977] 21 p.

Examined in the Development Information Center, AID, Washington, D.C.

4047

Mali agricultural sector assessment: final report, December 15, 1976. Ann Arbor, Center for Research on Economic Development, University of Michigan, [1976] xx, 239 p. illus.

HD2143.5.M34

Prepared for the Bureau for Africa, U.S. Agency for International Development, under contract AID/afr-C-1143.

Bibliography: p. 233–239.

Charles Steedman, team leader.

Issued also in microfiche. [Sahel Documents and Dissertations. Ann Arbor, University Microfilms International, 1980] 4 sheets (DLC-Micro Microfilm 5357 ML 047); and [Washington, U.S. Agency for International Development, 1976?] 3 sheets (DLC-Sci RR PN-AAE-453).

4048

Social anthropological and rural economic studies in Mali: the Dukolomba forest; the Bandaigara plateau, [by] Riitta K. Eskelinen [et al.] [Binghamton], Research Foundation of the State University of New York, 1979. 507 p. maps.

Prepared for the U.S. Agency for International Development under contract AID/afr-C-1045.

Annotation in *Sahel Bibliographic Bulletin*, v. 4, no. 1, 1980, p. 32–33.

A collection of field reports on social and economic conditions as related to livestock production in two regions of Mali.

Microfiche. [Sahel Documents and Dissertations. Ann Arbor, Mich., University Microfilms International, 1980] 6 sheets.

DLC-Micro Microfiche 5357 ML 084

4049

Zalla, Thomas. Mali country report. [s.l., 1976] 6 p.

At head of title: Master's program in agricultural economics for students from the Sahel.

Microfiche. [Washington, U.S. Agency for International Development, 1976?] 1 sheet.

DLC-Sci RR PN-AAF-316

Grain and Grain Storage

4050

Berg, Elliot. Reforming grain marketing systems in West Africa. Ann Arbor, Center for Research on Economic Development, University of Michigan, 1979. 50 p. (Michigan. University. Center for Research on Economic Development. Discussion paper, no. 79)

An examination of the foodgrain marketing problems of Mali.

Abstract in *A.I.D. Research and Development Abstracts*, v. 7, no. 3, 1980, p. 2.

4050 (cont.)

Microfiche. [Washington, U.S. Agency for International Development, 1979?] 1 sheet.

DLC-Sci RR PN-AAG-742

4051

Berthe, Mahamadou, *and* G. Olaf Meyer-Ruhle. Report on the first joint evaluation of Operation Mils-Mopti (AID project grant agreement 688-11-130-202) [Bamako?], 1977. [66] leaves (in various foliations)

Text in English or French.

Examined in the Documentation Center, Sahel Development Program, Agency for International Development, Washington, D.C.

4052

Guggenheim, Hans. Of millet, mice and men: traditional and invisible technology solutions to postharvest losses in Mali. *In* World food, pest losses, and the environment, edited by David Pimentel. [Boulder, Colo., Published by Westview Press for the American Association for the Advancement of Science, 1978] (AAAS selected symposium, 13) p. 109–162.   SB599.2.W67

"Some of the postharvest loss data presented in this paper were collected with the assistance of Hamidy Hama Diallo of the *Operation de Protection des Semences et Recoltes au Mali*, between December, 1976 and January, 1977 under USAID grant BKO 688-77-06."—p. 158.

4053

Guggenheim, Hans, *and* Hamidy H. Diallo. Grain storage in the Fifth Region of Mali. [Bamako?, 1977?] 173 p.

Prepared under a U.S. Agency for International Development grant.

Concerns the Dogon area.

Microfiche. [Sahel Documents and Dissertations. Ann Arbor, Mich., University Microfilms International, 1980] 3 sheets.

DLC-Micro Microfiche 5357 ML 038

4054

Jepson, Lance, *and* John Heard. Operation Mils-Mopti, Phase II. Washington, U.S. Agency for International Development, 1979. 136 p.

MiEM

Brief description in *Sahel Bibliographic Bulletin*, Apr./June 1982, p. 100.

4055

Johnson, Jerry J. Market gardening on the Dogon Plateau; Action Culture Maraichere: an analysis. [Bamako?], 1977. 41 leaves

Report prepared for the U.S. AID Mission to Mali.

"Action Culture Maraichere is a sub-activity of Operation Mils ..., a joint development effort between USAID and the Malian government that englobes five of the seven cercles in the Fifth Region of Mali with administrative headquarters in Mopti. The primary activity of Operation Mils is to increase millet production in the Fifth Region."—p. [1].

4056

Mali. [*Treaties, etc. United States, 1977 May 13*] Project grant agreement between the Republic of Mali and the United States of America for Operation Mils. *In* U.S. *Treaties, etc.* United States treaties and other international agreements, v. 29, 1976–77. [Washington, Dept. of State; for sale by the Supt. of Docs., U.S. Govt. Print. Off., 1981] p. 5129–5157. ([Treaties and other international acts series, 9093])   JX231.A34 v. 29

In English and French.

At head of title: AID project no. 688-11-130-202.

Signed at Bamako, May 13, 1977.

Project designed to increase the production and improve the marketing of grain.

4057

Mali. [*Treaties, etc. United States, 1978 Mar. 30*] Project grant agreement between the Government of the Republic of Mali and the United States of America for Action Riz-Sorgho. *In* U.S. *Treaties, etc.* Treaties and other international agreements, v. 30, 1978–79. [Washington, Dept. of State; for sale by the Supt. of Docs., U.S. Govt. Print. Off., 1980] p. 1856–1874. ([Treaties and other international acts series, 9296])   JX231.A34 v. 30

Signed at Bamako, Mar. 30, 1978.

In English and French.

Concerns a U.S. Agency for International Development grant for improving rice and sorghum production.

4058

Sako, Bafotigui, *and* Ronald W. Cotterill. An econometric analysis of supply responsiveness in traditional agriculture: millet, sorghum and rice farmers in Mali. East Lansing, Dept. of Agricultural Economics, Michigan State University, 1981. 85 p. (African Rural Economy Program. Working paper, no. 36)   MiEM

Bibliography: p. 83–85.

Printing financed by the U.S. Agency for International Development under contract AID/afr-C-1267.

4058 (cont.)

Copy examined in the Development Information Center, AID, Washington, D.C.

Livestock and Range Management

4059

Beazer, William F., *and* Josiah Dirck Stryker. Financing recurrent government expenditures for livestock development in Mali. [s.l.], 1976. [49] p. (in various pagings)

Report prepared for the Government of Mali under a U.S. Agency for International Development contract.

On cover: Mali Livestock Sector Grant.

Microfiche. [Washington, U.S. Agency for International Development, 1976?] 1 sheet (DLC-Sci RR PN-AAG-106); and [Sahel Documents and Dissertations. Ann Arbor, Mich., University Microfilms International, 1980] 1 sheet (DLC-Micro Microfiche 5357 ML 034).

4060

Bloch, Peter C., *and* Abou Bagayoko. Report on a study of the education and training component of the Mali Livestock Sector Grant. [s.l., 1975] 29 p.

Prepared for the U.S. Agency for International Development.

Microfiche. [Sahel Documents and Dissertations. Ann Arbor, Mich., University Microfilms International, 1980] 1 sheet.

DLC-Micro Microfiche 5357 ML 080

4061

Candler, Wilfred. Analytical model of the Mali livestock economy: scope of work. [s.l.], 1975. 37 p.

Prepared for the U.S. Agency for International Development under contract AID/afr-C-1903.

Examined in the Development Information Center, AID, Washington, D.C.

4062

Delgado, Christopher L. Livestock and meat production, marketing, and exports in Mali; a review of the evidence. Ann Arbor, Center for Research on Economic Development, University of Michigan, 1979. [220] p.

Prepared for the Regional Economic Development Services Office, West Africa, U.S. Agency for International Development.

On cover: "This is a rough draft in progress."

Examined in the Documentation Center, Sahel Development Program, AID, Washington, D.C.

4063

Evaluation of the productivities of Maure and Peul cattle breeds at the Sahelian Station, Miono, Mali. Addis Ababa, International Livestock Centre for Africa, [1978] 109 p. (International Livestock Centre for Africa. ILCA monograph, no. 1)

The Centre is supported in part by the U.S. Government.

Bibliography: p. 102–105.

Study undertaken in cooperation with the Institut d'économie rurale du Mali.

Abstract in *A.I.D. Research and Development Abstracts*, Feb. 1981, p. 18.

Microfiche. [Washington, U.S. Agency for International Development, 1978?] 2 sheets.

DLC-Sci RR PN-AAG-756

4064

Examination of AID-financed livestock activities in Mali. [Washington], Office of the Auditor General, U.S. Agency for International Development, 1975. 19 p.

Examined in the Development Information Center, AID, Washington, D.C.

4065

Grayzel, John A. Cattle raisers and cattle raising in the Douloloma forest area, October 1974–September 1975. [Eugene?], Dept. of Anthropology, University of Oregon, [1975?] 51 leaves. maps. (FAR 26478-N)

"Funded by the Research Foundation of the State University of New York ... for the project "Mali livestock' on behalf of the United States Agency for International Development and L'Office malien de bétail et viande."

Examined in the former Foreign Affairs Research Documentation Center, U.S. Dept. of State.

4066

—— Report on animal prices at the market of Bussain. [Washington?], U.S. Agency for International Development, 1975. 51 p.   MiEM

4067

Landfield, Sherwin. Evaluation report, Central Veterinary Laboratory (1961–1976), Ministry of Production, Bamako, Mali. [Washington?] Agency for International Development, 1976. [87] p. (in various pagings)

Microfiche. [Sahel Documents and Dissertations. Ann Arbor, Mich., University Microfilms International, 1980] 1 sheet.

DLC-Micro Microfiche 5357 ML 033

4068

Livestock sector evaluation, Mali—USAID, July–September 1978, [by] Maurice de Young [et al.] [Bamako, U.S. AID Mission, 1978] [275] p.

Microfiche. [Sahel Documents and Dissertations. Ann Arbor, University Microfilms International, 1980] 4 sheets.

DLC-Micro Microfiche 5357 ML 044

4069

Mali livestock project; annual report. 1st+ May 15, 1975/Aug. 23, 1976+ Minneapolis, Experience Incorporated.

Prepared for the Government of Mali under a U.S. Agency for International Development contract.

1st report (May 15, 1975/Aug. 23, 1976) examined in the Documentation Center, Sahel Development Program, AID, Washington, D.C.; 3d report (May 15, 1977/May 14, 1978) issued in microfiche. [Sahel Documents and Dissertations. Ann Arbor, Mich., University Microfilms International, 1980] 1 sheet (DLC-Micro Microfiche 5357 ML 093).

4070

Mali livestock sector grant—program proposal. [Washington?], U.S. Agency for International Development, 1975. 59 p.   MiEM

4071

Mali livestock sector redesign: USAID/team reports, July–September 1978, [by] Maurice de Young [et al.] [s.l.], U.S. Agency for International Development, 1979. 162 p.   MiEM

4072

Mali range survey; final report, prepared for the Government of the Republic of Mali under the auspices of the United States Agency for International Development. Washington, Earth Satellite Corporation, 1977. 1 v. (various pagings) illus., fold. map.

Bibliography: p. E-1–E-7.

A study using Skylab satellite imagery as the basis of a range survey.

On cover: Mali livestock sector studies.

Examined in the Development Information Center, AID, Washington, D.C.

4073

Problems of implementing A.I.D.'s livestock sector project activities in Mali. Washington, Area Auditor General, U.S. Agency for International Development, 1980. 39 leaves.

"Audit report number 80-67."

Examined in the Documentation Center, Sahel Development Program, AID, Washington, D.C.

4074

Report on development alternatives in the Dilly pastoral zone. Washington, International Consulting Division, Chemonics, 1981. 114 p. maps (fold. in pockets)

Prepared for the U.S. Agency for International Development.

Examined in the Development Information Center, AID, Washington, D.C.

4075

Stryker, Josiah Dirck. Livestock production and distribution in the Malian economy; supplementary report prepared for the U.S. Agency for International Development. [s.l.], 1973. [76] p. map.

Microfiche. [Washington, U.S. Agency for International Development, 1973?] 1 sheet (DLC-Sci RR PN-PAB-613); and [Sahel Documents and Dissertations. Ann Arbor, Mich., University Microfilms International, 1980] 1 sheet (DLC-Micro Microfiche 5357 ML 043).

4076

Suggested guidelines for improving the livestock marketing information service of Mali. [Washington?], Office of Food and Agriculture, U.S. Agency for International Development, 1974. 17 p.

Prepared in cooperation with the Office malien du bétail et de la viande, Ministère de la production, Bamako.

Microfiche. [Sahel Documents and Dissertations. Ann Arbor, Mich., University Microfilms International, 1980] 1 sheet.

DLC-Micro Microfiche 5357 ML 088

Rice

4077

McIntire, John. Resource costs and economic incentives in Malian rice production. [Stanford, Calif?], Food Research Institute, Stanford University, 1979. [69] p.

Prepared for the U.S. Agency for International Development under contract AID/afr-C-1235.

Examined in the Documentation Center, Sahel Development Program, AID, Washington, D.C.

4078

——— Rice policy in Mali. *In* Pearson, Scott R. Rice in West Africa: policy and economics. Stanford, Calif., Stanford University Press, 1981. p. 299–330. map.   HD9066.A462P4

4078 (cont.)

Publication results from a research project, "The Political Economy of Rice in West Africa," carried out jointly by the Food Research Institute, Stanford University, and the West Africa Rice Development Association between June 1976 and Sept. 1979, and funded by the U.S. Agency for International Development under contract AID/afr-C-1235.

4079

———— Rice production in Mali. *In* Pearson, Scott R. Rice in West Africa: policy and economics. Stanford, Calif., Stanford University Press, 1981. p. 331–360.　　　　　HD9066.A462P4

Publication results from a research project carried out jointly by the Food Research Institute, Stanford University, and the West Africa Rice Development Association and funded by the U.S. Agency for International Development (see more complete note in entry 4078).

Assistance Programs

4080

U.S. *AID Mission to Mali.* Mission disaster plan. Bamako, 1976.

Cited in *Mali: A Country Profile* (entry 4029), p. 46.

4081

———— United States Agency for International Development activities in Mali: a briefing paper. [Bamako?], 1981. 23 p.

Examined in the Development Information Center, AID, Washington, D.C.

4082

U.S. *Agency for International Development.* Annual budget submission: Mali. Washington, U.S. International Development Cooperation Agency.

Vols. for 1977+ examined in the Development Information Center, AID, Washington, D.C.

4083

———— Country development strategy statement: Mali. Washington, U.S. International Development Cooperation Agency. annual.

Vols. for 1981+ examined in the Development Information Center, AID, Washington, D.C.

4084

———— Sahel Recovery and Rehabilitation Program, Mali: proposal and recommendations. Washington, 1974. ca. 250 p. (in various pagings)

(Program assistance paper)
　　　　　HC547.M25U54　1974

Includes bibliographical references.

"The proposed assistance provides supplementary financing to the Government of Mali for the purpose of conducting immediate recovery and rehabilitation activities designed to assist in mitigating or forestalling emergency conditions created by the Sahelian drought."

4085

An Appraisal of the AID program in Mali. [Washington?], Operations Appraisal Staff, Bureau for Program and Policy Coordination, U.S. Agency for International Development, 1979. 49 p.

Examined in the Development Information Center, AID, Washington, D.C.

4086

Bingen, R. James. Research/studies in Sahel Francophone West Africa: Mali; an inventory of research, studies, and reports sponsored by the U.S. Agency for International Development. Washington, Sahel Development Program, U.S. Agency for International Development, 1977. [44] p.

Covers 36 projects undertaken in the period 1962–77.

Abstract for series on francophone West Africa and The Gambia in *A.I.D. Research and Development Abstracts*, Oct. 1977, p. 12–13.

Microfiche. [Washington, U.S. Agency for International Development, 1977?] 1 sheet.
　　　　　DLC-Sci RR PN-AAD-514

4087

Evaluation of Mali land use inventory project (688-0205), [by] James Bower [et al.] Bamako, U.S. AID Mission, 1980. 54 p.　　　　　MiEM

4088

Mali. [*Treaties, etc. United States, 1971 Apr. 17*] Mali, Peace Corps. Agreement effected by exchange of notes dated at Bamako December 23, 1969 and April 17, 1971; entered into force April 17, 1971. *In* U.S. *Treaties, etc.* United States treaties and other international agreements, v. 26, 1975. [Washington, Dept. of State; for sale by the Supt. of Docs., U.S. Govt. Print. Off., 1976] p. 2611–2621. ([Treaties and other international acts series, 8178])　　　JX231.A34 v. 26

In English and French.

4089

Mali. [*Treaties, etc. United States, 1974 Jan. 28*] Mali drought recovery and rehabilitation agreement signed at Bamako January 28, 1974; entered into

4089 (cont.)

force January 28, 1974; and amending agreements signed at Bamako January 28, 1975; entered into force January 28, 1975; and signed at Bamako June 30, 1975; entered into force June 30, 1975; and signed at Bamako August 22, 1975; entered into force August 22, 1975. *In* U.S. *Treaties, etc.* United States treaties and other international agreements, v. 28, 1976–77. [Washington, Dept. of State; for sale by the Supt. of Docs., U.S. Govt. Print. Off., 1978] p. 1–23. ([Treaties and other international acts series, 8641]) JX231.A34 v. 28

In English and French.

Grant agreement between the Government of Mali and the U.S. Agency for International Development for assistance in the fields of range management, livestock improvement, water resources, agricultural production, storage, transportation, and health.

4090

Mali. [*Treaties, etc. United States, 1974 Nov. 6*] Mali; agricultural commodities: transfer under Title II. Agreement signed November 6, 1974 and May 7, 1975; entered into force May 7, 1975, and amending agreements signed May 29, 1975; entered into force May 29, 1975, and signed at Washington and Bamako January 11 and February 2, 1977; entered into force February 2, 1977. *In* U.S. *Treaties, etc.* United States treaties and other international agreements, v. 29, 1976–77. [Washington, Dept. of State; for sale by the Supt. of Docs., U.S. Govt. Print. Off., 1980] p. 5746–5752. ([Treaties and other international acts series, 9147]) JX231.A34 v. 29

4091

Roush, James L. Development is a joint effort: discussion paper on improving the effectiveness of USAID-funded technical assistance to Mali. [s.l.], U.S. Agency for International Development, 1980. 67 p. MiEM

4092

Technical Assistance Information Clearing House. Development assistance programs of U.S. non-profit organizations in Mali. [New York], American Council of Voluntary Agencies for Foreign Service, 1976. 13 p. maps. (TAICH country report) DLC

The Clearing House is operated by the Council under a grant from the U.S. Agency for International Development.

4093

———— Development assistance programs of U.S. non-profit organizations; Mali. 3d ed. [New York], American Council of Voluntary Agencies for Foreign Service, 1980. 23 p. maps. (TAICH country report) DLC

Economic Conditions

4094

Foreign economic trends and their implications for the United States. Mali. 1969+ Washington, for sale by the Supt. of Docs., U.S. Govt. Print. Off. annual. (International marketing information series) HC10.E416

Continues *Economic Trends and Their Implications for the United States. Republic of Mali.*

Prepared by the U.S. Embassy, Bamako.

Vols. for 1969–77 distributed by the U.S. Bureau of International Commerce; vols. for 1978–79 by the U.S. Industry and Trade Administration; vols. for 1980 (i.e., FET 81-004)— by the U.S. International Trade Administration.

Not published, 1973–74?

The following issues for the period 1975–81 have been identified in L.C.:

FET 75-081.	1975.	8 p.
FET 76-106.	1976.	11 p.
FET 77-103.	1977.	9 p.
FET 78-108.	1978.	9 p.
FET 79-081.	1979.	9 p.
FET 81-004.	1981.	8 p.
FET 81-132.	1981.	8 p.

4095

Langellier, Jean-Pierre. Military regime seeks solution for troubled economy. *In* U.S. *Joint Publications Research Service.* JPRS 68749. [Springfield, Va., National Technical Information Service, 1977] (Translations on Sub-Saharan Africa, no. 1720) p. 44–52.

Translation of article in *Le Monde*, Paris, Feb. 12, 13–14, 1977.

Microfiche. [s.l., 1977] DLC-Micro JPRS 68749

4096

Ondobo, Claude. Traore defines national policy, economic goals. *In* U.S. *Joint Publications Research Service.* JPRS 72454. [Springfield, Va., National Technical Information Service, 1978] (Translations on Sub-Saharan Africa, no. 2039) p. 69–72.

Translation of interview with President Traoré, in *Demain l'Afrique,* Paris, Nov. 1978, p. 54–57.

Microfiche. [Washington, Supt. of Docs., U.S. Govt. Print. Off., 1979?] DLC-Micro JPRS 72454

4097

UDPM national council on state enterprises, party deficiencies. *In* U.S. *Joint Publications Research Service.* JPRS 75862. [Springfield, Va., National Technical Information Service, 1980] (Sub-Saharan Africa report, no. 2256) p. 120–123.

Translation of article on the Union démocratique du peuple malien, in *L'Essor*, Bamako, Apr. 12–13, 1980, p. 1, 4, 6.

Microfiche. [s.l., 1980]

DLC-Micro JPRS 75862

4098

Wolpin, Miles D. Legitimizing state capitalism: Malian militarism in Third World perspective. [s.l., 1979] 11 p.   DLC

Prepared for the Colloquium on Mali, sponsored by the U.S. Dept. of State, Nov. 1979.

Education

4099

Educational development in Mali since 1975. Bamako, National Ministry of Education, 1977. 14 p.

Report to the International Conference on Education, Geneva, Switz., 1977.

Abstract in *Resources in Education*, Mar. 1978, p. 143.

Microfiche. [Arlington, Va., ERIC Document Reproduction Service; prepared for Educational Resources Information Center, National Institute of Education, 1978] 1 sheet.

DLC-Micro ED146073

4100

Yena, Issa. Reform in basic education in Mali. *In* Educational reform and innovations in Africa: studies prepared for the Conference of Ministers of Education of African Member States of Unesco. Paris, Unesco, 1978. (Experiments and innovations in education, no. 34) p. 19–24.   LA1500.E38

Issued also in microfiche. [Arlington, Va., ERIC Document Reproduction Service; prepared for Educational Resources Information Center, National Institute of Education, 1978] 1 sheet.

DLC-Micro ED160036

Energy Resources— Production and Consumption

4101

Mali. [*Treaties, etc. United States, 1978 Aug. 26*] Project grant agreement between the Republic of Mali and the United States of America for Mali renewable energy. *In* U.S. *Treaties, etc.* United Stated treaties and other international agreements, v. 30, 1978–79. [Washington, Dept. of State; for sale by the Supt. of Docs., U.S. Govt. Print. Off., 1981] p. 4903–4938. ([Treaties and other international acts series, 9493])   JX231.A34 v. 30

Signed at Bamako Aug. 26, 1978.

A U.S. Agency for International Development project to "apply sources of renewable energy to tasks now largely accomplished by human muscle power," to "help alleviate Mali's dependence on costly fossil fuels and firewood," and to "gain a better understanding, based on scientific observation, of the technical, social and economic consequences of introducing renewable resources energy technologies in rural Africa."—p. 4914.

4102

Mali renewable energy project paper. Ann Arbor, Center for Research on Economic Development, University of Michigan, 1978. 41 p.   MiU-RE

Prepared for the U.S. Agency for International Development under contract AID/afr-C-1143.

4103

Mali renewable energy project paper. Appendices. Ann Arbor, Center for Research on Economic Development, University of Michigan, 1978. 150 p.   MiU-RE

Prepared for the U.S. Agency for International Development under contract AID/afr-C-1143.

Foreign Relations

4104

Gaudio, Attilio. Reported Libyan interventionary policy analyzed. *In* U.S. *Joint Publications Research Service.* JPRS 74631. [Springfield, Va., National Technical Information Service, 1979] (Sub-Saharan Africa report, no. 2178) p. 1–4.

Translation of article on reported Libyan threats toward Mali, in *Africa*, Dakar, Oct. 1979, p. 37–39.

Microfiche. [s.l., 1979]

DLC-Micro JPRS 74631

4105

Joint Cuban-Mali communique issued. *In* U.S. *Joint Publications Research Service.* JPRS 70663. [Springfield, Va., National Technical Information Service, 1978] (Translations on Sub-Saharan Africa, no. 1880) p. 67–71.

Translation of communique issued on the occasion of the visit of an official Malian delegation to Cuba, in *L'Essor*, Bamako, Dec. 19, 1977, p. 6.

4105 (cont.)
Microfiche. [Washington, Supt. of Docs., U.S. Govt. Print. Off., 1978]

DLC-Micro JPRS 70663

Health and Nutrition

4106
U.S. *Peace Corps. Mali.* Medical guide. [Bamako], 1976. 53 leaves. DPC

4107
Adams, Robert L. A report on a nutritional consultation with USAID/Mali. Arlington, Va., Medical Service Consultants, inc., 1979. 26 leaves.
Prepared under contract to the U.S. Agency for International Development.
Examined in the Documentation Center, Sahel Development Program, AID, Washington, D.C.

4108
Cole, David, Stephen Joseph, *and* Hanellore Vanderschmidt. Consultants' technical report: Mali rural health project. Visit for American Public Health Association—United States Agency for International Development—January 1976. [Washington?, 1976?] [80] leaves (in various foliations)
Examined in the Documentation Center, Sahel Development Program, AID, Washington, D.C.

4109
Imperato, Pascal J. Health and nutrition services of the Sahel R and R program in Mali. [Washington?] American Public Health Association, 1974. 54 p. map.
Prepared for the U.S. Agency for International Development under contract AID/csd 2604.
R and R: Recovery and rehabilitation.
Abstract in *A.I.D. Research and Development, Abstracts*, Apr. 1978, p. 30.
Microfiche. [Washington, U.S. Agency for International Development, 1974?] 1 sheet (DLC-Sci RR PN-RAB-634), and [Sahel Documents and Dissertations. Ann Arbor, Mich., University Microfilms International, 1980] 1 sheet (DLC-Micro 5357 ML 039).

Politics and Government

4110
Bennett, Valerie P. Military government in Mali. [s.l.], 1979. 10 p. DLC
Prepared for the Colloquium on Mali, sponsored by the U.S. Dept. of State, Nov. 1979.

"This paper was prepared for the Department of State as part of its external research program. Views or conclusions contained herein should not be interpreted as representing the official opinion or policy of the Department of State."

4111
Diallo, Tayire. President looks to restored democracy. *In* U.S. *Joint Publications Research Service.* JPRS 68749. [Springfield, Va., National Technical Information Service, 1977] (Translations on Sub-Saharan Africa, no. 1720) p. 36–43.
Translation of interview with Moussa Traoré, in *Afrique industrie infrastructures*, Paris, Feb. 1, 1977, p. 33–36.
Microfiche. [s.l., 1977]

DLC-Micro JPRS 68749

4112
Keita, Kasse. Nation suffers under repressions of military dictatorship. *In* U.S. *Joint Publications Research Service.* JPRS 68225. [Springfield, Va., National Technical Information Service, 1976] (Translations on Sub-Saharan Africa, no. 1690) p. 20–24.
Translation of article in *Africa*, Dakar, Oct. 1976, p. 41–43.
Microfiche. [s.l., 1976]

DLC-Micro JPRS 68225

4113
Reported eyewitness account of March student revolt. *In* U.S. *Joint Publications Research Service.* JPRS 75920. [Springfield, Va., National Technical Information Service, 1980] (Sub-Saharan Africa report, no. 2258) p. 67–70.
Translation of article in *Africa*, Dakar, May 1980, p. 31–41.
Microfiche. [s.l., 1980]

DLC-Micro JPRS 75920

4114
Traoré, Moussa. Traore: all should work together for national solidarity. *In* U.S. *Joint Publications Research Service.* JPRS 74789. [Springfield, Va., National Technical Information Service, 1979] (Sub-Saharan Africa report, no. 2191) p. 30–33.
Translation of speech by President Traoré recorded in *L'Essor*, Bamako, Sept. 22, 1979, p. 7–10.
Microfiche. [s.l., 1980]

DLC-Micro JPRS 74789

4115
Traore interviewed on inter-African, domestic affairs. *In* U.S. *Joint Publications Research Service.* JPRS 74452. [Springfield, Va., National Technical

4115 (cont.)

Information Service, 1979] (Sub-Saharan Africa report, no. 2170) p. 1–4.

Translation of interview with President Moussa Traoré, in *Revue africaine de strategie*, Paris, Oct.–Dec. 1979, p. 37, 39.

Microfiche. [Washington, Supt. of Docs., U.S. Govt. Print. Off., 1979]

DLC-Micro JPRS 74452

Population Studies

4116

Africa: Mali. Selected statistical data by sex. Washington, 1981. 31, 17 p.   DLC

Study supported by the U.S. Agency for International Development's Office of Women in Development and Office of Population.

Data assembled by the International Demographic Data Center, U.S. Bureau of the Census.

Among the tables, based on 1960–61 data (unless otherwise indicated), are the following: population by province, sex, and urban/rural residence (1976); population by ethnic group, sex, and urban/rural residence; population by religion, sex, and urban/rural residence; life expectancy; urban and rural populations by marital status, age, and sex; number of households; heads of households by age, sex, and urban/rural residence; number of literate persons by age, sex, and urban/rural residence; number of economically active persons by age, sex, and urban/rural residence.

4117

Colvin, Lucie G. Mali. *In* The Uprooted of the western Sahel: migrants' quest for cash in the Senegambia, [*by*] Lucie Gallistel Colvin [et al.] New York, Praeger, [1981] p. 260–286.

HB2125.5.A3U67

"The U.S. Agency for International Development (AID) funded this research."—p. iii.

4118

Profiles of Sahelian countries: Mali. Washington, Socio-Economic Analysis Staff, International Statistical Programs Center, U.S. Bureau of the Census, 1974. [40] leaves (in various foliations)

Prepared at the request of the U.S. Agency for International Development.

Concerns demographic projections.

Examined in the Documentation Center, Sahel Development Program, AID, Washington, D.C.

Other Subjects

4119

Feasibility study of the Kayes-Nioro du Sahel road. [New York?], Tippetts-Abbett-McCarthy-Stratton Engineers and Architects, 1980. 3 v.

Report submitted to the U.S. Agency for International Development.

Contents: Executive summary.—v. 1. Final report.—v. 2. Appendices.

Microfiche. [Washington, U.S. Agency for International Development, 1980?] (PN-AAJ-057-PN-AAJ-059); examined in the Development Information Center, AID, Washington, D.C.

4120

Grayzel, John A. The ecology of ethnic-class identity among an African pastoral people: the Doukoloma Fulbe. [Eugene?], Dept. of Anthropology, University of Oregon, 1977. 246 p.

"The research for this work was financed by the Research Foundation of the State [University] of New York under the supervision of Dr. Michael Horowitz and in cooperation with the United States Agency for International Development and L'Office malien du viande et bétail."—p. x.

Bibliography: p. 237–246.

Dissertation—University of Oregon.

Microfiche. [Sahel Documents and Dissertations. Ann Arbor, Mich., University Microfilms International, 1980] 3 sheets.

DLC-Micro Microfiche 5357 ML 023

4121

Perinbaum, B. Marie. Change and continuity in Malian history. College Park, Dept. of History, University of Maryland, [1979?] 6 leaves.

DLC

Presented at a U.S. Dept. of State briefing, Nov. 19, 1979.

4122

Stanley, Janet. The Dogon: art and ethnology; a bibliography. Washington, Museum of African Art, Smithsonian Institution, [1979?] 2 leaves.

DLC

Mauritania

General

4123

U.S. *Dept. of State.* Post report. Mauritania. [Washington?], 1979. 20 p. illus., map.

JX1705.A286 Spec. Format

L.C. has also report issued in 1973.

For a description of the contents of this publication, see the note to entry 936.

4124

U.S. *Dept. of State. Bureau of Public Affairs.* Background notes. Mauritania. [Washington, for sale by the Supt. of Docs., U.S. Govt. Print. Off.] 1981. 7 p. maps. (U.S. Dept. of State. Department of State publication 8169)   G59.U5

L.C. retains only the latest revision.

For a description of the contents of this publication, see the note to entry 937.

4125

Draft environmental report on Mauritania. Washington, Science and Technology Division, Library of Congress, 1979. 38 p. maps.

HC59.7.E6475 v. 2

On cover: "AID/DS/ST contract no. SA/TOA 1-77 with U.S. Man and the Biosphere Secretariat, Department of State, Washington, D.C."

Abstract in *A.I.D. Research & Development Abstracts*, July 1981, p. 29.

Bound with *Environmental and Natural Resource Management in Developing Countries: A Report to Congress. Appendix* (entry 399).

Issued also in microfiche. [Washington, U.S. Agency for International Development, 1979?] 1 sheet.   DLC-Sci RR PN-AAG-977

4126

Drobot, Lucy. Mauritania: a country profile. Arlington, Va., Evaluation Technologies, inc., 1978. 63 leaves. col. map.

Prepared for the Office of U.S. Foreign Disaster Assistance, U.S. Agency for International Development.

Bibliography: leaves 61–63.

Microfiche. Sahel Documents and Dissertations. [Ann Arbor, Mich., University Microfilms International, 1980] 2 sheets.

DLC-Micro 5357 MU 015

4127

Gerteiny, Alfred G. On the history, ethnology, and political philosophy of Mauritania. [s.l., 1977?] 21 leaves. (FAR 27730-S)

Paper presented at the Conference on Mauritania, sponsored by the U.S. Dept. of State, 1977.

Examined in the former Foreign Affairs Research Documentation Center, U.S. Dept. of State.

4128

Mango, Cecily. Mauritania, a country profile; prepared for the Office of U.S. Foreign Disaster Assistance, Bureau for Private and Development Cooperation, Agency for International Development, Department of State by Evaluation Technologies, Inc., under contract AID/SOD/PDC-C-0283. 2d ed. Washington, The Office, 1980. 55 p., 1 leaf of plates.

TD554.22.M36 1980

Bibliography: p. 53–55.

A general introduction, with emphasis on political structure, disaster preparedness, demography, health, nutrition, housing, economic conditions, agriculture, geography, transportation, power, and communications.

4129

The Peace Corps in Mauritania. [Washington, U.S. Govt. Print. Off., 1980] folder ([6] p.) illus., map.

DLC

"ACTION 4200.57."

An introduction to the country for Peace Corps Volunteers.

Agriculture

4130

Agricultural institutional framework. [Nouakchott?], Directorate of Studies and Programming, Ministry of Economy and Finance, 1981. 152 p. (Rural assessment and manpower surveys. OP-6)
DLC

Financed by the U.S. Agency for International Development in cooperation with Checchi and Company, Louis Berger International, inc., and Action Programs International.

Note: This document is part of a series of studies produced through the cooperation of the Government of Mauritania and the U.S. Agency for International Development in an effort to provide background information for the drafting of Mauritania's fourth plan of social and economic development (1981–1985). Initiated in 1978, the project involved Checchi and Company, Washington, D.C., Louis Berger International, East Orange, N.J., and Action Programs International, Santa Monica, Calif.

4131

Agricultural production: analysis of selected aspects of Mauritanian agriculture. [Nouakchott?], Directorate of Studies and Programming, Ministry of Economy and Finance, [1981] 81 p. (Rural assessment and manpower surveys. AS-4)
DLC

Financed by the U.S. Agency for International Development in cooperation with Checchi and Company, Louis Berger International, inc., and Action Programs International.

Background information on this document is given in the note to entry 4130.

4132

Agro-ecological zones of Mauritania. [Nouakchott?], Directorate of Studies and Programming, Ministry of Economy and Finance, [1980] [197] p. maps. (Rural assessment and manpower surveys. AS-1)
DLC

Financed by the U.S. Agency for International Development in cooperation with Checchi and Company, Louis Berger International, inc., and Action Programs International.

Background information on this document is given in the note to entry 4130.

4133

Country said to be threatened with famine. *In* U.S. *Joint Publications Research Service.* JPRS 74877. [Springfield, Va., National Technical Information Service, 1980] (Near East/North Africa report, no. 2064) p. 83–86.

Translation of article in *Chaab*, Nouakchott, Nov. 6, 1979, p. 1, 8.

Microfiche. [s.l., 1980]
DLC-Micro JPRS 74877

4134

Discussion on Mauritania rural sector assessment and national manpower study. Washington, U.S. Agency for International Development, 1977. 2 v.

A report on sessions held at the U.S. Dept. of State, Aug. 9–10, 1977.

Examined in the Documentation Center, Sahel Development Program AID, Washington, D.C.

4135

Dryland agriculture. [Nouakchott?], Directorate of Studies and Programming, Ministry of Economy and Finance, [1980] 140 p. (Rural assessment and manpower surveys. SS-2)
DLC

Bibliography: p. 137–140.

Financed by the U.S. Agency for International Development in cooperation with Checchi and Company, Louis Berger International, inc., and Action Programs International.

Background information on this document is given in the note to entry 4130.

4136

Irrigated agriculture. [Nouakchott?], Directorate of Studies and Programming, Ministry of Economy and Finance, [1981] 102 p. (Rural assessment and manpower surveys. SS-1)
DLC

Financed by the U.S. Agency for International Development in cooperation with Checchi and Company, Louis Berger International, inc., and Action Programs International.

Background information on this document is given in the note to entry 4130.

4137

Minister deplores deficit in rainfall, effect on crops. *In* U.S. *Joint Publications Research Service.* JPRS 76726. [Springfield, Va., National Technical Information Service, 1980] (Near East/North Africa report, no. 2212) p. 124–127.

Translation of interview with Mohamed ould Amar, Minister of Rural Development, in *Chaab*, Nouakchott, Sept. 6–7, 1980, p. 3.

Microfiche. [s.l., 1980]
DLC-Micro JPRS 76726

4138

Minister notes government's agricultural programs, policies. *In* U.S. *Joint Publications Research Service.* JPRS 76798. [Springfield, Va., National Technical Information Service, 1980] (Near East/North Africa report, no. 2218) p. 110–116.

Translation of interview with Mohamed ould Amar in *Chaab*, Nouakchott, Sept. 26–28, 1980.

4138 (cont.)

Microfiche. [s.l., 1980]

DLC-Micro JPRS 76798

4139

Minister notes government's efforts to alleviate food shortage. *In* U.S. *Joint Publications Research Service.* JPRS 76495. [Springfield, Va., National Technical Information Service, 1980] (Near East/North Africa report, no. 2187) p. 140–145.

Translation of interview with Mohamed ould Amar in *Chaab*, Nouakchott, July 18, 1980, p. 3.

Microfiche. [s.l., 1980]

DLC-Micro JPRS 76495

4140

Oasis agriculture. [Nouakchott?], Directorate of Studies and Programming, Ministry of Economy and Finance, [1980] 167 p. map. (Rural assessment and manpower surveys. SS-4)   DLC

Bibliography: p. 163–167.

Financed by the U.S. Agency for International Development in cooperation with Checchi and Company, Louis Berger International, inc., and Action Programs International.

Background information on this document is given in the note to entry 4130.

4141

The Public sector: organization and operation of rural development activities. [Nouakchott?], Directorate of Studies and Programming, Ministry of Economy and Finance, [1981] [140] p. maps. (Rural assessment and manpower surveys. AE-4-2)

DLC

Financed by the U.S. Agency for International Development in cooperation with Checchi and Company, Louis Berger International, inc., and Action Programs International.

Background information on this document is given in the note to entry 4130.

4142

Report of a terms of reference mission for a rural sector assessment in Mauritania. [s.l.], 1977. [72] leaves (in various foliations)

Prepared for the U.S. Agency for International Development.

Examined in the Documentation Center, Sahel Development Program, AID, Washington, D.C.

4143

Social change: social organization of agricultural production. [Nouakchott?], Directorate of Studies and Programming, Ministry of Economy and Finance, [1980] 87 p. (Rural assessment and manpower surveys. AS-8-2)   DLC

Bibliography: p. 84–87.

Financed by the U.S. Agency for International Development in cooperation with Checchi and Company, Louis Berger International, inc., and Action Programs International.

Background information on this document is given in the note to entry 4130.

4144

Staff summary report: an assessment of agro-forestry potential within the environmental framework of Mauritania. Report of working discussions among officials of the Government of the Islamic Republic of Mauritania, the United States Agency for International Development, and a panel of scientists convened by the National Academy of Sciences, Nouakchott, Mauritania, 23–28 April 1979. Washington, National Academy of Sciences, 1979. 21 leaves. illus., maps.

On cover: Advisory Committee on the Sahel, Board on Science and Technology for International Development, Commission on International Relations, National Academy of Sciences-National Research Council.

Examined in the Documentation Center, Sahel Development Program, AID, Washington, D.C.

Economic Aspects

4145

Framework for calculating rural GDP from basic production data. [Nouakchott?], Directorate of Studies and Programming, Ministry of Economy and Finance, 1981. 1 v. (unpaged) (Rural assessment and manpower surveys. OP-3)   DLC

Financed by the U.S. Agency for International Development in cooperation with Checchi and Company, Louis Berger International, inc., and Action Programs International.

Background information on this document is given in the note to entry 4130.

4146

Rural income in Mauritania. [Nouakchott?], Directorate of Studies and Programming. Ministry of Economy and Finance, [1981] [95] p. (Rural assessment and manpower surveys. AS-6)

DLC

Financed by the U.S. Agency for International Development in cooperation with Checchi and Company, Louis Berger International, inc., and Action Programs International.

Background information on this document is given in the note to entry 4130.

4147

Rural production. [Nouakchott?], Directorate of Studies and Programming, Ministry of Economy and Finance, 1981. 137 p. (Rural assessment and manpower surveys. OP-5)   DLC

Financed by the U.S. Agency for International Development in cooperation with Checchi and Company, Louis Berger International, inc., and Action Programs International.

Background information on this document is given in the note to entry 4130.

4148

Rural sector consumption patterns in Mauritania. [Nouakchott?], Directorate of Studies and Programming, Ministry of Economy and Finance, [1980] 139 p. map. (Rural assessment and manpower surveys. AS-5)   DLC

Financed by the U.S. Agency for International Development in cooperation with Checchi and Company, Louis Berger International, inc., and Action Programs International.

Background information on this document is given in the note to entry 4130.

Fisheries

4149

Fishery companies of Mauritania. [Casablanca?], U.S. Consulate General, Casablanca, 1976. 20 p.

Microfiche. [Springfield, Va., National Technical Information Service, 1977] 1 sheet.

          DLC-Sci RR PB261862

4150

Inland fisheries. [Nouakchott?], Directorate of Studies and Programming, Ministry of Economy and Finance, [1980?] 117 p. (Rural assessment and manpower surveys. SS-5)   DLC

Financed by the U.S. Agency for International Development in cooperation with Checchi and Company, Louis Berger International, inc., and Action Programs International.

Background information on this document is given in the note to entry 4130.

4151

Traditional maritime fisheries. [Nouakchott?], Directorate of Studies and Programming, Ministry of Economy and Finance, 1981. 112 p. map. (Rural assessment and manpower surveys. SS-6)

          DLC

Financed by the U.S. Agency for International Development in cooperation with Checchi and Company, Louis Berger International, inc., and Action Programs International.

Background information on this document is given in the note to entry 4130.

Livestock and Range Management

4152

Livestock subsector study. [Nouakchott?], Directorate of Studies and Programming, Ministry of Economy and Finance, [1980] 117 p. maps. (Rural assessment and manpower surveys. SS-3)

          DLC

Financed by the U.S. Agency for International Development in cooperation with Checchi and Company, Louis Berger International, inc., and Action Programs International.

Background information on this document is given in the note to entry 4130.

4153

———— Supplement: range management and development. [Nouakchott?], Directorate of Studies and Programming, Ministry of Economy and Finance, [1980] 117 p. maps. (Rural assessment and manpower surveys. SS-3a)   DLC

Financed by the U.S. Agency for International Development in cooperation with Checchi and Company, Louis Berger International, inc., and Action Programs International.

4154

Madland, Marc P., *and* Marguerite P. Madland. Selibaby range-livestock project: field study of the 10th region, July 1975–January 1976. End of tour report. [Nouakchott?], USAID/Mauritania, 1976. 171 p.

Examined in the Development Information Center, AID, Washington, D.C.

4155

Martin, Niels L., William M. Williamson, *and* Carey B. Singleton. Selibaby range-livestock project, Selibaby, Mauritania; technical consultants' report. New York, Near East Foundation, 1975. 30 p.

Prepared for the U.S. Agency for International Development.

Microfiche. [Sahel Documents and Dissertations. Ann Arbor, Mich., University Microfilms International, 1980] 1 sheet.

          DLC-Micro Microfiche 5357 MU 028

4156

OMVS/Mauritania forage research: project review paper. [Washington?, Agency for International Development, 1976?] [67] p. (in various pagings) maps.

A study of the means of improving the produc-

4156 (cont.)

tivity and standard of living of herders in the Kaedi region of Mauritania.

Examined in the Documentation Center, Sahel Development Program, AID, Washington, D.C.

4157

Singleton, Carey B. Mauritania's range and livestock project: findings and recommendations of field survey trip to Selibaby, Mauritania. [New York?], Near East Foundation, 1976. [30] leaves.

Prepared for the U.S. Agency for International Development.

Examined in the Documentation Center, Sahel Development Program, AID, Washington, D.C.

4158

Social change: the future of pastoralism. [Nouakchott?], Directorate of Studies and Programming, Ministry of Economy and Finance, [1980] 73 p. map. (Rural assessment and manpower surveys. AS-8-1)   DLC

Financed by the U.S. Agency for International Development in cooperation with Checchi and Company, Louis Berger International, inc., and Action Programs International.

Background information on this document is given in the note to entry 4130.

4159

Survey of cattle diseases in the Selibaby area, Mauritania, [by] Saydil M. Touré [et al.] [s.l., 1975?] [8] p.

Prepared for the U.S. Agency for International Development.

Microfiche. [Sahel Documents and Dissertations. Ann Arbor, Mich., University Microfilms International, 1980] 1 sheet.

DLC-Micro Microfiche 5357 MU 032

Assistance Programs

4160

U.S. *Agency for International Development.* Annual budget submission: Mauritania. Washington, U.S. International Development Cooperation Agency.

Vols. for 1977+ examined in the Development Information Center, AID, Washington, D.C.

4161

———— Country development strategy statement: Mauritania. Washington, U.S. International Development Cooperation Agency. annual.

Vols. for 1981+ examined in the Development Information Center, AID, Washington, D.C.

4162

———— Program assistance paper, proposal and recommendations: Sahel recovery and rehabilitation program, Mauritania. Washington, [1964] 1 v. (various pagings) maps.   DLC

4163

———— Renewable resource management. Mauritania. Project review paper. [Washington?], 1977. 83 p.   MiEM

4164

———— Sahel Recovery and Rehabilitation Program, Mauritania: proposal and recommendations. Washington, 1974. ca. 250 p. (in various pagings) (Program assistance paper)

HC547.M3U54   1974

Includes bibliographical references.

"The proposed assistance provides supplementary financing to the Government of Mauritania for the purpose of conducting immediate recovery and rehabilitation activities designed to assist in mitigating or forestalling emergency conditions created by the Sahelian drought."

4165

Bingen, R. James. Research/studies in Sahel francophone West Africa: Mauritania; an inventory of research, studies, and reports sponsored by the U.S. Agency for International Development. Washington, Sahel Development Program, U.S. Agency for International Development, 1977. [23] p.

Covers 13 projects undertaken in the period 1962–77.

Abstract for series on francophone West Africa and The Gambia in *A.I.D. Research and Development Abstracts*, Oct. 1977, p. 12–13.

Microfiche. [Washington, U.S. Agency for International Development, 1977?] 1 sheet.

DLC-Sci RR PN-AAD-515

4166

Consolidated statement on overall development strategies. [Nouakchott?], Directorate of Studies and Programming, Ministry of Economy and Finance, 1981. 54 p. (Rural assessment and manpower surveys. OP-1)   DLC

Financed by the U.S. Agency for International Development in cooperation with Checchi and Company, Louis Berger International, inc., and Action Programs International.

Background information on this document is given in the note to entry 4130.

4167

Dossier de projects. [Nouakchott?], Directorate of Studies and Programming, Ministry of Economy and Finance, 1981. 1 v. (various pagings) (Rural assessment and manpower surveys. PI-1)

DLC

Financed by the U.S. Agency for International Development in cooperation with Checchi and Company, Louis Berger International, inc., and Action Programs International.

Text in English.

Background information on this document is given in the note to entry 4130.

4168

Golding, Robert M. Evaluation of the emergency relief operation in Mauritania in 1978. [s.l.], 1978. [26] p. map.

Prepared for the U.S. Agency for International Development under contract AID/afr-C-1479.

A report on efforts of the Agency for International Development to provide food and animal feed as a result of low rainfall in 1977.

Microfiche. [Washington, U.S. Agency for International Development, 1978?] 1 sheet.

DLC-Sci RR PN-AAG-335

4169

Mauritania. *Ministère de l'économie et des finances. Direction des études et de la programmation.* Synthesis. [Nouakchott?], Directorate of Studies and Programming, Ministry of Economy and Finance, 1981. 90 p. (Rural assessment and manpower surveys. S-1)

DLC

"In 1978 the Government of the Islamic Republic of Mauritania and the United States Agency for International Development embarked on a very substantial undertaking to provide the Mauritanian central planning group with a head start on the drafting of the Fourth Plan of Social and Economic Development (1981–1985). An expatriate team of specialists was to assist in the identification of a development strategy and alternate paths of achieving it. In view of the almost total lack of adequate data and analytical bases for the task, the project called for a series of underlying studies to produce information on manpower and employment, the resources and production systems of the rural sector, and its diverse ethnic groups—how they function socially and economically. The combined effort is titled Rural Assessment and Manpower Survey, known widely by its acronym RAMS."—Foreword.

4170

Mauritania. [*Treaties, etc. United States, 1974 Feb. 26*] Mauritania drought recovery program.

Agreement signed at Nouakchott February 26, 1974; entered into force February 26, 1974. *In* U.S. *Treaties, etc.* United States treaties and other international agreements, v. 26, 1976. [Washington, Dept. of State; for sale by the Supt. of Docs., U.S. Govt. Print. Off., 1977] p. 3894–3910. ([Treaties and other international acts series, 8224])

JX231.A34 v. 26

In English and French.

Concerns a U.S. Agency for International Development grant agreement.

4171

Mauritania. [*Treaties, etc. United States, 1976 May 28*], Mauritania, agricultural commodities: transfer under Title II. Agreement signed at Nouakchott May 28, 1976; entered into force May 28, 1976. *In* U.S. *Treaties, etc.* United States treaties and other international agreements, v. 29, 1976–77. [Washington, Dept. of State; for sale by the Supt. of Docs., U.S. Govt. Print. Off., 1980] p. 5775–5780. ([Treaties and other international acts series, 9153])

JX231.A34 v. 29

In English and French.

4172

Mauritania. [*Treaties, etc. United States, 1978 Apr. 18*], Mauritania, agricultural commodities: transfer under Title II. Agreement signed at Nouakchott April 18, 1978; entered into force April 18, 1978; and amending agreement signed at Nouakchott April 18, 1978; entered into force April 18, 1978. *In* U.S. *Treaties, etc.* United States treaties and other international agreements, v. 30, 1978–79. [Washington, Dept. of State; for sale by the Supt. of Docs., U.S. Govt. Print. Off., 1980] p. 3067–3076. ([Treaties and other international acts series, 9397]

JX231.A34 v. 30

In English and French.

Authorizes the Commodity Credit Corporation to transfer and deliver food grain to Mauritania.

4173

Mauritania begins to develop with foreign aid, hopes for more input from U.S. business. Commerce America, Dec. 5, 1977: 25–26. illus.   HF1.C38

Issued by the U.S. Dept. of Commerce.

4174

Technical Assistance Information Clearing House. Development assistance programs of U.S. non-profit organizations: Mauritania. [New York], American Council of Voluntary Agencies for Foreign Service, 1978. 13 p. (TAICH country report)

DLC

The Clearing House is operated by the Council

4174 (cont.)

under a grant from the U.S. Agency for International Development.

"1st edition."

Ecology

4175

Environmental regeneration of southern third of Mauritania. [Nouakchott?], Directorate of Studies and Programming, Ministry of Economy and Finance, [1980] [239] p. maps. (Rural assessment and manpower surveys. AS-2) DLC

Bibliography: p. [237–239].

Financed by the U.S. Agency for International Development in cooperation with Checchi and Company, Louis Berger International, inc., and Action Programs International.

Background information on this document is given in the note to entry 4130.

4176

―――― Appendices. [Nouakchott?, 1980] 1 v. (unpaged) DLC

Financed by the U.S. Agency for International Development in cooperation with Checchi and Company, Louis Berger International, inc., and Action Programs International.

4176a

Gritzner, Jeffrey A. Staff report: environmental degradation in Mauritania: a report of working discussions held by officials of the Government of the Islamic Republic of Mauritania and the U.S. Agency for International Development, and a panel of scientists convened by the National Research Council, and subsequent activities undertaken by the staff of the Advisory Committee on the Sahel. Washington, National Academy Press, 1981. 102 p. MiEM

Funding provided by the U.S. Agency for International Development's Office of Science and Technology under contract AID/ta-C-1433.

"Includes detailed recommendations for 7 different ecological zones and a review of land use and environmental change since prehistoric times."—*Sahel Bibliographic Bulletin*, July/Sept. 1982, p. 149.

Economic Conditions

4177

Annotated statistical compendium. [Nouakchott?] Directorate of Studies and Programming, Ministry of Economy and Finance, 1981. 2 v.

(Rural assessment and manpower surveys. AE-4-3) DLC

Financed by the U.S. Agency for International Development in cooperation with Checchi and Company, Louis Berger International, inc., and Action Programs International.

Background information on this document is given in the note to entry 4130.

4178

Duteil, Mireille. Economic recovery possible if war ends. *In* U.S. *Joint Publications Research Service.* JPRS 73302. [Springfield, Va., National Technical Information Service, 1979] (Translations on Near East and North Africa, no. 1949) p. 29–32.

Translation of article on the impact of the conflict in Western Sahara on Mauritania; in *Demain l'Afrique*, Paris, Mar. 12, 1979, p. 56–57.

Microfiche. [Washington, Supt. of Docs., U.S. Govt. Print. Off., 1979]

DLC-Micro JPRS 73302

4179

Economic activities of the rural private sector. [Nouakchott?], Directorate of Studies and Programming, Ministry of Economy and Finance, 1980. [92] p. (in various pagings) (Rural assessment and manpower surveys. AE-4-1) DLC

Financed by the U.S. Agency for International Development in cooperation with Checchi and Company, Louis Berger International, inc., and Action Programs International.

Background information on this document is given in the note to entry 4130.

4180

Economic prospects for 1980 considered brighter. *In* U.S. *Joint Publications Research Service.* JPRS 76015. [Springfield, Va., National Technical Information Service, 1980] (Sub-Saharan Africa report, no. 2145) p. 216–219.

Article in *West Africa*, London, June 16, 1980, p. 1056–1058.

Microfiche. [s.l., 1980]

DLC-Micro JPRS 76015

4181

Foreign economic trends and their implications for the United States. Mauritania. 1977?+ Washington, for sale by the Supt. of Docs., U.S. Govt. Print. Off. annual. (International marketing information series) HC10.E416

Prepared by the U.S. Embassy, Nouakchott.

Vol. for 1977 distributed by the U.S. Bureau of International Commerce; vols. for 1978–79 by the U.S. Industry and Trade Administration; vols. for

4181 (cont.)

1981– by the U.S. International Trade Administration.

Not published in 1980.

The following issues have been identified in L.C.:

FET 77-109. 1977. 9 p.
FET 78-109. 1978. 11 p.
FET 79-055. 1979. 11 p.
FET 81-124. 1981. 15 p.

4182

Macro-economic simulation model for assessing development priorities. [Nouakchott?], Directorate of Studies and Programming, Ministry of Economy and Finance, 1981. 118 p. (Rural assessment and manpower surveys. OP-2)   DLC

Financed by the U.S. Agency for International Development in cooperation with Checchi and Company, Louis Berger International, inc., and Action Programs International.

Background information on this document is given in the note to entry 4130.

4183

Magassouba, Moriba. Mounting economic problems, moneylenders hesitate to invest. *In* U.S. *Joint Publications Research Service.* JPRS 70779. [Springfield, Va., National Technical Information Service, 1978] (Translations on Near East and North Africa, no. 1769] p. 98–101.

Translation of article in *Demain l'Afrique*, Paris, Feb. 6, 1978, p. 23.

Microfiche. [Washington, Supt. of Docs., U.S. Govt. Print. Off., 1978]

DLC-Micro JPRS 70779

4184

Mansour, Anne. SNIM director discusses Mauritanianization, company's progress. *In* U.S. *Joint Publications Research Service.* JPRS 76231. [Springfield, Va., National Technical Information Service, 1980] (Near East/North Africa report, no. 2165) p. 66–74.

Translation of interview with Baba ould Sidi Abdallah, general manager of the Société nationale industrielle et minière, in *Chaab*, Nouakchott, June 26–29, 1980.

Microfiche. [s.l., 1980]

DLC-Micro JPRS 76231

4185

Moulaye, Zeini. Nation suffering from after-effects of Saharan war. *In* U.S. *Joint Publications Research Service.* JPRS 75352. [Springfield, Va., National Technical Information Service, 1980] Near East/North Africa report, no. 2093) p. 64–67.

Translation of article in *Demain l'Afrique*, Paris, Jan. 28, 1980, p. 40–41.

Microfiche. [s.l., 1980]

DLC-Micro JPRS 75352

4186

President discusses serious economic situation. *In* U.S. *Joint Publications Research Service.* JPRS 70879. [Springfield, Va., National Technical Information Service, 1978] (Translations on Near East and North Africa, no. 1776) p. 99–102.

Translation of interview with President Moktar ould Daddah, in *Remarques africaines*, Brussels, Feb. 1978, p. 23–24.

Microfiche. [Washington, Supt. of Docs., U.S. Govt. Print. Off., 1978]

DLC-Micro JPRS 70879

4187

SNIM's objectives depend on factors outside its control. *In* U.S. *Joint Publications Research Service.* JPRS 76269. [Springfield, Va., National Technical Information Service, 1980] (Near East/North Africa report, no. 2168) p. 97–100.

Translation of article in *Le Monde diplomatique*, Paris, July 1980, p. 29.

SNIM: Société nationale industrielle et minière.

Microfiche. [s.l., 1980]

DLC-Micro JPRS 76269

Education

4188

Education as a development tool. [Nouakchott?], Directorate of Studies and Programming, Ministry of Economy and Finance, 1981. [58] p. (Rural assessment and manpower surveys. PI-2)

DLC

Financed by the U.S. Agency for International Development in cooperation with Checchi and Company, Louis Berger International, inc., and Action Programs International.

Background information on this documents is given in the note to entry 4130.

4189

Evaluation of the formal education system in relation to development objectives. [Nouakchott?], Directorate of Studies and Programming, Ministry of Economy and Finance, [1980] 243 p. (Rural assessment and manpower surveys. FS-3-2)   DLC

Financed by the U.S. Agency for International Development in cooperation with Checchi and Company, Louis Berger International, inc., and Action Programs International.

4189 (cont.)

Background information on this document is given in the note to entry 4130.

4190

———— Appendices. [Nouakchott?], Directorate of Studies and Programming, Ministry of Economy and Finance, [1980] 46 p. map.   DLC

Financed by the U.S. Agency for International Development in cooperation with Checchi and Company, Louis Berger International, inc., and Action Programs International.

4191

Hamden, D. O. Minister discusses progress of educational reform. *In* U.S. *Joint Publications Research Service.* JPRS 74819. [Springfield, Va., National Technical Information Service, 1979] (Near East/North Africa report, no. 2061) p. 56–60.

Translation of interview with Yahya ould Menkouss, Minister of Civil Service and Professional Training, in *Chaab*, Nouakchott, Sept. 22–24, 1979.

Microfiche. [s.l., 1980]
                DLC-Micro JPRS 74819

4192

Non-formal education. [Nouakchott?], Directorate of Studies and Programming, Ministry of Economy and Finance, [1981] [242] p. maps. (Rural assessment and manpower surveys. FS-3-3)
                DLC

Financed by the U.S. Agency for International Development in cooperation with Checchi and Company, Louis Berger International, inc., and Action Programs International.

Background information on this documents is given in the note to entry 4130.

Foreign Relations

4192a

Bennis, Abdellatif. Premier hopes for peace with all nations. *In* U.S. *Joint Publications Research Service.* JPRS 73462. [Springfield, Va., National Technical Information Service, 1979] (Translations on Near East and North Africa, no. 1962) p. 100–106.

Translation of interview with Prime Minister Ahmed Ould Bouceif of Mauritania in *Le Matin*, Casablanca, Apr. 21, 1979, p. 4.

Microfiche. [Washington, Supt. of Docs., U.s. Govt. Print. Off., 1979]
                DLC-Micro JPRS 73462

4193

Junqua, Daniel. President says nation cannot resist Algeria by own means. *In* U.S. *Joint Publications Research Service.* JPRS 70743. [Springfield, Va., National Technical Information Service, 1978] (Translations on Near East and North Africa, no. 1767) p. 54–57.

Translation of interview with President Moktar ould Daddah, in *Le Monde*, Paris, Jan. 19, 1978, p. 1, 5.

Microfiche. [Washington, Supt. of Docs., U.S. Govt. Print. Off., 1978]
                DLC-Micro JPRS 70743

4194

Nation's prestige damaged by Polisario success. *In* U.S. *Joint Publications Research Service.* JPRS 70671. [Springfield, Va., National Technical Information Service, 1978] (Translations on Near East and North Africa, no. 1762) p. 84–87.

Article in *West Africa*, London, Jan. 30, 1978, p. 181–182.

Microfiche. [Washington, Supt. of Docs., U.S. Govt. Print. Off., 1978]
                DLC-Micro JPRS 70671

4195

President discusses alleged Algerian aggression. *In* U.S. *Joint Publications Research Service.* JPRS 70638. [Springfield, Va., National Technical Information Service, 1978] (Translations on Near East and North Africa, no. 1760) p. 74–77.

Translation of interview with President Moktar ould Daddah, in *Remarques africaines*, Brussels, Dec. 1, 1977, p. 11–12.

Microfiche. [Washington, Supt. of Docs., U.S. Govt. Print. Off., 1978]
                DLC-Micro JPRS 70638

4196

President discusses Saharan, racial policies. *In* U.S. *Joint Publications Research Service.* JPRS 73638. [Springfield, Va., National Technical Information Service, 1979] (Translations on Sub-Saharan Africa, no. 1977) p. 49–53.

Translation of interview with President Moustapha ould Mohamed Saleck, in *Revue africaine de stratégie*, Paris, Apr.–June 1979, p. 4, 7, 9.

Microfiche. [Washington, Supt. of.Docs., U.S. Govt. Print. Off., 1979]
                DLC-Micro JPRS 73638

Geology, Hydrology, and Mineral Resources

The following items (entries 4197–99) are listed in chronological order:

4197

Stevens, Candice. The mineral industry of Mauritania. *In* Minerals yearbook, v. 3, 1977. [Washington, for sale by the Supt. of Docs., U.S. Govt. Print. Off., 1981] p. 629–632.
TN23.U612   1977, v. 3
Prepared by the U.S. Bureau of Mines.

4198

———— The mineral industry of Mauritania. *In* Minerals yearbook, v. 3, 1978–79. [Washington, U.S. Govt. Print. Off., 1981] p. 635–637.
TN23.U612   1978–79, v. 3
Prepared by the U.S. Bureau of Mines.

4199

Clarke, Peter J. The mineral industry of Mauritania. *In* Minerals yearbook, v. 3, 1980. [Washington, for sale by the Supt. of Docs., U.S. Govt. Print. Off., 1982] p. 653–658.   TN23.U612   1980, v. 3
Prepared by the U.S. Bureau of Mines.

Health and Nutrition

4200

The Food and nutritional situation in Mauritania. [Nouakchott?] Directorate of Studies, and Programming, Ministry of Economy and Finance, [1981] 94 p. map. (Rural assessment and manpower surveys. FS 1-1)   DLC
Financed by the U.S. Agency for International Development in cooperation with Checchi and Company, Louis Berger International, inc., and Action Programs International.
Background information on this document is given in the note to entry 4130.

4201

Health/nutrition. [Nouakchott?], Directorate of Studies and Programming, Ministry of Economy and Finance, 1981. 93, 79 p. (Rural assessment and manpower surveys. OP-8)   DLC
Bibliography: p. 90–93.
Financed by the U.S. Agency for International Development in cooperation with Checchi and Company, Louis Berger International, inc., and Action Programs International.

Background information on this document is given in the note to entry 4130.

4202

Malek, Emile, *and* David Goff. Mauritania: public health assessment of proposed dams, water-related diseases and community water supplies. Arlington, Va., CDM Five, 1981. [55] leaves (in various foliations) maps.
Prepared for the U.S. Agency for International Development.
Microfiche. [Washington, U.S. Agency for International Development, 1981?] 1 sheet (PN-AAJ-296); examined in the Development Information Center, AID, Washington, D.C.

4203

Rural health: outline of the Mauritanian health sector. [Nouakchott?], Directorate of Studies and Programming, Ministry of Economy and Finance, 1981. 93 p. maps. (Rural assessment and manpower surveys. FS 1-2)   DLC
Financed by the U.S. Agency for International Development in cooperation with Checchi and Company, Louis Berger International, inc., and Action Programs International.
Background information on this document is given in the note to entry 4130.

Labor

Background information on the following documents (entries 4204–7) is given in the note to entry 4130.

4204

Employment implications of alternative development strategies. [Nouakchott?], Directorate of Studies and Programming, Ministry of Economy and Finance, 1981. 53 p. (Rural assessment and manpower surveys. OP-7)   DLC
Financed by the U.S. Agency for International Development in cooperation with Checchi and Company, Louis Berger International, inc., and Action Programs International.

4205

Employment situation. [Nouakchott?], Directorate of Studies and Programming, Ministry of Economy and Finance, [1981] 98 p. maps. (Rural assessment and manpower surveys. FS-2)
DLC
Financed by the U.S. Agency for International Development in cooperation with Checchi and Company, Louis Berger International, inc., and Action Programs International.

4206

———— Supplement. [Nouakchott?], Directorate of Studies and Programming, Ministry of Economy and Finance, [1980] [77] p.   DLC

Financed by the U.S. Agency for International Development in cooperation with Checchi and Company, Louis Berger International, inc., and Action Programs International.

4207

Manpower skills. [Nouakchott?], Directorate of Studies and Programming, Ministry of Economy and Finance, [1980] 123 p. (Rural assessment and manpower surveys. FS-3-1)   DLC

Financed by the U.S. Agency for International Development in cooperation with Checchi and Company, Louis Berger International, inc., and Action Programs International.

Politics and Government

4208

"Democrats" see precipitous situation, blame Ould Daddah. *In* U.S. *Joint Publications Research Service.* JPRS 71577. [Springfield, Va., National Technical Information Service, 1978] (Translations on Sub-Saharan Africa, no. 1822) p. 66–70.

Translation of article in *El Moudjahid*, Algiers, July 3, 1978, p. 5.

Microfiche. [Washington, Supt. of Docs., U.S. Govt. Print. Off., 1978]

DLC-Micro JPRS 71577

4209

Duteil, Mireille. Demands, attitudes of blacks set forth. *In* U.S. *Joint Publications Research Service.* JPRS 73059. [Springfield, Va., National Technical Information Service, 1979] (Translations on the Near East and North Africa, no. 1926) p. 100–105.

Translation of article in *Demain l'Afrique*, Paris, Feb. 26, 1979, p. 32–34.

Microfiche. [Washington, Supt. of Docs., U.S. Govt. Print. Off., 1979]

DLC-Micro JPRS 73059

4210

———— Haidalla making some progress since withdrawing from war. *In* U.S. *Joint Publications Research Service.* JPRS 74409. [Springfield, Va., National Technical Information Service, 1979] (Near East/North Africa report, no. 2034) p. 48–51.

Translation of article in *Demain l'Afrique*, paris, Sept. 10, 1979, p. 55–56.

Microfiche. [s.l., 1979]

DLC-Micro JPRS 74409

4211

Prime Minister discusses government's aims, action. *In* U.S. *Joint Publications Research Service.* JPRS 77402. [Springfield, Va., National Technical Information Service, 1981] (Near East/North Africa report, no. 2267) p. 117–120.

Translation of interview with Prime Minister Ahmed ould Bneijara, in *Chaab*, Nouakchott, Dec. 17, 1980, p. 1, 3, 8.

Microfiche. [s.l., 1981]

DLC-Micro JPRS 77402

Population Studies

4212

Africa: Mauritania. Selected statistical data by sex. Washington, 1981. 31, 17 p.   DLC

Study supported by the U.S. Agency for International Development's Office of Women in Development and Office of Population.

Date assembled by the International Demographic Data Center, U.S. Bureau of the Census.

Among the tables, all based on 1965 data (unless otherwise noted), are the following: unadjusted population by age, sex, and urban/rural residence (1975); population by province, sex, and urban/rural residence; population by religion, sex, and urban/rural residence; life expectancy; rural population by marital status, age, and sex; number of households; heads of households by age, sex, and urban/rural residence; number of literate persons by age, sex, and urban/rural residence; number of rural persons enrolled in school by sex; economically active rural population by occupational status and sex.

4213

Colvin, Lucie G. Mauritania. *In* The Uprooted of the western Sahel: migrants' quest for cash in the Senegambia, [by] Lucie Gallistel Colvin [et al.] New York, Praeger, [1981] p. 244–259. map.

HB2125.5.A3U67

"The U.S. Agency for International Development (AID) funded this research."—p. iii.

4214

Demographic projections. [Nouakchott?], Directorate of Studies and Programming, Ministry of Economy and Finance, [1980] 138 p. maps. (Rural assessment and manpower surveys. AS-3)

DLC

Financed by the U.S. Agency for International Development in cooperation with Checchi and Company, Louis Berger International, inc., and Action Programs International.

4214 (cont.)

Background information on this document is given in the note to entry 4130.

4215

Profiles of Sahelian countries: Mauritania. Washington, Socio-Economic Analysis Staff, International Statistical Programs Center, U.S. Bureau of the Census, 1974. [41] leaves (in various foliations)

Prepared at the request of the U.S. Agency for International Development.

Concerns demographic projections.

Examined in the Documentation Center, Sahel Development Program, AID, Washington, D.C.

4216

Studies in social change: population movements and migrations in Mauritania. [Nouakchott?], Directorate of Studies and Programming, Ministry of Economy and Finance, [1980] 246 p. (Rural assessment and manpower surveys. AS-8-3)

DLC

Bibliography: p. 244–246.

Financed by the U.S. Agency for International Development in cooperation with Checchi and Company, Louis Berger International, inc., and Action Programs International.

Background information on this document is given in the note to entry 4130.

Social Conditions

4217

Basic human needs as a concept in the formulation of a development strategy. [Nouakchott?], Directorate of Studies and Programming, Ministry of Economy and Finance, 1981. 21 p. (Rural assessment and manpower surveys. OP-4)   DLC

Financed by the U.S. Agency for International Development in cooperation with Checchi and Company, Louis Berger International, inc., and Action Programs International.

Background information on this document is given in the note to entry 4130.

4218

Diongue, Aliou. Cultural conflict between blacks, Moors noted. *In* U.S. *Joint Publications Research Service.* JPRS 73325. [Springfield, Va., National Technical Information Service, 1979] (Translations on Near East and North Africa, no. 1951) p. 14–22.

Translation of article in *Le Soleil,* Dakar, Mar. 8–11, 1979.

Microfiche. [Washington, Supt. of Docs., U.S.

Govt. Print. Off., 1979]

DLC-Micro JPRS 73325

4219

Rubin, Edward. Comprehensive human resources development and its application to Mauritania. [s.l., 1975?] [13] p.

Prepared for the U.S. Agency for International Development.

Microfiche. [Sahel Documents and Dissertations. Ann Arbor, Mich., University Microfilms International, 1980] 1 sheet.

DLC-Micro Microfiche 5357 MU 009

Background information on the following documents (entries 4220–23) is given in the note to entry 4130.

4220

Sociological profiles: Black African Mauritania. [Nouakchott?], Directorate of Studies and Programming, Ministry of Economy and Finance, [1980] 69 p. (Rural assessment and manpower surveys. AS-7-1)   DLC

Bibliography: p. 68–69.

Financed by the U.S. Agency for International Development in cooperation with Checchi and Company, Louis Berger International, inc., and Action Programs International.

4221

Sociological profiles: the Moors. [Nouakchott?], Directorate of Studies and Programming, Ministry of Economy and Finance, [1980] 129 p. (Rural assessment and manpower surveys. AS-7-2)

DLC

Bibliography: p. 120-129.

Financed by the U.S. Agency for International Development in cooperation with Checchi and Company, Louis Berger International, inc., and Action Programs International.

4222

Studies in social change: the evolution of modes of accumulation and social change in Mauritania. [Nouakchott?], Directorate of Studies and Programming, Ministry of Economy and Finance, [1980] 113 p. (Rural assessment and manpower surveys. AS-8-4)   DLC

Financed by the U.S. Agency for International Development in cooperation with Checchi and Company, Louis Berger International, inc., and Action Programs International.

4223

Synthesis of sociologic studies. [Nouakchott?], Directorate of Studies and Programming, Ministry of Economy and Finance, [1980] 59 p.

4223 (cont.)

(Rural assessment and manpower surveys. AS-9)
DLC

Financed by the U.S. Agency for International Development in cooperation with Checchi and Company, Louis Berger International, inc., and Action Programs International.

Women

4224

Abeille, Barbara. A study of female life in Mauritania; prepared for Nouakchott, Mauritania USAID-Research and Development. Washington, distributed by Office of Women in Development, Agency for International Development, 1979. xvii, 51, 2 leaves. HQ1815.A64

Includes bibliographical references.

4225

Smale, Melinda S. Women in Mauritania: effects of drought and migration on their economic status and implications for development programs. [Washington], distribution by Office of Women in Development, Agency for International Development, International Development Cooperation Agency, 1980. xxvi, 163 p. illus.

HQ1815.S65

Prepared for the Office of Women in Development, AID, and the U.S. AID Mission to Mauritania by the Office of International Cooperation and Development, U.S. Dept. of Agriculture.

Bibliography: p. 157–159.

Abstract in *A.I.D. Research & Development Abstracts*, v. 9, no. 3, 1981, p. 28–29.

Issued also in microfiche. [Washington, U.S. Agency for International Development, 1980] 2 sheets. DLC-Sci RR PN-AAJ-464

Other Subjects

4226

Dunham, Daniel C. Alternative energy systems in rural Mauritania. Mt. Rainier, Md., Volunteers in Technical Assistance, inc., 1977. 61 p. illus.

Prepared for the U.S. Agency for International Development under grant AID/afr-G-1355.

Abstract in *Government Reports Announcements & Index*, Oct. 12, 1979, p. 121.

Microfiche. [Springfield, Va., National Technical Information Service, 1979] 1 sheet.
DLC-Sci RR PB-296364

4227

Francis, Timothy P., *and* Stephen Hanchey. Mauritanian Arabic. Brattleboro, Vt., Experiment in International Living, for ACTION/Peace Corps, 1979. 4 v. illus. (Peace Corps language handbook series) DPC

Contents: [v. 1.] Grammar handbook.—[v. 2] Literacy handbook.—[v. 3] Communication and culture handbook.—[v. 4] Teacher's handbook.

4228

Heyman, Juliane M. Report on literature search, documentation and related information on Mauritania. [s.l.], 1978. 57 leaves.

Prepared for the U.S. Agency for International Development under contract AID/afr-C-1428.

A report on those documentation centers in the United States, Europe, and West Africa that have material on Mauritania.

Examined in the Documentation Center, Sahel Development Program, AID, Washington, D.C.

Issued also in French (held by MiEM).

4229

Mauritania: shelter sector assessment, [by] Joseph M. Perta [et al.] Washington, National Savings and Loan League, 1979. [158] p. illus., maps.

Prepared for the Office of Housing, U.S. Agency for International Development.

In English and French.

Abstract in *A.I.D. Research and Development Abstracts*, Feb. 1981, p. 67.

Microfiche. [Washington, U.S. Agency for International Development, 1979?] 2 sheets.
DLC-Sci RR PN-AAG 801

4230

Reyna, Stephen P. Social soundness, the Guidimaka tracks and trails project (682-0214). Abidjan, Regional Economic Development Services Office, West Africa, [U.S. Agency for International Development], 1979. 34 p. MiEM

Niger

General

4231

U.S. *Dept. of State.* Post report. Niger. [Washington, Dept. of State, Publishing Services Division; for sale by the Supt. of Docs., U.S. Govt. Print. Off.] 1980. 12 p. illus., map. (*Its* Department and Foreign Service series, 201)

      JX1705.A286 Spec. Format

    L.C. has also reports issued in 1974 and 1978.

    For a description of the contents of this publication, see the note to entry 936.

4232

U.S. *Dept. of State. Bureau of Public Affairs.* Background notes. Niger. [Washington, for sale by the Supt. of Docs., U.S. Govt. Print. Off.], 1980. 7 p. illus., maps. (U.S. Dept. of State. Department of State publication 8293)   G59.U5

    L.C. retains only the latest revision.

    For a description of the contents of this publication, see the note to entry 937.

4233

Mango, Cecily. Niger: a country profile. Washington, Office of Foreign Disaster Assistance, Agency for International Development, 1980. 53 p., 1 leaf of plates.   DT547.22.M36

    "May 1980."

    "Prepared for the Office of U.S. Foreign Disaster Assistance, Bureau for Private and Development Cooperation, Agency for International Development, Department of State by Evaluation Technologies, inc., under contract no. AID/SOD/PDC-C-0283."—p. ii.

    Bibliography: p. 51–53.

    A general introduction, with emphasis on political structure, disaster preparedness, demography, health, nutrition, housing, economic conditions, agriculture, geography, transportation, power, and communications.

4234

The Peace Corps in Niger. [Washington, U.S. Govt. Print. Off., 1980] folder ([6] p.) illus., map.

        DLC

    "ACTION 4200.61."

    An introduction to the country for Peace Corps Volunteers.

4235

Speece, Mark. Draft environmental report on Niger. Tucson, Arid Lands Information Center, Office of Arid Lands Studies, University of Arizona, 1980. 160 p. maps.   AzU

    Sponsored by the U.S. Agency for International Development.

    On cover: "National Park Service Contract no. CX-0001-0-0003 with U.S. Man and the Biosphere Secretariat, Department of State, Washington, D.C."

    Bibliography: p. 139–160.

    Abstract in *A.I.D. Research & Development Abstracts*, July 1981, p. 36–37.

    Issued also in microfiche. [Washington, U.S. Agency for International Development, 1980?] 2 sheets.   DLC-Sci RR PN-AAJ-203

Agriculture

4236

U.S. *AID Mission to Niger.* Projet de développement rural du Département de Niamey, Phase II (AID-683-0240): avant-project. Niamey, 1980. 25 p.

        MiEM

4237

Conly, Shanti. [Agricultural development in Niger] Niamey, U.S. AID Mission to Niger, 1979. 2 v.

        MiEM

    Contents: Pt. 1. National and agricultural development strategies in Niger: a review of development plans, 1961–1983.—Pt. 2. Government policies and institutions affecting rainfed agriculture.

    Copy examined in the Documentation Center,

4237 (cont.)
Sahel Development Program, U.S. Agency for International Development, Washington, D.C.

4238
Ferguson, Nancy, *and* W. Gerald Matlock. Energy analysis of agriculture and renewable natural resources in Zinder, Niger. Tucson, Arid Lands Natural Resources Committee, University of Arizona, 1979. 66 p.   AzU

Issued as Appendix 3 of the *Final Report of the Natural Resource Planning Project for the Province of Zinder, Niger* (entry 4324).

Supported by the U.S. Agency for International Development.

Bibliography: p. 64–66.

Additional information on this document is given in entry 4324.

Issued also in microfiche. [Sahel Documents and Dissertations. Ann Arbor, Mich., University Microfilms International, 1980] 1 sheet.
DLC-Micro Microfiche 5357 NG 027

4239
Kountché, Seyni. Kountche: food situation not catastrophic, but tragic. *In* U.S. *Joint Publications Research Service.* JPRS 71133. [Springfield, Va., National Technical Information Service, 1978] (Translations on Sub-Saharan Africa, no. 1929) p. 41–46.

Translation of a presidential press conference reported in *Le Sahel*, Niamey, Apr. 11, 1978, p. 1.

Microfiche. [Washington, Supt. of Docs., U.S. Govt. Print. Off., 1978]
DLC-Micro JPRS 71133

4240
Nation's food situation following 1976 harvest analyzed. *In* U.S. *Joint Publications Research Service.* JPRS 68400. [Springfield, Va., National Technical Information Service, 1976] (Translations on Sub-Saharan Africa, no. 1698) p. 40–49.

Translation of article in *Le Sahel*, Niamey, Nov. 19, 1976.

Microfiche. [s.l., 1976]
DLC-Micro JPRS 68400

4241
Niger agricultural sector assessment. [Niamey?], USAID/Niamey, 1979. 2 v. maps.

Includes bibliographical references.

"The general nature of the following study is an assessment of the dry land agricultural sector of Niger."—p. v.

Contents: v. 1. Enger, Warren G. Synthesis.— v. 2, pt. A. Enger, Warren J., *and* Melinda S. Smale. Implications of foreign assistance on Niger's domestic investment capacity.—v. 2, pt. B. Enger, Warren J. The Government of Niger's agricultural strategy and the potential for meeting long-term goals.—v. 2, pt. C. Ferguson, Carl E. Agronomy and agricultural research.—v. 2, pt. D. Sutter, John W. Social analysis of the Nigerien rural producer.—v. 2, pt. E. Smale, Melinda S. Women in development issues in Niger.—v. 2, pt. F. Borsdorf, Roe. Marketing profile: cereals and cash crops.—v. 2, pt. G. Kiser, Harvey L. Cooperatives: report and analysis.

Microfiche. [Washington, U.S. Agency for International Development, 1979] (PN-AAJ-408–PN-AAJ-409); examined in the Development Information Center, AID, Washington, D.C.

4242
President's press conference on crops, electric power. *In* U.S. *Joint Publications Research Service.* JPRS 74789. [Springfield, Va., National Technical Information Service, 1979] (Sub-Saharan Africa report, no. 2191) p. 36–40.

Translation of report on President Seyni Kountché's press conference, in *Le Sahel*, Niamey, Oct. 15, 1979, p. 4–5.

Microfiche. [s.l., 1980]
DLC-Micro JPRS 74789

4243
Rural sector human resources development: project paper. [Niamey?], U.S. AID Mission to Niger, 1978. 122 p.   MiEM

"Project no. 683–0226."

4244
Sargent, Merritt W. Brief description of animal traction activities: Niamey Productivity Project, 1st phase. Niamey, U.S. AID Mission to Niger, 1977. 40 p.   MiEM

Issued also in microfiche. [Sahel Documents and Dissertations. Ann Arbor, Mich., University Microfilms International, 1980] 1 sheet.
DLC-Micro Microfiche 5357 NG 014

4245
Wentling, Mark G. A basic analysis of the average farm in the project zone. Niamey, 1978. 27 p.

The author, Project Officer for the U.S. AID Mission to Niger, prepared this paper for the Niamey Department Development Project.

Microfiche. [Sahel Documents and Dissertations. Ann Arbor, Mich., University Microfilms International, 1980] 1 sheet.
DLC-Micro Microfiche 5357 NG 012

Agricultural Education and Extension

4246

Charlick, Robert B. Agricultural extension and cooperation in rural Niger; interviews with participants in the farmer extension systems in Zinder and Maradi departments. [s.l., 1978] 135 p.

Report prepared for the Office of Development Resources, U.S. Agency for International Development.

Microfiche. [Sahel Documents and Dissertations. Ann Arbor, Mich., University Microfilms International, 1980] 2 sheets.

DLC-Micro Microfiche 5357 NG 004

4247

——— Planification et évaluation des activités d'information et d'organisation rurale dans le cadre du projet de productivité du Département de Niamey. Niamey, U.S. AID Mission to Niger, 1977. 91 p. MiEM

4248

Moulton, Jeanne B. *Animation rurale*: education for rural development. Amherst, Center for International Education, University of Massachusetts, [1977] [249] p. maps.

"This is a study of *animation rurale*, an out-of-school adult education program which has been implemented in most nations of French West Africa [sic]. The purpose of this study is to define the problems and issues of nonformal education programs designed to enhance rural development."—p. ix.

Niger is used as an example.

Abstract in *Resources in Education*, Apr. 1978, p. 111.

Microfiche. [Arlington, Va., ERIC Document Reproduction Service; prepared for Educational Resources Information Center, National Institute of Education, 1978] 3 sheets.

DLC-Micro ED147091

Some pages illegible on microfiche examined.

4249

Ryan, Carl A. Study of extension training and cooperatives in Niger. [s.l.], Agricultural Cooperative Development International, 1974. 16 p.

Prepared for the U.S. Agency for International Development under contract AID/csd-2219.

Examined in the Development Information Center, AID, Washington, D.C.

Economic Aspects

4250

Battles, Ralph U. Study of agricultural credit and cooperatives in Niger. [s.l.], Agricultural Cooperative Development International, 1975. 19 p.

Prepared for the U.S. Agency for International Development under contract AID/csd-2219.

Examined in the Development Information Center, AID, Washington, D.C.

4251

Kouamé, Koli L., *and* Frantz F. J. Reid. Rapport sur l'enquête socio-économique de six villages dans la zone du projet. Niamey, Project Productivité Niamey, USAID, 1978. 40 p. MiEM

"Resultat d'une enquête socio-économique de base dans les villages de Fandou-Béri, Bourbourkabé, Sadeizé Koira, Toudou, Gao-Alzana, et Diguina regroupant Zermas, Haoussas, Peuhls, et Touaregs, pour aider à l'élaboration de projet de développement rural."—*Sahel Bibliographic Bulletin*, Apr./June 1982, p. 103.

4252

Niamey Department development project: project paper. [Niamey?], U.S. AID Mission to Niger, 1977. [125] p. MiEM

"Project no. 683-0205."

4253

Schaetzen, Yves de. President Kountche discusses post-drought situation. *In* U.S. *Joint Publications Research Service*. JPRS 68023. [Springfield, Va., National Technical Information Service, 1976] (Translations on Sub-Saharan Africa, no. 1681) p. 36–41.

Translation of article in *Afrique industrie infrastructures*, Paris, Sept. 1, 1976, p. 38–41.

Microfiche. [s.l., 1976]

DLC-Micro JPRS 68023

4254

——— Rural development minister discusses agricultural projects, financing. In U.S. *Joint Publications Research Service*. JPRS 68009. [Springfield, Va., National Technical Information Service, 1976] (Translations on Sub-Saharan Africa, no. 1680) p. 37–45.

Translation of interview with Boulama Manga, Minister of Rural Development, in *Afrique agriculture*, Paris, Sept. 1976, p. 18–21.

Microfiche. [s.l., 1976]

DLC-Micro JPRS 68009

4255

Stewart, Bonnie A. The impact of the marketing organizations serving the agricultural sector in Zinder, Niger. [Tucson?], Dept. of Oriental Studies, University of Arizona, 1978. xv, 196 p. maps.

Research supported in part by the U.S. Agency for International Development.

Dissertation—University of Arizona.

Microfiche. [Sahel Documents and Dissertations. Ann Arbor, Mich., University Microfilms International, 1980] 3 sheets; and [Ann Arbor, Mich., University Microfilms International, 1979?] (DLC-Micro 79-06413).

(DLC-Microfiche 5357 NG 050)

4256

Stewart, Bonnie A., *and* W. Gerald Matlock. The agricultural marketing system in Zinder, Niger. Tucson, Arid Lands Natural Resources Committee, University of Arizona, 1979. 15 p.

AzU

Issued as Appendix 5 of the *Final Report of the Natural Resource Planning Project for the Province of Zinder, Niger* (entry 4324).

Supported by the U.S. Agency for International Development.

Additional information on this document is given in entry 4324.

Issued also in microfiche. [Sahel Documents and Dissertations. Ann Arbor, Mich., University Microfilms International, 1980] 1 sheet.

DLC-Micro Microfiche 5357 NG 005

4257

Thom, Derrick J. Niger's landlocked position: the problem of groundnut evacuation. [Logan, Utah State University, 1977] 28 p.

Funding for this study provided by the Foreign Field Research Program, Division of Earth Sciences, National Academy of Sciences-National Research Council.

Microfiche. [Sahel Documents and Dissertations. Ann Arbor, Mich., University Microfilms International, 1980] 1 sheet.

DLC-Micro Microfiche 5357 NG 071

Forests and Forestry

4258

Glakpe, E. K., *and* S. Smith. Wood resources, consumption and demand, and electrical energy options for Zinder, Niger. Tucson, Arid Lands Natural Resources Committee, University of Arizona, 1979. 34 p.   AzU

Issued as Appendix 4 of the *Final Report of the*

Natural Resource Planning Project for the Province of Zinder, Niger (entry 4324).

Supported by the U.S. Agency for International Development.

Additional information on this document is given in entry 4324.

Issued also in microfiche. [Sahel Documents and Dissertations. Ann Arbor, Mich., University Microfilms International, 1980] 1 sheet.

DLC-Micro Microfiche 5357 NG 121

4259

Meeting of Peace Corps/Niger & Niger Water and Forests Service. [1st]+ [1971?]+ [Niamey?], U.S. Peace Corps, Niger. annual.   DPC

Report of meeting between Peace Corps representatives and the staff of the Service des eaux et forêts of Niger.

Reports for 1973 (3d) and 1974 (4th) examined in DPC.

4260

Niger forestry and land-use planning project (no. 683-0230) [Niamey?], U.S. AID Mission to Niger, [1979?] 115 p. illus.

Examined in the Documentation Center, Sahel Development Program, U.S. Agency for International Development, Washington, D.C.

Grain and Grain Storage

4261

Niger. [*Treaties, etc. United States, 1975 Sept. 17*] Project agreement between the Department of State, Agency for International Development (AID), an agency of the Government of the United States of America, and the Ministry of Foreign Affairs and Cooperation, an agency of the Government of Niger. *In* U.S. *Treaties, etc.* United States treaties and other international agreements, v. 29, 1976–77. [Washington, Dept. of State; for sale by the Supt. of Docs., U.S. Govt. Print. Off., 1980] p. 5377–5427. ([Treaties and other international acts series, 9118])   JX231.A34 v. 29

In English and French.

Agreement concerning cereal production signed at Niamey September 17, 1975, and amending agreement signed at Niamey July 23, 1977.

4262

Niger cereals production project; USAID non-capital project paper. [Washington?], U.S. Agency for International Development, 1975 114 p.

MiEM

4263

Report on the second evaluation of the Niger Cereals Project, project number 683-0201, January 15–25, 1978. [s.l., 1978?] 73 leaves.

Evaluation sponsored by the U.S. Agency for International Development.

Examined in the Documentation Center, Sahel Development Program, AID, Washington, D.C.

4264

Sorghum improvement: annual report, Niger Cereals Project. [Niamey?]

Project supported by the U.S. Agency for International Development.

Vol. for 1978 issued in microfiche. [Sahel Documents and Dissertations. Ann Arbor, Mich., University Microfilms International, 1980] 1 sheet.
DLC-Micro Microfiche 5357 NG 115

4265

Williams, James E. Extension analysis. Niamey, 1978. 58 p.   MiEM

Prepared for the Niger Cereals Project, U.S. Agency for International Development, and the Government of Niger.

Livestock and Range Management

4266

Eddy, Edward D. Labor and land use on mixed farms in the pastoral zone of Niger. [Ann Arbor], Center for Research on Economic Development, University of Michigan, 1979. 493 p. illus., map.
        MiU

Prepared for the U.S. Agency for International Development under contract AID/afr-C-1169.

Bibliography: p. 491–493.

Issued also in microfiche. [Sahel Documents and Dissertations. Ann Arbor, Mich., University Microfilms International, 1980] 7 sheets.
DLC-Micro Microfiche 5357 NG 057

4267

——— Prospects for the development of cattle production on mixed farms in the pastoral zone of Niger: a summary. *In* Shapiro, Kenneth H. Livestock production and marketing the Entente states of West Africa: summary report. [Ann Arbor], Center for Research on Economic Development, University of Michigan, 1979. p. 328–437.   MiU

Study financed by the U.S. Agency for International Development under contract AID/afr-C-1169.

Issued also in microfiche. [Sahel Documents and Dissertations. Ann Arbor, Mich., University

Microfilms International, 1980] (DLC-Micro 5357 AS 162); and [Washington, U.S. Agency for International Development, 1979?] (PN-AAJ-217).

4268

Greene, Jake. Niger range management guide. [Niamey], Peace Corps, 1977. 47 p.   DPC

4269

Improved livestock production in Zinder, Niger: a scenario for development. Tucson, Arid Lands Natural Resources Committee, University of Arizona, 1979. 121 p.   AzU

Issued as vol. 3 of *Final Report of the Natural Resources Planning Project for the Province of Zinder, Niger* (entry 4324).

Supported by the U.S. Agency for International Development.

Additional information on this documents is given in entry 4324.

Issued also in microfiche. [Sahel Documents and Dissertations. Ann Arbor, Mich., University Microfilms international, 1980] 2 sheets.
DLC-Micro Microfiche 5357 NG 052

4270

Kinni, Amoul. Etude sur la commercialisation du bétail et de la viande dans le département de Zinder, Niger. Tucson, Arid Lands Natural Resources Committee, University of Arizona, 1979. 48 p.
      AzU

Issued as Appendix 7 of the *Final Report of the Natural Resource Planning Project for the Province of Zinder, Niger* (entry 4324).

Supported by the U.S. Agency for International Development.

Additional information on this documents is given in entry 4324.

Copy examined in the Documentation Center, Sahel Development Program, AID, Washington, D.C.

4271

Niger livestock field survey. Washington, U.S. Agency for International Development, 1976.

Cited in *The Economic, Social, and Physical Environment of the Department of Zinder, Republic of Niger* (HC547.N52Z553), leaf 118.

4272

Niger range and livestock: project paper. [s.l., Agency for International Development, 1977] [240] p.

Examined in the Documentation Center, Sahel Development Program, AID, Washington, D.C.

4273

Report, inventory and preliminary management plan for the Niger Range and Livestock Project. Minneapolis, Experience Incorporated, 1976. [256] p. (in various pagings) illus., maps.

Prepared for the U.S. Agency for International Development.

Microfiche. [Washington, U.S. Agency for International Development, 1976?] 3 sheets (DLC-Sci RR PN-RAB-626); and [Sahel Documents and Dissertations. Ann Arbor, Mich., University Microfilms International, 1980] 3 sheets (DLC-Micro Microfiche 5357 NG 105).

4274

Schneider, Robert R. Preliminary study of the livestock market in the western zone of the Niger range and livestock project. Williamstown, Mass., Dept. of Economics, Williams College, [1980] 59 p.

Prepared for the U.S. Agency for International Development under contract AID/afr-C-168.

Examined in the Development Information Center, AID, Washington, D.C.

4275

Sutter, John W. Pastoral herding in the Arrondissement of Tanout; a socio-economic study prepared for the Niger Range and Livestock Project, Livestock Service, Ministry of Rural Development. Zinder, 1978. 55 p.

Study funded by the U.S. Agency for International Development.

Microfiche. [Sahel Documents and Dissertations. Ann Arbor, Mich., University Microfilms International, 1980] 1 sheet.

DLC-Micro Microfiche 5357 NG 076

4276

Wardle, Christopher. Promoting cattle fattening amongst peasants in Niger. Ann Arbor, Center for Research on Economic Development, University of Michigan, 1979. 42 p. (Livestock production and marketing in the Entente states of West Africa. Working paper, no. 2)   MiU

Prepared for the U.S. Agency for International Development under contract AID/afr-C-1169.

Copy examined in the Development Information Center, AID, Washington, D.C.

Assistance Programs

4277

U.S. Agency for International Development. Annual budget submission: Niger. Washington, U.S. International Development Cooperation Agency.

Vols. for 1976/77+ examined in the Devel-

opment Information Center, AID, Washington, D.C.

4278

——— Country development strategy statement: Niger. Washington, U.S. International Development Cooperation Agency. annual.

Vols. for 1981+ examined in the Development Information Center, AID, Washington, D.C.

Vol. for 1981 issued also in microfiche. [Sahel Documents and Dissertations. Ann Arbor, University Microfilms International, 1980] 1 sheet.

DLC-Micro Microfiche 5357 NG 019

4279

——— Training for development management in Niger. [Washington?], 1975. 24 p.   MiEM

4280

Bingen, R. James. Research/studies in Sahel francophone West Africa: Niger; an inventory of research, studies, and reports sponsored by the U.S. Agency for International Development. Washington, Sahel Development Program, U.S. Agency for International Development, 1977. [56] p.

Covers 36 projects undertaken in the period 1962–77.

Abstract for series on francophone West Africa and The Gambia in *A.I.D. Research and Development Abstracts*, Oct. 1977, p. 12–13.

Microfiche. [Washington, U.S. Agency for International Development, 1977?] 1 sheet.

DLC-Sci RR PN-AAD-516

4281

Niger. [*Treaties, etc. United States, 1976 June 9*] Niger, agricultural commodities: transfer under Title II. Agreement signed June 9, 1976, entered into force June 9, 1976; and amending agreement signed at Niamey July 1, 1977, entered into force July 1, 1977. *In* U.S. *Treaties, etc.* United States treaties and other international agreements, v. 29, 1976–77. [Washington, Dept. of State; for sale by the Supt. of Docs., U.S. Govt. Print. Off., 1980] p. 5708–5712. ([Treaties and other international acts series, 9143])   JX231.A34 v. 29

4282

Niger. [*Treaties, etc. United States, 1978 Apr. 25*] Niger, agricultural commodities: transfer under Title II. Agreement signed at Niamey April 25, 1978; entered into force April 25, 1978. *In* U.S. *Treaties, etc.* United States treaties and other international agreements, v. 30, 1978–79. [Washington, Dept. of State; for sale by the Supt. of Docs., U.S.

4282 (cont.)

Govt. Print. Off., 1980] p. 3077–3127. ([Treaties and other international acts series, 9380])

JX231.A34 v. 30

Authorizes the Commodity Credit Corporation to transfer and deliver food grain to Niger.

4283

Niger: program summary. [Washington?], Office of Sahel and Francophone West Africa Affairs, Bureau for Africa, U.S. Agency for International Development, 1977. [21] leaves. illus., maps.

Examined in the Documentation Center, Sahel Development Program, AID, Washington, D.C.

4284

Report on examination of AID programs administered at the Regional Development Office/Niamey. [Washington], Office of the Auditor General, U.S. Agency for International Development, 1977. 17 p.

Examined in the Development Information Center, AID, Washington, D.C.

4285

Report on examination of the Sahel Recovery and Rehabilitation Program, Niger. [Washington], Office of the Auditor General, U.S. Agency for International Development, 1975. 27 p.

Examined in the Development Information Center, AID, Washington, D.C.

4286

SDP review seminar: Niger. Washington, Sahel Development Program, U.S. Agency for International Development, 1977. 78 p.   MiEM

4287

Sahel recovery and rehabilitation program, Niger: proposal and recommendations. Washington, U.S. Agency for International Development, [1974] 1 v. (various pagings) map.

At head of title: Program assistance paper.

Examined in the Documentation Center, Sahel Development Program, AID, Washington, D.C.

4288

Technical Assistance Information Clearing House. Development assistance programs of U.S. non-profit organizations in Niger. [New York], American Council of Voluntary Agencies for Foreign Service, 1976. 13 p. maps. (TAICH country report)   DLC

The Clearing House is operated by the Council under a grant from the U.S. Agency for International Development.

4289

―――― Development assistance programs of U.S. non-profit organizations: Niger. 3d ed. [New York], American Council of Voluntary Agencies for Foreign Service, 1980. 23 p. maps. (TAICH country report)   DLC

Communications and Transportation

4290

Abdoua, Mamadou J. Evaluation des effets produits par le bitumage de la route trans-Saharienne sur l'économie de la région de Zinder. Tucson, Arid Lands Natural Resources Committee, University of Arizona, 1979. 55 p.   AzU

Issued as Appendix 6 of the *Final Report of the Natural Resource Planning Project for the Province of Zinder, Niger* (entry 4324).

Supported by the U.S. Agency for International Development.

Additional information on this document is given in entry 4324.

Copy examined in the Documentation Center, Sahel Development Program, AID, Washingtion, D.C.

4291

Feasibility study for the raising of the bridge at Gaya and the construction of the port of Gaya: interim report. Pottstown, Pa., Sanders & Thomas, inc., [1975] 35 leaves.

Prepared for the U.S. Agency for International Development and the Government of Niger.

Examined in the Documentation Center, Sahel Development Program, AID, Washington, D.C.

4292

Road construction progress detailed. *In* U.S. *Joint Publications Research Service.* JPRS 71449. [Springfield, Va., National Technical Information Service, 1978] (Translations on Sub-Saharan Africa, no. 1959) p. 104–108.

Translation of article in *Sahel hebdo*, Niamey, May 29, 1978, p. 4–5.

Microfiche. [Washington, Supt. of Docs., U.S. Govt. Print. Off., 1978]

DLC-Micro JPRS 71449

4293

Silverman, Theresa. Tele-Niger: adapting an electronic medium to a rural African context. Washington, Clearinghouse on Development Communications, Academy for Educational Development, 1976. 45 p. (Clearinghouse

4293 (cont.)

Development Communications. Information bulletin, no. 8)

"The Clearinghouse ... is supported by the Technical Assistance Bureau of the U.S. Agency for International Development, Washington, as part of its program in educational technology and development communications."

Abstract in *Government Reports Announcements & Index*, June 22, 1979, p. 42.

Microfiche. [Springfield, Va., National Technical Information Service, 1979] 1 sheet.

DLC-Sci RR PB-292904

4294

Tourawa, Dubois. Air Niger's financial problems noted. *In* U.S. *Joint Publications Research Service.* JPRS 74827. [Springfield, Va., National Technical Information Service, 1979] (Sub-Saharan Africa report, no. 2193) p. 38–41.

Translation of article in *Sahel Hebdo*, Niamey, Oct. 8, 1979, p. 15–17.

Microfiche. [s.l., 1980]

DLC-Micro JPRS 74827

Economic Conditions

4295

Analysis of Niger's five year economic and social development plan, 1979–83. [Niamey], U.S. AID Mission to Niger, 1980. [98] p. (in various pagings)

Examined in the Development Information Center, U.S. Agency for International Development, Washington, D.C.

4296

Appraisal of the natural resource and economic situation of the Province of Zinder, Niger. Tucson, Arid Lands Natural Resources Committee, University of Arizona, 1979. 238 p.   AzU

Issued as vol. 2 of the *Final Report of the Natural Resource Planning Project for the Province of Zinder, Niger* (entry 4324).

Supported by the U.S. Agency for International Development.

Issued also in French.

Additional information on this document is given in entry 4324.

Issued also in microfiche. [Sahel Documents and Dissertations. Ann Arbor, Mich., University Microfilms International, 1980] 4 sheets.

DLC-Micro Microfiche 5357 NG 011

4297

Arnould, Eric J. Petty craft production and the underdevelopment process in Zinder, Niger.

Tucson, Arid Lands Natural Resources Committee, University of Arizona, 1979. 15 p.

AzU

Issued as Appendix 8 of the *Final Report of the Natural Resource Planning Project for the Province of Zinder, Niger* (entry 4324).

Supported by the U.S. Agency for International Development.

Additional information on this documents is given in entry 4324.

Issued also in microfiche. [Sahel Documents and Dissertations. Ann Arbor, Mich., University Microfilms International, 1980] 1 sheet.

DLC-Micro Microfiche 5357 NG 078

4298

Foreign economic trends and their implications for the United States. Niger. 1969?+ Washington, for sale by the Supt. of Docs., U.S. Govt. Print. Off. annual. (International marketing information series)   HC10.E416

Continues *Economic Trends and Their Implications for the United States. Niger.*

Prepared by the U.S. Embassy, Niamey.

Vols. for 1969?–77 distributed by the U.S. Bureau of International Commerce; vol. for 1979 by the U.S. Industry and Trade Administration; vol. for 1980– by the U.S. International Trade Administration.

Not published in 1975, 1979; apparently not published in 1973.

The following issues for the period 1974–81 have been identified in L.C.:

ET 74-032. 1974. 7 p.

FET 76–045. 1976. 9 p.

FET 77–093. 1977. 9 p.

FET 78–087. 1978. 9 p.

FET 80–012. 1980. 11 p.

FET 81–039. 1981. 12 p.

4299

Horenstein, Nadine R. Macro-economic trends; Niger. [Washington?], 1979. [78] p.

Prepared for the U.S. Agency for International Development.

Microfiche. [Washington, U.S. Agency for International Development, 1979?] 1 sheet (PN-AAH-372); examined in the Development Information Center, AID, Washington, D.C.

4300

Kountché, Seyni. President Kountche discusses socioeconomic problems, projects. *In* U.S. *Joint Publications Research Service.* JPRS 67366. [Springfield, Va., National Technical Information Service, 1976] (Translations on Sub-Saharan Africa, no. 1654) p. 57–62.

4300 (cont.)

Translation of speech recorded in *Le Sahel,* Niamey, Apr. 28, 1976, p. 1, 8.

Microfiche. [s.l., 1976]

DLC-Micro JPRS 67366

4301

McCollough, J. M., M. H. Collion, *and* Eric J. Arnould. Markets: a study of markets and prices in Zinder, Niger. Tucson, Arid Lands Natural Resources Committee, University of Arizona, 1979. 42 p.　　　　　　　　　　　　AzU

Issued as Appendix 10 of the *Final Report of the Natural Resource Planning Project for the Province of Zinder, Niger* (entry 4324).

Supported by the U.S. Agency for International Development.

Additional information on this documents is given in entry 4324.

Issued also in microfiche. [Sahel Documents and Dissertations. Ann Arbor, Mich., University Microfilms International, 1980] 1 sheets.

DLC-Micro Microfiche 5357 NG 062

4302

Objectives of 1978–1983 five year plan noted. *In* U.S. *Joint Publications Research Service.* JPRS 75359. [Springfield, Va., National Technical Information Service, 1980] (Sub-Saharan Africa report, no. 2225) p. 109–115.

Translation of article in *Le Sahel,* Niamey, Feb. 8, 1980, p. 3, 4, 8.

Microfiche. [s.l., 1980]

DLC-Micro JPRS 75359

4303

President discusses development programs, uranium. *In* U.S. *Joint Publications Research Service.* JPRS 70682. [Springfield, Va., National Technical Information Service, 1978] (Translations on Sub-Saharan Africa, no. 1884) p. 78–84.

Translation of interview with President Seyni Kountché in *Afrique industrie infrastructures,* Paris, Jan. 15, 1978, p. 42–49.

Microfiche. [Washington, Supt. of Docs., U.S. Govt. Print. Off., 1978]

DLC-Micro JPRS 70682

4304

Three-year investment plan analyzed. *In* U.S. *Joint Publications Research Service.* JPRS 68045. [Springfield, Va., National Technical Information Service, 1976] (Translations on Sub-Saharan Africa, no. 1682) p. 38–43.

Translation of interview with Moussa Bako, Minister of Public Works, Transportation, and

Urbanism, in *Afrique industrie infrastructures,* Paris, Sept. 1, 1976, p. 46–49.

Microfiche. [s.l., 1976]

DLC-Micro JPRS 68045

Foreign Relations

4305

Garba, Isaaka. Nigerian-Libyan cooperation said to be increasing. *In* U.S. *Joint Publications Research Service.* JPRS 70682. [Springfield, Va., National Technical Information Service, 1978] (Translations on Sub-Saharan Africa, no. 1884) p. 85–89.

Translation of article in *Sahel Hebdo,* Niamey, Jan. 22, 1978, p. 6–7, 21.

Microfiche. [Washington, Supt. of Docs., U.S. Govt. Print. Off., 1978]

DLC-Micro JPRS 70682

4036

Kountche regime's diplomacy said to be prudent, independent. *In* U.S. *Joint Publications Research Service.* JPRS 74107. [Springfield, Va., National Technical Information Service, 1979] (Sub-Saharan Africa report, no. 2147) p. 102–105.

Translation of article in *Demain l'Afrique,* Paris, July 30, 1979, p. 33–34.

Microfiche. [Washington, Supt. of Docs., U.S. Govt. Print. Off., 1979]

DLC-Micro JPRS 74107

4307

Weiss, Danielle. President discusses foreign relations, uranium resources. *In* U.S. *Joint Publications Research Service.* JPRS 75545. [Springfield, Va., National Technical Information Service, 1980] (Sub-Saharan Africa report, no. 2238) p. 30–37.

Translation of interview with President Seyni Kountché, in *Europe Outremer,* Paris, Oct. 1979, p. 9–13.

Microfiche. [s.l., 1980]

DLC-Micro JPRS 75545

Geology, Hydrology, and Mineral Resources

4308

Diallo, Hamidou. Review of progress, plans in mining sector. *In* U.S. *Joint Publications Research Service.* JPRS 71148. [Springfield, Va., National Technical Information Service, 1978] (Translations on Sub-Saharan Africa, no. 1930) p. 43–49.

Translation of article in *Sahel hebdo,* Niamey, Apr. 15, 1978, p. 21–26.

4308 (cont.)

Microfiche. [Washington, Supt. of Docs., U.S. Govt. Print. Off., 1978]

DLC-Micro JPRS 71148

4309

Hoepffner, M. Etude hydrologique des bassins de Tabelot (campagne 1977) [s.l.], 1978. [70] p.

MiEM

Study supported in part by the U.S. Agency for International Development.

Uranium

4310

Data on new uranium mining company provided. *In* U.S. *Joint Publications Research Service.* JPRS 65787. [Springfield, Va., National Technical Information Service, 1975] (Translations on Africa, no. 1617) p. 24–29.

Translation of article on the Compagnie minière d'Akouta (COMINAK), in *Afrique industrie infrastructures*, Paris, Sept. 1, 1975, p. 34–35.

Microfiche. [s.l., 1975]

DLC-Micro JPRS 65787

4311

Gaudio, Attilio. Uranium accounts for growing share of national revenues. *In* U.S. *Joint Publications Research Service.* JPRS 69889. [Springfield, Va., National Technical Information Service, 1977] (Translations on Sub-Saharan Africa, no. 1809) p. 29–33.

Translation of article in *L'Opinion*, Rabat, Aug. 27, 1977, p. 4.

Microfiche. [s.l., 1977]

DLC-Micro JPRS 69889

4312

Horenstein, Nadine. Uranium and the Nigerian economy. [Washington?], 1979, 49 p. map.

Prepared for the U.S. Agency for International Development.

Microfiche. [Washington, U.S. Agency for International Development, 1979?] 1 sheet (PN-AAH-373); examined in the Development Information Center, AID, Washington, D.C.

4313

Impact of uranium on economy discussed. *In* U.S. *Joint Publications Research Service.* JPRS 72308. [Springfield, Va., National Technical Information Service, 1978] (Translations on Sub-Saharan Africa, no. 2029) p. 35–53. illus.

Translation of article in *Demain l'Afrique*, Paris, Oct. 1978, p. 61–70.

Microfiche. [Washington, Supt. of Docs., U.S. Govt. Print. Off., 1978]

DLC-Micro JPRS 72308

4314

Sigisbert, Geneviève. Uranium production, other mining activities reviewed. *In* U.S. *Joint Publications Research Service.* JPRS 67676. [Springfield, Va., National Technical Information Service, 1976] (Translations on Sub-Saharan Africa, no. 1665) p. 17–31. illus., map.

Translation of article in *Europe Outremer*, Paris, Mar. 1976, p. 35–40.

Microfiche. [s.l., 1976]

DLC-Micro JPRS 67676

Health and Nutrition

4315

Boostrom, Eugene R., Gladstone Fairweather, *and* James Neal. Report on health consultancy in Niger; October–November 1976. [Washington?], American Public Health Association, [1976?] [157] leaves (in various foliations) map.

Prepared for the U.S. Agency for International Development under contract AID/afr-C-1253.

Examined in the Documentation Center, Sahel Development Program, AID, Washington, D.C.

4316

Lythcott, George I., Theresa Dupuis, *and* Richard V. Bernhart. Niger: DEIDS reconnaissance, Oct. 8–20, 1973. [Washington, 1973] [8] p. map.

Prepared for the U.S. Agency for International Development under contract AID/csd-3423.

Focus is on maternal and child health, family planning and nutrition, especially in rural areas.

Microfiche. [Washington, U.S. Agency for International Development, 1973?] 1 sheet.

DLC-Sci RR PN-AAB-574

4317

Maternal and child health/child spacing project, Republic of Niger; final report. [Geneva?], Organization for Rehabilitation through Training, [1975] [87] p. (in various pagings)

Prepared for the U.S. Agency for International Development under contract AID/afr-389.

On cover: American ORT Federation.

Covers field operations for the period Dec. 1972–Jan. 1975.

Abstract in *A.I.D Research and Development Abstracts*, Apr. 1978, p. 30.

Microfiche. [Washington, U.S. Agency for International Development, 1975?] 1 sheet.

DLC-Sci RR PN-RAB-632

4318

Niger. [*Treaties, etc. United States, 1978 June 1*]
Project grant agreement between the Republic of
Niger and the United States of America for rural
health improvement. *In* U.S. *Treaties, etc.* United
States treaties and other international agreements,
v. 30, 1978–79. [Washington, Dept. of State; for
sale by the Supt. of Docs., U.S. Govt. Print. Off.,
1980] p. 3083–3127. ([Treaties and other international acts series, 9381])   JX231.A34 v. 30

Signed at Niamey June 1, 1978.

At head of title: AID project no. 683-0208.

In English and French.

Politics and Government

4319

Decraene, Philippe. Political, economic development reported. *In* U.S. *Joint Publications Research
Service.* JPRS 72390. [Springfield, Va., National
Technical Information Service, 1978] (Translations
on Sub-Saharan Africa, no. 2034) p. 74–83.

Translation of article in *Le Monde*, Paris, Oct.
28–30, 1978.

Microfiche. [Washington, Supt. of Docs., U.S.
Govt. Print. Off., 1978]

DLC-Micro JPRS 72390

4320

Ibrahim, Cisse. Security director discusses police.
In U.S. *Joint Publications Research Service.* JPRS
67639. [Springfield, Va., National Technical Information Service, 1976] (Translations on Sub-
Saharan Africa, no. 1663) p. 33–36.

Translation of interview with Abdou Diori,
Director of National Security, in *Sahel Hebdo*,
Niamey, June 14, 1976, p. 16–17.

Microfiche. [s.l., 1976]

DLC-Micro JPRS 67639

Population Studies

4321

Africa: Niger. Selected statistical data by sex.
Washington, 1981. 31, 17 p.   DLC

Study supported by the U.S. Agency for International Development's Office of Women in Development and Office of Population.

Data assembled by the International Demographic
Data Center, U.S. Bureau of the Census.

The only statistical information provided is based
on 1960 data; for most headings, no data is recorded.

4322

Profiles of Sahelian countries: Niger. Washington,

Socio-Economic Analysis Staff, International
Statistical Programs Center, U.S. Bureau of the
Census, 1974. [41] leaves (in various folations).

Prepared at the request of the U.S. Agency for
International Development.

Concerns demographic projections.

Examined in the Documentation Center, Sahel
Development Program, AID, Washington, D.C.

Other Subjects

4323

U.S. *Information Agency. Office of Research.* Evaluation of *Courrier* news/feature bulletin in Niger.
[Washington?], 1977. 11 p.

"E-6-77."

Survey of readers of a weekly French language
bulletin issued by the agency in Niger.

Brief abstract in *American Statistics Index*,
1978, Abstracts, p. 899.

Microfiche. [Washington, Congressional Information Service, 1978?]

DLC-Micro ASI:78 9856-2.84

4324

Arizona. University. *Arid Lands Natural Resources
Committee.* Final report of the Natural Resource
Planning Project for the Province of Zinder, Niger.
Tucson, 1979. 3 v., 11 appendixes.   AzU

"The activities which are culminated in this final
report were supported by the U.S. Agency for
International Development, Office of Science and
Technology, grant AID/ta-G-1111 [and] Africa
Bureau contract AID/afr-G-1147."

Includes bibliographies.

AzU holds report uncataloged (cite C0134762).

Copy examined in the Documentation Center,
Sahel Development Program, AID, Washington,
D.C.

Note: The individual volumes and appendixes of the report
are cited separately in this guide; they can be identified through
the index under *Final Report of the Natural Resource Planning
Project for the Province of Zinder, Niger.*

4325

Crow, John E., *and* Helen K. Henderson. A report
of survey findings from three villages in Zinder,
Niger. Tucson, Arid Lands Natural Resources
Committee, University of Arizona, 1979. 52 p.

AzU

Issued as Appendix 9 of the *Final Report of the
Natural Resource Planning Project for the Province
of Zinder, Niger* (entry 4324).

Supported by the U.S. Agency for International
Development.

4325 (cont.)

Additional information on this document is given in entry 4324.

Copy examined in the Documentation Center, Sahel Development Program, AID, Washington, D.C.

4326

Description of final report and planning methodology. Tucson, Arid Lands Natural Resources Committee, University of Arizona, 1979. 26 p. AzU

Issued as vol. 1 of the *Final Report of the Natural Resource Planning Project for the Province of Zinder, Niger* (entry 4324).

Supported by the U.S. Agency for International Development.

Additional information on this document is given in entry 4324.

Issued also in microfiche. [Sahel Documents and Dissertations. Ann Arbor, Mich., University Microfilms, International, 1980] 1 sheet.

DLC-Micro Microfiche 5357 NG 023

4327

Final list of collected documents. Tucson, Arid Lands Natural Resources Committee, University of Arizona, 1979. 59 p. AzU

Issued as Appendix 11 of the *Final Report of the Natural Resource Planning Project for the Province of Zinder, Niger* (entry 4324).

Supported by the U.S. Agency for International Development.

Additional information on this document is given in entry 4324.

Issued also in microfiche. [Sahel Documents and Dissertations. Ann Arbor, Mich., University Microfilms International, 1980] 1 sheet.

DLC-Micro Microfiche 5357 NG 041

4328

Lindblad, Carl. Recommendations for the Niger rodent control project with proposed expanded ancilliary activities and training outline. [Niamey?], Peace Corps/Niger, 1978. 1 v. (various pagings)

Examined in the Development Information Center, U.S. Agency for International Development, Washington, D.C.

4329

Localization of an experimental ecological unit in the Maradi region of Nigeria [*sic*], [by] M. Mainguet [et al.] Washington, National Aeronautics and Space Administration, 1977. [335] p. maps. (U.S. National Aeronautics and Space Administration. NASA technical memorandum 75085)

Translation of French text.

Concerns a region in southern Niger.

Microfiche. [s.l., 1978] 4 sheets.

DLC-Sci RR N78-12553

4330

Matlock, W. Gerald, *and* Nancy Ferguson. Combatting desertification in Zinder. Tucson, Arid Lands Natural Resources Committee, University of Arizona, 1979. 26 p. AzU

Issued as Appendix 2 of the *Final Report of the Natural Resource Planning Project for the Province of Zinder, Niger* (entry 4324).

Supported by the U.S. Agency for International Development.

Additional information on this document is given in entry 4324.

Issued also in microfiche. [Sahel Documents and Dissertations. Ann Arbor, Mich., University Microfilms International, 1980] 1 sheet.

DLC-Micro Microfiche 5357 NG 017

4331

Ministers give details on 1981 budget. *In* U.S. *Joint Publications Research Service.* JPRS 76637. [Springfield, Va., National Technical Information Service, 1980] (Sub-Saharan Africa report, no. 2307) p. 49–55.

Translation of article in *Le Sahel*, Niamey, Sept. 22, 1980, p. 3–4, 5.

Microfiche. [s.l., 1980]

DLC-Micro JPRS 76637

4332

Niger. [*Treaties, etc. United States, 1975 July 21*] Agreement to provide certain social security benefits for certain employees of the United States of America in the Republic of Niger. *In* U.S. *Treaties, etc.* United States treaties and other international agreements, v. 26, 1976. [Washington, Dept. of State; for sale by the Supt. of Docs., U.S. Govt. Print. Off., 1977] p. 2758–2765. ([Treaties and other international acts series, 8194])

JX231.A34 v. 26

Signed at Niamey July 21, 1975.

In English and French.

4333

Stokelin, Freddie L. Marketing in Niger. Washington, U.S. Dept. of Commerce, International Trade Commission; [for sale by the Supt. of Docs., U.S. Govt. Print. Off.], 1981. 7 p. (Overseas business reports. OBR 81-15)

HF91.U482 1981, no. 15

International marketing information series.

Issued also in microfiche. [Washington, Congressional Information Service, 1981?]

DLC-Micro ASI:81 2046-6.11

4334

Urry, J. B., Nancy Ferguson, *and* D. A. Mouat. A natural resources analysis of the Province of Zinder, Niger using remote sensing techniques. Tucson, Arid Lands Natural Resources Committee, University of Arizona, 1979. 23 p.   AzU

Issued as Appendix 1 of the *Final Report of the Natural Resource Planning Project for the Province of Zinder, Niger* (entry 4324).

Supported by the U.S. Agency for International Development.

Additional information on this documents is given in entry 4324.

Issued also in microfiche. [Sahel Documents and Dissertations. Ann Arbor, Mich., University Microfilms International, 1980] 1 sheet.
DLC-Micro Microfiche 5357 NG 023

4335

Woman in Niger   her role in traditional society and the possibilities of her integration into the national economy. [Niamey?], USAID/Niger, 1974. 16 p.

Examined in the Development Information Center, AID, Washington, D.C.

4336

Wright, Albert. Solar energy program described. *In* U.S. *Joint Publications Research Service*. JPRS 70051. [Springfield, Va., National Technical Information Service, 1977] (Translations on Sub-Saharan Africa, no. 1824) p. 35–39.

Translation of article in *Le Sahel*, Niamey, Aug. 6, 1977.

Microfiche. [s.l., 1977]
DLC-Micro JPRS 70051

Nigeria

General

4337

U.S. *Dept. of State.* Post report. Nigeria. [Washington?], 1978. 40 p. illus., map. JX1705.A286 Spec. Format

Includes reports on Lagos, Ibadan, Kaduna, and Kano.

For a description of the contents of this publication, see the note to entry 936.

4338

U.S. *Dept. of State. Bureau of Public Affairs.* Background notes. Nigeria. [Washington, for sale by the Supt. of Docs., U.S. Govt. Print. Off.], 1980. 7 p. illus., maps (U.S. Dept. of State. Department of State publication 7953). G59.U5

L.C. retains only the latest revision.

For a description of the contents of this publication, see the note to entry 937.

4339

Nigeria, a country study; Foreign Area Studies, the American University; edited by Harold D. Nelson. 4th ed. Washington, for sale by the Supt. of Docs., U.S. Govt. Print. Off., c1982. xxviii, 358 p. illus., maps. DT515.22.N53 1982

Rev. ed. of: *Area Handbook for Nigeria,* [by] Harold D. Nelson. Rev. 3rd ed., 1972 (DT515.N37 1972).

Bibliography: p. 309–343.

Among the appendixes are the following:

Table 2. Censuses and estimates of the Nigerian population (p. 290).

Table 3. Major ethnolinguistic categories (in percent of total population) (p. 291).

Table 14. Federal election results, 1979 (p. 302–303).

Table 15. Daily newspapers of Nigeria, indicating estimated circulation and political affiliation (p. 304).

Table 16–18. Major military weapons (p. 305–308).

4340

A Nigerian notebook: units and resources for teachers and parents, early childhood and elementary, [by] Necia Harkless [et al.] [Lexington?], Nigerian Curriculum Development Project, College of Education, University of Kentucky, 1980. 75 p. illus., maps.

A resource book for teaching about Nigeria.

Microfiche. [Arlington, Va., ERIC Document Reproduction Service; prepared for Educational Resources Information Center, National Institute of Education, 1981] 1 sheet.

DLC-Micro ED197014

Agriculture

4341

Awa, Njoku E. Food production problems of small farmers in low-technology nations: some evidence from Nigeria. Ithaca, Dept. of Communication Arts, New York State College of Agriculture and Life Sciences, Cornell University, 1980. 16 p. map. (Cornell international agriculture monograph, no. 79)

Bibliography: p. 15–16.

Abstract in *A.I.D. Research & Development Abstracts,* v. 9, no. 4, 1981, p. 5.

Microfiche. [Washington, U.S. Agency for International Development, 1980?] 1 sheet.

DLC-Sci RR PN-AAJ-036

4342

Boyd, A. H. Report to Ahmadu Bello University, Institute for Agricultural Research, OAU Joint Cereal Grains Research Project 26, USAID/Lagos and AID/W—foundation seed project facilities for ABU/IAR. Mississippi State, Seed Technology Laboratory, Mississippi State University, 1975. [39] p. map.

Prepared under contract for the U.S. Agency for International Development.

Abstract in *A.I.D. Research and Development Abstracts,* Apr. 1976, p. 3.

4342 (cont.)

Microfiche. [Washington, U.S. Agency for International Development, 1975?] 1 sheet.

DLC-Sci RR PN-AAB-471

4343

Boyd, J. E. L., *and* E. A. Ayok. Farm equipment development project, Daudawa, N.C.S., Nigeria. Report for Nov. 1971 – Dec. 1973. London, Intermediate Technology Development Group, c1974. [113] p. illus..

N.C.S. North-Central State.

Abstract in *Appropriate Technology Information for Developing Countries*, 2d ed., 1979, p. 221.

Microfiche. [Springfield, Va., National Technical Information Service, 1979] 2 sheets.

DLC-Micro PB-297784

4344

Cassava's role as a food staple; a cross disciplinary systems analysis of nutrition problems in a cassava dependent culture, [by] Jay E. April [et al.] Boulder, University of Colorado, 1974. [189] p. (in various pagings)

Prepared for the Office of Nutrition, Bureau for Technical Assistance, U.S. Agency for International Development, under contract AID/CM/ta-C-73-44.

Focus is on southern Nigeria.

Abstract in *A.I.D. Research and Development Abstracts*, Apr. 1978, p. 20.

Microfiche. [Washington, U.S. Agency for International Development, 1974?] 2 sheets.

DLC-Sci RR PN-AAD-711

4345

Chong, Kwong-Yuan. A simulation policy analysis of the Western Nigerian cocoa industry. [East Lansing], Dept. of Agricultural Economics, Michigan State University, 1973. 155 p.

Bibliography: p. 152–155.

Thesis (Ph.D.)—Michigan State University.

In his acknowledgements, the author notes the "general financial support" of the U.S. Agency for International Development under contracts AID/csd-1557 and AID/csd-211d.

Microfiche. [Washington, U.S. Agency for International Development, 1973?] 2 sheets.

DLC-Sci RR PN-AAB-764

Microfilm. [Ann Arbor, Mich., University Microfilms International, 1973]

DLC-Micro 73-29678

4346

―――― Some illustrative policy runs using the Nigerian agricultural system simulation model for developmental planning. [East Lansing, Mich.?], 1973. 5 leaves.

"The work was performed under USAID contracts AID/csd-1557 and AID/csd-2975."

"Presented at the Sixth Hawaii International Conference on Systems Sciences, Honolulu, Hawaii, January 1973."

Microfiche. [Washington, U.S. Agency for International Development, 1973?] 1 sheet.

DLC-Sci RR PN-AAA-880

4347

Monu, Erasmus D. An appraisal of the contribution of rural sociological and agricultural extension research to the transfer of technology to small scale farmers in Nigeria. [s.l.], 1980. 37 p.

Paper presented at a meeting of the Rural Sociological Society, 1980.

Abstract in *Resources in Education*, Apr. 1981, p. 105.

Microfiche. [Arlington, Va., ERIC Document Reproduction Service; prepared for Educational Resources Information Center, National Institute of Education, 1981] 1 sheet.

DLC-Micro ED195365

4348

Nigeria. [*Treaties, etc. United States, 1980 July 23*] Memorandum of understanding on cooperation in the field of agriculture between the Government of the United States of America and the Government of the Federal Republic of Nigeria. [Washington, Dept. of State; for sale by the Supt. of Docs., U.S. Govt. Print. Off., 1981] 5 p. (Treaties and other international acts series, 9819)   DLC

Signed at Lagos July 23, 1980.

4349

Nigerian food supply: a summary. [Washington?], 1974. 10 p.

Study conducted by the U.S. Foreign Agricultural Service in cooperation with the National Association of State Departments of Agriculture.

Microprint. [New York, Readex Microprint, 1976] 1 sheet.   DLC-Micro Month. Cat. Govt. Pubs., 1975 no. 15746

4350

Norman, David W., David H. Pryor, *and* Christopher J. N. Gibbs. Technical change and the small farmer in Hausaland, Northern Nigeria. East Lansing, African Rural Economy Program, Dept. of Agricultural Economics, Michigan State University, 1979. 127 p. map. (African rural economy paper, no. 21)   HD2145.5.Z9N677

Published under U.S. Agency for International Development contract AID/afr-C-1260.

4350 (cont.)

Issued with the Dept. of Economics, Kansas State University, and the Institute for Agricultural Research, Ahmahu Bello University, Zaria, Nigeria.

Bibliography: p. 114–122.

Abstract in *A.I.D. Research and Development Abstracts*, v. 8, no. 2, 1980, p. 23.

Issued also in microfiche. [Washington, U.S. Agency for International Development, 1979?] 2 sheets (DLC-Sci RR PN-AAG-951); and [Sahel Documents and Dissertations. Ann Arbor, Mich., University Microfilms International, 1980] 2 sheets (DLC-Micro Microfiche 5357 AS 336).

4351

Program Planning Workshop on Cassava Dependent Food Systems in Nigeria, *Ibadan, 1975*. Proceedings. [Boulder], Taximetric Laboratory, University of Colorado, 1976. 17 p.

Sponsored by the U.S. Agency for International Development.

Workshop held at the International Institute of Tropical Agriculture, Ibadan, Nigeria, June 16–18, 1975.

Microfiche. [Washington, U.S. Agency for International Development, 1975?] 1 sheet.

DLC-Sci RR PN-AAE-314

4352

——— [Report] [s.l., 1975] [25] p. illus.

Sponsored in part by the U.S. AID Mission to Nigeria.

On cover: Program Planning Workshop, Food Nutrition Systems in Cassava Dependent Nigeria.

Rapporteurs: Taximetric Laboratory, University of Colorado.

Microfiche. [Washington, U.S. Agency for International Development, 1975?] 1 sheet.

DLC-Sci RR PN-AAE-738

4353

A Review of USAID projects in four major livestock producing states in Nigeria: an assessment of range management, [by] James D. Bates [et al.] Research Triangle, N.C., Statistics Research Division, Research Triangle Institute, 1975. 171 p. illus., map.

DLC

"RTI project 26U-853; final report."

On cover: U.S. Agency for International Development, Washington, D.C.

Covers Benue Plateau, North Central, North Eastern, and North Western states.

Abstract in *A.I.D. Research and Development Abstracts*, Jan. 1979, p. 10.

Issued also in microfiche. [Washington, U.S. Agency for International Development, 1975?] 2 sheets.

DLC-Sci RR PN-AAF-029

4354

Robinson, K. L., *and* A. O. Falusi. The present and potential role of fertilizer in meeting Nigeria's food requirements. Ithaca, Dept. of Agricultural Economics, New York State College of Agriculture and Life Sciences, Cornell University, 1974. 13 p.

Abstract in *A.I.D. Research and Development Abstracts*, Jan. 1976, p. 23–24.

Microfiche. [Washington, U.S. Agency for International Development, 1974?] 1 sheet.

DLC-Sci RR PN-AAB-266

4355

Shuler, Alexanderina V. Minikits and maxi yields. War on hunger, v. 10, Nov. 1976: 7–10. illus.

HD9000.1.W37 1976

Issued by the U.S. Agency for International Development.

Describes the seed and fertilizer "minikits" used on an experimental basis by maize and rice farmers in Nigeria.

4356

Starns, William W. Land tenure among the rural Hausa. Madison, Land Tenure Center, University of Wisconsin, 1974. 39 p. maps. (Wisconsin. University—Madison. Land Tenure Center. LTC, no. 104)

DT515.42.S8

Abstract in *A.I.D. Research and Development Abstracts*, July 1975, p. 32.

Issued also by the African Studies Program, University of Wisconsin (DT515.42.S8 1974).

Issued also in microfiche. [Washington, U.S. Agency for International Development, 1974?] 1 sheet.

DLC-Sci RR PN-AAB-071

4357

System simulation and agricultural development policy making, [by] Michael H. Abkin [et al.] [East Lansing, Dept. of Agricultural Economics, Michigan State University, 1973] 60 p.

Concerns agricultural development policy in Nigeria.

Abstract in *A.I.D. Research and Development Abstracts*, July 1975, p. 15.

Microfiche. [Washington, U.S. Agency for International Development, 1973?] 1 sheet.

DLC-Sci RR PN-AAA-986

4358

System simulation of agricultural development: some Nigerian policy comparisons. [East Lansing], Michigan State University Agricultural Sector Simulation Team, [1973] 49 p.

"The research reported here was done under

4358 (cont.)

U.S. Agency for International Development contracts AID/csd-1557 and AID/csd-2975."

Microfiche. [Washington, U.S. Agency for International Development, 1973?] 1 sheet.

DLC-Sci RR PN-AAB-762

4359

Wallace, Tina. The impact of a large-scale irrigation scheme on two wards in a small town in Kano State, Nigeria: its implications for rural development. *In* Southall, Aidan. Small urban centers in rural development in Africa. Madison, African Studies Program, University of Wisconsin-Madison, 1979. p. 241–256.

Concerns Chiromawa.

A grant from the Office of Urban Development, U.S. Agency for International Development, assisted in the preparation for publication of the papers collected in the study.

Microfiche. [Washington, U.S. Agency for International Development, 1980?] (PN-AAJ-064); examined in the Development Information Center, Agency for International Development, Washington, D.C.

Economic Aspects

4360

Ejiga, N. O. O., and K. L. Robinson. The economics of cowpea marketing in Nigeria. Ithaca, N.Y., Dept. of Agricultural Economics, New York State College of Agricultural and Life Sciences, Cornell University, 1981. 73 p. (Cornell international agriculture monograph, no. 82)

Bibliography: p. 66–69.

Abstract in *A.I.D. Research & Development Abstracts*, v. 9, no. 3, 1981, p. 34.

Microfiche. [Washington, U.S. Agency for International Development, 1981?] 1 sheet.

DLC-Sci RR PN-AAH-502

4361

Matlon, Peter J. Income distribution among farmers in Northern Nigeria: empirical results and policy implications. [East Lansing, African Rural Economy Program, Dept. of Agricultural Economics, Michigan State University, 1979] 11 p. (African rural economy paper, no. 18)   MiEM

Published under U.S. Agency for International Development contract AID/ta-C-1328.

Bibliography: p. 105–108.

Abstract in *A.I.D Research and Development Abstracts*, v. 7, no. 1, 1979, p. 4.

Issued also in microfiche. [Washington, U.S. Agency for International Development, 1979?] 2

sheets (DLC-Sci RR PN-AAG-617); and [Sahel Documents and Dissertations. Ann Arbor, Mich., University Microfilms International, 1980] 2 sheets (DLC-Micro Microfiche 5357 AS 141).

4362

—— The size distribution, structure, and determinants of personal income among farmers in the north of Nigeria. [Ithaca, N.Y.], Cornell University, 1977. xxiv, 491 p.

Field work for study supported by the U.S. Agency for International Development.

Microfiche. [Sahel Documents and Dissertations. Ann Arbor, Mich., University Microfilms International, 1980] 6 sheets.

DLC-Micro Microfiche 5357 AS 305

4363

Nigeria's producer prices for oilseeds hurt marketing. Foreign agriculture, Feb. 16, 1976: 8–9.

HD1401.F65   1976

Issued by the U.S. Foreign Agricultural Service.

4364

Norman, David W. Inter-disciplinary research on rural development; the experience of the Rural Economy Research Unit in Northern Nigeria. [Washington,], Overseas Liaison Committee, American Council on Education, 1974. 46 p. (American Council on Education. Overseas Liaison Committee. OLC paper, no. 6)

Bibliography: p. 43–46.

Activities of the Overseas Liaison Committee are supported in part through a contract with the U.S. Agency for International Development.

Discusses the activities of the Rural Economy Research Unit (RERU) of Ahmadu Bello University, Nigeria.

Microfiche. [Washington, U.S. Agency for International Development, 1974?] 1 sheet.

DLC-Sci RR PN-AAD-704

4365

Simmons, Emmy B. Economic research on women in rural development in Northern Nigeria. [Washington], Overseas Liaison Committee, American Council on Education, 1976. 34 p. (American Council on Education. Overseas Liaison Committee. OLC paper, no. 10)   DLC

Activities of the Overseas Liaison Committee are supported in part through a contract with the U.S. Agency for International Development.

Abstract in *A.I.D. Research and Development Abstracts*, Jan. 1978, p. 5.

Issued also in microfiche. [Washington, U.S. Agency for International Development, 1976?] 1 sheet.   DLC-Sci RR PN-AAD-705

Fisheries

4366

Danson, Kobina. Nigeria fishes for self-sufficiency: a new crash program to boost fish production is taking shape. Agenda, Oct. 1981: 19–20. illus.

HC59.7.A742   1981

Issued by the U.S. Agency for International Development.

4367

Johnson, Malcolm C. Fish-pond site selection, Mid-Western State, Nigeria. Auburn, Ala., International Center for Aquaculture, [1974] 13 p.

Based on a survey conducted during the period June 30–July 19, 1974.

Microfiche. [Washington, U.S. Agency for International Development, 1974?] 1 sheet.

DLC-Sci RR PN-RAA-971

4368

Ladipo, Olasupo O. General system analysis and simulation approach: a preliminary application to Nigerian fisheries. [East Lansing], Dept. of Agricultural Economics, Michigan State University, 1973. 315 p.

Bibliography: p. 310–315.

Dissertation—Michigan State University.

Microfiche. [Washington, U.S. Agency for International Development, 1973?] 4 sheets.

DLC-Sci RR PN-AAB-774

Microfilm. [Ann Arbor, Mich., University Microfilms International, 1973]

DLC-Micro 73-29736

Forests and Forestry

4369

Lambrecht, Dora. Nigeria and its wood: how a vital resource is disappearing. Agenda, Jan. 1978: 18–20.

HC59.7.A742   1978

Issued by the U.S. Agency for International Development.

4370

Nweke, Felix I. A systems analysis and simulation study of Nigerian forestry sector: wood consumption component. [East Lansing], Dept. of Agricultural Economics, Michigan State University, 1975. 291 p.

Bibliography: p. 288–291.

Field research supported by the U.S. Agency

for International Development through contracts AID/csd-2975 and AID/csd-2826.

Dissertation—Michigan State University.

Microfiche. [Washington, U.S. Agency for International Development, 1975?] 4 sheets; and [Ann Arbor, Mich., University Microfilms International, 1976?] (DLC-Micro 76-12501) (DLC-Sci RR PN-AAD-087)

Assistance Programs

4371

U.S. *Agency for International Development*. Annual budget submission: Nigeria. [Washington?]

Vol. for 1981 examined in the Development Information Center, AID, Washington, D.C.

4372

Beard, Eugene, *and* Richard V. Bernhart. Report on evaluation of Opportunities Industrialization Centre, Lagos, Nigeria, for Industrial Training Fund, Lagos, Nigeria. McLean, Va., Operations Analysis Division, General Research Corporation, 1974. 128 p.

"Report OAD-CR-65."

Prepared for the U.S. Agency for International Development under contract AID/CM/otr-C-73-198.

Abstract in *A.I.D. Research and Development Abstracts*, Sept. 1975, p. 23–24.

Microfiche. [Washington, U.S. Agency for International Development, 1975?] 2 sheets.

DLC-Sci RR PN-AAB-177

4373

Davis, Morris. Some political dimensions of international relief: two cases. International organization, v. 28. 1974: 127–140.   JX1901.I55

"The present commentary is part of a larger project on international relief as a political process which is being facilitated by National Science Foundation grant GS-31333."—p. 127.

Nigeria and Bangladesh are the case studies.

4374

Technical Assistance Information Clearing House. Development assistance programs of U.S. non-profit organizations: Nigeria. [New York], American Council of Voluntary Agencies for Foreign Service, 1979,. 35 p. maps. (TAICH country report)

HC517.N48T4a

The Clearing House is operated by the Council under a grant from the U.S. Agency for International Development.

Commerce

4375

U.S. *Industry and Trade Administration.* Industrial process controls: Nigeria. [Washington], 1979. 8 p. (Country market survey. CMS 79-211)

International marketing information series.

Examined in the Asia-Africa Division, Office of Country Marketing, U.S. Dept. of Commerce.

4376

Brooks, Willie. Nigeria is potential growth market for U.S. processed foods. Foreign agriculture, Apr. 7, 1975: 5–6, 13 illus.   HD1401.F65   1975

Issued by the U.S. Foreign Agricultural Service.

4377

Country commercial program for Nigeria; fiscal year 1976. [Washington?], U.S. Dept. of Commerce, [1975?] 29 p.

Issued in cooperation with the U.S. Dept. of State and the U.S. Embassy, Lagos.

Microprint. [New York, Readex Microprint, 1976] 1 sheet.   DLC-Micro Month. Cat. Govt Pubs., 1975 no. 11355

4378

Doing business in Nigeria sometimes complicated, but rewards can be worthwhile. Commerce America, Nov. 8, 1976: 24–25. illus.
HF1.C38

Issued by the U.S. Dept. of Commerce.

4379

Market for industrial process control equipment, Nigeria. Chislehurst, Eng., SIRA Institute, ltd., 1978. 59 p.

Prepared for Domestic and International Business Administration, U.S. Dept. of Commerce.

Abstract in *Government Reports Announcements & Index*, June 9, 1978, p. 26.

Microfiche. [Springfield, Va., National Technical Information Service, 1978] 1 sheet.
DLC-Sci RR DIB-78-04-511

4380

Market share reports. Country series: Nigeria, 1971–75. [Washington], U.S. Dept. of Commerce; for sale by the National Technical Information Service, Springfield, Va., [1977] 69 p.

Indicates the United States share of the market in Nigeria for various products compared to the shares for Belgium-Luxemburg, France, Federal Republic of Germany, Great Britain, Italy, Netherlands, Sweden, and Japan.

Microfiche. [Washington, Congressional Information Service, 1977?]
DLC-Micro ASI:77 2016-1.69

4381

Market share reports. Country series: Nigeria, 1975–79. [Washington], International Trade Administration, U.S. Dept. of Commerce; for sale by the National Technical Information Service, Springfield, Va., [1979] 69 p.

Includes same comparative data as in *Market Share Reports. Country series: Nigeria, 1971–75* (entry 4380).

Microfiche. [Washington, Congressional Information Service, 1979?]
DLC-Micro ASI:81 2046-2.69

4382

Moe, Lyle E. Nigeria's economic boom holds promise for U.S. farm sales. Foreign agriculture, Apr. 7, 1975: 2–4. illus.   HD1401.F65   1975

Issued by the U.S. Foreign Agricultural Service.

4383

Nigeria: a survey of U.S. export opportunities. Washington, International Trade Administration, U.S. Dept. of Commerce; [for sale by the Supt. of Docs., U.S. Govt. Print. Off.], 1981. 104 p. map.
DLC

4384

Nigeria: solar market conditions and potential. Washington, Systems Consultants, inc., 1981. 10 p.   DLC

On cover: Solar Energy Research Institute International Market Development Program (DOE).

Prepared under contract to the Solar Energy Research Institute, Golden, Colo., as part of the Export Information Task No. 1168.20 for the U.S. Dept. of Energy.

4385

Nigeria's import needs can help U.S. suppliers narrow huge trade gap. Commerce America, Apr. 24, 1978, 22–23. illus.   HF1.C38

Issued by the U.S. Dept. of Commerce.

4386

Rydlun, Rodney P. Marketing in Nigeria. [Washington], U.S. Dept. of Commerce, Domestic and International Business Administration; [for sale by the Supt. of Docs., U.S. Govt. Print. Off.], 1976. 37 p. (Overseas business reports. OBR 76-26)
HF91.U482   1976, no. 26

International marketing information series.

4386 (cont.)

Superseded by *Marketing in Nigeria* (Overseas business reports. OBR 79-11; entry 4387).

Issued also in microfiche. [Washington, Congressional Information Service, 1976?]

DLC-Micro ASI:76 2026-5:24

4387

Zassenhaus, Harold R. Marketing in Nigeria. [Washington], U.S. Dept. of Commerce, Industry and Trade Administration; [for sale by the Supt. of Docs., U.S. Govt. Print. Off.], 1979. 41 p. (Overseas business reports. OBR 79-11)

HF91.U482   1979, no. 11

International marketing information series.

Supersedes *Marketing in Nigeria* (Overseas business reports. OBR 76-26; entry 4386).

Communications and Transportation

4388

Nigeria. [*Treaties, etc. United States, 1975 June 4*] Nigeria telecommunication: embassy facilities. Agreement effected by exchange of notes dated at Washington November 19 and 22, 1974 and June 4, 1975; entered into force June 4, 1975. *In* U.S. *Treaties, etc.* United States treaties and other international agreements, v. 27, 1976. [Washington, Dept. of State; for sale by the Supt. of Docs., U.S. Govt. Print. Off., 1977] p. 3297–3300. ([Treaties and other international acts series, 8364])

JX231.A34 v. 27

Concerns radio links between the Ministry of External Affairs, Lagos, and the Nigerian Embassy, Washington, D.C.

4389

Nigeria. [*Treaties, etc. United States, 1978 Apr. 27*] Air transport agreement between the Federal Military Government of the Federal Republic of Nigeria and the Government of the United States of America. *In* U.S. *Treaties, etc.* United States treaties and other international agreements, v. 29, 1976–77. [Washington, Dept. of State; for sale by the Supt. of Docs., U.S. Govt. Print. Off., 1979] p. 3102–3115. ([Treaties and other international acts series, 8999])   JX231.A34 v. 29

Signed at Lagos, Apr. 17, 1978, entered into force definitively June 16, 1978, with memorandum of understanding signed at Lagos Nov. 4, 1977.

Concerns commercial air service between the two countries.

Economic Conditions

4390

U.S. *Bureau of International Commerce.* Nigeria: a survey of U.S. business opportunities. [Washington], U.S. Dept. of Commerce, Domestic and International Business Administration, Bureau of International Commerce; for sale by the Supt. of Docs., U.S. Govt. Print. Off., 1976. 190 p. illus. (Country market sectoral survey)

HC517.N48U53   1976

International marketing information series. Bibliography: p. 177–178.

4391

[U.S. *Central Intelligence Agency*] Nigeria; economic activity. [Washington, 1977] col. map.

G8841.G1   1977.U5

Scale not given.
"503485 10-77."

4392

U.S. *Congress. Senate. Committee on Banking, Housing, and Urban Affairs. Subcommittee on International Finance.* International financial conditions: hearings, Ninety-sixth Congress, first session ... December 12 and 14, 1979. Washington, U.S. Govt. Print. Off., 1980. 820 p.

KF26.B3946 1979e
J74.A23 96th
Cong., Sen. Comm.
Banking, v. 48

Adlai E. Stevenson, chairman.

An appended *Report to Congress on Foreign Government Treatment of U.S. Commercial Banking Organizations*, by the Dept. of the Treasury, includes a chapter on banking in Nigeria (p. 542–549).

4393

Abkin, Michael H., *and* Thomas J. Manetsch. Simulation approach to development planning with Nigerian and Korean applications. [East Lansing, Michigan State University, 1974] [34] p.

The "Nigerian model" is discussed specifically on p. 10–15.

Microfiche. [Washington, U.S. Agency for International Development, 1974?] 1 sheet.

DLC-Sci RR PN-AAB-759

4394

African development: international and regional paradigms; special report, [by] John J. Nash [et al.] Ft. Wadsworth, N.Y., 432 Military Intelligence Detachment (Strategic), 1977. [32] p. (FAR 28388-N)

4394 (cont.)

At head of title: Strategic Studies Institute, U.S. Army War College, Carlisle Barracks, Pa.

Focuses on Nigeria's participation in regional organizations concerned with economic cooperation. "We have done so because Nigeria appears to possess the energy, resources, versatility and leadership to become the eventual arbiter of conflicting interests in West Africa."—p. v.

Examined in the former Foreign Affairs Research Documentation Center, U.S. Dept. of State.

Issued also in microfiche. [s.l., Defense Documentation Center, 1978] 1 sheet (AD-B-024824L).

4395

Chu, Kong. The prospect for economic development in Nigeria. Atlanta, Georgia Institute of Technology, 1974. 16 p.

"This paper was prepared under a Georgia Tech program funded by the Agency for International Development."

Microfiche. [Washington, U.S. Agency for International Development, 1974?] 1 sheet.

DLC-Sci RR PN-AAA-607

4396

Foreign economic trends and their implications for the United States. Nigeria. 1969+ Washington, for sale by the Supt. of Docs., U.S. Govt. Print. Off. (International marketing information series)

HC10.E416

Semiannual, 1969–78, 1980+ ; annual, 1979.

Continues *Economic Trends and Their Implications for the United States. Nigeria.*

Prepared by the U.S. Embassy, Lagos.

Vols. for 1969–78 distributed by the U.S. Bureau of International Commerce; vols. for 1978–79 by the U.S. Industry and Trade Administration; vols. for 1980– by the U.S. International Trade Administration.

The following issues for the period 1973–81 have been identified in L.C.:

ET 73-064. 1973. 10 p.
ET 73-145. 1973. 9 p.
ET 74-086. 1974. 9 p.
ET 74-134. 1974. 9 p.
ET 75-049. 1975. 9 p.
FET 75-100. 1975. 9 p.
FET 76-016. 1976. 10 p.
FET 76-095. 1976. 10 p.
FET 77-009. 1977. 9 p.
FET 77-073. 1977. 10 p.
FET 78-025. 1978. 14 p.
FET 78-065. 1978. 10 p.
FET 79-031. 1979. 13 p.
FET 80-023. 1980. 10 p.
FET 80-097. 1980. 15 p.

FET 81-043. 1981. 9 p.
FET 81-127. 1981. 10 p.

4397

Mabawonku, Adewale F. An economic evaluation of apprenticeship training in western Nigerian small-scale industries. East Lansing, Dept. of Agricultural Economics, Michigan State University, 1979. 69 p. (African rural economy paper, no. 17)

HD4885.N6M3

"Published as part of Michigan State University's Off-Farm Employment Project, which is financed by the Office of Rural Development and Development Administration, Development Support Bureau, U.S. Agency for International Development (AID/ta-CA-2)."

On cover: African Rural Economy Program.

Bibliography: p. 61–66.

Abstract in *A.I.D. Research and Development Abstracts*, v. 7, no. 1, 1979, p. 13.

Issued also in microfiche. [Washington, U.S. Agency for International Development, 1979?] 1 sheet. DLC-Sci RR PN-AAG-616

4398

Nigeria. [*Treaties, etc. United States, 1975 Feb. 10*] Investment guarantee agreement between the Government of the United States of America and the Federal Military Government of the Federal Republic of Nigeria. *In* U.S. *Treaties, etc.* United States treaties and other international agreements, v. 26, 1975. [Washington, Dept. of State; for sale by the Supt. of Docs., U.S. Govt. Print. Off., 1976] p. 103–106. ([Treaties and other international acts series, 8012]) JX231.A34 v. 26

Signed at Lagos Aug. 3, 1974; entered into force Feb. 10, 1974 with agreed minute.

4399

Obasanjo, Olusegun. Obasanjo speech presenting 1979–80 budget. *In* U.S. *Joint Publications Research Service*. JPRS 73268. [Springfield, Va., National Technical Information Service, 1979] (Translations on Sub-Saharan Africa, no. 2092) p. 95–110.

Text of speech by the Nigerian Head of State in *Daily Times*, Lagos, Apr. 2, 1979.

Microfiche. [Washington, Supt. of Docs., U.S. Govt. Print. Off., 1979]

DLC-Micro JPRS 73268

4400

Rimlinger, Gaston V. Communalism and the gains from development: the case of Nigeria. Houston, Tex., Program of Development Studies, William Marsh Rice University, 1976. 55 p. (William Marsh

4400 (cont.)

Rice University. Program of Development Studies, Paper, no. 74)   HD82.W535 no. 74

Includes bibliographical references.

"This paper reports research related to AID contract no. AID/otr-C-1394, on Distribution of Gains, Wealth and Income from Economic and Political Development, Phase II."

Abstract in *A.I.D. Research and Development Abstracts*, July 1978, p. 32.

Issued also in microfiche. [Washington, U.S. Agency for International Development, 1976?] 1 sheet.   DLC-Sci RR PN-AAD-631

4401

Schatz, Sayre P. Nigeria: economic overview. [s.l.], 1979. 16 p.   DLC

On cover: "Presented at the United States Department of State, Washington, October 3, 1979."

4402

Spiliotes, Nicholas J. Indigenization, foreign investment and trade: implications for Nigerian foreign policy. [s.l.] 1979. [10] p.   DLC

On cover: "This paper was prepared for the Department of State as part of its external research program."

4403

Wall, Nelson C. Stimulating growth of small-scale industry; final report. Atlanta, Engineering Experiment Station, Georgia Institute of Technology, 1975–79. 5 v. illus.   GAT

Prepared for the U.S. Agency for International Development under contract AID/ta-C-1062.

Covers Brazil, Korea, and Nigeria.

Vol. issued in 1979 includes end-of-project report.

Vols. issued in 1976 and 1979 appear also in microfiche as follows: 1976 ([Washington, U.S. Agency for International Development, 1976?] 1 sheet. PN-AAH-470); 1979 ([Washington, U.S. Agency for International Development, 1979?] 2 sheets PN-AAG-723); both examined in the Development Information Center, AID, Washington, D.C.

Education

4404

Beckett, Paul A. University students and institutions in Nigerian society: a paper presented at the Department of State Colloquium on Nigeria, October 3, 1979. [s.l.], 1979. [16] p.   DLC

4405

Fafunwa, A. Babatunde. The growth and development of Nigerian universities. [Washington], Overseas Liaison Committee, American Council on Education, 1974. 41 p. (American Council on Education. Overseas Liaison Committee. OLC paper, no. 4)   LA1633.F32

Activities of the Overseas Liaison Committee are supported in part through a contract with the U.S. Agency for International Development.

Abstract in *A.I.D. Research and Development Abstracts*, Apr. 1978, p. 28.

Issued also in microfiche. [Washington, U.S. Agency for International Development, 1974?] 1 sheet.   DLC-Sci RR PN-AAD-602

4406

Federal Republic of Nigeria: report on major trends in education. Lagos, Federal Ministry of Education, [1977] [15] p.

Report presented to the International Conference on Education, Geneva, Switz., 1977.

Abstract in *Resources in Education*, Feb. 1978, p. 164.

Microfiche. [Arlington, Va., ERIC Document Reproduction Service; prepared for Educational Resources Information Center, National Institute of Education, 1978] 1 sheet.

DLC-Micro ED144898

4407

Future Nigerian-U.S. linkages in higher education, [by] James P. Dixon [et al.] Washington, Overseas Liaison Committee, American Council on Education, 1977. 123 p. map.

Prepared for the U.S. Agency for International Development under contract AID/sod C-15.

Among the appendixes are the following:

Elmer, Laurel. Past links between U.S. and Nigerian higher education. p. 50–52.

Includes a table indicating AID-sponsored links between American and Nigerian universities.

Dixon, James P. Development of medical education in Nigeria. p. 70–77.

Moore, J. Duain. Agriculture in Nigerian universities. p. 79–82.

McNown, John S. United States involvement with engineering education in Nigeria. p. 83–88.

Lewis, Arthur J. Teacher education in Nigerian universities. p. 89–92.

Also included are descriptions of the new Bayero University College, Kano; University of Calabar; University College, Port Harcourt; University of Ilorin; University of Jos; University of Maiduguri; and University of Sokoto (p. 97–123).

Abstract in *Resources in Education*, Sept. 1977, p. 95.

4407 (cont.)

Microfiche. [Arlington, Va., ERIC Document Reproduction Service; prepared for Educational Resources Information Center, National Institute of Education, 1977] 2 sheets.

DLC-Micro ED 138139

4408

Hawes, Hubert W. R., *and* A. O. Ozigi. Postgraduate teacher training: a Nigerian alternative; study prepared for the International Educational Reporting Service. Paris, Unesco Press, 1975. 53 p. illus. (Experiments and innovations in education; no. 20)

LB1731.H34

Abstract in *Resources in Education*, Aug. 1976, p. 208.

Issued also in microfiche. [Arlington, Va., ERIC Document Reproduction Service; prepared for Educational Resources Information Center, National Institute of Education, 1976] 1 sheet.

DLC- ED121784

4409

Ifenwanta, Samuel, *and* David C. Gardner. The importance of lifelong career development as perceived by Nigerian teachers and administrators. [s.l.], 1978. 17 p.

Abstract in *Resources in Education*, Aug. 1980, p. 5.

Microfiche. [Arlington, Va., ERIC Document Reproduction Service; prepared for Educational Resources Information Center, National Institute of Education, 1980] 1 sheet.

DLC-Micro ED183737

4410

Imogie, Abraham I. Post-independence universities in Nigeria: an example of dissatisfaction with colonial education systems in the Third World. [s.l.], 1978. 51 p.

Paper presented at the Second National Conference on the Third World, 1978.

Abstract in *Resources in Education*, 1980 annual cumulation, p. 281.

Microfiche. [Arlington, Va., ERIC Document Reproduction Service; prepared for Educational Resources Information Center, National Institute of Education, 1980] 1 sheet.

DLC-Micro ED176638

4411

Kalu, Wilhelmina J. Salvage operation: the head teacher and the future of special education in Nigeria. [s.l., 1978] 20 p.

Paper presented at the World Congress on Future Special Education, 1978.

A review of trends and national policy in Nigerian special education projects.

Abstract in *Resources in Education*, Jan. 1979, p. 80.

Microfiche. [Arlington, Va., ERIC Document Reproduction Service; prepared for Educational Resources Information Center, National Institute of Education, 1979] 1 sheet.

DLC-Micro ED158554

4412

Madu, Oliver V. A. The school system and the social development of Nigeria. New York, Sociology & Anthropology Dept., St. John's University, 1974. 23 p.

Paper presented at the Seventh World Conference of Sociology, 1974.

Abstract in *Resources in Education*, July 1975, p. 147.

Microfiche. [Arlington, Va., ERIC Document Reproduction Service; prepared for Educational Resources Information Center, National Institute of Education, 1975] 1 sheet.

DLC-Micro ED103317

4413

Margolis, Alan M. Nigeria: a study of the educational system of Nigeria and a guide to the academic placement of students in educational institutions of the United States. [Washington], International Education Activities Group of the American Association of Collegiate Registrars and Admissions Officers, 1977. 117 p. illus., map. (World education series)

LB2970.N55M37

"Publication of the World Education Series is assisted by grants from the Bureau of Educational and Cultural Affairs, United States Department of State."

Abstract in *Resources in Education*, Nov. 1978, p. 114–115.

4414

Mba, P. O. Priority needs of special education in developing countries—the case of Nigeria. [s.l.], 1978. [10] p.

Paper presented at the World Congress on Future Special Education, 1978.

Abstract in *Resources in Education*, Jan. 1979, p. 75.

Microfiche. [Arlington, Va., ERIC Document Reproduction Service; prepared for Educational Resources Information Center, National Institute of Education, 1979] 1 sheet.

DLC-Micro ED158487

4415

Mitchell, Robert E., James M. Seymour, *and* Howard F. Tuckman. Northern Nigeria teacher education project. [Washington], U.S. Agency for International Development, 1981. 51 p. (A.I.D. project impact evaluation report, no. 23)

Abstract in *A.I.D. Research & Development Abstracts*, v. 9, no. 3, 1981, p. 39.

Microfiche. [Washington, U.S. Agency for International Development, 1981?] 1 sheet.

DLC-Sci RR PN-AAJ-173

4416

Obebe, Bolarinde J. Federal Republic of Nigeria national policy on education: an educational task for a developing nation. [s.l., 1977] 17 p.

Abstract in *Resources in Education*, Sept. 1980, p. 192.

Microfiche. [Arlington, Va., ERIC Document Reproduction Service; prepared for Educational Resources Information Center, National Institute of Education, 1980] 1 sheet.

DLC-Micro ED186512

4417

—— New approaches to curriculum development in Nigerian schools. [s.l., 1977] 22 p.

Abstract in *Resources in Education*, Sept. 1980, p. 192.

Microfiche. [Arlington, Va., ERIC Document Reproduction Service; prepared for Educational Resources Information Center, National Institute of Education, 1980] 1 sheet.

DLC-Micro ED186513

4418

Odokara, E. O. Outreach: university's concern for communities around it. Nsukka, Division of Extra-Mural Studies, University of Nigeria, [1976] [67] p. illus.

On cover: "This book is an inventory of innovative continuing education services of the University of Nigeria, Nsukka, to the marginal masses of its surrounding communities."

Abstract in *Resources in Education*, Nov. 1977, p. 32.

Microfiche. [Arlington, Va., ERIC Document Reproduction Service; prepared for Educational Resources Information Center, National Institute of Education, 1977] 1 sheet.

DLC-Micro ED140072

4419

Pritchard, Mervyn W. Primary school inspection in Nigeria. Paris, International Institute for Educational Planning, c1975. 146 p. map. (International Institute for Educational Planning. IIEP research report, 12) LB2970.N55P74

On cover: "The organization and staffing of the primary school inspectorate: case studies-2."

Abstract in *Resources in Education*, July 1977, p. 62.

Issued also in microfiche. [Arlington, Va., ERIC Document Reproduction Service; prepared for Educational Resources Information Center, National Institute of Education, 1977] 2 sheets.

DLC-Micro ED135049

4420

Ross, Eugene L. Project analysis program—universities of Connecticut, Ife, and Massachusetts in cooperation with the United States Agency for International Development—final report of the project team. Ile-Ife, 1976. 63 leaves.

A review of a project analysis and management program at the Institute of Administration, University of Ife.

Examined in the Development Information Center, AID, Washington, D.C.

4421

Stickney, Benjamin D. Boarding schools: an alternative educational experience for disadvantaged children. [s.l.], 1977. 12 p.

Based on the author's experience as a Peace Corps teacher in Nigeria.

Abstract in *Resources in Education*, Feb. 1979, p. 201.

Microfiche. [Arlington, Va., ERIC Document Reproduction Service; prepared for Educational Resources Information Center, National Institute of Education, 1979] 1 sheet.

DLC-Micro ED160673

4422

Taiwo, Adediran A. A study of the nature of incidental physical science knowledge possessed by elementary school children in Western State of Nigeria. [New York], School of Education, New York University, 1975. 273 p.

Bibliography: p. 261–273.

Thesis (Ph.D.)—New York University.

Abstract in *Resources in Education*, July 1976, p. 185.

Microfiche. [Arlington, Va., ERIC Document Reproduction Service; prepared for Educational Resources Information Center, National Institute of Education, 1976] 4 sheets; (DLC-Micro ED 119996) and [Ann Arbor, Mich., University Microfilms International, 1975?] (DLC-Micro 76-01763)

Energy Resources— Production & Consumption

4423

[U.S. *Central Intelligence Agency*] Nigeria; petroleum. [Washington, 1977] col. map.

G8841.H8 1977.U5

Scale ca. 1 : 3,700,000.

"503486 10-77."

Depths shown by contours.

Shows oil fields, gas fields, oil pipelines, refineries, and concessions.

4424

U.S. *Dept. of Energy*. Report on the petroleum resources of the Federal Republic of Nigeria, prepared jointly by the U.S. Department of Energy & U.S. Geological Survey. [Springfield, Va., available from National Technical Information Service, 1979. [139] p. (in various pagings) maps. (Foreign Energy Supply Assessment Program series)

HD9577.N52U54 1979

"DOE/IA-0008."

4425

Asioudu, Phillip C. Impact of oil on economy discussed. *In* U.S. *Joint Publications Research Service*. JPRS 77137. [Springfield, Va., National Technical Information Service, 1981] (Sub-Saharan Africa report, no. 2342) p. 42–48.

Article in *New Nigerian*, Kaduna, Nov. 20, 21, 22, 1980.

Microfiche. [s.l., 1981]

DLC-Micro JPRS 77137

4426

Commissioner for Petroleum Col. M. Buhari interviewed. *In* U.S. *Joint Publications Research Service*. JPRS 70696. [Springfield, Va., National Technical Information Service, 1978] (Translations on Sub-Saharan Africa, no. 1885) p. 47–50.

Interview with the Commissioner for Petroleum, Nigerian National Petroleum Corporation, in *New Nigerian*, Kaduna, Jan. 20, 21, 1978.

Microfiche. [Washington, Supt. of Docs., U.S. Govt. Print. Off., 1978]

DLC-Micro JPRS 70696

4427

Energy crisis: Libya's and Nigeria's role. New York, School Services Division, African-American Institute, [1975] 13 p. map.

Abstract in *Resources in Education*, Apr. 1977, p. 129.

Microfiche. [Arlington, Va., ERIC Document Reproduction Service; prepared for Educational Resources Information Center, National Institute of Education, 1977] 1 sheet.

DLC-Micro ED132091

4427a

Gray, Beverly A. The Nigerian petroleum industry; a guide, compiled by Beverly Ann Gray, African Section, African and Middle Eastern Division. Washington, Library of Congress, 1978. 66 p. (Maktaba Afrikana series)   Z6972.G72

400 entries.

4428

Wilson, Ernest J. Critical issues of energy policy in Nigeria: policies of capture and distribution. [s.l.], 1979. 16 p.   DLC

On cover: "Prepared for U.S. State Department, October 1979, Washington, D.C."

Ethnology

4429

[U.S. *Central Intelligence Agency*] Nigeria; tribal groups. [Washington, 1977] col. map.

G8841.E1 1977.U5

Scale not given.

"503487 10-77."

4430

Cohen, Ronald. Oedipus Rex and Regina: the queen mother in Africa. Africa, v. 47, 1977: 14–30. illus.

PL8000.I6 1977

Research carried out in northeastern Nigeria with funds supplied in part by the National Science Foundation and the National Endowment for the Humanities.

4431

Salamone, Frank A. Behavioral implications of ethnic categories among Northern Nigerian schoolchildren. [s.l., 1974] [51] p. map.

Abstract in *Resources in Education*, Feb. 1976, p. 196.

Microfiche. [Arlington, Va., ERIC Document Reproduction Service; prepared for Educational Resources Information Center, National Institute of Education, 1976] 1 sheet.

DLC-Micro ED113287

4432

Talley, Odessa B. "The Igbo people of Nigeria as seen through *Things Fall Apart* by Chinua Achebe." Urbana, African Studies Program, University of Illinois, [1978] 18 p.

Report developed as part of an interdisciplinary

4432 (cont.)

workshop project in African curriculum development funded by the National Endowment for the Humanities.

Abstract in *Resources in Education*, 1980 annual cumulation, p. 2124.

Microfiche. [Arlington, Va., ERIC Document Reproduction Service; prepared for Educational Resources Information Center, National Institute of Education, 1980] 1 sheet.

DLC-Sci RR ED189003

Foreign Relations

4433

U.S. *President, 1977–1981 (Carter)* Lagos, Nigeria. Joint communique issued at the conclusion of meetings between the President and General Obasanjo. April 2, 1978. *In* U.S. *President.* Public papers of the Presidents of the United States. Jimmy Carter. 1978. [Washington, Office of the Federal Register, National Archives and Records Service; for sale by the Supt. of Docs., U.S. Govt. Print. Off., 1979] p. 664–667.   J80.A283 1978

4434

—— Lagos, Nigeria. Remarks of the President and Lt. Gen. Olusegun Obasanjo at the welcoming ceremony. April 1, 1978. *In* U.S. *President.* Public papers of the Presidents of the United States. Jimmy Carter. 1978. [Washington, Office of the Federal Register, National Archives and Records Service; for sale by the Supt. of Docs., U.S. Govt. Print. Off., 1979] p. 643–645.   J80.A283 1979

Note: Additional remarks by President Carter and Nigerian leaders on Apr. 2, 1978 are given on p. 645–664.

4435

—— Visit of Lieutenant General Obasanjo of Nigeria. Toasts of the President and Lieutenant General Obasanjo at a dinner honoring the Nigerian Head of State. October 11, 1977. *In* U.S. *President.* Public papers of the Presidents of the United States. Jimmy Carter. 1977. [Washington, Office of the Federal Register, National Archives and Records Service; for sale by the Supt. of Docs., U.S. Govt. Print. Off., 1978] p. 1772–1777.

J80.A283 1977

4436

—— Visit of Lieutenant General Olusegun Obasanjo of Nigeria. Remarks of the President and the Nigerian Head of State at the welcoming ceremony. October 11, 1977. *In* U.S. *President.* Public papers of the Presidents of the United States. Jimmy Carter. 1977. [Washington, Office of the

Federal Register, National Archives and Records Service; for sale by the Supt. of Docs., U.S. Govt. Print. Off., 1978] p. 1762–1763.

J80.A283 1977

4437

—— Visit of Lieutenant General Obasanjo of Nigeria. Remarks to reporters following the Nigerian Head of State's departure. *In* U.S. *President.* Public papers of the Presidents of the United States. Jimmy Carter. 1977. [Washington, Office of the Federal Register, National Archives and Records Service; for sale by the Supt. of Docs., U.S. Govt. Print. Off., 1978] p. 1781–1783.

J80.A283 1978

4438

—— Visit of President Shagari of Nigeria. White House statement, October 7, 1980. Weekly compilation of presidential documents, Oct. 13, 1980: 2104–2105.   J80.A284 1980

Note: The texts of toasts at a state dinner, Oct. 7, 1980, are given on p. 2108–2112.

4439

Clark, G. Edward. Soviet opportunities in the Third World: Nigeria. *In* Background studies: Soviet opportunities in the Third World. Arlington, Va., Strategic Studies Center, Stanford Research Institute, 1976. p. 191–269.

Prepared for the Office of the Deputy Chief of Staff for Operations and Plans, U.S. Army.

Microfiche. [s.l., Defense Documentation Center, 1980]   DLC-Sci RR AD-A079603

4440

DeLancey, Mark W. Nigeria: foreign policy alternatives: background notes at the beginning of civilian rule. [s.l.], 1979. [14] p.   DLC

Prepared for presentation at the U.S. Dept. of State, Oct. 3, 1979.

4441

Diggs, Charles C. The African viewpoint: remarks of the Nigerian head of state at Howard University. Congressional record, 95th Congress, 1st session, v. 123, Oct. 25, 1977: 35067–35068.

J11.R5 v. 123

Remarks in the U.S. House of Representatives.

Includes text of the Oct. 12, 1977 address by General Olusegun Obasanjo, Head of the Federal Military Government.

4442

Percy, Charles C. Foreign Relations Committee hosts Lieutenant General Obasanjo and other members of Nigerian delegation. Congressional

4442 (cont.)

record, 95th Congress, 1st session, v. 123, Oct. 12, 1977: 33381–33383.   J11.R5 v. 123

Remarks in the U.S. Senate.

Includes text of remarks by General Obasanjo.

4443

Visit to West Africa. *In* U.S. *Dept of State.* The Department of State bulletin, v. 80, no. 2042, Sept. 1980: 11–14. illus.   JX232.A33 v. 80

Text of address by Vice President Walter Mondale, Lagos, Nigeria, July 23, 1980, and text of a joint U.S.-Nigeria communique.

Geology, Hydrology, and Mineral Resources

4444

U.S. *Geological Survey.* Preliminary engineering geologic report on selection of urban sites in the Federal Capital Territory, Nigeria. [Reston, Va.?], 1977. 78 p. illus., maps (some fold. in pocket) (Project report, Nigerian investigations (IR) N-1)   DLC

"Prepared by the U.S. Geological Survey for the Federal Capital Development Authority of Nigeria."

4445

Ege, John R., Wallace R. Griffitts, *and* William C. Overstreet. Preliminary engineering geologic report on selection of urban sites in the Federal Capital Territory, Nigeria. [Reston, Va.], U.S. Geological Survey, 1977. 78 p. illus., maps (3 fold. in envelope) (U.S. Geological Survey. Reports—Open file series, no. 77–885)   DI-GS

U.S. Geological Survey. Project report: Nigerian investigations, (IR) N-1.

Prepared for the Federal Capital Development Authority of Nigeria.

4446

Harris, Keith L. The mineral industry of Nigeria. *In* Minerals yearbook, v. 3, 1972. [Washington, for sale by the Supt. of Docs., U.S. Govt. Print. Off., 1974] p. 609–614.   TN23.U612 1972, v. 3

Prepared by the U.S. Bureau of Mines

4447

———— The mineral industry of Nigeria. *In* Minerals yearbook, v. 3, 1973. [Washington, for sale by the Supt. of Docs., U.S. Govt. Print. Off., 1976] p. 653–660   TN23.U612 1973, v. 3

Prepared by the U.S. Bureau of Mines.

4448

———— The mineral industry of Nigeria. *In* Minerals yearbook, v. 3, 1974. [Washington, for sale by the Supt. of Docs., U.S. Govt. Print. Off., 1977] p. 683–689.   TN23.U612 1974, v. 3

Prepared by the U.S. Bureau of Mines.

4449

Jolly, Janice L. W. The mineral industry of Nigeria. *In* Minerals yearbook, v. 3, 1975. [Washington, for sale by the Supt. of Docs., U.S. Govt. Print. Off., 1978] p. 733–744.

TN23.U612 1975, v. 3

4450

———— The mineral industry of Nigeria. *In* Minerals yearbook, v. 3, 1976. [Washington, for sale by the Supt. of Docs., U.S. Govt. Print. Off., 1980] p. 783–793.   TN23.U612 1976, v. 3

Prepared by the U.S. Bureau of Mines.

4451

———— The mineral industry of Nigeria. *In* Minerals yearbook, v. 3, 1977. [Washington, for sale by the Supt. of Docs., U.S. Govt. Print. Off., 1981] p. 691–702.   TN23.U612 1977, v. 3

Prepared by the U.S. Bureau of Mines.

4452

———— The mineral industry of Nigeria. *In* Minerals yearbook, v. 3, 1978–79. [Washington, U.S. Govt. Print. Off., 1981] p. 691–700.

TN23.U612 1978–79, v. 3

Prepared by the U.S. Bureau of Mines.

4453

Morgan, George A. The mineral industry of Nigeria. *In* Minerals yearbook, v. 3, 1980. [Washington, for sale by the Supt. of Docs., U.S. Govt. Print. Off., 1982] p. 731–738.   TN23.U612 1980, v. 3

Prepared by the U.S. Bureau of Mines.

4454

Nigeria. [*Treaties, etc. United States, 1977 Feb. 4*] Memorandum of understanding between the Federal Capital Development Authority, Federal Republic of Nigeria, and U.S. Geological Survey, Department of Interior, Government of the United States. *In* U.S. *Treaties, etc.* United States treaties and other international agreements, v. 29, 1976–77. [Washington, Dept. of State; for sale by the Supt. of Docs., U.S. Govt. Print. Off., 1979] p. 256–267. ([Treaties and other international acts series, 8809])   JX231.A34 v. 29

Agreement dated Feb. 4, 1977.

4455

Peterson, L. R., *and* Gerald Meyer. Hydrologic reconnaissance evaluation of the Federal Capital Territory and surrounding areas, Nigeria. Reston, Va., U.S. Geological Survey, 1977. 30 leaves. maps. (U.S. Geological Survey. Open-file report, 77-596)   DLC

"Prepared in cooperation with the Federal Capital Development Authority of Nigeria."

Health and Nutrition

4456

Nigeria: DEIDS reconnaissance, Sept. 26 – Oct. 7, 1973, [by] Malcolm H. Merrill [et al.] [Washington, Division of International Health Programs, American Public Health Association], 1973. [14] p. map.

Prepared for the U.S. Agency for International Development.

Focus is on maternal and child health, family planning, and nutrition, especially in rural areas.

Microfiche. [Washington, U.S. Agency for International Development, 1973] 1 sheet.
DLC-Sci RR PN-AAB-559

4457

Smith, Victor E. Efficient resource use for tropical nutrition: Nigeria. East Lansing, Division of Research, Graduate School of Business Administration, Michigan State University, 1975. xxvi, 375 p. (MSU international business and economic studies)
TX360.N53S64

"This study was conducted under the auspices of the Consortium for the Study of Nigerian Rural Development, a contractor for the United States Agency for International Development. The final stages of the work, including the preparation of this report, were financed partially by the Midwest Universities Consortium for International Activities, by the Rockefeller Foundation, and by a 211d grant for USAID to the Agricultural Economics Department of Michigan State University. Use of the Michigan State University computing facilities was made possible in part because of the support of those facilities from the National Science Foundation."—p. xvii.

Bibliography: p. 371–375.

Issued also in microfiche. [Washington, U.S. Agency for International Development, 1975?] 5 sheets.   DLC-Sci RR PN-AAD-425

Housing and Urban Development

4458

Chaterjee, Lata. Housing development in Nigeria. [Washington], Office of Housing, Bureau for Science and Technology, U.S. Agency for International Development, 1981. 38 p.

Abstract in *A.I.D. Research & Development Abstracts*, v. 10, no. 1/2, 1982, p. 54.

4459

Cohen, Ronald. Conflict and development in a small urban African center. *In* Southall, Aidan. Small urban centers in rural development in Africa. Madison, African Studies Program, University of Wisconsin-Madison, 1979. p. 199–212. maps.

Concerns Biu, a town in northeastern Nigeria.

A grant from the Office of Urban Development, U.S. Agency for International Development, assisted in the preparation for publication of the papers collected in the study.

Microfiche. [Washington, U.S. Agency for International Development, 1980?] (PN-AAJ-064); examined in the Development Information Center, Agency for International Development, Washington, D.C.

4460

Dike, Azuka A. Growth and development patterns of Akwa and Nsukka, Nigeria. *In* Southall, Aidan. Small urban centers in rural development in Africa. Madison, African Studies Program, University of Wisconsin-Madison, 1979. p. 213–225.

A grant from the Office of Urban Development, U.S. Agency for International Development, assisted in the preparation for publication of the papers collected in the study.

Microfiche. [Washington, U.S. Agency for International Development, 1980?] (PN-AAJ-064); examined in the Development Information Center, Agency for International Development, Washington, D.C.

4461

Hannerz, Ulf. Town and country in southern Zaria: a view from Kafanchan. In Southall, Aidan. Small urban centers in rural development in Africa. Madison, African Studies Program, Univedsity of Wisconsin-Madison, 1979. p. 226–240.

A grant from the Office of Urban Development, U.S. Agency for International Development, assisted in the preparation for publication of the papers collected in the study.

Microfiche. [Washington, U.S. Agency for In-

4461 (cont.)

tcrnational Dcvclopment, 1980?] (PN-AAJ-064); examined in the Development Information Center, Agency for International Development, Washington, D.C.

4462

Trager, Lillian. Market centers as small urban places in western Nigeria. *In* Southall, Aidan. Small urban centers in rural development in Africa. Madison, African Studies Program, University of Wisconsin-Madison, 1979. p. 138–157.

A grant from the Office of Urban Development, U.S. Agency for International Development, assisted in the preparation for publication of the papers collected in the study.

Microfiche. [Washington, U.S. Agency for International Development, 1980?] (PN-AAJ-064); examined in the Development Information Center, Agency for International Development, Washington, D.C.

Language and Languages

4463

Kinyomi, Folashade O. A curricular plan for improving English instruction in secondary schools in Nigeria. [s.l.] 1980. 111 p.

Abstract in *Resources in Education*, July 1980, p. 90.

Microfiche. [Arlington, Va., ERIC Document Reproduction Service; prepared for Educational Resources Information Center, National Institute of Education, 1980] 2 sheets.

DLC-Micro ED183026

4464

Okonkwo, Chuka. Language in African education: a comparative analysis of the curricular elements of school texts. Buffalo, Comparative Education Center, Faculty of Educational Sciences, State University of New York, 1978. 46 p. (New York. State University, Buffalo. Comparative Education Center. Occasional paper, no. 2)

Essay taken from the author's doctoral dissertation, *Language and Education: An African Case*, submitted to the State University of New York, Buffalo.

"This study involves an examination of language and curricular contents of texts used in the former Eastern Nigeria and contemporary East Central State of Nigeria primary schools between 1957 to [sic] 1976."

Abstract in *Resources in Education*, Dec. 1978, p. 78.

Microfiche. [Arlington, Va., ERIC Document Reproduction Service; prepared for Educational

Resources Information Center, National Institute of Education, 1978] 1 sheet.

DLC-Micro ED157396

4465

Osaji, Debe. Language survey in Nigeria. Québec, International Center for Research on Bilingualism, 1979. 173 p. (International Center for Research on Bilingualism; B-81) P381.O67

Abstract in *Resources in Education*, Apr. 1980, p. 64.

Issued also in microfiche. [Arlington, Va., ERIC Document Reproduction Service; prepared for Educational Resources Information Center, National Institute of Education, 1980] 1 sheet.

DLC-Micro ED179113

4466

Taiwo, C. O. The mother tongue as a means of promoting equal access to education in Nigeria: problems and solutions. Paris, United Nations Educational, Scientific and Cultural Organization, 1976. 24 p.

An extension of the author's *The Mother Tongue as a Means of Promoting Equal Access to Education in Nigeria,* issued by UNESCO in 1972.

Abstract in *Resources in Education*, Oct. 1979, p. 98.

Microfiche. [Arlington, Va., ERIC Document Reproduction Service; prepared for Educational Resources Information Center, National Institute of Education, 1979] 1 sheet.

DLC-Micro ED171115

Libraries and Library Resources

4467

Bankole, Beatrice S. Problems in establishing a name authority file for Nigerian authors. [s.l.] 1979. 13 p.

Paper presented at the 1979 conference of the International Federation of Library Associations.

Abstract in *Resources in Education*, 1980 annual cumulation, p. 1670.

Microfiche. [Arlington, Va., ERIC Document Reproduction Service; prepared for Educational Resources Information Center, National Institute of Education, 1980] 1 sheet.

DLC-Micro ED186010

4468

Nwamefor, R. C. Security problems of university libraries in Nigeria. Overseas universities, Sept. 1974: 20–22. LB2331.5.O94 1974

Issued also in microfiche. [Arlington, Va., ERIC

4468 (cont.)

Document Reproduction Service; prepared for Educational Resources Information Center, National Institute of Education, 1975] 1 sheet.

DLC-Micro ED098961

4469

Nwoye, S. C. The consequences of extending a country's library legislation to the inclusion of academic libraries, with special reference to Nigeria. [s.l.], 1979. 30 p.

Paper presented at the 1979 conference of the International Federation of Library Associations.
Bibliography: p. 28–30.
Abstract in *Resources in Education*, Sept. 1980, p. 116.
Microfiche. [Arlington, Va., ERIC Document Reproduction Service; prepared for Educational Resources Information Center, National Institute of Education, 1980] 1 sheet.

DLC-Micro ED185994

Politics and Government

4470

U.S. *Congress. House. Committee on Foreign Affairs. Subcommittee on Africa.* Nigeria's return to civilian rule: hearing, Ninety-sixth Congress, first session, September 26, 1979. Washington, U.S. Govt. Print. Off., 1979. 52 p.

KF27.F625 1979g
J74.A23-96th
Cong., House Comm.
For. Aff., v. 50

Stephen J. Solarz, chairman.

In his opening remarks, Chairman Solarz notes that "Nigeria's return to civilian rule under an American-style constitution following 13 years of military rule is an enormously significant achievement which could potentially have major implications for the survival of constitutional democracy in Africa and the prospects for the return of civilian rule in other sub-Saharan countries."—p. 1.

4471

Cohen, Ronald. The pull of opposites: incorporation and autonomy in Nigeria. *In* African themes: Northwestern University Studies in honor of Gwendolen M. Carter, edited by Ibrahim Abu-Lughod. Evanston, Ill., Program of African Studies, Northwestern University, 1975. p. 149–173.   DT4.A343 1975

Research supported in part by the National Science Foundation and the National Endowment for the Humanities.

4472

Ikoku, S. G. Future role of armed forces in Nigeria discussed. *In* U.S. *Joint Publications Research Service.* JPRS 70667. [Springfield, Va., National Technical Information Service, 1978] (Translations on Sub-Saharan Africa, no. 1882) p. 24–30.

Article in *Sunday Times*, Lagos, Jan. 29, 1978, p. 8, 9.
Microfiche. [Washington, Supt. of Docs., U.S. Govt. Print. Off., 1978]

DLC-Micro JPRS 70667

4473

Jervis, Steven. Post-war attitude in Nigeria's eastern states. [s.l., 1975] 4 leaves. (FAR 22306-S)

Paper presented at the Colloquium on Nigeria, sponsored by the U.S. Dept. of State, 1975.
Examined in the former Foreign Affairs Research Documentation Center, U.S. Dept. of State.

4474

McGovern, George S. Nigeria: moving toward unity. Congressional record [daily ed.], 96th Congress, 2d session, v. 126, Mar. 24, 1980: S2882–S2884.

J11.R7 v. 126

Remarks in the U.S. Senate.
Includes article, "Lurching toward unity," by Pauline H. Baker, in the *Wilson Quarterly*.

4475

Manifesto of Great Nigerian People's Party (GNPP) *In* U.S. *Joint Publications Research Service.* JPRS 72745. [Springfield, Va., National Technical Information Service, 1979] (Translations on Sub-Saharan Africa, no. 2058) p. 32–40.

From *New Nigerian*, Kaduna, Jan. 5–6, 1979.
Microfiche. [Washington, Supt. of Docs., U.S. Govt. Print. Off., 1979]

DLC-Micro JPRS 72745

4476

Murphy, Sharon M. Voter registration drive in Nigeria: patterns of communication influence. [s.l., 1979] 14 p.

Paper presented at the annual meeting of the Association for Education in Journalism, 1979.
Abstract in *Resources in Education*, 1980 annual cumulation, p. 419.
Microfiche. [Arlington, Va., ERIC Document Reproduction Service; prepared for Educational Resources Information Center, National Institute of Education, 1980] 1 sheet.

DLC-Micro ED177580

4477

Obasanjo, Olusegun. Presidential address on national indiscipline. *In* U.S. *Joint Publications Research*

4477 (cont.)

Service. JPRS 69948. [Springfield, Va., National Technical Information Service, 1977] (Translations on Sub-Saharan Africa, no. 1815) p. 19–24.

Article in *New Nigerian*, Kaduna, Sept. 19, 1977, p. 8.

Microfiche. [s.l., 1977]

DLC-Micro JPRS 69948

4478

Problems of a Marxist-Leninist party in Nigeria discussed. *In* U.S. *Joint Publications Research Service.* JPRS 70863. [Springfield, Va., National Technical Information Service, 1978] (Translations on Sub-Saharan Africa, no. 1902) p. 62–66.

Article in *New Horizon*, Lagos, Jan./Feb. 1978, p. 6, 7, 20–22.

Microfiche. [Washington, Supt. of Docs., U.S. Govt. Print. Off., 1978]

DLC-Micro JPRS 70863

4479

Samuels, Michael A. How the new constitutional structure in Nigeria will work. [s.l.], 1979. 11 p.

DLC

Prepared for the Colloquium on Nigeria, U.S. Dept. of State, Oct. 3, 1979.

4480

Shagari, Shehu. Shagari speech to National Assembly. *In* U.S. *Joint Publications Research Service.* JPRS 74585. [Springfield, Va., National Technical Information Service, 1979] (Sub-Saharan Africa report, no. 2178) p. 65–69.

Text of President Shagari's speech to the National Assembly of Nigeria on Oct. 16, 1979, reported in the *Daily Times*, Lagos, Oct. 18, 1979, p. 3.

Microfiche. [s.l., 1979]

DLC-Micro JPRS 74585

4481

Successes and shortcomings of local governments discussed. *In* U.S. *Joint Publications Research Service.* JPRS 70896. [Springfield, Va., National Technical Information Service, 1978] (Translations on Sub-Saharan Africa, no. 1906) p. 14–21.

Article in *West Africa*, London, Feb. 13, 20, 27, and Mar. 6, 1978.

Microfiche. [Washington, Supt. of Docs., U.S. Govt. Print. Off., 1978]

DLC-Micro JPRS 70896

4482

Whitaker, C. S. Second beginnings: the new political framework in Nigeria. [s.l.], 1979. 29 p.   DLC

On cover: "Also presented as a part of testimony

for a hearing of the Subcommittee on Africa of the House Foreign Affairs Committee, U.S. Congress, House of Representatives, September 26, 1979, and the U.S. State Department Conference on Nigeria, October 3, 1979, Washington, D.C."

4483

——— The significance of constitutional innovation in Nigeria. [Washington?], 1978. 16 leaves. (FAR 29150-S)

Presented at a conference, Nigeria—Today and Tomorrow, sponsored by the U.S. Dept. of State, Sept. 1978.

Examined in the former Foreign Affairs Research Documentation Center, U.S. Dept. of State.

Population Studies

4484

Arowolo, Oladele O. Determinants of fertility among Yorubas of Nigeria. *In* Recent empirical findings on fertility: Korea, Nigeria, Tunisia, Venezuela, Philippines; investigators: Lee Hyo-Chai [and others] Washington, Interdisciplinary Communications Program, Smithsonian Institution, 1976. (Interdisciplinary Communications Program. Occasional monograph series, no. 7) p. 27–45.

HB903.F4R39

"ICP work agreement reports."

Prepared for the U.S. Agency for International Development under contract AID/csd-3598.

Issued also in microfiche. [Washington, U.S. Agency for International Development, 1976?] 2 sheets.   DLC-Sci RR PN-AAG-400

4485

Essang, Sunday M., *and* Adewale F. Mabawonku. Determinants and impact of rural-urban migration: a case study of selected communities in Western Nigeria. East Lansing, Dept. of Agricultural Economics, Michigan State University, 1974. 34 p. (African rural employment paper, no. 10)

HB2546.N5E8

"This paper has been published as part of a three year study of rural employment problems in Africa which is being financed under an AID/Washington contract (AID csd 3625) with the Department of Agricultural Economics at Michigan State University."

Issued also in microfiche. [Washington, U.S. Agency for International Development, 1974?] 1 sheet.   DLC-Sci RR PN-AAA-577

4486

Morgan, Robert W. Yoruban modernization and fertility in Lagos. *In* New perspectives on the

4486 (cont.)
demographic transition; investigators: Robert W. Morgan [and others] Washington, Interdisciplinary Communications Program, Smithsonian Institution, 1976. (Interdisciplinary Communications Program. Occasional monograph series, no. 4) p. 1–51.   HB871.N47
"ICP work agreement reports."
Prepared for the U.S. Agency for International Development under contract AID/csd-3598.
Issued also in microfiche. [Washington, U.S. Agency for International Development, 1976?] 3 sheets.   DLC-Sci RR PN-AAG-397

4487
Rierson, Michael. Country report: Nigeria. [Washington], Interdisciplinary Communication Program, Smithsonian Institution, 1976. [62] p.
Prepared for the U.S. Agency for International Development under contract AID/csd-3598.
Bibliography: p. [53–56].
Concerns research on analyses of population problems.
Microfiche. [Washington, U.S. Agency for International Development, 1976?] 1 sheet (PN-AAF-560); examined in the Development Information Center, AID, Washington, D.C.

Religion

4488
Nicolas, Guy. Contemporary changes in Islam examined. *In* U.S. *Joint Publications Research Service.* JPRS 77005. [Springfield, Va., National Technical Information Service, 1980] (Sub-Saharan Africa report, no. 2333) p. 81–88.
Translation of article on Islam in Nigeria, in *Le Monde diplomatique*, Paris, Nov. 1980, p. 36.
Microfiche. [s.l., 1980]
DLC-Micro JPRS 77005

4489
Paden, John N. Islam, constitutional change, and politics in Nigeria. [s.l.], 1979. 15 p. maps.
DLC
On cover: "This paper was prepared for the Department of State as part of its external research program."

Science and Technology

4490
Contributions to industrial development of science and technology institutions in Malaysia, Nigeria, and Colombia and opportunities for bilateral co-

operation (a cross-cultural comparative analysis) [by] G. E. Schweitzer [and others] [Ithaca, N.Y.], Program on Science, Technology, and Society, Cornell University, 1979. 30 p.
Prepared for the U.S. Dept. of State.
Microfiche. [s.l., Defense Technical Information Center, 1981] 1 sheet.
DLC-Sci RR AD-A092892

4491
Nigeria. [*Treaties, etc. United States, 1980 Sept. 22*] Agreement for scientific and technical cooperation between the Government of the United States of America and the Government of the Federal Republic of Nigeria. [Washington, Dept. of State; for sale by the Supt. of Docs., U.S. Govt. Print. Off., 1981] 8 p. (Treaties and other international acts series, 9865)   DLC
Signed at Lagos Sept. 22, 1980.

4492
Schweitzer, G. E., *and* H. T. Bergh. Contributions to economic development of science and technology institutions in Nigeria and opportunities for bilateral cooperation. [Ithaca, N.Y.], Program on Science, Technology and Society, Cornell University, 1979. [69] p. (in various pagings) illus.
On cover: "Final report to U.S. Department of State."
Bibliography: p. [65–69]
Microfiche. [s.l., Defense Technical Information Center, 1980] 1 sheet.
DLC-Sci RR AD-A089457

Other Subjects

4493
U.S. *Information Agency. Office of Research.* Evaluation of *Interlink* and *Topic* magazines in Nigeria. [Washington], 1977. 46 p.
"E-5-77."
Readership study of two agency publications.
Abstract in *American Statistics Index*, 1978, Abstracts, p. 898–899.
Microfiche. [Washington, Congressional Information Service, 1977?]
DLC-Micro ASI:78   9856-2:75

4494
U.S. *Information Agency. Research Service.* Partial results of the readership study of *Interlink* and *Topic* in Nigeria. [Washington?], 1976. [4] p.
DLC
"Research memorandum M-33-76."

4495

―――― VOA audience estimate for Nigeria. [Washington], 1974. 16 p. (FAR 21632-N)

Examined in the former Foreign Affairs Research Documentation Center, U.S. Dept. of State.

4496

Akinola, Joshua A. Nigeria: teaching resource units for use in American elementary and secondary schools. [East Lansing, African Studies Center, Michigan State University, 1978] 181 p.

Financed in part by the U.S. Office of Education.

Abstract in *Resources in Education*, May 1979, p. 176.

Microfiche. [Arlington, Va., ERIC Document Reproduction Service; prepared for Educational Resources Information Center, National Institute of Education, 1979?] 2 sheets.

DLC-Micro ED164373

4497

Ani, A. A. Suggestions for new tax formula reported. *In* U.S. *Joint Publications Research Service*. JPRS 70667. [Springfield, Va., National Technical Information Service, 1978] (Translations on Sub-Saharan Africa, no. 1882) p. 38–42.

Article in *Daily Times*, Lagos, Jan. 28, 1978, p. 32.

Microfiche. [Washington, Supt. of Docs., U.S. Govt. Print. Off., 1978]

DLC-Micro JPRS 70667

4498

Cohen, Ronald. The natural history of hierarchy: a case study. *In* Power and control: social structures and their transformation, edited by Tom R. Burns and Walter Buckley. London, SAGE, c1976. p. 185–214. HM24.P68

Study conducted in northeastern Nigeria with funds provided in part by the National Science Foundation and the National Endowment for the Humanities.

4499

Daily, Fred. Listening to international radio stations and to VOA in urban Nigeria, 1977. Washington, Office of Research, International Communication Agency, 1979. 35 p. DLC

"Research report R-15-79."

4500

Harris, Donald S., *and* Badru I. O. Rabiu. [Country labor profile]: Nigeria. *In* International labor profiles: comprehensive reports on the labor forces of 40 key nations, including data on wage and hour standards, labor organizations, social benefit pro-

grams, governmental regulations, and other labor-related topics. 1st ed. Detroit, Grand River Books, 1981. p. 214–220. illus., map. HD4901.I56

Report prepared by the Bureau of International Labor Affairs, U.S. Dept. of Labor.

4501

A Look at the U.S. team in Lagos. *In* U.S. *Dept. of State*. Newsletter, no. 215, Aug. – Sept. 1979: 42–45. illus. JX1.U542 1979

Mainly illustrations of activities of U.S. Embassy personnel.

4502

Nigeria. [*Treaties, etc. United States, 1976 Apr. 20*] Procedures for mutual assistance in the administration of justice in connection with the Lockheed Aircraft Corporation matter. *In* U.S. *Treaties, etc*. United States treaties and other international agreements, v. 27, 1976. [Washington, Dept. of State; for sale by the Supt. of Docs., U.S. Govt. Print. Off., 1977] p. 1055–1058. ([Treaties and other international acts series, 8243])

JX231.A34 v. 27

Agreement between Nigeria and the United States signed at Washington Apr. 20, 1976.

Concerns "alleged illicit acts pertaining to the sales activities in Nigeria of the Lockheed Aircraft Corporation and its subsidiaries or affiliates."

4503

Nigeria. [*Treaties, etc. United States, 1980 Sept. 22*] Memorandum of understanding on environmental protection between the United States Environmental Protection Agency and the Federal Ministry of Housing and Environment of Nigeria. [Washington, Dept. of State; for sale by the Supt. of Docs., U.S. Govt. Print. Off., 1981] 8 p. (Treaties and other international acts series, 9864)

DLC

Signed at Lagos Sept. 22, 1980.

Concerns exchanges of scientific, technical, and regulatory information concerning environmental protection and the exchange of specialists in this field "to enhance their professional development in environmental matters."—p. 3.

4504

Overstreet, William C. Provisional map showing land use based on interpretation of vegetation, Federal Capital Territory, Republic of Nigeria. Reston, Va., U.S. Geological Survey, 1977. map. G8843.F4G4 1977.O9

Scale 1 : 100,000.

Prepared for the Federal Capital Development Authority.

Senegal

General

4505

U.S. *Agency for International Development.* Selected bibliography on Senegal, together with a list of useful maps. [Washington?], 1978. 17 p.

Examined in the Development Information Center, AID, Washington, D.C.

4506

U.S. *Dept. of State.* Post report. Senegal. [Washington, for sale by the Supt. of Docs., U.S. Govt. Print. Off.], 1981. [20] p. illus., map. (U.S. Dept. of State. Department of State publication, 9231)

JX1705.A286 Spec. Format
Department and Foreign Service series, 273.
L.C. has also report issued in 1978.
For a description of the contents of this report, see the note to entry 936.

4507

U.S. *Dept. of State. Bureau of Public Affairs.* Background notes. Senegal. [Washington, for sale by the Supt. of Docs., U.S. Govt. Print. Off.] 1979. 6 p. illus., maps. (U.S. Dept. of State. Department of State publication 7820)   G59.U5
L.C. retains only the latest revision.
For a description of the contents of this publication, see the note to entry 937.

4508

Analytical bibliography of documents concerning Senegal. Bibliographie analytique des documents concernant le Sénégal. Dakar, Documentation Center, U.S. AID Mission to Senegal, 1981. 131 p.
MiEM

4509

Draft environmental report on Senegal. Tucson, Arid Lands Information Center, Office of Arid Lands Studies, University of Arizona, 1980. 105 p. maps.   AzU

Study sponsored by the U.S. Agency for International Development through the U.S. National Committee for Man and the Biosphere.

On cover: "National Park Service Contract No. CX-0001-0-0003 with U.S. Man and the Biosphere Secretariat, Department of State, Washington, D.C."

Bibliography: p. 87–105.

Abstract in *A.I.D. Research & Development Abstracts*, July 1981, p. 37.

Issued also in microfiche. [Washington, U.S. Agency for International Development, 1980?] 2 sheets.   DLC-Sci RR PN-AAJ-204

4510

The Peace Corps in Senegal. [Washington, U.S. Govt. Print. Off., 1980] folder ([6] p.) illus., map.
DLC
An introduction to the country for Volunteers.

4511

Philippi, Thomas. Senegal, a country profile; prepared for the Office of U.S. Foreign Disaster Assistance, Bureau for Private and Development Cooperation, Agency for International Development, Department of State by Evaluation Technologies, Inc., under contract AID/SOD/PDC-C-0283; written and research by Thomas Philippi. Washington, The Office, 1980. 66 p. 2 leaves of plates.   DT549.22.P48
Includes bibliography.
A general introduction, with emphasis on political structure, disaster preparedness, demography, health, nutrition, housing, economic conditions, agriculture, geography, transportation, power, and communications.

Issued also in microfiche. [Sahel Documents and Dissertations. Ann Arbor, Mich., University Microfilms International, 1980] 1 sheet.

DLC-Micro Microfiche 5357 SG 120

Agriculture

4512

U.S. *Peace Corps. Senegal.* Rural development. [Dakar?], 1976. 20 leaves.   DPC

4513

Bagley, Jay M. Appraisal of IBRD plan for Diagambal sprinkler irrigation project. [s.l.], 1977. 29 leaves. maps.

Prepared for the U.S. Agency for International Development.

IBRD: International Bank for Reconstruction and Development.

A project in the Senegal River delta.

Examined in the Documentation Center, Sahel Development Program, AID, Washington, D.C.

4514

Bakel crop production, Senegal; project paper. [Washington?. U.S. Agency for International Development, 1976] 2 v.

Examined in the Documentation Center, Sahel Development Program, AID, Washington, D.C.

4515

Brown, Don, *and* Axel Magnuson. Agricultural and rural development strategy for USAID/Senegal. Dakar, [U.S. AID Mission], 1980. 34 p.

MiEM

"Joint planning of U.S. assistance programs in Senegal: resource paper."

4516

Chaupin, Sammy L. Minister discusses agricultural production, programs. *In* U.S. *Joint Publications Research Service.* JPRS 75009. [Springfield, Va., National Technical Information Service, 1980] (Sub-Saharan Africa report, no. 2204) p. 81–87.

Translation of interview with Djibril Sene, Minister of Rural Development, in *Le Soleil*, Dakar, Dec. 17, 1979, p. 4.

Microfiche. [s.l., 1980]

DLC-Micro JPRS 75009

4517

Gellar, Sheldon. Analysis and evaluation of roles played by Promotion Humaine, regional development agencies and local institutions in promoting rural development in Senegal. Dakar, [U.S. AID Mission], 1980. 32 p.   MiEM

"Joint planning of U.S. assistance programs in Senegal: resource paper."

4518

Gellar, Sheldon, Robert B. Charlick, *and* Yvonne

Jones. Animation rurale and rural development: the experience of Senegal. [Ithaca, N.Y.], Rural Development Committee, Center for International Studies, Cornell University, [1980] 211 p. map. (Special series on animation rural, no. 2)

DLC

"After 20 years (1959–79), the theory of 'Animation Rurale' (AR), which emphasizes cooperative village control of economic institutions, has been discarded as a basis for rural development planning in Senegal."—Abstract.

Abstract in *A.I.D. Research & Development Abstracts*, v. 9, no. 3, 1981, p. 22.

Issued also in microfiche. [Washington, U.S. Agency for International Development, 1980?] 3 sheets.   DLC-Sci RR PN-AAJ-634

4519

Gilbert, Elon H., David W. Norman, *and* Fred E. Winch. Farming systems research: a critical appraisal. East Lansing, Dept. of Agricultural Economics, Michigan State University, 1980. 135 p. (MSU rural development paper, no. 6)

MiEM

Prepared for the U.S. Agency for International Development under contract AID/ta-CA-3.

Bibliography: p. 123–124.

"Includes a brief summary of the *Unités expérimentales* approach in Senegal."—*Sahel Bibliographic Bulletin*, v. 5, no. 4, 1981, p. 189.

4520

Gritzner, Jeffrey A. A preliminary assessment of environmental degradation and agricultural productivity in the Senegalese groundnut basin: a report to the Advisory Committee on the Sahel of the National Academy of Sciences. Washington, National Academy of Sciences, 1980. 81 p.

MiEM

4521

Kostinko, Gail, *and* Josué Dioné. An annotated bibliography of rural development in Senegal: 1975–1980. [East Lansing, Dept. of Agricultural Economics, Michigan State University, 1980] 73 p. (African rural economy paper, no. 23)   DLC

"Published under terms of Alternative Rural Development Strategies Cooperative Agreement AID/ta-CA-3 at Michigan State University funded by the Agency for International Development."

On cover: African Rural Economy Program.

277 entries.

4522

Lebeau, Francis. The plan de redressement: rural sector reform and its implications. Dakar, [U.S. AID Mission], 1980. 37 p.   MiEM

4522 (cont.)

"Joint planning of U.S. assistance programs in Senegal: resource paper."

4523

Sene, Ibrahima. Farmers' behavior towards new technology: the Senegalese case. East Lansing, Dept. of Agricultural Economics, Michigan State University, 1980. 43 p. (African Rural Economy Program. Working paper, no. 33)   MiEM

Publication financed by the U.S. Agency for International Development under contract AID/afr-C-1267.

Copy examined in the Development Information Center, AID, Washington, D.C.

4524

Senegal food and energy study; energy use and opportunities for energy-related improvements in the food system. Washington, Checchi and Co., 1980. [260] p. (in various pagings) maps.

Issued in collaboration with Brookhaven National Laboratory, Upton, N.Y.

Bibliography: p. B-1–B-6.

"The growth of agriculture, the mainstay of Senegal's economy, is contingent upon the acquisition of imported energy. This study examined the key constituents of the Senegalese food system in relation to energy supply and demand."—Abstract.

Abstract in *A.I.D. Research and Development Abstracts*, v. 9, no. 3, 1981, p. 59.

Microfiche. [Washington, U.S. Agency for International Development, 1980?] 3 sheets.

DLC-Sci RR PN-AAJ-274

4525

Senegal land conservation and revegetation, [by] Donald Burzlaff [et al.] [Dakar?, U.S. AID Mission, 1978?] 1 v. (various foliations of leaves)

Examined in the Documentation Center, Sahel Development Program, U.S. Agency for International Development, Washington, D.C.

4526

Ware, Theresa A. Wolof farmers and Fulani herders: a case study of drought adaptation in the Diourbel region of Senegal. [Ann Arbor], University of Michigan, 1979. 242 leaves.

Prepared under a grant from the African-American Scholars Council as part of its grant from the U.S. Agency for International Development.

Thesis (Ph.D.)—University of Michigan.

Microfiche. [Sahel Documents and Dissertations. Ann Arbor, Mich., University Microfilms International, 1980] 3 sheets (DLC-Micro Micro-

fiche 5357 SG 138); and [Ann Arbor, Mich., University Microfilms International, 1979] (DLC-Micro 79-16840).

Economic Aspects

4527

Franzel, Steven. An interim evaluation of two agricultural production projects in Senegal: the economics of rainfed and irrigated agriculture. East Lansing, Dept. of Agricultural Economics, Michigan State University, 1979. 65 p. (African Rural Economy Program. Working paper, no. 28)

MiEM

Prepared for the U.S. Agency for International Development under contract AID/afr-C-1260.

Issued also in microfiche. [Washington, U.S. Agency for International Development, 1979?] 1 sheet (DLC-Sci RR PN-AAG-631); and [Sahel Documents and Dissertations. Ann Arbor, Mich., University Microfilms International, 1980] 1 sheet (DLC-Micro Microfiche 5357 SG 069).

4528

Maddox, Michael M. A model of Senegal agricultural supply and demand. Arlington, Virginia Research Institute, inc., 1976. [36] p.

Prepared for the Office of Sahel and Francophone West Africa, U.S. Agency for International Development.

"Working paper no. 3/"

Microfiche. [Sahel Documents and Dissertations. Ann Arbor, Mich., University Microfilms International, 1980] 1 sheet.

DLC-Micro Microfiche 5357 SG 085

4529

—— A tool for integrated agricultural policy analysis in the Sahel. Arlington, Va., Virginia Research Institute, inc., 1977. [55] leaves (in various foliations)

A "preliminary model of agricultural supply and demand in Senegal" prepared for the Office of Sahel and Francophone West Africa, U.S. Agency for International Development.

Abstract in *A.I.D. Research and Development Abstracts*, Jan. 1979, p. 2.

Microfiche. [Washington, U.S. Agency for International Development, 1977?] 1 sheet (DLC-Sci RR PN-AAG-068); and [Sahel Documents and Dissertations. Ann Arbor, Mich., University Microfilms International, 1980] 1 sheet (DLC-Micro Microfiche 5357 AS 340).

4530

Senc, Pape M. Bud-Senegal's bankruptcy to have serious consequences. *In* U.S. *Joint Publications Research Service.* JPRS 74472. [Springfield, Va., National Technical Information Service, 1979] (Sub-Saharan Africa report, no. 2172) p. 118–121.

Translation of article on the closing of a large truck farming company, in *Le Soleil*, Dakar, Sept. 20, 1979, p. 4.

Microfiche [s.l., 1979]

DLC-Micro JPRS 74472

4531

Weiler, Edward M. Social cost-benefit analysis of the Nianga pilot project, Senegal. [Lafayette, Ind.?], Purdue University, 1979. 276 p. maps.

Thesis (M.S.)—Purdue University.

Concerns the economic viability of an irrigated agriculture project.

Abstract in *A.I.D. Research and Development Abstracts*, v. 7, no. 1, 1979, p. 10.

Microfiche. [Washington, U.S. Agency for International Development, 1979?] 3 sheets.

DLC-Sci RR PN-AAG-508

Grain and Grain Storage

4532

U.S. *Agency for International Development.* Sahel mid-term program: Senegal cereals production and agricultural extension program (SODEVA). [Washington, 1974?] 135 leaves. map.　　DPC

SODEVA: Société de développement et de vulgarisation agricole.

4533

Cereals project [and] Eastern Senegal livestock project, [by] Moustapha Dia [et al.] [s.l.], 1978. 47 leaves.

Apparently prepared by the U.S. Agency for International Development in cooperation with the Government of Senegal.

At head of title: "Evaluation report 'Promotion Humaine' projects."

Examined in the Documentation Center, Sahel Development Program, AID, Washington, D.C.

4534

Niane, Amadou D. Supply and demand of millet and sorghum in Senegal. East Lansing, Dept. of Agricultural Economics, Michigan State University, 1980. 77 p. (African Rural Economy Program. Working paper, no. 32)　　MiEM

Publication financed by the U.S. Agency for International Development under contract AID/afr-C-1267.

Bibliography: p. 76–77.

Copy examined in the Development Information Center, AID, Washington, D.C.

4535

Pedersen, John R., *and* Kenneth Steinke. Recommendations for implementation of an in-country training program for grain storage and preservation in Senegal. [Manhattan, Kan.?], 1978.

"Food and Feed Grain Institute. Technical assistance report, no. 74."

Cited in "Listing of Reports Printed under Contract AID/ta-C-1162," prepared by the Food and Feed Grain Institute, Kansas State University.

4536

Pfost, Harry B. Current storage situation for domestic grains in Senegal. Manhattan, Food and Feed Grain Institute, Kansas State University, [1979] 54 p. (Grain storage, processing and marketing, report no. 77)　　DLC

Prepared for the U.S. Agency for International Development under contract AID/ta-C-1152.

4537

Promotion humaine component to the Senegal cereals production project. Washington, U.S. Agency for International Development, 1975. 42 p.

MiEM

4538

Ross, Clark G. A village level study of producer grain transactions in rural Senegal. [Ann Arbor, Center for Research in Economic Development, University of Michigan], 1979. [79] p.　　MiU

Prepared for the U.S. Agency for International Development under a joint contract between Purdue University (AID/afr-C-1257) and the University of Michigan (AID/csd-2547).

Abstract in *A.I.D. Research and Development Abstracts*, v. 7, no. 3, 1980, p. 2.

Issued also in microfiche. [Sahel Documents and Dissertations. Ann Arbor, Mich., University Microfilms International, 1980] 1 sheet.

DLC-Micro Microfiche 5357 SG 137

4539

——— Grain demand and consumer preferences— Dakar, Senegal. Ann Arbor, Center for Research on Economic Development, University of Michigan, 1979. 26 p. (Michigan. University. Center for Research on Economic Development. Discussion paper, no. 80)　　MiU

Prepared for the U.S. Agency for International Development under contract AID/afr-C-1257.

Issued in cooperation with Purdue University

4539 (cont.)
and the Centre de recherche économique appliquée of the Université de Dakar.

Issued also in French (examined in the Documentation Center, Sahel Development Program, AID, Washington, D.C.).

Issued also in microfiche. [Sahel Documents and Disserations. Ann Arbor, Mich., University Microfilms International, 1980] 1 sheet.
DLC-Micro Microfiche 5357 SG 063

4540
Spencer, William P. Donald L. Pfost, *and* John R. Pedersen. Recommendations for grain storage and preservation in Senegal; prepared for the Agency for International Development, United States Department of State, AID/ta-C-1162, Technical assistance in grain storage, processing, and marketing and agribusiness development at the Food and Feed Grain Institute, Kansas State University, Manhattan, Kansas. Manhattan, Kan., The Institute, 1975. 132 p. illus. (Grain storage, processing and marketing report, no. 54)   SB190.S66

Includes bibliographical references.

Abstract in *A.I.D. Research and Development Abstracts*, July 1978, p. 26.

Issued also in microfiche. [Washington, U.S. Agency for International Development, 1975?] 2 sheets.   DLC-Sci RR PN-AAC-917

Livestock and Range Management

4541
Bakel range livestock project, Eastern Senegal. Logan, Consortium for International Development, Utah State University, [1975?] 377 leaves. fold. map.

Prepared for the U.S. Agency for International Development.

John M. Cheney, chief of party, Bakel Range Livestock Design Team.

Microfiche. [Washington, U.S. Agency for International Development, 1975?] 4 sheets (DLC-Sci RR PN-AAD-198); and [Sahel Documents and Dissertations. Ann Arbor, Mich., University Microfilms International, 1980] 5 sheets (DLC-Micro Microfiche 5357 SG 016).

4542
SODESP livestock production and resources management project. [Washington, Agency for International Development, 1978?] [200] p. maps.

SODESP: Société de développement de l'élevage dans la zone sylvo-pastorale (Senegal).

Examined in the Documentation Center, Sahel Development Program, AID, Washington, D.C.

4543
Senegal range and livestock development. [Washington?, U.S. Agency for International Development, 1976?] 33 p.

Examined in the Documentation Center, Sahel Development Program, AID, Washington, D.C.

4544
Shoemaker, Robert W. Senegal range and livestock development. [s.l., U.S. Agency for International Development, 1974] [182] p. (in various pagings)

Microfiche. [Sahel Documents and Dissertations. Ann Arbor, Mich., University Microfilms International, 1980] 3 sheets.
DLC-Micro Microfiche 5357 SG 122

Rice

4545
Craven, Kathryn, *and* A. Hasan Tuluy. Rice policy in Senegal. *In* Pearson, Scott R. Rice in West Africa: policy and economics. Stanford, Calif., Stanford University Press, 1981. p. 229–262.
HD9066.A462P4

Publication results from a research project, "The Political Economy of Rice in West Africa," carried out jointly by the Food Research Institute, Stanford University, and the West Africa Rice Development Association between June 1976 and Sept. 1979, and funded by the U.S. Agency for International Development under contract AID/afr-C-1235.

4546
Tuluy, A. Hasan. Costs and incentives in rice production in Senegal. *In* Pearson, Scott R. Rice in West Africa: policy and economics. Stanford, Calif., Stanford University Press, 1981. p. 263–295.
HD9066.A462P4

Publication results from a research project carried out jointly by the Food Research Institute, Stanford University, and the West Africa Rice Development Association and funded by the U.S. Agency for International Development (see more complete note in entry 4545).

Casamance Region

4547
Casamance integrated rural development; mid-term report. [Washington?], 1977. [60] leaves.

Apparently prepared for the U.S. Agency for International Development.

Examined in the Documentation Center, Sahel Development Program, AID, Washington, D.C.

4548

Casamance regional development. [s.l., Agency for International Development, 1978?] 7 v. map.

Examined in the Documentation Center, Sahel Development Program, AID, Washington, D.C.

4549

Casamance regional development program; terms of reference for a master plan for agricultural development of the lower Casamance. [s.l.], 1977. [49] leaves (in various foliations) map.   MiEM

Program supported by the Government of Senegal and the U.S. Agency for International Development.

Copy examined in the Documentation Center, Sahel Development Program, AID, Washington, D.C.

4550

Casamance regional development project: project review paper. [Dakar?, U.S. AID Mission, 1978?] 1 v. (various foliations of leaves) illus., maps.

Emphasis is on improving agricultural production.

Examined in the Documentation Center, Sahel Development Program, U.S. Agency for International Development, Washington, D.C.

4551

Rigoulot, Jean Pierre. An analysis of constraints on expanding rice output in the Casamance region of Senegal. East Lansing, Dept. of Agricultural Economics, Michigan State University, 1980. 65 p. (African Rural Economy Program. Working paper, no. 31)   MiEM

Publication financed by the U.S. Agency for International Development under contract AID/afr-C-1267.

Copy examined in the Development Information Center, AID, Washington, D.C.

Assistance Programs

4552

U.S. *AID Mission to Senegal.* Joint assessment of U.S. assistance programs in Senegal. Evaluation conjointe du programme d'aide américaine au Sénégal. Dakar, 1980. 2 v.   MiEM

"Final report."

Issued in conjunction with the Ministère du plan et de la coopération of Senegal.

4553

—— PL-480 Title III program for Senegal. Dakar, 1980. [200] p.   MiEM

Cover title: Program proposal: Senegal food for development program, PL480 Title III, FY 1980-FY1982.

Contents noted in *Sahel Bibliographic Bulletin*, Apr./June 1982, p. 113.

4554

U.S. *Agency for International Development.* Annual budget submission: Senegal. Washington, U.S. International Development Cooperation Agency.

Vols. for 1979+ examined in the Development Information Center, AID, Washington, D.C.

4555

—— Country development strategy statement: Senegal. Washington, U.S. International Development Cooperation Agency. annual.

Vols. for 1981+ examined in the Development Information Center, AID, Washington, D.C.

Vol. for 1981 issued also in microfiche. [Sahel Documents and Dissertations. Ann Arbor, Mich., University Microfilms International, 1980] 1 sheet.

DLC-Micro Microfiche 5357 SG 034

4556

—— Sahel recovery and rehabilitation program, Senegal: proposal and recommendations. Washington, [1974] 1 v. (various pagings) map.

At head of title: Program assistance paper.

Examined in the Documentation Center, Sahel Development Program, AID, Washington, D.C.

4557

Action (Service Corps). *Internal Audit Staff.* Review of Peace Corps activities in Senegal. [Washington?], 1973. 97 leaves.   DPC

4558

Bienen, Henry. Report on the political implications of the joint assessment and U.S. aid to Senegal. Dakar, [U.S. AID Mission], 1980. 31 p.

    MiEM

"AID's political influence is limited, and the micro impacts of AID projects have not been determined."—*Sahel Bibliographic Bulletin*, Apr./June 1982, p. 105.

4559

Bingen, R. James. Research/studies in Sahel francophone West Africa: Senegal; an inventory of research, studies, and reports sponsored by the U.S. Agency for International Development. Washington, Sahel Development Program, U.S. Agency for International Development, 1977. [77] p.

Covers 57 projects undertaken in the period 1962–77.

Abstract for series on francophone West Africa

4559 (cont.)

and The Gambia in *A.I.D. Research and Development Abstracts*, Oct. 1977, p. 12–13.

Microfiche. [Washington, U.S. Agency for International Development, 1977?] 1 sheet.

DLC-Sci RR PN-AAD-517

4560

Senegal. [*Treaties, etc. United States, 1975 May 28*] Senegal; agricultural commodities: transfer under Title II; agreement signed at Washington and Dakar November 6, 1974 and May 28, 1975; entered into force May 28, 1975; and amending agreement signed at Washington and Dakar March 2 and May 28, 1976; entered into force May 28, 1976. *In* U.S. *Treaties, etc.* United States treaties and other international agreements, v. 29, 1976–77. [Washington, Dept. of State: for sale by the Supt. of Docs., U.S. Govt. Print. Off., 1979] p. 1006–1010. ([Treaties and other international acts series, 8862]) JX231.A34 v. 29

Under Title II, Public Law 480, the Commodity Credit Corporation was authorized to transfer and deliver food to Senegal.

4561

Senegal. [*Treaties, etc. United States, 1975 Aug. 7*] Grant agreement between the Government of the Republic of Senegal and the Agency for International Development for the Sahel recovery and rehabilitation program. *In* U.S. *Treaties, etc.* United States treaties and other international agreements, v. 27, 1976. [Washington, Dept. of State; for sale by the Supt. of Docs., U.S. Govt. Print. Off., 1977] p. 2672–2691. ([Treaties and other international acts series, 8339]) JX231.A34 v. 27

Signed at Dakar Mar. 23, 1974, and amending agreements signed at Dakar Aug. 5 and Aug. 7, 1975; entered into force Aug. 7, 1975.

4562

Senegal. [*Treaties, etc. United States, 1978 Feb. 21*] Senegal, agricultural commodities: transfer under Title II. Agreement signed at Dakar February 21, 1978; entered into force February 21, 1978; and amending agreement signed at Dakar March 29, 1978; entered into force March 29, 1978. *In* U.S. *Treaties, etc.* United States treaties and other international agreements, v. 30, 1978–79. [Washington, Dept. of State; for sale by the Supt. of Docs., U.S. Govt. Print. Off., 1980] p. 3052–3062. ([Treaties and other international acts series, 9377]) JX231.A34 v. 30

Authorizes the Commodity Credit Corporation to transfer and deliver food grain to Senegal.

4563

Sylla, Abdoulaye N. Need for foreign aid in development struggle stressed. *In* U.S. *Joint Publications Research Service*. JPRS 74725. [Springfield, Va., National Technical Information Service, 1979] (Sub-Saharan Africa report, no. 2186) p. 81–84.

Translation of article in *Le Soleil*, Dakar, Oct. 1, 1979, p. 1, 2.

Microfiche. [s.l., 1979]

DLC-Micro JPRS 74725

4564

Technical Assistance Information Clearing House. Development assistance programs of U.S. non-profit organizations, Senegal. [New York], American Council of Voluntary Agencies for Foreign Service, 1977. 15 p. maps. HC547.S4T4a

The Clearing House is operated by the Council under a grant from the U.S. Agency for International Development.

4565

Teranga; Peace Coprs Senegal newsletter. 1976+ [Dakar?] monthly. DPC

4566

Weber, Mark S. Proposed USAID support for the private sector in assisting Senegalese development: an analysis of alternatives. Dakar, [U.S. AID Mission], 1980. 108 p. MiEM

"Joint planning of U.S. assistance programs in Senegal: resource paper."

"The informal sector is seen as the prime source of employment generation; AID and World Bank experiences in the Entente Council countries and in Lesotho are analyzed; economic conditions and institutions in Senegal are reviewed; recommends that AID start its programs in the urban informal sector."—*Sahel Bibliographic Bulletin*, Apr./June 1982, p. 114.

Commerce

4567

Chittum, J. Marc. Marketing in Senegal. [Washington], U.S. Dept. of Commerce, Domestic and International Business Administration; [for sale by the Supt. of Docs., U.S. Govt. Print. Off.], 1977. 16 p. (Overseas business reports. OBR 77–58) HF91.U482 1977, no. 58

International marketing information series.

4568

Senegal. [Brussels], International Union for the Publication of Customs Tariffs, 1978. 258 p. DLC-LL

4568 (cont.)

Issued as no. 168 (2d ed.) of the Union's *Bulletin international des douanes. International Customs Journal.*

Microfiche. [Springfield, Va., National Technical Information Service, 1978] 3 sheets.

DLC-Sci RR PB283560

Communications and Transportation

4569

Editor of monthly 'Promotion' fined. *In* U.S. *Joint Publications Research Service.* JPRS 74699. [Springfield, Va., National Technical Information Service, 1979] (Sub-Saharan Africa report, no. 2185) p. 122–126.

Translation of article on legal proceedings against Boubacar Diop, editor of *Promotion,* on charges of violating Senegal's press and libel laws, in *Le Soleil,* Dakar, Oct. 13–14, 1979, p. 2.

Microfiche. [s.l., 1979]

DLC-Micro JPRS 74699

4570

Kulakow, Allan. Accelerated impact project, rural satellite communications, USAID/Senegal. [s.l], Academy for Educational Development, inc., 1980. 112, [33] leaves. maps.

Prepared for the U.S. AID Mission to Senegal.

Concerns a proposal for a communications system linking Dakar with stations in Casamance.

Examined in the Documentation Center, Sahel Development Program, AID, Washington, D.C.

4571

TRSB microwave landing system demonstration program at Dakar, Senegal; final report. [Atlantic City, N.J. National Aviation Facilities Experimental Center]; available from National Technical Information Service, Springfield, Va., 1978. [44] p. (in various pagings)

Prepared for Systems Research & Development Service, U.S. Federal Aviation Administration.

"Report no. FAA-RD-78-21."

TRSB: Time Reference Scanning Beam.

Microfiche. [s.l., Defense Documentation Center, 1978] 1 sheet. DLC-Sci RR AD-A054645

Economic Conditions

4572

Colvin, Lucie G. Private initiatives in the Senegalese economy: potential modes of AID assistance. Dakar, [U.S. AID Mission], 1980. 34 p. MiEM

"Joint planning of U.S. assistance programs in Senegal: resource paper."

Discussion of employment.

4573

Foreign economic trends and their implications for the United States. Senegal. 1969+ Washington, for sale by the Supt. of Docs., U.S. Govt. Print. Off. annual. (International marketing information series) HC10.E416

Prepared by the U.S. Embassy, Dakar.

Vols. for 1969–77 distributed by the U.S. Bureau of International Commerce; vols. for 1978–80 by the U.S. Industry and Trade Administration; vols. for 1981– by the U.S. International Trade Administration.

The following issues for the period 1973–81 have been identified in L.C.:

ET 73-089. 1973. 12 p.
ET 74-099. 1974. 11 p.
FET 76-022. 1976. 11 p.
FET 77-018. 1977. 7 p.
FET 78-020. 1978. 7 p.
FET 79-026. 1979. 7 p.
FET 80-040. 1980. 11 p.
FET 81-070. 1981. 7 p.

4574

Keutu, Wa. PDS leader discusses nation's economic problems. *In* U.S. *Joint Publications Research Service.* JPRS 74987. [Springfield, Va., National Technical Information Service, 1980] (Sub-Saharan Africa report, no. 2203) p. 186–190.

Translation of interview with Abdoulaye Wade, secretary-general of the Parti démocratique sénégalais, in *Demain l'Afrique,* Paris, Dec. 1979, p. 50–51.

Microfiche. [s.l., 1980]

DLC-Micro JPRS 74987

4575

Magassouba, Moriba. Government's main concern to promote economic recovery. *In* U.S. *Joint Publications Research Service.* JPRS 74827. [Springfield, Va., National Technical Information Service, 1979] (Sub-Saharan Africa report, no. 2193) p. 122–125.

Translation of article in *Demain l'Afrique,* Paris, Oct. 22, 1979, p. 38–39.

Microfiche. [s.l., 1980]

DLC-Micro JPRS 74827

4576

President discusses government's economic policies. *In* U.S. *Joint Publications Research Service.* JPRS 70677. [Springfield, Va., National Technical In-

4576 (cont.)

formation Service, 1978] (Translations on Sub-Saharan Africa, no. 1883) p. 89–98.

Translation of interview with Léopold S. Senghor in *Afrique industrie infrastructures*, Paris, Jan. 1, 1978, p. 24–30.

Microfiche. [Washington, Supt. of Docs., U.S. Govt. Print. Off., 1978]

DLC-Micro JPRS 70677

4577

Schaetzen, Yves de. Minister defines decentralization policies. *In* U.S. *Joint Publications Research Service*. JPRS 65956. [Springfield, Va., National Technical Information Service, 1975] (Translations on Sub-Saharan Africa, no. 1621) p. 30–36.

Translation of interview with Louis Alexandrenne, Minister of Industrial Development, in *Afrique industrie infrastructures*, Paris, Aug. 1975, p. 14–15.

Microfiche. [s.l., 1975]

DLC-Micro JPRS 65956

4578

——— Planning minister discusses nation's economic assets, liabilities. *In* U.S. *Joint Publications Research Service*. JPRS 75920. [Springfield, Va., National Technical Information Service, 1980] (Sub-Saharan Africa report, no. 2258) p. 129–132.

Translation of interview with Louis Alexandrenne, Minister of Plan & Cooperation, in *Afrique industrie*, Paris, May 1, 1980, p. 38–40.

Microfiche. [s.l., 1980]

DLC-Micro JPRS 75920

4579

Seck, Ousmane. Minister rejects price analysis of opposition paper. *In* U.S. *Joint Publications Research Service*. JPRS 75359. [Springfield, Va., National Technical Information Service, 1980] (Sub-Saharan Africa report, no. 2225) p. 140–145.

Translation of article in *Le Soleil*, Dakar, Feb. 2–3, 1980, p. 1, 3, in which the Minister of Finance and Economy responds to an article on the cost of living in Senegal published in *Taxaw*.

Microfiche. [s.l., 1980]

DLC-Micro JPRS 75359

Education

4580

Carvin, Joseph. Education and training in Senegal. Dakar, [U.S. AID Mission], 1981. [140] p.

MiEM

"Joint planning of U.S. assistance programs in Senegal: resource paper."

Author recommends that the U.S. Agency for International Development promote literacy in local languages.

4581

Dione, Samba. Middle-level practical education in Senegal. *In* Educational reforms and innovations in Africa: studies prepared for the Conference of Ministers of Education of African Member States of Unesco. Paris, Unesco, 1978. (Experiments and innovations in education, no. 34) p. 11–18.

LA1500.E38

Issued also in microfiche. [Arlington, Va., ERIC Document Reproduction Service; prepared for Educational Resources Information Center, National Institute of Education, 1978] 1 sheet.

DLC-Sci RR ED160036

4582

LeBel, Phillip G. A linear planning model for education with applications to Senegal. [Boston], Boston University, 1977. xx, 223 leaves.

Field research supported by the National Science Foundation.

Thesis (Ph.D.)—Boston University.

Microfiche. [Sahel Documents and Disserations. Ann Arbor, Mich., University Microfilms International, 1980] 5 sheets.

DLC-Micro Microfiche 5357 SG 075

Microfilm. [Ann Arbor, Mich., University Microfilms International, 1977]

DLC-Micro 77-11407

4583

L'Enseignement moyen pratique au Sénégal; description et évaluation de la phase expérimentale. Post-primary practical education/training in Senegal; description and evaluation of the experiment. [Paris], Unesco, 1977. [86] p. (in various pagings) (United National Educational, Scientific and Cultural Organization. Educational financing-occasional paper no. 3)

Text in French.

Abstract in *Resources in Education*, July 1979, p. 165.

Microfiche. [Arlington, Va., ERIC Document Reproduction Service; prepared for Educational Resources Information Center, National Institute of Education, 1979] 2 sheets.

DLC-Sci RR ED167440

4584

Integrated services for youth job development. New York, International Division, National Board of YMCAs of the U.S.A., 1977. [89] leaves.

Report submitted to the U.S. Agency for International Development.

4584 (cont.)

Concerns vocational training in Senegal.
YMCAs: Young Men's Christian Associations.
Examined in the Documention Center, Sahel Development Program, AID, Washington, D.C.

Energy Resources— Production & Consumption

4585

Attempts to develop solar, other types of energy noted. *In* U.S. *Joint Publications Research Service.* JPRS 74987. [Springfield, Va., National Technical Information Service, 1980] (Sub-Saharan Africa report, no. 2203) p. 192–198.

Translation of article in *Le Soleil*, Dakar, Nov. 22, 1979, p. 6.

Microfiche. [s.l., 1980]

DLC-Micro JPRS 74987

4586

Diouf, Abdou. Premier opens national days of reflection on renewable energy. *In* U.S. *Joint Publications Research Service.* JPRS 75528. [Springfield, Va., National Technical Information Service, 1980] (Sub-Saharan Africa report, no. 2237) p. 128–133.

Translation of speech recorded in *Le Soleil*, Dakar, Feb. 22, 1980, p. 1, 3.

Microfiche. [s.l., 1980]

DLC-Micro JPRS 75528

4587

Diouf, Bara, *and* Ibrahima Gaye. Premier discusses para-public companies, energy program. *In* U.S. *Joint Publications Research Service.* JPRS 74699. [Springfield, Va., National Technical Information Service, 1979] (Sub-Saharan Africa report, no. 2185) p. 107–119.

Translation of interview with Abdou Diouf, Prime Minister of Senegal, in *Le Soleil*, Dalar, Oct. 13–14, 1979, p. 4–5.

Microfiche. [s.l., 1979]

DLC-Micro JPRS 74699

4588

Fall, Moustapha. Need for comprehensive energy policy stressed. *In* U.S. *Joint Publications Research Service.* JPRS 76979. [Springfield, Va., National Technical Information Service, 1980] (Sub-Saharan Africa report, no. 2331) p. 69–78.

Translation of article in *Le Soleil*, Dakar, Oct. 24, 25 26, 27, 1980.

Microfiche. [s.l., 1980]

DLC-Micro JPRS 76979

4589

Senegal fuelwood production. Dakar, U.S. AID Mission to Senegal, 1979. [110] p.　　　MiEM

4590

Ulinski, Carol A. Trip report: Senegal renewable energy project. [s.l.], 1978. 23 p.

Prepared for the U.S. Agency for International Development under contract AID/afr-C-1453.

Examined in the Development Information Center, AID, Washington, D.C.

4591

Working papers for a renewable energy project in Senegal, [by] Moustapha Kassé [et al.] [Ann Arbor], Center for Research on Economic Development, University of Michigan, 1979. [90] p. (in various pagings) illus., map.　　　MiU-RE

Prepared for the U.S. Agency for International Development under contract AID/afr-C-1143.

"Renewable energy" is defined as "energy produced directly by sun, wind, and biomass."

Foreign Relations

4592

Diouf, Bara. French president discusses Senegalese relations. *In* U.S. *Joint Publications Research Service.* JPRS 71335. [Springfield, Va., National Technical Information Service, 1978] (Translations on Sub-Saharan Africa, no. 1950) p. 64–68.

Translation of interview with President Valéry Giscard d'Estaing, in *Le Soleil*, Dakar, May 17, 1978, p. 3.

Microfiche. [Washington, Supt. of Docs., U.S. Govt. Print. Off., 1978]

DLC-Micro JPRS 71335

4593

President Senghor sets forth his African policy. *In* U.S. *Joint Publications Research Service.* JPRS 72680. [Springfield, Va., National Technical Information Service, 1979] (Translations on Sub-Saharan Africa, no. 2054) p. 104–108.

Translation of article in *Remarques Arabo-Africaines*, Brussels, Nov. 1978, p. 10–12.

Microfiche. [Washington, Supt. of Docs., U.S. Govt. Print. Off., 1979]

DLC-Micro JPRS 72680

Geology, Hydrology, and Mineral Resources

4594

Dudley, Earll D. A hydrologic review of the proposed Bakel-small perimeters, Senegal River basin, Senegal. [Washington?], U.S. Bureau of Reclamation, 1976. 28 leaves, [14] leaves of plates. illus., maps.   DI

4595

Rao, G. V. Final report of activities of water resources consultant during March–June 1977. Denver, Engineering Consultants, inc., [1977] 120 leaves. maps.

Prepared for the Regional Economic Development Service Office/West Africa, U.S. Agency for International Development.

The focus is on the development of a master plan for utilization of water and land resources in Lower Casamance, Senegal.

Examined in the Development Information Center, AID, Washington, D.C.

Health and Nutrition

4596

Menes, Robin J. Senegal. Washington, Division of Program Analysis, Public Health Service, 1976. xix, 144 p. map. (Syncrisis: the dynamics of health; an analytic series on the interactions of health and socioeconomic development, v. 19)

RA418.S98 v. 19

DHEW publication no. (OS) 76-50037.

Bibliography: p. 141–144.

Abstracts in *Government Reports Announcements & Index*, Oct. 26, 1979, p. 51–52, and *American Statistics Index*, 1976, Abstracts, p. 357.

Issued also in microfiche. [Washington, U.S. Agency for International Development, 1976?] 2 sheets (DLC-Sci RR PN-AAC-654); [Sahel Documents and Dissertations. Ann Arbor, Mich., University Microfilms International, 1980] 3 sheets (DLC-Micro Microfiche 5357 SG 132); and [Washington, Congressional Information Service, 1976?] (DLC-Micro ASI:76 4006-1.19).

4597

Preliminary report: environmental assessment and health component design, Bakel irrigated perimeter project—Senegal. [Washington?], American Public Health Association, 1977. 70 leaves.

Prepared for the U.S. Agency for International Development under contract AID/afr-C-1253.

Examined in the Documentation Center, Sahel Development Program, AID, Washington, D.C.

4598

Sabagh, Georges. Consultant proposals for the expansion of the evaluation phase of the Sine-Saloum project. [Washington?], American Public Health Association, 1977. 21 p.

Prepared for the U.S. Agency for International Development under contract AID/pha-C-1100.

Examined in the Development Information Center, AID, Washington, D.C.

4599

Senegal Rural Health Services Development Project. Final report. Columbia, Md., Westinghouse Health Systems, 1976. [32] p. (in various pagings)

Prepared for the U.S. Agency for International Development under contract AID/afr-C-1145.

Abstract in *A.I.D. Research and Development Abstracts*, Jan. 1979, p. 26.

Microfiche. [Washington, U.S. Agency for International Development, 1976?] 1 sheet.

DLC-Sci RR PN-AAF-421

4600

Senegal: the Sine Saloum rural health care project, by Richard F. Weber [et al.] [Washington?], U.S. Agency for International Development, 1980. [82] p. (in various pagings) illus., maps. ([A.I.D. project impact evaluation report, no. 9])

DLC

Includes bibliography.

Abstract in *A.I.D. Research & Development Abstracts*, July 1981, p. 46.

Issued also in microfiche. [Washington, U.S. Agency for International Development, 1980?] 1 sheets.   DLC-Sci RR PN-AAJ-008

Politics and Government

4601

Carvin, Joseph. Progress report of the administrative reform of 1971: the rural communes. Dakar, [U.S. AID Mission], 1980. [60] p.   MiEM

"Joint planning of U.S. assistance programs in Senegal: resource paper."

4602

Cottingham, Clem. Political change in Senegal. [s.l., 1973] 7 leaves. (FAR 18443-S)

Prepared for the Colloquium on Senegal, sponsored by the U.S. Dept. of State, Nov. 1973.

Examined in the former Foreign Affairs Research Documentation Center, U.S. Dept. of State.

4603

Creevey, Lucy. Muslim politics and ten years of development in Senegal. [s.l.], 1977. 36 leaves. (FAR 27009-N)

Prepared for the Colloquium on Senegal, sponsored by the U.S. Dept. of State, July 1977.

Examined in the former Foreign Affairs Research Documentation Center, U.S. Dept. of State.

4604

Diouf, Bara. Senghor denies that he plans to retire. *In* U.S. *Joint Publications Research Service*. JPRS 72390. [Springfield, Va., National Technical Information Service, 1978] (Translations on Sub-Saharan Africa, no. 2034) p. 115–119.

Translation of interview with President Senghor, in *Le Soleil*, Dakar, Oct. 23, 1978, p. 3.

Microfiche. [Washington, Supt. of Docs., U.S. Govt. Print. Off., 1978]

DLC-Micro JPRS 72390

4605

Final resolution passed by PS national council. *In* U.S. *Joint Publications Research Service*. JPRS 76584. [Springfield, Va., National Technical Information Service, 1980] (Sub-Saharan Africa report, no. 2304) p. 57–66.

Translation of article on the Parti socialiste sénégalais in *Le Soleil*, Dakar, July 21, 1980, p. 5.

Microfiche. [s.l., 1980]

DLC-Micro JPRS 76584

4606

Government's economic failures have political effects. *In* U.S. *Joint Publications Research Service*. JPRS 75441. [Springfield, Va., National Technical Information Service, 1980] (Sub-Saharan Africa report, no. 2229) p. 131–134.

Article in *West Africa*, London, Mar. 10, 1980, p. 431–433.

Microfiche. [s.l., 1980]

DLC-Micro JPRS 75441

4607

Kebe, Moctar. PAI leader discusses party's policies, tasks. *In* U.S. *Joint Publications Research Service*. JPRS 67984. [Springfield, Va., National Technical Information Service, 1976] (Translations on Sub-Saharan Africa, no. 1679) p. 44–48.

Translation of interview with Majhemout Diop, leader of the PAI, in *Le Sahel*, Dakar, Sept. 1, 1976. p. 5.

Microfiche. [s.l., 1976]

DLC-Micro JPRS 67984

4608

Magassouba, Moriba. Differences between socialism

of PS, PDS defined. *In* U.S. *Joint Publications Research Service*. JPRS 70782. [Springfield, Va., National Technical Information Service, 1978] (Translations on Sub-Saharan Africa, no. 1894) no. 99–104.

Translation of article in *Demain l'Afrique*, Paris, Feb. 6, 1978, p. 17–19.

PS: Parti socialiste sénégalais.

PDS: Parti démocratique sénégalais.

Microfiche. [Washington, Supt. of Docs., U.S. Govt. Print. Off., 1978]

DLC-Micro JPRS 70782

4609

—— Outcome of election to determine Senghor's retirement. *In* U.S. *Joint Publications Research Service*. JPRS 70114. [Springfield, Va., National Technical Information Service, 1977] (Translations on Sub-Saharan Africa, no. 1830) p. 54–63.

Translation of article in *Demain l'Afrique*, Paris, Sept. 1977, p. 17–21.

Microfiche. [s.l., 1977]

DLC-Micro JPRS 70114

4610

Possibility of unity among leftist groups called remote. *In* U.S. *Joint Publications Research Service*. JPRS 74967. [Springfield, Va., National Technical Information Service, 1980] (Sub-Saharan Africa report, no. 2201) p. 131–134.

Translation of article in *Le Politicien*, Dakar, Nov. 1979, p. 4.

Microfiche. [s.l., 1980]

DLC-Micro JPRS 74967

4611

President discusses multi-party system, Tunisian relations. *In* U.S. *Joint Publications Research Service*. JPRS 71570. [Springfield, Va., National Technical Information Service, 1978] (Translations on Sub-Saharan Africa, no. 1968) p. 106–115.

Translation of interview with Léopold S. Senghor, in *Dialog*, Tunis, June 17, 1978, p. 25–31.

Microfiche. [Washington, Supt. of Docs., U.S. Govt. Print. Off., 1978]

DLC-Micro JPRS 71570

4612

Sine, Babacar. Senghor not threatened by Marxists while they are disunited. *In* U.S. *Joint Publications Research Service*. JPRS 75680. [Springfield, Va., National Technical Information Service, 1980] (Sub-Saharan Africa report, no. 2246) p. 1–5.

Translation of article on the Parti africain de l'indépendance, in *Le Soleil*, Dakar, Mar. 22–23, 1980, p. 1, 3.

4612 (cont.)

Microfiche. [s.l., 1980]

DLC-Micro JPRS 75680

Population Studies

4613

Africa: Senegal. Selected statistical data by sex. Washington, 1981. 31, 17 p.   DLC

Study supported by the U.S. Agency for International Development's Office of Women in Development and Office of Population.

Data assembled by the International Demographic Data Center, U.S. Bureau of the Census.

Among the tables, all based on 1970 data (unless otherwise noted), are the following: unadjusted population by age, sex, and urban/rural residence (1976); population by region, sex, and urban/rural residence (1971); population by ethnic group, sex, and urban/rural residence (1970–71); life expectancy; infant mortality rates (1970–71); urban and rural populations by marital status, age, and sex; number of economically active persons by age, sex, and urban/rural residence; economically active population by occupational status, sex, and urban/rural residence (1970–71).

4614

Ba, Cheikh. Northern Senegal. *In* The Uprooted of the western Sahel: migrants' quest for cash in the Senegambia, [by] Lucie Gallistel Colvin [et al.] New York, Praeger, [1981] p. 113–135. map.

HB2125.5.A3U67

"The U.S. Agency for International Development (AID) funded this research."—p. iii.

4615

Chaudry, Susan L. Development of a plan for family planning training and educational activities in Senegal. [Washington?], American Public Health Association, 1976. 15 p.

Prepared for the U.S. Agency for International Development under contract AID/pha/C-1100.

Abstract in *A.I.D. Research and Development Abstracts*, Apr. 1978, p. 32–33.

Microfiche. [Washington, U.S. Agency for International Development, 1976?] 1 sheet.

DLC-Sci RR PN-RAB-633

4616

Colvin, Lucie G. Senegal. *In* The Uprooted of the western Sahel: migrants' search for cash in the Senegambia, [by] Lucie Gallistel Colvin [et al.] New York, Praeger, [1981] p. 83–112. map.

HB2125.5.A3U67

"The U.S. Agency for International Development (AID) funded this research."—p. iii.

4617

Faye, Jacques. Zonal approach to migration in the Senegalese peanut basin. *In* The Uprooted of the western Sahel: migrants' quest for cash in the Senegambia, [by] Lucie Gallistel Colvin [et al.] New York, Praeger, [1981] p. 136–160. maps.

HB2125.5.A3U67

"The U.S. Agency for International Development (AID) funded this research."—p. iii.

4618

Free, Michael J., *and* Margot L. Zimmerman. Family planning in Senegal: assessment and recommendations. Seattle, Program for the Introduction and Adaptation of Contraceptive Technology, 1979. [101] p. (in various pagings)

Prepared for the U.S. Agency for International Development.

Bibliography: p. E1–E2.

Examined in the Documentation Center, Sahel Development Program, AID, Washington, D.C.

4619

Hamer, Alice. Diola women and migration: a case study. *In* The Uprooted of the western Sahel: migrants' quest for cash in the Senegambia, [by] Lucie Gallistel Colvin [et al.] New York, Praeger, [1981] p. 183–203. map.   HB2125.5.A3U67

"The U.S. Agency for International Development (AID) funded this research."—p. iii.

4620

Profiles of Sahelian countries: Senegal. Washington, Socio-Economic Analysis Staff, International Statistical Programs Center, U.S. Bureau of the Census, 1974. [41] leaves (in various foliations)

Prepared at the request of the U.S. Agency for International Development.

Concerns demographic projections.

Examined in the Documentation Center, Sahel Development Program, AID, Washington, D.C.

4621

Soumah, Moussa. Regional migrations in southeastern Senegal, internal and international. *In* The Uprooted of the western Sahel: migrants' quest for cash in the Senegambia, [by] Lucie Gallistel Colvin [et al.] New York, Praeger, [1981] p. 161–182. maps.   HB2125.5.A3U67

"The U.S. Agency for International Development (AID) funded this research."—p. iii.

4622

Sow, Fatou. Migration to Dakar. *In* The Uprooted of the western Sahel: migrants' quest for cash in the Senegambia, [by] Lucie Gallistel Colvin [et al.] New York, Praeger, [1981] p. 204–243. map.

        HB2125.5.A3U67

    "The U.S. Agency for International Development (AID) funded this research."—p. iii.

4623

Tomaro, John. Population and development in Senegal: some thoughts on USAID's role and the place of family planning. Dakar, [U.S. AID Mission], 1980. 23 p.   MiEM

    "Joint planning of U.S. assistance programs in Senegal: resource paper."

Women

4624

Gaye, Ibrahima. Official discusses efforts to promote women's status. *In* U.S. *Joint Publications Research Service*. JPRS 75775. [Springfield, Va., National Technical Information Service, 1980] (Sub-Saharan Africa report, no. 2251) p. 79–83.

    Translation of interview with Maimouna Kane, Senegal's secretary of state for women's affairs, in *Le Soleil*, Dakar, Mar. 15–16, 1980, p. 4.

    Microfiche. [s.l., 1980]

        DLC-Micro JPRS 75775

4625

Women's development, [by] Isaac Nahmias [et al.] [Dakar?, U.S. AID Mission, 1978?] [125] leaves (in various foliations) illus.

    Examined in the Documentation Center, Sahel Development Program, U.S. Agency for International Development, Washington, D.C.

Other Subjects

4626

U.S. *Information Agency. Office of Research.* VOA audience estimate for Senegal, 1974. [Washington?], 1976. 19 p.   DLC

    "E-16-76."

    Issued also in microfiche. [Washington, Congressional Information Service, 1976?]

        DLC-Micro ASI:77 9856-2.32

4627

U.S. *Information Agency. Research Service.* Prelimi-nary audience estimate for Senegal. [Washington?] 1976. [2] leaves.   DLC

    Research memorandum M-9-76.

4628

Fall, Michael W. Rodent control in Senegal: present problems, future needs. Denver, Fish and Wildlife Service, 1976. 23 p.

    "Preliminary report."

    Examined in the Development Information Center, U.S. Agency for International Development, Washington, D.C.

4629

Maack, Stephen C. Urban change and quarter routinization in Pikine, Senegal. [New York], Columbia University, 1978. 778 leaves.

    Field research supported in part by the National Science Foundation and the National Institute of Mental Health.

    Thesis (Ph.D.)—Columbia University.

    An analysis of Dagoudane Pikine, a suburb of Dakar.

    Microfiche. [Sahel Documents and Dissertations. Ann Arbor, Mich., University Microfilms International, 1980] 9 sheets; (DLC-Micro Microfiche 5357 SG 134) and [Ann Arbor, Mich., University Microfilms International, 1979?] (DLC-Micro 79-04100).

4630

Seminaire de Télédetection; Senegal, *Dakar*, Mar, 31 – Apr. 10, 1980. Compte-rendus. [Brookings?], Remote Sensing Institute, South Dakota State University, 1980. 2 v.

    Issued for the U.S. Agency for International Development under contract AID/ta-C-1468.

    Text in English and French.

    Abstract in *A.I.D. Research & Development Abstracts*, v. 10, no. 1/2, 1982, p. 65.

4631

Wills, Dorothy D. Culture's cradle: social structural and interactional aspects of Senegalese socialization. Austin, University of Texas, 1977. 645 leaves.

    Study funded in part by the National Institute of Mental Health.

    Thesis (Ph.D.)—University of Texas.

    Study of child development and the place of children in the social structure.

    Microfiche. [Sahel Documents and Dissertations. Ann Arbor, Mich., University Microfilms International, 1980] 7 sheets; (DLC-Micro Microfiche 5357 SG 035) and [Ann Arbor, Mich., University Microfilms International, 1977?] (DLC-Micro 77-29116).

Sierra Leone

General

4632

U.S. *Dept. of State.* Post report. Sierra Leone. [Washington, Dept. of State, Publishing Services Division; for sale by the Supt. of Docs., U.S. Govt. Print. Off.], 1980. 16 p. illus., map. (*Its* Department and Foreign Service series, 185)

JX1705.A286 Spec. Format
Department of State publication, 9124.
L.C. has also report issued in 1976.
For a description of the contents of this publication, see the note to entry 936.

4633

U.S. *Dept. of State. Bureau of Public Affairs.* Background notes. Sierra Leone. [Washington, for sale by the Supt. of Docs., U.S. Govt. Print. Off.], 1980. 6 p. illus., maps. (U.S. Dept. of State. Department of State publication 8069)   G59.U5
L.C. retains only the latest revision.
For a description of the contents of this publication, see the note to entry 937.

4634

Kaplan, Irving. Area handbook for Sierra Leone; coauthors, Irving Kaplan [et al.] [1st ed. Washington, for sale by the Supt. of Docs., U.S. Govt. Print. Off.], 1976. 400 p. maps.

DT516.K36
"DA Pam 550-180."
"One of a series of handbooks prepared by Foreign Area Studies (FAS) of the American University.
Bibliography: p. 355–378.
Abstract in *Government Reports Announcement & Index*, Apr. 1, 1977, p. 25.
Issued also in microfiche. [s.l., 1977] 5 sheets.
DLC-Sci RR AD-A034792

4635

The Peace Corps in Sierra Leone. [Washington, U.S. Govt. Print. Off., 1980] folder ([6] p.) illus., map.
DLC
"ACTION 4200.67."
An introduction to the country for Volunteers.

Agriculture

4636

Barrows, Richard L. Individualized land tenure and African agricultural development: alternatives for policy. Madison, Land Tenure Center, University of Wisconsin-Madison, 1973. 30 p. (LTC paper, no. 85)
Prepared for the U.S. Agency for International Development under contract AID/csd-2263.
Uses the agricultural and tenure systems of the Mende and Limba in Sierra Leone as illustrations.
Microfiche. [Springfield, Va., National Technical Information Service, 1973] 1 sheet.
DLC-Sci RR PN-AAA-112

4637

Food flows and simulations, rural Sierra Leone, by Victor E. Smith [et al.] East Lansing, Dept. of Agricultural Economics, Michigan State University, 1981. 90 p. map. (MSU rural development series. Working paper, no. 19)   MiEM
"Report no. 7 Consumption Effects of Economic Policy Project, USAID Contract no. AID/DSAN-C-0008."
Bibliography: p. 89–90.

4638

Potts, Howard C. Seed handling and production for the ACRE project (Sierra Leone) Mississippi State, Seed Technology Laboratory, Mississippi State University, [1980] 33 p. illus.   MsSM
Prepared under a cooperative agreement with the U.S. Agency for International Development.
ACRE: Adaptive Crop Research and Extension Project.
Issued also in microfiche. [Washington, U.S. Agency for International Development, 1980?] 1

4638 (cont.)

sheet (PN-AAH-741); examined in the Development Information Center, AID, Washington, D.C.

4639

Spencer, Dunstan S. C. African women in agricultural development: a case study in Sierra Leone. East Lansing, Dept. of Agricultural Economics, Michigan State University, 1976. 36 p. (African Rural Economy Program. Working paper, no. 11)
HD6073.A4S557

Bibliography: p. 34–36.

Issued in cooperation with the Dept. of Agricultural Economics, Njala University College, Njala, Sierra Leone.

Abstract in *A.I.D. Research and Development Abstracts*, Jan. 1977, p. 37.

Issued also in microfiche ([Washington, U.S. Agency for International Development, 1976?] 1 sheet)   DLC-Sci RR PN-AAB-951

Economic Aspects

4640

Joint determination of food consumption and production in rural Sierra Leone: estimates of a household-firm model, [by] John Strauss [et al.] [East Lansing, Dept. of Agricultural Economics, Michigan State University], 1981. [80] p. (MSU rural development series. Working paper, no. 17)

Consumption Effects of Economic Policy. Project. Report no. 6.

Prepared for the U.S. Agency for International Development under contract AID/DSAN-C-0008.

Abstract in *A.I.D. Research & Development Abstracts*, v. 9, no. 3, p. 36.

Microfiche. [Washington, U.S. Agency for International Development, 1981?] 1 sheet.
DLC-Sci RR PN-AAJ-702

4641

King, Robert P., *and* Derek Byerlee. Income distribution, consumption patterns, and consumption linkages in rural Sierra Leone. Njala, Sierra Leone, Dept. of Agricultural Economics, Njala University College; East Lansing, Dept. of Agricultural Economics, Michigan State University, 1977. 95 p. illus. (African rural economy paper, no. 16)
HC517.S53C64

On cover: African Rural Economy Program.

Bibliography: p. 91–95.

"This paper has been developed as part of a two-year study of income distribution among rural households in Africa financed under a United States Agency for International Development

Contract (AID/ta-C-1328 with Michigan State University."

Abstract in *A.I.D. Research and Development Abstracts*, Apr. 1978, p. 4.

Issued also in microfiche. [Washington, U.S. Agency for International Development, 1977?] 2 sheets.   DLC-Sci RR PN-AAE-456

4642

Linsenmeyer, Dean A. Economic analysis of alternative strategies for the development of Sierra Leone marine fisheries. Njala, Sierra Leone, Dept. of Agricultural Economics, Njala University College; East Lansing, Dept. of Agricultural Economics, Michigan State University, 1976. 178 p. maps. (African Rural Economy Program. Working paper, no. 18)   SH315.S5L56

Bibliography: p. 174–178.

"Research partially funded by Agency for International Development Contract AID/csd 3625, Department of Agricultural Economics, Michigan State University, East Lansing, Michigan."

4643

May-Parker, Ibi I., *and* Carl Liedholm. Processing component of the Rural Employment Research Project, Njala University College: research statement. [East Lansing, Dept. of Agricultural Economics, Michigan State University], 1974. 9 p.

"This paper has been developed as part of a three year study of rural employment problems in Africa which is being financed under an AID/Washington contract (AID/csd 3625) with the Department of Agricultural Economics at Michigan State University."

Microfiche. [Washington, U.S. Agency for International Development, 1974?] 1 sheet.
DLC-Sci RR PN-RAA-523

4644

Michigan. State University, *East Lansing. Dept of Agricultural Economics.* Household food consumption in rural Sierra Leone, [by] Victor E. Smith [et al.] East Lansing, 1979. 111 p. (Michigan. State University, East Lansing. MSU rural development series. Working paper, no. 7)
TX360.S5M52   1979

"Consumption effects of economic policy project. Report no. 2."

Prepared for the U.S. Agency for International Development under contract no. AID/DSAN-C-0008.

Bibliography: p. 109–111.

Abstract in *A.I.D. Research and Development Abstracts*, v. 8, no. 2, 1980, p. 14.

Issued also in microfiche. [Washington, U.S.

4644 (cont.)

Agency for International Development, 1979?] 2 sheets.   DLC-Sci RR PN-AAH-104

4645

Rural employment in tropical Africa: summary of findings, by Derek Byerlee [et al.] Njala, Sierra Leone; East Lansing, Mich., African Rural Economy Program, Dept. of Agricultural Economics, Njala University College and Dept. of Agricultural Economics, Michigan State University, 1977. 176 p. (African Rural Economy Program. Working paper, no. 20)   HD5837.A6R87

"This report summarizes the results of the research project 'Rural Employment in Tropical Africa: A Network Approach: financed through USAID contract AID/csd 3625' (p. ix) initiated in 1972.

Focus is on Sierra Leone.

Abstract in *A.I.D. Research and Development Abstracts*, Oct. 1977, p. 3.

Issued also in microfiche. [Sahel Documents and Dissertations. Ann Arbor, Mich., University Microfilms International, 1980] 3 sheets (DLC-Micro Microfiche 5357 AS 275), and [Washington, U.S. Agency for International Development, 1977?] 2 sheets (DLC-Sci RR PN-AAD-176).

4646

Spencer, Dunstan S. C. Women in a developing economy: a West African case study. East Lansing, Dept. of Agricultural Economics, Michigan State University, 1979. 67 p.

Prepared for the U.S. Agency for International Development under contract AID/afr-C-1364.

Case study of women in the rural economy of Sierra Leone.

Abstract in *A.I.D. Research and Development Abstracts*, v. 9, no. 1, 1981, p. 31–32.

Microfiche. [Washington, U.S. Agency for International Development, 1979?] 1 sheet.
          DLC-Sci RR PN-AAH-579

4647

Spencer, Dunstan S. C., *and* Derek Byerlee. Small farms in West Africa; a descriptive analysis of employment, incomes, and productivity in Sierra Leone. East Lansing, African Rural Economy Program, Dept. of Agricultural Economics, Michigan State University, 1977. 80 p. map. (African Rural Economy Program. Working paper, no. 19)
          HD2146.5.S64

"This paper has been developed as part of a three year study of rural employment problems in Africa financed under a United States Agency for International Development contract (AID/csd 3625) with Michigan State University."

4648

—— Technical change, labor use and small farmer development; evidence from Sierra Leone. East Lansing, Dept. of Agricultural Economics, Michigan State University, 1976. [21] p. (African Rural Economy Program. Working paper, no. 15)
          MiEM

Research financed under U.S. Agency for International Development contract AID/csd-3625.

Issued in cooperation with the Dept. of Agricultural Economics, Njala University College, Njala, Sierra Leone.

Paper presented at annual meeting of the American Agricultural Economics Association, 1976.

Issued also in microfiche. [Washington, U.S. Agency for International Development, 1976?] 1 sheet.   DLC-Sci RR PN-AAD-483

4649

Spencer, Dunstan S. C., Derek Byerlee, *and* Steven Franzel. Annual costs, returns, and seasonal labor requirements for selected farm and nonfarm enterprises in rural Sierra Leone. [East Lansing, Dept. of Agricultural Economics, Michigan State University], 1979. 46 p. ([African Rural Economy Program] Working paper, no. 27)   MiEM

Published under terms of a U.S. Agency for International Development contract.

Issued in cooperation with the Dept. of Agricultural Economics, Njala University College, Njala, Sierra Leone.

Bibliography: p. 45–46.

Issued also in microfiche. [Washington, U.S. Agency for International Development, 1979?] 1 sheet.   DLC-Sci RR PN-AAC-638

4650

Strauss, John, Victor E. Smith, *and* Peter Schmidt. Determinants of food consumption in rural Sierra Leone: application of the Quadratic Expenditure System to the Consumption-Leisure Component of a Household-Firm Model. [East Lansing], Dept. of Agricultural Economics, Michigan State University, 1981. [43] p. (MSU rural development series. Working paper, no. 14)

"Published under Agency for International Development Contract AID/DSAN-C-0008, with Michigan State University."

Abstract in *A.I.D. Research & Development Abstracts*, v. 9, no. 3, 1981, p. 35–36.

Microfiche. [Washington, U.S. Agency for International Development, 1981?] 1 sheet.
          DLC-Sci RR PN-AAJ-701

4651

—— Single-equation estimation of food consumption choices in rural Sierra Leone. [East

4651 (cont.)

Lansing, Dept. of Agricultural Economics, Michigan State University], 1981. [114] p. (MSU rural development series. Working paper, no. 13)

Consumption Effects of Economic Policy Project. Report no. 4.

Prepared for the U.S. Agency for International Development under contract AID/DSAN-C-0008.

Abstract in *A.I.D. Research & Development Abstracts*, v. 9, no. 4, 1981, p. 35–36.

Microfiche. [Washington, U.S. Agency for International Development, 1981?] 2 sheets.

DLC-Sci RR PN-AAJ-563

4652

Ward, William A. Incorporating employment into agricultural project appraisal: a preliminary report. East Lansing, Dept. of Agricultural Economics, Michigan State University, 1975. [82] p. (African Rural Employment Research Network. Working paper, no. 6)   HD1521.W36

"This paper has been developed as part of a three-year study of rural employment problems in Africa which is being financed under an AID/Washington contract (AID/csd 3625) with the Department of Agricultural Economics at Michigan State University."

Bibliography: p. 67–79.

Includes illustrations from Sierra Leone.

Abstract in *A.I.D. Research and Development Abstracts*, Jan. 1976, p. 24–25.

Issued also in microfiche. [Washington, U.S. Agency for International Development, 1975?] 1 sheet.   DLC-Sci RR PN-AAB-246

Rice

4653

May-Parker, Ibi I. Problems of rice marketing in Sierra Leone. [East Lansing, Dept. of Agricultural Economics, Michigan State University, 1973] 13 p.
MiEM

Abstract in *A.I.D. Research and Development Abstracts*, July 1975, p. 22.

Microfiche. [Washington, U.S. Agency for International Development, 1973?] 1 sheet.

DLC-Sci RR PN-AAB-023

4654

Spencer, Dunstan S. C. Making optimum use of national resources: the case of the drive for self-sufficiency in rice production in Sierra Leone. [East Lansing, Dept. of Agricultural Economics, Michigan State University, 1973] 21 p.

Paper presented at the Third Annual Confer-

ence of the Sierra Leone Agricultural Society, Bo Teachers College, Sept. 6–9, 1973.

Abstract in *A.I.D. Research and Development Abstracts*, July 1975, p. 16.

Microfiche. [Washington, U.S. Agency for International Development, 1973?] 1 sheet.

DLC-Sci RR PN-AAA-988

4655

—— Rice policy in Sierra Leone. *In* Pearson, Scott R. Rice in West Africa: policy and economics. Stanford, Calif., Stanford University Press, 1981. p. 175–200.   HD9066.A462P4

Publication results from a research project, "The Political Economy of Rice in West Africa," carried out jointly by the Food Research Institute, Stanford University, and the West Africa Rice Development Association between June 1976 and Sept. 1979, and funded by the U.S. Agency for International Development under contract AID/afr-C-1235."

4656

—— Rice production in Sierra Leone. *In* Pearson, Scott R. Rice in West Africa: policy and economics. Stanford, Calif., Stanford Univeristy Press, 1981. p. 201–225. map.   HD9066.A462P4

Publication results from a research project carried out jointly by the Food Research Institute, Stanford University, and the West Africa Rice Development Association and funded by the U.S. Agency for International Development (see more complete note in entry 4655).

4657

Spencer, Dunstan S. C., Ibi I. May-Parker, *and* Frank S. Rose. Employment, efficiency and income in the rice processing industry of Sierra Leone. East Lansing, Mich., African Rural Economy Program, 1976. 78 p. illus. (African rural economy paper, no. 13)   HD9066.S52S65

Issued by the Dept. of Agricultural Economics, Michigan State University, in cooperation with the Dept. of Agricultural Economics, Njala University College, University of Sierra Leone.

"This paper has been developed as part of a three year study of rural development problems in Africa financed under a U.S. Agency for International Development Contract (AID/csd-3625) with Michigan State University."—p. ix.

Abstracts in *A.I.D. Research and Development Abstracts*, July 1977, p. 22; *Selected Appropriate Technologies for Developing Countries*, no. 1, p. 101; and *Government Reports Announcements & Index*, Sept. 16, 1977, p. 11.

Issued also in microfiche. [Washington, U.S. Agency for International Development, 1976?] 1

4657 (cont.)
sheet (DLC-Sci RR PN-AAC-755); and [Springfield, Va., National Technical Information Service, 1977] 1 sheet (DLC-Sci RR PB 268185).

Assistance Programs

4658
U.S. *Agency for International Development.* Annual budget submission: Sierra Leone. Washington, U.S. International Development Cooperation Agency.
Vols. for 1978+ examined in the Development Information Center, AID, Washington, D.C.

4659
—— Country development strategy statement: Sierra Leone. Washington, U.S. International Development Cooperation Agency. annual?
Vol. for 1983 examined in the Development Information Center, AID, Washington, D.C.

4660
U.S. *Peace Corps. Sierra Leone.* Peace Corps/Sierra Leone training manual for the 1973 education orientation program, July 16–September 8, 1973. [Freetown, 1973] 186 p.   DPC

4661
Action (Service Corps) *Internal Audit Staff.* Review of Peace Corps activities in Sierra Leone. [Washington?], 1973. 136 leaves.   DPC

4662
Anderson, G. William. Effectiveness and impact of the CARE/Sierra Leone rural penetration roads project (AID projects 636-0101, 636-0111, 636-0126) [Washington], Agency for International Development, 1980. [101] p. (in various pagings) illus., maps. (A.I.D. project impact evaluation paper, no. 7)   DLC
Includes bibliography.
CARE: Cooperative for American Relief Everywhere.
Abstract in *A.I.D. Research & Development Abstracts*, July 1981, p. 62–63.
Issued also in microfiche. [Washington, U.S. Agency for International Development, 1980?] 2 sheets.   DLC-Sci RR PN-AAH-751

4663
Hafner, Craig. Village based training. A pre-service training model developed in Sierra Leone. [Washington], Office of Programming & Training Coordination, [U.S. Peace Corps], 1979. 19 leaves.   DPC

4664
Hugo, Cornelius, *and* Kenneth L. Casavant. Assessment of the need, impact and proposed uses of 1980 PL 480 Title I rice sales to Sierra Leone. Manhattan, Food and Feed Grain Institute, Kansas State University, [1979] 80 p. (Grain storage, processing and marketing, report no. 80)   DLC
Prepared for the U.S. Agency for International Development under contract AID/ta-C-1162.

4665
Sierra Leone. [*Treaties, etc. United States, 1978 Aug. 31*] Agreement between the Government of the United States of America and the Government of the Republic of Sierra Leone for sales of agricultural commodities. *In* U.S. *Treaties, etc.* United States treaties and other international agreements, v. 30, 1978–79. [Washington, Dept. of State; for sale by the Supt. of Docs., U.S. Govt. Print. Off., 1980] p. 672–684. ([Treaties and other international acts series, 9210])   JX231.A34 v. 30
Signed at Freetown Aug. 31, 1978.

4666
Sierra Leone. [*Treaties, etc. United States, 1979 Aug. 23*] Agricultural commodities: agreement between the United States of America and Sierra Leone, signed at Freetown August 23, 1979, with memorandum of negotiations, and amending agreement effected by exchange of notes signed at Freetown September 5 and 6, 1979. [Washington, Dept. of State; for sale by the Supt. of Docs., U.S. Govt. Print. Off., 1980] 10 p. (Treaties and other international acts series, 9617)   DLC

4667
Sierra Leone. [*Treaties, etc. United States, 1980 Aug. 8.*] Agreement between the Government of the United States of America and the Government of the Republic of Sierra Leone for the sale of agricultural commodities under Public Law 480 Title I program. [Washington, Dept. of State; for sale by the Supt. of Docs., U.S. Govt. Print. Off., 1981] 8 p. (Treaties and other international acts series, 9840)   DLC
Signed in Freetown Aug. 8, 1980.

4668
Sierra Leone—tropical storm, June 1975. Washington, Office of Foreign Disaster Assistance, U.S. Agency for International Development, [1975?] 2 p. illus., maps. (Foreign disaster assistance report)   DLC

4669

Technical Assistance Information Clearing House. Development assistance programs of U.S. non-profit organizations: Sierra Leone. [New York], American Council of Voluntary Agencies for Foreign Service, 1977. 21 p. maps. (TAICH country report)   HC517.S5T52a

The Clearing House is operated by the Council under a grant from the U.S. Agency for International Development.

Economic Conditions

4670

Chuta, Enyinna J. A research proposal to study small-scale industries in rural areas of Sierra Leone. [s.l.], 1973. [13] p.

Microfiche. [Washington, U.S. Agency for International Development, 1973?] 1 sheet.
          DLC-Sci RR PN-RAA-510

4671

———— An economic analysis of small-scale industries in rural areas of Sierra Leone. East Lansing, Dept. of Agricultural Economics, Michigan State University, [1974] 39 p. maps.

Bibliography: p. [36]–39.

Microfiche. [Washington, U.S. Agency for International Development, 1974?] 1 sheet.
          DLC-Sci RR PN-RAA-509

4672

———— The economics of the gara (tie-dye) cloth industry in Sierra Leone. East Lansing, Dept. of Agricultural Economics, Michigan State University, 1978. 32 p. (African Rural Economy Program. Working paper, no. 25)   MiEM

"This Working Paper is a revised version of a paper presented at the 1977 Joint National Meeting of the Latin American Studies Association and the African Studies Association, Houston, Texas, November 1977. The research on this paper was financed by U.S. Agency for International Development contracts with Michigan State University (AID/csd-3625 and AID/ta-CA-2) and published under contract AID/ta-CA-2."

Abstract in *A.I.D. Research and Development Abstracts*, July 1978, p. 34.

Issued also in microfiche. [Washington, U.S. Agency for International Development, 1978?] 1 sheet.   DLC-Sci RR PN-AAF-318

4673

———— Techniques of production, efficiency and profitability in the Sierra Leone clothing industry. East Lansing, Dept. of Agricultural Economics, Michigan State University, 1980. 21 p. (African Rural Economy Program. Working paper, no. 30)
          MiEM

"Published as part of Michigan State University's Off-Farm Employment Project, which is financed by the Office of Rural Development and Development Administration, Development Support Bureau, U.S. Agency for International Development (AID/ta-CA-2)."

Copy examined in the Development Information Center, AID, Washington, D.C.

4674

Chuta, Enyinna, *and* Carl Liedholm. A progress report on research on rural small scale industry in Sierra Leone. Njala, Sierra Leone, Dept. of Agricultural Economics, Njala University College; East Lansing, Dept. of Agricultural Economics, Michigan State University, 1974. 41 leaves. map. (African Rural Employment Research Network. Working paper, no. 4)   HD2346.S5C47

Bibliography: leaves 39–40.

"This paper has been developed as part of a three-year study of rural employment problems in Africa which is being financed under a U.S. Agency for International Development Contract (AID/csd 3625) with Michigan State University."

Issued also in microfiche (Washington, U.S. Agency for International Development, 1974?] 1 sheet)   DLC-Sci RR PN-RAA-512

4675

———— The role of small scale industry in employment generation and rural development: initial research results from Sierra Leone. Njala, Sierra Leone, Dept. of Agricultural Economics, Njala University College; East Lansing, Dept. of Agricultural Economics, Michigan State University, 1975. 44 p. (African rural employment paper, no. 11)   HD2346.S5C48   1975

On cover: African Rural Employment Research Network.

Bibliography: p. 43–44.

"This paper has been developed as part of a three-year study of rural employment problems in Africa which is being financed under a U.S. Agency for International Development Contract (AID/csd 3625) with Michigan State University."

Abstract in *A.I.D. Research and Development Abstracts*, Jan. 1976, p. 24.

Issued also in microfiche ([Washington, U.S. Agency for International Development, 1975?] 1 sheet)   DLC-Sci RR PN-AAB-364

4676

Collier, John L. Economic structure and policies in Sierra Leone, 1961–70. [s.l., 1975] 16 leaves. (FAR 21120-N)

Prepared for the Colloquium on Sierra Leone, sponsored by the U.S. Dept. of State, Jan. 1975.

Examined in the former Foreign Affairs Research Documentation Center, U.S. Dept. of State.

4677

Employment growth and change in Sierra Leone small scale industry, 1974–1980, by Enyinna Chuta [et al.] East Lansing, Dept. of Agricultural Economics, Michigan State University, 1981. 23 p. (African Rural Economy Program. Working paper, no. 37)   MiEM

"Developed and published as part of Michigan State University's Off-Farm Employment Project, which is financed by the Office of Rural Development and Development Administration, Development Support Bureau, U.S. Agency for International Development (AID/ta-CA-2)."

4678

Employment-output conflicts, factor price distortions and choice of technique: empirical results from Sierra Leone, [by] Derek Byerlee [et al.] [East Lansing, Dept. of Agricultural Economics, Michigan State University], 1979. 35 p. (African Rural Economy Program. Working paper, no. 26)   MiEM

Research supported in part by the U.S. Agency for International Development and published under contract AID/ta-C-1328.

Abstract in *A.I.D. Research and Development Abstracts*, v. 7, no. 2, 1979, p. 7.

Issued also in microfiche. [Washington, U.S. Agency for International Development, 1979?] 1 sheet.   DLC-Sci RR PN-AAG-668

4679

Foreign economic trends and their implications for the United States. Sierra Leone. 1969+ Washington, for sale by the Supt. of Docs., U.S. Govt. Print. Off. annual. (International marketing information series)   HC10.E416

Continues *Economic Trends and Their Implications for the United States. Sierra Leone.*

Prepared by the U.S. Embassy, Freetown.

Vols. for 1969–77 distributed by the U.S. Bureau of International Commerce; vols. for 1978–79 by the U.S. Industry and Trade Administration; vols. for 1980– by the U.S. International Trade Administration.

The following issues for the period 1973–81 have been identified in L.C.:

ET 73-097. 1973. 8 p.

ET 74-095. 1974. 8 p.
FET 75-097. 1975. 7 p.
FET 76-113. 1976. 7 p.
FET 77-125. 1977. 8 p.
FET 78-106. 1978. 7 p.
FET 79-100. 1979. 7 p.
FET 80-108. 1980. 7 p.
FET 81-126. 1981. 11 p.

4680

Haen, Hartwig de. Aggregate policy models of the Sierra Leone economy with special emphasis on the small scale economy. [East Lansing?], 1974. 44 p.

"This paper has been developed as part of a three-year study of rural employment problems in Africa which is being financed under an AID/Washington contract (AID/csd-3625) with the Department of Agricultural Economics at Michigan State University."

Microfiche. [Washington, U.S. Agency for International Development, 1974?] 1 sheet.

DLC-Sci RR PN-RAA-514

4681

Haen, Hartwig de, Derek Byerlee, *and* Dunstan S. C. Spencer. Preliminary formulations of policy models of the Sierra Leone economy emphasizing the rural sectors. Njala, Sierra Leone, Dept. of Agricultural Economics, Njala University College; East Lansing, Dept. of Agricultural Economics, Michigan State University, 1974. 39 leaves. (African Rural Employment Research Network. Working paper, no. 3)   HC517.S5H33

"This paper has been developed as part of a three-year study of rural employment problems in Africa which is being financed under a U.S. Agency for International Development contract (AID/csd 3625) with Michigan State University."

Issued also in microfiche. [Washington, U.S. Agency for International Development, 1974?] 1 sheet.   DLC-Sci RR PN-RAA-517

4682

Liedholm, Carl, *and* Enyinna Chuta. The economics of rural and urban smallscale industries in Sierra Leone. Njala, Sierra Leone; East Lansing, Mich., African Rural Economy Program, Dept. of Agricultural Economics, Njala University College, University of Sierra Leone [and] Dept. of Agricultural Economics, Michigan State University, 1976. 129 p. (African rural economy paper, no. 14)

HD2346.S5L53

Bibliography: p. 127–129.

"This paper has been developed as part of a three year study of rural employment in tropical Africa financed under a United States Agency for

4682 (cont.)

International Development contract (AID/csd-3625) with Michigan State University."

Abstracts in *A.I.D. Research and Development Abstracts*, July 1977, p. 2, and in *Government Reports Announcements & Index*, Sept. 16, 1977, p. 31.

Issued also in microfiche. [Washington, U.S. Agency for International Development, 1976?] 2 sheets (DLC-Sci RR PN-AAC-756); [Arlington, Va., ERIC Document Reproduction Service; prepared for Educational Resources Information Center, National Institure of Education, 1977] 2 sheets (DLC-Sci RR ED134388); and [Springfield, Va., National Technical Information Service, 1977] 2 sheets. (DLC-Sci RR PB-268493).

4683

May-Parker, Ibi I., V. Sorenson, *and* John Shaffer. Initial working paper on incorporating the marketing dimension into the Sierra Leone "Rural Employment Research Project." [East Lansing, Dept. of Agricultural Economics, Michigan State University], 1974. 54 p.   MiEM

"This paper has been developed as part of a three year study of rural employment problems in Africa which is being financed under an AID/Washington contract (AID/csd 3625) with the Department of Agricultural Economics at Michigan State Univeristy."

Issued also in microfiche. [Washington, U.S. Agency for International Development, 1974?] 1 sheet.   DLC-Sci RR PB-RAA-522

4684

Timmer, C. Peter. The economics of marketing and processing in Sierra Leone; consultant's report. [East Lansing, Dept. of Agricultural Economics, Michigan State University], 1973. 7 p.

Microfiche. [Washington, U.S. Agency for International Development, 1973?] 1 sheet.   DLC-Sci RR PN-RAA-527

Education

4685

The Development of education in Sierra Leone, 1974/75-1975/76; report (part II). [Freetown?], Planning Unit, Ministry of Education, 1977. 13 p.

Report to the 36th session, International Conference on Education, Geneva, Switz., 1977.

Abstract in *Resources in Education*, Jan. 1978, p. 139.

Microfiche. [Arlington, Va., ERIC Document Reproduction Service; prepared for Educational

Resources Information Center, National Institute of Education, 1978] 1 sheet.   DLC-Micro ED143616

4686

Jones, Joseph. Teacher Corps/Peace Corps program, Sierra Leone: final report. Houston, Texas Southern University, 1976. 6 leaves.   DPC

Report submitted to the Peace Corps.

4687

Ketkar, Suhas L. Economics of education in Sierra Leone. Ann Arbor, Center for Research on Economic Development, University of Michigan, 1975. 37 p. (Michigan. University. Center for Research on Economic Development. Discussion paper, no. 47)

Abstract in *A.I.D. Research and Development Abstracts*, Sept. 1975, p. 19.

Microfiche. [Washington, U.S. Agency for International Development, 1975?] 1 sheet.   DLC-Sci RR PN-AAB-154

Geology, Hydrology, and Mineral Resources

The following items (entries 4688-95) are listed in chronological order:

4688

Stipp, Henry E. The mineral industry of Sierra Leone. *In* Minerals yearbook, v. 3, 1972. [Washington, for sale by the Supt. of Docs., U.S. Govt. Print. Off., 1974] p. 695-698.

          TN23.U612   1972, v. 3

Prepared by the U.S. Bureau of Mines.

4689

——— The mineral industry of Sierra Leone. *In* Minerals yearbook, v. 3, 1973. [Washington, for sale by the Supt. of Docs., U.S. Govt. Print. Off., 1976] p. 739-743.   TN23.U612   1973, v. 3

Prepared by the U.S. Bureau Mines.

4690

Jolly, Janice L. W. The mineral industry of Sierra Leone. *In* Minerals yearbook, v. 3, 1974. [Washington, for sale by the Supt. of Docs., U.S. Govt. Print. Off., 1977] p. 785-790.

          TN23.U612   1974, v. 3

Prepared by the U.S. Bureau of Mines.

4691

——— The mineral industry of Sierra Leone. *In* Minerals yearbook, v. 3, 1975. [Washington, for

4691 (cont.)

sale by the Supt. of Docs., U.S. Govt. Print. Off., 1978] p. 841–844.   TN23.U612   1975, v. 3

4692

Stevens, Candice. The mineral industry of Sierra Leone. *In* Minerals yearbook, v. 3, 1976. [Washington, for sale by the Supt. of Docs., U.S. Govt. Print. Off., 1980] p. 919–922.

TN23.U612   1976, v. 3

Prepared by the U.S. Bureau of Mines.

4693

—— The mineral industry of Sierra Leone. *In* Minerals yearbook, v. 3, 1977. [Washington, for sale by the Supt. of Docs., U.S. Govt. Print. Off., 1981] p. 821–824.   TN23.U612   1977, v. 3

4694

Stevens, Candice, *and* Phyllis A. Lyday. The mineral industry of Sierra Leone. *In* Minerals yearbook, v. 3, 1978–79. [Washington, U.S. Govt. Print. Off., 1981] p. 819–822.   TN23.U612   1978–79, v. 3

Prepared by the U.S. Bureau of Mines.

4695

Keyes, William F. The mineral industry of Sierra Leone. *In* Minerals yearbook, v. 3, 1980. [Washington, for sale by the Supt. of Docs., U.S. Govt. Print. Off., 1982] p. 855–857.

TN23.U612   1980, v. 3

Prepared by the U.S. Bureau of Mines.

Health and Nutrition

4696

Jenkins, Phyllis L. Peace Corps Sierra Leone health handbook. Rev. ed. [Washington?, Peace Corps?, 1976] 32 p. illus.   DPC

Cover title: What you need to know about tropical diseases and living well in Sierra Leone.

First ed., by Paul Goff, issued in 1973.

4697

Kolasa, Kathryn M. The nutritional situation in Sierra Leone. East Lansing, Dept. of Agricultural Economics, Michigan State University, 1979. 91 p. (Michigan. State University, East Lansing, MSU development working papers, no. 2)

TX360.S5K64

"AID/ta-CA-3."

"Project on Consumption Effects of Economic Policy. Report, no. 1."

Bibliography: p. 83–91.

Abstracts in *A.I.D. Research and Development Abstracts*, v. 7, no. 1, 1979, p. 18, and *Government*

Reports Announcements & Index, June 20, 1980, p. 2158.

Issued also in microfiche. [Washington, U.S. Agency for International Development, 1979] 2 sheets (DLC-Sci RR PN-AAG-612) and [Springfield, Va., National Technical Information Service, 1980] 2 sheets (DLC-Sci RR PB 80-155013).

4697a

Sierra Leone national nutrition survey, undertaken by the Government of Sierra Leone. Final report, October 1978, with the assistance of the UCLA Nutrition Assessment Unit, Division of Population, Family and International Health, School of Public Health, University of California, Los Angeles, California, U.S.A., in cooperation with the United States Agency for International Development. [Los Angeles?], 1978. 218 p. map.

Includes bibliographies.

Microfiche. [Washington, U.S. Agency for International Development, 1978?] 3 sheets (DLC-Sci RR PN-AAG-482); and [Washington, Congressional Information Service, 1978?] (DLC-Micro ASI:79 7206-8.5).

Politics and Government

4698

Country's political, economic conditions surveyed. *In* U.S. *Joint Publications Research Service*. JPRS 73098. [Springfield, Va., National Technical Information Service, 1979] (Translations on Sub-Saharan Africa, no. 2082) p. 146–155.

Article in *West Africa*, London, Feb. 19 and 26 and Mar. 5, 1979.

Microfiche. [Washington, Supt. of Docs., U.S. Govt. Print. Off., 1979]

DLC-Micro JPRS 73098

4699

Jordan, Robert S., *and* John P. Renninger. Sierra Leone politics since independence: an interpretation. [s.l., 1975] 6 leaves. (FAR 21123-N)

Paper presented at the Colloquium on Sierra Leone, sponsored by the U.S. Dept. of State, Jan. 1975.

Examined in the former Foreign Affairs Research Documentation Center, U.S. Dept. of State.

Population Studies

4700

Africa: Sierra Leone. Selected statistical data by sex. Washington, 1981. 32, 17 p.   DLC

Study supported by the U.S. Agency for In-

4700 (cont.)

ternational Development's Office of Women in Development and Office of Population.

Data assembled by the International Demographic Data Center, U.S. Bureau of the Census.

Among the tables, all based on 1963 data (unless otherwise noted), are the following: unadjusted population by age, sex, and urban/rural residence (1974); population by district, sex, and urban/rural residence (1974); population by ethnic group, sex, and urban/rural residence; population by nationality, sex, and urban/rural residence; life expectancy; number of literate persons by age, sex, and urban/rural residence; number of persons enrolled in school by age, sex, and urban/rural residence; number of economically active persons by age, sex, and urban/rural residence; economically active population by occupational status, sex, and urban/rural residence.

4701

Byerlee, Derek, *and* Joseph L. Tommy. An integrated methodology for research on migration: the Sierra Leone Rural-Urban Migration Survey. Njala, Dept. of Agricultural Economics and Extension, Njala University College, University of Sierra Leone, 1975. 11 p.

On cover: "The Sierra Leone Rural-Urban Migration Survey is being undertaken with financial support from the Population Council and a [AID] subcontract from Michigan State University to Njala University College."

Abstract in *A.I.D. Research and Development Abstracts*, Apr. 1979, p. 27.

Microfiche. [Washington, U.S. Agency for International Development, 1975?] 1 sheet.

DLC-Sci RR PN-RAA-508

4702

Byerlee, Derek, Joseph L. Tommy, *and* Habib Fatoo. Rural-urban migration in Sierra Leone; determinants and policy implications. East Lansing, African Rural Economy Program, Dept. of Agricultural Economics, Michigan State University, 1976. 113 p. illus. (African rural economy paper, no. 13)   HB2126.9.A3B93

Bibliography: p. 111–113.

Issued in cooperation with the Dept. of Agricultural Economics, Njala University College, University of Sierra Leone.

"This paper has been developed as part of a three year study of rural employment in tropical Africa financed under a United States Agency for International Development contract (AID/cad 3625) with Michigan State University. The research in Sierra Leone was carried out under a sub-contract to the Department of Agricultural

Economics and Extension, Njala University College, Sierra Leone, under AID/cad 3625."

Abstract in *A.I.D. Research and Development Abstracts*, July 1977, p. 4.

Issued also in microfiche. [Washington, U.S. Agency for International Development, 1976?] 2 sheets (DLC-Sci RR PN-AAC-755); and [Arlington, Va., ERIC Document Reproduction Service; prepared for Educational Resources Information Center, National Institute of Education, 1977] 2 sheets (DLC-Micro ED134387).

4703

Mills, L. R. Circular rural-urban migration: the case of rural absentees in central Sierra Leone. [East Lansing, Dept. of Agricultural Economics, Michigan State University, 1973] [24] p.

Abstract in *A.I.D. Research and Development Abstracts*, July 1975, p. 14.

Microfiche. [Washington, U.S. Agency for International Development, 1973?] 1 sheet.

DLC-Sci RR PN-AAA-983

Other Subjects

4704

Brown, J. Randall, *and* Milton E. Harvey. Regional specialization and optimal resource allocation: a logistic for efficient interregional transaction in Sierra Leone. [Kent, Ohio], Kent State University, [1978?] [38] leaves. maps.

Research supported by the National Science Foundation.

Examined in the National Science Foundation, Washington, D.C.

4705

McMaster, Robert L., Eric Chrisofferson, *and* Asaf Ashraf. Structural framework of continental shelf and slope off southwestern Sierra Leone, West Africa. *In* American Association of Petroleum Geologists. Bulletin, v. 59, Nov. 1975: 2161–2171. illus.   TN860.A3 v. 59

Study at the Graduate School of Oceanography, University of Rhode Island, supported by the Office of Naval Research under contract N00014-68-A-0215-003.

4706

Spitzer, Leo. The Creoles in Sierra Leone history: an outline of their intellectual and political reactions to colonialism. [s.l.], 1975. 12 leaves. (FAR 21122-N)

Prepared for the Colloquium on Sierra Leone, sponsored by the U.S. Dept. of State, Jan. 1975.

Examined in the former Foreign Affairs Research Documentation Center, U.S. Dept. of State.

Togo

General

4707

U.S. *Dept. of State.* Post report. Togo. [Washington, Dept. of State, Publishing Services Division; for sale by the Supt. of Docs., U.S. Govt. Print. Off., 1981] 16 p. illus., map. (*Its* Department and Foreign Service series, 220)

JX1705.A286 Spec. Format
Department of State publication, 9171.
L.C. has also report issued in 1975.
For a description of the contents of this publication, see the note to entry 936.

4708

U.S. *Dept. of State. Bureau of Public Affairs.* Background notes. Togo. [Washington, for sale by the Supt. of Docs., U.S. Govt. Print. Off.] 1981. 4 p. maps. (U.S. Dept. of State. Department of State publication, 8325) G59.U5
L.C. retains only the latest revision.
For a description of the contents of this publication, see the note to entry 937.

4709

The Peace Corps in Togo. [Washington, U.S. Govt. Print. Off., 1980] folder ([6] p.) illus., map.
DLC
"ACTION 4200.71."
An introduction to the country for Volunteers.

Agriculture

4710

Agricultural changes reported. *In* U.S. *Joint Publications Research Service.* JPRS 68710. [Springfield, Va., National Technical Information Service, 1977] (Translations on Sub-Saharan Africa, no. 1717) p. 120–126.
Translation of article in *Europe Outremer*, Paris, Oct. 1976, p. 29–31, 37.

Microfiche. [s.l., 1978]
DLC-Micro JPRS 68710

4711

Delouche, James C. Seed multiplication/quality control—Togo. [Mississippi State], Seed Technology Laboratory, Mississippi State University, 1977. 51 p.
Prepared for the U.S. Agency for International Development under contract AID/ta-C-1219.
Examined in the Development Information Center, AID, Washington, D.C.

4712

MacKenzie, Bruce. Modern management in Togolese rural development: a seminar on modern management processes applied to intersectorial rural development in the Republic of Togo, Lama-Kara, Togo—July 25 – August 5, 1980. New York, Center for International Public Issues, inc., 1981. [51] p. (in various pagings)
Supported by the U.S. Agency for International Development under contract AID/afr-C-1672.
Seminar conducted in collaboration with the Centre national de promotion des petites et moyennes entreprises of Togo.
Text in English or French.
Examined in the Development Information Center, AID, Washington, D.C.

Assistance Programs

4713

U.S. *Agency for International Development.* Annual budget submission: Togo. Washington, U.S. International Development Cooperation Agency.
Vols. for 1981+ examined in the Development Information Center, AID, Washington, D.C.

4714

—— Country development strategy statement: Togo; small program statement. Washington, U.S.

4714 (cont.)

International Development Cooperation Agency. annual.

Vols. for 1981+ examined in the Development Information Agency, AID, Washington, D.C.

4715

U.S. *Peace Corps. Togo.* PCV newsletter. v. 1+ Jan. 1975?+ [Lomé?]   DPC

4716

Leiberg, Leon, John W. McCollum, *and* Paul Smith. Peace Corps/Togo: country program evaluation. [s.l.], Social, Educational Research & Development, inc., 1977. [60] p. (in various pagings)
                                                                              DPC

Prepared for the Division of Evaluation, Action (Service Corps).

4717

Technical Assistance Information Clearing House. Development assistance programs of U.S. non-profit organizations: Togo. [New York], American Council of Voluntary Agencies for Foreign Service, 1976. 13 p. maps. (TAICH country report)
                                                     HC557.T6T4a Dec. 1976

The Clearing House is operated by the Council under a grant from the U.S. Agency for International Development.

4718

——— Development assistance programs of U.S. non-profit organizations: Togo. [New York], American Council of Voluntary Agencies for Foreign Service, 1982. 19 p. maps. (TAICH country report)   HC557.T6T4a 1982
"2nd edition."

4719

Togo. [*Treaties, etc. United States, 1977 Oct. 12*] Togo; agricultural commodities: transfer under Title II; agreement signed at Lome October 12, 1977; entered into force October 12, 1977. *In* U.S. *Treaties, etc.* United States treaties and other international agreements, v. 29, 1976–77. [Washington, Dept. of State; for sale by the Supt. of Docs., U.S. Govt. Print. Off., 1980] p. 5286–5288. ([Treaties and other international acts series, 9106])
                                                                  JX231.A34 v. 29

4720

Togo. [*Treaties, etc. United States, 1980 Mar. 10*] International military education and training (IMET) Agreement between the United States of America and Togo effected by exchange of notes dated at Lome March 10 and July 17, 1980. [Washington, Dept. of State; for sale by the Supt. of

Docs., U.S. Govt. Print. Off., 1981] 5 p. (Treaties and other international acts series, 9866)
                                                                              DLC

In English and French.

4721

Togo. [*Treaties, etc. United States, 1980 Mar. 28*] Finance: consolidation and rescheduling of certain debts: agreement between the United States of America and Togo signed at Lome March 28, 1980. [Washington, Dept. of State; for sale by the Supt. of Docs., U.S. Govt. Print. Off., 1980] 14 p. (Treaties and other international acts series, 9740)
                                                                              DLC

In English and French.

Economic Conditions

4722

Data on 1976–1980 plan. *In* U.S. *Joint Publications Research Service.* JPRS 68710. [Springfield, Va., National Technical Information Service, 1977] (Translations on Sub-Saharan Africa, no. 1717) p. 110–116.

Translation of article in *Europe Outremer*, Paris, Oct. 1976, p. 26–28.

Micrfocihe. [s.l., 1977]
                                                   DLC-Micro JPRS 68710

4723

Foreign economic trends and their implications for the United States. Togo. 1969+ Washington, for sale by the Supt. of Docs., U.S. Govt. Print. Off. annual. (International marketing information series)   HC10.E416

Continues *Economic Trends and Their Implications for the United States. Togo.*

Prepared by the U.S. Embassy, Lomé.

Vols. for 1969–77 distributed by the U.S. Bureau of International Commerce; vols. for 1978–79 by the U.S. Industry and Trade Administration; vols. for 1980– by the U.S. International Trade Administration.

The following issues for the period 1973–81 have been identified in L.C.:

ET 73-075. 1973. 11 p.
ET 74-082. 1974. 11 p.
ET 75-096. 1975. 8 p.
FET 76-089. 1976. 8 p.
FET 77-112. 1977. 13 p.
FET 78-091. 1978. 11 p.
FET 79-114. 1979. 11 p.
FET 80-107. 1980. 17 p.
FET 81-121. 1981. 14 p.

4724

Weiss, Danielle. President discusses search for economic independence. *In* U.S. *Joint Publications Research Service.* JPRS 68604. [Springfield, Va., National Technical Information Service, 1977] (Translations on Sub-Saharan Africa, no. 1711) p. 20–26.

Translation of interview with President Gnassingbé Eyadéma in *Europe Outremer*, Parts, Oct. 1976, p. 10–13.

Microfiche. [s.l., 1977]

DLC-Micro JPRS 68604

Language and Languages

4725

Kozelka, Paul R. Ewe (for Togo) Brattleboro, Vt., Experiment in International Living, for ACTION/Peace Corps, [1980] 4 v. illus. (Peace Corps language handbook series)   DPC

Contents: [1] Communication and culture handbook.—[2] Grammar handbook.—[3] Special skills handbook.—[4] Teacher's handbook.

4726

Sedlak, Philip A. S. Kabiye communication and culture handbook. Brattleboro, Vt., Experiment in International Living, [for] ACTION/Peace Corps, [1980?] 246 p. (Peace Corps language handbook series)

Held by the African Language Program Library, Yale University.

4727

———— Kabiye grammar handbook. Brattleboro, Vt., Experiment in International Living, [for] ACTION/Peace Corps, [1980?] 246 p. (Peace Corps language handbook series)

Held by the African Language Program Library, Yale University.

4728

———— Kabiye: special skills handbook. Brattleboro, Vt., Experiment in International Living, 1980. 263 p. (Peace Corps language handbook series)   CtY

Politics and Government

4729

Eyadéma, Gnassingbé. Eyadema warns against corruption, exploitation. *In* U.S. *Joint Publications Research Service.* JPRS 72438. [Springfield, Va., National Technical Information Service, 1978]

(Translations on Sub-Saharan Africa, no. 2037) p. 45–49.

Translation of speech recorded in *Togo-Presse*, Lomé, Nov. 7, 1978, p. 3, 5.

Microfiche. [Washington, Supt. of Docs., U.S. Govt. Print. Off., 1978]

DLC-Micro JPRS 72438

4730

Political, economic situation surveyed. *In* U.S. *Joint Publications Research Service.* JPRS 68721. [Springfield, Va., National Technical Information Service, 1977] (Translations on Sub-Saharan Africa, no. 1718) p. 49–53.

Translation of article in *France Eurafrique*, Paris, Dec. 1976, p. 6–8.

Microfiche. [s.l., 1977]

DLC-Micro JPRS 68721

4731

Resolutions of political commission. *In* U.S. *Joint Publications Research Service.* JPRS 68431. [Springfield, Va., National Technical Information Service, 1977] (Translations on Sub-Saharan Africa, no. 1700) p. 109–119.

Translation of resolutions of the Rassemblement du peuple togolais, in *Togo presse Denyigba*, Lomé, Nov. 30, 1976, p. 4–6.

Microfiche. [s.l., 1977]

DLC-Micro JPRS 68431

Population Studies

4732

Africa: Togo. Selected statistical data by sex. Washington, 1981. 31, 17 p.   DLC

Study supported by the U.S. Agency for International Development's Office of Women in Development and Office of Population.

Data assembled by the International Demographic Data Center, U.S. Bureau of the Census.

Among the tables, all based on the 1970 data, are the following: unadjusted population by age, sex, and urban/rural residence; population by province, sex, and urban/rural residence; population by ethnic group, sex, and urban/rural residence; life expectancy; urban and rural populations by marital status, age, and sex; number of literate persons by age, sex, and urban/rural residence; number of persons enrolled in school by age, sex, and urban/rural residence; number of economically active persons by age, sex, and urban/rural residence; economically active population by occupational status, sex, and urban/rural residence.

4733

Profiles of Sahelian countries: Togo. Washington, Socio-Economic Analysis Staff, International Statistical Programs Center, U.S. Bureau of the Census, 1974. [34] leaves.

Prepared at the request of the U.S. Agency for International Development.

Concerns demographic projections.

Examined in the Documentation Center, Sahel Development Program, AID, Washington, D.C.

Other Subjects

4734

U.S. *Agency for International Development. Office of Housing.* Republic of Togo, shelter sector assessment. [Washington], The Office, 1977. xxii, 130, [14] leaves. illus., maps.

HD7376.8.A3U54 1977

Based on a study conducted by National Savings and Loan League.

Bibliography: leaves [131]–[133].

Prepared by Joseph M. Perta, and others.

Abstract in *A.I.D. Research and Development Abstracts*, Oct. 1978, p. 39–40.

Issued also in microfiche. [Washington, U.S. Agency for International Development, 1977?] 2 sheets (PN-AAF-454); examined in the Development Information Center, AID, Washington, D.C.

4735

Atignon, Koffi. Reform of the education system in Togo. *In* Educational reforms and innovations in Africa: studies prepared for the Conference of Ministers of Education of African Member States of Unesco. Paris, Unesco, 1978. (Experiments and innovations in education, no. 34)

LA1500.E38

Issued also in microfiche. [Arlington, Va., ERIC Document Reproduction Service; prepared for Educational Resources Information Center, National Institute of Education, 1978] 1 sheet.

DLC-Micro ED160036

4736

Chittum, J. Marc. Marketing in Togo. [Washington], U.S. Dept. of Commerce, Industry and Trade Administration; [for sale by the Supt. of Docs., U.S. Govt. Print. Off.], 1977. 9 p. (Overseas business reports. OBR 77-70)

HF91.U482 1977, no. 70

International marketing information series.

4737

Salami, Amoussa. Port, airfield, railway projects outlined. *In* U.S. *Joint Publications Research Service.* JPRS 69864. [Springfield, Va., National Technical Information Service, 1977] (Translations on Sub-Saharan Africa, no. 1808) p. 108–112.

Translation of article in *Togo-Presse*, Lomé, Aug. 17, 1977, p. 1, 4.

Microfiche. [s.l., 1977]

DLC-Micro JPRS 69864

4738

Togo. [*Treaties, etc. United States, 1979 Jan. 30*] Agreement on procedures for mutual assistance between the United States Department of Justice and the Ministry of Justice of the Republic of Togo in connection with matters relating to the Gulfstream American Corporation, formerly known as Grumman American Aviation Corporation. *In* U.S. *Treaties, etc.* United States treaties and other international agreements, v. 30, 1978–79. [Washington, Dept. of State; for sale by the Supt. of Docs., U.S. Govt. Print. Off., 1980] p. 3477–3485. ([Treaties and other international acts series, 9401]) JX231.A34 v. 30

In English and French.

4739

Togo nutrition status survey, October 1976-January 1977, conducted by the Ministry of Rural Development, Government of Togo. [Washington, Office of Nutrition, Agency for International Development, 1977] 120 p.

Conducted with the assistance of the Center for Disease Control, U.S. Public Health Service, in cooperation with the U.S. Agency for International Development.

Microfiche. [Washington, Congressional Information Service, 1977?] (DLC-Micro ASI:79 7206-8.4); and [Washington, U.S. Agency for International Development, 1977?] 2 sheets (PN-AAG-240); examined in the Development Information Center, AID, Washington, D.C.

Upper Volta

General

4740

U.S. *Dept. of State.* Post report. Upper Volta. [Washington?], 1978. [25] p. illus., map.

JX1705.A286 Spec. Format

For a description of the contents of this publication, see the note to entry 936.

4741

U.S. *Dept. of State. Bureau of Public Affairs.* Background notes. Upper Volta. [Washington, for sale by the Supt. of Docs., U.S. Govt. Print. Off.] 1981. 4 p. maps. (U.S. Dept. of State. Department of State publication 8201, rev.)   G59.U5

L.C. retains only the latest revision.

For a description of the contents of this publication, see the note to entry 937

4742

The Peace Corps in Upper Volta. [Washington, U.S. Govt. Print. Off., 1980] folder ([6] p.) illus., map.

DLC

"ACTION 4200.73."

An introduction to the country for Volunteers.

4743

Turner, Sandra J. Draft environmental profile on Upper Volta. Tucson, Arid Lands Information Center, Office of Arid Lands Studies, University of Arizona, 1980. 138 p. maps.   DLC

Prepared for the U.S. Agency for International Development.

On cover: National Park Service Contract No. CX-0001-0-0003 with U.S. Man and the Biosphere Secretariat, Department of State, Washington, D.C.

Bibliography: p. 121 138.

Abstract in *A.I.D. Research & Development Abstracts*, July 1981, p. 37–38.

Issued also in microfiche. [Washington, U.S. Agency for International Development, 1980?] 2 sheets.   DLC-Sci RR PN-AAJ-205

4744

Upper Volta: a country profile; prepared for the Office of U.S. Foreign Disaster Assistance, Bureau for Private and Development Cooperation, Agency for International Development, Department of State by Evaluation Technologies, Inc., 1978. 53 p. col. map.   DLC

Bibliography: p. 52–53.

A general introduction, with emphasis on political structure, disaster preparedness, demography, health, nutrition, housing, economic conditions, agriculture, geography, transportation, power, and communications.

Issued also in microfiche. [Sahel Documents and Dissertations. Ann Arbor, Mich., University Microfilms International, 1980] 2 sheets.

DLC-Micro Microfiche 5357 UV 201

Agriculture

4745

U.S. *AID Mission to Upper Volta.* Upper Volta forestry education and development (686–0235): project paper. [s.l.], 1978. 77 p.   MiEM

4746

U.S. [*Treaties, etc. Upper Volta, 1978 June 8*] Project agreement between the Government of the Republic of Upper Volta and the Government of the United States of America for agricultural human resources development. Accord de subvention entre le Gouvernement de la République de Haute-Volta et le Gouvernement des Etats-Unis d'Amerique pour le développement des ressources humaines agricoles. *In* U.S. *Treaties, etc.* United States treaties and other international agreements, v. 30, 1978–79. [Washington, Dept. of State; for sale by the Supt. of Docs., U.S. Govt. Print. Off., 1980] p. 3186–3204. ([Treaties and other international acts series, 9388])   JX231.A34, v. 30

Signed at Ouagadougou June 8, 1978.

Concerns agricultural education.

4747

Agricultural human resources development (Upper Volta), [by] James L. Stallings [et al] Ouagadougou, U.S. AID Mission to Upper Volta, [1977?] 206 p.   MiEM

"Project paper. Project no. 686–0221."

4748

Delgado, Christopher L. An investigation of the lack of mixed farming in the West African savannah: a farming systems approach for Tenkodogo, Upper Volta. [Ann Arbor, Center for Research on Economic Development, University of Michigan, 1978] 71 p. (Michigan. University. Center for Research on Economic Development. Discussion paper, no. 74)   MiU

Financed by the U.S. Agency for International Development under contract AID/afr-C-1169.

Bibliography: p. 69–71.

A summary of the principal points in *Livestock Versus Foodgrain Production in Southeast Upper Volta* (entry 4749).

Abstract in *A.I.D. Research and Development Abstracts*, v. 7, no. 1, 1979, p. 3.

Issued also in microfiche. [Washington, U.S. Agency for International Development, 1978?] 1 sheet (DLC-Sci RR PN-AAG-425); and [Sahel Documents and Dissertations. Ann Arbor, Mich., University Microfilms International, 1980] 2 sheets. (DLC-Micro Microfiche 5357 UV 101).

4749

———— Livestock versus foodgrain production in southeastern Upper Volta: a resource allocation analysis. [Ann Arbor], Center for Research on Economic Development, University of Michigan, 1979. 427 p. map. (Livestock production and marketing in the Entente states of West Africa. Monograph, 1)   MiU

"This monograph is part of a three-year study of West African livestock economics undertaken ... for the United States Agency for International Development under contract AID/afr-c-1169."—Foreword.

Bibliography: p. 416–426.

Abstract in *A.I.D. Research & Development Abstracts*, v. 9, no. 4, 1981, p. 24.

Issued also in microfiche. [Washington, U.S. Agency for International Development, 1979?] 5 sheets (DLC-Sci RR PN-AAH-785); and [Sahel Documents and Dissertations. Ann Arbor, Mich., University Microfilms International, 1980] (DLC-Micro 5357 UV 102).

4750

———— The southern Fulani farming system in Upper Volta: a new old model for the integration of crop and livestock production in the West African savannah. [Ann Arbor], Center for Research on Economic Development, University of Michigan, 1978. 176 p. maps.

"Final report to U.S.A.I.D., contract REDSO/WA 77–107, September 15, 1978."

Microfiche. [Washington, U.S. Agency for International Development, 1978?] 2 sheets (DLC-Sci RR PN-AAG-895); and [Sahel Documents and Dissertations. Ann Arbor, Mich., University Microfilms International, 1980] 3 sheets (DLC-Micro Microfiche 5357 UV 188).

4751

Dougherty, George M. Report to USAID/Upper Volta and AID/W on Upper Volta Seed Multiplication Project. Mississippi State, Seed Technology Laboratory, Mississippi State University, 1975. 46 p.   MsSM

Prepared for the U.S. Agency for International Development under contract AID/ta-C-12-19.

Issued also in microfiche. [Washington, U.S. Agency for International Development, 1975?] 1 sheet.   DLC-Sci RR PN-AAG-109

4752

Frelastre, Georges. Agricultural policy changes reviewed. *In* U.S. *Joint Publications Research Service.* JPRS 77098. [Springfield, Va., National Technical Information Service, 1981] (Sub-Saharan Africa report, no. 2339) p. 90–96.

Translation of article in *Le Mois en Afrique*, Paris, Oct. – Nov. 1980, p. 66–73.

Microfiche. [s.l., 1981]

DLC-Micro JPRS 77098

4752a

Integrated rural development program for Seguenega, Upper Volta. [Washington?], 1978. [267] leaves (in various foliations)

Submitted to the U.S. Agency for International Development.

Examined in the Documentation Center, Sahel Development Program, AID, Washington, D.C.

4753

Johnson, Hariadene. Sahel medium-term project reviews: Upper Volta Seed Authority. [s.l.], U.S. Agency for International Development, 1974. 25 p.   MiEM

4754

Niena-Dionkele rice production. [Ouagadougou?, U.S. AID Mission, 1977?] [96] leaves. map.

                    MiEM

4755

Perry, Edward C. Urban functions in rural development in Upper Volta: report of a field visit. Washington, Office of Urban Development, Agency for International Development, 1978. [35] p. MiEM

Issued also in microfiche. [Sahel Documents and Dissertations. Ann Arbor, Mich., University Microfilms International, 1980] 1 sheet.

DLC-Micro Microfiche 5357 UV 203

4756

Popper, Roger, *and* George Burrill. An evaluation plan for rural water supply projects. Washington, Practical Concepts, inc., 1978. [57] p. (in various pagings)

Prepared for the U.S. AID Mission to Upper Volta.

Abstract in *A.I.D. Research and Development Abstracts*, v. 7, no. 1, 1979, p. 10.

Microfiche. [Washington, U.S. Agency for International Development, 1978?] 1 sheet.

DLC-Sci RR PN-AAG-538

4757

Potts, Howard C. Report to USAID/Upper Volta, AID/W and MRD/Upper Volta on short-term implementation of NSS technical program. Mississippi State, Seed Technology Laboratory, Mississippi State University, 1978. 36 p.

MsSM

MRD: Ministry of Rural Development.
NSS: National Seed Service.

Issued also in microfiche. [Washington, U.S. Agency for International Development, 1978?] 1 sheet. DLC-Sci RR PN-AAG-040

4758

Seed production and supply—Upper Volta. Washington, U.S. Agency for International Development, 1974. 50 p. MiEM

4759

Stickley, Thomas. The computer: an appropriate technology for managing a viable agricultural credit system in a low income country: Upper Volta. East Lansing, Dept. of Agricultural Economics, Michigan State University, 1980. 13 p.

MiEM

"Project report, no. 20."

Prepared under U.S. Agency for International Development contract AID/afr-C-1314.

Paper presented at the meeting of the American Agricultural Economics Association, 1980.

4760

Vollrath, Thomas L. An econological analysis of small farm modernization: adjustments to mechanization in Upper Volta. Knoxville, University of Tennessee, 1973] 97 p.

Financial support provided in part by the U.S. Agency for International Development under contract AID/csd-1927.

Thesis (M.S.)—University of Tennessee.

Microfiche. [Washington, U.S. Agency for International Development, 1973?] 2 sheets.

DLC-Sci RR PN-AAA-188

4761

White, T. Kelley. Report to USAID/Upper Volta and AID/W, Upper Volta Seed Multiplication Project. [s.l.], Experience, Incorporated, 1976. 32 p.

Prepared for the U.S. Agency for International Development under contract AID/afr-C-1130.

Microfiche. [Washington, U.S. Agency for International Development, 1976?] 1 sheet.

DLC-Sci RR PN-AAG-132

Eastern ORD

Note: The following items (entries 4762–96) specifically relate to the Organisme régional de développement (ORD) for the eastern region of Upper Volta ("ORD de l'Est") centered in Fada N'Gourma.

4762

U.S. *AID Mission to Upper Volta.* Eastern ORD annual plan. Ouagadougou.

ORD: Organisme régional de développement.

Report for 1975/76 cited in *An Analysis of the Eastern ORD Rural Development Project in Upper Volta* (entry 4779).

4763

U.S. *Agency for International Development.* Eastern ORD rural road construction. Washington, 1975.

Cited in *An Analysis of the Eastern ORD Rural Development Project in Upper Volta* (entry 4779).

4764

U.S. [*Treaties, etc. Upper Volta, 1977 June 30*] Project agreement between the Department of State, Agency for International Development (AID), an agency of the Government of the United States of America, and Ministry of Rural Development (Ministère du Développement Rural), an agency of the Republic of Upper Volta (République de Haute-Volta) *In* U.S. *Treaties, etc.* United States treaties and other international agreements, v. 29, 1976–77, [Washington, Dept. of State; for sale by the Supt. of Docs., U.S. Govt. Print. Off., 1980]

4764 (cont.)

p. 5363–5373. ([Treaties and other international acts series, 9117]) JX231.A34 v. 29

In English and French.

Signed at Ouagadougou, June 30 and July 1, 1977; entered into force July 1, 1977.

Concerns adjustments in project elements of the Integrated Rural Development Project to support the increased decentralization of the Eastern ORD.

4765

Animal traction credit in six intensive zones in the Eastern ORD of Upper Volta, [by] Vincent Barratt [et al.] Fada N'Gourma, ORD de l'Est, 1978. 44 p. MiEM

"Project report, no. 24."

4766

Assefa Mehretu. Area/regional planning for rural development strategies with special reference to the Eastern ORD of Upper Volta. East Lansing, Dept. of Agricultural Economics, Michigan State University, 1977. 38 p. MiEM

"Prepared under terms of contract AID/afr-C-1260, Agricultural Economics Services in the Sahel."

Bibliography: p. 33–38.

Abstract in *A.I.D. Research and Development Abstracts*, July 1978, p. 8–9.

Issued also in microfiche. [Washington, U.S. Agency for International Development, 1977?] 1 sheet. DLC-Sci RR PN-AAF-027

4767

—— Regional planning for rural development in the Eastern ORD of Upper Volta: consultant's report. East Lansing, Dept. of Agricultural Economics, Michigan State University, 1978. 68 p. MiEM

Prepared under terms of U.S. Agency for International Development contract AID/afr-C-1314.

4768

Assefa Mehretu, *and* David C. Wilcock. Eastern region of Upper Volta. East Lansing, Dept. of Agricultural Economics, Michigan State University, 1979. 56 p. MiEM

"Michigan State University Technical Assistance Team, ORD de l'Est, Fada N'Gourma, Upper Volta. Regional planning working paper, no. 1."

Prepared for the U.S. Agency for International Development under contract AID/afr-C-1314.

Bibliography: p. 54–56.

Issued also in French.

4769

Baker, Doyle C., *and* Gregory C. Lassiter. Crop production in the Eastern ORD: preliminary results from the 1978–79 micro-economic survey. Fada N'Gourma, Bureau de l'analyse économique et de la planification, ORD de l''Est, 1980. 52 p. MiEM

"Project report, no. 45."

4770

Barratt, Vincent. Animal traction in the Eastern ORD. East Lansing, Dept. of Agricultural Economics, Michigan State University, 1980. 39 p. MiEM

"Project report, no. 43."

Apparently prepared for the U.S. Agency for International Development.

4771

Buccola, Steven T. Consultant's report: Michigan State University Eastern ORD Project, Upper Volta. [s.l.], 1979. 48 p. MiEM

Prepared for the U.S. Agency for International Development under contract AID/afr-C-1314.

4772

Conditions de diffusion du crédit agricole et de mise en oeuvre d'activités de ORD de l'Est, Fada-N'Gourma, sous/secteurs de Namounou et Diabo. Ouagadougou, 1975. [65] p. MiEM

Financed by the U.S. Agency for International Development.

4773

Eastern ORD rural roads project paper. [Ouagadougou, U.S. AID Mission, 1977?] 112 leaves.

Examined in the Documentation Center, Sahel Development Program, U.S. Agency for International Development, Washington, D.C.

4774

Environmental analysis for selected rural road projects in the Eastern O.R.D., Upper Volta: Fada N'Gourma-Bilanga Road, Ougarou-Nassougou Road. [Chicago?], Environmental Seven Ltd., [1976] 1 v. (various foliations of leaves)

Prepared for the U.S. Agency for International Development under contract AID/otr-C-1450.

Examined in the Development Information Center, AID, Washington, D.C.

4775

Fotzo, Pascal T. Analyse préliminaire des enquêtes agro-économiques des bas-fonds de l'O.R.D. de l'Est, R.H.V. Fada N'Gourma, O.R.D. de l'Est, Bureau de l'analyse économique et de la planification, 1981. 33 p. MiEM

4775 (cont.)

Prepared for the U.S. Agency for International Development under contract AID/afr-C-1314.

4776

Hoskins, John A. Eastern O.R.D. farm market centers. Ouagadougou, [U.S. AID Mission, 1978?] [12] p.

Examined in the Documentation Center, Sahel Development Program, AID, Washington, D.C.

4777

Lassiter, Gregory C. Cropping enterprises in eastern Upper Volta. East Lansing, Dept. of Agricultural Economics, Michigan State University, 1981. 44 p. (African Rural Economy Program. Working paper, no. 35)　　　　　　MiEM

Publication financed by the U.S. Agency for International Development under contract AID/afr-C-1314.

Issued in cooperation with the Organisme régional de développement de l'Est, Fada N'Gourma, Upper Volta.

Copy examined in the Development Information Center, AID, Washington, D.C.

4778

Matlon, Peter J. Consultant's report: MSU Eastern ORD Project, Upper Volta. East Lansing, Dept. of Agricultural Economics, Michigan State University, 1979. 20 leaves.　　　　MiEM

Prepared for the U.S. Agency for International Development under contract AID/afr-C-1314.

In English and French.

Copy examined in the Documentation Center, Sahel Development Program, AID, Washington, D.C.

4779

Michigan. State University, *East Lansing. Dept. of Agricultural Economics*. An analysis of the Eastern ORD rural development project in Upper Volta: report of the M.S.U. mission, by Carl K. Eicher [et al.] East Lansing, 1976. 103 p. maps. (African Rural Economy Program. Working paper, no. 9)
　　　　　　　HD2135.U63　1976

"AID/afr-C-1182."

Bibliography: p. 92–95.

"From mid-October to mid-December 1975, at the request of USAID, four members of the Department of Agricultural Economics at Michigan State University (MSU) conducted a study mission in Upper Volta, Niger and Benin (Dahomey). The focus of this effort centered on the implementation and future development potential of Upper Volta's Eastern ORD rural development

organization which is receiving major material and technical assistance from USAID."—p. 1.

Abstract in *A.I.D. Research and Development Abstracts*, Jan. 1977, p. 37.

Issued also in microfiche. [Washington, U.S. Agency for International Development, 1976?] 2 sheets.　　　　DLC-Sci RR PN-AAB-949

4780

Michigan State University Contract Team, USAID Intergrated Rural Development Project, ORD de l'Est, Fada N'Gourma, Upper Volta; report. East Lansing, Dept. of Agricultural Economics, Michigan State University. semiannual.
　　　　　　　　　　MiEM

Prepared for the U.S. Agency for International Development under contract AID/afr-C-1314.

MiEM has Dec. 1978/May 1979; same issue examined in the Development Information Center, AID, Washington, D.C.

4781

Poulin, Roger J., Alice Morton, *and* Anita Mackie. Evaluation of the Eastern ORD Integrated Rural Development Project. [Abidjan?], Regional Economic Development Services Office, U.S. Agency for International Development, 1978. [52] leaves. map.

Microfiche. [Sahel Documents and Dissertations. Ann Arbor, Mich., University Microfilms International, 1980] 1 sheet.
　　　　DLC-Micro Microfiche 5357 UV 085

4782

Reyna, Stephen P. Social analysis, Eastern Region food production project 686-0244. Abidjan, Regional Economic Development Services Office, [U.S. Agency for International Development], 1979. 38 p.　　　　　　　　MiEM

Bibliography: p. 33–34.

4783

Rural enterprise development project activities report. Jan./June 1978–July/Dec. 1979. [s.l.], Partnership for Productivity/Upper Volta.
　　　　　　　　　　MiEM

"Project to provide loans to small business in the Eastern ORD."—*Sahel Bibliographic Bulletin*, v. 5, no. 4, 1981, p. 183.

4784

Stickley, Thomas. An analysis of the agricultural credit system of the Eastern ORD of Upper Volta: final report, June 1977 through 1980. East Lansing, Dept. of Agricultural Economics, Michigan State University, 1980. 23 p.　　MIEM

"Project report, no. 22."

4784 (cont.)

Prepared for the U.S. Agency for International Development under contract AID/afr-C-1314.

4785

————— Enquête préliminaire sur la situation du crédit agricole dans l'ORD de l'Est de la Haute-Volta. Preliminary inquiry into the agricultural credit situation in the Eastern ORD of Upper Volta. Fada N'Gourma, Organisme régional de développement de l'Est, 1977. 30 p.   MiEM

Financed by the U.S. Agency for International Development.

4786

————— Rural credit account of the Eastern ORD of Upper Volta, April 1974 through March 31, 1980. East Lansing, Dept. of Agricultural Economics, Michigan State University, 1980. 33 p.

MiEM

"Project report, no. 21."

Apparently prepared for the U.S. Agency for International Development.

4787

————— The cereal bank experience of the Eastern ORD of Upper Volta. East Lansing, Dept. of Agricultural Economics, Michigan State University, 1980. 6 p.   MiEM

"Project report, no. 11."

Prepared for the U.S. Agency for International Development under contract AID/afr-C-1314.

4788

Stickley, Thomas, *and* Edouard Tapsoba. Loan repayment delinquency in the Eastern O.R.D. of Upper Volta. Fada N'Gourma, USAID Integrated Rural Development Program in the Eastern ORD, 1979. 14 p.   MiEM

"Paper no. 9."

4789

Swanson, Richard A. Eastern ORD village names. Fada N'Gourma, Eastern ORD, 1977. 2 p.

MiEM

"Document no. 6."

Prepared for the U.S. Agency for International Development under contract AID/afr-C-1289.

Issued also in French.

4790

————— Gourmantché agriculture. Fada N'Gourma, Upper Volta, 1978. 52 p.

"Document no. 7."

Prepared under a U.S. Agency for International Development contract.

Microfiche. [Sahel Documents and Disser-

tations. Ann Arbor, Mich., University Microfilms International, 1980] 1 sheet.

DLC-Micro Microfiche 5357 UV 093

4791

————— Gourmantché agriculture. Pt. II. Cultivated plant resources & field management. Fada N'Gourma, Upper Volta, 1979. 207 p.

"Document no. 8."

Prepared under a U.S. Agency for International Development contract.

Microfiche. [Sahel Documents and Dissertations. Ann Arbor, Mich., University Microfilms International, 1980] 3 sheets.

DLC-Micro Microfiche 5357 UV 094

4792

Upper Volta Integrated Rural Development Project. Washington, U.S. Agency for International Development, 1974.

"Stacy Mission report."

Cited in *An Analysis of the Eastern ORD Rural Development Project in Upper Volta* (entry 4779).

4793

VanDyk, David W. Development of the audio-visual capacity of the Eastern ORD, Fada N'Gourma, Upper Volta. East Lansing, Dept. of Agricultural Economics, Michigan State University, 1980. 43 p.

MiEM

"Project report, no. 12E."

Prepared for the U.S. Agency for International Development under contract AID/afr-C-1314.

4794

Wilcock, David C. Inventaire socio-économique des villages de l'est. East Lansing, Dept. of Agricultural Economics, Michigan State University, 1981. [110] p.   MiEM

Prepared for the U.S. Agency for International Development.

"Computer generated census of socio-economic characteristics of 637 villages; includes data on population, infrastructure, school and health facilities, commerce in sorghum and millet, and non-farm employment."—*Sahel Bibliographic Bulletin*, v. 5, no. 4, 1981, p. 184.

4795

————— Rural small scale enterprises in eastern Upper Volta: survey results. East Lansing, Dept. of Agricultural Economics, Michigan State University, 1981. 68 p. (African Rural Economy Program. Working paper, no. 38)   MiEM

Publication financed by the U.S. Agency for International Development under contract AID/afr-C-1314.

4795 (cont.)

Issued in cooperation with the Organisme régional de développement de l'Est, Fada N'Gourma, Upper Volta.

Copy examined in the Development Information Center, AID, Washington, D.C.

4796

Zalla, Tom. A proposed structure for the medium-term credit program in the eastern ORD of Upper Volta. East Lansing, Dept. of Agricultural Economics, Michigan State University, 1976. 39 p. (African Rural Economy Program. Working paper, no. 10)   HD1440.U76Z35

Prepared for the U.S. Agency for International Development under contract AID/afr-C1182.

Abstract in *A.I.D. Research and Development Abstracts*, Oct. 1976, p. 20.

Issued also in microfiche. [Washington, U.S. Agency for International Development, 1976?] 1 sheet.   DLC-Sci RR PN-AAB-950

Grain and Grain Storage

4797

Lindblad, Carl. The potential role of Peace Corps volunteers in Upper Voltan rural grain storage programs. [Ouagadougou?], Peace Corps/Upper Volta, 1976. 7 p.

Examined in the Development Information Center, U.S. Agency for International Development, Washington, D.C.

4798

Sherman, Jacqueline R. Crop disposal and grain marketing in the Manga region of Upper Volta: a case study. Ann Arbor, Center for Research on Economic Development, University of Michigan, 1981. 106 p.   MiU-RE

Submitted under terms of U.S. Agency for International Development grant 90009N.

4799

Singh, Ram D. Major cropping patterns: SAFGRAD countries; Upper Volta facts and observations relevant to farming systems research (with special reference to three regions of Upper Volta) Ouagadougou, Farming Systems Research Unit—SAFGRAD, 1981. 70 p.   EiEM

Prepared for the U.S. Agency for International Development under contract AID/afr-C-1492.

SAFGRAD: Semi-Arid Food Grain Research and Development Program.

Livestock and Range Management

4800

U.S. *AID Mission to Upper Volta.* Upper Volta village livestock: project paper. Ouagadougou, 1976.

Cited in *An Analysis of the Eastern ORD Rural Development Project in Upper Volta* (entry 4779).

4801

Herman, Larry A. The livestock and meat marketing system in Upper Volta: an evaluation of economic efficiency. [Ann Arbor], Center for Research on Economic Development, University of Michigan, 1981. 266 p. (Livestock production and marketing in the Entente states of West Africa. Monograph, 4)   MiU

Prepared for the U.S. Agency for International Development under contract AID/afr-C-1169.

4802

———— The livestock and meat marketing system in Upper Volta: summary of an evaluation of economic efficiency. *In* Shapiro, Kenneth H. Livestock production and marketing in the Entente states of West Africa: summary report. [Ann Arbor], Center for Research on Economic Development, University of Michigan, 1979. p. 232–327.

MiU

Study financed by the U.S. Agency for International Development under contract AID/afr-C-1169.

Issued also in microfiche. [Sahel Documents and Dissertations. Ann Arbor, Mich., University Microfilms International, 1980] (DLC-Micro Microfiche 5357 AS 162); and [Washington, U.S. Agency for International Development, 1979?] (PN-AAJ-217).

4803

Herman, Larry A., *and* Marty Makinen. Livestock and meat production, marketing, and exports in Upper Volta. *In* Livestock and meat marketing in West Africa, [by] Edgar J. Ariza-Niño [et al.] v. 1. [Ann Arbor], Center for Research on Economic Development, University of Michigan, 1980. p. 35–204. maps.   MiU

Prepared for the Regional Economic Development Services Office, West Africa, U.S. Agency for International Development, under contract REDSO/WA 77-105.

For information on abstracts/reviews of this report, see entry 3161.

Issued also in microfiche. [Washington, U.S. Agency for International Development, 1980?]

DLC-Sci RR PN-AAJ-212

4804

Vengroff, Richard. Environmental uncertainty, survival strategies and livestock production in the Soudanian zones of Upper Volta. [s.l.], 1980. 29 p.
MiEM

Research funded by the U.S. Agency for International Development.

4805

Village livestock: project paper, [by] James A. Bennett [et al.] [Washington?, U.S. Agency for International Development, 1976?] [95] leaves (in various foliations)

Examined in the Documentation Center, Sahel Development Program, AID, Washington, D.C.

Assistance Programs

4806

U.S. *AID Mission to Upper Volta.* Upper Volta: Sahel Development Program strategy review paper. [Ouagadougou?], 1977. 54 p.   MiEM

4807

U.S. *Agency for International Development.* Annual budget submission: Upper Volta. Washington, U.S. International Development Cooperation Agency.

Vols. for 1977+ examined in the Development Information Center, AID, Washington, D.C.

4808

———— Country development strategy statement: Upper Volta. Washington, U.S. International Development Cooperation Agency. annual.

Vols. for 1981+ examined in the Development Information Center, AID, Washington, D.C.

Vol. for 1981 issues also in microfiche. [Sahel Documents and Dissertations. Ann Arbor, Mich., University Microfilms International, 1980] 1 sheet.
DLC-Micro Microfiche 5357 UV040

4809

———— Sahel recovery and rehabilitation program, Upper Volta. Washington, [1974] 1 v. (various pagings) maps.

At head of title: Program assistance paper.

Examined in the Documentation Center, Sahel Development Program, AID, Washington, D.C.

4810

U.s. *Agency for International Development. Area Auditor General/West Africa.* Report of audit of the PL 480 Title II Food for Peace Program, Upper Volta. [s.l.], 1979. 9 p.

"Audit report no. 4-686-79-2."

Examined in the Development Information Center, AID, Washington, D.C.

4811

U.S. *Agency for International Development. Office of Sahel and Francophone West Africa Affairs.* Upper Volta: program summary. [Washington?], 1978. 20 leaves. maps.

Examined in the Documentation Center, Sahel Development Program, AID, Washington, D.C.

4812

U.S. *Peace Corps. Upper Volta.* Upper Volta FY 1979: country management plan. [Ouagadougou], 1978. 30 p.   MiEM

4813

U.S. [*Treaties, etc. Upper Volta, 1975 Feb. 6*] Agreement between the Government of the United States of America and the Government of the Republic of Upper Volta on general conditions for the employment of Peace Corps Volunteers. *In* U.S. *Treaties, etc.* United States treaties and other international agreements, v. 26, 1976. [Washington, Dept. of State; for sale by the Supt. of Docs., U.S. Govt. Print. Off., 1977] p. 2682–2691. ([Treaties and other international acts series, 8183])   JX231.A34, v. 26

Signed at Ouagadougou Feb. 6, 1975.

In English and French.

4814

U.S. [*Treaties, etc. Upper Volta, 1977 Sept. 9*] Upper Volta; agricultural commodities: transfer under Title II. Agreement signed at Ouagadougou September 9, 1977; entered into force September 9, 1977. *In* U.S. *Treaties, etc.* United States treaties and other international agreements, v. 29, 1976–77. [Washington, Dept. of State; for sale by the Supt. of Docs., U.S. Govt. Print. Off., 1980] p. 5279–5288. ([Treaties and other international acts series, 9105])   JX231.A34 v. 29

4815

Bingen, R. James. Research/studies in Sahel francophone West Africa: Upper Volta; an inventory of research, studies, and reports sponsored by the U.S. Agency for International Development. Washington, Sahel Development Program, U.S. Agency for International Development, 1977. [30] p.

Covers 17 projects undertaken in the period 1962–77.

Abstract for series on francophone West Africa and The Gambia in *A.I.D. Research and Development Abstracts*, Oct. 1977, p. 12–13.

4815 (cont.)

Microfiche. [Washington, U.S. Agency for International Development, 1977?] 1 sheet.
DLC-Sci RR PN-AAD-518

4816

Reyna, Stephen P. Impact of l'Authorité des aménagements des vallées des Voltas. Abidjan, Regional Economic Development Services Office, West Africa, [U.S. Agency for International Development], 1980. [100] p. MiEM

4817

Technical Assistance Information Clearing House. Development assistance programs of U.S. non-profit organizations in Upper Volta. [New York], American Council of Voluntary Agencies for Foreign Service, 1974. 15 p. maps. (TAICH country report) HC547.U6T4a 1974

The Clearing House is operated by the Council under a grant from the U.S. Agency for International Development.

4818

——— Development assistance programs of U.S. non-profit organizations: Upper Volta. [New York], American Council of Voluntary Agencies for Foreign Service, 1977. 21 p. maps. (TAICH country report) HC547.U6T4a Nov. 1977

4819

Upper Volta: program summary. [Washington?], Agency for International Development, 1977. 21 leaves. map.

Examined in the Development Information Center, AID, Washington, D.C.

4820

Volta valley development project. [Ouagadougou?, U.S. AID Mission, 1978?] 79 leaves.

Concerns projects of the Authorité des aménagements des vallées des Voltas, an agency of the Government of Upper Volta.

Examined in the Documentation Center, Sahel Development Program, U.S. Agency for International Development, Washington, D.C.

Economic Conditions

4821

Foreign economic trends and their implications for the United States. Upper Volta. 1969+ Washington, for sale by the Supt. of Docs., U.S. Govt. Print. Off. annual. (International marketing information series) HC10.E416

Prepared by the U.S. Embassy, Ouaga-

dougou. Vols. for 1969–77 distributed by the U.S. Bureau of International Commerce; vols. for 1978–79 by the U.S. Industry and Trade Administration; vols. for 1980– by the U.S. International Trade Administration.

Apparently not published in 1973.

The following issues for the period 1974–81 have been identified in L.C.:
ET 74-026. 1974. 11 p.
FET 75-025. 1975. 10 p.
FET 76-027. 1976. 7 p.
FET 77-120. 1977. 6 p.
FET 78-107. 1978. 4 p.
FET 80-005. 1980. 9 p.
FET 80-103. 1980. 8 p.
FET 81-087. 1981. 8 p.

4822

Zoma, Emmanuel. Industrial, mining sectors examined. *In* U.S. *Joint Publications Research Service.* JPRS 69530. [Springfield, Va., National Technical Information Service, 1977] (Translations on Sub-Saharan Africa, no. 1780) p. 48–56.

Translation of article in *Afrique industrie infra-structures*, Paris, June 1, 1977, p. 42–45.

Microfiche. [s.l., 1977]
DLC-Micro JPRS 69530

Energy Resources— Production & Consumption

4823

Kern, Edward C. Solar energy alternatives for the United States Embassy and for rural development projects within the Republic of Upper Volta. Lexington, Lincoln Laboratory, Massachusetts Institute of Technology, 1978. 37 p. illus.
DLC

Prepared for the U.S. Dept. of Energy under contract no. EY-76-C-02-4094.

Issued also in microfiche. [s.l., 1978] 1 sheet.
DLC-Sci RR COO/4094-5

4824

Roberts, Allen F. A final evaluations of the social impact of the Tangaye (Upper Volta) solar energy demonstration. [Ouagadougou?], Ouagadougou Mission, Office of Rural Development, U.S. Agency for International Development, 1980. 120 p. MiEM

4825

Upper Volta harnesses the sun: solar energy makes life easier in Tangaye. Agenda, Nov. 1979: 12–13.
HC59.7.A742 1979

4825 (cont.)

Issued by the U.S. Agency for International Development.

Politics and Government

4826

Congress held to establish Voltan progressive front. *In* U.S. *Joint Publications Research Service.* JPRS 74827. [Springfield, Va., National Technical Information Service, 1979] (Sub-Saharan Africa report, no. 2193) p. 161–173.

Translation of article on the Union progressiste voltaïque, in *L'Observateur*, Ouagadougou, Nov. 5, 1979, p. 1, 4–10.

Microfiche. [s.l., 1980]

DLC-Micro JPRS 74827

4827

Decraene, Philippe. Power struggle ensues despite stability, steady progress. *In* U.S. *Joint Publications Research Service.* JPRS 68596. [Springfield, National Technical Information Service, 1977] (Translations on Sub-Saharan Africa, no. 1710) p. 22–30.

Translation of article in *Le Monde*, Paris, Jan. 16/17–18, 1977.

Microfiche. [s.l., 1977]

DLC-Micro JPRS 68596

4828

FPV reaction to UDV-RDA congress reported. *In* U.S. *Joint Publications Research Service.* JPRS 75859. [Springfield, Va., National Technical Information Service, 1980] (Sub-Saharan Africa report, no. 2255) p. 67–79.

Translation of article in *L'Observateur*, Ouagadougou, Mar. 31, 1980, p. 1, 6–12.

FPV: Front progressiste voltaïque-Rassemblement démocratique africaine.

Microfiche. [s.l., 1980]

DLC-Micro JPRS 75859

4829

Guirma returns to politics. *In* U.S. *Joint Publications Research Service.* JPRS 71010. [Springfield, Va., National Technical Information Service, 1978] (Translations on Sub-Saharan Africa, no. 1917) p. 145–153.

Translation of interview with Frederic Guirma, in *L'Observateur*, Ouagadougou, Mar. 16, 1978, p. 1, 4–7.

Microfiche. [Washington, Supt. of Docs., U.S. Govt. Print. Off., 1978]

DLC-Micro JPRS 71010

4830

Ilboudo, Patrick. UPV leader explains opposition view. *In* U.S. *Joint Publications Research Service.* JPRS 71786. [Springfield, Va., National Technical Information Service, 1978] (Translations on Sub-Saharan Africa, no. 1985) p. 113–124.

Translation of interview with Joseph Ki-Zerbo, in *L'Observateur*, Ouagadougou, July 20, 1978, p. 1, 3–9.

Microfiche. [Washington, Supt. of Docs., U.S. Govt. Print. Off., 1978]

DLC-Micro JPRS 71786

4831

El Kara, K. I., *and* L. Sawadogo. Proceedings of seventh UDV-RDA congress. *In* U.S. *Joint Publications Research Service.* JPRS 75862. [Springfield, Va., National Technical Information Service, 1980] (Sub-Saharan Africa report, no. 2256) p. 159–173.

Translation of article on a meeting of the Union démocratique voltaïque-Rassemblement démocratique africaine, in *L'Observateur*, Ouagadougou, Mar. 26–30, 1980.

Microfiche. [s.l., 1980]

DLC-Micro JPRS 75862

4832

Kone, Ahmed. Ki-Zerbo's new party examined. *In* U.S. *Joint Publications Research Service.* JPRS 74978. [Springfield, Va., National Technical Information Service, 1980] (Sub-Saharan Africa report, no. 2202) p. 66–69.

Translation of article on the Union progressiste voltaïque founded by Joseph Ki-Zerbo, in *Demain l'Afrique*, Paris, Nov. 19, 1979, p. 59–60.

Microfiche. [s.l., 1980]

DLC-Micro JPRS 74978

4833

Nation's democratic system, development examined. *In* U.S. *Joint Publications Research Service.* JPRS 75628. [Springfield, Va., National Technical Information Service, 1980] (Sub-Saharan Africa report, no. 2244) p. 78–81.

Article in *West Africa*, London, Apr. 14, 1980, p. 650–652.

Microfiche. [s.l., 1980]

DLC-Micro JPRS 75628

4834

Report on sixth UDV-RDA congress. *In* U.S. *Joint Publications Research Service.* JPRS 70863. [Springfield, Va., National Technical Information Service, 1978] (Translations on Sub-Saharan Africa, no. 1902) p. 213–220.

4834 (cont.)

Translation of article in *L'Observateur*, Ouagadougou, Feb. 16, 1978, p. 1, 6–8.

Microfiche. [Washington, Supt. of Docs., U.S. Govt. Print. Off., 1978]

DLC-Micro JPRS 70863

4835

Report on UNDD congress. *In* U.S. *Joint Publications Research Service.* JPRS 70782. [Springfield, Va., National Technical Information Service, 1978] (Translations on Sub-Saharan Africa, no. 1894) p. 170–177.

Translation of article in *L'Observateur*, Ouagadougou, Dec. 27, 1977, p. 1, 4, 5, 6, 7.

UNDD: Union nationale pour la défense de la démocratie.

Microfiche. [Washington, Supt. of Docs., U.S. Govt. Print. Off., 1978]

DLC-Micro JPRS 70782

4836

Reportage on Voltan progressive front. *In* U.S. *Joint Publications Research Service.* JPRS 74884. [Springfield, Va., National Technical Information Service, 1980] (Sub-Saharan Africa report, no. 2195) p. 171–176.

Translation of article on the Union progressiste voltaïque, in *L'Observateur*, Ouagadougou, Nov. 6, 1979, p. 1, 4, 6–7, 10.

Microfiche. [s.l., 1980]

DLC-Micro JPRS 74884

Elections

4837

Biographic details on four candidates given. *In* U.S. *Joint Publications Research Service.* JPRS 71270. [Springfield, Va., National Technical Information Service, 1978] (Translations on Sub-Saharan Africa, no. 1944) p. 141–147.

Translation of article on Joseph Ki-Zerbo, Aboubacar Sangoulé Lamizana, Joseph Ouedraogo, and Macaire Ouedraogo, in *L'Observateur*, Ouagadougou, Apr. 4, 1978, p. 4–6.

Microfiche. [Washington, Supt. of Docs., U.S. Govt. Print. Off., 1978]

DLC-Micro JPRS 71270

4838

Election results reported. *In* U.S. *Joint Publications Research Service.* JPRS 71449. [Springfield, Va., National Technical Information Service, 1978] (Translations on Sub-Saharan Africa, no. 1959) p. 119–123.

Translation of election results reported by de-

partment, in *L'Observateur*, Ouagadougou, May 30, 1978, p. 1, 5, 6, 7.

Microfiche. [Washington, Supt. of Docs., U.S. Govt. Print. Off., 1978]

DLC-Micro JPRS 71449

4839

Kabue, Buana. Coming presidential elections will decide fate of democratization process. *In* U.S. *Joint Publications Research Service.* JPRS 70261. [Springfield, Va., National Technical Information Service, 1977] (Translations on Sub-Saharan Africa, no. 1843) p. 134–140.

Translation of article in *Demain l'Afrique*, Paris, Nov. 1977, p. 16, 18.

Microfiche. [s.l., 1977]

DLC-Micro JPRS 70261

4840

Lamizana, Aboubacar Sangoulé. General Lamizana delivers campaign speech. *In* U.S. *Joint Publications Research Service.* JPRS 71449. [Springfield, Va., National Technical Information Service, 1978] (Translations on Sub-Saharan Africa, no. 1959) p. 119–123.

Translation of speech recorded in *L'Observateur*, Ouagadougou, May 11, 1978, p. 1, 5, 8.

Microfiche. [Washington, Supt. of Docs., U.S. Govt. Print. Off., 1978]

DLC-Micro JPRS 71449

4841

Magassouba, Moriba. Upper Volta election discussed. *In* U.S. *Joint Publications Research Service.* JPRS 71449. [Springfield, Va., National Technical Information Service, 1978] (Translations on Sub-Saharan Africa, no. 1959) p. 119–123.

Translation of article in *Demain l'Afrique*, Paris, June 1978, p. 52–53.

Microfiche. [Washington, Supt. of Docs., U.S. Govt. Print. Off., 1978]

DLC-Micro JPRS 71449

4842

Ouedraogo, Tenoga. Educator comments on political scene, upcoming election. *In* U.S. *Joint Publications Research Service.* JPRS 70643. [Springfield, Va., National Technical Information Service, 1978] (Translations on Sub-Saharan Africa, no. 1879) p. 144–148.

Translation of article in *L'Observateur*, Ouagadougou, Jan. 5, 1978, p. 6–7.

Microfiche. [Washington, Supt. of Docs., U.S. Govt. Print. Off., 1978]

DLC-Micro JPRS 70643

4843

UPV candidate speaks, holds press conference. *In* U.S. *Joint Publications Research Service.* JPRS 71246. [Springfield, Va., National Technical Information Service, 1978] (Translations on Sub-Saharan Africa, no. 1941) p. 171–175.

Translation of report on a press conference held by Joseph Ki-Zerbo, in *L'Observateur*, Ouagadougou, Mar 29, 1978, p. 8–11.

Microfiche. [Washington, Supt. of Docs., U.S. Govt. Print. Off., 1978]

DLC-Micro JPRS 71246

4844

Views of presidential candidates reported. *In* U.S. *Joint Publications Research Service.* JPRS 71335. [Springfield, Va., National Technical Information Service, 1978] (Translations on Sub-Saharan Africa, no. 1950) p. 139–144.

Translation of article reporting the views of Aboubacar Sangoulé Lamizana, Joseph Ouedraogo, Joseph Ki-Zerbo, and Macaire Ouedraogo, in *L'Observateur*, Ouagadougou, May 17, 1978, p. 5, 9, 10.

Microfiche. [Washington, Supt. of Docs., U.S. Govt. Print. Off., 1978]

DLC-Micro JPRS 71335

Population Studies

4845

Africa: Upper Volta. Selected statistical data by sex. Washington, 1981. 31, 17 p.   DLC

Study supported by the U.S. Agency for International Development's Office of Women in Development and Office of Population.

Data assembled by the International Demographic Data Center, U.S. Bureau of the Census.

Among the tables, all based on 1975 data (unless otherwise noted), are the following: adjusted population by age and sex; population by department, sex and urban/rural residence; life expectancy (1960–61); urban and rural populations by marital status, age, and sex; heads of households by age, sex, and urban/rural residence; number of literate persons by age, sex, and urban/rural residence; number of economically active persons by age, sex, and urban/rural residence.

4846

Finnigan, Gregory A. Population movement, labor migration, and social structure in a Mossi Village. [Waltham, Mass.], Dept. of Anthropology, Brandeis University, 1976. 264 leaves. maps.

Research supported by a grant from the U.S. National Institute of Mental Health.

Dissertation—Brandeis University.

Microfiche. [Sahel Documents and Dissertations. Ann Arbor, Mich., University Microfilms International 1980] 5 sheets.

DLC-Micro Microfiche 5357 UV 115

4847

Fleury, Jean-Marc. People on the move; the migration of people is more than a matter of chance. Agenda, Dec. 1979: 14–15. illus.

HC59.7.A742   1979

Issued by the U.S. Agency for International Development.

Upper Volta is used as an example.

4848

Gregory, Joel W. Underdevelopment, dependency, and migration in Upper Volta. [Ithaca, N.Y.], Cornell University, 1974. 320 leaves.

Research supported in part through a fellowship from the U.S. Office of Education.

Dissertation—Cornell University.

Microfiche. [Sahel Documents and Dissertations. Ann Arbor, Mich., University Microfilms International, 1980] 4 sheets.

DLC-Micro Microfiche 5357 UV 200

Microfilm. [Ann Arbor, Mich., University Microfilms International, 1974?]

DLC-Micro 74-18096

4849

Profiles of Sahelian countries: Upper Volta. Washington, Socio-Economic Analysis Staff, International Statistical Programs Center, U.S. Bureau of the Census, 1974. [41] leaves (in various foliations)

Prepared at the request of the U.S. Agency for International Development.

Concerns demographic projections.

Examined in the Documentation Center, Sahel Development Program, AID, Washington, D.C.

4850

Smith, James T. Economy and demography in a Mossi village. [Ann Arbor], University of Michigan, 1977. 375 leaves.

Study supported in part by a fellowship from the National Institute of Child Health and Human Development of the Department of Health, Education, and Welfare, and by a grant from the U.S. Agency for International Development.

Thesis (Ph.D.)—University of Michigan.

Microfiche. [Sahel Documents and Dissertations. Ann Arbor, Mich., University Microfilms International, 1980] 8 sheets (DLC-Micro Microfiche 5357 UV 052); and [Ann Arbor, Uni-

4850 (cont.)
versity Microfilms International, 1977?] (DLC-Micro 77-18729).

Women

4851
U.S. *AID Mission to Upper Volta*. Women's roles in development (Upper Volta): project review paper. Ouagadougou, 1975.
Cited in *An Analysis of the Eastern ORD Rural Development Project in Upper Volta* (entry 4779).

4852
Barnes, Carolyn. Strengthening Voltaic women's roles in development (Upper Volta) *In* International Conference on Women and Food, *University of Arizona, Tucson.* Jan. 8–11, 1978. Proceedings and papers. v. 2. [Tucson?], 1978. p. 71–74.
Conference sponsored by the Consortium for International Development with the support of a U.S. Agency for International Development grant.
Microfiche. [Washington, U.S. Agency for International Development, 1978?]
DLC-Sci RR PN-AAG-530

4853
Hoskins, Marilyn W., *and* Josephine Guissou. Social and economic development in Upper Volta: woman's perspective. [s.l.], Société africaine d'études et de développement, 1978. 36 p.
DLC
At head of title: Agency for International Development, Regional Economic Development Services Office West Africa (REDSO/WA 77-121).
Issued also in microfiche. [Sahel Documents and Dissertations. Ann Arbor, Mich., University Microfilms International, 1980] 1 sheet.
DLC-Micro Microfiche 5357 UV 187

4854
Strengthening women's roles in development. [Ouagadougou?, U.S. AID Mission, 1977?] [114] leaves.
Examined in the Documentation Center, Sahel Development Program, U.S. Agency for International Development, Washington, D.C.

4855
Taylor, Ellen. Women paraprofessionals in Upper Volta's rural development. [Ithaca, N.Y.], Rural Development Committee, Center for International Studies, Cornell University, [1981] 56 p. maps.
DLC
"Special series on paraprofessionals, no. 3."

"In cooperation with the U.S. Agency for International Development, the Rural Development Committee ... has undertaken research on the role of paraprofessionals in rural development."—p. iii.
Abstract in *A.I.D. Research & Development Abstract*, v. 9, no. 3, 1981, p. 30.
Issued also in microfiche. [Washington, U.S. Agency for International Development, 1981] 1 sheet.
DLC-Sci RR PN-AAJ-636

Other Subjects

4856
Berry, Eileen, Charles Hays, *and* Earl Scott. Onchocerciasis clearance in West Africa with special reference to Upper Volta. [Worcester, Mass.?] Clark University, [1978?] 48 leaves, 12 p. (Workshops in Environmantal Investigation. Techniques and procedures for project development. Case study, no. 2)
DLC
"Training course for preparing initial environmental examinations conducted on behalf of AID Training Contract RFP/50106 and prepared for workshops in February and May, 1978."

4857
Butler, Herbert W. Conceptualizing chiefship and chiefdom among the Mossi. [s.l., 1976] [27] leaves (FAR 26828-N)
Research supported by a grant from the National Institute of Mental Health.
Study presented at a Conference on Historic Site Archaeology, Gainesville, Fla., 1976.
Examined in the former Foreign Affairs Research Documentation Center, U.S. Dept. Of State.

4858
Evaluation of savanna water resources project: report, [by] George M. Coleman [et al.] McLean, Va., American Technical Assistance Corporation, 1977. [36] leaves (in various foliations)
Submitted to the U.S. AID Mission to Upper Volta and the U.S. Agency for International Development under contract AID/afr-C-1142.
Examined in the Documentation Center, Sahel Development Program, AID, Washington, D.C.

4859
Kalmogo, Léonard. Finance minister discusses new budget. *In* U.S. *Joint Publications Research Service.* JPRS 72497. [Springfield, Va., National Technical Information Service, 1978] (Translations on Sub-Saharan Africa, no. 2042) p. 82–89.
Translation of speech by the Minister of

4859 (cont.)

Finance, recorded in *L'Observateur*, Ouagadougou, Nov. 16, 1978, p. 1, 4–6.

Microfiche. [Washington, Supt. of Docs., U.S. Govt. Print. Off., 1978]

DLC-Micro JPRS 72497

4860

Press freedom in Upper Volta discussed. *In* U.S. *Joint Publications Research Service.* JPRS 72444. [Springfield, Va., National Technical Information Service, 1978] (Translations on Sub-Saharan Africa, no. 2038) p. 74–81.

Translation of article in *L'Observateur*, Ouagadougou, Nov. 13, 1978, p. 8–10.

Microfiche. [Washington, Supt. of Docs., U.S. Govt. Print. Off., 1978]

DLC-Micro JPRS 72444

4861

Report of the technical committee to establish a remote sensing center at Ouagadougou, Upper Volta. [Ouagadougou?], 1977, [110] p. (in various pagings)

Study supported in part by the U.S. Agency for International Development.

Examined in the Development Information Center, AID, Washington, D.C.

4862

Swanson, Richard A. Gurmantche taxonomies and paradigms. Fada N'Gourma, Eastern ORD, 1977. 39 p.   MiEM

"Document no. 5."

Prepared for the U.S. Agency for International Development under contract AID/afr-C-1289.

4863

——— Innovation analogies among the Gurma: development effort formulations as expanded through culturally perceived channels. Fada N'Gourma, Eastern ORD Integrated Rural Development Project, 1977. 5 p.   MiEM

Prepared for the U.S. Agency for International Development.

Issued also in French.

4864

——— Proverbs and riddles. [Fada N'Gourma?], 1977. 35 p.

Prepared under U.S. Agency for International Development contract AID/afr-C-1289.

A collection of Gourmantche tales "to help promote the program of rural literacy by encouraging reading of ethnic materials."

Microfiche. [Sahel Documents and Dissertations. Ann Arbor, Mich., University Microfilms International, 1980] 1 sheet.

DLC-Micro Microfiche 5357 UV 129

4865

Ténoga, Paul. Professor discusses origin, meaning of Voltan [sic] names. *In* U.S. *Joint Publications Research Service.* JPRS 72357. [Springfield, Va., National Technical Information Service, 1978] (Translations on Sub-Saharan Africa, no. 2032) p. 79–84.

Translation of article in *L'Observateur*, Ouagadougou, Oct. 25, 1978, p. 1, 6–8.

Microfiche. [Washington, Supt. of Docs., U.S. Govt. Print. Off., 1978]

DLC-Micro JPRS 72357

4866

Traditional sculpture from Upper Volta: an exhibition at the Museum of African Art, Smithsonian Institution, Washington, D.C. [Washington, Museum of African Art, Smithsonian Institution] 1979. [12] p. illus., maps.   DLC

Western Sahara

Note: In mid- 1983, the issues of the legal status and sovereignty of the former Spanish Sahara were unresolved. Moroccan occupation of the entire territory, following Mauritania's abandonment of its claims in 1979, was opposed by forces of the Saharan Arab Democratic Republic, proclaimed in 1976 by Polisario (Frente Popular para la Liberación de Saguia el Hamra y Río de Oro), the principal organization resisting Moroccan-Mauritanian rule. In U.S. Government publications, the term "Western Sahara" is used to indicate the entire region.

4867

[U.S. *Central Intelligence Agency*] Spanish Sahara. 8–74. [Washington, 1974] col. map.
G8900   1974.U5
Scale ca. 1 : 5,500,000.
"502 310."
Includes location map and maps of "Saharan peoples" and "Economic activity."

4868

Dessort, Francis. Main enemy said to be underdevelopment. *In* U.S. *Joint Publications Research Service.* JPRS 69355. [Springfield, Va., National Technical Information Service, 1977] (Translations on Near East and North Africa, no. 1674) p. 92–95.
Translation of article in *Remarques africaines,* Brussels, May 17, 1977, p. 14–15.
Microfiche. [s.l., 1977]
DLC-Micro JPRS 69355

4869

Waring, Mowton L. Spanish Sahara: focus of contention; a research report submitted to the faculty. Maxwell Air Force Base, Ala., Air War College, Air University, 1976. 118 leaves. maps. (FAR 24786-N)
"Professional study no. 6099."
Bibliography: leaves 108–118.
"The physical environment, historical evolution, and economic potential, particularly the lucrative phosphate industry, of the West African desert are described to establish the setting in which Spain, Morocco, Mauritania, Algeria, and rival liberation movements have been in contention for the territory."—p. iii.
Examined in the former Foreign Affairs Research Documentation Center, U.S. Dept. of State.
Issued also in microfiche. [s.l., 1976] 2 sheets (AD-B010587L).

4870

Zerhouni, Salmouni. Senegalese parliamentarian dis-

cusses Saharan problem. *In* U.S. *Joint Publications Research Service.* JPRS 72198. [Springfield, Va., National Technical Information Service, 1978] (Translations on Sub-Saharan Africa, no. 2020) p. 106–109.
Translation of article based on an interview with Habib Thiam of the Assemblée nationale, in *L'Opinion*, Rabat, Sept. 21, 1978, p. 1–2.
Microfiche. [Washington, Supt. of Docs., U.S. Govt. Print. Off., 1978]
DLC-Micro JPRS 72198

International Dimensions of Conflict

4871

Morocco, Algeria seen pressured to negotiate end to conflict. *In* U.S. *Joint Publications Research Service.* JPRS 75397. [Springfield, Va., National Technical Information Service, 1980] (Near East/North Africa report, no. 2096) p. 114–117.
Translation of article in *al-Nahār al-'Arabi wa al-duwalī*, Paris, Feb. 11–17, 1980, p. 24.
Microfiche. [s.l., 1980]
DLC-Micro JPRS 75397

4872

Munir, Muhammed. Internationalization of western Sahara conflict seen. *In* U.S. *Joint Publications Research Service.* JPRS 77356. [Springfield, Va., National Technical Information Service, 1981] (Near East/North Africa report, no. 2263) p. 97–100.
Translation of article in *al-Nahār al-'Arabi wa-al-duwalī*, Paris, Nov. 3–9, 1980, p. 19–20.
Microfiche. [s.l., 1981]
DLC-Micro JPRS 77356

4873

SDAR minister notes Spanish role in Saharan decolonization. *In* U.S. *Joint Publications Research Service.* JPRS 71044. [Springfield, Va., National

4873 (cont.)

Technical Information Service, 1978] (Translation on Near East and North Africa, no. 1789) p. 78–83.

Translation of interview with Mohamed Salem ould Salek, Minister of Information of the Saharan Arab Democratic Republic, in *Révolution africaine*, Algiers, Mar. 29 APr. 4, 1978, p. 27–31.

Microfiche. [Washington, Supt. of Docs., U.S. Govt. Print. Off., 1978]

DLC-Micro JPRS 71044

4874

Solarz, Stephen J. King Hassan's quagmire. Congressional record [daily ed.], 96th Congress, 2d session, v. 126, May 22, 1980: E2585–E2587.

J11.R7 v. 126

Extension of remarks in the U.S. House of Representatives concerning the Western Sahara.

Includes article from the *New York Times*.

4875

Stone, Richard B. Foreign Relations' Near East Subcommittee staff reports on the Sahara conflict, Tunisia, and Israel. Congressional record [daily ed.], 96th Congress, 2d session, v. 126, Dec. 4, 1980: S15636–S15645.

J11.R7 v. 126

Remarks in the U.S. Senate.

Includes staff report, *North Africa and the Conflict in the Western Sahara* (S15643–S15645).

4876

Ware, Lewis B. Decolonization and the global alliance in the Arab Maghrib: the case of Spanish Sahara. Maxwell Air Force Base, Ala., Directorate of Documentary Research, Institute for Professional Development, U.S. Air University, 1975. 53 p.

AMAU

"AU-204-75-IPD."

United States Policy

4877

U.S. *Congress. House. Committee on Foreign Affairs. Subcommittee on Africa.* Current situation in the Western Sahara, 1980: hearing Ninety-sixth Congress, second session, December 4, 1980. Washington, U.S. Govt. Print. Off., 1981. 24 p.

KF27.F625 1980f
J74.A23 96th
Cong., House Comm.
For. Aff., v. 143

Stephen J. Solarz, chairman.

Witness is Harold H. Saunders, Assistant Secretary of State for Near Eastern and South Asian Affairs.

4878

—— U.S. policy and the conflict in the western Sahara: hearings before the Subcommittees on Africa and on International Organizations of the Committee on Foreign Affairs, House of Representatives, Ninety-sixth Congress, first session, July 23 and 24, 1979. Washington, U.S. Govt. Print. Off., 1979. 209 p.

KF27.F625 1979f
J74.A23 96
Cong., House Comm.
For. Aff., v. 33

Stephen J. Solarz, chairman, Subcommittee on Africa.

Don Bonker, chairman, Subcommittee on International Organizations.

Among the appendixes are copies of United Nations and Organization of African Unity resolutions on the Western Sahara.

4879

U.S. *Congress. House. Committee on Foreign Affairs. Subcommittee on International Security and Scientific Affairs.* Proposed arms sale to Morocco: hearings before the Subcommittees on International Security and Scientific Affairs and on Africa of the Committee on Foreign Affairs, House of Representatives, Ninety-sixth Congress, second session, January 24 and 29, 1980. Washington, U.S. Govt. Print. Off., 1980. 80 p.

KF27.F64825 1980
J74.A23 96th Cong.
House Comm. For. Aff.
v. 60

Clement J. Zablocki, chairman, Subcommittee on International Security and Scientific Affairs.

Stephen J. Solarz, chairman, Subcommittee on Africa.

Principal witness is Harold H. Saunders, Assistant Secretary of State for Near Eastern and South Asian Affairs.

Among the appendixes is the following:

Appendix 2. List of countries recognizing the Saharan Arab Democratic Republic, submitted by the Dept. of State. p. 78.

4880

U.S. *Congress. House. Committee on International Relations. Subcommittee on International Organizations.* The question of self-determination in western Sahara; hearing before the Subcommittees on International Organizations and on Africa, Ninety-fifth Congress, first session, October 12, 1977. Washington, U.S. Govt. Print. Off., 1977. 82 p.

KF27.I5494 1977m
J74.A23 95th Cong.,
House. Comm. Inter.
Rel., v. 50

4880 (cont.)

Donald M. Fraser, chairman, Subcommittee on International Organizations.

Charles C. Diggs, Jr., chairman, Subcommittee on Africa.

Includes bibliographical references.

Among the appendixes are the following:

Appendix 1. Lippert, Anne. The Western Sahara: an emerging state in northwest Africa? (p. 47–61).

Appendix 3. Responses by the Department of State to questions submitted by Subcommittee Chairman Fraser (p. 66–82).

4881

U.S. *Congress. House. Study Mission to Morocco, the Western Sahara, Mauritania, Algeria, Liberia, Spain, and France.* Arms for Morocco? U.S. policy toward the conflict in the Western Sahara: report of a Study Mission to Morocco, the Western Sahara, Mauritania, Algeria, Liberia, Spain, and France, August 5–18, 1979, to the Committee on Foreign Affairs, U.S. House of Representatives, January 1980. Washington, U.S. Govt. Print. Off., 1979, i.e. 1980. 26 p. map.

E183.8.M8U54   1979

Included in the appendixes is the full text of the peace treaty signed on Aug. 5, 1979 between the Polisario Front and Mauritania (p. 18–19), plus recent Organization of African Unity and United Nations resolutions on the Western Sahara (p. 20–25).

4882

U.S. *Congress. Senate. Committee on Foreign Relations.* Proposed arms sales to Morocco: hearing, Ninety-sixth Congress, second session ... January 30, 1980. Washington, U.S. Govt. Print. Off., 1980, 43 p.   KF26.F6   1980
J74.A23 96th
Cong., Sen. Comm.
For. Rel., v. 34

Frank Church, chairman.

4883

Duteil, Mireille. Possible effects of U.S. military aid to Morocco explored. *In* U.S. *Joint Publications Research Service.* JPRS 74920. [Springfield, Va., National Technical Information Service, 1980] (Near East/North Africa report, no. 2066) p. 118–121.

Translation of article in *Demain l'Afrique*, Paris, Nov. 5, 1979, p. 32–33.

Microfiche. [s.l., 1980]

DLC-Micro JPRS 74920

4884

Joint report by Senators Church and Javits on the sale of arms to Morocco. Congressional record [daily ed.], 96th Congress, 2d session, v. 126, Feb. 5, 1980: S962–S963.   J11.R7 v. 126

Remarks in the U.S. Senate concerning S. Con. Res. 71 "to disapprove the sale of arms to Morocco."

Includes comments on the Western Sahara crisis.

4885

McGovern, George S. Morocco. Congressional record [daily ed.], 96th Congress, 1st session, v. 125, Oct. 22, 1979: S14887–S14889.

J11.R7 v. 125

Remarks in the U.S. Senate concerning Western Sahara.

Includes articles from the *Washington Post* and *New York Times*.

4886

Tsongas, Paul E. Arms to Morocco. Congressional record [daily ed.], 96th Congress, 1st session, v. 125, Oct. 30, 1979: S15481–S15482.

J11.R7 v. 125

Remarks in the U.S. Senate.

Includes articles from the *New York Times* and *Boston Globe.*

Military Dimensions of Conflict

4887

Germain-Robin, Françoise. Journalists accompany APLS to Western Sahara. *In* U.S. *Joint Publications Research Service.* JPRS 74691. [Springfield, Va., National Technical Information Service, 1979] (Near East/North Africa report, no. 2051) p. 41–45.

Translation of article on the Saharan People's Liberation Army, in *L'Humanité Dimanche*, Paris, Oct. 3–9, 1979.

Microfiche. [s.l., 1979]

DLC-Micro JPRS 74691

4888

———— Morocco accused of "fierce repression" of Saharans. *In* U.S. *Joint Publications Research Service.* JPRS 74780. [Springfield, Va., National Technical Information Service, 1979] (Near East/North Africa report, no. 2058) p. 140–143.

Translation of article in *L'Humanité Dimanche*, Paris, Oct. 24–30, 1979, p. 2, 23.

Microfiche. [s.l., 1980]

DLC-Micro JPRS 74780

4889

Hammūsh, Sa'īd. Sahara leader discusses war with Morocco, negotiations with Mauritania. *In* U.S. *Joint Publications Research Service.* JPRS 73752. [Springfield, Va., National Technical Information Service, 1979] (Translations on Near East and North Africa, no. 1987) p. 107–114.

Translation of interview with Mohamed Lamine, Head of Government of the Saharan Arab Democratic Republic, in *al-Sha'b*, Algiers, May 20–21, 1979.

Microfiche. [Washington, Supt. of Docs., U.S. Govt. Print. Off., 2979]

DLC-Micro JPRS 73752

4890

Mallet, Roland. Polisario said to be formidable fighting force. *In* U.S. *Joint Publications Research Service.* JPRS 71086. [Springfield, Va., National Technical Information Service, 1978] (Translations on Near East and North Africa, no. 1971) p. 101–107.

Translation of article in *Demain l'Afrique*, Paris, Apr. 8, 1978, p. 41–44.

Microfiche. [Washington, Supt. of Docs., U.S. Govt. Print. Off., 1978]

DLC-Micro JPRS 71086

4891

Miguez, Alberto. Saharan conflict said to be moving toward stabilization. *In* U.S. *Joint Publications Research Service.* JPRS 71432. [Springfield, Va., National Technical Information Service, 1978] (Translations on Near East and North Africa, no. 1814) p. 54–59.

Translation of article in *La Vanguardia*, Barcelona, May 19, 24, 30, 1978.

Microfiche. [Washington, Supt. of Docs., U.S. Govt. Print. Off., 1978]

DLC-Micro JPRS 71432

4892

Ostos, Manuel. Climate of insecurity said to exist in Moroccan zone. *In* U.S. *Joint Publications Research Service.* JPRS 71176. [Springfield, Va., National Technical Information Service, 1978] (Translations on Near East and North Africa, no. 1799) p. 149–155.

Translation of article in *El Pais*, Madrid, Apr. 18, 19, 1978.

Microfiche. [Washington, Supt. of Docs., U.S. Govt. Print. Off., 1978]

DLC-Micro JPRS 71176

4893

Polisario Secretary General on status, future of conflict. *In* U.S. *Joint Publications Research Service.*

JPRS 73626. [Springfield, Va., National Technical Information Service, 1979] (Translations on Near East and North Africa, no. 1975) p. 159–165.

Translation of interview with Mohamed Abdelaziz, Secretary General of Polisario, in *al-Mujāhid*, Algiers, Mar. 9, 1979, p. 12–14, 29.

Microfiche. [Washington, Supt. of Docs., U.S. Govt. Print. Off., 1979]

DLC-Micro JPRS 73626

4894

Results of ALPS operations November 1977-April 1978. *In* U.S. *Joint Publications Research Service.* JPRS 71459. [Springfield, Va., National Technical Information Service, 1978] (Translations on Near East and North Africa, no. 1816) p. 178–185.

Translation of article on operations of the "Saharan People's Army of Liberation," in *El Moudjahid*, Algiers, May 21, 1978, p. 4.

Microfiche. [Washington, Supt. of Docs., U.S. Govt. Print. Off., 1978]

DLC-Micro JPRS 71459

4895

SDAR premier discusses current offensive. *In* U.S. *Joint Publications Research Service.* JPRS 69069. [Springfield, Va., National Technical Information Service, 1977] (Translations on Near East and North Africa, no. 1651) p. 120–123.

Translation of report on a press conference by Prime Minister Mohammed Lamine, in *Jornal de Angola*, Luanda, Apr. 6, 1977, p. 1–2.

Microfiche. [s.l., 1977]

DLC-Micro JPRS 69069

4896

Salinas, Armando L. Spanish reporter describes visit to Western Sahara. *In* U.S. *Joint Publications Research Service.* JPRS 73583. [Springfield, Va., National Technical Information Service, 1979] (Translations on Near East and North Africa, no. 1972) p. 123–131.

Translation of article in *Mundo Obrero*, Madrid, Mar. 8–10, 1979.

Microfiche. [Washington, Supt. of Docs., U.S. Govt. Print. Off., 1979]

DLC-Micro JPRS 73583

4897

Samoza, Manuel. Polisario guerrilla war increasingly effective. *In* U.S. *Joint Publications Research Service.* JPRS 71044. [Springfield, Va., National Technical Information Service, 1978] (Translations on Near East and North Africa, no. 1789) p. 84–90.

Translation of article in *Prisma del Meridiano*, Havana, Feb. 1–15, 1978, p. 16–19.

4897 (cont.)

Microfiche. [Washington, Supt. of Docs., U.S. Govt. Print. Off., 1978]

DLC-Micro JPRS 71044

4898

Silva, Vicente J. Portuguese journalist reports on Western Sahara situation. *In* U.S. *Joint Publications Research Service.* JPRS 73042. [Springfield, Va., National Technical Information Service, 1979] (Translations on Near East and North Africa, no. 1925) p. 67–72.

Translation of article in *Expresso*, Lisbon, Jan. 20, 1979, p. 16, 17.

Microfiche. [Washington, Supt. of Docs., U.S. Govt. Print. Off., 1979]

DLC-Micro JPRS 73042

Political Dimensions of Conflict

4899

AOSARIO open letter to African heads of state. *In* U.S. *Joint Publications Research Service.* JPRS 76495. [Springfield, Va., National Technical Information Service, 1980] (Near East/North Africa report, no. 2187) p. 192–195.

Translation of a statement by the pro-Moroccan "Association des originaires du Sahara ancienne-ment sous domination espagnole," in *L'Opinion*, Rabat, Aug. 6, 1980, p. 3.

Microfiche. [s.l., 1980]

DLC-Micro JPRS 76495

4900

'Abbās, Muḥammad. Saharan prime minister fore-sees victory over Moroccan forces. *In* U.S. *Joint Publications Research Service.* JPRS 74345. [Springfield, Va., National Technical Information Service, 1979] (Near East/North Africa report, no. 2030) p. 75–79.

Translation of interview with Mohamed Lamine, Prime Minister of the Saharan Arab Republic, in *al-Sha'b*, Algiers, Aug. 22, 1979, p. 1, 7.

Microfiche. [Washington, Supt. of Docs., U.S. Govt. Print. Off., 1979]

DLC-Micro JPRS 74345

4901

Bayon, Felix. Polisario said to control far southeast of Hassan's kingdom. *In* U.S. *Joint Publications Research Service.* JPRS 74444. [Springfield, Va., National Technical Information Service, 1979]

(Near East/North Africa report, no. 2036) p. 87–96.

Translation of article in *El Pais*, Madrid, Sept. 18–20, 1979.

Microfiche. [Washington, Supt. of Docs., U.S. Govt. Print. Off., 1979]

DLC-Micro JPRS 74444

4902

Belghiche, Tayes. Saharan "prime minister" Lamine gives interview to Algiers paper. *In* U.S. *Joint Publications Research Service.* JPRS 74803. [Springfield, Va., National Technical Information Service, 1979] (Near East/North Africa report, no. 2060) p. 81–84.

Translation of interview with Mohamed La-mine, Prime Minister of the Saharan Arab Democratic Republic, in *El Moudjahid*, Algiers, Nov. 12, 1979, p. 5.

Microfiche. [s.l., 1980]

DLC-Micro JPRS 74803

4903

Benyakhlef, el-Hedi. SDAR Prime Minister re-views Saharan people's struggle. *In* U.S. *Joint Publications Research Service.* JPRS 74819. [Springfield, Va., National Technical Information Service, 1979] (Near East/North Africa report, no. 2061) p. 65–72.

Translation of interview with Prime Minister Mohamed Lamine of the Saharan Arab Democratic Republic in *al-Sha'b*, Algiers, Nov. 6, 1979, p. 1, 5.

Microfiche. [s.l., 1980]

DLC-Micro JPRS 74819

4904

Biro, Françoise. Current status of Saharan problem surveyed. *In* U.S. *Joint Publications Research Service.* JPRS 70263. [Springfield, Va., National Technical Information Service, 1977] (Trans-lations on Near East and North Africa, no. 1735) p. 100–106.

Translation of interview with Prime Minister Lamine in *Politique hebdo*, Paris, Oct. 31 – Nov. 6, 1977, p. 16–18.

Microfiche. [s.l., 1977]

DLC-Micro JPRS 70263

4905

Boloix, José. Reporter with Spanish Communist de-legation describes visit. *In* U.S. *Joint Publications Research Service.* JPRS 73812. [Springfield, Va., National Technical Information Service, 1979] (Near East/North Africa report, no. 1992) p. 100–104.

Translation of article in *Mundo Obrero*

4905 (cont.)

Semanal, Madrid, May 10–16, 1979, p. 16–18, reporting on the delegation's visit to Western Sahara

Microfiche. [Washington, Supt. of Docs., U.S. Govt. Print. Off., 1979]

DLC-Micro JPRS 73812

4906

——— Role of Polisario front in SDAR discussed. *In* U.S. *Joint Publications Research Service.* JPRS 73782. [Springfield, Va., National Technical Information Service, 1979] (Translations on Near East and North Africa, 1989) p. 98–106.

Translation of article in *Mundo Obrero*, Madrid, May 6, 8, and 9, 1979.

Microfiche. [Washington, Supt. of Docs., U.S. Govt. Print. Off., 1979]

DLC-Micro JPRS 73782

4907

Bū-Qattāyah, al-Ṣādiq. Interview with president of SDAR. *In* U.S. *Joint Publications Research Service.* JPRS 67563. [Springfield, Va., National Technical Information Service, 1976] (Translations on Near East and North Africa, no. 1535) p. 74–79.

Translation of interview with Mohamed Lamine, in *al-Mujahid*, Algiers, May 30, 1976, p. 8–9, 16.

Microfiche. [s.l., 1976]

DLC-Micro JPRS 67563

4908

al-Darwīsh, Qusayy S. Background, current Sahara situation reviewed. *In* U.S. *Joint Publications Research Service.* JPRS 74705. [Springfield, Va., National Technical Information Service, 1979] (Near East/North Africa report, no. 2053) p. 56–63.

Translation of article in *al-Dustūr*, London, Oct. 8–14, 1979, p. 20–22.

Microfiche. [s.l., 1979]

DLC-Micro JPRS 74705

4909

Doutrelant, Pierre M. Polisario military success clouded by refugee problems. *In* U.S. *Joint Publications Research Service.* JPRS 67805. [Springfield, Va., National Technical Information Service, 1976] (Translations on Near East and North Africa, no. 1551) p. 50–62.

Translation of article in *Le Monde*, Paris, Aug. 6–9, 1975.

Microfiche. [s.l., 1976]

DLC-Micro JPRS 67805

4910

Gaudio, Attilio. Setting up Saharan self-determination referendum difficult. *In* U.S. *Joint Publications Research Service.* JPRS 75667. [Springfield, Va., National Technical Information Service, 1980] (Near East/North Africa report, no. 2114) p. 114–117.

Translation of article in *Africa*, Dakar, Mar. 1980, p. 53, 54.

Microfiche. [s.l., 1980]

DLC-Micro JPRS 75667

4911

al-Ḥusanyī, Hudá. Events connected with Sahara problem related. *In* U.S. *Joint Publications Research Service.* JPRS 74517. [Springfield, Va., National Technical Information Service, 1979] (Near East/North Africa report, no. 2041) p. 1–6.

Translation of article in *al-Ḥawādith*, London, Sept. 21, 1979, p. 22, 23.

Microfiche. [s.l., 1979]

DLC-Micro JPRS 74517

4912

Ḥamdi, Māhir. Polisario political bureau discusses situation in Sahara. *In* U.S. *Joint Publications Research Service.* JPRS 72848. [Springfield, Va., National Technical Information Service, 1979] (Translations on Near East and North Africa, no. 1913) p. 45–49.

Translation of interview with al-Haritami al-Hasan in *al-Hurrīyah*, Beirut, Dec. 18, 1978, p. 31, 32.

Microfiche. [Washington, Supt. of Docs., U.S. Govt. Print. Off., 1979]

DLC-Micro JPRS 72848

4913

Polisario front official Ahmed Baba Miske talks about movement. *In* U.S. *Joint Publications Research Service.* JPRS 66911. [Springfield, Va., National Technical Information Service, 1976] (Translations on Near East and North Africa, no. 1488) p. 7–26.

Translation of interview in *el Djeich*, Algiers, Jan. 1976, p. 18–24.

Microfiche. [s.l., 1976]

DLC-Micro JPRS 66911

4914

Rizq, Jihād. Sacrificing Saharan people to save Hassan II deplored. *In* U.S. *Joint Publications Research Service.* JPRS 73825. [Springfield, Va., National Technical Information Service, 1979] (Near East/North Africa report, 1994) p. 153–157.

Translation of interview with Mohamed Lamine, Prime Minister of the Saharan Arab

4914 (cont.)

Democratic Republic, in *al-Nidā'*, Beirut, June 5, 1979, p. 6.

Microfiche. [Washington, Supt. of Docs., U.S. Govt. Print. Off., 1979]

DLC-Micro JPRS 73825

4915

SDAR premier discusses political program. *In* U.S. *Joint Publications Research Service*. JPRS 67531. [Springfield, Va., National Technical Information Service, 1976] (Translations on Near East and North Africa, no. 1532) p. 29–32.

Translation of interview with Mohamed Lamine, in *Voix ouvrière*, Geneva, May 15, 1976, p. 8.

Microfiche. [s.l., 1976]

DLC-Micro JPRS 67531

4916

Valenzuela, Fernando. Journalist visits Sahara, talks with Polisario leaders. *In* U.S. *Joint Publications Research Service*. JPRS 75329. [Springfield, Va., National Technical Information Service, 1980] (Near East/North Africa report, no. 2092) p. 156–166.

Translation of article in *Mundo Obrero*, Madrid, Jan. 23, 24, and 25, 1980.

Microfiche. [s.l., 1980]

DLC-Micro JPRS 75329

Western Indian Ocean

4917

U.S. *Agency for International Development.* Annual budget submission: Indian Ocean—Seychelles, Mauritius, Madagascar. Washington, U.S. International Development Cooperation Agency.

Vol. for 1981 covers Comoros, Madagascar, Mauritius, and Seychelles.

Vols. for 1981, 1983 examined in the Development Information Center, AID, Washington, D.C.

4918

U.S. *Central Intelligence Agency.* Indian Ocean atlas. [Washington], The Agency, 1976. 80 p. col. illus., col. maps.   G2850.U5 1976

Includes gazetteer and index.

Contents: Natural environment.—Resources. —Shipping.—Political relationships.—Islands in the sea.

4919

Faure, Gérard. Annotated check list of corals in the Mascarene Archipelago, Indian Ocean. Washington, Smithsonian Institution, 1977. 26 p. (Atoll research bulletin, no. 203)

QE565.A8 no. 203

4920

———— Annotated check list of Octocorallia in the Mascarene Archipelago, Indian Ocean. Washington, Smithsonian Institution, 1977. 13 p. (Atoll research bulletin, no. 204)

QE565.A8 no. 204

4921

Henderson, Faye. Island countries of the Indian Ocean: regional profile. Washington, Office of Foreign Disaster Assistance, Agency for International Development, 1980. 182 p., 1 leaf of plates, col. map.   DT468.H68

"July 1980."

"Prepared for the Office of U.S. Foreign Disaster Assistance, Bureau for Private and Development Cooperation, Agency for International Development, Department of State by Evaluation Technologies, Inc., under contract AID/SOD/PDC-C-028."—p. ii.

Bibliography: p. 178–182.

Among the countries and dependencies covered: Comoros, Madagascar, Mauritius, Réunion, and Seychelles.

Includes information on the government, economy, population, agriculture, transportation, energy resources, communications, disaster preparedness, health, nutrition, and housing for each country.

4922

Leymarie, Philippe. U.S. Indian Ocean strategy reviewed. *In* U.S. *Joint Publications Research Service.* JPRS 69733. [Springfield, Va., National Technical Information Service, 1977] (Translations on Sub-Saharan Africa, no. 1794) p. 1–12.

Translation of article in *Revue française d'études politiques africaines*, Paris, Jan./July 1977, p. 94–107.

Microfiche. [s.l., 1977]

DLC-Micro JPRS 69733

4923

Moine, Jacques. Indian Ocean socialism examined. *In* U.S. *Joint Publications Research Service.* JPRS 75091. [Springfield, Va., National Technical Information Service, 1980] (Sub-Saharan Africa report, no. 2211) p. 5–21.

Translation of article on a meeting of socialist organizations of the Comoros, Madagascar, Mauritius, Réunion, and Seychelles, in *L'Afrique et l'Asie modernes*, Paris, 4th quarter, 1979, p. 3–23.

Microfiche. [s.l., 1980]

DLC-Micro JPRS 75091

4924
Precarious state of Mayotte described. *In* U.S. *Joint Publications Research Service.* JPRS 75024. [Springfield, Va., National Technical Information Service, 1980] (Sub-Saharan Africa report, no. 2206) p. 6–15.

Translation of article in *Le Monde*, Paris, Dec. 29–31, 1979.
Microfiche. [s.l., 1980]

DLC-Micro JPRS 75024

Comoros

4925

U.S. *Dept. of State. Bureau of Public Affairs.* Background notes. Comoros. [Washington, for sale by the Supt. of Docs., U.S. Govt. Print. Off.] 1979. 4 p. maps. (U.S. Dept. of State. Department of State publication 8963)   G59.U5

    L.C. retains only the latest revision.

    For a description of the contents of this publication, see the note to entry 937.

4926

[Comoro Islands—diplomatic relations and recognition] *In* Boyd, John A. Digest of United States practice in international law. 1977. [Washington], Office of the Legal Adviser, Dept. of State; [for sale by the Supt. of Docs., U.S. Govt. Print. Off., 1979] (U.S. Dept. of State. Department of State publication, 8960)   JX21.R68   1977

4927

Rangers, Latimer. Exclusive presidential interview. *In* U.S. *Joint Publications Research Service.* JPRS 66963. [Springfield, Va., National Technical Information Service, 1976] (Translations on Sub-Saharan Africa, no. 1641) p. 7–11.

    Translation of interview with President Ali Soilih, in *Madagascar Matin*, Tananarive, Feb. 6, 1976, p. 6.

    Microfiche. [s.l., 1976]

DLC-Micro JPRS 66963

Madagascar

General

4928

U.S. *Dept. of State.* Post report. Madagascar. [Washington?], 1978. [17] p. illus., map.

JX1705.A286 Spec. Format

For a description of the contents of this publication, see the note to entry 936.

4929

U.S. *Dept. of State. Bureau of Public Affairs.* Background notes. Madagascar. [Washington, for sale by the Supt. of Docs., U.S. Govt. Print. Off.], 1982. 4 p. maps. (U.S. Dept. of State. Department of State publication, 8015)   G59.U5

L.C. retains only the latest revision.

For a description of the contents of this publication, see the note to entry 937.

4930

U.S. *Dept. of State. Office of the Geographer.* Madagascar: change in capital city name. Washington, 1977. 1 p.   DLC-G&M

"Geographic note GE-171."

4931

———— Madagascar: new long-form name. Washington, 1976. 1 p.   DLC-G&M

"Geographic note GE-158."

4932

Madagascar: a country profile. [Washington], prepared for the Office of U.S. Foreign Disaster Assistance, Bureau for Private and Development Cooperation, Agency for International Development, 1976. 35 leaves.   DLC

Prepared by Evaluation Technologies, inc., under U.S. Agency for International Development contract AID-otr-C-1553.

A general introduction, with some emphasis on political structure, demography, health, nutrition, economic conditions, agriculture, geography, transportation, communications, and power resources.

Agriculture

4933

Fisher, Denis. Agricultural training in Madagascar. *In* U.S. *Joint Publications Research Service.* JPRS 68680. [Springfield, Va., National Technical Information Service, 1977] (Translations on Sub-Saharan Africa, no. 1715) p. 31–34.

Translation of article in *Actuel développement*, Paris, Sept.–Oct. 1976, p. 43, 44.

Microfiche. [s.l., 1977]

DLC-Micro JPRS 68680

4934

Folsom, William B., *and* Dennis M. Weidner. Fisheries of the Malagasy Republic, 1974. Washington, U.S. Dept. of Commerce, National Oceanic and Atmospheric Administration, National Marine Fisheries Service, 1976. 23 p. illus. (Foreign fisheries leaflet, no. 76–1)

SH315.M24F64

"NOAA—S/T 76-2119."

Bibliography: p. 19.

Assistance Programs

4935

U.S. *Agency for International Development.* Disaster relief, case report: Malagasy Republic—cyclones, January and February 1976. Washington, Agency for International Development, [1977] [6] p. illus., map.   DLC

4936

EEC delegation arrives to discuss aid cooperation. *In* U.S. *Joint Publications Research Service.* JPRS 75884. [Springfield, Va., National Technical Information Service, 1980] (Sub-Saharan Africa report, no. 2257) p. 33–42.

4936 (cont.)

Translation of article in *Madagascar-Matin,* Antananarivo, Apr. 14, 1980, p. 2.

EEC: European Economic Community.

Microfiche. [s.l., 1980]

DLC-Micro JPRS 75884

4937

GDR cultural, scientific accord reported. *In* U.S. *Joint Publications Research Service.* JPRS 73090. [Springfield, Va., National Technical Information Service, 1979] (Translations on Sub-Saharan Africa, no. 2081) p. 86–89.

Translation of article in *Madagascar-Matin,* Antananarivo, Feb. 22, 1979, p. 1, 3.

GDR: German Democratic Republic.

Microfiche. [Washington, Supt. of Docs., U.S. Govt. Print. Off., 1979]

DLC-Micro JPRS 73090

4938

Romanian-Malagasy transportation agreement. *In* U.S. *Joint Publications Research Service.* JPRS 72555. [Springfield, Va., National Technical Information Service, 1979] Translations on Sub-Saharan Africa, no. 1046) p. 130–134.

Translation of article in *Madagascar-Matin,* Antananarivo, Nov. 30, 1978, p. 2.

A review of discussions concerning possible Romanian technical assistance.

Microfiche. [Washington, Supt. of Docs., U.S. Govt. Print. Off., 1979]

DLC-Micro JPRS 72555

4939

Technical Assistance Information Clearing House. Development assistance programs of U.S. non-profit organizations in Madagascar. [New York], American Council of Voluntary Agencies for Foreign Service, 1976. 9 p. maps. (TAICH country report)   HC547.M2T4a

The Clearing House is operated by the Council under a grant from the U.S. Agency for International Development.

Economic Conditions

4940

EEC official's press conference reported. *In* U.S. *Joint Publications Research Service.* JPRS 72693. [Springfield, Va., National Technical Information Service, 1979] (Translations on Sub-Saharan Africa, no. 2055) p. 35–43.

Translation of interview with Claude Cheysson, Commissioner of Development of the European Economic Community, Antananarivo, reported in *Madagascar-Martin*, Antananarivo, Dec. 8–9, 1978.

Remarks are primarily on the economy of Madagascar.

Microfiche. [Washington, Supt. of Docs., U.S. Govt. Print. Off., 1979]

DLC-Micro JPRS 72693

4941

Foreign economic trends and their implications for the United States. Madagascar. 1969+ Washington, for sale by the Supt. of Docs., U.S. Govt. Print. Off. annual. (International marketing information series)   HC10.E416

Prepared by the U.S. Embassy, Antananarivo (formerly Tananarive).

Vols. for 1969–77 distributed by the U.S. Bureau of International Commerce; vols. for 1978–79 by the U.S. Industry and Trade Administration; vols. for 1980– by the U.S. International Trade Administration.

Title varies: 1969–75, *Foreign Economic Trends and Their Implications for the United States. Malagasy Republic.*

The following issues for the period 1973–81 have been identified in L.C.:

ET 73-111. 1973. 11 p.

ET 74-075. 1974. 13 p.

ET 75-074. 1975. 8 p.

FET 76-087. 1976. 8 p.

FET 77-129. 1977. 7 p.

FET 78-072. 1978. 8 p.

FET 79-067. 1979. 10 p.

FET 80-092. 1980. 13 p.

FET 81-008. 1981. 11 p.

4942

Madagascar's socialist goals make business apprehensive, keep investment level down. Commerce America, July 19, 1976: 28–29.   HF1.C38

Issued by the U.S. Dept. of Commerce.

4943

Ravalitera, Pela. Long-term plan calls for socialist, revolutionary development. *In* U.S. *Joint Publications Research Service.* JPRS 70357. [Springfield, Va., National Technical Information Service, 1977] (Translations on Sub-Saharan Africa, no. 1853) p. 17–27.

Translation of article in *Madagascar-Matin,* Antananarivo, Nov. 15, 1977, p. 1, 2, 5.

Microfiche. [s.l., 1977]

DLC-Micro JPRS 70357

4944

Report on changing economic institutions. *In* U.S. *Joint Publications Research Service.* JPRS 72632.

4944 (cont.)

[Springfield, Va., National Technical Information Service, 1979] (Translations on Sub-Saharan Africa, no. 2051) p. 94–98.

Translation of article in *Le Monde diplomatique*, Paris, Dec. 1978, p. 27.

Microfiche. [Washington, Supt. of Docs., U.S. Govt. Print. Off., 1979]

DLC-Micro JPRS 72632

4945

Rising import, diminishing export figures for 1979. *In* U.S. *Joint Publications Research Service.* JPRS 75441. [Springfield, Va., National Technical Information Service, 1980] (Sub-Saharan Africa report, no. 2229) p. 80–84.

Translation of article in *Madagascar-Matin*, Antananarivo, Jan. 7, 8, 1980.

Microfiche. [s.l., 1980]

DLC-Micro JPRS 75441

4946

Roux, Christian. Reorganization of the economy since 1974. *In* U.S. *Joint Publications Research Service.* JPRS 76890. [Springfield, Va., National Technical Information Service, 1980] (Sub-Saharan Africa report, no. 2324) p. 32–49.

Translation of article in *Le Mois en Afrique*, Paris, Aug.–Sept. 1980, p. 81–97.

Microfiche. [s.l., 1980]

DLC-Micro JPRS 76890

Foreign Relations

4947

Ranaivosoa, Georges. French envoy projects improved French-Malagasy relations. *In* U.S. *Joint Publications Research Service.* JPRS 69679. [Springfield, Va., National Technical Information Service, 1977] (Translations on Sub-Saharan Africa, no. 1789) p. 26–43.

Translation of interview with Pierre Hunt, French Ambassador to Madagascar, in *Courrier diplomatique de l'Océan indien*, Tananarive, 2d quarter 1977, p. 18–29.

Microfiche. [s.l., 1977]

DLC-Micro JPRS 69679

4948

—— Soviet ambassador reviews relations since 1972. *In* U.S. *Joint Publications Research Service.* JPRS 69296. [Springfield, Va., National Technical Information Service, 1977] (Translations on Sub-Saharan Africa, no. 1762) p. 45–52.

Translation of interview with Aleksandr I.

Alekseyev, in *Courrier diplomatique de l'Océan indien*, Tananarive, first quarter, 1977, p. 15–19.

Microfiche. [s.l., 1977]

DLC-Micro JPRS 69296

4949

Reportage on visit of Vietnamese delegation. *In* U.S. *Joint Publications Research Service.* JPRS 77184. [Springfield, Va., National Technical Information Service, 1981] (Sub-Saharan Africa report, no. 2346) p. 48–54.

Translation of article in *Madagascar-Matin*, Antananarivo, Nov. 13–15, 17, 1980.

Microfiche. [s.l., 1981]

DLC-Micro JPRS 77184

Geology, Hydrology, and Mineral Resources

4950

Ambrosio, Suzann C. The mineral industry of Madagascar. *In* Minerals yearbook, v. 3, 1980. [Washington, for sale by the Supt. of Docs., U.S. Govt. Print. Off., 1982] p. 627–635.

TN23.U612   1980, v. 3

Prepared by the U.S. Bureau of Mines.

4951

Morse, David E. The mineral industry of Madagascar. *In* Minerals yearbook, v. 3, 1976. [Washington, for sale by the Supt. of Docs., U.S. Govt. Print. Off., 1980] p. 699–705.

TN23.U612   1976, v.3

Prepared by the U.S. Bureau of Mines.

4952

—— The mineral industry of Madagascar. *In* Minerals yearbook, v. 3, 1978–79. [Washington, U.S. Govt. Print. Off., 1981] p. 617–622.

TN23.U612   1978–79, v. 3

Prepared by the U.S. Bureau of Mines.

Labor

4953

Employment figures analyzed; reasons for unemployment given. *In* U.S. *Joint Publications Research Service.* JPRS 68710. [Springfield, Va., National Technical Information Service, 1977] (Translations on Sub-Saharan Africa, no. 1717) p. 22–28.

Translation of article in *Madagascar-Matin*, Tananarive, Jan. 18, 19. 1977.

4953 (cont.)

Microfiche. [s.l., 1977]

DLC-Micro JPRS 68710

4954

Malagasy-ILO relations, projects discussed. *In* U.S. *Joint Publications Research Service.* JPRS 74987. [Springfield, Va., National Technical Information Service, 1980] (Sub-Saharan Africa report, no. 2203) p. 65–71.

Translation of article in *Madagascar-Matin*, Antananarivo, Nov. 29–Dec. 11, 1979.

ILO: International Labor Organization.

Microfiche. [s.l., 1980]

DLC-Micro JPRS 74987

Politics and Government

4955

Adotevi, John B. Malagasy Socialist Party Secretary General discusses political crises. *In* U.S. *Joint Publications Research Service.* JPRS 65444. [Springfield, Va., National Technical Information Service, 1975] (Translations on Africa, no. 1608) p. 19–23.

Translation of interview with André Resampa of the Parti socialiste malgache, in *Le Soleil*, Dakar, July 15, 1975, p. 3.

Microfiche. [s.l., 1975]

DLC-Micro JPRS 65444

4956

Details of AREMA meeting given. *In* U.S. *Joint Publications Research Service.* JPRS 75051. [Springfield, Va., National Technical Information Service, 1980] (Sub-Saharan Africa report, no. 2208) p. 38–42.

Translation of article on the Avant-garde de la révolution malgache, in *Madagascar-Matin*, Antananarivo, Jan. 2, 1980, p. 1, 2, 3.

Microfiche. [s.l., 1980]

DLC-Micro JPRS 75051

4957

Dethomas, Bruno. New Ratsiraka regime faces many problems. *In* U.S. *Joint Publications Research Service.* JPRS 67195. [Springfield, Va., National Technical Information Service, 1976] (Translations on Sub-Saharan Africa, no. 1648) p. 8–16.

Translation of article in *Le Monde*, Paris, Apr. 2–3, 1976.

Microfiche. [s.l., 1976]

DLC-Micro JPRS 67195

4958

Head of National Assembly interviewed. *In* U.S. *Joint Publications Research Service.* JPRS 72555. [Springfield, Va., National Technical Information Service, 1978] (Translations on Sub-Saharan Africa, no. 2046)

Translation of interview with Lucien X. Michol-Andrianarahinjaka, in *Madagascar-Matin*, Dec. 1, 1978, p. 1–2, 4.

Microfiche. [Washington, Supt. of Docs., U.S. Govt. Print. Off., 1979]

DLC-Micro JPRS 72555

4959

Ratsiraka, Didier. President Ratsiraka gives speech, urges unity. *In* U.S. *Joint Publications Research Service.* JPRS 75314. [Springfield, Va., National Technical Information Service, 1980] (Sub-Saharan Africa report, no. 2223) p. 97–103.

Translation of speech recorded in *Madagascar-Matin*, Antananarivo, Jan. 12, 1980, p. 2.

Microfiche. [s.l., 1980]

DLC-Micro JPRS 75314

4960

—— President's new year address reported. *In* U.S. *Joint Publications Research Service.* JPRS 75051. [Springfield, Va., National Technical Information Service, 1980] (Sub-Saharan Africa report, no. 2208) p. 25–29.

Translation of speech recorded in *Madagascar-Matin*, Antananarivo, Jan. 2–3, 1980.

Microfiche. [s.l., 1980]

DLC-Micro JPRS 75051

4961

—— Text of President Ratsiraka's fifth anniversary day speech. *In* U.S. *Joint Publications Research Service.* JPRS 76254. [Springfield, Va., National Technical Information Service, 1980] (Sub-Saharan Africa report, no. 2281) p. 49–74.

Translation of speech recorded in *Madagascar-Matin*, Antananarivo, June 17–18, 1980.

Microfiche. [s.l., 1980]

DLC-Micro JPRS 76254

4962

Reportage on AKFM-KDRSM congress. *In* U.S. *Joint Publications Research Service.* JPRS 76659. [Springfield, Va., National Technical Information Service, 1980] (Sub-Saharan report, no. 2309) p. 31–36.

Translation of article on the Ankoton'ny Kongresi'ny Fahaleovantenan Madagaskara (Parti du congrès de l'indépendance de Madagascar), in *Madagascar-Matin*, Antananarivo, Aug. 18–19, 1980.

4962 (cont.)
Microfiche. [s.l., 1980]
DLC-Micro JPRS 76659

Religion

4963
Randriantsalama, André. Malagasy variant of Catholic theology discussed. *In* U.S. *Joint Publications Research Service.* JPRS 76649. [Springfield, Va., National Technical Information Service, 1980] (Sub-Saharan Africa report, no. 2308) p. 45–51.
Translation of article in *Madagascar-Matin*, Antananarivo, July 12, 14, 1980.
Microfiche. [s.l., 1980]
DLC-Micro JPRS 76649

4964
Report on Muslims in Madagascar in 1977. *In* U.S. *Joint Publications Research Service.* JPRS 70782. [Springfield, Va., National Technical Information Service, 1978] (Translations on Sub-Saharan Africa, no. 1894) p. 59–73.
Translation of article in *L'Afrique et l'Asie modernes*, Paris, 4th quarter 1977, p. 28–46.
Microfiche. [Washington, Supt. of Docs., U.S. Govt. Print. Off., 1978]
DLC-Micro JPRS 70782

Other Subjects

4965
Achievements of Air Madagascar technical division reported. *In* U.S. *Joint Publications Research Service.* JPRS 72847. [Springfield, Va., National Technical Information Service, 1979] (Translations on Sub-Saharan Africa, no. 2066) p. 7–10.
Translation of article in *Aviation Magazine International*, Paris, Jan. 15–31, 1979, p. 30–31.
Microfiche. [Washington, Supt. of Docs., U.S. Govt. Print. Off., 1979]
DLC-Micro JPRS 72847

4966
Activities of first PRC medical mission reported. *In* U.S. *Joint Publications Research Service.* JPRS 70114. [Springfield, Va., National Technical Infor-mation Service, 1977] (Translations on Sub-Saharan Africa, no. 1830) p. 12–21. illus.
Translation of article in *Madagascar-Matin*, Antananarivo, Sept. 23, 1977, p. 1–5.
PRC: People's Republic of China.
Microfiche. [s.l., 1977]
DLC-Micro JPRS 70114

4967
Africa: Madagascar. Selected statistical data by sex. Washington, 1981. 31, 17 p.   DLC
Study supported by the U.S. Agency for International Development's Office of Women in Development and Office of Population.
Data assembled by the International Demographic Data Center, U.S. Bureau of the Census.
Among the tables, all based on 1975 data (unless otherwise indicated), are the following: unadjusted population by age, sex, and urban/rural residence; population by province, sex, and urban/rural residence; life expectancy (1972); number of persons enrolled in school by age, sex, and urban/rural residence.

4968
Devillard, Jean-Marc. Massacre of Comorans at Majunga reported. *In* U.S. *Joint Publications Research Service.* JPRS 68710. [Springfield, Va., National Technical Information Service, 1977] (Translations on Sub-Saharan Africa, no. 1717) p. 1–4.
Translation of article in *Le Monde*, Paris, Jan. 16–17, 1977, p. 4.
Microfiche. [s.l., 1977]
DLC-Micro JPRS 68710

4969
Here's some of the magic of Madagascar. *In* U.S. *Dept. of State.* Newsletter, no. 221, Mar. 1980: 38–41. illus.   JX1.U542 1980
Mostly illustrations of activities of U.S. Embassy personnel in Antananarivo.

4970
Pichon, Michel. Recherches sur les peuplements à dominance d'anthozoaires dans les récifs coral-liens de Tuléar (Madagascar) Washington, Smithsonian Institution, 1978. xxxv, 447 p. (Atoll research bulletin, no. 222)   QE565.A8 no. 222
English abstract: p. i–xxxv.
Bibliography: p. 375–408.

Mauritius

General

4971

U.S. *Dept. of State.* Post report. Mauritius. [Washington, Dept. of State, Publishing Services Division; for sale by the Supt. of Docs., U.S. Govt. Print. Off.], 1980. 16 p. illus., map. (*Its* Department and Foreign Service series, 207)

JX1705.A286 Spec. Format

Department of State publication, 9152.

L.C. has also report issued in 1977.

For a description of the contents of this publication, see the note to entry 936.

4972

U.S. *Dept. of State. Bureau of Public Affairs.* Background notes. Mauritius. [Washington, for sale by the Supt. of Docs., U.S. Govt. Print. Off.], 1980. 4 p. illus., maps. (U.S. Dept. of State. Department of State publication 8023)

G59.U5

L.C. retains only the latest revision.

For a description of the contents of this publication, see the note to entry 937.

Assistance Programs

4973

U.S. *Agency for International Development.* Country development small program statement: Mauritius. [Washington?] annual?

Vol. for 1979 examined in the Development Information Center, AID, Washington, D.C.

4947

———— Disaster relief, case report: Mauritius-cyclone, February 6–7, 1975. Washington, [1976?] 4 p. illus., map. DLC

4975

Mauritius. [*Treaties, etc. United States, 1979, June 29*] Agreement between the Government of the United States of America and the Government of Mauritius for sales of agricultural commodities. *In* U.S. *Treaties, etc.* United States treaties and other international agreement, v. 30, 1978–79. [Washington, Dept. of State; for sale by the Supt. of Docs., U.S. Govt. Print. Off., 1980] p. 6079–6098. ([Treaties and other international acts series, 9541]) JX231.A34 v. 30

Signed at Port Louis June 29, 1979 with minutes of negotiations signed at Port Louis June 18, 1979.

4976

Mauritius. [*Treaties, etc. United States, 1980 July 11*] Agreement between the Government of the United States of America and the Government of Mauritius for the sale of agricultural commodities under the Public Law 480, Title I program. [Washington, Dept. of State; for sale by the Supt. of Docs., U.S. Govt. Print. Off., 1981] 8 p. (Treaties and other international acts series, 9811) DLC

Signed at Port Louis July 11, 1980; entered into force July 11, 1980 with minutes of negotiation.

Economic Conditions

4977

Benefits begin to accrue from sugar price increase. *In* U.S. *Joint Publications Research Service.* JPRS 75474. [Springfield, Va., National Technical Information Service, 1980] (Sub-Saharan Africa report, no. 2233) p. 53–56.

Translation of article in *Le Mauricien*, Port Louis, Feb. 20, 1980, p. 6.

Microfiche. [s.l., 1980]

DLC-Micro JPRS 75474

4978

Duval discusses economic reform, coming elections. *In* U.S. *Joint Publications Research Service.* JPRS 67504. [Springfield, Va., National Technical Information Service, 1976] (Translations on Sub-Saharan Africa, no. 1658) p. 14–24.

4978 (cont.)

Translation of interview with Gaetan Duval, leader of PMSD, in *Le Mauricien*, Port Louis, May 5–6, 1976.

Microfiche. [s.l., 1976]

DLC-Micro JPRS 67504

4979

Foreign economic trends and their implications for the United States. Mauritius. 1979+ Washington, for sale by the Supt. of Docs., U.S. Govt. Print. Off. annual. (International marketing information series)   HC10.E416

Prepared by the U.S. Embassy, Port Louis.

Vol. for 1979 distributed by the U.S. Industry and Trade Administration; vols. for 1981– by the U.S. International Trade Administration.

The following issues have been identified in L.C.:

FET 79-082. 1979. 7 p.

FET 81-038. 1981. 11 p.

4980

Mansoor, A. Success of devaluation examined. *In* U.S. *Joint Publications Research Service.* JPRS 75576. [Springfield, Va., National Technical Information Service, 1980] (Sub-Saharan Africa report, no. 2241) p. 25–31.

Article, in English, in *Le Mauricien*, Port Louis, Mar. 27, 1980, p. 6.

Microfiche. [s.l., 1980]

DLC-Micro JPRS 75576

4981

Patel, Sulaiman. Economic slowdown brings reconsideration of problems. *In* U.S. *Joint Publications Research Service.* JPRS 66792. [Springfield, Va., National Technical Information Service, 1976] (Translations on Sub-Saharan Africa, no. 1638) p. 30–34.

Translation of article in *L'Express*, Port Louis, Dec. 31, 1975, p. 1, 11.

Microfiche. [s.l., 1976]

DLC-Micro JPRS 66792

Education

4982

Bérenger, Paul. MMM: education in a mess. *In* U.S. *Joint Publications Research Service.* JPRS 73214. [Springfield, Va., National Technical Information Office, 1979] (Translations on Sub-Saharan Africa, no. 2088) p. 45–49.

Translation of editorial by the Secretary-General of the MMM, in *Le Peuple*, Port Louis, Mar. 7, 1979, p. 1, 4.

Microfiche. [s.l., 1979]

DLC-Micro JPRS 73214

4983

Desveaux, Jean-Mee. Student union leaders explain university strike. *In* U.S. *Joint Publications Research Service.* JPRS 73673. [Springfield, Va., National Technical Information Service, 1979] (Translations on Sub-Saharan Africa, no. 2119) p. 54–61.

Translation of interview with leaders of the Mauritius Student Union concerning disturbances at the University of Mauritius, reported in *Le Mauricien*, Port Louis, May 7, 1979, p. 5, 6.

Microfiche. [Washington, Supt. of Docs., U.S. Govt. Print. Off., 1979]

DLC-Micro JPRS 73673

4984

Mauritius. *Ministry of Education and Cultural Affairs.* Report on educational developments, 1974–1976; presented at the 36th session of the International Conference on Education, Geneva, September 1977. [Port Louis?, 1977?] 8 p.

Abstract in *Resources in Education*, Feb. 1978, p. 165.

Microfiche. [Arlington, Va., ERIC Document Reproduction Service; prepared for Educational Resources Information Center, National Institute of Education, 1978] 1 sheet.

DLC-Micro ED144901

Foreign Relations

4985

Jugernauth, Raj. Duval proposes defense pact with France. *In* U.S. *Joint Publications Research Service.* JPRS 71586. [Springfield, Va., National Technical Information Service, 1978] (Translations on Sub-Saharan Africa, no. 1971) p. 28–32.

Translation of interview with Gaeten Duval, leader of PMSD, in *The Nation*, Port Louis, June 19, 1978, p. 1, 4.

Microfiche. [Washington, Supt. of Docs., U.S. Govt. Print. Off., 1978]

DLC-Micro JPRS 71586

4986

Mauritius hopes for substantial American sugar quota. *In* U.S. *Joint Publications Research Service.* JPRS 66363. [Springfield, Va., National Technical Information Service, 1975] (Translations on Sub-Saharan Africa, no. 1630) p. 30–34.

Translation of wide-ranging interview with Pierre G. Balancy, Ambassador of Mauritius to the United States, on Mauritian-American re-

4986 (cont.)

lations, in *L'Express*, Port Louis, Nov. 5, 1975, p. 1, 8.

Microfiche. [s.l., 1975]

DLC-Micro JPRS 66363

Politics and Government

4987

Bérenger, Paul. MMM Secretary General addresses issues. *In* U.S. *Joint Publications Research Service.* JPRS 72198. [Springfield, Va., National Technical Information Service, 1978] (Translations on Sub-Saharan Africa, no. 2020) p. 50–54.

Translation of article in *Le Peuple*, Port Louis, Sept. 29, 1978, p. 1, 4.

MMM: Mouvement militant mauricien.

Microfiche. [Washington, Supt. of Docs., U.S. Govt. Print. Off., 1978]

DLC-Micro JPRS 72198

4988

Berenger talks about MMM political plans. *In* U.S. *Joint Publications Research Service.* JPRS 73365. [Springfield, Va., National Technical Information Service, 1979] (Translations on Sub-Saharan Africa, no. 2099) p. 30–34.

Translation of interview with Paul Béranger, Secretary-General of the Mouvement militant mauricien, in *The Nation*, Port Louis, Mar. 25, 1979, p. 1, 4.

Microfiche. [Washington, Supt. of Docs., U.S. Govt. Print. Off., 1979]

DLC-Micro JPRS 73365

4989

Boodhoo, Harish. Labor Party reorganization proposed. *In* U.S. *Joint Publications Research Service.* JPRS 70677. [Springfield, Va., National Technical Information Service, 1978] (Translations on Sub-Saharan Africa, no. 1883) p. 59–62.

Translation of articel in *The Nation*, Port Louis, Dec. 30, 1977, p. 2.

Microfiche. [Washington, Supt. of Docs., U.S. Govt. Print. Off., 1978]

DLC-Micro JPRS 70677

4990

Discontent revealed in survey of youths' political views. *In* U.S. *Joint Publications Research Service.* JPRS 73609. [Springfield, Va., National Technical Information Service, 1979] (Translations on Sub-Saharan Africa, no. 2115) p. 48–55.

Translation of article in *Le Mauricien*, Port Louis, Mar. 20–21, 1979.

Microfiche. [Washington, Supt. of Docs., U.S. Govt. Print. Off., 1979]

DLC-Micro JPRS 73609

4991

MMM has rejected Stalinism. *In* U.S. *Joint Publications Research Service.* JPRS 76526. [Springfield, Va., National Technical Information Service, 1980] (Sub-Saharan Africa report, no. 2300) p. 58–64.

Translation of interview with Paul Béranger, leader of the Mouvement militant mauricien, in *Le Mauricien*, Port Louis, July 28, 1980, p. 5–6.

Microfiche. [s.l., 1980]

DLC-Micro JPRS 76526

4992

MMM strategy analyzed by Labor [sic] Party leader. *In* U.S. *Joint Publications Research Service.* JPRS 76554. [Springfield, Va., National Technical Information Service, 1980] (Sub-Saharan Africa report, no. 2301) p. 43–49.

Translation of interview with James B. David of the Labour Party, in *The Nation*, Port Louis, July 27, 1980, p. 1–3.

Microfiche, [s.l., 1980]

DLC-Micro JPRS 76554

4993

Mauritian socialism outlined: "the third way." *In* U.S. *Joint Publications Research Service.* JPRS 72390. [Springfield, Va., National Technical Information Service, 1978] (Translations on Sub-Saharan Africa, no. 2034) p. 62–65.

Translation of article in *Le Peuple*, Port Louis, Nov. 8, 1978, p. 4.

Microfiche. [Washington, Supt. of Docs., U.S. Govt. Print. Off., 1978]

DLC-Micro JPRS 72390

4994

PSM first congress, PMSD meeting reported. *In* U.S. *Joint Publications Research Service.* JPRS 75775. [Springfield, Va., National Technical Information Service, 1980] (Sub-Saharan Africa report, no. 2251) p. 55–59.

Translation of article on the Parti socialiste mauricien and the Parti mauricien social démocrate, in *Le Mauricien*, Port Louis, Mar. 10, 1980, p. 1, 4.

Microfiche. [s.l., 1980]

DLC-Micro JPRS 75775

4995

Portraits of Mauritian political leaders. *In* U.S. *Joint Publications Research Service.* JPRS 67161.

4995 (cont.)

[Springfield, Va., National Technical Information Service, 1976] (Translations on Sub-Saharan Africa, no. 1646) p. 21–26.

Translation of article in *Le Monde*, Paris, Mar. 13, 1976, p. 22.

Microfiche. [s.l., 1976]

DLC-Micro JPRS 67161

4996

Prime Minister discusses defense, proposed republic. *In* U.S. *Joint Publications Research Service.* JPRS 71730. [Springfield, Va., National Technical Information Service, 1978] (Translations on Sub-Saharan Africa, no. 1981) p. 30–33.

Translation of interview with Seewoosagur Ramgoolam, in *The Nation*, Port Louis, July 15, 1978, p. 1, 4.

Microfiche. [Washington, Supt. of Docs., U.S. Govt. Print. Off., 1978]

DLC-Micro JPRS 71730

4997

Report on PMSD congress in Curepipe. *In* U.S. *Joint Publications Research Service.* JPRS 72510. [Springfield, Va., National Technical Information Service, 1978] (Translations on Sub-Saharan Africa, no. 2044) p. 76–79.

Translation of article in *Le Mauricien*, Port Louis, Nov. 13, 1978, p. 1, 4.

Microfiche. [Washington, Supt. of Docs., U.S. Govt. Print. Off., 1978]

DLC-Micro JPRS 72510

4998

Visit of French naval units protested. *In* U.S. *Joint Publications Research Service.* JPRS 70663. [Springfield, Va., National Technical Information Service, 1978] (Translations on Sub-Saharan Africa, no. 1880) p. 76–79.

Translation of article in *Le Militant*, Port Louis, Jan. 6, 1978, p. 1, 4.

Microfiche. [Washington, Supt. of Docs., U.S. govt. Print. Off., 1978]

DLC-Micro JPRS 70663

Other Subjects

4999

Africa: Mauritius. Selected statistical data by sex. Washington, 1981. 31, 17 p.   DLC

Study supported by the U.S. Agency for International Development's Office of Women in Development and Office of Population.

Data assembled by the International Demographic Data Center, U.S. Bureau of the Census.

Among the tables, all based on 1972 data (unless otherwise noted), are the following: unadjusted population by age, sex, and urban/rural residence; population by province, sex, and urban/rural residence; population by ethnic group (i.e., Hindu, Muslim, Sino-Mauritian); population by language, sex, and urban/rural residence; total population by marital status, age, and sex; number of households; heads of households by age, sex, and urban/rural residence; number of literate persons by age, sex, and urban/rural residence (1962); number of persons enrolled in school by age, sex, and urban/rural residence; number of economically active persons by age, sex, and urban/rural residence; economically active population by occupational status, sex, and urban/rural residence.

5000

DeChantel, Jean. The University of Mauritius Library: its development and evolution. Overseas universities, Sept. 1974: 14–17. illus.

LB2331.5.094

Issued also in microfiche. [Arlington, Va., ERIC Document Reproduction Service; prepared for Educational Resources Information Center, National Institute of Education, 1975] 1 sheet.

DLC-Micro ED098961

5001

A Market survey of prototype core housing units in Mauritius. [s.l.], Padco, inc., 1980. 83 p. illus.

Prepared for the Office of Housing, U.S. Agency for International Development, under contract AID/otr-C-1627.

Abstract in *A.I.D. Research & Development Abstracts*, v. 9, no. 3, 1981, p. 50.

Microfiche. [Washington, U.S. Agency for International Development, 1980?] 1 sheet.

DLC-Sci RR PN-AAJ-486

5002

Raiford, M. T. Feasibility study report: Mauritius Alternative Energy Project No. 698-0135. [Nairobi, U.S. AID Mission], 1979. 26 p.

Concerns solar energy and wind power.

Microfiche. [Washington, U.S. Agency for International Development, 1979] 1 sheet.

DLC-Sci RR PN-AAG-850

5003

Simmons, Emmy B., *and* Thomas T. Poleman. The food balance sheet as a parameter of tropical food economies: the case of Mauritius. Ithaca, New York State College of Agriculture and Life Sciences, Cornell University 1974. 77 p. illus.

5003 (cont.)
(Cornell international agriculture bulletin, 29)
TX360.M35S55
Research supported by the Foreign Demand and Competition Division, Economic Research Service, U.S. Dept. of Agriculture.

Abstract in *A.I.D. Research and Development Abstracts,* Jan. 1976, p. 22.
Issued also in microfiche. [Washington, U.S. Agency for International Development, 1974?] 1 sheet.   DLC-Sci RR PN-AAB-273

Réunion

5004

Creole as language of instruction. *In* U.S. *Joint Publications Research Service.* JPRS 76377. [Springfield, Va., National Technical Information Service, 1980] (Sub-Saharan Africa report, no. 2289) p. 59–62.

Translation of article in *Témoignages*, St. Denis, July 24, 1980, p. 10.

Microfiche. [s.l., 1980]

DLC-Micro JPRS 76377

5005

Elie Hourau discusses autonomy convention at Sainte-Anne. *In* U.s. *Joint Publications Research Service.* JPRS 70126. [Springfield, Va., National Technical Information Service, 1977] (Translations on Sub-Saharan Africa, no. 1831) p. 45–51.

Translation of series of interviews with the secretary-general of an autonomist youth front in Réunion concerning a meeting of autonomist groups from French overseas departments held in Ste.-Anne, Guadeloupe, in *Témoignages*, St.-Denis, Sept. 19–21, 1977.

Microfiche. [s.l., 1977]

DLC-Micro JPRS 70126

5006

MMM delegate protests expulsion from Reunion. *In* U.S. *Joint Publications Research Service.* JPRS 72324. [Springfield, Va., National Technical Information Service, 1978] (Translations on Sub-Saharan Africa, no. 2030) p. 47–51.

Translation of article in *Le Peuple*, Port Louis, Oct. 12, 1978, p. 1, 4, concerning the expulsion from Réunion of Claude de l'Estrac of the Mouvement militant mauricien.

Microfiche. [Washington, Supt. of Docs., U.S. Govt. Print. Off., 1978]

DLC-Micro JPRS 72324

5007

Proportional representation demanded. *In* U.S. *Joint Publications Research Service.* JPRS 73428. [Springfield, Va., National Technical Information

Service, 1979] (Translations on Sub-Saharan Africa, no. 2102) p. 50–53.

Translation of article in *Témoinages*, St. Denis, Mar. 28, 1979, p. 5.

Microfiche. [Washington, Supt. of Docs., U.S. Govt. Print. Off., 1979]

DLC-Micro JPRS 73428

5008

Results of 10 June elections given. *In* U.S. *Joint Publications Research Service.* JPRS 73877. [Springfield, Va., National Technical Information Service, 1979] (Sub-Saharan Africa report, no. 2133) p. 21–26.

Translation of article in *Témoignages*, St. Denis, June 12, 1979, p. 4.

Microfiche. [Washington, Supt. of Docs., U.S. Govt. Print. Off., 1979]

DLC-Micro JPRS 73877

5009

Reunionese Communist Party 20th anniversary celebrated. *In* U.S. *Joint Publications Research Service.* JPRS 73877. [Springfield, Va., National Technical Information Service, 1979] (Sub-Saharan Africa report, 2133) p. 27–37.

Translation of article in *Témoignages*, St. Denis, May 18–29, 1979.

Microfiche. [Washington, Supt. of Docs., U.S. Govt. Print. Off., 1979]

DLC-Micro JPRS 73877

5010

Unfairness of media discussed. *In* U.S. *Joint Publications Research Service.* JPRS 76842. [Springfield, Va., National Technical Information Service, 1980] (Sub-Saharan Africa report, no. 2321) p. 95–99.

Translation of article in *Témoignages*, St. Denis, Sept. 29, 1980, p. 4–5.

Microfiche. [s.l., 1980]

DLC-Micro JPRS 76842

5011

Vergès, Paul. Reportage on Paul Verges press conference. *In* U.S. *Joint Publications Research Service*. JPRS 73060. [Springfield, Va., National Technical Information Service, 1979] (Translations on Sub-Saharan Africa, no. 2079) p. 154–159.

Translation of press conference of the secretary-general of the Communist Party of Réunion, in *Témoignages*, St. Denis, Feb. 3/4, 1979, p. 3, 4, 5.

Microfiche. [Washington, Supt. of Docs., U.S. Govt. Print. Off., 1979]

DLC-Micro JPRS 73060

5012

——— Verges speaks out for autonomy, development. *In* U.S. *Joint Publications Research Service*. JPRS 70584. [Springfield, Va., National Technical Information Service, 1978] (Translations on Sub-Saharan Africa, no. 1872) p. 75–84.

Translation of speech recorded in *Témoignages*, St. Denis, Dec. 17–18, 1977, p. 4–5.

Microfiche. [Washington, Supt. of Docs., U.S. Govt. Print. Off., 1978]

DLC-Micro JPRS 70584

5013

Verges holds press conference on lengthy foreign mission. *In* U.S. *Joint Publications Research Service*. JPRS 72398. [Springfield, Va., National Technical Information Service, 1978] (Translations on Sub-Saharan Africa, no. 2035) p. 79–85.

Translation of interview with Paul Vergès, in *Témoignages*, St. Denis, Oct. 19, 20, 1978.

Microfiche. [Washington, Supt. of Docs., U.S. Govt. Print. Off., 1978]

DLC-Micro JPRS 72398

Seychelles

General

5014

U.S. *Dept. of State.* Post report. Seychelles. [Washington?], 1979. 12 p. illus., map.

JX1705.A286 Spec. Format

For a description of the contents of this publication, see the note to entry 936.

5015

U.S. *Dept. of State. Bureau of Public Affairs.* Background notes. Seychelles. [Washington, for sale by the Supt. of Docs., U.S. Govt. Print. Off.], 1981. 4 p. illus., maps. (U.S. Dept. of State. Department of State publication 8246, rev.)

G59.U5

L.C. retains only the latest revision.

For a description of the contents of this publication, see the note to entry 937.

5016

The Peace Corps in Seychelles. [Washington, U.S. Govt. Print. Off., 1980] folder ([4] p.) illus., map.

DLC

"ACTION 4200.66."

An introduction to the country for volunteers.

Assistance Programs

5017

Billings, Martin H. Seychelles small country program statement. Nairobi, REDSO/EA, [U.S. Agency for International Development], 1978. 41 leaves.

Examined in the Development Information Center, AID, Washington, D.C.

5018

Seychelles. [*Treaties, etc. United States, 1978 June 9*] Peace Corps agreement between the United States of America and Seychelles, effected by exchange of notes signed at Victoria May 31 and June 9, 1978.

In U.S. *Treaties, etc.* United States treaties and other international agreements, v. 30, 1978–79. [Washington, Dept. of State; for sale by the Supt. of Docs., U.S. Govt. Print. Off., 1980] p. 1916–1924. ([Treaties and other international acts series, 9300])

JX231.A34 v. 30

Fauna and Flora

5019

Battistini, R., *and* C. Jouannic. Recherches sur la géomorphologie de l'Atoll Farquhar (Archipel des Seychelles) Washington, Smithsonian Institution, 1979. [40] p. illus., maps. (Atoll research bulletin, no. 230)

QE565.A8 no. 230

5020

Donaldson, A., *and* B. A. Whitton. Algal flora of freshwater habitats on Aldabra. Washington, Smithsonian Institution, 1977. 26 p. map. (Atoll research bulletin, no. 215)

QE565.A8 no. 215

5021

—— Chemistry of freshwater pools on Aldabra. Washington, Smithsonian Institution, 1977. [28] p. illus., maps. (Atoll research bulletin, no. 213)

QE565.A8 no. 213

5022

Drew, Edward A. A photographic survey down the seaward reef-front of Aldabra Atoll. Washington, Smithsonian Institution, 1977. [17] p. illus., maps. (Atoll research bulletin, no. 193)

QE565.A8 no. 193

5023

Feare, Christopher J. Ecological observations on African banks, Amirantes. Washington, Smithsonian Institution, 1979. 7 p. (Atoll research bulletin, no. 227)

QE565.A8 no. 227

5024

—— Ecology of Bird Island, Seychelles. Washington, Smithsonian Institution, 1979. [38] p. illus., maps. (Atoll research bulletin, no. 226)

QE565.A8 no. 226

Bibliography: p. 26–29.

5025

Frith, C. B. Life history notes on some Aldabran land birds. Washington, Smithsonian Institution, 1977. [17] p. illus. (Atoll research bulletin, no. 201)

QE565.A8 no. 201

5026

Frith, D. W. A list of insects caught in light traps on West Island, Aldabra Atoll, Indian Ocean. Washinton, Smithsonian Institution, 1979. 11 p. (Atoll research bulletin, no. 225)

QE565.A8 no. 225

5027

Gillham, Mary E. Observations on vegetation of blue-faced booby colonies on Cosmoledo Atoll, Western Indian Ocean. Washington, Smithsonian Institution, 1977. 11 p. (Atoll research bulletin, no. 199)   QE565.A8 no. 199

5028

—— Vegetation of sea and shore-bird colonies on Aldabra Atoll. Washington, Smithsonian Institution, 1977. 19 p. (Atoll research bulletin, no. 200)   QE565.A8 no. 200

5029

Hnatiuk, R. J., *and* L. F. H. Merton. Vegetation of Aldabra, a reassessment. Washington, Smithsonian Institution, 1979. 22 p. (Atoll research bulletin, no. 239)   QE565.A8 no. 239

Bibliograpby: p. 21–22.

5030

Rosen, Brian R. Check list of recent coral records from Aldabra (Indian Ocean) Washington, Smithsonian Institution, 1979. [26] p. (Atoll research bulletin, no. 233)   QE565.A8 no. 233

5031

Stoddart, D. R., *and* L. U. Mole. Climate of Aldabra Atoll. Washington, Smithsonian Institution, 1977. [27] p. (Atoll research bulletin, no. 202)

QE565.A8 no. 202

5032

Stoddart, D. R., M. J. Coe, *and* F. R. Fosberg. D'Arros and St. Joseph, Amirante Islands. Washington, Smithsonian Institution, 1979. 48 p.

illus., maps. (Atoll research bulletin, no. 223)

QE565.A8 no. 223

Includes bibliographies.

An investigation of the ecology of the region.

5033

Webb, M. D. Fulgoroidea from Aldabra, Astove, and Cosmoledo atolls collected by the Royal Society Expedition, 1967–68 (Hemiptera-Homoptera) Washington, Smithsonian Institution, 1975. 10 p. (Atoll research bulletin, no. 177)

QE565.A8 no. 177

5034

Whitton, B. A., *and* A. Donaldson. Terrestrial and freshwater algae of three western Indian Ocean islands (Astove, Farquhar, and St. Pierre) Washington, Smithsonian Institution, 1977. 8 p. (Atoll research bulletin, no. 216)

QE565.A8 no. 216

5035

Whitton, B. A., *and* M. Potts. Blue-green algae (Cyanobacteria) of the oceanic coast of Aldabra. Washington, Smithsonian Institution, 1979. 8 p. (Atoll research bulletin, no. 238)

QE565.A8 no. 238

5036

—— Observation on redox potential in freshwater pools on Aldabra. Washington, Smithsonian Institution, 1977. [5] p. (Atoll research bulletin, no. 214)   QE565.A8 no. 214

5037

Wickens, G. E. The propagules of the terrestrial flora of the Aldabra Archipelago, western Indian Ocean. Washington, Smithsonian Institution, 1979. [39] p. illus. (Atoll research bulletin, no. 229)

QE565.A8 no. 229

Bibliography: p. 35–37.

Finance

5038

René, France Albert. President Albert Rene's budget speech for 1981 published. *In* U.S. *Joint Publications Research Service.* JPRS 77295. [Springfield, Va., National Technical Information Service, 1981] (Sub-Saharan Africa report, no. 2353) p. 51–71.

Article in *Nation*, Victoria, Dec. 26, 1980, p. 2–8.

Microfiche. [s.l., 1081]

DLC-Micro JPRS 77295

5039

—— President gives 1980 budget address. *In* U.S. *Joint Publications Research Service.* JPRS 75058. [Springfield, Va., National Technical Information Service, 1980] (Sub-Saharan Africa report, no. 2209) p. 74–88.

Article in *Nation*, Victoria, Dec. 26, 1979, p. 2, 3, 6, 7, 8.

Microfiche. [s.l., 1980]

DLC-Micro JPRS 75058

Politics and Government

5040

New constitution signed, explained. *In* U.S. *Joint Publications Research Service.* JPRS 73386. [Springfield, Va., National Technical Information Service, 1979] (Translations on Sub-Saharan Africa, no. 2100) p. 90–102.

From article in *Nation*, Victoria, Mar. 26, 30, and Apr. 3, 5, 1979.

Microfiche. [Washington, Supt. of Docs., U.S. Govt. Print. Off., 1979]

DLC-Micro JPRS 73386

5041

President announces new party structure. *In* U.S. *Joint Publications Research Service.* JPRS 71425. [Springfield, Va., National Technical Information Service, 1978] (Translations on Sub-Saharan Africa, no. 1957) p. 113–117.

Report of a statement by President France Albert René establishing the Seychelles People's Progressive Front, in *Nation*, Victoria, June 10, 1978, p. 1, 2, 7.

Microfiche. [Washington, Supt. of Docs., U.S. Govt. print. Off., 1978]

DLC-Micro JPRS 71425

5042

René, France Albert. President's speech marks 5 June celebration. *In* U.S. *Joint Publications Research Service.* JPRS 75976. [Springfield, Va., National Technical Information Service, 1980] (Sub-Saharan Africa report, no. 2262) p. 121–129.

Article in *Nation*, Victoria, June 5, 1980, p. 11–14, 41.

Microfiche. [s.l., 1980]

DLC-Micro JPRS 75976

5043

SPPF structures, roles explained. *In* U.S. *Joint Publications Research Service.* JPRS 75520. [Springfield, Va., National Technical Information Service, 1980] (Sub-Saharan Africa report, no. 2236) p. 63–67.

Article in *The People*, Victoria, Mar. 1980, p. 3, 4, 16.

SPPF: Seychelles People's Progressive Front.

Microfiche. [s.l., 1980]

DLC-Micro JPRS 75520

Other Subjects

5044

Africa: Seychelles. Selected statistical data by sex. Washington, 1981. 31, 17 p.   DLC

Study supported by the U.S. Agency for International Development's Office of Women in Development and Office of Population.

Data assembled by the International Demographic Data Center, U.S. Bureau of the Census.

Among the tables, all based on 1977 data (unless otherwise indicated) are the following: unadjusted population by age, sex, and urban/rural residence (1971); population by nationality, sex, and urban/rural residence; life expectancy (1971–75); number of literate persons by age, sex, and urban/rural residence (1960); number of persons enrolled in school 12 to 19 years old by age, sex, and urban/rural residence; number of economically active persons by age, sex, and urban/rural residence; economically active population by occupational status, sex, and urban/rural residence.

5045

Details of first development plan reported. *In* U.S. *Joint Publications Research Service.* JPRS 68829. [Springfield, Va., National Technical Information Service, 1977] (Translations on Sub-Saharan Africa, no. 1726) p. 48–51.

Translation of article in *Europe Outremer*, Paris, Nov. 1976, p. 13–15.

Microfiche. [s.l., 1977]

DLC-Micro JPRS 68829

5046

President Rene comments on OAU, nonalined meetings. *In* U.S. *Joint Publications Research Service.* JPRS 74519. [Springfield, Va., National Technical Information Service, 1979] (Sub-Saharan Africa report, no. 2174) p. 2–7.

Translation of interview with President France Albert René of Seychelles in *Révolution africaine*, Algiers, Sept. 14/20, 1979, p. 12–15.

OAU: Organization of African Unity.

Microfiche. [s.l., 1979]

DLC-Micro JPRS 74519

5047

Seychelles. [*Treaties, etc. United States, 1976 June 29*]
Seychelles tracking station: Mahe Island.
Agreement signed at Victoria June 29, 1976; entered into force June 29, 1976. *In* U.S. *Treaties, etc.*
United States treaties and other international agreements, v. 27, 1976. [Washington, Dept. of State; for sale by the Supt. of Docs., U.S. Govt. Print. Off., 1977] p. 3709–3722. ([Treaties and other international acts series, 8385])

JX231.A34 v. 27

Index

Note: This index combines personal and corporate authors, subjects, and titles in one alphabetical sequence, with numbers referring to entries in the text. Names of political leaders not established in Library of Congress catalogs are entered according to the form of name given in Chiefs of State and Cabinet Members of Foreign Governments *(JF37.U5; entry 816). For names of universities and other institutions of higher learning not established in the Library, the thirty-third (1982–83) edition of* The World of Learning *(AS2.W6) served as the primary source. United States government agencies are entered according to the latest form of entry established in the Library. Subject headings are based on the ninth edition (1980) of* Library of Congress Subject Headings *(Z695.U4749 1980), augmented to meet the specific requirements of this compilation.*

A

ACRE. *See* Adaptive Crop Research and Extension Project

AF-LOG, 28

AF Press Clips, 3

AFRIECON/SADAP Accessions Bulletin, 2057

AID. *See* United States-Agency for International Development

A.I.D. Evaluation Special Study (series), 542, 1186

A.I.D. Program Evaluation Discussion Paper (series), 38, 157, 874

A.I.D. Program Evaluation Report (series), 164

A.I. D. Project Impact Evaluation Report (series), 1560, 1567, 3963, 4415, 4600

A.I.D. Research & Development Abstracts, 17 (note)

ANRD. *See* Alianza Nacional de Restauración Democrática

AOSARIO. *See* Association des originaires du Sahara anciennement sous domination espagnole

AREMA. *See* Avant-garde de la révolution malgache

Abattoirs. *See* Slaughtering and slaughter-houses

'Abbās, Muḥammad, 4900

Abbott, Susan, 1673

Abbreviations, 13

'Abd al-'Azīz, Usāmah S, 1743

'Abd al-Raḥmān, Ja'far, 1784–85

'Abd al-Salām, Yūsuf, 1744

Abdel Rahman, Mustafa, 1747

Abdelaziz, Mohamed, 4893

Abdoua, Mamadou J., 4290

Abdu, Anwar, 1279

Abdulaziz, Mohamed H., 1348

Abebe Worku, 1472

Abeille, Barbara, 4224

Abercrombie, Frank D., 155, 3336

Abidjan, Ivory Coast, 3841

Abkin, Michael H., 4357, 4393

Abou-Bakr, Ahmed, 1745

Abu Bakr, 'Uthmān, 1513

Abu Ḥajj, Zayn-al-'Ābidīn, 1746

Abuja, Nigeria. *See* Nigeria—Federal Capital Development Authority

Abzug, Bella S., 2675

Acacia, 3300

Academy for Educational Development, 457, 475, 1973, 2431, 3393, 3396, 3480, 3878–79, 3882–92, 3895, 4570

Accessions List, Eastern Africa, 19

Accra, Ghana, 3846

Acheampong, Ignatius K., 3704

Achebe, Chinua, 4432

Achonu-Abidjan, E., 3200

Achour, Mouloud, 939

Acquisition of publications, from
    Africa, Southern, 2077
    Africa, Sub-Saharan, 779
    Benin, 3247
    Botswana, 2077
    Brazil, 2077
    Cape Verde, 3247, 3369, 3428
    Chad, 3427
    France, 3428
    The Gambia, 3243, 3369, 3428
    Germany (Federal Republic), 2077
    Ghana, 3243
    Great Britain, 789, 2077
    Guinea, 3247
    Guinea-Bissau, 3247
    Ivory Coast, 3247
    Kenya, 2077
    Lesotho, 2077
    Liberia, 3243
    Mali, 3247, 3369, 3427
    Mauritania, 3247, 3427
    Netherlands, 789, 2077
    Niger, 3247, 3427
    Nigeria, 3247
    Senegal, 3247, 3369, 3427–28
    Sierra Leone, 3247
    South Africa, 2077
    Sweden, 2077
    Togo, 3247
    Upper Volta, 3243, 3247, 3427–28
    Zambia, 2077

B

C

Educational assistance, Canadian, Tanzania, 1958

Educational assistance, Cuban, Angola, 2241

Educational broadcasting, Tanzania, 1951

Educational exchanges
  Africa, Sub-Saharan, with United States, 8, 468–69
  Nigeria, with United States, 4407, 4413

Educational outreach. *See* Adult education

Educational Reforms and Innovations in Africa, 1468, 1622, 1735, 1956, 3515, 4100, 4581, 4735

Educational television. *See* Television in education

Educational tests and measurements
  The Gambia, 3209
  Ghana, 3209
  Nigeria, 3209
  Sierra Leone, 3209

Edwards, Helen A., 1275

Edwards, Ralph S., 424–25

Ege, John R., 4445

Egerton Agricultural College, 1576, 1599

Eglin, Colin W., 2763

Egypt, foreign relations, Sudan, 1802, 1805–7, 1809, 1813–14
  treaties, 1812

Eicher, Carl K., 105, 108, 4779

Eicher, Jean-Claude, 3883

Eicher, Shirley F., 2355

Eighmy, Thomas H., 1638

Ejiga, N. O. O., 4360

Ekoola, Jean-Paul, 981

Election law
  Ivory Coast, 3910
  Mozambique, 2524

Elections
  Angola, 2281
  Mauritius, 4978
  Monrovia, Liberia, 4004
  Mozambique, 2524, 2538
  Namibia, 2600, 2611
  Nigeria, 4339
  Réunion, 5008
  Senegal, 4609
  Upper Volta, 4837–44
  Zimbabwe
    1979: 2946, 3007, 3067, 3095–3106
    1980: 3107–12
  See also Election law; and Politics and government under names of regions and countries, e.g., Zambia—politics and government

Elections: 1980, the Rhodesian Debacle, 3110

Electric power systems
  Africa, French-speaking, 543
  Africa, Sub-Saharan, 407
  Chad, 3554–55
  Djibouti, 1367
  Ethiopia, 1405
  The Gambia, 3626

Electric power systems (cont.)
  Ivory Coast, 3898
  Madagascar, 4932
  Mali, 4029
  Mauritania, 4128
  Mozambique, 2489
  Niger, 4233, 4242
  Senegal, 4511
  Somalia, 1697
  Upper Volta, 4744
  Zaire, 1145, 1167, 1180
  Zimbabwe, 3118

Electronic data processing. *See* Computer programs

Elementary education. *See* Education, primary

Elephants, 545–46

Elima (Kinshasa), 371

Elliott, Howard J. C., 3846

Elliott, Robert, 214

Ellis, Miller W., 1219–23, 2511–12, 2584–85, 2691–95, 2874–78

Elphick, Richard, 2800

Ely, Northcutt, 671

Emane, Obame, 1073

Embargo, United States
  against South Africa, 2637, 2640, 2751, 2754
  against Uganda, 2006
  See also Sanctions (International law)

Emery, K. O., 669, 2127

Emigation, Zimbabwe, 3053

Emigration and immigration of scientific and technical personnel. *See* Brain drain

Emiru Woldeyes, 1437

Emmanuel, Paul, 1247, 2709

Emmons, Marian, 861

Employees of Diplomatic Missions, 575 (note)

Employment. *See* Manpower

Employment Practices of U.S. Firms in South Africa, 2653

Endemic diseases. *See* names of specific diseases, e.g., Trypanosomiasis

Enea, Susan, 1361a

Energy policy
  Organization of African Unity, 535
  United States, 518

Energy resources
  Africa, Eastern, 1279, 1353
  Africa, Southern, bibliography, 2086
  Africa, Sub-Saharan, 521, 523, 532, 535–36, 664
  Africa, West, 3276
  Angola, 2165
  Cameroon, 291, 1020
  Cape Verde, 3521
  Comoros, 4921
  Ethiopia, 291, 532
  Ghana, 291, 525, 3774, 3783
  Ivory Coast, 519

Ethiopia (cont.)
foreign relations (cont.)
Sudan, 1294, 1303–4, 1803, 1809
Union of Soviet Socialist Republics, 635, 1297, 1310–11, 1324, 1327, 1516, 1520, 1537
United States, 1291, 1295, 1304, 1306, 1309, 1401, 1472, 1475–76, 1520, 1534
treaties, 1438–43
gazetteers, 1542a
history, 1401, 1403, 1474, 1504
industries, 1464
local government, 1491, 1503
nationalism and revolution–Eritrea, 1511–37
politics and government, 822, 826, 1305, 1346, 1400–1, 1405, 1485, 1489–1537
Ethiopian Manuscript Microfilm Library, 1545
Ethnic groups
Benin, 3509
Cape Verde, 3546
Chad, 3606
The Gambia, 3638
Ghana, 3758
Ivory Coast, 3915
Lesotho, 2443
Liberia, 4017
Malawi, 2460
Mali, 4116
Mauritius, 4999
Mozambique, 2544
Namibia, 2607
Nigeria, 4339, 4429
Rwanda, 1122
Senegal, 4613
Seychelles, 5045
Sierra Leone, 4700, 4706
South Africa, 2623, 2784–87
Swaziland, 2828
Togo, 4732
Western Sahara, 4867
Zimbabwe, 3032
See also names of individual ethnic groups, e.g., Masai
Ethnology. *See* Africa, Sub-Saharan—ethnology; and under names of regions and countries, e.g., Mali—ethnology
European Economic Community, assistance to Africa, Sub-Saharan, 329, 354, 4936, 4940
Evaluation Technologies inc., 1145, 1147, 1273, 1367, 1697, 3400, 3521, 3554, 4126, 4233, 4744, 4921, 4932
Evans, Robert B., 101
Evans, Stella, 3886
Ewbank, Douglas C., 3255
Ewe language, 4725
Ewert, D. Merrill, 474
Exchange control. *See* Foreign exchange—law

Exchange of persons programs, American, with Africa, Sub-Saharan, 8
Exchanges, educational. *See* Educational exchanges
Exiles. *See* Refugees
Experience Incorporated, 998, 1192, 1904, 4069, 4273, 4761
Experiment in International Living, 1996, 2392, 2827, 3242, 4725–28
Experiments and Innovations in Education (series), 1017, 1468, 1622, 1735, 1951, 1956, 4100, 4408, 4581
Export-Import Bank of the United States, 7, 225, 349, 1167, 1180, 2636, 2652
Eyadéma, Gnassingbé, 9, 3215, 3248, 4724, 4729
Eyenga Sana, 1249

F

FAN (Forces armées du nord) *See* Chad—civil war
FAPLA. *See* Forças Armadas Populares de Libertação de Angola
FATUS: Foreign Agricultural Trade of the United States, 333 (note)
FNLA. *See* Frente Nacional de Libertação de Angola
FPV. *See* Front progressiste voltaïque
FRELIMO. *See* Frente de Libertação de Moçambique
FROLINAT. *See* Front de libération nationale du Tchad
Fadiga, Abdoulaye, 3191
Fafunwa, A. Babtunde, 4405
Fahnballeh, H. Boima, 4003
Faïk, Sully, 1271
Fairbank, Alan W., 2465
Fairweather, Gladstone, 4315
Fall, Michael W., 4628
Fall, Moustapha, 4588
Falusi, A. O., 4354
Famil, Silmi, 1519
Family, Africa, Sub-Saharan, 480, 497
Family Health Care, inc., 2131, 2343, 2380, 2436, 2465, 2586, 2823, 2880, 3041, 3417–19, 3422, 3436, 3438
Family planning
Africa, French-speaking, 855
Africa, Sub-Saharan, 234, 837, 839, 841–43, 847
Benin, 3229a, 3232, 3644
Cameroon, 1001–2, 1004
Ethiopia, 1541
The Gambia, 3229a, 3232, 3644
Ghana, 838, 3257, 3279, 3739, 3760, 3770
Guinea-Bissau, 3838
Ivory Coast, 3279
Kenya, 838–39, 1632, 1669

H

I

J

K

L

M

Mauritania (cont.)
  Ministère de l'économie et des finances. Direction des études et de programmation (cont.)
    4216–17, 4220–23
    politics and government, 4123–24, 4128, 4208–11
      directories, 3483
    social conditions, 4130 (note), 4143, 4217–23, 4230
Mauritian Militant Movement. *See* Mouvement militant mauricien
Mauritius, 4971–5003
  armed forces, 4996
  bibliography, 19
  climate, 4971
  commerce, 333–34
    United States, 4979
  economic conditions, 4921, 4971–72, 4977–81
  economic policy, 424, 4978, 4981
  foreign relations, 4985–86
    France, 4985, 4998
    United States, 4972, 4986
      treaties, 4975–76
  history, 4972
  Ministry of Education and Cultural Affairs, 4984
  politics and government, 4921, 4971–72, 4987–98
Mauritius Student Union, 4983
Maxon, Richard, 3565–66
May, Jacques M., 3453
Maynes, Charles W., 2121
Mayotte, 4924
May-Parker, Ibi I., 4643, 4653, 4657, 4683
Mazonowicz, Douglas, 172
Mazrui, Ali A., 2017
Mba, P. O., 4414
Mbabane, Swaziland, 2802
Mbaye, Keba, 766
Mbitiru, Chege, 2600
Mbogoro, D. A. K., 1289
M'Bokolo, Elikia, 863
Mdluli, S. B., 2667
Measles, Zaire, 1232
Measures. *See* Weights and measures
Mecklenburg, Robert, 723
Medical assistance, American
  Africa, Central, 281
  Africa, Southern, directories, 2158
  Africa, Sub-Saharan, 176, 240, 290, 689, 715, 723, 738
    directories, 724
  Africa, West, 281, 3227
  Botswana, 715
  Cameroon, 690
  Cape Verde, 690
  Central African Republic, 690
  Ethiopia, 1440, 1442

Medical assistance, American (cont.)
  Ghana, 690
  Kenya, 1632, 1639
  Lesotho, 690
  Liberia, 690
  Mali, 690, 4109
  Niger, 690
  Senegal, 690
  Sudan, 690, 1824
  Tanzania, 690, 1936
  Zaire, 690
Medical assistance, Chinese, Madagascar, 4966
Medical education
  Kenya, 1641, 1643
  Nigeria, 4407
  See also Medical research
Medical instruments and apparatus, South Africa, 2645
Medical research, 688
  bibliography, 692
Medical Service Consultants, 1824, 4107
Medicine, preventive, Kenya, 1640
Medicine, traditional
  Africa, Sub-Saharan, 707
  Botswana, 2377
Meharry Medical College
  International Center for Health Sciences, 732
    about, 715
  Maternal and Child Health/Family Training and Research Center, 725
Mehrutu, Assefa. *See* Assefa Mehretu
Meir, Uwe H., 932
Melaku Worede, 1413
Mellor, John W., 1414, 1420, 1422
Mende, 4636
Menes, Robin J., 4596
Mengistu Haile-Mariam, 1296, 1318–19, 1467, 1503
  about, 1494, 1510
Menkerios, Haile, 1530
Menkouss, Yahya ould, 4191
Mentally ill, South Africa, care and treatment, 2709
Mercenary troops
  Africa, Sub-Saharan, 798
  Angola, 2136, 2273
  Zaire, 1250
  Zimbabwe, 2136
Merchant marine, Sudan, 1794
  See also Shipping
Meriwether, Delano, 2380
Merrick, Walter F., 2725
Merrill, Malcolm H., 4456
Merton, L. F. H., 5029
Merwin, Charles L., 3704
Messe, Xavier, 431
Meta Systems, inc., 667
Methane, South Africa, 2618

Method, Francis J., 2430
Meyer, Gerald, 4455
Meyer-Ruhle, G. Olaf, 4051
Miami University, Oxford, Ohio. European Center, 469
Mice. *See* Rodents
Michelini, Philip, 974–75, 1093–94, 1189–90, 2858, 3865–66
Michigan. University. *See* University of Michigan
Michigan State University, 377, 3144, 4393, 4701
    African Studies Center, 508, 3287, 4496
    Agricultural Sector Simulation Team, 4358
    Dept. of Agricultural Economics, 67, 74, 77, 95, 98–99, 108, 114, 118, 122, 353, 1152, 1159, 1415, 1417, 1423, 1893, 1990, 3123, 3133–35, 3139a–43, 3195, 3332, 3430, 3484, 3491, 3669, 4033, 4345, 4357, 4368, 4370, 4397, 4457, 4485, 4519, 4521, 4523, 4527, 4551, 4637, 4639–54, 4671–75, 4677, 4680–84, 4697, 4702–3, 4759, 4766–68, 4770, 4777–80, 4784–87, 4793–96
    Eastern ORD Project, 4771, 4778–96
    about, 4779–80
    Graduate School of Business Administration. Division of Research, 4457
    Non-Formal Education Information Center, 884
    Off-Farm Employment Project, 4672, 4677
    Sahel Documentation Center, 3287, 3369, 3427–28
    See also African Rural Economy Program
Michler, Walter, 1530
Michol-Andrianarahinjaka, Lucien X., 4958
Mickelwait, Donald R., 305, 877, 1765
Mickolus, Edward F., 815
Midamerica International Agricultural Consortium, 3933
Middleton, John, 3791
Midwest Universities Consortium for International Activities, 4457
Midwives
    Africa, Central, 718
    Africa, Sub-Saharan, 694, 696
    Africa, West, 718, 3228–29
    Botswana, 2378
    Cameroon, 718
    Mali, 718
    Niger, 718
    Senegal, 718
    Upper Volta, 718
Migrant labor
    Africa, Southern, 2052, 2133–35
    Africa, Sub-Saharan, 99, 126
    Africa, West, 3256, 3435
    Ethiopia, 95
    Ghana, 3765
    Lesotho, 2424, 2442
    Mali, 4117

Migrant labor (cont.)
    Mauritania, 4213, 4225
    Nigeria, 95
    Sahel, 3435
    Senegal, 4614, 4616–17, 4619
    Senegambia, 3432–34
    Sierra Leone, 95, 4699
    South Africa, 2786a
    Upper Volta, 4846
Miguez, Alberto, 4891
Military assistance, American
    Africa, Sub-Saharan, 175, 231, 236, 241, 245, 248, 253, 257, 274, 277, 303, 791–95, 1166
    Botswana, 2361
    Cameroon, 966
    Ethiopia, 795, 1438, 1459, 1474
    Kenya, 795, 1595, 1627
    Liberia, 4021
    Malawi, 2452
    Morocco, 795, 4879, 4881–84, 4886
    Nigeria, 795
    Somalia, 1704, 1709, 1719
    South Africa, 2751
    Togo, 4720
    Zaire, 253, 795, 1166, 1210, 1243
Military assistance, Arab nations, Africa, Sub-Saharan, 644
Military assistance, Bulgarian, Africa, Sub-Saharan, 321–25
Military assistance, Chinese, Africa, Sub-Saharan, 7, 321–27
Military assistance, Communist nations. *See*, e.g., Military assistance, Chinese; Military assistance, Soviet
Military assistance, Cuban
    Africa, Sub-Saharan, 327, 801, 804, 812, 2216
    Angola, 801, 2216, 2242–45, 2249, 2323, 2329
    Ethiopia, 1316, 1516
Military assistance, Czech, Africa, Sub-Saharan, 321–25
Military assistance, French, Africa, Sub-Saharan, 799, 2216
Military assistance, German (Democratic Republic), Africa, Sub-Saharan, 321–25
Military assistance, Hungarian, Africa, Sub-Saharan, 321–25
Military assistance, Polish, Africa, Sub-Saharan, 321–25
Military assistance, Romanian, Africa, Sub-Saharan, 321–25
Military assitance, Senegalese, Zaire, 1246
Military assistance, Soviet
    Africa, Sub-Saharan, 7, 321–25, 802, 2216
    Angola, 2216, 2256
    Ethiopia, 1316, 1516
    Somalia, 1715, 1720

Navies (cont.)
    South Africa, 2758
    Soviet, in Africa, 796, 3249
Navy Disease Vector Ecology and Control Center, 1483
Navy-yards and naval stations, Soviet, Somalia, 1715, 1722
Naẓīr, Ahmad M., 1523
Nchapi, M'ampiti F., 2440
Ndegwa, Philip, 1611
N'Djamena, Chad, 3552, 3583, 3595, 3603
Ndongo-Biyongo, Donato F., 1080
Ndonzuau Nzonzila, 2044
Neal, James, 4315
Neal, Stephen L., 2636
Near East Foundation, 4155
Near East/North Africa Report (series) *See* United States—Joint Publications Research Service
Nebraska. University. *See* University of Nebraska-Lincoln
Nedzi, Lucien N., 165
Nellum (Al L.) and Associates, 1910
Nelson, Gary, 3310
Nelson, Harold D., 1403, 1698, 2623, 4339
Nelson, Joan M., 1654
Nelson, Stephen D., 318, 3381
Netherlands, commerce
    Cameroon, 972–73
    Ethiopia, 1460–61
    Gabon, 1091–92
    Ghana, 3689–90
    Ivory Coast, 3862–63
    Kenya, 1609–10
    Liberia, 3957–58
    Nigeria, 4380–81
    South Africa, 2642–43
    Tanzania, 1943–44
    Uganda, 2007–8
    Zaire, 1187–88
    Zambia, 2856–57
    Zimbabwe, 2922–23
Nettleton, John G., 381
Neto, Agostinho, 2174–75, 2196–97, 2209–11, 2250, 2270, 2272, 2279, 2297–98, 2330
Netting, Robert M., 3311
Neumann, Alfred K., 3736
New Hampshire. University. *See* University of New Hampshire
New Mexico. University. *See* University of New Mexico
New Transcentury Foundation, 886
New York (State) State University at Binghamton. *See* State University of New York at Binghamton
New York (State) State University at Buffalo. *See* State University of New York at Buffalo

New York (State) State University at Stony Brook. *See* State University of New York at Stony Brook
New York State College of Agriculture and Life Sciences, 2011, 2047, 4341, 5003
    Dept. of Agricultural Economics, 2012, 3688, 3856, 4354, 4360
New York University. School of Education, 4422
New Zealand, commerce, Africa, West, 3149
Newbury, Catherine, 1237
Newman, Mark D., 67, 3312
Newsom, David D., 327, 589, 830, 2083
Newspapers. *See* Press
Newsweek, coverage of Africa, 913
Nguema, Francisco. *See* Masie Nguema Biyogo Negue Ngong
Nguema, Mba, 1075
Nguema Mbasogo, Teodoro O. *See* Obiang Nguema Mbasogo, Teodoro
Ngwube, Douglas, 205–6
Niamey, Niger, 4231
Niamey (*Département*), Niger, 4236, 4252
Niane, Amadou D., 4534
Nicholas, David D., 2465
Nichols, D. J., 849a
Nicholson, Sharon E., 682
Nickel, Ivory Coast, 3900
Nicolas, Guy, 864–65, 4488
Niger, 4231–4336
    climate, 4231
    commerce, 333–34
        United States, 4298, 4333
    economic conditions, 410, 3406, 4231–33, 4295–4304, 4311–13, 4319
    economic policy, 3411, 4295, 4302–4, 4331
    finance, public, 3411, 4331
    foreign relations, 4305–7
        Libya, 4305
        Togo, 3215
        treaties, 4261, 4281–82, 4318, 4332
    history, 4232
    industries, 4297
    police, 4320
    politics and government, 4231–33, 4319–20
        directories, 3483
    Service des eaux et fôrets, 4259
Niger River Basin, 3186, 3196
See also River Niger Commission
Nigeria, 4337–4504
    about, study and teaching, 4496
    armed forces, 803, 820, 4472
    climate, 4437
    commerce, 4375–87, 4402
        Belgium, 4380–81
        France, 4380–81
        Germany (Federal Republic), 4380–81
        Great Britain, 4380–81

Nutrition (cont.)
Réunion, 4921
Sahel, 3282, 3422
bibliography, 3425
Seychelles, 4921
Senegal, 3420, 4511
Sierra Leone, 4697–97a
Somalia, 1273, 1697
Sudan, 1273
Tanzania, 1273, 1993
Togo, 4739
Uganda, 1273
Upper Volta, 3420–21, 4744
Zaire, 1145, 1224
See also Hunger
Nutrition Training Seminar for Preschool Health
Program Supervisors (*1974*), 3738
Nwamefor, R. C., 4468
Nwankwo, Robert I., 382
Nweke, Felix I., 4370
Nwoye, S. C., 4469
Nyamboki, Cornelius, 1658
Nyarko, K., 3245
Nyerere, Julius K., 419, 861, 1966
about, 1967–68, 1984, 3093
Nyhan, Patricia, 3550
Nyquist, Thomas, 2794
Nziramasanga, Mudziviri, 2905, 2932
Nzongola-Ntalaja, 1238

O

OAU. *See* Organization of African Unity
OLC paper (series) *See* American Council on
Education. Overseas Liaison Committee
OMVS. *See* Organisation pour la mise en valeur du
fleuve Sénégal
OPEC. *See* Organization of Petroleum Exporting
Countries
OPIC. *See* Overseas Private Investment Cor-
poration
ORD (Organisme régional de développement) *See*
Agriculture—Upper Volta
Oakley, David, 3044
Oakley, Robert S., 1179
Obanya, Pai, 462
Obasanjo, Olusegun, 4399, 4433–37, 4441–42, 4477
Obebe, Bolarinde J., 4416–17
Obeck, Douglas K., 1546
Obeid, Mohammed, 1756
Obeng, H. B. 3658
Obi, Dorothy S., 785
Obiang Nguema Mbasogo, Teodoro, 1077
about, 1083
Obote, Apollo Milton, 2043

O'Brien, Conor C., 827
Ocaya, Anthony, 2004
Ocean Data Systems, inc., 1691, 3901
Oceanography
Africa, Southern, 2127
Africa, Sub-Saharan, 868–69
Africa, West, 3263
Mauritania, 3262
Western Saharan, 3262
Odell, Marcia, 2353
Odokara, E. O., 4418
Odubanjo, M. O., 65
Odynak, E. S., 1958
Office national des transports (Zaire) *See* Onatra
Ofusu-Amaah, S., 3736
Ogaden, conflict in, 1319, 1321, 1327, 1434, 1436
See also Ethiopia—foreign relations—Somalia;
Somalia—foreign relations—Ethiopia
Ogunfowora, O., 118
Ogunsheye, F. Adetowun, 786
Ohene-Darko, Regina, 3665
Ohio State University
Dept. of Agricultural Economics and Rural
Sociology, 68–72, 1466
Agricultural Finance Program, 70–72
Dept. of Geography, 1561
Dept. of Linguistics, 773, 775
The Oil Conspiracy, 2653
Oilseeds
Africa, Sub-Saharan, 34, 130, 182, 335
Nigeria, 4363
Ojokojo, James S., 809
Okedeji, Francis O., 845, 847, 850, 853
O'Keefe, Philip, 1362
Oklahoma. University. *See* University of Okla-
homa
Okonkwo, Chuka, 4464
Okumu, John J., 1651
Old age, Zambia, 2889
Olds, Hugh, 632
O'Leary, William, 843
O'Linn, Bryan, 2603
Oliveira, Manuel Rezende de, 2190
Olnick, Norman, 1448
Olson, Craig V., 1765
Olson, Howard C., 1976
Olson, R. V., 3145
O'Meara, Patrick, 3069
Omega Navigation Station, 4022
Omnibus Multilateral Development Institutions
Act (*1977*), 207
Omo River, Ethiopia, 532
Omondi, Lucia, 462
Onatra, 1259
Onchocerciasis, 196, 734, 3119, 3226
Ondo, Ngong, 1139

P

Roads (cont.)
   Upper Volta, 4763, 4773–74
   Zaire, 1153, 1178, 1233
   Zambia, 2390
Robbins, Richard D., 2906
Robert Dean Consultants, 2128
Roberts, Allen F., 4824
Roberts, Betty Jean, 1684
Roberts, Holden, 2319
Roberts, Kenneth E., 2140
Robertson, Barbara L., 2664
Robertson, Neville, 2664
Robinson, Howard T., 2549
Robinson, K. L., 4354, 4360
Robinson, Wayne, 1622a
Rocha, Carlos, 2195, 2201
Rockefeller Foundation, 743, 3374, 4457
Rodents
   Mali, 4052
   Niger, 4328
   Sahel, 3313
   Senegal, 4628
Roder, Wolf, 2907
Rodriques, Luiz, 2337
Roe, Emery, 2354
Roehrig, Matthew, 3792
Rogers, William D., 2114
Rojko, Anthony, 34
Romania, foreign relations
   Angola, 2196
   Madagascar, 4938
   See also Economic assistance, Romanian;
      Military assistance, Romanian
Rondos, Alex, 651–52, 3874, 3911–12
Roofing, Ghana, 3740
Roots, Logan H., 1232
Roper, D. Lee, 1363
Rose, Frank S., 4657
Rose, Irene, 1580–81
Rose, Tim, 1557, 2053
Rosen, Brian R., 5030
Rosenberg, Norman J., 3317
Rosenblum, Sam, 3979
Rosenfield, Patricia L., 733, 1977–78
Rosenthal, Benjamin S., 2685
Ross, Clark G., 4538–39
Ross, Doran H., 3785
Ross, Eugene L., 4420
Rossouw, S. F., 2799
Rotberg, Robert I., 2151, 2553, 2899
Roth, H. M., 1144
Rourk, J. Phillip, 120–21
Roush, James L., 4091
Rousseau, Rudolph, 1731
Roux, André le, 2591, 2605
Roux, Christian, 4946
Rouze, Anne, 3875–76

Rovine, Arthur W., 2083, 2562
Rowe, E. Thomas, 3365
Rowland, T. John, 3718
Royal Society Expedition (*1967–68*), 5033
Royal Society of Tropical Medicine and Hygiene,
   London, 1478, 1482
Rubber industry and trade, Angola, 2200
Rubin, Edward, 4219
Ruchti, James R., 778
Rudran, Rasanayagam, 2051
Rukandema, F. M., 2011
Rural Assessment and Manpower Surveys (series),
   4130–32, 4135–36, 4140–41, 4143, 4145–48,
   4150–53, 4158, 4166–67, 4169, 4175, 4179,
   4182, 4188–89, 4192, 4200–1, 4203–5, 4207,
   4214, 4216–17, 4220–23
Rural communities
   Africa, Sub-Saharan, 81, 124
      bibliography, 75
   Africa, West, 3140–41
   Ghana, 3788, 3791
   Ivory Coast, 3850
   Kenya, 81, 1565, 1569
   Mali, 4045
   Nigeria, 3139a, 3141, 3195, 4459–62
   Sierra Leone, 3139a, 3141
   Tanzania, 1889, 1894, 1896
   Upper Volta, 4755
   Zaire, 1154
   Zambia, 2841
Rural development. *See* Agriculture; Rural com-
   munities; Women in rural development
Rural employment
   Africa, Sub-Saharan, 114, 122
   Ethiopia, 122
   Nigeria, 122
   Sierra Leone, 122, 4643, 4645, 4647, 4652, 4675,
      4682
   Upper Volta, 4794
   See also Agricultural laborers; Migrant labor
Rural health services
   Ghana, 3725–37, 3739
   Liberia, 3999
   Mali, 4108
   Mauritania, 4203
   Niger, 4316, 4318
   Nigeria, 4456
   Senegal, 4599–4600
   See also Medical assistance, American
Rural sociology. *See* Sociology, rural
Rural-urban migration
   Africa, Sub-Saharan, 888, 920
   Africa, West, 3121
   Cameroon, 1003
   Nigeria, 4485
   Sierra Leone, 4701–3
   South Africa, 2786a

Rural-urban migration (cont.)
  Upper Volta, 4847–48
  Zambia, 2860, 2887
  See also Migrant labor
Rusch, William H., 294
Russel, Darrell A., 3655, 3659
Russell, Paul, 42
Russia. *See* Union of Soviet Socialist Republics
Russin, Antoinette, 2815
Rutidermatidae, 3211
Rwanda, 1117–32
  bibliography, 19
  census, 1128
  climate, 1120
  commerce, 333–34
  economic conditions, 410, 1120–21, 1123, 1127
  foreign relations, United States, 1121
    treaties, 1129–30
  history, 1120
  politics and government, 1120–21
Ryan, Carl A., 4249
Ryan, James G., 916
Rydlun, Rodney P., 4386

S

SADEX, 2059, 2164
SAFGRAD. *See* Semi-Arid Food Grain Research and Development Program
SARD. *See* Saharan Arab Democratic Republic
SCAUL. *See* Standing Conference of African University Libraries
SDAR. *See* Saharan Arab Democratic Republic
SPPF. *See* Seychelles People's Progressive Front
SRI International. Strategic Studies Center, 4, 2137
SWAPO. *See* South-West Africa People's Organisation of Namibia
Sabagh, Georges, 3439, 4598
Sabatini, Omero, 354
Sabbe, Osman Saleh, 1514–15, 1520, 1524, 1526, 1535
Sabotage, Mozambique, 2486
Sachsenmeier, Peter, 459–61
Saharan Arab Democratic Republic, 4873, 4879, 4889, 4895, 4900, 4902, 4914–15
  See also Polisario
Saharan People's Liberation Army, 4887, 4894
Sahel, 3281–3485
  bibliography, 3282, 3285–87, 3412
  climate, 3283, 3317
  economic conditions, 3282–83, 3404, 3406–13
  foreign relations
    Algeria, 3478
    Libya, 3478
    Morocco, 3478
    Tunisia, 3478

Sahel (cont.)
  history, 3284
  industries, 3282
  social conditions, 3390, 3465–69
Sahel (Niamey), 371
Sahel Bibliographic Bulletin, 3287
Sahel Crop Pest Management Conference (*1974*), 3318
Sahel Development Program. *See* United States—Agency for International Development—Sahel Development Program
Sahel Institute. *See* Institut du Sahel
Sahelian Social Development, 3284, 3297, 3311, 3320, 3468, 3479
Sai, Fred T., 839
St. Floris National Park, Central African Republic, 1043
St. John's University (Collegeville, Minn.) Monastic Manuscript Microfilm Library, 1545
St. John's University (New York) Sociology & Anthropology Dept., 4412
Sakaike, Tonic, 2115
Sako, Bafotigui, 4058
Salacuse, Jeswald W., 437
Salami, Amoussa, 4737
Salamone, Frank A., 4431
Salaries and allowances. *See* Officials and employees—salaries, allowances, etc. under names of countries, e.g., Mozambique—officials and employees—salaries, allowances, etc.
Salek, Mohamed Salem ould, 4873
Ṣāliḥ, Najib, 1390
Ṣāliḥīn, Muhammad K., 1789
Salinas, Armando L., 4896
Saline water conversion, Cape Verde, 3542
Salvador, Joaquim, 2732, 3065
Samoff, Joel, 1957
Samoza, Manuel, 4897
Samuels, Michael A., 625, 2970, 4479
San, 2162, 2370–73, 2606
San Pedro, Ivory Coast, 3861
Sanchez, Juan, 3505
Sanctions (International law), United States
  against Namibia, 2562
  against Rhodesia, 2946, 2954, 2975–3030, 3096, 3100, 3102
  against Uganda, 2019–20, 2032
  See also Embargo
Sand
  Africa, Southern, 402
  Africa, Sub-Saharan, 405
  Namib Desert, 405
  Sahara, 405
  Sahel, 402
Sand-dunes, Sahel, 3283
Sanders & Thomas, inc., 4291

Sangumba, Jorge, 2340
Sanitation, Cape Verde, 3521
Santini, Jim, 665
Santos, José E. dos, 2178, 2213, 2237, 2303–5, 2338
Santos, Lorena, 3837
Santos, Manuel dos, 3825
Santos, Marcelino dos, 2494–96
Sanyal, Bikas C., 1873
São Tomé e Principe, 1133–41
  economic conditions, 1133
  foreign relations, 1136, 1139
    Cuba, 1137
    Gabon, 1110
    United States, 1133
  politics and government, 1133, 1135–38, 1141
Sargent, Merritt W., 105, 3123, 3133–35, 3330, 3491, 3561, 4244
Sarsiellidae, 3211
Sassou-Nguesso, Denis, 1061, 1064
Satellites, Artificial. See Remote sensing
Saudi Arabia Development Fund, 1699
Saunders, Harold H., 4877, 4879
Saunders, Margaret O., 3322
Savimbi, Jonas, 2318, 2320, 2324
  about, 2304, 2325
Sayer, I. A., 2455
Scaife, Rugenal R., 3793
Scali, John A., 2565, 2569
Schaetzen, Yves de, 4253–54, 4577–78
Schatten, Fritz, 1509
Schatz, Sayre P., 438, 4401
Schatzberg, Michael G., 75, 1154, 1242
Schaufele, William E., 355–56, 1291, 1300, 2088, 2116, 2187–88, 2214, 2217, 2917
Schenkkan, Robert F., 457
Scherrer, J. Carole, 3459
Scheuer, James H., 838, 867
Scheyer, Stanley C., 3419
Schistosomiasis
  Africa, Sub-Saharan, 733–34, 739
  Ethiopia, 1477
  Tanzania, 733, 1977
Schlegel, David E., 3318
Schlegel, Priscilla M., 484
Schmidt, Nancy J., 499–501
Schmidt, Peter, 4650–51
Schneider, Michael J., 834
Schneider, Robert R., 4274
Schoen, Robert, 2787
Schoeneberger, Mary M., 1958
Schoepf, Brooke, 4043
Scholars' Guide to Washington, D.C. for African Studies, 29
Scholars' Guide to Washington, D.C. for Middle Eastern Studies, 29 (note)
Scholarships, 296, 416

Scholtz, Leopold, 2747
School attendance
  Africa, Sub-Saharan, 408
  Benin, 3509
  Botswana, 2386
  Chad, 3606
  Cameroon, 1000
  The Gambia, 3638
  Ghana, 3756
  Lesotho, 2443
  Liberia, 4017
  Madagascar, 4967
  Malawi, 2460
  Mauritania, 4212
  Mauritius, 4999
  São Tomé e Principe, 1134
  Seychelles, 5044
  Sierra Leone, 4698
  South Africa, 2786a
    Bophuthatswana, 2666
  Sudan, 1866
  Swaziland, 2828
  Tanzania, 1987a
  Togo, 4732
  Zambia, 2886
School children, food, Kenya, 1635
School enrollment. See School attendance
Schor, Sigmund, 1006
Schott, John R., 1591
Schreiber, Joseph F., 683
Schroeder, Harold J., 1216–17
Schruben, Paul G., 684
Schubert, J. S., 390
Schultheis, Michael J., 2012
Schuring, G. K., 2750
Schutz, Barry M., 3092
Schwarz, Paul A., 302
Schweiker, Richard S., 3024
Schweitzer, G. E., 4490, 4492
Scible, Robert H., 2757
Science
  Africa, Sub-Saharan
    directories, 872
    study and teaching, 447, 449, 451–52, 454
  Ghana, 3696, 3773, 3776
  Nigeria, 4491
    study and teaching, 4422, 4490, 4492
  Sahel, 3429
  Zimbabwe, 2918, 3113
Science Education Programme for Africa, 447, 449, 452, 454, 464
Scott, Earl, 4856
Scott, William E., 956–57
Scotton, James F., 1685
Scranton, Mary I., 2618
Scranton, William W., 2023, 2570, 2973

T

U

United States (cont.)
  International Military Education and Training
    Program
    Botswana, 2361
    Cameroon, 966
    Malawi, 2452
  International Trade Administration, 346–47,
    358, 944, 975, 982, 1047, 1092, 1098, 1127,
    1194, 1461, 1465, 1610, 1613, 1737, 1781,
    1793, 1944, 1949, 2008, 2425, 2456, 2639,
    2643, 2649, 2830, 2857, 2862, 2921, 2923,
    2931, 3513, 3533, 3687, 3690, 3811, 3832,
    3863–64, 3870, 3958, 4020, 4094, 4181, 4298,
    4333, 4383, 4396, 4573, 4679, 4723, 4821,
    4941, 4979
  Joint Chiefs of Staff, 277
  Joint Publications Research Service
    1975:
      Africa, Eastern, 1386, 1424, 1499, 1511
        1515, 1705, 1717–18, 1722
      Africa, Southern, 2309, 2320, 2326, 2334,
        2340, 2539
      Africa, Sub-Saharan, 13, 656, 770
      Africa, West, 3507, 3534–35, 3589, 3810,
        3825, 4310, 4577
      Western Indian Ocean, 4955, 4986
    1976:
      Africa, Central, 976, 978, 999, 1066, 1080,
        1084, 1097, 1099, 1115, 1138, 1265
      Africa, Eastern, 1373, 1384, 1387, 1391,
        1526
      Africa, Southern, 2190, 2195, 2201, 2205–6,
        2281, 2290, 2307, 2319, 2321, 2327,
        2344, 2481, 2488, 2513, 2529, 2546–47,
        2719
      Africa, Sub-Saharan, 435, 621
      Africa, West, 3315, 3464, 3508, 3540, 3598,
        3602, 3815, 3837–38, 4112, 4240,
        4253–54, 4300, 4304, 4314, 4320, 4907,
        4909, 4913
      Western Indian Ocean, 4927, 4957, 4978,
        4981, 4995
    1977:
      Africa, Central, 1053, 1062, 1065, 1128,
        1193, 1236, 1250–51, 1253–54, 1261,
        1264
      Africa, Eastern, 1288, 1307, 1311, 1317,
        1321, 1323, 1382, 1490, 1498, 1508,
        1522, 1524, 1527, 1536, 1732, 1736,
        1787, 1803, 1812, 1821, 1983, 1985,
        2043
      Africa, Southern, 2172, 2180, 2194, 2198,
        2202, 2212, 2244, 2279–80, 2286, 2289,
        2294, 2301, 2310, 2322, 2329, 2333,
        2337, 2484, 2486, 2501, 2521, 2524–26,
        2531, 2538, 2541–42, 2566–67, 2592,
        2594, 2603, 2855, 2885, 3091, 3114

United States (cont.)
  Joint Publications Research Service (cont.)
    1977 (cont.)
      Africa, Sub-Saharan, 554, 613, 624, 626,
        642, 833
      Africa, West, 3462, 3490, 3497–98, 3505–6,
        3539, 3541, 3585, 3812, 3814, 3833,
        3836, 3839, 3848, 3868, 3907, 3914,
        4095, 4111, 4311, 4336, 4477, 4710,
        4722, 4724, 4730–31, 4737, 4822, 4827,
        4839, 4868, 4904, 4922
      Western Indian Ocean, 4933, 4943, 4953,
        4966, 5005, 5045
    1978:
      Africa, Central, 943, 981, 1060, 1078, 1096,
        1101, 1110, 1139, 1209, 1214, 1244,
        1246–49, 1266
      Africa, Eastern, 1313, 1319, 1376, 1378,
        1385, 1486–87, 1492–93, 1495, 1502,
        1506, 1510, 1513, 1518, 1521, 1523,
        1528, 1531, 1535, 1659, 1716, 1743,
        1777, 1784–85, 1801–2, 1806–7, 1810–
        11, 1816, 1831, 1869, 1896, 2044
      Africa, Southern, 2122, 2168, 2174, 2176,
        2185, 2200, 2203, 2209, 2241, 2245,
        2267, 2271, 2274, 2277–78, 2282, 2286,
        2288, 2295, 2297, 2299–2300, 2302,
        2306, 2308, 2314, 2316, 2341–42, 2432,
        2479, 2494–95, 2498–2500, 2517, 2520,
        2532, 2537, 2545, 2548, 2595, 2598,
        2601, 2604, 2611, 2613, 2701, 2721,
        2730, 2734, 2736, 2745, 2761, 2771,
        2798, 2838, 2894, 2909, 2942, 3067,
        3073, 3087, 3094
      Africa, Sub-Saharan, 383, 584, 605, 609,
        620, 639, 649–50, 764, 774, 802, 879,
        1051
      Africa, West, 3193, 3203, 3276, 3495–96,
        3500, 3503, 3512, 3517, 3530, 3551,
        3580, 3597, 3601, 3617, 3636, 3797,
        3817, 3824, 3860, 3872–73, 3899, 3908,
        4096, 4105, 4183, 4186, 4193–95, 4208,
        4239, 4292, 4303, 4305, 4308, 4313,
        4319, 4426, 4472, 4478, 4481, 4497,
        4576, 4592, 4604, 4608, 4729, 4829–30,
        4834–35, 4837–38, 4840–44, 4860,
        4865, 4870, 4873, 4890–92, 4894, 4897
      Western Indian Ocean, 4870, 4873, 4890–
        92, 4894, 4897, 4958, 4964, 4985, 4987,
        4989, 4993, 4996–98, 5012, 5041
    1979:
      Africa, Central, 939, 983, 992, 1037–38,
        1059, 1061, 1070, 1072, 1083, 1109,
        1136, 1141, 1239
      Africa, Eastern, 1289, 1292, 1296, 1299,
        1308, 1318, 1320, 1325, 1344–45, 1383,
        1407, 1467, 1488, 1496–97, 1503, 1507,

V

Library of Congress Publications on Africa, 1965–1984

Note: *Library of Congress Publications in Print*, revised biennially and distributed free upon request by the Library's Central Services Division, lists currently available titles relating to Africa. It also cites a number of general publications that include references to Africana, such as *Newspapers Currently Received in the Library of Congress*.

Unless otherwise noted publications listed below were prepared in the Library's African Section. The source for each publication is indicated by the symbol below each listing.

Africa South of the Sahara: Index to Periodical Literature, 1900–1970. 1971. 8 reels.
Available on 35mm microfilm from G. K. Hall & Co., 70 Lincoln St., Boston, Mass. 02111; $365.00 in the U.S. and Canada; $401.00, export price

Africa South of the Sahara: Index to Periodical Literature. First supplement. 1973. 1 reel.
Available on 35mm microfilm from G. K. Hall & Co.; $110.00 in the U.S. and Canada; $121.00, export price

Africa South of the Sahara: Index to Periodical Literature. Second supplement. 1981. 3 v.
Available (in book edition or microfilm) from G. K. Hall & Co.; $220.00 in the U.S. and Canada; $242.00, export price

African Names and Naming Practices: A Selected List of References in English. 1977. p. 206–207.
Reprinted from the *Library of Congress Information Bulletin*, v. 36, Mar. 2, 1977.
D

African Newspapers in Selected American Libraries: A Union List. 3d ed. 1965. 135 p.
Ph (electrostatic print) $26.00
Ph (positive microfilm) $20.00
Compiled in the Library's Serial Division

The African Section in the Library of Congress. 1981. folder ([5] p.)
D

Africana Acquisitions: Report of a Publication Survey Trip to Nigeria, Southern Africa and Europe, 1972. 1973. 122 p.
F

Africana in the Library of Congress. [1977] folder ([5] p.)
OP

American Doctoral Dissertations on the Arab World, 1883–1974. 2d ed. 1976. 173 p.
F
Compiled in the Library's Near East Section

American Doctoral Dissertations on the Arab World: Supplement, 1975–1981. 1983. 200 p.
SuDocs (S/N 030-000-00145-1) $9.00
Compiled in the Library's Near East Section

Arab-African Relations, 1973–75: A Guide. 1976. 26 p. (Maktaba Afrikana series)
    Ph (electrostatic print) $10.00
    Ph (positive microfilm) $18.00

Arab-World Newspapers in the Library of Congress: A List. 1980. 85 p. (Near East series)
    SuDocs (S/N 030-000-00120-6) $5.50
    Compiled in the Library's Near East Section

Botswana, Lesotho, and Swaziland: A Guide to Official Publications, 1868–1968. 1971. 84 p.
    F

Contemporary Amharic Creative Literature: A Guide. 1981. 42 p. (Maktaba Afrikana series)
    D

East African Community: Subject Guide to Official Publications. 1976. 272 p.
    F

Folklore from Africa to the United States: An Annotated Bibliography. 1976. 161 p.
    SuDocs (S/N 030-001-00066-4) $10.00
    Compiled in the Library's Children's Literature Center

French-Speaking Central Africa: A Guide to Official Publications in American Libraries. 1973. 314 p.
    F

French-Speaking West Africa: A Guide to Official Publications. 1967. 201 p.
    Ph (electrostatic print) $32.00
    Ph (positive microfilm) $25.00

Ghana: A Guide to Official Publications, 1872–1968. 1969. 110 p.
    F

Islam in Sub-Saharan Africa: A Partially Annotated Guide. 1978. 318 p.
    SuDocs (S/N 030-001-00068-1) $14.00

Kenya: Subject Guide to Official Publications. 1978. 423 p.
    SuDocs (S/N 030-001-00073-7) $11.00

Liberia During the Tolbert Era: A Guide. 1983. 79 p. (Maktaba Afrikana series)
    D

Madagascar and Adjacent Islands: A Guide to Official Publications. 1965. 58 p.
    F

Nigeria: A Guide to Official Publications. 1966. 166 p.
    Ph (electrostatic print) $28.00
    Ph (positive microfilm) $22.00

The Nigerian Petroleum Industry: A Guide. 1978. 66 p. (Maktaba Afrikana series)
    D

Portuguese Africa: A Guide to Official Publications. 1967. 217 p.
    F

Recent Afro-Libyan Relations: A Selected List of References. 1981. 15 p. (Africana Directions series)
    D

The Rhodesias and Nyasaland: A Guide to Official Publications. 1965. 285 p.
　　F

La Section africaine de la Bibliothèque du Congrès. [1980] folder ([5] p.)
　　D

Spanish-Speaking Africa: A Guide to Official Publications. 1973. 66 p.
　　Ph (electrostatic print) $20.00
　　Ph (positive microfilm) $20.00

Sub-Saharan Africa: A Guide to Serials. 1970. 409 p.
　　F

Tanganyika African National Union: A Guide to Publications by and about TANU. 1976. 52 p. (Maktaba Afrikana series)
　　D

Uganda: Subject Guide to Official Publications. 1977. 271 p.
　　SuDocs (S/N 030-000-00064-8) $14.00

United States and Africa: Guide to U.S. Official Documents and Government-Sponsored Publications on Africa, 1785–1975. 1978. 949 p.
　　SuDocs (S/N 030-000-00098-6) $22.00

University of Malawi Publications: A Guide. 1980. 41 p. (Maktaba Afrikana series)
　　D

Zanzibar's Afro-Shirazi Party, 1957–1977: A Bibliography. 1978. 20 p. (Maktaba Afrikana series)
　　D

GUIDES IN PREPARATION

Africa South of the Sahara: Index to Periodical Literature. Third supplement
African Newspapers in the Library of Congress
Eastern Africa: Guide to the University Publications of Kenya, Tanzania and Uganda
A Guide to the University Publications of Zambia

Key to Symbols

D　Distributed free by the Library of Congress, African and Middle Eastern Division, African Section, Washington, D.C. 20540

F　Available free upon request to the Library of Congress, Central Services Division, Washington, D.C. 20540

OP　Out of print

Ph　For sale by the Library of Congress, Photoduplication Service, Washington, D.C. 20540. Checks should be made payable to the Chief, Photoduplication Service

SuDocs　For sale by the Superintendent of Documents, U.S. Government Printing Office, Washington, D.C. 20402. When ordering, cite the stock number which appears in parentheses after the symbol "SuDocs." Add 25% of the total price for foreign postage. Increases in cost make it necessary for the Superintendent of Documents to raise the selling price of many publications offered. As it is not feasible for the Superintendent of Documents to correct the prices manually in all publications stocked, the prices charged on your order may differ from the prices printed in the publications or those listed here